THE VICTORIA HISTORY
OF THE
COUNTIES OF ENGLAND

———

A HISTORY OF
YORKSHIRE EAST RIDING

VOLUME II

THE VICTORIA HISTORY
OF THE
COUNTIES OF ENGLAND

EDITED BY R. B. PUGH, D. LIT.

THE UNIVERSITY OF LONDON
INSTITUTE OF
HISTORICAL RESEARCH

Oxford University Press, Ely House, 37 Dover Street, London W1X 4AH

GLASGOW NEW YORK TORONTO MELBOURNE WELLINGTON
CAPE TOWN IBADAN NAIROBI DAR ES SALAAM LUSAKA ADDIS ABABA
DELHI BOMBAY CALCUTTA MADRAS KARACHI LAHORE DACCA
KUALA LUMPUR SINGAPORE HONG KONG TOKYO

ISBN 0 19 722738 4

© *University of London 1974*

PRINTED IN GREAT BRITAIN BY
ROBERT MACLEHOSE AND CO. LTD
THE UNIVERSITY PRESS, GLASGOW

INSCRIBED TO THE
MEMORY OF HER LATE MAJESTY
QUEEN VICTORIA
WHO GRACIOUSLY GAVE THE TITLE TO
AND ACCEPTED THE DEDICATION
OF THIS HISTORY

BRIDLINGTON, c. 1900: showing the Royal Prince's Parade, the Victoria Rooms, and the north pier

A HISTORY OF THE COUNTY OF

YORK

EAST RIDING

EDITED BY K. J. ALLISON

VOLUME II

PUBLISHED FOR
THE INSTITUTE OF HISTORICAL RESEARCH
BY
OXFORD UNIVERSITY PRESS
1974

Distributed by Oxford University Press until 1 January 1977
thereafter by Dawsons of Pall Mall

CONTENTS OF VOLUME TWO

		PAGE
Dedication		v
Contents		ix
List of Illustrations		x
List of Maps and Plans		xii
Editorial Note		xiii
Classes of Documents in the Public Record Office used		xiv
Note on Abbreviations		xv
Topography	Descriptions of buildings by MARGARET TOMLINSON	
Dickering Wapentake	By K. J. ALLISON and J. D. PURDY	1
Argam	By K. J. ALLISON	6
Bempton	By J. D. PURDY	8
Bessingby	By J. D. PURDY	16
Boynton	By J. D. PURDY	21
Bridlington	By K. J. ALLISON	29
Burton Agnes	By K. J. ALLISON	106
Burton Fleming	By K. J. ALLISON	119
Carnaby	By J. D. PURDY	125
Filey	By K. J. ALLISON	131
Flamborough	By J. D. PURDY	151
Folkton	By J. D. PURDY	164
Foston on the Wolds	By K. J. ALLISON	176
Foxholes	By J. D. PURDY	190
Fraisthorpe	By J. D. PURDY	199
Ganton	By J. D. PURDY	208
Garton on the Wolds	By J. D. PURDY	216
Harpham	By K. J. ALLISON	223
Hunmanby	By K. J. ALLISON	228
Little Kelk	By K. J. ALLISON	245
Kilham	By J. D. PURDY	247
Langtoft	By J. D. PURDY	263
Lowthorpe	By K. J. ALLISON	271
Muston	By K. J. ALLISON	278
Nafferton	By K. J. ALLISON	283
Wold Newton	By K. J. ALLISON	297
Reighton	By K. J. ALLISON	303
Rudston	By J. D. PURDY	310
Ruston Parva	By K. J. ALLISON	320
Thwing	By K. J. ALLISON	324
Willerby	By K. J. ALLISON	332
Index	By K. J. ALLISON	340
Corrigenda to Volume I		365

LIST OF ILLUSTRATIONS

Thanks are rendered to the Bridlington Public Library, the Committee for Aerial Photography of the University of Cambridge, *Country Life*, the Ministry of the Environment, the National Monuments Record, Aerofilms Ltd., C. H. Wood (Bradford) Ltd., Mr. F. F. Johnson, and B. T. Batsford Ltd. for permission to use material in their care or to use photographs in their possession as indicated below.

Bridlington sea-front, c. 1900. Photograph in Bridlington Public Library	*frontispiece*
Wolds landscape at Fordon. Photograph by J. K. St. Joseph, 1967, from the Cambridge University Collection, copyright reserved	*facing page* 32
Argam, deserted village site. Photograph by J. K. St. Joseph, 1969, from the Cambridge University Collection, copyright reserved	,, ,, 32
Rudston churchyard, prehistoric monolith. Photograph by Margaret Tomlinson, 1971	,, ,, 33
Flamborough Head, Danes' Dyke. Photograph by J. K. St. Joseph, 1948, from the Cambridge University Collection, copyright reserved	,, ,, 33
Boynton Hall. Photograph, *Country Life*, 29 July 1954	,, ,, 48
Sewerby Hall. Photograph by A. P. Baggs, 1972	,, ,, 48
Boynton Hall, staircase. Photograph, *Country Life*, 29 July 1954	,, ,, 49
Boynton church. Photograph by G. B. Wood, 1948, National Monuments Record	,, ,, 49
Arms of the borough of Bridlington	*page* 70
Buckton Hall in the 18th century. Drawing by F. F. Johnson	,, 84
Burton Agnes Hall. Photograph by G. B. Wood, 1949, National Monuments Record	*facing page* 112
Burton Agnes Hall, the gatehouse. Photograph, *Country Life*, 6 June 1953	,, ,, 112
Burton Agnes, old manor-house. Photograph by Ministry of Works	,, ,, 113
Bridlington, the Bayle. Photograph by H. Felton, 1953, National Monuments Record	,, ,, 113
Kilham, East Street. Photograph by Margaret Tomlinson, 1971	,, ,, 128
Bridlington, the harbour. Photograph by C. H. Wood (Bradford) Ltd.	,, ,, 128
Garton on the Wolds church, west end. Photograph by Margaret Tomlinson, 1971	,, ,, 129
Flamborough, Primitive Methodist chapel. Photograph by Gordon Barnes, 1970, National Monuments Record	,, ,, 129
Arms of the urban district of Filey	*page* 147
Bridlington, St. Mary's church, c. 1853. Photograph, National Monuments Record	*facing page* 192
Flamborough church, rood screen. Photograph by B. C. Clayton, c. 1930, B. T. Batsford Ltd., National Monuments Record	,, ,, 192
Bridlington, St. Mary's church, part of cloister arcade. Photograph by F. H. Crossley, National Monuments Record	,, ,, 193
Reighton church, font. Photograph by I. Coysh, National Monuments Record	,, ,, 193
Bridlington, St. Mary's church, north arcade. Photograph by H. Felton, 1953, National Monuments Record	,, ,, 193
Flamborough Head, cliffs and lighthouse, c. 1928. Photograph by Aerofilms Ltd.	,, ,, 208
Flamborough, old lighthouse. Photograph, National Monuments Record, 1971	,, ,, 208
Garton on the Wolds, Sykes monument. Photograph by Gordon Barnes, 1966, National Monuments Record	,, ,, 208
Garton on the Wolds church, interior. Photograph by Gordon Barnes, 1967, National Monuments Record	,, ,, 209
Rudston, Thorpe Hall dairy. Photograph by G. B. Wood, 1950, National Monuments Record	,, ,, 209
Bridlington, Alexandra Hotel. Photograph by Aerofilms Ltd., 1947	,, ,, 256
Filey, the Crescent. Photograph by Aerofilms Ltd.	,, ,, 256
Langtoft church, sedilia. Photograph by Gordon Barnes, 1966, National Monuments Record	,, ,, 257
Ganton church. Photograph by Margaret Tomlinson, 1971	,, ,, 257
Nafferton malting and corn-mill. Photograph by Margaret Tomlinson, 1971	,, ,, 272
Ruston Parva, Bracey Bridge water-mill. Photograph by J. S. Walker, 1971	,, ,, 272

LIST OF ILLUSTRATIONS

Bessingby, dovecot. Photograph by Margaret Tomlinson, 1971	*facing page* 273
Folkton, Manor Farm, barn. Photograph by Margaret Tomlinson, 1971	,, ,, 273
Carnaby House, wagon shed. Photograph by Margaret Tomlinson, 1971	,, ,, 273
Hunmanby, lock-up. Photograph by Margaret Tomlinson, 1971	,, ,, 273
Nafferton railway station. Photograph by Margaret Tomlinson, 1971	,, ,, 320
Bridlington, shop-front in High Street. Photograph by G. B. Wood, 1948, National Monuments Record	,, ,, 320
Bessingby, cottage. Photograph by Margaret Tomlinson, 1971	,, ,, 321
Reighton, Johnson's Farm. Photograph by J. S. Walker, 1971	,, ,, 321
Muston, house in Hunmanby Road. Photograph by Margaret Tomlinson, 1971	,, ,, 321
Garton on the Wolds, Manor Farm. Photograph by Margaret Tomlinson, 1971	,, ,, 321

LIST OF MAPS AND PLANS

The maps and plans were drawn by K. J. Wass from drafts by K. J. Allison and J. D. Purdy. All except those of Brigham, Fraisthorpe, Great Kelk, Kilham, and Reighton are based on Ordnance Survey maps with the sanction of the Controller of H.M. Stationery Office, Crown Copyright reserved. Those of Brigham, Fraisthorpe, Great Kelk, and Kilham, together with that of Sewerby and Marton (in part), are based on maps in the East Riding Record Office; that of Reighton is based on a map in the East Riding Registry of Deeds.

The Wapentake of Dickering	page 2
Bridlington, Modern Boundary Extensions	31
Bridlington, Growth of the Built-up Area	34
Street Plan, Bridlington, 1970	36
Street Plan, Bridlington, The Quay, 1970	38
Sewerby and Marton, 1802–50	94
Street Plan, Filey, 1970	133
Brigham before inclosure in 1767	177
Great Kelk, 1789	178
Fraisthorpe, Auburn, and Wilsthorpe, *c.* 1716	200
Kilham, 1729	248
Reighton before inclosure in 1820	304

EDITORIAL NOTE

THE arrangement of the Victoria History of the County of York in five distinct sets of volumes is described in the Editorial Note at the beginning of Volume I of the East Riding set. Under the sponsorship of the committee that was responsible for the compilation of that volume and also of *Yorkshire, The City of York* (published in 1961), preliminary work on the present volume was begun. In 1970, however, the committee was dissolved, and the East Riding County Council undertook the responsibility for compiling the remaining East Riding volumes, the county editor and assistant editor continuing in office. The City of York, one of the three main bodies represented on the former committee, continued to give financial support until the present volume had been written. The University of London gratefully acknowledges the generosity of the East Riding County Council and the City of York, as also that of the other contributors to the former joint fund.

It is impossible to mention personally here all those people who have helped in the compilation of this volume; their assistance has been greatly appreciated. Particular reference must, however, be made to the many facilities provided by the East Riding County Archivist, Mr. N. Higson, by the Acting Registrar of Deeds for the East Riding, Mr. C. N. Snowden, and by the Borough Librarian and Curator of Bridlington, Mr. S. T. Thompson. Grateful acknowledgement is also made of the permission to inspect records granted by parochial incumbents and, among others, the Minster Librarian and the Diocesan Registrar at York; the Archivists of the North Riding County Council and the Borthwick Institute of Historical Research, University of York; the Clerks of Bridlington Borough, Filey Urban District Council, the Commissioners of the Piers and Harbour at Bridlington, and the Lords Feoffees and Assistants of the Manor of Bridlington; and the Bridlington Harbour Master. The following people have kindly read and commented upon various articles in the volume: Alderman Miss Lucy M. Owston, the late the Revd. G. L. Barber, Mr. F. W. Fisher, Mr. M. E. Ingram, Mr. F. F. Johnson, and Mr. S. T. Thompson.

The *General Introduction* to the *History* (1970) outlines the structure and aims of the series as a whole.

LIST OF CLASSES OF DOCUMENTS IN THE PUBLIC RECORD OFFICE
USED IN THIS VOLUME
WITH THEIR CLASS NUMBERS

Chancery
    Proceedings
- C 1   Early
- C 3   Series II
- C 5   Six Clerks' Series, Bridges
- C 54   Close Rolls
- C 60   Fine Rolls
- C 66   Patent Rolls
- C 78   Decree Rolls
- C 93   Proceedings of Commissioners for Charitable Uses, Inquisitions and Decrees
- C 131   Extents for Debts

    Inquisitions post mortem
- C 132   Series I, Hen. III
- C 134   Edw. II
- C 135   Edw. III
- C 136   Ric. II
- C 138   Hen. V
- C 139   Hen. VI
- C 140   Edw. IV
- C 142   Series II
- C 143   Inquisitions ad quod damnum
- C 145   Miscellaneous Inquisitions
- C 211   Commissions and Inquisitions of Lunacy (Petty Bag Office)

    Chancery Files, Tower and Rolls Chapel
- C 257   Certiorari (Escheators etc.)
- C 260   Recorda

Court of Common Pleas
    Feet of Fines
- C.P. 25(1)   Series I
- C.P. 25(2)   Series II
- C.P. 40   Plea Rolls
- C.P. 43   Recovery Rolls

Exchequer, King's Remembrancer
- E 101   Accounts, Various
- E 112   Bills and Answers, etc.
- E 134   Depositions taken by Commission
- E 150   Inquisitions post mortem, Series II
- E 151   Inquisitions ad quod damnum
- E 159   Memoranda Rolls
- E 164   Miscellaneous Books, Series I
- E 178   Special Commissions of Inquiry
- E 179   Subsidy Rolls etc.
- E 190   Port Books

Exchequer, Augmentation Office
- E 301   Certificates of Colleges and Chantries
- E 303   Conventual Leases
- E 309   Enrolments of Leases
- E 310   Particulars for Leases
- E 315   Miscellaneous Books
- E 318   Particulars for Grants
- E 321   Proceedings of the Court of Augmentations

Ministry of Education
- Ed. 7   Public Elementary Schools, Preliminary Statements

Home Office
    Various, Census
- H.O. 107   Population Returns
- H.O. 129   Ecclesiastical Returns

Justices Itinerant, Assize and Gaol Delivery Justices, etc.
- J.I. 1   Assize Rolls, Eyre Rolls, etc.

Court of King's Bench (Crown Side)
- K.B. 26   Curia Regis Rolls
- K.B. 27   Coram Rege Rolls

Exchequer, Office of the Auditors of Land Revenue
- L.R. 2   Miscellaneous Books

Court of Requests
- Req. 2   Proceedings

Special Collections
- S.C. 2   Court Rolls
- S.C. 6   Ministers' Accounts

    Rentals and Surveys
- S.C. 11   Rolls
- S.C. 12   Portfolios

State Paper Office
- S.P. 5   Suppression Papers

    State Papers Domestic
- S.P. 16   Chas. I
- S.P. 29   Chas. II

Court of Star Chamber
- Sta. Cha. 2   Proceedings, Hen. VIII

Court of Wards
- Wards 7   Inquisitions post mortem

NOTE ON ABBREVIATIONS

Among the abbreviations and short titles used the following may require elucidation:

Acreage Returns, 1905	Board of Agriculture, Acreage Returns of 1905, from a MS. *penes* the Editor, Victoria History of the East Riding
'Annals of Bridlington'	Bridlington Public Library, scrapbook of cuttings from local newspapers, 59 vols., 1867–1942, compiled by W. Taylor and A. E. Matthewman
B.I.H.R.	University of York, The Borthwick Institute of Historical Research
Baines, *Hist. Yorks.* (1823)	E. Baines, *History, Directory and Gazetteer of the County of York*, vol. ii, East and North Ridings (1823)
Barley, *Par. Docs. E.R.*	*Parochial Documents of the Archdeaconry of the East Riding, an Inventory*, ed. M. W. Barley, Yorkshire Archaeological Society Record Series, vol. xcix (1939)
Boulter, 'Ch. Bells'	W. C. Boulter, 'Inscriptions on the Church Bells of the East Riding', *Yorkshire Archaeological Journal*, vol. ii (1873)
Bridlington Charty.	W. T. Lancaster, *Abstracts of the Charters and other documents contained in the Chartulary of the Priory of Bridlington* (1912)
Bulmer, *Dir. E. Yorks.* (1892)	T. Bulmer & Co. *History, Topography and Directory of East Yorkshire* (1892)
Char. Com. files	Records held by the Charity Commission at its Northern Office, Liverpool
1801 Crop Returns	School of Economic Studies, University of Leeds, typescript based on the original returns in the Public Record Office (H.O. 76/26), being an appendix to P. A. Churley, 'The Yorkshire Crop Returns of 1801', *Yorkshire Bulletin of Economic and Social Research*, vol. v (1953)
D. & C. York	The Dean and Chapter of York, York Minster Library
E.R.R.O.	East Riding Record Office, County Hall, Beverley
E.Y.C.	Yorkshire Archaeological Society Publications, Extra Series, *Early Yorkshire Charters*, ed. W. Farrer and Sir Charles Clay (1914–65)
Educ. Enquiry Abstract, 1835	*Abstract of Answers and Returns relative to the State of Education in England*, H.C. 62 (1835), xliii
Fasti Parochiales, iii	*Fasti Parochiales, vol. 3, Deanery of Dickering*, ed. N. A. H. Lawrance, Yorkshire Archaeological Society Record Series, vol. cxxix (1967)
G.R.O.	General Register Office, Somerset House
Hodgson, *Q.A.B.*	C. Hodgson, *Queen Anne's Bounty* (1845)
Lawton, *Rer. Eccles. Dioc. Ebor.*	G. Lawton, *Collectio Rerum Ecclesiasticarum de Diocesi Eboracensi* (1840)
Morris, *E. Yorks.*	J. E. Morris, *The East Riding of Yorkshire* (Little Guides, 3rd edn. 1932)
Purvis, *Bridlington Charters, etc.*	J. S. Purvis, *Bridlington Charters, Court Rolls and Papers* (1926)
9th Rep. Char. Com.	*Report of the Commissioners for Inquiry concerning certain Charities in England and Wales*, H.C. 258 (1823), ix
Rep. Com. Eccl. Revenues	*Report of the Commissioners appointed to Inquire into the Ecclesiastical Revenues of England and Wales* [67], H.C. (1835), xxii
3rd Rep. Poor Law Com.	*3rd Annual Report of the Poor Law Commissioners for England and Wales*, H.C. 546 (1837), xxxi
Rets. on Educ. of Poor, 1819	*Digest of Returns to the Select Committee on the Education of the Poor*, H.C. 224 (1819), ix (2)
Rets. rel. Elem. Educ. 1871	*Returns relative to Elementary Education*, H.C. 201 (1871), lv
Sheahan and Whellan, *Hist. York & E.R.*	J. J. Sheahan and T. Whellan, *History and Topography of the City of York, the Ainsty Wapentake, and the East Riding of Yorkshire*, vol. ii, East Riding (1856)

NOTE ON ABBREVIATIONS

T.E.R.A.S.	*Transactions of the East Riding Antiquarian Society*
White, *Dir. E. & N.R. Yorks.* (1840)	W. White, *History, Gazetteer and Directory of the East and North Ridings of Yorkshire* (1840)
White, *Dir. Hull & York* (1846)	F. White & Co. *General Directory of Kingston-upon-Hull and the City of York* (1846)
White, *Dir. Hull & York* (1858)	F. White & Co. *General Directory and Topography of Kingston-upon-Hull and the City of York* (1858)
Y.A.J.	*Yorkshire Archaeological Journal*
Y.A.S., MSS.	Yorkshire Archaeological Society, Leeds, manuscript collection
Yorks. Ch. Plate	Yorkshire Archaeological Society Publications, Extra Series, *Yorkshire Church Plate*, begun by T. M. Fallow, completed and edited by H. B. McCall, vol. i (1912)

Some of the publications of the Yorkshire Archaeological Society in its Record Series are cited by title alone. Two are listed above. Other titles and corresponding Record Series volume-numbers are as follows.

Yorks. Fines, i (vol. ii); ii (vol. v); iii (vol. vii); iv (vol. viii); *1327–47* (vol. xlii); *1347–77* (vol. lii); *1603–14* (vol. liii); *1614–25* (vol. lviii); *1218–31* (vol. lxii); *1232–46* (vol. lxvii); *1246–72* (vol. lxxxii); *1272–1300* (vol. cxxi); *1300–14* (vol. cxxvii)

Yorks. Deeds, i (vol. xxxix); ii (vol. l); iii (vol. lxiii); iv (vol. lxv); v (vol. lxix); vi (vol. lxxvi); vii (vol. lxxxiii); viii (vol. cii); ix (vol. cxi); x (vol. cxx)

Yorks. Inq. (*Inquisitions*), i (vol. xii); ii (vol. xxiii); iii (vol. xxxi); iv (vol. xxxvii); *Hen. IV–V* (vol. lix)

The following publications of the Surtees Society are also cited by title alone.

Test. Ebor. (*Testamenta Eboracensia*), i (vol. iv); ii (vol. xxx); iii (vol. xlv); iv (vol. liii); v (vol. lxxix); vi (vol. cvi)

THE WAPENTAKE OF DICKERING

THE GREATER part of the wapentake lies on the chalk hills of the Yorkshire Wolds at between 200 ft. and 500 ft. above sea-level. Eastwards the chalk reaches the sea in the high cliffs around Flamborough Head. A prominent feature of the Dickering wolds is a wide and deep valley, known as Grindalythe, through which the Gypsey Race flows to the sea at Bridlington. There is little other surface drainage, but the rolling hills are dissected by numerous steep-sided dry valleys. On the north the wolds end in a steep escarpment overlooking the Vale of Pickering, and a narrow strip of the vale lies within the wapentake. Southwards the wolds dip gently towards the Hull Valley and the Plain of Holderness, and the most southerly parishes in the wapentake include large areas of low-lying ground.

On the higher parts of the wolds the chalk lies close to the surface, but the southern slopes and the coastal belt from Filey to Flamborough Head are covered by boulder clay. The low-lying areas north and south of the wolds consist largely of boulder clay, sand, and alluvium. Open-field arable land and extensive sheepwalks occupied much of the wolds until the 18th and early 19th centuries. Parliamentary inclosure and subsequent improvement have produced a landscape of large and regular fields, with isolated farmsteads often protected by shelter-belts of trees. On the low-lying ground there was formerly much marsh, carr, and pasture. On wolds and low ground alike arable farming was predominant in 1971.

In prehistoric times the wolds were extensively settled and frequented, and the Dickering landscape was at one time marked by numerous embankments and barrows. Many of these earthworks have, however, been ploughed down, especially in the present century. By at least the early Bronze Age there was probably a trade route across northern Britain from Ireland to the continent which reached the sea in the Bridlington area.[1] The prehistoric trackways across the wolds may later have been followed by Roman roads. Two branches of the Roman road from York eventually lead to Bridlington, one reaching the coast along the valley of the Gypsey Race, the other, known as Wold Gate, along the ridge south of the Race.[2] Two or three Roman villas have been discovered in the wapentake near these roads.

From the 5th to the 9th century the area was extensively settled by both Anglians and Scandinavians. Most of their villages on the wolds lie in sheltered valleys and hollows, where meres or springs provided a supply of water. Noticeable features of the settlement pattern are a line of villages strung out along the valley of the Gypsey Race, another beneath the northern escarpment, and a third along the southern edge of the wolds. In the low-lying area to the south 'islands' of slightly higher ground provided the sites of most of the settlements. A dozen villages in the wapentake were depopulated during or after the Middle Ages, and several sites remain clearly visible on the ground. Most Dickering villages have been largely rebuilt in brick from the

---

[1] e.g. V. G. Childe, *Prehist. Communities of the Brit. Isles*, 117; *Y.A.J.* xxix. 365.

[2] I. D. Margary, *Roman Roads in Brit.* ii. 153–4; Mary Kitson Clark, *Gaz. of Roman Remains in E. Yorks.* 44–5.

18th century onwards, but much chalk building survives on the wolds and some cobble walling remains near the coast.

Agriculture has been the predominant occupation, but fishing has played a significant part in the economies of a few coastal settlements, and Bridlington Quay, Filey, and Flamborough retained small fishing fleets in 1971. Bridlington for long also enjoyed a flourishing oversea and coastal trade. The only prominent market centres were Kilham, though it has long lost this distinctive function, and the 'Old Town' of Bridlington, which has been submerged by the expansion of the seaside resort at the Quay. In the 19th century Filey, too, was developed as a resort and the growth of both towns was accelerated by the building of the railways linking them with Hull and with the line to York in 1846–7. In the 20th century holiday-making has affected all the coastal parishes.

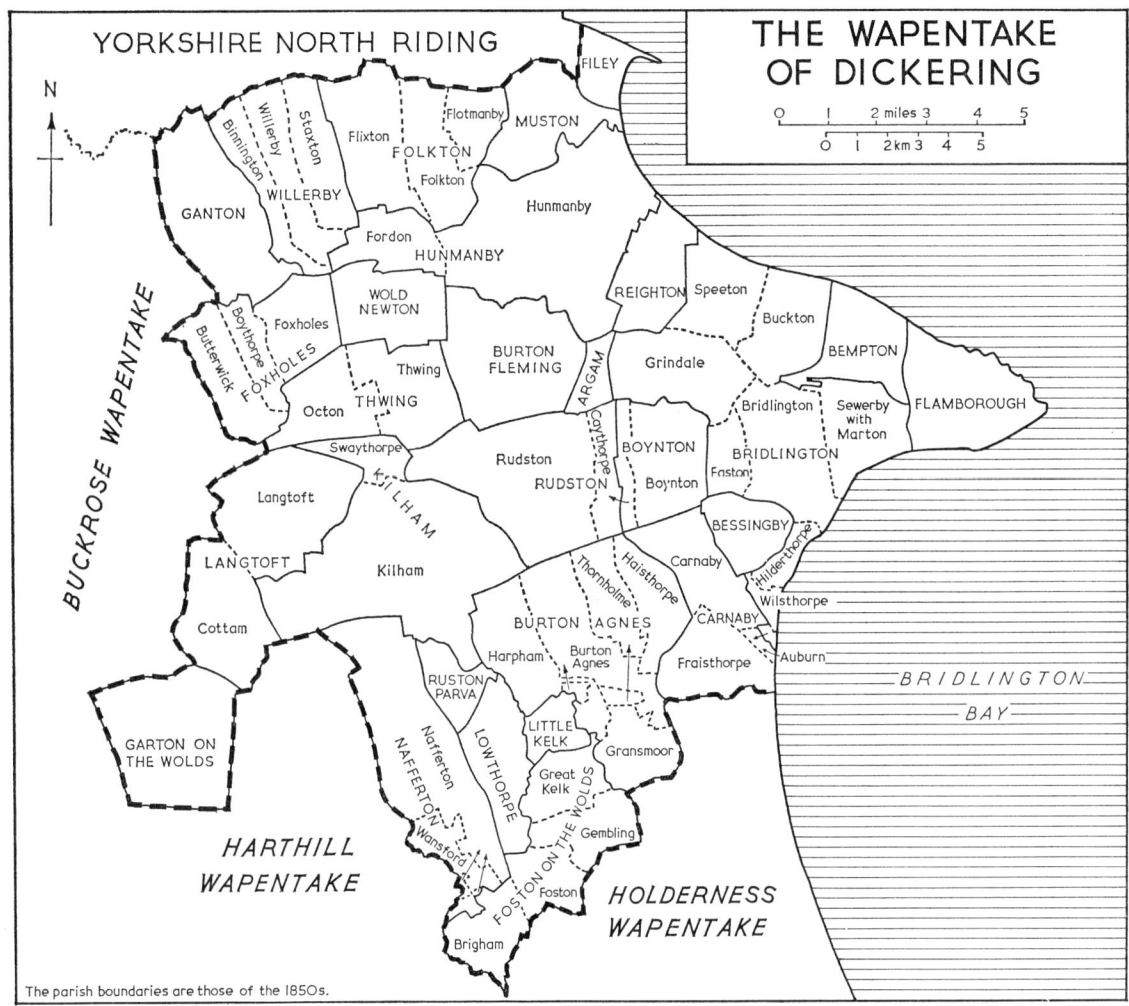

In 1086 the East Riding was the only part of Yorkshire which was divided into hundreds. The transformation of hundreds into wapentakes had already been completed in the other two ridings and was in various stages of completion in the rest of the Danelaw.[3] The change took place in the East Riding during the next 80 years and by the 1160s the 18 Domesday hundreds had been formed into 6 wapentakes.[4] Dickering

[3] I. Taylor, 'Wapentakes and Hundreds', *Domesday Studies*, i. ed. P. E. Dove, 67–76; F. W. Brooks, *Domesday Book and the E.R.* (E. Yorks. Loc. Hist. Ser. xxi), 17; see also *V.C.H. Yorks.* ii. 134.   [4] Brooks, *Domesday Bk. and E.R.* 18.

wapentake, first mentioned in 1166,[5] was broadly coextensive with the three Domesday hundreds of Hunthou, Turbar, and Burton.

Hunthou hundred covered the eastern part of the later wapentake, comprising the townships of Auburn, Bempton, Bessingby, Boynton, Bridlington, Buckton, Easton, Flamborough, Fraisthorpe, Grindale, Hilderthorpe, Marton, Reighton, Sewerby, Speeton, and Wilsthorpe, together with three detached townships in the north-west, Flixton, Foxholes, and Staxton.[6] All these townships subsequently remained in Dickering. The second element in the hundred name derives from 'haugr', meaning 'mound',[7] and the meeting-place may have been in Speeton township, the name of which means 'speech enclosure'.[8] The hundred gave its name to an area of common pasture stretching into several townships[9] and the name still survives in farm names. Huntoudale, mentioned in the late 13th century,[10] forms the boundary between Speeton and Buckton. The mound implied in the name may be the hill in Speeton parish between Huntoudale and the village.[11] Thus it is likely that the township of Speeton took its name from the hundred meeting-place.

Turbar hundred consisted of three separate portions.[12] The largest portion lay in the north of the later wapentake and contained the townships of Argam, Burton Fleming, Flotmanby, Folkton, Fordon, Hunmanby, Muston, and Wold Newton. The larger of the southern portions contained Brigham, Foston, Gembling, Great and Little Kelk, Nafferton, and Pockthorpe, and the smaller Garton and the greater part of Elmswell. In addition three places which were later depopulated, and the exact location of which is not known, Ledemare, Ricstorp, and Scloftone, lay in the northern group,[13] and one, Elestolf, in the southern group.[14] Elmswell, the smaller part of which lay in Driffield hundred in 1086,[15] was assessed in 1316 with St. Mary's liberty, York,[16] and later passed to Harthill wapentake, which had absorbed Driffield hundred. Wansford, not recorded in the Domesday survey, was part of Dickering wapentake by 1284–5.[17] Gembling and Great Kelk belonged wholly to the liberty of St. John, Beverley, in 1086.[18] They were not included in Dickering wapentake for taxation purposes in the Middle Ages, and in 1297 and 1334 both were assessed under the liberty of Beverley.[19] Throughout the Middle Ages they may have owed suit at the provost's court at Beverley[20] rather than at the wapentake court. A Gembling man certainly appeared before the provost's court in 1288–9.[21] Both townships appear in a list of the townships in Dickering wapentake in 1452[22] and were subsequently always reckoned in Dickering. Little Kelk's connexions with the manor of Lissett and the fee of Holderness perhaps explain why it was assessed with Holderness wapentake in 1297 and 1316.[23] Both connexions had ended by 1322,[24] however, and the township was subsequently regarded as part of Dickering. The name of Turbar hundred, which has not survived, derives in part from 'beorg', meaning 'hill',[25] and the meeting-place may have been at Spell Howe, in Flotmanby, the name of which means 'speech-mound'.[26]

---

[5] *Pipe R.* 1166 (P.R.S. ix), 48.   [6] *V.C.H. Yorks.* ii. 322.
[7] *P.N.E.R. Yorks.* (E.P.N.S.), 103.   [8] Ibid. 105.
[9] See pp. 47, 85, 88.
[10] *P.N.E.R. Yorks.* 103.
[11] Ex inf. Mr. H. G. Ramm, Royal Comm. on Historical Monuments, York, 1970.
[12] It has been suggested that this hundred originally formed part of the three surrounding hundreds. The northern block may have come from Hunthou; Brigham, Elmswell, Garton, Nafferton, and Pockthorpe, all within the soke of the manor of Driffield in 1086, from Driffield hundred; and Foston, Gembling, and Kelk from Burton. If that was so the original northern group of East Riding hundreds formed coherent units of almost equal size: ex inf. Mr. Ramm.   [13] See pp. 228, 278.
[14] *V.C.H. Yorks.* ii. 323; see below, p. 181 n.
[15] *V.C.H. Yorks.* ii. 320.   [16] *Feud. Aids*, vi. 204.
[17] Ibid. 31.   [18] *V.C.H. Yorks.* ii. 215.
[19] *Yorks. Lay Subsidy, 1297* (Y.A.S. Rec. Ser. xvi), 153, 156.
[20] The provost of Beverley held extensive rights of jurisdiction over the lands of the liberty: J.I. 1/1110 m. 154.
[21] G. Poulson, *Beverlac*, 585.
[22] E 179/202/127.
[23] *Yorks. Lay Subsidy, 1297*, 130, 132; *Feud. Aids*, vi. 162.
[24] See p. 245.
[25] *P.N.E.R. Yorks.* 86.
[26] Ibid. 116–17.

Burton hundred took its name from its principal township of Burton Agnes. It contained in 1086 the remainder of the townships, mostly in the centre and west, which make up Dickering wapentake. These were Binnington, Boythorpe, Burton Agnes, Butterwick, Carnaby, Caythorpe, Ganton, Gransmoor, Haisthorpe, Harpham, Kilham, Langtoft, Lowthorpe, Octon, Potter Brompton, Rudston, Ruston Parva, Swaythorpe, Thornholme, Thorpe, Thwing, and Willerby, together with 'Fornetorp', later depopulated.[27] Excluded in 1086 were Filey, which then lay in the North Riding, Cottam, then in Toreshou hundred,[28] and Wansford, not recorded in the Survey. All three had become part of Dickering by 1284–5,[29] although Lebberston and Gristhorpe, two townships of Filey, remained in the North Riding. The meeting-place is not known.[30]

The hundreds of Hunthou, Turbar, and Burton were probably grouped around the large manors of Bridlington, Hunmanby, and Burton Agnes respectively. Bridlington had 2 berewicks and soke in 10 townships in Hunthou, Hunmanby had 2 berewicks and soke in 3 townships in Turbar, and Burton Agnes had 3 berewicks and soke in 5 townships in Burton.[31] It seems likely that the detached portions of the hundreds originated in the connexion of certain detached lands with these manors in the pre-Conquest period.

In the Domesday Survey the Yorkshire assessment is given in terms of carucates and bovates and there is much to suggest that the division of lands was according to the carucal or duodecimal system. The assessments of the East Riding hundreds, for example, roughly approximate to 120, 180, or 240 carucates.[32] The hundreds of Hunthou, Turbar, and Burton amounted to 175, 182, and 260 carucates respectively.[33] There is also much evidence to suggest the duodecimal system in the assessments of manors and townships, singly or in relevant groupings. It has, however, been shown that a different, but equally reasonable, arrangement of the figures can often suggest a decimal arrangement.[34] The evidence, therefore, needs to be used with caution.

The wapentake remained in the hands of the Crown until at least the mid 17th century.[35] In 1552[36] and 1567[37] the office of wapentake bailiff, traceable from c. 1220,[38] was granted for life to successive holders, the second of whom was rewarded out of the issues of this and other wapentakes.

Wapentake courts are first recorded in the late 12th century.[39] About 1280 the wapentake met after Michaelmas[40] and in 1303 it was said to meet once a year.[41] The meeting-place is not certainly known but as the wapentake met in 1192 at Burton Fleming and in 1298 at Rudston a place near the boundary of those two townships is probable. The place may well have been the oval-shaped prehistoric earthwork known as Maiden's Grave,[42] which was surrounded by a much larger ditched enclosure into which four tracks originally led.[43] The wapentake name probably derives from the Old English 'dica-hring', meaning 'dike-circle',[44] a name which might be applied to that site. Alternatively, Maiden's Grave is close to the large and prominent Argam Dikes, and 'dike-circle' may mean 'the ring by the dike'. The site lies half-way between the two villages, just within Burton Fleming parish.[45] On at least one occasion, however, in

[27] V.C.H. Yorks. ii. 323; see below, p. 324.
[28] V.C.H. Yorks. ii. 310, 325.
[29] Feud. Aids, vi. 27, 32.
[30] It may have been at Rudston Beacon, near the boundary of Burton Agnes and Rudston, a spot centrally situated in the hundred and at the junction of ancient tracks.
[31] V.C.H. Yorks. ii. 197–8, 272. In most of those places the soke land was not the whole of the township.
[32] V.C.H. Yorks. ii. 135.
[33] Ibid. 189.
[34] H. C. Darby and I. S. Maxwell, Domesday Geog. of N. Eng. 180–2.
[35] E 317/Yorks./6.
[36] Cal. Pat. 1550–3, 295.
[37] Ibid. 1556–9, 82.
[38] B.M. Harl. Chart. 55F. 13.
[39] Bridlington Charty. 102.
[40] J.I. 1/1063 m. 21.
[41] Cal. Inq. p.m. iv, p. 105.
[42] Antiquity, xxxviii. 218.
[43] Ex inf. Mr. Ramm; see below, p. 119.
[44] P.N.E.R. Yorks. 85.
[45] Ex inf. Mr. Ramm. Alternatively it has been suggested that the meeting-place was at Rudston Beacon, where there are earthworks which might have been described as a 'dike-circle': P.N.E.R. Yorks. 85.

1449, the wapentake met at 'le stane' of Rudston, presumably the prehistoric monolith in the churchyard.[46] In 1651 the wapentake court, described as a court baron, met every three weeks.[47]

The payment of each township's share of the wapentake fine was from early times part of the court's business.[48] By the late 13th century, however, about a third of the townships paid nothing and were presumably quit of summons to the wapentake court. Such were Bartindale, Bempton, Bessingby, Buckton, Burton Agnes, Caythorpe, Cottam, Filey, Flamborough, Fordon, Gransmoor, Haisthorpe, Harpham, Hilderthorpe, Kilham, Langtoft, Lowthorpe, Newsham, Ruston Parva, Speeton, Thornholme, Wansford, and Wilsthorpe.[49]

[46] *Cal. Pat.* 1446–52, 306.
[47] E 317/Yorks./6.
[48] *Bridlington Charty.* 204; *Cal. Inq. p.m.* ix, p. 438; x, pp. 16, 23, 34; xi, p. 72.
[49] *Feud. Aids*, vi. 26 sqq.

ARGAM

The small and compact parish of Argam lies on the eastern flank of the valley of the Gypsey Race, some 4 miles north-east of Bridlington.[1] The village, which was probably a Scandinavian settlement,[2] was depopulated in the Middle Ages and only three isolated farm-houses remain. The parish boundary in the north and west follows the bottoms of two dry valleys. The area of the parish is 559 a.[3] The civil parish of Argam was joined to that of Grindale in 1935.[4]

The typically open wolds landscape is relieved only by a few small plantations. The land rises from 125–150 ft. above sea-level in the west to over 250 ft. in the north-east and south-east; between these areas of high ground, another dry valley, in which the village lay, extends across the parish. Argam is crossed by the road from Burton Fleming to Grindale, and other roads lead northwards to Reighton and southwards to Rudston. A field lane forming part of the boundary with Grindale is called Witch Lane.[5] The extensive earthworks marking the site of the village lie close to the prehistoric Argam Dikes, which cross Argam from north to south and formerly stretched for nearly 5 miles between Reighton and Rudston.[6] In the 18th century the banks were known as Old War Dike.[7] The remaining farm-houses, known as Argam or Argam Grange, Finley Hill, and Little Argam, are all 18th- or 19th-century buildings.

The village, which was always small, had been reduced to a single cottage by 1632[8] and there was still only one family in 1743.[9] The population was 21 in 1801 and remained at 20–40 throughout the 19th century.[10] It was 34 in 1931, when a separate figure is last available.[11]

MANOR AND OTHER ESTATES. In 1086 there were two estates in Argam, each of one carucate, belonging to the king and the count of Mortain respectively. The king's land had been held in 1066 by Carle.[12] It was later granted to the Gants and the overlordship descended from them to the Tattershalls.[13] The Mortain estate passed to the Paynels and then the archbishops of Canterbury as overlords, and a mesne lordship was held from them by the Meynells.[14]

Early in the 12th century the Crown estate was apparently held in demesne by a family taking its name from the village. Malger of Argam is mentioned then.[15] By 1284–5 William of Argam held both the Crown and the Canterbury estates.[16] The Argams retained the manor of *ARGAM* until the death of Sir William Argam about 1403, when it passed to his daughter Gillian, wife of John of Aske.[17] In 1428 it was still held by Aske,[18] but in 1432 Sir Thomas Cumberworth, son of Sir William Argam's second daughter Sibyl, was described as 'of Argam'.[19] At the death of Sir Thomas in 1451 Argam passed to his great-nephew Sir Robert Constable, of Flamborough,[20] and descended with Flamborough until the attainder of another Sir Robert Constable in 1537.[21]

In 1538 land in Argam was let by the Crown to John Bell,[22] but the property seems to have been restored soon after to Constable's heirs. In 1549 Robert Constable, Sir Robert's grandson, quitclaimed Argam to John Eglesfield,[23] who had married Anne, Sir Robert's daughter.[24] In 1557 Eglesfield and his wife and William Strickland and his wife Elizabeth quitclaimed the manor to William Edwyn and Bartholomew Abbott.[25]

The manor was subsequently split up. In 1563 Abbott conveyed half of it to William Webster,[26] who held it at his death in 1575, when his son William was aged seven.[27] His widow Anne married John Dixon and in 1592, in the course of a dispute between William Webster the younger and Dixon, she declared that her second husband had assigned her interest in Argam to one Wingate, owner of the Argam fee in Reighton.[28] Argam did not belong to Webster at his death in 1619.[29]

Probably during the 17th century the estate was acquired by the Jarratt family,[30] and in 1719 it belonged to John Jarratt.[31] In 1747 it passed to William Readhead.[32] When John Bell bought it in 1792 it was described as the manor of Argam and comprised 208 a.[33] The Bells retained it until 1873, when Richard Bell sold it, comprising 305 a., to Robert Holtby.[34] In 1919 David Holtby sold it to Abel Marr;[35] it was known by this time as Argam Grange and has remained in the Marr family.

The other half of the manor was itself divided by 1603 into two parts, one of which was in the possession of John Wright of Caythorpe, at his death in 1606.[36] He left it to Peter Paulyn with remainder to Robert Ellis, who died seised of it in 1622.[37] Ellis's son Robert died in 1644 and his estates were sequestrated, but in 1649 his heir, another Robert and then a minor, petitioned against their sale: his title to Argam was, he said, 'drawn in question by one Paulyn'.[38] At the death of Robert Ellis, apparently in

---

[1] This article was written in 1970.
[2] *P.N.E.R. Yorks.* (E.P.N.S.), pp. xxiv, 108.
[3] O.S. Map 6" (1854).
[4] *Census*, 1931.
[5] O.S. Map 6" (1854).
[6] *V.C.H. Yorks.* ii. 60; O.S. Map 6" (1854); see plate facing p. 32.
[7] Registry of Deeds, Beverley, BC/596/931.
[8] B.I.H.R., C.P., H. 1885, 1921.
[9] *Herring's Visit.* i. 193.
[10] *V.C.H. Yorks.* iii. 488.
[11] *Census.*
[12] *V.C.H. Yorks.* ii. 204, 226, 323.
[13] *Cal. Inq. p.m.* iv, p. 108; *Cal. Close*, 1307–13, 101; *Feud. Aids*, vi. 28, 141, 211, 228, 265–6.
[14] *Cal. Inq. p.m.* iii, p. 428; *Feud. Aids*, vi. 28.
[15] *Bridlington Charty.* 12.
[16] *Feud. Aids*, vi. 28.
[17] C.P. 25(1)/279/149 nos. 21, 49.
[18] C.P. 40/622 m. 218d.; E 179/202/104; *Feud. Aids*, vi. 265–6.
[19] B.M. Lansd. MS. 207c, f. 230; *Cal. Pat.* 1429–36, 275.
[20] C 139/143/29.
[21] See p. 154.
[22] *L. & P. Hen. VIII*, xiii (1), p. 140.
[23] *Yorks. Fines*, i. 141.
[24] W. Flower, *Visit. Yorks.* (Harl. Soc. xvi), 107.
[25] *Yorks. Fines*, i. 209.
[26] Ibid. 282.
[27] C 142/177/57.
[28] E 134/34 Eliz. Hil./16.
[29] C 142/373/37.
[30] P.C.C. 277 Berkley.
[31] Registry of Deeds, Beverley, F/334/720.
[32] Ibid. S/446/1100.
[33] Ibid. BR/196/320.
[34] Ibid. LC/122/162.
[35] Ibid. 195/436/386.
[36] C 145/669/19.
[37] C 142/393/144; /775/48; C 60/531 no. 45.
[38] *Royalist Composition Papers*, iii (Y.A.S. Rec. Ser. xx), 71.

1712, the estate was left to his wife for her lifetime and then to his daughters Margaret, Elizabeth, and Mary.[39] Margaret and her husband William Dent sold their share to Matthew Noble, Elizabeth's husband, in 1735.[40] This two-thirds of the estate passed to the Nobles' daughter Elizabeth, who married John Greenhill, and in 1767 they conveyed it to Richard Jordan.[41] John Greame acquired it in 1828 from William Jordan; it was then called Grindale or Finley Argam and comprised 132 a.[42] The Greames and Lloyd Greames retained it until 1952, when the 155-acre Finley Hill farm was sold to Ernest and Alfred Sellers.[43] Robert Ellis's third daughter married Robert Fulthorpe, and in 1737 they sold their share of the estate to Willey Reveley.[44] It may have subsequently passed to John Greame, who already held land in Argam by 1799.[45]

The remaining portion of the manor belonged in 1603 to Thomas Pearson, who devised it that year to his daughter Anne, who married Robert Knowsley of Burton Fleming.[46] Knowsley apparently died in 1638 and the estate passed to his daughter Elizabeth, wife of Charles Stutville.[47] By 1722 another Charles Stutville had been succeeded by his sister Jane, who married John Close; their daughter Jane married Thomas Grimston and the Argam estate thus passed to the Grimstons. It comprised about 150 a. in 1711.[48] Thomas Grimston sold the greater part of the estate, comprising 97 a., to John Farthing in 1804.[49] Farthing died in 1822, leaving Argam to his daughter Franky, wife of James Hopkinson. In 1855 she sold it, described as Little Argam, to Robert Carrick and in 1880 John Carrick sold it to Richard Holtby.[50] After Holtby's death in 1896 the estate was held by trustees, including Richard Holtby Stocks (d. 1928); it passed to Richard Stocks and others in 1930 and was sold to John Reed in 1941.[51]

Lands and tithes belonging to Argam church were apparently seized by the Crown at the time of the dissolution of the chantries.[52] The tithes are said to have been granted to Percival Gunson in 1572–1573,[53] and the 'chapel of Argam', with the 4-acre Parson's close, 10 a. in Burton Fleming, and 100 a. in Rudston, were granted to Anthony Collins and Henry Mapleton in 1585 and to Thomas Pearson and James Fletcher in 1634.[54] In 1632 the rectorial estate was said to be worth £40.[55] In the 18th and 19th centuries Parsonage close, of c. 20 a., belonged to the Readheads and the Bells,[56] and the close may have been part of the 35 a. of glebe that were said to exist in the 19th and 20th centuries.[57]

ECONOMIC HISTORY. The king's estate was said in 1086 to belong to Burton Fleming[58] and it was perhaps used as a grazing ground attached to that manor, for the name means 'at the shielings'.[59] After being assessed jointly with Bartindale, Argam does not appear in taxation records after the 15th century.[60] The period and cause of its depopulation are not known.

Closes called North field and South field in 1538[61] may possibly indicate the former existence of open fields. Only a shepherd lived at the site in 1632.[62] All the land lay in closes in the 18th century. In 1780 William Readhead's estate included swarth land, then used as a sheep-walk.[63] The Stutville estate in 1711 included a pasture close of about 120 a. called the Outgrounds,[64] and the Grimstons used at least part of this estate as a rabbit warren in 1755–8.[65] There have usually been 3 farmers in the 19th and 20th centuries.[66]

A windmill is mentioned in the mid 16th century.[67]

LOCAL GOVERNMENT. No manorial records and no parochial records before 1835 are known. Argam joined the Bridlington union in 1836.[68]

CHURCH. When Walter de Gant granted to Bardney abbey the church of Hunmanby and its dependent chapels in 1115, he included in the gift a carucate of land in Argam, where he intended to found a chapel.[69] Probably c. 1180–90 Ralph, abbot of Bardney, granted the chapel, with the tithes from a carucate belonging to Malger of Argam, to Malger's son William, in return for a pension of 10s. a year.[70] William subsequently resigned the chapel into the hands of his grandfather, then abbot of Bardney. In 1257 another William of Argam presented his son Thomas to the chapel and his right to do so was upheld against a claim by the abbey.[71] About 1269 a vicarage was ordained, the vicar being assigned the tithes of sheaves and small tithes, subject to the payment of the abbey's pension.[72] The ordination apparently did not take effect, however, and the living was later generally regarded as a rectory. The church had been demolished by 1632.[73] In 1870 the rectory was united with the curacy of Sewerby with Marton and Grindale.[74] The benefice of Argam and Grindale was in 1958 transferred to Rudston, and in 1963 all three were united with Boynton.[75] In 1970, however, Argam

---

[39] Regy. of Deeds, A/659/939.
[40] Ibid. O/232/574.
[41] Ibid. AI/139/285.
[42] Ibid. ED/149/170.
[43] Ibid. 910/461/394.
[44] Ibid. O/438/1081.
[45] E.R.R.O. Land Tax 1799.
[46] C 142/310/77.
[47] P.C.C. 273 Aylett (will of Anne Knowsley); *Regs. of Burton Fleming 1538–1812*, ed. G. E. Park and G. D. Lumb (Yorks. Par. Reg. Soc. ii), 30.
[48] Regy. of Deeds, A/619/882; H/329/682.
[49] Ibid. CG/290/460.
[50] Ibid. DM/240/281; /393/470; HI/231/278; NA/108/170.
[51] Ibid. 84/143/142 (1896); 95/382/353 (1897); 370/147/116; 408/361/283; 646/457/383.
[52] See p. 8.
[53] H. Grove, *Alienated Tithes*, p. cxxxii.
[54] C 66/1263 m. 1; C 66/2649 no. 4.
[55] B.I.H.R., C.P., H. 1885, 1921.
[56] Regy. of Deeds, BC/596/931; LC/122/162.
[57] Directories.
[58] *V.C.H. Yorks.* ii. 204.
[59] *P.N.E.R. Yorks.* 108.
[60] E 179/202/127.
[61] *L. & P. Hen. VIII*, xiii (1), p. 140.
[62] B.I.H.R., C.P., H. 1885, 1921.
[63] Regy. of Deeds, BC/596/931.
[64] Ibid. A/619/882.
[65] E.R.R.O., DDGR/42/5, 8, 11, 13, 15; /43/2.
[66] Directories.
[67] S.C. 6/Hen. VIII/4324; *Yorks. Fines*, i. 141, 209.
[68] *3rd Rep. Poor Law Com.* 167.
[69] B.M. Cott. MS. Vesp. E. xx, f. 54b; Dugdale, *Mon.* i. 628–9.
[70] B.M. Cott. MS. Vesp. E. xx, f. 195.
[71] Ibid. ff. 195–195d.
[72] *Reg. Giffard* (Sur. Soc. cix), 56.
[73] See below.
[74] York Dioc. Regy., Orders in Council 292.
[75] Ibid. 747, 781.

and Grindale were made a separate living, to be held in plurality with Burton Fleming.[76]

The advowson descended with the manor, the Argam family presenting until 1349, John of Aske in 1390 and 1425, Sir Thomas Cumberworth in 1433, and the Constables between 1497 and 1543.[77] Like the manor the advowson was then divided into three. Thus half of it was conveyed by Bartholomew Abbott to William Webster in 1563,[78] and Webster, Robert Ellis, and Robert Knowsley were the patrons in 1606.[79] John Gregory, of Hull, is recorded as patron in 1585–7;[80] he has not been traced as a landowner in the parish, and this is also the case with John Fletcher and George Jackson, who with Knowsley were named as patrons in 1632.[81] Charles Stutville held the advowson in 1700,[82] and by 1812 it had descended to Thomas Grimston; the Grimstons kept it until at least 1857.[83] In 1870, however, it passed to the Lloyd Greames, the patrons of Sewerby with Marton and Grindale.[84]

The church was valued at £4 13s. 4d. in 1291, reduced to £3 6s. 8d. in the new taxation.[85] In 1438 Sir Thomas Cumberworth, the patron, was licensed to grant the rector, in order to augment his income, £2 rent in Huttoft and Clixby (Lincs.), a house, a toft, and 80 a. of land in Rudston and Burton Fleming, and £1 10s. rent in Flixton.[86] The church was worth £4 in 1535.[87] The church and its appurtenant lands were apparently deemed at the time of the dissolution of the chantries to be a chantry and were alienated from the rectory. Nevertheless the rector was paid a stipend, amounting to a fifteenth of the estimated value of the rectory, by the lay rector in 1632,[88] and this continued to be the case in the 18th century.[89] The stipend was subsequently redeemed for £80.[90] The living was augmented with £200 from Queen Anne's Bounty in both 1714 and 1749.[91] In 1829–31 the average net income was £21.[92] When Argam and Grindale were made a separate living in 1970, £100 was allocated from the income of Rudston and £100 from Burton Fleming.[93] Sir Marmaduke Constable (d. 1520) assigned a 20-acre close to the rector,[94] but it was subsequently held by the lay rectors.[95]

The village being depopulated and the church destroyed, institution to the living was said in 1632 to have been by cutting sods on the supposed site of the church and presenting them to the incumbent; the then rector's predecessor had read prayers at the site.[96] The archbishop left it to the rector's choice whether he should preach one sermon a year in the fields, and the incumbent in 1743 said that he had chosen to do so; he also held the livings of Burton Agnes and Barmston.[97] The rector in 1835 also held Farlington with Marton (Yorks. N.R.), Warter, and South Cave.[98]

The church was dedicated to St. John the Baptist; its site is not known.

NONCONFORMITY. None known.

EDUCATION. No evidence.

CHARITIES FOR THE POOR. None known.

BEMPTON

THE parish of Bempton, roughly square in shape, lies on the coast about 3 miles north-west of Flamborough Head.[1] It is situated entirely on the wolds, which end at the sea in high chalk cliffs. Both Bempton and its hamlet of Newsham were probably Anglian settlements.[2] The village lies about a mile from the sea, and the site of Newsham, which has been depopulated, adjoins it to the south. A field near by was known as Old Walls in 1841,[3] and earthworks marking the site of the hamlet include a prominent hollow way.

In the south-west the parish boundary follows the line of what seem to be several former open-field strips, with the result that a long narrow area of Sewerby township protruded into Newsham field. In the south-east of the parish the boundary is formed for about ¾ mile by an unnamed stream which rises near the village. The stream may have also formed part, at least, of the boundary between Bempton and Newsham. The eastern boundary with Flamborough is formed by the prehistoric Danes' Dyke.[4] The area of the ancient parish is 1,970 a. Since 1935 Bempton has been combined with Buckton, together with 671 a. from Sewerby parish, as the civil parish of Bempton.[5]

The landscape of Bempton is typical of the wolds, with large arable fields extending up the almost treeless slopes. Several of the fields towards the sea are divided by earth banks. The main area of woodland is Dykes plantation, which runs for over ½ mile along Danes' Dyke, and there are smaller areas north of the village. Most of the parish lies at over 200 ft. above sea-level and in the south-west the land rises to over 300 ft. East of the village it falls to

---

[76] Ex inf. Revd. Dr. W. B. Johnston, Burton Fleming, 1970.
[77] *Fasti Parochiales*, iii. 2–3.
[78] *Yorks. Fines*, i. 282.
[79] 'Kindersley' is presumably an error for Knowsley here: *Fasti Parochiales*, iii. 3.
[80] Ibid.
[81] B.I.H.R., C.P., H. 1885, 1921.
[82] Registry of Deeds, Beverley, A/619/882.
[83] P.R.O. Inst. Bks.; E.R.R.O., DDGR/42/11, 13; /43/30.
[84] *York. Dioc. Cal.*
[85] *Tax. Eccl.* (Rec. Com.), 326.
[86] *Cal. Pat.* 1436–41, 17, 231.
[87] *Valor Eccl.* (Rec. Com.), v. 124.
[88] B.I.H.R., C.P., H. 1885, 1921.
[89] Ibid. TER. J. Argam, 1726, 1743; *Herring's Visit.* i. 193.
[90] H. Grove, *Alienated Tithes*, 647.
[91] Hodgson, *Q.A.B.* 438.
[92] *Rep. Com. Eccl. Revenues*, 932–3.
[93] Ex inf. Revd. Dr. Johnston, 1970.
[94] *Test. Ebor.* v. 90.
[95] See p. 7.
[96] B.I.H.R., C.P., H. 1885, 1921.
[97] *Herring's Visit.* i. 193.
[98] *Rep. Com. Eccl. Revenues*, 932–3.
[1] This article was written in 1969.
[2] *P.N.E.R. Yorks.* (E.P.N.S.), 106–7.
[3] *Y.A.J.* xxxviii. 65.
[4] See p. 151.
[5] *Census*, 1931.

under 175 ft. along the stream, and the village itself lies around the 225-foot contour. Further north the ground rises to over 350 ft. at Standard hill, and at the sea the chalk cliffs are mainly between 275 ft. and 300 ft. in height; in the extreme north-west they are over 325 ft.

These spectacular cliffs are the most notable feature of Bempton's landscape, forming part of a long stretch of chalk cliffs extending from Flamborough Head to Speeton. They hold one of the largest sea-bird colonies on the mainland of Britain. Razorbills, kittiwakes, and particularly guillemots are the most numerous species, but a wide variety of birds, many of them uncommon, nest on and around the cliffs.[6] In the early 20th century the road from Bempton village to the cliffs was said to be 'traversed by ornithologists from all over the country'.[7]

Fowling rights on the cliffs were held in the 16th century by William Strickland,[8] and in the 17th and 18th centuries by the trustees of the Ringley charity, by whom they were lost in the early 19th century owing to an error in copying an earlier deed.[9] In the 19th century the right to gather eggs from the cliffs from Speeton to Flamborough belonged to the farmers tenanting the adjacent lands, and they conceded this privilege to the men who worked for them.[10] The procedure of collecting eggs by descending the cliffs on a rope was known as 'climming' and it became a minor local industry and tourist attraction in the 19th and earlier 20th centuries. Climming was carefully organized and regulated. The participants were formed into gangs, each of which had its own area of cliff. About 1825–1830 there were four gangs, one of which worked Bempton cliffs, but c. 1850, when the industry was suffering from the depredations of tourists shooting birds in large numbers, there were only two gangs for the whole of the cliffs. This large-scale destruction, which led to a great diminution in the numbers of several species of birds on the cliffs, was a main cause of the passing of the Sea Birds Preservation Act of 1869.[11] By 1906 there were again four gangs, each then consisting of four men — the 'climmer' and three 'top men' to manage the ropes. There was a strict season for climming, from mid May to early July, and certain parts of the cliffs were left untouched to ensure a permanent supply of new birds. The average daily take of each gang at the beginning of the 20th century was 300–400 eggs. The eggs were mainly sold locally for food, or sent to the West Riding for use in the manufacture of patent leather. Well-marked eggs, however, were sold to collectors. In 1834 eggs were sold for 6d. a score, but by 1906 the price had risen to 1s. for 12–16 eggs. Good specimens in the latter year fetched up to 7s. 6d. or more each.[12] Climming declined after the Second World War and was finally made illegal in 1954.[13]

A stream rises south of the village, at what was known in the 19th century as the Lambing spring,[14] and flows eastwards across the south of the parish. A small pond, known as the Mere, was artificially created on the village green in the later 19th century. It was formerly used for washing sheep.[15]

In the more westerly of the two fields which form the site of the former village of Newsham lies the gravestone of Henry Jarratt (d. 1721), who was said to have committed suicide and been refused burial in consecrated ground.[16]

The village stands around the junction of two roads and a number of back lanes, which form a complicated street pattern. The Speeton–Flamborough road forms the main village street, known as High Street. It is crossed by the road from Sewerby to Bempton cliffs, sections of which are known as Newsham Hill as it enters the parish, Forty Foot Lane south of the village green, Church Lane and Shop Hill Lane in the village itself, Scarsea Gate as it leaves the village northwards, and Cliff Lane as it nears the sea. The triangular village green lies near the church at the southern end of the village. Gillus Lane, leading from the north end of the green to High Street, may have taken its name from a guild-house.[17] A lane known as Back Side leads from the western end of High Street around the northern side of the village, rejoining the Flamborough road further east. One section of this lane is known as the Jawbones. Poor People's Lane leads off the north side of High Street, and Bolam Lane, known as 'le Burlyn' and 'le Bolryn' in the early 14th century,[18] leads south from High Street to Bempton mill. Two minor roads north of the village are Blakehowe and Stonepit Lanes. The railway line from Filey to Bridlington, opened in 1847, cuts across the south-west corner of the parish and there is a station there.

The buildings in the village are mainly of the 18th to the 20th century. The chief material is brick, but there is much patching with chalk and cobbles and several outbuildings are entirely of these materials. Several houses in High Street are chalk-built with brick fronts. Opposite the church is an 18th-century brick house with tucked gables, and 18th- and earlier-19th-century houses stand by the green. A row of three-storeyed brick cottages of a storey and a half, dated 1724, with a dentil brick eaves course, stands near the Flamborough road in the east of the village. The most substantial dwelling is Bempton House, a building of c. 1840, on the corner of Poor People's Lane and High Street, and Coverley House, at the west end of High Street, is also of the earlier 19th century.

Modern development, including many bungalows and shacks, has taken place in the north, east, and west of the village. There are a dozen Council houses in the Jawbones and Back Side. Bempton has also been extended westwards by modern housing along the road to Buckton, although the two villages are still physically separate. An innkeeper was mentioned in 1558,[19] and since at least 1823 there has been one inn, the White Horse.[20] A Royal Air Force camp to

---

[6] T. H. Nelson, *Birds of Yorks.* i, p. xxix; ii. 689–90, 711 sqq.; *Hull Daily Mail*, 4 Feb. 1970; *V.C.H. Yorks.* i. 348 etc.
[7] Nelson, op. cit. i. 114.
[8] E 164/38 f. 237.
[9] E.R.R.O., DDX/25/9; see below, p. 12.
[10] For details see Nelson, *Birds of Yorks.* ii. 712–18; S. Leng, *Experiences and Reminiscences of a Cliff Climber*.
[11] 32 & 33 Vic., c. 17.
[12] Nelson, op. cit. ii. 713–14, 717, 719; see also Hull Scientific and Field Naturalists Club, *Trans.* iii. 1–26; *Yorks. Notes & Queries*, v. 64.
[13] Protection of Birds Act, 2 & 3 Eliz. II, c. 30.
[14] O.S. Map 6" (1853).
[15] E. H. Rudkin, *Bempton cum Newsholme cum Buckton*, 40; O.S. Map 6" (1853 and subsequent edns.).
[16] *T.E.R.A.S.* vi. 25.   [17] See p. 14.
[18] *P.N.E.R. Yorks.* (E.P.N.S.), 107.
[19] *Wills in the York Regy. 1554–1568* (Y.A.S. Rec. Ser. xiv), 153.   [20] Directories.

the north of the village was built in 1940 and used until 1967.[21]

There are five isolated farm-houses in the parish, Bempton Grange, Wandale, Metlands, Butterwicks, and Newsham Farms, all of which probably originated after the late-18th-century inclosure. The sail-less tower of a windmill, probably of the early 19th century, stands near Newsham Farm. In 1829 an 'old beacon' apparently stood on or near Standard hill.[22]

Bempton was rarely separately assessed to taxes and Newsham never. In 1377, together with Buckton, Bempton had 187 poll-tax payers,[23] and in 1670, again with Buckton, it had 81 households. Of the latter, 40 were discharged from payment of the hearth tax. In 1674 the number of those discharged is not given, but of the 41 chargeable households 27 had only one hearth each, 9 had 2, 2 had 3, one had 4, one had 6, and one had seven.[24] In 1743 there were 50 families in Bempton alone,[25] and in 1764 about 40.[26] The population in 1801 was 222 and it gradually increased to 346 by 1861. By 1901 it had declined to 284.[27] In 1931 the population was 298.[28]

MANORS AND OTHER ESTATES. Only one estate was recorded in the entry for Bempton in Domesday Book, a manor of 6 carucates held in 1066 by Ligulf and in 1086 by the count of Mortain. The hamlet of Newsham was not mentioned, but together with the remainder of the land of Bempton it was included in the entry for Buckton. In 1086 the king held 5 carucates and 6 bovates in Buckton, the count of Mortain 3 carucates and 6 bovates, and Hugh, earl of Chester, 2½ carucates. Thus in 1086 there was a total of 18 carucates in the three townships.[29] In 1284–5 there were assigned to the same three townships 9 carucates of the Canterbury fee, 5 carucates of the Brus fee, 6 carucates of the Gant fee, 1½ carucate of the honor of Chester, and 2½ carucates of the endowment of Bempton church — a total of 24 carucates. This suggests that 6 carucates of the Gant fee in Bempton were omitted from the Domesday Survey.[30]

The lands of the count of Mortain passed, like those at Boynton,[31] to the Paynels and later to the archbishops of Canterbury, whose overlordship is last mentioned in 1428.[32] Similarly the Meynells held a mesne lordship under the Paynels and the archbishops until at least the early 14th century.[33] In 1299 Nicholas de Meynell held 5 carucates of the Canterbury fee in Bempton and 2 carucates in Newsham.[34]

The capital manor of *BEMPTON* seems to have originated in land held of the Canterbury fee by the Buckton family in the 13th century. William of Buckton held land there in 1251,[35] and in 1299 Walter of Buckton held 5 carucates in Bempton of Nicholas de Meynell.[36] William of Buckton was returned in 1316 as lord of both Buckton and Bempton.[37] In the early 14th century Walter held 9 bovates and William 6 bovates of the Canterbury fee in Bempton.

Arnold, the son of Walter of Buckton, had died by 1341[38] and five years later his son Walter held 17 bovates of the Canterbury and Brus fees.[39] Peter Buckton received a grant of free warren in his manor of Bempton in 1400.[40] During the following century the Buckton family's holding in Bempton seems to have greatly decreased. At his death in 1530 William Buckton held only 4 bovates there, still of the Meynell fee.[41] William's daughter Ursula married John Collingwood[42] and their son Sir Cuthbert Collingwood in the later 16th century was said to hold Bempton manor.[43] Robert Collingwood, Cuthbert's grandson, in 1614–15 sold property in Bempton to Robert Robinson,[44] and in 1617 Collingwood sold what was presumably the remainder of his property there to Sir Thomas Blakiston.[45] The latter sold it in the same year to Henry Robinson, who had obtained Robert Robinson's land in Bempton in 1616.[46] After 1600 the property was not described as a manor. At inclosure in 1767 John Robinson, of Buckton, received an allotment of 32 a.[47] The land subsequently descended with Buckton manor[48] in the Robinson, and later the Foulis, families until 1869 when, following the death of Mark Robinson Foulis, it was sold to G. R. Wrangham.[49] It was resold in two lots the same year.[50]

A second manor of *BEMPTON* may have originated in the 14 bovates held of the Canterbury fee in the early 14th century by Ingram of Boynton.[51] It is possible that it had passed by the mid 14th century to the Sewerby family. In 1377 John Sewerby held 4½ carucates.[52] By 1428 part, at least, may have passed to Robert Hatfield, who then held 18 bovates.[53] The land descended in the Hatfield family, lords of the manor of Hatfield, in Holderness, until the early 16th century, when it passed to William, son of Sir Marmaduke Constable, of Flamborough, on William's marriage with Maud (d. 1560), daughter of John Hatfield.[54] In 1581 the manor, by then consisting of only about 8 bovates, was sold either by John Constable of Hatfield or his brother William to Christopher Maltby,[55] whose grandson, another Christopher, sold it in 1613 to Robert Robinson.[56] It had probably passed by 1648

---

[21] Ex inf. Ministry of Defence, 1970.
[22] J. Phillips, *Illustrations of Geol. of Yorks.* i [p. 197].
[23] E 179/202/62 m. 21.
[24] E 179/205/514, 521.
[25] *Herring's Visit.* i. 114.
[26] B.I.H.R., Bp. V. 1764/Ret. 53.
[27] *V.C.H. Yorks.* iii. 488.
[28] *Census*, 1931.
[29] *V.C.H. Yorks.* ii. 226, 322 and n.
[30] *Feud. Aids*, vi. 29.
[31] See p. 22.
[32] *Feud. Aids*, vi. 265.
[33] B.M. Add. MS. 26729, f. 112.
[34] *Cal. Inq. p.m.* iii, p. 428.
[35] K.B. 26/145 m. 35d.
[36] *Cal. Inq. p.m.* iii, p. 428.
[37] Ibid.; *Feud. Aids*, vi. 170.
[38] *Cal. Inq. p.m.* viii, p. 223.
[39] *Feud. Aids*, vi. 229.
[40] *Cal. Chart. R.* 1341–1417, 408.
[41] C 142/52/92.
[42] W. Flower, *Visit. Yorks.* (Harl. Soc. xvi), 41–2.
[43] C 142/263/27, 50.
[44] *Yorks. Fines, 1614–25*, 25.
[45] Ibid. 75.
[46] Ibid. 41, 75.
[47] Registry of Deeds, Beverley, AK/2/2.
[48] See p. 83.
[49] Regy. of Deeds, HC/272/274; KL/222/299; /235/312.
[50] Ibid. KL/261/345; KM/244/318.
[51] B.M. Add. MS. 26729, f. 112.
[52] E.R.R.O., DDLG/42/3.
[53] *Feud. Aids*, vi. 265.
[54] Poulson, *Hist. Holderness*, i. 442.
[55] E 134/37 & 38 Eliz. Mich./30; *Yorks. Fines*, ii. 175.
[56] *Yorks. Fines, 1603–14*, 221.

to John Jarratt, who died in that year possessed of lands in Bempton,[57] and in 1686 Henry Jarratt held the manor there.[58] In 1750 John Jarratt held it, including a manor-house and 12 bovates,[59] and at inclosure in 1767 his daughter Betty Jarratt was awarded about 200 a.[60] In 1774 she married Henry Broadley[61] and the property descended in the Broadley family until 1833, when the manor-house and 140 a. were conveyed by the devisees of John Broadley to Samuel Coverley.[62] In 1847 the manor passed to Anne Champion, one of Samuel's two coheirs,[63] and it descended in the Champion family until 1905. Maud Champion then vested the property, consisting of 164 a., in trustees[64] who seem to have dispersed it by the early 1920s.[65]

Other land in Bempton, which followed the descent of Caythorpe manor, seems to have been held in the 15th century by the Argam family, from whom it had descended by 1504 to Thomas Fairfax.[66] John Constable died possessed of this land in 1542,[67] and it apparently then passed to Sir Robert Constable, of Flamborough, as BEMPTON was included in a list of manors forfeited by him in 1537.[68] Two years later the manor was held of William Constable, of Caythorpe, by Ralph Ellerker.[69]

About 1570 Constable sold it to William Webster, whose son, another William, was involved in a dispute over his manorial rights in 1594–5 during which it was stated by several deponents that although in the past courts had been held by Ralph Ellerker and the plaintiff's father there was not and never had been a manor. Land called 'Forty Oxgang' in Bempton was, however, said to be subject to the manor of Caythorpe, and to have paid a 'free rent' to its lord.[70] The land was nevertheless still called a manor in 1608, when William Webster obtained a quitclaim from William Constable.[71] On his death in 1619 Webster's property in Bempton included 12 bovates and over 200 a. of land.[72] His son, another William, sold the property, still described as a manor, to Thomas Hardwick and Francis Perkins in 1632.[73]

By 1724 some at least of this land seems to have come into the possession of Henry Tymperon, part of whose estate then consisted of 5 bovates in 'the Forty Oxgang Fall'. It passed in that year to Henry Maister by marriage with Tymperon's daughter Mary.[74] At inclosure in 1767 Henry Maister received an allotment of 309 a., the largest awarded.[75] This estate descended to Arthur Maister, who in 1813 sold it in several lots, of which the largest, about 200 a., was bought by John Dawson.[76]

An estate in Bempton, which may be identified with that of 5 carucates and 6 bovates described under Buckton in 1086, when it was in the king's hands,[77] had passed to the Brus fee by the early 12th century.[78] In 1284–5 and 1302–3 it consisted of 5 carucates but in 1428, when the Brus overlordship is last mentioned, it consisted of only 10 bovates.[79] The Mauley family held a mesne lordship of this land by the mid 13th century. On the death of Roger de Mauley in 1265 his heirs were his three daughters.[80] The eldest married William de Graystoke, and her share in the lordship descended to William, Lord Dacre of Graystoke, who held 2 bovates in Bempton in 1563.[81] His son Francis Dacre sold his property there to Anne, countess of Arundel, Lord William Howard, and others.[82] Howard's grandson, William Howard, died possessed of it in 1644.[83] Roger de Mauley's second daughter had married Robert de Somervile by 1272,[84] and in the earlier 14th century the Somerviles held 14 bovates in Bempton.[85] The descent has not been traced further. The third daughter married Robert of Thwing, and in 1268 he held 6 bovates in Bempton.[86] In 1346 Thomas Thwing held land of the Brus fee there and in 1374 he, or another Thomas Thwing, held land there of Marmaduke Lumley.[87] The lordship seems to have subsequently descended in the Lumley family, and in 1396 Elizabeth, one of the coheirs of Thomas Thwing, quitclaimed the Bempton holding to Ralph Lumley, who held it at his death in 1400.[88] The descent has not been traced further.

The Brus fee seems never to have been organized as a manor, and the land was generally held by various small tenants, particularly after the 13th century. In the 12th century, however, Morcar seems to have held a substantial part of the fee,[89] as did William of Rudston in the 13th century.[90] In 1428 the 10 bovates of the Brus fee were held by three small tenants.[91]

Land in Bempton apparently omitted from the Survey in 1086 passed to the Gant fee and later to the Tattershalls. In 1284–5 6 carucates in Bempton, Buckton, and Newsham were held of the Gant fee[92] and in 1346 two estates in Bempton, of 3 carucates and 5 bovates and 1½ carucate, were held of the Tattershalls.[93]

The Grindale family held land in Bempton of this fee in the early 13th century,[94] and in 1346 Sir

[57] Cat. Yorks. Wills at Somerset Ho. 1649–60 (Y.A.S. Rec. Ser. i), 145.
[58] C.P. 43/414 rot. 35.
[59] E.R.R.O., DDHO/43/11; DDX/31/537.
[60] Regy. of Deeds, AK/2/2.
[61] E.R.R.O., DDX/31/543.
[62] Regy. of Deeds, ET/225/263.
[63] Ibid. GG/92/115.
[64] Ibid. 218/117/102.
[65] Ibid. 229/4/4; /7/7; /182/162; 230/56/48; 231/151/123; 232/445/370.
[66] B.M. Add. MS. 26737, f. 60; Flower, Visit. Yorks. 117; Y.A.J. xix. 185; see below, p. 313.
[67] C 142/65/79.
[68] T.E.R.A.S. viii. 66–7.
[69] C 142/61/57.
[70] E 134/37 & 38 Eliz. Mich./30.
[71] Yorks. Fines, 1603–14, 83.
[72] C 142/373/37.
[73] C.P. 25(2)/521/8 Chas. I Trin. pt 2, no. 13.
[74] E.R.R.O., DDLG/2/20.
[75] Regy. of Deeds, AK/2/2.
[76] Ibid. CU/409/458; /447/518; /576/706; /577/707; CW/360/525.
[77] V.C.H. Yorks. ii. 322 and n.
[78] Bridlington Charty. 1.
[79] Feud. Aids, vi. 29, 141, 266.
[80] E.Y.C. ii, p. 36.
[81] Castle Howard MSS., Box 24, Survey of Estates, 1563.
[82] Yorks. Fines, 1603–14, 73, 91.
[83] C 142/774/15.
[84] E.Y.C. ii, p. 36.
[85] B.M. Add. MS. 26729, f. 116; Abbrev. Rot. Orig. (Rec. Com.), ii. 114.
[86] E.Y.C. ii, p. 36; Yorks. Fines, 1246–72, 153.
[87] Feud. Aids, vi. 211; Cal. Inq. p.m. xiv, pp. 53–9.
[88] Cal. Close, 1396–9, 49; Yorks. Inq. Hen. IV–V, 38.
[89] Bridlington Charty. 1, 48.
[90] Yorks. Inq. i. 100–2.
[91] Feud. Aids, vi. 266.
[92] Ibid. 29.
[93] Ibid. 211.
[94] E.R.R.O., DDCC/111/1.

Marmaduke Grindale held 1½ carucate there.[95] In that year also John de Toucotes held 12 bovates of the Tattershall fee. There is no further evidence for the descent of these holdings. The rest of the fee was divided between six small tenants.[96]

In the early 15th century Anthony St. Quintin held land in Bempton,[97] although the origin and extent of the estate are not known. In 1562 land there was sold by Gabriel St. Quintin to Robert Vicarman,[98] and Ralph Vicarman sold property there to Leonard Acklam in 1622.[99] The latter already held land in Bempton which had been in the possession of John Pickfurth in 1545,[1] and which Thomas Pickfurth had sold to Thomas Acklam in 1581.[2] The Acklam estate, which consisted of 9 bovates by the mid 18th century, descended in the family until 1767, when it was sold by John Acklam to Mathew Smith, who already held land in Bempton.[3] At the inclosure of that year Smith was allotted 172 a.[4] In 1786, after his death, Smith's estate was sold to Isaac Cook.[5] In the same year Cook sold to George Walmsley about 75 a. and in 1803 another 61 a. of the estate.[6] Thomas Walmsley had received about 60 a. at inclosure and, with further purchases from Arthur Maister[7] and others, the Walmsley family increased its estate to about 400 a. by 1851.[8] In 1857 George Walmsley sold 61 a. to John Barber[9] and between 1877 and 1882 most of the remainder of the Walmsley estate was sold in separate lots.[10]

Morcar granted one bovate in Bempton to Bridlington priory between 1120 and 1135, and the priory later granted it to Morcar's grandson Asketil of Buckton in exchange for 2 other bovates there. In the 12th century also Ankerin of Bempton gave 2 bovates to the priory, and Walter of Boynton gave one.[11] In the early 14th century the priory held 3 bovates in Bempton of the Canterbury fee[12] and in 1535 its property was worth about £2.[13] In 1563 the land was let by the Crown to Martin Garrett and in 1572 to William Clapton,[14] but there is no further evidence for its descent.

Six bovates in Bempton were bought in the late 16th or early 17th century by Nathan Walworth, of Ringley (Lancs.).[15] The land was originally used to maintain a chapel and a preacher at Ringley but by the 18th century it supported the poor of that parish.[16] In 1635 the land was estimated at about 120 a.[17] but at inclosure in 1767 the trustees of the Ringley charity were awarded only 84 a.[18] It continued to be held by the trustees until 1917 when it was sold to F. E. Scaife. He sold it in 1926 to William Waind.[19]

Newsham is not mentioned in the Domesday Survey and the first reference to it occurs in 1284–5, though it was not then described separately from Buckton and Bempton.[20] In 1299 the township consisted of 2 carucates and belonged to the Canterbury fee.[21] During the 13th century Stephen de Meynell gave the lordship of Newsham to Bridlington priory.[22] The priory still held it in 1441[23] but there is no mention of its holding any land in Newsham in 1535.[24] Under the priory a mesne lordship was held in the 13th century by Osbert de Arches[25] and it passed to his daughter Maud and her husband William de Cauntelo.[26] The demesne tenants in 1299 were William of Argam, who held 1½ carucate, and John of Heslerton, who held ½ carucate.[27] The latter estate probably descended to Thomas of Heslerton, who held lands in Bempton in 1353,[28] but its descent has not been traced further.

The Newsham estate of William of Argam seems to have followed the descent of Argam manor.[29] In 1428 8 bovates were said to be held by Dame Catherine Cressy.[30] She had, however, apparently died before 1400,[31] and there was some confusion as to the succession in this period.[32] The Argam lands in Newsham had passed to Robert Constable, of Flamborough, by 1441,[33] although it was not until 10 years later that Argam manor descended to Robert Constable's son, another Robert, from the grandson of Dame Catherine.[34] The Newsham land then descended in the Constable family until the attainder of Sir Robert Constable in 1537. In 1569 the Crown granted the land to Francis Barnshaw and his son Martin.[35] It seems to have passed by 1574 to Thomas Clarke, who in that year sold it to Sir George Bowes and Edmund Smithson. A year later Bowes sold the land to Anthony Welbury, who sold it in the same year to William Webster.[36] In 1582 it was for once called the manor of *NEWSHAM*.[37] In 1635 William Webster held 12 bovates there,[38] at least some of which passed to John Jarratt, who was described in 1648 as 'of Newsham'.[39] It subsequently descended with the manor of Bempton in the Jarratt, Broadley, Coverley, and Champion families,[40] and at inclosure in 1843 Samuel Coverley was awarded 43 a. in lieu of 3

---

[95] *Feud. Aids*, vi. 227.
[96] Ibid. 226.
[97] *T.E.R.A.S.* xxi. 63–4; E.R.R.O., DDSQ/12/2, 5, 7–9.
[98] *Yorks. Fines*, i. 270.
[99] Ibid. *1614–25*, 193.
[1] E 179/203/227.
[2] *Yorks. Fines*, ii. 163.
[3] Regy. of Deeds, AJ/170/345.
[4] Ibid. AK/2/2.
[5] Ibid. BL/267/404.
[6] Ibid. BM/54/100; CF/97/148.
[7] Ibid. CU/409/458.
[8] H.O. 107/2367.
[9] Regy. of Deeds, HO/166/208.
[10] Ibid. MF/308/341; /309/342; /410/496; MG/107/161; /162; /251/365; NA/401/491; NB/156/259; NC/389/588.
[11] *Bridlington Charty.* 1, 48.
[12] B.M. Add. MS. 26729, f. 112.
[13] *Valor Eccl.* (Rec. Com.), v. 120.
[14] E 310/28/164 nos. 9, 46.
[15] E.R.R.O., DDX/25/9.
[16] Regy. of Deeds, AK/2/2.
[17] E.R.R.O., DDX/25/9.
[18] Regy. of Deeds, AK/2/2.
[19] Ibid. 182/33/27; 321/589/476.
[20] *Feud. Aids*, vi. 29.
[21] *Yorks. Inq.* iii. 114–15.
[22] *Bridlington Charty.* 53.
[23] C 139/103/28.
[24] *Valor Eccl.* v. 120.
[25] Ibid.; *Yorks. Inq.* iii. 114–15.
[26] *Bridlington Charty.* 53.
[27] *Yorks. Inq.* iii. 118.
[28] *Parl. Rep. Yorks.* i (Y.A.S. Rec. Ser. xci), 107.
[29] See p. 6.
[30] *Feud. Aids*, vi. 265. She is here referred to, apparently mistakenly, as Lady Catherine Hercy.
[31] C 66/362 m.1.
[32] See p. 6.
[33] C 139/103/28.
[34] C 139/143/29.
[35] *Cal. Pat.* 1566–9, 437.
[36] *Yorks. Fines*, ii. 51, 75, 79.
[37] Ibid. 188.
[38] C 142/527/48.
[39] *Cat. of Yorks. Wills at Somerset Ho. 1649–60*, 145.
[40] See p. 11.

bovates. The devisees of John Coverley also received an allotment of 34 a. The remainder of the Websters' land seems to have been divided among several small owners.[41]

The tithes of Bempton and Newsham, valued at about £10 in the early 16th century,[42] belonged to Bridlington priory until the Dissolution.[43] They were then kept in hand and let under the name of a rectory successively to Robert Puckering in 1538 and 1568,[44] Robert Grey in 1589–90,[45] and George Young in 1606.[46] In 1613 the rectory was granted to Francis Morrice and Francis Philips.[47] By 1623 it was in the possession of Dixy Hickman, who sold it that year to Phineas Hodgson.[48] In 1650 it was worth £120.[49] It descended in the Hodgson family until 1710, when William Hodgson sold it to the then lessee William Burton.[50] At the inclosure of Bempton in 1767 the tithes there were commuted for a rent-charge of £80 and land worth £70.[51] In 1808 the trustees of Robert Burton sold the whole rectory to Robert Broadley, lord of the capital manor.[52] In 1840 the tithes of Newsham, then still uninclosed, were commuted for £90 yearly.[53]

ECONOMIC HISTORY. There seem always to have been many small freeholders in Bempton. In 1338 an agreement was reached between Marmaduke of Grindale and eleven free tenants over their right of access, with their carts and animals, to Bempton moor. Marmaduke confirmed their right to have a roadway through his land called 'Ovenham' and stipulated that the road was to be 40 ft. wide with a wall on each side. These walls, for which he gave three feet of land on each side of the road, were to be built by the freeholders and maintained by them jointly with Marmaduke's tenants.[54] Fifteen small tenants, probably freeholders, held land in Bempton in 1346. Two held 4 bovates, one held 3, and 3 held 2, all of the Tattershall fee, and one held 3½ bovates, 2 held 3, 3 held 2, one held 1½, and 2 held ½ bovate, all of the Canterbury fee.[55] Bridlington priory's estate was held in 1536–7 by free tenants at a rent of about £2.[56]

In the 16th century there were said to be 100 bovates of land in the open fields of Bempton, probably including Newsham.[57] Bempton and Newsham, however, seem to have had separate fields. Newsham field was first mentioned in 1557.[58] Although Bempton was inclosed in 1767, Newsham field remained open until nearly 80 years later.[59] In 1802 it was said to contain 16 bovates, each consisting of 12 a.,[60] and 218 a. were inclosed in 1843.[61]

In 1563 there were five fields in Bempton — North, South, East, West, and Bowland fields.[62] East field was also mentioned in 1747.[63] At inclosure in 1767, when the fields of Bempton, including meadow and pasture, were said to contain about 80 bovates, the six open-field areas were called Sike, Metland, Market Dale, West and Long Land fields, and the Buttericks.[64] Long Land field, however, was not mentioned in the details of the allotments and seems to have been an alternative name for Metland field.[65]

The common meadows and pastures of Bempton were extensive. The Neat pasture was mentioned in 1563, and a holding of 2 bovates in that year had rights in the 'common town pasture' for 2 oxen, 3 cows, 2 horses, and 40 sheep.[66] Some meadow land probably lay along the stream in the south of the parish, but the main area of pasture and meadow was probably always in the north of the parish towards the sea. At inclosure in 1767 four areas of pasture were named: the Low pasture, the Standard, which presumably lay around Standard hill in the north-west of the parish, the Moor, first mentioned in 1338,[67] in the north-east, and the West Cliff.[68] In the 19th and 20th centuries land near the sea north of the Moor has been known as the Leys,[69] a name first recorded in 1771, when the ground was also called the Marrfurrs.[70] In 1969, however, there was ridge-and-furrow in this area, suggesting that it was laid to pasture from the open fields.

There is some evidence of early inclosure. An area which had probably been taken in from the open fields was known as 'Ovenham' in the 12th century,[71] and in 1338 it was said to be 'at the north head of the village'.[72] In the late 19th century a close north of the village was known as Next Ownham.[73] In 1251 four closes (*hovenams*), including one 'that lies to the shade', were mentioned.[74] Some 'old inclosed grounds' belonged to the Broadley manor in the 18th century.[75]

The open fields and other common lands of Bempton were inclosed in 1767[76] under an Act of 1765.[77] In all, 1,507 a. were allotted. Betty Jarratt, the lady of the manor, received about 200 a., Henry Maister 309 a., and Mathew Smith 172 a. The impropriator, Robert Burton, received 174 a., mostly in lieu of tithes. There were 2 allotments of 80 a.–100 a., 3 of 50 a.–80 a., 7 of 20 a.–50 a., 4 of 10 a.–20 a., and 19 of under 10 a.

Newsham was inclosed in 1843 under the General Inclosure Act of 1836.[78] In all, 218 a. were divided between nine proprietors, the largest allotment being the 43 a. awarded to Samuel Coverley, lord of the

[41] Regy. of Deeds, FG/430/15.
[42] *Miscellanea*, iii (Y.A.S. Rec. Ser. lxxx), 4, 16, 32.
[43] See p. 14.
[44] *L. & P. Hen. VIII*, xiii (1), p. 134; *Cal. Pat. 1566–9*, 324.
[45] C 66/1355 m. 35.
[46] *Cal. S.P.Dom. 1603–10*, 320.
[47] H. Grove, *Alienated Tithes*, p. cxxxii.
[48] *Yorks. Fines. 1614–25*, 218.
[49] T.E.R.A.S. ii. 56.
[50] Regy. of Deeds, A/336/478.
[51] Ibid. AK/2/2.
[52] E.R.R.O., DDHB/62/20.
[53] B.I.H.R., TA. 526S.
[54] *Bridlington Charty.* 49.
[55] *Feud. Aids*, vi. 226, 229.
[56] S.C. 6/Hen. VIII/4430.
[57] *Miscellanea*, iii (Y.A.S. Rec. Ser. lxxx), 13.
[58] B.I.H.R., Prob. Reg. xv (1), f. 244.
[59] Registry of Deeds, Beverley, BB/397/52; FG/430/15.
[60] E.R.R.O., DDHB/57/70.
[61] Regy. of Deeds, FG/430/15.
[62] Castle Howard MS., Box 24, Survey of Estates, 1563.
[63] E.R.R.O., QSF East. 1747, B. 1, 4.
[64] Regy. of Deeds, AK/2/2.
[65] E.R.R.O., DDCV/Parcel 1.
[66] Castle Howard MS., Box 24, Survey of Estates, 1563.
[67] *Bridlington Charty.* 49.
[68] Regy. of Deeds, AK/2/2.
[69] O.S. Map 6″ (1853, 1958).
[70] E.R.R.O., DDSY/4/105.
[71] *Bridlington Charty.* 48. The name comes from the word *offnama*, meaning an inclosure or intake.
[72] *Bridlington Charty.* 49.
[73] Regy. of Deeds, NL/389/588.
[74] *Yorks. Fines, 1246–72*, 34.
[75] E.R.R.O., DDHO/43/22.
[76] Regy. of Deeds, AK/2/2.
[77] 6 Geo. III, c. 26 (Priv. Act).
[78] Regy of Deeds, FG/430/15.

manors of Bempton and Newsham. There were 3 allotments of 30 a.–40 a., one of 20 a.–30 a., 3 of 10 a.–20 a., and one of under 10 a.

In 1801 505 a., about a quarter of the total area of the parish, were under crops, oats accounting for 263 a. and wheat for 122 a.[79] In 1856 Bempton was said to have some of the richest grazing and feeding pastures in the riding,[80] and in 1892 about half the land was still said to be in pasture.[81] The number of farms, many of them very small, has remained large, between 1823 and 1937 varying between ten and sixteen.[82] In 1851, out of 15 farms, 4 were over 150 a., one was of 100 a.–150 a., 5 were of 50 a.–100 a., and 5 were under 50 a.[83] In 1937 there were still 4 farms of 150 a. or over, and 9 smaller ones.[84] A market gardener was recorded in 1893, and by 1901 there were three in the parish.[85]

A windmill existed in Newsham in 1441,[86] and in the early 16th century the tithe of Newsham mill was valued at 2s.[87] There was still a mill there in 1692[88] and throughout the 19th century.[89] It apparently ceased to be used between 1905 and 1909,[90] but the stump of the tower remained in 1969.

LOCAL GOVERNMENT. No manorial records and no parochial records before 1835 are known. Bempton joined the Bridlington union in 1836.[91]

CHURCH. A chapel may have been built at Bempton c. 1200, the date of the earliest surviving parts of the fabric. Until 1441 Bempton was a chapelry of Bridlington parish, but an agreement was then reached between the inhabitants and Bridlington priory by which the chapel was made parochial. The inhabitants were to have burial rights and they were to provide a chaplain and keep the building in repair. The priory was to pay 13s. 4d. a year to help to provide the chaplain.[92] A commission was issued the same year for the consecration of the chapel and burial ground.[93] The living continued as a curacy until the mid 19th century,[94] since when it has been regarded as a vicarage.[95] In 1919 Buckton township was transferred from Bridlington parish to Bempton.[96]

The provision of curates apparently devolved upon the priory, for after the Dissolution they were nominated by the lay rectors[97] until the curacy became perpetual. The advowson then descended with the rectory and in 1786 Robert Burton was patron.[98] It passed with the rectory in 1808 to the Broadley, later the Harrison-Broadley, family and Mrs. D. Harrison-Broadley was patron in 1969.[99]

In 1525–6 the chaplain of Bempton received £4 a year.[1] In 1650 the curate's stipend was £13 6s. 8d.,[2] and this payment, which continued throughout the 18th and 19th centuries, formed the whole income of the benefice until 1766.[3] It was still paid by the impropriator in 1897.[4] The living was augmented by £200 from Queen Anne's Bounty in each of the years 1766, 1787, 1796, 1824, and 1832.[5] The average net income of the benefice in 1829–31 was £51.[6] In 1851 it was the same[7] but by 1861 had risen to about £78.[8] In 1867 the benefice was endowed out of the Common Fund with £15 a year,[9] and a year later it was reported to receive about £30 from the Ecclesiastical Commissioners.[10] In 1884 the net value of the living was about £153, 'having been £181 a few years ago'.[11]

The earliest acquisition of glebe land was between 1766 and 1770, when Bounty money was used to buy about 12 a. in Bempton.[12] By 1809 more Bounty money had been used to buy 11 a. in Beeford and 11 a. in Aldbrough.[13] Some of the Bempton land was sold in 1927 and 1958, and all the Beeford land in 1961.[14] Bempton had no parsonage house until 1845–6, when a large white-brick one was built near the church.[15]

In the 15th and 16th centuries there were references to the guilds of St. Mary and St. Helen, Corpus Christi, and St. Michael.[16] In 1569 'the guild house' was let to Richard Sharpe,[17] and a year later lands in Bempton 'given to the guild there' were granted to Hugh Counsell and Robert Pistor.[18] The lands of a former chantry in Bempton, consisting of a house and about 24 a., were let to Alice Perkins in 1573.[19] In 1556 several inhabitants deposed that Bempton church had recently been in danger of being pulled down through being wrongly returned as a chantry. To avert this they had paid £1 13s. 4d. to the surveyor of Crown property in the East Riding.[20]

From at least the late 17th century until 1845–6, when the parsonage house was built, the curates of Bempton did not reside. They held other livings in

[79] 1801 Crop Returns.
[80] Sheahan and Whellan, *Hist. York & E.R.* ii. 441.
[81] Bulmer, *Dir. E. Yorks.* (1892), 108–9.
[82] Directories.
[83] H.O. 107/2367.
[84] *Kelly's Dir. N. & E.R. Yorks.* (1937), 405–6.
[85] Ibid. (1893), 361; (1901), 407–8.
[86] C 139/103/28.
[87] *Miscellanea*, iii. 4.
[88] C.P. 43/438 rot. 207.
[89] H.O. 107/2367; directories. By 1850 it was called Buckton Mill: O.S. Map 6" (1853).
[90] *Kelly's Dir. N. & E.R. Yorks.* (1905), 420; (1909), 431–2.
[91] *3rd Rep. Poor Law Com.* 167.
[92] *Bridlington Charty.* 47. The date is given as 1444 in *V.C.H. Yorks.* iii. 203.
[93] *Fasti Parochiales*, iii. 7.
[94] Lawton, *Rer. Eccles. Dioc. Ebor.* 287; Sheahan and Whellan, *Hist. York & E.R.* ii. 441.
[95] Bulmer, *Dir. E. Yorks.* (1892), 108–9; *Crockford* (1967–8).
[96] York Dioc. Regy., Order in Council 522.
[97] See p. 13.
[98] Notes in church.

[99] Ex inf. Revd. H.A.M. Pickard, vicar, 1969.
[1] *Y.A.J.* xxiv. 77.
[2] *T.E.R.A.S.* ii. 56.
[3] B.I.H.R., TER. J. Bempton n.d. to 1764; Hodgson, *Q.A.B.* 434.
[4] Par. rec., Glebe terrier, 1897 (in Vicarage).
[5] Hodgson, *Q.A.B.* 434; Lawton, *Rer. Eccles. Dioc. Ebor.* 287.
[6] *Rep. Com. Eccl. Revenues*, 918–19.
[7] H.O. 129/24/524.
[8] B.I.H.R., TER. J. Bempton 1861.
[9] *Lond. Gaz.* 30 July 1867, p. 4228.
[10] B.I.H.R., TER. J. Bempton 1868.
[11] Ibid. Bp. V. 1884/Ret.
[12] Ibid., TER. J. Bempton 1770, 1809; Hodgson, *Q.A.B.* 435.
[13] B.I.H.R., TER. J. Bempton 1809.
[14] Regy. of Deeds, 346/583/486; 1125/554/499; 1207/312/292.
[15] Sheahan and Whellan, *Hist. York & E.R.* ii. 441.
[16] B.I.H.R., Prob. Reg. ii, f. 474; *Y.A.J.* xxiv. 75 n.
[17] E 310/27/162 no. 26.
[18] *Cal. Pat.* 1569–72, 38.
[19] E 310/29/169 no. 32.
[20] E.R.R.O., DDCC/139/65.

the 18th century, including Flamborough, Grindale, Speeton, and Bridlington, and they lived at Bridlington.[21] From at least 1865 to 1877 the curate was also the incumbent of Speeton.[22] In 1743 the curate, described as 'an old crazed man' who lived at Hornsea, had an assistant curate whose stipend he paid.[23] The curate in 1764 reported that his assistant had left him abruptly and he had not been able to engage another.[24] In 1851 there was an assistant curate, the incumbent living at Romford (Essex).[25]

A noteworthy incumbent of Bempton was Edward John Burrow (curate 1810–16), a writer on various topics, among them sea-shells, art (including two treatises on the Elgin Marbles), and theology.[26]

A service was held each Sunday in 1743 and, although it is not recorded how often communion was administered, 60 people had received it the previous Easter.[27] In 1764 services were still weekly and communion was administered three times a year, usually to about sixty people.[28] By 1865 communion was administered six times a year and the average number receiving was twelve. The congregation, however, which was said to be 'decidedly increasing, the church a few years ago having been nearly abandoned', consisted on average of 120 people.[29] Communion was administered only four times a year to 10–12 people in 1868.[30] In 1877 and 1884 it was administered every six weeks to 9–12 people, and in the latter year the average congregation was only 30–40.[31] By 1894 there were two services each Sunday, and by 1900 communion was administered once a week.[32] In 1969 there were two, sometimes three, services each Sunday.

From 1865 to 1900 the vicars often reported the difficulties they faced in a parish 'so wedded to dissent'. In 1865 the vicar estimated that even of those who attended church about four-fifths were Methodists, and in 1877 there were said to be 'very few bona fide members of the church'.[33] In 1900 there was 'no prospect of any attending ... church folk are almost nil'. Although the nonconformists helped to keep the church 'fairly well in a material way', it was impossible to exert pastoral authority when the prevailing attitude was that 'one place is as good as another'.[34]

The church of ST. MICHAEL is built of stone, partly rough-cast externally, and of 19th-century red brick. It consists of chancel, nave, north and south aisles, west tower, and south porch. Of the original church, dating from c. 1200, there remain only the two nave arcades and the base of the tower with its tower arch. The arcades, of four bays, are partly built of chalk and have semicircular arches on cylindrical and octagonal piers. There is also a 13th-century bowl-shaped font with stiff-leaved foliage decoration and a cylindrical shaft. The much restored upper stage of the tower, which is octagonal with longer cardinal sides, dates from the 14th century; it has windows with Decorated tracery and an embattled parapet.

In 1829 the chancel was rebuilt in red brick at the expense of Henry Broadley, lay rector.[35] There is now no chancel arch and a wooden screen, probably also of 1829, separates the nave from the chancel; a Royal Arms surmounts the screen. The chancel windows are plain and square-headed, except for the east window which contains unusual tracery. In 1856 there was said to be a west gallery,[36] but this has since been removed. In 1865 the vicar mentioned the bad effects in the parish of the 'external meanness of the church and its dilapidated condition', which was so serious that it 'ought to be rebuilt or at least restored'.[37] Restoration was carried out in 1868–70, when the south aisle was rebuilt, the church was repewed, and a brick clerestory was added.[38] In 1892 the church tower was repaired, and a stone wall was built on the west and south sides of the churchyard. Further restoration was carried out in 1906–14; the north aisle was reroofed, the south side of the clerestory was rebuilt in stone, with round windows, and two stained-glass windows were placed in the chancel.[39] In 1946 the church was again in urgent need of restoration; the chancel roof was said to be in danger of collapse, and there was decay in the aisle arcades.[40] In 1949 repairs were carried out with the aid of a grant from the Incorporated Church Building Society,[41] during which the south aisle was formed into a side chapel.[42] In 1960 more repairs were carried out.[43]

In 1552 there were two bells[44] and in 1969 still two, one of which is inscribed 'Johannis de Thynge Prior' and dates from about 1361.[45] The plate consists of two silver cups, one with a cover, a pewter flagon, and a 17th-century brass alms-dish. The cup with a cover was made in York in 1620 by Peter Pearson and the other in London in 1729, perhaps by Thomas Sadler.[46] The burial and marriage registers begin in 1597 and the register of baptisms in 1605; they are complete.[47]

Additions to the churchyard were made in 1894 and 1949.[48]

NONCONFORMITY. In 1623 one and in 1637 two non-communicants were reported in the parish.[49]

---

[21] B.I.H.R., Bp. V. 1764/Ret. 53; E. H. Rudkin, *Bempton cum Newsholme cum Buckton*, 28; *Herring's Visit.* i. 114.
[22] B.I.H.R., V. 1868/Ret. 42; V. 1877/Ret.
[23] *Herring's Visit.* i. 114, 218.
[24] B.I.H.R., Bp. V. 1764/Ret. 53.
[25] H.O. 129/24/524.
[26] *D.N.B.*
[27] *Herring's Visit.* i. 114.
[28] B.I.H.R., Bp. V. 1764/Ret. 53. In the Flamborough return the curate stated that a service was held at Flamborough and Bempton on alternate Sundays: ibid. 190.
[29] Ibid. V. 1865/Ret. 44.
[30] Ibid. V. 1868/Ret. 42.
[31] Ibid. V. 1877/Ret.; Bp. V. 1884/Ret.
[32] Ibid. Bp. V. 1894/Ret.; Bp. V. 1900/Ret. 25.
[33] Ibid. V. 1865/Ret. 44; V. 1877/Ret.
[34] Ibid. Bp. V. 1900/Ret. 25.

[35] Bulmer, *Dir. E. Yorks.* (1892), 108–9; stone on church.
[36] Sheahan and Whellan, *Hist. York & E.R.* ii. 441.
[37] B.I.H.R., V. 1865/Ret. 44.
[38] Ibid. and Churches index.
[39] Tablets in church.
[40] Rudkin, *Bempton*, 4.
[41] Notice in church.
[42] Par. rec., Faculty, 1948 (in Vicarage).
[43] Ibid. Letter.
[44] *Inventories of Ch. Goods*, 30.
[45] Boulter, 'Ch. Bells', 215.
[46] *Yorks. Ch. Plate*, i. 215–16.
[47] Barley, *Par. Docs. E.R.* 11.
[48] York Dioc Regy., Sentence of consecration.
[49] H. Aveling, *Post Reformation Catholicism in E. Yorks. 1558–1790* (E. Yorks. Loc. Hist. Ser. xi), 59.

In the early 18th century the pastor of Bridlington Baptist church baptized converts from Bempton[50] but no dissenters or meeting-places were reported in the parish in 1764.[51] The Methodists had five members at Bempton in 1789.[52] In 1805 a house was licensed for worship.[53] Protestant dissent increased greatly in the 19th century and in 1868 'nearly all' the inhabitants were Wesleyan or Primitive Methodists.[54] The first chapel in Bempton, a small brick building situated midway between Bempton and Buckton villages,[55] was built in 1825 by the Wesleyans.[56] It was replaced by a new chapel on the same site about 1903,[57] built of red brick and terra cotta. It was still used in 1969.

In 1843 the Primitive Methodists built a chapel in Bolam Lane.[58] It was enlarged in 1862[59] and in 1889 there were 48 members.[60] It is a plain square building, mainly of brick but with a chalk rear wall. The chapel had fallen out of use before 1964[61] but was still standing in 1969.

EDUCATION. In 1618–19 an unlicensed schoolmaster taught at Bempton.[62] There were two schools in 1819, containing altogether 32 pupils, each of whom paid 1½d. a week.[63] There were still two schools in 1835, when 12 boys and 15 girls were taught at their parents' expense.[64] In 1854 a National school was built by subscription.[65] This was maintained by a local rate, which varied from 3d. to 6d. a week according to the means of those paying, and also by a weekly sum from the parents.[66] In 1865 the average number of children attending the school was said to be 20. The Methodists also held a school which, in 1865, had been 'established for many years'. It, too, was maintained at the parents' expense, and the average attendance was about 50.[67]

In 1871–2 a new National school was built to accommodate 88 pupils.[68] In 1892 the average attendance was about 70.[69] The vicar and archdeacon were trustees and in 1894 it was said to be 'practically a church school though the scholars are all Methodists'.[70] Between 1908 and 1912 attendance varied between 78 and 81.[71] In 1912 a new school was built to accommodate 112 pupils.[72] Between 1914 and 1938 attendance varied between 61 and 78.[73] In 1969 the average number on the roll was 40.[74]

The former National school, built in 1854, is a red-brick building with stone-mullioned windows and a mainly chalk rear wall. It stands at the corner of the churchyard. In 1936 it was used as the Church Institute reading room[75] and in 1969 as the Men's Institute.

In 1884 the vicar reported that evening schools had been attempted, 'but in vain'.[76]

CHARITIES FOR THE POOR. Francis Walmsley, by will proved in 1782, left 6s. a year to be given in penny loaves each month to the poor of Bempton. This, together with a similar bequest to the poor of Flamborough,[77] was charged on two houses in Bridlington Quay. The money was paid in 1822 to the overseers, who distributed it, no longer in the form of loaves, to the poor whom they thought most in need.[78] The whole income was distributed to one recipient each year in 1943–6.[79]

In 1823 the Poor's Stock consisted of £10 from two 'ancient benefactions'. It was held by the overseers and produced 8s. a year interest, which was given to poor widows,[80] and it was still distributed in 1856.[81] No more is known of it.

John Lamplough, by will proved in 1896, left £100, the interest on which was to be given each Christmas to the poor at the vicar's discretion.[82] Between 1899 and 1915 about £2 was regularly distributed among from 6 to 8 people,[83] and the income was still £2 in 1962.[84]

Elizabeth Walmsley, by will proved in 1923, left £270 for charitable purposes. The income from £200 of this was to be used to provide a tea each Christmas for all women over the age of 65 in Bempton and Buckton, and any money left over was to be used for a sick fund for the poor. The income from £60 was to be used to provide a tea for children under the age of 13 'in summer so that they can have games in a field', and the income from the remaining £10 was to provide a prize each year for the most industrious child in Bempton school. The same woman also left £200 to found a scholarship at Bridlington High School for girls whose parents were residents of Bempton or Buckton, £200 to provide and maintain a clock in the church tower, and £500 to establish a sick fund for the poor of Bempton and Buckton.[85] In 1962 the total income of the charity (excluding the scholarship endowment) was about £27, of which about £17 was distributed to the poor, about £6 used to maintain the clock, and £5 used to provide prizes for the day and Sunday schools.[86]

---

[50] *Baptists of Yorks.* (1912), 64.
[51] B.I.H.R., Bp. V. 1764/Ret. 53.
[52] E.R.R.O., MRP/1/7.
[53] G.R.O. Worship Returns, Vol. v, no. 1976.
[54] B.I.H.R., V. 1868/Ret. 42.
[55] Bulmer, *Dir. E. Yorks.* (1892), 108–9.
[56] H.O. 129/24/524.
[57] G.R.O. Worship Reg. no. 39870.
[58] Ibid. no. 16430; H.O. 129/24/524.
[59] Bulmer, *Dir. E. Yorks.* 108–9.
[60] H. Woodcock, *Sketches of Prim. Meth. on Yorks. Wolds*, 68.
[61] G.R.O. Worship Reg. no. 16430.
[62] B.I.H.R., Schools index.
[63] *Rets. on Educ. of Poor, 1819*, 1076.
[64] *Educ. Enquiry Abstract, 1835*, 1079.
[65] Sheahan and Whellan, *Hist. York & E.R.* ii. 441.
[66] E.H. Rudkin, *Bempton cum Newsholme cum Buckton*, 39.
[67] B.I.H.R., V. 1865/Ret. 44.
[68] *Rets. Rel. Elem. Educ. 1871*, 474.
[69] Bulmer, *Dir. E. Yorks.* (1892), 108–9.
[70] B.I.H.R., Bp. V. 1894/Ret.
[71] *Bd. of Educ. List 21* (H.M.S.O.).
[72] Ed. 7/135. The Local Authority, in 1913–14, reported that there was accommodation for 130 pupils: E.R. Educ. Cttee. *Mins.* 1913–14, 79.
[73] *Bd. of Educ. List 21*.
[74] Ex inf. Chief Educ. Officer, County Hall, Beverley, 1969.
[75] B.I.H.R., Bp. V. 1936/Ret. 262.
[76] Ibid. Bp. V. 1884/Ret.
[77] See p. 164.
[78] *9th Rep. Char. Com.* 721.
[79] Char. Com. files.
[80] *9th Rep. Char. Com.* 721.
[81] Sheahan and Whellan, *Hist. York & E.R.* ii. 441.
[82] Par. rec., Extract from will (in Vicarage).
[83] Ibid., Vestry Min. Bk. 1855–1917 (in church).
[84] Char. Com. files.
[85] Par. rec., Copy of will.
[86] Char. Com. files.

BESSINGBY

The compact parish of Bessingby is situated on the southern edge of the wolds, adjoining Bridlington, mostly occupying a ridge of higher ground between the Plain of Holderness and the valley of the Gypsey Race.[1] The village was probably a Scandinavian settlement.[2] It is still physically separate from Bridlington, but in the 20th century the town has begun to encroach upon the parish and Bessingby has been incorporated in the borough.

Watercourses form most of the parish boundary. In the north the Gypsey Race separates Bessingby from Easton and Bridlington, and the southern and eastern boundaries with Hilderthorpe and Bridlington are formed by Bessingby beck as it flows northwards to meet the Race. About 800 yds. of the beck up to its junction with the Gypsey Race have been covered in during the 20th century. In the northwest the boundary follows the lower slopes of the valley of the Gypsey Race for about $\frac{3}{4}$ mile before turning up the valley side. The western boundary with Carnaby then runs straight over the wold. The area of the ancient parish is 1,270 a. In 1877 about 20 a. were transferred to the Bridlington local government board district and in 1923 about 355 a. were added to Bridlington borough. In 1935 6 a. were transferred to Carnaby civil parish and the remainder of Bessingby, comprising 899 a., also became part of the borough.[3]

The landscape of the parish exhibits the familiar features of both wolds and plain, and until inclosure in the later 18th century there was the usual distinction between open arable fields on the wold slopes and pasture and carr land on the plain. The wold rises to a height of more than 200 ft. above sea-level in the west of the parish, with a steep fall in the north to between 25 ft. and 50 ft. in the valley of the Gypsey Race. A Romano–British settlement has been found on the wold slopes $\frac{1}{2}$ mile from the site of Bessingby village.[4] The plain south of the village is also below 50 ft. High wood lies on the wold slopes north of the village and there are two smaller plantations on the plain. Bessingby Hall, which stands in a small park known in the 18th and 19th centuries as Hall close or Hall field,[5] lies between the village and the Driffield–Bridlington road. The hall, on the higher ground in the north of the park, commands an open view across the plain to the sea. The park has included about 40 a. of ornamental grounds and plantations probably since the late-18th-century inclosure.[6] Ridge-and-furrow suggests that part of it is former open-field land.

There are several earthworks in the parish, the most prominent of which are two parallel banks, about 400 yds. long, on the plain to the east of the park. From the western end of this pair, and at right-angles to it, two other parallel banks run south-eastwards as far as Middle wood. This pattern suggests that the banks may have originated as field boundaries, and they may be connected with 'the new fosse' which Bridlington priory constructed in Lamb Holme in the 12th or 13th century.[7] Another embankment runs up the wold slopes as far as High wood, starting from a point near the Bridlington road. In 1850 there was a 'fish pond' at the eastern end of the more prominent pair of banks.[8]

The main Driffield–Bridlington road runs across the parish on the lower wold slopes and continues over the Gypsey Race towards the Old Town area of Bridlington. From it Bessingby Lane leads eastwards to Bridlington Quay. The unpaved village street borders the park on the south and is connected to the Bridlington road by two other unpaved roads, along the west and east sides of the park, the latter known as Brick Kiln Balk. The former in the 18th and early 19th centuries continued southwards into Hilderthorpe. The village street formerly continued eastwards towards Bridlington but in 1969 only a footpath remained. The Bridlington road crosses the Gypsey Race by a modern bridge, but there has been a crossing there since at least the 16th century, when there is reference to 'the bridge called Bessingby cawsey'.[9] In 1648 the Bridlington town feoffees bought timber to repair 'Bessingby bridge'.[10] Bessingby Lane is carried over the Hull–Bridlington railway line, which runs through the south of the parish, by a 19th-century iron bridge. Two roads on the wolds are Wold Gate, which runs across the north of the parish, and Butterfly Lane, a field track connecting the Bridlington road with Wold Gate.

Most of the farm-houses and cottages in Bessingby are of the 18th century or later. The main building material is brick, some of which no doubt came from the brick-kiln at one time in use in the parish, but limestone and chalk are also found in the earlier buildings.

At the west end of the village a large dovecot bears a date-stone inscribed 'C.R. 1670', and underneath, more faintly, '1747', the latter possibly a restoration date.[11] The exterior walls are built mainly of chalk ashlar, but the lower courses are largely brick, there is a dentil brick string-course, and the upper part of one gable-end is clad in brick. A shallow plinth also contains cobbles. The interior walls, including a partition wall, are of brick and are entirely lined with nesting holes. There are several windows with stone sills and lintels and on the roof a weather-boarded cupola.

On the southern perimeter of the park is a cottage, probably of the early 18th century, of a storey and a half with a dark-pantiled roof and gabled dormers. The front is of red brick with stone quoins, stone-mullioned windows, and a central porch with a segmental stone arch. The key-stone of the arch is dated 1805 and it is possible that the front of the cottage was restored at this period. Near by is another red-brick cottage, built in the 18th century and unaltered.[12] Both Cottage Farm and

---

[1] This article was written in 1969.
[2] *P.N.E.R. Yorks.* (E.P.N.S.), 100.
[3] The figures for the additions to the borough in 1877 and 1923 have been calculated. In 1923 558 a. were so added, but part of this area was from the township of Hilderthorpe which had been in Bessingby civil parish: *Census*, 1931. See below, p. 30.
[4] *Y.A.J.* xxxvii. 438–40.
[5] E.R.R.O., DDCV/Parcels 90, 114; O.S. Map 6" (1854).
[6] E.R.R.O., DDCV/Parcel 114.
[7] *Bridlington Charty.* 26; see below, p. 19.
[8] O.S. Map 6" (1854).
[9] E 310/29/169 no. 65.
[10] *T.E.R.A.S.* ix. 84.
[11] See plate facing p. 273.
[12] See plate facing p. 321.

Manor Farm, towards the east end of the village street, are 18th-century brick buildings. The latter, which bears a date-stone of 1754, has a roof of dark pantiles. Near by are 18th-century barns of chalk and brick. A terrace of four and one pair of 19th-century semi-detached houses stand at the west end of the village street, and Church Farm bears the inscription 'Built 1765, rebuilt 1901'. The only isolated farm is Wandales, in the north of the parish, which probably originated after the late-18th-century inclosure. Bridlington Grammar School moved from the town to its present position, in the east of the parish, in 1899. The 20th-century development associated with the growth of Bridlington includes the 86-acre West Hill housing estate, begun by Bridlington corporation in 1949, and an industrial estate.[13]

There were 65 poll-tax payers at Bessingby in 1377.[14] Even with those of Easton included there were only 28 households in 1674, of which 3 were discharged from the hearth tax; one had 8 hearths, 3 each had 4, 2 had 3, 2 had 2, and 17 had only one.[15] In 1743 there were 13 families in the parish[16] and in 1764 20.[17] The population in 1801 was 87, and until 1871 it varied only between 66 and 99. By 1881, however, it had risen to 141 and by 1901 to 382.[18] In 1921 it was 329. The boundary changes of 1923 left Bessingby with an area which had had a population of 112 in 1921, and there were 106 inhabitants in 1931.[19]

MANOR AND OTHER ESTATES. In 1086 Bessingby consisted of one estate of 8 carucates, which was soke of Bridlington manor and held by the king.[20] It was subsequently granted either to Gilbert de Gant or to Gilbert's son Walter, and Walter was the overlord in the early 12th century.[21] The Gant fee later passed to the Tattershalls, of whom Bessingby was held in 1306 and 1335.[22]

Walter de Gant's estate in Bessingby was held of him by his constable, William FitzNiel, who by 1124 had granted one carucate there, formerly held by Saxo, to Bridlington priory. Forno, another of Walter's sub-tenants, at the same time granted the priory 2 bovates.[23] The remainder of Bessingby had been granted to the priory by Walter's son Gilbert de Gant by 1153.[24] The priory held *BESSINGBY* manor until 1537.[25]

Following the suppression of the priory the manor was retained by the Crown until the early 17th century. It was let to James Cookeson in 1553, James Cancellor and John Moore in 1565,[26] Edward Styring in 1583,[27] and Francis Styring and his son Thomas in 1593.[28] In 1605 the king granted the manor to Prince Charles,[29] but eight years later it was resumed by the Crown[30] and granted in 1616 to George Villiers, later duke of Buckingham.[31] In 1618 Villiers sold it to the tenant, Thomas Styring.[32]

In 1659 Thomas Styring's son Francis conveyed the manor to Richard Staveley.[33] It was devised by Michael Staveley, by will of 1724, to his executors and in 1726 it was conveyed to Thomas Goulton.[34] In 1765, when it comprised about 315 a., the manor was sold by Christopher Goulton to John Hudson,[35] and in the same year Hudson bought 17 bovates from Peter Crosyer.[36] At inclosure in 1768 Hudson was allotted 545 a.[37] The Hudsons' estate was subsequently considerably increased by purchases from Robert Grimston, Samuel Robson, the trustees of John Greame, Sir William Strickland, and others.[38] By 1868, when it was sold by the Hudsons to George Wright, the estate consisted of 1,067 a.[39] After the death of A. G. W. Wright in 1923 the estate was administered by trustees until 1932,[40] when it passed to Wright's son G. W. J. H. Wright.[41] Some land towards Bridlington has been sold for building purposes in the 20th century[42] but in 1969 G. W. J. H. Wright still owned the greater part of Bessingby.

A manor-house was mentioned in the 13th century[43] and also in the early 16th century, when it was let by the priory to Herbert St. Quintin and later to Henry Pulley.[44] In the late 17th century the manor-house had eight hearths.[45] The name Bessingby Hall occurs as early as 1767,[46] but the present house was designed by Thomas Cundy in 1807 for Harrington Hudson (d. 1848).[47] It is a yellow-brick building of two storeys, five bays long. The central bay of the main, south-facing, front is slightly recessed and contains the entrance, which is approached by a semicircular flight of steps. The semicircular Grecian Doric portico has a stone balustrade forming a balcony to the first-floor window. The roof has a parapet and moulded eaves. The interior has been altered but some original work remains.

The Rudston family seems to have held an estate in Bessingby over a long period. Robert of Rudston had land there before 1369,[48] and in 1423 William Rudston was in dispute with the priory.[49] Thomas Rudston held 4 bovates of the priory in 1533–4,[50]

---

[13] See pp. 40, 57, 79.
[14] E 179/202/62 m. 12.
[15] E 179/205/521.
[16] *Herring's Visit.* i. 111.
[17] B.I.H.R., Bp. V. 1764/Ret. 54.
[18] *V.C.H. Yorks.* iii. 488.
[19] *Census,* 1931.
[20] *V.C.H. Yorks.* ii. 197, 322.
[21] B.M. Cott. MS. Aug. ii, f. 56.
[22] *Cal. Inq. p.m.* iv, pp. 261, 265; vii, p. 470.
[23] *Bridlington Charty.* 12.
[24] Ibid. 26.
[25] *Feud. Aids,* vi. 32, 169.
[26] C 66/1011 m. 25.
[27] C 66/1228 m. 43.
[28] E 310/30/180 no. 17.
[29] C 66/1674 m. 25.
[30] C 66/1993 m. 8.
[31] C 66/2090 m. 7.
[32] C 54/2420 m. 39.
[33] C.P. 25(2)/615/1659 Mich. no. 2.
[34] Registry of Deeds, Beverley, I/440/965; /441/966; /442/967.
[35] Ibid. AG/233/470; /234/471.
[36] Ibid. /316/608.
[37] Ibid. AK/35/4.
[38] Ibid. AP/394/716; CD/123/180; CF/216/342; EP/389/450.
[39] Ibid. KF/282/388; /283/389.
[40] Ibid. 276/170/141; 321/205/173.
[41] Ibid. 444/325/252.
[42] Ibid. 183/396/345; 187/305/267; 190/482/413; see below, p. 40.
[43] *Bridlington Charty.* 27.
[44] *L. & P. Hen. VIII,* x, p. 413; *Miscellanea,* iii (Y.A.S. Rec. Ser. lxxx), 1.
[45] E 179/205/521.
[46] E.R.R.O., DDGR/42/17; M.E. Ingram, *Leaves from a Family Tree,* 108.
[47] H.M. Colvin, *Biog. Dict. Eng. Architects, 1660–1840,* 162.
[48] *Cal. Pat.* 1367–70, 449.
[49] *Monastic Notes,* i (Y.A.S. Rec. Ser. xvii), 24.
[50] *Miscellanea,* iii. 1.

and in 1623 John Rudston had 14 bovates.[51] The land apparently later passed to the Grimstons and at inclosure in 1768 Robert Grimston was allotted 171 a.[52] In 1772 Grimston sold it to John Hudson.[53]

Bessingby church was appropriated by Bridlington priory, probably in the 12th century.[54] In 1538 the church was valued at £10 14s. 4d.[55] The rectory was let by the Crown to Brian Leighton in 1538,[56] James Cookeson in 1553,[57] John Carlile in 1576 and 1587,[58] and John Carlile's son Thomas, John Warcoppe, and Edward Ruston in 1595.[59] It was then granted in fee in 1610 to Francis Morrice and Francis Philips,[60] who sold it the following year to Francis Styring. Thomas Styring sold it in 1624 to Samuel Buck and William Pearson.[61] 'Mr. Buck and Mr. Pearson' were the impropriators in 1650, when the value of the rectory was £90.[62]

The rectory subsequently descended in moieties.[63] Buck's share had passed by 1768 to another Samuel Buck, who at the inclosure of that year received an allotment of 54 a., worth £31 5s. a year, in lieu of his half of the tithes.[64] The other moiety was conveyed by Thomas Pearson in 1669 to Sir Francis Boynton,[65] and it subsequently seems to have become dispersed among the various proprietors of Bessingby.[66] At inclosure the owners of the land were said to hold this half of the tithes.[67] In 1843 the chief landowner, Harrington Hudson, merged the tithes on 1,041 a.[68]

ECONOMIC HISTORY. There is some evidence of the services performed by the priory's customary tenants. In 1264 a tenant of 4 bovates was bound to pay 5s. and do six plough-works a year and to act concurrently as reeve, the priory feeding him the while. He might, however, commute the services for 9s.[69] In 1543 the king used the services of the former priory's tenants for work on the harbour and piers at Bridlington. For one day the tenants, with ten carts, had to carry stone to the harbour.[70] Copyholders and tenants-at-will paid rents totalling £18 in 1536–7; free rents then amounted to only 3s.[71] and in 1544 only three people were said to hold freely.[72]

In the early 16th century there were 50 bovates of land in the open fields.[73] The 'town field' of Bessingby was mentioned in 1593.[74] At inclosure in 1768 there were three fields: West, Middle, and East or Tethering fields.[75] In 1853 the wold slopes north of the village were described as High field, and the area south of the village as Low field,[76] but there is no evidence that the open fields had extended to the plain.

The low-lying southern part of the parish towards Bessingby beck was from early times occupied by meadow, pasture, and carr, and there was more meadow land in the eastern part of the parish, along the Gypsey Race, described in the 13th century as extending to 'the principal stream dividing the meadows of Bridlington and Bessingby'.[77] In the 18th century this area was known as the ings.[78] In the 16th century there was pasture and meadow land near the bridge over the Gypsey Race.[79] Land in Lamb Holme is referred to in the 12th or 13th century.[80] This name may originally have denoted an island of higher land in a low-lying meadow on which lambs gathered.[81] The same grant also mentions the new fosse of Bridlington priory in Lamb Holme. 'The grassgrounds' formed part of the manor in the 16th and 17th centuries,[82] and other pastoral areas of the parish were known as 'Rawgholme' and Holme Butts; there was also grazing on the common meres and balks.[83] Common grazing in the open fields was allotted by beastgates in the 17th century.[84]

There is no evidence of any inclosed land before the 16th century. By 1544 the manor contained several closes, including Bessingby Cotes, Plowme garth, and Bullesse garth.[85] Subsequently there are many references to closes,[86] one of which, Collis garth, was said in 1596 to comprise five selions[87] and may therefore have been taken from the open fields. In 1650 Thomas Styring, lord of the manor, was said to have recently inclosed a flat of land there.[88]

The open fields, commons, and wastes, totalling about 1,080 a., were inclosed in 1768[89] under an Act of 1766.[90] John Hudson, as lord of the manor, was allotted 545 a., Robert Grimston 171 a., John Greame 83 a., and Thomas Yates 35 a. Samuel Buck received 54 a. in lieu of half the tithes. Four others received allotments of 5 a. or less.

Between 1805 and 1810 Harrington Hudson bought four cottages with their garths and demolished them to make an orchard.[91] It was during this period that the present hall was built. By 1843 the manor was divided into 3 large farms of 177 a., 330 a., and 407 a., 2 holdings of between 25 a. and 50 a., and 5 of under 10 a.[92] The three farms, Wandale, Church, and Manor farms, still occupied most of the land in the parish in 1969.

---

[51] C 142/674/79.
[52] Regy. of Deeds, AK/35/4.
[53] Ibid. AP/394/716.
[54] See p. 20.
[55] Dugdale, *Mon.* vi. 291.
[56] *L. & P. Hen. VIII*, xiii (2), p. 282.
[57] C 66/1142 m. 10.
[58] E 310/29/174 no. 37; E.R.R.O., DDLG/3/1.
[59] C 66/1431 m. 32.
[60] E.R.R.O., DDLG/3/5.
[61] *Yorks. Fines, 1614–25*, 254.
[62] *T.E.R.A.S.* ii. 56.
[63] E.R.R.O., DDLG/50/6.
[64] Regy. of Deeds, AK/35/4.
[65] E.R.R.O., DDGR/13/8.
[66] Regy. of Deeds, H/8/6; AG/234/471.
[67] Ibid. AK/35/4.
[68] Ibid. KF/279/384.
[69] *Bridlington Charty.* 27.
[70] E.R.R.O., DPX/57, Bessingby, p. 17.
[71] S.C. 6/Hen. VIII/4430.
[72] S.C. 6/Hen. VIII/4436.
[73] *Miscellanea*, iii (Y.A.S. Rec. Ser. lxxx), 16.
[74] E 310/30/180 no. 17.
[75] Registry of Deeds, Beverley, AK/35/4.
[76] O.S. Map 6" (1854).
[77] *Bridlington Charty.* 21.
[78] E.R.R.O., DDCV/Parcel 114.
[79] E 310/29/169 no. 65.
[80] *Bridlington Charty.* 26.
[81] *P.N.E.R. Yorks.* 325.
[82] S.C. 6/4436; C 66/2097 no. 19.
[83] S.C. 6/4436; C 66/2097 no. 19; E 310/28/167 no. 17; /30/179 no. 42.
[84] E.R.R.O., DDGR/13/8.
[85] S.C. 6/4436.
[86] e.g. E 310/29/169 no. 65; /30/180 no. 17.
[87] Ibid. /30/179 no. 42.
[88] E 134/1650 Trin./1.
[89] Regy. of Deeds, AK/35/4.
[90] 6 Geo. III, c. 26 (Priv. Act).
[91] Regy. of Deeds, CK/59/104; CN/236/362; CO/35/63; CR/144/180.
[92] Ibid. KF/279/384.

Lime-burning and brick-making were carried on in the 19th century; in 1850 a lime-kiln was situated on Bessingby Hill, and there was a brickworks near Bessingby Lane. Brick-making is also recorded by the name of the road along the eastern boundary of the park, Brick Kiln Balk,[93] and the field to the east was called Brick Kiln close in 1769.[94]

There was a water-mill, worth 13s. 4d. a year, in Bessingby in 1418, presumably situated on the Gypsey Race.[95] A windmill was mentioned in 1565[96] and Windmill close in 1766.[97]

LOCAL GOVERNMENT. No manorial records and no parochial records before 1835 are known. Bessingby joined the Bridlington union in 1836.[98]

CHURCH. A church existed at Bessingby in the first quarter of the 12th century, when it was granted to Bridlington priory.[99] No vicarage was ordained and the living remained a curacy. It was still referred to as a perpetual curacy in the earlier 19th century,[1] but has since been regarded as a vicarage.[2] In the Middle Ages curates were presumably provided by the priory and after the Dissolution they were provided and paid by the impropriators.[3] In 1659 the advowson was included in the sale of the manor by Francis Styring to Richard Staveley,[4] and it subsequently followed the descent of the manor.[5]

In 1537 the stipend paid by the Crown to the curate of Bessingby was £5 6s. 8d.[6] This sum constituted the entire income of the benefice up to 1748.[7] By 1764 the stipend fell to £4 16s. 8d. and that payment continued until at least 1861.[8] The living was augmented by £200 from Queen Anne's Bounty in 1748, 1773, 1786, 1808, and 1819, and by a parliamentary grant of £400 in 1824.[9] In 1764 the income of the benefice was £8 16s. 8d.,[10] in 1818 £33,[11] and in 1829–31 an average of £59 net.[12] In 1851 the net income was about £51.[13]

The earliest acquisition of glebe land was between 1764 and 1770, when Bounty money was used to buy 9 a. in Beeford, and between 1781 and 1809 more Bounty money was used to buy 4 a. in Bempton.[14] Bessingby does not seem to have had a parsonage house until 1958, when the present Vicarage was built near the new chapel of St. Mark on the West Hill housing estate.[15]

A guild dedicated to St. Mary Magdalene existed in Bessingby church in 1521,[16] and in 1549 its 'guildhouse' with a small amount of land was granted to Edward Pese and William Wynlove.[17] In 1570 lands of the former guild were granted to Hugh Counsell and Robert Pistor.[18]

The living has normally been held in conjunction with others since at least the early 18th century. In 1743 and 1764 the curate also held Boynton, where he lived, Carnaby, and Fraisthorpe with Auburn.[19] In 1835 he also held the rectory of Kirkbride (Cumb.) and the vicarage of Reighton, where he lived.[20] Between 1865 and 1877 the incumbent still held the vicarage of, and lived at, Reighton.[21] In 1936 the living was held with St. Mary's, Bridlington,[22] and in 1967–8 with Carnaby.[23] An assistant curate was employed at Bessingby in 1716, for much of the later 18th and early 19th centuries, and in 1876–9.[24] There was also an assistant curate in 1936.[25]

In 1636–7 the king presented Christopher Bradley to the curacy. He was ejected about 1650 but returned at the Restoration and was buried at Bessingby in 1679.[26] One of the more noteworthy of the clergy of Bessingby was William Scoresby (1789–1857), assistant curate in 1825–7, the distinguished mariner, explorer, and scientist.[27]

In 1743 a service was held at Bessingby only once every six weeks because 'the parishioners resort constantly to Carnaby . . . which has always been the custom here'. Communion was administered three times a year and had been received by sixteen people the previous Easter.[28] In 1764 there had been no service held in the church for three years because of its disrepair. Bessingby people attended Carnaby church, and 'some few' received communion there.[29] By 1865 there was a service each Sunday, but communion was administered only twice a year and the average number receiving was seven.[30] By 1877 communion was administered once a month and received by 8–10 people.[31] In 1969 there was a service each week, and two every fourth week.

The present church of ST. MAGNUS, built in 1893–4,[32] consists of nave, chancel, north and south aisles, and central tower with spire. The medieval church had been dedicated to St. Mary Magdalene.[33]

The original church was slightly to the south of the present one. In 1759 it was said to be 'so ruinous that the minister durst not venture to do duty in it',[34] and in 1764 'the body of the church was

---

[93] O.S. Map 6″ (1854).
[94] E.R.R.O., DDCV/Parcel 114.
[95] *Yorks. Inq. Hen. IV–V*, 144.
[96] E.R.R.O., DDLG/52/1.
[97] Ibid. DDCV/Parcel 114.
[98] *3rd Rep. Poor Law Com.* 167.
[99] *Bridlington Charty.* 12, 25–6, 431–2.
[1] *Rep. Com. Eccl. Revenues*, 918.
[2] *Kelly's Dir. N. & E.R. Yorks.* (1872), 315; *Crockford*.
[3] See p. 19.
[4] C.P. 25(2)/615/1659 Mich. no. 2.
[5] Registry of Deeds, Beverley, F/113/244; AG/234/471; *Rep. Com. Eccl. Revenues*, 918; *Crockford*.
[6] *L. & P. Hen. VIII*, xiv(2), p. 78; *Miscellanea*, iii (Y.A.S. Rec. Ser. lxxx), 34.
[7] B.I.H.R., TER. J. Bessingby n.d., 1716, 1743; *T.E.R.A.S.* ii. 56.
[8] B.I.H.R., TER. J. Bessingby 1764 to 1861.
[9] Hodgson, *Q.A.B.* 434.
[10] B.I.H.R., TER. J. Bessingby 1764.
[11] Lawton, *Rer. Eccles. Dioc. Ebor.* 287.
[12] *Rep. Com. Eccl. Revenues*, 918–19.
[13] H.O. 129/24/524.
[14] B.I.H.R., TER. J. Bessingby 1764, 1770, 1781, 1809.
[15] Ex inf. the Vicar, 1969.
[16] *Test. Ebor.* v. 133–4.
[17] *Cal. Pat.* 1549–51, 81. In the particulars for this grant the names are given as Pease and Wilson: E 318/1854.
[18] *Cal. Pat.* 1569–72, 38.
[19] B.I.H.R., Bp. V. 1764/Ret. 54; *Herring's Visit.* i. 111.
[20] *Rep. Com. Eccl. Revenues*, 918–19.
[21] B.I.H.R., V. 1865/Ret. 45; V. 1868/Ret. 43; V. 1871/Ret. 44; V. 1877/Ret.
[22] Ibid. Bp. V. 1894/Ret.; Bp. V. 1936/Ret. 263.
[23] *Crockford*.
[24] E.R.R.O., DPX/57, Bessingby, p. 15.
[25] B.I.H.R., Bp. V. 1936/Ret. 263.
[26] E.R.R.O., DPX/57, Bessingby, p. 14.
[27] *D.N.B.*
[28] *Herring's Visit.* i. 111.
[29] B.I.H.R., Bp. V. 1764/Ret. 54.
[30] Ibid. V. 1865/Ret. 45.
[31] Ibid. V. 1877/Ret.
[32] B.I.H.R., CD. 533; foundation stone.
[33] e.g. *Test. Ebor.* vi. 46–7.
[34] E.R.R.O., DDGR/42/11.

quite fallen down'.[35] A consolidation of the parish with Carnaby was proposed by the incumbent, who held both livings, but was successfully opposed by his parishioners.[36] A faculty was granted in 1765 to rebuild the church, to shorten it from 51 ft. to 31 ft., and to remove the tower.[37] This work was carried out at the expense of the landowners, and in particular of Christopher Goulton, the lord of the manor, who contributed about half.[38] The rebuilt church was a small, plain, brick structure, consisting of chancel and nave, with a small belfry.[39]

A new church was erected in 1893–4 with money bequeathed for the purpose by George Wright.[40] It is of sandstone and was designed by T. L. Moore in the Decorated style.[41] The central, embattled, tower has an octagonal spire. The bells, organ, pulpit, and lectern were given by Alfred Wright, who also gave the east window in memory of his uncle.[42] A brass inscription to William Pearson (d. 1668) and his wife Susanna were probably made by Thomas Mann, of York.[43] A marble tablet to Anne, wife of Harrington Hudson (d. 1818), representing a lady expiring in the arms of her attendants, is by R. J. Wyatt, of London. There are various other tablets to the Hudson family.

The church still contains the original circular Norman font, decorated with a round-headed arcade and the whole covered with chevrons and other ornamentation. In one bay of the arcade is a carving of the tree of life and in another a pair of animals.[44]

In 1552 the church contained three bells, one of which was broken,[45] and by 1764 there were only two.[46] The church as rebuilt in 1765 had one bell.[47] The present church contains eight tubular bells, but on the floor of the nave there stands an old bell, probably of the 15th or 16th century.[48] The plate consists of a cup, made in York in 1570 probably by Robert Beckwith, and a paten, made in London in 1704 by Seth Lofthouse.[49] The registers date from 1698 and are largely complete.[50] The churchyard was consecrated in 1895.[51]

In 1958 a chapel, dedicated to *ST. MARK*, was built on the West Hill estate. It is a large rectangular brick building and it is also used as a church hall. In 1969 two services were held each Sunday, with three every fourth week.

NONCONFORMITY. In 1676 three protestant dissenters were recorded in Bessingby,[52] but there is no evidence of organized dissent at a later date.

EDUCATION. A school may have existed at Bessingby in 1638–9, when Christopher Bradley, the curate, was licensed to teach.[53] A school certainly existed by 1690, when the curate recommended Edward Moore, 'of whose sobriety, learning and conformity . . . to the Church of England I am assured', asking that he might be licensed to teach there.[54] In 1819 a school at Bessingby was attended by one boy and 4 or 5 girls, and 10 children from the village attended school at Carnaby.[55] There was no school by 1835, however,[56] and in 1871 Bessingby children went to schools in Bridlington and Carnaby.[57]

CHARITIES FOR THE POOR. None known.

BOYNTON

THE parish of Boynton, roughly rectangular in shape, lies about 2½ miles west of Bridlington in the valley of the Gypsey Race and upon the wolds which surround it, with most of its area on the wold slopes on the north side of the valley.[1] The village, which is mainly situated in a small side valley, was probably an Anglian settlement.[2] Evidence of early settlement near the site of the village is provided by Romano-British remains of the 4th century and several Anglian burials, found in the main valley to the west of Boynton.[3] Since at least the early 16th century about a third of Caythorpe township, adjoining Boynton on the west, has been regarded as part of Boynton parish.[4] Thus the western parish boundary with Rudston is a relatively late one, and this may explain why, for most of its length as it runs over the wolds, it is undefined. The northern boundary with Grindale partly follows dry valley bottoms, and the southern boundary with Carnaby is formed by Wold Gate.[5] The area of the ancient parish is 2,613 a. Since 1935 Easton has been included in the civil parish of Boynton.[6]

The landscape of Boynton exhibits a marked contrast between the rolling, almost treeless, wold

[35] B.I.H.R., Bp. V. 1764/Ret. 54.
[36] E.R.R.O., DDGR/42/11.
[37] Lawton, *Rer. Eccles. Dioc. Ebor.* 287.
[38] E.R.R.O., DDGR/42/11.
[39] Bulmer, *Dir. E. Yorks.* (1892), 109–10.
[40] E.R.R.O., DPX/57, Bessingby, p. 22; foundation stone.
[41] E.R.R.O., DPX/57, Bessingby, p. 22; *Kelly's Dir. N. & E.R. Yorks.* (1897), 390.
[42] E.R.R.O., DPX/57, Bessingby, p. 22.
[43] *Y.A.J.* xxiv. 274.
[44] *T.E.R.A.S.* x. 111.
[45] *Inventories of Ch. Goods*, 32.
[46] B.I.H.R., TER. J. Bessingby 1764.
[47] Bulmer, *Dir. E. Yorks.* (1892), 109–10.
[48] *T.E.R.A.S.* iv. 72–3; Boulter, 'Ch. Bells', 215.
[49] *Yorks. Ch. Plate*, i. 216.
[50] E.R.R.O.
[51] B.I.H.R., CD. 533.
[52] Bodl. MS. Tanner 150, ff. 27 sqq.
[53] B.I.H.R., Schools index.
[54] B.I.H.R., Nom/SM. 1690.
[55] *Rets. on Educ. of Poor, 1819*, 1076, 1078.
[56] *Educ. Enquiry Abstract, 1835*, 1079.
[57] *Rets. rel. Elem. Educ. 1871*, 474.
[1] This article was written in 1969.
[2] *P.N.E.R. Yorks.* (E.P.N.S.), 99–100.
[3] Ex inf. Mr. T. C. M. Brewster, 1971.
[4] E.R.R.O., Land Tax, 1783; B.I.H.R., TA. 218S; O.S. Map 6" (1854); *Valor Eccl.* v. 122.
[5] See p. 1.
[6] *Census*, 1931.

to the north, and the well-wooded southern part of the parish. There is much woodland in the valley and on the lower wold slopes, particularly on the southern side of the valley, as a result of extensive planting by the Stricklands in the 18th and 19th centuries. Other plantations lie in Binsdale, a small valley about ½ mile west of the village; it is referred to, as Bildesdale, in the late 12th century.[7]

The wolds rise to over 325 ft. above sea-level in the north-west of the parish and much of the wold land north of the Gypsey Race lies at over 275 ft. Around the northern boundary the land falls to 200–250 ft. The wolds south of the Race rise steeply to over 250 ft. in the south-west of the parish. Most of the open-field land lay on the northern valley slopes before inclosure in 1783, although some was on the southern side of the valley in the area now occupied by Sands wood.[8] This area was presumably named from the deposit of sand which overlies the chalk, and which was formerly dug from a pit near Sands wood; there are also several chalk quarries on the wolds. Apart from the extensive area of woodland, the land is now devoted almost entirely to arable farming, the only permanent grass lying in the valley bottom along the Gypsey Race. Fishponds wood contains extensive ponds.

Boynton Hall, a late-16th-century building with substantial 18th-century alterations and additions, is situated at the southern end of the village on the low-lying ground south of the Race.[9] The house is surrounded by parkland and plantations, and the southern valley side rises steeply behind it. The Stricklands, owners of the hall and lords of the manor until 1950, dominated the life of the village for about 400 years.

The Rudston–Bridlington road runs across the parish on the lower wold slopes north of the Gypsey Race. Surviving earthworks show that the road formerly took a more southerly and direct line from near Binsdale to the Easton boundary, and thus ran south of the village through what is now parkland. The road was diverted by Sir George Strickland in 1768.[10] Part of the old course lay in the valley bottom and was probably subject to flooding by the Gypsey Race. The road which forms the village street runs north across the wolds to Grindale, and a minor road leads from the Rudston road in the west of the parish southwards over the wolds to Carnaby. The village street formerly continued southwards as a more direct road to Carnaby and this too was blocked in 1768; a hollow way in the park south of the hall is presumably a remnant of it. In 1844 George Hudson, the 'Railway King', proposed a York–Bridlington line passing through Boynton along the valley, but the scheme was successfully opposed by Sir George Strickland.[11]

The village lies mainly along the Grindale road, stretching from the church and the entrance to the park in the south as far as North Wood Farm. There are two isolated farms in the parish, Charleston in the north and Binsdale in the east, which probably originated after inclosure in the late 18th century. There are several modern buildings, including the wooden village hall which has stood in Boynton since 1949, but the village has not been extended at either end in modern times. In the Middle Ages, however, it probably stretched further south upon land near the Gypsey Race, now incorporated in the park, for in 1327 nine waste tofts were said to be subject to flooding by the stream.[12]

Many of the buildings in the village are 17th- and 18th-century cottages and houses, built of brick and chalk and often whitewashed. Some of the chalk buildings have tucked gables of brick. A cottage with an attached smithy is situated near the crossroads; the cottage is a one-storey building with dormers, mainly of white-washed chalk but patched with brick, and its windows and doorways have arched heads.

An early-18th-century brick outbuilding of the Vicarage has a crow-stepped and tucked gable and a projecting course at the eaves. Beyond the Vicarage and the church is the main entrance to the park. A large 18th-century brick building stands by the stream about 300 yds. east of the hall. This was probably a manufactory built by Sir George Strickland before 1770.[13] It consists of a taller central block with a lower recessed wing on either side, all of two storeys with half-hipped roofs and each containing two bricked-up circular openings in the north elevation. There are similar openings in the south elevation, as well as a round-headed loading bay on the first floor. Near by is a small round brick building, on a stone plinth, with a semicircular projection marking the position of a chimney. This may have been connected with the manufactory.[14]

In 1377 there were 100 poll-tax payers at Boynton.[15] In 1674 14 households were discharged from paying the hearth-tax and of the 15 that were taxed, 10 had only one hearth each, one had 2, 2 had 3, and only the Vicarage and Boynton Hall had more.[16] In 1743 there were 23 families[17] and in 1764 21.[18] The population was 66 in 1801; until 1891 it varied only between 100 and 128, with the exception of 1881 when it was 156. In the 20th century it fell from 161 in 1901[19] to 131 in 1921, before rising to 140 in 1931. Little growth subsequently took place and in 1951, even with Easton included, there were only 147 inhabitants in the civil parish.[20]

MANOR AND OTHER ESTATES. Four estates are recorded in Boynton in 1086, comprising 4, 3, 2, and half a carucate respectively. The two smaller estates were soke of Bridlington manor.[21]

The 4-carucate estate had been held in 1066 by Torchil and belonged to the count of Mortain by 1086.[22] The count's lands were forfeited for rebellion in 1088 and passed to the Paynel fee, which was later granted to the archbishop of Canterbury.[23] The archbishop's overlordship is last mentioned in 1428.[24] A mesne lordship under the Paynels and the

[7] E.R.R.O., DDWB/4/2.
[8] See p. 25.
[9] See p. 23.
[10] E.R.R.O., QSV/1/5 p. 434.
[11] J. T. Ward, *E. Yorks. Landed Estates in the 19th Cent.* (E. Yorks. Loc. Hist. Ser. xxiii), 7.
[12] *Cal. Inq. p.m.* vii, p. 14.
[13] See p. 26.
[14] Perhaps a drying-house. It was wrongly thought to be a pigeon-house in 1850, when another 'pigeon-house', now demolished, stood close by: O.S. Map 6" (1854).
[15] E 179/202/62 m. 25.
[16] E 179/205/521.
[17] *Herring's Visit.* i. 110.
[18] B.I.H.R., Bp. V. 1764/Ret. 78.
[19] *V.C.H. Yorks.* iii. 488.
[20] *Census.*
[21] *V.C.H. Yorks.* ii. 197, 204, 226.
[22] Ibid. 226.
[23] See p. 181.
[24] *Feud. Aids*, vi. 265.

archbishops was held by the Meynell family from at least the late 12th century until the death of Nicholas de Meynell in 1342.[25] In 1352 two mesne lords are mentioned, John Darcy, whose wife Elizabeth was Nicholas de Meynell's daughter, and Robert of Bolton, whose wife Alice was a more distant Meynell heiress.[26] The Bolton interest seems to have descended to William de Percy, Alice's son by a later marriage,[27] and the Percy lordship was last mentioned in 1389.[28] In 1418 the mesne lordship was divided between Elizabeth and Margery, daughters of Philip Darcy.[29] Margery married Sir John Conyers and the Conyers interest was mentioned until 1541.[30] Elizabeth married Sir James Strangways[31] and the Strangways retained half the lordship until 1541, when it was sold to William, Lord Dacre and Greystock.[32] The apparently undivided mesne lordship was later acquired by Edward, earl of Rutland, who died possessed of it in 1587.[33] It was last mentioned in the early 17th century.[34]

The Meynells appear to have retained much of BOYNTON manor in demesne. In the early 14th century Nicholas de Meynell held 6 carucates in demesne[35] and in 1316 he was returned as the sole lord of Boynton.[36] By 1428 the estate had apparently passed to Thomas, Lord Swynford, who then held 5 carucates,[37] and later in the 15th century it seems to have been acquired by the Newport family.[38] In 1549 Thomas Newport sold the manor to William Strickland.[39] During the 16th century Strickland bought other property from James Savage, Robert Hellard and Peter Ranson, and Thomas Boynton,[40] and during the 18th century from Sir Griffith and Francis Boynton and Pocklington Grammar School.[41] At inclosure in 1783 Sir George Strickland was allotted all the land in Boynton except a few acres of glebe.[42]

At the death of Sir Charles Strickland in 1909 the estate was settled for life upon his son Walter (d. 1938). In 1944 it was vested in Sir Charles' great-nephew C. H. Marriott (d. 1945) and in 1947 in Marriott's nephew James, who had changed his name to Strickland.[43] The property was sold to J. T. T. Fletcher in 1951.[44] In 1952 he sold about 715 a. to the timber company of J. Taylor Ltd., of Driffield,[45] and the rest of the estate was sold in smaller lots.[46] The company sold Boynton Hall in 1954 to W. S. Cook,[47] who was the owner in 1969, and most of its remaining property in Boynton in 1955 to H. J. Taylor, who granted it to his grandson J. D. T. Megginson in 1965.[48] The house has been divided into flats.

Boynton Hall was built by William Strickland (d. 1598) or his son Walter, probably in the late 16th century.[49] It was from the first a three-storeyed building, though the uppermost was formerly a gabled attic floor. It was H-shaped, with embattled turrets in the four internal angles. The original main entrance, in the south front, is thought to have been through one of these turrets. It would have given access to a screens passage across the end of the great hall, the hall itself occupying the whole of the central block and rising through two storeys. The turrets on the north front accommodated stairs, one of which remains. The walls were constructed of red brick, richly diapered with blue vitrified bricks, and the quoins and the continuous string-courses between the storeys were of stone. Also of stone was the facing of the two lower floors in the recessed centres of the north and south fronts. This work was done with re-used medieval stone, possibly fetched from Bridlington priory after its suppression. The house had 23 hearths in 1674.[50]

The first significant alterations were made c. 1700. The south front was given a symmetrical appearance by moving the entrance to the centre of the recessed middle portion and inserting new windows both there and in the flanking turrets.[51] It was probably at this period that the hall was divided horizontally by an inserted ceiling. The interior was considerably altered in 1700–4, by tradition following a fire in the late 17th century. The earliest surviving fittings are of this date, including the fine oak staircase in the west wing, with twisted balusters and a heavy moulded hand-rail.[52] Over it and of the same period is an enriched plaster ceiling and both the stair-well and a room in the west wing are lined with handsome bolection-moulded panelling. One bedroom contains a bolection-moulded 'Queen Anne' fire-place.

The exterior of the house was extensively remodelled by Sir William Strickland (d. 1735) in the 1730s, but much of the earlier brick- and stone-work remained as a background to the new classical detailing. The original mullioned windows were all replaced by sashes, and a Venetian window, of the Doric order, was inserted above the doorway on the south front; the doorway and its flanking windows were also remodelled and on the top floor a three-light lunette window was placed in a central gable. Another Venetian window, this time of the Ionic order, was inserted at the centre of the west front, with a circular window above it and a round-headed rusticated doorway below. Lord Burlington is known to have been concerned in these alterations, but, in Strickland's absence, the local clerk-of-works failed to carry out all his instructions. In particular, Lord Burlington supplied designs for 'a Palladian roof and an attic storey', but, when

---

[25] K.B. 26/71 m. 7; *Cal. Pat. 1292–1301*, 498; *Complete Peerage*, v. 285, where Nicholas is referred to as William.
[26] C 135/2/7; C 135/76/33; C 135/113/25.
[27] C 136/54/3; C 136/100/46.
[28] *Cal. Inq. Misc.* v, p. 123.
[29] *Cal. Pat. 1422–9*, 422.
[30] C 142/6/89; C 142/72/24.
[31] *Cal. Inq. p.m. Hen. VII*, i, pp. 111, 187.
[32] *Yorks. Fines*, i. 92.
[33] C 142/217/128.
[34] C 142/429/136; *Complete Peerage*, vi. 465.
[35] B.M. Add. MS. 26729, f. 112d.
[36] *Feud. Aids*, vi. 168.
[37] Ibid. 265.
[38] See p. 25.
[39] *Yorks Fines*, i. 135–6, 145.
[40] Ibid. 177, 258; E.R.R.O., DDWB/4/26.
[41] See p. 25.
[42] Registry of Deeds, Beverley, BB/397/52.
[43] Ibid. 125/64/57; 677/266/209; 759/118/106; 870/49/39.
[44] Ibid. 899/91/77.
[45] Ibid. 921/78/64.
[46] Ibid. 920/88/80; /90/81; 921//77/63; /81/65; 83/66; etc.
[47] Ibid. 970/125/104.
[48] Ibid. 1000/147/126; 1453/224/201.
[49] See plate facing p. 48. The house is described and illustrated in *Country Life*, 22 and 29 July 1954, and in *E. Yorks. Georgian Soc. Trans.* iii (3), 35–53; iv (1), 27–32.
[50] E 179/205/521.
[51] B.M. Lansd. MS. 914, f. 259 (drawing of S. front by Sam. Buck, c. 1720); *E. Yorks. Georgian Soc. Trans.* iii (3), 37 (reconstruction of original S. front).
[52] See plate facing p. 49.

Strickland returned, he found an 'old-fashioned roof and many other material alterations from the plan'.[53] It was apparently at this period, nevertheless, that the original gables disappeared and a full third storey was added to the building. Internal fittings introduced by Strickland included two chimneypieces probably designed by William Kent.

Later in the 18th century the house was altered for the third time. John Carr is thought to have been employed by Sir George Strickland between 1765 and 1780 for much of this work. The recessed centre of the north front was filled in, thus finally obscuring the original H-plan. Between the brick ends of the two former wings the new façade projects slightly and is built largely of re-used stone. At the centre is a three-storeyed and three-sided bay window, flanked by three tiers of round-headed windows. Below the existing Venetian window on the west front a central stone porch with Tuscan columns *in antis* was added *c.* 1780. Internally columns were introduced to screen off the end bays of the hall, which was used to house a collection of antique sculpture.

John Carr is also thought to have been responsible for the brick service wing built on the east side of the house at this time. It replaced two ranges of stables and offices which had formerly occupied the site.[54] The new wing is of two low storeys and is connected to the house by a curved wall. The north front, facing a courtyard, has a central pediment, the windows below it being set in three arched recesses rising through both storeys. There is a similar arcaded treatment on the west side overlooking the garden.

To the south-west of the house is a small, square, red-brick garden house, built in the 16th century. About 1770 it was given Gothic features, including a castellated parapet, pointed windows, and quatrefoil and star-shaped openings. The late-18th-century work at Boynton also included a tower, beyond the parish boundary, known as Carnaby Temple.[55]

To the west of the garden house is a three-sided block of outbuildings of red brick with stone dressings, evidently built in the late 18th century when the original stable range to the east of the house was demolished. The east wing remains substantially unaltered and has a central stone doorway, stone quoins, and a dentilled brick eaves course. The north wing has two large openings, apparently for carriages, and the west wing contained stables. The block is now used as farm buildings. Near by are the remains of an ice-house, and west of the stables is a square, two-storeyed, building which may have been a granary. It is built largely of chalk, with some brick, and has a pyramidal roof; the window openings are pointed and there are small circular openings below the eaves.

The 18th-century gateway to the park consists of two rusticated stone piers with ball finials and curved red-brick supporting walls. The lodge cottage, just inside the entrance, is an 18th-century building of a storey and a half, largely built of chalk, and whitewashed. It has tucked gables, a dentilled brick eaves course, and pointed windows and doors. In one gable-end a pointed recess contains an attic window. The irregularly-shaped and well-wooded park which surrounds the hall extends as far as Wold Gate to the south and, west of the village street, as far as the Rudston road to the north. The Gypsey Race flows eastwards through the park and is crossed by several bridges, the most notable of which is a low 18th-century brick bridge of five arches. At the southern edge of the park Fondbrig carries Wold Gate over a dry gulley in the valley side. This is an 18th-century ornamental bridge, built of brick with rough-hewn stone dressings. The northern side consists of a high wall with an arched opening in the parapet and, below the road level, a brick recess surmounted by a moulded stone decoration.

The 3-carucate estate in Boynton had been held in 1066 by Ulf, Archil, and Chenut and in 1086 was in the possession of the king.[56] It was later granted to the count of Aumale, whose overlordship was last mentioned in 1521.[57] Before 1127 the estate was granted to Alan de Mounceaux, whose descendants retained a mesne lordship until the end of the 15th century.[58]

Alan's son Ingram de Mounceaux granted a chief house and 3 carucates in Boynton *c.* 1200 to William of Boynton,[59] and after the death of Ingram of Boynton *c.* 1320 the property passed to his eldest son Walter. It subsequently descended in the Boyntons of Barmston and later of Burton Agnes. In the 16th century Thomas Boynton sold some of the land to William Strickland[60] and in 1755 the rest, including 16 bovates and known as Yates's farm, was conveyed by Sir Griffith and Francis Boynton to Sir George Strickland.[61] It was thus incorporated in the capital manor. Other land, amounting to 15 bovates in 1428,[62] was retained by the Mounceaux family until the later 15th century, when it passed to Sir Martin del See. In 1497 it was inherited by Sir Martin's daughter Margaret, widow of Henry Boynton,[63] and so was presumably reunited with the rest of the Mounceaux property.

The two smaller Domesday estates were in the king's hands in 1086 and subsequently became part of the Gant fee, which later passed to the Tattershalls.[64] A mesne lordship was held from at least the early 13th century by the Grindale family, descending in the early 14th century to Roger de Somerville.[65] A second mesne lordship belonged to another branch of the Grindale family and was mentioned as late as 1352.[66] Thirteenth-century tenants of the Grindales included Thomas of Caythorpe and Ralph de Wyerne.[67] Various grants of land in the Tattershall fee were made to Bridlington priory,[68] which retained 7 bovates in Boynton until the late 13th century when they were exchanged with Walter of Buckton for land elsewhere.[69] In 1286 Walter

---

[53] J. Lees-Milne, *Earls of Creation*, 163 n.
[54] B.M. Lansd. MS. 914, f. 259.
[55] See p. 126.
[56] *V.C.H. Yorks.* ii. 204.
[57] E.R.R.O., DDCC/141/66.
[58] K.B. 27/933 rot. 36; *Bridlington Charty.* 182.
[59] E.R.R.O., DDWB/4/3.
[60] Ibid. /26.
[61] Regy. of Deeds, X/184/417.
[62] *Feud. Aids*, vi. 267.

[63] E.R.R.O., DDCC/3/22; C 142/58/16; C 142/62/44.
[64] *V.C.H. Yorks.* ii. 197; *Cal. Close*, 1307–13, 102; *Cal. Inq. p.m.* vii, p. 470. It was sometimes described as the Mauley fee: e.g. *Cal. Inq. p.m.* xii, p. 220; *Feud. Aids*, vi. 225.
[65] K.B. 26/142 m. 14 d.; B.M. Add. MS. 26729, f. 113.
[66] *Bridlington Charty.* 53, 184; *Cal. Inq. p.m.* ix, p. 459.
[67] *Bridlington Charty.* 103, 182–4.
[68] Ibid. 182–4.
[69] Ibid. 85.

sold 5 bovates to Robert of Boynton,[70] and by 1352 the Boynton family had 15 bovates of the Tattershall fee, 8 of them held of Marmaduke Grindale and 7 of the prior of Bridlington.[71]

The Boynton family thus had a substantial interest in both the Aumale and the Tattershall fees. It also acquired land in the Canterbury fee, amounting to 14 bovates in 1352, when Roger Boynton died possessed of it.[72] The Boyntons' estate subsequently descended to Roger's great-grandson Robert Boynton, and thence to Robert's sister Elizabeth and her husband Thomas Newport. In 1428 Thomas still had 14 bovates of the Canterbury fee and 8 of the Tattershall fee.[73] Later in the 15th century the Newports apparently acquired the Meynell's demesne land in the Canterbury fee and so became lords of the manor.[74]

Another part of the Canterbury fee was held in 1428, when it comprised 10 bovates, by Thomas Lound.[75] Another Thomas Lound apparently conveyed the property in the early 16th century to Richard Hill, who devised it in 1523–4 to John Dowman.[76] In 1514 Dowman had founded the grammar school at Pocklington[77] and he gave the Boynton land to support the schoolmaster and usher.[78] At inclosure in 1783 the school exchanged the property, including 16 bovates, with Sir George Strickland for an estate in Pocklington.[79]

Two bovates in the parish were given by Alice of Boynton to Nun Appleton priory (Yorks. W.R.).[80] After the Dissolution the land was let by the Crown to Richard Young in 1567, William Strickland in 1578, and William Wilson in 1601.[81] A 'land' in Boynton belonged in the late 12th century to the Knights Templars[82] and may have passed on their suppression in 1312 to the Hospitallers, who in 1539–40 had a cottage and garden in Boynton.[83]

Boynton rectory, which belonged to Bridlington priory from the 12th century,[84] was worth £10 13s. 4d. in 1291 and 1428.[85] After the Dissolution it was let by the Crown to John Banaster and James Bourchier in 1538,[86] to William Godolgham in 1546, to Richard Whalley in 1566, and to Walter Whalley in 1569.[87] It was granted in fee in 1605 to John Lindley and one Starkey.[88] By 1637 it had passed to William Hustler and it was held by his heirs in 1650, when the tithes were worth £50.[89] By 1685 it belonged to Sir William Strickland[90] and at inclosure in 1783, when the Stricklands became sole landowners, the tithes were extinguished.[91]

ECONOMIC HISTORY. For only one of the four estates recorded in 1086 does the Domesday Survey give any information about the economic circumstances; the estate of 3 carucates, held in 1086 by the king, was then worth £1 and there was land for one plough.[92]

Information about the customary and free tenants and their holdings in the Middle Ages is scanty. Four bond holdings were mentioned about 1255,[93] and land was held by villein tenure (*villenagiis*) in 1335.[94] In 1368 the rents of cottars in the Tattershall fee amounted to £1 17s., about a tenth of the total value of the manor, and the rents of tenants-at-will totalled £18 10s., or virtually all of the remainder.[95] Freeholders were apparently few: there was none in the Tattershall fee in 1368.[96] The only evidence for the size of tenant holdings dates from 1346, when one tenant held 4 bovates, 4 held 2, and one held one, all of the Tattershall fee.[97]

Late-12th-century references to North Langes probably indicate strips or lands in the open fields.[98] In 1413 8 bovates in 'the fields of Boynton' were known as 'the landdale'.[99] In 1613 East field and South field were mentioned, and subdivisions of the open fields were known as the Wandales, the Cadales, the Mellands, the Charylls, Easton Dales, the Warlatts, the Sands, and the East and West Braimes.[1] Butts of land in the Hards and High field were referred to in 1685,[2] and in 1777 Westerdales formed part of the open fields.[3] The names of the fields were not given at inclosure in 1783.

The low-lying land along the Gypsey Race presumably provided meadow and pasture from early times, although in the early 14th century some land there was said to be subject to flooding.[4] It was probably in the valley bottom that East and West ings, said to contain 32 bovates of meadow land in 1613, were situated.[5] The Cow pasture was mentioned in 1716[6] and the Town pasture in 1783.[7] Another area of pasture was known in both the 17th and 18th centuries as Mason garths.[8] In the mid 19th century and later the area on the wold slopes between Binsdale and the Grindale road was known as Boynton sheepwalk[9] and land on the upper wold slopes in the north-west of the parish was known as Boynton Whins.[10]

In the 14th century the area of land under cultivation in the parish seems to have been decreasing. In 1327 nine 'tofts and lands' on the estate of John of Boynton were waste,[11] and in 1352, out of a

---

[70] *Yorks. Fines, 1272–1300*, 75.
[71] *Cal. Inq. p.m.* ix, p. 459.
[72] Ibid.
[73] G. Poulson, *Hist. Holderness*, i. 197; *Feud. Aids*, vi. 265, 267.
[74] See p. 23.
[75] *Feud. Aids*, vi. 265.
[76] C 1/1022/64–5.
[77] P. C. Sandys and C. M. Haworth, *Hist. of Pocklington Sch., E. Yorks., 1514–1950*, 8.
[78] C 1/1022/65.
[79] Regy. of Deeds, BB/397/52.
[80] J. Burton, *Mon. Ebor.* 277; *Cal. Chart. R. 1226–57*, 343.
[81] E 310/28/167 no. 45; E 310/31/183 no. 12; E 310/33/199 no. 28.
[82] E.R.R.O., DDWB/4/1.
[83] *Miscellanea*, iv (Y.A.S. Rec. Ser. xciv), 94.
[84] See p. 26.
[85] *Tax. Eccl.* (Rec. Com.), 326; *Feud. Aids*, vi. 327.
[86] *L. & P. Hen. VIII*, xiii (1), p. 562.
[87] *Cal. Pat. 1563–6*, 382; *1566–9*, 346.
[88] H. Grove, *Alienated Tithes*, p. cxxxiii.

[89] C 5/12/15; *T.E.R.A.S.* ii. 55–6.
[90] B.I.H.R., TER. J. Boynton 1685.
[91] Regy. of Deeds, BB/397/52.
[92] *V.C.H. Yorks.* ii. 204, 322.
[93] E.R.R.O., DDWB/4/7b.
[94] Ibid. /22.
[95] *Cal. Inq. p.m.* xii, p. 220.
[96] Ibid.
[97] *Feud. Aids*, vi. 225.
[98] E.R.R.O., DDWB/4/2; *P.N.E.R. Yorks.* (E.P.N.S.), 326.
[99] E.R.R.O., DDWB/4/24.
[1] Ibid. /27.
[2] B.I.H.R., TER. J. Boynton 1685.
[3] Registry of Deeds, Beverley, BB/397/52.
[4] *Cal. Inq. p.m.* vii, p. 14.
[5] E.R.R.O., DDWB/4/27.
[6] B.I.H.R., TER. J. Boynton 1716.
[7] Regy. of Deeds, BB/397/52.
[8] Ibid. U/481/922; E.R.R.O., DDWB/4/27.
[9] O.S. Map 6" (1854 and later edns.).
[10] O.S. Map 6" (1854).
[11] *Cal. Inq. p.m.* vii, p. 14.

total of 29 bovates held by Roger of Boynton, 20 were waste. He also held a waste toft and a ruinous windmill.[12] The Black Death may have been partly responsible for the decay but the earlier mention of waste and the fact that in 1354 the tax quota was reduced by only about 8 per cent[13] suggest that the decline was of longer standing.

Peter de Mauley had a park in Boynton in 1376,[14] and in the 14th century John of Boynton had 11 a. of 'marshy inclosure', presumably near the Gypsey Race.[15] In 1613 crofts were situated in North Pittes, which was later described as an inclosed 'flat' or furlong.[16] The Stricklands were probably responsible for some inclosure. A field was known as New Inclosure[17] in the mid 18th century, and by 1764 Sir George Strickland's demesne lands were all inclosed. The latter consisted of closes lying 'south of his house up to the Wold Gate', and others called Mill Hill close and Dogkennel close.[18]

The remaining open fields and commons, amounting to about 2,000 a., were inclosed in 1783[19] under an Act of 1777.[20] The whole of Boynton, except 16 bovates and several pasture closes in the possession of Pocklington Grammar School, was owned by Sir George Strickland, who was also the impropriator of the rectory. Under the award, Strickland obtained the school's land by exchange and he was allotted the whole of Boynton, except for 8 a. awarded to the vicar in lieu of part of the vicarial tithes.

In the 18th century, particularly after inclosure, and in the early 19th century Sir George Strickland (1729–1808) and his son Sir William (1753–1834) were actively engaged in improving the estate.[21] By 1770 Sir George Strickland had been using sainfoin on his wold land for many years and had increased its value from 2s. or 2s. 6d. to about £1 an acre.[22] By 1812 380 a. of plantations had been laid out on the wold slopes to the north and south of the hall and in the park surrounding it.[23] Following the abolition of common grazing at inclosure, the Stricklands also paid much attention to livestock improvement. Their success is revealed by the prices paid for their stock. In 1808 94 lots were sold for over £2,000.[24] Sir William's experiments with South Down sheep, however, failed.[25] About 1816, during the agricultural depression, he reported 'a great want of employment among the labouring poor', and he claimed that local farmers were living off their capital, or being bought out at ruinous prices.[26]

From the late 18th to the 20th centuries there have usually been from three to five farms in Boynton.[27] In 1851 the two largest farms, Binsdale and Charleston, contained 700 a. and 500 a. respectively, and there were two farms of between 250 a. and 400 a.[28]

A woollen manufactory, intended to provide employment for the poor, existed in Boynton by 1770. Sir George Strickland had been 'induced to found a building large enough to contain looms ... and space for women and children to spin'. At one time it had employed 'upwards of 150 hands' but in 1770 there were said to be 'under a dozen'.[29] It had probably closed by 1812.[30] The building stands about 300 yds. east of the hall, near the Gypsey Race. It was apparently powered by water from a mill race, now filled in. It later became the estate saw-mill[31] and in 1969 was used as a piggery.

A mill existed in the mid 13th century[32] and a miller was mentioned about the same time.[33] In 1352 a windmill was said to be ruinous,[34] but in 1549 the manor still contained a windmill.[35] A field was known in 1751 as Mill Hill close.[36]

LOCAL GOVERNMENT. There are surviving churchwardens' accounts from 1740 onwards, overseers' accounts for 1735–1800, and constables' accounts for 1740–93.[37] Both the churchwardens and the overseers were two in number. A poor-rate was first levied in 1738 at ½d. in the pound, which raised £1, and a poorhouse was mentioned in that year for the first and only time. Until about 1770 the rate generally varied between 1d. and 4½d., raising between £2 and £8. From 1770 to 1800, however, the rate was usually higher, several times reaching 1s. in the pound and averaging about 6d. The money was mostly used to provide out-relief. In 1797 two special rates of 9½d. and 2s. 7d. raised a total of £117 to pay for a lawsuit concerning settlement. In 1836 Boynton joined the Bridlington union.[38]

There was one constable. A rate levied to meet his expenses varied between ½d. and 4½d. The average amount raised was about £4. The main item of expenditure was payments to travellers with passes, and others included the cost of delivering warrants, organizing searches, and compensating victims of robbery.

CHURCH. A church existed in Boynton by 1120–7, when Stephen, count of Aumale, confirmed the gift of it to Bridlington priory.[39] It had been given to the priory either by Stephen himself or by Geoffrey Despenser.[40] A vicarage had been ordained by 1268, when the first recorded vicar was presented.[41]

[12] *Cal. Inq. p.m.* ix, p. 459.
[13] E 179/202/53.
[14] *Parl. Rep. Yorks.* i (Y.A.S. Rec. Ser. xci), 125.
[15] C 135/2/7.
[16] E.R.R.O., DDWB/4/27; Regy. of Deeds, BB/397/52.
[17] Regy. of Deeds, U/481/922.
[18] B.I.H.R., TER. J. Boynton 1764.
[19] Regy. of Deeds, BB/397/52.
[20] 17 Geo. III, c. 72 (Priv. Act).
[21] A. Harris, *Rural Landscape of E.R. Yorks.* 77; J. T. Ward, *E. Yorks. Landed Estates in the 19th Cent.* (E. Yorks. Loc. Hist. Ser. xxiii), 18–19; O. Wilkinson, *Agric. Revolution in E.R. Yorks.* (E. Yorks. Loc. Hist. Ser. v), 13–14.
[22] A. Young, *Six Months' Tour Through N. of Eng.* ii. 8.
[23] H. E. Strickland, *Gen. View Agric. E.R.* 177–8. Tree-planting had begun as early as 1725, when Sir William planted 100 larches from Switzerland, then a novelty in the area: *E. Yorks. Georgian Soc. Trans.* iii (3), 53.
[24] Wilkinson, *Agric. Rev. E.R. Yorks.* 13.
[25] Ward, *E. Yorks. Landed Estates in 19th Cent.* 19.
[26] Wilkinson, *Agric. Rev. E.R. Yorks.* 19.
[27] E.R.R.O., Land Tax, 1783; directories.
[28] H.O. 107/2367.
[29] Young, *Tour Through N. of Eng.* ii. 7–8.
[30] There is no mention of it in Strickland, *Gen. View Agric. E.R.*
[31] O.S. Map 25" (1892).
[32] E.R.R.O., DDWB/4/7b.
[33] Ibid. /5.
[34] *Cal. Inq. p.m.* ix, p. 459.
[35] *Yorks. Fines*, i. 145.
[36] Regy. of Deeds, U/481/922.
[37] Par. recs., in church.
[38] *3rd Rep. Poor Law Com.* 167.
[39] *Bridlington Charty.* 181; *E.Y.C.* iii, p. 50.
[40] *Bridlington Charty.* 1–2.
[41] *Reg. Giffard* (Sur. Soc. cix), 53.

From the late 17th century until the mid 19th century, however, Boynton was regarded as a curacy. In 1963 the benefice was united with that of Rudston with Grindale and Argam.[42]

The advowson was retained by Bridlington until the Dissolution, although in 1501 Sir Robert Constable, presumably lessee of the rectory, made a presentation. The Crown presented several times during the later 16th century[43] before granting the advowson to John Lindley, who died possessed of it in 1613.[44] In 1621 Walter Strickland presented[45] and, although the Crown presented in 1625 and 1666,[46] the advowson followed the descent of the manor until 1951, when it was transferred to the archbishop of York.[47]

The vicarage was worth £5 in 1291[48] and 1428.[49] In 1535 its net value was £7 14s. 2d.,[50] and in 1650 it was worth £30.[51] An attempt made in 1654 to augment the living out of Burton Agnes rectory failed.[52] In 1829–31 the average net income was £141.[53] In 1884 it was said to have recently decreased to about £190.[54]

The valuation of 1535 included corn and hay tithes in Caythorpe, hay tithes in Boynton, and wool and lamb tithes in both places.[55] By 1685 the hay tithe of Caythorpe had been commuted for 3s. 4d. a year, and by 1716 the same tithe on Sir William Strickland's land at Boynton had been commuted for £2 a year. The other tithes in Boynton were let to Sir George Strickland in the later 18th century.[56] At inclosure in 1783 the vicar received for half the tithes an allotment of 50 a., worth £18; 8 a. were in Boynton and 42 a. in Burton Fleming. The land was sold in 1921.[57] For the other half he received a rent-charge of £18 a year from Sir George Strickland.[58] The vicar continued to receive a third of the tithes in Caythorpe until 1843, when they were commuted for £115 a year.[59]

In 1284–5 the church was said to be endowed with 7 bovates[60] but there is no later reference to the land. In 1685 the vicarage had two butts in Boynton, one in the Hards and the other in High field. By 1716 the glebe was said to consist of one acre in High field and two gates in the Cow pasture, and in 1764 the vicar claimed land in the Hards but added that 'we cannot tell where that is'.[61] The glebe may have accounted for part of the vicar's allotment at inclosure.

There may have been a vicarage house in 1306, when 'the houses of the vicarage' were ordered to be handed over to the vicar,[62] and there certainly was in 1535.[63] It contained five hearths in 1674.[64] In 1764 it was described as a brick-built house of two storeys and attics, with a tiled roof, containing eight principal and more than fifteen minor rooms. The outbuildings included a dovecot, a coal-house, a brew-house, and a coach-house; with the exception of the brick dovecot they were all built of stone, presumably chalk.[65]

The surviving house, which is now a private dwelling, is an L-shaped building of red brick standing to the north of the church. The oldest part is the east range, which probably dates from the early 18th century. It is of two storeys, with cellars and attics, having sliding sash windows and a string-course between the storeys. The west wing, projecting towards the road, was added later in the 18th century and the south front appears to have been remodelled at the same time. These alterations probably took place before 1764, in view of the substantial size of the house at that date. The new wing may have replaced an earlier outbuilding which would account for some surviving chalk in its north wall and a stone floor found below the present wooden one. Both at the gable-end of this wing and near the east end of the south front are boldly-projecting ground-floor bay windows with ramped parapets. Several other ground-floor windows were replaced in the earlier 19th century. Internally the house contains 18th-century panelling and a much-altered staircase of the same period. The stables and other outbuildings are of brick with some chalk.

There were two chantries in the church, one dedicated to St. Michael and the other to St. Lawrence.[66] One of these probably originated in 1324, when the king licensed John of Boynton to grant a house and lands in Boynton and Rudston for the support of a chaplain to celebrate in Boynton church.[67]

Sir William Strickland (d. 1673) was a prominent parliamentarian and during his time there were several changes in the incumbency. William Camplesham was forced to leave the living in 1647 and was restored only in 1660. The intruded ministers were James Calvert (1652–5), W. Etherington (1655–8), and Simon Langthorne, who was ejected at the Restoration.[68] Calvert was still in the parish in 1683, when he was described as 'a nonconformist parson belonging to Mr. Strickland's family'.[69]

The vicars of Boynton have been resident from at least the early 18th century, and probably earlier. From at least 1743 until 1950 the living was held with that of Carnaby, and for much of the 18th century the vicar also held the curacy of Bessingby.[70]

In 1743 one service was held at Boynton each Sunday. Communion was administered three times a year, and about sixteen people received it the previous Easter.[71] By 1764 it was administered four times a year, and the average number of communicants was again sixteen.[72] In 1868 there was still a weekly service and communion was administered six times a year to about thirteen people. Three years

---

[42] York Dioc. Regy., Orders in Council 781.
[43] *Fasti Parochiales*, iii. 4.
[44] C 142/337/109.
[45] Inst. Bks.; *Fasti Parochiales*, iii. 4.
[46] Inst. Bks.; E.R.R.O., DPX/57, Boynton, p. 9.
[47] York Dioc. Regy., Orders in Council 709.
[48] *Tax. Eccl.* (Rec. Com.), 326.
[49] *Feud. Aids*, vi. 327.
[50] *Valor Eccl.* (Rec. Com.), v. 120.
[51] *T.E.R.A.S.* ii. 55–6.
[52] *Cal. S.P. Dom.* 1654, 249; see below, p. 111.
[53] *Rep. Com. Eccl. Revenues*, 920.
[54] B.I.H.R., Bp. V. 1884/Ret.
[55] *Valor Eccl.* v. 122.
[56] B.I.H.R., TER. J. Boynton 1685, 1716, 1764, 1781.
[57] Regy. of Deeds, 235/334/281; 863/128/113.
[58] Ibid. BB/397/52.
[59] B.I.H.R., TA. 218S.
[60] *Feud. Aids*, vi. 29.
[61] B.I.H.R., TER. J. Boynton 1685, 1716, 1764.
[62] *Reg. Greenfield*, iii (Sur. Soc. cli), 123.
[63] *Valor Eccl.* v. 122.
[64] E 179/205/521.
[65] B.I.H.R., TER. J. Boynton 1764.
[66] *Y.A.J.* xx. 258.
[67] *Fasti Parochiales*, iii. 3–6.
[68] *Walker Revised*, ed. A. G. Matthews, 390.
[69] *Cal. S.P. Dom.* 1683, 169.
[70] See pp. 20, 129, 207.
[71] *Herring's Visit.* i. 110.
[72] B.I.H.R., Bp. V. 1764/Ret. 78.

later communion was administered eight times a year, and by 1871 once a month, when the average number of communicants was only seven.[73] In 1884, when communion was administered every three weeks, the number receiving was said to depend a good deal on whether Sir Charles Strickland and his family were in residence at the hall. The vicar also in 1884 attributed the smallness of his congregation, which averaged about 30, to the proximity of Bridlington, which 'entices the poor people there on Sundays to attend the Salvation Army as well as for holiday purposes'. By 1894 there were two services each Sunday.[74] The seating arrangements in the church, consisting of box-pews facing each other across the aisle, were said in 1900 to be a great hindrance to parochial work and to be responsible for 'the almost entire absence of the cottagers from the services'. A family entering church was divided, the men, women, and children sitting in different pews, and this treatment, 'which is based on the feudal system', was strongly resented. The vicar likened the church to 'a chapel to a nobleman's house' and, although it was adequate for the purposes of the Strickland family when it was at Boynton, 'the bulk of the population . . . are being lost to the church'. By 1936 communion was administered every two weeks.[75] In 1969 there was a service every week but communion was administered only once a month.

The church of *ST. ANDREW* stands at the southern end of the village adjoining the park. It was largely rebuilt in brick about 1768 but the 15th-century stone tower has been left standing. The tower has Perpendicular windows at the belfry stage and an embattled parapet with four crocketed pinnacles. It bears a close resemblance to the church tower at Carnaby,[76] even to the tracery of its west window. There is a niche containing a modern figure of St. Andrew on the south-eastern buttress.

Little is known of the rest of the church before its 18th-century rebuilding. In the late 16th century the chancel was reported to be 'in wonderful great decay' and unusable in winter.[77] It was presumably repaired, as nothing more is heard of the state of the fabric until 1767, when Sir George Strickland sought permission to rebuild owing to the serious deterioration of the fabric.[78] Accordingly about 1768 the nave and chancel were entirely rebuilt, on the old foundations, perhaps to designs by John Carr of York.[79]

The entrance to the new church was through the base of the medieval tower, the lower stage forming a porch and the ringing chamber above it being converted into a west gallery, open to the nave. The gallery was used as the Strickland family pew[80] and has a coved plaster ceiling and a curving staircase leading up from the nave. The body of the church consists of three compartments, divided by screens of clustered columns and low railings. As originally planned the central compartment contained the altar and served as the chancel, while further east was the mortuary chapel of the Strickland family; this had a separate entrance in its south wall. In style the elegant interior is mainly classical, with plaster cornices and coved ceilings.[81] The windows, however, have pointed heads and lead glazing of Gothic design. Gothic tracery also adorns the pulpit, formerly a two-decker. The east window contains heraldic glass of 1768 by William Peckitt of York. The Norman-style font either has been recut or is an 18th-century replacement.

At a restoration by John Bilson in 1910 an attempt was made to modify the 'feudal' character of the interior, which had then become unacceptable. Alterations included the replacement of the old high-backed pews with new seating facing east. At the same time the altar was moved to the east end of the Strickland chapel, converting it into a new chancel.

There are many memorials of the Strickland family in the former chapel, including two elaborate painted and gilded monuments to Sir William (d. 1673) and his wife, and to Elizabeth (d. 1674), wife of Sir Thomas Strickland.[82] There is also an 18th-century cenotaph, attributed to William Kent, which was never inscribed and which includes a portrait medallion on its sarcophagus; it was probably erected by Sir William, 4th Bt. (d. 1735). A second monument to Sir William and his wife was set up by Sir George, 5th Bt. There were formerly older monuments in the church to the Newport family, including a tomb and a brass to Sir Robert Newport and his wife (both d. 1383), but these were removed, probably during the 18th-century rebuilding.[83]

The church contained two bells in 1552.[84] In 1704 it was reported as 'not having a good bell',[85] and this probably led to the casting of a new one. By 1764 there were two[86] and one of the surviving bells is inscribed '1705'.[87] The plate consists of a cup made in York in 1821 by Barber and Whitwell, and two plates made in London by John le Sage in 1719 and 1720. All three were given to the church in 1821 by Sir William Strickland.[88] The registers date from 1563 for burials, 1573 for baptisms, and 1588 for marriages, and are complete.[89]

NONCONFORMITY. In 1706 there were said to be eight Roman Catholics in the parish.[90] The vicar in 1743, however, reported no dissenters of any kind.[91] In 1765 one Roman Catholic, John Constable, was reported.[92] In 1865 there were 'a few' dissenters, but they had no meeting-place and they attended the parish church.[93]

EDUCATION. A school existed at Boynton in the late 17th century, and at least one pupil from it

---

[73] B.I.H.R, Bp. V. 1865/Ret. 69; V. 1868/Ret. 67; V. 1871/Ret. 66.
[74] Ibid., Bp. V. 1884/Ret.; Bp. V. 1894/Ret.
[75] Ibid., Bp. V. 1900/Ret. 42; Bp. V. 1936/Ret. 264.
[76] See p. 130.
[77] B.I.H.R., Churches index.
[78] Ibid. Bp. 3/113.
[79] Ibid. FAC. 1767/2; *Arch. Jnl.* cv. 85–6.
[80] B.I.H.R., Bp. V. 1894/Ret.
[81] See plate facing p. 49; *E. Yorks. Georgian Soc. Trans.* iv (1), pl. facing p. 28; *Country Life*, 22 July 1954, fig. 9.
[82] *Country Life*, 22 July 1954, figs. 10, 11.
[83] Bulmer, *Dir. E. Yorks.* (1892), 112–14.
[84] *Inventories of Ch. Goods*, 28.
[85] B.I.H.R., Churches index.
[86] Ibid. TER. J. Boynton 1764.
[87] Boulter, 'Ch. Bells', 215.
[88] *Yorks. Ch. Plate*, i. 225–6.
[89] Barley, *Par. Docs. E.R.* 17.
[90] H. Aveling, *Post Reformation Catholicism in E. Yorks. 1558–1790* (E. Yorks. Loc. Hist. Ser. xi), 59.
[91] *Herring's Visit.* i. 110.
[92] Aveling, op. cit. 59.
[93] B.I.H.R., V. 1865/Ret. 69.

went to the university between 1660 and 1699.[94] The vicar, William Kenyon, was licensed to teach in 1685.[95] In 1698 a pupil described it as a private school.[96] A school-house was mentioned in 1753[97] but there was no school in 1819, although a dame school had recently ceased to exist. The vicar stated that funds existed at Bridlington for the support of a school at Boynton, but that they were 'most wretchedly misapplied'. Seven children attended school at Carnaby at their parents' expense.[98] In 1865 13–14 children attended a dame school at Boynton, but some of the older children still went to Carnaby.[99] In 1871 a new school was built at Carnaby for the use of Boynton and Fraisthorpe parishes, as well as Carnaby.[1] In 1884, however, the vicar reported that a school had been started in Boynton and had 'already effected a great improvement in the manners, morals, and general education of the children'.[2] The school seems to have been short-lived, for 10 years later the vicar regarded the establishment of a school in the parish as a 'most pressing need'.[3]

In 1906 it was reported that there were about 30 children of school age in Boynton, with no provision for their education.[4] In 1909 a school was therefore built in Boynton with accommodation for about 60 pupils, on land given by Sir Charles Strickland.[5] Up to 1914 attendance varied between 42 and 47, but between 1918 and 1938 it declined to between 12 and 27.[6] In 1965 the pupils from Rudston school, on its closure, were transferred to Boynton,[7] and in 1969 the average number of pupils enrolled was 36.[8]

Evening classes in reading, writing, the Scriptures, and elementary geography and history were conducted between c. 1856 and c. 1865 by Mary Simpson, the vicar's daughter, largely for the benefit of farm lads.[9]

CHARITIES FOR THE POOR. In 1743 the vicar of Boynton reported that £1 a year was paid to the overseers for poor relief 'out of a farm called Emmet Land in this Riding'.[10] Nothing more is known of this charity.

In 1803 Elizabeth, probably wife of Sir George Strickland, left £50, the interest of which was to be used for the relief of poor persons in Boynton and Carnaby chosen by the vicar of Boynton; it was not to be used to discharge the poor-rates. By 1823 the capital included an accumulated interest of £10 and also £50 'formerly given by some person unknown for the poor of Boynton'; the interest was distributed as intended.[11] In 1880 the incumbent found that the income was being misapplied as a clothing club bonus. Until 1903 the income of about £3 a year was distributed together with the income of the Strickland Charity in Fraisthorpe to the poor of all three parishes. In 1925–7 the income was still about £3 but by 1965 it was only 7s., which was paid into the church funds.[12]

BRIDLINGTON

Growth of the Town, p. 33. Domestic Buildings, p. 40. Manor, p. 44. Priory Buildings, p. 45. Agriculture, p. 46. The Harbour, p. 47. Fishing, p. 50. Shipping and Trade, p. 51. Markets and Fairs, p. 54. Industry, p. 56. The Resort, p. 58. Social Institutions, p. 62. Public Services, p. 64. Transport, p. 67. Local Government, p. 68. Churches, p. 70. Roman Catholicism, p. 75. Protestant Nonconformity, p. 75. Education, p. 78. Charities for the Poor, p. 80. Townships: Buckton, p. 82. Easton, p. 85. Grindale, p. 87. Hilderthorpe, p. 90. Sewerby and Marton, p. 92. Speeton, p. 101. Wilsthorpe, p. 104.

It was said in 1537 that 'Bridlington stands in a far corner of the shire adjoining to the sea where no resort is of strangers except such as dwell about the same that come to the market there'.[1] For over two centuries more Bridlington, or Burlington as it was often called, remained a quiet market town with a small harbour. Since the mid 18th century, however, the adjacent sea and the resort of strangers have combined to transform it into a fashionable wateringplace and latterly a popular place for seaside holidays.[2] The old market town stood on the lowest slopes of the wolds, a mile inland from 'Bridlington Quay' and the harbour at the mouth of the Gypsey Race. The distinction between 'the Old Town' and 'the Quay' has always been maintained, though the two settlements have coalesced with the growth of the resort, and it will be convenient to use the terms in this account. The Quay lies on the sheltered southern flank of Flamborough Head and it has benefited from the protection which Bridlington Bay has for centuries afforded to shipping. The chalk cliffs of the headland, moreover, enhance the setting of the resort, which on its southern side is bordered by the relatively featureless clay-lands of Holderness.

The south-eastern section of Bridlington township, near the sea and the Gypsey Race, is in fact part of the plain of Holderness and lies between 25 ft. and 50 ft. above sea-level. This area was mostly occupied by the Moor before inclosure in 1771. From the Old Town northwards, however, the wold slopes rise steadily to the boundary of the township,

---

[94] E.R.R.O., DDX/25/9 p. 4.
[95] B.I.H.R., Schools index.
[96] E.R.R.O., DDX/25/9 p. 4.
[97] Par. rec. Overseers' accts. 1735–74, in church.
[98] *Rets. on Educ. of Poor, 1819*, 1077.
[99] B.I.H.R., V. 1865/Ret. 69.
[1] *Rets. rel. Elem. Educ. 1871*, 474; see below, p. 131.
[2] B.I.H.R., Bp. V. 1884/Ret. [3] Ibid., Bp. V. 1894/Ret.
[4] E.R. Educ. Cttee. *Mins.* 1906–7, 287; 1907–8, 59, 152.
[5] Ibid. 1907–8, 237; 1908–9, 295; Ed. 7/135; *Bd. of Educ. List 21* (H.M.S.O.).
[6] *Bd. of Educ. List 21*.

[7] E.R. Educ. Cttee. *Mins.* 1965–6, 148.
[8] Ex inf. Chief Educ. Officer, County Hall, Beverley, 1969.
[9] C. B. Freeman, *Mary Simpson of Boynton Vicarage* (E. Yorks. Loc. Hist. Ser. xxviii), *passim*.
[10] *Herring's Visit.* i. 110. The farm was presumably Emmotland, in N. Frodingham.
[11] *9th Rep. Char. Com.* 721.
[12] Char. Com. files.
[1] *L. & P. Hen. VIII*, xii (1), p. 593; partly printed in Purvis, *Bridlington Charters, etc.* 4.
[2] This article was written in 1969–70.

where the highest ground exceeds 325 ft. The slopes are dissected by three prominent dry valleys, with a fourth, smaller, valley at the western boundary. The extensive open fields covered much of the wold slopes before inclosure, with common pasture in the extreme north-west.

Since the cliffs both north and south of the Quay are composed of boulder clay and sand, erosion remained a constant problem until the sea front was protected by adequate defences in the later 19th century. The earliest defences were built on the north side and they resulted in increased erosion to the south. It has been estimated that immediately south of the harbour the cliffs receded by about 230 yds. in 1805–85. One estate there, with a frontage to the sea of 1,200 yds., lost 26 a. in 30 years. On the north side of the harbour the cliffs receded by only about 30 yds. in 1771–1852,[3] but several cliff-top houses in the Quay were lost during this period. A row of houses was taken down in 1819, two houses were lost in 1837, and in 1840 a nearby resident complained of the cliff that 'tons and tons are washing down and the high road if [the erosion is] not stopped will soon be impassable'.[4] In the 20th century the sea-walls and promenades have prevented further erosion, but they have themselves occasionally suffered damage by the sea, as during the storms which caused the east coast floods of 1953.[5]

The ancient parish of Bridlington, irregular in shape, extended for some 5 miles north of the town and for nearly 3 miles south of it, occupying 12,432 a. in all.[6] Eight outlying villages and hamlets lay within the parish and five of them are still distinct from the town: these are Buckton, Easton, Grindale, Speeton, and Wilsthorpe. Much of Hilderthorpe, however, has become part of the built-up area in the 19th and 20th centuries, and Sewerby and Marton are threatened by the most recent expansion of the town. All the townships are treated in separate sections at the end of this account, but the suburbs lying in Hilderthorpe and Sewerby with Marton are dealt with as part of the town. Part of the township of Auburn also lay within the ancient parish, but it is described elsewhere.[7]

The township of Bridlington itself contributed 2,519 a. to the area of the parish, including both the Old Town and the Quay. It lay entirely to the north of the Gypsey Race, except for a tiny projection beyond the stream to bring the south pier of the harbour within the township. After 1863 the newly-formed local government board enjoyed authority over the whole township. The board's district was extended in 1877 to include small adjoining areas in Hilderthorpe and Sewerby townships and Bessingby parish, which were already becoming built-upon; the new south pier marked the limit in Hilderthorpe.[8]

In 1894 the district was further extended into Sewerby and Hilderthorpe,[9] and in 1899 the newly-created borough had an area of 2,746 a.[10]

The borough was first extended in 1923, when 847 a. were added: 289 a. from Sewerby with Marton, just over 200 a. from Hilderthorpe, and about 355 a. from Bessingby parish. These additions resulted in a total area of 3,593 a.[11] Further extensions were made in 1935, involving 889 a. from Bessingby, 17 a. from Flamborough, 36 a. from Fraisthorpe with Auburn and Wilsthorpe, and 1,072 a. from Sewerby with Marton civil parishes: these additions totalled 2,014 a. and brought the area of the borough to 5,701 a.[12] No subsequent changes have taken place.

In wealth and size Bridlington was apparently exceeded by several villages in the wapentake during the Middle Ages. Its tax assessment in 1334 was surpassed by those of Hunmanby and Kilham, but Bridlington had the largest number of poll-tax payers in 1377: 379 compared with Kilham's 363.[13] It seems likely that Bridlington, although close to Kilham in wealth, had outstripped its rivals in size by the 16th and 17th centuries and that it had a high proportion of poor inhabitants. The Crown commissioner at the suppression of the priory remarked that he had never before seen such needy people as there were 'in these parts'.[14] There were 180 tenants of the manor in 1630, but only about 30 held any land,[15] and landless cottagers were still numerous in the 18th century.[16] In 1670, moreover, 113 out of 332 households were discharged from paying the hearth tax in Bridlington, including the Quay; Hunmanby and Kilham had only 155 and 131 households respectively. In 1672 352 households were recorded and 122 were discharged from the tax; of those assessed, 100 had only one hearth each, 59 had 2, 32 had 3, 23 had 4, and 16 had between 5 and eleven.[17] In 1743 there were 'about 527' families in the parish[18] and in 1764 about 550.[19]

The combined population of the Old Town and the Quay was 3,130 in 1801. The town grew steadily during most of the 19th century, the biggest intercensal increase, 677, occurring in 1841–51: this may reflect the arrival of the railway in 1846, but the increase was followed by a small decrease in population in 1851–61. By 1891 there were 6,840 inhabitants, but a much more rapid growth was at hand and by 1901 the population had increased to 9,528. There was, moreover, a similar growth in the population of Hilderthorpe township as the built-up area of Bridlington spread south of the Gypsey Race: from 194 in 1861 Hilderthorpe's population increased to 1,475 in 1881 and 2,518 in 1901.[20] The population of the whole borough was 12,482 in 1901.[21] In the 20th century the population increased

---

[3] T. Sheppard, *Lost Towns of the Yorks. Coast*, 200–1; *Proc. Geol. Soc. Yorks.* N.S. viii. 27.
[4] J. Thompson, *Hist. Sketches of Bridlington*, 153; White, *Dir. E. & N.R. Yorks.* (1840), 370; Purvis, *Bridlington Charters, etc.* 207–8.
[5] *Bridlington Free Press*, 6 Feb. 1953; *Hull Daily Mail*, 29 and 31 Jan. 1953.
[6] O.S. Map 6" (1854).
[7] See p. 199.
[8] 'Annals of Bridlington', vol. 5, pp. 54, 69.
[9] Bridlington Town Hall, loc. govt. bd. mins., vol. 7, p. 114; E.R.R.O., CCO 5.
[10] O.S. Map 6" (1894); *Census*, 1921.
[11] *Census*, 1931. The addition from Bessingby C.P., which included much of Hilderthorpe, was stated as 558 a. but the contributions of the 2 places to this figure have had to be calculated.
[12] *Census*, 1931. A discrepancy of 94 a. between the area of the borough after the additions of 1923 and before those of 1935 has not been accounted for.
[13] E 179/202/62 mm. 36, 40.
[14] *L. & P. Hen. VIII*, xii (2), p. 32.
[15] See p. 46.
[16] See p. 47.
[17] E 179/205/504, 514.
[18] *Herring's Visit.* i. 112. This figure apparently refers to the whole parish, though there are separate entries for Grindale and Speeton.
[19] B.I.H.R., Bp. V. 1764/Ret. 89.
[20] *V.C.H. Yorks.* iii. 488.
[21] *Census*.

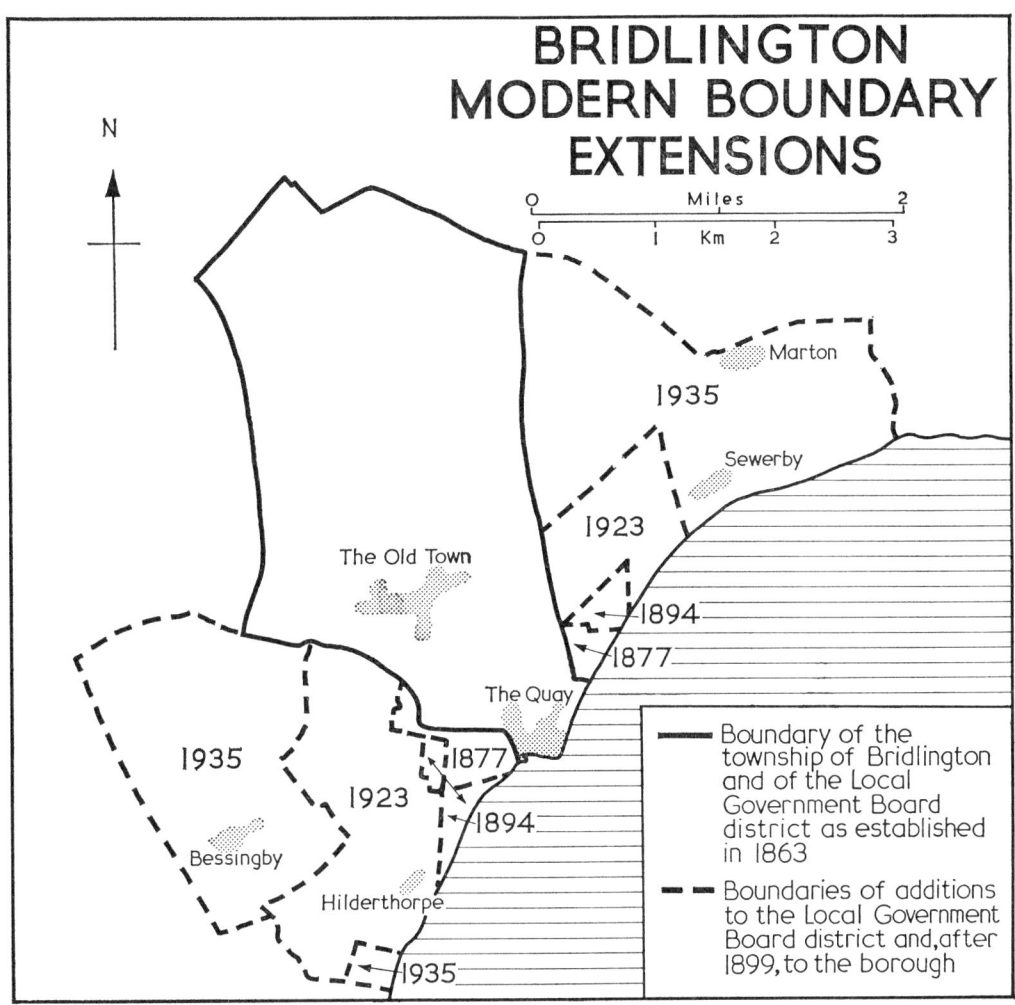

from 14,334 in 1911 to 19,705 in 1931,[22] 24,661 in 1951, and 26,023 in 1961.[23]

During prehistoric times the country near Bridlington was extensively settled, and prehistoric routes across the wolds may later have been followed by Roman roads; it is possible, moreover, that a harbour at the mouth of the Gypsey Race was used during the Roman occupation. Wold Gate may have continued eastwards to such a harbour; and the remains of paved roads found between the Old Town and Sewerby[24] suggests that the road along the valley of the Race may have led to a signal station at Flamborough.[25] From this road to Flamborough another road perhaps led to the harbour, conceivably following the line of a road later known as Fortyfoot Road;[26] the harbour site now lies beneath the sea, and erosion has doubtless removed any trace of a Roman settlement there. The name Castleburn, applied to the medieval predecessor of Bridlington Quay,[27] could derive from an encampment at the mouth of the stream. Roman coins have been found in the Bridlington area, some of them on the beach, together with a burial and pottery.[28]

Etymology suggests that Bridlington was an Anglian settlement.[29] Its principal part was no doubt that which was to become the Old Town in modern times, lying on the line of the suggested Roman road to Flamborough. A subsidiary settlement may have early developed by the sea, for the harbour is mentioned soon after 1100;[30] it is not referred to as 'the Quay' until the early 16th century,[31] but 'Castleburn' first occurs in the 13th century.[32] Domesday Book gives little indication that Bridlington possessed an urban character in 1086, apart from the mention of four burgesses; no other inhabitants are recorded and the Crown's chief estate in the town had declined in value from £32 to 8s. since 1066.[33] There is no reason to suppose that Bridlington was in any sense a borough and it is as a small market town that it appears in the Middle Ages.

[22] A population of 22,764 was recorded in 1921, but the census was taken in June when there were many visitors present.
[23] Census.
[24] Mary Kitson Clark, Gaz. of Roman Remains in E. Yorks. 69; see below, p. 92.
[25] See p. 153.
[26] Kitson Clark, op. cit. 69; Thompson, Hist. Sketches of Bridlington, 2.
[27] See below.
[28] Kitson Clark, op. cit. 49–51, 58–9, 69.
[29] P.N.E.R. Yorks. (E.P.N.S.), 102.
[30] See p. 47.
[31] P.N.E.R. Yorks. 103; Miscellanea, iii (Y.A.S. Rec. Ser. lxxx), 55.
[32] Bridlington Charty. 18. Ships were wrecked at Castleburn in 1318: Cal. Inq. Misc. ii, p. 94.
[33] V.C.H. Yorks. ii. 197; H. C. Darby and I. S. Maxwell, Domesday Geog. of N. Eng. 225–6.

Soon after 1086 the Crown estates in Bridlington passed to the Gants and in the early 12th century they were among the endowments made by Walter de Gant when he founded Bridlington priory.[34] This Augustinian house became one of the wealthiest religious foundations in Yorkshire and its presence must have profoundly influenced the development of Bridlington. It was the priory, moreover, which secured the grant of a market and fair in 1200, thus establishing the main economic function of the town. The priory became a notable place of pilgrimage after the canonization in 1401 of a former prior, John of Thwing. His shrine was visited by Henry V in 1421.[35] The endowments of the house included Bridlington church and this was largely rebuilt by the canons in the later 13th century; the nave was used by the townspeople and the chancel by the canons.

The last prior of Bridlington, William Wood, was attainted of treason and executed in 1537, after taking part in the Pilgrimage of Grace; the priory's property was thus forfeited to the Crown and the house was suppressed that year.[36] In 1538 Sir Matthew Boynton was given the stewardship of the priory's possessions in Yorkshire and Lincolnshire,[37] and Humphrey Chawney was made bailiff of the town and manor of Bridlington.[38] Boynton was given the right to appoint an under-steward, and he may therefore have been responsible for appointing Sir Marmaduke Constable, who was described as steward of Bridlington in 1539.[39]

The Crown was involved in considerable expense after the forfeiture of the priory in repairing both the harbour[40] and property in the town. An incomplete account records the expenditure of nearly £15 on property repairs in the 10 months following Wood's attainder.[41] There was, nevertheless, a considerable 'decay' in the rents which the Crown was able to collect from the town. The manor as forfeited was found to be worth about £196[42] but in 1541–2 over £29 rent could not be collected from waste property, in 1542–3 nearly £27, and in 1545–6 over £28.[43] The property involved lay in streets in the market town and at 'the seaside', alternatively referred in these accounts as the Quay or Castleburn. The burden of repairing the harbour was transferred to a group of townsmen in 1566, when they took a lease of the manor, but the decay of rents was apparently taken into account in fixing the lessees' rent at nearly £153.[44] It was probably failure to repair the harbour adequately which led to the forfeiture of this lease. Other leases followed, however, and a group of townsmen again held the manor from 1595 to 1623; eventually, in 1630, the manor was sold to the townsmen and a group of lords feoffees took over the administration of the town.

During the 16th and early 17th centuries Bridlington frequently saw signs of the activities of enemy ships along the coast.[45] By 1588 there were beacons near the Quay, giving light to Flamborough and Fraisthorpe, to warn of the approach of ships.[46] A rate was laid in 1613 for the beacons and again in 1625, when Bridlington and its townships, together with Bessingby and Boynton, raised money for 'the building of the watch-house'.[47] In 1596 and again in the 1630s the port was instructed to raise ship-money to help to provide vessels.[48] Bridlington played little part in the Civil War, though one of the most celebrated events in the town's history took place in 1643, when Queen Henrietta Maria landed at the Quay with arms and ammunition collected in Holland and the harbour was bombarded by parliamentary ships. The queen stayed in the town for several days before setting out for York.[49] It is said that a battery was constructed on either side of the harbour as a result of this incident.[50]

For the remainder of the century, and especially during the Dutch wars, Bridlington was much concerned with naval activities and military precautions. Ships were convoyed along the coast, sheltering in the bay and sometimes entering the harbour; enemy ships appeared offshore, prisoners and prizes were brought to the town, and Bridlington men and ships suffered at the hands of the Dutch; and much naval intelligence was sent from Bridlington, a service in which John Bower, a merchant of the Quay, was employed.[51]

For its own defence Bridlington had a few guns, apparently mounted in batteries flanking the harbour: fire from Dutch ships was answered from 'the forts' in 1666[52] and a fort north of the harbour was built in 1667.[53] The fort seems to have been repaired and manned in 1672,[54] when at one time the English and French fleets were stationed offshore; many sick seamen were landed at the Quay and much money was spent in the town on provisions.[55] Work was again carried out to fortify the town in 1678 and 1702.[56] Bridlington was next stirred in 1779, when the American naval captain John Paul Jones drove coasters into the harbour before fighting an engagement with English warships off Flamborough Head.[57] The fort was repaired and manned in 1794 and again during the Napoleonic War.[58]

---

[34] For the priory see *V.C.H. Yorks.* iii. 199–205.
[35] See J. S. Purvis, *St. John of Bridlington; D.N.B.*
[36] *Mon. Suppression Papers* (Y.A.S. Rec. Ser. xlviii), 40–7, 50–1, 53–7; *L. & P. Hen. VIII*, xii, *passim.* See also J. S. Purvis, *Dissolution of Bridlington Priory.*
[37] *L. & P. Hen. VIII*, xii (1), p. 409.
[38] Ibid. p. 568; xiv (1), p. 309. His name is often spelt 'Chawner' or 'Chaloner'.
[39] Ibid. xiv (2), p. 78.
[40] See p. 47.
[41] S.P. 5/832/10, printed in Purvis, *Bridlington Charters, etc.* 19–25.
[42] Purvis, op. cit. 17.
[43] S.C. 12/4/13, 14; E 315/382; printed in *Miscellanea,* iii. 43–63.
[44] See p. 44.
[45] *L. & P. Hen. VIII*, xix(2), pp. 131–2, 326; *Acts of P.C.* 1556–8, 295; 1627–8, 387–8; *Cal. S.P. Dom.* Add. 1566–79, 536; 1629–31, 466; 1631–3, 423.
[46] J. Nicholson, *Beacons of E. Yorks.* 8.
[47] E.R.R.O., DDLG/43/1.
[48] *Acts of P.C.* 1596–7, 151, 326; *Cal. S. P. Dom.* 1634–5, 243; 1638–9, 87–8.
[49] *V.C.H. Yorks.* iii. 421; Thompson, *Hist. Sketches of Bridlington,* 107–10.
[50] Thompson, op. cit. 110. Purvis, *Bridlington Charters, etc.* 313 also refers to a fort before 1650.
[51] *Cal. S.P. Dom.* 1649–50 etc., *passim.*
[52] Ibid. 1666–7, 114, 116, 259–60.
[53] Ibid. 1667, 1, 22–3, 40, 43, 48, 76–7, 90, 224, 285, 370.
[54] Ibid. 474, 489, 547; 1667–8, 14; 1671–2, 263, 554, 580; 1672–3, 236, 604–5.
[55] Ibid. 1672–3, 480.
[56] Ibid. 1678 and Addenda 1674–9, 139, 163, 599–600; 1691–2, 53; 1702–3, 292, 388.
[57] Thompson, *Hist. Sketches of Bridlington,* 117–21; S.E. Morison, *John Paul Jones,* 221 sqq.
[58] E.R.R.O., DDX/17/25, 32, 37, 40; R.W.S. Norfolk, *Militia, Yeomanry and Volunteer Forces of the E.R. 1689–1908* (E. Yorks. Loc. Hist. Ser. xix), 15, 24.

FORDON: showing typical dry valleys and open farm-land on the wolds

ARGAM: the site of the deserted village

FLAMBOROUGH: Danes' Dyke, from the south

RUDSTON: the prehistoric monolith

Part of it went over the cliff in 1813 and the rest was demolished soon after; the feoffees levelled it in 1818 and sold bricks from it in 1823. The battery on the south side of the harbour is said to have been destroyed by erosion c. 1805.[59] A painting of the fort c. 1800 shows a kidney-shaped building on the cliff edge, with moat, drawbridge, bank, and stockade.[60]

The 16th, 17th, and 18th centuries had also seen a marked growth in Bridlington's seaborne trade which may have boosted the prosperity and population of the Quay. The Old Town continued to depend upon its market and the provision of miscellaneous goods and services both to the town and to the near-by countryside. It was not until about 1750 that the first visitors began to give the Quay a reputation as a watering-place. The resort developed steadily thereafter, and more rapidly when the railway from Hull was opened in 1846. The 19th century saw a decline in the regional importance of the market and the near-extinction of trade at the harbour, though fishing has continued to make a notable, if relatively small, contribution to the town's economy. The resort, however, grew apace in the late 19th and early 20th centuries; during the same period, moreover, the Quay began to attract 'professional gentlemen' of Hull as summer residents and eventually businessmen from the West Riding to settle there.[61] In 1921 over 2,800 residents of Bridlington worked in Hull and the West Riding, and in 1951 over 1,100, including 15 per cent. of the working male population. The number of retired men in 1951 was nearly twice the national average, illustrating another aspect of the town's residential function.[62]

With the transformation of the Quay, the lords feoffees of the manor eventually ceased to administer the affairs of the town, giving way to a local government board in 1863. The town was incorporated as a borough in 1899 and large additions to its area have subsequently been made. It has remained largely dependent upon the holiday trade, though the development of light industry has been encouraged since the Second World War in an attempt to reduce the unemployment which is characteristic of seaside resorts.

GROWTH OF THE TOWN. In the Middle Ages most of the houses in the Old Town lay on either side of a long, curving, street which ran the length of the town from east to west. In the early 16th century this street was divided into Kirkgate and Westgate, but the central section later became High Street, and Kirkgate came to continue northwards as Pinfold Lane. North Back Lane and South Back Lane ran behind the main street, marking the limit of the house-plots and garths.

Three side roads joined the main street: from the end of Kirkgate Nungate led eastwards to become the Sewerby road; from the junction of Kirkgate and the original Westgate St. John's Gate led southwards towards the Quay; and from Westgate the wide Market Place led northwards to become the Hunmanby road. At the centre of the town a short side street known as Bayle Gate ran up to the priory gatehouse or Bayle. In 1539 the manorial rents included about £37 from tenants in Westgate, £13 from Kirkgate, £24 from St. John's Gate, £8 from Bayle Gate, £6 from Nungate, and £4 from tenants by the churchyard.[63] The absence of Market Place from this and other early-16th-century documents has led to the suggestion that it was a later addition to the town,[64] but another document of the period mentions three shops in the market-place and Market Place appears, with the other streets, in a rental of 1545–6.[65]

The antiquity of High Green and Low or Church Green is not known. High Green lies at the north-east end of the town near Nungate; it contained a large pond which was not filled in until 1900–1.[66] Low Green must have lain within the priory precincts, but it was presumably through the Bayle and across the green that most townspeople reached the priory church. The extensive conventual buildings of the priory lay mostly on the south side of the church, but, with the exception of the gatehouse, little trace of them now remains.[67]

Applegarth Lane, leading off Low Green near the Bayle, presumably dates from after the suppression of the priory. The name apparently refers to a priory orchard, and near-by land called Applegarthdale was inclosed by the canons c. 1262.[68] A close called Applegarth is frequently mentioned in the 16th century and later, and Applegarth Lane is recorded in 1672.[69] The inclosure made c. 1262 is perhaps the large, rectangular, area which was still surrounded by a ditch and embankment in modern times.[70] It was apparently part of this bank which was levelled in the early 19th century and found to contain the foundations of a wall.[71] Partly within the inclosure was the priory fishpond, mentioned in 1258,[72] which was known until the 16th century as the 'Great Pond', and was later called the 'River' or 'Long River'.[73] The pond has been filled in, but near by there are two mounds, supposed to mark the site of archery butts and known as Butt Hills. Finally, somewhere to the south of the priory the canons had a water-mill to which they constructed a watercourse in the 13th century;[74] this was apparently the dike, called the Main Drain in the 19th century, which left the Gypsey Race south-west of the Old Town and eventually rejoined it near the Quay.[75]

Beyond the priory's inclosure were roads known in the 13th century as Fiskergate and Dreggergate;[76]

---

[59] Lords Feoffees' Rec., Bayle, Bridlington, acct. bk. 1794–1852; Thompson, op. cit. 155–6.
[60] Purvis, *Bridlington Charters, etc.* 313.
[61] Bridlington Town Hall, loc. govt. bd. mins., vol. 4, p. 162 (1883); 'Annals of Bridlington', vol. 19, p. 170 (1902).
[62] *Census;* K. L. Mayoh, 'Comparative Study of Resorts on Coast of Holderness' (unpubl. M.A. thesis, Univ. of Hull, 1961), 61, 208–10.
[63] Purvis, *Bridlington Charters, etc.* 26.
[64] J. Thompson, *Hist. Sketches of Bridlington*, 122–3.
[65] *Miscellanea*, iii (Y.A.S. Rec. Ser. lxxx), 3, 63.
[66] 'Annals of Bridlington', vols. 17, p. 33; 18, p. 212.
[67] See p. 45.

[68] *Bridlington Charty.* 16–17.
[69] Purvis, *Bridlington Charters, etc.* e.g. 27, 276.
[70] O.S. Map 6" (1854) shows the 'ancient inclosure' and 'embankment'. It was of more than 30 a.: O.S. Map 25" (1912).
[71] Thompson, *Hist. Sketches of Bridlington*, 151. When a section of the bank was levelled during the First World War, however, no trace of walls was found: Purvis, *Dissol. of Bridlington Priory*, 22.
[72] *Bridlington Charty.* 20.
[73] Purvis, *Bridlington Charters, etc.* e.g. 26, 69, 302.
[74] *Bridlington Charty.* 18–20.
[75] O.S. Map 6" (1854).
[76] *Bridlington Charty.* 16–17, 22.

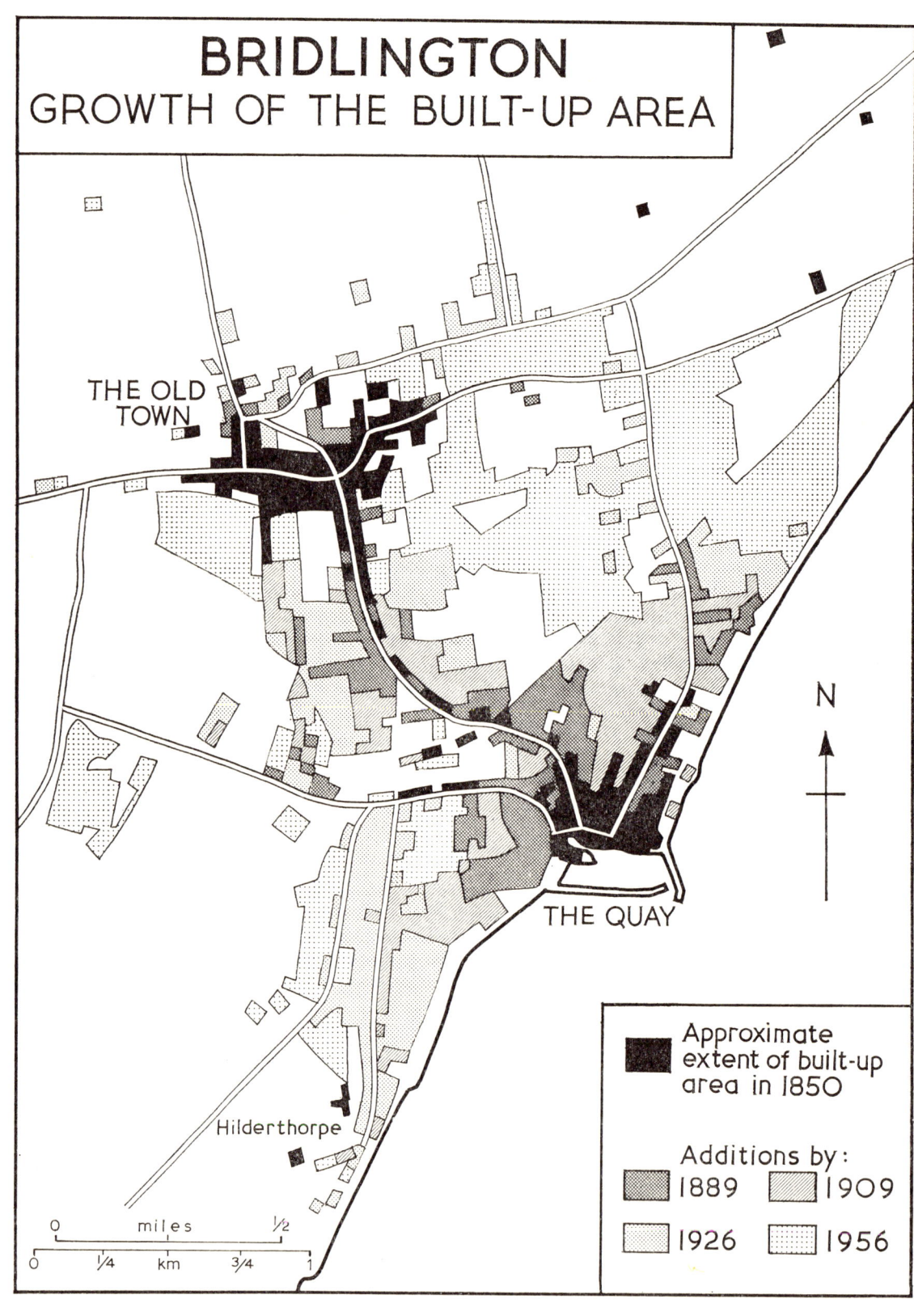

both probably have a derivation connected with fishing,[77] and they presumably led from the Old Town to the Quay. Little is known of the topography of the medieval settlement at the Quay. Rents from manorial tenants there amounted to about £12 in 1539, but no street names are mentioned;[78] the property there about this time included the 'beach houses' and the 'herring houses'.[79]

The number of houses in Bridlington had increased to about 350 by the 1670s; in 1672, for example, there were 232 in the Old Town and 120 at the Quay.[80] An approximately equal proportion of houses in the two settlements belonged to the poor: 78 and 83 per cent respectively were either discharged from paying the hearth tax or had only one or two hearths each. There were larger houses in both places, too, Eleanor Beaucock's[81] in the Old Town with twelve hearths and John Bower's at the Quay with eleven being the largest of all; two other merchants, John Rickaby and Bartholomew Anderson, had houses with six hearths at the Quay.

By the early 19th century the Old Town had grown little beyond its early limits, but besides much rebuilding and refronting of houses there seems to have been some building on the plots behind the houses. In 1796, for example, five houses were offered for sale in Westgate, with a large garden said to be convenient for building a new street or row of houses; when put up for sale again in 1812 this was described as nearly 3,500 sq. yds. of building land.[82] Maps of the period clearly illustrate this process of accretion.[83] The old centre of the Quay was similarly being altered by rebuilding and infilling.

Of the Quay it was written in 1821 that during the previous 50 years it had 'from an inconsiderable village become a neat, lively, and populous town'.[84] Ten years later the 'narrow, crooked and irregular' streets of the Old Town were contrasted with those of the Quay, 'remarkably spacious and the houses in general modern and neatly built'.[85] The two settlements were still separate, but on the road between them there were soon 'many neat and convenient houses on either side which bids fair for a union of the two towns'.[86] By 1850 Christ Church, the gasworks, and the railway station were also among the buildings standing near Quay Road. By 1874 the road was 'fringed with villa residences and private dwellings',[87] and in 1873 Gravel Pits was given the more fitting name of Midway Green.[88]

During the earlier 19th century the extension of the Quay itself was confined to building along the Promenade, running northwards from the town. A few houses, among them Fort Hall and Sea Breezes, had already been built by 1828,[89] and by 1850 such groups as Victoria Terrace, Bridlington Place, Providence Place, Ocean View, and Belle Vue reached almost to the township boundary.[90] Beyond the boundary Mark Barr built the first houses in Sewerby Terrace, each accommodating 12 to 15 visitors, between 1855 and 1859,[91] and the adjacent Alexandra Hotel was built in 1863–6.[92] The development of the land between the Promenade and the sea front proceeded steadily after the 1860s, mostly to provide resort accommodation. At the southern end, behind the new Sea Wall Parade, the local board laid out a new street (later Marlborough Terrace) in 1866–7 and offered for sale 34 building sites there and in the Esplanade and Cliff Street. The sites were bought by G. W. Travis, of Sheffield, who moved to Bridlington in 1869, and houses were built in 1869–71, including those forming the Crescent;[93] Cliff Square and much old property were replaced. The work was superintended by the architect Joseph Earnshaw, who also left Sheffield in 1869 to settle in Bridlington.[94] Further north 24 building sites near Fort Hall Terrace were sold in 1861.[95] The laying out of the Beaconsfield estate, belonging to Robert Beauvais and Thomas Harland, began in 1869 and the first houses were being built there in 1870, when 50 building sites were for sale.[96] Holy Trinity Church was also built there. Part of the estate was nevertheless still not built upon in 1890,[97] development perhaps having been delayed by the late completion of adequate defences along its sea front.[98] By 1890 further development had, however, taken place beyond the Alexandra Hotel in that part of Sewerby annexed to the local board's district in 1877. It comprised houses along St. Anne's and Flamborough Roads, and included St. Anne's Convalescent Home.[99]

The development of estates inland from the sea front also began at the Quay in the 1870s. Near Christ Church and adjoining Quay Road, the Wellington Road estate was begun by the Revd. James Thompson in 1875. Several 'villa residences' had been built by 1878,[1] and the Wellington, or Temperance, Hall was completed in 1877 to designs by Earnshaw, who had also laid out Wellington Road.[2] The near-by Field House estate was built by Earnshaw and Robert Bailey: Victoria Road was laid out in 1886 and houses were being built in 1886–7.[3] The Roman Catholic church was built

[77] P.N.E.R. Yorks. (E.P.N.S.), 102.
[78] Purvis, Bridlington Charters, etc. 26.
[79] S.C. 6/4430; Miscellanea, iii. 5, 55.
[80] E 179/205/504.
[81] 'Lady Beaucock' of the tax return was Eleanor, formerly wife of Wm. Hustler, of Bridlington, who by 1651 had married Dr. Edward Beaucock, of York: C 5/434/19.
[82] Hull Advertiser, 12 Nov. 1796; 15 Feb. 1812.
[83] J. Wood, Plan of Bridlington (1828); O.S. Map 60" (1854).
[84] J. Thompson, Hist. Sketches of Bridlington, 151.
[85] T. Allen, Hist. Yorks. iv. 34, 41.
[86] J. Furby, Excursions from Bridlington Quay (3rd edn.), 35.
[87] Popular Guide to Bridlington Quay (1874), 12.
[88] 'Notes on Work of Bridlington Local Govt. Bd.' (MS. notebk. in Bridlington Pub. Libr.), 115.
[89] J. Wood, Plan of Bridlington. See p. 42. For one built shortly before 1821 see Hull Advertiser, 2 Feb. 1821. Fort Hall was demolished in 1937: 'Annals of Bridlington', vol. 54, pp. 61, 155.

[90] O.S. Map 6" (1854).
[91] Registry of Deeds, Beverley, HI/78/99; IA/377/484; Hull Advertiser, 14 May 1859.
[92] Hull Advertiser, 5 Dec. 1863; 14 July 1866; Hull News, 29 Aug. 1864.
[93] 'Notes on Work of Loc. Govt. Bd.', 28, 39–40, 44–5, 47, 66–7, 73; Regy. of Deeds, KQ/393/519–20; 'Annals of Bridlington', vols. 2, p. 102; 9, p. 88.
[94] 'Annals of Bridlington', vol. 31, p. 69.
[95] E.R.R.O., DDCV/parcel 15.
[96] 'Notes on Work of Loc. Govt. Bd.', 55, 60–1, 80; 'Annals of Bridlington', vols. 2, p. 39; 31, p. 69; Regy. of Deeds, KI/376/518.
[97] O.S. Map 6" (1894).
[98] See p. 60.
[99] See p. 66.
[1] Regy. of Deeds, KQ/45/55; 'Annals of Bridlington', vols. 4, p. 79; 6, p. 53.
[2] 'Annals of Bridlington', vol. 5, pp. 32, 66; 31, p. 69.
[3] Bridlington Town Hall, Building Inspector's Office, drawing no. 267; 'Annals of Bridlington', vols. 10, pp. 3, 60, 85; 31, p. 69.

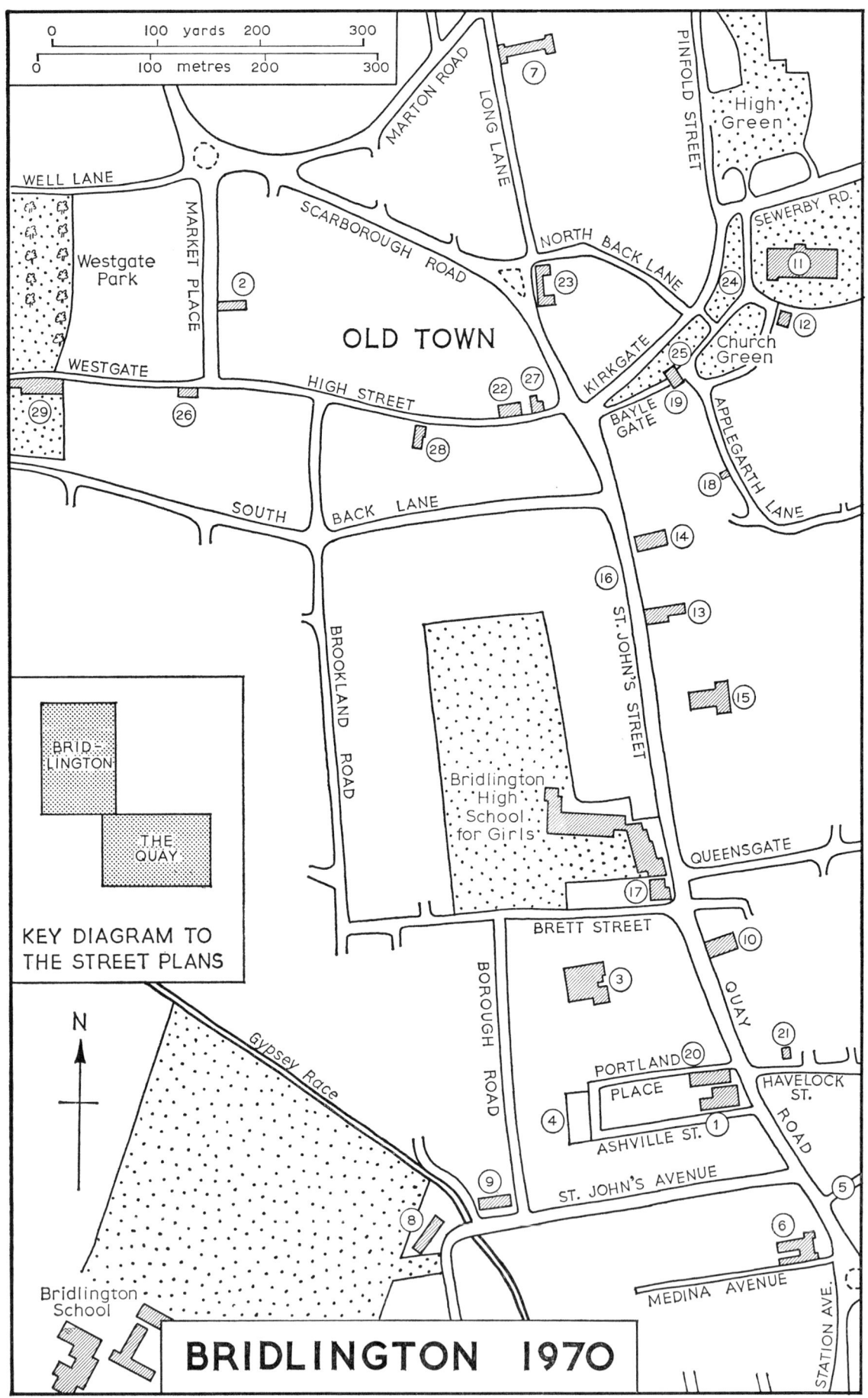

there a few years later. From these two estates, Trinity Road was made, joining up with the Promenade near Holy Trinity Church and running across land belonging to Cowton's charity.[4] Other new roads where building had begun by 1890 were North and Princess Streets, off Chapel Street; Princess Street was the work of G. W. Travis.[5] By this time, too, Quay Road was more or less continuously built up from the Quay to the Old Town, and development was beginning in streets behind the main road. In 1873, for example, approval was given for villas to be built in St. John's Avenue and terraced 'cottages' in Medina Avenue.[6] The Masonic Hall was put up in St. John's Avenue, to designs by William Bakewell, in 1875.[7] Beyond the Gypsey Race several houses had been built by 1890 in that part of Bessingby which had been annexed to the local board's district in 1877.[8]

On the south side of the Gypsey Race, in Hilderthorpe, practically no building had taken place by 1850.[9] In the 1870s, however, development began west of the harbour with a group of streets centred on Railway (later Windsor) Crescent, which lay beside a disused tramway.[10] Much of this was the work of Joseph Earnshaw.[11] By 1890 there were more terraces around West Street, and a mission church and a board school had been built.[12] This area was annexed to the local board's district in 1877. Further south in Hilderthorpe development was contemplated as early as 1866, when Albert Town, Yorkshire, Ltd. bought 10 a. of land and issued a prospectus of its plans.[13] The company gave up the project by 1870,[14] but two years later Godfrey Rhodes, of Leeds, bought the land and 41 a. more, and in 1875 he issued his own prospectus for 'South Burlington'.[15] Rhodes's attempt to build an adequate sea-wall beside the estate was unsuccessful, however,[16] and in 1894 he sold the land to Walter Battle[17] without any development having been achieved. Rhodes was unfortunate because his efforts coincided with a period of slackening demand for building sites.[18] One improvement effected by the local government board at this period which was of benefit to Hilderthorpe residents was the erection in 1882 of a permanent bridge to replace a wooden one over the Gypsey Race, at the bottom of Beck Hill.[19]

The development of the town continued rapidly between 1890 and the First World War. In 1901 it was said that around Quay Road, between the Old Town and the Quay, there was 'a constant succession of links in the shape of new houses, grouped in formal streets and terraces'.[20] On the east side of Quay Road the new streets included Havelock Crescent and Oxford, Cambridge, and Carlton Streets. On the west side there were similar developments in Brett Street, St. John's Walk, and other streets around the municipal complex of works depot, cattle market, fire and police stations, nursery garden, and electricity works. Further south the group of streets around Midway Avenue was forming.[21] Most of the houses built in these areas around Quay Road were residential, with modest terraces predominant, but there was some resort accommodation, too. On the north side of the Old Town several private houses were being built on Marton Road, and near by the first Council houses in the town were built in Watson's Balk in 1912–13; the latter

[4] O.S. Map 6″ (1894). See p. 81.
[5] O.S. Map 6″ (1894); 'Annals of Bridlington', vol. 9, p. 88; Bridlington Town Hall, Building Inspector's Office, drawing no. 57 (1878).
[6] 'Annals of Bridlington', vol. 3, pp. 47, 86, 88; Bridlington Free Press, 27 June 1874.
[7] 'Annals of Bridlington', vol. 4, pp. 47, 53.
[8] Ibid. 3, p. 72; O.S. Map 6″ (1894); Bridlington Town Hall, Building Inspector's Office, drawing no. 13 (1878).
[9] O.S. Map 6″ (1854).
[10] Kelly's Dir. N. & E.R. Yorks. (1872), 338; (1879), 366; see below, p. 68.
[11] 'Annals of Bridlington', vol. 31, p. 69.
[12] O.S. Map 6″ (1894); Bridlington Town Hall, Building Inspector's Office, drawing no. 142 (1880).
[13] Regy. of Deeds, IZ/265/327; 'Annals of Bridlington', vol. 1, pp. 9, 21.
[14] Regy. of Deeds, KQ/279/361; /281/362; /282/363.
[15] Ibid. LB/101/144; /102/145; 'Annals of Bridlington', vol. 4, p. 65.
[16] See p. 60. [17] Regy. of Deeds, 66/168/154 (1894).
[18] 'Annals of Bridlington', vols. 6, p. 53; 8, p. 94.
[19] Bridlington Town Hall, loc. govt. bd. mins., vol. 4, pp. 38, 70. [20] J. S. Fletcher, Picturesque Hist. Yorks. 395.
[21] O.S. Map 6″ (1912); Bridlington Town Hall, Building Inspector's Office, drawing no. 1223.

BRIDLINGTON 1970

KEY

1. Court House and Police Station
2. Corn Exchange
3. Electricity Works
4. Site of Cattle Market (closed 1969)
5. Site of Gasworks (1833–58)
6. Lloyd Hospital
7. Union Workhouse
8. Yorkshire Foresters' Convalescent Home
9. Masonic Hall
10. Temperance Hall
11. St. Mary's (Priory) Church
12. Rectory (1971)
13. Former Methodist church (rebuilt 1803)
14. St. John's Methodist Church
15. Burlington Methodist Church
16. Site of Zion Chapel (built c. 1700)
17. Zion Chapel (1906)
18. Former Baptist chapel (1699)
19. Site of Baptist chapel (demolished 1873)
20. Baptist chapel (1874)
21. Friends' meeting-house
22. Convent
23. Former Boys' and Girls' National School
24. Site of Infants' National School
25. The Bayle
26. Hebblethwaite House
27. Craven House
28. The Toft
29. The Avenue

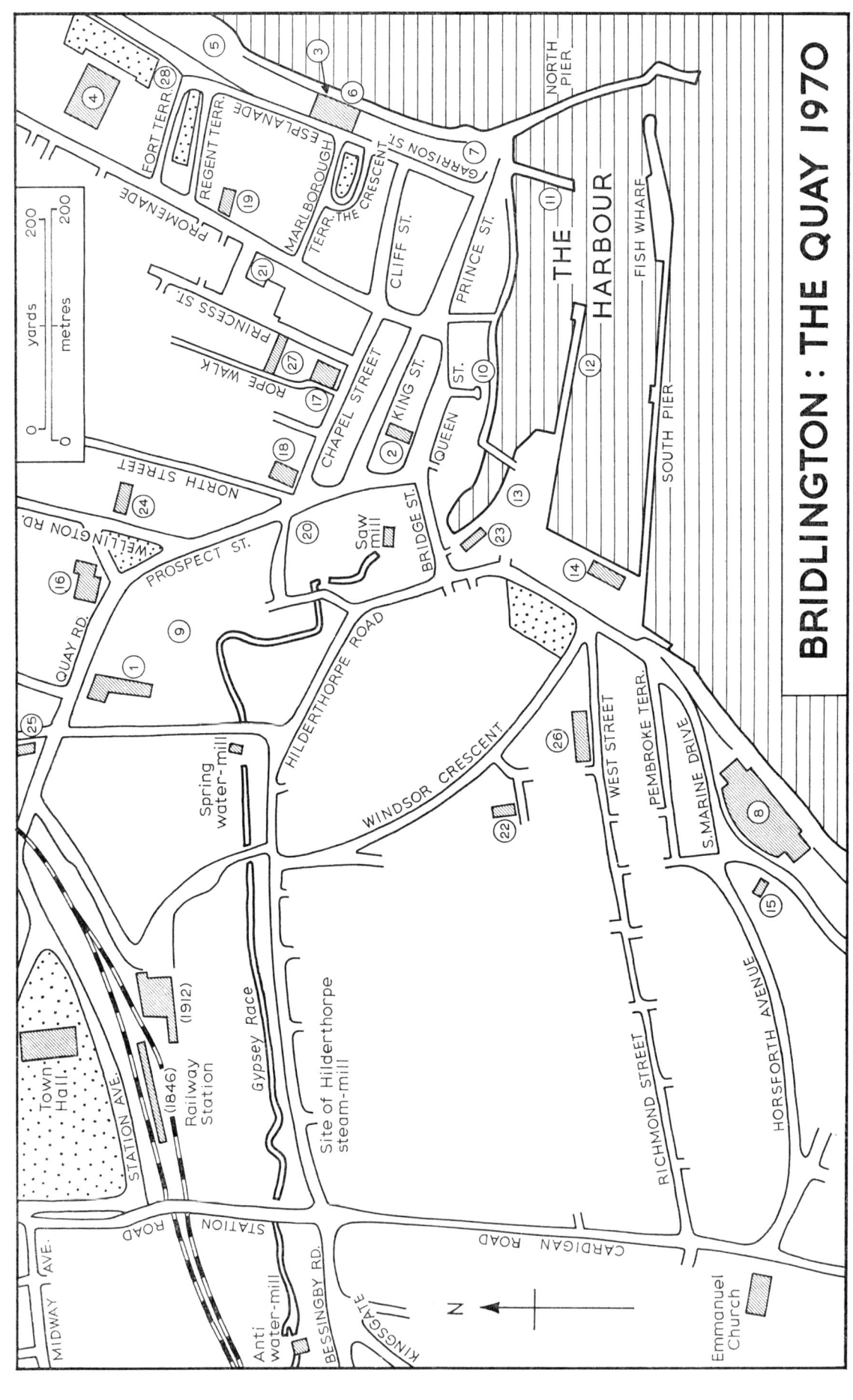

were needed to rehouse families from property demolished in St. John Street and near St. Mary's Church.[22]

At the Quay this period saw the completion and extension of the estates along the sea front and inland from the Promenade. Trinity Road was laid out, for example, according to plans made by Earnshaw in the 1890s, as was near-by Tennyson Avenue, on the line of the former Jemmy Temmy Lane.[23] By 1909 most of the area bounded by the railway and Sands Lane on the north and west had been built over. In Hilderthorpe the ill-fated Albert Town estate at last got under way after 1890. Yet another grand scheme was unsuccessfully launched in 1895,[24] but Walter Battle sold the land in 1896 to Whitaker Bros., of Horsforth, near Leeds, and during that year they built a sea-wall and the adjoining Spa.[25] In 1897 and the next few years Whitakers were selling plots and houses in Horsforth Avenue, Belgrave Road and Square, Cardigan Road, Marine Drive, and elsewhere.[26] Although roads were laid out over the whole estate, which was annexed to the local board's district in 1894, it was not quickly built up, much remaining to be done in 1909.[27] Walter Battle's own contribution in the 1890s was the development of an estate around near-by Richmond Street.[28] Further south, beyond the area of the Albert Town estate, J. W. Pitt acquired land in 1898 which became known as the Belvedere estate. In 1902 he was said to be planning to build 'villas' behind his new sea-wall, and by 1909 several houses had been built in Belvedere Road.[29]

The period between 1890 and 1914 also saw steps taken to improve existing roads in various parts of the town. Trees were planted along several roads in the 1890s[30] and after incorporation in 1899, and the latter event was also marked by the laying-out of Midway Green as Victoria Gardens and the renaming of Prospect Gardens as Wellington Gardens.[31] Quay Road was also improved by a scheme of widening which involved the demolition of about 60 houses; work began in 1903 and was not finished until 1912.[32] In the Old Town two new streets were made: Waterworks Street, between High Street and North Back Lane, and Gordon Road, between High Street and South Back Lane, providing a link with Ings Lane (now Brookland Road).[33] At the Quay a road was made beside the harbour in 1892–3[34] and at the same time a slipway leading from Prince Street to crane wharf was stopped up.[35] Clough Bridge was widened and renamed Bridge Street in 1903–4, and Cross Street was widened in 1904–5.[36]

After the First World War new housing estates began to be laid out in the area between Quay Road, Forty Foot Lane, and the railway. Queensgate was constructed across the area and both Council and private houses were built in the 1920s, including some on the corporation's Postill estate.[37] Forty Foot Lane, renamed Fortyfoot Road about this time, was made into a dual carriageway in 1922.[38] In Hilderthorpe building continued on the roads that were already laid out, and much of the area between Cardigan Road and Kingsgate was built up by 1926.[39] Kingsgate had been opened in 1923 as a new main approach road to Bridlington from the south.[40]

[22] 'Annals of Bridlington', vols. 29, pp. 256–8, 272; 30, pp. 6, 193.
[23] Bridlington Town Hall, Building Inspector's Office, drawings nos. 405, 577, 600, 601, 603, 620, 666, 704, 884.
[24] 'Annals of Bridlington', vol. 14, pp. 233–4.
[25] Regy. of Deeds, 80/185/170 (1896); see below, p. 60.
[26] Regy. of Deeds, 88/283/271 etc. (1897); 7/144/126 etc. (1898); 13/47/40 etc. (1899).
[27] O.S. Map 6" (1912).
[28] Regy. of Deeds, 79/521/484 (1896); 99/133/129; /365/352 (1898); 10/128/123; 11/62/57 (1899).
[29] Ibid. 3/279/233 (1898); 'Annals of Bridlington', vol. 19, p. 170.
[30] Bridlington Town Hall, loc. govt. bd. mins., vols. 6, p. 408; 7, p. 108.
[31] 'Annals of Bridlington', vol. 16, pp. 201, 203.
[32] Ibid. vols. 20, p. 132; 25, p. 81; 29, p. 134; E. R. Matthews, *Bridlington and some of its Municipal Works and Undertakings*, 9.
[33] 'Annals of Bridlington', vols. 7, p. 322; 8, p. 202.
[34] See p. 49.
[35] Bridlington Town Hall, loc. govt. bd. mins., vol. 6, pp. 295, 306.
[36] 'Annals of Bridlington', vols. 20, p. 295; 21, pp. 14, 262.
[37] Bridlington Corp. *Counc. Procs. and Cttee. Mins.* 1918–19, procs. p. 92, mins. p. 305; 1925–6, 26; 'Annals of Bridlington', vol. 43, pp. 20, 389; O.S. Map 6" (1929).
[38] 'Annals of Bridlington', vol. 39, p. 301.
[39] O.S. Map 6" (1929).
[40] 'Annals of Bridlington', vol. 40, p. 249.

BRIDLINGTON: THE QUAY 1970

KEY

1. Head Post Office
2. Public Library
3. Royal Prince's Parade
4. Grand Pavilion
5. Site of Grand Pavilion (1906–36)
6. Floral Pavilion
7. Site of Victoria Rooms
8. Spa Royal Hall and Theatre
9. Site of People's Palace
10. Site of Queen's Square baths
11. Crane Wharf Jetty
12. Chicken Run Jetty
13. Former Langdale's Wharf
14. Royal Air Force boat shed
15. Lifeboat House
16. Christ Church
17. Quay Methodist Church
18. Central Methodist Church
19. Trinity Congregational Church
20. Site of Union Chapel
21. Site of United Methodist Free Church chapel
22. Former Hilderthorpe Mission Church
23. Sailors' Bethel
24. Wellington Hall
25. Former Quay Girls' School
26. Technical Institute
27. Former Wesleyan Schools
28. Site of Fort Hall

Around the Old Town more private building took place in the 1920s along Scarborough, Marton, and Sewerby Roads and on Bempton Lane. On the south side of the Old Town the corporation began the South Back Lane estate in 1930 and 400 houses had been built by 1934.[41] Other Council houses were built near Sewerby Road, Marton Road, and St. John Street in the later 1930s,[42] and private housing was extended northwards beyond Fortyfoot Road[43] and as far as Limekiln Lane. By the Second World War houses were creeping further up the wold slopes around Bempton Lane, and new roads had also been laid out in Hilderthorpe on the west side of Kingsgate.[44] Between the wars these extensive schemes had effectively united the Old Town and the Quay. Both the private and the Council housing of this period was purely residential, with little purpose-built resort accommodation. A prominent addition to the sea-front buildings was the Expanse Hotel, erected in North Marine Drive in 1937.[45]

The chief street improvements of this period were the widening of the north end of St. John Street, completed in 1939,[46] and the remodelling of Waterworks Street and North Back Lane to provide an easy route from St. John Street to Scarborough Road, completed in 1934.[47] Other improvements included the building of bridges over the Gypsey Race at the ends of Springfield and Midway Avenues in 1931 and 1938.[48] The surrounds of St. Mary's Church and Church Green were also opened up by the extensive demolition of old property at various times, but especially in 1921.[49]

The earlier pattern of development was continued after the Second World War. The most noteworthy additions were private estates on the north side of the town, between Sewerby Road and Marton Gate, and a large Council estate on the south side, in Bessingby. The private estates were laid out after 1956.[50] The corporation's West Hill estate in Bessingby was built on land acquired by compulsory purchase; the first house was opened in 1949[51] and about 840 houses had been built by 1970.[52] On the fringes of the built-up area there were several caravan camps in 1970, the chief ones being those in Limekiln Lane and near Marton Road.

By 1969 the Old Town had become something of a quiet backwater, little visited, even at the height of the season, by holiday-makers at the resort. In spite of the spread of new building around it, it still retained its identity, its early street pattern, and many of its older houses. The greater part of it was designated a conservation area in 1969.[53]

DOMESTIC BUILDINGS. The houses of the medieval town were no doubt timber-framed and plastered. When repairs were carried out in 1537 payments were made to wrights, tilers, thatchers, and other workmen for erecting timber frames, for working lime and sand, for daubing, and for thatching with straw; the timber included pairs of 'forks' and 'cripple forks' (crucks), wall plates, 'sidewivers' (purlins), 'naystres', spars, balks, and laths.[54] No framed houses could be identified in 1970, although in one or two cases there were indications of former timber construction. Many such houses may have survived into the 17th and 18th centuries, and some were doubtless destroyed by fire in 1657, when ten houses were burnt, and in 1723, when '54 bays of building' were lost.[55] After the 16th century chalk blocks and cobbles were probably extensively used for walling, and remnants of these materials may still be seen. Several cottages completely built of cobbles still stood in Nungate until the 1960s.[56] Dressed stone from the priory buildings was also used: some survives in houses on the north side of High Street, and farm buildings around High Green contain sandstone blocks as well as chalk and cobbles. Bricks may have been made locally as early as 1508, when there is a mention of Robert Clay of 'Brykkylsay' at Bridlington,[57] and by the later 17th century the heaping of bricks in the streets and on the Moor was an offence frequently presented in the manorial courts.[58] In the 19th century there were brickworks in Bempton and Mill Lanes, north of the Old Town, and south of the Gypsey Race, in Bessingby.[59]

THE OLD TOWN. The streets of the Old Town contain a motley collection of houses of which the oldest may date from the 16th century; some are substantially unaltered but many were wholly or partially refronted in the 18th and earlier 19th centuries or completely rebuilt at a later date. The most notable survival is High Street, a narrow curving street closely built-up on both sides. In spite of alterations it retains a predominantly Georgian appearance, with many façades of architectural quality and a number of bow-fronted shops. The oldest houses are probably a group near the centre of the north side, nos. 42–50 (even nos.). Medieval stonework, perhaps taken from the priory, is visible in the lower walls; otherwise the frontages were completely remodelled at the end of the 18th century. One projecting party wall, corbelled forward at first-floor level, suggests that the upper storeys may originally have been timber-framed and jettied.

Several of the smaller refronted houses in High Street have steeply-pitched roofs and may be of 17th-century origin. There is ample evidence that towards the end of the century larger residences with richly-fitted interiors were being built for wealthy owners. The most complete façade of this

---

[41] 'Annals of Bridlington', vols. 47, p. 59; 48, pp. 23, 283; 51, p. 143.
[42] Ibid. vols. 52, p. 296; 55, pp. 248–9.
[43] In 1933 68 a. here were sold to developers: Regy. of Deeds, 465/208/165.
[44] O.S. Map 6" (1938).
[45] Ex inf. the Manager, 1971.
[46] 'Annals of Bridlington', vols. 55, p. 295; 56, p. 66.
[47] Ibid. 51, p. 176.
[48] Ibid. 48, p. 266; F. A. Slim and H. L. Gee, *Bridlington, 1899–1949*, [96].
[49] 'Annals of Bridlington', vols. 38, pp. 296, 454; 41, p. 25; 49, p. 307.

[50] In 1956 88 a. here were sold to developers: Regy. of Deeds, 1030/526/466.
[51] Bridlington Corp., *Counc. Proc. and Cttee. Mins.* 1946–7, 126; 1949–50, 74; O.S. Map 6" (1951–3).
[52] Ex inf. Town Clerk, 1970.
[53] E.R.C.C. *Mins.* 1968–9, 259.
[54] Purvis, *Bridlington Charters, etc.* 19–25; see *Y.A.J.* xxxvii. 57 for terms, but 'naystres' are unexplained.
[55] *Cal. S.P. Dom.* 1658–9, 78; E.R.R.O., QSF Midsummer 1723, D.31.
[56] Photographs in Bridlington Pub. Libr.
[57] B.I.H.R., Prob. Reg. vii, f. 29.
[58] Purvis, *Bridlington Charters, etc.* 255–6, etc.
[59] O.S. Map 6" (1854, 1894).

period is at nos. 7–9 Westgate, the former home of the Hebblethwaite family. It is two storeys high and eight bays long, designed symmetrically and built entirely of dark red brick. A rainwater-head bears the initials W.H. There are uniform mullioned and transomed windows and a coved cornice enriched with acanthus leaves. Moulded brick dressings include quoins, a string-course breaking forward above the ground-floor windows, a pediment over the former central doorway, and a shouldered architrave with flanking consoles to the central window on the first floor. The original doorway has been converted to a window and entrances, replacing windows, have been made at both ends of the front; their pediments are modern but one opening contains the original oak door. At the east end of the house, occupied by the Midland Bank, the floor between the storeys has been removed to form a banking hall. The lower walls have bolection-moulded oak panelling and a chimney-piece flanked by foliage carving; the richly ornamented plasterwork of the former upper room does not appear to be original. A panelled room at the rear has a ceiling with a central wreath in high relief. In the western half of the house is an oak staircase with heavy turned balusters and ball-capped newels.

No. 16 High Street (Craven House) was also a substantial house of late-17th-century origin; the front was remodelled c. 1800 but some rich brickwork survives at the back. No. 43 High Street (the Toft) was probably built in 1673, a date formerly visible on a rainwater-head.[60] It was refronted towards the middle of the 19th century when the attics were converted into a full top storey. One original mullioned and transomed window remains at the rear and until recently there was a domed lantern crowning the staircase projection in the angle between the main block and a back wing. Internally there are many original fittings of unorthodox but exuberant design, richly carved with swags and garlands. They include door-cases in the entrance hall and, on the first floor, panelling and a chimney-piece in the so-called white drawing room; there are also two enriched ceilings. The staircase has ball-capped newels and heavy turned balusters. The fittings in one ground-floor room and in part of the rear wing date from the 18th century. Eighteenth-century panelling, brought from elsewhere, was inserted in two rooms on the top floor in 1970. No. 45 High Street, next to the Toft, carries a date tablet of 1693. The two-storeyed front, which has a dentil eaves cornice and dormer windows, was altered and converted into a shop c. 1800. The entry at the side of the house, continuing as a path leading to South Back Lane, is paved with narrow bricks set on edge in a herringbone design, the bricks perhaps being of Dutch origin.

Other houses in High Street retaining late-17th- or early-18th-century features include no. 34 and the Board inn (no. 62). In Westgate the much altered Star inn, nos. 11–15, and West End House may be structurally of the same period, as are some surviving cottages in Market Place (nos. 19–21). A row of two-storeyed houses on the north-west side of Kirkgate appears to date from c. 1700. The row includes Lourdes House (nos. 15 and 17), which retains a stone plinth, a moulded brick string-course, and a doorway with a pulvinated frieze. No. 4 Kirkgate, which has a steep roof and re-used sandstone in its back wall, may be older.

The most imposing early-18th-century house is the Avenue, in Westgate, probably built for the Prickett family in 1714; the date appears on two elaborate lead rainwater-heads. The brick front, which is of three storeys and five bays, was altered and given a classical porch in the early 19th century. Original features include brick angle pilasters and moulded brick cornices above the windows. At the rear are two full-height projecting bays. The interior was much altered when the house became a hospital; some of the panelling is now in Bridlington High School, but several chimney-pieces and plaster ceilings remain. A service wing adjoining the house was evidently raised to two storeys during the alterations of c. 1820. At the same time a stable block was built west of the wing; it has a large central archway with rusticated and vermiculated surround, surmounted by a pediment. The avenue of trees from which the house took its name formed an axial approach on the opposite side of Westgate and is now incorporated in Westgate Park. A house in High Street (nos. 51 and 53) has several features in common with the Avenue and is of similar date. The two-storeyed front is of seven bays with full-height angle and intermediate pilasters. The ground floor has been altered by the insertion of shops but the interior retains a contemporary staircase and panelling. No. 64 High Street has a three-storeyed frontage of the later 18th century, with a particularly elaborate pedimented door-case; its frieze is enriched with swags and medallions and its pilasters have acanthus capitals, lion masks, and pendants.

The late 18th century and the years around 1800 saw much rebuilding and refronting in the Old Town. Several new houses of the period were designed by John Matson, architect, who was living at the Quay between 1790 and 1823.[61] It was the period when bowed shop-fronts, of which several good examples survive, were inserted in High Street. That at no. 70 consists of two bow windows on coved supports, the double doorway between them having a Gothic fan-light and decorative glazing to the upper panels. A similar front at nos. 42–4 has Gothic enrichment to the main cornice and to those of the two windows. There are also double bows at no. 46[62] and, on the opposite side of the street, at no. 45. No. 67 has an early-19th-century shop-front consisting of large flat-fronted bow windows with delicate glazing-bars of painted brass. There is also a good 19th-century shop-front at nos. 59–61. The building activity of c. 1800 also involved the insertion of a number of new door-cases in High Street. A typical example, ornamented with fluting and oval paterae, is that at no. 28. No. 16 (Craven House) was given a new symmetrical front in 1806 when the interior was remodelled;[63] the pedimented door-case has reeded pilasters with fluted capitals and a tympanum enriched with swags and lion masks. The Dominican convent is the largest house in the street, having a frontage of nine bays set back behind

---

[60] The interior is illustrated in F. F. Johnson, 'The Toft. High Street, Bridlington', *E. Yorks. Georgian Soc. Trans*, ii (4), facing pp. 33, 38, 40, 44.

[61] H. M. Colvin, *Biog. Dict. Eng. Architects, 1660–1840*, 381. [62] See plate facing p. 320.
[63] F. F. Johnson, 'Craven House, Bridlington', *E. Yorks. Georgian Soc. Trans*. i (2), 35.

cast-iron railings; the building may date from the 18th century but most of its features, including the Tuscan doorway, are alterations of c. 1825. Among mid-19th-century classical doorways in High Street are those at nos. 29, 34, and 43. At Westgate Lodge a pedimented doorway of c. 1800 has a frieze, perhaps original, decorated with vine leaves and grapes.

In Market Place, a wide street where considerable demolition had taken place by 1970, many of the houses were built in the earlier 19th century. They include no. 1, which has a shop-front consisting of flat-fronted bow windows, and nos. 9 and 17, both with two-storeyed projecting bays. Coverley House is a three-storeyed building of the late 18th century, its front altered and given a Tuscan porch some 40 years later. No. 26, on the opposite side of the street, is a double-fronted house of yellow brick with a recessed central bay, faced with rusticated stucco; an iron balustrade flanks the entrance steps. No. 27 (Levisham House) dates from soon after 1800 and has a central doorway with pediment, fan-light, and reeded pilasters. At no. 38 there is a bow window rising through both storeys and a door-case with an open pediment and fluted pilasters. Among buildings in Market Place which have been rebuilt or cleared away are the Nag's Head inn and several houses with bowed shop-fronts.[64] St. John Street (formerly St. John's Gate), which leads south to become Quay Road and to connect the Old Town with the Quay, contains a few small 18th- and early-19th-century buildings with later alterations and inserted shops. Further north-east, most of the early houses in Bayle Gate, Kirkgate, Pinfold Street, and Nungate (later Sewerby Road) have been demolished and only a few old farm buildings survive at High Green.

THE QUAY. At the Quay the street improvements and rebuilding and alteration of houses in the 19th and 20th centuries have left scant remains of earlier buildings. One or two individual houses in King Street, Queen Street, and Prince Street have the low eaves and steep roofs which suggest that they belonged to the old village. The first buildings of the seaside town date from the very late 18th and early 19th centuries. A few can be recognised by their bow windows and Georgian doorways, and a shop in King Street still contains an 'Adam' ceiling. On the Promenade no. 45 is a three-storeyed house with a bow to its two upper floors and no. 17A has a late-18th-century door-case with fluted and reeded pilasters, oval paterae, and an open pediment. Twin doorways at nos. 4 and 5 Queen Square also incorporate the fluting and paterae which are characteristic of Bridlington door-cases at this period. In Prospect Street a pair of three-storeyed red-brick fronts (nos. 10 and 12 Wellington Road) survive from an otherwise altered row; they have rusticated quoins, string-courses, and twin doorcases with semicircular fan-lights and reeded pilasters. Also in Prospect Street was Cottesmore House, demolished in 1966, which was a double-fronted two-storeyed building with a pedimented doorway flanked by bay windows.[65]

During the earlier 19th century lodging-houses were being built in the older streets of the Quay. About 1800, for example, at least three of the houses in New Buildings (the west side of Manor Street) were erected.[66] The original houses that remain in this row have shop-fronts inserted in the ground floors; they are three-storeyed, with or without attics, and most are single-fronted. No. 13, however, is five bays long with a central doorway and has bay windows through all three floors in the end bays. No. 6 (Barclays Bank) was the centrepiece of New Buildings; it was originally two separate houses, converted into one for Sir Henry Boynton c. 1810–15 when it was refronted in stone and given bow windows rising through all the storeys.[67] Extensive alterations to the façade in 1898 included the removal of the ground-floor bows.[68] Other early lodging-houses similar to those in Manor Street survive, usually much altered, in King and Queen Streets, the Promenade, and elsewhere.

Of the larger houses built around the fringes of the Quay in the late 18th or early 19th century, a notable survivor is Field House (no. 20 Victoria Road).[69] It is a two-storeyed house standing back from the adjacent streets in its own grounds. The entrance front of the larger section was originally on the south side, flanked at the angles by bowed projections rising through both storeys; the central doorway was later moved to the east front. The south-east bow was evidently designed to enclose a sunk bath which, in the early 19th century, was served by a chalybeate spring. The bath survives beneath the floor boards. An adjacent house, to which the larger building was apparently added, is of 18th-century origin; its fluted Doric portico was made into a porch in the mid 19th century, when bay windows were also added. In the 1890s Field House was used as a massage and hydropathic establishment.[70]

Along Quay Road, between the Quay and the Old Town, there are a few survivors of houses built before 1850. They are mostly on the north-east side and are disguised under later alterations and modern shop-fronts. Of York Place, for example, the yellow-brick upper storeys of nos. 88–94 (even nos.) can be recognized. Nos. 96–102 are detached houses of yellow brick and there are two short rows of smaller houses of the late 18th and early 19th centuries. The Crown Hotel has a three-storeyed mid-19th-century stucco front, with a cast-iron balcony, and nos. 170 and 172 comprise a red-brick pair with twin doorways in a recessed central bay, flanked by attached Doric columns. Medina Cottage, on the opposite side of the street, is a double-fronted house with a Tuscan porch surmounted by a cast-iron balcony, the central first-floor window being flanked by moulded jambs terminating in volutes.

Around the Promenade most of the pre-1850 houses have been replaced. A few much-altered fronts may survive in the row that included Bridlington and Providence Places, and Sea Breezes remains behind a later façade. Just to the west of the Promenade, in Tennyson Avenue, a group of early-19th-century houses still stands: Belle Vue House, Belle

[64] Photograph in Bridlington Pub. Libr.
[65] Photograph in Bridlington Pub. Libr.
[66] *Hull Advertiser*, 3 July 1819.
[67] Ex inf. Mr. F. F. Johnson, 1971.
[68] O.S. Map 60″ (1853); *Illus. Guide to Bridlington Quay and District*, 38 (photo. of house before alterations); Bridlington Town Hall, Building Inspector's Office, drawing no. 1093.
[69] F. F. Johnson, 'Field Ho., Bridlington Quay, E. Yorks.', *E. Yorks. Georgian Soc. Trans.* ii (3), 33–5.
[70] Bulmer, *Dir. E. Yorks.* (1892), 139.

Vue Cottage, and Belle Vue, the last-named comprising a dignified red-brick terrace of four three-storeyed houses with moulded round-headed door surrounds. The few houses built south of the Gypsey Race before 1850 included some rows of mean brick cottages in Hilderthorpe Road, demolished in 1970.

Among the earliest buildings surviving from the development of the sea front after the mid 19th century are some of the plain stucco-fronted houses in Sewerby Terrace. In the centre of the terrace is the Alexandra Hotel of 1863–6, designed by W. B. Stewart, of Scarborough,[71] in an ornate Renaissance style inspired by that of the French Second Empire. It has an imposing stucco front of four storeys above a semi-basement and consists of a central block of nine bays, flanked by tower-like three-bay wings. French influence is particularly strong in the treatment of the slate mansard roof, with its two tiers of round-headed and circular attic windows. A decorative panel round a central dormer is crowned by two recumbent figures flanking a shell-like motif bearing the letters 'AH'. Other features of the front include vermiculated quoins, pedimented window-heads, eaves brackets, mask keystones, bay windows, a classical porch, and a continuous cast-iron balcony at first-floor level.

No elaborate layout was attempted in the siting of the sea-side terraces which were the most spectacular feature of Bridlington's next phase of development. They were erected mainly along the sea front and in the short streets at right-angles to it. Uniform in plan, they consisted of single-fronted houses of three or four storeys with basements below and attics above, each house having its bay window rising at least to the first floor. Variations occurred only in the size of the houses and in their elevational treatment. The stucco-fronted terraces built by G. W. Travis c. 1870 were designed by Joseph Earnshaw. They are somewhat similar in style to the Alexandra Hotel but less elaborate. Perhaps the most typical examples are the Crescent and Marlborough Terrace, which are four-storeyed and have moulded architraves, eaves brackets, mansard roofs, and ornamental dormers. Others were built in the Promenade, the Esplanade, and Cliff Street. Fort and Regent Terraces, built in the early 1870s,[72] have less pretentious three-storeyed frontages of red brick; the former is largely unaltered but the ground-floor bays of the latter have been replaced by shop-fronts.

The stucco-fronted terraces on the Beaconsfield estate further north were the next to be built.[73] Albion Terrace (dated 1878) and Royal Crescent, both designed by Joseph Earnshaw, are the most architecturally ambitious, while Bright Crescent is plainer and Gladstone Crescent on a smaller scale. In the next decade variegated brick frontages tended to replace those of ornamental stucco, but a multi-storey bay window to each house remained almost universal. Several semi-detached houses in York Road, built by 1890, have twin-gabled fronts of red or white brick with dressings of the contrasting colour. An irregular pair of yellow-brick houses at the end of the road near the sea has decorative barge-boards as well as red-brick and stone dressings.

Groups of three- and four-storeyed houses in St. Anne's Road, also built by 1890, include some faced with stucco and others of variegated brick.

Of the larger, detached, houses built near the sea front between 1850 and 1890 several survive in and near St. Anne's Road. They include the stuccoed Danes' Lea and Sunny Bank, and the Tudor-style Red House, of red brick with stone dressings. On the Promenade no. 69 (the Victoria Hotel) is an imposing double-fronted house, having a contemporary wing with an ogee-shaped pediment and a cupola. Canton Villas, on Flamborough Road, include one highly decorative pebble-dashed and stuccoed house, with vermiculated quoins and a hexagonal tower.

Inland from the sea front Wellington Road was laid out by Joseph Earnshaw in the later 1870s and 1880s. The first houses, built at the south end of the road, were large detached or semi-detached residences of red or white brick with a great variety of ornament and, for the first and almost the last time, a few Gothic Revival features; particularly striking examples are nos. 1, 32, and 34. In Victoria Road the semi-detached houses of the later 1880s are smaller and those in Princess Street consist of red-brick terraced pairs. North Street contains more modest terraces, while the two-storeyed cottages of North View Terrace, west of the Promenade, were evidently not designed to accommodate visitors.

The infilling along Quay Road at this period includes a distinctive group of six houses (nos. 60–70, even) of brick and stucco with bow-fronted ground-floor windows and plentiful stone dressings. The new streets off Quay Road contained both large semi-detached houses of red, grey, or yellow brick, such as those in St. John's Avenue, and small red-brick terraces; one of the latter, in Portland Place, is dated 1878. After 1890 many other streets in this area were built up with modest houses of multi-coloured brick, arranged in terraces and short rows.

The period between 1890 and the First World War saw rapid development north of the Quay. The new streets exhibit a great variety of houses designed for residential and, especially, resort accommodation. The most spacious streets, with the largest houses, include the post-1890 section of Wellington Road and the whole of Trinity Road and Tennyson Avenue. Here the houses are detached or semi-detached with short terraces intermixed, all of red, white, or yellow brick and most of them with multi-storey bay windows. In other streets the houses are more modest but show the same variation of colour, grouping, and height. Towards the end of the period some of the larger houses in Swanland Avenue, Park Avenue, and Flamborough Road introduce such innovations as half-timbered or tile-hung gables. Throughout the area the lodging- and boarding-houses are thus characterized by variety of colour and design, by numerous floors, and by spacious bay windows, giving street after street the unmistakable air of a resort.

In Hilderthorpe, where development began later and was less rapid in its early stages, several three-storeyed terraces of multi-coloured brick had been built in the Windsor Crescent and West Street area by 1890. The only sea-side terrace to compare with

---

[71] *Hull Advertiser*, 29 Aug. 1864. See plate facing p. 256.

[72] *Kelly's Dir. N. & E.R. Yorks.* (1872), 336–7.
[73] Ibid. (1879), 363–4.

the more ambitious groups further north is Pembroke Terrace; it consists of eleven three-storeyed houses of red brick and stucco with bay windows to three floors and heavy stone ornament to porches and windows. At the turn of the century the inland streets round Richmond Street and Horsforth Avenue were being built up with characteristic resort houses similar to those on the opposite side of the Gypsey Race. A distinctive 'Norwegian chalet' style makes its appearance in Cardigan Road and at the corner of Horsforth Avenue, the houses being of brick, rough-cast, and timber, with wide overhanging eaves. The most impressive sea-front group is in Marine Drive near the Spa; it consists of an irregular terrace of red brick and rough-cast, varying between four and six storeys in height, the façade embellished with three-storeyed bay windows and ornamental gables.

MANOR. In 1086 the greater part of Bridlington was in the king's hands: he had in all 13 carucates, 9 of which had been held in 1066 by Morcar and 4 by Carle. A third estate, of 5 carucates, belonged to the count of Mortain, and this had been held in 1066 by Torchil.[74] Bridlington was the centre of a great royal estate at this time, with berewicks at Hilderthorpe and Wilsthorpe and soke in thirteen other townships.[75] After the Survey the king's estates in Bridlington passed to the Gants and the Mortain estate passed, like Boynton, to the Paynels and subsequently to the archbishops of Canterbury, under whom a mesne lordship was held by the Meynells.[76]

Early in the 12th century Walter de Gant gave all 13 carucates of his estate as part of the endowment of Bridlington priory. A further carucate was given to the priory at the same period by Jordan Paynel and in 1286 William de Cauntelo, presumably as demesne lord of part of the Paynel estate, gave 4 carucates more.[77] In 1284–5 the priory was said to hold 15 carucates of the Gant and Canterbury fees,[78] and in 1299 it held 6 carucates of the Canterbury fee from Nicholas de Meynell.[79] The priory retained the manor of BRIDLINGTON until its possessions were forfeited to the Crown in 1537 after the attainder of the last prior.[80]

After the suppression of the priory various parcels of its former property in Bridlington were let by the Crown,[81] but no leases of the manor itself were granted until 1566, when it was let to Thomas Waferer and eleven other inhabitants of the town for 40 years at a rent of nearly £153.[82] This lease was forfeited, apparently because of the failure of the lessees to perform covenants contained in it,[83] and in 1591 the manor was let to John Stanhope.[84] In 1595, however, a 41-year lease was granted to William Wood and eleven other inhabitants.[85] This was followed in 1623 by the granting of the manor in fee to Sir John Ramsay, still for the annual payment of £153.[86] His brother Sir George Ramsay sold the manor in 1630 to thirteen inhabitants of the town, the fee-farm rent remaining the same.[87]

The manor was subsequently owned and the town governed by a body of feoffees, on behalf of the inhabitants, under the terms of a deed drawn up in 1636.[88] The lords feoffees have ever since retained ownership of some manorial property and they still fulfil certain functions, although most of their administrative powers were surrendered in the later 19th century.[89] Apparently from the outset the feoffees sold the houses and land of the manor to the tenants, each of whom continued to pay his share of the fee-farm rent.[90] There were thus no outstanding landowners at the time of inclosure in 1771, with the exception of James Hebblethwaite: and much of his estate derived from his ownership of the rectory.[91]

The rectorial estate belonged to the priory until its suppression. The church was valued at £66 13s. 4d. in 1291.[92] In the early 16th century tithe corn alone was worth £6[93] and in 1538–9 the rectory was valued at £40.[94] The rectory was let by the Crown to John Avery in 1538 and to John Calverley in 1551.[95] It was farmed by both Avery and Calverley to the Boyntons of Barmston. Matthew Boynton bequeathed the lease to his daughters at his death in 1540.[96] The rectory was next let, together with the manor, to twelve inhabitants of the town in 1566, at a rent of £32. It was also included in Stanhope's lease in 1591 and in the 1595 lease to twelve townsmen, both at the same rent.[97] A grant said to have been made by the Crown to Henry Best and Robert Holland in 1594–5[98] perhaps did not take effect. The townsmen in 1600 farmed the rectory to Francis Boynton for £70.[99] In 1611 the Crown granted it in fee to Francis Morrice and Francis Philips,[1] and in 1613 they conveyed it to Sir Francis Boynton.[2] It was farmed by Boynton to Melchoir Gibbon for some years from 1613 onwards.[3]

Sir Matthew Boynton is said to have let the rectory to Robert Palmer and William Bower in 1632,[4] and in 1637 he sold it to Henry Fairfax.[5] In 1650 the tithes were worth £170.[6] The rectory next passed to David, earl of Buchan, on his marriage with Frances Fairfax in 1697.[7] Buchan retained it until 1729, when he conveyed it to Leonard Bower

---

[74] *V.C.H. Yorks.* ii. 197, 204, 226, 322.
[75] Ibid. 147, 197.
[76] See p. 22.
[77] *Bridlington Charty.* 1, 13.
[78] *Feud. Aids*, vi. 55.
[79] *Yorks. Inq.* iii. 117; *Cal. Inq. p.m.* iii, p. 428.
[80] See p. 32.
[81] The reversions of these leases were included in the 1566 lease, in which the earlier leases are recited.
[82] *Cal. Pat.* 1563–6, 447–9.
[83] See p. 48.
[84] Purvis, *Bridlington Charters, etc.* 38–40.
[85] Ibid. 41–52.
[86] Ibid. 52–61.
[87] Ibid. 65–85.
[88] Ibid. 86–105.
[89] See p. 68.
[90] e.g. Purvis, op. cit. 105–9.
[91] See pp. 45, 47.

[92] *Tax. Eccl.* (Rec. Com.), 303–4.
[93] *Miscellanea*, iii (Y.A.S. Rec. Ser. lxxx), 16, 32.
[94] M. Prickett, *Hist. Ch. Bridlington* (1836 edn.), 96.
[95] Ibid. 99; Purvis, *Bridlington Charters, etc.* 31; *Acts of P.C.* 1550–2, 228. See also C 3/38/79.
[96] *Test. Ebor.* vi. 100–1. See also C 1/1311/54, 55.
[97] Purvis, *Bridlington Charters, etc.* 40, 46; *Cal. Pat.* 1563–6, 447–9.
[98] H. Grove, *Alienated Tithes*, p. cxlvii. Their christian names are given in C 66/1516 m. 32.
[99] E.R.R.O., DDWB/15/82b.
[1] E.R.R.O., DDDA/3/7; Purvis, *Bridlington Charters, etc.* 200.
[2] Prickett, *Hist. Ch. Bridlington* (1836 edn.), 100.
[3] Lords Feoffees' Rec., Bayle, Bridlington, receipts.
[4] T. Allen, *Hist. Yorks.* iv. 4.
[5] C.P. 25(2)/523/13 Chas. I Mich. pt. 2, no. 38.
[6] *T.E.R.A.S.* ii. 53.
[7] *Complete Peerage.* See also C 5/568/6.

and Miles Barnes.[8] The lords feoffees agreed with Bower in 1729 that composition rents amounting to £309 a year should be paid in lieu of tithes for a period of four years.[9] Despite being involved in transactions concerning the rectory in 1729 and 1738,[10] Bower remained the impropriator[11] until 1759, when he and Gertrude Burdett conveyed it to James Hebblethwaite.[12] At inclosure in 1771, when the tithes were worth £385, Hebblethwaite was allotted 265 a. in lieu of half of them and rent-charges of £192 10s. for the rest; he also received a non-rectorial allotment of 157 a.[13]

The Hebblethwaites kept the land and rents until 1825, when Harriet Hebblethwaite devised them to Margaret Harland.[14] In 1838 Margaret sold to John Kirby most of the non-rectorial estate allotted to James Hebblethwaite in 1771,[15] and it seems likely that she conveyed the rectorial estate to him as well, for Kirby was named as impropriator between 1849 and 1865.[16] In 1872 Kirby sold 272 a. of former Hebblethwaite land to Christopher Hutchinson, making no mention of the tithe rents,[17] and in 1913 the trustees of J. H. Hutchinson sold 281 a., known as West Huntow farm, to the East Riding county council.[18] The land comprised in these last two transactions included some of the rectorial estate. In 1881 the tithe rents were secured to the benefice, which thus became a rectory.[19]

PRIORY BUILDINGS. Much of the priory was demolished after its suppression, the only buildings to survive being the nave of the church, which had always been used for parochial purposes, and the Bayle or gatehouse.

After the Dissolution the nave of the priory church became the parish church of St. Mary the Virgin and, as such, is described elsewhere.[20] The fabric dates mainly from the 13th century with some 15th-century rebuilding at the south-west corner. The crossing, the transepts with eastern aisles, and the aisled chancel were set obliquely beyond the east end of the present church, having a pronounced slant northwards. All have disappeared, but there are traces of the foundations of both transepts and some remains of the south transept where it joined the nave. The discovery of extensive foundations, notably when the east and south sides of the church-yard were cleared for burials early in the 19th century, revealed that the crossing and chancel had extended at least 125 ft. beyond the east end of the nave.[21] At the Dissolution the choir was said to be 58 paces long. Over the crossing the 'steeple' was described as 'tower fashion', high, and 'dangerously in decay'. There was a fine gilded reredos behind the high altar, and between it and the east window was the shrine of St. John of Bridlington 'in a fair chapel on high', approached by a stone stairway on each side. Under the shrine were five chapels.[22]

Among the many fragments of worked stone recovered from the churchyard at various periods, the most notable belonged to an elaborately carved cloister arcade which evidently ante-dated the 13th-century rebuilding of the church. Five bays of the arcade were reassembled and set up in the church in 1910–12.[23] The undercut decoration of the hood-moulds and the capitals of the twin shafts, some with 'linen-fold' and beaded ornament, are fine examples of the very last phase of Romanesque carving in the north of England, dating from c. 1180.[24]

The cloister lay south of the priory nave. The position of the north walk outside the wall of the existing aisle is indicated by the surviving corbels which supported the cloister roof and by two impressive doorways which led from the cloister into the church; there is a large arched recess beside the most easterly door. Attached to the aisle wall further west are some remains of the west range of the cloister in which the prior's lodgings were situated. They include traces of an undercroft vault and the bases of one row of the piers which supported it. A stair, approached by a small doorway from the cloister walk, is now enclosed in a buttress, and at a higher level on the aisle wall is the outline of a fire-place. The general layout of the claustral buildings was recorded soon after the Dissolution.[25] The prior's lodgings in the west range had a first-floor hall with service rooms to the south and his private chambers and chapel to the north. The frater occupied the south side of the cloister and on the east side was the entrance to the chapter-house with the dorter at a higher level. The chapter-house had 'nine fair lights' around it and may therefore have been a free-standing polygonal structure with ten sides. Buildings to the east of the dorter included an old frater, the infirmary with its chapel, the treasury, and a 'new chamber'. Also recorded at this time were a malthouse, barn, and other outbuildings to the north of the priory and a bakehouse and brew-house to the south. The guest lodgings and stables lay near the gatehouse.

The surviving gatehouse, or Bayle, was perhaps built in or soon after 1388, when a licence to crenellate was granted to the priory.[26] It is approached from the west by the street called Bayle Gate and was formerly hemmed in by the buildings which lined the narrow street. After the clearance of houses in the earlier 20th century, however, the Bayle was left standing on an island site. It is a rectangular structure of sandstone and chalk, with angle and intermediate buttresses. The interior walls are of chalk but various materials, including brick, have been used in restoration work.[27] Any battlements

[8] Regy. of Deeds, L/15/24; /16/25, 26.
[9] Purvis, *Bridlington Charters, etc.* 133–5.
[10] Regy. of Deeds, L/17/27; /18/28; P/217/562.
[11] B.I.H.R., TER. J. Bridlington 1743, 1749.
[12] Regy. of Deeds, AA/244/501.
[13] Ibid. AN/121/11.
[14] Ibid. EA/339/420.
[15] Ibid. FF/1/1.
[16] B.I.H.R., TER. J. Bridlington 1849 to 1865.
[17] Regy. of Deeds, MA/259/1872.
[18] Ibid. 153/524/454; E.R.C.C. *Mins.* 1912–13, 506.
[19] Par. Recs., memorandum bk. of work done, 1846 onwards.
[20] See p. 72.

[21] T. Allen, *Hist. Yorks.* iv. 11; M. Prickett, *Hist. Ch. Bridlington* (1836 edn.), 49, 108.
[22] From a survey of c. 1541, printed in *Archaeologia*, xix. 270 sqq.
[23] *Y.A.J.* xxi. 174; xxii. 238.
[24] L. Stone, *Sculpture in Brit. in Middle Ages*, 81–2.
[25] *Archaeologia*, xix. 272–5. A reconstruction of the layout is shown in drawings by J. S. Purvis in St. Mary's Ch. and in a model at Sewerby Hall Mus.
[26] *Cal. Pat.* 1385–9, 439. See plate facing p. 113.
[27] It has been restored at various times from the 17th century onwards, most fully in 1933. A rainwater head is dated 1792. Arms of the feoffees on the west face were put up in the 19th century replacing others placed there successively in 1663 and 1797.

which may have crowned the parapet are now missing and the windows, mostly square-headed with ogee-headed lights, are either modern or restored. On the outer, or west, face is a main archway with a smaller entrance beside it; they are both pointed and have continuous mouldings carried down the jambs, the larger arch being enriched with ball-flower ornament. The east front has a single wide arch with much-weathered quatrefoil panels to the jambs. Above the gateway passage is a vault with moulded stone ribs, carved bosses, and chalk infilling. The diagonal ribs spring from angle corbels, of which three are carved with figures of musicians and the fourth with a crowned king; all are somewhat defaced. From the side walls of the passage pointed doorways originally gave access to the two ground-floor rooms, a prison on the north and a porter's lodge on the south.[28] Two similar doorways led to spiral staircases which communicated with a first- and second-floor room on each side and to a single large chamber, or court-room, occupying the whole of the top floor; one original stone staircase remains.[29]

AGRICULTURE. There was said to be land for nine ploughs on the king's estates in Bridlington in 1086, but much had apparently been laid waste since the Conquest for the value of the manor had fallen from £32 in 1066 to 8s. There is also mention of 8 a. of meadow in 1086.[30]

Little is known of the agricultural arrangements in the township during the ownership of the manor by Bridlington priory. There are brief references to open-field land, to common pasture in the Moor, to the ox pasture, and to demesne and tenants' meadow land lying between the town and the Gypsey Race.[31]

In the early 16th century the priory cultivated 68 of its 115 open-field bovates in demesne.[32] The other 47 were let to tenants, but it seems that many inhabitants had little or no land and suggestions were made at the suppression of the priory in 1537 for the demesne lands to be widely distributed among them. The duke of Norfolk recommended to Thomas Cromwell that the inhabitants should have all the demesnes at farm and should not alienate their shares, 'whereby it shall not come to one man's hands, and thereby many men shall be relieved'. He suggested that the inhabitants should also be sold the priory cattle and that they should have 'the grass ground' as well as the arable land.[33] Shortly afterwards the Crown commissioner reported that he had offered the demesnes and the standing corn to the inhabitants but had sold nothing because they would not give enough.[34] The manor as a whole was not immediately farmed out by the Crown and the methods of management of the steward and bailiff are not known. An undated rental, perhaps from early in Elizabeth I's reign, shows 'all the manor lands', comprising 679 a., let to tenants.[35]

The Crown lease of the manor to twelve inhabitants in 1566 suggests that the duke of Norfolk's recommendations had in fact been heeded. The lessees were bound in covenants to allot land to inhabitants who had none, and to let the demsene arable and pasture lands to tenants for 21 years or less, no man to have more than 4 bovates.[36] Similar provisions were made in the lease to twelve inhabitants in 1595.[37] After the manor had been sold to thirteen townsmen in 1630, a 'deed of management' was drawn up between those thirteen feoffees and some 180 tenants. Only 31 inhabitants then held open-field land; their holdings totalled 104 bovates, of which about 40 were described as 'town land' and about 60 as demesne, apparently preserving the distinction between land cultivated in demesne and land let to tenants before the Dissolution. Of the 31 landholders 2 had a ½ bovate, one had one, 5 had 2, 8 had 3, one had 3½, 5 had 4, one had 4½, and 8 had five. Ten of the feoffees held land, each with 3 or more bovates.[38] After 1630 the feoffees sold to each man his holding of land or other property, subject to the payment of a proportion of the Crown's fee-farm rent and to the payment of pier-rates.[39]

Such sales of property contained a schedule of the common rights to be enjoyed in the township. First, each cottager had two beast-gates in the 'great' and 'little' moors of the Quay from 3 May to 11 November, and ten sheep-gates in Sheep Huntow, the fallow fields, and the wastes and commons; both husbandmen and cottagers also kept animals in the moors from 11 November to 25 March, after which the ground was laid until 3 May. Secondly, the owner of each bovate of town land had a quarter of a beast-gate in the moors from 3 May to 11 November and 20 sheep-gates. Thirdly, the owner of each bovate of demesne land, although having no beast-gates, had 30 sheep-gates. Fourthly, 'the town's hursell' of cattle, perhaps a common herd, had eatage in West Leys and Haverdale Heads from harvest to 25 February. Fifthly, the same herd had eatage in the ings, Lamb Hills, and other grounds, inclosed or otherwise, on the south side of the beck from 1 August to 25 March. Finally, the town's herd of swine was kept in the fields 'as formerly they have been'.[40]

In an early-17th-century rental all the open-field land was described as lying in East and West fields,[41] and there are frequent references in the 17th century to divisions of the open fields called Broad, Oxgang, Great Town, and Little Town Dales. In 1729 there were 42, 18, 32, and 17 bovates respectively in the four 'dales', a total of 109,[42] and at inclosure in 1771 there were 36, 21, 32, and 17, a total of 106. The allotments made at inclosure were, however, described as lying in East, West, Hill, and Ducky Dike fields. Allotments totalling 230 a. were made in East, 282 a. in West, 242 a. in Hill, and 197 a. in Ducky Dike fields; a further 233 a. were indis-

---

[28] *Archaeologia*, xix. 271.
[29] The doorways have been altered and moved: R. Horspool, *The Bayle at Bridlington;* J. S. Purvis and M. E. Ingram, *The Bayle, Bridlington*. For the post-Dissolution uses to which the building has been put see below, pp. 62, 65, 68, 77–9.
[30] *V.C.H. Yorks.* ii. 192, 204.
[31] *Bridlington Charty.* 16, 21.
[32] *Miscellanea*, iii (Y.A.S. Rec. Ser. lxxx), 10.
[33] *L. & P. Hen. VIII*, xii (1), p. 593, partly printed in Purvis, *Bridlington Charters, etc.* 4.
[34] *L. & P. Hen. VIII*, xii (2), p. 32, quoted in ibid. 4–5.
[35] Purvis, op. cit. 27
[36] *Cal. Pat.* 1563–6, 447–9; B.M. Lansd. MS. 65/17, printed in Purvis, op. cit. 30–1.
[37] Purvis, op. cit. 48–9. [38] Ibid. 97–104.
[39] There are said to be 200 of such 'leases'; one is printed in ibid. 105–9.
[40] An example is printed in ibid. 110–11. See also E.R.R.O., DDCV/parcel 91.
[41] Lords Feoffees' Rec., Bayle, Bridlington.
[42] Purvis, op. cit. 135.

tinguishably taken from East, Hill, and Ducky Dike fields, and several allotments were from open fields and other areas.[43] It is not possible to equate dales and fields, but the dales may have been named from the four prominent valleys cut into the wold slopes, and the long and narrow fields were similarly aligned, running up and down the slopes north of the Old Town. The varying quality of land within this large open-field area is suggested by the various values attributed to demesne land and the rents received for tenants' land in the early 16th century. Sixty-six bovates were worth 10s. each, 34 8s. each, and 15 only 6s. each.[44]

The Moor in 1771 lay to the south-east of the Old Town, stretching to the sea and to the Gypsey Race. Allotments totalling 158 a. were taken solely from it. The common pastures called Huntow and Old Moor in 1771 lay in the extreme north-west, high on the wolds, contiguous with pastures known as Huntow in neighbouring townships.[45] Near by, along the northern margin of Bridlington, was Norlands, perhaps also common pasture. Allotments made solely from Huntow and Old Moor amounted to 88 a. and from Norlands 173 a. The common meadows in the ings lay along the Gypsey Race south of the Old Town, and 47 a. were allotted solely from them in 1771. An area known as New Pasture, mentioned as early as 1731,[46] lay close to the Old Town; it may have been taken out of West field but it was presumably used in common until 1771, when 39 a. and more were allotted there. Oxmires, covering 17 a., seems to have been taken from East field.[47]

Rights of common, or 'cottage rights', in the various fields, pastures, and meadows were held in 1771 by about 130 people, more than 90 of whom had no land at all. The total number of rights was more than 230. No individual held more than 13 and 70 men had one, or only a fraction of one, common right. The owners of open-field land presumably had beast- and sheep-gates, as specified in sales of land,[48] but details are not given in the inclosure award. One man, however, though he held no land, had acquired 20 sheep-gates in Huntow and 30 in the fallow fields.[49]

In addition to crofts and garths there were various closes in the area around the Old Town by the 16th century. More than twenty meadow and pasture closes, with a total area of more than 120 a., are mentioned in the Elizabethan rental.[50] They include Butt, North, Spring, Oak, Dead, and Moor closes, Haverdale Heads, and the twenty-acre Replekeld, which was later subdivided and usually called Ripplegills.[51] In some cases these were apparently not whole-year closes. Several inhabitants enjoyed the use of Butt close in respect of their open-field holdings,[52] for example, and in 1639 it was alleged that High and Low Leys and Haverdale Heads were occupied in severalty from 25 March until harvest and then in common.[53] The existence of part-year common rights in these and other areas has also been referred to earlier.[54] The Leys, or Ley closes, lay on either side of the road from the Old Town towards Easton, and Haverdale Heads was further west, in the valley of the Gypsey Race; common rights in these grounds were extinguished at inclosure in 1771.[55]

The commonable land remaining at inclosure in 1771,[56] under an Act of 1768,[57] amounted to 2,011 a., and allotments totalling about 1,950 a. were made. The outstanding allottee was James Hebblethwaite, the impropriator of the rectory, who received 265 a. in lieu of tithes and 157 a. for his own land and common rights. Only one other allotment exceeded 100 a., that of 139 a. received by Beverley corporation in lieu of the estate which it acquired c. 1740 under the will of Anne Routh.[58] There were 8 allotments of between 50 a. and 99 a., 14 of 20 a.–49 a., and 12 of 10 a.–19 a. As many as 119 allotments were of under 10 a., mostly received by the landless cottagers in lieu of their common rights.

The numbers of farmers recorded in Bridlington since inclosure have been about 10–20, often with half a dozen market gardeners and several cow-keepers as well.[59] Of the 18 farmers in 1851, 13 had under 50 a. and only 3 as much as 150 a.–300 a.[60] This pattern of mainly small farms was subsequently preserved. Much of the former Hebblethwaite estate and all of the Beverley corporation land were, moreover, converted to smallholdings when the East Riding county council bought 281 a. of West Huntow farm in 1913 and 141 a. of North Mount farm in 1919.[61] A large proportion of the area north of the Old Town was still farmland in 1969, most of it in arable cultivation.

THE HARBOUR. The port of Bridlington belonged to the Gants at the end of the 11th century and was given, as part of the manor, to the priory.[62] In 1446 the right to anchorage, quayage, and groundage in the port was granted to the priory by the Crown.[63] There is no evidence relating to the maintenance of the harbour by the priory, but at the Dissolution the Crown was obliged to undertake prompt and extensive repairs. Enquiries were made in 1537 about the use of stone from the priory buildings; local men advised that stone alone would not withstand the sea and that it would be best to use timber and stone, as before.[64] Heavy charges were incurred for work carried out during the next six years.[65] Much of the work was done by men of

---

[43] Registry of Deeds, Beverley, AN/121/11.
[44] *Miscellanea*, iii. 10.
[45] See pp. 85, 88.
[46] E.R.R.O., QSF Easter 1731, B. 16.
[47] Regy. of Deeds, AN/121/11.
[48] See p. 46.
[49] Regy. of Deeds, AN/121/11.
[50] Purvis, *Bridlington Charters, etc.* 27–9.
[51] e.g. C 142/534/103; E.R.R.O., DDCV/parcel 91.
[52] e.g. E.R.R.O., DDBV/8/18; DDX/91/8, 11.
[53] Purvis, op. cit. 119.
[54] See p. 46.
[55] Regy. of Deeds, AN/121/11.
[56] Ibid.
[57] 8 Geo. III, c. 17.
[58] *10th Rep. Char. Com.* (H.C. 103), pp. 683–4 (1824), xiii. See below, p. 71.
[59] Directories.
[60] H.O. 107/2367.
[61] Regy. of Deeds, 153/524/454; 195/337/298. An additional 31 a. in Sewerby were included in the Routh estate and in the sale of 1919.
[62] *Bridlington Charty.* 1.
[63] *Cal. Chart. R. 1427–1516*, 67.
[64] *L. & P. Hen. VIII*, Add. i, pp. 416–17.
[65] Ibid. xiv (2), p. 78, quoted in Purvis, *Bridlington Charters, etc.* 166; *L. & P. Hen. VIII*, xv, p. 11; E 101/459/5, 6, printed in *Miscellanea*, iii (Y.A.S. Rec. Ser. lxxx), 63–71.

Bridlington and near-by villages,[66] fulfilling labour services owed to the manor.

By the end of 1554 further work needed to be done, more particularly as the result of a gale in October of that year. In the north pier ten 'rooms', or compartments of the timber framework, were decayed. Trees and old timber were used, and nearly £7 was 'delivered in prest to divers honest men of the same town', suggesting an assessment made by a group of responsible townsmen.[67] It is clear that the piers at this period, and no doubt much earlier, consisted of a timber framework filled with stone.

The lessees of the manor in 1566 took upon themselves the repair and maintenance of the harbour, and they were allowed £100 for the purpose, as well the old materials of the piers, stone from the priory site, and 120 trees. Assessments, or pier-rates, were also authorised in the town.[68] In addition, tolls were collected on goods shipped or landed and duties taken from ships using the harbour.[69] A survey made in 1580 showed that some work had recently been done but that much more was needed.[70] There is little doubt that the harbour was not kept in adequate repair by the lessees, but the reasons for their failure are far from clear.[71] In 1581 the lessees themselves claimed to have spent about £1,000 since 1566.[72] The non-repair of the harbour nevertheless seems to have been the main reason for the forfeiture of the 1566 lease.

The harbour was surveyed again in 1590 and reported to be generally in good repair, but with some defects. A significant point was the removal by the sea of two rooms at the landward end of the south pier: this was subsequently to be one of the most constant difficulties. The commissioners responsible for the survey commented that assessments had usually been collected by quay wardens, and they recommended that six such wardens should be appointed at the next manor court.[73] The piers had deteriorated by 1591, when they were surveyed once more.[74] Maintenance of the harbour was included in the leases of the manor in 1591 and 1595, and in the grant of 1623, and the same responsibility was transferred to the town feoffees in 1630.[75]

Periodic repairs were no doubt necessary during the 17th century, as in 1663–4 when many men provided labourers, horses, and carts to take stone and timber to the harbour.[76] The townspeople, moreover, several times petitioned the Crown for financial assistance,[77] and in 1672 it was alleged that the storm damage of 1663 would cost £4,000 to put right and that afterwards £150 a year would be needed.[78] A duty to be collected at Newcastle and Sunderland, on ships loaded there, was granted in 1672 for 21 years to raise the £4,000.[79] Passing tolls on coal loaded at those ports were granted in the first Bridlington Piers Act of 1697, after much damage had been done to the piers the previous year, and they were to be collected until 1704. In 1715 the various tolls and duties were renewed and they were continued by successive Acts thereafter.[80]

The harbour was badly decayed in 1717, when the commissioners responsible for enforcing the Acts recorded that all £344 collected in tolls and duties since 1715 had been spent and £402 more besides; a further £137 was needed for work in the coming winter. The commissioners also made an estimate of the cost of rebuilding both piers completely: £8,272 for the south pier and £1,133 for the north.[81] The county justices thereupon authorized the levying of eight pier-rates in the town, and 46 similar rates were levied between 1718 and 1728.[82] The rebuilding may thus have been carried out, but the state of the piers still caused much concern in the mid century and large quantities of timber were used for repairs.[83]

In 1764 it was decided to build a stone causeway to protect the landward end of the south pier and in 1765 to build a new north pier entirely of stone. These plans were soon abandoned, however, and in 1770 timber was ordered to be used at the root of the south pier to stop the sea from entering the harbour.[84] John Smeaton examined the piers in 1778; he suggested ways of combating worm in the timbers and also recommended that stone be used to protect the landward end of the north pier to keep the sea from eroding into the harbour.[85] A sixty-foot stone extension of the north pier was proposed in 1786 and agreed upon in 1792, but its completion was deferred in 1796 after the foundations had been finished. It was completed in modified form and cased in stone on the seaward side between 1801 and 1805. A further 180 ft. of the pier was similarly cased in 1805–8. No work in stone was attempted in the south pier and a timber breakwater to protect the landward end was ordered in 1810.[86]

The replacement of the old piers with stone structures and the enlargement of the harbour were eventually achieved in the 19th century. Work began in 1816 under the supervision of David Matthews, in accordance with plans drawn up two years earlier by Simon Goodrick. The harbour was deepened and a dam built to retain tide water and produce a scouring effect when it was let out. By 1820 the dam had failed and been removed. Much of the crane wharf was rebuilt in 1819. The new north pier, begun in or soon after 1816, was not finished until 1843; it was 608 ft. long, nearly 100 ft. longer than

---

[66] *Miscellanea*, iii. 66–7; *L. & P. Hen. VIII*, xiv (2), p. 234, printed in full in Purvis, *Bridlington Charters, etc.* 165–6. See above, p. 19.
[67] E 101/459/7, printed in *Miscellanea*, iii. 71.
[68] Purvis, *Bridlington Charters, etc.* 30.
[69] The 'ancient rate' of tolls and duties is given in ibid. 180–2.
[70] B.M. Lansd. MS. 31/27, printed in ibid. 168–9.
[71] Ibid. 30/5; 31/27, 67; 65/17, printed in ibid. 29–35, 170–5.   [72] Ibid. 31/68, printed in ibid. 175–7.
[73] E 178/2714, quoted in J. S. Purvis, 'Bridlington Piers and Harbour' (TS. in Bridlington Pub. Libr.), 3–4.
[74] E 178/2725.
[75] Purvis, *Bridlington Charters, etc.* 40, 47, 58, 81.
[76] Ibid. 177–8.
[77] Ibid. 184–8.
[78] S.P. 29/309/166, abstracted in ibid. 188–90.

[79] Ibid. /167, abstracted in ibid. 190–1.
[80] 8 & 9 Wm. III, c. 29; 1 Geo. I, stat. 1, c. 49; 5 Geo. I, c. 10; 7 Geo. I, c. 14; 26 Geo. II, c. 10; 29 Geo. III, c. 23; 56 Geo. III, c. 60; 1 Vic. c. 110; 18 & 19 Geo. V, c. 69. Passing tolls everywhere were abolished in 1861 by 24 & 25 Vic. c. 47.
[81] E.R.R.O., Quarter Sess. Order Bk., printed in Purvis, *Bridlington Charters, etc.* 193–5.
[82] Purvis, op. cit. 196–7. Similar rates were regularly levied thereafter: ibid. 200.
[83] Harbour Comrs., general min. bk. 1755–1837 (in Harbour Master's office), *passim*.
[84] Ibid. 25 June 1764, 20 Sept. 1765, 16 May 1770.
[85] Ibid. 11 Sept. 1778; E.R.R.O., DDX/16/142.
[86] Harb. Comrs., gen. min. bk. 1755–1837, 12 Sept. 1786, 25 July 1792, 22 Aug. 1796, 22 May 1798, 31 Aug. 1801, 17 Sept. and 2 Nov. 1805, 26 Apr. 1810.

BOYNTON HALL: the south front

SEWERBY HALL: the south front

BOYNTON CHURCH: the west end

BOYNTON HALL: the principal staircase

the old pier. The new south pier was built in 1843–8, in accordance with the plans of James Walker; it was about 1,500 ft. long, compared with the 1,100 ft. of the old pier. It was in a more southerly position and the area of the harbour was consequently increased from 5½ a. to 12 a. The only major alteration subsequently made to the piers was the lengthening of the north pier by about 120 ft. in 1866.[87]

Regular maintenance and improvement work by the harbour commissioners continued, but financial difficulties prohibited much large-scale development. Dredging to deepen the harbour began in 1884[88] and a new fish wharf at the west end of the harbour was erected in 1885; in 1888–9 a wharf there was built for Langdale's Chemical Manure Co.[89] In 1892–3 a board room for the commissioners and a new harbour master's house were built near the crane wharf, and at the same time the local board made a new road along the north side of the harbour.[90] Further dredging was carried out in 1904 and, on about the line of the old south pier, a jetty later known as the Chicken Run was built. The immediate object was to improve conditions for the regatta held that year.[91] Demands for better accommodation for fishing boats and fish buyers increased after the First World War as the industry grew with the use of motor boats.[92] In 1915 the commissioners had refused to allow the extended use of the crane wharf as a fish market and ordered all large boats to land their catches at the narrow south pier, where there was no cover for buyers.[93] The commissioners could not afford the necessary improvements and government aid was refused in 1919 and 1921.[94] Some improvement was made possible in 1924, when the town corporation was given permission to take 25,000 cu. yds. of mud and sand from the harbour to fill behind its new sea-wall. In 1926 the commissioners sold Langdale's Wharf, which they had bought in 1900, in order to finance limited improvements.[95]

After long discussions about the best means of improving the harbour, during which a corporation take-over was strongly urged,[96] an Act of 1928 was passed reconstituting the commissioners and giving them borrowing powers.[97] The 30 commissioners appointed under the earlier Acts were local gentlemen and prominent townsmen, with several of the lords feoffees in addition. They were now reduced to 22. Eleven of the old commissioners remained but they were joined by nominees of public bodies, together with a local fish salesman.

The much-needed improvements were made by the new commissioners in 1930–1. The seaward end of the south pier was widened to form a fish wharf and covered accommodation was provided there. At the same time the Chicken Run jetty was reconstructed and lengthened.[98] Extensive dredging took place in 1934–7, and a long-term dredging programme began in 1943.[99] The fish wharf and shelter were improved and extended in 1949–51, a new Chicken Run jetty was built in 1950–1,[1] and the crane wharf jetty was rebuilt in concrete in 1958–9.[2] An ice plant was erected on the fish wharf in 1966, and further reconstruction work there was carried out in 1968–9.[3] The harbour's facilities were then fully used by fishing boats, trading vessels, pleasure craft, and private sailing boats.[4]

A scheme by the corporation to make a new road across the western end of the harbour and to improve the harbour surrounds was first mooted in 1931. A similar proposal was made in 1958 and improvements were eventually undertaken in 1968–9.[5] The work included the demolition of property on the northern side of the harbour and the construction of a wider and longer Harbour Road there; the building of a bridge linking this road with the former Langdale's Wharf, which the corporation had acquired in 1930;[6] and the building of a raised footpath from the bridge to South Cliff Road.

Since the late 1920s the Royal Air Force has occupied a site at the west end of the harbour for the accommodation of launches, and its buildings there have been extended at various times.[7]

Although they have never been launched in the harbour itself, the life-boats stationed at Bridlington may be appropriately described here.[8] The first lifeboat was acquired in 1805[9] and replaced in 1824 by a boat given to the local fishermen. A new boat was provided in 1850 and soon afterwards the Royal National Life-boat Institution took over its management. The boat-house was in Chapel Street.[10] In 1865 the R.N.L.I. introduced a new boat, after Count Bathyanny had given another to the fishermen. The former boat did not survive 'the great gale' of 10 February 1871, when known losses among the coal fleet sheltering in the bay were 30 ships and 70 men. Within a year, however, there were three life-boats: a new R.N.L.I. boat, the

---

[87] Ibid. 5 Nov. 1816, 27 Aug. 1817, 23 July and 16 Sept. 1819, 25 Sept. 1820, 27 Sept. 1842, 26 Sept. 1843, 25 Sept. 1848, 12 May 1865, 24 Sept. 1866; *Letter to R. P. Braine*, 1847 (copy in Harb. Master's office); Purvis, *Bridlington Charters, etc.* pl. facing p. 162 (appar. based on map in Harb. Master's office); *2nd Rep. Tidal Harbours Com.*, H.C. 692, pp. 389–96 (1846), xviii (1).
[88] Harb. Comrs., gen. min. bk. 1873–1904 (in Harb. Master's office), 27 Mar. 1884, 28 Apr. 1886.
[89] Ibid. 29 Sept. 1885, 15 Nov. 1888; abstract of general accts. 1837–92 (in Harb. Master's office).
[90] Ibid. gen. min. bk. 1873–1904, 27 Sept. 1892, 25 Aug. 1893.
[91] Ibid. 4 Mar. 1904; 'Annals of Bridlington', vol. 21, pp. 74 etc.
[92] See p. 51.
[93] Harb. Comrs., gen. min. bk. 1904–28, 15 Oct. 1915, 10 Jan. 1918, etc.
[94] Ibid. 30 Sept. 1919, 12 Aug. 1921.
[95] Ibid. gen. min. bk. 1873–1904, 20 Sept. 1900; 1904–28, 29 Apr. 1924, 2 Mar. 1926.
[96] Ibid. 1904–28, *passim*.   [97] 18 & 19 Geo. V, c. 69.

[98] Harb. Comrs., gen. min. bk. 1928–67 (in office of Clerk to the Comrs.), 25 Apr. 1930, 14 Jan. and 17 Apr. 1931.
[99] Ibid. 21 Jan. 1935, 24 Jan. 1938, 25 Jan. 1943.
[1] Ibid. 25 Apr. 1949, 24 Apr. 1950, 29 Jan. and 7 May 1951.
[2] Ibid. 12 May 1958, 4 May 1959.
[3] Ibid. 23 May 1966; gen. min. bk. 1967-date (in office of Clerk to the Comrs.), 24 Sept. 1968, 11 Feb. 1969.
[4] See plate facing p. 128.
[5] Harbour Comrs., gen. min. bk. 1928–67, 17 Apr. 1931; 30 Sept. 1958; gen. min. bk. 1967-date, 7 May 1968.
[6] Ibid. 1928–67, 27 Sept. 1960; 'Annals of Bridlington', vol. 47, p. 28.
[7] Harb. Comrs., gen. min. bk. 1928–67, 19 Nov. 1928, 21 Jan. 1933, 26 Sept. 1950, 29 Jan. 1951.
[8] Unless otherwise stated this paragraph is based on G. Simpkin, 'The Lifeboats of Bridlington' (1955) (TS. in Bridlington Pub. Libr.), *passim*.
[9] *Hull Advertiser*, 28 Sept. 1805.
[10] J. Wood, *Plan of Bridlington* (1828); O.S. Map 60" (1853).

fishermen's boat, and a third one presented by the Revd. Y. Lloyd Greame in view of the dissatisfaction felt at the performance of the R.N.L.I. boat in 1871. The third boat was managed by the Sailors' and Working Men's Club and was housed in Cliff Street. The R.N.L.I. boat-house was transferred to South Cliff, near the harbour.[11] There was subsequently much rivalry between the R.N.L.I. and the S.W.M.C. crews. The fishermen's boat was wrecked in 1886 and that of the S.W.M.C. in 1898; thenceforth a single boat was stationed at Bridlington. The boat-house was moved from South Cliff Road, behind the harbour, to its present site in South Marine Drive in 1904.[12]

FISHING. Before the 19th century there are only fragmentary references to fishing from the port. Fishermen no doubt worked from the Quay in the Middle Ages, as others did from Filey, Flamborough,[13] Scarborough,[14] and Whitby.[15] There were 'herring houses' at the Quay in the 1530s, and fish shipped coastwise from Bridlington in the early 16th century may have been locally caught.[16] Fishing cobles were occasionally bequeathed by local men, by two inhabitants of Hilderthorpe, for example, in 1525 and 1541, and by two Bridlington men in 1558 and 1609.[17] It was also reported in 1581 that there had been an increase of 'two fishers', each of 34 tons, at Bridlington.[18] Some Bridlington boats fished at a distance from the port in the 17th century, like a coble fishing at Great Yarmouth in 1658. Others worked in the bay, like a coble which landed a fish $22\frac{1}{2}$ ft. long in 1677.[19] By the early 18th century many barrels of English-caught cod and herring were being sent to London,[20] and again some of these were no doubt landed by Bridlington fishermen. Finally, in 1801 a boat at Bridlington was said to have been let for the herring fishery.[21] Only in the later 19th century, however, does the history of the industry emerge from obscurity.

Four main methods of fishing have been employed at Bridlington in the later 19th and 20th centuries: inshore trawling, chiefly for plaice, from March to October; drift-net fishing for herrings; line-fishing, especially for cod, from October to March; and potting for crabs and lobsters, from March to June.[22] A few people have also been employed working shrimp nets along the shore. Inshore fishing in the bay has always been carried on from small boats called cobles but larger boats, called smacks, yawls, or keels, have been used further afield.[23] Motors began to be fitted in these sailing boats about 1914 and soon purpose-built motor boats were in use as well, gradually replacing the sails.

More than 300 boats were fishing off Bridlington in 1902, but only 84 boats belonged to the port in that year.[24] Earlier figures are incomplete, but the number of first-class boats belonging to Bridlington was 7 in 1889, 18 in 1890, and 11 in 1898,[25] compared with only 4 in 1902. Only a proportion of the Bridlington boats was at work in any one year. In 1903, for example, 49 were fishing and 38 were idle.[26] By 1912 there were still 80 boats belonging to the port, 8 of them first-class, and 172 men were employed in them; there were also 7 men shrimping along the shore.

At the end of 1914 6 herring boats fitted with motors were line-fishing, and a year later 25 motor boats were lining. Trawling from motor boats in the bay was allowed in 1918, when it was said that 'very few sailing boats are left'. Early in 1920 there were 53 motor boats at Bridlington, though 'a good many' were laid up because they could not pay their way. The increased price of transporting fish from the port caused some men to revert from motor boats to cobles and others to turn increasingly to taking out pleasure parties. There were 38 motor boats in 1921 and 34 in 1922, together with 14 cobles and small boats, and 142 fishermen were employed in 1921.[27] Because of the scarcity of fish many men turned to pleasure trips or to relief work, such as road-making, during the next few years. By 1928 the number of boats was down to 24 motor cobles and 14 sailing cobles, and 144 men were employed. There was a further fall in the number of boats in the 1930s.[28]

After the industry had recovered from the disruption of the Second World War, 14 keel boats and 15 motor cobles were employing 133 men in 1947. The total number of boats increased to 48 by 1952, and in 1951 there were 183 fishermen;[29] it fell to 30 in 1956, but rose again to 46 in 1963.[30] In 1969 there were 41 boats all told, of which 35 were keels, manned by about 150 fishermen.[31]

The numbers of boats belonging to the port give some indication of the varying prosperity of the industry, though under-employment of boats and men regularly occurred. The amount of fish landed at Bridlington by British boats clearly indicates the use made of the port,[32] as do the tolls paid on fish landed there.[33] Bad weather accounts for much of the small-scale year-to-year variation in the amount of fish landed, but other factors help to explain the longer-term trends. Much-reduced landings of wet fish in 1905–9, for example, were at least partly caused by over-fishing in the limited area of the bay

---

[11] *Kelly's Dir. N. & E.R. Yorks.* (1872), 332; O.S. Map 25″ (1893).
[12] 'Annals of Bridlington', vol. 21, p. 102. The building carries the date 1903.
[13] See pp. 141, 158.
[14] See P. Heath, 'North Sea Fishing in the 15th Cent.', *Northern Hist.* iii. 53–69.
[15] *Bridlington Charty.* 77–9; *Whitby Charty.* i (Sur. Soc. lxix), 4, 311.
[16] *Miscellanea*, iii (Y.A.S. Rec. Ser. lxxx), 42–3; see above, p. 35.
[17] B.I.H.R., Prob. Reg. xi, ff. 152, 597; xv (3), f. 259; xxxi, f. 2.
[18] *Cal. S.P. Dom.* 1581–90, 3.
[19] Ibid. 1658–9, 454; 1677–8, 403.
[20] See p. 52.
[21] E.R.R.O., DDGR/43/21.
[22] Unless otherwise stated the following paragraphs are based on North Eastern Sea Fisheries Cttee. *Mins.*

[23] See also E. W. White, *Brit. Fishing Boats and Coastal Craft; Pt. I: Historical Survey* (H.M.S.O.), 15.
[24] Bd. of Trade, *Sea Fisheries: 15th Ann. Rep. of Inspectors* [for 1900], 118.
[25] W. Garstang, *The Impoverishment of the Sea*, 68.
[26] Bd. of Agric. and Fisheries, *Ann. Rep. . . . relating to Sea Fisheries for 1903*, 50–1.
[27] *Census*, 1921.
[28] Ibid. 1931.
[29] Ibid. 1951.
[30] Min. of Agric. and Fisheries, *Sea Fisheries Statistical Tables*, 1952–63.
[31] Ex inf. Capt. R. Spear, Harbour Master, 1969.
[32] See Bd. of Agric. and Fisheries, *Ann. Reps. . . . relating to Sea Fisheries*, Pt. II Tables, 1886–1918; Min. of Agric. and Fisheries, *Sea Fisheries Statistical Tables*, 1919–69; North Eastern Sea Fisheries Committee, *Mins.* 1903–4 onwards.
[33] See Harbour Comrs., gen. acct. bks. 1790–1928 (in Harbour Master's Office); 1929–69 (in office of Clerk to the Comrs.); annual *Statement of Accounts*.

within which trawling was allowed. In 1909, when more than 20 cobles were trawling, it was said to be quite impossible for so many boats to make a living within the permitted area. The threatened prohibition of all trawling, however, led to 116 fishermen signing an undertaking in 1912 to stay within the limits, though they did not always do so.

A great increase in landings during the First World War is partly explicable by a temporary extension of the trawling area. The large landings both during and after the war were also encouraged by the use of motor boats: before motor trawling began some 2,200 cwt. of plaice were caught in the bay in 1911–15, but after the introduction of motor boats almost 5,000 cwt. were landed in 1916–20. This increased activity in the bay helped to produce a scarcity of fish in the 1920s which, as already mentioned, caused considerable under-employment. The vastly-increased landings made after the Second World War have largely been the result of the gradual abandonment of line-fishing for the more remunerative trawling beyond the bay from keel boats. The reduced number of cobles still trawled and potted in the bay itself. Among other recent developments are the use of Seine nets on Bridlington boats and a revival of the catching of salmon.

Among landings at Bridlington by boats of other ports were those of herrings from deep-sea steam trawlers. While Bridlington boats have long caught small herrings in the bay, the deep-sea herrings were landed by East Anglian and Scottish boats. In the early years of the present century Scottish fisher-girls and fish buyers spent a short season in Bridlington, and more than 100 boats were sometimes in the harbour on Sundays, when the Scots fishermen came ashore.[34] The herring season gradually declined in importance, and when Bridlington was used for the landing of deep-sea herrings in 1962 it was said to be the first time 'for many years'. In 1962 77 boats landed and in 1963 70, but numbers dwindled thereafter.[35]

Foreign boats have rarely landed fish at Bridlington, though Danish boats regularly did so in the 1940s. Foreign landings actually exceeded British landings in 1945–6 but they became of little significance after 1950.

Fishing boats paid duties for their use of the harbour, under the various harbour Acts,[36] and in the late 19th century a special duty was imposed on fishing boats.[37] Comprehensive tolls on fish landed were not, however, collected. In 1860 a toll was introduced for fish landed on the beach from 'strange' boats, thus avoiding the harbour,[38] but the revenues from it were small and collection appears to have lapsed soon after 1900. Fish tolls were reimposed in 1918, to strengthen the commissioners' hand in applying for a government grant towards harbour improvements,[39] and they are separately recorded after 1928. The revenues clearly reflect the boom in the industry after the Second World War.

SHIPPING AND TRADE. Little is known of the use made of the port in the Middle Ages by either coastal or oversea shipping. Bridlington priory was a large wool-grower, supplying it to the king in 1339,[40] for example, and said to rank fourth among the Yorkshire monasteries in the 14th century with an annual stock of 50 sacks.[41] Some of this wool was exported from Bridlington, and in 1339 and 1341 there is mention of the prior's ship, the *Mariole*, and of the use of it to ship wool abroad.[42] In 1447 the priory had licence to export up to 30 sacks of wool custom-free, a privilege renewed in 1452, though there is no indication of the port of shipment.[43] It is, however, perhaps indicative of the minor importance of Bridlington that it was not among the ports of the south and east coasts taxed by John in 1203–5, and also that it was little used by the king in the late 13th and early 14th centuries for the despatch of corn to Scotland; even corn bought at Bridlington in 1298 was sent down-river to Hull.[44] Bridlington was considered fit, together with Beverley, to provide a balinger for the king's service in 1402,[45] but it may have been built elsewhere.

By the early 16th century there are clear indications of both the coastal and the oversea trade of the port. More than 20 coal ships paid groundage at Bridlington in 1541–2, as well as a similar number from France ('Frans ships') and two carrying barley and salt; men from Hull, Lincoln, and York all paid toll for barley and fish.[46] A lawsuit *c*. 1530 between Philip Hanby, of Bridlington Quay, and a London fishmonger for whom he had obtained barley, peas, beans, and other goods, probably reflects the coastwise traffic in foodstuffs to the capital.[47] Several Bridlington men described themselves as merchants at this period[48] and the port certainly had some ships of its own. In 1528–9 eight crayers at Bridlington and Whitby were found to be available for campaigns in Scotland,[49] and in 1544 there was a similar report of ten ships belonging to Bridlington, of between 26 and 80 tons each.[50] A little later, in 1565, Bridlington was chosen along with Hull for the licensed export of malt, grain, and pulses.[51]

A more detailed picture of the port's shipping and trade begins to emerge in the late 16th century.[52] A small but steady coasting trade was then carried on, mainly with the ports on the north-east coalfield but with an occasional ship sailing south. The outward cargoes were largely foodstuffs, above all corn and malt, and the inward were coal. In the outward trade there were 11 sailings in the winter six months

---

[34] e.g. 'Annals of Bridlington', vol. 16, pp. 186, 191–2; 17, pp. 206, 246; 19, p. 261; 20, p. 233; 22, p. 230.
[35] Ex inf. Harbour Master, 1969. These landings followed the designation of Bridlington as a herring port.
[36] See p. 48.
[37] Harbour Comrs., cttee. min. bk. 1837–61 (in Harbour Master's Office), 30 Oct. 1860.
[38] Ibid. gen. min. bk. 1837–73, 28 Apr. and 12 May 1865.
[39] Ibid. 1904–28, 10 Jan. and 30 May 1918.
[40] *Cal. Pat.* 1338–40, 289, 296.
[41] *Miscellanea* (Thoresby Soc. xxxiii), 9.
[42] *Monastic Notes*, i (Y.A.S. Rec. Ser. xvii), 22; *Cal. Close*, 1339–41, 208–9.
[43] *Cal. Chart. R.* 1427–1516, 119, 121.
[44] *Pipe R. 1204* (P.R.S. n.s. xviii), 218; *Y.A.J.* xlii. 140–1.
[45] *Cal. Close*, 1399–1402, 239.
[46] E 315/382, printed in *Miscellanea*, iii (Y.A.S. Rec. Ser. lxxx), 42–3.
[47] C 1/656/33.
[48] B.I.H.R., Prob. Reg. ix, f. 210; xi, ff. 284, 595, 618.
[49] *L. & P. Hen. VIII*, iv (2), p. 2223.
[50] Ibid. xix (1), p. 117.
[51] *Cal. S.P. Dom.* 1601–3 and Addenda 1547–65, 559.
[52] Based on port bks. for Michaelmas 1577 to Easter 1578 (E 190/307/9), Mich. 1578 to East. 1579 (ibid./13), Mich. 1593 to Mich. 1594 (/309/5, 14), and Mich. 1599 to Mich. 1600 (ibid./10, 16).

of 1577–8, with 552 qr. of malt, 477 qr. of barley, 32 qr. of other grain, some butter and cheese, and a little wool and cloth; 8 of these shipments went to Newcastle and only one southwards—to Sandwich. In the same six months of 1578–9 there were only 4 outward sailings. In the year 1593–4 there were 16, of which 12 were to Newcastle and 2 to London; the cargoes comprised 350 qr. of malt, 150 qr. of barley, and 306 qr. of other grain and pulses. There were as many as 32 outward sailings in the year 1599–1600, 26 of them to Newcastle and none to the south, and the cargoes amounted to 885 qr. of malt, 536 qr. of barley, 214 qr. of wheat, and 169 qr. of pulses. The inward sailings were all of colliers from Newcastle. In the year 1593–4 there were 36, carrying 567 chaldrons of coal, with a little iron and several iron pots. And in the winter six months of 1599–1600 20 sailings brought in 308 chaldrons of coal.[53] The average amount of coal brought in during five full years between 1584 and 1600 was 691 chaldrons.[54] The trade was carried on at this period in small ships of between 5 and 60 tons, only a few of which belonged to Bridlington.

During the course of the 17th century the coasting trade was greatly expanded and, although its main directions remained the same, both outward and inward cargoes were more varied.[55] There was little new in the 12 outward sailings in 1624–5, 10 of them to Newcastle, with cargoes consisting almost entirely of malt (635 qr.) and grain and pulses (521 qr.); and there were only 8 outward sailings in 1633–4. But in 1644–5, when 5 out of 13 sailings were southwards, there were butter (80 firkins), hides, tallow, wool, cloths, and coal in the cargoes, besides 380 qr. of malt and 363 qr. of grain and beans. The number of sailings increased to 21 in 1654–5, 4 of them southwards, and their goods included 1,060 qr. of malt,[56] 655 qr. of barley, 623 qr. of other grain and pulses, and 40 barrels of butter. In 1666–7 almost all of the 49 sailings were northwards, and 15 were now to Sunderland besides 18 to Newcastle; 1,851 qr. of malt, 1,970 qr. of barley, and 189 qr. of other grain and pulses accounted for most of their cargoes. There was a similar number of sailings, 43, in 1674–5, but the mounting trade of the later years of the century is shown in the 103 outward sailings of 1684–5.

The inward trade similarly increased during the century and it is noteworthy how many inward sailings there were compared with those outward: the colliers seem to have frequently gone north without a cargo and thus were not recorded in the port books. Throughout the period Newcastle and Sunderland were of roughly equal importance; coal and salt still dominated the cargoes but hides, wool, cloth, stockings, timber, glass, grindstones, lead, soap, and butter all appeared frequently, if in small quantities. In 1624–5 there were 70 inward sailings, with 846 chaldrons of coal and 141 weys of salt, and in 1633–4 54 sailings. In 1635–6 1,019 chaldrons of coal were brought in.[57] In 1644–5 there were 36 sailings, with 570 chaldrons of coal and 197 weys of salt, and by 1654–5 as many as 90, with 1,274 chaldrons of coal and 55 weys, 20 barrels, and 56 bowls of salt. In 1666–7 there were only 39 sailings, with 668 chaldrons of coal and 121 weys of salt, but sailings later rose to 96 in 1674–5 and 134 in 1684–5. It is noticeable that the coastal trade of this century was increasingly conducted in Bridlington ships, about 20 of them by the second half of the century; they accounted for most of the sailings, each ship making 2 or 3 voyages in the course of the year.

The high level reached by Bridlington's coastal trade in the late 17th and early 18th centuries was marked by the growing importance of London as a market for the north's foodstuffs.[58] Thus there were 55 outward sailings in 1700–1, 96 in 1703–4, and 68 in 1705–6; and while many were still to the north-eastern ports, there were 23, 38, and 33 respectively to London. The traditional commodities still bulked large in their cargoes: in 1700–1, 5,042 qr. of malt, 1,730 qr. of barley, and 2,339 qr. of other grains and pulses; in 1703–4, 8,518 qr. of malt, 6,425 qr. of barley, and 5,268 qr. of other grain and pulses; and in 1705–6, 9,730 qr. of malt, 1,590 qr. of barley, and 2,046 qr. of other grain and pulses. But London was also taking more butter, as well as increasing quantities of fish and ale. In those three years respectively 51 firkins, 217 firkins, and 605 firkins and 463 qr. of butter were shipped. Of fish, 45 barrels, 19 firkins, and 3 casks went out in 1700–1, 65 barrels and 3 firkins in 1703–4, and 117 barrels in 1705–6. The variety of measures for ale defy summary. The sailings of 1721–2 confirm the new character of Bridlington's outward trade, for all but 4 of the 40 sailings were to London. Besides 16,848 qr. of malt and 1,450 qr. of oats and beans the cargoes included a variety of foods and beverages, such raw materials as hides and unwrought copper, and many kinds of household goods; some of these miscellaneous items had been imported from the continent for re-shipment to London.

The inward coasting sailings of the early 18th century were still largely from Newcastle and Sunderland, carrying mainly coal, cinders, and salt, but with noteworthy quantities of glass, flag and step stones, grindstones, and tobacco pipes. There were 94 sailings in 1700–1, 73 in 1703–4, and 67 in 1705–6. In the first of these years 1,245 chaldrons of coal and 121 chaldrons and 2,290 bowls of cinders were carried; in the second 931 chaldrons of coal and 77 chaldrons and 4,200 bowls of cinders; and in the third 821 chaldrons of coal and 77 chaldrons and 4,120 bowls of cinders. Salt amounted to 121 tons and 42 bushels in 1700–1, 104½ tons in 1703–4, and 66 tons, 34 weys, and 158 bushels in 1705–6. In each of the first two years a single sailing from Hull brought in a variety of raw materials and manufactured goods, including groceries, spirits, and tobacco; iron, lead shot, and sand; and timber, flax, and tar. In 1721–2 there were 81 inward sailings, with 1,138

---

[53] The total for the whole year is said to have been 869 chaldrons: Bertha Hall, 'The Trade of Newcastle and the N.E. Coast, 1600–40' (unpublished Ph.D. thesis, Univ. of London, 1933), 200, 203.
[54] J. U. Nef, *Rise of the Brit. Coal Indy.* ii. 383.
[55] Based on port bks. for full years from Christmas to Christmas 1624–5 (E 190/315/10), 1633–4 (/317/5), 1644–5 (/318/12), 1654–5 (/319/2), 1666–7 (/320/7), 1674–5 (/322/1), and 1684–5 (/328/9; /329/8). Fragmentary papers concerning paid and unpaid tolls c. 1630–50 are in Lords Feoffees' Rec., Bayle, Bridlington; see also Purvis, *Bridlington Charters, etc.* 178–80.
[56] Here and later one last of malt or grain is reckoned as comprising 10 qr.
[57] Hall, thesis cit., 204.
[58] Based on port bks. for full years from Christmas to Christmas 1700–1 (E 190/336/2; /337/1), 1703–4 (/338/10; /339/7), 1705–6 (/340/1; /341/7), and 1721–2 (/355/6; /356/3).

chaldrons of coal, 89 chaldrons and 2,870 bowls of cinders, and 46 tons of salt. One sailing from Hull and one from London brought luxury goods and materials. As in the earlier period Bridlington-owned ships dominated the trade.

The coasting trade, above all in coal and corn, clearly played a large part in the economy of Bridlington during the 17th and 18th centuries.[59] Although some of the coal was subsequently re-shipped from the port, much was doubtless distributed in the town and in the countryside behind; labourers working as far away as Elmswell were sometimes allowed the use of horses to fetch coal from Bridlington. Salt was similarly distributed, and corn was collected from farmers over a wide area.[60] The tonnage of coasting vessels belonging to Bridlington reached a high level in the 18th century; there were over 3,000 tons in 1716, over 2,000 in 1723, and over 1,000 in 1730, 1744, and 1751.[61]

Oversea trade was conducted on a small scale in the early 17th century.[62] In the year 1608–9, for example, there were no outward sailings, and in 1613–14 only one ship, Bridlington-owned, left the port, carrying 90 kerseys to Lisbon. In 1618–19 there were 6 outward sailings, but in 1622–3 only one. The number of sailings was up to 18 in 1633–4, and the cargoes included 492 chaldrons of coal, 52 cloths, and some butter. The inward trade was generally a little more active. In the winter six months of 1602–3 5 ships entered the port, 4 of them carrying about 60 weys of salt from Kirkcaldy, in Scotland; only one was from the continent, with 750 deals from Norway. In 1608–9 there were 5 sailings, from the Low Countries and Norway, and in 1613–14 there were 10 sailings, 2 of them in Bridlington ships, all from the Low Countries. The goods included raw materials which had come from around the Baltic, among them 2,450 deals, 2,100 spars, and 165 balks and joists; vegetables from the Low Countries; and exotic foodstuffs from southern Europe and the East. In 1618–19 there were 13 sailings, 9 of them from Norway. There were 8 sailings in 1622–3, one of them from Scotland with 400 Norwegian deals and spars, and one from Emden and 6 from the Low Countries, all with corn, beans, and hops; one ship was Bridlington owned. In 1633–4 there were 9 inward sailings.

In the later 17th century the oversea trade was greatly expanded.[63] In 1669–70 there were 25 outward sailings, 22 of them made by 12 ships belonging to Bridlington. Most were to the Low Countries, with a few to Norway and France. The chief goods carried were 233 northern cloths and 326 firkins of butter, and there were 15 chaldrons of coal. Much corn was exported to the Low Countries in the 1670s.[64] There were 35 sailings from Bridlington in 1700–1, though the destinations are not stated, and foodstuffs accounted for the bulk of the cargoes: 746 qr. of malt, 3,230 qr. of grain and beans, and 3,078 firkins of butter. The inward trade similarly flourished. There were 35 sailings in 1669–70, many from the Low Countries but several from France and 15 from Norway. Timber was still the most prominent import: over 8,000 deals, 6,200 balks and spars, 16,000 laths, and more besides. In 1700–1 there were 22 inward sailings, with over 6,800 deals and many other kinds of timber among the cargoes. In both years there was again a variety of manufactured goods, raw materials, and foodstuffs.

The amount of oversea trade conducted during the 18th century no doubt fluctuated very much from year to year.[65] In 1710–11 there were only 6 outward and 7 inward sailings. Exports comprised 29 cloths, 411 qr. of grain, flour, and rapeseed, 75 barrels of fish, and 17 chaldrons of coal; and nearly 14,000 deals and much other timber formed the bulk of the imports. In contrast there were as many as 24 outward and 15 inward sailings in 1721–2. Exports, to the Low Countries, Norway, and Sweden, comprised 90 cloths, 2,707 qr. of malt, 912 qr. of grain and flour, and 394 chaldrons of coal. Imports from Norway and Sweden were largely of timber, but now with some brass wire and iron. The sailings into the Baltic are noticed here for the first time, and so is one from Lisbon, with wine, figs, and 2,500 oranges and lemons, luxury goods of the kind which were usually brought coastwise from London or from the entrepôt of the Low Countries.

Many local men seem to have taken part in the trade of the port as masters of ships or shippers of goods, and often as both. Throughout the 17th century and into the 18th, however, successive members of the Bower, Rickaby, and Woolfe families were always prominent, and in the early 18th century Richard Hardcastle emerges as an especially active merchant.[66] In 1700 Edward Bower, John Rickaby's maltster, and Richard Hardcastle all gave evidence on Richard Woolfe's behalf when he was accused of customs offences regarding malt shipped to Rotterdam.[67] Several of these men were makers as well as shippers of malt.[68] The extent of the trading interest of John Bower, who made his will in 1676, was such that he ordered the sale of 'so much of my shipping' as would raise £2,000, to support legacies.[69]

The same merchants sometimes also served as customs officers at Bridlington. A 'legal quay' for the landing of customable goods was apparently established in 1559, and the appointed area was described in 1680 as comprising the inside length of the north pier, the ground alongside the cartway leading from the pier towards the town, and a 60-yard stretch of the beach northwards from the pier. The limits of the port were then from Flamborough Head to Barmston, but in 1730 they extended as far south as Spurn Head. Bridlington was always reckoned a member of the port of Hull.[70]

By the later 18th century the port's trade was

---

[59] See also T. S. Willan, *Eng. Coasting Trade, 1600–1750.*
[60] *Farming Bk. of Hen. Best of Elmswell* (Sur. Soc. xxxiii), 100, 115.
[61] B.M. Add. MS. 11,255, quoted by Willan, op. cit. 220.
[62] Based on port bks. for Mich. 1602 to East. 1603 (E 190/311/11), and for full years from Christmas to Christmas 1613–14 (/313/8) and 1622–3 (/315/3). Details for 1608–9, 1618–19, and 1633–4 are from Hall, thesis cit. 221–3.
[63] Based on port bks. for full years from Christmas to Christmas 1669–70 (E 190/320/10) and 1700–1 (/336/3).
[64] *Cal. S.P. Dom.* 1675–6, 378–9, 427; 1676–7, 2, 235, 414, 457, 517, 542.
[65] Based on port bks. for full years from Christmas to Christmas 1710–11 (E 190/344/11) and 1721–2 (/355/9).
[66] Port bks., *passim.*
[67] E 134/12 Wm. III Mich./28.
[68] See p. 56.
[69] E.R.R.O., DDBR/15/2.
[70] E 134/12 Wm. III Mich./28; E 159/576, Hil. 12; E 178/6305.

declining: Arthur Young in 1770 wrote of 'a slight trade that maintains ten or a dozen ships'.[71] Bridlington nevertheless remained a valuable harbour of refuge. In the 19th century upwards of 200 or 300 ships at one time might shelter in the bay, and the harbour was extensively used for refuge by fishing boats and coasters as well as by ships trading at Bridlington. As many as 496 ships, excluding fishing vessels, entered the harbour in 1844, 761 in 1845, and 825 in 1846.[72] Between 1849 and 1860 the number varied between 242 and 433, of which those entering for trading accounted for between 82 and 111. In addition, over 100 fishing vessels of 40–50 tons were said to enter for refuge each year.[73] The use of the harbour steadily fell off in the latter part of the century. The development of steam-ships reduced the need for refuge and it became increasingly difficult for these larger boats to enter the harbour safely. The growth of railway traffic after 1846 also had serious consequences for the trade of the port.

A significant proportion of Bridlington's trade was handled in locally-owned ships. In the 1820s and 1840s there were 16 or 17 shipowners in the town. By 1858 the number had fallen to 4 and in 1872 there was only one. Until at least 1858 there was also one 'trading vessel' owned at Bridlington.[74] The latter was presumably a ship running a regular service between Bridlington and local ports: the last such ship is said to have been the *Banshee*, sailing between Hull and Scarborough and calling at Bridlington.[75] The decline in local trade is also reflected in shipbuilding: the last ship built at Bridlington was launched in 1843,[76] though some fishing cobles continued to be made.

The coastwise shipment of corn to the northern collieries and to London was one of the chief components of Bridlington's trade in the 19th century. About 54,000 qr. are said to have been sent to London in the year ending 6 April 1811.[77] Over 21,000 qr. were shipped in the year ending 25 July 1817 and over 31,300 qr. in 1821–2. The trade temporarily fell off in the 1820s and only 3,300 qr. were shipped in 1826–7, but the total had increased to 15,400 qr. in 1831–2, 26,300 qr. in 1836–7, and 37,700 qr. in 1841–2. The subsequent decline was permanent. In 1846–7, after the railway line from Hull was opened providing competition with the coasters, 13,800 qr. of corn were shipped. By 1851–2 the total was only 6,700 qr. and by 1856–7 only 1,000 qr. The trade seems to have ceased altogether in the 1890s.[78] Other exports included old horses sent to the continent. Goods shipped into Bridlington in the 19th century included timber from the Baltic and North America, coal, bones, stone, bricks, and foodstuffs.[79]

The inward shipment of goods continued in the early 20th century on a reduced scale. The commodities brought in included timber, iron, coal, stone, bones, bricks, slates, china clay, phosphates, and foodstuffs. The number of shipments, however, greatly decreased: there were 36 in the year ending 25 July 1907, 28 in 1911–12, 11 in 1916–17, 14 in 1921–2, 15 in 1926–7, and 9 in 1931–2.[80] After the Second World War the trade was boosted in the 1950s by the import of potash for the local firm of Cross Bone Fertilisers Ltd. The tonnage was also swollen in 1966 by the import of aluminium slabs to be processed and re-shipped by R. J. Shepherd (Engineers).[81] The number of entrances into the harbour by coasters was 7 in the year ending 31 March 1956; it jumped to 23 in 1959–60 and 52 in 1960–1, exceeding 50 again in 1961–2 and 1962–3, before falling to 34 in 1963–4 and 21 in 1964–5. It was still more than 20 in 1967–8,[82] when dredging was carried out to provide a new berth for coasters, freeing for fishing boats the berth used previously.[83]

MARKETS AND FAIRS. From the early Middle Ages the Old Town of Bridlington had some local importance as a market centre. The first grant of market rights was made to the priory in 1200 and comprised a fair on 14 and 15 August and a Saturday market.[84] Three further fairs were granted in 1446: on 7–9 September, 10 October, and 10–12 May.[85]

A fair on 10 October is included in a list of East Riding fairs in 1641.[86] In the 18th and 19th centuries fairs were held on the Monday before Whit Sunday and on 21 October, and they were noted for cattle and for linen or woollen cloth and toys.[87] By the early 19th century,[88] and perhaps long before, they were pleasure fairs as well. Generally known as the Spring and October Fairs, they continued into the 20th century, with business giving way entirely to pleasure. The Spring Fair was the smaller and it died out in the 1920s; the October Fair was still held in 1969. Until c. 1900 there was also a statute fair for the hiring of servants, held on the Tuesday nearest to 14 November; it, too, was also a pleasure fair.[89]

Since about 1900 both Wednesday and Saturday have been market days for the general market[90] and a separate corn market continued to be held on Saturdays. A market for cattle on alternate Saturdays was begun in 1837,[91] and apparently re-established

---

[71] *Six Months' Tour through N. of Eng.* ii. 7.
[72] *Letter to R. P. Braine*, 1847 (copy in Harbour Master's office).
[73] *The Advantages of Bridlington. . . as a Harb. of Refuge*, 1857 with MS. additions (copy in Harb. Master's office).
[74] Directories; J. S. Purvis, 'Bridlington Piers and Harb.' (TS. in Bridlington Pub. Libr.), 8–9. Nine vessels belonged to the port in 1854: Sheahan and Whellan, *Hist. York & E.R.* ii. 453.
[75] 'Annals of Bridlington', vol. 31, p. 30.
[76] Purvis, 'Piers and Harb.', 9.
[77] H. E. Strickland, *Gen. View Agric. E.R.* (1812), 280–1.
[78] Harb. Comrs., gen. min. bk. 1755–1837, 31 Aug. 1825; corn toll bks. 1816–38, 1839–93 (in Harb. Master's office).
[79] Ibid. coastwise and foreign tolls, 1819–37; collector's bk. 1841 (in Harb. Master's office).
[80] Ibid. tonnage dues on strange vessels, 1906–33 (in Harb. Master's office).
[81] Ibid. gen. min. bk. 1928–67 (in office of Clerk to the Comrs.), 27 Sept. 1966; cttee. mins. 1945–52 (in Harb. Master's Office), 4 Dec. 1950.
[82] Ex inf. Capt. R. Spear, Harbour Master, 1969.
[83] Harb. Comrs., gen. min. bk. 1967–date (in office of Clerk to the Comrs.), 24 Jan. 1968.
[84] *Bridlington Charty.* 2.
[85] *Cal. Chart. R.* 1427–1516, 67.
[86] *Farming Bk. of Hen. Best of Elmswell* (Sur. Soc. xxxiii), 114.
[87] *Yorks. Fairs and Mkts.* (Thoresby Soc. xxxix), 148, 174; *1st Rep. Royal Com. Mkt. Rights and Tolls*, Vol. i [C.5550], p. 217, H.C. (1888), liii; H. E. Strickland, *Gen. View Agric. E.R.* (1812), 277.
[88] e.g. Lords Feoffees' Rec., Bayle, Bridlington, min. bk. 1804–62 (sub 1834); acct. bk. 1852–90 (sub 1861); 'Annals of Bridlington', vol. 1, p. 147 (1869).
[89] Directories; 'Annals of Bridlington', vol. 15, p. 259.
[90] Directories; 'Annals of Bridlington', vol. 18, p. 334.
[91] Lords Feoffees' Rec., min. bk. 1804–62 (sub 1837).

in 1864.[92] It seems to have lapsed by 1899, when a new cattle market was set up by the urban district council, held at first on Tuesdays and later on Mondays;[93] this was closed in 1969.[94]

Tolls from the market and fairs were received by the priory until its suppression. They were let to William Blancher in 1549 and subsequently included in all the 16th-century leases and grants of the manor.[95] There is little evidence of the amounts raised. Tolls and 'gainage' of ships together brought in 19s. 11d. in 1539,[96] and the toll of the market amounted to about 8s. in 1541–2.[97] In the early 19th century the tolls were farmed by the feoffees for £18 a year, raised to £24 in 1817. They were then kept in hand and £39 was received in 1838 and £31 in 1861.[98] In the 1880s and early 1890s the average receipts for tolls from both markets and fairs were £63 a year.[99] The total in 1898 was £93, comprising £75 from the markets and £18 from fairs and hirings.[1] The lords feoffees sold the market tolls to the town council, and assigned their right to hold fairs, for £1,800 in 1899.[2] In the year ending November 1902 the corporation received as much as £174 from market tolls and £43 from the fairs.[3]

Markets were held in the Old Town, in the wide street known as Market Place, probably until c. 1910.[4] Stalls were set up there for the benefit of Bridlington and country tradesmen. Among the latter, shoemakers from Malton, Hornsea, Scarborough, Kelk, Brigham, Fisholme, and Muston, butchers from Gransmoor, Seaton, Filey, Hornsea, Hunmanby, Lebberston, and Foston, and oatmealmen from Nafferton, Hornsea, and Harpham are all mentioned in the 17th century.[5] In 1821 butchers' stalls were set up at the bottom of Market Place, and also along the western part of High Street where they were sheltered from the north winds that blew down Market Place; butter, eggs, and poultry were then sold on Cross Hill, as the bottom end of Market Place was called. Cross Hill was no doubt the site of the former market cross and in 1821 it was occupied by a house and shop.[6] The building was later known as Centre House and was demolished in 1913.[7] There were also stocks and a pillory in Market Place. A market bell was fixed to the pillory in the late 18th century, but it fell into disuse and was removed in 1810.[8] A corn exchange was built on the east side of Market Place in 1824;[9] corn had previously been sold in the open and the market-place is occasionally referred to as the corn market.[10] The exchange seems to have become little used by corn dealers during the 1870s[11] and the corn market was held at the Black Lion inn, High Street, by 1896.[12] The exchange still stood in 1969. Its stone-built façade is in the Gothic style, with pointed windows and doorway; the name is carried on a carved panel and a pediment bears the feoffees' arms.

It is not known when markets were, in addition, first held at the Quay, but it seems likely in any case that they were preceded by some informal open-air selling. In 1869 the feoffees made charges for stalls placed in King Street by adjacent house- and shop-owners, and it was said that this practice had gone on for 40–50 years.[13] In 1865 fish stalls set up in Queen Street and on Ship Hill near by were creating a nuisance, and they were ordered to be placed on the slipway leading from Prince Street to the harbour;[14] again, such stalls are likely to have long been used at the Quay. The feoffees were taking tolls in 1885 for such amusements as waxworks and shooting galleries set up in Queen Street.[15] By the 1890s a Saturday market was being held in King and Prince Streets,[16] and thereafter these streets were regular places of assembly for general markets. They continued after the ending of the Old Town markets, and King Street was still a market-place in 1969; Prince Street ceased to be used in 1949.[17] The corn market continued to be held at the Black Lion until the Second World War; wool and occasionally animals were also sold there in 1928.[18] The cattle market was held in 1864 at the north end of Market Place;[19] from 1899 onwards it was held next to the corporation depôt in Portland Place, off Quay Road.[20]

The fairs were for long held on High and Low or Church Greens. The cattle fair was in 1837 extended to include horses and sheep and it was ordered that horses should be sold on Low Green, sheep on High Green.[21] By 1864, however, sheep were sold in a hired field,[22] and horses had been moved to High Green by 1884. In the latter year it was ordered that the next Spring Fair, on 26 May, and all subsequent fairs for beasts and sheep should be held in a field at the corner of the Bessingby and Easton roads, at the west end of the Old Town; horse fairs were to continue on High Green.[23] Some indication of the number of animals which had crowded onto the greens is given in 1878; tolls were paid, apparently at the fair on 3 June, for 255 beasts, 534 sheep, and an unspecified number of horses.[24] Is is said that an annual fair was also held

---

[92] Char. Com. files, 1864 Report on Bridlington Chars., pt. 2; 'Notes on Work of Bridlington Loc. Govt. Bd.' (MS. notebk. in Bridlington Pub. Libr.), 14.
[93] 'Annals of Bridlington', vol. 16, p. 174; *Rep. on Mkts. and Fairs in Eng. and Wales* (Min. of Agric. and Fish.), 1928, iii. 154.
[94] Bridlington Corp. *Counc. Procs. and Cttee. Mins.* 1968–9, p. 251.
[95] *Cal. Pat.* 1563–6, 447–9; Purvis, *Bridlington Charters, etc.* 39, 44–5, 54, 75, 88.   [96] Purvis, op. cit. 26–7.
[97] E 315/382, printed in *Miscellanea*, iii (Y.A.S. Rec. Ser. lxxx), 43.
[98] Lords Feoffees' Rec., acct. bks. 1794–1890. For accts. of 1878 see Purvis, op. cit. 310; a schedule of the tolls etc. in 1857 is printed in ibid. 138–9.
[99] 'Annals of Bridlington', vol. 15, p. 28.
[1] Ibid. 16, p. 125.   [2] Ibid. pp. 60, 180.
[3] Bridlington Corp. *Counc. Procs. and Cttee. Mins.* 1901–2, cttee. mins. submitted 24 Dec., p. 13.
[4] Ex inf. Town Clerk, Bridlington, 1969.
[5] Purvis, *Bridlington Charters, etc.* 129–33, 226–8, 233–4, 242, 252, 254, 267–8, 275.
[6] J. Thompson, *Hist. Sketches of Bridlington*, 124. There are references to the cross in Purvis, op. cit. 156.
[7] 'Annals of Bridlington', vol. 30, p. 328.
[8] Thompson, *Hist. Sketches*, 126; *T.E.R.A.S.* iii. 44.
[9] *Hull Advertiser*, 6 Feb., 10 Dec. 1824.
[10] E.R.R.O., QSF Mich. 1744, B.2.
[11] Lords Feoffees' Rec., Bayle, Bridlington, acct. bk. 1852–90.   [12] 'Annals of Bridlington', vol. 15, p. 144.
[13] Ibid. 2, p. 39.
[14] 'Notes on Work of Loc. Govt. Bd.', 20–1.
[15] Bridlington Town Hall, loc. govt. bd. mins., vol. 4, p. 398.
[16] Ibid. 7, p. 24; 'Annals of Bridlington', vol. 15, p. 23.
[17] Ex inf. Town Clerk, Bridlington, 1969.
[18] *Rep. on Mkts. and Fairs in Eng. and Wales*, iii. 154.
[19] Char. Com. files, 1864 Rep., pt. 2.
[20] 'Annals of Bridlington', vol. 16, p. 174; Bridlington Corp. *Counc. Procs. and Cttee. Mins.* 1968–9, p. 251.
[21] Lords Feoffees' Rec., min. bk. 1804–62 (*sub* 1837).
[22] Char. Com. files, 1864 Rep., pt. 2.
[23] Purvis, *Bridlington Charters, etc.* 138.
[24] Ibid. 310.

on the north pier in the 19th century.[25] High Green was still the meeting-place of the pleasure fair in 1969.

INDUSTRY. In the Middle Ages and later there existed in Bridlington a range of crafts and trades characteristic of a market town and port. There was, for example, the occasional brewer, glover, mason, glazier, brazier, and chandler,[26] and a group of mercers, woollen drapers, and skinners.[27] A small manufacture of cloth also seems to have become established. A Bridlington man paid aulnage on two cloths in 1378–9,[28] a dyer is recorded in 1458,[29] and several weavers worked in the town in the 16th and 17th centuries.[30] Corn-milling was carried on at the water-mills on the Gypsey Race which belonged to the priory in the Middle Ages.[31]

The most prominent of the town's trades in the 17th and 18th centuries were corn-dealing and malt-making, upon which the seaborne trade in grain and malt was based. Several maltsters are mentioned in the 17th century[32] and some merchants and ship-masters were maltsters too: Richard Woolfe and Richard Hardcastle, for example, both had malt-kilns in the early 18th century.[33] The Prickett family, which acquired much property in the town at this period, also had several malt-kilns by the late 18th century.[34] In 1761 there are said to have been more than sixty kilns in Bridlington, but with the decline of the trade of the port there were a mere six, and those only partially employed, by 1823.[35] Brewers and coopers similarly declined in numbers. In 1823 there were 5 brewers besides the specialist maltsters, but by 1840 only 6 brewers and maltsters combined, and by 1858 only three.[36] The last malting in the town closed soon after 1900.[37] There were still 13 corn merchants in 1823, but by 1840 there were 8 and by 1858 only two.

The corn-milling industry had some small part in the seaborne trade of the port but its growth in the late 18th and early 19th centuries was more concerned with the needs of the local population. Bridlington priory had owned six mills near to the town: windmills known as 'Colome' Mill, in East field, Bridge Mill, near the Gypsey Race west of the Old Town, Hilderthorpe Mill, and Convent Mill; and two water-mills 'hard by the sea shore'. The mills had brought the priory rents of £12 in the early 16th century.[38] Colome and Convent Mills were let to William Cordell in 1557, and all were let with the manor in 1566.[39] In 1591 Bridge Mill was found to be decayed, Colome Mill out of repair, and Convent Mill well maintained.[40] All six mills were included in the leases of the manor made in 1591 and 1595, but in 1614 they were separated from it and granted in fee to William Whitmore and Edward Sawyer.[41] The water-mills were probably at the sites on the Gypsey Race occupied by two of the later water-mills. A third water-mill was subsequently built further upstream, probably by 1761, when Thomas Bradley, miller, was accused of erecting a sluice and flooding the Moor.[42] At least one windmill was still at work in 1721.[43]

The sites of Bridge[44] and Hilderthorpe windmills were certainly abandoned, and the location of the other early windmills is not precisely known. By 1793, however, there were at least two windmills, one at the Quay, near Spring water-mill, the other near Bradley's water-mill.[45] The second of these, later known as the Anti-Monopoly Mill, was rebuilt in 1800.[46] By 1823 Moses Dukes had built New, or Dukes's, Mill in Bempton Lane,[47] and in 1825 William Gibson and Francis Spink built Spink's Mill in Mill Lane.[48] About that time, too, a windmill was erected at the Quay, near the Esplanade,[49] but it apparently did not last until the 1850s. Black Mill, near Marton Road, had appeared by 1846[50] and another near Forty Foot Lane by 1851.[51] Thus in 1853 there were seven windmills,[52] three of which were worked in conjunction with the water-mills.

In the mid 19th century steam power began to be introduced by Bridlington millers. By 1846 the water-mill near the harbour had steam,[53] and so did Dukes's windmill by 1858 and Spring Mill by 1889.[54] Like most small country mills, however, the Bridlington mills declined and went out of use in the later 19th and early 20th centuries. A miller is last mentioned at the harbour water-mill in 1872.[55] The mill may have been rebuilt in 1873[56] and by 1882 it was described as the 'steam saw mills'; it was subsequently known as the Victoria Saw Mills, and

---

[25] Purvis, *Bridlington Charters, etc.* 164.
[26] B.I.H.R., Prob. Reg. xiii, f. 203; xvii, ff. 77, 353; xxxix, f. 48; xlv, f. 164; li, f. 19; lx, f. 44.
[27] Ibid. v, f. 401; viii, ff. 40, 112; xxxix, f. 459; xlix, f. 288; li, f. 63; liv, f. 188; lvii, f. 410; lviii, ff. 313, 427; lix, ff. 9, 66, 245; bdles. of wills for May 1649–50, Mar. 1650–1; E.R.R.O., DDLG/5/12, 24.
[28] *Early Yorks. Woollen Ind.* (Y.A.S. Rec. Ser. lxiv), 37.
[29] B.I.H.R., Prob. Reg. ii, f. 392.
[30] Ibid. xvi, f. 78; xxx, f. 3; xxxii, f. 598; xxxvi, f. 11; xlv, ff. 285, 421; l, f. 407; lii, f. 462; lx, f. 46; bdle. of wills for Dec. 1646–7.
[31] *Bridlington Charty.* 12, 19.
[32] B.I.H.R., Prob. Reg. xliv, ff. 176, 483; xlv, f. 52; bdles. for 1639–40 and 1640–1; Somerset Ho., P.C.C. 60 Bent.
[33] Purvis, *Bridlington Charters, etc.* 182–4; see above, p. 53.
[34] Registry of Deeds, Beverley, AR/174/341; AW/98/151; AZ/252/398.
[35] J. Thompson, *Hist. Sketches of Bridlington*, 127; Baines, *Hist. Yorks.* ii. 172–3.
[36] Directories.
[37] It is last mentioned in 1909: *Kelly's Dir. N. & E.R. Yorks.* (1909), 473.
[38] Purvis, *Bridlington Charters, etc.* 26, 39; *Miscellanea* iii (Y.A.S. Rec. Ser. lxxx), 3.
[39] *Cal. Pat.* 1557–8, 17–18; 1563–6, 447–9.
[40] E 178/2725.
[41] Purvis, op. cit. 39, 44, 78.
[42] E.R.R.O., QSF Mich. 1761, B.4. The Bradleys still had this mill in 1771: Regy. of Deeds, AN/121/11 and map of 1793.
[43] E.R.R.O., QSF East. 1721, D.9–10.
[44] The mill mound was bulldozed in 1969; pottery found suggests that it was last used in the first quarter of the 16th cent.: ex inf. Mr. J. R. Earnshaw, Sewerby Hall Mus., 1970.
[45] Lords Feoffees' Rec., Bayle, Bridlington, map of 1793.
[46] E. Mellor, 'Mills and Milling' (TS. in E.R.R.O.), p. 11.
[47] Regy. of Deeds, DX/150/169; Baines, *Hist. Yorks.* ii. 176.
[48] Regy. of Deeds, EK/165/180; /166/181; /285/317; *Hull Advertiser*, 29 Aug. 1828.
[49] Regy. of Deeds, EP/292/345; J. Wood, *Plan of Bridlington* (1828).
[50] White, *Dir. Hull & York* (1846), 433.
[51] H.O. 107/2367.
[52] O.S. Map 6" (1854).
[53] White, *Dir. Hull & York* (1846), 433; E.R.R.O., DDCV/parcel 16; it is said to have been built in 1837: Sheahan and Whellan, *Hist. York & E.R.* ii. 447.
[54] White, *Dir. Hull & York* (1858), 673; *Kelly's Dir. N. & E.R. Yorks.* (1889), 357.
[55] *Kelly's Dir. N. & E.R. Yorks.* (1872), 336.
[56] Date on building.

it may have been worked by electricity by 1890, when it supplied power to light the Royal Prince's Parade.[57] The building was used as workshops in 1969. Spring Mill, later called Lowson's Mill or Bridlington Mills, remained at work, still powered by water, until the First World War.[58] It still stood in 1969. A miller is last mentioned at the third water-mill, known as the Anti-Mill (like the windmill which was worked with it) or Medforth's Mill, in 1864; it was subsequently used for the manufacture of manure and is said to have been worked until 1904;[59] it, too, still stood in 1969. The last of the windmills to remain at work were Dukes's Mill and Black Mill, where millers are last mentioned in 1905 and 1913 respectively.[60] Little trace of any of the windmills remained in 1969.

In the later 19th century a varied business was conducted at several of the mills. The Colsons, for example, at the harbour water-mill, were corn, seed, and oil-cake merchants as well as millers in 1872. The water-mill known as Anti or Medforth's Mill took its name from Robert Medforth, who was the miller there in 1864. By 1879, however, Medforth and Hutchinson were corn, seed, cake, and manure merchants at 'Hilderthorpe Mills',[61] a designation which seems to have encompassed both the water-mill and a steam-mill at the junction of Hilderthorpe Road and Station Avenue. The steam-mill had been used for seed- and bone-crushing from at least the 1850s,[62] and artificial manure was being made at Anti Mill in 1868.[63] The steam-mill may have been rebuilt in 1885,[64] and Medforth and Co. continued there as feed distributors in 1969.

At the Quay in the 18th century there were probably many men still engaged in ancillary trades connected with shipping and fishing, but their numbers subsequently decreased. The building of ships is mentioned in the late 17th century,[65] and seventeen ships are recorded as having been built between 1765 and 1843, when the last was launched.[66] The trade was already said to be stagnating in 1823, when there were 3 shipbuilders, 2 sail-makers, one block- and mast-maker, and 2 ropers; one ropery had been established in 1789 but had since declined.[67] Only a dozen men were engaged in these occupations in 1851.[68]

The decline of the corn and malt trades early in the 19th century, and milling later, and the reduction of trades allied to shipping removed some of the most distinctive elements from the town's economy. By the later 19th century the Old Town still had many of the characteristics of the market town, providing goods and services for the surrounding rural area; it was, however, becoming increasingly dependent upon the holiday industry at the Quay, where fishing and the entertainment of visitors were the dominant occupations. There was little of an industrial character among the typical country-town trades, crafts, and professions. Soap-boiling and hat-making were mentioned in 1821,[69] and in 1823 there were 2 weavers, a worsted spinner, and 2 dyers, one of whom was also a worsted manufacturer. There was a flaxdresser and linen-manufacturer in 1846 and 2 dyers in 1872.[70] About 1850 there were also 2 iron- and brass-founders and by 1872 several agricultural implement manufacturers as well.[71] The numbers employed in these trades, however, cannot have been great.

By the 20th century the holiday industry dominated the town's economy to a marked degree. In 1921 2,859 men and women out of a working population of 9,988 were in the 'personal service' occupational group, which includes café, hotel, and boarding-house keepers and domestic servants; in 1931 2,507 out of 8,765 were in that group, and in 1951 2,079 out of 9,591.[72] As many as 13 per cent of the male working population and 45 per cent of the female were employed in personal services in Bridlington in 1951, compared with a national average of $4\frac{1}{2}$ per cent and 20 per cent respectively.[73] This dependence on a single industry, which was both unstable and seasonal, inevitably caused unemployment. Attention was drawn to the problem as early as 1905, it was emphasized by the First World War, and it was clearly seen in the 1920s and 1930s.[74] There was, however, little diversification of employment before the Second World War, though one noteworthy addition was a fertilizer works, later Cross Bone Fertilizers Ltd., which was established in Pinfold Lane, north of the Old Town, in 1917.[75]

After the war three small clothing and engineering works were established on scattered sites in the town, but the most significant development was the formation of an industrial estate by the corporation in 1946.[76] It was allotted some 35 a. on the southern edge of the town, formerly in Bessingby parish. Three sites on the estate were occupied by 1950 and 200 people were employed. In 1952, however, the largest firm failed and employment fell to 20; the firm, which had previously occupied a site at the harbour, moved to the estate in 1946 and at first made fishing cobles before turning over to coach bodies. An engineering firm moved to the estate from a site in the town in 1955, a shell-fish processing

---

[57] Bridlington Town Hall, loc. govt. bd. mins., vols. 4, p. 70; 6, pp. 16, 22, 128, 298.
[58] Directories.
[59] Mellor, 'Mills and Milling', p. 25. See below.
[60] *Kelly's Dir. N. & E.R. Yorks.* (1905), 458; (1913), 491.
[61] Ibid. (1872), 336; (1879), 366; *Slater's Dir. Yorks.* (1864), 70.
[62] H.O. 107/2367; O.S. Map 6" (1854).
[63] 'Notes on Work of Bridlington Loc. Govt. Bd.' (MS. notebk. in Bridlington Pub. Libr.), 42.
[64] Date on remaining office block.
[65] Purvis, *Bridlington Charters, etc.* 281.
[66] J. S. Purvis, 'Bridlington Piers and Harbour' (TS. in Bridlington Pub. Libr.), 9.
[67] J. Thompson, *Hist. Sketches of Bridlington*, 156; Baines, *Hist. Yorks.* ii. 175–6, 179.
[68] H.O. 107/2367.
[69] Thompson, op. cit. 127–8.

[70] Baines, *Hist. Yorks.* ii. 177, 181; White, *Dir. Hull & York* (1846), 433; *Kelly's Dir. N. & E.R. Yorks.* (1872), 334–5.
[71] White, *Dir. Hull & York* (1858), 675; *Kelly's Dir. N. & E.R. Yorks.* (1872), 331; H.O. 107/2367.
[72] Census.
[73] K. L. Mayoh, 'Comparative Study of the Resorts on the Coast of Holderness' (unpubl. M.A. thesis, Univ. of Hull, 1961), 205.
[74] e.g. E.R.C.C. *Mins.* 1904–5, 333; 1914–15, 490–1; Harb. Comrs., gen. min. bk. 1928–67 (in office of Clerk to the Comrs.), 1 Oct. 1928; 'Annals of Bridlington', vol. 38, pp. 405, 409.
[75] Ex inf. Cross Bone Fertilisers Ltd.; *Kelly's Dir. N. & E.R. Yorks.* (1921), 473.
[76] This paragraph is largely based on H. D. Watts, 'Industrial Geog. of Rural E. Yorks.' (unpubl. M.A. thesis, Univ. of Hull, 1964), 57–72.

plant was built in 1956, and a bedspread manufacturer moved from the West Riding in 1959. By the end of 1962 ten firms had been established since 1946 and 350 people were employed. There were ten firms on the estate in 1970 and three others in Pinfold Lane, where an engineering works was established in 1966[77] near the fertilizer factory.

The industrial estate achieved only limited success in increasing male employment and alleviating seasonal unemployment, and in 1966 the town lost the status of a Development District which it had enjoyed since 1958. Unemployment in January varied between about 5 and 8 per cent in the 1950s and 1960s, and it was over 9 per cent in February 1970.[78]

THE RESORT. It was probably during the later 18th century that visitors were first attracted to Bridlington Quay to bathe in the sea.[79] Arthur Young in 1770 wrote of 'the resort of some company to the Quay for bathing',[80] and in 1772 a sick child was taken to Bridlington for two months to bathe, and it is said to have benefited from it. A visitor in 1775 also took pleasure in looking at ships through a telescope.[81] One regular visitor was John Courtney, of Beverley, who spent his first holiday at Bridlington in 1796 and went again in several subsequent years.[82] The first guide to the resort was published in 1805, and by 1813 the Quay was being recommended for the hot and cold baths, bathing machines, sea breezes, coastal scenery, shipping in the bay, near-by places of historic interest, inns and shops, billiards, cards and balls, and beach, with its shells, stones, and fossils.[83] Such attractions as these have ever since sustained it, at first as a fashionable watering-place and later as a popular seaside resort. Bridlington was not apparently noted as a 'spa', with medicinal waters, though there were several chalybeate springs around the Quay.[84]

It was a 'genteel company', including a sprinkling of the aristocracy, which at first spent the season at Bridlington. In 1808, for example, the duke and duchess of Leeds, Marchioness and Lady Harriet Townsend, Earl and Countess Fitzwilliam, Viscount Milton, Earl Moira, and Sir Thomas and Lady Vavasour were among the visitors.[85] The duke and duchess of Newcastle arrived early in July 1813 and did not travel to Hull, on their way south, until 21 August.[86] And in September 1844 the duke of Newcastle and Lords Charles and Robert Clinton were among those present.[87] Many visitors advertised their presence by including their names in lists published in the Hull, and later also the Bridlington, newspapers, but many others apparently remained anonymous. There were reported to be nearly 1,000 visitors on 17 August 1838 and 'several thousand' on 8 September 1843,[88] though only 460 names were given in the list for 9 September 1843.[89] The named visitors rarely stayed for less than a month and the 'season' lasted from mid June to early October. In 1844, for example, about 100 names were listed on 20 June, over 300 on 4 July, 400 on 11 July, 500 or more from 25 July to 6 September, and still nearly 300 on 26 September.[90]

It is clear from the early lists of visitors that Bridlington drew its custom from a limited area. On 15 July 1843, for example, of the 237 visitors listed 19 per cent were from Hull, 61 per cent from elsewhere in Yorkshire, and 16 per cent from the north-east Midlands; and a week later, when there were 244 visitors, the corresponding percentages were 17, 50, and 27.[91] This pattern was no doubt largely dictated by the difficulties of travel to Bridlington, and for many visitors a circuitous journey was necessary. When Charlotte Brontë visited Bridlington in 1839, coach, train, coach again, fly, and post-chaise were involved in the journey from Haworth.[92]

The existing inns in the Old Town and the Quay were soon supplemented by new accommodation. Rooms were no doubt offered to visitors in many of the older houses, but some houses were being specially built for the purpose before the turn of the century. A newly-built house near the north cliff, for example, offered for sale in 1799, had four 'lodging rooms',[93] and by 1813 there were 69 'principal lodging-houses', as well as 'several other houses... which have very neat and comfortable accommodations for small families or individuals'.[94] Existing inns were improved, like the New Inn, taken over in 1805 by a landlord who had been butler to the Sykes family at Sledmere. And the first 'complete hotel' was provided the same year when the former residence of Col. Pitts at the Quay was converted into the George hotel.[95] The lists given in directories may not be complete, but there were at least 107 inns and lodging-houses in 1823, 101 in 1831, 135 in 1840, and 165 in 1846.[96]

The amenities of the Quay were steadily improved during the earlier 19th century. Benjamin Milne's hot baths, 'fitted up in the first style of elegance', were opened in 1803, and new baths were built in 1815. Ground was acquired in 1822 for a library and reading room and a bowling green, and in 1823 the latest improvements were said to be a ball-room and subscription reading room. The number of bathing machines was increased in 1827 and the theatre, which had existed for more than twenty years, was newly fitted-up.[97] In 1828 the site of the fort on the

---

[77] Ex inf. R. J. Shepherd (Engineering) Ltd.
[78] Ex inf. Employment Exchange, Bridlington.
[79] In writing this section extensive use has been made of the material and references contained in K. L. Mayoh, 'Comparative Study of the Resorts on the Coast of Holderness' (unpubl. M.A. thesis, Univ. of Hull, 1961). Mr. Mayoh's co-operation is gratefully acknowledged.
[80] *Six Months' Tour through N. of Eng.* ii. 7.
[81] E.R.R.O., DDGR/42/22, 25.
[82] Ibid. DDX/60/3–4 (details kindly supplied by Mr. N. Higson).
[83] J. Coates, *Descriptive Poem, with a List of the Lodging Houses* (2 edns.).
[84] J. Thompson, *Hist. Sketches of Bridlington*, 154–5; O.S. Map 6" (1854).
[85] *Hull Advertiser*, 3 Sept. 1808.
[86] Ibid. 10 July, 21 Aug. 1813.
[87] Ibid. 27 Sept. 1844.
[88] *Hull Advertiser*.
[89] *Burlington & E.R. Advertiser*.
[90] Mayoh, thesis cit. 38–40.
[91] Ibid. 33. The 'N.E. Midlands' includes Notts., Lincs., and Derb.
[92] F. R. Pearson, *Charlotte Brontë on the E. Yorks. Coast* (E. Yorks. Loc. Hist. Ser. vii), 10–11; see below, p. 67.
[93] *Hull Advertiser*, 24 Aug. 1799.
[94] Coates, *Descriptive Poem*.
[95] *Hull Advertiser*, 6 Aug. 1803; 11 May, 22 June 1805.
[96] Mayoh, thesis cit., facing p. 154.
[97] *Hull Advertiser*, 4 June 1803; 13 May 1815; 11 Oct. 1822; 6 Aug. 1823; 4 May, 7 Sept. 1827; Thompson, *Hist. Sketches of Bridlington*, 159. A theatre is mentioned in 1814: *Hull Advertiser*, 13 Aug. 1814.

north cliff was used to form the Esplanade, intended as a select public walk and provided with a newsroom and shelter called the Colonnade.[98] A museum, belonging to Arthur Strickland, was opened in 1834.[99] The older baths were replaced in 1844 by Bishop's Improved Baths, erected near the Esplanade: they contained 'all the modern improvements', with separate suites of rooms for men and women.[1] The new piers completed in the 1840s were an added attraction and a brass band was playing on the south pier during the season in 1843.[2] The final improvement during this period was the erection of public rooms, the Victoria Rooms, near the north pier in 1846. This was a castellated building in the Gothic style, designed by Worth & Frith, of Sheffield, and it included a room for balls, concerts, and promenading, a newsroom, a reading room, and a billiard room.[3] The amenities of the resort at this time are perhaps best summed up by the assertion that 'Bridlington attracts numbers of that class of visitors for whom Hornsea is too quiet and Scarborough too gay'.[4]

It was at this point that the railway arrived to boost the holiday trade: the line from Hull was opened late in 1846 and that north to join the York–Scarborough line a year later.[5] The effect of the railways is shown in the lengthening lists of visitors. There were 799 on 8 August 1850 compared with 537 on 15 August 1844: an increase of nearly 50 per cent.[6] Reduced railway fares were offered in 1854 and the town was said to be sometimes 'exceedingly thronged' with visitors from the Midlands and the West Riding. These fares were for 14- or 28-day periods and they doubtless played a part in changing the nature of the 'season'.[7]

The Quay was, indeed, no longer the fashionable watering-place of the earlier years of the century. Day excursion trains ran from the West Riding as early as 1873, and 5,000 visitors were estimated to have arrived by such trains on August Bank Holiday Monday in 1879; 2,000 came from Hull alone on Whit Monday in 1885.[8] General summer train services were increased in 1885, and a more direct route to the West Riding was provided in 1890.[9] The length of visitors lists also continued to increase: to 945 on 7 Aug. 1866 and 2,527 on 7 Aug. 1880; a little earlier in the 1894 season, on 30 June, the number was 1,404.[10] The residential visitors, however, frequently complained in letters to Bridlington newspapers of the scandalous behaviour of trippers.[11] One such holiday-maker, the rector of Fisherton Anger (Wilts.), found the town in July 1896 'overrun, two or three times a week, with trippers from Sheffield, Leeds, York and Hull', and a year later he reported that the town was 'much spoiled' by trippers, 'some of whom are of the rougher sort'.[12] Visitors from such distant places as Wiltshire were still in a small minority, about 10 per cent in four visitors lists between 1850 and 1894. Hull contributed an average of 16 per cent, the West Riding 50 per cent, the rest of Yorkshire 10 per cent, and the north-east Midlands 14 per cent. Hull's share over this period appears to have increased significantly and that of the Midlands to have decreased.[13]

The 'season' was not immediately changed by the arrival of the railway. In 1860, as in 1844, there was no pronounced peak and for six weeks between late July and early September nearly 1,000 visitors were listed. By 1880, however, a change was apparent: August had become the main season and there was a marked peak of 3,500 visitors in the last week.[14] The number of boarding-houses in business during the season seems to have varied a good deal from year to year, even allowing for the deficiencies of directories. A notable increase above the level of the 1840s took place in the 1860s and 228 hotels and boarding-houses were mentioned in 1867. By the 1890s there were generally 300 to 400, and as many as 458 were recorded in 1892.[15] Whereas most of the earlier lodging-houses had been converted dwelling-houses in the older centre of the Quay, by about 1860 purpose-built boarding-houses were becoming commoner. There were also a few larger, more select, hotels being built in the later 19th century, notably the grandiose Alexandra in 1866.[16]

The improvement of the resort's amenities during the second half of the century was largely concerned with the construction of sea defences, which was fundamental to the development of the sea front for the cliffs north and south of the Quay were subject to constant erosion.[17] The sea front north of the harbour was the first to be protected, initially by small private undertakings and after the 1860s by larger public works. The front to the south was entirely unprotected until the 1880s and no public works were carried out until well into the 20th century.

The early defences between the north pier and Bishop's baths consisted of a sloping timber wall; from the baths to the Fort Hall estate there was a brick wall, and in 1859 the wall along the Fort Hall estate was itself converted from timber to brick.[18] Further north the owners of the Beaconsfield estate built a wall to protect their own property and Mark Barr built another brick wall close to Sands Cut.[19] Most of the front that was in use in the mid century thus had some sort of protection. The first more extensive works were carried out by the local board of health in 1866–7.[20] With the aid of an improvement-rate the board built the Sea Wall Parade. This combined sea defence and promenade, built of stone, stretched for 720 ft. between the

---

[98] *Hull Advertiser*, 13 June, 15 Aug. 1828; 24 July 1829; J. Furby, *Excursions from Bridlington Quay* (1st edn.), 4–5.
[99] White, *Dir. E. & N.R. Yorks.* (1840), 370.
[1] *Burlington & E.R. Advertiser*, 11 July 1844.
[2] *Hull Advertiser*, 7 July 1843; see above, p. 48.
[3] Ibid. 9 June 1848; J. Varley, *Guide to Bridlington Quay* (2nd edn.), 20. See frontispiece.
[4] W. White, *A Month in Yorks.* (1858), 77–8.
[5] See p. 67.
[6] *Bridlington & E.R. Advertiser*, 15 Aug. 1844; *Bridlington Quay Mercury*, 8 Aug. 1850.
[7] Varley, *Guide* (2nd edn.), 20; W. W. Tomlinson, *N.E. Rly.* 547; Mayoh, thesis cit. 60.
[8] 'Annals of Bridlington', vols. 6, p. 88; 9, p. 67.
[9] Ibid. 9, p. 53; see below, p. 67.
[10] Mayoh, thesis cit. 127 and facing p. 128.
[11] Ibid. 133.
[12] *Fisherton Anger Par. Mag.* Aug. 1896, Sept. 1897.
[13] Mayoh, thesis cit. facing p. 128.
[14] Ibid. 166–7.
[15] Ibid. facing p. 154.
[16] See p. 43.
[17] See p. 30.
[18] Varley, *Guide* (4th edn.), 14; *Proc. Inst. Civil Engineers*, clix. 67. The Fort Hall estate had a timber wall by 1821: E.R.R.O., DDLG/5/69.
[19] *Hull & E.R. Times*, 9 Apr. 1921.
[20] See frontispiece. For the work of the board see p. 69.

Victoria Rooms and the Fort Hall estate; about 2 a. of ground was reclaimed behind it and laid out as gardens. It was renamed the Royal Prince's Parade in 1888, after a visit by Prince Albert. As an additional protection five groynes were built in 1868 in front of the new wall.[21] Next, the wooden Victoria Sea Defences were built by the board in 1869–70 to protect 370 ft. of the front further north, to fill a gap between two of the private brick walls.[22]

In 1879–81 the board constructed a stone wall, later called the Alexandra Sea Wall, extending for 1,020 ft. north of Sands Cut, to protect the Sewerby estate.[23] The board had earlier refused to provide a new wall to replace that built by the owners of the Beaconsfield estate, but damage by the sea there in 1881 and 1886 led to many protests, including one from 120 Sheffield people.[24] The Beaconsfield Sea Wall was consequently built by the board and opened in 1888; it was 1,020 ft. long and included a colonnade for shelter.[25] At the same time an iron bridge was built over Sands, by then called Trinity, Cut.[26] The board had thus constructed a continuous defence and promenade for most of the sea front within the town boundaries. The urban district council then built the wooden Sewerby Sea Defences, 915 ft. in 1896 and 246 ft. in 1899, and fifteen groynes were added between 1899 and 1905 to prevent the erosion of the beach.[27]

Nothing was done on the south side of the harbour until 1879, when Godfrey Rhodes began work on a wall in front of his estate.[28] It was damaged during construction and, after parts of it had collapsed, Rhodes tried unsuccessfully in 1883 to sell it and the land reclaimed behind it to the local board.[29] Eventually Whitaker Bros. built the Spa Wall there in 1896, together with a lower wall extending 2,280 ft. further south; the latter was later known as the South Cliff Sea Wall. Whitakers also erected seven groynes.[30]

Among the resort's amenities the Victoria Rooms, which were bought by the local board in 1879,[31] continued to accommodate all kinds of entertainments during the second half of the century. Bishop's Baths remained in use until the 1860s but were removed during the construction of the Sea Wall Parade. In 1874, however, new baths were built beside the harbour, in Queen's Square.[32] Two roller-skating rinks were opened for brief periods, one on the Sea Wall Parade and the other, the Empress, built in 1876 near the cliffs on the Beaconsfield estate; the Empress was removed when the Beaconsfield Sea Wall was built.[33] By 1890 there was also a switchback railway near Carr (later Sands) Lane.[34] A recreation ground, with a cycle-racing track, was established in Oliver's Lane in 1884[35] and subsequently acquired by the trustees of George Dukes, who by will proved in 1893 made a bequest to provide a recreation ground.[36]

Two new attractions appeared in 1896. The first was the New Spa, south of the harbour, which included a promenade, a theatre, and a 'glass dome' for concerts, standing behind Whitaker Bros.' new sea-wall.[37] In 1898 the near-by 'Hydro', in Marine Drive, was opened by Bridlington Hydropathic Ltd.[38] The second attraction was the People's Palace, built in 1896 in Quay Road by a private company; it was designed by Joseph Earnshaw and provided a concert hall, ball-room, and bowling green.[39] Even in 1823 it had been said of the Quay that 'the sources of amusement here are somewhat circumscribed';[40] with the changing character of the resort and the coming of trippers there was a serious lack of popular amusements and the Palace was therefore welcomed.[41] One resort amenity was notably absent at Bridlington, a 'promenade pier'. After piers had been opened the previous year at Withernsea and Hornsea, agitation began in 1879 for Bridlington to keep in step, and a company was formed for the purpose in 1882.[42] Attempts to have a pier built on the north beach were still being made in 1900,[43] but nothing was achieved. Among the special events staged during the later 19th century were regattas in the bay,[44] and both boating and fishing became increasingly popular.

After 1900 Bridlington's popularity was maintained and the numbers of hotels and boarding-houses continued to increase, at least until the First World War. More than 500 such establishments were listed in directories in 1901, 650 in 1905, over 700 in 1909, and 922 in 1913. The war proved a serious setback and afterwards the altering character of 'the seaside holiday' brought changes in the established pattern of facilities, in Bridlington as elsewhere. In 1921 there were about 700 hotels and boarding-houses. The small numbers shown in later directories are not a reliable guide,[45] but in 1959–60 there were only about 500 registered with the corporation. The

---

[21] Varley, *Guide* (6th edn.), 16–17; *Hull & E.R. Times*, 9 Apr. 1921; *Proc. Inst. Civil Engineers*, clix. 67–8.

[22] 'Notes on Work of Bridlington Loc. Govt. Bd.' (MS. notebk. in Bridlington Pub. Libr.), 47, 49; *Proc. Inst. Civil Engineers*, clix. 66.

[23] Bridlington Town Hall, loc. govt. bd. mins., vol. 3, pp. 240, 413; *Proc. Inst. Civil Engineers*, clix. 65.

[24] 'Annals of Bridlington', vol. 8, p. 79.

[25] *Proc. Inst. Civil Engineers*, clix. 66.

[26] Bridlington Town Hall, loc. govt. bd. mins., vol. 5, p. 259.

[27] *Proc. Inst. Civil Engineers*, clix. 65; *1st Rep. Royal Com. on Coast Erosion, Vol. 1, Pt. 2* [Cd. 3684], Mins. of Evidence p. 206, H.C. (1907), xxxiv.

[28] 'Annals of Bridlington', vol. 6, p. 87. For Rhodes's plans see above, p. 37.

[29] Bridlington Town Hall, loc. govt. bd. mins., vol. 4, pp. 176–7; 'Annals of Bridlington', vols. 7, p. 62; 8, p. 49.

[30] 'Annals of Bridlington', vol. 15, pp. 83–9; *Proc. Inst. Civil Engineers*, clix. 67, 71.

[31] 'Annals of Bridlington', vol. 7, p. 2.

[32] Ibid. 4, p. 24.

[33] Ibid. 5, p. 30; T. Cape, *Brief Sketches... of Bridlington Quay* (1877), 26; (1879), 26; W. Taylor, *Brief Hist. of Bridlington Loc. Bd.* 4.

[34] O.S. Map 25″ (1893). It was demolished in 1912: 'Annals of Bridlington', vol. 29, p. 342.

[35] Bulmer, *Dir. E. Yorks.* (1892), 129.

[36] Char. Com. files; 'Annals of Bridlington', vol. 14, p. 147.

[37] 'Annals of Bridlington', vol. 15, pp. 83–9, 96; Registry of Deeds, Beverley, 88/451/432 (1897).

[38] Regy. of Deeds, 8/189/178 (1898). It closed in 1916: 'Annals of Bridlington', vol. 33, p. 66.

[39] 'Annals of Bridlington', vol. 15, pp. 25, 92.

[40] Baines, *Hist. Yorks.* ii. 174.

[41] W. Pochin, *Reliable Guide to Bridlington Quay* (1897), 7.

[42] 'Annals of Bridlington', vol. 6, p. 102; Bridlington Town Hall, loc. govt. bd. mins., vol. 3, p. 188; Mayoh, thesis cit. 110–12.

[43] Harbour Comrs., gen. min. bk. 1873–1904 (in Harbour Master's Office), 23 Mar. 1900. An Act was obtained: 63 & 64 Vic., c. 193.

[44] *The Royal Yorks. Yacht Club, 1847–1947, passim;* 'Annals of Bridlington', vol. 5, p. 82.

[45] For various reasons boarding-houses were increasingly omitted from directories.

decline of the boarding-house trade is partly attributable to the decreasing demand for such accommodation, partly to the loss of cheapness, which had earlier been its great virtue. Some boarding-houses have been converted to 'holiday flats' and the hotels and boarding-houses that remain are open for a shorter 'season' each year. For residential visitors Easter, Whitsuntide, and the August Bank Holiday became the peak periods of the season.[46]

The numbers of day visitors, however, continued to increase and there have been growing numbers of caravan visitors around the fringes of the town.[47] A sample survey taken in 1960 showed as many as 49 per cent day visitors, compared with 39 per cent staying for 2–7 days and only 13 per cent for longer periods.[48] Over 40 per cent of this sample travelled by car and 25 per cent by bus and coach; large car parks at the north and south ends of the sea front have been provided to relieve parking on promenades and near-by streets, with coach parks nearer the town centre. The remaining 30 per cent used trains[49] and services from Hull were still being maintained in 1969 after closure of the allegedly uneconomic line had been successfully resisted. The 1960 sample survey also showed the continuing regional nature of Bridlington's attraction: 64 per cent were from the West Riding and 15 per cent from the north-east Midlands. Hull contributed only 5 per cent, but its share of the tripper trade is more clearly shown in the 21 per cent of Hull people among those arriving by train on August Bank Holiday Saturday the same year. Outside the resort's traditional catchment areas, north-west England has provided increasing numbers of visitors.[50]

The improvement of the sea defences and promenades continued after 1900. The Royal Prince's Parade was extended in 1904–6 to replace the old brick walls, and at the same time the Victoria Terraces were built, replacing the wooden defences of 1869.[51] The wooden Sewerby Sea Defences were similarly replaced by a stone wall in 1929–31, with North Marine Drive constructed behind it.[52] Extending northwards from this wall for about 800 ft., the Sewerby Sea Wall was built in 1964–5.[53]

On the south side of the harbour the corporation bought the Spa Wall in 1919, and then extended it as the Princess Mary Promenade in 1925–8.[54] Thr corporation also bought the 600-ft. Pitt's, or Belvedere, Wall in 1925: this had been built, together with nine groynes, to protect J. W. Pitt's Belvedere estate in 1901–2.[55] Finally, in 1953 the corporation bought another privately-built wall, Wiseman's Wall, which linked Pitt's Wall with the Princess Mary Promenade.[56] The last improvement to the sea-front promenades was the construction in 1969 of a harbour footpath, incorporating a bridge over the harbour, to link the promenades on the north and south sides of the town.[57]

On the Royal Prince's Parade the Floral Pavilion was erected beside the existing bandstand in 1904, and in 1906 the Grand Pavilion was built on the Parade extension.[58] The Parade continued as a centre of varied entertainment, with illuminations, firework displays, and galas, and until its demolition in 1936 the Grand Pavilion was used for concerts and films. To preserve the view of the bay created by the removal of the Grand Pavilion the site was converted to a boating lake and a new Grand Pavilion was built in Victoria Terrace Gardens; opened in 1937, it contained a theatre and dance hall.[59] Further north, behind the Beaconsfield Wall, a new skating rink was opened in 1909;[60] the Floral Hall was built on the same site in 1921 but was destroyed by fire in 1923.[61]

At the New Spa the theatre was burnt down in 1906 but rebuilt the following year.[62] The Spa continued to be operated by a private company until 1914; it was then leased by the corporation, which in 1919 went on to buy the undertaking. The 'glass dome' was replaced by the Spa Royal Hall in 1926, and the hall was rebuilt after being destroyed by fire in 1932.[63] A boating lake was built near by, and for a time it was converted to a skating rink and outdoor dance floor. The People's Palace briefly became the New Hippodrome skating rink in 1909.[64]

Various gardens have been laid out along the sea front since 1900, and in 1921 the corporation took over the six-acre Dukes Park, which was much used by visitors.[65] Additions have been made to its facilities and by 1969 it covered nearly 12 a.[66] Avenue Park recreation ground was opened in 1924, and in 1925 the corporation bought the golf course at the south end of the town which had been run privately since its construction in 1902.[67] A large-scale extension of holiday amenities followed the corporation's purchase of Sewerby House and its estate in 1934; they were opened to the public in 1936 and improvements have been continually made. The house contains a museum and art gallery, one room being devoted to exhibits connected with Amy Johnson, the aviator, who was a native of Hull. A golf course, various other sporting facilities, and a zoo are among the attractions in the grounds.[68] Queen's Park, near Fortyfoot Road, was opened in 1937.[69] The corporation's acquisition of sea-front land continued with the purchase of about 400 a. in Flamborough, including a golf course, in the

---

[46] Mayoh, thesis cit. 153–60, 170.
[47] For caravan camps see pp. 40, 93, 105.
[48] Mayoh, thesis cit. 175.
[49] Ibid. 136.
[50] Ibid. 122 and facing pp. 125, 128, 147.
[51] E. R. Matthews, *Bridlington and some of its Municipal Works and Undertakings*, 12–13.
[52] F. A. Slim and H. L. Gee, *Bridlington, 1899–1949*, [13], [16].
[53] Bridlington Corp., *Counc. Proc. and Cttee. Mins.* 1964–5, 314.
[54] Slim and Gee, op. cit. [13].
[55] 'Annals of Bridlington', vol. 19, p. 170; *Proc. Inst. Civil Engineers*, clix. 68, 71.
[56] Ex inf. Town Clerk, Bridlington, 1968.
[57] See p. 49.
[58] 'Annals of Bridlington', vols. 21, p. 129; 23, p. 181.
[59] Ibid. 53, p. 342; 54, pp. 194, 199.
[60] Ibid. 26, p. 187.
[61] Ibid. 38, p. 165; 40, p. 287.
[62] Ibid. 23, p. 256; 24, p. 62.
[63] Ibid. 43, pp. 207, 217; 49, pp. 21, 216; Slim and Gee, op cit. [9].
[64] 'Annals of Bridlington', vol. 26, p. 129.
[65] Char. Com. files.
[66] Ex inf. Town Clerk, 1970.
[67] Slim and Gee, op. cit. [11–12]; 'Annals of Bridlington', vol. 19, p. 164.
[68] Slim and Gee, op. cit. [20]; F. F. Johnson, *Sewerby Hall and Park* (4th edn.), 25 sqq.
[69] 'Annals of Bridlington', vol. 54, p. 239.

1930s.[70] The corporation had thus come to control nearly all the open space on the sea front for some 8 miles around the town.[71]

Musical entertainment has long been prominent on the sea front. The local government board had provided bands on the Royal Prince's Parade, including Professor J. M. Wilson's group, which was engaged in 1867.[72] An orchestra prospered, with growing repute, in the bandstand on the Parade and later in the Floral Pavilion up to the Second World War; its conductors included in 1930–2 Alfred Barker, 'one of the greatest orchestral leaders Britain ever had'. Afterwards it diminished in size and eventually became an all-purposes band. In contrast, Herman Darewski, who arrived at the Spa in the early 1920s, is said to have represented the nadir of resort music. His intention was to 'jazz up' the Spa, and he introduced dancing and thought up 'stunts' for the Royal Hall.[73]

Moving pictures became increasingly popular between the two world wars. They were shown at the Victoria Rooms in 1909, at the People's Palace in 1910, and in the Grand Pavilion and the Temperance Hall, in St. John Street, in 1911.[74] In 1912 the popularity of these entertainments led to the People's Palace becoming the Palace Picture House, and the Temperance Hall the Picturedrome.[75] By 1915 the Spa, too, was showing pictures and by 1924 there was a picture theatre alongside the café and ball-room at the Winter Gardens on the Promenade. Similarly, in 1931, films were introduced at the Oriental Lounge, also on the Promenade, where there had long been a café, concert room, and ball-room.[76] In the mean time the Picturedrome had become the Adelphi in 1924, and it was again renamed as the Roxy in 1935.[77] A purpose-built cinema, the Regal, was opened on the Promenade in 1938,[78] and the Palace, Lounge, Roxy, and Winter Gardens all continued as cinemas up to the Second World War. The Palace did not survive the war. The Lounge and the Roxy were both licensed for the last time in 1964,[79] leaving the Winter Gardens and the Regal (as the A.B.C.) still functioning in 1969. The Roxy became a 'bingo' hall.

Orchestras and cinemas illustrate the constantly changing character of the entertainments provided during the 20th century. Pierrots, concert parties, and orchestral music gave way to dancing, variety shows, and films; later, amusement arcades were constructed on the Esplanade and elsewhere, and gaming, including 'bingo', has appeared more recently. The Grand Pavilion and the Spa Royal Hall and theatre nevertheless remained the chief centres of entertainment in 1969. The Pavilion is a plain stuccoed building, distinguished only by an arcade of high arches facing the sea. The Royal Hall is a more elaborate structure of concrete and glass, and, like the adjoining theatre, it presents ornamental doorways to the promenade. Several of the older resort buildings have not survived. The Victoria Rooms were burnt down in 1933[80] and both the People's Palace and the Queen's Square baths were bombed in the Second World War.[81] Of the People's Palace, only the heavily rusticated Classical entrance from Prospect Street remained in 1969, surmounted by the name and a segmental pediment enclosing the feoffees' arms.[82]

SOCIAL INSTITUTIONS. Some social institutions, including places of entertainment, have been dealt with elsewhere.[83] This section describes some of the local societies, the libraries, and the newspapers of the town.

SOCIETIES. Several friendly societies were established in Bridlington in the early 19th century, including the Female Union Society in 1802, meeting at the Black Lion inn in the Old Town, the Amicable Society in 1820,[84] and the Benevolent Society for Bridlington and Quay in 1825.[85] A co-operative venture, the anti-monopoly corn mill, was also begun about this time.[86] A meeting was called in 1800 to consider the establishment of subscription mills,[87] though the Anti Mill is first referred to by name only in 1846.[88] The temperance movement was represented in the town by the Bridlington and Quay Temperance Society, which was founded in 1835 and built a hall in St. John Street in 1854.[89] After the hall had become a cinema,[90] the society acquired a house in Quay Road in 1918 and erected a hall behind it in Springfield Avenue in 1931,[91] which was still in use in 1969. A second hall, designed by Joseph Earnshaw, was built by the Albert Temperance Society in Wellington Road in 1876–7; it was acquired by the Salvation Army in 1887.[92]

The Bridlington and Quay Mechanics' and Scientific Institution was also established in the 1830s. At the first meeting, in 1838, it was resolved to have a library, a museum, and lectures,[93] and the library is recorded in the 1840s.[94] The institution rented the Bayle for meetings until 1852.[95] It then became inactive, and in 1854 the Bridlington Mutual Improvement Society was founded to take its place.[96] In 1858 the Londesborough Lodge of Freemasons was established, meeting in the Victoria

[70] See p. 155.
[71] Slim and Gee, op. cit. [33].
[72] Bridlington Town Hall, loc. govt. bd. mins., *passim*; 'Annals of Bridlington', vol. 1, pp. 27–8.
[73] K. Young, *Music's Great Days in the Spas and Watering Places*, 92, 143–6; H. Darewski, *Musical Memories*, 63–74; Floral Pavilion, 1967 Centenary Celebration Concert, Souvenir Programme (copy in Bridlington Pub. Libr.).
[74] 'Annals of Bridlington', vols. 26, p. 312; 27, p. 238; 28, p. 312.
[75] Ibid. 29, pp. 3–4, 227.
[76] Ibid. 32, p. 353; 41, p. 118; 48, p. 30.
[77] Ibid. 41, p. 287; 52, p. 224.
[78] Ibid. 55, p. 209.
[79] E.R.C.C. *Mins.* 1963–4, 281, 394.
[80] 'Annals of Bridlington', vol. 50, p. 271.
[81] Photographs in Bridlington Pub. Libr.
[82] With the adjoining shops it was built a few years after the main building: Bridlington Town Hall, Building Inspector's Office, drawing no. 1106 (1899).

[83] See pp. 58 sqq.
[84] E.R.R.O., QDC/2/18, 23.
[85] Copy of rules, in Bridlington Pub. Libr.
[86] See p. 56.
[87] Lords Feoffees' Rec., Bayle, Bridlington, handbill in Museum.
[88] White, *Dir. Hull & York* (1846), 433.
[89] 'Annals of Bridlington', vol. 6, p. 2; Sheahan and Whellan, *Hist. York & E.R.* ii. 452; *Hull Advertiser*, 18 Nov. 1854.
[90] See above.
[91] Registry of Deeds, Beverley, 193/225/193; 'Annals of Bridlington', vol. 48, p. 190.
[92] 'Annals of Bridlington', vol. 5, pp. 32, 66; see below, p. 77.
[93] Copy of *Rules*, in Hull Pub. Libr.
[94] White, *Dir. Hull & York* (1846), 435.
[95] Lords Feoffees' Rec., Bayle, Bridlington, acct. bk. 1794–1852.
[96] Sheahan and Whellan, *Hist. York & E.R.* ii. 452.

Rooms; a hall was built in St. John's Avenue in 1875 and enlarged in 1925, and other lodges were established in 1919, 1922, and 1949.[97] The Victoria Sailors' and Working Men's Club was founded in 1865 with premises in Cliff Street; these were enlarged and refronted in 1877,[98] and were still in use in 1969.

One society early established to foster a particular field of interest was the Agricultural Society, founded in 1835 and holding an annual show. By the 1850s there was also a Floral and Horticultural Society.[99] Various societies were formed in the late 19th and early 20th centuries, including the Musical Society (1893), the Literary and Debating Society (1898), the Amateur Operatic and Dramatic Societies (1908), and the Literary and Philosophical Society (1925).[1] Of these the Literary and Debating Society is said to have developed from the Wesleyans' Mutual Improvement Society, which had existed for 14 years; the Primitive Methodists had a similar society.[2] Finally, the Augustinian Society was founded in 1920 to foster antiquarian research;[3] it meets in the Bayle, where it has established a museum of local antiquities in conjunction with the lords feoffees.[4]

LIBRARIES. From the early 19th century onwards there were various circulating libraries in the town.[5] It was not until 1925, however, after much public agitation, that the Public Libraries Acts were adopted and a 'free' library opened.[6] It was housed from 1926 in the information bureau in Quay Road, where it was open on two, later three, evenings a week. Nearly all the books were non-fiction.[7] Eventually a former bank in King Street was adapted for the library and opened in 1937; there was then a lending stock of about 6,000 books.[8] By 1949 the stock had increased to 19,000 and the library included a children's department, opened in 1945, periodicals and reference rooms, opened in 1946, and a separate local collection. An extension to the building, reaching back to Queen Street, was erected in 1966.[9]

NEWSPAPERS.[10] The town was served in 1836–7 by the *Scarborough, Whitby and Bridlington Chronicle*,[11] but the first specifically Bridlington papers appeared in June 1843. The *Burlington Reporter and Burlington Quay Fashionable Advertiser*[12] was printed by William Forth, and the *Burlington and East Riding Advertiser*[13] by John and Thomas Keddy.[14] By 1849 the *Reporter* was printed by Rachel Hickson.[15] It seems subsequently to have lapsed and then been revived by Mrs. Hickson, for in 1853 she began to print the *Burlington Reporter and Weekly List of Visitors at the Quay*, with June 1843 as the reputed date of establishment.[16] The *Bridlington and Quay Advertiser and List of Visitors*, printed by Hudson Beauvais, first appeared in 1847,[17] and in 1849 it was replaced by the *Bridlington and Quay Advertiser and Improved List of Visitors*. In its first number, on 11 June,[18] the latter claimed to have been established in June 1843 and it referred to the *Reporter* as its only rival: it seems, therefore, that Beauvais had absorbed the Keddys' paper.

Several new papers appeared in the 1850s and 1860s. The *Bridlington Quay List of Visitors and General Advertiser* was first printed in 1850 by H. Varley and appeared only in the 'season'.[19] By August that year John Varley was printing it as the *Bridlington Quay Mercury, General Advertiser and Weekly List of Visitors*,[20] and by 1854 John Varley & Sons had renamed it the *Bridlington Quay Mercury and Weekly List of Visitors*; it was still being printed, by T. F. Varley, in 1868.[21] In 1854 John Furby began the monthly *Bridlington and Quay Advertiser and Miscellany of Useful and Entertaining Knowledge*.[22] The *Bridlington and Quay News and Tradesmen's Herald*, also printed by Furby, appeared from 1855 to 1858.[23]

Two other papers which began in the 1850s enjoyed a long existence. The *Bridlington Quay Observer* was founded in 1859 and continued until 1899. It was printed, in the 'season' only, successively by George Furby, J. W. Furby, and Richard Brown.[24] The *Bridlington Free Press and Illustrated Advertiser* also first appeared in 1859; it was later known as the *Bridlington Free Press, Bridlington Quay News and East Riding General Advertiser*, and in 1954 it became the *Bridlington Free Press and Chronicle*, under which title it was still published in 1969.[25] It was printed successively by W. W. Coopland (1859–65), William

---

[97] *Hist. Londesborough Lodge. . . 1858–1958, passim.*
[98] 'Annals of Bridlington', vol. 5, p. 64; date on building.
[99] Sheahan and Whellan, *Hist. York & E.R.* ii. 452.
[1] 'Annals of Bridlington', vols. 16, pp. 91, 93; 26, pp. 69, 140; 42, p. 234.
[2] Ibid. 9, p. 44; Bridlington Pub. Libr., MS. hist. of the society (1948).
[3] 'Annals of Bridlington', vol. 37, p. 217.
[4] For the museum see J. S. Purvis and M. E. Ingram, *The Bayle, Bridlington.*
[5] e.g. *Hull Advertiser*, 25 Apr. 1912; directories.
[6] 'Annals of Bridlington', vols. 40, p. 132; 42, pp. 183, 259. [7] Ibid. 42, p. 259; 43, pp. 290, 327–8.
[8] Ibid. 54, p. 180.
[9] F. A. Slim and H. L. Gee, *Bridlington, 1899–1949*, [66]; ex inf. Mr. S. T. Thompson, Borough Librarian, 1969.
[10] Partly based on G. E. Laughton and Lorna R. Stephen, *Yorks. Newspapers*, and K. L. Mayoh, 'Comparative Study of Resorts on Coast of Holderness' (unpubl. M.A. thesis, Univ. of Hull, 1961), App. B.
[11] Laughton and Stephen, op. cit. 43.
[12] Copies for 3 June to 7 Oct. 1843 are in Bridlington Pub. Libr. In 1844 it was known successively as the *Burl. Rep. and Burl. Quay, Driffield, Kilham, and Hunmanby Advert.* and the *Burl. Rep. and Burl. Quay and Driff. Fashionable Advert.*: copies in ibid.

[13] Some copies from 1843 and 1844 are in ibid.
[14] The Keddys' press was registered that year: E.R.R.O., QDL/10.
[15] Part of an un-numbered copy in 'Bridlington Newspapers etc.' (scrapbk. in Bridlington Pub. Libr.).
[16] *Bridlington Free Press*, 2 Jan. 1959.
[17] Nos. 1–17 are in 'Bridlington Newspapers etc.'.
[18] In Bridlington Pub. Libr.
[19] *Bridlington Free Press*, 2 Jan. 1959.
[20] No. 6 (8 Aug. 1850) is in Bridlington Pub. Libr. John Varley's press was registered in 1847: E.R.R.O., QDL/15.
[21] A few copies, ranging from 20 July 1854 to 22 Sept. 1868, are in Bridlington Pub. Libr. (several in 'Bridlington Newspapers etc.'). A complete file from 29 June 1858 to 22 Sept. 1868 is in the B.M. Newspaper Libr., Colindale.
[22] No. 1 is in 'Bridlington Newspapers etc'.
[23] All copies except those for Jan.–Apr. 1857 are in the B.M. John Furby registered a press in 1808: E.R.R.O., QDL/2.
[24] The files in the B.M. are complete except for the years 1870–3 and 1897. There are a few copies in Bridlington Pub. Libr.
[25] Bridlington Pub. Libr. holds complete files from 1925 (except for 1936), together with a few earlier copies. Complete files from 1859 onwards, except for 1884, 1897, and 1910, are in the B.M.

Furby (1865–7), William Taylor (1867–87), E. P. Rogers (1887–96), and Green & Son (1896–8). It has since been printed at Scarborough.

In 1874 Charles Forster began the *Bridlington and Quay Gazette* and it continued until 1914,[26] printed by Forster's widow and then his son C. E. Forster.[27] For a time Charles Forster also printed, in the 'season' only, the *Bridlington Illustrated Gazette*. Another new paper, the *Bridlington and Quay Advertiser*, appeared briefly in 1896–7.[28] Finally, the *Bridlington Chronicle and East Coast Advertiser* was founded in 1897 and continued until 1954,[29] when it was incorporated in the *Free Press*. It was printed by William Forster until 1946 and then by H. J. Taylor.[30]

PUBLIC SERVICES. Both the Old Town and the Quay relied on wells and springs for their water until the mid 19th century. At the Quay the chief source was a spring next to the harbour, discovered in 1811 by Benjamin Milne. It flowed as the tide rose, discharging throughout the period of high tide, and by 1821 a constant supply was assured by pumping the water to a 1,200-gallon cistern.[31] In 1839 the feoffees contributed towards the maintenance of five pumps in the Old Town and two at the Quay, one of them the spring pump.[32] After 1863 the pumps were repaired by the local board, which was taking steps to improve the cistern at the harbour spring in 1863–4. Some of the pumps continued to be used after 1865, when a water undertaking was established,[33] and the harbour spring was maintained until at least 1881.[34]

The Bridlington and Quay Water Co. was formed in 1865, after agreement had been reached with the local board for laying pipes under the streets.[35] A pumping station and reservoir were built the same year at the junction of Marton Road and Mill Lane, close to the Old Town, and another station was built at a higher level in Mill Lane in 1872. The undertaking was bought by the town council in 1899.[36]

New plant, including two engines, was opened at the higher works in 1912, and the reservoir there was covered over in 1925.[37] A new engine house and borehole were constructed at the higher works in 1933, with a 500,000-gallon reservoir near Scarborough Road. This not only met all the needs of the town but also made possible a much improved supply to Sewerby and Marton: the areas lying at a higher level than Sewerby church had hitherto not been supplied at all.[38] Under an Act of 1933 the supply area was extended to include most of Bridlington rural district, the work being carried out in 1936–8. Part of this area was supplied from the works at Bridlington but much of it from a new pumping station and boreholes at Burton Agnes.[39] Although Bridlington supplied water in bulk to Flamborough, the installations there and at Muston, Folkton, and Hunmanby belonged to the rural district council until 1959, when they were acquired by Bridlington corporation.[40] The town's water undertaking was transferred to the East Yorkshire (Wolds Area) Water Board in 1962.[41]

The first gasworks in the town were built in Quay Road in 1833,[42] and the Burlington Gas Light Co. was formed in 1836.[43] In 1858–9 the works were rebuilt[44] on a new site off Quay Road, in what is now Moorfield Road. New plant was installed there about 1937 and the works were extended in 1949, after nationalization.[45] The amount of gas produced rose from 70 mill. cu. ft. in 1898 to 216 in 1936 and 347 in 1948.[46] In 1957 mains were laid to supply gas to Driffield. Gas production at Bridlington ceased in 1968 when natural gas, from beneath the North Sea, was introduced. The gasholders, however, remained in use,[47] and offices and showrooms in Quay Road, opened in 1931,[48] were also still in use in 1969.

Electric lighting was first used in public places in 1890, when the local board arranged for the lighting of the Royal Prince's Parade, and the system was extended along North Cliff in 1894.[49] Power was supplied in 1890 and later from the Victoria Saw Mills.[50] In 1900 the corporation was itself empowered to make electricity and it began to do so in 1905, when a generating station and offices were opened in Brett Street, off Quay Road.[51] There were 442 electric street lamps soon after the station was opened,[52] and at first most of the output was used in the streets and at the Parade and the Spa.[53] The

---

[26] Its title had various additions later on, such as *E. Yorks. Advert. and Illustrated Visitors List*. There are a few copies in Bridlington Pub. Libr. and a complete file, except for 1896, in the B.M.
[27] Slim and Gee, *Bridlington, 1899–1949*, [90].
[28] All copies are in the B.M.
[29] Variant titles included the *Bridlington and Quay Chron., Hilderthorpe News and General Intelligencer*. A complete file from 1938 to 1954, together with a few earlier copies, is in Bridlington Pub. Libr. A complete file, except for 1912, is in the B.M.
[30] Slim and Gee, op. cit. [90].
[31] Accts. for work done, 1811–13, in Lords Feoffees' Rec., Bayle, Bridlington; J. Thompson, *Hist. Sketches of Bridlington*, 159–60.
[32] Purvis, *Bridlington Charters, etc.* 305.
[33] 'Notes on Work of Bridlington Loc. Govt. Bd.' (MS. notebk. in Bridlington Pub. Libr.), 3, 5, 10, 123.
[34] Bridlington Town Hall, loc. govt. bd. mins., vol. 3, p. 354.
[35] 'Notes on Work of Loc. Govt. Bd.', 15–17.
[36] Bridlington Town Hall, loc. govt. bd. and U.D.C. mins., vol. 8, p. 311.
[37] 'Annals of Bridlington', vols. 29, pp. 209–10, 270; 42, p. 244
[38] Ibid. vol. 50, pp. 104, 109.
[38] Ibid. vol. 50, pp. 104, 109.
[39] Ibid. vols. 53, p. 161; 55, p. 291; Bridlington Corp., *Programme of Official Inauguration* (1938).

[40] *Counc. Proc. and Cttee. Mins.* 1949–50, 204.
[41] Ibid. 1961–2, 345.
[42] 'Annals of Bridlington', vol. 1, before p. 1; *Hull Advertiser*, 25 Jan. and 12 July, 1833; White, *Dir. Hull & York* (1846), 425–6.
[43] *Deed of Settlement* (1859) (copy in Bridlington Pub. Libr.). The Co. had become the Bridlington G.L. Co. by 1859 and was renamed the Bridlington Gas Co. in 1886.
[44] J. Varley, *Guide to Bridlington Quay* (1864), 21.
[45] F. A. Slim and H. L. Gee, *Bridlington, 1899–1949*, [80–1].
[46] Ibid. [81]; 'Annals of Bridlington', vol. 54, p. 282.
[47] *Bridlington Free Press*, 29 Mar. and 2 Aug. 1968.
[48] 'Annals of Bridlington', vol. 48, p. 63.
[49] Bridlington Town Hall, loc. govt. bd. mins., vols. 6, pp. 16, 22, 39–40; 7, p. 175; 'Annals of Bridlington', vol. 14, p. 55; W. Taylor, *Brief Hist. of Bridlington Loc. Bd.* 6.
[50] Bridlington Town Hall, loc. govt. bd. mins., vols. 6, pp. 16, 22, 128, 298.
[51] Unless otherwise stated the rest of this paragraph is based on *Official Opening of New Premises and Showrooms* (1939) and other material kindly supplied by Mr. C. R. Taylor, District Manager, Yorks. Elect. Bd., Bridlington.
[52] *Bridlington Elect. Works* (n.d. c. 1905), 18 (copy in Bridlington Pub. Libr.).
[53] E.R. Matthews, *Bridlington and some of its Municipal Works and Undertakings*, 18.

generating station was closed in 1932 and the town's supply was taken from the electricity grid. New offices and showrooms in Quay Road were opened in 1939 but destroyed by bombs in 1941.[54]

It is said that a draper named Hustler paved the streets and otherwise improved the town c. 1680.[55] Much work was done by the feoffees in the late 18th and early 19th centuries. Flagging of the streets began in 1798, when parts of St. John Street and High Street were dealt with, and the former was completed in 1799. Regular expenditure on flagging was incurred thereafter, with a noteworthy burst of activity in the 1840s: Market Place, High Street, 'the West End' of the town, and unspecified places at the Quay were all flagged then, and several public subscriptions were raised to help to meet the cost.[56] There was still no street lighting in 1821, privately-provided lamps having been wantonly destroyed,[57] but oil lamps were fixed in the Old Town in 1824 and the feoffees regularly contributed towards their upkeep.[58] Gas lighting in the streets was introduced in 1838, when gas inspectors were appointed.[59] Responsibility for street paving and lighting was assumed by the local board in 1863.

The maintenance of open sewers from the Old Town to the Gypsey Race was for long the responsibility of the feoffees.[60] As the town, and more particularly the Quay, expanded in the 19th century, however, a piecemeal system of covered drains was gradually constructed at the expense of private landowners and local authorities. As late as 1870, for example, the owner of the Beaconsfield estate was told to provide his own drainage, using a groyne across the foreshore, but the local board was willing to contribute towards the drain along his promenade.[61] Much of the town's sewage, however, still found its way to the harbour and the sea along the Gypsey Race.[62] Various schemes to improve the drainage system were considered by the board in the 1870s[63] before that of Brierley and Holt of Blackburn was settled upon in 1878. In a report on the existing sewers they mentioned drains in Market Place, High Street, West Gate, Kirkgate, and St. John Street, in the Old Town, and in Cliff Street, at the Quay. The scheme was completed by 1885, with 6½ miles of new sewers and an outfall on the south foreshore, near the harbour.[64] By 1899 a further 12 miles of sewers had been laid and a new outfall constructed at the north end of the town, near Sands Lane.[65] In that year the borough surveyor prepared a scheme to remodel the system, including the provision of over 2 miles of surface-water sewers, the rebuilding and enlargement of existing sewers, the reconstruction of the old and the making of a new screen chamber at the harbour, and the laying of a new outfall sewer under the south pier and over the sands to discharge near the old outfall. The work was completed by 1912, together with the improvement of the drainage of Hilderthorpe.[66] Work on a new disposal scheme began in 1952 and had been largely completed by 1971, with the exception of the final disposal of the foul effluent. New spine sewers were laid throughout the town and the discharge of foul effluent was concentrated at the harbour outfall.[67]

Scavengers responsible for cleansing the streets were appointed by the feoffees,[68] whose courts were much concerned to prevent and to punish the deposit of dung and rubbish in the streets and other public places.[69] Similar measures were later adopted by the local board until scavenging was put out to contractors. After complaint about the accumulation of night-soil in a field in Fortyfoot Lane, the board resolved in 1865 to provide a 'receptacle' for it near the Flamborough road. In 1873 a scavenger was appointed for the Christ Church district and he was to use the Flamborough road manure yard.[70] The night-soil problem was, of course, resolved by the improved sewerage system constructed after 1878 and the installation of water closets. There were only 690 water closets in 1878 but 3,427 by 1912.[71]

In 1899 scavenging was taken over from private contractors by the corporation. Various rubbish dumps were used in the early 20th century before dumping at Haverdale Heads began in 1927. In 1936 the corporation brought into use part of the 28 a. on the opposite side of the Gypsey Race which it had bought for the purpose in 1931–2.[72]

The parish constables responsible for maintaining order in Bridlington were replaced by men of the newly-formed East Riding constabulary in 1857.[73] Lock-ups, or kidcotes, in the Bayle and at the Quay[74] sufficed for securing prisoners until 1843–4, when a police station and lock-up were built in Nungate, in the Old Town.[75] In 1881 a new station and court house were built in Ashville Street, on the corner of Quay Road, designed by Smith and Brodrick of Hull in the 'Queen Anne' style and constructed of red brick with yellow-brick dressings.[76] Additions have since been made to the buildings.

The first fire engine in the town was acquired in 1767 and was kept in St. Mary's Church in the early 19th century.[77] An engine at the Quay was mentioned as early as 1823, both engines being under the control of the feoffees.[78] In 1866, after the establishment of

[54] Slim and Gee, *Bridlington, 1899–1949*, [69].
[55] J. S. Fletcher, *Picturesque Hist. Yorks.* (1901), 396.
[56] Lords Feoffees' Rec., Bayle, Bridlington, acct. bk. 1794–1852.
[57] Thompson, *Hist. Sketches of Bridlington*, 123.
[58] Lords Feoffees' Rec., acct. bk. 1794–1852; *Hull Advertiser*, 6 and 27 Feb. 1824.
[59] Bayle Mus., Bridlington, printed notice of 1838; *Hull Advertiser*, 30 Oct. 1838.
[60] Purvis, *Bridlington Charters, etc.* 155, 246, 264, 275.
[61] 'Notes on Work of Bridlington Loc. Govt. Bd.' (MS. notebk. in Bridlington Pub. Libr.), 58–9.
[62] Ibid. 68, 106.
[63] e.g. ibid. 111, 125, 129–31.
[64] Bridlington Corp., local govt. bd. mins., vols. 3, pp. 93, 187, 306–7, 335; 4, e.g. pp. 129–30, 379; Matthews, *Municipal Undertakings*, 4–5.
[65] Loc. govt. bd. mins., vols. 5, pp. 59–60, 100, 346; 6, pp. 4, 105, 241; Matthews, op. cit. 5; 'Annals of Bridlington', vol. 16, p. 165.
[66] Matthews, op. cit. 5; 'Annals of Bridlington', vol. 29, p. 282.
[67] Ex inf. Town Clerk, 1970.
[68] Purvis, *Bridlington Charters, etc.* 220.
[69] e.g. ibid. 259–60, 262–4.
[70] 'Notes on Work of Bridlington Loc. Govt. Bd.' 20–1, 114.
[71] Matthews, *Municipal Undertakings*, 4.
[72] 'Annals of Bridlington', vol. 48, p. 325; Registry of Deeds, Beverley, 440/378/294; 447/70/55; Bridlington Corp., *M.O.H. Ann. Rep. 1936*, 41.
[73] E.R.R.O., QAP/3/1.
[74] Lords Feoffees' Rec., Bayle, Bridlington, acct. bk. 1794–1852 (*sub* 1838); O.S. Map 60" (1854).
[75] E.R.R.O., QAP/5/7–10.
[76] 'Annals of Bridlington', vol. 7, p. 98; Bridlington Corp., Building Inspector's Office, drawing no. 150 (1880).
[77] Thompson, *Hist. Sketches of Bridlington*, 138; *Hull Advertiser*, 8 Oct. 1812.
[78] Lords Feoffees' Rec., Bayle, Bridlington, acct. bk. 1794–1852; min. bk. 1804–62.

the water undertaking, fire-plugs began to be fitted in the streets.[79] One of the engines was kept in the Bayle and one at the Quay.[80] They were taken over by the local board in 1874 and the feoffees agreed to pay £25 a year towards the board's fire service; in the following year the board secured the services of the volunteer life company, formed to help at shipwrecks, as a volunteer fire brigade.[81] In 1894, however, the board began to recruit full-time firemen,[82] and when the town was incorporated in 1899 a brigade consisting of a captain and eleven men was established.[83] A new engine had been bought in 1883 and the first steam engine was acquired in 1899.[84] The Quay engine was in 1893 moved to Portland Place, to the board's depot, where the other equipment was kept.[85] A fire station was built there in 1901.[86] The first motor fire engine was bought in 1912.[87] After forming part of the National Fire Service during the Second World War, the brigade passed under the control of the county council in 1948.[88] A new station, in Bessingby Road, was built in 1960–1.[89]

The insufficiency of St. Mary's churchyard led to the formation of a burial board in 1873[90] and a cemetery in Sewerby Road, with chapels and lodge, was designed by Alfred Smith of Nottingham. It covered 8 a.[91] and was consecrated in 1883.[92] The cemetery was taken over by the corporation in 1904[93] and extensions[94] have brought the total area to about 19 a.[95] The two chapels, in the Gothic style, are connected by an arcade surmounted by a tall turret and spire.

A postal service to Bridlington[96] was established some time between 1635 and 1651,[97] and it is said that a daily service was introduced by the efforts of Benjamin Milne, who came to the town in 1791.[98] A receiving office was opened in the Old Town in the later 18th century, and the post office was in High Street in the early 19th century. An office at the Quay was opened in 1841 and became a head post office in 1875, when it was in Prince Street. A new head office was built in Queen Street about 1900[99] and was replaced by a new building in Quay Road in 1929.[1] The office was destroyed by bombs in 1940 but was rebuilt on the same site and reopened in 1952.[2]

A telegraph service was first operated in Bridlington by a private company, perhaps the Electric and International Telegraph Co.; it was taken over by the Post Office in 1870 and offices were opened that year in both the Old Town and the Quay. The National Telephone Co. opened an exchange in Bridlington in 1896, which was taken over by the Post Office in 1912.[3]

Three hospitals, the Lloyd, Avenue, and Bempton Lane Hospitals, came under the control of the Leeds Regional Hospital Board when the National Health Service was established in 1948, and all still existed in 1969. As in other seaside resorts there is a comparatively large number of convalescent and other homes in the town.

The Lloyd Hospital was founded in 1868 by Alicia Lloyd, sister of Yarburgh Lloyd Greame, who gave £1,200.[4] It was opened that year in a rented house in Quay Road and was supported by the endowment and by public subscription; in 1870 the Bridlington charity trustees granted £45 to maintain three beds. From the first honoraria were paid to the medical and dispensing staff. In 1871 the hospital moved to another house in Quay Road and this had accommodation for sixteen in-patients the following year. A new hospital, designed by Smith and Brodrick of Hull, was completed and opened in 1876; it is a two-storeyed Gothic building of red brick with stone dressings. The north wing was extended in 1894, increasing the accommodation from fifteen to 30 beds. After the loss of the lifeboat run by the S.W.M.C. in 1898[5] the lifeboat committee gave the remaining funds of £172 to the hospital on condition that sailors over 30 years old hurt while at work should be treated free. The hospital was enlarged in 1926, increasing the accommodation by 20 beds. Just before nationalization the assets of the hospital included nearly £27,000 stock, besides £8,000 in a 'new hospital' fund. The old buildings were still in use in 1969.[6]

The Avenue Hospital was opened in the house known as the Avenue, in Westgate, in 1932 by the East Riding county council. It was intended as a hospital for the sick poor and at first accommodated about 40 patients.[7] A maternity annexe was opened in 1939.[8] In 1967 there were 66 beds.[9]

Bempton Lane Hospital was opened as the borough sanatorium in 1904, with eighteen beds.[10] It was used for general medical cases as well as for infectious diseases after 1950, and in 1967 it was a geriatric hospital, with 72 beds.[11]

St. Anne's Convalescent Home was opened in two

---

[79] 'Notes on Work of Bridlington Loc. Govt. Bd.' (MS. notebk. in Bridlington Pub. Libr.), 33–4.
[80] *Kelly's Dir. N. & E.R. Yorks.* (1872), 332.
[81] 'Notes on Work of Loc. Govt. Bd.', 127, 130, 133a, 136; 'Annals of Bridlington', vol. 15, p. 37.
[82] Bridlington Town Hall, loc. govt. bd. mins., vol. 7, p. 84; 'Annals of Bridlington', vol. 14, p. 30.
[83] 'Annals of Bridlington', vol. 16, pp. 20, 167.
[84] Ibid. p. 20; loc. govt. bd. mins., vol. 4, p. 152.
[85] Loc. govt. bd. mins., vol. 6, pp. 355–6.
[86] Ibid. vol. 18, p. 126.
[87] *Kelly's Dir. N. & E.R. Yorks.* (1913), 479.
[88] E.R.C.C. *Mins.* 1947–8, 352.
[89] Ibid. 1960–1, 268, 377.
[90] 'Notes on Work of Bridlington Loc. Govt. Bd.' (MS. notebk. in Bridlington Pub. Libr.), 100–1, 104, 122; 'Annals of Bridlington', vol. 3, p. 65.
[91] *Kelly's Dir. N. & E.R. Yorks.* (1897), 414.
[92] 'Annals of Bridlington', vol. 4, p. 71; B.I.H.R., CD. 477.
[93] 'Annals of Bridlington', vol. 21, p. 211.
[94] York Dioc. Regy., Sentences of consecration; 'Annals of Bridlington', vols. 22, p. 220; 31, p. 226; 46, p. 230; 52, p. 336; Bridlington Corp. *Counc. Proc. and Cttee. Mins.* 1962–3, 325.

[95] Slim and Gee, *Bridlington, 1899–1949*, [73].
[96] Unless otherwise stated this paragraph is based on R. Ward, *Postal Hist. of Bridlington and Bridlington Quay.*
[97] See also *Cal. S.P. Dom.* 1671–2, 221; 1672, 434.
[98] Thompson, *Hist. Sketches of Bridlington*, 159.
[99] 'Annals of Bridlington', vol. 46, p. 118; Bridlington Town Hall, Building Inspector's Office, drawing no. 866.
[1] 'Annals of Bridlington', vol. 46, p. 121.
[2] Ibid. vol. 57, p. 212.
[3] Ex inf. the Archivist, P.O. Records, London.
[4] This account is based on *The Lloyd Hospital, Bridlington, 1868–1968* (copy in Bridlington Pub. Libr.).
[5] See p. 50.
[6] *Hospitals Year Bk. 1969*, 64.
[7] 'Annals of Bridlington', vol. 49, pp. 141, 353; E.R.C.C. *Mins.* 1932–3, 47, 370.
[8] 'Annals of Bridlington', vol. 56, p. 46.
[9] Bridlington Corp. *M.O.H. Ann. Rep. 1967*, 10.
[10] 'Annals of Bridlington', vols. 20, p. 76; 21, p. 90; Matthews, *Bridlington and some of its Municipal Works and Undertakings*, 15.
[11] Bridlington Corp. *M.O.H. Ann. Rep. 1950*, 11; *1967*, 10.

houses in Carr Lane in 1869 or 1870, near the iron church of St. Anne which was erected in Flamborough Road in the former year.[12] The prime mover in these projects was Capt. E. Barnes.[13] He then began to build a new home in Hilderthorpe,[14] but it was eventually erected in Flamborough Road, to designs by Joseph Earnshaw, and the first part of it was opened in 1878.[15] The old iron church is said to have been re-erected next to the home in 1888,[16] but it was replaced by a brick church in 1897.[17] Home and church were destroyed by bombs in 1941. Money received in compensation was used to build twelve almshouses on the site in 1961 and eight more in 1965. They are known as St. Anne's Homes[18] and were designed by F. F. Johnson.

The Yorkshire Foresters' Orphanage and Convalescent Home was opened in St. John's Avenue in 1899. It was designed by R. J. Beale and is built of red brick with stone dressings. The orphanage had been founded in 1887 but children were at first boarded out. The building was enlarged in 1927.[19]

Burlington House, in Marton Road, is the former union workhouse, known from 1930 to 1948 as the Bridlington County Institution.[20]

The Annie and Nellie Woodcock Homes, in Limekiln Lane, were opened in 1962 in a house acquired under the will of Nellie Woodcock, proved in 1958, bequeathing her residuary estate for a home for Methodists. Another house, in St. George's Avenue, was opened in 1965.[21]

Three homes have been opened by the East Riding county council. Danes Lea old people's home, in St. Anne's Road, was opened in a former nursing home in 1951.[22] The Parker Home for children, in Marton Road, was opened in 1950 in a house devised for the purpose by H. J. Parker, by will proved in 1947.[23] Carr Head old people's home, in Sands Lane, was built on the site of the Tudor Convalescent Home and opened in 1969.[24]

TRANSPORT. Although a network of local roads converged upon Bridlington, only one road into the town was ever turnpiked and that for a short period. The road from Beverley via White Cross was turnpiked in two sections, in 1761 and 1767; the second Act dealt with the section from White Cross to Bridlington, but it was never renewed and the erosion of the cliffs south of the town no doubt made the road dangerous.[25] Mile-stones were certainly provided and the first one from the Old Town terminus of the turnpike still stands in Cardigan Road.[26]

By the late 18th century a regular mail service to Bridlington had been established,[27] as well as the first passenger-coach service. In 1791 a coach ran twice a week to Hull and by 1823 there were two coaches running between Scarborough, Bridlington, and Hull, at least one of them daily in summer and three times a week in winter.[28] In 1831 there was a daily coach between those places, with three extra coaches in summer; by 1840 there was also a thrice-weekly service to Leeds and by 1846 daily services in summer to York and by omnibus to Hull.[29] The arrival of the railway in 1846 soon brought the coach services to an end, and omnibuses ran from principal inns and hotels to meet the trains at Bridlington station.[30] The coaching inns had included the Lord Nelson and the Globe, in the Old Town, and the Britannia and the Stirling Castle, at the Quay.

Bridlington was the centre of an extensive network of carrier services. About thirty carriers served country towns and villages in the 1820s and 1830s, nearly fifty in the mid century, and still nearly thirty in the 1890s. The number had fallen to about a dozen in the 1930s. These services were based on numerous inns, with the Star and the Black Lion always prominent.[31]

Besides the omnibuses running to the station there were hackney carriages in use in the town by the 1860s,[32] and a horse-bus service between the Old Town and the Quay is said to have been started c. 1880 by the Williamson family.[33] A half-hourly bus service between High Street and Prince Street was certainly operated from 1889 onwards.[34] Although the corporation was authorised in 1920 to provide a bus service[35] it never did so, and buses were run in and around the town by several private companies. The last local firms involved were Williamson & Son and the White Bus Co., which ceased operation in 1951 and 1955 respectively.[36] The East Yorkshire Motor Services Ltd. was alone in the field in 1969.

A railway line between Bridlington and Hull was opened in 1846 and a line north to Filey linking Bridlington with the line to York, in 1847. A more direct route from the West Riding than that via Hull was provided in 1890, when the line from Driffield to Market Weighton was opened, giving a connexion with Selby.[37] The line from Hull to Bridlington and beyond remained open in 1969.

The inhabitants of the Old Town had in 1844

---

[12] 'Annals of Bridlington', vols. 1, p. 145; 26, p. 129.
[13] Ibid. 2, p. 34.
[14] Ibid. p. 85; 3, p. 8.
[15] Ibid. 5, p. 1; 6, p. 53; 31, p. 70.
[16] *Kelly's Dir. N. & E.R. Yorks.* (1893), 388.
[17] 'Annals of Bridlington', vols. 15, pp. 197–8; 26, p. 129.
[18] Ibid. 58, p. 95; Char. Com. files.
[19] 'Annals of Bridlington', vols. 16, pp. 129, 185; 44, p. 171.
[20] It became Burlington House in 1948: E.R.C.C. *Mins.* 1948–9, 166.
[21] Char. Com. files; ex inf. Messrs. Harland, Turnbull & Roberts, Bridlington, 1970.
[22] Bridlington Corp. *M.O.H. Ann. Rep. 1950*, 11; *1951*, 11.
[23] Char. Com. files; E.R.C.C. *Mins.* 1950–1, 164.
[24] E.R.C.C. *Mins.* 1968–9, 198.
[25] K. A. MacMahon, *Roads and Turnpike Trusts in E. Yorks.* (E. Yorks. Loc. Hist. Ser. xviii), 27; see below, p. 201.
[26] Two mile-posts from the eroded section of the road survive, one in Hull Museums and one in the Bayle, Bridlington.
[27] See p. 66.
[28] R. G. Battle, *Dir. Hull* (1791), 66; Baines, *Hist. Yorks.* ii. 181.
[29] W. White, *Dir. Hull etc.* (1831), 240; *Dir. E. & N.R. Yorks.* (1840), 378; White, *Dir. Hull & York* (1846), 439; see above, p. 58.
[30] e.g. White, *Dir. Hull & York* (1858), 678.
[31] Directories.
[32] 'Notes on Work of Bridlington Loc. Govt. Bd.' (notebk. in Bridlington Pub. Libr.), 14.
[33] G. Hardwick, *Bygone Bridlington*, 64.
[34] Directories. [35] 10 & 11 Geo. V, c. 65.
[36] Ex inf. Secy., E. Yorks. Motor Services Ltd., Hull, 1970.
[37] K. A. MacMahon, *Beginnings of E. Yorks. Rlys.* (E. Yorks. Loc. Hist. Ser. iii), 8, 12, 25. For earlier proposals see Bridlington Pub. Libr. *Gateway*, Oct. 1949, 4; *Hull Advertiser*, 31 Jan., 14, 25, 28 Feb., 18 Apr., and 2 May 1834.

opposed the building of the railway station at Spring Gardens, near the Quay, arguing that visitors to the market town should have greater consideration than those to the resort, and that the company would in any case need a tramway to link the station with the harbour for goods traffic.[38] Though the station was in fact built 300 yds. short of Spring Gardens, it was hardly at the midway point between Old Town and Quay which the objectors had favoured.[39] By 1851 a tramway had been built from the station to the harbour, crossing the Gypsey Race into Hilderthorpe; the line was derelict by 1866 but the track was not removed until 1917.[40]

The original station was a long, single-storeyed, building of grey brick with stone dressings, having a Tuscan portico and at least one rusticated archway in the main façade. The portico was removed in 1892[41] but the much-altered remains of the building still stood in 1969. Public accommodation at the station was improved in 1874[42] and a new stationmaster's house was built at about the same time.[43] In 1892–3 a new excursion platform was built and the surrounds of the station were much altered.[44] What amounts to a new station was built to the east of the old one in 1912; the buildings are of red brick with stone dressings, and several additional platforms were provided.[45]

LOCAL GOVERNMENT. THE MANOR. Throughout the Middle Ages the town was governed by the prior as lord of the manor of Bridlington, and he enjoyed various privileges. He had been granted by Henry I sac, soc, toll, team, infangtheof, and quittance of tolls;[46] in 1392 he was further granted court leet and view of frankpledge, the assize of bread and ale, the chattels of felons and fugitives, waifs and strays, and wreck of the sea between Earl's Dike and 'Flamborough dike';[47] and in 1446 and 1452 he was granted more franchises, including quittance of suits at county and wapentake courts, the power to appoint coroners, and cognizance of pleas of novel disseisin and mort d'ancestor, and of other pleas moved in any of the king's courts.[48] The prior's three-weekly court[49] was held in the priory gatehouse,[50] and there too was the prison which was granted in 1446. After the prior's attainder the court was held ten times in the year beginning at Michaelmas 1537, on behalf of the Crown. On one occasion fines were collected for 21 infringements of the assize of bread and payments were made by 57 bakers, tipplers, butchers, hucksters, and alehouse-keepers. The court was also concerned with many pleas of debt, as well as the usual domestic and agricultural offences.[51]

The manorial courts were subsequently held by the Crown and by various lessees and grantees until in 1630 the manor was sold to thirteen inhabitants of the town.[52] In 1636 the so-called 'Bridlington town deed' was drawn up, constituting the thirteen inhabitants as feoffees to act on behalf of all the townsmen, with the help of twelve assistants. When the feoffees were reduced by death to six their number was to be made up from the assistants and new assistants were to be elected.[53] One of the thirteen feoffees was regarded as the 'chief lord' and each year he took a lease of the manor from the other feoffees to hold in trust.[54] The feoffees were empowered by the town deed to collect pier-rates, and in the 18th century these were paid over to the commissioners appointed to administer the harbour Acts.[55]

There are few surviving court rolls before the date of the town's purchase of the manor: they exist for only 1619 and 1622–4.[56] From 1631 to 1829 there is a long, though incomplete, series of rolls.[57] Two courts were held each year in the 17th and early 18th centuries, but thereafter there was usually only one; the meeting-place was still the former priory gatehouse, known as the town's house or town's hall. The enforcement of agricultural and market regulations, the prevention of nuisances in the streets and elsewhere, and the maintenance of order among the inhabitants provided much work for the earlier courts, but in the 18th century little business was recorded. The common oven of the town is several times mentioned in the rolls. It had existed before the Dissolution and was repaired soon after;[58] all inhabitants were obliged to use it under the terms of the deed of 1636, but later they apparently paid compositions to use their own ovens.[59]

A host of officers was appointed at the courts: in 1638, for example, 4 constables, 4 quay (or pier) wardens, 2 bread and butter weighers, 2 ale-finers, 4 market searchers (2 for flesh and 2 for leather), 2 channel sweepers, and a pinder were chosen, and there were also bylawmen, though not appointed at that particular court. Some officers served for either Bridlington (i.e. the Old Town) or the Quay. Thus in 1668 one of the 4 constables and one of the 5 quay wardens were for the Quay; and of the 7 bylawmen 3 were for the open fields, 3 for the Moor, and one for the Quay. The remaining officers chosen that year were 4 affeerors, a neatherd, a swineherd, and all the others who had been appointed in 1638. There were also up to 10 viewers and triers of leather. The numbers of some officers were variable, but few additional posts were filled: surveyors of highways are, however, sometimes recorded, as in

---

[38] 'Annals of Bridlington', vol. 1, before p. 1; Brit. Tpt. Hist. Rec. (York), Y.N.M. 4/8.
[39] O.S. Map 60" (1853).
[40] Ibid. 25" (1893); K. Hoole, *Regional Hist. of Rlys. of Gt. Brit.* iv (*The North-East*), 57.
[41] B.R. (York), architect's dept., B. 64/70/193.
[42] 'Annals of Bridlington', vol. 4, p. 17.
[43] B.R. (York), arch. dept., B. 64/70/190.
[44] 'Annals of Bridlington', vol. 13, pp. 6, 105–6; *Gateway*, Winter 1949, 10; O.S. Map 25" (1893, 1911).
[45] 'Annals of Bridlington', vol. 29, p. 135; B.R. (York), arch. dept., E. 66/70/211.
[46] *Cal. Chart. R.* 1300–26, 187.
[47] Ibid. 1341–1417, 331–2.
[48] Ibid. 1427–1516, 67, 120.
[49] e.g. *Yorks. Inq.* iv. 85.
[50] *Archaeologia*, xix. 271.
[51] Lords Feoffees' Rec., Bayle, Bridlington.
[52] See p. 44.
[53] The deed is printed in Purvis, *Bridlington Charters, etc.* 86–105.
[54] There are many of these among the Lords Feoffees' Rec.
[55] See p. 48.
[56] All the court rolls are among the Lords Feoffees' Rec. Transcripts of several rolls, and extracts from and abstracts of other rolls and court papers, are printed in Purvis, op. cit. 229–99. The following account is largely based on Purvis.
[57] They are listed in Purvis, op. cit. 210–11.
[58] *Miscellanea*, iii (Y.A.S. Rec. Ser. lxxx), 3, 48–9.
[59] Purvis, op. cit. 97, 266, 272.

1702 when three were chosen. Some constables' accounts survive from c. 1640 to 1670.[60]

Although there are no court rolls after 1829, the subsequent proceedings of the court are recorded in jury books covering the period 1805–83. These contain lists of fines and a succession of 'views' by which the jury arbitrated in disputes concerning boundaries, trespass, and nuisances. It became known as the 'muck middens jury'. The last jury was sworn and the last view recorded at a court held in 1883, though there is a separate list of amercements for 1888.[61] The local government board agreed to take over the lords feoffees' pinfolds at Bridlington and the Quay in 1886.[62] The work of the feoffees' in administering the town during the 19th century is revealed in their minute and account books[63] and is described elsewhere.[64]

After 1863 the feoffees gradually surrendered their administrative powers to the local government board and to the urban district and borough councils. They retained, however, some of the property of the manor and their income from rents was used for the general good of the town; pier-rates, too, continued to be collected and passed on to the harbour commissioners. In 1864 the total income, excluding pier-rates, was £189 and in 1967 it was over £4,000.[65] Twice-yearly meetings continued to be held at the Bayle in 1970 and the numbers of feoffees and assistants have been maintained as laid down in 1636.[66]

THE VESTRY. Little is known of the work of the vestry before the later 18th century, but there are surviving accounts of the overseers of the poor for 1630–41 as well as for 1760–83[67] and vestry minutes for 1764–1831.[68]

The rate levied by the overseers in the 1630s is not recorded. Their income in 1636[69] included monthly assessments totalling nearly £4, a rent-charge of £2 from Robert Prudom's charity, interest of £1 on the town stock, nearly £5 in benefactions, and 12s. 6d. given by three men 'for [their] drunkenness'. There was £14 in the town stock in 1638–40. Weekly money payments were made to more than 60 people and clothing was given to nearly 30, while 5 boys were put out as apprentices. The average yearly expenditure by the overseers was about £41.

In the 1760s and 1770s there were three overseers of the poor. A poor-rate was levied twice a year and it was frequently about 5d. in the pound. Thus rates of 5d. raised about £67 in the Old Town and £11 in the Quay in 1760, and £81 in the Old Town and £13 in the Quay in 1780. Much of the money was spent on out-relief but the workhouse, or 'town's house', is frequently mentioned.

The workhouse, standing beside Church Green, is first mentioned in 1743, when two newly-built houses were leased for the purpose.[70] When the Bridlington poor law union was formed in 1836 the owner of the parish workhouse would not allow it to be altered for use by the union. In 1847–8 a new workhouse, designed by Charles Tilney of York, was built on Marton Road; it consisted of a long two-storeyed range in yellow brick, with two entrance lodges. It catered for more than 30 townships comprising the union, but from a third to a half of the inmates were generally from Bridlington.[71]

There is little record of the work of the parish surveyors of highways, but the surveyor in 1732 was allowed to raise an assessment of £33; his expenses between July 1730 and July 1731 had amounted to £19.[72] Churchwardens' accounts for 1669 show the contribution of all eight townships to the Bridlington assessment.[73] The church-rate in 1637, like the constables' rate in 1646, consisted of 4d. for each house or cottage, 6d. for each bovate of demesne land, 4d. for each bovate of town land, 4d. for each cow, and 8d. for every 20 sheep.[74]

The vestry minutes show the way in which, in the later 18th century, the church-rate was apportioned among the townships in the parish. The Old Town and the Quay were assessed together; Sewerby paid a third of the Bridlington assessment; Buckton, Speeton, and Grindale each paid half the Sewerby assessment; Easton and Hilderthorpe each paid a fifth of the Sewerby assessment; Wilsthorpe paid half the Easton assessment; and Auburn paid a fifth of the Wilsthorpe assessment. There were normally four churchwardens—three for Bridlington and the other sometimes for the Quay, sometimes for one or other of Easton, Hilderthorpe, or Wilsthorpe.

THE TOWN COUNCIL. In 1863 the Local Government Act of 1858 was adopted and a local board established for the township of Bridlington, including the Old Town and the Quay.[75] It consisted at first of nine elected representatives, among them Thomas Prickett as chairman, with a clerk and a treasurer; three additional members were elected after 1877, when parts of Sewerby, Bessingby, and Hilderthorpe were annexed to the board's district. The district was further extended in 1894. The first board meetings were held in the corn exchange, but rented rooms in High Street were used from 1864 until 1893, when meetings were transferred to the Victoria Rooms. Of the original nine board members at least five were already feoffees; subsequently it was not unusual for men to be members of both bodies and several board members were also harbour commissioners. Thomas Prickett (d. 1885), for example, was the board's chairman for over 14 years and was a long-serving feoffee and harbour commissioner.[76]

Much of the board's time was devoted to improvements to sea defences, promenades, and sewerage,[77]

---

[60] Ibid. 144–56.
[61] Ibid. 299–309.
[62] Bridlington Town Hall, loc. govt. bd. mins., vol. 5, pp. 13–14.
[63] Min. bks. 1804 onwards, acct. bks. 1794 onwards: Lords Feoffees' Rec.
[64] See p. 64 sqq.
[65] Char. Com. files.
[66] See e.g. 'Annals of Bridlington', vols. 20, p. 84; 57, p. 116.
[67] Lords Feoffees' Rec., Bayle, Bridlington.
[68] Par. Recs., in vestry.
[69] Most of the acct. for this year is printed in Purvis, *Bridlington Charters, etc.* 157–61.

[70] E.R.R.O., DDLG/5/44.
[71] E.R.R.O., Bridlington poor law union min. bks., *passim*.
[72] E.R.R.O., QSF Mich. 1737, C. 26–7.
[73] Purvis, op. cit. 146–7. [74] Lords Feoffees' Rec.
[75] The following paragraphs are based on the board's minutes, in Bridlington Town Hall; 'Notes on Work of Bridlington Loc. Govt. Bd.' (for the period 1863–77) (MS. notebk. in Bridlington Pub. Libr.); and W. Taylor, *Brief Hist. of Bridlington Loc. Bd.*
[76] Loc. govt. bd. mins., vol. 4, p. 367; 'Annals of Bridlington', vol. 9, p. 70. [77] See pp. 59–60, 65.

and among the early committees appointed were the sanitary, improvement, and parade committees. Considerable attention was also given to the cleansing, repair, drainage, and lighting of the streets, as well as to road improvements.[78] The board took over the work of the former highways board and of the gas inspectors, and committees were formed for highways and for watching and lighting. The inspection of plans for new houses began in 1864, and steps were taken the same year to control hackney carriages, pleasure boats, bathing machines, and common lodging-houses. A special committee was also formed to deal with nuisances ranging from the dropping of orange peel to the making of artificial manure. The office of surveyor and clerk of works was created in 1877, incorporating the work of the surveyor of new buildings and the inspector of nuisances. A medical officer of health was first appointed in 1872. While much of the board's work was of an uncontroversial nature, there was lengthy dispute over the major questions of sea defences and sewerage, and on these and other matters the board was frequently in conflict with the town feoffees and the harbour commissioners, as well as with private landowners.

From the beginning the board levied a regular general district rate, as well as an occasional highway rate. In 1865 the board's area was divided into two rating districts, broadly corresponding to the Quay and the Old Town, and these each raised in addition an 'improvement rate' in the ratio of three to one. Large loans, raised on security of the rates, were nevertheless necessary to enable improvements to be carried out, and by 1870 the board's loan debt amounted to £38,900. The system was changed in 1877 when additional areas were annexed to the board's district and one general district rate was levied everywhere; there was great controversy about the equity of this arrangement. At the end of its existence the board had a debt of £3,000.

Under the Local Government Act of 1894 the board became the urban district council, holding its first meeting in the Victoria Rooms in January 1895.[79] The new council had fifteen members, including most of the last members of the board, and its first chairman was G. G. O. Sutcliffe. The board's committees were continued.

In 1899 the urban district council's desire for incorporation was satisfied and the town became a borough. It was divided into three wards, Bridlington, Hilderthorpe, and Quay, each of which was to have two aldermen and six councillors. Many of the old councillors were elected to the new council and the first mayor was Robert Medforth. When the boundaries were extended in 1923 the number of wards was increased to six: Old Town East, Old Town West, Hilderthorpe South, Hilderthorpe North, Quay South, and Quay North.[80] In 1950 Hilderthorpe North and South were replaced by Hilderthorpe and Bessingby wards.[81] The numbers of aldermen and councillors have remained unchanged.

The Victoria Rooms continued to be the meeting-place of the town council until 1932, but most corporation departments were transferred in 1925 when White Lodge, an early-Victorian villa on Quay Road,[82] was brought into use as corporation offices. Eventually an imposing new town hall, designed in the neo-Georgian style by P. M. Newton, the borough architect, and built of red brick with lavish stone dressings and a central cupola, was erected on the site of White Lodge and opened in 1932.[83]

The officers of the new council included a part-time borough treasurer until 1927, when the office became full-time, but from 1900 until 1918 the town clerk was also borough accountant and a separate accountant was appointed from 1918 to 1927.[84] The first borough architect was appointed in 1931.[85] In addition to the general increase in its activities as the town developed,[86] the corporation also acted as a Part III local education authority from 1903 until 1944.[87] Among the corporation departments several have been concerned with the promotion of the resort and the conduct of entertainment there. The Spa and the Parade were run by separate committees until 1946, when they came under the control of a new entertainments committee. Publicity was conducted by the town clerk's department until 1946 and then by a separate committee until 1962; it has since been the concern of a combined entertainments and publicity committee.[88]

BRIDLINGTON BOROUGH. *Per pale sable and argent, three Gothic capital letters B counterchanged, on a silver embattled chief, two bars wavy azure.*

The insignia of the borough include the mayor's chain and badge, acquired in 1899, the mayoress's chain, presented in 1930, and the mace, given in 1936. Arms were assumed in 1899 and granted in 1934.[89]

CHURCHES. The church of Bridlington is first mentioned in 1086.[90] It was given to the priory which was established there, probably in 1113,[91] by Walter de Gant. No vicarage was ordained and the

---

[78] See p. 65.
[79] The following paragraphs are based on the U.D.C. minutes, in the Town Hall, and the printed borough council minutes, in Bridlington Pub. Libr.
[80] 13 and 14 Geo. V, c. 44.
[81] Bridlington Corp. *Counc. Proc. and Cttee. Mins.* 1950–1, 429.
[82] It had previously been known as Rose Cottage and Roseville: O.S. Map 60″ (1854); 25″ (1893).
[83] 'Annals of Bridlington', vol. 49, p. 132.
[84] F. A. Slim and H. L. Gee, *Bridlington, 1899–1949*, [38].
[85] Bridlington Corp. *Counc. Proc. and Cttee. Mins.* 1930–1, 994.
[86] See pp. 64–6. [87] See p. 78.
[88] Bridlington Corp., *Year Bks.*; Slim and Gee, op. cit. [63].
[89] 'Annals of Bridlington', vols. 16, p. 209; 47, p. 131; 52, p. 133; 53, p. 313.
[90] *V.C.H. Yorks.* ii. 197.
[91] *E.Y.C.* ii, pp. 427–8; *Y.A.J.* xxix. 241–2.

church was served by a parochial chaplain provided by the priory.[92] Such a chaplain is first mentioned in 1346;[93] in 1525–6 his net income was £5 a year, and six other chaplains in the church each received £4.[94] There were medieval chapels in the parish at Buckton, Grindale, Sewerby, and Speeton, all but Buckton becoming separate parishes in modern times.[95] Bempton, too, was a chapelry of Bridlington, but it attained parochial status in the 15th century.[96] After the Dissolution the church at Bridlington was served by curates,[97] and it remained a perpetual curacy until the mid 19th century.[98] By 1872 it was styled a vicarage and in 1881 it became a rectory.[99]

After the Dissolution the 'advowson' of Bridlington was mistakenly referred to in a Crown grant to the archbishop of York in 1558,[1] but the grant in any case presumably lapsed on the accession of Elizabeth I. Curates were probably chosen by the impropriators until 1768, when the patronage was assigned to the Revd. Matthew Buck, in consideration of a donation to the living,[2] and it later passed to his brother Samuel. After Samuel Buck's death in 1806 the advowson was held by his daughters Anne and Catherine and their respective husbands Sir Francis Wood and the Revd. Alexander Cooke.[3] In 1835 Wood and Cooke sold the advowson to the Revd. Charles Simeon,[4] whose trustees still held it in 1969.

After the Dissolution the incumbent received a stipend of £8 from the impropriator,[5] and it continued to be paid in the 17th, 18th, and 19th centuries. Fees amounted to £15 in the late 17th century[6] and in 1696 Henry Cowton devised 5s. a week out of land in Bridlington, Sewerby, and Marton for the incumbent to preach a sermon and read prayers on Wednesdays;[7] £13 a year was normally received for this sermon.[8]

The living was augmented from Queen Anne's Bounty in 1747 and 1769, each time with £200, and in 1817 with £600; a parliamentary grant of £1,200 was given in 1812.[9] The augmentation of 1769 was to meet a benefaction of £200 given by the Revd. Matthew Buck.[10] The average net value of the living in 1829–31 was £143 a year.[11] An endowment of £7 a year was given in 1868 and increased to £230 a year in 1869.[12] In 1884 the net income was £350.[13]

At inclosure in 1771 the curate received an allotment of 1 a. in lieu of a sheaf of barley from each bovate in the township.[14] Glebe land at Keldholme (in Kirkbymoorside, Yorks. N.R.) had been bought with Bounty money by 1764, and more at Bonwick (in Skipsea) by 1777. By 1825 more grant money had been spent on land at Beeford,[15] and by 1889 there was said to be 66 a. of glebe.[16] Some of the land was sold in 1918.[17] In the 18th century curates rented a house in Bridlington in which to live.[18] There was no parsonage house until 1850–1, when a large, grey-brick, building was erected in Well Lane; £1,000 was given in 1862 to meet the cost.[19] A new Rectory was built near the church in 1970.

There is no record of chantries in the church, but a tailors' light in the nave was mentioned in 1535,[20] and guilds of the Virgin and the Holy Trinity are recorded in the late 15th century.[21] Two 'guild houses' and land belonging to the former guild were in 1548 granted by the Crown to Michael Stanhope and John Bellow.[22] Five bovates formerly belonging to Holy Trinity guild were included in the 16th-century leases of the manor; they were nevertheless granted to Sir Francis Knowles in 1590 and sold by him the same year to John Stanhope. In 1594 Stanhope granted 2 of these bovates to Robert Collinson and it was apparently all 5 bovates which Collinson conveyed to John Moore in 1619.[23] In 1721 Christopher Moore's widow Anne Routh devised the land to Elizabeth Weeton, with remainder to Beverley corporation. The corporation held it from c. 1740 until 1919, when it was sold to the East Riding county council.[24]

An assistant curate is first mentioned in 1871 and there has subsequently normally been one, though there were two in 1936.[25]

A Puritan influence in the town may have been exercised by Sir Matthew Boynton. William Crashaw, curate early in the 17th century and later vicar of Burton Agnes, was a Puritan, and in 1634 the Bridlington churchwardens, along with those of Barmston and Burton Agnes, were questioned about the preachers using their pulpits.[26] Later in the century a Presbyterian, William Luck, was ejected from the living.[27]

Services were held at St. Mary's twice on Sundays and Wednesdays, and once on Fridays, in 1743; communion was administered once a month to between 50 and 70 people.[28] By 1764 the only service was on Wednesdays.[29] In 1851 there were three on Sundays[30] but in the 1860s two services were held on Sundays and one on Wednesdays.[31] By

[92] The priory's right to serve the church by a stipendiary priest was confirmed in 1310: *Reg. Greenfield*, iii (Sur. Soc. cli), 173.
[93] *Yorks. Deeds*, ix. 162–3.
[94] *Y.A.J.* xxiv. 77.
[95] See pp. 85, 89, 99, 103.
[96] See p. 14.
[97] B.I.H.R., C.P., H. 4159; TER. J. Bridlington 1749 etc.; Bp. 4A/19, 20; *Fasti Parochiales*, iii. 7.
[98] *Rep. Com. Eccl. Revenues*, 922–3; White, *Dir. Hull & York.* (1858), 666.
[99] Par. Recs., memorandum bk. of work done, 1846 onwards; *Kelly's Dir. N. & E.R. Yorks.* (1872), 331.
[1] *Cal. Pat.* 1557–8, 420.
[2] Lawton, *Rer. Eccles. Dioc. Ebor.* ii. 289.
[3] Registry of Deeds, Beverley, DU/335/392; *Rep. Com. Eccl. Revenues*, 922–3; Baines, *Hist. Yorks.* ii. 171.
[4] Regy. of Deeds, EZ/395/398.
[5] *L. & P. Hen. VIII*, xiv (2), p. 78.
[6] B.I.H.R., TER. J. Bridlington n.d. etc.; Purvis, *Bridlington Charters, etc.* 40.
[7] *9th Rep. Char. Com.* 727.
[8] B.I.H.R., TER. J. Bridlington 1716 etc.
[9] Hodgson, *Q.A.B.* 435.
[10] Ibid.; B.I.H.R., TER. J. Bridlington 1770.
[11] *Rep. Com. Eccl. Revenues*, 922–3.
[12] *Lond. Gaz.* 1 May 1868, p. 2500; 30 Apr. 1869, p. 2557.
[13] B.I.H.R., Bp. V. 1884/Ret.
[14] Regy. of Deeds, AN/121/11.
[15] B.I.H.R., TER. J. Bridlington 1764, 1777, 1825.
[16] *Kelly's Dir. N. & E.R. Yorks.* (1889), 346.
[17] Regy. of Deeds, 190/563/487; 191/112/90.
[18] B.I.H.R., Bp. V. 1764/Ret. 89; *Herring's Visit.* i. 113.
[19] *Lond. Gaz.* 22 July 1862, p. 3652; *Hull Advertiser*, 26 Apr. 1850; White, *Dir. Hull & York* (1858), 666.
[20] B.I.H.R., Prob. Reg. xi, f.193.
[21] Ibid. iv, ff. 218, 236.
[22] *Cal. Pat.* 1548–9, 38.
[23] E.R.R.O., DDBV/8/1,8; Purvis, *Bridlington Charters, etc.* 39.
[24] Regy. of Deeds, 195/337/298; *10th Rep. Char. Com.* (H.C. 103), pp. 683–4 (1824), xiii.
[25] B.I.H.R., V. 1871/Ret. 76; Bp. V. 1936/Ret. 268.
[26] R. A. Marchant, *Puritans and the Ch. Courts in Dioc. York, 1560–1642*, 122, 241–2.
[27] See p. 75.
[28] *Herring's Visit.* i. 113.
[29] B.I.H.R., Bp. V. 1764/Ret. 89.
[30] H.O. 129/24/524.
[31] B.I.H.R., V. 1865/Ret. 79; V. 1868/Ret. 77.

1871 there was an additional Sunday service, and by 1877 another was held in a licensed room.[32] In 1884 there were three services on Sundays, one on Wednesdays, and one on Fridays, with a weekly mission service in the school-room.[33] The number of communicants at the monthly communions in the 1860s was about forty, and about the same number received the twice-monthly communions in 1871. By 1877 communion was administered weekly to about twenty people. In 1969 there were three and sometimes four services each Sunday.

A Methodist chapel in St. John Street was acquired for use as the Priory Church Institute in 1885[34] and renovated in 1894,[35] when there were also two mission rooms in the parish.[36] The Institute was sold in 1958[37] and the church rooms in 1969 were on Church Green.

The church of ST. MARY THE VIRGIN, generally known as the Priory Church, is a large and imposing building, entirely constructed of stone, and with the exception of the gatehouse is all that remains of Bridlington priory.[38] The present church is the nave of the medieval priory church and it was used for parochial purposes even before the Dissolution. The crossing and central tower, the transepts, and the chancel of the medieval church have all been demolished, along with the conventual buildings of the priory. The existing church is an aisled building, 185 ft. long and of ten bays, the three easternmost bays being used as the chancel. The post-Reformation east wall is set obliquely across the end of the chancel, reflecting the northward slant of the banished eastern half of the priory church. At the south-east angle are indications of the former transept and along the south wall some traces of the cloister which adjoined the medieval nave. The north porch has survived, together with parts of the two western towers which stand above the most westerly bays of the existing aisles.[39]

Little is left of the Norman church, though it has been suggested that the lowest courses of stone in the north-west tower and at the west end of the north wall are of that period.[40] The church was rebuilt in the 13th century, apparently in several stages; the final stage shows characteristics of the Decorated style and may have been completed very early in the 14th century.[41] The only later medieval work is at the south-west corner of the church which, with the west end of the nave, was rebuilt or remodelled in the 15th century.

Rebuilding of the nave evidently started at the north-west corner. The round-headed west doorway of the tower and the jambs of the window above are of the early 13th century; the upper part of the tower is of later date. The outer wall of the north aisle, with boldly projecting gabled buttresses and lancet windows, was built about the middle of the 13th century. There are indications that the length of wall east of the porch, where some of the lancets are paired, was the last to be completed. The vaulted porch has a modern superstructure, but the interior contains the most elaborate Early English work in the church. The side walls are lined with trefoil-headed arcading and both the outer arch and the inner doorway are richly moulded. Most of the capitals are carved with foliage but those to the jamb-shafts east of the doorway have the heads of a king, a queen, and perhaps an archbishop.[42] Inside the church the north and south arcades, with their composite piers and deeply-moulded arches of three orders, are part of the mid-13th-century rebuilding.[43] In the west bay of the north aisle, however, the pier and responds supporting the tower may be of slightly earlier date. The three piers at the west end of the south aisle were altered in the 15th century. Surviving shafts and springers in both aisles suggest that stone vaulting was intended but never carried out.

The triforium and clerestory above the north arcade mark the next building phase, dating from the later 13th century. The clerestory windows and the arched bays of the triforium below are all of four lights, their heads filled with Geometrical tracery. On the south side the work may be slightly later. Only five original clerestory windows survive, that at the east end being blocked and the three west windows being of 15th-century date. The five windows have similar tracery to those opposite but are much taller. There is no proper triforium but 15th-century arcaded screens form a shallow gallery across the windows below transom level. The south aisle dates largely from c. 1300. Its form was dictated by the contiguity of the conventual buildings. Only the five eastern bays have windows, set high to clear the roof of the cloister which ran below them. The two elaborate doorways which survive originally led from the cloister into the aisle. Further west, where the west range of the cloister joined the church, there are no aisle windows and a few traces of the range are still visible.[44] In the late 13th or early 14th centuries at least two more stages were added to the north-west tower and it may have been completed to its full height at this period. The windows, including that above the west doorway with earlier jambs, have Geometrical tracery and there is wall arcading in the Decorated style at the second stage. The carved band which ornaments the parapets above the nave clerestories is continued round the tower and is evidently of the same date.

It is possible that some such catastrophe as the fall of the south-west tower may account for its rebuilding, and the modification of adjacent parts of the church, in the 15th century. The west doorway of the tower has an ogee canopy and is flanked by wall arcading which is carried round the buttresses. The two stages above have Perpendicular windows

---

[32] B.I.H.R., V. 1871/Ret. 76; V. 1877/Ret.
[33] Ibid., Bp. V. 1884/Ret.
[34] 'Annals of Bridlington', vols. 9, p. 85; 10, p. 2.
[35] Ibid. 14, p. 53.
[36] B.I.H.R., Bp. V. 1894/Ret.
[37] Char. Com. files.
[38] See plate facing p. 192. For details of the demolished parts of the priory church and conventual buildings see p. 45.
[39] For the existing church see M. Prickett. Hist. Ch. Bridlington (1836 edn.) with 7 plates and a plan; J. W. Lamb, Guide to Bridlington Priory Ch. (revised edn., c. 1955); Morris, E. Yorks, 115–18.

[40] Lamb, Guide, 13, 20.
[41] The former choir appears to have contained many lancet windows (Archaeologia, xix. 272), suggesting that the banished eastern half of the church also dated from the 13th century; rebuilding of the whole fabric may thus have been almost continuous for close on 100 years.
[42] It has been suggested that the heads commemorate the visit to York in 1251 of Henry III and Queen Eleanor for the marriage of Alexander III and Margaret by Archbp. Gray: Lamb, Guide, 13.
[43] See plate facing p. 193.
[44] For further details of the monastic remains on the south side of the church see p. 45.

and more wall arcading; the top-most stage is a 19th-century addition. The most dramatic of the 15th-century alterations was the reconstruction of the west wall of the nave, its upper part almost entirely filled with a huge Perpendicular window, 55 ft. high, 27 ft. wide, and of nine lights.[45] Below it externally is elaborate arcading and a richly-moulded central doorway under a crocketed canopy. A curious feature of the window is that above transom level the glass and tracery are set inwards by about 9 ins. Internally the transom rests on an arcaded stone screen which runs across the base of the window and helps to support the mullions and tracery above. Other 15th-century work in the church includes the somewhat similar screens which take the place of a triforium across the earlier clerestory windows on the south side. The three most westerly windows of the clerestory are entirely of the 15th century and at the same period the corresponding piers of the arcade below were rebuilt or refaced and ornamented with Perpendicular panelling; the 13th-century western respond has survived.

At the east end of the church the western arch of the former crossing was walled in after the Dissolution. The two east windows then inserted were replaced in 1862 by the present Geometrical window.[46] Massive buttresses enclose the two western piers of the former tower, one of which contains a spiral staircase. The arches at the east ends of both existing arcades have been distorted, presumably by the thrust formerly exerted by the great central tower, despite the fact that their piers are of extra size. An internal buttress against the north-west pier of the crossing was evidently built as an attempt to counteract this pressure.

The church was extensively restored in the 19th century. A loft was erected in 1808 at the request of an innkeeper at the Quay, who wanted it for his summer visitors.[47] This was presumably the 'Quay Loft', on the north side of the church, which was taken down and rebuilt in 1823.[48] Preparations for the restoration of the west window of the nave, the west front, and part of the roof began in 1846 and the work was done in 1848. The rest of the roof was renewed and the church repewed in 1855–8. Together with various other renovations, these works were supervised first by Edmund Sharpe and afterwards by G. G. (later Sir Gilbert) Scott.[49]

More restoration was carried out in the 1860s. At this time the west front of the church presented a curiously unfinished appearance. The flanking towers, of markedly different design, were in poor condition and reached no higher than the clerestory parapets.[50] Either they had never been completed to their intended height before the Dissolution or the top stages had subsequently been removed. The stump of the south tower was crowned with 'a paltry octagonal turret of brickwork', placed there about the middle of the 18th century to house three new bells.[51] In 1875–6 Scott restored the west front and added top storeys to both towers, in each case repeating the style of the work below. The elaborate belfry stage of the south tower has lofty Perpendicular windows, crocketed buttresses, wall arcading, and an ornate parapet with angle and intermediate pinnacles.[52] Restoration of the church, which included the replacement of the upper storey of the north porch, continued until 1884.[53]

The medieval church furnishings were apparently dispersed at the Dissolution. A screen probably went to Flamborough, where it still survives.[54] Bench-ends, the work of the 'Ripon school' of wood-carvers, are now in Leake and Over Silton (Yorks. N.R.) churches. Two of them have been copied for the 20th-century stalls at Bridlington: they are the stalls of John Hampton (prior 1510–21) and Peter Hardy (sub-prior).[55] The pulpit was erected in 1850, with additions in 1960. The 19th-century reredos is of Caen stone. The font, of Frosterley marble, probably dates from the 14th century. Fragments of carved stone from the medieval priory, including parts of a 12th-century cloister arcade,[56] are housed in the aisles.

There are four noteworthy tombstones. In the south aisle is a black slab of Tournai marble, which was perhaps the tomb cover of Walter de Gant, the founder of the priory. It is carved in flat relief with representations of a church, a lion, two dragons, and a fox and a bird drinking from a jug.[57] Near by are incised slabs to Robert Charder, a canon (d. 1535), and Robert Burstwick, prior (d. 1493).[58] In the north aisle is a much-decorated blue slab to William Bower (d. 1671), which records his foundation of a knitting school.[59]

There are many monumental stones and brasses, including those to James Hebblethwaite (the impropriator, d. 1773), Cornelius Rickaby (curate, d. 1786), and various members of the Creyke, Greame, Rickaby, and Prickett families. That of John Greame (d. 1798) is by Fisher of York, and those of John Greame (d. 1841) and Yarburgh Yarburgh (d. 1856) are by Skelton of York. Other 18th-century monuments are by Pycock of Hull (1787, 1788), and 19th-century monuments include several by the Earles (1803, 1813, 1840) and W. D. Keyworth (1848) of Hull.

Miscellaneous items of note include a medieval stone offertory box with a bracket for an image near by, and a carved pedestal and holy water stoup, near another bracket, all in the chancel; a fragment of a carving of the crucifixion and a pre-Reformation wooden money box, both in the south aisle; an Elizabethan iron chest, in the nave; and the Royal Arms of Anne and ten hatchments of local families, in the aisles. The first organ was installed in 1789 to replace a quartet of instruments, and new organs were erected in 1834 and 1899.

The priory church had seven bells in the central

---

[45] cf. the design of the great E. and W. windows at Beverley Minster, the former dating from c. 1416: *Test. Ebor.* iii. 57.
[46] T. Allen, *Hist. Yorks.* iv. 9; Par. rec., Memorandum bk. of work done, 1846 onwards (in vestry).
[47] *Y.A.J.* xxxvii. 193–4; Lawton, *Rer. Eccles. Dioc. Ebor.* 289.
[48] Par. rec., Vestry min. bk. 1805–31.
[49] Ibid. Schedule of work (1846); Plan for reseating (n.d.); Mem. bk. of work done; *Hull Advertiser*, 17 Oct. 1857.
[50] See plate facing p. 192.
[51] Allen, *Hist. Yorks.* iv. 8.
[52] It was perhaps inspired by the 15th-cent. W. towers of Beverley Minster.
[53] Par. rec., Mem. bk. of work done; B.I.H.R., FAC. 1876/1; Bp. V. 1884/Ret.
[54] See p. 162.
[55] *Y.A.J.* xxix. 160, 163–5.
[56] See p. 45 and see plate facing p. 193.
[57] Prickett, *Hist. Ch. Bridlington*, plates, no. [8]; *Y.A.J.* xlii. 334, fig.
[58] The latter's coffin was found on the site of the S. transept in 1821: Prickett, op. cit. 27.
[59] See p. 79.

tower.[60] Later, the parish church had only three, and in 1764 these were sold and replaced by three new ones, made by James Harrison of Barrow;[61] one of these was recast in 1783.[62] In 1902 eight bells made by Taylors of Loughborough were installed.[63] The medieval church plate was confiscated at the Dissolution.[64] New plate was bought in 1788[65] but subsequently stolen, and all the surviving plate is modern. A silver chalice was given by Frances Cottrell-Dormer in 1880, another by Thomas Prickett in 1885, and a silver paten by Robert Medforth in 1885.[66]

The registers begin in 1564 and are complete except for marriages between 1619 and 1633. All the earlier registers include entries for the various townships in the parish.[67]

The churchyard was enlarged in 1813 by the addition of land on the south and east sides of the church,[68] and it was enclosed by a wall in 1854.[69] It was again extended in 1863[70] but was largely closed in 1884.[71]

The church and churchyard benefit from the charities of Mary Tassell (by will proved in 1910), who gave £200, Alice North (1931), who gave £300, A. L. Barnes-Lawrence (1934), and Thomas Prickett (1935), as well as from a fund established in 1884 and another founded at an unknown date.[72]

Christ Church, in Quay Road, was consecrated in 1841 as a chapel-of-ease to St. Mary's[73] and a district chapelry was assigned to it out of St. Mary's parish in 1843.[74] It was described as a perpetual curacy in 1857,[75] but by 1872 it was styled a vicarage.[76] The patron was and remains the incumbent of St. Mary's. The parish was enlarged in 1870, when a small part of Sewerby and Marton was included in it, and again in 1924, when a part of St. Mary's parish was transferred to it.[77]

The church was endowed with £40 a year in 1843[78] and by 1851 7 a. of glebe in Bridlington had been acquired. The total income in 1851 was £153, of which £90 was from pew rents.[79] A further endowment of £33 a year was given in 1876,[80] and in 1884 the net value of the living was £237 a year.[81] The church benefits from the charities of Mary Riby (by will proved in 1883), who gave £500, Thomas Gray (1921), who gave £100, and Sarah Hobson (1925), who devised a house.[82] A grant towards a parsonage house was given in 1843, and by 1857 a house had been built behind the church.[83]

In the 19th century two services were held each Sunday and another on Thursdays during the season at the resort.[84] In 1874 the mission church of St. Hilda was built in Thorpe Street, Hilderthorpe, and it was enlarged in 1899. Two services were held there each Sunday in summer, one at other times, in 1894. By 1905 it was no longer used for worship[85] and it subsequently became part of Hilderthorpe school. In the 20th century there has been an assistant curate.[86]

CHRIST CHURCH was built on a site given by John Rickaby to designs by Scott (later Sir Gilbert Scott) and Moffatt.[87] It is of stone, in the Early English style, and consists of chancel, nave, aisles, and west tower. Enlargements were carried out in 1851 and a spire was added to the tower in 1859;[88] six bells were made in 1858–9 by Naylor Vickers & Co. of Sheffield.[89] A new peal of eight tubular bells was made by Harrington and Latham of Coventry in 1901.[90] The church contains a 14th-century font with a carved 17th-century cover, both brought from York Minster.[91] A parish room, called the Wycliffe Room, was built in 1884[92] and a church hall in 1911.[93]

Holy Trinity Church, in the Promenade, was consecrated in 1871 as a chapel-of-ease to Christ Church,[94] and a consolidated chapelry was assigned to it out of Christ Church parish in 1874.[95] It was styled a vicarage and is in the patronage of the archbishops of York.[96]

The church was endowed with £46-odd in 1877[97] and by 1884 the living was worth £300 net.[98] The minister also benefits from the charity of Mary Holiday (by will proved in 1913), who gave £300.[99] A Vicarage was built in Tennyson Avenue in 1892–3.[1]

In 1877 two services were held each Sunday, with a third in summer to meet the needs of visitors. By 1884 there were three services every Sunday and one on Wednesdays, with extra services in the season: the average congregation was said to be increased from 500 to 1,100 in summer. By 1900 there was an assistant curate.[2]

The church of *HOLY TRINITY* was built largely at the cost of the Revd. Y. G. Lloyd Greame of Sewerby to designs by Smith and Brodrick of Hull.[3] It is of stone, in a late-13th-century style, and

---

[60] Prickett, op. cit. 108.
[61] Par. rec., Vestry min. bk. 1764–1804 (in vestry); Boulter, 'Ch. Bells', 215.
[62] Par. rec., Vestry min. bk. 1764–1804.
[63] Lamb, *Guide*, 27.
[64] *L. & P. Hen. VIII*, xii (2), p. 53.
[65] Par. rec., Vestry min. bk. 1764–1804.
[66] *Yorks. Ch. Plate*, i. 227.
[67] For separate township registers see pp. 90, 104.
[68] B.I.H.R., CD. 66; Par. rec., Vestry min. bk. 1805–31.
[69] Par. rec., Mem. bk. of work done, 1846 onwards.
[70] Sheahan and Whellan, *Hist. York & E.R.* ii. 450.
[71] Par. rec., Mem. bk. of work done.
[72] Char. Com. files.
[73] B.I.H.R., CD. 198; H.O. 129/24/524.
[74] *Lond. Gaz.* 26 May 1843, p. 1742.
[75] B.I.H.R., TER. J. Bridlington 1857.
[76] *Kelly's Dir. N. & E.R. Yorks.* (1872), 331.
[77] York Dioc. Regy, Orders in Council 294, 554.
[78] *Lond. Gaz.* 3 Oct. 1843, p. 3216.
[79] H.O. 129/24/524; B.I.H.R., TER. J. Bridlington 1857.
[80] *Lond. Gaz.* 12 May 1876, p. 2927.
[81] B.I.H.R., Bp. V. 1884/Ret.
[82] Char. Com. files.
[83] B.I.H.R., TER. J. Bridlington 1857; *Lond. Gaz.* 3 Oct. 1843, p. 3216.
[84] B.I.H.R., V. 1865/Ret. 80; V. 1868/Ret. 78.
[85] Ibid., Bp. V. 1894/Ret.; Char. Com. files; *Kelly's Dir. N. & E.R. Yorks.* (1905), 448.
[86] B.I.H.R., Bp. V. 1900/Ret. 50; Bp. V. 1936/Ret. 265.
[87] Regy. of Deeds, FP/72/69; *Kelly's Dir. N. & E.R. Yorks.* (1889), 351.
[88] *Hull Advertiser*, 4 July 1851; 2 July 1859.
[89] Boulter, 'Ch. Bells', 215. The 2 bells existing before the spire was built were removed to Flamborough: see below, p. 163.
[90] 'Annals of Bridlington', vol. 18, p. 207.
[91] Ex inf. Sir Nikolaus Pevsner, 1970.
[92] 'Annals of Bridlington', vol. 9, p. 41.
[93] Stone on building.
[94] B.I.H.R., CD. 408.
[95] York Dioc. Regy., Orders in Council 315.
[96] Crockford.
[97] *Lond. Gaz.* 11 May 1877, p. 3088.
[98] B.I.H.R., Bp. V. 1884/Ret.
[99] Char. Com. files.
[1] Bridlington Town Hall, Building Inspector's Office, drawing no. 507.
[2] B.I.H.R., V. 1877/Ret.; Bp. V. 1884/Ret.; Bp. V. 1900/Ret. 51.
[3] 'Annals of Bridlington', vol. 2, p. 4.

consists of chancel, nave, aisles, and north-west tower with spire and pinnacles. There are three bells, presented by the Revd. Lloyd Greame.[4] A parish room was built in 1892–3.[5]

The church of Emmanuel, in Cardigan Road, Hilderthorpe, was opened in 1903 as a chapel-of-ease to Christ Church.[6] It was consecrated in 1916[7] and a district chapelry assigned to it out of Christ Church parish the same year.[8] It was styled a vicarage and is in the patronage of trustees, among them the rector of St. Mary's and the vicar of Christ Church.[9] The parish was enlarged in 1924, when part of Christ Church was transferred to it.[10] A house bought for a Vicarage in 1918 was replaced by another, bought in 1962.[11] The church benefits from the charity of Laura Harcourt, who gave £1,000 in 1890 for mission work in the Hilderthorpe part of the parish.[12]

The church of EMMANUEL was built on a site given by A. G. W. Wright of Bessingby[13] and designed in a simple Gothic style by Brodrick, Lowther, and Walker of Hull.[14] It is built of red brick, with stone and terracotta dressings, and consisted at first of nave, aisles, and temporary chancel. It was completed in 1928, with chancel, tower, vestries, and side chapel, designed by W. S. Walker, Son and Field.[15] A building was bought for a parish hall in 1917, and a new hall was built in 1928.[16]

ROMAN CATHOLICISM. Few recusants were discovered at Bridlington in the 16th to 18th centuries,[17] and when Roman Catholics' houses were searched for arms in 1678 there were only three 'poor houses' to be examined in the town.[18]

There is no reference to organized Roman Catholicism until 1886, when meetings were first held in the Victoria Rooms and then an iron church, dedicated to St. William, was built in Wellington Road. It was designed by J. C. Hawes.[19] It was replaced in 1893–4 by the church of Our Lady and St. Peter, in Victoria Road, designed in a Gothic style by Smith, Brodrick, and Lowther of Hull.[20] It is of red brick with stone dressings and consists of chancel, nave, aisles, and side chapels.

By 1895 a house in Wellington Road was used as a Dominican Convent school.[21] The school moved to a house in High Street about 1930.[22]

PROTESTANT NONCONFORMITY. Early nonconformity in Bridlington was fostered by the teachings of the ejected minister of St. Mary's, William Luck, in the 1660s. The congregation which Luck founded was Presbyterian, and Zion Chapel remained Presbyterian for much of the 18th century. Later the chapel became Independent, perhaps c. 1770 when the views of an Arian minister caused dissention among the congregation. There was a small group of Quakers in the town by the late 1660s, and before the end of the century a Baptist church was also established. Methodism came to be established in Bridlington c. 1770, and Wesleyans and Primitives were the strongest nonconformist churches in the 19th century, when the Friends died out and both the Independents and the Baptists reached a low ebb.

In the late 18th and early 19th centuries various buildings were registered for worship by unidentified groups of dissenters. Some were dwelling houses, as in 1732, 1765, 1771 (two), 1773, 1774, 1800 (two), 1805, and 1822.[23] Others were described as chapels when registered in 1804 and 1812, and two were newly-erected buildings in 1777 and 1833.[24] Several were in makeshift premises: a granary in 1816, a room in the Swan yard in 1820, a malt-kiln in 1821, and the old playhouse at the Quay in 1827.[25]

By tradition the Baptist church in Bridlington began with the conversion of Robert Prudom by a Scotsman sheltering in the harbour on his way home from London, where he had himself been converted. Prudom established the church in 1698 with 22 members[26] and their meeting-place was built in 1699[27] in Applegarth Lane, near St. Mary's Church. Forty-two new members were added before Prudom's death in 1708. The following year David Prudom's house in Bayle Gate, next to the Bayle, was licensed as a meeting-house and it was conveyed to the church in 1714. A chapel was subsequently built on the site to replace the tiny meeting-house in Applegarth Lane.

George Braithwaite became minister in 1713 and 62 people were baptised by him before he moved to London in 1734. A less successful period seems to have been followed, and the church was depleted by the formation of Baptist churches at Hull in 1736 and Scarborough in 1770.[28] Thirty-five Baptist families were reported in 1743, and '26 or more' in 1764.[29] Between 1767 and 1794, however, about ninety members were added, and between 1795 and 1845 about seventy more, despite the opening of other churches at Hunmanby in 1817 and Kilham in 1821.[30] In 1823 the Baptists shared with the Independents the new Union Chapel at the Quay.[31]

---

[4] *Kelly's Dir. N. & E.R. Yorks.* (1889), 352.
[5] B.I.H.R., Bp. V. 1894/Ret.; Bridlington Town Hall, Building Inspector's Office, drawing no. 507.
[6] *Kelly's Dir. N. & E.R. Yorks.* (1905), 448.
[7] York. Dioc. Regy., Sentence of consecration.
[8] Ibid. Orders in Council 514.   [9] Ex inf. the vicar, 1971.
[10] York. Dioc. Regy., Orders in Council 554.
[11] *Kelly's Dir. N. & E.R. Yorks.* (1925), 485; Char. Com. files.   [12] Char. Com. files.
[13] *Kelly's Dir. N. & E.R. Yorks.* (1905), 448.
[14] *The Builder*, 6 Sept. 1902.
[15] *Kelly's Dir. N. & E.R. Yorks.* (1905), 448; (1929), 452; stone on building.
[16] Ibid. (1925), 485; (1933), 420; stone on building.
[17] B.I.H.R., C.P., H. 1608–9; H. Aveling, *Post Reformation Catholicism in E. Yorks. 1558–1790* (E. Yorks. Loc. Hist. Ser. xi), 59.   [18] *Cal. S.P. Dom.* 1678, 479.
[19] 'Annals of Bridlington', vol. 10, p. 27; Bridlington Town Hall, Building Inspector's Office, drawing no. 284; *Kelly's Dir. N. & E.R. Yorks.* (1893), 388.
[20] 'Annals of Bridlington', vols. 13, p. 108; 14, p. 60.
[21] *Cook's Dir. Bridlington* (1895), 75.
[22] 'Annals of Bridlington', vols. 47, p. 197; 49, p. 187.
[23] G.R.O. Worship Returns, Vol. v, nos. 395, 1579–80, 1910, 3672; vii, nos. 44, 47; B.I.H.R., DMH. 1771/27, 30; 1773/19.
[24] G.R.O. Worship Rets., Vol. v, nos. 1879, 2630, 4309; B.I.H.R., DMH. 1777/20.
[25] G.R.O. Worship Rets., Vol. v, nos. 3021, 3431, 3597, 4081.
[26] *Baptists of Yorks.*, ed. C. E. Shipley, 63; R. H. Brennan, *Bridlington Bapt. Ch. 1698–1948*, 4–5.
[27] H.O. 129/24/524. Their register of baptisms begins in 1698: *Lists of Non-parochial Regs. and Recs. in the Custody of the Registrar-General. . . 1859*, 81.
[28] Brennan, *Bapt. Ch.* 7–11, 16, 17.
[29] B.I.H.R., Bp. V. 1764/Ret. 89; *Herring's Visit.* i. 112.
[30] Brennan, *Bapt. Ch.* 13, 17, 18; *Baptists of Yorks.* 207.
[31] Baines, *Hist. Yorks.* ii. 175.

The chapel in Bayle Gate was used until 1873. It was then demolished but the adjoining burial ground, together with the former meeting-house and burial ground in Applegarth Lane, were restored in 1938[32] and still remained in 1969. A new chapel, designed by Samuel Musgrave of Hull in the Gothic style, was built in Quay Road in 1874. It is of white brick, with red-brick and stone dressings, and has 500 sittings.[33]

The chapel benefits from the charities of Henry Dailes (by will dated 1750), George Baron (1842), William Sellar (1846), and Christopher Baron (1851), which had combined assets of £259 in 1937, and of Elizabeth Martin (by will proved in 1926), who gave £600.[34]

By 1669 there was already a group of Friends in Bridlington, meeting in the house of Zachary Smayles.[35] Thenceforth Bridlington was one of the regular meeting-places of the Kelk Monthly Meeting and in the 18th century it became the most frequent, and eventually the sole, meeting-place.[36] One Quaker in 1700 was the prominent merchant Richard Hardcastle.[37] There were said to be thirteen Quaker families in the town in 1743,[38] but fewer in 1764,[39] and in 1773 the remaining members chose to be joined to the Owstwick Monthly Meeting.[40]

Meetings were apparently being held once more by 1828, when a meeting-house existed in St. John Street.[41] Its registration for worship was cancelled in 1861,[42] when the Quakers 'died out',[43] and there seems to have been no meeting-house in the town until 1903, when the present wooden building was erected in Havelock Street on the site of the Society's old burial ground.[44]

Methodism is said to have been introduced into the district by Thomas and William Robinson, who moved to the Quay from North Shields in 1769. John Wesley sought directions from them before his first visit in 1770, when he preached in the Quay to 'many plain and many genteel' people. In 1772 he found the room appointed for his meeting too small, and he eventually moved to the market-house after the ringing of the church bells had obliged him to leave St. Mary's churchyard. Wesley was in Bridlington again, at the Old Town or the Quay, in 1774, 1777, 1779, 1782, 1784, 1786, 1788, and 1790, on the last occasion in Zion Congregational Chapel.[45]

The Methodists had 102 members in Bridlington in 1787 and about 80 in 1788–91.[46]

The first chapel in the Old Town is said to have been built by 1775, and to have been rebuilt in 1803 and enlarged in 1805.[47] It was used until 1884, subsequently becoming the Priory Church Institute; part of its stuccoed façade survived in 1969 above a shop-front. This building was replaced in 1884 by Burlington Methodist Church, further south along St. John Street. Designed by Joseph Earnshaw, it is the most grandiose of the town's nonconformist chapels; it is built of white brick with stone dressings in an Italianate style, and its twin towers are crowned with cupolas. It has 650 sittings.[48]

The earliest Methodist chapel at the Quay was built in Cliff (now Chapel) Street in 1795, and was enlarged in 1818 and 1820. It was replaced by Quay Methodist Church, built on the same site in 1873 to designs by William Botterill of Hull. It is of white brick, with stone dressings, in a Renaissance style and has an ornate front with tall Corinthian pilasters, a central pediment, and angle towers surmounted by cupolas; there are nearly 1,100 sittings.[49] The ornate yellow-brick Sunday schools adjoin the chapel in Princess Street. The chapel benefits from the charity of John Webster (by will proved in 1926), who gave £25.[50]

A second Wesleyan chapel at the Quay was built on the Promenade in 1852, to designs by George Truelove.[51] It had apparently passed to the Reform Methodists by 1865,[52] and was deregistered in 1876,[53] perhaps on account of the increased accommodation in the new Chapel Street building.

Two Primitive Methodist chapels were opened in the 1830s. One was built in 1833, on the west side of St. John Street, and rebuilt in 1849,[54] on the east side. In 1877 St. John's Methodist Church was built on the same site. It was designed by William Freeman of Hull,[55] is built of red brick with stone dressings, and has round-headed windows and twin turrets with pyramidal roofs; it contains 600 sittings.[56] There were 320 members in 1889.[57] The church was closed in 1970.[58]

The second early chapel built by the Primitives was put up in 1833 on the Esplanade. It was in use in 1851[59] but was disused by 1867 and demolished in 1869.[60] It was apparently replaced by a new chapel, built in Chapel Street in 1870 to designs by Joseph

---

[32] Brennan, *Bapt. Ch.* 24 and illus. facing p. 14.
[33] Ibid. 20 and illus. facing p. 15; 'Annals of Bridlington', vols. 3, p. 85; 4, p. 32.
[34] Char. Com. files.
[35] G. L. Turner, *Original Recs. of Early Nonconf.* i. 152. Smayles died in 1670. Two men were buried in the Quaker burial ground in 1674 and 1681: B.I.H.R., Prob. Reg. lv, f. 68; lix, f. 245.
[36] E.R.R.O., DDQR/12–15, 26, mins. etc. of the Kelk (later Bridlington) Monthly Meeting. It is said to have become the Bridlington M.M. in 1712: *V.C.H. Yorks.* iii. 66.
[37] E 134/12 Wm. III Mich./28.
[38] *Herring's Visit.* i. 112.
[39] B.I.H.R., Bp. V. 1764/Ret. 89.
[40] E.R.R.O., DDQR/14.
[41] J. Wood, *Plan of Bridlington* (1828). The meeting is said to have reopened in 1810: *V.C.H. Yorks.* iii. 67.
[42] G.R.O. Worship Reg. no. 5525.
[43] B.I.H.R., V. 1865/Ret. 79.
[44] *Kelly's Dir. N. & E.R. Yorks.* (1905), 447; O.S. Map 6" (1854). It was registered in 1954: G.R.O. Worship Reg. no. 64512.
[45] *Jnl. of John Wesley*, ed. N. Curnock, v. 372 and n., 473; vi. 30, 148, 241, 353, 518; vii. 170, 404; viii. 75.

[46] E.R.R.O., MRP/1/7.
[47] E. Mellor, 'Dissent and Nonconf. in Bridlington' (TS. in E.R.R.O.), 12
[48] *Kelly's Dir. N. & E.R. Yorks.* (1889), 346; Bridlington Town Hall, Building Inspector's Office, drawing no. 216; 'Annals of Bridlington', vols. 8, p. 57; 9, p. 24.
[49] *Kelly's Dir. N. & E.R. Yorks.* (1889), 352; 'Annals of Bridlington,' vol. 3, pp. 31, 74.
[50] Char. Com. files.
[51] *Hull Advertiser*, 18 June and 20 Aug. 1852; White, *Dir. Hull & York* (1858), 671.
[52] B.I.H.R., V. 1865/Ret. 80.
[53] G.R.O. Worship Reg. no. 58.
[54] H.O. 129/24/524; Registry of Deeds, Beverley, EW/63/72. It was still shown in its old position in 1850: O.S. Map 60" (1853).
[55] 'Annals of Bridlington', vol. 5, pp. 36, 80.
[56] *Kelly's Dir. N. & E.R. Yorks.* (1889), 346.
[57] H. Woodcock, *Sketches of Prim. Meth. on Yorks. Wolds*, 53.
[58] Ex inf. Mr. S. T. Thompson, 1971.
[59] H.O. 129/24/524.
[60] 'Notes on Work of Bridlington Loc. Govt. Bd.' (MS. notebk. in Bridlington Pub. Libr.), p. 39; 'Annals of Bridlington', vol. 1, p. 124.

Wright of Hull, and seating 320 people.[61] Central Methodist Church was built on the enlarged site in 1879 to seat 750 people. It was designed by William Freeman in an Italianate style,[62] and has a red-brick gabled front with grey-brick and stone dressings, flanked by projecting angle turrets. There were 212 members in 1889.[63] The church was closed in 1969.[64]

The final Methodist chapel was that built on the Promenade by the United Methodist Free Churches in 1872. It was designed by Joseph Earnshaw[65] with 500 sittings, and built of brick, with a stuccoed front.[66] It was deregistered in 1958[67] and subsequently demolished.

After his ejection from the curacy at the parish church in 1662, William Luck applied for a licence as a Presbyterian preacher the same year[68] and held meetings in his own house.[69] That house was licensed for his use in 1672, together with the 'Court House' in the Bayle.[70] The curate of St. Mary's and others had opposed Luck's use of the Court House, suggesting a meeting-place further from the church 'and better if not near the town'.[71] In 1676 Luck was presented for keeping a meeting-house[72] and he is said to have used a brewery not far from the church.[73] Most of the 30 dissenters reported in 1676 and the 25 people fined in 1684 for attending a conventicle[74] may have been in his congregation. Luck died c. 1690 and was succeeded by Richard Whitehurst (d. 1697) and John Benson (d. 1720). Benson is said to have built a chapel on the site of the brewery in 1698.[75]

Zion Chapel, in St. John Street, was built soon after 1700[76] and there were 300 hearers in the town in 1715.[77] Twenty-nine Presbyterian families were reported in 1743 and '20 or more' in 1764.[78] An Arian minister, John Smith, arrived after 1745 and his views led to a split in the congregation c. 1770, when he was excluded from the chapel and preached elsewhere in the town. The chapel was enlarged by Samuel Lyndall (minister 1788–97)[79] and Wesley preached there in 1790.[80]

There were further difficulties c. 1832, when the trustees refused to admit J. Benson as minister. The majority of the congregation consequently worshipped with him in the Bayle, and another minister used the chapel. Both men withdrew before 1837 so that the congregation might be reunited.[81] Zion Chapel continued in use throughout the 19th century, though the Independent congregation was described as weak in the 1860s and in 1894.[82] The building, which was of brick and stucco, was restored in 1886 and had 300 sittings.[83] It was replaced in 1906 and its site used by the Congregationalists as a burial ground. The new chapel, designed by Joseph Sheperdson and seating 230 people,[84] is of red brick with stone dressings.

The minister of Zion Chapel benefits from the charities of Matthew Prudom (by will dated 1715), who devised land, Leonard Chamberlain (1716), who gave £100, Edward Huddleston (by will proved in 1729), who devised land, and George Agars (1841), who gave £100.[85]

The first Congregational chapel to be built in the Quay was Union Chapel, near the end of Prospect Street, about 1817, but services there ended in 1840.[86] Trinity Congregational Church, on the Promenade, was opened in a former skating rink in 1877, but a new building was put up on the site in 1879[87] to seat over 700 people. It was renovated in 1911.[88] The church, designed by Joseph Earnshaw, is of red brick with white-brick and stone dressings, in an Italianate style. The chapel benefits from the charity of Robert Cox (by will proved in 1953), who devised two houses.[89]

The Salvation Army in 1881 registered the Temperance Hall (known as Wellington Hall), in Wellington Road;[90] in 1887 it bought the hall and it was reopened, after alterations, the same year.[91] Also in 1881 the Army registered for worship the Bath Saloon, in Queen's Square at the Quay, but this was disused by 1895.[92] A hall in Market Place, in the Old Town, was registered in 1935 but disused before 1954.[93]

An undenominational Sailors' Bethel stood near the crane wharf until 1892, when it was demolished during improvements there. The same year a temporary building was put up on a wharf at the west end of the harbour[94] and this was used until its demolition in 1933.[95] Services were then held in the former St. Hilda's mission church, Thorpe Street, until 1934, when premises near Clough Wharf, Bridge Street, were acquired.[96] The new premises

---

[61] 'Annals of Bridlington', vols. 1, p. 144; 6, p. 82.
[62] Ibid. 6, p. 82; *Kelly's Dir. N. & E.R. Yorks* (1889), 352.
[63] Woodcock, *Prim. Meth. on Yorks. Wolds*, 61.
[64] *Hull Daily Mail*, 4 July 1969.
[65] 'Annals of Bridlington', vols. 3, pp. 8, 52; 31, p. 69.
[66] *Kelly's Dir. N. & E.R. Yorks*. (1889), 352.
[67] G.R.O. Worship Reg. no. 21130.
[68] A. E. Trout, 'Hist. Zion Cong. Ch. Bridlington', *Hull & E.R. Cong. Mag.* July 1929, 3.
[69] Turner, *Original Recs. of Early Nonconf*. i. 152.
[70] Ibid. i. 354, 483, 520, 575, 622; ii. 644; A. Gordon, *Freedom after Ejection*, 222; B. Dale, *Yorks. Puritanism and Early Nonconf.* 271; *Cal. S.P. Dom.* 1672, 25, 236.
[71] Trout, 'Hist. Zion Ch.' 3; Dale, *Yorks. Puritanism*, 98; *Cal. S.P. Dom.* 1672, 143.
[72] Dale, *Yorks. Puritanism*, 98.
[73] Trout, 'Hist. Zion Ch.' 3.
[74] Bodl. MS. Tanner 150, ff. 27 sqq.; E.R.R.O., DDLG/5/32.
[75] Trout, 'Hist. Zion Ch.' 3; Dale, *Yorks. Puritanism*, 98. The Independents' registers of baptisms and burials begin in 1698: *Lists of Non-parochial Regs. and Recs. in the Custody of the Registrar-General . . . 1859*, 81.
[76] 1702 according to Dale, *Yorks. Puritanism*, 98; endowed in 1706 according to J. G. Miall, *Cong. in Yorks*. 244.
[77] Trout, 'Hist. Zion Ch.' 5.
[78] B.I.H.R., Bp. V. 1764/Ret. 89; *Herring's Visit*. i. 112.
[79] Trout, 'Hist. Zion Ch.' 5.
[80] *Jnl. of John Wesley*, ed. Curnock, viii. 75.
[81] Miall, *Cong. in Yorks*. 245.
[82] B.I.H.R., V. 1865/Ret. 79; V. 1868/Ret. 77; Bp. V. 1894/Ret.
[83] *Kelly's Dir. N. & E.R. Yorks*. (1889), 346, which gives the date of building as 1705.
[84] *Building News*, 3 Aug. 1906; *Kelly's Dir. N. & E.R. Yorks*. (1909), 458.
[85] Char. Com. files. For Chamberlain see *V.C.H. Yorks. E.R.* i. 338.
[86] Trout, 'Hist. Zion Ch.' *Hull & E.R. Cong. Mag.* Aug. 1929, 3. It was called 'lately built' in 1820: Regy. of Deeds, DH/155/181.
[87] 'Annals of Bridlington', vols. 5, p. 78; 6, pp. 59, 81.
[88] *Kelly's Dir. N. & E.R. Yorks*. (1889), 352; (1913), 476.
[89] Char. Com. files.
[90] G.R.O. Worship Reg. no. 25393.
[91] 'Annals of Bridlington', vol. 10, pp. 59, 87.
[92] G.R.O. Worship Reg. no. 25396.
[93] Ibid. 56409.
[94] Harbour Comrs., gen. min. bk. 1873–1904, 26 Aug. and 27 Sept. 1892.
[95] 'Annals of Bridlington', vol. 50, pp. 21, 31.
[96] Ibid. 51, pp. 86, 90.

had been warehouses until 1893, when they were converted to the Albert Hall dance hall.[97]

The Assemblies of God registered a room in Station Road in 1934, but it had ceased to be used by 1954.[98] The Brethren registered Gospel Hall, St. John's Walk, in 1939.[99] A house in Victoria Road was registered by the Christian Scientists in 1940.[1] Kingdom Hall, Quay Road, was registered by the Jehovah's Witnesses in 1941 and replaced by a house in York Road in 1961.[2] The Evangelical Free Church registered Princess Hall, Princess Street, in 1954.[3] The building was part of the former Wesleyan day school.[4] A Spiritualists' meeting-place was registered at a house in Trinity Road in 1957,[5] and the Christian Spiritualists registered a room on the Promenade in 1962.[6] The Christadelphians registered a hall in St. Wilfrid Road in 1965.[7]

EDUCATION. The first recorded schools in Bridlington are the boys' grammar school, which existed by at least the 16th century, and the knitting school, founded in 1671. There were no doubt other small and ephemeral schools; as early as 1564, for example, the grammar-school master's monopoly in the town was protected when an unlicensed teacher was forbidden 'to meddle with teaching any school' there.[8]

The first National school was opened in 1818, but there were other schools at this time of which little is known. A 'Lancasterian' school is said to have been established in 1810,[9] and in 1819 there were 'several' other day schools with about 430 pupils all told.[10] By 1835, in addition to the grammar, knitting, and National schools, there were two infants' schools, one of them begun in 1828, with 132 boys and 118 girls, supported by subscriptions and quarterage; five day schools, with 86 boys and 46 girls; one day and boarding school, begun in 1822, with 16 girls; and one boarding school, begun in 1828, with 10 girls, the seven last-mentioned schools all dependent on parents' payments.[11] There were subsequently usually a dozen small private 'academies' in the town[12] but these are not included in the following account.

A school board was formed in 1879 and it built two new schools, besides taking over one National school. The board was replaced by Bridlington corporation as the authority for elementary education in 1903 and the East Riding county council took over from the corporation in 1944. Five new council schools have been built, and in 1905 the town and county councils established the Girls' High School.

There were several attempts to provide adult education in the later 19th century. In 1865, for example, the vicar of St. Mary's reported that 'some years' previously he had run an adult evening school with more than 90 in attendance, and that for the last three years he had kept a winter night school for about 20 men. The curate of Christ Church stated the same year that a private evening school in his parish had recently closed. There was an evening class there once a week in 1877.[13] An evening school was opened in 1905,[14] eventually becoming the Evening Institute and in 1947 the Technical Institute. From 1935 to 1954 all the evening classes were held in St. George's Boys' and Girls' Schools, with various buildings, including St. Mary's Church Institute, used during the day-time. In 1954 the former Hilderthorpe board school was adapted for use by the Technical Institute, but some classes were still held at the St. George's schools.[15]

GRAMMAR SCHOOL. A school was probably kept at the priory in the Middle Ages. In the 15th century the canons were exempted from the payment of clerical subsidies on condition that they kept twelve choristers, with a master to teach them grammar and song.[16] There may have been a secular school soon after the Dissolution, for a schoolmaster at Bridlington is mentioned in 1563 and regularly thereafter. In the 1630s he held the school in the chancel of the church.[17] Boys were going from the school to the University of Cambridge in 1630 and it was presumably this school which benefited from an endowment made in 1636.[18]

William Hustler, by an indenture of that year, set aside a rent-charge of £40 from the manor of Broughton (Yorks. N.R.) to be used after his death to maintain a schoolmaster and usher in a school of his appointment, otherwise for the master and usher at Bridlington. The master was to receive £26 13s. 4d. a year, the usher £13 6s. 8d.[19] The salaries were regularly paid until 1727 but the owners of Broughton subsequently refused payment, partly because of the doubt about which school should benefit,[20] and it was decreed in Chancery in 1741 that the £40 should be paid to Bridlington.[21] The school was probably from the first held in the Bayle.[22]

The only curate of Bridlington who seems to have served at the school was Cornelius Rickaby, who became master in 1735; in 1743 he had 20 pupils.[23] Rickaby's successor held the mastership for 30 years, but at his death in 1816 had been absent for 26 of them. His usher took the whole of the endowment, but he did not teach either. After complaint by the townspeople, it was ordered in Chancery that the office of usher should be abolished, that the whole £40 should be paid to the master, and that the children, who were not to exceed 20 in number, should be taught grammar, reading, writing, and

---

[97] 'Annals of Bridlington', vols. 13, p. 89; 51, p. 21.
[98] G.R.O. Worship Reg. no. 55189.
[99] Ibid. 58645.   [1] Ibid. 59333, 66683.
[2] Ibid. 59659, 68326.
[3] Ibid. 64274.
[4] See p. 80.
[5] Worship Reg. no. 65998.
[6] Ibid. 68730.
[7] Ibid. 70273.
[8] Bridlington School, *Jubilee Celebrations, 1899–1949*, 8; J. S. Purvis, *Tudor Par. Docs. Dioc. York*, 107–8.
[9] J. Lawson, *Endowed Grammar Schs. of E. Yorks.* (E. Yorks. Loc. Hist. Ser. xiv), 1; *Hull Advertiser*, 2 June 1810.
[10] *Rets. on Educ. of Poor, 1819*, 1077.
[11] *Educ. Enquiry Abstract, 1835*, 1080.

[12] Directories.
[13] B.I.H.R., V. 1865/Ret. 79, 80; V. 1868/Ret.
[14] E.R. Educ. Cttee. *Mins.* 1905–6, 185, 187.
[15] Ex inf. Chief Educ. Officer, County Hall, Beverley, 1970.
[16] Lawson, *Grammar Schs.* 7–8.
[17] B.I.H.R., Schools index; *Jubilee Celebrations*, 8–9.
[18] Lawson, *Grammar Schs.* 12.
[19] The indenture is transcribed and discussed in A. Thornton, *Bridlington School. . . 1636–1936*, 6 sqq.
[20] E.R.R.O., DDX/120/1, nos. 70, 77.
[21] *9th Rep. Char. Com.* 722.
[22] In 1656 the crew of a captured ship were put in 'the school-house' for security: *Cal. S.P. Dom. 1656–7*, 122.
[23] E.R.R.O., DDX/120/1, no. 77; *Herring's Visit.* i. 113.

arithmetic free.[24] Before the period of neglect, the number of pupils had been as high as 80.[25] In 1835 there were 45 boys, those not on the foundation paying quarterage,[26] and in 1864 there were 30, 10 of them paying 7s. 6d. a quarter. After the National school was opened in the Bayle in 1818, the grammar school was held in a building at the corner of North Back Lane and Gill's Lane in 1850, and in 1864 it was kept in a room in the corn exchange in Market Place. In the latter year it was described as no better and perhaps worse than a good National school;[27] a year later, when it was found to be merged with the master's private 'academy', it was reported that the school 'hinders rather than promotes the civilisation of the place'. The school was closed on the death of the master in 1866.[28]

The school lapsed until an adequate endowment was provided under a Scheme of 1894. The grammar school was to have the income from Hustler's endowment, together with that of the knitting school, the infants' school at the Quay, the educational part of the charities of Henry Cowton and others, and funds contributed by the lords feoffees of the manor. The income included interest on £5,046 stock which had accumulated in the funds of the three schools. The lords feoffees were to give £50 a year for five years from the opening of the school, but in 1898 it was arranged that this might be raised to £60 or replaced by a lump sum of not less than £1,800 in the event of the market and fair tolls being sold.[29] The sum of £1,800 was duly given.[30]

A site just outside the town, in Bessingby parish, was bought in 1895 and the school, designed by John Bilson of Hull, was opened in 1899 with 50 boys.[31] An annual grant was made to the school by the county council, which also, together with the town corporation and the lords feoffees, gave money for extensions to the buildings. The chief extensions were a science block (1902), an enlargement of the main block (1903), dining hall and kitchens (1912), a hall (1924), and additions to the science block and classrooms (1927). In 1918 the county council bought the house in Westgate known as the Avenue and let it at a nominal rent to the grammar school, as accommodation for boarders, until 1931. The name was changed to Bridlington School in 1921.[32] Before the First World War the number of pupils increased to over 150 and by 1921 it was 426. It subsequently fell to under 300 in 1931, recovered to about 380 in the late 1930s, and then dropped to about 260 in 1940. The number rose steadily after the Second World War to over 560 in 1948; it was 535 in April 1969.[33] The school was recognized as a voluntary controlled secondary school in 1945.[34]

KNITTING SCHOOL. By an indenture of 1671 William Bower settled land in trust in Bridlington and Birdsall upon the lords feoffees for the support of a master to teach poor children to card and spin wool and knit stockings. The master was to provide the wool and to have the profit of the children's work during their first 18 months of instruction; thereafter each child was to have a sixth of its own profits. There were to be twelve children, each remaining in the school for 2–5 years. A third of the rent from the Birdsall estate was to be paid to the master and the rest divided among the children.[35]

The endowment included a house in Bridlington, in Kirkgate, backing upon Church Green, where the mistress lived and kept the school. Only one instance is known of a master being appointed, in 1793. The girls' share of the Birdsall rent was distributed in the form of a weekly wage. The rent increased from £24 in 1785 to £50 in 1872. The wage rose from 5d. in 1785 to 1s. in 1830, but thereafter was reduced on account of expenses. The girls each paid 1d. a week out of their wage in the 19th century for instruction in reading. The school closed in 1872,[36] and in 1894 its endowments were transferred to the Grammar School.[37]

NATIONAL AND CHURCH SCHOOLS. The local branch of the National Schools Society was formed in 1817, supported by benefactions and subscriptions.[38] Its school was opened in the Bayle the following year, when 159 boys were admitted, and a girls' school was begun in 1822. New schoolrooms for boys and girls were built in North Back Lane in 1826,[39] and in 1835 the average number of pupils was 110 boys and 103 girls; quarterage of 1s. each child was being paid in 1835.[40] An infants' schoolroom, in North Back Lane, is said to have been built in 1838, the school having been started in 1828.[41] A National school for infants was built in Church Green in 1857.[42] The numbers on the books at the three National schools were 323 boys and girls and 82 infants in 1865; the average attendance was 270 boys and girls and 105 infants in 1868, and in 1877 there were 238 boys and girls and 160 infants at the schools.[43] An annual government grant was received by 1854–5.[44] The average attendance in 1908 was 502 in all three departments and in 1910 476.[45] The schools were replaced in 1910 by Burlington Council School: the boys' and girls' building was

---

[24] 9th Rep. Char. Com. 722–3; Lawson, Grammar Schs. 25.
[25] Rets. on Educ. of Poor, 1819, 1077.
[26] Educ. Enquiry Abstract, 1835, 1080.
[27] Char. Com. files, 1864 Report on Bridlington Chars., pt. I; O.S. Map 60″ (1853).
[28] Lawson, Grammar Schs. 28; Thornton, Bridlington Sch. 16.
[29] Char. Com. files.
[30] Thornton, Bridlington Sch. 18.
[31] Ibid.; 'Annals of Bridlington', vol. 17, p. 37.
[32] Thornton, Bridlington Sch. 18–21.
[33] Ibid. 21; Jubilee Celebrations, 22–3; ex inf. Chief Educ. Officer.
[34] E.R. Educ. Cttee. Mins. 1945–6, 145.
[35] 9th Rep. Char. Com. 724–5.
[36] Ibid. 726; Educ. Enquiry Abstract, 1835, 1080; M. Lawson, 'The Knitting Sch.', Bridlington Augustinian Soc. Jnl. no. 3, 19–27. Lawson used the sch. acct. bk. of 1785–1872.
[37] See above.
[38] Par. Recs., Nat. Sch. Bridlington, bk. of procs. 1817–23 (in vestry).
[39] E. Mellor, 'Educ. in Bridlington' (TS. in Bridlington Pub. Libr. and E.R. County Libr., Beverley), 1; J. Thompson, Hist. Sketches of Bridlington, 166; White, Dir. E. & N.R. Yorks. (1840), 368.
[40] Educ. Enquiry Abstract, 1835, 1080.
[41] White, Dir. E. & N.R. Yorks. (1840), 368; O.S. Map 60″ (1853).
[42] E.R.R.O., SGP; Par. Recs., architect's drawings (in vestry).
[43] B.I.H.R., V. 1865/Ret. 79; V. 1868/Ret. 77; V. 1877/Ret.
[44] Rep. of Educ. Cttee. of Council, 1854–5 [1926], p. 240, H.C. (1854–5), xlii.
[45] Bd. of Educ. List 21 (H.M.S.O.).

still standing in 1969, but the infants' school had been demolished.

The first infants' school at the Quay was begun in 1827,[46] and another, in Christ Church parish, was founded in Chapel Row in 1836. A National school for boys and girls, in Quay Road, was begun in 1850.[47] The numbers attending were 120 boys and girls and 130 infants in 1865, 123 and 127 in 1868, and 133 and 63 in 1877.[48] An annual government grant was received by 1854–5.[49] In 1879 the National school was handed over to the new school board and became Quay Girls' School.[50] The infants' school was closed at about the same time and its assets were later transferred to the Grammar School.[51]

A Wesleyan day school was built between Rope Walk and Princess Street, at the Quay, in 1840, and there were 79 children there in 1847. Boys, girls, and infants used the same building until 1894–5, when a separate infants' department was built.[52] An annual government grant was received by 1854–5.[53] The average attendance in 1908 was 208, but it fell to 132 in 1914 and the school was closed the following year.[54] The 1840 and 1894–5 buildings still stood in 1969, the latter known as Princess Hall.[55]

BOARD SCHOOLS. A school board for Bridlington, the Quay, Hilderthorpe, Bessingby, and Easton was formed in 1879[56] and took over the National school in Quay Road the same year, renaming it Quay Girls' School and retaining it until 1903. The second board school, in West Street, Hilderthorpe, was opened in 1882[57] with some 130 boys and 60 infants. The building of the former St. Hilda's mission church was also used for more than 30 years up to 1953.[58] A girls' class was started in 1918, and in 1927 the school became a junior school when children over 11 years old were transferred elsewhere. The average attendance in 1900 was about 340,[59] and in 1908 it was 311; it fell to 240 in 1913 but then increased to 398 in 1922, before falling again to 252 in 1938.[60] The school closed in 1953 when Hilderthorpe County Primary School was built.[61] The Central Board School was opened in Oxford Street in 1903, and Quay Girls' School consequently closed; it was still standing in 1969. The average attendance at the Central school was 523 in 1905,[62] 858 in 1908, and 923 in 1911. It fell to as little as 675 in 1927, but was 914 in 1932 and 850 in 1938.[63] The senior girls were in 1938 transferred to the new St. George's Senior Girls' School, and in 1953 some of the Central School pupils were transferred to Hilderthorpe County Primary School.[64] The school had been renamed Oxford Street School in 1920, and in 1948 it became Moorfield County Primary School.[65] The average number of children on the roll in 1969 was 712.[66]

COUNCIL SCHOOLS. The first school built by Bridlington corporation, as a Part III education authority after 1903, was Burlington School, opened in 1910 in Marton Road to replace St. Mary's National schools. The average attendance in 1912 was 526; after falling to 437 in 1919 it increased to 500 in 1922 and was 508 in 1938.[67] The average number on roll in 1969 was 475.[68] St. George's Senior Boys' School was opened in St. Alban Road in 1935, and in 1938 it had an average attendance of 330.[69] In 1938 St. George's Senior Girls' School was built close by, and a gymnasium block for both schools was built in 1939.[70] After 1944 both schools became secondary, and in 1965 they became the lower section of Headlands School.[71]

Under the Education Act of 1944 the county council assumed Bridlington's powers as the L.E.A. It built one primary school in 1953, in Rosebery Avenue, Hilderthorpe, replacing the old Hilderthorpe School and drawing some pupils from Moorfield School.[72] A new secondary school was provided in 1965, when Headlands School was opened in Sewerby Road; the new building housed the upper section of the school, the lower occupying the old St. George's Secondary School buildings. The total number on the roll in April 1969 was 1,156.[73]

GIRLS' HIGH SCHOOL. Bridlington High School for Girls was established and partly supported by the East Riding county council and Bridlington corporation. It was opened in 1905 in a former private house, the Elms, in St. John Street, adapted and enlarged by John Bilson of Hull; there were 20 pupils.[74] Extensions to the buildings were provided by the county council and opened in 1910, 1927, and 1932. On the last occasion the former façade of the Elms was replaced.[75] A final extension, including a new science block, was completed in 1958.[76] The number of pupils had increased to 350 by 1925 and 550 by 1947.[77] In April 1969, when the school enjoyed 'maintained' status, there were 533 girls on the roll.[78]

CHARITIES FOR THE POOR. Apart from the endowments for schools,[79] about a dozen charities were founded for the benefit of the poor in Bridlington between the late 17th and mid 19th centuries. In

[46] White, *Dir. E. & N.R. Yorks*, (1840), 368.
[47] Regy. of Deeds, GO/397/448; White, *Dir. Hull & York* (1858), 667.
[48] B.I.H.R., V. 1865/Ret. 80; V.1868/Ret. 78; V. 1877/Ret.
[49] *Rep. of Educ. Cttee. of Council, 1854–5*, p. 240.
[50] Mellor, 'Educ. in Bridlington', 6, 8.
[51] See p. 79.
[52] Mellor, 'Educ. in Bridlington', 2, 12; Bridlington Town Hall, Building Inspector's Office, drawing no. 606.
[53] *Rep. of Educ. Cttee. of Council, 1854–5*, p. 240.
[54] *List 21*.   [55] See p. 78.
[56] *Lond. Gaz.* 16 May 1879, p. 3379.
[57] Mellor, 'Educ. in Bridlington', 6.
[58] Char. Com. files.
[59] E.R.R.O., SLB. log bks. 1882–1953.
[60] *List 21*.
[61] Mellor, 'Educ. in Bridlington', 12.
[62] Ibid. 8–9; 'Annals of Bridlington', vol. 20, p. 124.
[63] *List 21*.
[64] Mellor, 'Educ. in Bridlington', 11–12.
[65] Bridlington Corp. *Mins. of Cttees. and Counc. 1919–20*, Counc. Mins., p. 44; E.R. Educ. Cttee. *Mins.* 1948–9, 68.
[66] Ex inf. Chief Educ. Officer.
[67] *List 21*.
[68] Ex inf. Chief Educ. Officer.
[69] 'Annals of Bridlington', vol. 52, p. 261; *List 21*.
[70] 'Annals of Bridlington', vols. 55, p. 135; 56, p. 26.
[71] Ex inf. Chief Educ. Officer.
[72] E.R. Educ. Cttee. *Mins.* 1953–4, 29.
[73] Ibid. 1965–6, 182; ex inf. Chief Educ. Officer.
[74] 'Annals of Bridlington', vols. 22, p. 214; 23, p. 24; 44, p. 29.
[75] Ibid. 27, p. 287; 44, pp. 196, 204; 48, p. 106; 49, p. 310.
[76] B.H.S. *Magazine*, Dec. 1957 and Dec. 1958.
[77] Ibid. Dec. 1947; 'Annals of Bridlington', vol. 48, p. 37.
[78] Ex inf. Chief Educ. Officer.   [79] See pp. 78–9.

the period 1824–46 distributions known as the 'Little Dole', 'Great Dole', 'Lady Day Dole', and 'Michaelmas Dole' were made, totalling £187 in 1825, £159 in 1835, and £136 in 1845. In addition, the 'Coal Dole' amounted to 608, 701, and 1,060 bags respectively in those three years.[80] The total income from the various charities in 1864 was £319. Ten of them were administered by the curate and churchwardens of St. Mary's and the income of these was distributed in 'Sunday Bread', worth £16, 'Wednesday Bread', worth £17, the 'Coal Dole', worth, with an addition from the church offertory and poor box, £15, and various other doles, worth £172. The Sunday and Wednesday bread doles were each given to 32 people in 1864, the coal doles to 150 people of Bridlington, 89 of the Quay, and 8 of Sewerby in 1862, and the miscellaneous doles to 379 people of Bridlington and 326 of the Quay in 1864. Two charities were administered by the overseers of the poor, who distributed coal to about 300 people in 1863. The final charity was run by trustees and an average of about 30 people a year received 5s. doles in 1853–62.

All of these charities were reported to the Charity Commissioners in 1864 to be in 'a very unsatisfactory state'; they were said to 'demoralise the people', who 'consider it a privilege to beg'.[81] Consequently a Scheme was devised in 1870 for the joint management of the charities of Benjamin Woolfe, Henry Cowton, Ann Watson, William and Joseph Hudson, Timothy Woolfe, Thomas and Mary Dale, Mary Stead, Jane Woolfe, Robert Prudom, Ann Yates, and Isaac Wall. They were known as 'the charities of Henry Cowton and others' and were to be used for gifts in money or kind to the needy, to support hospitals and schools, and to provide exhibitions. In 1894 part of the endowments was separated to be used for educational purposes.[82] The rest continued to be jointly administered, later under the name of 'the Bridlington Charities', and the charities of George Harrison, Marmaduke Peasegood, and William Blackburn were subsequently added. The total income in 1970 was £2,655, and £1,625 was distributed, mainly in coal.[83]

Robert Prudom, before 1636, gave a rent-charge of £2 for the poor, but it was reported in 1823 as lost.[84]

Benjamin Woolfe, by will of 1682, left £50, the interest to be used for the poor. The endowment was used to buy a three-acre close, which yielded £12 rent in 1864.[85]

Henry Cowton, by will dated 1696, devised two houses and 8 bovates of land in Sewerby and Marton, and 3 bovates and half a close in Bridlington, to trustees. Of the income from this property, £6 a year was to be paid to the poor of Bridlington, £17 6s. 8d. a year to the minister of Bridlington for a weekly sermon and services,[86] 6s. 8d. a week for bread for those attending the sermon and services, and 1s. a week to the parish clerk for distributing the bread. He also bequeathed the reversion of £500 to be laid out in land for the poor of Bridlington. The residue of his estate was to be used for the poor of Bridlington, the Quay, and Hunmanby. By 1823 the charity property consisted of two houses and 137 a. in Sewerby and Marton, let for £117, and 10 a. in Bridlington, let for £54. The payments then made, totalling nearly £39, were £6 to the poor of Bridlington, distributed in money or coal, £13 to the minister, about £17 for bread for those at the services, and £2 12s. to the clerk. Of the money distributed from the residue, $\frac{3}{5}$ went to Bridlington and the Quay.[87] By 1864 the income was £204.[88] In 1970 it was £612.[89]

Ann Watson, by will dated 1720, directed that £1 6s. should be used to buy bread for the poor of Bridlington. In 1823 it was distributed monthly to the poor attending services at St. Mary's.[90]

George Parkin, by will dated 1723, devised two houses and other property for the benefit of certain named persons, who were to supply 40 bushels of coal a year for 20 poor widows. In 1823 it was found that this had not been done for more than 30 years.[91]

William Hudson, by will dated 1731, devised his houses and garths to his son Joseph, who was to pay £5 a year to the poor of Bridlington and the Quay. Joseph Hudson, by indenture of 1771, added a further charge of £5 on the property, and he also augmented the charity by another rent-charge, of £4 a year. In 1823 the whole sum of £14 was distributed together.[92] The income in 1970 was £4.[93]

Timothy Woolfe, a London fishmonger and son of Richard Woolfe of Bridlington Quay,[94] by will dated 1734, gave £500 to be put to charitable uses in and around the town. In 1760 a 31-acre close in Ulrome was conveyed to trustees in satisfaction of the legacy. In 1823 the rent of £56 was distributed to the poor of Bridlington and the Quay.[95]

Thomas and Mary Dale in 1756 granted £110 to be laid out in land for the benefit of the poor of Bridlington; £100 of the money was raised from the estate of Mary Stead, of whom Mary Dale was executrix, who died before carrying out an intention to bequeath such a sum. The money was used to buy 2 a. in Bridlington, and the rent of nearly £16 was distributed in 1823.[96] The income in 1970 was £3.[97]

Jane Woolfe, by indenture of 1775, devised 4 a., the rent to be given to the poor. In 1823 over £25 was distributed in Bridlington and the Quay. By 1864 the endowment consisted of £666 stock and the income was £20.[98] The income of 'Woolfe's Charity' in 1970 was £70.[99]

Ann Yates, in 1795, bequeathed £100 for the poor of Bridlington. In 1823 the money was out on loan and the 5 per cent interest was applied with the Hudsons' charity. In 1864 £108 stock produced

---

[80] Par. Recs., dole bk. 1824–46 (in vestry).
[81] Char. Com. files, 1864 Report on Bridlington Chars., pt. I.
[82] See p. 79.
[83] Ex inf. Clerk to Bridlington Charity Trustees, 1971.
[84] 9th Rep. Char. Com. 731; Purvis, Bridlington Charters, etc. 158.
[85] Char. Com. files, 1864 Rep. pt. I; E. Mellor, 'Some Local Chars. in. . . Bridlington' (TS. in E.R.R.O.), 25.
[86] See p. 71.
[87] 9th Rep. Char. Com. 726–8.
[88] Char. Com. files, 1864 Rep. pt. I.

[89] Ex inf. Clerk to B.C.T. 1971.
[90] 9th Rep. Char. Com. 731; V.C.H. Yorks. E.R. i. 346.
[91] 9th Rep. Char. Com. 732.
[92] Ibid. 729–30.
[93] Ex inf. Clerk to B.C.T. 1971.
[94] Monument in St. Mary's Ch. Bridlington.
[95] 9th Rep. Char. Com. 730.
[96] Ibid. 731.
[97] Ex inf. Clerk to B.C.T. 1971.
[98] Char. Com. files, 1864 Rep. pt.1; 9th Rep. Char. Com. 730.
[99] Ex inf. Clerk to B.C.T. 1971.

an interest of £3.[1] The income in 1970 was £3.[2]

Isaac Wall, by will dated 1795, bequeathed £1,000 stock, the interest to be given to the poor of Bridlington and the Quay in bread and coal. In 1823 £30 was distributed.[3] The income in 1970 was £25.[4]

Yarburgh Yarburgh, by will dated 1855, bequeathed £1,000 for the poor, $\frac{2}{5}$ of which was to go to Bridlington. In 1864 Bridlington's share of the endowment was represented by £406 stock and the interest was £12.[5] In 1960 the total endowment was £742 stock and the income of £16 was distributed in money, coal, and provisions, $\frac{2}{5}$ of it still in Bridlington.[6]

Ann Barker, by will dated 1865, bequeathed £450 to be used for coal, blankets, or provisions for the poor. In 1930 the income of £12 from £480 stock was distributed in clothing, in 1931 in groceries.[7]

Thomas Owston, by will proved in 1888, bequeathed £300 for the benefit of 20 poor families attending St. Mary's Church. In 1931 the endowment was £273 stock and the income £7; 7s. 6d. was given to each of eighteen people.[8]

George Harrison, by will proved in 1918, bequeathed money to buy fuel for the poor of Hilderthorpe. In 1960 it was represented by £625 stock.[9] The income in 1970 was £37.[10]

William H. Blackburn, by will proved in 1923, directed that after the death of his wife and daughter $\frac{1}{6}$ of his residuary estate should be paid to St. Mary's Church and $\frac{2}{6}$ to the trustees of the Bridlington Charities. In each case the income was to be used to buy coal, clothing, or food for the poor of the Old Town Ward.[11] Blackburn's wife and daughter died in 1926 and 1951 respectively, and the trustees of the Bridlington Charities received a first payment of £2,000 in 1965; the income in 1970 was £76.[12]

Marmaduke Peasegood, by will proved in 1938, devised his residuary estate of over £4,300 to be administered with the Bridlington Charities. In 1970 the income was £171.[13]

Alice Hopper, by will proved in 1947, bequeathed £250 to buy a house for women in reduced circumstances. In 1950 it was directed that until a house was acquired the money should be used to pay the rent of such women.[14]

A charity known as Benevolence was established in 1950 to continue the work of the former Bridlington and District Nursing Association. Holidays are provided for poor people and cash payments made to the needy. Income from invested voluntary contributions amounted to £119 in 1962 and payments of £274 were made that year.[15]

Henry Blake, by will proved in 1952, bequeathed £1,280 to provide old inhabitants of Bridlington with extra comforts and amenities. In 1971 the endowment was represented by £1,168 stock and the interest of £72 was paid to Burlington House and Danes Lea old people's homes. In 1968 £1,556 stock was added to this fund by a bequest of Florence Duckmanton; the income was £96 in 1971.[16]

A rent-charge of £4 given by an unknown person before 1786 had been lost by 1823.[17]

BUCKTON

The township of Buckton, covering 1,984 a.,[18] lies on the northern side of Flamborough Head, some 3 miles from Bridlington. The village, which was an Anglian settlement,[19] stands a mile from the sea and is barely separated from Bempton village. The township boundary follows only one notable natural feature, the bottom of a small dry valley towards Speeton. Buckton was in 1935 merged with Bempton civil parish.[20]

The typical wolds countryside of the southern part of Buckton gives way towards the sea to a bleaker landscape, where exposure to the weather inhibits tree and bush growth and where in places banks replace hedges as field boundaries. Over much of the township the pattern of long and narrow fields is suggestive of an early inclosure, and there was certainly no inclosure by Act of Parliament.[21] Much of Buckton lies between 300 ft. and 350 ft. above sea-level, but north-westwards the land rises to over 425 ft. at the sea, and here the entire length of the township's coastline is marked by the sheer chalk cliffs which continue into Speeton and Bempton.[22] The lowest ground in the township, around 225 ft., is at the village site itself, in a valley which runs westwards from Bempton. In Buckton the valley divides, one branch continuing westwards, the other turning north towards the sea.

Buckton is crossed by the main road from Flamborough to Filey, and by the Bridlington–Filey railway line. Towards Filey the main road is known as Speeton Gate. From the village minor roads run south towards Bridlington and south-west towards Grindale, the latter formerly known as Sheep Walk Lane.[23] Howdy Cow Lane follows the small valley towards the sea.

The houses of the village stand along the Flamborough–Filey road, the Bridlington road, and a short back lane connecting them. In the centre of the village and on the east and west sides prominent earthworks mark the sites of former houses and garths. The farm-houses and cottages are mostly brick buildings of the 18th to the 20th century and

---

[1] Char. Com. files, 1864 Rep. pt. 1; *9th Rep. Char. Com.* 730.
[2] Ex inf. Clerk to B.C.T. 1971.
[3] *9th Rep. Char. Com.* 731.
[4] Ex inf. Clerk to B.C.T. 1971.
[5] Char. Com. files, 1864 Rep. pt. 1; see below, p. 100. The remaining $\frac{3}{10}$ was to go to Heslington, near York.
[6] Char. Com. files.
[7] Ibid.
[8] Ibid.
[9] Ibid.
[10] Ex inf. Clerk to B.C.T. 1971.
[11] Char. Com. files.
[12] Ex inf. Clerk to B.C.T. 1971.
[13] Ex inf. Clerk to B.C.T. 1971.
[14] Char. Com. files.
[15] Ibid.; ex inf. Mr. P. A. Smith, Bridlington, 1970.
[16] Ex inf. Director of Social Services, County Hall, Beverley, 1972; see above, p. 67.
[17] *9th Rep. Char. Com.* 731.
[18] O.S. Map 6" (1854).
[19] *P.N.E.R. Yorks.* (E.P.N.S.), 103.
[20] *Census*, 1931.
[21] See p. 85.
[22] For egg-collecting on these cliffs see p. 9.
[23] O.S. Map 6" (1854).

none is especially noteworthy. In 1747 Robert Grimston wrote to Hannah Robinson of her father's expenses in building and repairing houses, barns, and stables at Buckton, 'that made it appear almost a new town',[24] but this is not apparent now. One or two houses incorporate work in chalk and cobbles, as do many of the farm buildings. A chalk, cobble, and brick building at Grange Farm resembles those at Speeton.[25] The only outlying buildings, apart from Buckton Hall, are High Huntow Farm, Buckton Barn, and Mill Farm, all in the south of the township. The windmill known as Buckton mill stands just over the boundary into Bempton.[26] Buckton Hall stands in the west of the township, a mile distant from the village and ¾ mile from the sea.[27]

No early population figures are available, for Buckton was rarely separately assessed or reported upon. In 1801 there were 111 inhabitants. By 1811 the number had increased to 162 and there were about 180 inhabitants in 1841–61. For the rest of the century the population stood at between 140 and 150,[28] but it subsequently increased to 180 in 1921 and was still as high as 174 in 1931.[29]

No charities are recorded at Buckton but the women and children of the township benefited from the charities of Elizabeth Walmsley at Bempton.[30]

MANORS AND OTHER ESTATES. The entry for Buckton in Domesday Book includes much of the land in Bempton, as well as all of Newsham.[31] The king held 5 carucates and 6 bovates, the count of Mortain 3 carucates and 6 bovates, and Hugh, earl of Chester, 2 carucates and 4 bovates.[32] Six carucates which later became part of the Gant fee were apparently omitted from the Domesday entry.[33] It is not clear what contribution each of the townships made to these estates.

The estate of the count of Mortain passed like that at Boynton to the Paynels and later to the archbishops of Canterbury. Under these overlords a mesne lordship was held by the Meynell family. The Meynell fee comprised 9 carucates in 1284–5,[34] and Nicholas de Meynell held 4 carucates in Buckton of the archbishop of Canterbury in 1299.[35]

The capital manor of *BUCKTON* originated in land held of the Canterbury fee by the Buckton family. In 1241 William of Buckton was laying claim to 4 bovates which had belonged to his father Ernald, and in the same year William acknowledged that he held land of the Meynell fee from Simon of Hales.[36] The Bucktons' manor is mentioned in 1287.[37] William of Buckton held 4 carucates of the Meynell fee in 1299, 4 others being held by Thomas of Hales,[38] and in 1316 William of Buckton was returned as lord of the township.[39] Arnald of Buckton had 20 bovates in 1335,[40] and more than one member of the family had land in Buckton at that time.[41]

The manor was held by the Bucktons until the death of William Buckton in 1530; he then held 32 bovates of the Meynell fee. He was succeeded by his daughter Ursula,[42] who married John Collingwood.[43] Robert Collingwood conveyed the manor in 1617 to Sir Thomas Blakiston, and he sold it the same year to Henry Robinson.[44] Blakiston had bought other land in Buckton in 1616 from Thomas Stockton,[45] and this was presumably included in the sale to Robinson. More land was added to the estate by the Robinsons; they had acquired land from Thomas Ogle in 1609, and William Belwood's land was bought in 1617.[46] Most of the township eventually came into the family's possession.

The Robinsons held Buckton until the death of John Robinson in 1769. He was succeeded by his daughter Hannah, wife of Sir William Foulis, and the estate later descended to John Robinson Foulis (d. 1826) and Mark Foulis.[47] The latter held over 1,800 a. in the township,[48] but at his death in 1868[49] the estate was split up. The hall, manor, and 415 a. of land were in 1869 sold to William and Joseph Jackson, who had long been the tenants.[50] Joseph Jackson sold them to F. A. Hutchinson in 1906, and C. F. Hutchinson to W. A. Marr in 1947.[51] In 1968 H. W. Marr sold the hall, manor, and 325 a. to Charles Bealby and other members of the Bealby family.[52]

Buckton Hall was built for John Robinson in 1744–5,[53] probably replacing an earlier house belonging to the Robinsons, though the site of this is unknown. The hall, a tall square building with the main front facing south, was originally at the centre of a symmetrical composition: to the east and west curving screen walls with rusticated doorways linked it to identical outbuildings, but of these features only the eastern screen wall and the western outbuilding remain.[54] Also on the eastern side of the house was a large garden surrounded by a wall with deep V-shaped embrasures; only one section of the wall still stands.[55]

The hall itself was originally a four-storeyed building, with attics in the double-pitched roof which ended in twin gables to east and west. After a fire in 1919, however, a flat roof was constructed. The lowest floor is a semi-basement, with brick vaulting,[56] which contained store-rooms and servants' quarters.

---

[24] E.R.R.O., DDGR/45/7.
[25] See p. 101.
[26] See p. 14.
[27] See below.
[28] *V.C.H. Yorks.* iii. 488.
[29] *Census.*
[30] See p. 16.
[31] See p. 10.
[32] *V.C.H. Yorks.* ii. 197, 219, 226, 322. It was believed that other entries related to this Buckton (ibid. 322) but they in fact refer to Buckton in Settrington: H. C. Darby and I. S. Maxwell, *Domesday Geog. of N. Eng.* 482–4.
[33] See p. 10.
[34] *Feud. Aids*, vi. 29.
[35] *Yorks. Inq.* ii. 115, 118; *Cal. Inq. p.m.* iii, pp. 428–9.
[36] J.I. 1/1047 mm. 14d, 35d.
[37] *Yorks. Deeds*, x. 38.
[38] *Cal. Inq. p.m.* iii, pp. 428–9.
[39] *Feud. Aids*, vi. 170.
[40] *Cal. Inq. p.m.* vii, p. 403.
[41] E.R.R.O., DDSC/17; *Yorks. Fines, 1300–14*, 76.
[42] C 142/52/92.
[43] W. Flower, *Visit. of Yorks.* (Harl. Soc. xvi), 41–2.
[44] *Yorks. Fines, 1614–25*, 75.
[45] Ibid. 66; *1603–14*, 123.
[46] Ibid. *1603–14*, 107; *1614–25*, 88. See also C 3/324/41; /413/91; /459/20, 21, 23, 24, 34; C 5/25/70, 71.
[47] *E. Yorks. Georgian Soc. Trans.* ii (2), 27.
[48] Registry of Deeds, Beverley, HM/19/18.
[49] Ibid. KF/395/540.
[50] Ibid. KL/222/299. Other sales are in /223/301; /224/302; etc.
[51] Ibid. 88/467/444 (1906); 749/184/147; 1033/8/8; 1293/81/75.
[52] Ibid. 1542/176/134.
[53] It is described in *E. Yorks. Georgian Soc. Trans.* ii (2), 27–33; *Country Life*, 24 Sept. 1948, 628–30.
[54] See fig. 1.
[55] Illus. in *Country Life*, 24 Sept. 1948, 630.
[56] Illus. in ibid.

BUCKTON HALL IN THE 18TH CENTURY

The chief elevation is of five bays, the central bay breaking forward and containing the doorway. It is faced with chalk ashlar, deeply channelled on the central bay and flat elsewhere. The dark freestone of the lavish dressings provides a strong contrast to the whiteness of the chalk. Freestone is used for the rusticated quoins, for the string-courses between the floors, for the Gibbs surround of the doorway, and for the architraves and key-blocks of the windows. The façade is crowned by a pulvinated frieze and a cornice, with a pediment over the central bay. Above the cornice is a brick and stone parapet, divided by pilasters. The architectural features of the front, together with its strong vertical emphasis, suggest a building of the early, rather than the mid, 18th century. It is thought that this may be due to the old-fashioned taste of John Robinson, who was 70 years old when Buckton Hall was built.[57]

The other three elevations of the house are of red brick and comparatively plain. On the east side, however, there is a central doorway surmounted by a Venetian window which formerly lit the main staircase; above that again is a bulls-eye window. The fire of 1919[58] destroyed not only the roof but also the interior of the house, which included fine doors, chimney-pieces, ceilings, and staircase. The building has been carefully restored externally, though the interior of the uppermost floors is no longer fitted-up. The remaining outbuilding, the stables, is also built of chalk with freestone dressings, and has rusticated quoins and door and window surrounds; inside, a wooden arcade with Doric columns separates the stalls.[59]

A second estate, sometimes referred to as the manor of BUCKTON, may also have originated, as in Bempton,[60] in the Canterbury fee. Again like its counterpart in Bempton, this estate passed to the Hatfield family and, by 1525,[61] to the Constables. It was sold by Christopher Constable to Christopher Maltby in 1581,[62] but its further descent has not been traced. The Constables apparently retained some property in Buckton during the 17th century.[63]

The Crown estate of 1086 passed into the Brus fee and some land in Buckton formed part of it, though most may have been in Bempton.[64] The Mauleys had a mesne lordship in it and in 1265 William of Rudston was the demesne tenant under Roger de Mauley.[65] When Roger died that year his heirs were his three daughters, one of whom married William de Greystock. In 1418 Ralph, baron Greystock, enjoyed rent from property in Buckton.[66] No more is known of this estate.

The fee apparently omitted from the Survey in 1086 passed to the Gants and later to the Tattershalls. In 1304 William of Buckton was returned as holding 6 carucates in Buckton under the Tattershalls,[67] but this presumably included land in Bempton.

Property in Buckton acquired by Bridlington priory seems to have included land from several different fees. Four bovates were given in the early 12th century by Goro, one of Walter de Gant's men.[68] Other gifts, made by Robert of Buckton, John of Buckton, Malger of Buckton, Alexander Despenser, and John the knight of Rudston, included 8 more bovates.[69] A further 4 bovates and 40 a. of land were granted to the priory by Thomas Storour and others in 1401.[70] The priory's property was worth £2 8s. in 1535.[71]

The tithes of Buckton belonged, with those of the mother-church, to Bridlington priory.[72] After the Dissolution the chapel was in 1538 let to Robert Wharton.[73] In 1561 it was let to Thomas Warcopp and in 1579 half of it to Richard Marks.[74] In 1594 Tristram, Robert, and Randall Carliell had a grant of it.[75] The tithes, which were worth £60 in 1650,[76] were held by the Carliells until 1700, when Henry Carliell conveyed them to John Burdett.[77] Later in 1700 Burdett sold them to Humphrey Robinson[78] and they subsequently descended with the capital manor. When they were commuted in 1843 only 89 a. were still subject to their payment and for these a rent-charge of £16 12s. was awarded to Mark Foulis.[79]

---

[57] Illus. in *Country Life*, 24 Sept. 1948, 628–9.
[58] 'Annals of Bridlington', vol. 36, p. 139.
[59] Illus. in *Country Life*, 24 Sept. 1948, 628–9.
[60] See p. 10.
[61] *Yorks. Fines*, i. 44.
[62] Ibid. ii. 175.
[63] See p. 85.
[64] See p. 11.
[65] *Yorks. Inq.* i. 102; *Cal. Inq. p.m.* i, p. 201.
[66] *Yorks. Inq. Hen. IV–V*, 144.
[67] *Cal. Inq. p.m.* iv, p. 108.
[68] *Bridlington Charty.* 1.
[69] Ibid. 49–51.
[70] *Cal. Pat.* 1399–1401, 529.
[71] *Valor Eccl.* (Rec. Com.), v. 120; *Miscellanea*, iii (Y.A.S. Rec. Ser. lxxx), 13.
[72] See p. 71.
[73] *L. & P. Hen. VIII*, xiii (2), p. 409.
[74] E.R.R.O., DDLG/6/3, 6.
[75] Ibid. /8.
[76] *T.E.R.A.S.* ii. 53.
[77] C.P. 25(2)/896/12 Wm. III Trin. no. 13.
[78] C.P. 43/469 rot. 96.
[79] B.I.H.R., TA. 579S.

ECONOMIC HISTORY. The open fields and moor of the township are referred to in an agreement between John and Walter Buckton in 1359. John pardoned Walter and his tenants for digging turves in Buckton moor, and Walter granted John a roadway, reserving to himself the right to turn his horses, carts, and harrows upon it when his adjoining 12 bovates were reaped or sown.[80] In the early Middle Ages there were intakes in that part of the township towards Speeton: this land was known as West Ovenham.[81] Other early inclosure is suggested by a reference to Walter Buckton's close, with a ditch around it, in 1359.[82]

The names and location of the open fields are uncertain, but in the early 16th century there were said to 80 bovates there.[83] By 1655 a third of the manor included 30 bovates of open-field land and about 250 a. of closes.[84] The date when the remaining commonable lands of Buckton were inclosed is not known, but recent inclosures in the township are mentioned in 1729 and 1733.[85] There may have been a large area of common pasture in the south, where, besides Huntow, there were fields still known as the Sheep Walk in 1850. The 'sheep walks in the Huntow and Brackens' belonging to two open-field bovates are mentioned in 1733.[86] There were still several stretches of unimproved rough pasture in the 19th century, especially in the area known as Howdy Cows along the small valley running towards the sea.[87] In 1843 there were 1,304 a. of arable land and 619 a. of meadow and pasture, 42 a. of the latter called Cliff leys or Butcher's close.[88] The Foulis estate included eight farms, of between 160 a. and 380 a., in 1856, as well as 20 cottages.[89] There were usually six farmers in Buckton in the 19th and early 20th centuries, but by 1937 there were ten.[90]

A windmill formed part of the Buckton family's manor in 1341[91] and Bridlington priory enjoyed the tithe of Buckton mill in the early 16th century.[92] No more is known of it. A miller is still listed among the inhabitants of the village in 1840[93] but she is similarly listed under Bempton, and the windmill called Buckton mill was, in fact, just over the boundary into Bempton parish.[94]

CHURCH. Buckton township remained in Bridlington parish until 1919, when it was annexed to Bempton.[95] In the Middle Ages Buckton had its own chapel, dedicated to St. Lawrence, first mentioned in 1293.[96] A chaplain was no doubt provided by the priory: there were two chaplains, each receiving £4 net a year, in 1525–6, one of them presumably responsible for the chantry.[97] The chapel probably fell into decay during the 16th century, after the chantry was suppressed.[98]

Arnald of Buckton had licence in 1304 to give 10 tofts and 9 bovates of land in Burton Fleming to Bridlington priory to support a chaplain celebrating daily in Buckton chapel.[99] The chantry was worth £4 6s. 8d. in 1535.[1] The property was granted to Francis Barker and Thomas Browne in 1571.[2]

NONCONFORMITY. Members of the Constable family were reported recusant in the earlier 17th century and in 1676 a popish priest was caught in their house.[3] No nonconformist church was ever established in Buckton.

EDUCATION. In the earlier 19th century a school was held in a building provided by the trustees of Mark Foulis. By 1823 it was endowed with £2 a year from the Foulis estate. In 1835 parents subscribed as well; it was then attended by 12 children. Another school, begun in 1818 and supported entirely at the parents' expense, was attended by 15 children in 1835.[4] The first of these schools was still mentioned in 1856,[5] but it had ceased to exist by 1871, when the children of Buckton went to Bempton.[6]

EASTON

The township of Easton, covering 734 a.,[7] lies little more than a mile west of the Old Town of Bridlington, in the valley of the Gypsey Race. It was probably an Anglian settlement.[8] Almost the whole of the township is north of the Race, which forms part of the southern boundary; on the east and north the boundary follows small valleys cut into the wold slopes. The township was in 1935 merged for civil purposes with Boynton.[9]

Apart from the low-lying ground near the Race, mostly below 25 ft. above sea-level, Easton consists almost entirely of wold land, rising to nearly 300 ft. in the north of the township. It is mostly used for arable farming and the large wolds fields are interrupted by only a single long plantation running along the slope above the village. The main road along the valley of the Gypsey Race from Bridlington runs through Easton; maps show the course of an

---

[80] E.R.R.O., DDSC/17.
[81] J.I. 1/1517 m. 18; *Bridlington Charty.* 51.
[82] E.R.R.O., DDSC/17.
[83] *Miscellanea*, iii (Y.A.S. Rec. Ser. lxxx), 16.
[84] C 78/1150 no. 22.
[85] Registry of Deeds, Beverley, L/21/37; N/265/586.
[86] Ibid. N/263/583.
[87] O.S. Map 6" (1854).
[88] B.I.H.R., TA. 579S.
[89] Regy. of Deeds, HM/19/18.
[90] Directories.
[91] *Cal. Inq. p.m.* viii, p. 223.
[92] *Miscellanea*, iii. 4.
[93] White, *Dir. E. & N.R. Yorks.* (1840), 371.
[94] Bempton Mill likewise stands just into Sewerby, where millers are also separately recorded.
[95] York Dioc. Regy., Orders in Council 522.
[96] *Yorks. Inq.* ii. 151.
[97] *Y.A.J.* xxiv. 77–8.
[98] The chapel is mentioned in 1556 among property delivered to the crown: E.R.R.O., DDCC/139/65.
[99] *Yorks. Inq.* ii. 151; iv. 12–13; *Cal. Pat.* 1301–7, 215.
[1] *Valor Eccl.* (Rec. Com.), v. 122.
[2] *Cal. Pat.* 1569–72, 237.
[3] H. Aveling, *Post Reformation Catholicism in E. Yorks. 1558–1790* (E. Yorks. Loc. Hist. Ser. xi), 59.
[4] *9th Rep. Char. Com.* 732; *Educ. Enquiry Abstract, 1835*, 1081; E. H. Rudkin, *Bempton cum Newsholme cum Buckton*, 39.
[5] Sheahan and Whellan, *Hist. York & E.R.* ii. 455.
[6] *Rets. rel. Elem. Educ. 1871*, 474.
[7] O.S. Map 6" (1854).
[8] *P.N.E.R. Yorks.* (E.P.N.S.), 104.
[9] *Census*, 1931.

old road, not visible on the ground in 1969, diverging from the present line to run close to the stream,[10] where it was perhaps liable to flooding. In the north the Bridlington–Grindale road crosses the township.

The village now consists of only four houses on the main road. The oldest is an 18th-century farmhouse of chalk and brick, two are of the 1930s, and the other, Eastfield Farm, was built in 1961 when an older house was demolished.[11] This older house was that in which Charlotte Brontë stayed on visits to Easton in 1839 and 1849.[12] There is one isolated farm-house, high on the wold slopes.

Easton was a small village in the Middle Ages, with only 10 adults paying the poll tax in 1377,[13] and thereafter there can never have been many more houses than the three which comprised the hamlet in the 19th century. The population was 21 in 1801 and it subsequently until 1931 varied between 17 and 38.[14]

There is no record of a chapel at Easton and no known Nonconformist meeting-place apart from a house registered for worship in 1815.[15] There was never a school and no charities are recorded.

ESTATES. In 1086 the whole of Easton was in the hands of the king. One estate, of 5 carucates, had been held by Morcar in 1066 and it belonged to the manor of Bridlington. A second, of one carucate, was held by Elaf in 1066.[16] Most if not all of *EASTON* subsequently belonged to the Gants and later the Tattershalls.[17] There appears to have been an intermediate lordship under the Tattershalls, held by Hugh de Cardoyl in 1304, the heir of Thomas de Cailly in 1323, and Constantine Clifton in 1353.[18]

In 1284–5 the Gant land was held in four estates: Adam Ulrome and William of Buckton together had $3\frac{1}{2}$ carucates, 2 bovates lay in the Kyme fee, and 2 carucates and 2 bovates belonged to Bridlington priory.[19] No more is known of the Kyme fee. The Ulromes held their land, described as 11 or sometimes 13 bovates, until at least 1353,[20] but its descent has not been traced further. The Bucktons held 7 bovates in 1303 and 1346,[21] and 14 in 1375 when John Buckton granted to three men the reversion of 7 bovates and also the service of 7 more which were held by Richard Easton.[22] In 1377 Richard conveyed his 7 bovates to Sir Robert Boynton,[23] and the other 7 were given to Bridlington priory.[24]

The land held by Bridlington priory in 1284–5 had been acquired in the early 12th century. Henry I confirmed to the priory his own gift of $1\frac{1}{2}$ carucate and that of 2 bovates made by Ralph and Gocelin Buc, men of Walter de Gant. Gocelin's daughters later gave a further 5 bovates.[25] The 7 bovates given in 1377 by Richard Easton may not have been the only addition to the priory's land in the township. By the Dissolution its estate there was worth £8 2s. 8d.[26]

The priory's land at Easton was let by the Crown in 1566 to Stephen Leckenby,[27] and in 1589 the Stricklands were disputing the ownership of 9 bovates with Nicholas King and others.[28] William Strickland had acquired other land in Easton in 1562 and Walter Strickland in 1579.[29] The whole of the township eventually passed into the possession of the Stricklands, and they were the sole landowners in 1783.[30] The estate descended in the family until 1951[31] and it was sold as two farms, of 346 a. and 381 a., in 1952 and 1953.[32]

The tithes of the township belonged to Bridlington priory until the Dissolution; in the early 16th century the corn tithes were worth over £3.[33] They were subsequently included in the 16th-century grants of tithes in Hilderthorpe and elsewhere.[34] In 1650 the tithes, worth £30, belonged to one Wright,[35] and in 1702 a fifth of the Easton tithes were conveyed from George to Charles Cowart.[36] They are not mentioned again.

ECONOMIC HISTORY. Some decline in the size and prosperity of the village may have taken place in the early 14th century and at the time of the Black Death. Thus there were 7 taxpaying households in 1297, the tax quota was reduced by 15 per cent in 1354, and there were only 10 adults paying the poll tax in 1377.[37] Positive evidence of decay is provided by the estate of Hugh Ulrome, who in 1353 had a chief-house in ruins, 6 waste tofts, and 11 bovates of land lying waste.[38]

Nothing is known of the open-field arrangements nor of the dates at which inclosure took place. There were said to be 50 bovates in the township in the early 16th century.[39] Certain closes there are mentioned in 1548.[40] A mill is recorded in 1303.[41] In modern times the township consisted of two farms on the Strickland estate;[42] there are now three, High Field farm having been taken out of East (later Eastfield) farm in 1955.[43]

---

[10] e.g. O.S. Map 6" (1854).
[11] Local inf. and date-stone.
[12] F.R. Pearson, *Charlotte Brontë on the E. Yorks. Coast* (E. Yorks. Loc. Hist. Ser. vii), 12, 20.
[13] E 179/202/62 m. 19.
[14] *V.C.H. Yorks.* iii. 488; *Census*.
[15] G.R.O. Worship Returns, Vol. v, no. 2903.
[16] *V.C.H. Yorks.* ii. 197, 204, 322.
[17] *Feud. Aids*, vi. 29, 228, 265–6; *Cal. Inq. p.m.* iv, pp. 261, 265–6; vii, p. 470.
[18] *Cal. Inq. p.m.* iv, p. 108; vi, p. 225; x, pp. 16–17.
[19] *Feud. Aids*, vi. 29.
[20] Ibid. 169, 228; *Cal. Inq. p.m.* vi, p. 225; x, pp. 16–17.
[21] *Feud. Aids*, vi. 228; *Yorks. Fines, 1300–14*, 35.
[22] *Yorks. Deeds*, ii. 64–65.
[23] C.P. 25(1)/277/140 no. 12.
[24] *Cal. Pat.* 1377–81, 8.
[25] *Bridlington Charty.* 1, 24.
[26] *Valor Eccl.* v. 120–1; *Miscellanea*, iii (Y.A.S. Rec. Ser. lxxx), 12, 28.
[27] *Cal. Pat.* 1563–6, 483.
[28] E 134/32 Eliz. Hil./2.
[29] *Yorks. Fines*, i. 258, 269; ii. 142.
[30] E.R.R.O., Land Tax 1783.
[31] See p. 23.
[32] Registry of Deeds, Beverley, 871/615/482; 922/134/120; 945/160/133. These sales were by J. T. T. Fletcher: see above, p. 23.
[33] *Miscellanea*, iii (Y.A.S. Rec. Ser. lxxx), 16.
[34] See p. 92.
[35] *T.E.R.A.S.* ii. 54.
[36] C.P. 25(2)/983/1 Anne East.
[37] E 179/202/53; E 179/202/62 m. 19; *Yorks. Lay Subsidy, 1297* (Y.A.S. Rec. Ser. xvi), 139, 142.
[38] *Cal. Inq. p.m.* x, pp. 16–17.
[39] *Miscellanea*, iii (Y.A.S. Rec. Ser. lxxx), 16.
[40] *Cal. Pat.* 1553, 327.
[41] C.P. 25(1)/269/78 no. 43.
[42] Directories.
[43] Regy. of Deeds, 945/160/133; 1007/318/283; /320/284.

GRINDALE

The township of Grindale occupies 2,429 a.[44] of open wold country, 3 miles north-west of Bridlington and 3 miles from the sea at Speeton.[45] The village was probably a Scandinavian settlement, lying in a 'green valley'.[46] It does in fact lie in a prominent valley running from east to west across the township, and several smaller side valleys are cut into the wold slopes. Part of the southern boundary with Boynton is marked by a long curving hedge-bank on the lower slopes of the main east-west valley. Grindale was a chapelry of Bridlington until the 19th century, but it has long enjoyed some degree of ecclesiastical independence.[47] In 1935 Argam was merged with it for civil purposes.[48]

The open landscape of the township is broken only by a few plantations and it is dominated by the large regular fields that were created at inclosure in 1844. Almost all the land is arable, though some of the small fields around the village are under grass. The main valley is dry except for the village pond and a pool at Keld spring. The valley bottom varies from 150 ft. above sea-level in the west of the township to 250 ft. in the east. The ground rises, in places steeply, to 250 ft. or more over much of the wold ground, and 340 ft. is reached in the north-east of the township. The road from Bridlington to Burton Fleming follows the main valley, and minor roads lead over the wolds to Reighton, Bempton, and Boynton; the Reighton road follows the most prominent of the side valleys, known as Gosling Slack. Evidence of early settlement on the wold slopes in Grindale is provided by an Iron-Age cemetery discovered near North Dale[49] and the remains of a Roman villa.[50]

The village lies on both sides of the valley, around the large pond or mere. All round the village earthworks and soil- or crop-marks indicate the houses and garths of a more extensive settlement. Most of the present village lies close to the main street at the north end of the site. The cottages and farm-houses are probably all of the 18th century or later. Most are built of brick, but several houses and many farm buildings are wholly or partly of chalk; one cottage contains some cobbles. The six farm-houses in the village are of the late 18th and the earlier 19th centuries. There are about ten Council houses. The only outlying buildings are two post-inclosure farms in the north-east of the township, North Dale and East Leys.

Grindale had only about 40 poll-tax payers in 1377,[51] and there were 28 households in 1670, 7 of them discharged from the hearth tax. Of the 19 households assessed to the hearth tax in 1674 18 had only one hearth and the other had four.[52] In 1743 there were said to be about 14 families in the township[53] and in 1764 8 or more.[54] The population was 88 in 1801. After falling to 69 in 1811, it increased to a maximum of 202 in 1871; the greatest inter-censal increase, from 116 in 1841 to 153 in 1851, took place in the years around the inclosure of 1844. By 1901 the population had dropped to 154.[55] It fluctuated in the early 20th century between 183 in 1911 and 153 in 1931, and in 1961, even after the inclusion of Argam in the civil parish, it was only 138.[56]

MANOR AND OTHER ESTATES. The larger of the two Domesday estates in Grindale, 8 carucates, belonged to the king and was soke of Bridlington manor. The second, 4 carucates, belonged to the archbishop of York.[57]

The Crown estate subsequently passed to the Gants and later the Tattershalls.[58] In 1284–5 7½ carucates of it were held by Walter of Grindale, and this estate constituted the manor of GRINDALE. By 1346 the Grindale family held 6 carucates and 2 bovates, and there were also four small holdings in the Tattershall fee. The Grindales were apparently no longer in possession in 1428, when the 6 carucates then said to comprise the Tattershall fee were held by John Hellercar, with 5 carucates, and Walter Gower.[59]

The manor is next mentioned in 1547, when it was conveyed by Sir Edward Gower to Richard Hutchinson.[60] Richard's son Thomas conveyed it to Anthony and William Gamage in 1577,[61] and in 1605 it included 209 a. of land.[62] The same or another Anthony Gamage conveyed the manor in 1635 to Sir Anthony Browne, who sold it in 1651 to John Hirst. At his death in 1657 Hirst left the manor in equal shares to his nephews William Steele, Richard Hirst, and Samuel Hoyle, and in 1675 their successors conveyed it to Robert Greame.[63] In 1745 the Greames bought a further 3 closes and 5 bovates from Benjamin Hudson, who had himself bought them the previous year from William Huitson.[64] By 1783 John Greame was by far the largest landowner in the township,[65] and in 1786 he acquired the rectorial estate as well;[66] in 1794 he had 73 bovates out of a total of 103 in the open fields.[67] At inclosure in 1844 Yarburgh Greame received allotments totalling 1,587 a.,[68] and in 1853 he bought the prebendal estate.[69] The Lloyd Greames held their land in Grindale until 1952, when nearly 1,800 a. were sold as five separate farms.[70]

Several small holdings of land, deriving from the

---

[44] O.S. Map 6" (1854).
[45] This article was written in 1969.
[46] *P.N.E.R. Yorks.* (E.P.N.S.), 104.
[47] See p. 89.   [48] *Census,* 1931.
[49] Ex inf. Mr. T. C. M. Brewster, 1971.
[50] Mary Kitson Clark, *Gaz. of Roman Remains in E. Yorks.* 85.
[51] E 179/202/62 m. 46.
[52] E 179/205/514, 521.
[53] *Herring's Visit.* ii. 17–18.
[54] B.I.H.R., Bp. V. 1764/Ret. 220.
[55] *V.C.H. Yorks.* iii. 488.
[56] *Census.*
[57] *V.C.H. Yorks.* ii. 197, 211, 322.
[58] *Feud. Aids,* vi. 28, 227, 265–6; *Yorks. Inq.* iv. 35; *Cal. Inq. p.m.* iv, p. 107.
[59] *Feud. Aids,* vi. 28, 227, 265–6.
[60] C 142/125/49; *Yorks. Fines,* i. 129. They had had dealings about the manor in 1541: *Yorks. Fines,* i. 95.
[61] *Yorks. Fines,* ii. 107. See also C 142/125/49; /142/155.
[62] C 142/287/3.
[63] E.R.R.O., DDLG/16/74, 83, 85, 92.
[64] Registry of Deeds, Beverley, S/132/308; /214/516. These bovates adjoined other land already belonging to the Greames.
[65] E.R.R.O., Land Tax, 1783.
[66] See p. 88.
[67] E.R.R.O., DDCV/parcel 22.
[68] Ibid. Enrolment Bk. H.
[69] See p. 88.
[70] Regy. of Deeds, 908/368/322; 909/86/79; /173/155; /235/207; 914/373/326.

former Crown estate of 1086, were acquired by the Stricklands in the late 18th and early 19th centuries,[71] amounting in all to 29 bovates.[72] At inclosure in 1844 Sir George Strickland was allotted 571 a.[73] The estate was retained by the Stricklands until 1949, when it was sold as two separate farms.[74]

The Domesday estate of the archbishop of York helped to support the prebend of Grindale in York Minster. In 1654 the land was sold by parliamentary trustees to Matthew Allured,[75] but it was recovered by the prebend at the Restoration. At inclosure in 1844 106 a. were allotted to the prebend, but in 1853 they were sold to Yarburgh Greame[76] and became part of the Greame estate. The Greames had leased the land since at least 1688.[77]

In the Middle Ages the tithes of Grindale belonged to Bridlington priory,[78] and in the early 16th century the corn tithes were worth £7 or £8.[79] After the Dissolution, together with those in certain other Bridlington townships, they were included in several 16th-century leases.[80] In the 17th century they passed to the Hustler family and were worth £50 a year in 1650.[81] The Hustlers remained impropriators[82] until 1782, when James Hustler's heirs conveyed the estate to Marmaduke Prickett. Four years later Prickett sold it to John Greame.[83] The tithes were commuted in 1841 for £286 10s., payable to the Greames.[84] Some land had also belonged to the priory in right of Grindale chapel. In 1284–5 4 bovates were described as the endowment of the 'church'[85] and they may have been the 4 bovates given to the priory by Ralph of Grindale before 1135; Walter of Grindale later gave another bovate.[86] In the early 16th century these 5 bovates were worth £1.[87]

ECONOMIC HISTORY. The Domesday Survey gives little information about the Crown estate in Grindale, but that of the archbishop, which had land for two ploughs, was waste in 1086 after being worth £1 10s. in 1066.[88] Grindale's tax quota was much reduced in 1354 and also in 1452; a decline in the size and wealth of the village in the century after the Black Death may account for the extensive earthworks which mark the sites of former houses. The excavation of one house-site has revealed the footings of a 17th-century building, and medieval and 17th-century pottery was found.[89]

The manorial estate was worth £30 in 1303, when it was held by Walter of Grindale;[90] Walter had paid easily the largest tax assessment in 1297: 7s. 6d. out of 13s. 5d. for the whole village.[91] In 1545 the manor may have been in the occupation of Robert Barmby, who then had by far the largest subsidy assessment, but there was no outstanding taxpayer in 1601–2.[92] Much of the prebendal estate was held in demesne by the prebendary about 1295.[93] Early in Elizabeth I's reign Grindale was let to the archbishop's secretary, and he sold the lease.[94]

The rents and services of the customary tenants on the prebendal estate are revealed by a survey made about 1295. There were then 21 tenants, 5 of them holding 2 bovates each, 3 holding 1½, 5 holding one, and one holding ½ bovate; the other 7 tenants had no land but between them held 8 tofts and 8 crofts. Their rents totalled about £4 12s. Each landholder was required to cart hay once a year, to reap in autumn for one day, and to find a cart for one day; he owed heriot, merchet, and leyrwite to the lord, as well as suit of mill and of court. The toft-holders did only the day's reaping.[95]

The open-field arable land lay on the wold slopes around the valley. There is no indication of its total area until the early 16th century, when there were said to be 80 bovates in Grindale.[96] The prebendal estate alone had included 36 bovates in 1295, for there were 16 bovates in demesne as well as those held by tenants. Other land may have been taken in from the waste for temporary cultivation at this period, as the prebendal demesne also included intakes, the 'ovenames'.[97] John Greame's estate in 1766 comprised 68 bovates, made up of 551 a. of 'infield tillage' and 140 a. of 'outfield tillage'.[98] In 1794 there were 103 bovates in the whole township,[99] and in 1841 1,155 a. of arable were subject to the payment of tithes.[1] At inclosure in 1844 allotments were made in lieu of 99 bovates.[2]

Meadow land presumably lay in the valley, though there are few references to it. About 1295 the prebendal demesne included 10 a. of meadow, of which only 4 a. on average could be mown.[3] The permanent pasture lay on the highest ground in the township. In 1766 John Greame's estate included 816 a. of 'leys and whinny ground'.[4] In 1794 the pastures were known as Huntow and West Swarth, and they were used in alternate years for horses and for oxen or cows.[5] Huntow pasture was in the north-east of Grindale adjoining pastures in Buckton and Bridlington also known as Huntow.[6] Even after inclosure in 1844 two closes, called Grindale Whins, remained as rough grazing.[7] In 1841 1,047 a. of common pasture were subject to the payment of tithes.[8]

On several occasions in the 17th and 18th centuries agreements were made for the stinting of the

---

[71] E.R.R.O., Land Tax, 1783–1832; DDHB/57/184; DDLG/16/132.
[72] Ibid. DDCV/parcel 22.
[73] Ibid. Enrolment Bk. H.
[74] Regy. of Deeds, 806/404/329; 809/522/426.
[75] E.R.R.O., DDLG/16/12.
[76] Ibid. Enrolment Bk. H; Regy. of Deeds, HA/247/266.
[77] E.R.R.O., DDLG/16/95–102, 106.
[78] e.g. *Miscellanea*, iv (Y.A.S. Rec. Ser. xciv), 6.
[79] *Miscellanea*, iii (Y.A.S. Rec. Ser. lxxx), 16, 32.
[80] See p. 92.
[81] *T.E.R.A.S.* ii. 54. See also E.R.R.O., DDX/120/1.
[82] B.I.H.R., TER. J. Grindale 1685 to 1781.
[83] Registry of Deeds, Beverley, BI/521/813.
[84] B.I.H.R., TA. 629L.
[85] *Feud. Aids*, vi. 28.
[86] *Bridlington Charty.* 1–2, 53.
[87] *Miscellanea*, iii. 30; *Valor Eccl.* (Rec. Com.), v. 120–1.
[88] *V.C.H. Yorks.* ii. 197.
[89] *Med. Archaeol.* x. 216.
[90] *Yorks. Inq.* iv. 35.
[91] *Yorks. Lay Subsidy, 1297* (Y.A.S. Rec. Ser. xvi), 142.
[92] E 179/203/227; E 179/204/373.
[93] *Miscellanea*, iv (Y.A.S. Rec. Ser. xciv), 5–6.
[94] *V.C.H. Yorks.* iii. 381.
[95] *Miscellanea*, iv. 5–6.
[96] *Miscellanea*, iii (Y.A.S. Rec. Ser. lxxx), 16.
[97] *Miscellanea*, iv. 5–6.
[98] E.R.R.O., DDLG/16/126b.
[99] Ibid. DDCV/parcel 22.
[1] B.I.H.R., TA. 629L.
[2] E.R.R.O., Enrolment Bk. H.
[3] *Miscellanea*, iv. 5–6.
[4] E.R.R.O., DDLG/16/126b.
[5] Ibid., DDCV/parcel 22.
[6] See pp. 47, 85.
[7] O.S. Map 6" (1854).
[8] B.I.H.R., TA. 629L.

commonable grounds in Grindale. In 1689 the stint was fixed at 10 sheep for each bovate, house, or cottage and one horse or beast for each bovate.[9] In 1775 the customary practice of occupiers feeding unlimited numbers of sheep in the fallow fields from 1 May to 11 November was ended: in future they were to be allowed 12 sheep for each house and 12 for each bovate. A second agreement, in 1794, concerned stints in the fallow fields and pastures. One ox or cow in the pastures and 10 sheep in the fields were to be allowed for each house or cottage, 10 sheep in the fields for each bovate, one horse in the pastures for every 2 bovates, and 2 oxen or cows in the pastures for every 3 bovates. The agreement was reached by 9 owners and 16 tenants, and it was to last until two thirds of the owners of land wanted to change it. There were 103 bovates and 19 cottage rights. The third agreement was made in 1795; it concerned use of the balks and headlands in the open fields and the time of laying the beast pastures. To prevent animals trespassing upon the corn, they were not to be fed on balks and headlands from 1 May until after harvest time, except that each occupier might keep one horse on his 'respective headland' during harvest time. Animals were to be kept off the pastures between 5 April and 12 May so that they might be laid to improve them.[10] At inclosure in 1844 allotments were made in lieu of 27 common rights.[11]

Little early inclosure was carried out in the township. John Greame's estate included 84 a. in closes in 1766.[12] In 1844, apart from the crofts and garths around the village, there were three ancient inclosures adjoining Argam[13] and a fourth next to the Bridlington road.[14] The open fields remained in common cultivation until 1844, but some concerted action to improve the husbandry was taken on at least one occasion, in 1775. The occupiers then agreed that 'we will annually sow down upon our respective oxgangs of land in one of the eight fields ... a crop of turnips yearly and the year after a crop of clover with barley'.[15] Thus the earlier open fields, the names of which are not known, had already been subdivided to improve the rotation of crops.[16] On one farm in 1837 the 128 a. of arable included 29 a. under turnips and 27 a. under clover.[17]

Inclosure took place in 1844, under the General Inclosure Act of 1836.[18] All told 2,317 a. of commonable lands were dealt with. Yarburgh Greame was allotted 1,587 a., Sir George Strickland 571 a., and the prebendary 106 a. The only two other landowners received 22 a. and 7 a. respectively. During the later 19th and 20th centuries there have been 7-9 farmers in the township.[19]

A windmill is mentioned only once, about 1295.[20] In 1872 agricultural implements were made by Thomas Robson, who is said to have invented the straw elevator for stacking corn.[21]

LOCAL GOVERNMENT. Surviving records of the Grindale manorial court include verdicts for 1670–1719 and 1757–1861, call rolls for 1694, 1698, and 1739–1862, and surrenders and admissions for 1673–1865.[22] The verdicts are mainly concerned with entry fines and agricultural matters. Bylawmen are first mentioned in 1689. In the later 18th and earlier 19th centuries the officers usually appointed were 2 bylawmen, a pinder, and 2 constables, one each for the freehold and copyhold 'manors'. After 1841 only one constable was appointed and after 1848 apparently none at all.

CHURCH. Although never formally separated from the parish of Bridlington, Grindale has long had some degree of independence, with its own chaplain, benefice income, and patron. It was thought in 1650 fit to be a parish.[23] By the 19th century it was regarded as a distinct perpetual curacy, and in 1854 it was united with the curacy of Sewerby.[24] In 1870 that curacy together with that of Grindale was united with the rectory of Argam.[25] In 1958 Grindale and Argam were transferred to Rudston,[26] and Boynton was added to this benefice in 1963.[27] In 1970, however, Grindale and Argam were made a separate living, to be held in plurality with Burton Fleming.[28]

The parochial chaplain of Grindale, mentioned as early as 1346,[29] was presumably provided by Bridlington priory. At the Dissolution his stipend was paid out of the priory's lands.[30] Later the nomination of the curate belonged to the impropriator: in 1764, for example, James Hustler had it.[31] Thus it passed to Marmaduke Prickett and thence to the Greame family,[32] which held it until it was transferred to the archbishop in 1929.[33]

The impropriators provided a stipend of £5 for the curates.[34] It was five times augmented with £200 from Queen Anne's Bounty: in 1749, 1767, 1786, 1808, and 1824.[35] The average annual income in 1829–31 was £57 net,[36] and in 1851 the living was worth about £80.[37] When Argam and Grindale were made a separate living in 1970, £100 was allotted to it from the income of Rudston and £100 from Burton Fleming.[38] Glebe land was acquired with Bounty money: by 1764 land at Keldholme (in

[9] E.R.R.O., DDLG/16/1.
[10] Ibid., DDCV/parcel 22; DDLG/16/4.
[11] Ibid. Enrolment Bk. H.
[12] Ibid. DDLG/16/126b.
[13] Called West closes in 1850: O.S. Map 6" (1854).
[14] E.R.R.O., Enrolment Bk. H.
[15] Ibid., DDCV/parcel 22.
[16] The names of the 8 fields are given in the inclosure allotment bk.: ibid., DX/14.
[17] Ibid. DDLG/16/134.
[18] The award (ibid., Enrolment Bk. H) is not dated but the map (ibid., IA Grindale) is dated 1844. There also survive the allotment and survey bks. (ibid., DX/13, 14). See also ibid. DDLG/16/151–2.
[19] Directories.
[20] Miscellanea, iv. 5–6.
[21] Kelly's Dir. N. & E.R. Yorks. (1872), 542.
[22] E.R.R.O., DDLG/16/1–3.
[23] T.E.R.A.S. ii. 54.

[24] York Dioc. Regy., Orders in Council 124.
[25] Ibid. 292.
[26] Ibid. 747.
[27] Ibid. 781.
[28] Ex inf. Revd. Dr. W. B. Johnston, Burton Fleming, 1970.
[29] Yorks. Deeds, ix. 162–3; he was not the same individual who was chaplain of Bridlington at the time. See also Yorks. Sessions of the Peace (Y.A.S. Rec. Ser. c), 38.
[30] L. & P. Hen. VIII, xiv (2), p. 78.
[31] B.I.H.R., Bp. V. 1764/Ret. 89.
[32] H.O. 129/24/524; Rep. Com. Eccl. Revenues, 938–9.
[33] York Dioc. Regy., Orders in Council 595.
[34] B.I.H.R., TER. J. Grindale 1685 etc.; T.E.R.A.S. ii. 54.
[35] Hodgson, Q.A.B. 441.
[36] Rep. Com. Eccl. Revenues, 938–9.
[37] H.O. 129/24/524.
[38] Ex inf. Revd. Dr. Johnston, 1970.

Kirkbymoorside, Yorks. N.R.) had been bought and by 1777 land at Bonwick.[39]

The curates of Grindale lived elsewhere and also had charge of other cures. Bempton, Bridlington, Burton Fleming, Flamborough, Reighton, Rudston, and Speeton were all at various times held by the curate of Grindale in the 17th, 18th, and early 19th centuries.[40] In 1743, for example, the assistant curate of Bempton, who lived in Bridlington, was curate at Grindale,[41] and he was later curate of Bempton, Bridlington, Flamborough, and Grindale. The incumbents of the united benefices after 1854 lived elsewhere.[42]

There was only one service at Grindale each month in 1743 and 1764, and Holy Communion was administered only thrice and once a year respectively in those years. There were 8–10 communicants in 1743.[43] By 1851 there was a service each Sunday,[44] and in 1865 communion was received once every two months by about nine people.[45] In 1871 communion was administered once every six weeks, and in 1877 once a month.[46] By 1884 there was a weekly service on Wednesday as well as Sunday, and monthly communion was received by about twenty people.[47] In 1969 there was one service each Sunday.

The church of ST. NICHOLAS[48] was built by Y. G. Lloyd Greame in 1874.[49] It replaced a building which had been erected by John Greame in 1830 on the foundations of an older chapel.[50] The 1830 building, consisting of a nave and chancel, was described as of brick and low and mean.[51] Nothing is known of the earlier chapel, but two fonts, one a disused rough bowl and the other a restored tub font, survive in the present church. Minor repairs were done to the chapel in 1721.[52]

The stone-built church of 1874 was designed by Smith and Brodrick of Hull[53] in the Early English style; it consists of nave and chancel, with a small belfry at the west end.

There was one bell in the chapel in 1552[54] and there is still one, undated, bell in the modern church.[55] The plate includes a silver cup and paten cover, made in York in 1570, and a base metal cup, given by Thomas Bell in 1856. There are also silver vessels presented by Y. G. Lloyd Greame: chalice, paten, plate, and flagon, with London hallmarks for 1873.[56]

A register survives for the period 1591–1775, including baptisms, burials, and marriages. Later registers include baptisms from 1818 and burials and marriages from 1874.[57] There are Grindale baptismal entries for 1843–6 in the Speeton register.[58]

NONCONFORMITY. There was said to be one family of Anabaptists in Grindale in 1743, and 'some few' in 1764.[59] A Wesleyan Methodist chapel was built in 1826, and in 1851 it was said that a Primitive Methodist chapel had existed for six years.[60] No more is known of the Primitives. The Wesleyan chapel was subsequently rebuilt, perhaps in 1861 when it was registered for worship. It had ceased to be used by 1954,[61] and in 1969 it served as a village hall. The building was designed by R. G. Smith of Hull.[62]

EDUCATION. There was apparently no school at Grindale until a National school was built by the Lloyd Greames in 1858. It was supported by subscription and by school pence, the latter paid by 45 children in 1874.[63] An annual government grant was received by 1876–7.[64] The attendance was about 25 in 1865 and 1871.[65] It gradually fell in the 20th century from 42 in 1908 to 30 in 1919 and 26 in 1938.[66] The school was transferred to the county council in 1927.[67] It was closed in 1958, when there were fewer than 20 on the roll,[68] and the children were transferred to Boynton.[69] The school and school-house were still standing in 1969.

HILDERTHORPE

The township of Hilderthorpe, covering 455 a. in 1850,[70] lies by the sea immediately south of Bridlington. It was a Scandinavian settlement.[71] The medieval village became depopulated and prominent earthworks mark its site, north of Hilderthorpe Hall.[72] In the 20th century, however, the northern section of Hilderthorpe, as far south as the village site, has been developed as part of Bridlington: these developments are described in the relevant sections of this article dealing with the town and resort. For civil purposes Hilderthorpe was split up in 1894. That part of the township which was included in the district of the Bridlington local board was regarded as a separate civil parish, and

---

[39] B.I.H.R., TER. J. Grindale 1764, 1777.
[40] E.R.R.O., DPX/58, Grindale, pp. 8–9.
[41] Herring's Visit. i. 218; ii. 17–18.
[42] See p. 100.
[43] B.I.H.R., Bp. V. 1764/Ret. 220; Herring's Visit. ii. 17–18.
[44] H.O. 129/24/524.
[45] B.I.H.R., V. 1865/Ret. 464.
[46] Ibid. V. 1871/Ret. 417; V. 1877/Ret.
[47] Ibid. Bp. V. 1884/Ret.
[48] In 1541 it was described as the chapel of the Blessed Virgin Mary: Yorks. Fines, i. 95.
[49] Inscription in church.
[50] H.O. 129/24/524.
[51] e.g. Sheahan and Whellan, Hist. York & E.R. ii. 456.
[52] B.I.H.R., Churches index.
[53] E.R.R.O., DDLG/16/146(a).
[54] Inventories of Ch. Goods, 33.
[55] Boulter, 'Ch. Bells', 123.
[56] Yorks. Ch. Plate, i. 257.
[57] Barley, Par. Docs. E.R. 57. The earliest register is at St. Mary's Church, Bridlington, the others are at Grindale.
[58] E.R.R.O.
[59] B.I.H.R., Bp. V. 1764/Ret. 220; Herring's Visit. ii. 17–18.
[60] H.O. 129/24/524.
[61] G.R.O. Worship Reg. no. 14277.
[62] Kelly's Dir. N. & E.R. Yorks. (1872), 542.
[63] Ed. 7/135.
[64] Rep. of Educ. Cttee. of Council, 1876–7 [C. 1780–I], p. 900, H.C. (1877), xxix.
[65] B.I.H.R., V. 1865/Ret. 464; Rets. rel. Elem. Educ. 1871, 474.
[66] Bd. of Educ. List 21 (H.M.S.O.).
[67] E.R. Educ. Cttee. Mins. 1926–7, 176.
[68] E.R.R.O., SLB. Log Bks. 1876–1958.
[69] E.R. Educ. Cttee. Mins. 1957–8, 235. A few children (from North Dale Fm.) went to Speeton: E.R.R.O., SLB. Admissions Reg. 1874–1958.
[70] O.S. Map 6″ (1854).
[71] P.N.E.R. Yorks. (E.P.N.S.), 103.
[72] For an air photo. see Y.A.J. xxxviii, facing p. 63; M. W. Beresford, Lost Villages of Eng. facing p. 274.

the rest became part of Bessingby civil parish.[73] In 1923, however, the whole of Hilderthorpe was merged with Bridlington civil parish and included in the borough.[74]

The township is low-lying, scarcely anywhere reaching 25 ft. above sea-level, and the boulder-clay cliffs are correspondingly low. The ancient township boundary mostly followed watercourses, including Bessingby beck on the east and the Gypsey Race on the north. Near the sea, however, the boundary ran a little to the south of the Gypsey Race so that the south pier of the harbour lay within Bridlington. The right to take a payment for the groundage of ships driven ashore in Hilderthorpe and Wilsthorpe was said in 1722 to have long belonged to the Stricklands of Boynton.[75] Erosion by the sea has considerably reduced the area of the township, notably in the 19th century.[76]

Only two houses at the village site survived into modern times. One, Flat Top Farm, was an 18th-century house which was demolished in 1966.[77] The other, variously called Hilderthorpe House, Lodge, or Hall, stood on J. W. Pitt's estate. The estate was used as a golf course from 1902 onwards, and in 1925 Pitt sold it to Bridlington corporation; the house has become the club-house.[78] The present building was erected in the late 19th century. It is a large, red-brick, house of two storeys, with a prominent three-storeyed corner tower.

The former coast road leading to Bridlington[79] left the sea near Hilderthorpe village and ran northwards towards the Old Town; it was known as Hilderthorpe Lane in the 19th century and later as Cardigan Road. The only other old road in the township ran beside the Gypsey Race and led to the harbour. Kingsgate, the new road into Bridlington opened in 1923,[80] approaches the town through Hilderthorpe.

There were 56 poll-taxpayers in 1377[81] and 13 able-bodied men were mustered in 1539.[82] Eight households were liable to or exempt from the hearth tax in 1670, and of the 3 households charged to the tax in 1674, 2 had 3 hearths each and one had six.[83] In 1801 the population of Hilderthorpe and Wilsthorpe together was still only 40, but by the 1830s the growth of Bridlington was beginning to affect the township: in 1861 there were 194 inhabitants and thereafter the number increased rapidly as part of Hilderthorpe became built-over.[84]

Little is known of the local government of the township, but a manorial court for Hilderthorpe and Wilsthorpe was held on behalf of the king in 1545, and offences concerning such matters as stock and affray brought in fines totalling 14s.[85]

ESTATES. In 1086 there were three estates in Hilderthorpe: the smallest, of ½ carucate, belonged in both 1066 and 1086 to a king's thegn, Clibert; the king himself held 2½ carucates, which Morcar had held in 1066; and the count of Mortain had 3½ carucates.[86]

It was perhaps the estate of Clibert which comprised the ½ carucate given by Henry I to Bridlington priory.[87] The Crown estate of 2½ carucates passed after 1086 to the Gants and later to the Tattershalls.[88] The gift of 2 bovates to the priory by Matthew, a man of Walter de Gant, was confirmed by Henry I, and Gilbert de Gant granted the priory 2 carucates in Hilderthorpe, described as appurtenant to the vill of Bessingby. A further 2 bovates were given to the priory by John son of Arundel of Hilderthorpe, and 2 bovates more by Robert Buscel in 1246.[89] By 1284–5 the priory held the whole of the Gant fee in the township[90] and it retained this estate until the Dissolution, when it was worth about £2 11s.[91]

The Mortain estate of 1086 seems subsequently to have been given to Watton priory. Robert Constable is known to have granted 4 bovates to the priory in the 13th century,[92] and the priory had 3 carucates and 3 bovates at Hilderthorpe in 1284–5.[93] Swine priory, too, apparently had land in the township in 1449.[94] Another holding, comprising 2 bovates, belonged to Sir John Mounceaux in 1353; it passed to the del See family and after the death of Sir Martin del See in 1494 it was inherited by his daughter Joan, wife of Peter Hildyard.[95]

It has not been possible to connect the later holdings in Hilderthorpe with the medieval estates. In the early 18th century the largest holdings were apparently those of the Tympertons and the Rickabys. John Tymperton, who held his estate by 1711–12, conveyed closes totalling about 200 a. and 24 bovates to Mark Kirkby in 1728.[96] Kirkby died in 1748 and one of his heirs, Richard Sykes, secured the property the following year.[97] In 1814 Sir Mark Sykes granted it to Harrington Hudson.[98] Another part of the Tymperton estate, comprising 5 closes and 8 bovates, passed c. 1765 to Robert Hodgson through his wife Jane, great-granddaughter of John Tymperton.[99] It was acquired by Sir Christopher Sykes in 1778[1] and was included in the sale to Hudson in 1814. Several sales of land were made by Hudson in the 1860s and 1870s, including those which formed the Albert Town estate.[2] The largest sale, however, was of 197 a. to George Wright in 1874.[3] In 1932 most of this land passed to G. W. J. H. Wright,[4] who still owned it in 1969.

In 1717 John Rickaby devised most of his

---

[73] E.R.R.O., CCO 5; see above, p. 69.
[74] *Census*, 1931.
[75] E 134/8 & 9 Geo. I Trin./6.
[76] See p. 30.
[77] Photograph in Bridlington Pub. Libr.
[78] See p. 61.
[79] See p. 201.
[80] See p. 39.
[81] E 179/202/62 m. 18.
[82] *L. & P. Hen. VIII*, xiv. (1), p. 309.
[83] E 179/205/514, 521.
[84] *V.C.H. Yorks.* iii. 488.
[85] S.C. 2/211/56.
[86] *V.C.H. Yorks.* ii. 197, 226, 286, 322.
[87] *Bridlington Charty.* 1.
[88] *Feud. Aids.* vi. 32; *Cal. Inq. p.m.* iv, pp. 108, 261.
[89] *Bridlington Charty.* 1–2, 12, 26–9; *Yorks. Fines, 1232–46*, 145.
[90] *Feud. Aids*, vi. 32.
[91] *Valor Eccl.* (Rec. Com.), v. 120–1; *Miscellanea*, iii (Y.A.S. Rec. Ser. lxxx), 12, 28.
[92] *V.C.H. Yorks.* iii. 254; *T.E.R.A.S.* xii. 5.
[93] *Feud. Aids*, vi. 32.
[94] *Cal. Pat.* 1446–52, 306.
[95] E.R.R.O., DDWB/20/10, 27; DDCC/3/16, 22. See below, p. 105.
[96] Registry of Deeds, Beverley, A/527/753; E/66/115; K/554/1189.
[97] E.R.R.O., DDSY/108/3.
[98] Regy. of Deeds, CY/358/527.
[99] Ibid. AE/126/250; /127/251; AG/60/125.
[1] Ibid. AZ/246/393.   [2] See pp. 37, 39.
[3] Regy. of Deeds, LM/382/476.   [4] Ibid. 444/325/252.

property in Hilderthorpe to his sister Hester Mirfield,[5] and by 1764 it had passed to Thomas Grant by marriage to Dorothy Mirfield; it then comprised 65 a. in closes and 16 bovates.[6] The Grants retained the property until 1841, when 72 a. in closes and 28 a. of open-field land were conveyed to Charles Hudson.[7] In 1858 Hudson sold it to Luke Warters, in 1871 it was acquired by William Jarrett, and in 1898 he sold it to J. W. Pitt.[8] Several building plots were sold by Pitt before he conveyed 84 a., as well as land along the cliff top and a sea-wall, to Bridlington corporation in 1925.[9]

The tithes of the township were enjoyed by Bridlington priory until the Dissolution. They were subsequently included in various leases of tithes in several of the Bridlington townships. Leases were taken by John Banaster and James Bourchier in 1538, Thomas Raynnowe in 1545, William Godolgham in 1546, Richard Whalley in 1566, and Walter Whalley in 1569.[10] The tithes were subsequently granted away by the Crown and in 1631 William Smithson acquired them from John Garforth.[11] In 1650 the tithes of Hilderthorpe and Wilsthorpe together were said to belong to John Buck and John Weaver and to be worth £35.[12] The tithes were acquired in 1659 by Thomas Rickaby, Richard Ellis, and Bartholomew Anderson from Robert Winne.[13] They are not mentioned again.

ECONOMIC HISTORY. In 1086 there were six villeins and land for one plough on the half-carucate estate at Hilderthorpe.[14] After the Black Death the township was relieved of more than 60 per cent of its tax quota, but later tax returns suggest that the depopulation of the village was gradual and long drawn out.[15]

In the 18th century a single tenant held the Sykes estate in Hilderthorpe,[16] and there were normally two or three farmers in the township in the 19th century.[17] Much of the land was in open-field cultivation in the 18th century, but the date of inclosure is not known: it was not complete even in the later 19th century, for about 25 a. of open-field land on the former Grant estate are mentioned as late as 1871.[18] By the 18th century, however, there were numerous closes, too. On the Tymperton estate in 1728, for example, there were 15 closes, 11 of them totalling 179 a., as well as 24 bovates in the open fields.[19] The Grants had 6 closes, totalling 65 a., as well as 16 bovates, in 1764.[20]

CHURCH. There is no evidence that Hilderthorpe ever had its own chapel. It remained in the parish of St. Mary's, Bridlington, until 1843, when it was included in the new parish of Christ Church Bridlington Quay. In 1916 it became the separate parish of Emmanuel, Hilderthorpe.[21]

SEWERBY AND MARTON

The township of Sewerby with Marton lies on the southern side of Flamborough Head, less than 2 miles from Bridlington. It occupies 2,116 a.[22] Sewerby was probably a Scandinavian and Marton an Anglian settlement.[23] Remains of a possible Roman camp were in the 1890s visible on the clifftop near Sewerby House, and an embanked road which formerly led towards Bridlington may also have been Roman.[24] The discovery of an Anglian cemetery, perhaps of the 6th century,[25] suggests early settlement near the later village sites. The village of Sewerby stands less than ¼ mile from the sea and little more from the suburbs of Bridlington, which now cover a substantial area in the southwest of the township.[26] Some modern development has also taken place in the village itself, and since 1934 the grounds of Sewerby House have been gradually developed by Bridlington corporation with entertainments for visitors to the resort; a cliff-top promenade links these grounds with the town. The small village of Marton lies about ½ mile north of Sewerby. Until new building took place in the 20th century, little remained of the old village. It was small even in the Middle Ages, but earthworks survive on the north side of the road to Flamborough to indicate its former extent. Though further away from Bridlington, some holiday development has taken place in the village and many houses are scattered along the roads leading to the town. Between Sewerby and Marton is the extensive parkland around the former Greame and Creyke family mansions, and much of the north and west of the township is still open farmland.

The township boundary in the south-west has long followed a roadway, and this is now one of the main avenues through the suburbs of Bridlington. On the west the line of this road is continued as a field-road. Towards the east a stream in a deeply-cut valley divides Sewerby from Flamborough and Bempton. The civil parish of Sewerby with Marton remained distinct until 1935, but it had already been reduced in size. The extreme south-western corner of the township lay within the district of Bridlington local board, established in 1863, and within the urban district which replaced it in 1895. A slightly larger area, 84 a., lay within the borough which was created in 1899. In 1923 a further 289 a. of Sewerby with Marton was taken into the borough, and in 1935 1,072 a. more. The remainder, comprising 671 a., was merged with Bempton civil parish in 1935.[27]

---

[5] Regy. of Deeds, F/119/257; P/431/1097.
[6] Ibid. AG/167/335.
[7] Ibid. FR/99/117.
[8] Ibid. HR/230/282; KW/17/25; 3/279/233 (1898).
[9] Ibid. 316/193/159; /195/160.
[10] *L. & P. Hen. VIII*, xiii (1), p. 562; xx (1), p. 212; xxi (1), p. 766; *Cal. Pat.* 1563–6, 382; 1566–9, 346.
[11] C.P. 25(2)/520/7 Chas. I Mich. no. 15.
[12] *T.E.R.A.S.* ii. 55.
[13] C.P. 25(2)/615/1659 Mich. no. 18.
[14] *V.C.H. Yorks.* ii. 286.
[15] E 179/202/53; see above, p. 91.

[16] E.R.R.O., DDSY/26/1, 2; /97/3; /107/18, 19, 25, 28.
[17] Directories.
[18] Regy. of Deeds, KW/17/25.
[19] Ibid. K/554/1189.
[20] Ibid. AG/167/335.
[21] See p. 75.
[22] O.S. Map 6" (1854).
[23] *P.N.E.R. Yorks.* (E.P.N.S.), 104.
[24] Mary Kitson Clark, *Gaz. of Roman Remains in E. Yorks.* 128.
[25] *Med. Archaeol.* iv. 137.
[26] These are considered as part of the town: see pp. 35, 40.
[27] *Census.* For the growth of Bridlington see above, p. 30.

Over much of the township the landscape of large rectangular fields is that created by the inclosure of 1811, though a substantial area in the east had been inclosed in the mid 17th century.[28] The landscape contrasts strongly with that on the more exposed northern side of Flamborough Head, for in Sewerby and Marton there are plentiful hedgerow trees and some plantations, no doubt reflecting the activities of the Greames and Creykes whose estates covered a large part of the township. At the eastern extremity of Sewerby is the steep-sided and wooded valley which forms the boundary with Flamborough; the earthwork known as Danes' Dyke lies on its further side.

The ground reaches a height of about 275 ft. above sea-level in the north-west and about 200 ft. in the north-east, falling steadily southwards towards the sea. Sewerby village lies at about 100 ft. and the chalk cliffs eastwards from the village are little lower. In the south-west the ground falls to under 50 ft. and part of this area was carr-land before inclosure; the low cliffs there are of boulder clay. The rocky foreshore in front of the chalk cliffs gives way to a broad beach which forms the North Sands of Bridlington. The right to take a payment for the groundage of ships driven ashore at Sewerby was said in 1722 to have long belonged to the Stricklands of Boynton; John Greame had laid claim to it, after acquiring the Carliells' manor in 1714.[29]

The modern road pattern is to a large extent the creation of the inclosure commissioners in the early 19th century. Of the earlier roads there is mention of Seagate, in or near Sewerby village, in the Middle Ages and in the early 18th century.[30] Dumpuddle Lane is recorded in 1734.[31] In 1343 two roads were called Martongate and Brechegate,[32] and the name Marton Gate was applied to the Bridlington–Marton road in the 19th century. In 1850 the roads around the two villages also included Sewerby, Jewison's, Short, and Sheep Rake Lanes; High Sewerby Road led across the parkland to Leys Road (the remnant of a longer Leys Road) and on to The Moor Road; and Sands and Carr Lanes crossed the former common pastures near the sea. Frith Lane led into the parkland from the east end of Sewerby village.[33]

The most striking feature of the landscape is the parkland of Marton Hall and Sewerby House, which was largely created during the earlier 19th century. Some noteworthy changes to the road pattern and village layout were involved in the imparking. It is possible that certain changes were made about 1710 by the Carliells' tenant at Sewerby, John Greame.[34] When Elizabeth Carliell sold the property to Greame in 1714 it included the manor-house, a house in its yard and a close behind it, and ten 'cottages, tofts or crofts where houses have formerly stood'.[35] Thus the surrounds of the house may already have been 'improved' before the alterations of the 19th century.[36]

Until final inclosure in 1811 the main village street of Sewerby divided at its eastern end, one branch running in front of Sewerby House and leading to the moor, the other running across the Leys and past Marton Hall, on its way to the moor and to Flamborough.[37] The inclosure commissioners stopped up parts of these roads, allotting them in 1811 to Greame and Creyke, and in their places new roads were laid out giving a wide berth to both mansions. Within this new framework an extensive area of parkland and plantations had been created by 1850. At Sewerby this involved the removal of perhaps a dozen houses and the re-alignment of the road connecting the head of the village street with the back lane. Some new cottages were apparently built in the village to rehouse displaced families, notably a terrace lying at right-angles behind the village street. Some 26 a. of plantations were added in 1841–5 to the 13 a. already existing.[38] G. G. Scott's church and school were additional ornaments to the surrounds of the park.[39]

Apart from the mansions there are few buildings of note in either village. Sewerby lay mainly along the single main street until its expansion in the 20th century. The vista at the east end of the street is closed by the gatehouse of Sewerby House. The 18th- and 19th-century terraced cottages of the village are mostly of brick, with some chalk and cobbles; one incorporates dressed ashlar. In the present century some gaps between houses have been filled, the village has been extended towards Bridlington, and developments have taken place both north and south of the main street. In the 1930s Cliff Estate, North Cliff, and Riviera Estate, consisting of bungalows and chalets, were built between the village and the sea.[40] A large caravan camp now occupies the land behind Charity (or Cowton's) Farm, the only farm-house in the village. The Ship inn is a mid-19th-century building in the back lane. The Bottle and Glass is mentioned in 1823 but the Ship is recorded in its place in 1840.[41] Near the inn is a village hall, probably the building rented from the Lloyd Greames as a reading room in 1894.[42]

The chief buildings in Marton village are Marton Manor and Marton Grange, the former known as the Grove until c. 1900. The Manor appears to be an 18th-century house, altered and raised to three storeys in the 19th century; its farm buildings include a massive brick barn with tie-rod heads dated 1775. The Grange is a 19th-century house with chalk, cobble, and brick farm buildings similar to those at Speeton.[43] Near by is a small brick tower which formerly housed a hydraulic ram.[44] There are also several 20th-century houses to the east of the village, two of them near the site of the former brickyard, as well as a caravan camp. More 20th-century houses line the roads west of the village, where an 'ancient enclosure'[45] was scarcely visible in 1969, and there is a caravan camp there, too.

---

[28] See p. 98. [29] E 134/8 & 9 Geo. I Trin./6.
[30] Registry of Deeds, Beverley, K/613/1310; *Yorks. Deeds*, vi. 125.
[31] Regy. of Deeds, M/450/738.
[32] *Yorks. Deeds*, v. 130. For the Breach see below, p. 98.
[33] O.S. Map 6" (1854); see maps on p. 94.
[34] See p. 95.
[35] Registry of Deeds, Beverley, E/194/337.
[36] This evidence does not support a suggestion that the whole village was moved out of the park in the 18th cent.: *Y.A.J.* xxxviii. 68.
[37] See maps on p. 94, based on E.R.R.O., DDLG/30/897; Regy. of Deeds, 1811 (inclosure map); O.S. Map 6" (1854).
[38] E.R.R.O., DDLG/30/902. [39] See p. 100.
[40] O.S. Map 6" (various edns.).
[41] Baines, *Hist. Yorks.* ii. 387; White, *Dir. E. & N.R. Yorks.* (1840), 372. The ship had been built since 1838: E.R.R.O., DDLG/30/633–5.
[42] B.I.H.R., Bp. V. 1894/Ret.
[43] See p. 101.
[44] O.S. Map 6" (1854).
[45] Ibid. (all edns.).

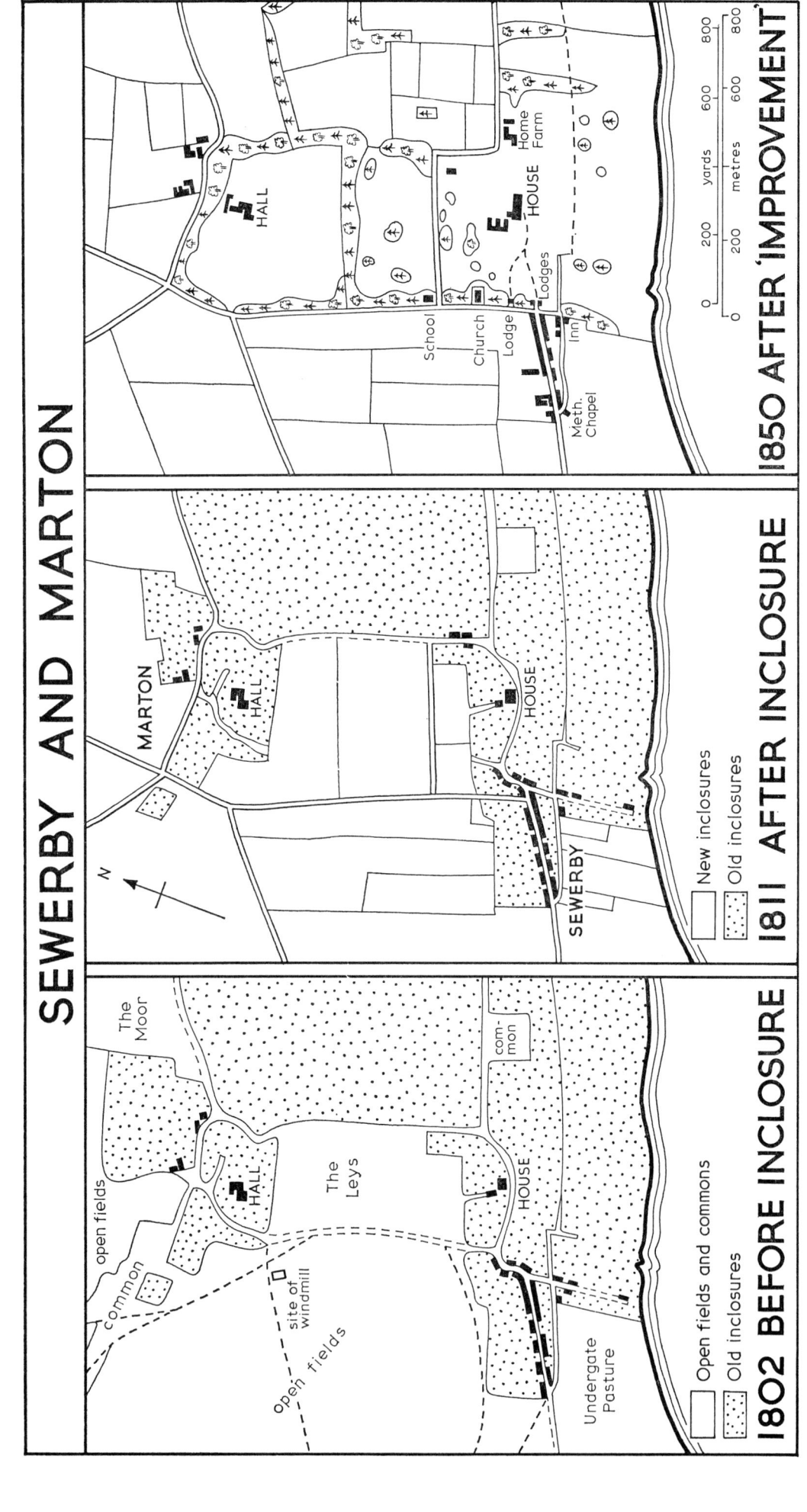

Numerous outlying farm-houses were built in the 19th century after inclosure. They include Sands House on the Sewerby to Bridlington road; Danes' Dyke Farm in the east; High (formerly Greame's) Barn towards Bempton, a yellow-brick farm range with living accommodation in one end; Field House on the Bempton road; and Sewerby Cottage, Marton Lodge, and Sewerby Fields, all near the Marton–Bridlington road. In the extreme north-west is the stump of Speeton windmill and the mill-house. Flamborough railway station stands next to the Marton–Bempton road and next to it is a 19th-century terrace called Marton Cottages. The railway line was opened in 1847; the station was closed to goods traffic in 1964 and to passengers in 1970.[46] Close by is the extensive factory of Flamborough Maltings, completed in 1964.[47]

No poll-tax figures are available for Sewerby and Marton.[48] In 1674 25 out of 49 households were discharged from paying the hearth tax; of the 24 that were assessed, 11 had one hearth, 7 had 2, 3 had 3, and one each had 4, 5, and 6 hearths.[49] The population of the township in 1801 was 279. Between 1811 and 1821 it rose from 248 to 317, and in 1831–61 it was about 350. During the later 19th century the expansion of Bridlington into Sewerby began, and by 1891 there were 628 inhabitants.[50] In the 20th century the population of the township, excluding the areas taken into the borough of Bridlington, rose from 306 in 1911 to 383 in 1931.[51]

MANORS AND OTHER ESTATES. There were eight holdings in Sewerby and Marton in 1086. Three of these belonged to the count of Mortain: two contained a total of 6½ carucates in Sewerby, held separately by Carle and Torchil in 1066 and together by Richard in 1086; the third, consisting of one carucate in Marton, was held by Carle in 1066 and by the count in 1086.[52] The king also had three holdings. One consisted of 6 carucates in Marton and was soke of the manor of Bridlington. The other two were held by his thegn Clibert in both 1066 and 1086; they consisted of 1½ carucate in Sewerby and 2 carucates in Marton.[53] The seventh holding, 1½ carucate in Sewerby, was soke of the manor of Flamborough and belonged to Hugh, earl of Chester.[54] Finally, 3 carucates in Marton belonged to the archbishop of York.[55]

The Mortain estate of 1086 later passed like Boynton to the Paynel family and subsequently to the archbishops of Canterbury.[56] A mesne lordship was held under them by the Meynells, and in 1284–5 the Meynell fee comprised 5 carucates and 6 bovates in Sewerby.[57]

In the 12th century at least part of the Meynell fee may have been held in demesne by the Gras family, for in 1188 Agnes of Rotsea, daughter of William le Gras, granted more than 4 bovates to Osbert of Sewerby.[58] Subsequently the demesne lords of Sewerby under the Meynells were members of the family that took its name from the village.[59] The Osbert already mentioned granted land there to Bridlington priory.[60] Robert of Sewerby had 3 carucates in the township in 1234[61] and William had 4 carucates and 2 bovates in 1299.[62] Robert of Sewerby was lord of the manor of SEWERBY in 1316,[63] and the family held it until the death of William of Sewerby in 1450.[64]

Before 1453 William's daughter and heir Margaret married Geoffrey Pigot.[65] Their son Ranulph Pigot died childless in 1503 and was succeeded by the three daughters of his brother Thomas.[66] Sewerby was apparently divided between Margaret, who married James Metcalfe, and Elizabeth, whose third husband was Sir Charles Brandon. In 1545 Brandon sold part of his share to Marmaduke Thwayt and George Metham, and in 1552 Thomas Thwayt sold it to Sir William Fairfax and others; Fairfax in turn sold it to Ralph Creyke in 1588[67] and it thus became part of the Creykes' estate at Marton.[68]

Margaret Pigot's share was sold by her son Sir Christopher Metcalfe to Ralph Raysing in 1565.[69] In the same year Raysing acquired other property in Sewerby from Christopher Thwing, which the latter had bought in 1555 from Elizabeth Brandon.[70] In 1567 Raysing sold the manor to John Carliell.[71] The Carliells retained it[72] until 1714, when Elizabeth Carliell and her son Henry sold it to John Greame; it then included the manor-house where the Carliells had lived, but which was already occupied by Greame, and 4 bovates of land.[73] The Greame family already had other land in Sewerby and they subsequently acquired more.[74] John Greame was allotted 843 a. at inclosure in 1811,[75] and further additions were made to the estate by the 1830s.[76]

At the death in 1856 of Yarburgh Greame, who had taken the surname Yarburgh in 1852, Sewerby passed to his sister Alicia (d. 1867) for life and then to her son Y. G. Lloyd, who took the additional surname Greame.[77] When the estate was finally broken up and sold by Yarburgh Lloyd Greame between 1930 and 1950 it comprised nearly 1,400 a. The house and 411 a. were sold to Bridlington corporation in 1934,[78] and other large sales were of Field House Farm, with 251 a., in 1936, and Marton

---

[46] Ex inf. Divisional Manager, Brit. Rail (E.R.), Doncaster, 1971.
[47] *Bridlington Free Press*, 6 Nov. 1964.
[48] The certificate for Marton is mutilated: E 179/202/62 m. 41.
[49] E 179/205/521.
[50] *V.C.H. Yorks.* iii. 489.
[51] Census.
[52] *V.C.H. Yorks.* ii. 226.
[53] Ibid. 197, 286–7.
[54] Ibid. 219.
[55] Ibid. 212.
[56] See p. 22.
[57] *Feud. Aids*, vi. 29.
[58] *Bridlington Charty*. 36.
[59] *Yorks. Deeds*, vi. 188–91 gives pedigree.
[60] *Bridlington Charty*. 36–8.
[61] *Yorks. Fines, 1232–46*, 20.
[62] *Cal. Inq. p.m.* iii, pp. 428–9.
[63] *Feud. Aids*, vi. 170; *Cal. Inq. p.m.* vii, p. 402.
[64] *Test. Ebor.* ii. 136 n.
[65] Ibid. iii. 161.
[66] Ibid. iv. 213–14.
[67] *Yorks. Fines*, i. 115, 165; iii. 106.
[68] See p. 96.
[69] *Yorks. Fines*, i. 315.
[70] E.R.R.O., DDLG/30/84, 88, 92.
[71] *Yorks. Fines*, i. 330.
[72] e.g. C 145/516/43; *Y.A.J.* xxxiii. 313.
[73] Registry of Deeds, Beverley, E/194/337.
[74] E.R.R.O., DC/20/1, 2; DDLG/30/174, 178, 405, 412, 434, 475, 504, 611, 624.
[75] Regy. of Deeds, CQ/111/4.
[76] E.R.R.O., Land Tax; DDLG/30/546, 583, 659.
[77] J. T. Ward, *E. Yorks. Landed Estates in the 19th Cent.* (E. Yorks. Loc. Hist. Ser. xxiii), 47; F. F. Johnson, *Sewerby Hall and Park* (4th edn.), 21
[78] Regy. of Deeds, 509/31/24.

Manor Farm, with 309 a., in 1947.[79] Bridlington corporation has retained the chief estate.

It seems likely that the later Sewerby House stood on the same site as the medieval manor-house of the Sewerby family. A new chapel attached to the manor-house was mentioned in 1414,[80] and in 1468 the house included a chapel.[81] The house of the Carliells, probably also on the same site, had seven hearths in the late 17th century.[82] Panelling and a chimney-piece of this period were evidently preserved when the house was rebuilt and still survive in a room on the top floor. There are also several early doorways, including one of Tudor design, in the semi-basement.

The house was rebuilt c. 1714–20 by John Greame (d. 1746).[83] The early-18th-century structure, which was of three storeys above a semi-basement, survives as the central block of the present house. The entrance front, facing south, was originally of red brick with stone dressings; it is seven bays long and has closely-set sash windows with stone architraves and key-blocks. The three central bays, flanked by stone quoins, break slightly forward and are surmounted by a pediment. Inside several panelled rooms of this period survive, together with a fine cantilevered staircase of oak with three twisted balusters to each step. Also of the early 18th century is the first stable building, to the west of the house, built of brick, two storeys high, with rusticated stone quoins and doorway and a heavily-rusticated, round-headed, central window extending into an open pediment.[84] Greame's son, another John (d. 1798), made few additions to the house, but c. 1750 he built a privy that was approached through a shellwork grotto.

The house was considerably altered, probably in 1807–8, by John Greame's nephew and heir, also John.[85] A two-storeyed bow-fronted wing was added at each end, together with an elegant semicircular portico in the centre, and the building was painted to resemble stone. Care was evidently taken to repeat some of the features of the original house and to unite old and new in a harmonious whole; the work may have been by the Bridlington architect John Matson, though the plans drawn in 1807 are signed by Thomas Johnson, of Leeds. The east wing was extended at the rear c. 1830. A new stable block, enclosing a courtyard on three sides, was built in the 1820s, the design in keeping with that of the earlier stables and the house. It is of two storeys, and built of brick with rusticated stone quoins. The south front has a recessed Doric portico with a pediment, later crowned by an Italianate stone clock-tower of 1847. The long west elevation consists of three slightly recessed sections separated by two pedimented sections, each of the latter containing a round-headed archway, a semicircular window, and a bulls-eye, all heavily rusticated.[86]

The final alterations were made to the house by Yarburgh Greame, apparently in 1848, to designs by H. F. Lockwood, of Hull.[87] The bow-fronted wings were raised another storey and the cornice and central pediment rebuilt over the whole façade; the pediment contains the Greame arms. Probably during the same period the round-arched classical gateway to the stable yard was built, together with a balustrade in front of the house[88] and a single-storeyed conservatory adjoining the east wing. The impressive gatehouse, which gives access to the grounds from the head of the village street, is of about the same date. It is built of yellow brick with stone dressings and incorporates two flanking lodges; the central archway is surmounted by a Doric entablature and pediment. Lockwood was probably the architect of much of the mid-19th-century work at Sewerby, including the gatehouse.[89] Home Farm was built during the earlier 19th century,[90] and near by in the parkland is a mid-century dovecot of yellow brick with stone dressings. Since 1931 the house (now styled Sewerby Hall) and park have been developed by Bridlington corporation with recreational facilities and attractions for visitors.

The Crown estate of 1086 subsequently passed to the Gants and later to the Tattershalls as overlords. During the 12th century part of this land was held in demesne by the Neville family: in 1160–76 Alice de Gant confirmed to Geoffrey de Neville 2 carucates in Marton which his father Ralph had previously held of Walter de Gant.[91] The last of the Nevilles was William, who died without heirs in the mid 13th century, and the estate descended through the two daughters of Roger de Neville (d. before 1227). The first, Maud, married William Malbis. Two-and-a-half carucates were said to belong to the Malbis fee in 1284–5,[92] and Richard Malbis held the land in 1304.[93] The second of Roger de Neville's daughters, Hawise, married Walter of Lowthorpe. After the death of Thomas of Lowthorpe by 1279 his property passed to his daughters Cecily and Margery, and by 1290–1 they had married respectively Robert and John of Heslerton.[94]

It is not certain how the parts of the manor were reunited, nor is it clear how the estate passed to its later owners, the Creykes. At least part of the manor may have been acquired by Thomas Creyke of Beverley (d. 1488) by marriage with Joan, daughter and coheir of Anthony Arden of Marton (d. 1455). Thomas Creyke's son Robert was 'of Beverley and Marton'. Robert's son William married Agnes, daughter of John Heslerton,[95] and it is possible that another part of the estate thus passed to the Creykes. Other land was added in 1588.[96]

---

[79] Regy. of Deeds, 560/537/415; 760/418/345.
[80] B.I.H.R., Churches index.
[81] *Test. Ebor.* iii. 161–8. [82] E 179/205/2.
[83] See plate facing p. 48. For a full architectural description see F. F. Johnson, *Sewerby Hall and Park* (4th edn.), *passim*.
[84] The original ground-floor windows have been replaced by Bridlington corporation since 1931.
[85] E.R.R.O., DDLG/30/911 (plans of 1807); a rainwater-head on the west wing is inscribed 'J. G. 1808'.
[86] The south front contains 2 bow windows inserted by Bridlington corporation.
[87] E.R.R.O., DDLG/30/843.
[88] The centre of the balustrade has been removed by Bridlington corporation.

[89] There are plans for the conservatory, a summer house, and a cottage, drawn for Yarburgh Greame by Lockwood, together with unsigned plans for the gatehouse: E.R.R.O., DDLG/30/913–14, 916–18. Measured drawings of the gatehouse in the National Monuments Record tentatively ascribe the design to 'Pritchard of York'.
[90] The house has recently been rebuilt.
[91] *E.Y.C.* ii, p. 461.
[92] *Feud. Aids*, vi. 29.
[93] *Cal. Inq. p.m.* v, p. 54.
[94] Ibid. See below, p. 273.
[95] *Dugdale's Visit. Yorks.*, ed. J. W. Clay, ii. 448, which contains (447 sqq.) a pedigree of the Creykes; *Test. Ebor.* ii. 195–6.
[96] See p. 95.

Ralph Creyke was allotted 200 a. at inclosure in 1811[97] and the family retained the estate until the 20th century. Some 230 a., comprising Marton Lodge farm, were sold in 1913,[98] and the hall with 34 a. of land were sold to Florence Gane in 1931.[99] The Gane family still owned the hall in 1969.

Marton Hall was built by Gregory Creyke, probably in or soon after 1672, the year of his marriage,[1] perhaps on the site of an earlier house.[2] It is of brick with stone dressings and is a square two-storeyed building with a five-bay frontage. The exterior was much altered in the late 18th and 19th centuries but original features include stone quoins, a moulded brick string-course breaking forward above the ground-floor windows, and, on the north wall, a stone tablet bearing the arms of Creyke. Internally there are several late-17th-century panelled rooms, two having chimney-pieces flanked by garlands. The finest feature is the staircase of c. 1672, which has carved and twisted balusters and enriched strings; above it is a cornice decorated with swags and an ornate ceiling with a central wreath. The wide entrance doorway on the west front is an insertion of the late 18th or early 19th century; it has engaged columns and pilasters, a Doric entablature, and a segmental fanlight with Gothic glazing below an open pediment. At about the same period rooms on the south side of the house were remodelled and a two-storeyed bay window was added. The building has been used as a private school since 1912.[3]

Another part of the Crown land was held by the Marton family. Ernald of Marton held land from Simon de St. Liz in 1166,[4] and this estate apparently comprised 2 carucates in 1284–5.[5] In the early 14th century it belonged to John of Marton. In 1304 he held one carucate in demesne, while the other was held under him by Bridlington priory.[6] The descent of this land has not been traced further.

A further carucate of Crown land was held by Stephen of Thorpe in 1344;[7] under him, most of the land, 5 bovates, had been held by Robert of Sewerby in 1335.[8] This land presumably descended as part of the Sewerby family's manor.

The archbishop of York's estate of 1086 later formed part of the endowment of the prebendary of Bugthorpe.[9] Known as the manor of *MARTON*, it was held from the prebendary by John Hotham in 1414.[10] Sir Francis Hotham still held the manor in 1546,[11] but in 1568 John Hotham conveyed it to Thomas Preston and William Clerke.[12] From Richard Preston it passed to Thomas Bird in 1617, and from Bird to William Hustler in 1621.[13] The Hustlers retained it until 1782, when Evereld Hustler sold it to John Greame[14] and it became part of the Greame's Sewerby estate.

Another estate was held from the prebendary in the early 17th century by the Blakelock family. Thus Robert Blakelock in 1606 held a manor-house with 14 bovates of land, and other property including 6 more bovates.[15] His sons Edward and Ralph still held it in 1616,[16] but it was perhaps his share of this estate which Ralph sold to John Cooke in 1622.[17] Its descent has not been traced further.

The estate belonging to Hugh, earl of Chester, in 1086 as soke of Flamborough manor was by 1284–5 held by William of Flamborough.[18] Though the details are confused, it is clear that estates in Sewerby and Marton were held in the early Middle Ages both by the Constable family, lords of Flamborough, and by the Flamborough family. Some of this land apparently passed to the Sewerby family.[19] Another part of it, 6 bovates, was given before 1303 by Robert Constable to his daughter Lettice, who married Thomas de Houton.[20] William de Houton held this land at his death in 1355,[21] but soon afterwards it passed to the Langdales.[22] Thomas Langdale granted land, said to be 80 a., to Richard Shippabotham in 1554,[23] and Richard's son Robert Shippabotham still held 6 bovates of the Constables at his death in 1579.[24] Other land in Sewerby was attached to the Constables' manor of Flamborough[25] and descended with it to the Stricklands.[26] In 1803 Sir George Strickland conveyed his Sewerby property, including 8 bovates, to John Greame,[27] and it was merged in the Greames' manorial estate.

By various gifts Bridlington priory built up a substantial estate in Sewerby and Marton. At least 7 bovates were given by the Marton family, at least 6 bovates by the Sewerbys, and more by the Flamboroughs and others.[28] By the early 16th century the priory had at least 19 bovates and its property in Sewerby was worth £6.[29] Various leases were made by the Crown after the Dissolution and former priory land may later have comprised several of the smaller landholdings in the township. Some of the priory land was granted in 1596 to Francis Skelton, and in 1601 it passed from Edward Bee and Justinian Povey to William Greame in 1601,[30] and this no doubt became part of the Greame's manorial estate in the 18th century.

In the Middle Ages the tithes belonged to the priory and in the early 16th century the corn tithes

---

[97] Regy. of Deeds, CQ/111/4.
[98] Ibid. 151/501/417.
[99] Ibid. 429/579/463.
[1] The arms of Creyke and his wife appear on the staircase ceiling. In 1674 Creyke was charged tax on one hearth and on 6 more 'new built': E 179/205/521.
[2] Ex inf. Mr. F. F. Johnson, 1971.
[3] *The Martonian*, 1955, 2–4.
[4] *E.Y.C.* ii, p. 430.
[5] *Feud. Aids*, vi. 29.
[6] *Cal. Inq. p.m.* iv, p. 108.
[7] Ibid. viii, p. 350.
[8] Ibid. vii, p. 402.
[9] *Miscellanea*, iv (Y.A.S. Rec. Ser. xciv), 11.
[10] *Yorks. Inq. Hen. IV–V*, 100, 152–3.
[11] *Test. Ebor.* vi. 246.
[12] *Yorks. Fines*, i. 362.
[13] Ibid. *1614–25*, 101, 171.
[14] Regy. of Deeds, BF/62/103.
[15] C 142/291/74.
[16] E.R.R.O., DPX/21.
[17] *Yorks. Fines*, 1614–25, 202.
[18] *Feud. Aids*, vi. 29.
[19] E.R.R.O., DDCC/App. A, pp. 33 (no. 2), 36 (no. 2), 37 (no. 1), 38 (no. 2), 39 (no. 1), 41 (nos. 1–3); *Yorks. Deeds*, iv. 132–5.
[20] *Yorks. Deeds*, iv. 133, 135.
[21] *Cal. Inq. p.m.* x, pp. 188–9.
[22] E.R.R.O., DDCC/149/26; *Yorks. Deeds*, v. 133. See also C 1/332/23.
[23] *Yorks. Fines*, i. 176; *Yorks. Deeds*, iv. 137.
[24] C 142/185/58.
[25] E.R.R.O., DDHA/4/62.
[26] See p. 154.
[27] Regy. of Deeds, CF/367/577.
[28] *Bridlington Charty.* 2, 31–40; *Yorks. Fines, 1232–46*, 38.
[29] *Miscellanea*, iii (Y.A.S. Rec. Ser. lxxx), 4, 12; *Valor Eccl.* (Rec. Com.), v. 120.
[30] C.P. 43/75 rot. 41; E.R.R.O., DDLG/30/405.

alone were worth over £15.[31] After the Dissolution the tithes were included, with those of various other Bridlington townships, in several 16th-century leases.[32] In the 17th century some of the tithes passed to the Hustler family and were worth £30 a year in 1650.[33] In the 1670s the tithes were farmed from the Hustlers by Eleanor Beaucock and in the 1690s by John Dawson and John Robinson, all of whom were involved in disputes over their payment.[34] The tithes were in 1782 sold by Evereld Hustler to John Greame,[35] and at inclosure in 1811 his nephew was allotted 322 a. for his part of the tithes. For the remaining part, the descent of which has not been traced, George Darley was allotted 63 a.[36]

ECONOMIC HISTORY. The Domesday Survey gives some small indication of the condition of the villages in 1086. The archbishop's estate, in Marton, had land for two ploughs, and those of the king's thegn Clibert each had land for one. The archbishop's estate had fallen little in value since the Conquest, from 10s. in 1066 to 8s. 4d. in 1086; Clibert's estate in Sewerby, however, had been worth 10s. in 1066 but was waste in 1086, and his Marton land was also waste; so were the large estates of the count of Mortain in Sewerby and of the king in Marton.[37]

Robert of Sewerby, in a grant of his manor-house and lands c. 1308, mentioned his seven serfs (*nativi*),[38] and in 1335 he had 23 bovates of land and 6 a. of meadow in demesne and received over £3 in rents from serfs and cottars.[39] In 1368 John of Sewerby let a tenement where the lessees were to build a new house, and he agreed to provide 4 posts, a hearth, 20 spars, and straw for thatching.[40] In 1377 John of Sewerby let the manor-house, open-field land, the park, and meadow called the 'frith'. With the meadow went hay-harvest boon-works, and the stock included in the lease were 4 cattle, 6 horses, 21 swine, and 77 sheep and lambs.[41] The tenants of Bridlington priory's land did day-works for the repair of Bridlington harbour.[42]

There is no evidence that the two villages ever had separate field systems and most references are to 'the fields of Sewerby and Marton'. The early number and names of the fields are uncertain, but North field is mentioned in 1618 and 1634,[43] East field in 1652,[44] and North, East, and South fields in 1675.[45] Lands abutting on the sea and in Huntcliffe in 1634 were probably part of East field, and in the same year a bovate 'upon the Breach' is mentioned, as well as land in the Gowdie Marr. Part of East field was inclosed in the mid 17th century and by 1773 the arable land lay in Little field (to the north of Marton), Bempton Mill field (in the north-west),

Undergate field (to the west of Sewerby), the Town Lays (between the two villages), the Brache, Aunams, the Westerdales, and the Far and Near Dogdales.[46] The last five areas may have comprised a separate field, lying between Undergate and Bempton Mill fields, where a field is shown on a map of 1802. The fields are not named on the map but are marked 'fallow', 'bean', 'barley', and 'wheat'.[47] The references to the Breach, or Brache, and Aunams, probably corruptions of 'breck' and 'avenham', suggest intakes of land that may have been only periodically cultivated. The total extent of openfield land was put at 130 bovates in the early 16th century[48] and at 133 bovates, besides 'a considerable quantity of odd land', in 1773.[49] At inclosure in 1811 allotments totalling 1,154 a. were made from the open fields.[50]

In 1773 there were three 'flats or parcels of pasture land in the open fields', one of them called the Town Lays or Leys.[51] The Leys are first mentioned in 1652, when a part of them was apparently inclosed,[52] but they still contributed 43 a. to the area of the open fields in 1811.

The chief areas of common pasture were the moor, Undergates pasture, and the carr. The moor lay in the extreme east, towards Flamborough, and access to it across the land inclosed in the 17th century was provided through Marton village and from Sewerby. Allotments totalling 176 a. were made from the moor at inclosure in 1811. Undergates pasture lay between the Sewerby–Bridlington road and the sea, and the carr adjoined it to the south, on the most low-lying land in the townships. Allotments totalling 183 a. were made from Undergates pasture in 1811, and the carr then comprised 36 a.[53]

Early grants of pasture for 100 and 200 sheep to Bridlington priory[54] probably involved rights in the open fields, as well as in the common pastures. No specific references have been found to pasturage in the moor, but beast-gates in the Undergates and the carr were held in right of each bovate of open-field land. Such beast-gates are recorded in 1618 and later.[55]

The first inclosures took place c. 1650, when part of East field was inclosed by agreement between more than 20 inhabitants.[56] A survey made in 1650 records 130 a. in 'Linames', 66 a. in Huntcliffe, and 64 a. in Dowgarth,[57] and this may have been the total extent of the lands that were inclosed. In 1651 part of Dowgarth and a section of Huntcliffe known as the New close formed the allotments of several of the participants in the inclosure.[58] A year later Randall Carliell's allotment consisted of 40 a. in Huntcliffe and 14 a. at Guildas Pits.[59] When the final inclosure took place in 1811, 95 a. of ancient inclosures were involved in exchanges, 70 a. of them

---

[31] *Miscellanea*, iii. 32.
[32] See p. 92.
[33] *T.E.R.A.S.* ii. 53; see also E.R.R.O., DDX/120/1.
[34] B.I.H.R., C.P., H. 2945, 3194, 3198, 3202, 3420, 4480–8.
[35] Registry of Deeds, Beverley, BF/62/103.
[36] Ibid. CQ/111/4.
[37] *V.C.H. Yorks.* ii. 198, 212, 226, 286–7.
[38] *Yorks. Deeds*, vi. 127.   [39] C 135/38/20.
[40] *Yorks. Deeds*, v. 132.
[41] Ibid. vi. 128–9.
[42] E 310/33/200 no. 13.
[43] E.R.R.O., DDBV/8/4.
[44] Ibid. DC/20/1.
[45] Ibid. DDLG/30/461a.

[46] Ibid. /896.
[47] Ibid. /897.
[48] *Miscellanea*, iii (Y.A.S. Rec. Ser. lxxx), 16.
[49] E.R.R.O., DDLG/30/896.
[50] Registry of Deeds, Beverley, CQ/111/4.
[51] E.R.R.O., DDLG/30/896.
[52] See below.
[53] Regy. of Deeds, CQ/111/4 and inclosure map.
[54] *Bridlington Charty.* 33.
[55] e.g. E.R.R.O., DDBV/8/4; Regy. of Deeds, D/210/347; CF/367/577.
[56] E.R.R.O., DC/20/2; DDX/41/1; DDLG/42/28.
[57] Ibid. DDLG/30/175.
[58] Ibid. /174, 178.
[59] Ibid. DDX/41/1.

in the Lynhams.⁶⁰ The area known as the Lynhams lay in the north-east, adjoining Bempton; in 1734 one close there was alternatively called Lynham or Gilderspit close.⁶¹ The other ancient inclosures in 1811 were mostly to the east of the village in an arc around the moor, including almost all the cliff-top land as far as the Flamborough boundary.⁶²

The remainder of the open fields and common pastures were inclosed in 1811, under an Act of 1802.⁶³ A total of 1,624 a. of commonable ground were dealt with; allotments totalling 1,515 a. were made, and 36 a. were sold to cover the expenses of the inclosure. John Greame received 843 a., 322 a. of them in lieu of tithes, and 200 a. went to Ralph Creyke. Two other allotments exceeded 100 a., those of William Carliell (116 a.) and George Darley (105 a., including 63 a. in lieu of tithes), and the remaining allotments were 3 of between 30 a. and 60 a., 5 of between 10 a. and 30 a., and 4 of under 10 a. each.

The number of farmers in Sewerby and Marton has usually been about ten since inclosure, and one of them was often also a miller. The number increased in the 1930s and there were 15 farmers and 2 market-gardeners in 1937.⁶⁴

The only non-agricultural occupation of note is fishing, though it seems never to have been followed by many Sewerby men. The fish tithes were let separately from the other tithes in the 16th century.⁶⁵ Several 'fishers' of Sewerby are mentioned in 1441,⁶⁶ and a fishing coble was bequeathed by a Sewerby man in 1482.⁶⁷

A mill in Sewerby is first mentioned in the early 14th century⁶⁸ and often thereafter. In 1619 the windmill stood in the fields of Sewerby 'nigh unto Bempton', probably on the site close to the boundary with Bempton which has been occupied in the 18th century and later by Speeton, or Bempton, mill.⁶⁹ A miller there is last recorded in 1937,⁷⁰ and the mill was derelict in 1969. A second mill, in Marton, is mentioned in 1723⁷¹ and shown on a plan of 1773: it was a post mill and stood near the north end of the Leys.⁷² There were lime-kilns in several quarries on the wolds in the township in the 19th century, and also at the cliffs at the end of Sands Lane.⁷³ Old brickworks were recorded in 1850 on what had been the moor, and by 1909 there was a brickworks on the north side of the Marton–Flamborough road which was in use until at least 1933.⁷⁴

LOCAL GOVERNMENT Surviving parish records include overseers' accounts for the period 1755–1836, constables' accounts for 1718–1836, surveyors' accounts from 1836 until the 1890s, and churchwardens' accounts for 1848–1914.⁷⁵

An isolated note of 1598 recorded that 20 people in Sewerby and Marton were taxed for poor relief, and that payments were made to 16 adults, 13 children, and 6 widows who were the mothers of most of the children.⁷⁶ The accounts of the two overseers record assessments made from 1755 onwards, but the rate is not mentioned until 1804, when it was 1s. in the pound and produced £95 from 26 people. Thereafter the rate was usually less than 1s., but it reached 1s. 10d. in 1819–20. The town stock stood at £12 in 1755 and £5 in 1804. Relief was provided in the form of weekly money payments, occasional payments in special circumstances, and grants for rent, food, fuel, and clothing. Weekly payments were made to 8 people in 1755 and 17 in 1804. The town house, or poorhouse, is first mentioned in 1756; £19 was spent on 'building the town house' in 1775, and £47 on 'erecting a new poor house and repairs of the others' in 1827–8. After Sewerby became part of the Bridlington poor-law union the four cottages that comprised the poorhouses were sold.⁷⁷

The accounts of the single constable similarly record assessments from the beginning but rates only from 1804, when a rate of 2½d. in the pound produced £20 from 26 people. The rate was usually between 2d. and 4d. until 1816, when the constable began to draw his revenue from the overseers' assessment. Expenditure included payments for cleansing the 'town's well'.

The two surveyors usually levied rates totalling from 9d. to 1s. in the pound, though in 1858–9 they reached as much as 2s. 6d. A shilling rate raised about £150. Other income was obtained by letting the roadside herbage.

CHURCH. A chapel at Sewerby, in the parish of Bridlington, is first mentioned in 1319, when Robert of Sewerby was licensed to grant land in Sewerby and Burton Fleming to Bridlington priory to maintain a chaplain who would celebrate daily in the chapel.⁷⁸ The 14th-century chapel apparently fell into disuse, for in 1449 Thomas Warter bequeathed £10 to build a chapel, if the prior would give licence, and £10 to maintain a priest there for 10 years. The chapel may have been built but it was not consecrated until 1468, after Elizabeth of Sewerby had left the residue of her estate to keep a regular chaplain at Sewerby. It was then licensed for service on account of Elizabeth's bequest and because of the distance from Sewerby to the parish church at Bridlington.⁷⁹ The chapel was, it seems, treated as a chantry chapel in the 16th century. 'Marton chapel', presumably the same building, is mentioned in 1552,⁸⁰ and in 1556 it was included in a list of property delivered to the Crown surveyor.⁸¹

A new church was built by Yarburgh Greame and consecrated in 1848.⁸² The curacy was united with

⁶⁰ Regy. of Deeds, CQ/111/4. ⁶¹ Ibid. M/450/738.
⁶² Ibid. inclosure map.
⁶³ 42 Geo. III, c. 106 (Local and Personal); the award is in Regy. of Deeds, CQ/111/4, together with a copy of the map; the pre-inclosure and inclosure maps, both drawn in 1802, are in E.R.R.O., DDLG/30/346, 897.
⁶⁴ Directories.
⁶⁵ e.g. Cal. Pat. 1563–6, 382.
⁶⁶ Ibid. 1436–41, 463.
⁶⁷ B.I.H.R., Prob. Reg. v, f. 71.
⁶⁸ C 135/38/20; Yorks. Deeds, vi. 127.
⁶⁹ E.R.R.O., DDLG/30/149, 896; Regy. of Deeds, D/210/347; F/189/415.
⁷⁰ Kelly's Dir. N. & E.R. Yorks. (1937), 529.
⁷¹ Regy. of Deeds, H/498/1009.
⁷² E.R.R.O., DDLG/30/896.
⁷³ Ibid. /772, 778; O.S. Map 6" (1854).
⁷⁴ Ibid.; Kelly's Dir. N. & E.R. Yorks. (1933), 535.
⁷⁵ E.R.R.O., DDLG/30/856–8, 865–85.
⁷⁶ Ibid. /43/1.
⁷⁷ Ibid. memo. at end of overseers' accts.; /30/669, 859.
⁷⁸ Monastic Notes, ii (Y.A.S. Rec. Ser. lxxxi), 8.
⁷⁹ Test. Ebor. ii. 136; iii. 161.
⁸⁰ Inventories of Ch. Goods, 34.
⁸¹ E.R.R.O., DDCC/139/65.
⁸² B.I.H.R., CD. 218.

that of Grindale in 1854.[83] In 1870 the curacy of Sewerby with Marton and Grindale was united with the rectory of Argam; in the same year a small part of Sewerby was transferred to Christ Church parish, Bridlington.[84] Sewerby and Marton became a separate living in 1958.[85] The patronage belonged to the Greame family until transferred to the archbishop in 1929.[86]

In 1868 the church of Sewerby with Marton was endowed with four holdings of stock: (i) £3,600, the interest from which was to be applied to the use of the incumbent, the clerk, and the sexton; (ii) £350 for repairs to the church; (iii) £50 for general purposes; and (iv) £1,000 for the incumbent.[87] A parsonage house was being built in 1865, though the incumbent was resident in Sewerby even before that.[88] The house was used by the incumbent of the joint living after 1870[89] but it was sold in 1955[90] and in 1969 was known as Sewerby Grange. It is a large yellow-brick building in the Gothic style. Since 1955 the living has been held with Holy Trinity, Bridlington, where the incumbent has resided.[91]

A service was held at Sewerby each Sunday in 1851 and 1865, with Holy Communion once a month. In 1868 and 1871 there were two services on alternate Sundays in summer.[92] By 1884 there were two every Sunday, with a third twice a month and another on Thursdays, and the church was said to be often over-full during the Bridlington 'season'.[93] The average attendance at communion was about twenty in the 1860s and 1870s, and about thirty in 1884. Communion was administered weekly in 1936.[94] There were three services each Sunday in 1969.

The church of *ST. JOHN THE EVANGELIST*, built in 1848, was designed by G. G. (later Sir Gilbert) Scott. It appears that the unusual Norman style of the building was the choice of Yarburgh Greame and not of Scott, who later complained about the 'fads' of his employer.[95] The church consists of nave, chancel, north transept, south porch, and bell-turret at the junction of nave and chancel. The west end, facing the road, is decorated with wall arcading; Norman zig-zag and other ornament, remarkably correct in detail, is also concentrated on the south doorway, the upper stage of the turret, and the chancel arch. There are Royal Arms of Victoria and monuments to Thomas Greame (d. 1779), John Greame (d. 1841), and Yarburgh Yarburgh (d. 1856).

There were two bells in the old chapel in 1552.[96] The pair of bells in the new church were cast by C. & G. Mears of London in 1847.[97] The burial ground was consecrated in 1859.[98]

NONCONFORMITY. A barn in Sewerby was licensed for worship in 1800 and a house in 1818.[99] A Wesleyan Methodist chapel was built in 1825,[1] and it was presumably this building that was registered for worship in 1854.[2] It stood on the back lane at the west end of the village but was demolished after a new chapel was built and registered in 1962.[3] The new red-brick chapel and hall stand a little to the west of the old chapel site, adjoining the road to Bridlington.

In 1889 the Primitive Methodists were said to use a cottage in Sewerby and to have 24 members.[4]

EDUCATION. There were two schools in Sewerby in 1835, supported by subscription, which were attended by 12 boys and 14 girls.[5] A new school was built by Yarburgh Greame in 1849 and opened in 1850.[6] The yellow-brick building, with stone dressings, is in the Gothic style and was designed by G. G. (later Sir Gilbert) Scott.[7] The school was at first supported by the patron and by school pence[8] but it received an annual government grant by 1876–1877.[9] The endowment consisted of half the income from £2,000, bequeathed by Yarburgh Yarburgh in 1856.[10] The attendance was about 50 in the 1860s and 1870s,[11] but in the 20th century it has varied between only 28 in 1908 and 46 in 1914 and 1932; in 1938 it was 32.[12]

In 1948 the school was temporarily closed because of its structural condition and the children were sent to Flamborough school; it was permanently closed in 1949[13] and has since been in private occupation.

CHARITIES FOR THE POOR. Richard Raine in 1772 gave £5 for the poor, and in 1823 the overseers distributed the 5s. interest.[14] Yarburgh Yarburgh, by will dated 1855, bequeathed £1,000 for the poor, three-tenths of which was to go to Sewerby. The income from a further £1,000 was directed to be paid to the schoolmaster at Sewerby. Money and goods were distributed in 1960.[15]

---

[83] York Dioc. Regy., Orders in Council 124.
[84] Ibid. 292, 294.
[85] Ibid. 747.
[86] Ibid. 595.
[87] B.I.H.R., TER. J. Sewerby 1868.
[88] Ibid. V. 1865/Ret. 464; E.R.R.O., DDLG/30/840.
[89] B.I.H.R., Bp. V. 1884/Ret.
[90] Regy. of Deeds, 998/330/291.
[91] *Crockford* (1967–8).
[92] B.I.H.R., V. 1865/Ret. 464; V. 1868/Ret. 413; V. 1871/Ret. 417; H.O. 129/24/524.
[93] B.I.H.R., Bp. V. 1884/Ret.
[94] Ibid., Bp. V. 1936/Ret. 308.
[95] E.R.R.O., DDLG/30/824; F. F. Johnson, *Sewerby Hall and Park* (4th edn.), 21.
[96] *Inventories of Ch. Goods*, 34.
[97] Boulter, 'Ch. Bells', 218.
[98] B.I.H.R., CD. 301.
[99] G.R.O. Worship Rets., Vol. v, nos. 1562, 2726.

[1] H.O. 129/24/524.
[2] G.R.O. Worship Reg. no. 2386.
[3] Ibid. no. 68533.
[4] H. Woodcock, *Sketches of Prim. Meth. on Yorks. Wolds*, 61.
[5] *Educ. Enquiry Abstract, 1835*, 1081.
[6] H.O. 129/24/524; stone on building.
[7] F. F. Johnson, *Sewerby Hall and Park* (4th edn.), 21.
[8] Ed. 7/135.
[9] *Rep. of Educ. Cttee. of Council, 1876–7* [C. 1780–I], p. 910, H.C. (1877), xxix.
[10] E.R.R.O., SLB. Sewerby correspondence file.
[11] B.I.H.R., V. 1865/Ret. 464; *Rets. rel. Elem. Educ. 1871*, 476.
[12] *Bd. of Educ. List 21* (H.M.S.O.).
[13] E.R. Educ. Cttee. *Mins.* 1948–9, 66, 198; 1949–50, 6.
[14] *9th Rep. Char. Com.* 732.
[15] Char. Com. files; see above, p. 82.

SPEETON

The township of Speeton, covering 1,844 a.,[16] lies on the northern shoulder of Flamborough Head, about 4 miles from both Bridlington and Filey. It was an Anglian settlement and the name, 'speech enclosure', suggests that it was the meeting-place of the Domesday hundred of Huntou.[17] The village itself lies north of the Filey–Flamborough road and only ½ mile from the sea. Only one section of the township boundary follows any notable natural feature, the valley known as Maiden's Grave Slack which separates Speeton from Reighton in the south-west. Speeton was in 1935 merged with Reighton civil parish.[18]

Much of the southern part of the township is typical of the open wolds landscape; there are few trees, and the large fields, mostly arable, are those created by the inclosure of 1794. Most of this area is between 300 ft. and 350 ft. above sea-level, but Maiden's Grave Slack, running across the township from the south-west, is only 250 ft. in the valley bottom. In the north, however, the chalk reaches a height of up to 425 ft. in a series of prominent hillocks, known as Speeton Hills, lying from west to east across the township; individual sections are called Beacon, Bonfire, Mill, Strenk, Pickle, and Cow Pasture hills.[19] Most of the present village lies in the shelter of these hillocks.

The high ground falls away as a steep north-facing escarpment, which for most of its length looks over a gently-undulating shelf of clay land before the sea is reached. In the extreme east, however, the escarpment itself reaches the sea and forms, for nearly ½ mile, the high chalk cliffs which continue into Buckton and Bempton.[20] The clay shelf produces cliffs of a very different kind. They are shapeless and unstable, and although in places up to 200 ft. high they may be 1,000 ft. wide. Cut into these cliffs, and running back into the clay shelf, is the steep-sided and tree-covered Speeton Gap or Ravine. The various beds comprising the Speeton Clay are renowned for their fossil content. In front of the chalk cliffs the foreshore is rocky, but along the clay section the rock gives way to a stretch of sand. Ships have often been driven upon these cliffs in bad weather.[21]

Two main roads cross the township: that from Flamborough to Filey and, further south, the Bridlington–Filey road. These are linked by the straight New Road, perhaps created at inclosure, which crosses the Bridlington–Filey railway line; the latter was opened in 1847. At one time a track, now lost, provided a shorter route to Bridlington church for wedding and burial parties from Speeton.[22] From the Flamborough–Filey road Wide Lane leads into the village.

Most of the houses of the present village stand on the slightly sheltered southern slope of Speeton Hills, but the village formerly extended to the northern slopes as well.[23] A large area of earthworks on the north side was levelled and destroyed in 1960.[24] Cobble Lane leads northwards from the village to become Green Lane and then Raikes Lane. Near these lanes, which are now in part grassed over, is Garend, or Garth's End, pond.[25] There are also indications of former crofts and garths on the south side of the village.

Several of the farm-houses and cottages in the village, including Manor Farm, appear to be 18th-century houses, subsequently altered and extended; they are built of brick and chalk. The farm-buildings include examples of the local practice of using cobbles for the lower walls and chalk for the upper, with brick used decoratively in quoins and around window and door openings. There are a few late-19th- and 20th-century private houses, as well as seventeen Council houses along Wide Lane. The coastguard station, on the side of Bonfire hill, is a large two-storeyed brick building, erected soon after 1904.[26] Near by there are slight traces of the site of the windmill, which was demolished in 1921; it was a three-storeyed tower mill with an ogee-shaped cap.[27] The only isolated houses in the township are the railway station, Southfield Farm, and Greenland Farm, with a few 20th-century houses and bungalows.

Although Beacon and Bonfire hills are two distinct hillocks to the west of the village,[28] it seems that beacons and bonfires were both kindled on the same hill in later years. The post of the beacon still stood in 1886 but it was apparently removed so that a bonfire could be built on the site to celebrate the Jubilee in 1887. There was also a bonfire in 1897, and others at the coronations of Edward VII and George V[29] and at the Jubilee in 1935.[30]

No poll-tax certificate has been identified. There were 28 households in 1674; 14 were discharged from the hearth tax, and of the others 10 had only one hearth each, 3 had 2, and one had three.[31] About 10 families were recorded in 1743[32] and about 12 in 1764.[33] In 1801 the population was 104 and it varied between 111 and 160 during the rest of the century; it stood at 146 in 1901.[34] Numbers varied little thereafter and in 1931 the population was 165.[35]

MANORS AND OTHER ESTATES. In 1086 Speeton consisted of two estates, one of 4 carucates, belonging to the king, which was soke of the manor of Bridlington, the other of 6 carucates, belonging to the count of Mortain. The second of these had been held in 1066 by Ligulf.[36] Subsequently Speeton passed to the Gants and later the Tattershalls.[37]

In the later 12th century 3 carucates in Speeton were given to Bridlington priory by Gilbert de Gant,[38] and in 1182 Thomas de Alost surrendered

---

[16] O.S. Map 6″ (1854).
[17] P.N.E.R. Yorks. (E.P.N.S.), 85–6, 105.
[18] Census, 1931. [19] O.S. Map 6″ (1854); 25″ (1954).
[20] For egg-collecting on these cliffs see p. 9.
[21] G. Alcock, Speeton Par. & Ch. 50–1. [22] Ibid. 23–4.
[23] As shown on a map of 1772: E.R.R.O., IA Speeton.
[24] Med. Archaeol. v. 333.
[25] Alcock, Speeton, 9; O.S. Map 6″ (1854).
[26] When the site was acquired for the purpose: E.R.R.O., DDLO/Box 3.
[27] Alcock, Speeton, 10; photo. in church.
[28] O.S. Map 6″ (1854). [29] Alcock, Speeton, 43.
[30] Ex inf. the vicar, 1971. [31] E 179/205/521.
[32] Herring's Visit. iii. 135.
[33] B.I.H.R., Bp. V. 1764/Ret. 49.
[34] V.C.H. Yorks. iii. 489.
[35] Census.
[36] V.C.H. Yorks. ii. 197, 226.
[37] Feud. Aids, vi. 29; Cal. Inq. p.m. iv, p. 108.
[38] Bridlington Charty. 2, 41.

his rights in the township to the priory, in return for a carucate in Fraisthorpe.[39] In 1284–5 the priory was said to hold 3½ carucates of the Gant fee,[40] and at the Dissolution the manor of SPEETON was worth £12 a year.[41]

Several leases of the manor were made by the Crown in the 16th century: it was let to Christopher Newport and Thomas Metham before 1561, to Thomas Warcopp in 1561, to Francis Skelton in 1575–6, and to Gregory Skelton in 1587–8.[42] In 1598–9, however, Speeton was granted in fee to Henry Best and Robert Holland.[43]

William Fisher was dealing with the manor in 1611[44] and the Fishers retained it until 1630, when Gideon Fisher conveyed it to Sir Michael Wharton.[45] The Whartons held Speeton until another Sir Michael died in 1725, leaving his estates in undivided shares to his sisters and heirs Mary Pennyman, Elizabeth Pelham, and Susanna Newton. In 1775, however, the estates were divided and Speeton fell to the share of Michael Newton: he got 1,688 a. there, together with common rights.[46] In 1812 trustees for the sale of Newton's estates sold to William Denison the 1,723 a. which had been allotted at inclosure in 1794.[47] Denison was succeeded in 1849 by his brother-in-law Lord Albert Conyngham, who then took the name Denison and became Lord Londesborough in 1850.[48]

The earls of Londesborough retained Speeton until 1909–10, when the estate was sold in four separate lots. Manor Farm, comprising 539 a. and still including the manor, went to Valentine Prodham.[49] The farm was sold by Blanche Prodham to Robert and David Rogerson in 1948.[50]

A second estate, sometimes called a moiety of the manor of SPEETON, may have originated with Gilbert de Gant's grant in the mid 12th century of half of Speeton, 'that is, in tofts and crofts', to Tero son of Malger.[51] By 1284–5 Thomas of Speeton held 2½ carucates of the Gant fee.[52] This was presumably the manor granted by five chaplains to John of Speeton in 1362.[53] By 1455 the estate belonged to the Portington family, and in the early 16th century Thomas Portington alleged that the prior of Bridlington's men had entered his moiety of the manor.[54] The Portingtons held it until 1586, when it was acquired by Michael Wharton and Edward Lawson.[55] The estate was united with the capital manor when the latter also passed to the Whartons in 1630.

The tithes of the township were let to Robert Puckering in 1538.[56] They were later included in the 16th-century leases of the manor, and they were acquired by Sir Michael Wharton in 1630.[57] Wharton was involved in disputes over their payment in 1639–40.[58] The tithes were valued at £50 in 1650.[59] No later mention of them has been found.

ECONOMIC HISTORY. Some indication of the medieval economy of the township is given in a brief account for Bridlington priory's grange, covering a five-week period in 1349. It indicates a combination of arable farming and stock rearing: during that time 3 ploughmen and 3 shepherds were employed, there were expenses for threshing and mowing, and 106 animals were received: 65 pigs, the rest cattle of various kinds.[60] A lease of the manor, with the tithe corn of the township, made by the priory in 1536 suggests a similar situation. The rent was mostly payable in kind: 18 qr. of wheat, 19 qr. of barley, 8 qr. of oats, a fat swine, and 4 other swine or 2 oxen.[61]

The open-field land extended across the whole of the southern part of Speeton. Its various sections were called East, Cross, Mill, and Beacon fields in 1772, and North, East, Cross, West, Bean, Mill South, and Beacon fields at inclosure in 1794.[62] There may earlier have been three fields, called the corn, barley, and pease fields in 1647.[63] The chalk hillocks and the escarpment have perhaps always provided rough pasture, as they still did in 1850,[64] and the moor lay in the north-east, against the sea. Below the escarpment, on the shelf between the chalk and the sea, were the Low fields, which provided common pasture in the 18th century. The inclosure commissioners also dealt with the Cliff, probably common pasture near the sea.

Pains made at a manorial court in 1647 included regulations for the pasturing of sheep and cattle in Low field and provided that one gate should be enjoyed for each house and 3½ for each bovate of land.[65] When a survey of the former Wharton estates was made before the partition of 1775 there were no common rights attached to the five large farms, each of which had between 250 a. and 450 a. But nine houses or cottages, each with only 2 a.–9 a. of land, all had such rights. Two houses each had ½ cattle-gate in Low field and 9 sheep-gates in the moor and the Rakes; 6 had one cattle-gate and 18 sheep-gates; and one had 2 cattle-gates and 36 sheep-gates.[66] The Rakes, which were not specifically mentioned in the inclosure award, lay on the hillock north-east of the village.[67]

Little early inclosure took place in the township. Gilbert of Speeton, probably in the 12th century, released his rights in a close which the canons had surrounded with a wall,[68] but this appears to have been only a small area near the village. Several 'New

---

[39] *E.Y.C.* ii, p. 494.
[40] *Feud. Aids*, vi. 29.
[41] *Valor Eccl.* (Rec. Com.), v. 120.
[42] C 66/1141 m. 40; C 66/1312 m. 35; *Cal. Pat.* 1560–3, 78.
[43] C 66/1516 m. 32.
[44] *Yorks. Fines, 1603–14*, 157.
[45] C.P. 25(2)/520/6 Chas. I East. no. 14.
[46] 15 Geo. III, c. 49 (Priv. Act).
[47] Registry of Deeds, Beverley, BG/415/65; CU/120/121.
[48] J. T. Ward, *E. Yorks. Landed Estates in the 19th Cent.* (E. Yorks. Loc. Hist. Ser. xxiii), 17–18.
[49] Regy. of Deeds, 119/515/457; /541/482; 121/7/7; /68/64.
[50] Ibid. 773/481/415.
[51] *Yorks. Deeds*, ix. 162.
[52] *Feud. Aids*, vi. 29.
[53] *Yorks. Deeds*, ix. 164.
[54] *Yorks. Sta. Cha. Proc.* ii (Y.A.S. Rec. Ser. xlv), 147.
[55] *Yorks. Fines*, iii. 52.
[56] *L. & P. Hen. VIII*, xiii (1), p. 134.
[57] See above. [58] B.I.H.R., CP., H. 2612.
[59] *T.E.R.A.S.* ii. 53.
[60] B.I.H.R., Mon. 3; B. Waites, 'Aspects of 13th and 14th Cent. Arable Farming on Yorks. Wolds', *Y.A.J.* xlii. 139–40. [61] L.R. 2/408 f. 5d.
[62] E.R.R.O., IA Speeton; Regy. of Deeds, Beverley, BG/415/65.
[63] E.R.R.O., DDMC deed no. 202.
[64] O.S. Map 6″ (1854).
[65] E.R.R.O., DDMC deed no. 202.
[66] 15 Geo. III, c. 49 (Priv. Act).
[67] E.R.R.O., IA Speeton; O.S. Map 6″ (1854).
[68] *Bridlington Charty.* 44.

closes' lay between Low field and the Cliff in 1772.[69] The remaining commonable lands were inclosed in 1794[70] under an Act of the previous year.[71] Allotments totalling 1,732 a. were made, all but 9 a. going to Michael Newton as lord of the manor: 6 a. were awarded to the prebend of Grindale and 3 a. to another proprietor.

In 1801 575 a. were reported under crops, 290 a. being sown with oats.[72] There have been five or six farmers in the township in the 19th and 20th centuries, one of them also the miller until the turn of the century.[73] The windmill, which is mentioned in the early 16th century,[74] was worked until soon after 1900.[75]

LOCAL GOVERNMENT. Meetings of the manor court are recorded in 1546, when offences concerning such matters as straying stock and affray brought in fines totalling nearly 11s.,[76] and 1742.[77] A series of pains, mostly dealing with agricultural affairs, was made at a manorial court in 1647 and several times confirmed, the last occasion being in 1772.[78]

CHURCH. The surviving fabric shows that there has been a chapel at Speeton since at least Norman times. It long remained technically in Bridlington parish, but by the 18th century it was regarded as a perpetual curacy. In 1919 it was united with Reighton.[79]

The parochial chaplain of Speeton, mentioned in 1451,[80] was presumably provided by Bridlington priory. The curacy was later in the gift of the owners of the chief manor; thus the presentation was acquired by William Denison in 1832[81] and the earl of Londesborough had it in 1868.[82] After Speeton was united with Reighton, the earl of Londesborough had one turn in four, and after an exchange with Skerne in 1929 the archbishop of York had the fourth turn.[83]

The Crown provided a stipend for the curates, amounting to £3 12s. when first mentioned in 1650[84] and always a little over £3 in the 17th century and later.[85] The income was four times augmented from Queen Anne's Bounty, in 1734, 1758, 1765, and 1805, each time with £200.[86] In 1851 the curacy was said to have a permanent endowment of only £50,[87] and in 1865 the three principal farmers, 'acting annually in rotation', gave liberally to the offertory.[88]

Glebe land was bought in the 18th century with Bounty money. In 1742 10 a. was acquired at Middleton (Yorks. N.R.) and by 1770 25 a. had been bought at Bewholme. By 1770 the curate also received four-fifths of the rent of 3 a. allotted at the inclosure of Middleton.[89] This was said in 1861 to be 'at present lost to the living', but by then the glebe also included 3 a. at Beverley.[90]

The curates lived elsewhere and usually held other livings. In 1743 and 1764, for example, the curate lived at Hunmanby.[91] In the 17th century and later the incumbents of Flamborough and Bempton often served at Speeton,[92] and in the late 19th century the vicar of Bempton had charge of it.[93]

In the Middle Ages there was a chantry in the chapel, dedicated to St. Leonard, and it had property in Harpham.[94]

There was only one service every six weeks at Speeton in 1743 and one each month in 1764; in both years communion was administered only twice and in 1743 it was received by about forty people.[95] By 1851 there was a service each Sunday,[96] and in 1865 communion was received six times a year by about ten people.[97] In 1868 and 1871 communion was received four times a year,[98] but by 1877 only once every six weeks[99] and in 1884 and 1900 once every seven or eight weeks. In 1900 only five or six people, all Methodists, took communion.[1] By 1936 it was administered once a month.[2] One service was held each Sunday in 1970.

The small church of ST. LEONARD, consisting of chancel, nave, and west tower, stands in a field at the east end of the village, now surrounded by a wall but without a churchyard.[3] It is built of stone, with a little chalk, and in part rests on a double plinth, the lower half of which is of cobbles. The building is largely of early Norman origin. The upper part of the chancel appears to have been rebuilt and both nave and chancel are housed under a continuous roof. There are no surviving openings on the north side of the church, but in the south wall are two square-headed windows, one in the nave and one in the chancel; the chancel also has a restored lancet. The early-12th-century chancel arch, of a single order, is semicircular and rests on a plain chamfered abacus. The circular font is also Norman. An *agnus dei*, perhaps of c. 1120–5, found over the modern south door in 1965, has been reset inside the church;[4] next to it is a stone carved with a cross, formerly on the outside of the west wall. In the chancel there are two trefoil-headed recesses in the

---

[69] E.R.R.O., IA Speeton.
[70] Regy. of Deeds, BG/415/65.
[71] 33 Geo. III, c. 97 (Priv. Act).
[72] 1801 Crop Returns.
[73] Directories.
[74] *Miscellanea*, iii (Y.A.S. Rec. Ser. lxxx), 4.
[75] *Kelly's Dir. N. & E.R. Yorks.* (1901), 562, mentions a miller but ibid. (1905), 582, does not. It was described in 1909 as disused: E.R.R.O., DDLO/Box 3.
[76] S.C. 2/211/127.
[77] E.R.R.O., CSR/20/37.
[78] E.R.R.O., DDMC deed no. 202.
[79] York Dioc. Regy., Orders in Council 524.
[80] B.I.H.R., Prob. Reg. ii, f. 224.
[81] Regy. of Deeds, Beverley, CU/120/121.
[82] B.I.H.R., V. 1868/Ret. 464.
[83] York Dioc. Regy., Orders in Council 568; *York Dioc. Cal.* 1930.
[84] *T.E.R.A.S.* ii. 53.
[85] B.I.H.R., TER. J. Speeton 1685 to 1861.
[86] Hodgson, *Q.A.B.* 453.
[87] H.O. 129/24/524.
[88] B.I.H.R., V. 1865/Ret. 509.
[89] The rest went to Folkton vicarage: G. Alcock, *Speeton Par. and Ch.* 31.
[90] B.I.H.R., TER. J. Speeton 1743, 1764, 1770, 1781, 1861.
[91] Ibid. Bp. V. 1764/Ret. 49; *Herring's Visit.* iii. 135.
[92] Alcock, *Speeton*, 26–7.
[93] B.I.H.R., V. 1865/Ret. 509; V. 1868/Ret. 464; V. 1871/Ret. 470; V. 1877/Ret.; Bp. V. 1884/Ret.
[94] See p. 225.
[95] B.I.H.R., Bp. V. 1764/Ret. 49; *Herring's Visit.* iii. 135.
[96] H.O. 129/24/524.
[97] B.I.H.R., V. 1865/Ret. 509.
[98] Ibid. V. 1868/Ret. 464; V. 1871/Ret. 470.
[99] Ibid. V. 1877/Ret.
[1] Ibid. Bp. V. 1884/Ret.; Bp. V. 1900/Ret. 371.
[2] Ibid. Bp. V. 1936/Ret. 294.
[3] Morris, *E.R. Yorks.* 315.
[4] Described and illustrated in *Y.A.J.* xli. 590.

north wall, one with a crudely-carved stone above it. In the chancel east wall, which has no window, is the remains of a late medieval canopied niche with a bracket at its base; beside it is a projecting square money box.

The west end of the church contains two modern lancets flanking the tower. The small tower consists of three stages, separated by a stone string-course and each stepped back from the stage below. The third stage is capped with a concave pyramidal roof, and is pierced with round-headed bell openings. Internally the bell-rope hangs in a small arched recess.

Perhaps in the 18th century the church was provided with box pews and a three-decker pulpit and the font was moved into the chancel. During restoration work in 1911 the pews, pulpit, and plaster ceiling were removed; the new pulpit is part of a stall given to St. Mary's Church, Bridlington, in 1857. The church was also restored in 1965.[5]

There is one undated bell.[6] The plate consists of a silver cup, made in York in 1645 by Christopher Mangey, and two pewter plates.[7] A register of baptisms, burials, and marriages survives for 1636–1792. Entries for 1792–1863 may be found in the Bempton registers. There are separate Speeton registers from 1837, for baptisms, and 1863, for burials and marriages.[8]

NONCONFORMITY. The first record of dissent in the township is the licensing of a Wesleyan Methodist chapel in 1849;[9] it is said to have been built two years earlier.[10] Later in the century the Church of England ministers spoke of the prevalence of dissent, and in 1865 the minister said that 'nearly all the inhabitants attend both church and chapel'.[11] There was a similar situation in the early 20th century, when the afternoon service at the church had a congregation only in alternate weeks.[12] In 1894 all the Sunday-school children were Methodists.[13] In 1925 the early Wesleyan chapel was replaced by a new one,[14] an ornate, largely red-brick, building.

EDUCATION. About 1830 a school was being held at the east end of the church.[15] Subsequently a school was held in a house near the boundary with Reighton, later known as Speeton Grange. About 1865–70 the chancel of the church again housed a school.[16] In 1865 the average attendance was about 12, and the master was supported by school pence and by his trade as a tailor; the three principal farmers also provided money, 'acting annually in rotation'.[17] The average attendance was 25 in 1868, but the curate then stated that the school would probably soon be discontinued, despite financial support by himself and the farmers, because Lord Londesborough would not increase his contribution; the children, he said, would have to go to Reighton.[18] By 1871 the school had been closed.[19]

In 1875 a school board was formed for Reighton and Speeton and a school was built in 1876 to serve both places;[20] it stands on the road between them, a short distance inside Speeton township. Its income derived from school pence in 1877,[21] but an annual government grant was given from 1878.[22] The average attendance in 1890–1905 was about 50.[23]

The school was enlarged in 1908.[24] The average attendance was 51 in 1908 and about 40–60 thereafter; it was again 51 in 1938.[25] The average number on the roll in 1969 was 37.[26]

CHARITIES FOR THE POOR. In 1823 the town stock consisted of £2 10s. arising from two benefactions, and the interest of 2s. 6d. was distributed by the overseers.[27] No more is known of it.

WILSTHORPE

The township of Wilsthorpe, covering 276 a. in 1850,[28] lies on the coast south of Bridlington. It was a settlement of Scandinavian origin.[29] The village was depopulated in the Middle Ages: part of its site has been eroded by the sea, but earthworks still remain around the site of the single farm-house which stood until the 1920s. Since the 1930s, however, it has been much developed as a place for holidays, and chalets and caravans cover much of the land adjoining the cliffs. Wilsthorpe was included in the civil parish of Fraisthorpe until 1935, when most of it was transferred to Carnaby civil parish and 36 a. was taken into the borough of Bridlington.[30]

The township is low-lying and little more than 25 ft. above sea-level. Its boundary is partly formed by watercourses. The low boulder-clay cliffs have been steadily eroded by the sea: about 40 yds. are said to have been lost between 1810 and 1833, and a house was destroyed in the early 20th century.[31] Wilsthorpe farm-house, on the site of the former village, was then the only building in the township. In the 1920s, however, a dozen houses were built for

---

[5] Alcock, *Speeton*, 17–19; restorations recorded in church.
[6] Boulter, 'Ch. Bells', 218.
[7] *Yorks. Ch. Plate*, i. 318; Alcock, *Speeton*, 32.
[8] Barley, *Par. Docs. E.R.* 139. The earliest register is at St. Mary's Church, Bridlington, the baptismal register is in E.R.R.O., and the register from 1863 onwards is at Reighton Vicarage.
[9] B.I.H.R., DMH. 1849/7.
[10] H.O. 129/24/524.
[11] B.I.H.R., V. 1865/Ret. 509; V. 1868/Ret. 464.
[12] Alcock, *Speeton*, 19.
[13] B.I.H.R., Bp. V. 1894/Ret.
[14] G.R.O. Worship Reg. no. 50013; stone on building.
[15] M. Prickett, *Hist. Ch. Bridlington* (1831 edn.), 53.
[16] Alcock, *Speeton*, 24.
[17] B.I.H.R., V. 1865/Ret. 509.
[18] Ibid. V. 1868/Ret. 464.
[19] *Rets. rel. Elem. Educ. 1871*, 476.
[20] E.R.R.O., SB. Reighton Mins. and Accts. 1875–1903; date on building.
[21] Ed. 7/135.
[22] E.R.R.O., SB. Reighton Mins. and Accts. 1875–1903.
[23] Directories.
[24] E.R. Educ. Cttee. *Mins.* 1908–9, 295.
[25] *Bd. of Educ. List* 21 (H.M.S.O.).
[26] Ex inf. Chief Educ. Officer, County Hall, Beverley, 1969.
[27] *9th Rep. Char. Com.* 732.
[28] O.S. Map 6" (1854).
[29] *P.N.E.R. Yorks.* (E.P.N.S.), 88.
[30] *Census*, 1931.
[31] T. Sheppard, *Lost Towns of Yorks. Coast*, 198.

smallholders, three of them on the village site. Wilsthorpe farm-house itself has been demolished.

The former coast road leading to Bridlington[32] passed through Wilsthorpe. After it was eroded by the sea the only road in the township was that leading inland to Carnaby. This now crosses Kingsgate, a new road into Bridlington opened in 1923.[33]

In 1377 47 adults paid the poll tax[34] and in 1539 6 able-bodied men were mustered.[35] In the 19th century the population returns were combined with those of Hilderthorpe.[36]

MANORS AND OTHER ESTATES. In 1086 there were two estates in Wilsthorpe, both of 2 carucates; one was held by the king, the other by Drew de Bevrère. Before the Conquest they had been held by Morcar and Harold respectively.[37]

After 1086 the Crown estate became part of the Gant and later the Tattershall fees.[38] It had been a berewick of Bridlington in 1086 but by 1147–53 it was said to belong to the vill of Bessingby. At this latter date it was granted by Gilbert de Gant to Bridlington priory.[39] The priory held the estate until the Dissolution, when it was worth £5 2s.[40] In 1560 24 bovates of former priory land were granted by the Crown to Thomas Wood and Thomas Fale.[41] The manor of WILSTHORPE was subsequently sold by Wood to William Dyneley (d. 1586).[42] In 1593 Henry Dyneley conveyed part of his Wilsthorpe property to William Tanckard,[43] and in 1595 William Green bought the manor-house and a tenement there.[44] At the death of Green's nephew, another William, in 1605 Wilsthorpe passed to his daughter Elizabeth,[45] who later married Sir John Buck.[46] Their son John in 1654 conveyed the manor to Sir William Strickland of Boynton.[47] The land was held by the Stricklands until the death of Sir Charles Strickland in 1909, and in 1921 the trustees of the Boynton estate sold the whole of Wilsthorpe to the East Riding county council for use as smallholdings.[48] Most of it was still owned by the council in 1969.

Drew de Bevrère's estate passed to the counts of Aumale, Drew's successors as lords of Holderness.[49] In 1086 it was described as a berewick of Cleeton.[50] By 1358 Swine priory already had at least one bovate of this fee,[51] and in 1428 it had 8 bovates at Wilsthorpe.[52] At the Dissolution the priory's estate was worth about £1.[53] In 1560 6½ bovates of former Swine land were granted to Thomas Wood and Thomas Fale[54] and they subsequently descended with the former Crown estate.

In 1346 other land of the Aumale fee was held by Sir John Mounceaux and Thomas of Caythorpe,[55] and in 1428 John Mounceaux and John Bound had 4 bovates each.[56] Maud, the daughter of Mounceaux's son Thomas, married Brian del See.[57] The estate thus passed to the del Sees, and at the death of Sir Martin del See it was inherited by his daughter Joan, wife of Peter Hildyard.[58] It is not known when this land was acquired by the Stricklands. It may have been as late as the early 18th century if this estate was the reputed manor which the Grimston family claimed to own in 1699 and to have had since 1650.[59]

The Bound land of 1428 was apparently acquired by Bridlington priory. Soon after 1500 Thomas Bound alleged that while he was a ward of the prior his 1½ bovate in Wilsthorpe was 'deceitfully' taken to the use of the priory.[60]

The tithes of Wilsthorpe were enjoyed by Bridlington priory until the Dissolution, and in the early 16th century the corn tithes were worth, together with those of Hilderthorpe, £4 13s. 4d.[61] The tithes were let to John Bell in 1538.[62] It is said that they were sold to Best and Holland in 1594–5,[63] and they were in 1600 in the possession of the Greens, who owned the manor at that time. William Green then referred to his title to the last four years of one Weycoe's patent of the tithes.[64] In 1650 the tithes of Hilderthorpe and Wilsthorpe belonged to John Buck and John Weaver and were worth £35.[65] They were conveyed by Buck, along with the manor, to Sir William Strickland in 1654[66] and are not mentioned again.

ECONOMIC HISTORY. Wilsthorpe received no relief after the Black Death, and in 1377 there were 47 adults paying the poll tax.[67] When the former possessions of Bridlington and Swine were granted to Wood and Fale in 1560, eight tenants were said to hold the same number of houses and 30½ bovates of land.[68] In the early 19th century Strickland's land was occupied by a single tenant[69] and there continued to be only one farm until the county council bought the land for smallholdings in 1921.[70]

The development of land near the cliffs for holiday-makers began in the 1930s, when sales by the county council included about 35 a. to Bridlington corporation.[71] Some of the land has been used for chalets and caravans, and the corporation caravan site occupies that part of Wilsthorpe taken into the borough in 1935. Also in the 1930s a ten-acre strip of land along the cliff edge was let by the county

[32] See p. 201.
[33] See p. 39.
[34] E 179/202/62 m. 16.
[35] L. & P. Hen. VIII, xiv (1), p. 309.
[36] See p. 91.
[37] V.C.H. Yorks. ii. 197, 269, 322.
[38] Cal. Inq. p.m. iv, pp. 108, 261; vii, pp. 469–70.
[39] E.Y.C. ii, pp. 449–51; Bridlington Charty. 26.
[40] Valor Eccl. (Rec. Com.), v. 120; Miscellanea, iii (Y.A.S. Rec. Ser. lxxx), 12, 28.
[41] Cal. Pat. 1558–60, 455–6.
[42] C 142/213/91.
[43] Yorks. Fines. iii. 191.
[44] C 142/168/133; Yorks. Fines, iv. 26.
[45] Wards 7/29/71; C 3/403/121.
[46] G.E.C. Baronetage, iii. 141.
[47] C.P. 25(2)/614/1654 East. no. 12.
[48] Registry of Deeds, Beverley, 234/562/466. See above, p. 23.
[49] V.C.H. Yorks. ii. 171–2; Feud. Aids, vi. 32.
[50] V.C.H. Yorks. ii. 269.
[51] Cal. Inq. Misc. iii, p. 96.
[52] E 179/202/104.
[53] E 315/401 f. 379; Valor Eccl. v. 114.
[54] E 318/Box 48/2566; Cal. Pat. 1558–60, 455–6.
[55] Feud. Aids. vi. 211.
[56] E 179/202/104.
[57] Test. Ebor. ii. 83.
[58] G. Poulson, Holderness, ii. 201; E.R.R.O., DDCC/3/22.
[59] C 5/283/90.
[60] Monastic Chancery Proc. (Y.A.S. Rec. Ser. lxxxviii), 22–3.
[61] Miscellanea, iii. 16, 32.
[62] L. & P. Hen. VIII, xiii (1), p. 140.
[63] H. Grove, Alienated Tithes, p. cxlvii.
[64] B.I.H.R., Prob. Reg. xxxi, f. 136.
[65] T.E.R.A.S. ii. 55.
[66] C.P. 25(2)/614/1654 East. no. 12.
[67] E 179/202/53; E 179/202/62 m. 16.
[68] E 318/Box 48/2566.
[69] E.R.R.O., Land Tax; DDX/3/3.
[70] Directories.
[71] Bridlington Corp. Counc. Proc. & Cttee. Mins. 1931–2, 69, 599.

council for building,[72] and eight houses and several chalets were erected.

CHURCH. A chapel is mentioned in 1538 and the advowson of a parish church in 1558,[73] but there is no certain evidence of an early place of worship. Wilsthorpe was included in the new parish of Christ Church, Bridlington Quay, in 1843 and it became part of the newly-created parish of Emmanuel, Hilderthorpe, in 1916.[74] A mission church was opened at Wilsthorpe in 1936 and used until 1968, with a break during the Second World War.[75]

BURTON AGNES

BURTON AGNES lies on the southern edge of the wolds, nearly 6 miles from Bridlington and on one of the main roads to the east Yorkshire coast.[1] The parish extends over a mile north of the road to Wold Gate, which forms the parish boundary for more than 2 miles. South of the Bridlington road it extends 3 miles across the Plain of Holderness, where its boundaries mostly follow watercourses. The parish includes the townships of Thornholme and Haisthorpe, also on the Bridlington road, and Gransmoor, on the plain. Burton was an Anglian settlement, but the townships were all Scandinavian.[2] It was probably with reference to Agnes of Aumale (d. before 1176), second wife of Adam de Brus (II), that Burton received its distinctive suffix.[3] The ancient parish also included the chapelry of Harpham, but that had assumed certain parochial functions by the 18th century and it is treated separately here.[4] The total area of the parish in 1850 was 8,707 a., of which Burton Agnes township accounted for 2,575 a., Thornholme for 1,345 a., Haisthorpe for 1,390 a., Gransmoor for 1,253 a., and Harpham for 2,144 a.[5] In 1884 small areas were transferred from Burton Agnes to Gransmoor and Harpham, and from Thornholme to Burton Agnes.[6] In 1935 Haisthorpe was transferred to Carnaby civil parish.[7]

The north of the parish is rolling and almost treeless wold, rising to 250 ft.–300 ft. above sea-level along Wold Gate. There were formerly several quarries there, notably a large tree-filled pit north of Burton Agnes village. The large, mostly arable, fields were laid out at the inclosure of the open fields in the mid 19th century. In marked contrast, hedgerow trees and plantations give a well-wooded appearance to the south of the parish, on the boulder clay, alluvium, and gravel of the plain. The general level of the plain is only 25 ft.–50 ft. Much of this area was moor, carr, and meadow until the 18th and 19th centuries. Most of the low-lying ground in Haisthorpe was occupied after 1944 by Carnaby airfield.[8]

The village is dominated by Burton Agnes Hall, built in the early 17th century to replace a medieval manor-house which in part still exists. The life of the parish has equally been dominated by the owners of the hall, above all by the Griffith family, who were lords of the manor for 300 years, and the Boynton family, who held it for nearly 250 years. In Gransmoor and Thornholme this role was taken by the St. Quintins of Harpham. The hall stands on rising ground above the village[9] and commands an extensive view across the plain to the sea. Celia Fiennes, staying with her cousin Sir Griffith Boynton in 1697, remarked that from the gallery windows 'you view the whole country round, and discover the ships under sail though at a good distance'.[10] Parkland and plantations north of the hall occupy part of the open-field land which was inclosed by Sir Griffith Boynton in 1722, and it was perhaps at that time that a double ditch, still visible round the west side of the park, was made.

Until the 19th century the village houses lay closely along the main road below the hall, around the cross-roads formed by its junction with the road from Gransmoor and with what is now a cul-de-sac leading to the old Rectory, church, and hall. More recent building has extended the village along the main road, along the Gransmoor road, and along a road leading over the wold to Rudston. The course of the Rudston road has twice been changed. Until the 18th century it continued from its present line north of the park directly into the centre of the village. After the inclosure of 1722 and the laying out of the park, the road was diverted to join a more westerly track up the wold, and at the same time New Lane was made round the eastern side of the inclosed ground.[11] By its new course the road eventually reached the Bridlington road along two steep and winding back lanes; these were replaced by a new and easier road, made by Sir Henry Boynton in 1861.[12] Near the village cross-roads is a prominent pond, from which Mill beck flows eastwards across the parish. The beck fed several fishponds near the village[13] and it was presumably at the beck that a washing-stone was set in the 17th century: above it nobody might wash 'puddings, fish, clothes, or any other filthy thing'.[14]

The character of the village in the 20th century has been affected by the presence of the Bridlington road, which now carries heavy traffic through the village. By 1937 there was a garage;[15] the Blue Bell

---

[72] Regy. of Deeds, 582/321/260.
[73] *L. & P. Hen. VIII*, xiii (1), p. 140; *Cal. Pat.* 1557–8, 401.   [74] See pp. 74–5.
[75] Ex inf. Revd. J. L. Badger, Emmanuel Ch., 1970.
[1] This article was written in 1961, with some revision to 1971.
[2] *P.N.E.R. Yorks.* (E.P.N.S.), 88.
[3] *E.Y.C.* ii, p. 35.
[4] See p. 226.
[5] O.S. Map 6" (1854).
[6] *Census*, 1891. Moorhouse field was transferred to Harpham, Thornholme Moor farm (142 a. in 1840: B.I.H.R., TA. 312M) to Burton Agnes, and Silkholmes (56 a. in 1840: ibid.) to Gransmoor.   [7] *Census*, 1931.
[8] Ex inf. Ministry of Defence, 1969.
[9] The open ground between the hall and the village street was called Ryegate Hill in 1840 and Maypole Hill in 1850: B.I.H.R., TA. 312M; O.S. Map 6" (1854).
[10] *Journeys of Celia Fiennes*, ed. C. Morris, pp. xx, 90.
[11] E.R.R.O., DDCV/Parcel 91; O.S. Map 6" (1854).
[12] E.R.R.O., DDCV/Parcel 120; HD/66.
[13] O.S. Map 6" (1854).
[14] *Miscellanea*, ii (Y.A.S. Rec. Ser. lxxiv), 90.
[15] *Kelly's Dir. N. & E.R. Yorks.* (1937), 435.

has been adapted to attract new trade; and 100,000 people visited the hall between 1949 and 1956.[16] The road has been improved for traffic by the cutting back of the hillside near the cross-roads, and this involved the demolition of alms-houses and some old cottages in 1939.

Apart from the manor-house and the hall, no domestic buildings survive from before the 18th century, and there is little visible work in chalk. Of the 18th-century cottages two are dated 1767. One of the many 19th-century houses is dated 1857 and bears the initials of Sir Henry Boynton. The initials of the Wickham–Boyntons appear on several 20th-century houses, together with dates ranging from 1912 to 1938. There are also 14 Council houses on the Gransmoor road and 24 on the Rudston road. Buildings outside the village in 1854 included Mill House, on the wold slopes, and three farms on the plain. The railway station was presumably built in 1846, when the line to Bridlington was opened, and there is a warehouse of the same period beside the line. By 1892 there was a farm on the wolds and another stood on the ground transferred to Burton Agnes in 1884.[17]

The hamlet of Thornholme is strung out along the main road, ½ mile north-east of Burton Agnes. Earthworks suggest that the houses were formerly more continuous. One of the 18th-century cottages is dated 1782, there are numerous 19th-century houses, and two buildings bear the initials of William H. St. Quintin and the dates 1912 and 1919. Haisthorpe lies ¾ mile further north-east, partly on the main road but with most of its houses along two minor roads on the wold slope and another on the plain. Foundations have been found suggesting that Haisthorpe, too, was once larger. The 20th-century additions include 12 Council houses. The hamlet of Gransmoor lies 2½ miles south-east of Burton Agnes. Shrinkage is again suggested by prominent earthworks at the western end of the hamlet.[18] There are five scattered farm-houses.

In 1377 there were 182 payers of the poll tax in Burton Agnes, with a further 180 in the hamlets.[19] From the 16th century onwards there has been a high proportion of cottages in the parish. Thus in Burton Agnes in 1506 there were 18 houses and 37 cottages;[20] in 1653 11 houses and 37 cottages;[21] in 1700 13 houses and 38 cottages;[22] and in 1805 7 houses and 33 cottages.[23] From the late 15th to the early 17th centuries there were about 10 houses and half a dozen cottages in Haisthorpe;[24] in 1656 8 houses and 14 cottages;[25] and in 1736 3 houses and 11 cottages.[26] At Thornholme there were 5 farmhouses and 6 cottages in 1796.[27] In 1670 56 households in Burton Agnes were assessed to or discharged from the hearth tax, as well as 25 in Haisthorpe and 24 in Thornholme; Gransmoor was combined with Harpham. In 1674 out of 73 houses taxed in Burton Agnes, Haisthorpe, and Thornholme, excluding the hall and Haisthorpe manor-house, 64 had only one hearth. In Thornholme none was larger; in Haisthorpe 2 had 2 hearths each; in Burton Agnes one had 2, 4 had 3, and 2 had five.[28] Perhaps typical of the cottages in the 16th century was that of Henry Barmby of Thornholme: it contained only parlour, 'house', and milk-house.[29]

In 1743 there were said to be 74 families in the parish and in 1764 127.[30] In 1801 the population was 502. It increased to a maximum of 723 in 1861, fell to 597 in 1901, and subsequently exceeded 600 even after the transfer of Haisthorpe to Carnaby civil parish in 1935; it was 582 in 1961. The population of Burton Agnes itself has been comparatively steady. It exceeded 300 by 1821 and has since varied between 317 and 350. Numbers in Haisthorpe have varied between 103 and 157 since 1811, and in Thornholme between 82 and 119. In Gransmoor they rose from 49 in 1801 to 114 in 1871, but had fallen to 89 in 1921.[31]

MANORS AND OTHER ESTATES. Burton Agnes was assessed at 12 carucates in 1086 and, with the berewicks of Boythorpe, Gransmoor, and Harpham (13 carucates), was held by the king, and from him by an unnamed rent-payer. Its soke extended over Haisthorpe, Thornholme, Langtoft, Thwing, and Potter Brompton. Before the Conquest the estate had belonged to Morcar.[32] It is thought that the rent-payer in 1086 may have been Geoffrey Bainard, who gave the church to St. Mary's abbey, York, in 1100–25.[33] Burton Agnes was subsequently given to Robert de Brus[34] and the overlordship descended in the Brus family until the death of Peter de Brus in 1272.[35] It presumably then fell to the share of Peter's daughter Lucy and her husband Marmaduke of Thwing,[36] and subsequently descended in the Thwing and Lumley families.[37]

The demesne lord of *BURTON AGNES* in the later 12th century was probably Roger de Stutville, who was holding lands in Yorkshire under Adam de Brus (II) in 1172.[38] His son Anselm de Stutville died by 1199 and Burton Agnes passed to his sister and coheir Alice, widow of Roger de Merlay (I). The inheritance was disputed by a second sister, Agnes, wife of Herbert de St. Quintin.[39] Roger de Merlay (III) succeeded to his father's lands in 1239,[40] however, and in 1265 Burton Agnes was divided between two of his daughters and coheirs, Mary, wife of William de Greystock, and Isabel, who later

---

[16] *Burton Agnes Hall, An Illus. Survey* (n.d. priv. print.).
[17] O.S. Map 6″ (1854, 1892).
[18] Called Old Garths on O.S. Map 6″ (all edns.).
[19] E 179/202/62 m. 24.
[20] *Cal. Inq. p.m. Hen. VII*, iii, pp. 65–66.
[21] E.R.R.O., DDWB/5/81.
[22] Ibid. /85.
[23] Ibid. DDCV/Parcel 100.
[24] Ibid. DDWB/10/4; *Cal. Inq. p.m. Hen. VII*, ii, pp. 38–9; iii, pp. 87–8.
[25] E.R.R.O., DDWB/20/56.
[26] Ibid. /10/21.
[27] Y.A.S. MSS., MS. 709b.
[28] E 179/205/514, 521.
[29] B.I.H.R., C.P., I. 895.
[30] Ibid. Bp. V. 1764/Ret. 103; *Herring's Visit.* i. 37.
[31] *V.C.H. Yorks.* iii. 489; *Census.*
[32] *V.C.H. Yorks.* ii. 198.
[33] *E.Y.C.* ii, p. 34.
[34] *V.C.H. Yorks.* ii. 291. Brus's wife Agnes may have been Bainard's daughter: *E.Y.C.* ii, p. 12.
[35] *E.Y.C.* ii, p. 15 and *V.C.H. Yorks. N.R.* ii. 336 give lineage.
[36] *Cal. Inq. p.m.* i, pp. 265–7; ii, p. 189.
[37] Ibid. viii, p. 87; x, p. 220; xiv, p. 59; xv, p. 97; *Cal. Inq. p.m. Hen. VII*, iii, pp. 65–6; see below, p. 326.
[38] *Pipe R.* 1172 (P.R.S. xviii), 62.
[39] *Abbrev. Plac.* (Rec. Com.), 76; *Pipe R.* 1199 (P.R.S. N.S. x), 53; *E.Y.C.* ii, p. 35; ix, pp. 29–30; *Cur. Reg. R.* vi. 76, 235; viii. 173, 207, 366.
[40] *Ex. e Rot. Fin.* (Rec. Com.), i. 322; *E.Y.C.* ix, pp. 30–1.

married Robert de Somerville.[41] In 1294 John de Greystock exchanged his share in the manor with Robert de Somerville[42] and the Somervilles held the manor until 1355.[43] The Greystocks, however, retained some land in Burton Agnes; a bovate there was held in 1317 by Robert son of Ralph as heir of Mary and William de Greystock's son John, and in 1323 by Ralph de Greystock.[44] Part of the Greystock land in Thornholme subsequently passed to the Constables of Wassand, and that in Burton Agnes may have done so too, for in 1617 Philip Constable sold a house, 2 closes, and 2 bovates to the lord of Burton Agnes.[45]

In 1355 Philip de Somerville was succeeded by his daughter Joan and her husband Rhys ap Griffith,[46] and Burton Agnes remained in the Griffith family until 1654.[47] Then, on the death of Sir Henry Griffith, it passed to Sir Francis Boynton of Barmston, son of Sir Henry's sister Frances.[48] The manor descended in the Boynton family until 1899, when it passed from Sir Henry Somerville Boynton to his daughter Cycely; in the same year she married Thomas Lamplough Wickham, afterwards Wickham-Boynton.[49] Mr. Marcus Wickham-Boynton owned the estate in 1971.

The old manor-house stands between the hall and the church.[50] It owes its present external appearance, that of a rectangular three-storeyed brick building with sash windows, largely to alterations carried out in the 17th and 18th centuries. The original stone structure, however, dates from c. 1170–80 and thus was probably built by Roger de Stutville. Like several other surviving houses of the period it consists of a simple rectangle, containing a vaulted undercroft below and a hall on the first floor; a stone stair within the north-west angle connects one with the other. Original masonry is visible externally only in the west and north walls. At the west end a 12th-century plinth and small window, lighting the staircase, survive. In the north wall is a restored ground-floor window and a blocked doorway to the hall, the latter originally reached by an external stair. Near the centre of the wall is a corbelled flue projection, partly of 12th-century date, which indicates the existence of an early fire-place in the hall. Internally the vaulted undercroft consists of two aisles, each of four bays, divided by cylindrical piers with moulded bases and 'water-leaf' capitals. Much of the masonry, including the chamfered vaulting ribs, is of chalk. The original spiral stair rises to the hall and may formerly have continued upwards to the roof. In the hall itself only fragments of 12th-century work have survived, but the floor, of stone slabs, is partly original.

The old building was remodelled in the 15th century, probably by Sir Walter Griffith (d. 1481). The walls were raised in height and a new arch-braced collar-beam roof, which is still in position, was constructed. Other 15th-century features include an external string-course and the remains of a large traceried window, both at the west end. It may be assumed that additions had been made to the house during the Middle Ages but no structures adjoining it have survived. When the new Burton Agnes Hall was built in 1601–10, the 12th-century building became service quarters and was presumably altered for the purpose. The brick facing on the south and east walls may have been added in the 17th century to match the new building. The most drastic alterations seem to have taken place in the following century, when the old house was used as a laundry. The undercroft suffered the insertion of a doorway and the destruction of its north-east bay. Across the hall a new ceiling was constructed giving the building an extra storey, and new partitions, fire-places, and a staircase were inserted; a stone set in the east wall of the hall is inscribed 1712, suggesting a date for the work. The present stone-framed sash windows which light all three storeys are of the same period. In 1948 the building came into the guardianship of the Ministry of Works, and it was subsequently restored. Work included the removal of the extra floor in the hall, the opening-up and restoration of the medieval roof, the replacement of the damaged vault in the undercroft, and the exposure and repair of several original openings. In an outbuilding near the old manor-house is a 12th-century well, with a donkey wheel which may be of the 17th century.

Dates on and in the building suggest that the new hall was built c. 1601–10, and it was thus the work of Sir Henry Griffith.[51] Its design has been attributed to Robert Smythson.[52] The building, which is of red brick with stone dressings, takes the form of a square block with a small internal courtyard. In this respect it breaks away, like Smythson's other great houses, from the typical H- or E-shaped Elizabethan plan. The principal, or entrance, front faces south and this half of the building is of three full storeys, while further north the top storey consists only of gabled attics; as a result the east and west fronts have an irregular sky-line. The principal rooms are on the south and east sides, the great hall, with a screens passage across its west end, occupying the centre of the south range. The top floor of this range houses the long gallery, which formerly stretched for 115 ft. across the whole width of the building. The west wing contains the kitchen and offices.[53]

The symmetrical south front is flanked by two short projecting wings, each terminating in a three-storeyed semicircular bay below a gable. Between the wings are two square projections, also three-storeyed; one contains the entrance porch leading to the screens passage and the other, which balances it, forms an oriel at the upper end of the hall. To compensate for the insignificant position of the doorway, the east side of the porch bay is entirely of stone and carries three superimposed orders, Ionic,

---

[41] *Cal. Inq. p.m.* i, p. 200; *Cal. Close*, 1279–88, 106; 1288–1296, 217.
[42] E.R.R.O., DDWB/20/5.
[43] e.g. ibid. /5/12; *T.E.R.A.S.* xviii. 69, 111–12; *Feud. Aids*, vi. 169; *Cal. Inq. p.m.* viii, p. 87.
[44] *Cal. Inq. p.m.* vi, pp. 30, 307.
[45] E.R.R.O., DDWB/5/72a; DDRI/Box 1.
[46] *Yorks. Fines, 1327–47*, 140; *Cal. Inq. p.m.* x, p. 220; *Cal. Close*, 1354–60, 133.
[47] For lineage see *Misc. Gen. et Her.* i. 64; *Visit. Yorks. 1584–5 and 1612*, ed. J. Foster, 524; Burke, *Ext. and Dorm. Baronetcies* (1838), 229. The Griffith baronetcy was created in 1627.
[48] *G.E.C. Baronetage*, i. 114.
[49] Burke, *Peerage* (1959), 273–4 gives lineage.
[50] Ministry of Works guide. See plate facing p. 113.
[51] See plate facing p. 112.
[52] M. Girouard, 'The Smithson Family, their Work and Drawings' (unpubl. Ph. D. thesis, London Univ. 1957), 168.
[53] For a plan see Sir Nikolaus Pevsner, *The planning of the Elizabethan Country House* (Inaugural Lecture delivered at Birkbeck College, 1960), p. 12. The house is described in *Country Life*, 6, 11, 18 June 1953.

Corinthian, and Composite, together with the arms of the Griffith family and of Elizabeth I. On the corresponding side of the other bay are three niches, one above the other, containing statues placed there by the present owner of the house. Above each bay is a flourish of strapwork and finials. The east and west sides of the house are plainer, but both have embattled five-sided bays near their angles. The storeys are divided by continuous stone string-courses on all fronts.

Much of the elaborate 17th-century carved woodwork, plaster, and alabaster survive throughout the house. Outstanding are the hall, the lower drawing room, and a bedroom in the east wing. In the hall the most notable features are the screen, with many reliefs of biblical and allegorical subjects, and the overmantel, the upper section of which was brought from the Boynton's Elizabethan house at Barmston at its demolition in the 18th century. The main staircase is unusual, with continuous newel posts linked by a series of arches and with a very narrow well. The long gallery above the front range originally had an enriched barrel ceiling. Two-thirds of the gallery was divided into small rooms in the 19th century and the rest dismantled; the latter section was restored in 1951–2 with the ceiling a copy of the original. The house had 32 hearths in 1674.[54]

The most significant alterations to the house were made by Sir Griffith Boynton (d. 1730). They included the refitting of several rooms, notably the upper drawing room on the east side and the Chinese room, which is lined with cut screens of painted lacquer. He also inserted large Palladian windows at the two ends of the long gallery and replaced many of the other mullioned and transomed windows in the house with sashes.

The date 1610 for the completion of the original house is suggested by the presence of that date on the overmantel in a bedroom and on the gatehouse. The gatehouse stands to the south of the house, placed axially in relation to the main front.[55] Between the two is a wide grass forecourt, studded with clipped yews; there was a bowling green there in 1697.[56] The three-storeyed embattled gatehouse, of red brick with stone dressings, has taller octagonal turrets with domed roofs at the four angles. On its outer face the central round-arched gateway is flanked by stone arcading and surmounted by a stone entablature carrying the arms of James I and two allegorical figures. The buildings round the stable yard, which lies west of the house, are dated 1859.

Among several small estates in Burton Agnes was that of the Cawoods. It may have originated in 1470, when William Cawood obtained from Edward Skeryn 3 bovates and other property there in exchange for land in Wetwang.[57] In 1507 Walter Cawood held his property in Burton Agnes and Thornholme in socage from Walter Griffith.[58] Walter Cawood in 1578 devised his 'mansion place', 5 bovates, and other land in Burton Agnes to his wife.[59] In 1597 Marmaduke Cawood sold 5½ bovates to Henry Griffith.[60]

Three crofts in Burton Agnes were granted to North Ferriby priory by Roger de Merlay in the early 13th century.[61] 'South croft called Ferriby croft' and 'Northferybecroft' were held by the Griffiths in the mid 15th century[62] and 'Prest crofts' were rented by them from the priory in the 1480s and 1490s.[63] After the Dissolution Ferriby crofts were acquired by the Griffiths;[64] they lay south-west of the village.[65]

In 1086 Gransmoor consisted of 4 carucates forming a berewick of Burton Agnes and held by the king, and 2 carucates held by Ernuin the priest.[66] Like Burton Agnes, the larger estate was granted to Brus[67] and held by Stutvilles. After Anselm de Stutville's death by 1199 it apparently passed to his sister Alice, and descended from her to the Merlays and Greystocks; the larger part of it was, however, held from them by the St. Quintins of Harpham.[68] The estate, sometimes described as the manor of GRANSMOOR,[69] descended in the St. Quintin family[70] until 1788. Sir William St. Quintin then sold it to Isaac Leatham,[71] author of *A General View of the Agriculture of the East Riding of Yorkshire* (1794). In 1810 Leatham sold it to Thomas Duesbery,[72] and he in 1837 devised it to his nephew William Duesbery Thornton, who later took the name of Duesbery.[73] In 1900 the Revd. C. L. T. Duesbery sold the estate, then consisting of 1,372 a., to J. T. T. Cliff.[74] In 1915 the latter sold 217 a. to A. H. Taylor and in 1920 301 a. to W. E. Y. Putman.[75] Cliff died in 1953[76] and in 1956 his trustees sold the rest of the estate in separate lots.[77]

Of the 2 carucates held in 1086 by Ernuin the priest one was apparently acquired by Robert de Brus[78] and it may have descended with his chief estate in Gransmoor. It is possibly to be identified with land held by under-tenants of the Merlays and Greystocks.[79] The other carucate became part of the fee of the Gants of Hunmanby; it was held by a succession of under-tenants before, by 1284–5, being granted to Bridlington priory.[80] At the Dissolution the priory owned property in Gransmoor worth £1 10s. 8d.[81]

In 1086 Haisthorpe consisted of 4 carucates as

---

[54] E 179/205/521.
[55] See plate facing p. 112.
[56] *Journeys of Celia Fiennes*, 90.
[57] E.R.R.O., DDWB/5/50.
[58] *Cal. Inq. p.m. Hen. VII*, iii, p. 301.
[59] B.I.H.R., Prob. Reg. xxi, f. 95.
[60] E R.R.O., DDWB/6/4; C 2/Jas. I/G 12/2.
[61] E.R.R.O., DDWB/5/2a.
[62] Ibid. /47, 48.
[63] Ibid. /54, 56, 61.
[64] Ibid. /64, 66, 84, 85; /20/44.
[65] B.I.H.R., TA. 312M, where they are called Priest closes.
[66] *V.C.H. Yorks.* ii. 198, 287, 323.
[67] Ibid. 198, 291.
[68] *Cal. Inq. p.m.* i, pp. 200–201; vi, pp. 30, 307; *Feud. Aids*, vi. 31.
[69] e.g. *Yorks. Fines*, iii. 2.
[70] See p. 224.
[71] E.R.R.O., DDDU/Bdle. 2; Registry of Deeds, Beverley, BN/85/130.
[72] Regy. of Deeds, CP/305/467. Duesbery was already in possession in 1809: E.R.R.O., DDDU/Bdle. 2; Land Tax.
[73] E.R.R.O., DDCC/134/76.
[74] Regy. of Deeds, 27/124/117 (1900).
[75] Ibid. 171/132/109; 217/309/275.
[76] Ibid. 1051/58/55.
[77] Ibid. 1047/494/421; 1050/555/500; 1051/58/55; /275/246.
[78] *V.C.H. Yorks.* ii. 287, 292; *E.Y.C.* ii, p. 34.
[79] *Cal. Inq. p.m.* i, pp. 200–201; vi, pp. 30, 307.
[80] *E.Y.C.* ii, p. 432; *Feud. Aids*, vi. 31; *Bridlington Charty.* 160–2.
[81] *Valor Eccl.* (Rec. Com.), v. 120.

soke of Burton Agnes and held by the king, and 2 carucates held by the archbishop of York.[82] The larger estate was given to Robert de Brus[83] and, like Burton Agnes, was held by the Stutvilles, Merlays, Somervilles, and Griffiths.[84] By 1265 the under-tenant was William of Haisthorpe[85] and in 1312 John of Haisthorpe held the manor of *HAISTHORPE*;[86] he was allowed a private oratory there in 1313–14.[87] The manor was still held by the Haisthorpes in 1356.[88] By 1414 the manor had passed to John Thornholme[89] and it remained in the Thornholme family until 1599.[90] In that year John Thornholme left two coheirs, Catherine, widow of Sir William Calverley, and Margaret, wife of Robert Saltmarsh.[91] Margaret and Robert quitclaimed the manor to Catherine in 1601,[92] and in 1611 William Calverley sold it to Henry Griffith.[93] It subsequently descended with Burton Agnes and in 1943 the Haisthorpe estate contained 1,248 a.[94] The Air Ministry bought 554 a. in 1948 for Carnaby airfield and the rest of the estate was sold, in separate lots, in 1952.[95]

The manor, comprising Haisthorpe Hall, 18 bovates, and some closes, was in 1631 let by Sir Henry Griffith to Henry Bushell.[96] Bushell devised the lease to his elder son Francis in 1662, together with other land that he had bought from Sir Henry.[97] The lease may have been surrendered after the death of Bushell's younger son Charles. In 1726 the 'lands of the late Charles Bushell' included 4 closes in Burton Agnes itself.[98]

The archbishop's estate was held by St. John's college, Beverley, in 1086,[99] and in 1284–5 and 1309 it was said to lie within the liberty of St. John.[1] In 1283 and 1316 the under-tenant was John de Crepping,[2] whose father had probably held it before.[3] The estate may have been merged with Haisthorpe manor in the 14th century. In 1343 John de Crepping alleged that John of Haisthorpe had disseised him of part of his free tenement there, and in 1348 John of Haisthorpe obtained seisin of 2 bovates in Haisthorpe which his father had been granted by John de 'Cressinges'.[4]

Among several small estates in Haisthorpe was one of 6 bovates and other land which belonged to the Pearsons of Lowthorpe in the 17th century. They sold it to Thomas Norton,[5] who held it in the early 18th century.[6] It was sold to the Revd. George Colbatch in 1731[7] and bought by Sir Griffith Boynton in 1758.[8]

Bridlington priory had property worth 2s. 8d. in Haisthorpe at the Dissolution.[9]

The medieval manor-house, which in 1333 was 'enclosed with walls and ditches',[10] may be represented by the moated site at the south end of the village. The farm-house near by was apparently its successor and was said in 1855 to be partly ancient.[11] It may have been the manor-house which was let to Henry Bushell in 1631[12] and the house, occupied by 'Mr. Bushell', which contained nine hearths in 1674.[13] Haisthorpe Hall, at first called Haisthorpe Lodge,[14] at the north end of the village was built c. 1850 and was occupied in 1855 by Mary, widow of Sir Henry Boynton.[15]

In 1086 Thornholme consisted of 7 carucates as soke of Burton Agnes, held by the king.[16] It was subsequently granted to Brus[17] and held by the Stutvilles. After the death of Anselm de Stutville by 1199 Thornholme, like Gransmoor, passed to his sister Alice and descended from her to the Merlays and Greystocks; most of Thornholme, however, was held from them by the St. Quintins of Harpham.[18] The estate, sometimes referred to as the manor of *THORNHOLME*,[19] descended in the St. Quintin family[20] until the death of Violet H. St. Quintin in 1943. It then consisted of 1,174 a.[21] In 1944 it was sold by her trustees to M. W. Wickham-Boynton.[22] In 1948 he sold 154 a. to the Air Ministry for Carnaby airfield; the remainder was sold in separate lots in 1949.[23]

Several smaller estates were for certain periods held separately from the St. Quintin lands. At Roger de Merlay's death in 1265, when the chief estate passed to Mary wife of William de Greystock, other land fell to a second coheir, Isabel, who later married Robert de Somerville.[24] Land in Thornholme was held by the Griffiths,[25] who succeeded the Somervilles at Burton Agnes, and the Boyntons. They also acquired property there in 1597 when 7 bovates and 6 closes were sold to Henry Griffith as part of the Cawood estate.[26] In the early 19th century the Boynton property was apparently acquired by William St. Quintin.[27]

---

[82] *V.C.H. Yorks.* ii. 198, 325.
[83] Ibid. 291.
[84] C 3/72/17; *Abbrev. Plac.* (Rec. Com.), 222; *Feud. Aids,* vi. 31; *Cal. Inq. p.m.* i, p. 200; viii, p. 88; *Hen. VII,* iii, pp. 87–8.
[85] *Cal. Inq. p.m.* i, p. 200.
[86] *T.E.R.A.S.* xviii. 111–12.
[87] *Reg. Greenfield,* iii (Sur. Soc. cli), 208, 222.
[88] *Cal. Inq. p.m.* viii, p. 88.
[89] E.R.R.O., DDWB/10/1.
[90] For lineage see *Visit. Yorks. 1584–5 and 1612,* 166.
[91] C 142/669/10.
[92] *Yorks Fines,* iv. 164.
[93] E.R.R.O., DDWB/10/5; *Yorks. Fines, 1603–14,* 165.
[94] Regy. of Deeds, 668/410/356.
[95] Ibid. 797/473/395; 925/487/397 et sqq.
[96] E.R.R.O., DDBV/20/1.
[97] B.I.H.R., Prob. Reg. xlv, f. 233.
[98] Ibid. TER. J. Burton Agnes 1726.
[99] *V.C.H. Yorks.* ii. 215.
[1] J.I. 1/1112 rot. 5; *Feud. Aids,* vi. 31; *Cur. Reg. R.* xiii. 45.
[2] *Cal. Chart. R. 1257–1300,* 266; *Feud. Aids,* vi. 169.
[3] Robt. de Crepping (fl. 1249) held land in Haisthorpe: K.B. 26/135 rot. 3.
[4] K.B. 27/336 rot. 139; K.B. 27/354 rot. 46d.
[5] Y.A.S. MSS., MS. 709a.
[6] He took part in the inclosure of 1723: see p. 113.
[7] E.R.R.O., DDWB/10/18.
[8] Ibid. DDHB/7/7; DDWB/10/25, 26.
[9] *Valor Eccl.* v. 120.
[10] *T.E.R.A.S.* xviii. 85.
[11] Sheahan and Whellan, *Hist. York & E.R.* ii. 461.
[12] E.R.R.O., DDBV/20.
[13] E 179/205/521.
[14] Sheahan and Whellan, op. cit. ii. 461; O.S. Map 6" (1854, 1892).
[15] Sheahan and Whellan, op. cit. ii 461.
[16] *V.C.H. Yorks.* ii. 198.
[17] Ibid. 291.
[18] There were several smaller under-tenants: *Cal. Inq. p.m.* i, pp. 200–201; vi, pp. 30, 307; *Feud. Aids,* vi. 31.
[19] e.g. C.P. 43/673 rot. 304; C.P. 43/929 rot. 343.
[20] See p. 224.
[21] Regy. of Deeds, 533/40/34; 676/589/476.
[22] Ibid. 683/189/162.
[23] Ibid. 797/473/395; 926/373/316; 948/320/272; /321/273; 951/227/198; 952/134/122.
[24] E.R.R.O., DDWB/20/8; *Feud. Aids,* vi. 169; *Cal Inq. p.m.* viii, p. 88; *Cal. Close, 1337–9,* 83.
[25] E.R.R.O., DDWB/18/11; /20/44, 56; *Cal. Inq. p.m. Hen. VII,* iii, pp. 65–6.
[26] E.R.R.O., DDWB/6/4.
[27] E.R.R.O., Land Tax.

Another estate was that apparently formed out of the Greystock lands and held by the Salvin family by 1353.[28] In 1533 William Salvin sold property in Thornholme to Marmaduke Constable of Wassand, and in 1546 he conveyed it to the Crown.[29] It was granted to Edward Wingate in 1590,[30] bought by Robert Robinson in 1608, and acquired by William St. Quintin in 1613.[31]

Bridlington priory was c. 1199–1219 given two tofts in Thornholme by Agnes and Alice de Stutville.[32] The property was worth 4s. at the Dissolution.[33]

The rectory, which was given to St. Mary's abbey, York, in the 12th century,[34] was valued at £33 6s. 8d. in 1291,[35] reduced to £23 6s. 8d. in 1339.[36] It was held by the abbey until the Dissolution and granted to the archbishop of York in 1545.[37] In 1568 it was let by the archbishop to Walter Griffith,[38] and in 1647, when it was let to Sir Henry Griffith, its value was about £220; after Sir Henry had compounded for delinquency in 1649 several proposals were made for using the income of the rectory to assist other parishes, and one for settling part of it on Burton Agnes school.[39] The tithes in Burton Agnes were leased by Sir Francis Boynton in 1664 and by Sir William St. Quintin in 1722, and the St. Quintins were the lessees in Harpham in 1770.[40] The tithes of Haisthorpe and Gransmoor were held by John Pearson in 1665.[41] The tithes were commuted in 1840 for £887, comprising £522 in Burton Agnes and Haisthorpe, £190 in Gransmoor, and £176 in Thornholme; the archbishop's lessees were then William St. Quintin in Burton Agnes, Haisthorpe, and Thornholme, and William Duesbery in Gransmoor.[42] The tithes in Harpham were extinguished at inclosure in 1776.[43] It was presumably rectorial glebe in Burton Agnes which was described as a manor in 1316, when the abbot of St. Mary's was granted protection for his servants carrying corn thence to York.[44] In 1647 there was said to be a bovate of rectorial glebe,[45] but in 1840 there were only 3 roods.[46]

ECONOMIC HISTORY. By 1086 Burton was the centre of a large estate.[47] Together with its berewicks it had been worth £24 before the Conquest, but in 1086 a rent-payer rendered only 10s. to the king and the soke was waste.[48] Burton Agnes was a comparatively large village in the Middle Ages and its local importance perhaps owed something to a Tuesday market and an annual fair, on 10–17 November, granted to Roger de Merlay (III) in 1257.[49] In 1265 the market profits were valued at 10s.[50] but no more is heard of either market or fair.

There were several under-tenants of the lords of the manor in the 13th and 14th centuries,[51] and the smaller free tenants in Burton Agnes and Thornholme numbered 14 in 1265, paying rents of from 1d. to £2 4s.[52] In 1336 Roger de Somerville received rents from 5 free tenants in Thornholme and one in Gransmoor.[53] A free tenant of Alexander de St. Quintin at Gransmoor, Walter Freman, had ploughing, mowing, and carting services remitted in 1239–40, but his rent and foreign service were confirmed.[54] In the 16th century freeholders were apparently less numerous, and few of them took part in the early-18th-century inclosures.[55] In Burton Agnes in 1791 and 1805 there were only 4 and one freeholders respectively,[56] and in 1840 there was only one landowner in the entire parish, apart from the owners of the manors and chief estates.[57]

Little is known of the customary tenants and their lands. In 1265 38 bovates were held in bondage and 6 in drengage; each tenant was obliged to mow in autumn for 14 days, carry corn with 2 carts for one day, undertake 2 ploughings and 3 harrowings, provide 2 fowls at Christmas, and make an annual aid totalling 4s. 6d. to the lord. In addition 48 cottars paid nearly £4 rent and 3 men held land at will.[58]

Not until 1700 is there a comprehensive record of the size of tenant farms in Burton Agnes. Then, of 13 tenants one had 10½ bovates, one had 9, one had 8, 2 had 7, 2 had 6, one had 5, 3 had 4, and one only closes; the thirteenth had one bovate and a smith's shop.[59] In Haisthorpe in 1508 3 tenants each had 3 bovates, and 2 had 4;[60] in 1656 2 farmers had 5 bovates, 5 had 4, and one had 3;[61] by 1736, one had 13 bovates and 2 had eight.[62] Several of the cottagers in the 16th century and later were described as grassmen.[63]

The open fields of Burton Agnes, Thornholme, and Haisthorpe lay mainly on the wold slopes and by the 19th century there was only one small extension south of the Driffield-Bridlington road. North of the road in 1850 lay West, Middle, and East fields in Burton Agnes, High and Low fields in Thornholme, and West, East, and High fields in Haisthorpe;[64] in 1796 the fields of Thornholme had been West, Middle, and East.[65] In the Middle Ages, however, the fields had extended further south. Low Wandales in Burton Agnes, for example, had probably

---

[28] G. Wrottesley, *Ped. from Plea R.* 73.
[29] *Yorks. Fines*, i. 66, 125.
[30] C 66/1350 m. 25.
[31] *Yorks. Fines, 1603–14*, 90, 209.
[32] *Bridlington Charty.* 162; *E.Y.C.* ix, pp. 133–4.
[33] *Valor Eccl.* v. 120.
[34] See p. 114.
[35] *Tax. Eccl.* (Rec. Com.), 304.
[36] *Cal. Pat.* 1338–40, 255.
[37] *L. & P. Hen. VIII*, xx (1), p. 215.
[38] B.I.H.R., C.P., G. 1398.
[39] Lambeth Pal. MS. 918, xvii, f. 1; *T.E.R.A.S.* ii. 58; *Cal. Cttee. for Compounding*, 162, 1375–7; *Cal. S.P. Dom.* 1654, 249; 1655–6, 239.
[40] E.R.R.O., DDWB/5/92; /10/10; B.I.H.R., TER. J. Burton Agnes 1770.
[41] B.I.H.R., Prob. Reg. xlvii, f. 369v.
[42] Ibid. TA. 312 M.
[43] See p. 226.
[44] *Cal. Pat.* 1313–17, 555.
[45] Lambeth Pal. MS. 918, xvii, f.1.
[46] B.I.H.R., TA. 312 M.
[47] See p. 107.
[48] *V.C.H. Yorks.* ii. 198.
[49] *Cal. Chart. R.* 1226–57, 468.
[50] *Yorks. Inq.* i. 101.
[51] *Cal. Inq. p.m.* i, p. 200; viii, p. 88.
[52] *Yorks. Inq.* i. 101.
[53] E.R.R.O., DDWB/18/2, 4; /20/8.
[54] *Yorks. Fines, 1232–46*, 87.
[55] See p. 113.
[56] E.R.R.O., DDCV/Parcel 100.
[57] B.I.H.R., TA. 312 M. See also E.R.R.O., Land Tax.
[58] *Yorks. Inq.* i. 100–101.
[59] E.R.R.O., DDWB/5/85.
[60] *Cal. Inq. p.m. Hen. VII*, iii, p. 210.
[61] E.R.R.O., DDWB/20/56.
[62] Ibid. /10/21.
[63] B.I.H.R., Prob. Reg. xxi, f. 94; E.R.R.O., DDCV/Parcel 100. For grassmen see *Y.A.J.* xl. 389.
[64] O.S. Map 6" (1854).
[65] Y.A.S. MSS., MS. 709b.

been part of them,[66] and in Haisthorpe there had been two additional fields, Low and South-east, and West field formerly extended south of the main road as well.[67] Low field had been converted to pasture by 1677, when beast-gates were held in place of open-field land.[68] The open fields of Gransmoor were entirely on the plain; there were three, called Langham, South, and Moor fields.[69] Burton Agnes manor contained 73 bovates in 1265[70] and 74 in 1506,[71] 800 a. of arable in 1653, and 7 bovates of demesne and 71½ of tenants' land in 1700.[72] Haisthorpe manor contained 600 a. of arable in 1497,[73] 46 bovates in both 1506 and 1603,[74] 18 bovates of demesne and 33 of tenants' land in 1656,[75] and 13 bovates of demesne and 29 of tenants' land in 1736.[76] At Gransmoor Sir William St. Quintin had 685 a. in the three fields in 1700.[77] In 1716 the vicarial glebe lay in 20 furlongs in Burton Agnes; the vicar owned all four strips in each furlong, and the furlongs were all surrounded by Sir Griffith Boynton's land.[78] When Boynton inclosed 85 a. in the fields in 1722 he had to acquire only 11 a. of glebe and a few acres from Sir William St. Quintin to achieve sole ownership.[79]

The common meadows lay south of the open fields and a share in them was attached to open-field holdings. In 1623, for example, a Thornholme man devised a bovate of corn together with its meadow,[80] and in 1685 the 8 bovates of vicarial glebe in Burton Agnes carried the right to 16 lands in the meadows. The latter in 1685 included the ings, the 'Inghay' carr, and the Holmes; in 1726 the glebe lay in the ings, the 'Inner' carr, the Holmes, and the Fishpools.[81] The common meadows in the townships apparently included the Town ings in Thornholme.[82]

A broad belt of moor extended across the parish, between the arable fields and meadows of Burton Agnes, Thornholme, and Haisthorpe on the north and those of Gransmoor on the south. The moor belonged to Burton Agnes manor, and rights of pasture there were mentioned in the early 13th century.[83] Common rights there were also enjoyed by the inhabitants of Harpham,[84] and the prior of Bridlington in 1439 surrendered to Walter Griffith similar rights which he had enjoyed in respect of his lands in neighbouring Fraisthorpe.[85] The respective rights of Walter Griffith and John St. Quintin on the moor and elsewhere were defined in 1465. Each was to appoint a pinder for Thornholme and they were to share the profits arising from offences there, whether they were taken to the court at Burton Agnes or to that at Harpham. St. Quintin's tenants in Thornholme, Gransmoor, and Harpham were to have right of commonage on Burton moor and in the fields and waste grounds of Burton Agnes; Griffith's tenants were to have similar rights in Harpham and and Gransmoor; and Griffith and St. Quintin were to share commonage in Thornholme.[86]

The moor included areas of marsh, turbary, and carr, and besides pasturage it also provided whins,[87] turf,[88] and fowl.[89] Pasturage was for all kinds of animals. In the early 13th century, for example, Roger de Merlay granted the right to feed 8 oxen, 6 cows, 100 sheep, and 2 horses there.[90] That part of the moor lying around Burton Mere, however, was known as the Horse carr, and horse-gates were enjoyed there in the 17th and 18th centuries.[91] In the 17th century pasturage in open fields and commons was stinted. In 1632 husbandmen and cottagers were allowed 20 sheep for each house and 20 for each bovate of land, and those who rented cottages were in 1633 limited to 40 sheep and 6 horned beasts 'within the territories of Burton Agnes'. In the latter year inhabitants were forbidden to tether animals in West or Middle fields and strangers in any field. The tethering of cattle on balks in the sown fields was forbidden in 1681 and it was ordered in 1688 that anyone taking in sheep 'to winter in the fallows' should keep them on his own ground.[92]

Many areas of demesne pasture lay around the moor. Some were let to tenants,[93] and others were used in common for certain periods of the year. In 1465, for example, various meadows, carrs, and closes were common from early September to the middle of March, and some were in addition common for the whole of every third year.[94] Among the property let was a cottage called the Moor House, which appears to have been a dairy farm in the 15th and 16th centuries. In 1454 Walter Griffith let it together with a croft, a carr, 10 cows, and 5 calves; similar leases were made in 1495 and 1497,[95] and a 'dairyman' lived there in 1553.[96]

Early inclosure produced a number of closes in addition to the crofts and garths around the village. In 1465, for example, Burton Agnes manor included the Old and New Coney Garths, the Horse close, the Calf close, Silkholme, and Owram close.[97] Owram (or Worm) and Silkholmes, as they were called in 1840, lay beyond the moor,[98] and the Coney Garth was north of the village in 1722.[99] By 1700 the closes included the Great and Upper Cow pastures, Wandale closes, and Cawood closes,[1] and in 1716 the Intacks and Seagrows.[2] There was a 58-acre New close at Gransmoor by 1700.[3]

Large-scale inclosure of common fields, moors,

---

[66] B.I.H.R., TA. 312 M.
[67] That part of West field which was inclosed in 1723: E.R.R.O., DDWB/10/16. [68] Ibid. /12.
[69] Ibid. DDSQ uncalendared; O.S. Map 6" (1854).
[70] Yorks. Inq. i. 100.
[71] Cal. Inq. p.m. Hen. VII, iii, pp. 65–6.
[72] E.R.R.O., DDWB/5/81, 85.
[73] Cal. Inq. p.m. Hen. VII, ii, pp. 38–9.
[74] Ibid. iii, pp. 87–8; E.R.R.O., DDWB/10/4.
[75] E.R.R.O., DDWB/20/56. [76] Ibid. /10/21.
[77] Ibid. DDSQ uncalendared.
[78] B.I.H.R., TER. J. Burton Agnes 1716.
[79] E.R.R.O., DDWB/5/93, 94.
[80] B.I.H.R., Prob. Reg. xxxvii, f. 378.
[81] Ibid. TER. J. Burton Agnes 1685, 1726.
[82] E.R.R.O., DDWB/5/88. [83] Ibid. /2a, 6.
[84] Ibid. /2b, 49, 67; Yorks. Sta. Cha. Proc. (Y.A.S. Rec. Ser. xli), 156–7.
[85] E.R.R.O., DDWB/5/45. [86] Ibid. /49.

[87] B.I.H.R., TER. J. Burton Agnes 1716; Miscellanea, ii (Y.A.S. Rec. Ser. lxxiv), 95.
[88] E.R.R.O., DDWB/5/43, 67; Yorks. Inq. i. 101.
[89] B.I.H.R., Prob. Reg. xvi, f. 37.
[90] E.R.R.O., DDWB/5/2a.
[91] Ibid. /88, 99; /20/39, 41; /23/17; DDBV/20/1.
[92] Miscellanea, ii. 87–9.
[93] e.g. B.I.H.R., Prob. Reg. xi, f. 729; xxviii, f. 56; E.R.R.O., DDWB/8/2.
[94] E.R.R.O., DDWB/5/49; T.E.R.A.S. xviii. 111–12.
[95] E.R.R.O., DDWB/5/47, 58, 59.
[96] B.I.H.R., Prob. Reg. xiii, f. 968.
[97] E.R.R.O., DDWB/5/49.
[98] B.I.H.R., TA. 312M. Owram was called Wharram in the mid 19th century and an embankment cross there was Wharram Hill: O.S. Map 6" (1854).
[99] E.R.R.O., DDCV/Parcel 91. [1] Ibid. DDWB/5/85.
[2] B.I.H.R., TER. J. Burton Agnes 1716; TA. 312M.
[3] E.R.R.O., DDSQ uncalendared.

The south front

The gatehouse

BURTON AGNES HALL

Burton Agnes Manor-House: the undercroft

Bridlington: the priory gatehouse

and meadows took place in the 18th century. The inclosure of Gransmoor was being planned in 1700, when Sir William St. Quintin's tenants were anxious lest they should not be able to pay their rents if the fields were inclosed and laid to grass.[4] The inclosure nevertheless took place, 'in or about the year 1702'.[5] In 1719 Sir Griffith Boynton, Sir William St. Quintin, and the other freeholders inclosed Burton moor and certain meadows and carrs in Burton Agnes, Thornholme, and Haisthorpe. In all 1,821 a. were allotted, Boynton receiving 887 a. and St. Quintin 763 a. Among the grounds involved were the Firth and Longstone carr in Haisthorpe, Haisthorpe common carr, Arnott carr in Thornholme, and Horse carr, Cow carr, and Ferriby crofts, all in Burton Agnes, as well as the moor.[6] In 1722 Sir Griffith Boynton was said to have 'lately' inclosed 85 a. in the open fields of Burton Agnes, comprising 57 a. in East field and 28 a. in Middle field; Sir William St. Quintin carried out an unspecified inclosure in Thornholme at the same time. The inclosures were facilitated by small exchanges of land between Boynton and the vicar and between Boynton and St. Quintin.[7] At least in Thornholme the date of these inclosures may have been 1714: St. Quintin's open-field and other land was then surveyed and 'the division... accomplished'.[8] In 1723 Sir Griffith Boynton and four freeholders in Haisthorpe inclosed part of West field, and lands in East or South-east field which included various parcels of meadow and pasture. Of the 340 a. allotted Boynton received 280 a.[9] Finally, in 1758 Sir Griffith Boynton and the vicar inclosed, in Burton Agnes, meadow called Fish Pools, the ings. Ferriby Groves, and the Holmes, and pasture called Inner carr, in which they had cow-gates. Boynton received 180 a. and the vicar 17 a.[10]

As the result of these inclosures most of the low-lying ground was improved in the 18th century. Several remnants were dealt with in the later 19th century. The Moorhouse field, after having been used as an undivided pasture, was by 1824 tilled in separate parcels by several tenants;[11] it was inclosed between 1854 and 1892.[12] There were still 113 a. unimproved in the Horse carr in 1840 and these too were inclosed, and Burton Mere drained, between 1854 and 1892.[13] The greater part of the open-field land in Burton Agnes, Thornholme, and Haisthorpe was not involved in the earlier inclosures but survived on the wold slopes until the 1850s. The circumstances of its final inclosure are not known.[14]

There was a marked predominance of tillage in 1840. Of the tithable land in Burton Agnes 1,823 a. were arable, 420 a. meadow and pasture, and 59 a. woodland; in Thornholme 1,165 a. were arable, 136 a. meadow and pasture, and 14 a. woodland; in Haisthorpe 1,186 a. were arable, 157 a. meadow and pasture, and 8 a. woodland; and in Gransmoor 980 a. were arable, 185 a. meadow and pasture, and 60 a. woodland. Sir Henry Boynton then owned 2,227 a. in Burton Agnes, but only about 270 a. were held as a home farm. Nearly 30 tenants held land or houses, including 9 substantial farms ranging in size from 110 a. to 260 a. There were also 30 cottagers. In Haisthorpe Sir Henry owned 1,231 a. and Dame Mary Boynton the rest; there were 4 tenants, with farms of from 122 a. to 469 a., and about a dozen cottagers. In Thornholme William St. Quintin was the sole landowner; 5 farms were of from 142 a. to 295 a. and there were 9 smaller holdings and cottages. In Gransmoor William Duesbery was the sole landowner; 4 farmers held from 175 a. to 369 a. each and there were 7 smaller holdings and cottages.[15] In 1872 there were still 9 principal farmers in Burton Agnes and 4 in each township, and the numbers have subsequently varied only slightly.[16]

There were brickworks in Burton Agnes in the later 19th and early 20th centuries.[17] Gravel has been obtained commercially from a quarry in Gransmoor since 1944.[18] A water-mill at Thornholme is mentioned in the 13th century,[19] and a water-mill and a windmill at Burton Agnes are first mentioned in 1265.[20] The mills in Burton Agnes belonged to the manor and in the 17th century tenants were obliged to have their corn ground there.[21] The mills still functioned in 1840 but had apparently ceased to do so by 1850 when 'Old Mill' stood by the pond near the centre of the village and Mill House marked the site of the windmill, north of the park.[22] There was no trace of either in 1961. There may also have been windmills in Haisthorpe and Gransmoor: Mill close in Haisthorpe is mentioned in 1631 and Mill closes lay at the north end of the village in 1840, when there was also a Mill Hill close in Gransmoor.[23]

LOCAL GOVERNMENT. In the late 13th century the lords of Burton Agnes claimed gallows, infangtheof, the assize of bread and ale, pillory, and tumbril.[24] The manorial court of Burton Agnes is first mentioned in 1312[25] and that of Haisthorpe in 1350.[26] The only known medieval court records are the proceedings of two courts held in Haisthorpe in 1414.[27] Gransmoor may have fallen under the jurisdiction of the St. Quintins' court at Harpham, as Thornholme certainly did.[28]

There are references to bylawmen and to their

[4] Ibid.
[5] B.I.H.R., TER. J. Burton Agnes 1716.
[6] E.R.R.O., DDWB/5/88; the award was confirmed by a Chancery Decree: ibid. /23/39; see also B.I.H.R., Bp. 3/74.
[7] E.R.R.O., DDWB/5/93, 94. Elsewhere St. Quintin's inclosure is said to have involved the Holmes: ibid. /18/17.
[8] E.R.R.O., DDSQ uncalendared.
[9] Ibid. DDWB/10/15–17. [10] Ibid. /5/97.
[11] 11th Rep. Com. Char. H.C. 433, p. 719 (1824), xiv.
[12] O.S. Map 6" (1854, 1892).
[13] Ibid.; B.I.H.R., TA. 312M.
[14] In a glebe terrier of 1865 the open fields were said to have been inclosed 'by the Tithe Commissioners' in 1857: B.I.H.R. TER. J. Burton Agnes 1865. Canon Isaac Taylor wrote in 1886 that the fields were inclosed 'about thirty years ago' and that they remained open 'until 1856': *Domesday Studies*, ed. P. E. Dove, i. 59, 180. There is no known inclosure award.

[15] B.I.H.R., TA. 312M. [16] Directories.
[17] O.S. Map 6" (1854, 1892); *Kelly's Dir. N. & E. R. Yorks.* (1909), 482.
[18] Ex inf. secretary, W. Clifford Watts, Ltd., Bridlington, 1969.
[19] *Cur. Reg. R.* vi. 235; *Yorks. Inq.* i. 100.
[20] E.R.R.O., DDWB/5/9–11, 15; *Yorks. Inq.* i. 100–101.
[21] *Miscellanea*, ii. 93–4. For lessees of the mills see B.I.H.R., Prob. Reg. xvi, f. 77 (1559); E.R.R.O., DDWB/5/99 (1766).
[22] B.I.H.R., TA. 312M; White, *Dir. E. & N. R. Yorks.* (1840), 378; O S. Map 6" (1854).
[23] E.R.R.O., DDBV/20; B.I.H.R., TA. 312M.
[24] J.I. 1/1110 m. 144.
[25] E.R.R.O., DDWB/5/12.
[26] *Yorks. Deeds*, v. 84.
[27] E.R.R.O., DDWB/10/1.
[28] Ibid. /5/49.

supervision of fields and pastures in 1465 and 1572,[29] and there survives a book of bylaws made at a court held in 1632 and added to on subsequent occasions until 1710.[30] The bylaws were agreed upon in 1632 by the jury 'and all the assembly there', and a list of about a dozen names accompanies some of the later orders. The jury apparently had other duties too, for a testator in 1632 wished that her property should be repaired 'according to the judgment and view of the jury... of Agnes Burton'.[31] In one order of 1632 the court is described as 'the bylaw' and all husbandmen and cottagers were ordered to attend. The bylawmen themselves were four in number, three of them being husbandmen each of whom was given a pick made by the constable. Other officers mentioned were pinders, a swine-herd, ale-tasters, and constables.

Courts were still being held at Burton Agnes in the late 19th century, many call rolls surviving for 1791–1875. In 1791 five bylawmen, a constable, a deputy constable, and a pinder were appointed, but the number of bylawmen was still normally four. Several pains were still in force, those listed in 1817, for example, dealing with sewers, rubbish, and wandering animals.[32] Court papers relating to the St. Quintin manor at Thornholme show that two bylawmen, a pinder, and one or two constables were being appointed there in the 19th century.[33]

In the 17th century the parish officers were apparently to some extent subjected to the manor court, for in 1632 the overseers, churchwardens, and constables were all ordered to present their accounts to the jury on the day before the court held at Easter.[34] Churchwardens' accounts survive from 1765 onwards.[35] Organized relief of the poor is first mentioned in 1591, when a testator left 4d. to 'every one of the poor allowed within the town of Burton Agnes and relieved in the book of the poor there'.[36] Accounts of the overseers of the poor, apparently for Burton Agnes only, survive for the period 1768–1825.[37] An annual rate was levied which at 2d. in the pound raised about £6 from 40 people in 1771. Relief given included weekly money payments to 5 persons. The poorhouses were rebuilt in 1775 and the cost was met partly by the use of £42 of the town stock; only £8 remained in the stock thereafter. The rate was steadily increased after c. 1790. At 11d. in the pound it raised £61 in 1795 and at 2s. 10d. in the pound £245 in 1821. About 15 people received weekly payments in the 1820s.

Gransmoor appears to have administered its own relief, and a rate-book survives for 1656–1803.[38] From 1656 to 1667 a rate was levied, in 1661, for example, 23 persons paying from 1d. to 10d. each. From 1668 to 1739 the only income was from the town stock. After 1740 a rate varying from ½d. to 6d. in the pound was levied on householders and cottagers, and up to seven people contributed each year. The town stock stood at £12 10s. until 1787 and £10 thereafter, and was lent to two or three men. Expenditure was less than £1 until the mid 18th century but then rose, apparently as the result of the provision of a poorhouse. In 1792 £10 was spent and in 1793 £20, of which £5 was for the rent and charges of the poorhouse. From one to six people were relieved each year from 1671 to 1803. The township had one overseer.

In 1836 Burton Agnes joined the Bridlington union.[39]

CHURCH. Burton Agnes church was first mentioned c. 1100–15, when it was given by Geoffrey Bainard to St. Mary's abbey, York, together with two-thirds of the demesne tithes.[40] The church was apparently not fully appropriated to the abbey until after 1220, when it was arranged that after the death of Michael Belet, then parish priest, a fixed stipend of £10 13s. 4d. should be paid to the vicar.[41] Vicarial tithes were subsequently received by the incumbents, and before 1868 the rents paid in lieu of rectorial tithes were acquired as well and the living became a rectory that year.[42] Both Gransmoor and Haisthorpe had medieval chapels, as did Harpham; the latter early assumed certain parochial functions, however, and came to be regarded as a separate parish.[43]

The advowson of Burton Agnes belonged to St. Mary's abbey until the Dissolution. It was granted in 1539 to Charles, duke of Suffolk,[44] and in 1545, shortly before the duke's death, to the archbishop of York.[45] The right of presentation was at first exercised by the heirs of the duke of Suffolk, but the archbishop presented in 1600 and was immediately in dispute with the Crown, which claimed the advowson by wardship of one of the duke's heirs. Archbishops and heirs both presented during the 17th century and the dispute was not settled until c. 1702–3, when judgement was given against the archbishop.[46] By 1723 the advowson had been acquired by the St. Quintin family,[47] which retained it until at least 1786.[48] In the 1830s and 1840s it was held by Robert Raikes,[49] from at least 1856 until 1867 by the Revd. Augustus Duncombe,[50] in 1869–71 by trustees, in 1872–7 by the Revd. John Robinson, and from 1878 until 1898 by John and then J. H. Denney. In 1899 it passed to E. F. Coates,[51] later Sir Edward Coates (d. 1921). In 1925,

---

[29] E.R.R.O., DDWB/5/49, 67.
[30] Printed in *Miscellanea*, ii (Y.A.S. Rec. Ser. lxxiv), 87–99. A transcript of bylaws for 1545, seen by M. W. Barley ('E. Yorks. Manorial Bylaws', *Y.A.J.* xxxv. 35–6), could not be traced in 1961.
[31] B.I.H.R., Prob. Reg. xli, f. 852.
[32] E.R.R.O., DDCV/Parcel 100.
[33] Call rolls and jury papers, 1803–1914: Y.A.S. MSS., DD. 89.
[34] *Miscellanea*, ii. 89.
[35] E.R.R.O., PR. 1860–1.
[36] B.I.H.R., Prob. Reg. xxv, f. 856.
[37] E.R.R.O., PR. 1859.
[38] B.I.H.R., MD. 10.
[39] *3rd Rep. Poor Law Com.* 167.
[40] *E.Y.C.* ii, p. 33.
[41] *Fasti Parochiales*, iii. 9–11; *Reg. Gray* (Sur. Soc. lvi), 136.
[42] *Lond. Gaz.* 26 June 1868, p. 3591.
[43] See p. 226.
[44] *L. & P. Hen. VIII*, xiv (1), p. 261, where it is mistakenly said to be late of Bridlington priory.
[45] Ibid. xx (1), p. 216; xxi (2), p. 163. Confirmed in 1556: *Cal. Pat. 1555–7*, 188.
[46] B.I.H.R., Bp. 3/64, 72–3; Lawton, *Rer. Eccles. Dioc. Ebor.* 291; Bacon, *Liber Regis*, 1129. For the duke's heirs see *Complete Peerage*, sub Suffolk, Derby, Chandos, Bridgwater, Huntingdon.
[47] E.R.R.O., DDSQ/16/3.
[48] Ibid. /12/27; Bacon, *Liber Regis*, 1129; Sir John Thompson presented *pro hac vice* in 1734.
[49] *Rep. Com. Eccl. Revenues*, 922–3; Lawton, *Rer. Eccles. Dioc. Ebor.* 291.
[50] Sheahan and Whellan, *Hist. York & E. R.* ii. 459; *York Dioc. Cal.*
[51] *York Dioc. Cal.*

when it was vested in Sir Edward's trustees, it was exchanged with the patronage of Brafferton and Nunnington (Yorks. N.R.), held by the Crown and exercised by the Lord Chancellor.[52]

In all available figures for the income of the benefice the chapelry of Harpham is included with Burton Agnes. The vicarage was valued at £20 in 1291,[53] reduced to £13 6s. 8d. in 1339.[54] It was worth £20 6s. 2d. net in 1535, out of which a pension, doubtless the vicar's stipend, of £10 13s. 4d. was paid to St. Mary's abbey.[55] In 1650 the vicarage was worth £65,[56] in 1703 over £120,[57] and in 1829–31 the average net value was £897.[58] The incumbent in 1884 stated that his income had fallen to £600–£700.[59] The net income in 1925 was £979.[60] Tithes accounted for the greater part of the income. After the inclosure of 1702 those of Gransmoor were paid by composition.[61] The tithes were in 1840 commuted for £751, comprising £444 in Burton Agnes and Haisthorpe, £171 in Gransmoor, and £136 in Thornholme.[62] Those in Harpham had been extinguished at inclosure in 1776.

The church was endowed with 8 bovates of land in Burton Agnes and 2 in Harpham in 1284–5,[63] and there was still the same amount of glebe in 1535.[64] In the 17th and 18th centuries the glebe included 8 bovates in the open fields of Burton Agnes, with its appurtenant meadow land, as well as a right of common in the fields and on the moor. In 1758, when the meadows were inclosed, the vicar was allotted 17 a., and when the moors were inclosed in 1719 he received 27 a.[65] In 1840 there were 130 a. of vicarial glebe in Burton Agnes,[66] and in 1865, after the inclosure of the open fields, 125 a.[67] At Harpham 90 a. had been allotted to the vicar at inclosure in 1776 in lieu of tithes and glebe.[68] The glebe was sold in 1913.[69]

The Vicarage was apparently a large house in 1600, when it contained eight principal rooms and more than twenty smaller rooms, outhouses, and farm buildings.[70] It was assessed on five hearths in 1674,[71] and in 1716 was built of chalk and thatched.[72] The house was rebuilt under a faculty granted in 1760 and in 1764 was described as brick-built and tiled.[73] It was bought by Marcus Wickham-Boynton after the Second World War and part of the house was rented from him by the rector. A new and smaller Rectory was built near by on the Rudston road in 1954 and the old house was subsequently privately occupied.[74]

A chantry of St. Mary in Burton Agnes church was founded in 1313 by Roger de Somerville, who endowed it with 2 houses, 2 bovates, 16 a. of land, and 20 cart-loads of peat in Burton Agnes and Thornholme.[75] The advowson was held by the lords of Burton Agnes manor, as was the advowson of Braceford hospital, in Harpham, which was attached to the chantry.[76] By 1390 the endowed property was forfeited to the Crown on the grounds that the chantry had been founded without the king's licence.[77] In 1397 it was granted for life to Thomas Brigg, and it was let in 1436 to William Dales and in 1449 to William St. Quintin.[78] In 1535 the income of the chantry was £5 8s. 8d.[79] After the Dissolution the chantry property was let to John Jackson in 1563,[80] and it was later held by the Griffiths.[81] Leases of parts of the property of the chantry and the hospital were made to Sir James Croft in 1582 and to Henry Griffith in 1584, but all was in 1590 granted to John Rant and Thomas Hulton.[82] Henry Griffith held it in 1625,[83] but no more is known of it.

Lights founded in the church included those instructed to be put on the 'Judasses' in 1466, on the altar of St. Nicholas in 1505, before the images of Our Saviour and the Virgin Mary in 1521, and before the image of Our Lady in the 'side closet' in 1536.[84] Two obits were founded in 1531 by Sir Walter Griffith, and one by Robert Tovie in 1535, endowed with the rent of a close.[85] A guild of the Virgin Mary is mentioned in 1505.[86]

A chapel at Gransmoor existed by 1347, when a chantry was founded there,[87] and it probably still stood in 1545, when bequests were made to it.[88] The chantry was founded by Walter of Harpham and endowed with 2 houses, 5 bovates, and 13s. 4d. rent in Gransmoor and Thornholme. In 1360 Walter gave an additional 2 tofts and 2 bovates in Harpham.[89] He himself presented the chaplain in 1363 and instructed that future presentations should be made by Sir William St. Quintin for one turn and St. Mary's abbey, York, for two. The last known presentation was made by the king in 1544.[90] The chantry was valued at £3 16s. 4d. in 1535, when its endowment had been decreased by a house and 2 tofts.[91] The chantry property, lately held by William St. Quintin, was let in 1563 to Walter

---

[52] York Dioc. Regy., Orders in Council 571.
[53] *Tax. Eccl.* (Rec. Com.), 304.
[54] *Cal. Pat.* 1338–40, 255.
[55] *Valor Eccl.* v. 9, 123.
[56] *T.E.R.A.S.* ii. 57.
[57] Lawton, *Rer. Eccles. Dioc. Ebor.* 291.
[58] *Rep. Com. Eccl. Revenues*, 922–3.
[59] B.I.H.R., Bp. V. 1884/Ret.
[60] York Dioc. Regy., Orders in Council 571.
[61] B.I.H.R., TER. J. Burton Agnes 1716.
[62] Ibid. TA. 312M.
[63] *Feud. Aids*, vi. 31.
[64] *Valor Eccl.* v. 123.
[65] B.I.H.R., TER. J. Burton Agnes *passim*; E.R.R.O., DDWB/5/88, 97.
[66] B.I.H.R., TA. 312M.
[67] Ibid. TER. J. Burton Agnes 1865.
[68] See p. 226.
[69] Regy. of Deeds, 149/555/409.
[70] B.I.H.R., Consistory Wills, Wm. Greene, 25 Apr. 1600.
[71] E 179/205/521.
[72] B.I.H.R., TER. J. Burton Agnes 1716.
[73] Ibid. 1764; Lawton, *Rer. Eccles. Dioc. Ebor.* 291.
[74] Ex inf. Revd. G. Dibbs, rector, 1961.
[75] *Cal. Pat.* 1313–17, 29. The grant was confirmed by Philip de Somerville in 1349 with the addition of pasture for 2 cows: E.R.R.O., DDWB/6/2.
[76] E.R.R.O., DDWB/5/51 (1479); *Yorks. Fines*, 1327–47, 140; *Cal. Pat.* 1385–9, 514; 1388–92, 200; *V.C.H. Yorks.* iii. 304–5.
[77] C 257/52 no. 41; C 257/53 no. 26.
[78] *Cal. Fine R.* 1430–7, 292; 1445–52, 90, 107.
[79] *Valor Eccl.* v. 124.
[80] *Cal. Pat.* 1560–3, 618.
[81] E.R.R.O., DDWB/5/65; /20/37.
[82] Ibid. /20/37; C 66/1346 m. 9.
[83] E.R.R.O., DDWB/20/44.
[84] B.I.H.R., Prob. Reg. vi, f. 194; ix, f. 205; xi, f. 200; *Test. Ebor.* ii. 272–3. For other lights see Prob. Reg. x, f. 24; xi, ff. 132, 441, 462, 753; xiii, ff. 119, 142, 295.
[85] B.I.H.R., Prob. Reg. xi, f. 145; *Test. Ebor.* v. 287–9.
[86] B.I.H.R., Prob. Reg. vi, f. 194.
[87] *Cal. Pat.* 1345–8, 363.
[88] B.I.H.R., Prob. Reg. xiii, f. 118. See also ibid. ix, f. 421 (1528); x, f. 24 (1530); xi, f. 145 (1535).
[89] *Cal. Pat.* 1345–8, 363, 371; 1358–61, 440
[90] *Fasti Parochiales*, iii. 101–2.
[91] *Valor Eccl.* v. 123.

Griffith; he transferred his interest in 1564 to Gabriel St. Quintin, whose son George obtained a renewal of the lease in 1580.[92] In 1582 the property was granted to Sir James Croft.[93] In 1590 the reversion was granted to Sir Francis Knowles[94] and sold in turn to Lord Stanhope and George St. Quintin; the land was held by William St. Quintin in 1611, when it included Chantry close in Thornholme.[95] No more is known of the chantry lands, but in 1840 a piece of ground at the east end of Thornholme village was called Chantry garth.[96] A new chapel at Gransmoor, a small brick building at the west end of the village, was built in 1839 by W. D. T. Duesbery.[97]

Nothing is known of the early history of a chapel at Haisthorpe. In 1587 the ruined chapel and Chapel garth, previously held by a member of the Thornholme family, were let to Thomas Shotton.[98]

From at least the 17th century[99] the parish was administered with the help of a curate, normally resident in Harpham. In the 18th century several incumbents also held other livings.[1] Thus in 1743 Thomas Dade held the rectories of Barmston and Argam; he lived at Burton Agnes and his curate at Barmston, and he served Harpham himself.[2] In 1764 William Cayley lived half the year at Burton Agnes and half at York, where he had a 'residentiarship' in the minster; his curate lived in the Vicarage while Cayley was in York and for the remaining six months at Lowthorpe.[3] There are few known cases of non-residence earlier than Cayley's in 1764.[4]

Noteworthy incumbents include Richard Green (d. 1564), who founded the school,[5] and William Green (d. 1600), who bequeathed £100 to the poor of the parish.[6] Timothy Welfitt (d. 1702) apparently mismanaged both his own and the parish affairs. At his death his debts totalled £206 and his glebe was neglected, 'the land being not ordered according to good husbandry'.[7] During the previous year he had been engaged in a lawsuit in which he was alleged to have taken upon himself sole responsibility for the letting of the farm which supported Green's charity.[8] In the late 19th century John Denny (vicar 1877–94) was in prolonged dispute with his fellow trustees of Green's charity, especially with Sir Henry Boynton concerning the conduct of the school. His successor found his work hampered by the fact that 'my predecessor neglected his duties for seventeen years'.[9] Thomas Dade (d. 1759) was the father of the local antiquary William Dade, who was born at Burton Agnes c. 1740; William's collections were incorporated in Poulson's *History of Holderness*. Robert Wilberforce (vicar 1840–54) was appointed archdeacon of the East Riding in 1841, but in 1854 he was received into the Roman Catholic church. Another tractarian, the author and hymn-writer James Skinner, was assistant curate during the first years of Wilberforce's incumbency.[10]

William Crashawe, vicar 1608–26, Edward Riggs, assistant curate in 1622, and Thomas Calvert, vicar in 1632, were all Puritans. In 1634 the churchwardens were ordered to rail the Holy Table.[11] In 1643 the assistant curate, Thomas Callis, was ejected for loyalty to the king and conformity to the Church,[12] and James Birkhead, vicar in 1644, was also ejected.[13]

In 1743 a service was normally held in the church twice each Sunday; communion was administered five times a year and was received by 60–70 people.[14] Only one Sunday service was held in 1764 because the incumbent was responsible for both Burton Agnes and Harpham, and about 70 persons communicated four times a year.[15] By 1851 two services were held in the church and one in the chapel at Gransmoor.[16] In 1864 communion was received by about 20 people monthly at Burton Agnes but had only just begun to be administered at Gransmoor.[17] Communion was held twice monthly in 1884, with an average of eleven communicants. In 1894 three Sunday services were held in the church and one in the chapel. In 1936 communion was administered weekly,[18] and in 1961 three Sunday services were held in the church but only two each month at Gransmoor.

The church of *ST. MARTIN*, built mostly of stone, consists of chancel, nave, north and south aisles, south porch, and west tower. The south entrance is approached through an avenue of clipped yews, their branches forming a canopy overhead. Nothing survives of the original church, which was replaced c. 1125–50. Of this second building, which was without aisles, there remain parts of the nave walls and, possibly, the much-altered chancel arch. The circular font, decorated with interlacing arcades, may also be of 12th-century origin but has been largely recut.

A north aisle was added to the church c. 1200, the arcade, which was cut through the thick Norman wall, having circular piers, scalloped capitals, and pointed arches of a single unmoulded order. A south aisle was built in the 13th century; the arcade of this date was constructed in a new and less massive wall, only the responds to east and west of it being of the original Norman width. A blocked 12th-century window is visible high up in the western respond and 12th-century corbels have been reset in the aisle above the arcade. The north aisle was rebuilt and widened early in the 14th century by Roger de Somerville, perhaps to accommodate the chantry which he founded in 1313.[19] In 1317 he was licensed to transfer his wife's body to the new aisle which he had made,[20] and his own tomb occupies a recess in the north wall.

---

[92] C 3/141/57; C 66/1189 m. 10.
[93] E.R.R.O., DDWB/20/37.
[94] C 66/1358 m. 22.
[95] C 2/Jas. I/G 12/2.
[96] B.I.H.R., TA. 312M.
[97] White, *Dir. E. & N. R. Yorks.* (1840), 379.
[98] C 66/1287 m. 17.
[99] *Miscellanea*, i (Y.A.S. Rec. Ser. lxi), 152.
[1] E.R.R.O., DPX/57, Burton Agnes, pp. 11–12.
[2] *Herring's Visit.* i. 38, 109, 193; ii. 91.
[3] B.I.H.R., Bp. V. 1764/Ret. 103.
[4] See *Reg. Gray* (Sur. Soc. lvi), 67; *Cal. Papal Reg.* vii. 345.
[5] See p. 118.
[6] B.I.H.R., Prob. Reg. xxxi, f. 136.
[7] Ibid. C.P., H. 4731.
[8] C 5/215/29.
[9] B.I.H.R., Bp. V. 1884/Ret.; Bp. V. 1894/Ret.; Char. Com. files.
[10] *D.N.B.*
[11] R. A. Marchant, *Puritans and the Ch. Courts in Dioc. York, 1560–1642*, 122, 237, 241, 272.
[12] *Miscellanea*, i (Y.A.S. Rec. Ser lxi), 152.
[13] *Walker Revised*, ed. A. G. Matthews, 389.
[14] *Herring's Visit.* i. 38.
[15] B.I.H.R., Bp. V. 1764/Ret. 103.
[16] H.O. 129/24/524.
[17] B.I.H.R., V. 1865/Ret. 93.
[18] Ibid. Bp. V. 1884/Ret.; Bp. V. 1894/Ret.; Bp. V. 1936/Ret. 269.
[19] See p. 115.
[20] *Reg. Greenfield*, v (Sur. Soc. cliii), 272.

The south aisle, narrower than the north, may have been rebuilt at about the same time; the east windows of both aisles have cusped interlacing tracery, typical of the earlier 14th century.

In the late 15th or early 16th century a clerestory was added to the nave and the tower was built; the capitals of the lofty tower arch are carved with badges of the Griffith family. It may also have been during this period that a chapel was built on the north side of the church, perhaps that mentioned in 1506 and that 'new chapel' in which Sir Walter Griffith asked to be buried in 1531.[21] This chapel was later demolished but a four-centred arch leading to it from the east bay of the north aisle is still visible externally. The present entrance to the church is by the 19th-century south porch but there is also a disused west door in the tower and others in the north aisle and the chancel.

The chancel was in need of repair in the 1720s,[22] and Sir William St. Quintin was granted permission in 1730 to rebuild and shorten it.[23] A complete rebuilding at this time would account for the fact that no medieval work survives in the present chancel. Also in 1730 the vicar and churchwardens agreed to repair the church at the expense of Sir Griffith Boynton.[24] Many of the surviving fittings in the church appear to date from this period, including the box pews and the former gallery front, reset below the tower arch to support the organ. Of the same date is the Boynton pew, placed in the easternmost bay of the north arcade and formerly extending further into the north aisle; it is surmounted by a classical arch and a pediment. Two other large pews, to accommodate servants from the hall and the Vicarage, have been removed from a corresponding position south of the chancel arch.[25] In 1766 a quantity of bricks (21,000) was used during work on the church. The north wall was repaired in 1825 and in 1848–9 work was done on the roof. It was at this time, during the incumbency of Robert Wilberforce, that the chancel was again largely rebuilt; the south and east walls, with their Gothic windows, date entirely from the 19th century, but earlier brickwork is still visible externally in the north wall. In 1856 the north aisle and the foundations of the tower were being repaired.[26] Extensive repairs to the nave and chancel were begun in 1948.[27] Part of the income arising from Green's charity was applied to church repairs; £2 a year was received in the 1760s and £4 in the later 18th and early 19th centuries.[28]

The so-called Griffith 'dormitory' at the east end of the north aisle contains a number of monuments, some probably moved there from the demolished chapel. The earliest is the chest tomb of Sir Roger Somerville (d. 1337) and his brother Sir Philip (d. 1355); a former brass commemorating Sir Roger has now disappeared.[29] There are also a fine alabaster tomb chest, carved with figures of saints and supporting the recumbent effigies of Sir Walter Griffith (d. 1481) and his first wife, a floor slab to Sir Henry Bushell of Haisthorpe (d. 1602), a tablet to Sir Henry Griffith (d. 1620) and his wife, and a canopied monument to Sir Henry Griffith (d. 1654) and two wives, believed to be the work of Edward Marshall or his son, or perhaps their joint effort.[30] The last-mentioned monument incorporates a tomb chest, carved with piled-up skulls and bones, on which rest three black-painted stone coffins. Heraldic glass and portraits in the east window of the aisle have been moved there from the west tower window.[31] Elsewhere in the church are tablets to George Burghope, vicar (d. 1727), Sir Griffith Boynton (d. 1761), Sir Griffith Boynton (d. 1778), Thomas Dade, vicar (d. 1759), and Ann wife of William Cayley, vicar 1760–84, and there is a stone bust of Robert Wilberforce, vicar 1840–55. The east window was presented by Wilberforce in 1844.

There have been four bells since at least 1552.[32] Two are dated 1601 and one 1634.[33] The plate includes a silver cup of 1710 and paten of 1724, and plated cup, paten, flagon, and almsdish; the plated cup and flagon bear the arms of Raikes and Williamson, the plated paten and dish of Raikes alone.[34] The set was given by Robert Raikes of Welton House in 1834;[35] the Williamson arms may be those of the family of Ann, wife of William Cayley (vicar 1760–84).[36] The registers date from 1700 for baptisms and 1701 for marriages and burials; there is a gap for baptisms and burials in 1787–1800.[37]

In 1888 a burial ground was opened on the Rudston road.[38]

NONCONFORMITY. Two cases of recusancy were reported in the parish in the 1560s, there were two non-communicants in 1666,[39] and two recusants were recorded in 1676.[40] There were also twelve protestant dissenters in 1676, and others were recorded in the early 18th century.[41] In 1743 there was a family of Anabaptists at Haisthorpe.[42] Houses were licensed for worship at Burton Agnes in 1798, 1800, 1819, and 1824, and at Haisthorpe and Gransmoor in 1809.[43] The Methodists had a dozen members at Haisthorpe in 1787–91.[44]

A Wesleyan Methodist chapel was built in 1837 near the centre of Burton Agnes village, on ground given by Sir Henry Boynton. A Primitive Methodist chapel was built in Haisthorpe in 1888,[45] and an adjoining Sunday school was added in 1911.[46] A

---

[21] *Test. Ebor.* iv. 243; v. 287.
[22] B.I.H.R., ER. V/CB. 15; ER. V/Ch. P. 1729.
[23] Ibid. ER. V/Ch. P. 1729; Bp. 75; Lawton, *Rer. Eccles. Dioc. Ebor.* 292.
[24] E.R.R.O., PR. 1847, register 1700–1801, loose paper of 1730.
[25] G. Dibbs, *Ch. of St. Martin, Burton Agnes.*
[26] E.R.R.O., PR. 1860, churchwardens' accts. 1765–1882.
[27] Ibid. 1861, churchwardens' accts. 1883–1950, pp. 264–265.
[28] E.R.R.O., PR. 1860, churchwardens' accts. 1765–1882; see below, p. 118.
[29] *Arch. Jnl.* cv. 84.
[30] *Burton Agnes Hall, An Illus. Survey* (n.d. priv. print.).
[31] Dibbs, *Ch. of St. Martin.*
[32] *Inventories of Ch. Goods,* 29.
[33] Boulter, 'Ch. Bells', 216.
[34] *Yorks. Ch. Plate,* i. 231.
[35] E.R.R.O., PR. 1847, memo. in register 1700–1801.
[36] Monument in church.
[37] E.R.R.O.
[38] B.I.H.R., CD. 505.
[39] *Y.A.J.* xxxv. 164; H. Aveling, *Post Reformation Catholicism in E. Yorks. 1558–1790* (E. Yorks. Loc. Hist. Ser. xi), 58.
[40] Bodl. MS. Tanner 150, ff. 27 sqq.
[41] Ibid.; B.I.H.R., ER. V/Ch. P. 1729.
[42] *Herring's Visit.* i. 37.
[43] G.R.O. Worship Returns, Vol. v, nos. 1417, 1537, 2299, 2330, 3276, 3882.
[44] E.R.R.O., MRP/1/7.
[45] Inscriptions on buildings.
[46] *Kelly's Dir. N. & E. R. Yorks.* (1921), 487.

Primitive Methodist chapel was built in Thornholme in 1892 and a Wesleyan chapel in Gransmoor in 1924.[47]

In 1851 the Primitive Methodists held cottage meetings[48] and were a source of much annoyance to the vicar.[49] In 1865 the vicar asserted that 'the population of the parish is almost entirely Wesleyan' and that, in addition to the chapel, cottages in the townships were used for meetings.[50] The estate bailiff was said to be the 'chief man' at the chapel in 1884, when two or three preachers lived in the parish.[51] The rector in 1900 said that he 'never came into a place so full of dissenters.'[52] In 1961 services were still held in Burton Agnes, Haisthorpe, and Thornholme.

EDUCATION. There may have been a school as early as 1540, when a Burton Agnes man left money for a boy 'to find him at the school',[53] and there was a schoolmaster in 1563.[54] The school was endowed by Richard Green, vicar, by will proved in 1564. The master was to have a salary of £8 a year. Green also left £3 each to keep three boys at the school and wished that one of them, John Green, should later become the schoolmaster.[55] This John Green did.[56] In 1600 William Green, vicar, left £50 each to his brother's three sons to keep them at the school and prepare them for the university.[57] The school had received an additional endowment of £3 6s. 8d. from Robert Vickarman by will proved in 1565.[58]

The school's income was £11 4s. in 1743, in addition to entering money; about 30 children were then taught to read and instructed in the catechism.[59] In 1764 the income was £8 from Green's charity and £3 4s. from lands of Sir Griffith Boynton, presumably Moorhouse field.[60] There were about 50 pupils in 1819.[61] Reading, writing, and arithmetic were taught to 30–40 children in 1824. They paid quarterage and entering money, and the master's stipend was £20 13s. 4d.[62]

The school was described as being near the vicarage in 1743 and as 'an ancient building' adjoining the church in 1824.[63] It was replaced in 1834[64] by a new building in the corner of the churchyard[65] which was not demolished until c. 1956.[66]

In 1835 there were 45 boys and 25 girls at the school.[67] By 1850 it received an annual government grant.[68] The average attendance was about 35 in 1871.[69] Since 1847 only boys had attended, a separate girls' school having been built by the vicar in that year; its only income in 1849 was £7 10s. from school pence.[70] About 45 girls attended in 1871,[71] when the school apparently closed.

In 1871 Sir Henry Boynton built a new school on the Rudston road, accommodating 140 children. By 1877 the average attendance was 28 boys and 39 girls and infants; the income of £76 in 1875 included £22 from Green's charity.[72] The average attendance remained at about 60 until the 1920s but was only 39 in 1938;[73] it was about 40 in 1961, when the children of Haisthorpe went to Carnaby and those of Gransmoor to Lissett.[74]

The school became 'controlled' in 1949 and a third of the educational part of the income from Green's charity was subsequently applied to the Sunday school. In 1959, however, it was decided that the terms of the Scheme for the charity should be strictly adhered to and the whole of the educational part of the income applied to the Sunday school.[75] In 1966 the building was extended to accommodate 120, and pupils from Harpham and Carnaby were transferred to it.[76] The average number on the roll in 1969 was 95.[77]

Of the townships only Gransmoor has ever had a school. In 1871 8 boys and 11 girls attended a school there,[78] and an evening school was held in 1868. An evening school was also held at Burton Agnes in the 1860s.[79]

CHARITIES FOR THE POOR. Richard Green, vicar, by will proved in 1564,[80] instructed his executors to spend £200 to buy land to maintain a free school. After payment of the schoolmaster's salary, half of the remaining income from the land was to go to the poor and half to the upkeep of the church.[81] In 1615 £10 a year was paid to the schoolmaster and churchwardens.[82] Later Sir Henry Griffith held £100 of the endowment and he set aside Moorhouse field, New ings, and Ferriby crofts for the benefit of the poor and the school.[83] The endowment was used in or soon after 1701 to buy a 37-acre farm called Willerby Haggs (Kirk Ella).[84]

By 1824 the income was divided equally between school, poor, and church.[85] That division was confirmed by a Scheme of 1863, and in 1895 a portion of the poor's share was said to be allotted

---

[47] Inscriptions on buildings.
[48] H.O. 129/24/524.
[49] H. Woodcock, *Sketches of Prim. Meth. on Yorks. Wolds*, 81.
[50] B.I.H.R., V. 1865/Ret. 93.
[51] Ibid. Bp. V. 1884/Ret.
[52] Ibid. Bp. V. 1900/Ret. 63.
[53] Ibid. Prob. Reg. xi, f. 462.
[54] Ibid. Schools index.
[55] Ibid. Prob. Reg. xxx, f. 37; see below.
[56] Ibid. xxv, f. 1357.
[57] At the university they were to have a further £100 each until they got fellowships: ibid. xxxi, f. 136.
[58] B.I.H.R., Prob. Reg. xvii, f. 443.
[59] *Herring's Visit.* i. 37.
[60] B.I.H.R., Bp. V. 1764/Ret. 103; see below, p. 119.
[61] *Rets. on Educ. of Poor, 1819*, 1078.
[62] *11th Rep. Char. Com.* H.C. 433, p. 719 (1824), xiv.
[63] *Herring's Visit.* i. 37; *11th Rep. Char. Com.* 718. In 1825 the church was repaired 'on the north side the low part from the west end to the school room': E.R.R.O., PR. 1860.
[64] E.R.R.O., PR. 1848, acct. in register 1801–12.
[65] It is marked on O.S. Map 6" (1854).
[66] Ex inf. Revd. G. Dibbs, rector, 1961.
[67] *Educ. Enquiry Abstract, 1835*, 1081.
[68] *Mins. of Cttee. of Council for Educ.* [1215] H.C., p. 491 (1850), xliii.
[69] *Rets. rel. Elem. Educ. 1871*, 474–5.
[70] Ed. 7/135.
[71] *Rets. rel. Elem. Educ. 1871*, 474–5.
[72] Ed. 7/135; date on building.
[73] *Bd. of Educ. List 21* (H.M.S.O.).
[74] Ex inf. the rector, 1961.
[75] Ex inf. Chief Educ. Officer, County Hall, Beverley, and the rector, 1961.
[76] E.R. Educ. Cttee. *Mins.* 1963–4, 96–7; 1964–5, 199; 1966–7, 128.
[77] Ex inf. Chief Educ. Officer, 1969.
[78] *Rets. rel. Elem. Educ. 1871*, 474–5.
[79] B.I.H.R., V. 1865/Ret. 93; V. 1868/Ret. 90.
[80] B.I.H.R., Prob. Reg. xxx, f. 37.
[81] See pp. 117–18.
[82] C 93/6/5.
[83] E.R.R.O., DDWB/5/84; see below.
[84] C 5/215/29; *11th Rep. Char. Com.* H.C. 433, pp. 718–9 (1824), xiv.
[85] *11th Rep. Char. Com.* 718–9.

to each township, two-fifths to Burton Agnes and one-fifth each to Gransmoor, Haisthorpe, and Thornholme. In 1920 the farm was sold and by 1960 the charity was represented by £3,840 stock. In 1931 the income was still sub-divided as in 1895.[86] The income in 1960 was about £140 and the poor's share was distributed in cash.[87] The income in 1971 was £250, of which £86 was distributed to the aged and needy.[88]

There were bedehouses in Burton Agnes in 1506[89] and the poor 'bedwomen' were mentioned in 1538.[90] These houses may have ceased to exist before 1706, when alms-houses were built under the terms of the will of Elizabeth, widow of William Boynton. Her son Sir Griffith Boynton endowed them with a house, 5 bovates, and closes in Haisthorpe in 1714, when they were described as 'newly erected', and he directed that £10 8s. a year should be paid to the occupants.[91] There were usually four poor widows. The alms-houses were demolished in 1939;[92] they stood on the south side of the Bridlington road, just to the west of the cross-roads.[93]

The Moorhouse field charity apparently originated when Sir Henry Griffith set aside this and other grounds for the purposes of Green's charity.[94] Later a rent-charge of £8 4s. 9d. was levied on tenants of Moorhouse field and in 1824 it was paid to the overseers and divided equally between the poor and the school.[95] Payment temporarily lapsed in the late 19th century but £8 4s. was still shared among the occupants of the alms-houses in 1937. After the demolition of the alms-houses the rent-charge was in 1941 redeemed by Thomas Wickham-Boynton for £328, which was invested in stock. By a Scheme of 1942 the income was directed to be distributed to the poor.[96] In 1960 £8 was distributed.[97]

In 1716 George Burghope, vicar, gave £35, a third of the interest on which was to be used after his death for an annual sermon and two-thirds given to the poor. In 1720 Burghope gave a further £35 in trust for the poor.[98] Income from both gifts was received by the churchwardens in 1729.[99] The charity existed in 1764[1] and interest was paid until 1801, when it lapsed. By 1824 £20 of the endowment had been recovered and distributed outright to the poor;[2] no more is heard of the rest.

The Town Stock of Haisthorpe consisted in 1824 of £56, which was lent to the farmers of the township. The interest was distributed to the poor by the overseers.[3] In 1935 the charity was known as 'the Town Stock or Ellen White's charity' and the capital was invested.[4] Distribution of the income ceased in 1956 but payments were revived in 1962, when its income was less than £5 a year.[5]

BURTON FLEMING

BURTON FLEMING lies on the wolds 6 miles north-west of Bridlington.[1] It was an Anglian settlement. The distinctive suffix, which it has borne since the 12th century, commemorates the Gant family, lords of the manor. From at least the 14th century it has been alternatively known as North Burton.[2] The village itself lies in the valley of the Gypsey Race but most of the compact parish occupies the adjoining wold slopes. In the north parts of the parish boundary with Hunmanby follow prehistoric earthworks. The area of the parish is 3,909 a.[3]

Within Burton Fleming the Gypsey Race, having flowed eastwards from its source, turns south towards Rudston. A large area of the valley floor lies at 100 ft.–150 ft. above sea-level. The valley sides rise, gently for the most part, to reach heights of 300 ft.–350 ft. on the wolds in the north and west. Numerous dry valleys dissect the wold slopes, the most prominent being those along the eastern parish boundary and in the north-west of the parish, the latter leading to Cans Dale in Hunmanby. The wold slopes were largely occupied by open-field land, and the regular field-pattern throughout the parish reflects the inclosure of 1769. Arable farming now predominates on the wolds and in the valley alike, and the open landscape is broken only by shelter-belts of trees around several of the isolated farm-houses.

Burton Fleming was apparently a centre of prehistoric activity. A Bronze-Age henge, later known as Maiden's Grave, stood near the Gypsey Race to the south-east of the village. Only slight indications of it were visible in 1970. It was apparently surrounded by a triangular inclosure of Iron-Age or Romano-British date, with at least four trackways leading into it. Iron-Age burials have been found within the inclosure.[4] It may subsequently have been used as the wapentake meeting-place,[5] and it has been suggested that the name Stodefald, or 'horse inclosure', recorded in 1299, may refer to Maiden's Grave.[6] An Iron-Age cemetery in Rudston extends into Burton Fleming.[7]

The village lies mainly on the north bank of the Gypsey Race. At its centre, near the church, is a wide space formed by the oblique crossing of two main roads, one running from Fordon in the north-west to Rudston and the other from Hunmanby in the north to Thwing. The road from Wold Newton

---

[86] Char. Com. files.
[87] Ex inf. the rector, 1961.
[88] Ex inf. the rector, 1972.
[89] *Test. Ebor.* iv. 243.
[90] B.I.H.R., Prob. Reg. xi, f. 324.
[91] E.R.R.O., DDWB/5/86; the income was unchanged in 1743: *Herring's Visit.* i. 37.
[92] Char. Com. files.
[93] O.S. Map 6" (1854).
[94] See p. 118.
[95] *11th Rep. Char. Com.* 719.
[96] Char. Com. files.
[97] Ex inf. the rector, 1961.
[98] B.I.H.R., TER. J. Burton Agnes 1809.
[99] Ibid. ER. V/Ch. P. 1729.
[1] Ibid. Bp. V. 1764/Ret. 103.
[2] *11th Rep. Char. Com.* 719–20.
[3] Ibid. 720.
[4] Char. Com. files.
[5] Ex inf. Char. Com.
[1] This article was written in 1970.
[2] *P.N.E.R. Yorks.* (E.P.N.S.), 112.
[3] O.S. Map 6" (1854).
[4] *Antiquity*, xxxviii. 218–19.
[5] Ex inf. Mr. H. G. Ramm, Royal Commission on Historical Monuments, York, 1970. See p. 4.
[6] *Bridlington Charty.* 66; *P.N.E.R. Yorks.* 112.
[7] See p. 310.

to Grindale, mostly in the valley bottom, crosses the parish and runs through the village alongside the Race. The Fordon road led to Burton Fleming windmill and hence is known as Mill Road, and the Thwing road climbs the wolds as White Hill Road. On White Hill the latter branches and Nine Dikes Road leads towards Kilham. The road from Wold Newton to Hunmanby crosses the north-west corner of the parish, and that from Rudston to Hunmanby lies along the eastern parish boundary.

The most densely built-up streets in the village are those south of the cross-roads and known as Front Street (i.e. the Thwing road) and Back Street (the Rudston road). Behind Front Street, marking the limit of the crofts and garths, is Back Lane. The street running beside the Race is called Butchers Lane and, further east, South Street. Three small unnamed lanes link the main crossing roads. A mere lies at the roadside north of the church, and there are other ponds near the manor-house and in Back Street. The deeply-cut course of the Race where it enters the village is known as Penny Hole, and Penny bridge carries the Thwing road across it.

The houses and cottages date from the 18th century onwards, and many of the older ones are partly or wholly built of chalk, including two single-storeyed cottages. Chalk farm buildings include a barn with brick tucked gables, quoins, and plinth at Manor Farm. Apart from the manor-house,[8] where Queen Henrietta Maria is thought to have stayed for one night in 1643 on her way from Bridlington to York,[9] the most noteworthy house is North Burton Hall. It is an earlier-19th-century building of seven bays, completely stuccoed, with pilaster strips at the end of the main front and an entrance porch. A late-18th-century brick farm-house north-west of the church has a two-storeyed frontage of three bays and a doorway with a fanlight and open pediment. The smaller 19th-century houses include a terrace of eight brick cottages on the Thwing road, and there are 24 Council houses in Back Lane and a few others elsewhere. There is one public house, the Star. In 1823 there were two inns, the Board and the Volunteer; by 1840 these had been replaced by the Star and the Buck, the latter being last mentioned in 1879.[10]

The chief outlying farm-houses, Maiden's Grave Farm, North Burton Grange, West Field House, and Refuge, are all of the late 18th or 19th century. A windmill ¾ mile north-west of the village stood in ruins until well into the 20th century.

In 1377 there were 147 poll-tax payers in Burton Fleming.[11] In 1670 there were 52 households; in 1674 21 households were discharged from the hearth tax and of those that were charged 23 had only one hearth each, 3 had 2, and one had nine.[12] There were said to be 42 families in 1743[13] and 40 in 1764.[14] The population in 1801 was 237; it rose steadily to 574 in 1851, but had fallen to 422 by 1901, chiefly as the result of a drop of 118 between 1881 and 1891.[15] There was a further decrease after 1931 and there were 365 inhabitants in 1961.[16]

MANOR AND OTHER ESTATES. In 1086 all 16 carucates in Burton Fleming belonged to the king; 14½ carucates had been held by Carle before the Conquest, and 1½ carucate by Chilbert.[17] The manor subsequently became part of the Gant fee and was included in Gilbert de Gant's confirmation, in the early 12th century, of the gifts made by his father and his father's men to Bridlington priory.[18] In 1284–5 the priory was said to hold 12 out of 18 carucates at Burton Fleming.[19] The overlordship descended in the Gant and Tattershall families.[20]

Bridlington priory continued to hold the manor of *BURTON FLEMING* and apparently acquired all the remaining land in the parish. Five carucates were held in 1284–5 by Hugh FitzRalph as mesne lord under the Gants, and in 1308–9 by Geoffrey Beriot.[21] One carucate of Beriot's holding passed to John of Carleton, who granted it to the priory in Edward I's reign.[22] The priory had various other grants,[23] including those of Arnald, son of Walter of Buckton, who was licensed to grant 10 tofts and 9 bovates of land to it in 1304 to support a chantry at Buckton,[24] and of James of Wassand, who granted it 3 bovates which Peter de Friboys had given him for waging a duel at York.[25] In the early 14th century the priory held all 18 carucates in Burton Fleming,[26] and in 1535 its property there was worth about £30.[27]

The manor-house and demesnes had been let to Thomas Pulley, the priory's bailiff, in 1533, and after the Dissolution they were let in 1567 to Griffith Lewes and Hugh Matthew.[28] In 1585 a lease to Robert Knowsley included 13 bovates[29] and a reversionary lease of the same premises was made to Elizabeth Smithson in 1591.[30] In 1605 the king granted the manor to Prince Charles,[31] and it was leased by Knowsley in 1606.[32] It was resumed by the Crown and in 1616 granted to George Villiers, later duke of Buckingham.[33] Two years later Villiers sold it to Robert Knowsley.[34] Knowsley apparently died in 1638.[35] He was succeeded by his daughters Isabel, Frances, Anne, and Elizabeth.

Isabel married first Robert Ellis (d. 1644) and secondly Alan Lamont; with Alan she made a settlement of her share of the manor in 1646.[36]

---

[8] See p. 121.
[9] Her stay in the village is recorded in the parish register: E.R.R.O., PR. 931. See above, p. 32.
[10] Baines, *Hist. Yorks.* (1823), ii. 184; White, *Dir. N. & E.R. Yorks.* (1840), 380; *Kelly's Dir. N. & E.R. Yorks.* (1879), 371.
[11] E 179/202/62 m. 20.
[12] E 179/205/514, 521.
[13] *Herring's Visit.* i. 111.
[14] B.I.H.R., Bp. V. 1764/Ret. 104.
[15] *V.C.H. Yorks.* iii. 489.
[16] *Census.*
[17] *V.C.H. Yorks.* ii. 204.
[18] Ibid. 185; *Bridlington Charty.* 10, 54.
[19] *Feud. Aids*, vi. 27–8.
[20] Ibid.; *Cal. Inq. p.m.* iv, pp. 108, 257; vii, p. 469; *Cal. Close, 1307–13*, 100.
[21] *Feud. Aids*, vi. 27–8; *Cal. Inq. p.m.* iv, p. 261.
[22] *Cal. Close, 1272–9*, 485; *Bridlington Charty.* 55, 60; *Cal. Inq. p.m.* ii, p. 158.
[23] B.M. Harl. Chart. 55E. 25; *Bridlington Charty.* 5–6, 55–60.
[24] See p. 85.
[25] *Bridlington Charty.* 58.
[26] B.M. Add. MS. 26729, f. 114d.
[27] *Valor Eccl.* (Rec. Com.), v. 120.
[28] *Cal. Pat.* 1566–9, 73; *Valor Eccl.* v. 121.
[29] C 66/1256 m. 22.
[30] C 66/1372 m. 45.
[31] C 66/1669 m. 1; C 66/1674 m. [24].
[32] L.R. 2/229 f. 239.
[33] C 66/2090 no. 7; C 66/2115 no. 1.
[34] C 54/2419 no. 56.
[35] *Regs. of Burton Fleming* (Yorks. Par. Reg. Soc. ii), 35.
[36] C 142/775/48; C.P. 25(2)/525/22 Chas. I Mich. no. 49.

Frances Knowsley and her husband Cuthbert Lascelles quitclaimed their share to Lamont in 1649.[37] Lamont's heirs, including another Alan Lamont, apparently his grandson,[38] conveyed the manor to Sir William Strickland in 1733.[39] At inclosure in 1769 Sir George Strickland was allotted 523 a., as well as 101 a. for tithes.[40] Sir George Strickland (1782–1874) married Mary, daughter of Charles Constable of Wassand, and a settlement seems to have been made on their son Henry Strickland-Constable (1821–1909).[41] The Strickland-Constables sold 125 a. in Burton Fleming in 1959,[42] but they still owned Manor Farm in 1970.

Robert Knowsley's daughter Anne married John Knowsley, and at inclosure another John Knowsley was allotted 671 a., as well as 272 a. for tithes.[43] The larger part of the estate, 526 a., was conveyed by Robert Knowsley to John Farthing in 1791.[44] Farthing died in 1822, leaving Burton Fleming like Argam to his daughter Franky, wife of James Hopkinson. In 1855 she sold 104 a. to Robert Carrick, and this subsequently descended with the land in Argam.[45] In 1857 Franky sold the rest of the estate, described as 428 a., to Robert Holtby, and it subsequently passed to Tom Featherston in 1919 and to Joseph Harrison in 1931.[46] The Harrisons still held it in 1970.[47]

Knowsley's fourth daughter Elizabeth married Charles Stutville.[48] In 1705 Stutville conveyed 10 bovates to William Bower, who had acquired another 4 bovates from John Smith in 1697.[49] In 1754 Leonard and John Bower sold all 14 bovates to Thomas Wharram,[50] and at inclosure in 1769 Wharram was allotted 262 a., as well as 130 a. for tithes.[51] T. M. Wharram sold all 392 a. to Tom Woodcock in 1875,[52] and in 1878 it was acquired by J. W. Macdonald.[53] The estate has since remained in the possession of the Bosville Macdonalds of Thorpe Hall, Rudston.[54] They sold 323 a. to T. E. Wells & Son in 1954 but retained a farm of 134 a.[55]

The manor-house, now Manor Farm, may have been built in the 17th century by the Knowsleys. The main block was largely altered and given a stucco front in the mid 19th century, but the original chalk is still exposed on the rear wall. This wall has stone quoins at one angle and a blocked window opening with stone surround. A dovecot built in 1636[56] no longer exists. The house had nine hearths in 1674.[57]

Much land in the parish was separated from the manor after the Dissolution. When Villiers sold the manor to Robert Knowsley in 1618, for example, he excepted property which he had recently sold to James Barugh and others.[58] By the time of the inclosure of 1769 several proprietors had built up sizeable estates, the most noteworthy being those of the Milners and the Osbaldestons. Part of the Milners' estate was acquired in 1723, when 6 bovates and 6 closes were conveyed to John Milner by Thomas Barugh.[59] In 1769 Thomas Milner was awarded 441 a.[60] The estate was divided during the 19th century, but a large part of it, 337 a., passed to Christopher Wilson, who sold it in 1841 to William Beckett.[61] It subsequently passed to Christopher Wilkinson and in 1858 he conveyed it, under the name of North Burton Grange, to Sir Thomas Legard.[62] The Legards had also acquired, in 1853, a 134-acre holding which largely comprised John Marshall's allotment at inclosure.[63] When the Legard's estate was divided and sold in 1911, the 355 a. of Grange Farm went to Harold Wrigley, and in 1919 he sold it to members of the Pickering family.[64]

The Osbaldestons acquired several holdings in Burton Fleming in the 18th century, including 8 bovates from Thomas Winteringham in 1734, one from Thomas Thompson in 1756, 3 from John Sawdon in 1758, and 7 from John Warcup in 1768.[65] At inclosure in 1769 F. W. Osbaldeston was allotted 370 a.[66] Between 1870 and 1881 a further 195 a., which had been allotted (as 185 a.) to Thomas Barugh in 1769, were added to the estate.[67] The 576-acre estate was sold by Robert Osbaldeston-Mitford to Sir H. D. Readett Bayley in 1920;[68] T. D. R. Readett Bayley died in 1957 and the estate was in the hands of his trustees in 1970.[69]

Among the estates built up after inclosure was that of the Bouch family. By 1848 John Bouch had 133 a. and the house known as North Burton Hall.[70] To this Jeffrey Bouch in 1854 added 152 a.,[71] which had been allotted to Francis Lundy in 1769. The Bouches held the estate until 1919, when the hall and 288 a. were sold to John Byass. They were acquired by Thomas Harrison in 1942.[72]

Several small estates in Burton Fleming were held by religious houses. Nostell priory was given one carucate by Hugh de Muscamp;[73] Nunkeeling priory received one bovate from John de Friboys, which was worth 3s. 4d. in 1535;[74] Swine priory had 2 bovates, given by Isabel de Friboys, which were worth 3s. 9d. in 1535;[75] and the Knights Hospitallers of Beverley had some property there in 1539–40[76]

---

[37] C.P. 25(2)/612/1649 Mich. no. 26; P.C.C. 273 Aylett (will of Anne Knowsley); *Regs. of Burton Fleming*, 25, 31.
[38] *Regs. of Burton Fleming*, 50, 54, 55.
[39] Registry of Deeds, Beverley, M/394/621.
[40] Ibid. AN/312/16.
[41] Burke, *Peerage* (1963), 567.
[42] Regy. of Deeds, 1133/133/121.
[43] Ibid. AN/312/16.
[44] Ibid. BP/491/804.
[45] See p. 7.
[46] Regy. of Deeds, HO/240/305; 204/566/499; 424/457/378.
[47] See ibid. 604/372/278; 859/255/222.
[48] See p. 7.
[49] E.R.R.O., DDBM/3/11, 13.
[50] Ibid. /21.
[51] Regy. of Deeds, AN/312/16.
[52] Ibid. LW/321/488.
[53] Ibid. MP/127/174.
[54] See p. 314.
[55] Regy. of Deeds, 992/208/189; 1002/377/325.
[56] B.I.H.R., TER. J. Burton Fleming 1716.
[57] E 179/205/521.
[58] C 54/2419 no. 56.
[59] Regy. of Deeds, A/635/1286.
[60] Ibid. AN/312/16.
[61] Ibid. FQ/192/208.
[62] Ibid. HT/8/11.
[63] Ibid. HD/116/159.
[64] Ibid. 134/290/265.
[65] Ibid. O/44/84; Z/108/243; AA/87/178; AL/191/349.
[66] Ibid. AN/312/16.
[67] Ibid. BL/93/103; BQ/380/599; KS/206/278; NI/236/347; E.R.R.O., DDHU/2/1 etc.
[68] Regy. of Deeds, 209/184/157.
[69] Ibid. 1073/418/368.
[70] Ibid. GN/7/10.
[71] Ibid. HD/365/428.
[72] Ibid. 195/359/263; 651/131/115.
[73] *E.Y.C.* ii, p. 454; iii, p. 131.
[74] *Valor Eccl.* v. 115; Burton, *Mon. Ebor.* 386.
[75] *Bridlington Charty.* 62; *Valor Eccl.* v. 114; *Cal. Pat.* 1446–52, 306.
[76] *Miscellanea*, iv (Y.A.S Rec. Ser. xciv), 93.

which was restored to them when the order was briefly revived in 1558.[77] The subsequent ownership of these holdings has not been traced, but the bovate formerly belonging to Nunkeeling is mentioned in 1608[78] and 2 bovates called 'Swine land' are referred to as late as 1719.[79]

The great tithe of Burton Fleming was granted to Bardney abbey in 1115,[80] but in 1299 the corn and hay tithes on Bridlington priory's demesnes in the parish were transferred to the priory in return for concessions elsewhere.[81] At the Dissolution Bardney's corn and hay tithes were worth £12 and its lamb tithes were included in the value of Hunmanby rectory.[82] Bardney's tithes were let to various members of the Constable family[83] and then in 1590 to Richard Knowsley. In 1594 they were granted for life to William Knowsley,[84] and Richard bought them outright in 1599.[85] Robert Knowsley acquired Bridlington priory's tithes along with the manor in 1618;[86] they had been worth £8 in 1535.[87]

Knowsley thus had most of the rectorial tithes. Like the manor they were divided among his daughters and in 1650, when they were worth £96 a year, they belonged to John Knowsley, Cuthbert Lascelles, and Alan Lamont.[88] Demesne tithes were included in Lascelles' quitclaim of his share of the manor to Lamont in 1649 and in the sale of the manor by Lamont's heirs to Sir William Strickland in 1733.[89] It is not clear whether these were all of the demesne tithes or only part of them, the rest descending with the other shares of the manor. The tithes formerly belonging to Bardney are usually distinguished in the 17th and 18th centuries as the tithes of the Bondage field. Half of them belonged to the Knowsleys.[90] The other half were conveyed by Cuthbert Lascelles to Robert Hovy for life in 1657 with remainder to Alan Lamont, and in 1677 Lamont released them to John Bower.[91] The Bowers conveyed these tithes in 1754 to Thomas Wharram.[92] At inclosure in 1769 allotments were made for the various great tithes to John Knowsley, who received 204 a. for half his share and a rent-charge of about £14 for the rest, Sir George Strickland, who got 101 a. and about £21, and Thomas Wharram, who got 130 a. and about £31.[93] These allotments descended with the recipients' other estates in the parish. Rents of about £10 for part of the great tithes were paid to the Osbaldeston-Mitfords in the 19th century,[94] but it is not known how they acquired them.

Bardney abbey's lamb tithes were still annexed to Hunmanby rectory after the Dissolution and descended with it to Richard Osbaldeston in 1623.[95] At inclosure in 1769 F. W. Osbaldeston was allotted a rent-charge of £25 for these tithes.[96]

ECONOMIC HISTORY. In 1086 there was land for seven ploughs on the larger estate in Burton Fleming and for one on the smaller.[97] Bridlington priory's grange, comprising the whole township, produced nearly 450 qr. of corn, peas, and malt in 1355–6, more than half of it barley. Receipts from sales of corn were over four times as much as those from livestock, mainly pigs.[98] One of the monks accounted in 1355–6, and a chaplain of Burton Fleming was described as the priory's bailiff there in 1378.[99] The priory was experiencing difficulty with its tenants at Burton Fleming in 1426, when inquiry was ordered into the withdrawal of customs and services by certain bondmen.[1]

At the Dissolution the manor was out at farm to the priory's bailiff,[2] and he and 26 other tenants paid rents totalling £42. With the manor-house went 13 bovates of land and 21 householders had altogether 134½ bovates; 5 cottagers held only odd butts of land. Apart from the demesne, the largest holding comprised 11 bovates and the smallest 3, and the average size was about 6 bovates. The lease also included the demesne tithes and a windmill.[3] In 1608, when Robert Knowsley held a lease of the manor and the demesne tithes, the composition of tenant holdings was still much the same.[4]

East field is referred to as early as 1170–5,[5] and the demesne lands belonging to the priory lay in 1299 in 17 *culturae* and 2 intakes, or ovenams, in various parts of East and West fields.[6] It is possible, however, that the demesnes were later separated from the rest of the open-field land. In 1608 there were 31½ bovates of demesne; the remaining 123 bovates lay in 'the bondage or town field', and the former Bardney abbey tithes were from land similarly described.[7] A physical separation of demesne and tenant land is thus suggested, and in the 17th and 18th centuries there are frequent references to bovates in the Bondage field. These are sometimes distinguished from bovates in Hall Dale,[8] which apparently refers to part of the demesne land. When an agreement was made in 1663 between the various tithe-owners and the rest of the inhabitants, the tithes of the Bondage field were distinguished from those of 'the demesnes and Hall Dale'.[9] The Bondage field was no doubt subdivided for the purposes of rotation, and in 1608 many holdings lay 'in two fields'.[10]

There are few references to common pasture and meadow in the parish. Pasture for 120 sheep was among the gifts made to Bridlington priory.[11] Waste called the 'meres' was let by the priory in the early 16th century.[12] Certain intakes were apparently used as common pasture, at least in the 17th century. Two cows belonging to a tenant of the

---

[77] *Cal. Pat.* 1557–8, 319.
[78] L.R. 2/229 f. 244.
[79] E.R.R.O., DDBV/9/1.
[80] See p. 123.
[81] *Bridlington Charty.* 66–9.
[82] E.R.R.O., DDHU/9/12.
[83] C 66/1172 m. 7; *Cal. Pat.* 1560–3, 568.
[84] C 66/1424 m. 18.
[85] *Cal. S.P.Dom* 1598–1601, 342.
[86] See p. 120.
[87] *Valor Eccl.* v. 120.
[88] *T.E.R.A.S.* ii. 58.
[89] See p. 121.
[90] e.g. Regy. of Deeds, D/108/172; H/652/1323.
[91] E.R.R.O., DDBM/3/4–6, 9–10.
[92] Ibid. /21.
[93] Regy. of Deeds, AN/312/16.
[94] E.R.R.O., DDHU/2/40; /17/13–15.
[95] Ibid. /9/50; see below, p. 236.
[96] Regy. of Deeds, AN/312/16.
[97] *V.C.H. Yorks.* ii. 204.
[98] B.I.H.R., Mon. 1.
[99] *Monastic Notes*, i (Y.A.S. Rec. Ser. xvii), 24.
[1] *Cal. Pat.* 1422–9, 402.
[2] *Miscellanea*, iii (Y.A.S. Rec. Ser. lxxx), 11, 25; see above, p. 120.
[3] S.C. 12/10/35.
[4] L.R. 2/229 ff. 234–59.
[5] *E.Y.C.* ii, p. 460.
[6] *Bridlington Charty.* 66.
[7] L.R. 2/229 ff. 234–59.
[8] e.g. E.R.R.O., DDBM/3/2–3; DDBV/9/1; Registry of Deeds, Beverley, M/394/621; O/44/84.
[9] See p. 123.
[10] L.R. 2/229 ff. 234–59.
[11] *Bridlington Charty.* 60, 64.
[12] S.C. 12/10/35.

manor were being kept there in 1623,[13] and in 1647 open-field land was sold together with common of pasture in the 'Ownhams'.[14] There are various references to the Ownhams, distinguishing them from land in the Bondage field.[15]

The early inclosures probably lay around the village, in the valley of the Gypsey Race. In 1608 about twenty tenants each had some inclosed meadow, amounting to about 14 a. all told.[16] In the 18th century there were several demesne closes, including Coney garth and Great close.[17] Most tenants presumably kept some stock, and about one hundred and fifty cattle died of 'distemper' in Burton Fleming between February 1748 and June 1749.[18]

Most of the parish remained open until 1769, when it was inclosed[19] under an Act of the previous year.[20] The award dealt with a total of 3,652 a. Three allotments were made to men who owned estates deriving from the manor: Sir George Strickland got 523 a., as well as 101 a. for tithes, John Knowsley got 671 a., with 272 a. for tithes, and Thomas Wharram got 262 a., with 130 a. for tithes. Other large allotments were received by F. W. Osbaldeston (370 a.), Thomas Milner (441 a.), Thomas Barugh (185 a.), Francis Lundy (150 a.), Richard Marshall (110 a.), and John Marshall (108 a.). There were 3 allotments of between 80 a. and 99 a., and 5 of under 25 a. In the 19th and 20th centuries there have been 10–15 farmers in Burton Fleming.[21]

A windmill belonging to the manor is frequently mentioned from the late 13th century onwards.[22] By the mid 19th century the mill also had steam power.[23] A miller is last mentioned in 1905.[24]

LOCAL GOVERNMENT. At a court held on behalf of the Crown in 1546 various agricultural and domestic offences were presented, as well as an infringement of the 'bylaw'.[25] It was presumably the custody of the court leet and view of frankpledge of Burton Fleming which was granted to George Stanhope in 1660 under the name of 'Durton' or 'Darton' Fleming.[26] At a court held by Sir George Strickland in 1837 2 affeerors, 2 constables, and a pinder were appointed.[27]

A glimpse of parochial administration in the 17th century is given by the settlement in 1663 of a dispute between the impropriators and the vicar on the one hand and the rest of the inhabitants on the other. It was agreed that impropriators and vicar should contribute a sixth of all 'monthly assessments' laid on the lordship by Parliament and a fifth of the poor-rates. Such contributions were to be shared between the owners of the tithes of the Bondage field, who were to pay three-fifths, the owners of the lamb tithes and the vicar, one-fifth, and the owners of the demesne tithes, one-fifth. The owners of the Bondage field tithes also agreed to render a quarter of barley each year to the churchwardens and this was to exempt both impropriators and vicar from repairing any part of the church and from contributing to the constable's rate in respect of their tithes.[28]

Burton Fleming joined the Bridlington union in 1836.[29]

CHURCH. Burton Fleming was a dependent chapelry of Hunmanby in 1115, when it was given along with the mother church to Bardney abbey.[30] It was separated from Hunmanby in 1269 and a vicarage ordained.[31] It did not, however, become fully parochial immediately; in 1662, for example, it contributed towards the repair of Hunmanby church,[32] and burials took place at Hunmanby until 1828.[33] The chapelry of Fordon was transferred from Hunmanby to Burton Fleming in 1858.[34]

Bardney regularly presented to the living up to the Dissolution, though in 1350 a presentation was made by John of Stockwith by lease from the abbey. John Rockley, by a grant from the abbey, presented in 1543.[35] A Crown grant of the advowson to the archbishop of York in 1558[36] presumably lapsed on the accession of Elizabeth I. The advowson may have descended in the 16th century with the lamb tithes,[37] for Ralph Westrop presented in 1602.[38] It would thus have passed to Richard Osbaldeston in 1623 and he was certainly dealing in it in 1625.[39] It was therefore perhaps by mistake that the advowson was linked with the manor in deeds of 1618 and 1646.[40] The patronage thenceforth belonged to the Osbaldestons and Osbaldeston-Mitfords and passed with their estate in Burton Fleming to Sir H. D. Readett Bayley in 1920.[41] Bayley sold it in 1925 to Harrogate College,[42] and it passed to the Martyrs' Memorial Trust in 1952.[43]

The vicarage was valued at £5 in 1291[44] and £6 4s. net in 1535.[45] It was said to be worth £13 13s. 4d. in 1650[46] but in 1685 the vicar put the whole profits at only £6.[47] By 1809 the income had in-

---

[13] E.R.R.O., DDGR/34/4.
[14] Hull Univ. MS. DP/88.
[15] e.g. E.R.R.O., DDBM/3/2; DDBV/9/1; Regy. of Deeds, M/394/621.
[16] L.R. 2/229 ff. 234–59.
[17] B.I.H.R., TER. J. Burton Fleming 1716.
[18] E.R.R.O., PR. 932, p. 5.
[19] Regy. of Deeds, AN/312/16.
[20] 8 Geo. III, c. 49 (Priv. Act).
[21] Directories.
[22] e.g. C 66/2002 no. 2; S.C. 12/10/35; L.R. 2/229 f. 239; B.I.H.R., TER. J. Burton Fleming 1716; E.R.R.O., DDBD/13/1–3; /93/4, 73, 75; Cal. Inq. p.m. ii, p. 158; Miscellanea, iii. 4.
[23] Sheahan and Whellan, Hist. York & E.R. ii. 462.
[24] Kelly's Dir. N. & E.R. Yorks. (1905), 470.
[25] S.C. 2/211/21.
[26] C 66/2937 no. 12.
[27] E.R.R.O., DDX/3/10.
[28] Ibid. PR. 931, pp. 76–7, printed in Regs. of Burton Fleming (Yorks. Par. Reg. Soc. ii), 45–6.
[29] 3rd Rep. Poor Law Com. 167.
[30] Dugdale, Mon. i. 628–9.
[31] Reg. Giffard (Sur. Soc. cix), 56.
[32] B.I.H.R., C.P., H. 4838; and see E 134/42 & 43 Eliz. Mich./29.
[33] See p. 243.
[34] York. Dioc. Regy., Orders in Council 157.
[35] Fasti Parochiales, iii. 16; Cal. Pat. 1360–4, 74.
[36] Cal. Pat. 1557–8, 420.
[37] See p. 122.
[38] Fasti Parochiales, iii. 17.
[39] E.R.R.O., DDHU/9/50, 53.
[40] C 54/2419 no. 56; C.P. 25(2)/525/22 Chas. I. Mich. no. 49.
[41] Registry of Deeds, Beverley, 209/184/157.
[42] Ibid. 318/410/342.
[43] York. Dioc. Cal.
[44] Tax. Eccl. (Rec. Com.), 304.
[45] Valor Eccl. (Rec. Com.), v. 123.
[46] T.E.R.A.S. ii. 59.
[47] B.I.H.R., TER. J. Burton Fleming 1685.

creased to £58 a year[48] and by 1829–31 to an average of £84,[49] largely as the result of gifts of £200 from Queen Anne's Bounty in both 1767 and 1786 and of a further £200 parliamentary grant in 1810.[50] After the allotment of land formerly belonging to Folkton rectory in 1856 and the transfer of Fordon chapelry from Hunmanby parish, the income of Burton Fleming had risen to £285 net by 1884.[51]

At inclosure in 1769 the vicar was allotted 68 a. and £15 rent in lieu of tithe.[52] Apart from a ½-acre close, first recorded in 1685,[53] there was no glebe land until c. 1770, when 8 a. in Dringhoe was bought with Bounty money.[54] In 1856 102 a. in Octon, formerly belonging to Folkton rectory, were allotted to Burton Fleming; the transference of Fordon from Hunmanby added another 55 a. to Burton Fleming's glebe.[55] The Octon and Fordon glebe was sold in 1921.[56]

There was a vicarage house in 1535.[57] In 1571 the vicar was found to allow a victualling house to be kept in it,[58] and it was in decay in 1578.[59] It no longer existed by 1685[60] and it was not until 1884 that a Vicarage at the north end of the village was built.[61]

Non-residence of incumbents was usual in the 18th and 19th centuries until the building of the Vicarage. In 1743 a neighbouring clergyman served the cure, and in 1764 the vicar lived at Boynton and had an assistant who lived at Langtoft. The vicar in 1743 was also vicar of Rudston and of Hayton with Bielby, as well as assistant curate at Millington.[62] In 1835 there was an assistant curate and the vicar was also rector of Dickleburgh (Norf.).[63] The vicar lived at Hunmanby in 1868 and he had an assistant curate in 1875–7.[64]

There was said to be no service at all in 1578.[65] Services in 1743 are not recorded, but communion was then administered four times a year to about fifty people.[66] In 1764 there was a weekly service three weeks out of four. Services were still weekly in 1851, but by 1865 there were two services on alternate Sundays; communion was celebrated four times in both of those years, about thirty people receiving it in 1764 and fourteen in 1865.[67] By 1884 communion was celebrated monthly, and there were two celebrations each month in 1936.[68] In 1970 one service was held each week.

The church of ST. CUTHBERT, originally built of stone but extensively renovated with brick and incorporating some cobbles, consists of nave, chancel, west tower, and south porch.[69] A former south aisle has been removed. Of the 12th-century church there remain the jambs and shaft capitals of the chancel arch, set into the wall on either side of a later pointed arch. The arcade of the former aisle, embedded in the present south wall of the nave, is of the same date. Three circular piers are visible, one with a scalloped capital and another with a capital bearing primitive carved ornament. The semicircular arches have chamfered orders with spur stops. A narrow single-light window in the south wall of the nave, deeply-splayed inside, may be a relic of the early church though it has been renovated in brick. The circular 12th-century font has four carved heads on the base. The incomplete south doorway, also of the 12th century, probably had an arch of three orders; on the west side the carved abaci of the jamb shafts survive. The chancel, which is of stone ashlar, may have been built in the 14th century, but the square-headed east window is a 15th-century insertion. The squat four-stage tower is probably also of the 14th century. It contains one two-light window of that date and four narrow slit openings.

By the late 16th century the chancel was 'in decay'.[70] The church was perhaps reroofed in 1576, this date being cut into one of the beams.[71] In 1663 it was said that the tower and bells were 'not likely to stand a year'.[72] It was apparently after an adverse report in 1720[73] that the south aisle was removed, the arcade blocked, and the south wall, chancel, and porch extensively repaired with brick. Two pointed, wood-framed, windows were inserted in the blocked arcade and three square, two-light, windows of stone in the north wall; there is a similar window in the chancel. A pointed, iron-framed, window in the south wall of the nave perhaps dates from the early 19th century. The whole interior of the building is lime-washed. The church was restored in 1887[74] and 1930.[75]

There is a monument to Thomas Wharram (d. 1829), a Royal Arms of 1724, and a charity board of 1793. One of the two bells is dated 1720 and was made by Samuel Smith, the younger, of York.[76] The plate consists of a silver cup and electro-plated paten, flagon, and alms-dish, the last three all dated 1875.[77] The registers begin in 1538 and are complete.[78]

The churchyard was consecrated in 1828.[79]

NONCONFORMITY. A family of Anabaptists was reported in 1743,[80] and there were a few Baptists in 1865.[81] A Wesleyan Methodist chapel was licensed

---

[48] Ibid. 1809.
[49] *Rep. Com. Eccl. Revenues*, 922–3.
[50] Hodgson, *Q.A.B.* 436; the parl. grant is given as £315 in B.I.H.R., TER. J. Burton Fleming 1853, 1857.
[51] B.I.H.R., Bp. V. 1884/Ret.
[52] Regy. of Deeds, AN/312/16.
[53] B.I.H.R., TER. J. Burton Fleming 1685.
[54] Ibid. 1770.
[55] Ibid. 1865; *Lond. Gaz.* 8 Aug. 1856, pp. 2739–42.
[56] Regy. of Deeds, 235/238/200; 236/225/183.
[57] *Valor Eccl.* v. 123.
[58] J. S. Purvis, *Tudor Par. Docs. of Dioc. York*, 195.
[59] B.I.H.R., V. 1578–9/CB. 1.
[60] Ibid. TER. J. Burton Fleming 1685.
[61] Bulmer, *Dir. E. Yorks.* (1892), 155.
[62] B.I.H.R., Bp. V. 1764/Ret. 104; *Herring's Visit.* i. 111.
[63] *Rep. Com. Eccl. Revenues*, 922–3.
[64] B.I.H.R., V. 1868/Ret. 91; V. 1877/Ret.
[65] Ibid. V. 1578–9/CB. 1.
[66] *Herring's Visit.* i. 111.
[67] B.I.H.R., Bp. V. 1764/Ret. 104; V. 1865/Ret. 95; H.O. 129/24/524.
[68] B.I.H.R., V. 1868/Ret. 91; V. 1871/Ret. 91; V. 1877/Ret.; Bp. V. 1884/Ret.; Bp. V. 1936/Ret. 270.
[69] Morris, *E. Yorks.* 130.
[70] B.I.H.R., V. 1575/CB. 1; V. 1578–9/CB. 1; V. 1600/CB. 1.
[71] Sheahan and Whellan, *Hist. York & E.R.* ii. 462; a panel bearing the date was preserved when the roof was renewed in 1970.
[72] B.I.H.R., ER. V/CB. 1.
[73] Ibid. ER. V/CB. 15.
[74] Bulmer, *Dir. E. Yorks.* (1892), 155.
[75] Plaque in nave.
[76] Boulter, 'Ch. Bells', 216; *V.C.H. Yorks.* ii. 452.
[77] *Yorks. Ch. Plate*, i. 231–2.
[78] E.R.R.O. The earlier books have been printed: *Regs. of Burton Fleming* (Yorks. Par. Reg. Soc. ii).
[79] B.I.H.R., CD. 146A.
[80] *Herring's Visit.* i. 111.
[81] B.I.H.R., V. 1865/Ret. 95.

in 1807,[82] and in 1851 there were said to be two buildings used by the Wesleyans, one built in 1800 and the other c. 1803.[83] One of these stood in Back Street, just south of the cross-roads.[84] A new building, in Front Street, was licensed in 1883[85] and this, known as St. John's Methodist Church, was still in use in 1970. It is of red and yellow brick, with blue-brick and stone dressings. A Primitive Methodist chapel, in a lane joining Front and Back Streets, was built in 1838.[86] There were 32 members in 1889.[87] The chapel was replaced in 1903[88] by a new red-brick chapel in Front Street and this was in use in 1970, when the old building was still standing.

The parish incumbents complained of the strength of the Methodist churches in the late 19th century, and in 1900 the vicar alleged that 'all the wealth and influence is on the side of dissent. If we do anything they do more and can beat us.'[89]

EDUCATION. By 1835 there were two day schools in Burton Fleming, where 23 boys and 20 girls were taught at their parents' expense.[90] A school was built by subscription in 1843 and supported by school pence.[91] Only 31 children were in attendance in 1871,[92] and it was said in 1868 that all the farmers had governesses to teach their children at home.[93] The school, which was affiliated to the British Society,[94] stood at the cross-roads south of the church.[95]

A school board was formed in 1873 and a new school built, in Back Street, the following year; the old building was then demolished.[96] The school was improved by the county council in 1904 and 1913.[97] The average attendance was 90–100 in 1908–14 and usually between 70 and 80 in the 1920s and 1930s.[98] The average number on the roll in 1970 was 27.[99]

CHARITIES FOR THE POOR. Thomas Sawdon, by will proved in 1774, left £30, the interest to be distributed in bread to poor people attending church. Two shillings a month was expended in 1798 and also in 1823, when bread worth 8d. was distributed on each of three Sundays in each month.[1] No distribution was made for a period in the early 20th century, but bread was again distributed in 1930–1, when stock worth £31 produced about 12s. income.[2] Distribution stopped again during the 1930s and no more is known of the charity.[3]

CARNABY

CARNABY lies 2½ miles from Bridlington and is one of a string of villages situated at the southern edge of the wolds.[1] It may have been a Scandinavian settlement.[2] The northern boundary of the parish is formed by the road known as Wold Gate, and on the wold slopes the eastern boundary with Haisthorpe is formed by a green road called Hunger Hills Balk. South of the Bridlington road the elongated parish extends into the Plain of Holderness, where part of its boundary follows watercourses, among them that known variously as Bessingby or Auburn beck. The ancient parish originally included both Auburn and Fraisthorpe but they subsequently became distinct curacies and are dealt with separately here. The area of Carnaby itself was 1,944 a.[3] Since 1935 Carnaby civil parish has included Haisthorpe and Wilsthorpe townships and part of Bessingby civil parish.[4]

The landscape of Carnaby is similar to that of neighbouring Burton Agnes, with the same contrast between the mainly treeless wold slopes, with their large arable fields, and the more wooded and pastoral plain to the south. Chalk was formerly dug from several pits near Wold Gate, and there is still a large overgrown pit north of the village. The southern part of the parish is low-lying, generally only 25 ft. to 50 ft. above sea-level. The village itself lies around the 100-foot contour. To the north the land rises fairly steeply to nearly 250 ft. in the north-west and much of the wold ground lies at over 200 ft. In the north-east the parish extends beyond Carnaby wold and includes ground on the southern slopes of the valley of the Gypsey Race. The wold slopes were occupied by the open-field land of the parish until inclosure in the early 18th century, and much of the low-lying ground was common moor and carr. The disused Carnaby airfield has occupied a large area of the low-lying ground since 1944.[5] The only extensive area of woodland is Hallowkiln wood in the north-east, which is a southerly extension of woodland in Boynton.

The village stands around the junction of the main Bridlington road with Moor Lane, which runs southwards towards Fraisthorpe and Wilsthorpe. Until the 1920s this minor road carried traffic from Beverley through Carnaby village on its way to Bridlington. In 1923, however, a new road, known as Kingsgate, was opened, running across the southern part of the parish directly north-eastwards to Bridlington.[6]

[82] G.R.O., Worship Returns, Vol. v, no. 2078.
[83] H.O. 129/24/524.
[84] O.S. Map 6" (1854).
[85] G.R.O. Worship Reg., no. 27209.
[86] H.O. 129/24/524; date on building.
[87] H. Woodcock, *Sketches of Prim. Meth. on Yorks. Wolds*, 71.
[88] G.R.O. Worship Reg., no. 39491. The building carries the date 1902.
[89] B.I.H.R., Bp. V. 1884/Ret.; Bp. V. 1894/Ret.; Bp. V. 1900/Ret. 64.
[90] *Educ. Enquiry Abstract, 1835*, 1081.
[91] Ed. 7/135.
[92] *Rets. rel. Elem. Educ. 1871*, 474.
[93] B.I.H.R., V. 1868/Ret. 91.
[94] *Kelly's Dir. N. & E.R. Yorks.* (1872), 342.
[95] O.S. Map 6" (1854).
[96] E.R.R.O., SB. Sch. Bd. Mins. 1873–1903.
[97] E.R. Educ. Cttee. *Mins.* 1904–5, 277; 1913–14, 322.
[98] *Bd. of Educ. List 21* (H.M.S.O.).
[99] Ex inf. Chief Educ. Officer, County Hall, Beverley, 1970.
[1] E.R.R.O., PR. 933 (notes in par. reg.); *9th Rep. Char. Com.* 732.
[2] Char. Com. files.
[3] Ex inf. the vicar, 1972.

[1] This article was written in 1968.
[2] *P.N.E.R. Yorks.* (E.P.N.S.), 86. See also *T.E.R.A.S.* xxv. 25–6.
[3] O.S. Map 6" (1854).
[4] *Census*, 1931.
[5] Ex inf. Ministry of Defence, 1969.
[6] E.R.C.C. *Mins.* 1922–3, 26; F. A. Slim and H. L. Gee. *Bridlington, 1899–1949*, [9].

These are the only roads on the plain. On the wold slopes two minor roads run northwards: Temple Lane, formerly Hopkin Lane, which now leads only to Temple Farm; and Church Lane, which leads into Boynton. In the village a back lane to the north of the main street connects Temple and Church Lanes; sections of it are known as Turkey Lane and School Hill. At the bottom of School Hill stands a modern cross inscribed 'Carnaby medieval market stone. Reconstructed 1968'.

Although there are some modern buildings, including a petrol station, along the main street, the village does not seem to have been extended at either end at least during the last 100 years. Most of the houses and cottages are of the late 18th and 19th centuries, mainly built of brick but also with extensive use of chalk. Most of the farm-houses are situated in the village itself. They include Carnaby House, a late-18th- or early-19-century stuccoed brick building, two storeys high and three bays long, with quoins and a string-course. The central doorway is flanked by reeded half-columns set on tall bases and there is a somewhat similar doorway on the east side of the house. The farm buildings include a noteworthy 19th-century wagon shed with a central dovecot.[7] Hill Farm, also in the village, is chalk-built with a pedimented porch and dated 1822. The only isolated farm on the wolds is Temple Farm, and in the south of the parish there are four farm-houses built between 1888 and 1926.[8] The railway station, at the south end of the village, was probably built when the Hull-Bridlington line was opened in 1846.

Another isolated building is Carnaby Temple, an octagonal red-brick tower of two storeys and a basement, which stands at the summit of the wold slopes north of Temple Farm. It was built by Sir George Strickland in the late 18th century, probably as a look-out tower. There are round-headed windows in each face of each storey, many now blocked up. From the centre of the roof, which has a double slope and is covered with green slates, rises an octagonal brick cupola with arcaded sides, crowned by a ball finial. The interior walls were originally covered with frescoes bearing dates from 1771. An extension and chimney-stack were added at a later date when the building was inhabited by farm workers. In the late 19th century it was used as a store-house.[9] During the Second World War it was used for military purposes, and was afterwards left dilapidated.[10]

In 1377 173 people paid the poll tax at Carnaby.[11] In 1544 there were 30 houses and 10 cottages in the manor.[12] Forty-four houses were assessed to or discharged from the hearth tax in 1674. Of those assessed 25 had only one hearth, 2 had 2, 2 had 4, and one had 5 hearths.[13] By 1723 the manor contained only 10 houses and 16 cottages,[14] and only 29 families were reported in 1743[15] and 25 in 1764.[16] In 1801 the population was 129. It had risen to 161 by 1851[17] and 189 by 1911. There were 191 inhabitants in 1931.[18]

MANORS AND OTHER ESTATES. In 1086 there were two estates in Carnaby, comprising 13 carucates (including one carucate in Auburn), held of the king by two rent-payers. Before 1066 the whole estate had belonged to Chilbert.[19] Carnaby subsequently became part of the Percy fee and the overlordship descended with the main branch of the Percy family.[20] Their overlordship is last mentioned in 1638.[21]

The earliest known under-tenants of the manor of *CARNABY* belonged to a minor branch of the Percy family, whose main estates lay at Sutton upon Derwent, Bolton Percy (Yorks. W.R.), and Carnaby.[22] Robert son of Picot de Percy, a Domesday tenant of William de Percy, is the first of the family whom it is possible to connect with Carnaby, through his gift of its church to Bridlington priory between 1147 and 1153.[23] His son William was described as 'of Carnaby' in 1199 and 1204–10,[24] and William's son Robert was granted ½ carucate in Carnaby by John of Rudston in 1216–22.[25] Robert held 7 carucates there of the Percy fee in 1234–6.[26] After the death of Peter de Percy in 1318[27] the manor was held by his widow Isabel, who by 1323 had married Philip de Neville. Peter de Percy's daughter Eustacia, a minor at her father's death, had inherited the manor by 1335–6, when her husband was Walter of Heslerton.[28] In 1346 Walter held 9 of the 10 carucates of the Percy fee in Carnaby.[29] After the death of his son, another Walter, by 1368 his wife Euphemia held the manor for life.[30] In 1394, after her death, the manor passed to Ralph de Percy, son of Henry, earl of Northumberland.[31]

By 1428 the manor was in the possession of Sir William Hilton, who held 9 carucates there,[32] and it remained in the Hilton family until in 1573 it was conveyed by William Hilton to Thomas Layton.[33] The connexion of the Layton family with Carnaby seems to have been of short duration and they may have conveyed their estate to the Strickland family soon after 1573.[34] Walter Strickland held the manor at his death in 1635,[35] and it descended like Boynton in the Strickland family until 1951.[36] In 1921 about 400 a. of the estate were sold to the East Riding county council[37] and most of this land was still

---

[7] See plate facing p. 273.
[8] O.S. Map 6" (1854, 1892, 1928).
[9] Bulmer, *Dir. E. Yorks.* (1892), 160.
[10] *Hull Daily Mail*, 4 Feb. 1964.
[11] E 179/202/62 m. 47.
[12] *Yorks. Fines*, i. 112.
[13] E 179/205/521.
[14] Registry of Deeds, Beverley, H/481/976.
[15] *Herring's Visit.* i. 158.
[16] B.I.H.R., Bp. V. 1764/Ret. 116.
[17] *V.C.H. Yorks.* iii. 489.
[18] *Census.*
[19] *V.C.H. Yorks.* ii. 287.
[20] C 142/208/167; *Percy Charty.* (Sur. Soc. cxvii), 471; *Cal. Inq. p.m.* i, p. 205; vi, p. 237; xii, p. 226; *Feud. Aids*, vi. 31, 142, 230.
[21] C 142/553/45.
[22] *Whitby Charty.* ii (Sur. Soc. lxxii), 707–8; *E.Y.C.* xi, p. 10.
[23] *Bridlington Charty.* 429.
[24] *E.Y.C.* i, p. 493; xi, p. 81.
[25] B.M. Harl. Chart. 55F. 13.
[26] *Percy Charty.* 471.
[27] *Cal. Inq. p.m.* vi, p. 82.
[28] *Yorks. Fines, 1327–1347*, 95, 118.
[29] *Feud. Aids*, vi. 230.
[30] *Cal. Close, 1364–8*, 417.
[31] Ibid. 1392–6, 210.
[32] *Feud. Aids*, vi. 266–7; for a pedigree of the Hiltons see G.E.C. *Baronetage*, iv. 305.
[33] *Yorks. Fines*, ii. 38.
[34] The manor was not among the possessions of Thomas Layton at his death in 1584, nor does it appear that his son Charles held it after him: C 142/207/93; C 142/367/93.
[35] C 142/553/45.
[36] See p. 23.
[37] Registry of Deeds, Beverley, 234/562/466.

owned by the council in 1968. In 1947 200 a. were sold to the Air Ministry.[38] The remainder of the estate was split up in 1952 and sold in separate lots.[39]

In 1368 Walter Heslerton's manor-house stood in the Park,[40] and an area of moats and earthworks called the Park still marks the site.[41] Hall close, near Manor Farm, may be the site of a later house, for by the later 16th century the manor-house stood in Hall garth.[42]

The descent of the second estate of 1086 is more obscure, but it probably passed with the manor into the Percy fee.[43] A small estate, consisting of one carucate, was held from the Percies by Colin de Mauleverer in 1234–6.[44] This had passed by the late 13th century to Roger Mauleverer,[45] and in 1315 Nicholas Mauleverer held one carucate of Henry de Percy.[46] The family which took its name from this parish seems to have been originally a tenant of the Mauleverers, but soon after 1316 it became the owner of the estate.[47] In 1326 Beatrice, widow of Durand of Carnaby, brought a suit against the Uppiby family, which was then a tenant of St. Leonard's hospital, York, for the recovery of land in Carnaby.[48] Roncanus Carnaby held one carucate of land there of the Percy fee in 1368,[49] and in 1429 John Carnaby held 8 bovates there.[50] Subsequently the family moved to Northumberland.[51] The greater part of its estate was probably absorbed into the fee of St. Leonard's hospital in the 15th century.

The larger of two ecclesiastical fees in Carnaby was that of the hospital of St. Leonard which in the early 12th century consisted of one carucate of land.[52] In 1429 the hospital held 10 bovates in Carnaby of the Percies.[53] The former possessions of the hospital in 1557 included a manor-house and 16 bovates of land.[54] They were granted in the same year to James Lambert and George Cotton,[55] and eventually passed in 1595 from Henry Dynely to William Green.[56] Green's nephew's daughter Elizabeth married Sir John Buck, who in 1630 was in possession of the lands,[57] and in 1632 Samuel Buck died seised of them.[58] The Buck family retained the estate until the death of another Samuel Buck in 1806.[59] His estates remained in the hands of his devisees, Sir Francis Lindley Wood and the Revd. Alexander Cooke, who married Buck's daughters Anne and Catherine respectively. In 1835 the Carnaby estate was conveyed to Wood. It then consisted of 272 a. of land.[60] The estate remained in the family until 1895 when Charles Lindley, Viscount Halifax, conveyed it, then described as Carnaby House farm, to the tenant H. P. Robinson.[61] In 1899, however, Robinson conveyed it to his creditors, who two years later sold it to A. G. W. Wright of Bessingby.[62] It subsequently descended like Bessingby.[63] In 1954 79 a. were sold to the Air Ministry.[64]

A smaller estate in Carnaby was held by Bridlington priory. In the early 13th century William de Percy gave the priory 2 bovates adjoining land which it already had as part of the endowment of the church.[65] In 1305–6 Robert de Percy secured to the priory common pasture for its cattle.[66] In 1535 the priory's lands in Carnaby were valued at £1 16s. a year[67] and included 4 bovates.[68] They were let to Robert Brewster in the early 16th century,[69] in 1563 to Thomas Marten,[70] in 1572–3 to Edward Elrington,[71] in 1586 to Richard Mawe,[72] and in 1593 to Thomas Brewster.[73] In 1632 they were in the possession of Samuel Buck,[74] and they subsequently descended with his estate.

The great tithes belonged to Bridlington priory from the 12th century.[75] The rectory was valued at £16 in 1291 and 1428,[76] and at £12 in 1535.[77] In 1537 the tithes were let by the Crown to Thomas Brigham,[78] who in 1542 devised them to his son Ralph.[79] The rectory was let to John Carliell in 1546[80] and 1564,[81] and the reversion to Richard Statham in 1577.[82] In 1593 it was let to Ralph Tucker, Gamaliel Stevenson, and Nathaniel Peacock.[83] The rectory was granted in fee along with the advowson in 1609 to Francis Philips and Richard Moore,[84] who seem to have sold it to Sir Walter Strickland; he died possessed of it in 1635.[85] In 1650 the tithes were worth £110 a year.[86] They were presumably extinguished at inclosure in the early 18th century.[87]

ECONOMIC HISTORY. In 1066 Chilbert's estate of 13 carucates had land for seven ploughs, but there were only nine villeins with three ploughs in 1086, when the land was held of the king by two

---

[38] Ibid. 775/63/47.
[39] Ibid. 915/313/276 etc.; sale catalogue *penes* Mr. D. Thompson, Carnaby, 1968.
[40] *Cal. Inq. p.m.* xii, p. 181.
[41] O.S. Map 6" (1854).
[42] C 54/921 m. [3].
[43] Robt. de Percy was returned as sole lord in 1316: *Feud. Aids*, vi. 169.
[44] *Percy Charty.* 471.
[45] Ibid. 131.
[46] *Cal. Inq. p.m.* v, p. 318.
[47] C.P. 40/264 m. 239 d.; *Percy Charty.* 131; *Bridlington Charty.* 176; *Cal. Inq. p.m.* v, p. 318.
[48] C.P. 40/264 m. 239d; /275 m. 44.
[49] *Cal. Inq. p.m.* xii, p. 226.
[50] E 179/202/104.
[51] *T.E.R.A.S.* vii. 7.
[52] B.M. Cott. MS. Nero D. iii, f. 37.
[53] E 179/202/104.
[54] E 318/2185; B.M. Harl. MS. 606, f. 115.
[55] *Cal. Pat.* 1557–8, 273.
[56] *Y.A.J.* xxxvi. 438; *Yorks. Fines*, ii. 66; iii. 191; iv. 26.
[57] C 3/403/121. See above, p. 105.
[58] C 142/726/100.
[59] Regy. of Deeds, DU/335/392.
[60] Ibid. EX/336/375.
[61] Ibid. 73/114/110 (1895).
[62] Ibid. 15/168/163 (1899); 35/7/7 (1901).
[63] See p. 18.
[64] Regy. of Deeds, 989/469/405.
[65] *Bridlington Charty.* 7, 175.
[66] Ibid. 175.
[67] *Valor Eccl.* (Rec. Com.), v. 120.
[68] C 142/726/100; S.C. 6/Hen. VIII/4420, 4436.
[69] S.C. 6/Hen. VIII/4436.
[70] E 310/28/164 no. 38.
[71] E 311/16 f. 201.
[72] E 310/27/158 no. 73.
[73] E 310/31/187 no. 92.
[74] C 142/726/100.
[75] See p. 129.
[76] *Tax. Eccl.* (Rec. Com.), 326; *Feud. Aids*, vi. 327.
[77] *Valor Eccl.* v. 120.
[78] S.C. 12/17/6.
[79] *Test. Ebor.* vi. 159.
[80] *L. & P. Hen. VIII*, xxi (1), p. 356.
[81] *Cal. Pat.* 1563–6, 174.
[82] C 66/1161 m. 31; B.M. Add. Chart. 39984 no. 43.
[83] C 66/1398 m. 33.
[84] C 66/1797 m. 12.
[85] C 142/553/45.
[86] *T.E.R.A.S.* ii. 55.
[87] See p. 128.

rent-payers.[88] A grant to Robert de Percy in 1299 of a Thursday market and two six-day fairs, one from 23 to 28 June and the other from 28 August to 2 September,[89] may have enhanced the local importance of Carnaby in the Middle Ages. Nothing more is known of them.

There is no certain evidence of the names or position of the open fields, but in the 1850s, long after inclosure, an area called High field lay to the north of the village on the wolds and one of its subdivisions was called Temple field. To the south of the village, on the plain, lay West and East Low fields.[90] Near Low field lay Flashdales, a name first recorded in 1306[91] and meaning 'strips of land in the marsh',[92] and the Tofts, also first mentioned in 1306, when it was arable land.[93] In 1801 there were 502 a. under crops, notably wheat (137 a.).[94]

The meadow land and common pastures probably lay in the low-lying area towards Bessingby beck. In 1218–19 it was recorded that a few years before the villeins of Robert de Percy and St. Leonard's hospital had ploughed up the common and that whoever would not plough it had been forced to pay 1s. for every acre unploughed.[95] Carnaby moor, which was probably rough grazing and carr land, lay in the extreme south of the parish, extending to the Fraisthorpe boundary, and there was apparently a substantial amount of furze and heathland, some perhaps on the wold slopes.[96] From about 1520 until at least 1583 the lord of the manor paid 3s. 4d. a year to the vicar for the tithe of whins growing in the areas known as Eastermore Rowgham and Westmore.[97] Sir George Strickland (1729–1808) and his son Sir William (1753–1834) were both great improvers,[98] and it was probably they who had substantially reduced the acreage of waste in the parish by 1849: there were in that year 1,500 a. of arable land, 350 a. of meadow and pasture, 60 a. of woodland, and 90 a. of waste.[99]

Some inclosure had taken place in the Middle Ages. In 1306 Norman of Carnaby reserved to the prior of Bridlington the tithes of a new inclosure, called Sandwath, which he had made 'in the field of Carnaby... on the east side abutting upon that arable land called le Toftes',[1] and in the same year Robert de Percy granted that 'the new inclosure which abuts upon Flaiskedaile' might remain unfenced to allow Bridlington priory to have common there for its beasts at all times of the year.[2] Large-scale inclosure probably occurred between 1716 and 1726, but no detailed evidence has been found. Between those dates the vicar's glebe and tithes were converted into a stipend, and in 1764 this was said to have been settled when the fields were inclosed.[3]

In 1783 nearly all the land in Carnaby, except for the estate of Samuel Buck, belonged to Sir George Strickland.[4] The bulk of it was let to five substantial tenant-farmers. In 1839 the Stricklands had six tenants who each paid over £100 rent a year, and twelve who each paid between 15s. and £11.[5] In 1851 there were 3 farms of 300 a. or over, 2 of 200 a. to 300 a., and 2 of 150 a. to 200 a.[6] The number of large farms has subsequently changed little. Throughout the 19th and 20th centuries there have been 6 or 7, with 2 or 3 smaller ones. Between 1929 and 1933 the number of small farms increased to 8 and by 1937 to 9,[7] presumably as a result of the acquisition of about 400 a. of land in the south of the parish by the East Riding county council in 1921 for use as smallholdings.[8]

In the 19th century there were, as elsewhere, many itinerant farm-lads in the village. In 1884 the vicar estimated that out of a population of 190 there were 30–40 of them. He reported that many farmers had failed or given up their leases. Their farms were either taken in hand by the landlord, who settled a hind at the farm-house, or taken over by men of a lower social class, often dissenters in religion.[9]

There was a limeburner in 1858 and a brickmaker between 1897 and 1909.[10] A windmill is mentioned in 1368[11] and 1544,[12] and in 1573 there was a windmill and a water-mill,[13] the latter presumably situated on Bessingby beck.

LOCAL GOVERNMENT. The assize of bread and ale was claimed by the lord of the manor in the late 13th century.[14]

Churchwardens' accounts survive for 1744–98 and 1861–95, and constables' accounts for 1743–97 and 1799–1863.[15] In the earlier period there were three churchwardens. Throughout the 18th century the constables' rate usually varied between 1d. and 3d., producing from £3 to £8, and in 1800–35 it was generally between 3d. and 5d. The upkeep of the village well was a recurring expense in both periods. Rates of 6d. in 1812 and 5¾d. in 1830 each raised £50–60, about half of which was spent on new wells.

There are also surviving overseers' accounts for 1799–1836 and vestry minutes for 1822–36.[16] The select vestry consisted of eight members, mostly substantial farmers, seven of whom served for the whole period. In 1799 two poor-rates of 1s. 1½d. in the pound raised a total of £127, which was used mainly to provide weekly relief in money and kind. Subsequently the yearly rate varied from 6d. to 1s. 5d. After 1822 13–16 people were normally given relief each year, but in 1824 23 and in 1825 19 were relieved. The roundsman system was also employed.

---

[88] V.C.H. Yorks. ii. 287.
[89] Cal. Chart. R. 1257–1300, 478.
[90] O.S. Map 6" (1854).
[91] Bridlington Charty. 175.
[92] P.N.E.R. Yorks. 86.
[93] Bridlington Charty. 176.
[94] 1801 Crop Returns.
[95] Rolls of Justices in Eyre for Yorks. (Selden Soc. lvi), pp. xxviii, 394.
[96] Yorks. Fines, i. 112; ii. 38.
[97] Select 16th-Cent. Causes in Tithe (Y.A.S. Rec. Ser. cxiv), 134–8.
[98] J. T. Ward, E. Yorks. Landed Estates in the 19th Cent. (E. Yorks. Loc. Hist. Ser. xxiii), 18–19.
[99] B.I.H.R., TA. 277AS.
[1] Bridlington Charty. 176.
[2] Ibid. 175.
[3] See p. 129. The vicar attributed inclosure to an Act of Parliament, perhaps because inclosure Acts were commonplace in his own time.
[4] E.R.R.O., Land Tax, 1783.
[5] E.R.R.O., DDX/3/3, 14.
[6] H.O. 107/2367.
[7] Directories.
[8] Regy. of Deeds, 234/562/466.
[9] B.I.H.R., Bp. V. 1884/Ret.
[10] Directories.
[11] C 135/198/12.
[12] Yorks. Fines, i. 112.
[13] Ibid. ii. 38.
[14] J.I. 1/1110 m. 154.
[15] E.R.R.O., PR. 2311–4.
[16] Ibid. 2315–6.

KILHAM: East Street

BRIDLINGTON: the harbour and sea-front, from the south

FLAMBOROUGH: the Primitive Methodist chapel

GARTON ON THE WOLDS CHURCH: the west front

In 1829, for example, three men were given from 10d. to 1s. 6d. a day 'for [their] work in going round the town'.

Carnaby joined the Bridlington union in 1836, and the parish poorhouse was sold three years later.[17]

CHURCH. Carnaby church is first mentioned between 1148 and 1153, when it was granted by Robert de Percy to Bridlington priory.[18] In the 12th and 13th centuries it had two dependent chapels, at Fraisthorpe and Auburn, but these later became separate curacies.[19] A vicarage was ordained before 1268.[20]

The advowson belonged to the priory. In 1346–7, however, Walter of Heslerton, lord of the manor, claimed that William de Percy had presented in Richard I's reign, and that the advowson had consequently descended directly to Walter's wife Eustacia. Judgement was given in favour of the priory,[21] which retained the advowson until the Dissolution.[22] The Crown presented in 1556.[23] A grant to the archbishop of York in 1558[24] presumably lapsed on the accession of Elizabeth I, and in 1568 and 1600 the Crown again presented.[25] In 1609 the advowson was granted to Francis Philips and Richard Moore;[26] they probably sold it to Sir Walter Strickland, who held it in 1635 and whose son Sir William presented in 1637.[27] In 1661–2, however, a presentation was made by Robert Wittie.[28] The advowson subsequently descended with the manor until 1951, when it was transferred to the archbishop of York.[29]

The vicarage was worth £10 in 1291[30] and 1428,[31] and £7 in 1525–6.[32] In 1535 its net value was £7 8s. 10d.[33] and it was worth £40 in 1650[34] and 1726.[35] In 1816 the living was augmented with £200 from Queen Anne's Bounty,[36] and the average net income in 1829–31 was £44.[37] A further £200 augmentation was received in 1829,[38] and by 1857 the value of the living was £53.[39] Its value, including Fraisthorpe and Auburn, was said in 1884 to have recently fallen to £90 net, and by 1894 it was about £60.[40]

In the post-Dissolution leases of the rectory the tithes of the former lands of St. Leonard's hospital were reserved to the vicarage.[41] They contributed more than two-thirds of the value of the living in 1685.[42] The vicar still received them in 1716, but by 1726 they and the other perquisites of the vicarage had been converted into a stipend of £40 a year,[43] probably at the inclosure which had apparently taken place in the mean-time.[44] Until then there had been 2 bovates of glebe land and a vicarage house and cottage, all mentioned in 1535.[45]

There was a guild at Carnaby in 1521,[46] and in 1571 a 'guild house' was included in a Crown grant.[47] A building of that description was mentioned as late as 1723.[48] Two torches were left to the church in 1420 by Joan Mounceaux, wife of the lord of Barmston manor.[49]

The incumbents of Carnaby have frequently held other livings. In 1567 the vicar was also rector of Burghwallis (Yorks. W.R.),[50] and in 1743 he was also curate of Fraisthorpe and Bessingby and vicar of Boynton.[51] Subsequently the living was usually held with Boynton and Fraisthorpe and by 1851 it had been united with the latter. The vicar lived at Boynton throughout this period and often had an assistant curate at Carnaby.[52] There was an assistant curate in 1900.[53] Fraisthorpe was separated from Carnaby in 1929,[54] and in 1950 the living ceased to be held with Boynton.[55] In 1968 the vicar of Carnaby also held the living of, and resided at, Bessingby.

One noteworthy incumbent was John Otes (vicar 1568–1600), who was involved in many disputes with his parishioners.[56] In 1575, for instance, it was alleged that against their consent he had appointed his son as parish clerk and that the latter had unlawfully conducted a burial.[57] In 1583 he was in dispute over the tithes of whins, which his parishioners claimed were not due in kind since for the previous 60 years they had been commuted into a yearly money payment.[58] In 1575 his understanding of Latin was said to be mediocre, although he catechized diligently and was reported to be pious (*religiosus*).[59]

Incumbents during the interregnum were Peter Clark (vicar 1637–46), who was ejected from Kirby Underdale in 1662,[60] Caleb Wilkinson (vicar from 1646 probably until 1650),[61] and Jeremiah Garthwaite (who was the 'preaching minister' from 1650 to 1661).[62]

In 1743 a service was held in the church once every Sunday. The vicar also held a service at Boynton, 'to which several of my parishioners resort,

---

[17] Registry of Deeds, Beverley, FK/214/242; *3rd Rep. Poor Law Com.* 167.
[18] *E.Y.C.* xi, p. 115.
[19] See p. 206.
[20] *Reg. Giffard* (Sur. Soc. cix), 191, 210.
[21] C.P. 40/349 m. 216.
[22] B.I.H.R., C.P., E. 94; *Fasti Parochiales*, iii. 18.
[23] *Fasti Parochiales*, iii. 19.
[24] *Cal. Pat.* 1557–8, 420.
[25] *Fasti Parochiales*, iii. 19.
[26] C 66/1797 m. 12.
[27] *Miscellanea*, i (Y.A.S. Rec. Ser. lxi), 152.
[28] *Fasti Parochiales*, iii. 20.
[29] York Dioc. Regy., Orders in Council 709.
[30] *Tax. Eccl.* (Rec. Com.), 326.
[31] *Feud. Aids*, vi. 327.
[32] *Y.A.J.* xxiv. 65.
[33] *Valor Eccl.* (Rec. Com), v. 122.
[34] *T.E.R.A.S.* ii. 55.
[35] B.I.H.R., TER. J. Carnaby 1726.
[36] Hodgson, *Q.A.B.* 436.
[37] *Rep. Com. Eccl. Revenues*, 924.
[38] Lawton, *Rer. Eccles. Dioc. Ebor.* 293–4.
[39] B.I.H.R., TER. J. Carnaby 1857.
[40] Ibid., Bp. V. 1884/Ret.; Bp. V. 1894/Ret.
[41] E 315/408 f. 6; C 66/1161 m. 31; *L. & P. Hen. VIII*, xxi (1), p. 356.
[42] B.I.H.R., TER J. Carnaby 1685.
[43] Ibid. 1716, 1726.
[44] See p.128.
[45] *Valor Eccl.* v. 120.
[46] B.I.H.R., Prob. Reg. ix, f. 205.
[47] *Cal. Pat.* 1569–71, 237.
[48] Regy. of Deeds, Beverley, H/499/1010.
[49] *Test. Ebor.* i. 398.
[50] J. S. Purvis, *Tudor Par. Docs. of Dioc. York*, 24.
[51] *Herring's Visit.* i. 158.
[52] E.R.R.O., DPX/57, Carnaby, p. 6; B.I.H.R., V. 1865/Ret. 104; V. 1868/Ret. 100; V. 1871/Ret. 66; V. 1877/Ret.; Bp. V. 1884/Ret.; Bp. V. 1894/Ret.
[53] Ibid., Bp. V. 1900/Ret. 74.
[54] York Dioc. Regy., Orders in Council 593.
[55] Ex inf. the Revd. E. Dancy, Rudston, 1970.
[56] *Select 16th-Cent. Causes in Tithe* (Y.A.S. Rec. Ser. cxiv), 134.
[57] Purvis, *Tudor Par. Docs. of Dioc. York*, 191.
[58] *Sel. Causes in Tithe*, 134–8.
[59] Purvis, *Tudor Par. Docs. Dioc. York*, 120.
[60] *Calamy Revised*, ed. A. G. Matthews, 118.
[61] *Walker Revised*, ed. A. G. Matthews, 400.
[62] *Fasti Parochiales*, iii. 20.

which has always been a custom here'. Communion was administered three times a year and was received by about twenty people.[63] In 1764 a service was held at Carnaby every Sunday morning and at Boynton in the afternoon. Communion was administered four times a year but the number commonly receiving it had fallen to twelve.[64] By 1851 services were held in the morning and afternoon alternately.[65] Communion was administered six times a year in 1865 and eight in 1868, though the average number of communicants fell from 14 to 9 in those years. In 1871 it was administered monthly, in 1884 every six weeks, with 6–8 people receiving, and in 1936 on alternate Sundays.[66] In 1968 one service was held each Sunday.

The church of ST. JOHN THE BAPTIST consists of chancel, nave, south aisle, and west tower. It is built mainly of stone with some flint and cobble, but parts of the structure have been rebuilt in brick. Only the circular font, which has carved ornament within a pattern of lozenges and a cable moulding above,[67] has survived from the Norman church. The earliest parts of the existing fabric, the south aisle, the aisle arcade, and the tower arch, are of 13th-century date. There may have formerly been a north aisle, too, but it no longer exists. The present north wall of the nave is of brick, probably of the 18th century. There are two paired lancet windows and a single lancet in the south aisle. One of the two-light windows contains an early example of plate tracery, made by piercing the spandrel with an inverted trefoil. The aisle arcade consists of five pointed arches supported by octagonal piers, three of the moulded capitals having nail-head ornament. The most westerly bay of the aisle has been converted into an entrance passage into the church, possibly when the south porch was removed c. 1830.[68] The arch of this bay is separated from the rest of the arcade by a short length of wall, suggesting an extension of the church westwards in the 13th century. The arch responds match those of the tower arch; this arch is all that survives of the original 13th-century tower. The present tower, which was built in the 15th century, is of three stages, topped by an embattled parapet. It contains Perpendicular windows at the belfry stage and a west window with a narrow embattled transom.

In the late 16th century and for much of the 17th the nave and, especially, the chancel were in disrepair.[69] Restoration began around 1680[70] and in 1719 the chancel repairs were said to be almost completed.[71] The chancel was wholly rebuilt of brick, 'in the coarsest style',[72] and is now small and plain, with a wooden ceiling. It contained a small east window which is now blocked up. The chancel arch, which is unusually wide and low, may be of 13th-century origin but the mouldings of its responds have been obliterated, perhaps during the rebuilding of the chancel. At the same period or subsequently the north wall of the nave was completely rebuilt in brick and the south aisle wall was extensively patched in the same material.[73] In 1830 more repairs were carried out, the south porch was probably removed, the brick clerestory was added, the aisle was reroofed, and new square-headed windows were inserted in the north wall.[74] In the nave these windows were later replaced by traceried Gothic windows, but one still survives in the chancel. In 1966 the slates of the roof were replaced by tiles, and a new ceiling was put into the nave.[75]

Two probably 13th-century grave slabs with incised crosses are built into the wall of the aisle.[76] There is an incised inscription on the second arcade pier from the east marking the burial place of Walter Uppiby. This is said to be of 13th- or early-14th-century date,[77] and the Uppiby family certainly held land in Carnaby in the early 14th century.[78] A wall plaque in the nave commemorates Isabella Humphrey (d. 1910), mistress of the school in Carnaby for 37 years. The 19th-century Gothic pulpit is of stone and highly ornate.

In 1552 there were three bells.[79] There were still three in 1968, two dated 1630 and one 1693; one of the former was made by John Conyers.[80] In 1855 the later bell was badly cracked but it was restored in 1892 through the efforts of the vicar, who raised funds and brought over a German craftsman to carry out the work.[81]

The plate consists of a silver cup and base-metal paten and flagon. The cup, which was given by Elizabeth Strickland in 1685, was made in 1683 in York by Mark Gill.[82] The registers date from 1653 and are complete.[83]

NONCONFORMITY. In 1676 eleven dissenters were recorded [84] but it was said in 1743 that there was none.[85] The Methodists had 16 members at Carnaby in 1787 and from 10 to 13 in 1788–91.[86] Houses were licensed for worship in 1790 and 1805.[87] In 1851 a cottage was used as a Wesleyan meeting-place and attendance was put at 25.[88] In 1865 and 1868 private houses were said to be used by the Methodists, including Primitives. In 1868 the vicar remarked that 'most of my parishioners are dissenters'.[89] The Wesleyan chapel was built in 1876.[90] It has a red-brick front with stone dressings, and was deregistered in 1964.[91]

---

[63] *Herring's Visit.* i. 158.
[64] B.I.H.R., Bp. V. 1764/Ret. 116.
[65] H.O. 129/24/524.
[66] B.I.H.R., V. 1865/Ret. 104; V. 1868/Ret. 100; V. 1871/Ret. 66; Bp. V. 1884/Ret.; Bp. V. 1936/Ret. 264.
[67] *T.E.R.A.S.* x. 111.
[68] M. Prickett, *Hist. Ch. Bridlington* (1831 edn.), pl. 15.
[69] B.I.H.R., Churches index.
[70] E.R.R.O., DPX/57, Carnaby, p. 2.
[71] B.I.H.R., Churches index.
[72] *Y.A.J.* xxvi. 290–1.
[73] In 1968 the south wall was still in poor structural condition.
[74] E.R.R.O., DPX/57, Carnaby, p. 2.
[75] Ex inf. Mrs. D. Thompson, Carnaby, 1968; *Hull Daily Mail*, 13 Oct. 1965.
[76] *Y.A.J.* xlii. 335, 340.
[77] Ibid. xxi. 186.
[78] See p. 127.
[79] *Inventories of Ch. Goods*, 27.
[80] *Y.A.J.* ii. 216.
[81] E.R.R.O., DPX/57, Carnaby, pp. 17–18.
[82] *Yorks. Ch. Plate*, i. 234.
[83] The registers of baptisms and burials to 1812 and marriages to 1837 are in E.R.R.O.
[84] Bodl. MS. Tanner 150, ff. 27 sqq.
[85] *Herring's Visit.* i. 158.
[86] E.R.R.O., MRP/1/7.
[87] B.I.H.R., DMH. 1790/17; G.R.O. Worship Returns, Vol. v, no. 1911.
[88] H.O. 129/24/524.
[89] B.I.H.R., V. 1865/Ret. 104; V. 1868/Ret. 100.
[90] Date on building.
[91] G.R.O. Worship Reg. no. 23542. It is said to have closed c. 1950: ex inf. Mr. Redshaw, Carnaby, 1969.

EDUCATION. The vicar of Carnaby was licensed to teach in 1563.[92] There is no later reference to a school until 1819, when 25 to 30 children, 10 of whom were from Bessingby and 7 from Boynton, were taught at the expense of their parents.[93] In 1835, when 18 boys and 7 girls attended, the school was partly supported by an endowment of £5 a year from the vicar, Francis Simpson.[94] In 1856 the school was said to have been built by Sir William Strickland (1753–1834).[95] In 1865 it was supported almost entirely by the vicar,[96] and in 1868, when there were about 30 pupils, it also received a subscription from the assistant curate and £10 from Sir George Cholmley.[97] In 1871 a new school was built to accommodate 70 children, for the use of Boynton and Fraisthorpe parishes as well as Carnaby.[98] A special rate of 3d. in the pound at all three places raised about £102 in 1871 to meet expenses.[99]

It was decided in 1879 to levy a voluntary 1d. rate to support the school, which was also to receive £5 a year from Sir Charles Strickland[1] as well as quarterage.[2] In 1879–80 the school also received its first annual government grant.[3] In 1901 the average attendance was 52, and it subsequently varied between 45 and 74; in 1938 it was 59.[4] There was a steady decline in the number of children on the roll from 62 in 1952 to 20 in 1965.[5] The school was closed in 1967 and most of the remaining 17 children were transferred to Burton Agnes.[6] It still stood in 1968.

An evening school was held at Carnaby from c. 1856 by the vicar's daughter, Mary Simpson.[7]

CHARITIES FOR THE POOR. The Poor's Money, or Stock, consisted in 1823 of £25, part of a benefaction of £50 given by unknown persons, which was in the hands of a farmer. The remainder of the £50 had been lost 'many years' before. The interest was regularly distributed by the overseers among widows and other poor people, 'being such as endeavour to keep off the parish.[8] The charity was, however, lost in 1842 when the principal was spent on a pump, which was described as 'of far more benefit to the farmers than to the poor'.[9]

The poor of Carnaby also shared with those of Boynton the proceeds of Strickland's charity.[10]

FILEY

Growth of the Town, p. 134. Domestic Buildings, p. 136. Manors and other Estates, p. 138. Agriculture, p. 140. Fishing and Shipping, p. 141. Market and Fairs, p. 142. Industry, p. 143. The Resort, p. 143. Social Institutions, p. 145. Public Services, p. 145. Local Government, p. 146. Churches, p. 147. Roman Catholicism, p. 149. Protestant Nonconformity, p. 149. Education, p. 150. Charities for the Poor, p. 151.

THE fishing village of Filey began to attract visitors in the early 19th century and it quickly became a fashionable resort.[1] The town did not grow to the same extent as Bridlington, however, and its commercial development has been more restrained. The old village was for a time physically separate from the streets of 'New Filey', which were laid out to the south of it, and the town remained small and compact until well into the 20th century. One of the most distinctive features of the place is Filey Brigg, a promontory of rocks, mostly covered by the tides, which juts out from the headland known as Carr Nase. In the lee of the Brigg are the sheltered water of Filey Bay and the sands that stretch southwards as far as Speeton cliffs, while to the north-west of Carr Nase are the high cliffs that continue into the North Riding.

The parish of Filey includes the townships of Gristhorpe, Lebberston, and Newbiggin, which lie entirely in the North Riding. Though this account is largely concerned with Filey itself, it also includes the three townships. The village of Filey and the 19th-century resort lay in the East Riding, but that part of Filey township north of Filey beck was transferred from the North to the East Riding only in 1889.[2] Curiously the parish church stands on the north side of the beck, apart from the village. The total area of the ancient parish in 1850 was 3,312 a., of which Gristhorpe accounted for 872 a., Lebberston 1,277 a., Newbiggin 330 a., and Filey 833 a.[3] Filey's acreage was later reduced to 831 a., probably by erosion by the sea. The local government board from 1868 and the urban district council after 1895 enjoyed authority only over Filey township, but the urban district was enlarged to 2,108 a. in 1935 by the transference of 932 a. from Hunmanby, 327 a. from Muston, and 18 a. from Reighton.[4] The holiday facilities in the extended area are not physically part of the town and they are described under the parishes from which the extensions were made.[5]

The limestone and grit of the Middle Oolite which outcrop in the Brigg and in the cliffs to the north-west are covered with boulder clay over much of the parish. Numerous streams dissect the claylands in both Filey and the townships, and Gristhorpe and Lebberston extend southwards to the river Hertford in the Vale of Pickering. In Filey itself the chief streams are Filey beck and Dams Goit, which join to flow down the deep and steep-

---

[92] B.I.H.R., Schools index.
[93] *Rets. on Educ. of Poor, 1819*, 1078.
[94] *Educ. Enquiry Abstract, 1835*, 1082.
[95] Sheahan and Whellan, *Hist. York & E.R.* ii. 462.
[96] B.I.H.R., V. 1865/Ret. 104.
[97] Ibid. V. 1868/Ret. 100.
[98] Bulmer, *Dir. E. Yorks.* (1892), 159; *Rets. rel. Elem. Educ. 1871*, 474.
[99] E.R.R.O., PR. 2312.
[1] Ibid. SLB. Manager's min. bk., p. 1.
[2] Ibid., p. 4.
[3] *Rep. of Educ. Cttee. of Council, 1879–80* [C. 2562-1], H.C., p. 724 (1880), xxii.
[4] E.R.R.O., SLB. Manager's min. bk., p. 73; *Bd. of Educ. List 21* (H.M.S.O.).
[5] E.R.R.O., SLB. School reg. 1936–67, p. 173.
[6] Ibid. Fifteen children were transferred to Burton Agnes and two to Bridlington.
[7] See p. 29.
[8] *9th Rep. Char. Com.* 733.
[9] Char. Com. files.
[10] See p. 29.
[1] This article was written in 1970.
[2] E.R.R.O., LGO/1.
[3] O.S. Map 6" (1854).
[4] *Census*, 1931.
[5] See pp. 230, 278, 305.

sided Church Ravine to the sea. The stream in the ravine was culverted in 1871.[6] On the southern township boundary another stream reaches the sea in a smaller but well-marked ravine. Much of Filey township is less than 150 ft. above sea-level, but the ground rises gradually north of Filey beck to over 200 ft. at the limestone cliffs, and the cliffs reach 275 ft. in Gristhorpe. The boulder clay cliffs facing Filey Bay are under 100 ft. high; the construction of sea defences in the later 19th century has prevented further erosion there.

The wet and boggy character of the low-lying part of the township in early times is suggested by the place-name, for Filey was probably the 'cotton grass clearing'; the name is a combination of Anglian and Scandinavian elements. 'Brigg' probably derives from the Scandinavian 'jetty' or 'landing-place'.[7] There is no evidence to support the suggestion that the Romans constructed an artificial breakwater at the Brigg, but there was a Roman signal station on Carr Nase. It dated from the 4th century and showed signs of having been destroyed by burning.[8] Five large socketed stones, which probably supported the watch-tower, were placed in Crescent Gardens and later moved to the grounds of the public library, in Southdene.[9] Traces of possible Roman roads have been found under both the Scarborough and the Muston roads.[10]

Shingle and stone have been taken from the shore and from the Brigg since at least the 12th century, when Ralph de Neville granted Bridlington priory the right to take stone from his quarry at Filey, with free access over the rocks at 'le Hok' and elsewhere.[11] Most of the material has been used for road-making and for building, but in 1835 two Roman-cement manufacturers of Sculcoates, near Hull, were authorized to remove stones called 'oolite doggers and basalts' from the shore in Filey, Hunmanby, and Reighton.[12] Stone from the Brigg was used during the 19th and early 20th centuries at Bridlington harbour, Scarborough, Rudston, and Hunmanby,[13] for example, as well as Filey, and such depredations encouraged erosion in the bay. When sea walls were built to protect the cliffs below the town, much of the local stone was used,[14] and gravel was still taken in the early 20th century.[15]

Filey village lay alongside Church Ravine, with access to the shore down the ravine and also along a road descending the cliffs just south of the village. Only two roads lead inland, one south-westwards towards Muston and Hunmanby, the other north-westwards through Filey's townships and on towards the Vale of Pickering. The latter road divides at Gristhorpe, a branch leading along the coast to Scarborough. The hamlets all lay close to the main road: Newbiggin is now represented only by two isolated farms but Gristhorpe and Lebberston are fair-sized villages. The railway from Seamer Junction to Filey was opened in 1846; it passes through all the townships and there was a station at Gisthorpe, closed in 1959.[16] The line from Bridlington to Filey was opened in 1847.

Filey was one of the larger villages in the wapentake in the Middle Ages and in 1377 there were 165 poll-tax payers.[17] The poverty of the fishing community is suggested by the hearth-tax returns of the 1670s. Only 14 households were charged and as many as 35 exempted in 1670; the number of pauper households, moreover, was not stated that year but its size is indicated by a total of 77 households of all kinds in the return of 1672. Of the 17 households charged in 1674 8 had only one hearth each, 7 had 2, one had 3, and one had four.[18] There were reported to be about 120 families in Filey in 1743[19] and 105 in 1764.[20]

The population was 505 in 1801, and still only

---

[6] See p. 147. [7] *P.N.E.R. Yorks.* (E.P.N.S.), 111.
[8] Mary Kitson Clark, *Gaz. of Roman Remains in E. Yorks.* 82.
[9] Filey U.D.C. Offices, U.D.C. mins. 1944, pp. 1478–9.
[10] *Y.A.J.* xxxiv. 99–100.
[11] *Bridlington Charty.* 80.
[12] E.R.R.O., DDHU/9/81.
[13] *Filey Post*, 8 Apr. 1905; see below, pp. 229, 315.
[14] E.R.R.O., DDHU/9/83.
[15] Hunmanby Par. Counc. Rec., Scrapbk. p. 73.
[16] K. Hoole, *Regional Hist. of Rlys. of Gt. Brit.* iv (*The North-East*), 58. [17] E 179/202/62 m. 14.
[18] E 179/205/504, 514, 521. [19] *Herring's Visit.* i. 217.
[20] B.I.H.R., Bp. V. 1764/Ret. 187.

FILEY 1970

KEY

1. Council Offices (formerly Cliff Cottage)
2. Former council offices
3. Police Station
4. Post Office
5. Fire Station
6. Pumping Station (water)
7. Coble Landing
8. Lifeboat House
9. Public Library
10. Pavilion Theatre
11. Sun Lounge
12. Coastguard Station
13. Trinity Methodist Church
14. Ebenezer Methodist Church
15. Albert Hall
16. Site of Wesleyan chapel
17. Church Hall (former Infants' School)
18. Former Wesleyan School
19. Site of Vicarage
20. North Cliff Villa (now Newland House)
21. South Cliff Villas and former Convent School
22. Clarence Place
23. Cliff House
24. Rutland Terrace
25. Ackworth House (former Spa Saloon)
26. Downcliff House
27. Royal Crescent Hotel
28. Foord's Hotel
29. Site of Royal Hotel
30. Spring Row
31. Site of Mosey's Yard
32. Site of cross

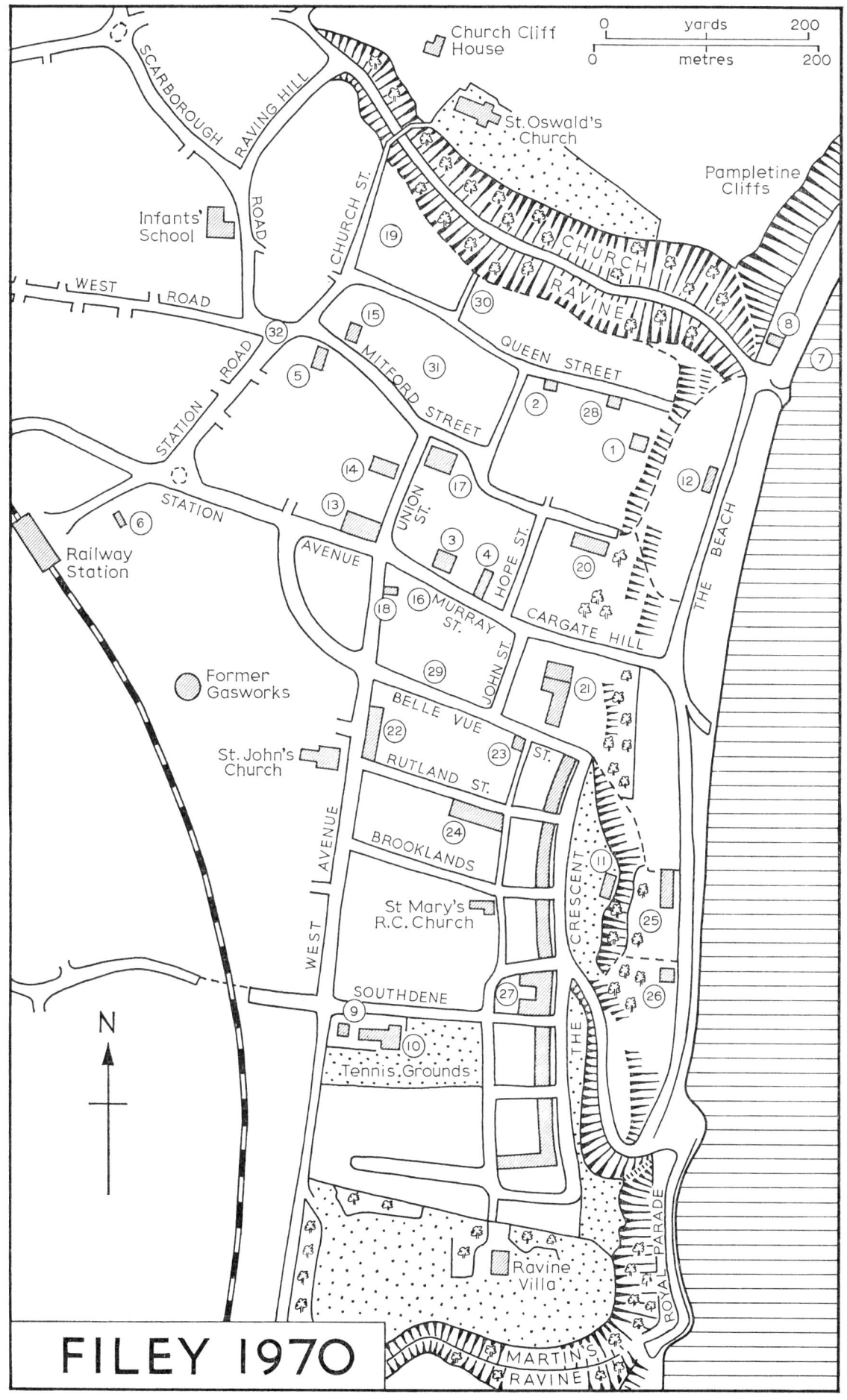

579 in 1811 when the growth of the resort had yet to begin. In 1821 there were 773 inhabitants but only about 30 were added by 1831. The development of New Filey is reflected in the rise to 1,231 in 1841 and 2,267 in 1871, with an average inter-censal increase of about 370. The rate of increase slackened in the 1870s and 1880s, but the population rose by 522 in the 1890s to 3,003 in 1901.[21] In 1931 the population was 3,733, including about 200 in the areas which were to be transferred to Filey in 1935. By 1951 the population was as high as 4,765, and it was 4,703 in 1961.[22]

Gristhorpe had a population of 129 in 1801. It rose to 217 in 1831 and subsequently was usually about 200, reaching 235 in 1961. At Lebberston there were 126 inhabitants in 1801. The population topped 170 in 1831 and 1851 but thereafter varied between 110 and 157; in 1961 it was 128.[23]

GROWTH OF THE TOWN. The old village of Filey lay mostly along a single main street (known by 1850 as King Street, in 1890 in part as Queen Street, and now wholly as Queen Street),[24] which ran back from the cliff top just south of Church Ravine. The ravine marked the end of the crofts and garths on the north side of the street, and on the south side the garths reached as far as a winding back lane (Back Street in 1850, Chapel Street, Mitford Street, and Alma Terrace in 1890, and now wholly Mitford Street). The back lane continued, later known as Black Cliff Head and Cliff Top, until it returned to the main street at its eastern end. By 1791 houses were built almost continuously along both sides of the street and also along one side of what later became known as Church Street, which lay across the western end of the main street.

A back lane (now Ravine Hill) led behind Church Street down into the ravine. At its south end Church Street opened into a triangular open space where the medieval market was held,[25] and at its north end a foot-bridge gave access to the church, across the ravine. There may have been a bridge at that point as early as 1454–5, when 'Kirkbridge' was mentioned.[26] A stone bridge there was washed away during a storm in 1857[27] and later replaced by an iron one. Beyond the bridge the only building apart from the church was Church Cliff House, the rectorial farm-house; earthworks and foundations near by suggest that there was an earlier house on the site.

In 1791 an alley led from the north side of the main street to a footpath (later called Sand Hill), which ran down the cliff to a foot-bridge over the beck and so to the sea-shore. A second alley (later Spring Row) led from the street to the ravine. On the south side of the street a narrow lane (Bettons Lane in 1850, Reynolds Street by 1890) led through to the back lane. There were, however, few buildings in any of the lanes in 1791. It was from the back lane that 'the road to the sands',[28] later called Carr Gate (now Union Street, Murray Street, and Cargate Hill), led down to a wide landing-place at the sea-shore, apparently the chief landing-place for the village in 1791.

During the earlier 19th century the layout and extent of the village changed little and it remained for a time physically separate from the streets of 'New Filey', which began to be developed to the south in the 1830s. One of the most striking changes in the village between 1791 and 1850 was the building of rows of small cottages, no doubt mainly for fishermen, in yards opening on to both sides of the main street, and also behind Church Street. One such terrace was in Spring Row, and on either side of the street were openings called Mosey's Yard, that on the south side containing 26 cottages.[29] Many of the fishermen's cottages had tan-houses, bark-houses, or beating chambers, where nets were treated to harden them.[30]

During the same period a few houses in the main street were rebuilt as lodging-houses, one at the seaward end of the street before 1840, for example.[31] Several 'villas' and other houses were also built around the village: some in the back lanes, like Rose and Cliff Cottages and the house later known as North Cliff Villa, others on the roads leading out of the village, like Grove Villa, on the Scarborough road. Several of these cottages, overlooking the sea, were described in 1828 as 'recently erected in the true Devonian style of domestic architecture'.[32] The site of North Cliff Villa was acquired by William Voase, a Hull wine merchant, in 1825 and the house was sold, after his death, in 1845.[33]

The first buildings erected in the resort of New Filey were a pair of houses on the cliff top, later known as South Cliff Villas, and a bath house on the corner of Sand Road and a lane leading towards Muston: these were built before 1833 by H. J. Shepherd, who was said in 1828 to be converting a field into a garden.[34] The lane to Muston later became Slea Lane, but it was sometimes known as Bentley's Lane; in 1837–8 Henry Bentley, a West Riding brewer, built Ravine Villa, with its lodge, stables, and grounds, overlooking the stream at the southern extremity of the township.[35] The systematic development of the area, however, was largely the work of J. W. Unett, a Birmingham solicitor.[36] In 1835 Unett bought 11 a. of the former Newton estate, together with an adjoining 5 a. on which South Cliff Villas and the bath house stood,[37] and a year later he acquired another 4 a. immediately

---

[21] *V.C.H. Yorks.* iii. 489.
[22] *Census.* The figure of 4,549 for 1921 was inflated by the presence of visitors.   [23] *V.C.H. Yorks.* iii. 519; *Census.*
[24] E.R.R.O., IA Filey, inclosure map, 1791; O.S. Map 6" (1854); 25" (1891). There is a reference to King St. as early as 1776: E.R.R O., DDX/130/1. This and some other name changes subsequently mentioned were made in 1891: *Filey Post,* 14 Mar. 1891.   [25] See p.143.
[26] B.I.H.R., Prob. Reg. ii, f. 311. For 'Churchbridge' in 1690 see E.R.R.O., DDHU/10/1 (89).
[27] *Filey Chronicle,* 9 Aug. 1857. Illus. in J. Cole, *Hist. and Antiquities of Filey* (1828), facing p. 41.
[28] So called in deeds of the 1840s (when New Filey was beginning to be developed), which also sometimes called it Sand Road.

[29] E.R.R.O., DDX/130/22, 23 etc.
[30] Ibid. /6, 39; Registry of Deeds, Beverley, IA/38/52. Later, red or tanned water from barked nets caused a nuisance on footpaths: e.g. *Filey Post,* 20 July 1901.
[31] Regy. of Deeds, FP/249/256.
[32] Cole, *Hist. Filey,* 124.
[33] Regy. of Deeds, DU/180/231; GF/337/386.
[34] Ibid. ET/243/282; Cole, *Hist. Filey,* 126.
[35] Regy. of Deeds, FE/245/241; GK/91/104; E.R.R.O., DDUN/Box 3; White, *Dir. E. & N.R. Yorks.* (1840), 381.
[36] The development of his estate may be traced in E.R.R.O., DDUN. These records were uncalendared in 1970 and references to the registered deeds are therefore often given here.
[37] Regy. of Deeds, EZ/350/336; see below, p. 138.

to the west and 15 a. to the south.³⁸ He thus owned most of the land between Sand Road on the north and the site of Bentley's villa on the south, stretching back from the sea front to the Muston lane.

Within a few years new streets had been laid out and plots were being sold and built up. The principal street, now the Crescent, ran along the cliff top overlooking the bay; behind it were Back Road (now South Crescent Road), North (now Belle Vue) Street, Middle (now Rutland) Street, South Street (now part of Brooklands), and John Street. The old Sand Road, from the bath house to John Street, was renamed Murray Street. From 1837 onwards Unett sold various building plots, sometimes with houses built or erecting, and builders of Scarborough and Bridlington, as well as Filey, shared in the development.³⁹ The houses in the streets behind the sea front were modest, but already in the 1840s the first block of the Crescent was being built; several of the impressive houses there were put up by John Barry, architect, and W. E. Woodall, both of Scarborough.⁴⁰

By 1850 the total extent of Unett's development was still only limited. Most continuously built over was the block of land between Murray Street, North Street, John Street, and Slea Lane, where, besides many small houses, there were the Royal Hotel, a Methodist chapel, the baths, and a school. Several houses there were built on land bought from Unett by Henry Spink.⁴¹ Only the centre of the Crescent had been developed, and in the streets behind there was little more than Rutland Terrace,⁴² in Middle Street, Clarence Place, in Slea Lane, and Cliff House, in North Street.⁴³ Cliff House was built by Francis Smith, probably in 1842.⁴⁴

The further growth of Filey was doubtless encouraged by the opening of the railway lines in 1846–7, giving a connexion with York and with Hull.⁴⁵ The station was built near the Muston road, conveniently placed for both the old village and the resort; by 1850 a new road (Station Road by 1890, later Station Avenue) had been made to give more direct access to New Filey from the station.

Building in the Crescent continued in the 1850s, when J. W. Unett (d. 1856) and his sons John and George sold more houses and plots.⁴⁶ By 1864 the Crescent was nearly complete, with more than 30 houses⁴⁷ and the Crescent, later the Royal Crescent, Hotel. The hotel was built in 1853 by J. W. Unett for a lessee to move into the following year.⁴⁸ The northernmost block of the Crescent was put up in 1850–1 by Henry Spink,⁴⁹ who also built three houses behind it, in North Street, in 1853.⁵⁰ The land between the Crescent and the cliffs was laid out by J. W. Unett as North and South Crescent Gardens, and these were used by the owners and occupiers of all the property in the Crescent.⁵¹

By 1861 the Belle Vue Hotel, at the north end of the Crescent, and South Crescent Villa (later Lodge), at the south end, had been built.⁵² Behind the south end a pair of houses known as St. Martin's Villas was built in 1874 and next to it a house was put up in 1879 for A. T. Clay, a Rastrick (Yorks. W.R.) businessman.⁵³ The Crescent itself was completed only in 1890, when houses forming the southern end were built by Edwin Martin, a Huddersfield man who a year before had bought the Ravine Villa estate.⁵⁴

By 1890, then, the whole of the Crescent had been built, as well as several groups of houses immediately behind in North, Rutland, and Melville Streets and in South Crescent. Wilkes Street (later Unett Street, now Southdene) had also been laid out. For the most part, however, the back streets were not built up, and along Slea Lane (i.e. the lane to Muston) the only houses to have appeared since 1850 were the scattered rows of Ravine Terrace and Ravine Bank, at the south end, and Windsor Terrace and Clarence Parade,⁵⁵ further north. St. John's church, opened in 1871 to meet the needs of New Filey, stood on the west side of Slea Lane. The period 1850–90 also saw the building of more than a dozen houses facing the sea at the foot of the cliffs below the Crescent.⁵⁶ They included Downcliff House and Ackworth House, the latter built as a baths saloon before 1863.⁵⁷ Downcliff House was apparently built by John Unett for his own use.⁵⁸ Other houses were built in a similar situation, below the cliffs on the north side of Carr Gate. Among them were William Graburn's Sea Breeze Villa, built c. 1860, three cottages which Graburn built near by, Belvedere, and Kingston Cottage.⁵⁹

By 1890, too, the physical separation of the old village and New Filey had ended. Building began in Union Street in the 1850s. During the 1870s one side of the street was completely built up, including two large Methodist chapels, and the terraces of Hope Street⁶⁰ provided a link between the old back lane of the village and Murray Street. More terraces and groups of houses appeared in the back lane, Chapel Street, and Alma Terrace; others were

---

³⁸ Ibid. FA/172/188; /352/367; /353/368; Unett actually bought an undivided six sevenths of the 15 a. but it was partitioned in 1849: ibid. GP/349/376.
³⁹ Ibid. FH/148/139; FK/340/384; FL/321/288; FN/293/288; FP/69/64; /112/120; FX/52/69; /289/344; GC/328/391; /354/412; etc.
⁴⁰ Ibid. FS/244/284; GD/299/350; GF/77/94. See plate facing p. 256.
⁴¹ Regy. of Deeds, FH/148/139; FL/20/25; GR/236/286; /237/287.
⁴² Ibid. GH/146/142.   ⁴³ O.S. Map 6″ (1854).
⁴⁴ Regy. of Deeds, FS/48/54. Not 1824 as in F. R. Pearson, *Charlotte Brontë on the E. Yorks. Coast.* (E Yorks. Loc. Hist. Ser. vii), 22.
⁴⁵ K. A. MacMahon, *Beginnings of E. Yorks. Rlys.* (E. Yorks. Loc. Hist. Ser. iii), 12.
⁴⁶ Regy. of Deeds, HB/407/494; HD/96/139; HI/50/70; /51/71; /102/136; HY/335/406; /393/484; /394/485; IA/373/477. A monument to J. W. Unett is in the parish church.
⁴⁷ Filey U.D.C. Offices, Crescent Gdns. cttee. mins. 1854–1914.

⁴⁸ E.R.R.O., DDUN/Box 3; E. W. Pritchard, *Observations on Filey as a Watering Place*, 21.
⁴⁹ Regy. of Deeds, GS/389/493; GW/154/194.
⁵⁰ Ibid. HA/167/177; /168/178; HB/274/354.
⁵¹ E.R.R.O., DDX/34/5; Filey U.D.C. Offices, Crescent Gdns. cttee. mins. 1854–1914.
⁵² W. S. Cortis, *Hist. and Descrip. Guide to Filey*, 26.
⁵³ Filey U.D.C. Offices, loc. govt. bd. mins. 1868–81, p. 344; Regy. of Deeds, LL/78/110; /79/111; MR/351/453.
⁵⁴ Loc. govt. bd. mins. 1881–91, p. 351; Regy. of Deeds, 29/259/245 (1889); *Filey Post*, 12 July 1890; date on corner house.
⁵⁵ Clarence Parade was built c. 1881: loc. govt. bd. mins. 1881–91, p. 66.
⁵⁶ O.S. Map 25″ (1891). See plate facing p. 256.
⁵⁷ Regy. of Deeds, IL/36/45.
⁵⁸ e.g. ibid. NN/97/145; *Kelly's Dir. N. & E.R. Yorks.* (1872), 362.
⁵⁹ Regy. of Deeds, HM/47/49; KD/82/112; KL/345/454.
⁶⁰ e.g. ibid. KM/369/506; LM/2/3; MN/329/517–18; MO/18/24; *Filey Chronicle*, 4 Sept. 1858.

built in Reynolds Street and Mariner's and Clifford's Terraces, lying between the back lane and Queen Street. To the west of the village several short rows appeared in Somerville (now Station) Road, West Parade (the old Common Right Lane of 1850), and the Scarborough road. Although Filey had thus become a small town, there had as yet been little change in King and Queen Streets, which still retained much of their village character.

Between 1890 and the First World War new development largely took the form of the infilling of empty sites in existing streets. Behind the Crescent, for example, the blocks of land between Belle Vue and Rutland Streets and between Rutland Street and Brooklands were completely built over. The houses there included more than 30 put up in 1899–1900 by M. H. Fell in terraces fronting on to Rutland Street, Brooklands, and West Avenue (formerly Slea Lane and West Street).[61] Fell had already built ten houses in Rutland Street in 1896–7.[62] Another terrace was built during this period in Southdene and a few new houses and shops elsewhere in the area behind the Crescent.[63] In 1903 it was said that the Unett estate alone, which was then practically built over, had 65 separate tenements on it.[64]

In the area between the old village and New Filey development was also taking place at this time on the land of E. L. Osbaldeston-Mitford. In 1904–5 plots were being sold in the block between Union, Murray, and Mitford Streets; and also, further west, in Station and Somerville Roads,[65] though the latter area was mostly built-up after the First World War. Beyond Somerville Road the development of more modest housing was beginning in Norman Avenue (now Crescent) and near-by streets. On the Muston road there were two or three isolated new houses, built on plots sold in 1899 by Edwin Martin.[66] On the sea front, too, there were several noteworthy changes. Terraces were completed on either side of Ackworth House,[67] the coastguard houses were rebuilt,[68] and the old North Cliff Villa was replaced by a grand new house. The villa was bought by Elinor Clarke in 1890, and she also acquired land to the north of it, Belvedere — another villa — to the east, and Foord's Hotel, near by in Queen Street.[69] The new North Cliff Villa was built in 1891–2[70] and Belvedere was demolished to extend the grounds. Miss Clarke, 'the wealthiest resident', died in 1905 and the house was sold to G. N. de Yarburgh Bateson.[71] The adjacent villa called Sea Breezes was also rebuilt, probably soon after 1905,[72] and was subsequently called Deepdene.

After the First World War private building continued around Station Avenue and Station Road, and along West Avenue and Muston Road.[73] Other private developments included Belle Vue Crescent, between Station and West Avenues, and the Croft, off Scarborough Road.[74] It was also in the years between the World Wars that house-building by the urban district council began. In the early 1920s about twenty houses were built in the Gardens, on Scarborough Road, and about 1930 nearly a hundred were put up on the Newlands housing estate, further west. Beyond the Newlands, about eighty houses were built on the Newthorpe estate in the late 1930s, as well as about forty bungalows in West Vale, off West Avenue, and other houses in Ravine Hill.

Council development continued after the Second World War with the erection of 75 more dwellings on the Newlands and Newthorpe estates in the later 1940s. A new housing estate was begun about 1950 on the east side of Muston Road and about two hundred houses and flats were built there by 1955. At the same time the demolition began of the yards and places behind Queen Street, seventeen of which had been condemned in 1935. They were replaced in the 1960s by fifteen houses between Queen Street and Church Ravine and 30 houses and flats, together with an old people's centre, to the south of Queen Street. Private development after 1939 included more houses along Muston Road,[75] but the most extensive private building of this period has been on the land of Grange Farm, to the west of Muston Road, which was acquired by the council in 1960 and subsequently sold to developers. Also privately built, in 1970, were the luxury flats of St. Oswald's Court, on the site of the Vicarage in Queen Street. Building was then still in progress on another private housing estate, on the north side of Scarborough Road.[76]

DOMESTIC BUILDINGS. The oldest surviving houses in Filey are built of the local stone, often in the form of rubble rather than ashlar. Cobbles are also to be seen in a few cottages, and several boundary walls are entirely built of them. From at least the 18th century brick was widely used, and there were brickworks in Filey in the 19th and 20th centuries. Many of the bricks are of a distinctive type, presumably made in the local kilns; they are yellow or pink in colour, mottled and striped with red. Such bricks were also sometimes used in near-by villages.

In the old village centre some houses survive from the 18th and possibly the 17th centuries, but generally much altered in more recent times. There are, for example, several two-storeyed stone cottages in both Queen and Church Streets which probably have a 17th-century origin; one (nos. 8 and 10 Queen Street) incorporates a round-headed window with a moulded stone surround and a hood-mould, and has a stone bearing arms, initials,[77] the date 1696, and the inscription 'The fear of God be in you'.

---

[61] Regy. of Deeds, e.g. 88/1/1 (1897); 10/215/201 (1889); 18/418/382; 23/159/138 (1900).
[62] Ibid. 80/114/108; /319/296; 87/107/102 (1896); 95/59/53 (1897).
[63] O.S. Map 6" (1913); *Filey Post*, 27 Mar. 1897.
[64] E.R.R.O., DDX/34/5.
[65] Regy. of Deeds, 72/114/94 (1904); 72/13/5; /170/148; /302/271; /428/389; /458/419; /459/420 (1905); 93/328/311 (1907); *Filey Post*, 3 Sept. 1904; 11 Feb. 1905.
[66] Regy. of Deeds, 9/499/461; 11/267/244 (1899).
[67] O.S. Map 6" (1913).
[68] *Filey Post*, 29 July 1912.
[69] Regy. of Deeds, 34/434/417; 35/32/32; 41/204/189 (1890); 86/399/380 (1896).
[70] Filey U.D.C. Offices, loc. govt. bd. mins. 1881–91, p. 373; *Filey Post*, 17 Oct. 1891; *Kelly's Dir. N. & E.R. Yorks.* (1893), 421. [71] Regy. of Deeds, 91/41/38 (1906).
[72] *Filey Post*, 18 Nov., 9 Dec. 1905.
[73] O.S. Map 25" (1929).
[74] Ibid. 6" (1938). [75] Ibid. (1958).
[76] These 2 paragraphs are largely based on Filey U.D.C. Offices, TS. list of 'Items from Council Mins.'.
[77] I.M.N., said to refer to John and Mary Norwood: ex inf. Mr. F. W. Fisher, Filey, 1971.

Several 18th-century cottages are of painted brick. The most noteworthy early cottages, however, a row of stone-built fishermen's houses in Queen Street, were demolished in the 1960s. Other, less modest, 18th-century houses form a group at the north end of Church Street, stepped downhill towards the ravine. At least one is built wholly of stone and another has a front of chequered brick. Nos. 33 and 35 form a three-storeyed house with plinth, quoins, and side walls of stone. The altered front carries a date tablet of 1716 but the top storey was probably added in the 19th century. Further south in Church Street the Station Hotel, and nos. 1–13 adjoining it, are stone buildings of 18th- or early-19th-century origin.

Many houses in Queen Street were refronted or completely rebuilt in the 19th century, among them Foord's Hotel and the former Ship Inn (no. 78). The Ship has a stone front, with plinth and quoins, added to an older building, and Foord's Hotel has a Greek Doric doorway with bay windows on both the floors above it. One other noteworthy building of the late 18th or early 19th century is Church Cliff House, on the north side of the ravine. It is a square house, two-storeyed and built of brick with stone dressings; the east front is six bays long and incorporates a round-headed staircase window, and the south front is of five bays with a dignified Georgian doorway at the centre. North of the house stands a square stone dovecot surmounted by a cupola.

The rows of small fishermen's cottages, built in yards behind the village streets in the earlier 19th century, had mostly been cleared away by 1970. Several of the houses built in the same period near the cliff top at the east end of the village still survive, but few call for special mention. They include Cliff Cottage, which housed the urban district council offices from 1949 until 1971 and has been much altered; it is a two-storeyed 'villa', with bay windows overlooking the sea. Rose Cottage, in Mitford Street, also survives, but the early house which became North Cliff Villa was subsequently completely rebuilt.[78]

The earliest houses built in New Filey included South Cliff Villas (before 1833) and Ravine Villa (1837–8), and both still stood in 1970. The semi-detached pair of South Cliff Villas is three storeys high, with a seven-bay front towards the sea; the houses were extensively altered, however, during their use as a convent school. Ravine Villa is a large, stuccoed, house, with a five-bay front; on the ground floor there are three square projecting bays, each having a three-light window divided by pilasters supporting a pediment. The south front has a Greek Doric porch with a balustrade.

The 1840s saw the building of the first houses in the Crescent, and others followed in the 1850s. These stucco-fronted terraces are built on two slight curves and stretch for 400 yds. along the cliff top, overlooking the sea. The earlier blocks precede similar large-scale developments at Bridlington by 20 or 30 years and architecturally are still in the Regency tradition. The later terraces show no significant change of style and the whole group forms by far the most impressive feature of the resort. The terraces are of varying heights, three or four storeys high, with or without basements and attics. Most of the individual houses are two bays wide, but in the earliest terrace (nos. 8–14), built in the 1840s, they have three bays; this terrace has Greek Doric porches with fluted columns and other neo-classical details. There is a continuous cast-iron balcony at first-floor level, and over-all rustication on the ground floor. Nos. 1–7, the most northerly block (1851), has similar rustication and an end elevation with Corinthian pilasters and a pediment. The former Royal Crescent Hotel (1853), nine bays long and occupying one block at the centre of the Crescent, is especially elaborately treated. It has a Venetian window over a central porch, a cast-iron balcony at first-floor level, and four ornate lamp standards on the pavement in front. The remainder of the Crescent, south of the hotel, dates from the 1850s to 1890 and has the same general characteristics as the other terraces.

Behind the Crescent, and on a less ambitious scale, Rutland Terrace (1847) is three-storeyed and stuccoed with a full-height bow-fronted bay window to each house; it is one of the earliest in style and least altered examples of resort architecture in the town. Clarence Place (1840s) is of red brick with Greek Doric doorways. Other stucco-faced houses of the mid century include rows, pairs, and single houses in Melville Terrace, Belle Vue Street, and Murray Street; among them are the Belle Vue Hotel and the Three Tuns. South Crescent Villa (now the White Lodge Hotel) (c. 1850) has been extensively altered. In South Crescent Avenue the semi-detached pair called St. Martin's Villas (1874) has gable-ends facing the street and pointed windows and doorways.

The houses put up at the foot of the cliffs below the Crescent in the period 1850–90 include Downcliff House, entirely stone-built, and Ackworth House, designed in the Renaissance style with a slate mansard roof. On the north side of Carr Gate the houses built below the cliffs at this period have mostly been demolished. Of the smaller houses built between the village and New Filey in the 1870s, those in Hope Street consist of modest terraces of yellow and mottled brick, with many shop-fronts later inserted.

The infilling in the area behind the Crescent between 1890 and the First World War included several terraces of red, yellow, white, or mottled brick. Similar houses were built along the Beach, including an ornate white-brick terrace on the north side of Ackworth House which incorporates multi-coloured brick and stone decorations. Further north North Cliff Villa was rebuilt in 1891–2; the new house (called Newland House in 1970) and its stable block were designed by W. H. Brierley of York[79] in the domestic Tudor style, and built entirely of stone on a grand scale. The growth of resort and residential housing on the west side of the town includes little that is noteworthy.

Of the townships lying north-west of Filey Lebberston contains few older buildings and Lebberston Hall dates from the late 19th century. Gristhorpe consists mainly of a single street, its white-washed stone houses and cottages set back above grass banks, giving it a look characteristic of many North Riding villages. The buildings are of a

[78] See below

[79] *Filey Post*, 11 Mar. 1905.

storey and a half or two storeys, several of them recently altered for use as holiday cottages. One house is dated 1684 and another has a tablet of 1665 to which the date 1747 has been added. Gristhorpe Hall, on the south side of the street, is an 18th- or early-19th-century house with later additions. The two-storeyed stucco front has flanking screen walls, a central pediment, and a Tuscan porch. The south elevation, also flanked by screen walls, is of stone with a two-storeyed bay window at the centre. Gristhorpe Lodge is an 18th-century house of stone and brick with an extension dated 1900.[80]

MANORS AND OTHER ESTATES. In 1086 the whole 18 carucates of Filey and its townships was soke of the royal manor of Falsgrave (Yorks. N.R.). Six separate estates were recorded: Filey and Lebberston each consisted of 6 carucates, Gristhorpe of 4 carucates, and the vills which made up the later manor of Newbiggin — 'Eterstorp', 'Rodebestorp', and 'Scagetorp' — contained 6, 4, and 6 bovates, respectively. Falsgrave had been held by Tosti before the Conquest.[81]

The estate in Filey subsequently passed under the overlordship of the Gants and later the Tattershalls. It was for long associated with Muston and the manor of *FILEY* was held, like Muston, by the Cockfield, Neville, Malbis, Beckwith, Maltby, and Warton families.[82] At the division of the former Warton estates in 1775 Michael Newton received 169 a. in Filey,[83] and at inclosure in 1791 he was allotted 122 a.[84]

Trustees for the sale of Newton's estate disposed of the property in 1813–14, the greater part, nearly 150 a., going to John Hall in 1814.[85] Much of this land passed to H. J. Shepherd in 1822, P. D. Cooke in 1825, and Susanna Tatham and T. H. Shepherd in 1833.[86] It was broken up about this time. In 1835 97 a. were bought by Elizabeth Taylor and other purchases included 11 a. by J. W. Unett,[87] who used it for resort development.[88]

Land in Filey also descended with part of the manor of Muston[89] from the Nevilles to the Heslertons; Robert of Heslerton had 6 tofts and 9½ bovates there at his death in 1309,[90] and another Robert had 10 bovates in 1346.[91] Some of this land apparently passed, like Muston, to the St. Quintins,[92] who also obtained Newbiggin.[93] Gabriel St. Quintin sold land in Lebberston to Robert Lowson in 1558, in Lebberston and Gristhorpe to Robert Vicarman in 1562, and in Filey to John Kyllyn in 1565, and William St. Quintin sold property in Lebberston to Edward Leppington and Thomas Stephenson in 1611.[94]

Again as in Muston little of the Gant land in Filey seems to have descended with the manor of Hunmanby. The lords of Hunmanby held courts for Filey in the 16th and 17th centuries, however,[95] and in the 19th and early 20th centuries the Mitfords and Osbaldeston-Mitfords were regarded as lords of the manor of Filey.[96] Until they acquired the rectory in the late 18th century[97] the Osbaldestons had little land in the parish. Humphrey Osbaldeston bought 1½ bovate in 1787, and for this he was awarded 17 a. at inclosure in 1791.[98] When the Osbaldeston-Mitford estate was sold in 1920 there were only 8 a. in Filey, apart from the beach and foreshore.[99]

Other land in Filey belonged, like the Crown estate in Muston, to the Buckton and Constable families.[1] Both had land in Filey in 1428[2] and William Buckton held 6 bovates in Filey as of the manor of Muston in 1507.[3] In 1601 William Constable died seised of property in Filey and his son Christopher had a quarter of the reputed manor in 1622.[4] The manor still belonged to the family in 1693,[5] but the property was subsequently split up.[6] Three bovates of it, together with land in Muston, passed from Sir Robert Constable to the Grindalls and then the Osbaldestons in the 18th century, and were sold to Thomas Robinson in 1775.[7]

Bridlington priory received a grant of ½ carucate of land in Filey from Ralph de Neville in 1160–5.[8] It apparently became attached to Filey church, which the priory also held.[9] The gift of a house and mill in Filey to St. Peter's hospital, York, was confirmed in 1148.[10] A house there was given by Gilbert de Gant to Thornton abbey (Lincs.) c. 1139–47.[11] A house called the hermitage, together with lands in Filey and Muston, was granted to the executors of Thomas Paynell in 1563.[12]

The Domesday estate in Gristhorpe was later soke of Pickering manor.[13] The demesne tenant in the 13th century was the Morpeth family, which gave land there to Bridlington priory. In 1275 Roger of Morpeth sold what was apparently the reversion, after his death, of 18 bovates and other property there and in Lebberston to Robert of Place.[14] Morpeth still held one carucate and 6 bovates in Gristhorpe in 1284–5,[15] however, the rest of the township then belonging to Bridlington. Robert Place seems to have been in possession of the Morpeth holding in 1301.[16] The widow of Sir William Place was seeking dower in Gristhorpe and

---

[80] Gristhorpe Lodge is said to have borne the date 1753 and Gristhorpe Hall to have been built on the site of an older house in 1800: Sheahan and Whellan, *Hist. York & E.R.* ii. 466.
[81] *V.C.H. Yorks.* ii. 196, 310.
[82] See p. 279.
[83] 15 Geo. III, c. 49 (Priv. Act).
[84] Registry of Deeds, Beverley, BG/310/43.
[85] Ibid. CW/443/621; E.R.R.O., DDHU/3/6 (map).
[86] Regy. of Deeds, DP/351/380; DX/19/16; ET/243/282.
[87] Ibid. EX/371/414; EZ/350/336.
[88] See p. 134.
[89] See p. 279.
[90] *Cal. Inq. p.m.* v, p 54.
[91] *Feud. Aids*, vi. 228.
[92] *Yorks. Fines, 1347–77*, 118.
[93] See p. 139.
[94] *Yorks. Fines*, i. 221, 270, 314; *1603–14*, 159.
[95] See p. 146.
[96] Directories.
[97] See p. 140.
[98] Regy. of Deeds, BG/310/43; BN/183/253.
[99] Ibid. 209/184/157; see below, p. 232.
[1] See p. 280.
[2] E 179/202/104; *Feud. Aids*, vi. 266.
[3] *Cal. Inq. p.m. Hen. VII*, iii, pp. 165–6.
[4] C 142/269/20; C 142/524/23.
[5] C.P. 43/441 rot. 191.
[6] Regy. of Deeds, D/121/196; E/99/171; /162/277.
[7] Ibid., AU/185/280; /375/612.
[8] *Bridlington Charty.* 76; *E.Y.C.* ii, p. 465.
[9] See p. 147.
[10] *E.Y.C.* i, p. 150.
[11] Ibid. ii, p. 429.
[12] *Cal. Pat.* 1563–6, 53.
[13] *Feud. Aids*, vi. 79.
[14] *Yorks. Fines, 1272–1300*, 6.
[15] *Feud. Aids*, vi. 79.
[16] *Yorks. Lay Subsidy 1297* (Y.A.S. Rec. Ser. xxi), 63.

elsewhere in 1387.[17] His son William's heirs died without issue and the family lands reverted to William Sewerby, son of Sir William Place's sister Margaret.

Another William Sewerby granted several manors, including *GRISTHORPE*, to his daughter Margaret Pigot,[18] who died seised of it in 1485.[19] In 1512 the manor passed to the four daughters and coheirs of Thomas Pigot.[20] Margery died without issue in 1518 and the estate was divided between Margaret, wife of James Metcalfe, Joan, who married first Sir Giles Hussey and later Sir Thomas Folkingham, and Elizabeth, who married successively Sir James Strangeways, Francis Neville, and Sir Charles Brandon.[21]

In the late 16th century land in Gristhorpe and Lebberston was being acquired by George Beswick, and in 1601 he bought Gristhorpe manor from Edmund Cootes.[22] Gristhorpe descended in the Beswick family until the 1920s. By 1929 Mrs. E. S. Jones was said to be chief landowner and lady of the manor.[23]

In the 13th century Robert of Morpeth confirmed a grant of land to Bridlington priory, and in 1256 his son William quitclaimed 6 bovates to the priory.[24] By 1284–5 Bridlington had 2 carucates and 2 bovates in Gristhorpe, and it still had 2 carucates in 1401–2.[25] At the Dissolution the priory's land there was worth about £3.[26] A house, 4 a. of land, and common of pasture in Gristhorpe were given by Roger son of Uctred of Gristhorpe to Fountains abbey in 1175.[27]

After 1086 Lebberston was included in the fee of Sir Roger Bigod and was held under him by William de Forz, count of Aumale, by 1234.[28] A mesne tenancy of this land was held in the early 13th century by the Ayton family, apparently represented by William of 'Aston' in 1208[29] and John of 'Eston' in 1284–5.[30] Six bovates were sold to Simon of Hale by William of Ayton, but before 1245 this holding, described as eight tofts and a carucate of land, was given by Simon to Rievaulx abbey.[31]

The largest lay holding under John of Eston in 1284–5 was the 2 carucates of John Bard[32] of Osgodby (Yorks. N.R.). Its descent followed that of Osgodby manor[33] until at least the 17th century.[34]

Other land in Lebberston was held by Henry of Cayton, who died before 1206, when his widow quitclaimed her dower in a carucate there to her son-in-law Oliver of Croom.[35] William of Cayton granted the homage and service of Oliver's son Thomas to Bridlington priory, and Henry son of Henry of Cayton granted 2 bovates to the priory.[36]

In 1208 Henry of Folkton obtained 2 bovates in Lebberston from William of Aston.[37] A tenant of the Folktons was William of Osgodby,[38] who granted 4 bovates to Bridlington priory[39] and 2 bovates to St. Peter's hospital, York.[40]

Rievaulx abbey still held its carucate in Lebberston in 1284–5.[41] At the Dissolution the land was let to Robert Lawson,[42] but its further descent has not been traced.

Bridlington priory secured other gifts of land in Lebberston in addition to those already mentioned, and by 1284–5 it had 3 carucates there.[43] In 1523–4 the prior claimed 16 bovates in Lebberston[44] and at the Dissolution the priory's land there was worth nearly £3.[45] In 1553 the Crown granted houses and rents in Lebberston, late of the priory, to Philip Lovell and Robert Foster.[46] This property was presumably the manor of *LEBBERSTON* which belonged to Robert Foster in 1567.[47] Houses and lands in the township were sold by Leonard Foster to Robert Brooke in 1596, and by Henry Brooke to William Lamplugh in 1624.[48] The manor was conveyed by another William Lamplugh to James Hebden in 1743.[49]

St. Peter's (later St. Leonard's) hospital retained its land in Lebberston until the Dissolution and by 1614 the property belonged to Christopher Coulson, whose father Robert was said to have bought it from James Nundie or Lundie.[50] In 1653 Fairlie Coulson compounded for lands there worth about £25 a year.[51]

The Domesday estates which later comprised Newbiggin were subsequently also soke of Pickering manor.[52] In 1187 the land was apparently in the king's hands[53] and by 1284–5 the 2 carucates there belonged to Robert of Wyerne.[54] In 1308 Robert was licensed to have a chapel in the manor-house.[55] The Wyernes retained the land until the late 14th century, when Agnes, daughter of Robert 'Warren', is said to have married Thomas de St. Quintin of Harpham.[56] Anthony St. Quintin held Newbiggin in 1428.[57] The manor of *NEWBIGGIN* was in 1567 granted by Gabriel St. Quintin to the borough of

[17] C.P. 40/508 m. 335; G. Wrottesley, *Ped. from the Plea R.* 349.
[18] C 1/546/39.
[19] *Cal. Inq. p.m. Hen. VII*, i, p. 103.
[20] C 142/27/31.
[21] C 142/33/79; C 142/56/53; C 142/95/70; *Test. Ebor.* iv. 213.
[22] E 179/261/19; *Yorks. Fines*, iv. 15, 26, 173.
[23] Directories.
[24] *Bridlington Charty.* 286.
[25] *Feud. Aids*, vi. 79, 178, 621.
[26] *Valor Eccl.* (Rec. Com.) v. 120.
[27] *Fountains Charty.* i. 345.
[28] *Yorks. Fines, 1232–46*, 29; *Feud. Aids*, vi. 82.
[29] *Yorks. Fines, John* (Sur. Soc. ii), 120.
[30] *Feud. Aids*, vi. 79, 82.
[31] *Rievaulx Charty.* (Sur. Soc. lxxxiii), 203, 230, 396. Robt. de Roos confirmed the gift: ibid. 26; *Cal. Chart. R. 1226–57*, 360.
[32] *Feud. Aids*, vi. 79, 82.
[33] *V.C.H. Yorks. N.R.* ii. 433.
[34] C.P. 25(2)/755/21 Chas. II Mich. no. 14.
[35] *Yorks. Fines, John*, 102.
[36] *Cal. Pat. 1307–13*, 439; *Bridlington Charty.* 5.
[37] *Yorks. Fines, John*, 120.
[38] B.M. Stowe Chart. 462.
[39] *Cal. Pat. 1307–13*, 439; *Bridlington Charty.* 292–3.
[40] B.M. Stowe Chart. 462.
[41] *Feud. Aids*, vi. 79.
[42] *Rievaulx Charty.* 317.
[43] *Bridlington Charty.* 5, 291 sqq.; *Feud. Aids*, vi. 79.
[44] C 1/513/3.
[45] *Valor Eccl.* v. 120.
[46] *Cal. Pat. 1553*, 193.
[47] C 142/147/166; E 134/12 Jas. I Mich./27.
[48] *Yorks. Fines*, iv. 57; *1614–25*, 245.
[49] C.P. 25(2)/1247/16–17 Geo. II Trin. no. 484.
[50] E 134/12 Jas. I Mich./27.
[51] *Royalist Composition Papers*, iii (Y.A.S. Rec. Ser. xx), 76.
[52] *Feud. Aids*, vi. 79.
[53] *Pipe R. 1187* (P.R.S. xxxvii), 91.
[54] *Feud. Aids*, vi. 79, 178.
[55] *Reg. Greenfield*, iii (Sur. Soc. cli), 140.
[56] G. Poulson, *Hist. Holderness*, ii. 268. See also B. M. Cott. MS. Vit. C. vi, f. 215; W. Flower, *Visit. Yorks.* (Harl. Soc. xvi), 96.
[57] E 179/202/104.

Kingston upon Hull.[58] The latter retained it until 1685, when it was conveyed to William Dickinson.[59]

Filey rectory was given to Bridlington priory in the early 12th century.[60] Fish tithes were payable in the 12th century, but between c. 1120–9 and 1192 the tithe of Filey fish landed at Whitby was enjoyed by Whitby abbey.[61] In 1291 the rectory was valued at £20.[62] It was let by the priory to Henry Salvan and William Walker in 1530 and to Thomas Brigham in 1536.[63] After the Dissolution it was let by the Crown to Robert Lutton in 1542[64] and to William Lutton in 1555.[65] It was granted by the Crown to the archbishop of York in 1558[66] but was presumably resumed by Elizabeth I. In 1568 it was let to Robert Rampston and Freman Young,[67] in 1580 to Tristram, Barbara, and Humphrey Farley,[68] and in 1595 to Reynold Farley.[69] It was granted in fee in 1601 to William Green[70] and he was succeeded in 1605 by his daughter Elizabeth, who later married Sir John Buck.[71] The payment of tithes to the Bucks was disputed on several occasions in the later 17th century.[72] In 1650 the tithes were worth £180 to Lady Buck, £120 from the townships and £60 from Filey itself.[73]

The rectory was apparently divided into three parts c. 1700 and they descended for a time like the corresponding parts of West Flotmanby manor.[74] In 1787 Edward Dowsett's trustees sold two parts of the rectory to Humphrey Osbaldeston.[75] Elizabeth Buck had sold the other part to F. W. Osbaldeston in 1763.[76]

The rectorial estate was extensive. At the inclosure of Filey in 1791 Osbaldeston was allotted, for his two thirds of the rectory held in fee simple, the 'parsonage house', 277 a., 10 houses, several small closes, part of 6s. 7d. tithe-rent from ancient inclosures, and part of the tithe of fish and seaweed. For his third held in tail he received 83 a., 15 houses, several closes, and the rest of the tithe-rent and tithes.[77] At Humphrey Osbaldeston's death in 1835 the two thirds of the rectory passed, like his other personal estates,[78] to Theodosia Brooke and then in 1871 to the Firmans. After H. B. Firman's death in 1930, the 320-acre Church Cliff farm was sold in 1932 to Tom and Sarah Smith. The Smiths sold it to the Church Cliff Farming Co. Ltd. in 1945. Over 100 a. was sold to the urban district council in 1965 and most of the remainder to J.D.T., Diana, and Carol Megginson in 1968.[79]

The other third of the rectorial estate descended after 1835 in the Osbaldeston-Mitford family.[80]

The sale of two thirds of the rectory to Humphrey Osbaldeston in 1787 excluded the tithes of 104 a. in Gristhorpe which were sold in the same year to George Beswick. By 1847 the tithes on 759 a. in Gristhorpe had already been merged and those on another 160 a. were merged that year; tithes due to George Beswick on 140 a. were commuted for a rent-charge of about £8.[81] By 1847, too, most of the tithes in Lebberston had been merged and those on 58 a. were merged in that year; tithes due to William Bottomley on 8 a. were commuted for about 7s.[82] The sale of 1787 also excluded the tithes of Newbiggin; they were worth £18 a year and were said to have lately belonged to General Harvey.[83]

Half a carucate of land given to Bridlington priory by Ralph de Neville[84] apparently came to be attached to the church. At the inclosure of Filey in 1791 there were 18½ bovates of glebe land and it was for this as well as for tithes that Humphrey Osbaldeston received his allotments.[85]

AGRICULTURE. Most of the land on the north side of Filey beck was occupied by two open fields, Church and Great fields. To the south of the village, and stretching from the cliffs inland to the Muston road, was Little field. Nothing is known of the extent or organization of the fields in the Middle Ages and a precise acreage cannot be determined from the inclosure award of 1791: there were, however, more than 400 a. of open-field land at that date.[86]

The carrs and marshes of the Vale of Pickering extended through Lebberston and Gristhorpe[87] into the westerly part of Filey township. There, lying around Carr Goat drain, this wet ground formed the common moor, which covered perhaps 70 a.–80 a. in 1791.[88] The stream was known as Dams Goit in 1850[89] and near it lay Filey Dam and Filey marsh, where fishing was enjoyed by the lord of Muston manor in 1579.[90] The Great Dam, of 3 a., was mentioned in 1726.[91] Another area of common pasture was the Ox pasture, lying around the north and west sides of Church and Great fields, mostly adjoining the cliff top.[92] In 1787 thirteen beast-gates on 'the moors' belonged to the rectory in right of houses in the village.[93] Common Right Road (later part of West Road) gave access from the village to the common moor.[94]

---

[58] *Yorks. Fines*, i. 336.
[59] L. M. Stanewell, *Calendar of Ancient Deeds etc.* (Hull Corp.), 145.
[60] See p. 147.
[61] *E.Y.C.* ii, pp. 222, 467.
[62] *Tax. Eccl.* (Rec. Com.), 304.
[63] E 315/108 f. 6d.; E/315/408 f. 6; *Valor Eccl.* (Rec. Com.), v. 120.
[64] *L. & P. Hen. VIII*, xvii, p. 60.
[65] *Cal. Pat.* 1554–5, 284.
[66] Ibid. 1557–8, 420.
[67] Ibid. 1566–9, 222.
[68] C 66/1187 m. 36.
[69] *Cal. S.P. Dom.* 1595–7, 9. For enquiries about the leases see E 134/42 Eliz. Trin./13; 42 & 43 Eliz. Mich./29; E 178/2836.
[70] C 66/1556 m. 20; *Yorks. Fines*, iv. 174.
[71] C 142/287/8; *Dugdale's Visit. Yorks.* (Sur. Soc. xxxvi), 70.
[72] B.I.H.R., R. AS. 21B/90–92; C.P., H. 2549, 3498, 4803–4, 4854–5, 4930.
[73] *T.E.R.A.S.* ii. 59.
[74] See p. 168.
[75] Regy. of Deeds, BM/392/647.
[76] Ibid. AE/44/95–6.
[77] Ibid. BG/310/43.
[78] See p. 232.
[79] Regy. of Deeds, 461/360/295; 697/453/382; 1473/497/430; 1550/188/167.
[80] See p. 138.
[81] B.I.H.R., TA 589S.
[82] Ibid. 124S.
[83] Regy. of Deeds, BM/392/647; E.R.R.O., DDCV/parcel 92.
[84] See p. 138.
[85] Regy. of Deeds, BG/310/43.
[86] E.R.R.O., IA Filey, inclosure map; Registry of Deeds, Beverley, BG/310/43.
[87] *Honour and Forest of Pickering*, ii (N.R. Rec. Soc. N.S. ii), 173; iii (N.R. Rec. Soc. N.S. iii), 18–20.
[88] E.R.R.O., IA Filey; Regy. of Deeds, BG/310/43.
[89] O.S. Map 6" (1854).
[90] *Yorks. Fines*, ii. 144.
[91] Regy. of Deeds, I/422/930.
[92] E.R.R.O., IA Filey; Regy. of Deeds, BG/310/43.
[93] Regy. of Deeds, BM/392/647.
[94] O.S. Map 6" (1854).

It was reported in 1517 that William Battom occupied three 'husbandholdings' at Filey with the result that two of the houses were ruined and ten people had been evicted.[95] Apart from garths behind the main streets of the village, the old inclosures in 1791 covered a limited area south of the back lane and towards the common moor; they also included the area known as the Dams. About 20 a. of closes then belonged to the rectory.[96] The open fields and commons of Filey were inclosed in 1791[97] under an Act of 1788.[98] The largest allotment, comprising 376 a., went to Humphrey Osbaldeston, all but 17 a. of it in lieu of his rectorial estate. Michael Newton received 122 a. and Christopher Foster 101 a. There were 2 allotments of 34 a., one of 16 a., one of 9 a., and 7 of under 2 a. each. The smallest allotments were probably in lieu of cottage rights and they included the interest of eleven other cottagers who sold out before the award was made. Thus John Wilson's allotment of 2 a. included the interest of seven others. A small allotment to the poor of Filey was later used as the site of the National school. Gristhorpe is said to have been inclosed in 1702.[99]

None of the low-lying grounds in Filey township remained to be dealt with by the commissioners for the Muston Drainage Act, but large areas in the south of Gristhorpe and Lebberston were improved in the early 19th century by the commissioners.[1] In 1801 there were only 871 a. under crops in the whole parish,[2] and much of the lower ground continued subsequently to be used as pasture. In the 19th and 20th centuries there have usually been fewer than 6 farmers in Filey but generally 10–15 in Gristhorpe and about 10 in Lebberston.[3]

FISHING AND SHIPPING. The importance of fishing from Filey at an early date cannot be doubted but, as in the case of Bridlington, there is little evidence.[4] As early as c. 1120–9, however, Filey men were certainly landing catches at Whitby as well as Filey,[5] and this was still the case in 1192;[6] in the 1190s Grimsby was also a landing-place for Filey men.[7] By 1231 boats were going out to 'Doggedraue' and 'Crokesi',[8] the former perhaps the Dogger Bank. There are occasional references to Filey fishermen in the 15th and 16th centuries.[9] In 1622 three men were presented at the Hunmanby manor court for throwing their 'fish guts' into the street at Filey,[10] and during a dispute about the payment of tithes in 1625–6 it was alleged that John Gamage, during the year, had caught 73,000 fish, including 40,000 herrings.[11]

Much more is known of fishing from Filey in the 19th century, when four main methods were employed. First, from about the end of January to early June larger boats known as yawls or luggers, which had been laid up at Scarborough during the winter, went line-fishing on the Dogger Bank and elsewhere for cod, halibut, haddock, and other fish. Secondly, from June to the end of November the yawls turned to herring fishing and were joined by a fleet of large cobles. Thirdly, the cobles alone continued fishing locally during the winter. And fourthly, from April to July cobles went around the Brigg for crabs and lobsters.[12] As at Bridlington, sailing cobles were used at Filey until about 1914, when motor cobles were gradually introduced: the first was built and launched at Filey in 1913.[13]

During the herring season the larger boats worked all along the east coast, sailing in the autumn as far as Great Yarmouth. In 1805 12 Filey boats went to Yarmouth[14] and in 1828 it was said that 10–12 boats still made the trip;[15] fewer did so during the lean years of 1840–50, however, and subsequently the Filey boats found good fishing nearer home.[16] In 1860 9 of the village's 23 yawls were lost in a single storm, but by 1867 there were 35 yawls belonging to Filey; each carried 6 men and 2 or 3 boys.[17] The large herring cobles, with crews of 3, numbered about 20 in the 1860s.[18] About 60 smaller cobles were said in 1868 to be used for local fishing and for carrying aboard the yawls.[19] Over 100 men and boys were said in 1840 to be engaged in fishing.[20] About 100 men took part in the dangerous winter fishing in 1861 and there were altogether about 180 adult fishermen in 1868.[21]

By the early 20th century Filey fishermen and others from further afield were illegally using trawls in Filey Bay, and in 1905 136 Filey men petitioned unsuccessfully for trawling to be legalized. In 1915 53 men, described as 'the large majority of inshore fishermen at Filey fishing at home', obtained leave to trawl for the duration of the war,[22] and the practice was subsequently continued. A few yawls were still working from Filey at this period — four were following the crab and lobster fishing in 1913, for example — but the scarcity of fish resulted in a reduction in the number of cobles engaged in line-fishing from 26 in 1913 to 14 in 1914.[23] By 1923 four or five motor boats were based on Filey and were used for trawling, line-fishing, and potting for crabs and lobsters; smaller boats were used for salmon and trout fishing. In 1928 17 motor cobles and 50 men worked from Filey, and there were still 17 boats in 1945. The number of motor cobles subsequently fell to 13, with 39 men, in 1948, 12 in 1952, and 10 in 1958. Between 1959 and 1961, however, there was a recovery from 9 to 15 boats. In 1970 there were still a dozen.[24]

The fluctuating fortunes of the fishing community

---

[95] *T.R.H.S.* N.S. vii. 250.
[96] E.R.R.O., IA Filey; Regy. of Deeds, BG/310/43.
[97] Regy. of Deeds, BG/310/43; E.R.R.O., IA Filey, map.
[98] 28 Geo. III, c. 13 (Priv. Act).
[99] J. Cole, *Hist. and Antiquities of Filey*, 146.
[1] E.R.R.O., DDCB/12/6; DDSY/11/2; /103/10. See below, p. 280. [2] Crop Returns, 1801.
[3] Directories. [4] See p. 50.
[5] *Whitby Charty.* i (Sur. Soc. lxix), 311; *E.Y.C.* ii, pp. 222–3. [6] *Bridlington Charty.* 77.
[7] Ibid. 79; *E.Y.C.* ii, p. 467. [8] *Bridlington Charty.* 78.
[9] B.I.H.R., Prob. Reg. ii, f. 311; iv, f. 59; xxviii, f. 93.
[10] S.C. 2/211/66. [11] B.I.H.R., C.P., H. 4854.
[12] W. S. Cortis, *Hist. and Descrip. Guide to Filey* (1861), 52–5.

[13] *Filey Post*, 8 Nov. 1913. See above, p. 50.
[14] Gent. Mag. Libr. *Eng. Topog.* xiv. 222.
[15] J. Cole, *Hist. and Antiquities of Filey*, 96.
[16] Cortis, *Guide*, 54–5.
[17] Ibid. 52–3; G. Shaw, *Our Filey Fishermen* (1867), 44–5.
[18] Cortis, *Guide*, 53; Shaw, *Fishermen*, 111–12.
[19] A. Pettitt, *Filey Handbk.* 39, 43.
[20] White, *Dir. E. & N.R. Yorks.* (1840), 381.
[21] Cortis, *Guide*, 55; Pettitt, *Handbk.* 51.
[22] N.E. Sea Fisheries Cttee. *Mins.* 1904–5, 325; 1914–15, 27. [23] Ibid. 1913–14, 52, 135–6.
[24] Ibid. 1922–3, 102; 1923–4, 7; 1927–8, 24–5; 1928–9, 76; 1944–5, 99; 1947–8, 91; 1951–2, 165; 1957–8, 148; 1960–1, 172; 1970–1, 138; M. Andrews, *The Heart of Filey* (1949), 14.

are reflected in the amount of fish landed at Filey.[25] The fishermen experienced similar difficulties to those encountered at Bridlington and Flamborough, and the Filey men, too, have increasingly turned to 'pleasuring' during the present century.[26] Other difficulties are peculiar to Filey. Boats have always had to be hauled to and from the slipway at the Coble Landing and launched from the beach, and fish have had to be unloaded by means of small boats and then carried back across the sands. Horses were eventually replaced by tractors for boat-hauling.[27] Even in the 1960s the size of boats which could be launched from the beach was limited and the fishermen were therefore unable to convert more extensively from line-fishing to trawling.[28]

Frequent shipwrecks occurred on the coast around Filey from the Middle Ages onwards[29] and, though the bay was much used for shelter, shipping would have greatly benefited from a harbour there. A local tradition holds that the Spittal rocks, running southwards from the Brigg, represent the remains of a Roman breakwater,[30] and in the early 17th century there are references to Filey pier. A Crown petitioner in 1637 spoke of the long-ruined pier and asked for a countrywide collection of money to enable him to create a harbour and maintain a light at Filey.[31] The use of the bay by ships continued[32] and plans for a harbour are said to have been drawn up in 1741.[33]

It was mainly to provide adequate facilities for local fishermen, as well as to encourage trade and to provide refuge for passing ships, that the construction of a harbour, protected by piers, was repeatedly proposed during the later 19th century.[34] The only improvements made, however, have been to the Coble Landing itself. The landing was first substantially built in 1870–1, with a timber wall and stone filling, and this structure lasted until it was rebuilt in stone in 1930.[35]

A life-boat was first provided at Filey in 1823, with a house on the landing near Sand Lane, and it was handed over to the Royal National Life-boat Institution in 1853.[36] Preparations for the building of a new sea wall in 1892–4[37] included the erection of a new life-boat house at the Coble Landing,[38] and this was still used in 1970.

The lords of the manor of Filey and Hunmanby for long enjoyed rights on the sea-shore and took any profits accruing from shipping. In 1278, for example, Gilbert de Gant and Richard de Malbis were entitled to whales that came ashore, reserving the heads and tails to the Crown.[39] The right to wreck of the sea was confirmed to Thomas Beckwith in 1447.[40] Little is known of shipping at Filey in the Middle Ages, though in 1275–6 seven men, including the prior of Bridlington, were alleged to have taken wool — 164 sacks in all — to the 'port' of Filey.[41]

The owners of the Lennox manor at Hunmanby were entitled in 1600 to 6d. for the groundage of ships 'landed in Filey pier', besides two bushels of coal from each coal ship.[42] Coal from the northern coalfield was probably for long the chief commodity landed at Filey. The carriage of coal from Filey to Muston was one condition on which a sale of land was made in 1625,[43] and in the 1830s coal ships accounted for all the groundage dues paid to Bertram Osbaldeston-Mitford. There were 50 such cargoes in 1836–7, 56 in 1837–8, 50 in 1838–9, and 65 in 1839–40.[44] In the years 1872 to 1878 vessels discharged cargoes on the sands 99 times, an average of only about 14 a year; 73 of the landings were by William Cammish's 38-ton *Maria* and the cargoes were chiefly of coal, with some timber.[45] Payments were made for 68 landings in 1884–9.[46] Throughout the 19th century there was a handful of shipowners and mariners in the town, who presumably engaged in this trade as well as in fishing.[47]

Apart from the profits received from wrecks and from shipping, the lords of the manor benefited from their customary right to fish with a drag net: as in Hunmanby, this was exercised until the present century.[48] They also profited from the removal of stone and shingle from the shore,[49] and from the gathering of sea-weed, which was burnt to make kelp. The impropriator had difficulty in collecting tithes on sea-weed in 1680–1,[50] for example, and there are references to men being allowed by the lords of the manor to collect the weed in 1783 and again as late as 1912.[51] In the early 20th century other profits from the beach included charges for the letting of sites and stands for entertainments, which were shared between the lords of the manor and the urban district council.[52]

MARKET AND FAIRS. A market to be held on Fridays was granted to Ralph de Neville in 1221.[53] Ten years later Gilbert de Gant complained that his own market at Hunmanby was prejudiced by that held at Filey by Ralph de Neville and Simon of Cockfield, though they denied it.[54] In 1240 the

---

[25] See Bd. of Agric. and Fisheries, *Ann. Reps. . . . relating to Sea Fisheries*, Pt. II, Tables, 1886–1918; Min. of Agric. and Fisheries, *Sea Fisheries Statistical Tables*, 1919–64; N.E. Sea Fisheries Cttee. *Mins.* 1903–4 onwards.
[26] See pp. 51, 159.
[27] Cortis, *Guide*, 56; Andrews, *Heart*, 15.
[28] N.E. Sea Fisheries Cttee. *Mins.* 1963–4, 154.
[29] e.g. *Cal. Pat.* 1247–58, 666; 1301–7, 216; 1307–13, 422; 1313–17, 598; 1330–4, 576; *L. & P. Hen. VIII*, xvii, p. 211.
[30] Mary Kitson Clark, *Gaz. of Roman Remains in E. Yorks.* 82.
[31] *Cal. S.P. Dom.* 1637–8, 17, 371; G. de Boer, *Hist. of the Spurn Lighthouses* (E. Yorks. Loc. Hist. Ser. xxiv), 14.
[32] *Cal. S.P. Dom.* 1652–3, 579; 1659–60, 550; 1666–7, 109; 1672–3, 605.
[33] Cortis, *Guide*, 22.
[34] E.R.R.O., DDHU/3/16, 19, 20, 22–6; 27 & 28 Vic., c. 93; 36 & 37 Vic., c. 63; 41 & 42 Vic., c. 114; 43 & 44 Vic., c. 189; 52 & 53 Vic., c. 210.
[35] E.R.R.O., DDX/16/35; Filey U.D.C. Offices, loc. govt. bd. mins. 1868–81, pp. 37–8, etc.
[36] Cole, *Hist. Filey*, 98–102; Cortis, *Guide*, 62; O.S. Map 6" (1854).
[37] See p. 144.
[38] O.S. Map 25" (1891).
[39] *Plac. de Quo Warr.* (Rec. Com.), 189; *Cal. Inq. Misc.* i, p. 336; *Yorks. Inq.* i. 184.
[40] *Cal. Chart. R.* 1427–1516, 75; *Cal. Pat.* 1446–52, 46, 446.
[41] *Rot. Hund.* (Rec. Com.), i. 115.
[42] E.R.R.O., DDHU/9/32, p. 2.
[43] Ibid. /52.
[44] Ibid. /17/15. [45] Ibid. /3/21. [46] Ibid. /28.
[47] Directories.
[48] e.g. Hunmanby Par. Counc. Rec., Scrapbk. p. 38; see below, p. 229.
[49] See p. 132.
[50] B.I.H.R., C.P., H. 3498.
[51] Hun. Par. Counc. Rec., Scrapbk. pp. 34, 73.
[52] E.R.R.O., DDHU/9/356.
[53] *Rot. Litt. Claus.* (Rec. Com.), i. 446.
[54] *Bracton's Note Bk.* ed. Maitland, ii, p. 386; *Cur. Reg. R.* xiv. 224.

market which William de Neville had been holding on Sundays was transferred to Fridays, and at the same time Neville was granted an annual fair on 23–24 August.[55] Gilbert de Gant then complained again that Hunmanby market was prejudiced, alleging that William had stopped his former practice of allowing to Gilbert part of the tolls collected at Filey. The matter was settled, however, by an agreement that the tolls should be equally divided between them.[56] In 1256 it was the turn of Scarborough to be jealous of Filey's market but its attempt to have the market suppressed evidently failed.[57] Richard de Malbis claimed the right to hold the market and fair in 1293.[58] A Friday market for meat, butter, and poultry was still held during the 19th century,[59] and in 1861 stalls were still erected on one of the traditional fair days, though it was said that the custom was being gradually transferred to the anniversary of the Odd Fellows' Society.[60] The market was probably held in the triangular open space where Church Street and the Scarborough and Muston roads met. The cross was said in 1828 to have been moved not long before to a new position a few yards away,[61] but the pedestal was still in its old place in 1850.[62] The shaft was removed and lost later in the century.[63]

INDUSTRY. Ancillary trades based on fishing and shipping have for long provided some employment in Filey. There have presumably been a few boat-builders at most periods, like the shipwright mentioned in 1501.[64] A boat-building yard lay by the shore near Sand Road in 1869;[65] in the later 19th century there were three or four boat-builders, and still one in the 1920s.[66] A ropemaker was often recorded, too, in the 19th century and there was a ropery in Common Right Road in 1850 and another behind Queen Street in 1890.[67] For much of the 19th century there were six or more fish merchants in the town, and a few fish-curers as well.[68]

A mill in Filey was given, with the church, to Bridlington priory in the 12th century, and the gift of a mill there to St. Peter's hospital, York, was confirmed in 1148.[69] A windmill was recorded in the 16th century[70] and in the 19th century there was a wind corn-mill in Common Right Road, a miller being last recorded in 1892.[71] The first reference to brickmaking was in 1837, when land was let for a brickfield,[72] and in 1850 there were three brickyards close to the town.[73] Two yards were still worked in the early 20th century by the Filey Estate Brick Co. and the Seadale Brick Co., the latter last mentioned in 1913.[74]

Other small industrial establishments in the town included a mineral water works, which was in existence at least from 1889 to 1913.[75] After the Second World War the need to provide additional employment in the resort led to the establishment of a small industrial site off Muston Road. Several firms built premises there in the 1950s and 1960s.[76]

RESORT. By the end of the 18th century there were a few visitors to Filey as a watering-place but little had been done, it seems, to provide for them. In 1805 it was said that this would be one of the leading places for sea-bathing in the north of England if buildings were erected for visitors, 'but these accommodations are few and not likely to be increased'.[77] The New Inn, in the main street, may have been opened about this time, but in 1823 the Ship and the Pack Horse were the only other inns in the village. Lodgings in village houses, however, were being let.[78] The New Inn was later called the Hotel, the New Hotel, and Foord's Hotel. The Britannia had appeared by 1828 and the Hope by 1840,[79] but all the inns were still in the old village.

By 1828 Filey was nevertheless providing other facilities for its visitors, some of whom arrived on the Royal Union coach from Hull or the Original British Queen from Scarborough, which passed through the village three times a week. The 'spa well' on Carr Nase had been discovered, cobles were available for pleasure trips, and there were two bathing machines on the beach. A surgeon, William Munro, had, moreover, a portable tin warm bath for hire at his house.[80] By 1840 it could be claimed that Filey had risen to 'considerable celebrity' as a bathing place in the previous 20 years.[81]

Much of that celebrity had been attained only since 1835, when J. W. Unett began to develop the resort of 'New Filey'. It was perhaps a little earlier that William Voase built his summer retreat, and certainly by 1833 a small bath house had been built.[82] Unett let the baths to William Munro in 1836 and sold them to him two years later.[83] In the later 1830s Henry Bentley's villa was built and in the 1840s the first block of houses in the Crescent. Other terraces and some individual houses also appeared in the 1840s.[84]

At one such house, Cliff House, in North (later Belle Vue) Street, Charlotte Brontë stayed in 1849 and 1852, and between these visits she found Filey 'much altered; more lodging-houses, some of them very handsome, have been built'.[85] The railway lines were opened in 1846–7 and omnibuses from Foord's and Taylor's Hotels met the trains in 1853.[86] Edwin

[55] J.I. 1/534 m. 3.
[56] *Yorks. Fines, 1232–46*, 102.
[57] *Cal. Pat. 1247–58*, 477.
[58] *Plac. de Quo Warr.* (Rec. Com.), 207.
[59] J. Cole, *Hist. and Antiquities of Filey*, 3; E. W. Pritchard, *Observations on Filey as a Watering Place* (1853 edn.), 20–1; directories.
[60] W. S. Cortis, *Hist. and Descrip. Guide to Filey*, 18.
[61] Cole, *Hist. Filey*, 3 n. [62] O.S. Map 6" (1854).
[63] *T.E.R.A.S.* iv. 10. [64] *Cat. Anct. D.* vi, C 5330.
[65] E.R.R.O., DDUN/Box 4.
[66] Directories.
[67] Ibid.; O.S. Map 6" (1854); 25" (1891).
[68] Directories; A. Pettitt, *Filey Handbk.* (1868), 50.
[69] *Bridlington Charty.* 12; *E.Y.C.* i, p. 150.
[70] E 310/28/168 f. 29.
[71] O.S. Map 6" (1854); Bulmer, *Dir. E. Yorks.* (1892), 185.

[72] E.R.R.O., DDUN/Box 3. [73] O.S. Map 6" (1854).
[74] *Kelly's Dir. N. & E.R. Yorks.* (1913), 530.
[75] Ibid. (1889), 386; (1913), 529.
[76] Filey U.D.C. Offices, counc. mins. *passim*.
[77] *Gent. Mag. Libr. Eng. Topog.* xiv. 221–2.
[78] Baines, *Dir. Yorks.* (1823), ii. 204.
[79] J. Cole, *Hist. and Antiquities of Filey* (1828), 130; White, *Dir. E. & N.R. Yorks.* (1840), 382; *Dir. Hull & York* (1858), 681.
[80] Cole, *Hist. Filey*, 109, 113–14, 128–9.
[81] White, *Dir. E. & N.R. Yorks.* (1840), 381.
[82] See p. 134.
[83] E.R.R.O., DDUN/Box 3; Registry of Deeds, Beverley, FR/17/19. [84] See pp. 134–5.
[85] F. R. Pearson, *Charlotte Brontë on the E. Yorks. Coast* (E. Yorks. Loc. Hist. Ser. vii), 21–2, 24.
[86] E. W. Pritchard, *Observations on Filey as a Watering Place* (1853), 33.

Taylor then had the Royal Hotel, in North Street, but in 1854 he leased from Unett the newly-built Crescent (later Royal Crescent) Hotel.[87] The Crescent Hotel had hot and cold baths, open to all visitors to the resort, supplementing the facilities at Munro's hot baths in Murray Street.[88] Two new inns, the Grapes and the Three Tuns, had appeared by the 1850s and the number of lodging-houses rose from a mere eight in 1840 to 49 in 1858.[89] By the latter year visitors could identify each other in the *Filey Chronicle and Weekly List of Visitors*.[90]

In 1868 it was claimed that there were 40 lodging-houses facing the sea near the Crescent Hotel, as well as others in the streets behind and in the village; the Royal Hotel and another new establishment, the Belle Vue, were said to have been converted into private houses, but it was reckoned that Filey could offer accommodation to about 1,100 visitors, 120 of them in the Crescent Hotel.[91] Forty lodging-houses were listed in 1872 and 79 in 1879.[92] By this time several new villas had been built by wealthy summer migrants, and Voase's house, later called North Cliff Villa, had been enlarged after Sir Thomas Legard of Ganton bought it in 1845.[93]

Charlotte Brontë in 1852 had found scarcely any visitors in Filey in the first week of June, and in 1868 the season was said to run from late June until early October.[94] In 1871 there were already 175 entries in the first list of visitors published, on 2 July; by the first week in August there were just over 300 entries, and thereafter the number fell to about 275 on 3 September and 100 on 15 October.[95]

Filey was very much a fashionable resort. One local writer claimed in 1867 to have seen Earl Russell, Cardinal Wiseman, and the archbishop of York on the Brigg in one day; he referred to the presence of six or seven members of parliament staying in the town at the same time the previous summer, to Jenny Lind having lodged in the same house as Charlotte Brontë, and to the duchess of Cambridge having made a special visit to see the Brigg.[96] Entries in the visitors' lists certainly indicate that Filey attracted a different type of visitor from Bridlington during the second half of the century. The lists for the peak week of the season in 1857, 1870, and 1890, for example, suggest that only 6 per cent of visitors came from Hull, 19 per cent from the West Riding, 12 per cent from the rest of Yorkshire, and 13 per cent from the north-east Midlands. But as many as 17 per cent came from London and 12 per cent from the home counties and the south of England.[97]

The protection of the sea front against erosion began during the early stages of the development of the resort. South of Sand Road a wall was built by J. W. Unett to protect the undercliff below the Crescent. Much of its 300-yard length was swept away in the 1850s, but another wall, 200 yds. long, was built *c.* 1854.[98] Robert Mitford said in 1852 that 'some few years since' he had built a wall from Filey beck to Sand Road to protect the cliff,[99] and the local board put up a barrier there in the 1870s;[1] these had apparently gone by 1890.[2] The first sea walls were of wood with a stone filling.

While their promenades were thus secured, visitors were provided with few special facilities in the mid century. Events like concerts were held in such buildings as the Royal Hotel in the 1850s,[3] but by 1863 the Spa Saloon had been built on the sea front below the Crescent; it accommodated all kinds of entertainments, and in 1874 it consisted of a hall, reading and reception rooms, 6 bath rooms, and 6 lodging rooms.[4] By 1876 there was also a skating rink, in John Street.[5] A band was hired to play in the Crescent Gardens during the season,[6] subscriptions for the purpose being collected from visitors and residents, who in some years were slow in coming forward.[7] Otherwise, the natural attractions sufficed.

In the later years of the century and in the early 1900s the number of lodging-houses steadily increased. In 1889 112 lodgings were listed, in 1893 119, in 1897 152, in 1901 186, and in 1905 226. There may, however, have been a falling-off in the number of visitors even before the First World War, for only 190 lodgings appear in 1909 and 172 in 1913.[8] Facilities were much extended during this period and the sea defences greatly improved. A wall was built below the south end of the Crescent in 1885, various property-owners subscribing towards it and Osbaldeston-Mitford providing stone.[9] It was still, however, largely a timber structure, and it stretched from Crescent Hill southwards to the Bentleys' Ravine Villa estate.[10] Another wooden barrier was built in 1889 along the Ravine Villa frontage[11] by Edwin Martin, after he had bought the estate that year.[12] Finally, Unett's wall of the 1850s was bought in 1878 by the local board[13] and work began on a new 700-yard wall in 1892, Osbaldeston Mitford again giving stone from the shore.[14] The completed wall, stretching from the Coble Landing near Filey beck to Crescent Hill, was opened in 1894.[15]

The Spa Saloon, after failing to pay its way in the 1880s, was used solely as a lodging-house by 1890 and was known as Ackworth House. It was later enlarged and became a private hotel in 1897.[16]

---

[87] E.R.R.O., DDUN/Box 3.
[88] W. S. Cortis, *Hist. and Descrip. Guide to Filey* (1861), 40.
[89] White, *Dir. E. & N.R. Yorks.* (1840), 382; *Dir. Hull & York* (1858), 681–2.
[90] See p. 145.
[91] A. Pettitt, *Filey Handbk.* (1868), 7, 35.
[92] Directories.
[93] Regy. of Deeds, GF/337/386; Pettitt, *Handbk.* 34.
[94] Pearson, *Brontë on Coast*, 24; Pettitt, *Handbk.* 34.
[95] *Filey Post*, 1871, *passim*.
[96] G. Shaw, *Rambles about Filey* (1867), p. iv.
[97] *Filey Chronicle*, 8 Aug. 1857; *Filey Post*, 6 Aug. 1870; 23 Aug. 1890. See above, p. 59.
[98] E.R.R.O., DDUN/Box 3; Pritchard, *Observations on Filey*, 22.
[99] E.R.R.O., DDHU/9/83.
[1] Filey U.D.C. Offices, loc. govt. bd. mins. 1868–81, pp. 84, 98, 146–9.
[2] O.S. Map 25″ (1891).
[3] *Filey Chronicle*, 15 Sept. 1855.
[4] Regy. of Deeds, IL/36/45; E.R.R.O., DDUN/Box 3.
[5] G. Shaw, *Guide to Filey* (1878), 89.
[6] E.R.R.O., DDX/34/5; *Filey Chronicle*, 4 Aug. 1855.
[7] *Filey Post, passim*.
[8] Directories.
[9] E.R.R.O., DDHU/9/83; DDX/34/7.
[10] O.S. Map 25″ (1891); County Libr., County Hall, Beverley, postcards (n.d.); A. N. Cooper, *Guide to Filey* (n.d., 1st edn.), illus. facing p. 4.
[11] E.R.R.O., DDHU/3/24; DDX/16/35.
[12] Regy. of Deeds, 29/259/245 (1889).
[13] Ibid. MQ/198/299.
[14] E.R.R.O., DDHU/3/29–32.
[15] Ibid. DDX/16/35.
[16] Filey U.D.C. Offices, loc. govt. bd. mins. 1881–91, p. 322; O.S. Map 25″ (1891); *Filey Post*, 24 Nov. 1888; 28 Aug. 1897.

Entertainments were held elsewhere, dancing at the skating rink, for example, in 1888.[17] After 1876 the former Methodist chapel in Murray Street became the Victoria Rooms and a great variety of events took place there; it was enlarged in 1891 and renamed the Victoria Hall.[18] After 1900 the new infants' school in Mitford Street was also much used to stage entertainments.[19] Crescent Gardens were improved in 1891 and a shelter provided below the bandstand, which was later known as the Kiosk.[20] Ernest Taylor (alias Andie Caine) and his pierrots began performing at Filey in 1896,[21] and c. 1910 Caine opened the Alfresco Pavilion on ground called the Sylvan Glade, in South Crescent Road.[22] The Grand Hall and Picture Palace was opened in Union Street in 1910.[23]

Games facilities improved, too, in these years. A tennis club was formed in 1886 and its tennis and croquet ground behind the Crescent was much used by visitors.[24] So was the golf course, opened in 1897 north of the town, between the church and Carr Nase. Two years later the club moved to a new course south of the town, lying in the parishes of Muston and Hunmanby.[25]

After the First World War Filey, like Bridlington, experienced the difficulties and changes which confronted most seaside resorts.[26] In the early 1920s 140–150 lodging-houses were still listed,[27] but their numbers later decreased. Holiday flats in Filey and caravan camps around the town, however, provide much accommodation, and Butlin's holiday camp was opened 2 miles south of Filey after the Second World War.[28]

The Grand Cinema was joined in 1938 by the Brigg,[29] in Station Avenue, and Caine's hall in South Crescent Road continued in use, known in 1933 as the Royal Hippodrome.[30] In 1925 the pavilion at the tennis ground in Southdene was enlarged by the urban district council and used as a concert and dance hall; it was known as the Pavilion Theatre in 1970. The council also improved Crescent Gardens, which it bought in 1920, and new covered accommodation called the Sun Lounge was built there in 1961.[31] More holiday facilities were provided in the house and grounds at Ravine Villa after the council acquired it in 1930. Other acquisitions by the council included the foreshore south of the Brigg in Filey, Muston, and Hunmanby in 1927; the remainder of the foreshore and the Brigg itself in 1953; and Carr Nase and much cliff-top land north of the town in 1965.[32] The sea defences and promenades were improved in 1929, when major repairs were needed to the wall opened in 1894, and in 1954–5, when a new wall and promenade called the Royal Parade were constructed from Crescent Hill southwards. The latter replaced the old timber barriers, which were badly damaged during the storms of 1953.[33]

SOCIAL INSTITUTIONS. A friendly society was established in Filey 'several years' before 1828,[34] and later in the century a temperance society, freemasons, Shepherds, and Oddfellows were all holding meetings in the town.[35] The Freemasons' Hall, in Rutland Street, was built and opened in 1909–10.[36] A mechanics' institute was founded in 1858, meeting in a house in Clarence Place.[37] Various societies were established in the late 19th and early 20th centuries, including a debating society in 1886.[38] A museum was established by the local history society in 1970, in cottages in Queen Street.

A free library is said to have been founded in 1825[39] but later in the century there were only circulating and subscription libraries in the town. James Knaggs's circulating library, for example, existed by 1855.[40] The county council established a branch library at Filey in 1933, housed in a new building in Southdene.[41]

The town's first newspaper was the *Filey Chronicle and Weekly List of Visitors*, established in 1855. It was called the *Filey Chronicle and General Advertiser* in 1858. The paper was published, during the 'season' only, until c. 1865, at first by James Knaggs and later by M. T. Kendall.[42] A second paper, the *Filey Advertiser*, apparently first appeared in 1863, published by A. Halliday, but lasted only a few years.[43] The *Filey Post and Weekly List of Visitors* was established in 1865 by G. R. Jackson and appeared, throughout the year, until 1918. Jackson published it from Driffield after 1885, as did his executors from 1894.[44] After 1918 Filey had no paper until 1931, when the *Filey News and Hunmanby Herald* was established by Lister Reekie. It survived until 1955, when it was incorporated with the *Scarborough Mercury*.[45]

PUBLIC SERVICES. In the early 19th century the whole village took its water from a spring on the north side of the beck below the churchyard.[46] To provide for the growing town the Filey Waterworks Co. was formed in 1856 and began to supply water that year. A reservoir was built in 1858 near springs at Rosedale, in Hunmanby parish. Besides Filey the company supplied those parts of Hunmanby and Muston close to the line of the mains.[47] A second

---

[17] *Filey Post*, 15 Dec. 1888.   [18] Ibid. 2 May 1891.
[19] Ibid. *passim*.   [20] Ibid. 6 June 1891; 26 May 1900.
[21] Ibid. 1 July 1905.
[22] Ibid. 16 Feb., 11 May 1907; 16 July 1910; O.S. Map 25" (1928).
[23] *Filey Post*, 30 Dec. 1911.
[24] Ibid. 27 Mar. 1886; O.S. Map 25" (1891).
[25] *Filey Post*. 5 June 1897; 22 Apr., 27 May, 5 Aug. 1899.
[26] See p. 60.   [27] Directories.   [28] See p. 230.
[29] Ex inf. Clerk to the Council, County Hall, Beverley, 1971.   [30] *Kelly's Dir. N. & E.R. Yorks.* (1933), 468.
[31] Filey U.D.C. Offices, U.D.C. mins.
[32] Regy. of Deeds, 209/184/157; 334/539/415; 343/23/18; 400/53/40; 941/511/447; 1473/497/430.
[33] E.R.R.O., DDX/16/35.
[34] J. Cole, *Hist. and Antiquities of Filey*, 127.
[35] The Oddfellows' lodge is said to have been established in 1835 and the temperance society in 1840: *Allison's Filey Guide* (1856), 12, 37.

[36] Stone on building; *Filey Post*, 2, 9 July 1910.
[37] *Filey Chronicle*, 17 July, 16 Oct. 1858.
[38] *Filey Post*, 8 May 1886.
[39] Cole, *Hist. Filey*, 128.
[40] *Filey Chronicle*, 1855, *passim*.
[41] E.R. Educ. Cttee. *Mins.* 1932–3, 38; 1933–4, 39.
[42] *Newspaper Press Dir.* 1857–65. Copies for 1855–8 are in the B.M. Newspaper Libr., Colindale.
[43] *Newspaper Press Dir.* 1864–8.
[44] Ibid. 1865 sqq. A complete file of the *Post* from 3 July 1869 to 8 June 1918 is at Colindale.
[45] *Newspaper Press Dir.* 1931 sqq. Copies from 3 Jan. 1953 to 14 May 1955 are at Colindale.
[46] Baines, *Hist. Yorks.* (1823), ii. 204; J. Cole, *Hist. and Antiquities of Filey*, 123; O.S. Map 25" (1891).
[47] E.R.R.O., DDHU/9/339–40, 346–7; Filey Waterworks Act 1856, 19 & 20 Vic., c. 19; *Filey Chronicle*, 2 Aug. 1856. The minutes of an informal cttee. and then of the company, 1854–86, are in Filey U.D.C. Offices.

reservoir was built at Rosedale in 1886[48] and the supply area was extended to Gristhorpe and Lebberston in 1891.[49] The company was acquired by the urban district council in 1898.[50] As late as 1889 the Rosedale supply had to be supplemented by water from private wells and public springs in Filey.[51] A deep well was sunk, however, near Filey railway station in 1891,[52] and the water pumped to the Rosedale reservoirs. Further boreholes have since been sunk, close to the first. The undertaking was transferred to the East Yorkshire (Wolds Area) Water Board in 1962.[53] The Rosedale reservoirs were no longer used in 1970, when a new reservoir to serve the area was being constructed in Muston parish.[54]

A first attempt to light the town with gas was made soon after 1846 before the task was successfully accomplished in 1852.[55] The Filey Gas Co. was bought by the waterworks company in 1859,[56] and so the supply of gas was also the responsibility of the U.D.C. after 1898. The gasworks stood from the beginning near the railway station. After nationalization production at Filey ceased in 1961 and gas was supplied from the grid; North Sea gas was introduced in 1968.[57]

Electricity was supplied to Filey from Scarborough in 1930.[58]

Alarm about the inadequate sewerage of the town was caused in 1855 when two children on holiday there died, apparently of diarrhoea. J. W. Unett immediately arranged for Pigot Smith, the superintendent engineer of the Birmingham drainage works, to visit Filey, and a nuisance removal committee was appointed by the vestry to administer the work. The drainage was laid in 1856–7. All the private sewers which formerly discharged upon the beach were intercepted by a single main sewer, which led to Church Ravine and thence to an outfall at low-water mark on the beach.[59]

Further works were undertaken, perhaps c. 1880, and an outfall was constructed near the Spa Saloon. In 1895–6, however, a scheme was carried out with a single outfall from Church Ravine.[60] A new scheme was carried out in the town itself in the 1950s, including a pumping station at Coble Landing, and in the council's extended area to the south of the town in the early 1960s.[61]

The parish constables were supplemented by a member of the newly-formed East Riding Constabulary in 1857.[62] An old lock-up, probably on the Muston road just south of Church Street, was demolished c. 1866.[63] The police station was later situated in Hope Street, but in 1892 it was replaced by a new station, in Murray Street.[64] The red-brick building, with paired and round-headed windows, was still in use in 1970.

A fire engine was bought by the local board in 1891 and a brigade with twelve firemen established. The first station was at the Beach.[65] A new station was opened in Queen Street c. 1900,[66] but in 1946 it was moved to Butlin's holiday camp.[67] In 1948 the brigade passed under the control of the county council and in 1950 premises in Mitford Street were converted to a fire station.[68]

Additions to St. Oswald's churchyard sufficed for the town until 1954, when a cemetery east of Grange Avenue was consecrated.[69]

In the later 19th century the post office in Filey was situated successively in King and Murray Streets. After 1900 it was for a time in Union Street before being moved to a purpose-built office in Murray Street in 1913.[70]

A telegraph service was established at the post office in 1870.[71] The National Telephone Co. installed a telephone service at Filey in 1906,[72] and it was taken over by the Post Office in 1912.[73]

Several houses in the town have been used as private convalescent homes. They include the former North Cliff Villa, used as a home since the 1920s[74] and known in 1970 as Newland House. An old people's home was built by the county council in Station Avenue and opened in 1970.[75]

LOCAL GOVERNMENT. THE MANOR. In the late 13th century the lord of Filey claimed the assize of bread and ale, pillory, and tumbril.[76] From the 17th century and later there are surviving presentments by the Filey jury at manorial courts held at Hunmanby. In the late 17th century there were elected a constable, a pinder, 2 ale-tasters, and 3 bylawmen for Filey, and in the period 1790–1850 2 constables and a pinder were usually appointed.[77] A short list of pains was made in 1690.[78]

THE VESTRY. Filey joined the Scarborough union in 1837.[79] There may have been a parish poorhouse in the early 19th century, for the 'poor houses' were still recorded, in Betton's Lane, in 1850.[80] The vestry continued to appoint 4 or more constables until 1872, and 2 surveyors of highways and 2 gas inspectors until 1868, when their work was taken

---

[48] E.R.R.O., DDHU/9/348, 354; Bulmer, *Dir. E. Yorks.* (1892), 180.
[49] Filey Water and Gas Act 1891, 54 & 55 Vic., c. 28.
[50] Ibid. 1898, 61 & 62 Vic., c. 230.
[51] *Filey Post*, 7 Dec. 1889.
[52] Ibid. 26 Sept. 1891.
[53] Filey U.D.C. Offices, U.D.C. mins.
[54] Ex inf. Miss L. M. Owston, Hunmanby, 1971.
[55] W. S. Cortis, *Hist. and Descrip. Guide to Filey* (1861), 27.
[56] Registry of Deeds, Beverley, GI/102/7.
[57] Ex inf. N.E. Gas. Bd., Filey and Hull, 1970–1.
[58] Ex inf. District Manager, N.E. Elect. Bd., Scarborough, 1968.
[59] Filey U.D.C. Offices, nuisance removal cttee. min. bk. 1855–66, *passim*; *Filey Chronicle*, 29 Sept., 6 Oct. 1855; 5 July 1856; see below, p 147.
[60] Filey U.D.C. Offices, local govt. bd. mins. 1868–81, pp. 283, 369; 1891–7, pp. 83, 189, 251, 296; *Filey Post*, 9 Jan. 1897.
[61] Filey U.D.C. Offices, U.D.C. mins.
[62] E.R.R.O., QAP/3/1.
[63] Filey U.D.C. Offices, vestry min. bk. 1864–89 (*sub* 1866).
[64] *Filey Post*, 23 Jan., 15 Oct. 1892.
[65] *Filey Post*, 14 Feb., 28 Nov. 1891.
[66] *Kelly's Dir. N. & E.R. Yorks.* (1901), 495.
[67] Filey U.D.C. Offices, U.D.C. mins. 1947, p. 214.
[68] E.R.C.C. *Mins.* 1949–50, 212, 348.
[69] York Dioc. Regy. (Minister), Sentence of consecration.
[70] Registry of Deeds, Beverley, 140/301/267; /302/268; directories; *Filey Post*, 7 June 1913.
[71] Ex inf. the Archivist, P.O. Records, London, 1971.
[72] *Filey Post*, 14 Apr. 1906.
[73] Ex inf. P.O. Archivist.   [74] Directories.
[75] E.R.C.C. *Mins.* 1969–70, 214, 328.
[76] *Plac. de Quo Warr.* (Rec. Com.), 207.
[77] E.R.R.O., DDHU/10/1 (e.g. 78, 85, 87, 95, 102); /29, 32, 36, 40, 43, 65; S.C. 2/211/64–6.
[78] E.R.R.O., DDHU/10/1 (89).
[79] *3rd Rep. Poor Law Com.* 174.
[80] O.S. Map 6″ (1854).

over by the local board. Four churchwardens were appointed, one of them for Gristhorpe and one for Lebberston. The vestry also established a nuisance removal committee in 1855; it consisted of thirteen men, including William Graburn as chairman, a secretary, and an inspector. Committee members were elected at vestry meetings until the local board took over their work. The committee carried out a drainage scheme and in 1856 levied a rate of 1s. in the pound, reduced to 6d. in subsequent years, on people using the new sewers. Money raised by the highway rate also went towards the work.[81]

THE TOWN COUNCIL. In 1868 the Local Government Act of 1858 was adopted and a local board established for the township of Filey.[82] It consisted of nine elected representatives, including the Revd. Arthur Pettitt as chairman, with a clerk and a treasurer. Several of the members had served on the nuisance removal committee. The first board meeting was held in the Royal Hotel, North Street, and a room in Queen Street was appointed as the office. Subsequently, however, the offices were said to be in North Street and they remained there for the life of the board.[83]

The board took over the work of the surveyors of highways and the gas inspectors, and the first committees appointed were for highways, nuisance removal, and general improvement. The joint office of surveyor and inspector of nuisances was also established in 1868, and a scavenger was appointed the following year. A medical officer of health was first appointed in 1873. Much of the board's time was devoted to sewerage, lighting, and sea defences.[84] General improvements to the town included the planting of trees in Station Road and West Street and the laying out of ornamental walks in Church Ravine, which the board bought in 1869. Work in the ravine, completed in 1871, also involved the culverting of the stream, the construction of a roadway, and the erection of an iron bridge leading to the church. Reynolds Street was widened in 1877 and several streets were flagged. From its early years the board also inspected plans for new houses.

Under the Local Government Act of 1894, the board became the urban district council, holding its first meeting in January 1895.[85] Meetings continued at first to be held in North Street but in 1897–8 the council built the offices in Queen Street which had been projected by the board. There were nine councillors, including four of the last members of the board, and the first chairman was Nicholas Maley.

The offices remained in Queen Street until 1940, when a house in West Avenue was leased for the purpose, but in 1949 they were moved to the Cottage (formerly Cliff Cottage) behind Queen Street. The former office building in Queen Street was used by various government departments. The Cottage, altered and enlarged, was used until 1971, when the offices were moved to the former convent school in John Street. Additional committees were set up as the activities of the council increased in the 20th century.[86] They included, from 1920, a pleasure grounds committee, and an entertainments manager was first appointed in 1946. The number of councillors was increased to twelve in 1923.

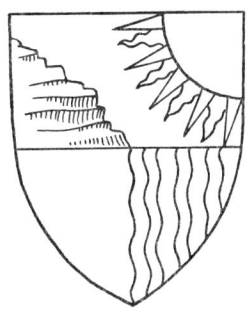

FILEY URBAN DISTRICT. *Per fess, in chief azure a representation of Filey Brig proper with the sun shining thereon or, the base per pale wavy gold and also azure three pallets wavy argent on the last*
[Granted 1952]

CHURCHES. The church at Filey was part of Walter de Gant's foundation endowment of Bridlington priory in the early 12th century.[87] No vicarage was ordained, and the church was served by priests supplied by the priory.[88] Curates were similarly supported by the impropriators after the Dissolution and the living remained a perpetual curacy until the later 19th century, when it became a vicarage.

The advowson was exempted from the 16th-century Crown leases of the rectory but it was included in the grant of 1601 and thereafter descended with the rectory.[89] After 1835 the Brookes and later the Firmans had two turns and the Osbaldeston-Mitfords and later the Bayleys had one. Their turns were sold to trustees in 1926–7[90] and the advowson has since belonged to the parochial church council.[91]

The parochial chaplain received £4 13s. 4d. in 1526 and a second chaplain £1.[92] In the late 17th century 8½ bovates of land were recorded as belonging to the living,[93] but this may have been rectorial glebe allowed to the use of the curate by the impropriator; it is not mentioned again. A stipend, usually said to be £15, was paid by the impropriator in the 18th century.[94] The curacy was augmented from Queen Anne's Bounty in 1780, 1791, and 1796, on each occasion by £200; parliamentary grants totalling £600 were made in 1810, to meet a benefaction of £400 from Humphrey Osbaldeston, and another of £1,000 in 1814.[95] In 1829–31 the average

---

[81] Filey U.D.C. Offices, vestry min. bk. 1864–89; nuisance removal cttee. min. bk. 1855–66.
[82] *Lond. Gaz.* 19 June 1868, p. 3434. The following paragraphs are based on the board's minutes, in Filey U.D.C. Offices.
[83] G. Shaw, *Guide to Filey* (1878), 89; directories.
[84] See p. 144.
[85] The following paragraphs are based on the council's minutes, in the U.D.C. Offices, together with a TS. list of 'Items from Council Mins.'.
[86] See p. 146.

[87] *Bridlington Charty.* 12.
[88] *Reg. Greenfield*, iii (Sur. Soc. cli), 173.
[89] See p. 140.
[90] Registry of Deeds, Beverley, 318/169/141; 343/437/370.
[91] Directories; *Crockford*.
[92] *Y.A.J.* xxiv. 78.
[93] B.I.H.R., TER. J. Filey n.d.
[94] Ibid. 1716 etc.; Regy. of Deeds, BG/310/43; *Herring's Visit.* i. 217.
[95] Hodgson, *Q.A.B.* 439; Lawton, *Rer. Eccles. Dioc. Ebor.* ii. 296.

net income was £95.[96] It was augmented with £20 a year in 1851,[97] and in 1892 it was said that Elinor Clarke had 'recently' given £5,000.[98] In 1884 the income was £343.[99]

By 1817 57 a. of glebe land at Misson (Notts.) had been bought with Bounty money.[1] There is no record of a parsonage house until one was built, in Church Street, by Theodosia Brooke, Admiral Mitford, and the Revd. T. N. Jackson in 1845.[2] This was sold in 1967 and a house bought in Belle Vue Crescent;[3] the old building was later demolished.

The church benefits from the charity of Jane Spink, who by will proved in 1897 bequeathed £50 for a lending library at St. Oswald's. Under a Scheme of 1935 the income is used for Sunday-school prizes.[4]

A statue of Our Lady in Filey church was mentioned in 1502, when William Blackburn, bailiff of the Percy estate at Hunmanby, left money for a light to burn before it; he also left £12 for a priest to celebrate for him for three years.[5]

In 1743 the curacy of Filey was supplied by the vicar of Folkton, who was then also vicar of Hunmanby; Filey was served by an assistant curate who had charge of three other places as well.[6] The vicar of Hunmanby employed an assistant curate who served Folkton and Filey in 1764.[7] The incumbent in 1835 also had Filey served by an assistant curate.[8] The vicar of Filey was non-resident in 1865 and resident in 1871, in both years having the services of an assistant.[9]

Modern incumbents include A. N. Cooper (vicar 1880–1935), who was noted for his preaching and for his walks from Filey to distant parts of England and Europe. He wrote several books on his church and on the neighbourhood.

A weekly service was held in 1743 and communion was administered three times a year, 100 people having received it the previous Easter.[10] By 1765 communion was administered four times a year to about sixty people.[11] In 1851 two services were held each Sunday in summer, when congregations were said to be doubled by visitors to the resort.[12] Before 1865 communion services had been increased to six a year but monthly celebrations were then being tried. There were 24–30 communicants in winter and 32–40 in summer. In the 1860s and later there were apparently two Sunday services the whole year. In 1877 communion was administered twice a month. By 1884 there were four services on Sundays, and A. N. Cooper claimed an out-of-season congregation of 500, rising to 1,200 in the summer; communion was administered weekly to about forty people. There were only two Sunday services in 1894.[13] In 1970 there were three.

The church of ST. OSWALD is of stone and consists of clerestoried nave, north and south aisles, chancel, transepts, central tower, and north and south porches.[14] The early Norman church was apparently partly rebuilt at the end of the 12th century: the nave, aisles, and clerestory all date from that period. The five-bay arcades have pointed arches and the columns are alternately octagonal and round. The clerestory windows, however, are round-headed and there is a similar opening in the north aisle. Externally there is a chamfered corbel-table above the clerestory. At the west end a sixth bay of each arcade is formed by a large pier and a respond, and these were clearly intended to support a tower which was never built. The piers have three clustered shafts on the sides facing towards the nave, but the other sides are plain. The round-headed south door is also of c. 1200 and the bowl-shaped font may belong to the same period.

In the earlier 13th century the easternmost, seventh, bay of the nave was removed, together with the early Norman chancel, and the present chancel, transepts, and central tower were built. The irregular piers of the tower have been described as a 'singular botch', and the tower is wider than the nave. It is possible that a complete rebuilding of the church on the scale of the new eastern half was intended but that, for some reason, the older nave was allowed to remain. Single lancet windows in the chancel and transepts appear to be original, but the east window, consisting of three grouped lancets, as well as the paired lancets at the end of each aisle, are 19th-century work. The chancel floor is two steps lower than the rest of the church. The trefoil-headed piscina in the chancel and triple sedilia in both chancel and south transept are typical of the earlier 13th century. So, too, are the shafted and moulded doorways in the chancel.

Externally the chancel and transepts had a coved corbel-table which was carried round the tower, a continuous string-course, and buttresses with volutes at their heads and bases. Only in a few places have these survived without restoration. The two-light belfry openings of the tower, each set under a single arch with an unpierced tympanum, are of an unusually early character for the 13th century. Indications of earlier and more steeply-pitched roofs remain on all four faces of the tower.

The external walls of the aisles have been so much altered that little original work remains. Whether the present 19th-century windows are copies of the former ones cannot be said. They consist mainly of paired lancets, but one window in the south aisle has tracery of 13th-century character. There are signs that the south aisle formerly had a much lower eaves level. The north aisle wall is known to have been rebuilt and the north porch is modern.

Other features include a cross in the interior wall above the south door and a double niche externally above the same door; the insertion of the niche has destroyed part of the moulding. A fragment of an

---

[96] *Rep. Com. Eccl. Revenues*, 934–5.
[97] B.I.H.R., TER. J. Filey 1857.
[98] Bulmer, *Dir. E. Yorks.* (1892), 182.
[99] B.I.H.R., Bp. V. 1884/Ret.
[1] Ibid., TER. J. Filey 1817 etc.
[2] Ibid. 1861.
[3] Regy. of Deeds, 1484/341/306; 1509/501/435.
[4] Char. Com. files.
[5] *Test. Ebor.* iv. 202–3.
[6] *Herring's Visit.* i. 217.
[7] B.I.H.R., Bp. V. 1764/Ret. 187.
[8] *Rep. Com. Eccl. Revenues*, 934–5.
[9] B.I.H.R., V. 1865/Ret. 182; V. 1871/Ret. 167; V. 1877/Ret.; Bp. V. 1884/Ret.; Bp. V. 1894/Ret.
[10] *Herring's Visit.* i. 217.
[11] B.I.H.R., Bp. V. 1764/Ret. 187.
[12] H.O. 129/24/525.
[13] B.I.H.R., V. 1865/Ret. 182; V. 1871/Ret. 167; V. 1877/Ret.; Bp. V. 1884/Ret.; Bp. V. 1894/Ret.; A. Pettitt, *Filey Handbk.* (1868), 35–6.
[14] Morris, *E. Yorks.* 159–61; G. A. Poole and J. W. Hugall, *Chs. of Scarborough, Filey, and Neighbourhood* (1848), 109 sqq.; J. Bilson, *St. Oswald's, the Parish Ch. of Filey*.

Anglian stone, with an interlaced pattern, is used as a step in the tower stair.[15] In the porch is an old bench-end with a poppy-head. A small stone effigy, thought to represent a canon of Bridlington,[16] has been built into the wall of the south aisle, and there is a Royal Arms in the north aisle.

The church was restored in 1839 and again in 1885–6. On the latter occasion the north aisle wall and parts of the transepts were rebuilt, the nave and aisles were reroofed, and the floor was lowered.[17]

The monuments include several 18th-century tablets to members of the Beswick family, of Gristhorpe and elsewhere. There are monuments by Skelton of York and others.[18]

There were four bells in 1552[19] but only three by 1764.[20] They are dated 1675, 1682, and 1700 and all were made by Samuel Smith, the elder, of York.[21] The oldest item of plate is a late-17th-century silver cup, made in York. Two silver cups, made in London in 1807, were presented by C. G. Wheelhouse in 1894. The 20th-century items include a plate given by A. V. Machin in 1909.[22]

The registers begin in 1600 for baptisms and 1695 for marriages and burials, but there are large gaps. Entries of baptisms are missing for 1612–93, 1712–15, and 1740–88; of marriages for 1696–1703, 1708–12, 1720–4, and 1732–53; and of burials for 1696, 1703–5, and 1740–88.[23]

The churchyard was extended in 1840, 1873, and 1923.[24]

A chapel dedicated to St. Bartholomew existed in Filey in the early Middle Ages,[25] and its ruins were in 1566 granted by the Crown to Francis Barker and Thomas Blackway.[26] Thereafter the parish church of St. Oswald was sufficient for the needs of the village until the 19th century, when the development of the resort began. An iron church was erected in West Street in 1857,[27] and the permanent building of ST. JOHN THE EVANGELIST was opened as a chapel-of-ease to the parish church in 1871.[28] It is in a 13th-century style, and consists of nave, chancel, and transepts.

In 1861 there were two weekly services at the iron church[29] and in 1868 two on week-days as well.[30] There were two Sunday services at the new church in 1877, when it was open from July to October.[31] There were also two in 1970, with an additional one in summer.

Medieval chapels are recorded in none of the townships, and no action was taken on the recommendation in 1650 that together they should be made into a separate parish.[32] Services were held in hired rooms there in 1894.[33]

A temporary iron church of ST. THOMAS, in the cure of the vicar of Filey, was built at Gristhorpe by W. M. B. Beswick in 1897.[34] One service was held each Sunday in 1970.

ROMAN CATHOLICISM. Farley Coulson and his wife were presented for recusancy in 1633, 1640, and 1653.[35] There is no record of organized Roman Catholicism in the town until the Revd. E. Roulin, in 1904 or 1905, was sent from Ampleforth as chaplain to the Sisters living in Filey. A chapel at the convent was at first used for worship, but in 1905 a temporary building was put up in Brooklands.[36] A permanent church of St. Mary, on the same site, was opened in 1906, designed by Father Roulin in the 'Italian' manner; it is built largely of bright red brick and consists of nave, chancel, and bell-turret. An extension was opened in 1961.[37]

The Sisters of Charity established the Convent of the Sacred Heart in John Street in 1904 and opened a school there in 1905.[38] They bought the former South Cliff Villas near by in 1907, altered and extended them in 1911, and bought two adjoining houses in 1938 and 1947.[39] The convent school continued to be housed there until 1969, when the Sisters sold the property.[40] The Sisters of Mercy acquired a house in South Crescent Road in 1943[41] and subsequently built a chapel beside it.

PROTESTANT NONCONFORMITY. The only dissenters reported in 1743 were one family of Quakers,[42] and there is only one record, in 1817, of a house licensed for worship in Filey.[43]

Methodists are said to have visited Filey in 1806 and four years later to have formed a society which had fifteen members in 1823. The subsequent conversion of the fishing community has been attributed largely to the work of 'Johnny' Oxtoby.[44] The first building used as a chapel by the Wesleyans, in Mosey's Yard off Queen Street, was acquired in 1811.[45] It was replaced by a new chapel, in Murray Street, in 1838[46] and this was enlarged in 1859.[47] Trinity Methodist Church, in Union Street, was built in 1876.[48] The Murray Street building subsequently became the Victoria Rooms (later Hall)[49]

---

[15] Y.A.J. xxi. 258.
[16] Ibid. xxxvii. 195–7 and illus.
[17] White, Dir. E. & N.R. Yorks. (1840), 381; Bulmer, Dir. E. Yorks. (1892), 180; A. N. Cooper, Filey and its Church (2nd edn., 1889), 30.
[18] Monuments to Robt. Shepherd (d. 1813), Geo. Beswick (d. 1829), J. W. Unett (d. 1856), and Wm. Watt (d. 1858).
[19] Inventories of Ch. Goods, 21.
[20] B.I.H.R., TER. J. Filey 1764.
[21] Boulter, 'Ch. Bells', 216; V.C.H. Yorks. ii. 452.
[22] Yorks. Ch. Plate, i. 80.
[23] Barley, Par. Docs. E.R. 48.
[24] B.I.H.R., CD. 195; York Dioc. Regy., Sentences of consecration.
[25] Bridlington Charty. 77.
[26] Cal. Pat. 1563–6, 475.
[27] W. S. Cortis, Hist. and Descrip. Guide to Filey (1861), 37 and map.
[28] Filey Post, 19 Aug. 1871.
[29] Cortis, Guide to Filey, 38.
[30] Pettitt, Filey Handbk. 35–6.
[31] B.I.H.R., V. 1877/Ret.
[32] T.E.R.A.S. ii. 59.
[33] B.I.H.R., Bp. V. 1894/Ret.
[34] Filey Post, 17 July 1897.
[35] H. Aveling, Post Reformation Catholicism in E. Yorks. 1558–1790 (E. Yorks. Loc. Hist. Ser. xi), 59.
[36] Filey Post, 22 Oct., 26 Nov. 1904; 8 Apr. 1905.
[37] Ibid. 9 Sept. 1905; notes in church.
[38] Filey Post, 28 Jan. 1905. Inscription on building: 'Magister Adest 1904–1954'.
[39] Registry of Deeds, Beverley, 97/422/377 (1907); 607/454/351; 764/177/149; Filey Post, 24 June 1911.
[40] Regy. of Deeds, 1636/520/414; local inf.
[41] Regy. of Deeds, 667/147/129.
[42] Herring's Visit. i. 217.
[43] B.I.H.R., DMH. Reg. 1, p. 50.
[44] G. Shaw, Our Filey Fishermen (1867), 16–18.
[45] Char. Com. files; W. S. Cortis, Hist. and Descrip. Guide to Filey (1861), 38; A. N. Cooper, Guide to Filey (1st edn., n.d.), 27.
[46] White, Dir. E. & N.R. Yorks. (1840), 381.
[47] Cortis, Guide, 38.
[48] Kelly's Dir. N. & E.R. Yorks. (1879), 393; date on building.
[49] Cooper, Guide, 27.

and has since been demolished. Trinity Church is a large stone building, designed in an early Gothic style with a turret and spire. It was restored after a fire in 1918 and reopened in 1923.[50] The church benefits from the charity of Jane Spink, who by will proved in 1897 bequeathed £500 to it.[51]

The first Primitive Methodist chapel was built in Chapel (later Mitford) Street in 1823[52] and enlarged in 1843 and 1859.[53] Known as Bethesda Chapel,[54] it was replaced by Ebenezer Methodist Church, in Union Street, built in 1870.[55] The Primitives had 269 members in 1889.[56] Bethesda Chapel became the Albert Hall[57] and still stood in 1970, a stuccoed building having round-headed windows with Gothic glazing bars. Ebenezer Church is built of red brick with stone dressings in an ornate Italian style. In the early 20th century the Primitives also held cliff-top services, especially for the fishermen.[58]

In 1860 the Independents bought a site for a chapel, but it was never used.[59]

The Methodists were described in 1865 as dividing their attendance between chapel and parish church, and in 1877 dissent was alleged by the vicar to have an 'immense hold' on the parish.[60]

By 1892 the Plymouth Brethren were meeting in the Albert Hall and they continued there until at least the 1930s, besides holding street services.[61] In 1944 they registered for worship a room in Belle Vue Street, but this had ceased to be used before 1954.[62] The Town Mission, which had been 'originally introduced as the Christian Army', also met in the Albert Hall in 1892.[63] The Friends met at the Mechanics' Institute in 1858, at the Masonic Hall in 1913, and still in Rutland Street in 1929.[64] A Salvation Army hall in West Avenue, perhaps the former Wesleyan school, is mentioned in 1933, but by 1937 the Army met in the Albert Hall.[65] Kingdom Hall, in Mitford Street, was registered by the Jehovah's Witnesses in 1946 but was disused by 1954,[66] and the Christian Science Society began to hold meetings in Rutland Street in 1960.[67]

In the townships a Wesleyan chapel was built at Gristhorpe in 1826[68] and by 1877 there was a Primitive Methodist chapel there, too.[69] The latter stood in Back Lane;[70] the former, lying between Gristhorpe and Lebberston, still served the two villages in 1970.

EDUCATION. The curate of St. Oswald's church was reported in 1595 to be teaching without a licence.[71]

In 1819 a school in Filey was attended by 40–50 children.[72] It was succeeded by a Church of England National school in 1831, held at first in a Methodist chapel which was found to be 'very inconvenient'. Apparently in 1832 a school was built by a Mrs Watson, of Filey, on a site belonging to the parish.[73] The building housed mixed, infants', and sewing schools and was attended by 90 boys and 70 girls in 1835. It was supported by subscriptions and school pence. Two other schools were attended by 9 boys and 21 girls in 1835.[74] The National school may have been rebuilt in 1839 and it was enlarged in 1846 to accommodate about 200 children.[75] It received an annual parliamentary grant by 1859.[76] The school stood on the Scarborough road.[77]

A new National school was built, on the old site, in 1874, still with accommodation for boys, girls, and infants.[78] In 1865 the infants' school and the girls' sewing school together had 110 pupils and the National school had 80; in 1877 the infants' school had 60–70 and the National school c. 100.[79] The National school was enlarged in 1892[80] and the infants' school was separated from it in 1900, when a new building was erected in Mitford Street.[81]

A Wesleyan school was apparently built near the Murray Street chapel in 1842,[82] and in 1857 a larger school was erected behind the chapel, fronting upon West Street.[83] By 1859 it received an annual parliamentary grant.[84] The National and Wesleyan schools provided the bulk of the school accommodation in the town: in 1871, for example, they had between them 296 places, while a private school school had only 14.[85]

By 1905 the National and Wesleyan schools had insufficient accommodation to meet the town's needs. The National school was extended, and a new County school was built in 1908 on West Road and opened the following year.[86] The Wesleyan school, with an attendance of about 180, thereupon closed.[87] It may have been used in the 1930s by the Salvation Army[88] and had been converted into shops by 1970. Attendance at the National school was 379 in 1908 and remained at 360–400 until 1914. It fell to 315–40 in the 1920s and then declined to 228 in 1938. The County school had an attendance of 187 in 1911,

---

[50] *Kelly's Dir. N. & E.R. Yorks.* (1921), 513; (1925), 534.
[51] Char. Com. files.
[52] Cortis, *Guide*, 38. Registered in 1824: G.R.O. Worship Returns, Vol. v, no. 3928; B.I.H.R. DMH. Reg. 1, p. 478.
[53] Registry of Deeds, Beverley, HY/200/266; Cortis, *Guide*, 38; Sheahan and Whellan, *Hist. York & E. R.* ii. 466.
[54] e.g. *Lond. Gaz.* 20 Jan 1863, p. 332.
[55] Date on building; G. Shaw, *Rambles about Filey* (2nd edn. 1886), 42.
[56] H. Woodcock, *Sketches of Prim. Meth. on Yorks. Wolds*, 154.
[57] Bulmer, *Dir. E. Yorks.* (1892), 182.
[58] E.R.R.O., DDX/74/1, p. 2.
[59] Char. Com. files; Regy. of Deeds, IC/85/118; Cortis, *Guide*, 38.
[60] B.I.H.R., V. 1865/Ret. 182; V. 1877/Ret.
[61] E.R.R.O., DDX/74/1, p. 12; Bulmer, *Dir. E. Yorks.* (1892), 183; *Kelly's Dir. N. & E.R. Yorks.* (1933), 465.
[62] G.R.O. Worship Reg. no. 60959.
[63] Bulmer, *Dir. E. Yorks.* (1892), 182.
[64] *Filey Chronicle*, 25 Sept. 1858; *Kelly's Dir. N. & E.R. Yorks.* (1913), 529; (1929), 495.
[65] *Kelly's Dir. N. & E.R. Yorks.* (1933), 465; (1937), 457.
[66] G.R.O. Worship Reg. no. 61384.
[67] Ibid. no. 67732.

[68] Date on building. Given as 1820 in White, *Dir. E. & N.R. Yorks.* (1840), 382.
[69] B.I.H.R., V. 1877/Ret.
[70] O.S. Map 25" (1891).
[71] J. S. Purvis, *Tudor Par. Docs. of Dioc. York*, 194.
[72] *Rets. on Educ. of Poor, 1819*, 1080.
[73] E.R.R.O., DDX/25/10.
[74] Ed. 7/135; *Educ. Enquiry Abstract, 1835*, 1084.
[75] W. S. Cortis, *Hist. and Descrip. Guide to Filey* (1861), 38–9.
[76] *Rep. of Educ. Cttee. of Counc. 1858–9* [2510], p. 667, H. C. (1859 Sess. 1), xxi (I).
[77] O.S. Map 6" (1854).
[78] E.R.R.O., SGP 22 (undated plans); *Kelly's Dir. N. & E.R. Yorks.* (1889), 385.
[79] B.I.H.R., V. 1865/Ret. 182; V. 1877/Ret.
[80] *Kelly's Dir. N. & E.R. Yorks.* (1893), 421.
[81] Ibid. (1901), 478; *Filey Post*, 3 Mar. 1900.
[82] Registry of Deeds, Beverley, FU/64/711.
[83] E.R.R.O., SGP 23 (undated plans); *Kelly's Dir. N. & E.R. Yorks.* (1889), 385.
[84] *Rep. of Educ. Cttee. of Counc. 1858–9*, p. 667.
[85] *Rets. rel. Elem. Educ. 1871*, 476.
[86] Ed. 7/135; E.R. Educ. Cttee. *Mins.* 1905–6, 58, 216; 1909–10, 44.
[87] *Bd. of Educ. List 21* (H.M.S.O.).
[88] See above.

but it fell to 106 in 1927 before rising to 180–90 in the 1930s;[89] accommodation there was already insufficient in 1939.[90]

Filey's schools were reorganized in 1946, when the County school became a temporary mixed secondary school and the National school became a junior mixed school; the infants' school retained its earlier function.[91] A new secondary school was eventually built in Muston Road and opened in 1961; the total number on the roll in 1970 was 414. The old County school thereafter housed the junior school and the infants moved into the National school. The average number on the roll in 1970 was 229 juniors and 173 infants.[92] The infants' school in Mitford Street was closed and in 1970 was used as a parish hall.

It was reported in 1865 that an adult evening school had been tried at Filey with little success. Adult classes were also held in 1884.[93]

In the townships there were schools at Lebberston and Gristhorpe in 1819, attended by about 20 and 35 children respectively.[94] Children from those places, however, later attended schools at Cayton and Filey respectively, but the new chapel at Gristhorpe, built in 1897, was used as an infants' school because of the long walk to Filey.[95]

CHARITIES FOR THE POOR. Like Muston Filey received £1 a year under the will of Elisha Trott, dated 1697; the payment was charged on the same land at Flotmanby.[96] In 1926–7 the £1 was used to buy coal for eight people.[97]

By the early 19th century the quarter-acre poor's land in Muston had become appropriated to Filey. A rent-charge of 8s. a year was paid out of it for several years before c. 1810, when it was raised to 12s. The land was bought by Christopher Russell in 1813 and he disputed the amount of the rent-charge: no payment was made after 1817.[98]

The Filey Fishermen's United Charities were formed in 1911 from the Fishermen's Net fund, established in 1868, and the Fishermen's charity, which had been administered under a Scheme of 1898. The net fund is used to replace nets or other gear lost at sea, and the Fishermen's charity benefits poor fishermen and their families by subscriptions, money payments, and gifts of food and other goods. In 1911 the net fund had £410 stock and the Fishermen's charity £352 in cash. The combined income in 1928–31 was £32 a year. In 1965–6 £1,089 stock produced an income of £39; 15s. was given to each of 48 people, and one man received £7 to replace gear.[99]

A. V. Machin, by will proved in 1924, bequeathed £400 in stock to provide coal and groceries for fifteen poor people of Filey. The income in 1928–31 was £10 a year.[1]

Florence Cammish, by will proved in 1964, left her residuary estate to provide for elderly residents of the town, at the discretion of trustees.[2]

At Lebberston there was a town stock of £6 10s. in 1823. It was then reported that £8 10s. formerly belonging to the poor of Gristhorpe had been lost c. 1800.[3]

FLAMBOROUGH

THE parish of Flamborough, which occupies the most easterly 3 miles of Flamborough Head, covers 3,081 a. and lies about 3 miles north-east of Bridlington.[1] The first element of the name is Scandinavian, perhaps meaning 'a spit or tongue of land'.[2] The parish is bounded on three sides by high chalk cliffs, and the only access from the sea is by two small coves, North and South Landings. The spectacular coastal scenery has led to its increasing popularity with visitors, and considerable modern holiday development has taken place. The old village centre lies on the more sheltered southern side of the headland, beside a small stream, about 1½ mile and ½ mile respectively from North and South Landings, and about 2 miles from the tip of the headland. The western parish boundary with Bempton and Sewerby is formed by the earthwork known as Danes' Dyke, which runs from north to south across the entire width of the promontory. In 1935 17 a. in the south-west, adjoining Sewerby, were transferred to the borough of Bridlington.[3]

Flamborough lies entirely on the wolds, for the most part at a height of over 125 ft. above sea-level. The landscape is open, wind-swept, and mainly treeless, with only a few small windbreaks and plantations. The village itself lies between 125 ft. and 150 ft. The ground rises in the west to over 175 ft. around Danes' Dyke, and in the north-west it reaches over 275 ft. on Metlow hill and also at the cliffs. East of the village much of the ground towards the tip of the promontory lies between 125 ft. and 150 ft. South of the village Beacon hill reaches over 175 ft. The regular modern field pattern of most of the parish results from the late-18th-century inclosure. Around Micklemires and the site of Carr Farm, however, the irregular fields may reflect the early inclosure of these areas. Most of the parish is now under arable cultivation. Danes' Dyke is a major landmark. It consists of an earth bank, about 18 ft. high, which runs for 2½ miles across the promontory, enclosing an area of about 5 square miles. A ditch on its western side, up to 60 ft. wide, is formed by a natural ravine for about a mile at the southern end, but to the north it was artificially constructed. Excavations have produced surface finds of the late Neolithic and early Bronze Ages,[4]

---

[89] *List 21.*
[90] E.R. Educ. Cttee. *Mins.* 1939–40, 40.
[91] Ibid. 1946–7, 143–4.
[92] Ex inf. Chief Educ. Officer, County Hall, Beverley, 1970.
[93] B.I.H.R., V. 1865/Ret. 182; Bp. V. 1884/Ret.
[94] *Rets. on Educ. of Poor, 1819,* 1080.
[95] *Filey Post,* 17 July 1897.
[96] See p. 282.
[97] Char. Com. files.

[98] *9th Rep. Char. Com.* 733.
[99] Char. Com. files.
[1] Ibid.   [2] Ibid.
[3] *9th Rep. Char. Com.* 733.

[1] This article was written in 1969.
[2] *P.N.E.R. Yorks.* (E.P.N.S.), 105–6; *Introd. to Survey of Eng. Place-Names* (E.P.N.S.), i. 68.
[3] *Census,* 1931.
[4] *V.C.H. Yorks.* ii. 54; F. & H. W. Elgee, *Archaeol. of Yorks.* 235. See plate facing p. 33.

but it seems likely that the dyke is of Iron-Age or Dark-Age date.

Except in the north-west the cliffs are mainly between 125 ft. and 150 ft. high. On the north side of the headland they are deeply indented, with many caves and stacks. Several of these features have names of Scandinavian origin, such as Breil Nook, Stottle Bink, Swinshers, Selwicks Bay, and Thornwick Nab.[5] 'Stack' and 'scar', which are elements in many names of coastal features, are also thought to be Scandinavian.[6] Of the caves the largest is Robin Lythe's Hole at North Landing, said to have been named after a smuggler.[7] On the more sheltered south side of the headland the cliffs are regular, with few indentations.

The cliffs, particularly on the north side, are the nesting-grounds of large numbers of sea-birds.[8] The earliest reference to fowling was in 1294–5, when Bridlington priory held rights there.[9] In the 16th century the rights belonged to the manor, and in 1537 and 1570 they were worth £1.[10] In 1561 it was said that 'great plenty of fowl' was obtained on the cliffs.[11] By the 19th century the rights were held by the tenants of adjoining land, and eggs were collected by gangs of 'climmers' as at Bempton.[12]

Two roads enter Flamborough from the west. That from Bempton, once Flamborough Gate, is now called Bempton Lane; the other, Bridlington (formerly Mill) Road, was straightened and widened in 1907 at the point where it crosses Danes' Dyke.[13] From the village three roads lead to the sea. That to North Landing, formerly North Sea Lane, is now North Marine Road and the others are Lighthouse and South Sea Roads. There are many field lanes in the parish, and a minor road leads south from Bridlington Road into Bridlington corporation's Danes' Dyke estate.[14]

The nucleus of the village formerly lay around the church, in the area where the main roads converge,[15] but a gradual extension northwards seems to have occurred as a result of the predominant role of North Landing in the life of the village. The lanes south of the church are now less densely built up, and earthworks east of Beacon Farm may mark the site of former houses. The village now lies mainly north of the church along Tower Street, High Street, and North Street, and there are several side lanes which form a complicated street pattern. In 1319 four streets were called Robin, Caster, Francis, and Fathogg Lanes;[16] none of these names has survived, though Caster may be the present Carter Lane. A back lane, known as Garth Ends in the mid 19th century and Chapel Street later, was extended northwards in 1930 to join North Marine Road.[17] South of the church are Lily Lane, West Street, Butlers Lane, Church Lane, and Water Lane. The last of these takes its name from Hartendale Gutter, a stream which runs near by.

Several ponds in the village formerly included the large North Mere, which lay at the north end of South Sea Lane. In 1938 it was filled in and replaced by North Mere Green.[18] South Mere, now known as Town End Pond, lies in the west of the village, near Bridlington Road.[19] Earthworks, described as old fish ponds in 1850, lie in a field east of Water Lane and south of Bridlington Road. They consist of three rectangular depressions surrounded by banks. Fishponds belonged to the manor in 1559.[20]

Few buildings in Flamborough are earlier than the 18th century. In the early 19th century many houses were said to be built of clay and cobbles,[21] and about 1885 the village was described as largely consisting of chalk-built cottages.[22] Brick is now the chief material, but many buildings still contain some cobbles and chalk, with several outbuildings entirely chalk-built. Manor Cottage, near the church, which has 18th-century and later features, is a one-storeyed building, with attics, built of chalk and brick. At the north end of Tower Street an 18th-century chalk cottage has rear dormers and a brick hood-mould over one window. Other 18th-century houses and cottages, of chalk and brick, stand mainly in the south of the village, which to some degree retains an agricultural atmosphere. They include Sunny Cottage, a stuccoed two-storeyed farm-house with a band between the storeys.

Flamborough was extended and enlarged during the 19th century and there are buildings of this period in various parts of the village, particularly in the north where the fishermen mainly lived. Chapel Street, High Street, and North Street, with closely-built rows of small plain cottages, have an almost urban appearance. In High Street many of the fishermen's cottages have been converted into shops and cafés in the 20th century. A long terrace of earlier-19th-century cottages at the south end of High Street has regularly-spaced pilasters, and there are smaller ranges of the same type further north. Victoria Terrace is a row of cottages at right-angles to High Street. More noteworthy is a pair of large Victorian semi-detached houses, built of chalk with brick dressings. At the north end of North Street and Chapel Street are several 'villas' and lodging-houses, built in the later 19th century. Several farm-houses in the south of the village also date mostly from the 19th century: these are Crofts, Hartendale, Grove, Beacon, and Church Farms. Much 20th-century building has taken place, both before and after the Second World War, partly as 'in-filling' in the village but mainly along the roads leading out of it. Between 1939 and 1963 an estate of 145 Council houses and flats was built on the east side of the village.[23]

Public houses include the Dog and Duck inn which, though much altered, is of the 18th century, and the Ship Hotel, in High Street, which dates from the early 19th century and has a doorcase with fluted columns and a modillioned cornice head.

---

[5] G. Hardwick, *The Story of Flamborough*, 12; T. Holderness, *E. Riding Sketches* (loose leaves in County Libr., County Hall, Beverley); *Flamborough: Village and Headland*, ed. R. Fisher, 9, 75. See plate facing p. 208.
[6] Holderness, *E.R. Sketches*.
[7] Sheahan and Whellan, *Hist. York & E.R.* ii. 469.
[8] Very few birds nest south of Selwicks Bay: *E. Yorks. Field Studies*, i (1968), 1.
[9] B.M. Add. R. 75569.
[10] E 315/288/1; *Cal. Pat. 1569–72*, 76.
[11] E 310/29/173 no. 8.
[12] See p. 9.
[13] E.R.C.C. *Mins*. 1906–7, 361; 1907–8, 166.
[14] See p. 155.
[15] T. Jefferys, *Map of the County of York*, 1772.
[16] *T.E.R.A.S.* viii. 58.
[17] E.R.C.C. *Mins*. 1930–1, 396.
[18] Ex inf. Mr. T. P. Cross, Flamborough, 1970.
[19] O.S. Map 6" (1854); 2½" (1953).
[20] E 310/31/185 no. 21.
[21] White, *Dir. E. & N.R. Yorks.* (1840), 383.
[22] Holderness, *E.R. Sketches*.
[23] Ex inf. Clerk to the Council, Bridlington R.D.C., 1970.

Since the early 19th century there have been 6 to 8 public houses. In 1831 these were the Ball, the Board, the Globe, the Dog and Duck, the North Star, the Rose and Crown, the Ship, and the Strickland Arms.[24] By 1840 the first three had closed and the Sea Birds inn had appeared. By 1846 the Strickland Arms had closed, and in the 1850s the Thornwick Hotel made its appearance.[25] Part of the Cliffe farm-house, near South Landing, has also recently become a public house.

There are several meeting-rooms in the village. The Victoria Institute, in Chapel Street, was built in 1887 by a Mrs. Creyke as a reading and recreation room.[26] It was still in use in 1969. The Memorial Hall, in South Sea Lane, was built by subscription in 1938.[27] The church hall was built north of the church in 1964.[28] Following the erection of a new Wesleyan chapel in 1889, the former chapel in Chapel Street was renamed the Liberal Hall and used as a reading and recreation room.[29] It has since been demolished. The village had a brass band in the earlier 20th century.[30] The Flamborough Fishermen's Fund was instituted in 1809 and existed until at least the 1830s.[31] The Flamborough Fishermen's Coble Insurance Association was established in 1884.[32] A monument at the south end of Chapel Street, erected in 1909, commemorates the crew of the coble *Two Brothers* who died trying to save another boat.

There are about ten outlying farm-houses in the parish, all probably originating after inclosure. Of these Hill Farm has recently been converted into holiday flats. The 18th-century Dyke Cottages stand in the south-west of the parish. Near the sea many bungalows and chalets have been built and several caravan camps opened.[33]

There was probably a Roman signal station on Beacon hill; 4th-century pottery has been found there and six large sandstone blocks, destroyed by quarrying, were apparently similar to those found at the signal-station site at Filey.[34] The hill takes its name from beacons which stood there from the 16th century. There were three of them in 1588, taking light from Bridlington and passing it to Rudston.[35] They were repaired in 1755.[36] One beacon still stood in 1834, but by 1887 it had gone.[37] There was also, in 1796, a flag-signal station on the headland to give warning of French warships.[38]

The cliffs around the headland have long been hazardous for passing ships and for Flamborough's own fishing boats. The first lighthouse to be built was that put up by Sir John Clayton in 1674, though voluntary dues from ships sailing by proved inadequate and the light was never kindled.[39] The tall octagonal tower of chalk still stands about 1,000 yds. from the tip of the headland. From c. 1840 until the turn of the century it was used as a marine telegraph station.[40] It has always been a navigational landmark for vessels entering Bridlington Bay, and in 1969 it was still said to be a useful guide to local fishermen.[41]

From 1770 to 1806 174 ships were wrecked off Flamborough Head and the adjoining coast, and eventually Benjamin Milne, collector of customs at Bridlington, convinced Trinity House of the need for a light on the headland. In 1806 the present brick lighthouse was built by John Matson of Bridlington about 400 yds. from the point.[42] About 350 yds. east of the lighthouse, on the extreme point of the headland, a signal-gun station was built by Trinity House in 1859. A cannon was fired in fog until 1877, when a rocket was substituted.[43] Between 1909 and 1913 a siren was installed.[44] In 1959 a toposcope was erected near the lighthouse, with a plaque commemorating the engagement with John Paul Jones off the headland in 1779.[45] By 1871 a volunteer company had been formed to manage rocket life-saving apparatus which was acquired a few years before.[46] The company still existed in 1969.

A station of the Royal National Life-boat Institution was established in 1871. There has been a life-boat at North Landing ever since, and until 1938 there was another at South Landing. The brick houses built for them in 1871 still stand and that at North Landing is still in use.[47] The rocky nature of the landings has always made it difficult to launch and recover life-boats and fishing cobles. Near the life-boat slipway at North Landing is a small brick building which was erected in 1875 to house a steam-engine, converted to oil power in the 1920s, used for hauling up cobles.[48] In 1924 a slipway was built for the cobles and the Flamborough Harbour Commission was established to maintain it.[49]

It was partly to combat smuggling that a coast-guard station was established at Flamborough between 1831 and 1840. By 1846 the officers occupied a row of eight cottages in Lighthouse Road,[50] but c. 1908 these were replaced by a row of six larger cottages on the opposite side of the road.[51] The earlier cottages still stood in 1969.

---

[24] W. White, *Dir. Hull etc.* (1831), 251.
[25] White, *Dir. E. & N.R. Yorks.* (1840), 385; *Dir. Hull & York* (1846), 443; (1858), 438.
[26] *Flamborough*, ed. Fisher, p. x.
[27] Registry of Deeds, Beverley, 592/362/296; date on building.
[28] Date on building.
[29] *Flamborough*, ed. Fisher, p. x.
[30] F. Brearley, *Hist. Flamborough*, 203–6.
[31] E.R.R.O., DDLG/12/1.
[32] *Flamborough*, ed. Fisher, 174–5.
[33] See p. 160.
[34] Mary Kitson Clark, *Gaz. of Roman Remains in E. Yorks.* 83–4; ex inf. Mr. T. C. M. Brewster, 1971; see above, p. 132.
[35] J. Nicholson, *Beacons of E. Yorks.* 35.
[36] E.R.R.O., QSF Mich. 1755, D. 8; Mich. 1756, D. 5.
[37] Nicholson, *Beacons*, 35. An 'old beacon', said in 1829 to stand at the N. end of Danes' Dyke, was apparently not in Flamborough: ibid. 37; J. Phillips, *Illustrations of Geol. of Yorks.* i [p. 197]; see above, p. 10.
[38] R. W. S. Norfolk, *Militia, Yeomanry and Volunteer Forces of E.R. 1689–1908* (E. Yorks. Loc. Hist. Ser. xix), 29.
[39] G. de Boer, *Hist. of Spurn Lighthouses* (E. Yorks. Loc. Hist. Ser. xxiv), 18 sqq.; see plate facing p. 208.
[40] Directories.
[41] *Hull Daily Mail*, 16 Aug. 1969.
[42] *Flamborough*, ed. Fisher, 52. See plate facing p. 208.
[43] Holderness, *E.R. Sketches*.
[44] *Kelly's Dir. N. & E.R. Yorks.* (1909), 512; (1913), 532.
[45] *Hull Daily Mail*, 13 Sept. 1958; 13 Feb. and 24 Sept. 1959. See above, p. 32.
[46] MS. notes *penes* Mrs. C. Cross, Flamborough, 1970; directories.
[47] Ex inf. R.N.L.I., London, 1969.
[48] *Flamborough*, ed. Fisher, 44; *Kelly's Dir. N. & E.R. Yorks.* (1925), 538; (1929), 498.
[49] N.E. Sea Fisheries Cttee. *Mins.* 1923–4, 27.
[50] White, *Dir. Hull etc.* (1831), 251; *Dir. E. & N.R. Yorks.* (1840), 384; *Dir. Hull & York* (1846), 443.
[51] *Flamborough Guide*, ed. Readhead, 28.

Several customs survived at Flamborough in the late 19th century, one of which, called Raising Herrings, was held to ensure a good fishing season. While the men were at sea their women folk disguised themselves, often in men's clothing, and went round the village receiving alms. A 'sword dance' was performed at Christmas, and a 'ribbon dance' at weddings.[52]

In 1377 Flamborough had 278 poll-tax payers,[53] and in 1674 102 households, of which 62 were exempted from the hearth tax. Of the 40 households which paid tax in 1674 25 had only one hearth each, 7 had 2, 4 had 3, one had 5, one had 7, one had 8, and one had twelve.[54] The unusually high proportion of exempt households suggests that there were many poor inhabitants, as does a bequest of food to 92 poor people by Sir Marmaduke Constable in 1520.[55] In 1743 there were said to be about 120 families in Flamborough,[56] and in 1764 90 or more.[57] The population in 1801 was 731 and it gradually increased to 1,390 in 1881.[58] It declined to 1,169 in 1911, rose to 1,325 in 1921, and declined again to 1,198 in 1939. Since the Second World War the population has increased sharply. In 1951 it was 1,585 and in 1961 1,706.[59]

MANOR AND OTHER ESTATES. In 1086 there were two estates in Flamborough. The larger consisted of 15 carucates and had been held as a manor by Earl Harold in 1066. In 1086 it was in the possession of Hugh, earl of Chester.[60] The manor formed part of the honor of Chester until at least 1519,[61] and land in Flamborough was still said to be held of the honor in 1638.[62]

The demesne tenant of the larger estate in 1086 was Hugh son of Norman.[63] Some time after 1086 it passed to William son of Niel, whose father had been created constable of Chester by Earl Hugh.[64] William, who died between 1125 and 1130, was succeeded by his son, another William, who had died by 1139. The latter seems to have had an illegitimate son, Robert the Constable (fl. 1146–8, 1185), who succeeded to his father's estate in Flamborough. This Robert was the ancestor of the Constable family of Flamborough, whose name almost certainly derived from the family's descent from the constables of Chester.[65] The Constable family retained the manor of FLAMBOROUGH until 1537,[66] when Sir Robert Constable was executed for his part in the Pilgrimage of Grace and his property was forfeited to the Crown.[67]

Before 1551 the Crown let the manor-house and demesne, consisting of 10 bovates and several closes, to Alan King[68] and in 1559 to Matthew Keck.[69] In 1562 the manor was let to Robert Puckering and eleven other inhabitants of Flamborough.[70]

Puckering already held land in the parish[71] and in 1540–1 he had been the Crown's bailiff of the manor.[72] In 1570 the lease was renewed,[73] and the lessees were also granted additional rents from the manor, and the right to hold a court.[74] In 1573 the queen, on the petition of Robert Constable, grandson of Sir Robert (d. 1537), granted the reversion of the manor to Michael Fenwick and William Mawburne, to the use of and with remainder to Constable.[75] In 1582 the queen granted the manor to Robert Constable's son, another Robert,[76] and regranted it to him in 1585.[77]

William Constable sold the manor in 1636 to Sir Henry Griffith of Burton Agnes.[78] In 1650 Griffith sold it to Walter Strickland,[79] who seems to have been a member of the Westmorland branch of the family. He died childless in 1671 and the estate passed to another Walter Strickland, second son of Sir Thomas Strickland of Boynton.[80] At inclosure in 1767 Walter Strickland was awarded 1,032 a.[81] His nephew, another Walter, died childless in 1793 leaving the manor to his widow for life, with remainder to Walter, third son of Sir George Strickland of Boynton.[82] Walter succeeded to the manor in 1807[83] and it descended in this branch of the family until 1870, when another Walter Strickland devised his Flamborough property to his sister Frances Elizabeth, widow of Charles Cottrell-Dormer.[84] In 1906 Clement Cottrell-Dormer was succeeded by his brother J. H. Upton.[85] In 1908 the manorial estate consisted of over 1,500 a.[86] Upton sold the manor in 1914 to R. G. H. Boulton[87] who, up to 1920, increased the estate by purchase.[88] Between 1921 and 1924 Boulton sold part of his estate[89] and in the latter year he sold the manorial rights, together with about 138 a. and a house in the village called Manor House, to Herbert Wood-

---

[52] *Flamborough*, ed. Fisher, 143–6.
[53] E 179/202/62 m. 5.
[54] E 179/205/521.
[55] *Test. Ebor.* v (Sur. Soc. lxxix), 91.
[56] *Herring's Visit.* i. 218.
[57] B.I.H.R., Bp. V. 1764/Ret. 190.
[58] *V.C.H. Yorks.* iii. 489.
[59] Census.
[60] *V.C.H. Yorks.* ii. 219.
[61] C 142/34/28.
[62] C 142/564/161.
[63] *V.C.H. Yorks.* ii. 219.
[64] *T.E.R.A.S.* viii. 53, 55; *E.Y.C.* xii, pp. 142–3.
[65] *E.Y.C.* xii, pp. 142–6; it has been suggested that the first Robert was the son of William son of Niel: *T.E.R.A.S.* xii. 1–3. Earlier accts. of the origin of the Constable family, of Flamborough, are inaccurate: *T.E.R.A.S.* vii. 15–16; viii. 51–69; E.R.R.O., DDEV/11/2.
[66] For pedigrees see *E.Y.C.* xii, facing p. 145; J. Foster, *Pedigrees . . . of Yorks.* iii; W. Flower, *Visit. Yorks.* (Harl. Soc. xvi), 63–6. The last two are inaccurate for the 12th and 13th centuries.
[67] *V.C.H. Yorks.* iii. 412–14; *Monastic Suppression Papers* (Y.A.S. Rec. Ser. xlviii), 39.
[68] S.C. 11/732.
[69] E 310/31/185 no. 21.
[70] C 66/1065 m. 33; E 310/29/173 no. 8; E.R.R.O., DX/131/h.
[71] S.C. 11/732.
[72] E 315/285/35.
[73] *Cal. Pat.* 1569–72, 76.
[74] E 309/Box 3/19 Eliz./4; C 66/1065 m. 33; E.R.R.O., DX/131/s.
[75] E.R.R.O., DX/131/w; DDHA/4/36; C 66/1096 m. 21; C 66/1213 m. 6.
[76] E.R.R.O., DX/131/ii; C 66/1217 mm. 25–32, 35; C 142/263/36.
[77] E.R.R.O., DX/131/iii; C 142/263/20(1).
[78] C.P. 25(2)/522/12 Chas. I Trin. no. 39.
[79] *Royalist Composition Papers*, iii (Y.A.S. Rec. Ser. xx), 160.
[80] *Flamborough: Village and Headland*, ed. R. Fisher, 99.
[81] Registry of Deeds, Beverley, AH/295/6.
[82] *Flamborough*, ed. Fisher, facing p. 96.
[83] *Flamborough*, ed. Fisher, 100. He was first of the family of Strickland, of Cokethorpe Park (Oxon.).
[84] *Flamborough*, ed. Fisher, 100–1.
[85] G. Hardwick, *Story of Flamborough*, 5.
[86] Regy. of Deeds, 101/158/142.
[87] Ibid. 157/538/466.
[88] Ibid. /542/467; /543/468; 189/271/240; 208/391/339.
[89] Ibid. 231/476/396; 245/45/37; 271/194/166; 287/263/208; /264/209, etc.

house.[90] Boulton was declared bankrupt in 1924 and by 1928 the remainder of his estate had been sold in separate lots.[91] In 1935 Herbert Woodhouse sold the 136-acre Danes' Dyke estate to Bridlington corporation,[92] but he retained Manor House until 1953, when he sold it to Mary Harker.[93]

Bridlington corporation also bought about 200 a. on Flamborough Head in 1939 from William Jowitt.[94] This land, which lay south of Lighthouse Road, had been sold, as Lighthouse or Head Farm, in 1924 by Boulton to William Coates. Coates had sold it in 1938–9 to Jowitt.[95] A further 71 a., north of Lighthouse Road, was bought by the corporation in 1939 from the trustees of G. W. Clark (d. 1906).[96]

The fortified manor-house of the Constables stood a short distance to the north of the church, but the only remains apart from earthworks are parts of a square tower which may date from the 14th century. In 1315 William the Constable was licensed to have an oratory,[97] presumably in the manor-house. Marmaduke Constable received licence to crenellate his house at Flamborough in 1351.[98] Leland described it in the early 16th century as 'taken rather for a manor place than a castle'.[99] At the death of Sir Robert Constable in 1537 it included the tower, a hall, a 'great parlour', a 'lord's parlour', a chapel, a court-house, a mill-house, and a 'great barn'.[1] The tower survived, and in 1798 it still contained a vaulted undercroft which was used as a cattle shed; chalk was then being removed and burnt for lime.[2] About 1885 the undercroft was described as about 14 ft. high, and the vaulting consisted of eight stone ribs with chalk blocks between.[3] Access to a former first-floor room was by a spiral staircase, approached through an ogee-headed doorway.[4] In 1969 parts of three walls of the tower were still standing, the outer skin of chalk ashlar largely removed, exposing the rough chalk blocks beneath. Inside, on the east and west walls, there are indications of the arches of the vaults, and on the south wall is part of the springing of a vault. There is a small doorway in the east wall and the remains of what seems to have been a window in the west wall.

A farm-house known as Manor House probably stands on the site of the house occupied by lords of the manor in the 16th century and later. In 1674 the Stricklands' manor-house had twelve hearths.[5] The surviving house dates from the early 19th century; it is mainly rough-cast, but some chalk is visible at the rear. After Frances E. Cottrell-Dormer succeeded to the manor, she built Danes' Dyke House in 1873, close to the sea in the south-west corner of the parish.[6] It had been demolished by 1969.

The second estate recorded in 1086 consisted of 1½ carucate, held of the king by Clibert, who had also held it before the Conquest.[7] It had probably passed by the 12th century to the family which took its name from the village. Niel of Flamborough is mentioned in 1189–90,[8] and in 1218 Gregory of Flamborough held 3 bovates there.[9] Between 1231 and 1249 Agnes of Newton, daughter of Otes of Flamborough, gave 2½ bovates to Robert the Constable.[10] In 1273 Vivian, son of Lawrence of Flamborough, claimed a holding which was almost identical with that held in 1218 by Gregory of Flamborough.[11] By 1276 Vivian's son Theobald had succeeded his father.[12] This seems to be the last reference to a member of the family. In 1284–5 the land in Flamborough not held by the Constables or by the church, amounting to over 5 carucates, was held by several unnamed people.[13]

Another holding in the 13th century was that of William Westingby, who in 1268 held a capital messuage and more than 3 bovates. His whole estate seems to have consisted of 8 bovates, some meadow, and a mill. His holding was later divided between John of Stapleton and John of Butterwick, who each received 3 bovates, and Julia of Seaton, who received two. The mill was divided between them.[14] None of these holdings has been traced further.

The origin of an estate of 3 carucates held in 1428 by Dame Catherine Cressy is unknown.[15] It seems likely that it descended like Argam manor and land in Newsham to Robert Constable of Flamborough by the mid 15th century,[16] and subsequently became incorporated in his manor.

In the later 16th century Thomas Preston held an estate of 20 bovates.[17] In 1609–12 Richard Preston sold 8 bovates and other land to Melchior Gibbon,[18] and the estate descended in the Gibbon family until about 1705, when it was sold to Henry Woolfe. Richard Woolfe sold it in 1721 to Matthew Smith,[19] and he in 1724 to John Grimston.[20] At inclosure in 1767 Robert Grimston received an allotment of 266 a.[21] Between 1770 and 1772 he sold his Flamborough land in several small lots.[22]

It is not known how the estate of the Ogle family originated. John Ogle (d. 1605) is said to have come to the parish from Northumberland in the mid 16th century.[23] In 1639 George Ogle died seised of 3 houses, 21 cottages, 3 closes, and 13¼ bovates.[24] The estate subsequently came to be divided between two branches of the family, and at inclosure in 1767 John Ogle received an allotment of 169 a. and William Ogle 118 a.[25] The estates descended in the Ogle family until the early 20th century. In 1918 18 cottages and houses and the 181-acre Ocean View farm were sold by the Revd. H. L. Ogle to R. G. H.

---

[90] Ibid. 287/267/212.
[91] Ibid. 298/164/131; 337/55/46 sqq.; /71/56; 339/71/58; 366/125/102; /486/393, etc.
[92] Ibid. 538/658/497.   [93] Ibid. 931/468/407.
[94] Ibid. 621/594/459; /596/460; 629/289/216.
[95] Ibid. 287/390/316; 603/600/461; 621/129/103.
[96] Ibid. 630/451/375.
[97] *Reg. Greenfield*, iii (Sur. Soc. xli), 245.
[98] *Cal. Pat.* 1350–4, 75, 225.
[99] Leland, *Itin.* ed. Toulmin Smith, i. 61.
[1] E 178/2564.
[2] T. Hinderwell, *Hist. and Antiquities of Scarborough*, 248.
[3] Holderness, *E.R. Sketches*.
[4] MS. notes *penes* Mrs. C. Cross, Flamborough, 1970.
[5] E 179/205/521.   [6] *Flamborough*, ed. Fisher, 101.

[7] *V.C.H. Yorks.* ii. 286.
[8] *Pipe R.* 1189 (Rec. Com.), 74.
[9] *Ex. e Rot. Fin.* (Rec. Com.), i. 19.
[10] E.R.R.O., DDCC/App. A/p. 46, no. 2.
[11] C.P. 40/2A m. 16d.   [12] J.I. 1/1054 m. 12d.
[13] *Feud. Aids*, vi. 29.   [14] *T.E.R.A.S.* xviii. 79.
[15] *Feud. Aids*, vi. 267.   [16] See pp. 6, 12.
[17] B.M. Add. MS. 26718, f. 46.
[18] C 2/Jas. I/G 4/65.
[19] Regy. of Deeds, H/256/544; I/139/308.
[20] Ibid. I/139/309; E 134/18 Geo. II Mich./8.
[21] Regy. of Deeds, AH/295/6.
[22] Ibid. AM/322/525; AP/177/288; /342/610; /611; /343/612; /613.
[23] *Flamborough*, ed. Fisher, 91.   [24] C 142/597/25.
[25] Regy. of Deeds, AH/295/6.

Boulton,[26] and in 1921 the 97-acre North Moor farm was sold by the Revd. P. H. D. Ogle to Muriel Tress.[27]

About 1640 Nathan Walworth of Ringley (Lancs.) bought a house and 2 bovates in Flamborough, the proceeds of which were to maintain a schoolmaster at Ringley.[28] At inclosure in 1767 the trustees of the Ringley charity were awarded 39 a.[29] In 1969 the land, known as Ringley Hills, still formed part of the endowment of the school.[30]

From the 12th century the church of Flamborough belonged to Bridlington priory.[31] Tithes payable in the early 13th century and later included those of fish.[32] By 1135 the church had been given a bovate of land in Flamborough,[33] and in 1284–5 it had 6 bovates, held of William the Constable.[34] The rectory was valued at £16 13s. 4d. in 1291[35] and 1428.[36] About 1533 it was held of the priory by Sir Marmaduke Constable at a rent of £32,[37] which was also its gross value in 1535.[38]

After the Dissolution the rectory was let by the Crown to John Wright in 1538,[39] Richard Foster in 1551,[40] John Cardell and Ralph Sherman in 1568,[41] and Edward Wingate in 1594.[42] In 1599–1600 it was granted in fee to Sir Miles Sandys and Edward Rhodes,[43] but by 1610 it had passed to Sir Thomas Wilsford.[44] Edward Wilsford held it in 1650, when it was valued at £208.[45] In 1753–4 a lawsuit was brought against the fishermen by the impropriator alleging that they refused to pay the full fish tithes. The fishermen, however, upheld their claim to exemption from tithes on certain kinds of fish and their right to take, tithe-free, enough fish to cover the expenses of each trip.[46] At inclosure in 1767 Robert Wilsford received a rent-charge of £287 10s. for tithes and an allotment of 120 a. in lieu of 6 bovates of glebe land and 3 cottage rights.[47] In 1815 Robert Wilsford Coupland sold about £168 of the composition rent, together with the glebe land, to Walter Strickland.[48]

Bridlington priory's estate included other land besides the glebe. Robert the Constable and William the Constable each granted one bovate to it in the 12th or 13th century,[49] and in 1298 the priory held 5 bovates under William the Constable.[50] The land descended with the rectory.

ECONOMIC HISTORY. The larger of the two Domesday estates, consisting of 15 carucates, was said to be one league long and half a league broad. There was land for eight ploughs, but in 1086 there was only one plough and one bordar. The value of the estate had fallen from £24 before the Conquest to 10s. The smaller estate, consisting of 1½ carucate, was said to contain land for one plough, but in 1086 it was waste.[51]

The manor was worth £66 13s. 4d. in 1488[52] and about £120 in 1537. In the latter year nearly £90 of the income came from the rents of tenants-at-will and about £20 from the demesne lands. Other sources of income were the farm of the mill, common oven, and fowling rights, the toll on anchorage of ships, and various small rents.[53] After 1537 the manor seems to have been neglected, and about 1540 it was said that it 'decays very sore and will do every day more and more except remedy be found betimes'.[54] By 1551 twelve cottages 'at the sea side' and twelve in the village had decayed, and the pier had been destroyed by the sea.[55] Although still in decay the manor was again valued at £120 in 1561–1562.[56]

Fishing has always had a part in the economy of Flamborough[57] and many of the manorial tenants in the Middle Ages were fishermen, apparently holding little or no land. In the 13th century the fishermen were accustomed to give a proportion of their catch each day to the lord of the manor.[58] In the 16th century many of the tenants-at-will were probably fishermen. There were 96 such tenants in 1551, and 72 of them held a cottage only, at rents of from 4s. to 10s. Of the 24 tenants who had land, one held 6 bovates, 8 held 4, 2 held 2, one held 1¾, 8 held one, 2 held ¾, and 2 held ½ bovate.[59] There were probably never many freeholders. In 1537 their rents amounted to only about £2 10s.,[60] and in 1551 and 1561 only about £1 14s. In 1551 11 people held freely at rents of between 2d. and 11s. 8d.[61] In 1783 there were 30 freeholders in the parish, but of these only 14 were assessed at over £1 for the land tax and most of the others at less than 10s.[62]

The tenants used common ovens in the 16th century. In 1537 there was only one, valued at £2, but in 1540 there were two.[63] In 1551 these 'bakehouses', which were formerly 'upheld by the ships belonging to the pier', were decayed.[64] By 1570 there was again only one bakehouse.[65] The tenants also owed suit at the manorial mill.[66]

Bridlington priory's estate was organized as a grange, and accounts for it survive from the period 1278–1357.[67] The priory's own land as well as the tithes apparently produced much corn: in 1278–9, for example, nearly 300 qr., including 113 qr. of oats and large amounts of wheat, maslin, and malted barley. Most of the grain was sent to the priory but sales sometimes amounted to nearly £20. There were frequent expenses for carts, presumably for the carriage of corn. Sheep and other animals were

---

[26] Regy. of Deeds, 189/271/240; /273/241.
[27] Ibid. 240/377/319. See F. Brearley, *Hist. Flamborough*, 79.
[28] E.R.R.O., DDX/25/9; see above, p. 12.
[29] Regy. of Deeds, AH/295/6.
[30] Ex inf. Counc. T. Woodhouse, Flamborough, 1969.
[31] See p. 160.   [32] B.M. Add. R. 75458.
[33] *Bridlington Charty*. 1.   [34] *Feud. Aids*, vi. 29.
[35] *Tax. Eccl.* (Rec. Com.), 304.   [36] *Feud. Aids*, vi. 327.
[37] *Miscellanea*, iii (Y.A.S. Rec. Ser. lxxx), 20.
[38] *Valor Eccl.* (Rec. Com.), v. 120.
[39] *L. & P. Hen. VIII*, xiii (2), pp. 407–8.
[40] E 310/29/172 no. 23.
[41] *Cal. Pat.* 1566–9, 221.   [42] C 66/1414 m. 23.
[43] C 66/1544 m. 6; H. Grove, *Alienated Tithes*, p. cxxxiii.
[44] C 142/319/190.   [45] *T.E.R.A.S.* ii. 53.
[46] F. Brearley, *Hist. Flamborough*, 31–3.
[47] Regy. of Deeds, AH/295/6.
[48] Ibid. CY/200/288; *Flamborough*, ed. Fisher, 94–5.
[49] *Cal. Pat.* 1307–13, 443–4; *Bridlington Charty*. 177.
[50] *Monastic Notes*, i (Y.A.S. Rec. Ser. xvii), 21.
[51] *V.C.H. Yorks.* ii. 219, 286, 322.
[52] *Cal. Inq. p.m. Hen. VII*, i, p. 151.
[53] E 315/288/1; S.C. 6/Hen. VIII/4323.
[54] E 315/285/38.
[55] S.C. 11/732; see below, p. 158.
[56] E 310/29/173 no. 8.   [57] See p. 158.
[58] *T.E.R.A.S.* viii. 57.   [59] S.C. 11/732.
[60] S.C. 6/Hen. VIII/4323.
[61] S.C. 11/732; E 310/29/173 no. 8.
[62] E.R.R.O., Land Tax 1783.
[63] E 315/285/35; E 315/288/1.
[64] S.C. 11/732.   [65] C 66/1065 m. 33.
[66] S.C. 11/732; E 310/29/173 no. 8; E.R.R.O., DX/131/h.
[67] B.M. Add. R. 75458–71, 75569–70.

often mentioned, though not in large numbers. During a dispute with the priory in 1298, however, William the Constable impounded 198 of its sheep.[68] The grange was apparently in the charge of the priory's under-cellarer and his total receipts were usually about £40–£60.

There are many early references to open-field land in the parish,[69] including ground called Mayde Lands in 1260.[70] The name Maidlands still survives for an area west of the village. By the 16th century there were four fields, known in 1572 as East, West, South, and North fields.[71] There were still four fields at inclosure in 1767, but East field was then also known as Lighthouse field, and West field and South field had become respectively Dykes field and Beacon field.[72]

In 1377 it seems that a three-course rotation was followed, for of the 8½ carucates then held by Sir Marmaduke Constable two thirds were sown and one third lay fallow.[73] In the 16th century, however, one field was fallowed every four years 'by ancient custom'.[74] The full extent of the open fields before 1767, when there were 107 bovates, is never revealed.[75] In the mid 16th century the manor included 65 bovates, as well as 'grass farms'.[76] The size of a bovate was then 12 a.[77]

There were extensive common pastures in Flamborough. About 1319 Bridlington priory was confirmed in its right of common for all animals throughout the year on the common moor and pasture.[78] The acreage of the common pastures at inclosure in 1767 cannot be determined, but they covered about a quarter of the parish. North moor and the Stacks lay in the east around Selwicks Bay, Horsekills lay near the sea to the north of the village, and West moor lay to the south-west, adjoining Danes' Dyke.[79] There were then about 160 common rights, of which 79 belonged to Walter Strickland as lord of the manor.[80]

In the mid 16th century the whins and furze growing on North moor and on Danes' Dyke were let with the manorial demesne.[81] In 1767 the lord of the manor still owned 20 parts in 21 of them, the remaining part belonging to Robert Grimston.[82] There was some marshland in the early 14th century.[83] A rabbit warren called Flamborough Dikes, presumably situated on and around Danes' Dyke, is mentioned in 1730 and the 1750s.[84]

Much meadow land was inclosed in the Middle Ages. By the 13th century Bridlington priory held three plots in lieu of the tithe of meadow in the manorial demesne: one lay 'on the east side of Herteshevede', the second contained 6 selions and lay 'on the west side of... Linghoudayls or Feukesmars', and the third lay in an area called 'Galighlyth'.[85] In the 16th century both 'Hartyshed' and 'Lingtonedalleas' were 'grass farms' in South field.[86] In the late 13th century an inclosed meadow was part of the holding of William Westingby.[87] New meadow land was being created by the lords of the manor in the early 14th century. William the Constable, about 1309, took in from the waste and inclosed two plots of meadow, one called the Westmar, the other 'lying beside Walwort'.[88] In the mid 16th century Walworth was a demesne close in North field.[89] William's son Robert inclosed, again from the waste, plots of meadow called 'Sandhoughleghs', 'Scalehouleghs', the Dykes, 'Ploughsemlands', and 'Smermerhill', and two unnamed plots.[90] In the earlier 16th century 'Plowsomlandes' was another grass farm in South field. The names of other grass farms suggest that they too contained, or had contained, meadow land; Westleas, in West field, and Stangleas and Holmeleas, in North field.[91] Micklemire, sometimes called Mickleings, a demesne close of 10 a. in the mid 16th century, may also have been meadow.[92] The name still survives for an area of irregular closes northeast of the village.[93] In 1319 the prior of Bridlington upheld his right to pasture animals after mowing in certain meadows belonging to Robert the Constable,[94] and one area which may have been meadow land remained in common until inclosure in 1767, namely the Holmes which lay near North Landing and contained less than 50 a.[95]

In the mid 16th century the demesne also contained several pasture closes. These included South moor, which lay near the sea south of the village and contained 50 a., Langspitte, which contained 36 a., and West close, of 8 a.[96] About 1260 a plot of cultivated land called Boulton croft is mentioned.[97] In the mid 16th century several demesne closes were probably arable: they included Pond close, Fishcroft, Hell close, and, in North field, New close, as well as Bolton croft.[98] In 1767 there were about 358 a. of old inclosure, of which Walter Strickland held 134 a.[99]

Areas within all four open fields were known as 'grass farms' or 'grassings' in the mid 16th century. These were probably laid down to augment the supply of meadow and pasture, but there is no evidence of their size or of their duration if they were not permanent closes. They were held in 1551 by 26 people at rents of between 6d. and 18s.[1]

The remaining open fields and commons of Flamborough were inclosed in 1767,[2] under an Act of 1765.[3] In all, 2,527 a. were allotted. Walter Strickland, as lord of the manor, was allotted 1,032 a.

[68] *Monastic Notes*, i (Y.A.S. Rec. Ser. xvii), 21.
[69] *Bridlington Charty.* 177; *T.E.R.A.S.* xviii. 79–80.
[70] E.R.R.O., DDCC/App. A/p. 34, no. 1.
[71] C 66/1096 m. 21.
[72] Regy. of Deeds, AH/295/6.　　　[73] C 136/2/15.
[74] E 310/29/173 no. 8; S.C. 6/Hen. VIII/4325.
[75] Regy. of Deeds, AH/295/6.
[76] S.C. 11/732; E 310/29/173 no. 8; see below.
[77] E.R.R.O., DX/131/h.
[78] *Bridlington Charty.* 180.
[79] E.R.R.O., IA Flamborough (map).
[80] Regy. of Deeds, AH/295/6.
[81] E 310/31/185 no. 21; E.R.R.O., DX/131/h.
[82] Regy. of Deeds, AH/295/6.
[83] *Yorks. Fines, 1327–47*, 136.
[84] E.R.R.O., QSF Mich. 1758, D. 1; DDLG/30/269, 823.
[85] *Bridlington Charty.* 181.
[86] S.C. 6/Hen. VIII/4324.
[87] *T.E.R.A.S.* xviii. 79.
[88] *Bridlington Charty.* 181.
[89] E 310/29/173 no. 8.
[90] *Bridlington Charty.* 181.
[91] S.C. 6/Hen. VIII/4324.
[92] E.R.R.O., DX/131/h; C 66/1065 m. 33.
[93] O.S. Map 2½" (1953).
[94] *Bridlington Charty.* 180–1.
[95] Regy. of Deeds, AH/295/6.
[96] E.R.R.O., DX/131/h.
[97] Ibid. DDCC/App. A/p. 34, no. 1.
[98] Ibid. DX/131/h.
[99] Regy. of Deeds, AH/295/6.　　　[1] S.C. 11/732.
[2] Regy. of Deeds, AH/295/6; E.R.R.O., IA Flamborough (map).
[3] 5 Geo. III, c. 23 (Priv. Act).

and Robert Grimston 266 a. The impropriator, Robert Wilsford, received 120 a., as well as a rent-charge. Five other men received substantial allotments: Henry Yates got 176 a., John Ogle 169 a., Beilby Thompson 149 a., and James Legard and William Ogle 118 a. each. In addition there were 3 allotments of 50 a.–100 a., 3 of 20 a.–50 a., 2 of 10 a.–20 a., and 15 of under 10 a.

In 1801 818 a. were under crops, about a quarter of the area of the parish. Oats were then growing on 297 a., wheat on 213 a., and turnips or rape on 113 a.[4] In the 19th and 20th centuries there have usually been from 14 to 17 farms in Flamborough, though there were only 9 in 1889 and a dozen in the 1920s.[5] In 1851 5 farms had an acreage of 150 or over,[6] and in the 1930s there were still 5 or 6 farms of that size.[7]

There was a mill in Flamborough by 1209[8] and two by 1218. A water-mill was explicitly mentioned c. 1260.[9] A windmill belonged to the manor in the early 16th century.[10] In 1551 Robert Puckering, lessee of the manor, also held a horse-mill which he was reported to have recently built,[11] and 10 years later the manor contained two horse-mills, in addition to the windmill.[12] In 1767 a windmill was situated in the west of the parish, near the Bridlington road, then called Mill Road.[13] The mill, a post mill, was blown down in 1839, and another in the village is said to have been burnt down a few years later;[14] it was presumably the ruined windmill which lay south of North Mere in 1850. Yet another mill was built in 1848 between North Mere and North Sea Lane,[15] but it had gone by 1889.[16]

In 1731 a market and fair were said to be appurtenant to the manor.[17] There is no further reference to the market, but during the 19th century a fair was held in Flamborough on Whit Tuesday.[18] Before the Sea Birds Act of 1869 it was described as 'a thoroughly murderous carnival', with visitors to the fair engaging in wholesale and indiscriminate shooting of sea-birds. About 1884 it was reported that since the passing of the Act the fair had greatly declined.[19] It is not known when it ceased.

Flamborough was a port of some significance from at least the early 14th to the later 16th century. In 1323 the king addressed orders to the keepers of the port and in 1342 he ordered the bailiffs of Flamborough to watch for spies attempting to leave it. The master of a Flamborough ship was accused of piracy in 1464.[20] The pier is first mentioned in 1400, when Robert Constable left £40 for its maintenance,[21] and it was again referred to in 1473.[22] It is reputed to have stood at South Landing.[23] In 1531 Sir Robert Constable reaffirmed his accustomed right of way between his manors of Flamborough and Holme upon Spalding Moor, in particular for carts carrying timber to repair the pier.[24] A toll on the anchorage of ships at the pier was part of the manorial revenue in the early 16th century.[25] In 1544 Flamborough's contingent of ships to serve in an expedition to Scotland comprised two of 30 and two of 40 tons.[26] George Emerson was trading from the port in 1544–7,[27] and John Willos (d. 1540), who owned a coble, and Thomas Bratoft (d. 1543) were described as 'shippers'.[28]

After the death of Robert Constable in 1537 the port fell into decay. By 1551 the pier had been destroyed by the sea;[29] it was 'well and substantially' rebuilt, but about 1569 it was again destroyed.[30] In 1570 the lease of the manor held by Robert Puckering and other inhabitants was renewed on condition that they rebuild the pier within four years.[31] They intended to rebuild it 'in a more convenient place', with a depth of 8 ft. of water at the harbour mouth,[32] but there is no further reference to it and it may never have been built.

Fishing at Flamborough was recorded as early as 1209, when there were at least nine boats there.[33] An agreement was made in 1267 between Robert the Constable and the fishermen on one hand and the prior of Bridlington on the other, following a dispute over fish tithes. Fish were divided into those given to the lord of the manor each day, and those the fishermen shared among themselves, the latter called 'scist fish'. The agreement provided that tithe should be paid before this division was made and that, in calculating the amount of tithe, which seems to have been paid in cash, no allowance was to be made for expenses, except bait. If a boat was lost in a storm a new one was to be provided 'in common'. Each Martinmas the priory was to give the crew of each boat twelve white loaves and 6d. for something to eat with them. Each fisherman was also to receive 4 gallons of ale, and each skipper (*gubernatori*) 8 gallons, to be drunk at once or not, as each man pleased. In return the priory was to be quit of all further obligations to the fishermen. Despite this agreement about fifty years later 69 fishermen refused to pay fish tithes, and in 1314 they took their case to law where judgement was given for the priory.[34]

In the mid 16th century the lord of the manor received tolls from fishermen and panniermen.[35] In 1550 fishing boats from Flamborough are mentioned,[36] and in 1563 unspecified fishermen were prevented from working around Flamborough

[4] 1801 Crop Returns.
[5] Directories.
[6] H.O. 107/2367.
[7] Kelly's Dir. N. & E.R. Yorks. (1933), 469; (1937), 462.
[8] B.M. Add. R. 75458.
[9] E.R.R.O., DDCC/App. A/p. 3, nos. 1, 2; *Ex. e Rot. Fin.* (Rec. Com.), i. 19.
[10] S.C. 6/Hen. VIII/4324; S.C. 11/732.
[11] S.C. 11/732.
[12] E 310/29/173 no. 8.
[13] Regy. of Deeds, AH/295/6.
[14] *Flamborough*, ed. Fisher, 32; Holderness, *E.R. Sketches*.
[15] Extracts from diary of John Hall (b. 1796), *penes* Mr. T. P. Cross, Flamborough, 1970; O.S. Map 6" (1854).
[16] O.S. Map 6" (1894).
[17] C.P. 43/592 rot. 232.
[18] Sheahan and Whellan, *Hist. York & E.R.* ii. 471.
[19] Holderness, *E.R. Sketches*.
[20] *Cal. Close*, 1323–7, 147; 1341–3, 486; *Cal. Pat.* 1461–7, 348.
[21] *Test. Ebor.* i. 264–5.
[22] *Cal. Pat.* 1467–77, 409.
[23] *Y.A.J.* xxi. 175.
[24] *Sta. Cha. Proc.* iii (Y.A.S. Rec. Ser. li), 25.
[25] E 310/31/185 no. 21; S.C. 6/Hen. VIII/4324.
[26] *L. & P. Hen. VIII*, xii (1), p. 1307; xix (1), pp. 61, 76; *Y.A.J.* xxi. 175.
[27] C 1/1118/22.
[28] B.I.H.R., Prob. Reg. xi, ff. 534, 678.
[29] S.C. 11/732.
[30] E 178/2564; E 310/29/173 no. 17.
[31] C 66/1065 m. 33.
[32] E 310/29/173 no. 17.
[33] B.M. Add. R. 75458.
[34] *Bridlington Charty.* 178–80; see below, p. 156.
[35] E 310/31/185 no. 21; E.R.R.O., DX/131/h.
[36] *Cal. Pat.* 1549–51, 420.

Head by the presence of foreign boats.[37] In 1581 two new fishing vessels, of 35 or 40 tons each, had recently been added to the Flamborough boats.[38] Provision was made in the inclosure award of 1767 for the fishermen to have access to the shore to gather bait,[39] and in 1794 about twenty Flamborough fishermen were drowned in a storm. In 1819 it was said that the Flamborough fishermen 'chiefly confine themselves to their own coasts, and seldom send more than four boats to the herring fishery at Yarmouth'.[40] In 1851 there were 123 fishermen in the parish.[41]

At the beginning of the 20th century three classes of inshore fishing were carried on from Flamborough: winter line-fishing, crab and lobster fishing, and herring fishing.[42] Small boats called cobles were used and they sailed mainly from North Landing, except when the wind was unfavourable and South Landing was used.[43] Most fishermen were said to keep a coble at each landing.[44]

Line-fishing took place from about mid October until Good Friday. Three men formed the crew of each coble, and the fish caught were mainly cod. Each crew sold its own catch by auction on the beach to local dealers. The fish was then carried to the cliff-top by donkeys, repacked, and carted to the railway station at Sewerby. The long journey to the station was said to be a serious hindrance, increasing the cost of marketing and detracting from the freshness of the fish.[45] Between 1886 and 1900 several unsuccessful attempts were made to have a tramway built from the cliff-top to the station.[46]

The crab and lobster season followed that for line-fishing, and until 1906 it continued until August. In that year the close season for crabs was abolished, and thereafter crabbing continued until October or even later. Smaller cobles with a crew of two were used, each crew working 30–40 pots.[47]

Drift-net fishing for herring started on 1 August and lasted until early October.[48] Larger cobles, crewed by four men, were used and the catch was generally landed at Scarborough or Bridlington because of the journey to the station. On account of low prices, however, herring fishing from Flamborough was already declining by the 1890s. In 1894 it was said that whereas there had formerly been about thirty herring boats there were then only fifteen.[49] By 1902 only twelve boats were reported,[50] and 20 years later herring fishing was said to have recently ceased.

In 1912 there were 155 fishermen and 114 boats, 91 of which were the smallest class of coble. The scarcity of fish, for which the growth of steam-trawling beyond Bridlington Bay since the beginning of the century was held responsible, was already threatening the inshore line-fishing. In 1912 98 Flamborough fishermen also unsuccessfully petitioned for trawling within the bay to be stopped. In 1913 many fishermen were said to be making a loss, a situation which occurred many times in the next 30 years, and the number of cobles engaged in line-fishing had fallen from 38 in 1912 to 33. The weight of wet fish landed at Flamborough fell by nearly a half between 1890 and 1914.[51] The fishing community often experienced great hardship, and soup kitchens were opened in the 1890s and in 1909.[52]

Despite a temporary rise in the price of fish during the First World War and the gradual introduction of motor-powered cobles from 1914 onwards, line-fishing continued to decline. Fish remained scarce and the weight landed in 1914–24 was only about a half of that in the previous decade. Moreover, while the cost of equipment rose the price of fish had fallen by the early 1920s to pre-war levels. In 1922 only 6 motor cobles and 36 sailing cobles remained. Five years later there were 11 motor but only 17 sailing cobles, and the number of fishermen was only 62.

Crab and lobster fishing became increasingly important as line-fishing declined. In 1934 about 2,000 pots were worked, and in 1937 crabbing was said to be more profitable even in the winter season. In 1919 some Flamborough fishermen also began inshore trawling, though nothing more is heard of it until 1931. Trawling was subsequently carried on at irregular intervals. In the 1920s many fishermen also supplemented their incomes during the summer by taking visitors on pleasure trips.

Since the Second World War both line-fishing and potting have continued to decline, and the number of boats fell from about 16 in 1940 to 9 in 1947; in the latter year only 27 men were engaged full-time. Between 1953 and 1961 at least one coble trawled each year, and in 1960 Flamborough fishermen obtained permission to trawl between Speeton and Flamborough Head. A recent development has been the growth of salmon fishing, first reported at Flamborough in 1959. Subsequently between one and five boats have worked salmon nets each year from South Landing. Since 1945 'pleasuring' has also greatly increased. In 1968 there were seven boats and about a dozen fishermen.[53]

From about the beginning of the 20th century Flamborough has increasingly attracted holidaymakers. The first refreshment rooms and holiday apartments appeared between 1889 and 1893, and by 1901 there were several people providing miscellaneous services for visitors.[54] From about 1900 until the First World War the privately-owned *Flamborough Guide* was published at intervals,[55] and by 1913 there were ten apartments and three refresh-

---

[37] Hist. MSS. Com. *12th Rep. App. IV, Rutland, I*, 88.
[38] *Cal. S.P. Dom.* 1581–90, 3.
[39] Regy. of Deeds, AH/295/6.
[40] J. Bigland, *Topog. and Hist. Description of Co. Yorks.* 417.
[41] H.O. 107/2367.
[42] This acct., unless otherwise stated, is based on the minutes of the North Eastern Sea Fisheries Cttee., 1890–1969.
[43] *Flamborough*, ed. Fisher, 47.
[44] *Flamborough Guide*, ed. Readhead, 14.
[45] *Flamborough*, ed. Fisher, 48.
[46] E.R.R.O., DDLG/30/383, 852; Flamborough Head Tramways Act, 50 & 51 Vic., c. 96.
[47] *Flamborough*, ed. Fisher, 48.
[48] *Flamborough Guide*, ed. Readhead, 14.
[49] *Flamborough*, ed. Fisher, 49.
[50] Bd. of Agric. and Fisheries, *Ann. Rep. relating to Sea Fisheries*, 1902, 117.
[51] See Bd. of Agric. and Fisheries, *Ann. Reps. . . . relating to Sea Fisheries*, pt. II, Tables, 1886–1918; Min. of Agric. and Fisheries, *Sea Fisheries Statistical Tables*, 1918–69; North Eastern Sea Fisheries Cttee. *Mins.* 1903–4 onwards.
[52] MS. notes *penes* Mrs. C. Cross, Flamborough, 1970; *Hull Daily News*, 8 Apr. 1909.
[53] Ex inf. Clerk to Flamborough Coble Club, 1970.
[54] *Kelly's Dir. N. & E.R. Yorks.* (1889), 388; (1893), 424; (1901), 482.
[55] Directories.

ment rooms.[56] Between the two wars holiday development continued, both in the village and along the coast. By 1933 there were seven refreshment rooms and cafés and a golf course had been constructed near the end of the headland.[57] A cricket pitch and tennis courts had appeared by 1936, when a guide-book to Flamborough was published.[58] In the 1930s bungalows and chalets proliferated; a holiday camp was established around Thornwick Bay between 1933 and 1937;[59] and North Landing was described in 1938 as 'a miniature China Town'.[60] In the late 1930s a plan to build over 1,000 bungalows on Flamborough Head provoked much public opposition, and to prevent development in the area Bridlington corporation in 1939 bought 270 a. on the headland. About twenty bungalows, however, had already been built.[61] The main development since the Second World War has been a great increase in the number of caravans. In 1951 a caravan site was established near the end of the headland and by 1961 there were three more around North Landing and Thornwick Bay. The county council then recommended that they should all be resited further inland, and by 1969 three new sites were occupied, although two of the old ones still remained.[62]

Because of its large population and the demands of visitors in modern times, Flamborough has had a wide variety of miscellaneous occupations. In the late 16th century a mercer, a tanner, and two weavers were recorded[63] and there was a weaver in 1823.[64] In 1851 about seventy people, excluding those connected with the fishing industry, followed a non-agricultural trade or craft.[65] Chalk-quarrying, lime-burning, and brick-making provided employment in the late 18th and 19th centuries. Chalk was taken from the cliffs,[66] as well as from inland quarries, and there were many lime-kilns in the parish.[67] A brick kiln was recorded in 1783,[68] Brick Kiln close was mentioned in 1822,[69] and in 1850 there was a brickyard south of the Bempton–Flamborough road[70] which continued in use until the First World War.[71] A sand and gravel quarry south of the village has been worked commercially since 1934.[72] Also recorded in the 19th century were a 'riding officer' in 1840, a tinner from 1840 to 1879,[73] and a guano merchant in 1851.[74] A boat-builder was mentioned from 1872 to 1937.[75]

LOCAL GOVERNMENT. In the Middle Ages and later Flamborough manor, presumably because of its early association with the honor of Chester,[76] had various privileges and liberties, the most noteworthy of which was the right of sanctuary both for felons and debtors. The right was confirmed when the manor was restored to Robert Constable in 1582.[77] The lord of the manor also claimed infangtheof[78] and the right to 'wrecks of sea', which in 1292–3 he stated to have long been held by his family.[79] The manorial bailiffs accounted for all revenues accruing from the privileges and tolls of the manor to the exclusion of the sheriff and officers of Admiralty.[80] It was claimed in 1540–1 that about twelve years previously Robert Constable had held an Admiralty court at Flamborough quay and 'declared his charter there openly'.[81] The lord of the manor held courts baron and leet and view of frankpledge in 1569–70.[82]

Vestry minutes survive for the period 1795–1858, when the vestry was an open one,[83] and there are accounts of the churchwardens for 1732–93, the overseers of the poor for 1718–1802, and the surveyors of highways for 1779–1802.[84] Churchwardens' accounts also exist for 1793 onwards.[85] There were two churchwardens, two surveyors, and two overseers. The poor-rate was 4d. in the pound in 1733 and 3d. in 1737–8. Most of the money raised was used to provide weekly relief, and there were parish poorhouses, first mentioned in 1731 and rebuilt in brick in 1781. Flamborough joined the Bridlington union in 1836.[86]

CHURCH. A church at Flamborough was first mentioned in a charter of c. 1094–1100, which records that it was given by Hugh, earl of Chester, to Whitby abbey.[87] The charter is probably spurious[88] and there is no further evidence that Whitby held Flamborough church. By 1130, when it was next mentioned, the church had been given by William son of Niel to Bridlington priory.[89] No vicarage was ordained and in 1310 the archbishop of York expressly confirmed the priory's right to serve the church by stipendiary priests.[90] During the later 14th century it seems that an arrangement arose whereby the church was served, at least in part, by the priest of St. Catherine's chantry, who was presented by the lord of the manor and instituted by the archbishop, thus acquiring a sort of vicarial status.[91] On at least two occasions in the early 15th century the chantry-priest exchanged livings with the vicar of another parish.[92] It seems, however, that

---

[56] *Kelly's Dir. N. & E.R. Yorks.* (1913), 533.
[57] Ibid. (1933), 469.   [58] *A Guide to Flamborough.*
[59] *Kelly's Dir. N. & E.R. Yorks.* (1933), 469; (1937), 462.
[60] 'Annals of Bridlington', vol. 55, p. 67.
[61] Ibid. p. 171; vol. 56, pp. 88, 158, 184.
[62] E.R.C.C. *Mins.* 1951–2, 105; 1960–1, 283, 286–7; 1963–4, 297; 1965–6, 81; ex inf. County Planning Officer, County Hall, Beverley, 1969.
[63] B.I.H.R., Prob. Reg. xv (1), f. 94; xvii, f. 297; xx, f. 90; xxviii, f. 13.
[64] Baines, *Hist. Yorks.* (1823), ii. 206.
[65] H.O. 107/2367.
[66] W. White, *A Month in Yorks.* 88; F. Brearley, *Hist. Flamborough,* 197.
[67] O.S. Map 6" (1854).
[68] Brearley, *Hist. Flamborough,* 195.
[69] E.R.R.O., DDFA/13/11.   [70] O.S. Map 6" (1854).
[71] Ex inf. Mr. T. P. Cross, Flamborough, 1970.
[72] Ex inf. W. Clifford Watts Ltd., Bridlington, 1969.
[73] Directories.   [74] H.O. 107/2367.
[75] Directories.   [76] See p. 154.
[77] E.R.R.O., DDEV/11/1; see above, p. 154.
[78] J.I. 1/1110 f. 127.
[79] *Plac. de Quo Warr.* (Rec. Com.), 220.
[80] E 315/285/37.   [81] Ibid.
[82] E 311/13/137.   [83] E.R.R.O., PR. 2355.
[84] It has not been possible to locate these records, which are in private hands. There are extracts from them in F. Brearley, *Hist. Flamborough,* 51–2, 67–9, 127–9, 160–3, and in E. Mellor, 'Flamborough' (TS. in Bridlington Pub. Libr.), 1–12. Extracts by Mellor are also in E.R.R.O., DDX/25/11.   [85] E.R.R.O., PR. 2355–6.
[86] *3rd Rep. Poor Law Com.* 167.
[87] *Whitby Charty.* i (Sur. Soc. lxix), 28; *E.Y.C.* ii, pp. 193–4.
[88] It is possible that the church had in fact been given to Whitby abbey and lost to it shortly afterwards. Alternatively it has been suggested that the charter might be genuine, but that 'Fleinesburg' had been mistakenly inserted by the scribe in place of 'Midelesburg': *E.Y.C.* ii, p. 193 n; *Whitby Charty.* i, p. xlvii.
[89] *Bridlington Charty.* 177.
[90] *Reg. Greenfield,* iii (Sur. Soc. cli), 173.
[91] *Fasti Parochiales,* iii. 99–101.   [92] Ibid. 19, 66.

Bridlington priory recovered its right to appoint priests, and in both 1441 and 1525–6 there was a parochial chaplain in Flamborough as well as the chantry-priest.[93] The living was styled a curacy until the 19th century, when it came to be regarded as a vicarage.[94]

After the Dissolution curates were at first appointed by the impropriators. Thus the advowson was let by the Crown in 1538 along with the rectory to John Wright,[95] who immediately sold his interest to Sir Marmaduke Constable.[96] A similar lease was made to Richard Foster in 1551.[97] A grant of the advowson to the archbishop of York in 1558[98] presumably lapsed on the accession of Elizabeth I. In 1582 and 1585 it was included in the Crown grant of the manor to Robert Constable,[99] and he died in possession in 1600.[1] By 1652–3, however, the patron was the impropriator, Edward Wilsford.[2] The advowson subsequently seems to have descended in the Wilsford family until 1815 when Robert Wilsford Coupland sold it to Walter Strickland, the lord of the manor.[3] It then descended with the manor and in 1969 the patron was Gerald Woodhouse.[4]

In 1208–9 the chaplain received a stipend of £3 16s. 8d. from Bridlington priory.[5] In 1525–6 the parochial chaplain received £6.[6] From the Dissolution to 1767 the stipend paid by the impropriator constituted virtually the entire income of the benefice. It was £30 in 1646[7] and £48 in 1650.[8] By 1685, however, the curate was paid only £8. By 1716 the stipend had risen to £16, and the impropriator continued to pay this sum throughout the 18th and 19th centuries.[9] In both 1767 and 1796 the living was augmented with £200 from Queen Anne's Bounty, and in 1814 with a parliamentary grant of £1,400.[10] The average net income of 1829–1831 was £81.[11] In 1861 the benefice received a grant of £25 a year from the Ecclesiastical Commissioners, and a further £24 in the form of a tithe rent-charge on 41 a. of land from Walter Strickland.[12] In 1883 the net value of the living was said to have fallen to £102.[13] It was augmented in 1894 by an anonymous gift of £920, and by grants of £700 from the Ecclesiastical Commissioners and £300 from the Diocesan Church Extension Society.[14]

Vicarial glebe was first acquired between 1770 and 1777, when land in Bonwick was bought with Bounty money.[15] Between 1817 and 1825 land at Beeford was bought with Bounty and grant money.[16] In 1897 the total amount of glebe was said to be 44 a.[17] There was no parsonage house until 1843, when, with the financial help of Walter Strickland, the present large yellow-brick Vicarage was built near the church.[18]

A chantry dedicated to St. Catherine was founded by Marmaduke Constable in 1359, endowed with a toft and £4 rent from the manor for a chaplain to celebrate daily in the church.[19] Until the Dissolution the chantry-priests were presented by the Constable family, lords of the manor, and instituted by the archbishop of York.[20] In 1525–6 the chantry was valued at £5 6s. 8d.[21] In 1570 the former chantry property, consisting of 11 cottages and 6 bovates, was let, with the manor, to Robert Puckering and others.[22] It was reserved to the Crown when Robert Constable was granted the manor in fee in 1582 and 1585,[23] but Constable was given a lease of it in 1584.[24]

Two other chantries, dedicated to St. Thomas and St. Mary Magdalene, were founded in the church, probably in the 13th or 14th century, by Robert the Constable, who gave a house for their support.[25] In 1376 Marmaduke Constable left two torches to the altar of St. Mary.[26] A cottage and a plot of land, given to support an obit, were let after the Dissolution together with the property of St. Catherine's chantry.[27]

A guild of St. Margaret was mentioned in 1566, when its former property in the parish, consisting of a house, 3 cottages, and 2 bovates, was let to Stephen Leckenby.[28] One of the cottages was known as the guild-house.[28] In 1576 it was let, again with the 2 bovates, to John Uerske and Francis Greenham,[29] and it was mentioned again in 1633.[30]

Before the parsonage house was built in 1843 the incumbents rarely, if ever, lived on their cure and often employed assistant curates. In 1743 the curate, 'an old crazed man', lived at Hornsea and the assistant curate at Bridlington.[31] In 1764 the curate himself lived at Bridlington.[32] The incumbents held other livings from the late 17th to the early 19th century, including Bempton, Grindale, and Bridlington, as well as the mastership of Bridlington Grammar School.[33]

---

[93] B.I.H.R. Churches index; *Y.A.J.* xxiv. 78.
[94] *Rep. Com. Eccl. Revenues*, 934; Sheahan and Whellan, *Hist. York & E.R.* ii. 470; *Kelly's Dir. N. & E.R. Yorks.* (1872), 364.
[95] C 54/418 no. 10; *L. & P. Hen. VIII*, xiii (2), pp. 407–8.
[96] C 54/418 no. 10.
[97] E 310/29/172 no. 23.
[98] *Cal. Pat.* 1557–8, 420.
[99] E.R.R.O., DX/131/ii, iii; *Yorks. Fines*, ii. 189; iii. 44.
[1] Wards 7/101/3.
[2] C.P. 25(2)/613/1652–3 Hil. no. 43; see above, p. 156.
[3] Registry of Deeds, Beverley, CY/200/288; *Flamborough: Village and Headland*, ed. R. Fisher, 34–5. There is no evidence to support the statements that the advowson belonged alternately to the lord of the manor and the archbishop, made in Ecton, *Thesaurus* (1788 edn.), 535, and Lawton, *Rer. Eccles. Dioc. Ebor.* 297.
[4] Ex inf. Counc. T. Woodhouse, Flamborough, 1969; see above, p. 154.
[5] B.M. Add. R. 75458.
[6] *Y.A.J.* xxiv. 69.
[7] *Royalist Composition Papers*, ii (Y.A.S. Rec. Ser. xviii), 134.
[8] *T.E.R.A.S.* ii. 53.
[9] B.I.H.R., TER. J. Flamborough 1716 etc.
[10] Hodgson, *Q.A.B.* 439.
[11] *Rep. Com. Eccl. Revenues*, 934.
[12] B.I.H.R., TER. J. Flamborough 1865; *Lond. Gaz.* 15 Oct. 1861, pp. 4065, 4067.
[13] B.I.H.R., Bp. V. 1884/Ret.
[14] *Flamborough*, ed. Fisher, 35.
[15] B.I.H.R., TER. J. Flamborough 1770, 1777.
[16] Ibid. 1817, 1825.
[17] *Kelly's Dir. N. & E.R. Yorks.* (1897), 459.
[18] *Flamborough*, ed. Fisher, 35.
[19] *Cal. Pat.* 1358–61, 214; *Black Prince's Reg.* iv. 293.
[20] *Fasti Parochiales*, iii. 8, 19, 66, 99–101.
[21] *Y.A.J.* xxiv. 69.
[22] E.R.R.O., DDHA/4/124; E 311/13 no. 137; *Cal. Pat.* 1569–72, 76.
[23] Wards 7/101/3.
[24] E 310/32/192 no. 55; C 66/1252 m. 13.
[25] *Bridlington Charty.* 178; J. Burton, *Mon. Ebor.* 226.
[26] *Test. Ebor.* i. 97–9.
[27] E 310/32/192 no. 55; *Cal. Pat.* 1569–72, 76.
[28] E 310/31/183 no. 54. The guild had also owned property in Bempton.
[29] C 66/1138 m. 15.
[30] S.C. 12/27/25 f. 15.
[31] *Herring's Visit.* i. 218.
[32] B.I.H.R., Bp. V. 1764/Ret. 190.
[33] Ibid., TER. J. Flamborough 1685, 1770; *Herring's Visit.* i. 218; *Rep. Com. Eccl. Revenues*, 934; J. Lawson, *Endowed Grammar Schs. of E. Yorks.* (E. Yorks. Loc. Hist. Ser. xiv), 21.

One noteworthy incumbent was Andrew Marvell (curate, 1609–12), the father of the poet, who seems to have been a moderate Puritan.[34] Several instances of neglect of duty were reported in the 17th and 18th centuries. In 1640, 1704, and 1757 the incumbent was said to have failed to hold the requisite number of services,[35] and in 1764 he was also accused of not administering communion at the great festivals, not burying the dead in due time, and not churching women or catechizing children.[36]

In 1743 communion was administered three times a year, and about one hundred and twenty people were said to have received it the previous Easter.[37] In 1764 a service was held on alternate Sundays, unless it fell on the first Sunday in the month which was 'from time immemorial excepted on account of the smallness of the stipend'. About seventy people had received communion the previous Easter.[38] About 1865 communion was administered some eight times a year to 7–12 people.[39] By 1868 there were two services each Sunday, and communion was administered monthly to about ten people.[40] In 1877 and 1884 communion was administered on alternate Sundays to 10–13 people,[41] and in 1936 every Sunday.[42] In 1969 there were four services each Sunday.

The church of ST. OSWALD consists of aisled chancel, nave with north and south aisles, west tower, and south porch. It has been much restored. The building is largely of limestone, but the north aisle wall is of cobbles. Of the aisleless Norman church, built c. 1100, there remain the rebuilt chancel arch and the tub font, the latter decorated with incised lozenges and, round the top, a double-roll cable moulding. The nave aisles were added in the 13th century, the south aisle being the earlier of the two. A door at the west end of the north aisle is now blocked. The nave arcades are each of four bays, with pointed arches on octagonal piers. The three-bay chancel arcades also originated in the 13th century. Until 1897 an Early English pointed arch existed in the west wall of the nave,[43] suggesting that there was also a tower by about 1300, and there may have been a west porch too.[44] The square-headed nave windows have Decorated tracery and are probably 19th-century replacements, while the clerestory, added in the 16th century, was also replaced later.[45]

In 1600 'the steeple' was in decay[46] and by 1640 it had fallen 'almost to the bottom'. In 1665 the poverty of the parish is said to have prevented its rebuilding.[47] The fallen masonry was not removed until 1846, when some at least was used in the churchyard wall.[48] In 1632–3 an extensive restoration took place. The pulpit was repaired, the pews were renewed in the body of the church and the 'loft', both aisles were paved, and the church was generally 'beautified'.[49] In the later 17th century the chancel was said to be out of repair, but it was 'very well repaired' in 1687.[50] The brick clerestory and the extensive brickwork in the south aisle, which both existed until the late-19th-century restoration, may have dated from this time.[51] In 1720 repairs to the outside walls were carried out,[52] and in 1825 the church was repewed and a west gallery built.[53] Until 1845 the north chancel aisle was used as a schoolroom;[54] it is now the vestry.

In 1864–9 much of the church was rebuilt. The cost of restoring the nave was raised by public subscription, while the impropriator, Walter Strickland, paid for the restoration of the chancel.[55] The architect was R. G. Smith of Hull.[56] The chancel and chancel aisles were almost entirely rebuilt and faced with stone externally; the Norman chancel arch, which was subsiding, was rebuilt; the nave and north aisle were reroofed; arches were inserted between the nave and chancel aisles; three new windows were inserted in the north aisle; the west gallery was removed; and a stone bell-turret, containing three bells, was built to replace the existing wooden one.[57]

The south porch was built in 1893 in memory of Walter Strickland and his wife Katherine.[58] In 1896–8 the present west tower was built in the Perpendicular style. It has three stages, with an embattled parapet, and on the south face is a canopied niche containing a figure of St. Oswald. Both the porch and tower were designed by C. Hodgson Fowler. The tower clock was given in memory of Frances E. Cottrell-Dormer (d. 1892).[59] The south chancel aisle has been made into a Lady Chapel in the 20th century, and a chapel in the north aisle of the nave was dedicated in 1963.[60] On the south wall of the Lady Chapel is a large rectangular piscina, much restored.

The church is rich in fittings, of which the most striking are the late-15th- or early-16th-century rood screen and loft. These are products of the 'Ripon school' of wood-carvers and, although extensively restored, still retain much original work, with traces of colouring.[61] The screen consists of six two-centred bays, with a four-centred door-head, and each bay contains elaborate tracery. The loft, one of only two extant examples in Yorkshire, originally contained fifteen canopied niches. In 1866 it was removed and placed above the tower arch, but it was returned to its proper place in 1895.[62] It is almost certain that the loft was not made for

---

[34] E.R.R.O., PR. 2335; R. A. Marchant, *Puritans and Ch. Courts in Dioc. York, 1560–1642,* 321; *D.N.B.*
[35] E.R.R.O., DPX/57, Flamborough, p. 2.
[36] B.I.H.R., Bp. 20D/90.
[37] *Herring's Visit.* i. 218.
[38] B.I.H.R., Bp. V. 1764/Ret. 190.
[39] Ibid., V. 1865/Ret. 186.
[40] Ibid., V. 1868/Ret. 171.
[41] Ibid., V. 1877/Ret.; Bp. V. 1884/Ret.
[42] Ibid., Bp. V. 1936/Ret. 277.
[43] F. Brearley, *The Parish Ch. of St. Oswald, Flamborough,* 11; *Y.A.J.* xv. 488–9.
[44] The base of a north wall remains under the footpath, and there are foundations parallel to the present west wall, about 6 ft. from it: Brearley, *Parish Ch.* 11.
[45] Morris, *E.R. Yorks.* 162.
[46] B.I.H.R., Churches index.
[47] E.R.R.O., DPX/57, Flamborough, p. 2.
[48] Brearley, *Parish Ch.* 11.
[49] E.R.R.O., PR. 2335. The details are wrongly given in *T.E.R.A.S.* i, pp. xiv–xv.
[50] B.I.H.R., Churches index.
[51] *Y.A.J.* xv. 488–9.
[52] B.I.H.R., Churches index.
[53] Brearley, *Parish Ch.* 15.
[54] J. Lawson, *Primary Educ. in E. Yorks. 1560–1902* (E. Yorks. Loc. Hist. Ser. x), 16.
[55] Brearley, *Parish Ch.* 18.
[56] Ex inf. Sir Nikolaus Pevsner, 1971.
[57] B.I.H.R., Churches index; Brearley, *Parish Ch.* 17–18.
[58] Tablet in porch.
[59] Brearley, *Parish Ch.* 18–19.
[60] Ibid. 22.
[61] Ibid. 7, 45–50. For a detailed description of the screen and loft, together with illus., see *Y.A.J.* xxiv. 128–32. See plate facing p. 192.
[62] Plaque under screen.

Flamborough,[63] but came from Bridlington priory at the Dissolution. There are three early-16th-century wooden parclose screens in the chancel which also seem to have come from Bridlington.[64]

Monuments include the plain chest tomb of Marmaduke Constable (d. 1520),[65] and another plain chest tomb with a marble top. A fragment of a stone effigy apparently shows the upper part of a skeleton with the breast open and what is traditionally held to be a toad at the heart.[66] There are several monuments to the Strickland, Wilsford, and Ogle families, including one to Walter Strickland (d. 1671).

There was a pair of organs in the church in 1552.[67] A bass violin was bought by subscription in 1812 and strings two years later. A 'psalm-master' was employed in 1807 and 1810 'for instructing to sing'.[68]

The church contained only one bell from at least 1552 until the restoration of 1864-8,[69] when three were provided.[70] Of these one was dated 1789 and the others, cast in the earlier 19th century by Mears of London, came from Christ Church, Bridlington.[71] In 1898 the present four bells by Mears and Stainbank of London were hung.[72] The plate consists of a silver cup of 1725, a set of silver vessels, given by Walter Strickland in 1869, a miniature silver communion set, given by A. E. Sunley, and a silver salver, given by Miss L. I. Broadley.[73] The silver cup was made in London by M. Arnett and E. Pococke. There are also a paten, a flagon, and two basins of pewter.[74] The burial and baptismal registers begin in 1564. The former are complete except for the years 1641-52 and 1699-1702, and the latter except for 1675-84. The marriage register, which begins in 1567, has gaps for 1602-53 and 1658-73.[75]

A new burial ground, opposite the church, was consecrated in 1878, and additions were made to the churchyard in 1918 and 1936.[76]

NONCONFORMITY. A single non-communicant is recorded in Flamborough in 1594 and 1604.[77] Although the pastor of Bridlington Baptist church is said to have baptized converts from Flamborough in the early 18th century,[78] no dissenters were reported in 1743.[79] In 1764 there was one Presbyterian[80] and in 1787 the Methodists had three members at Flamborough.[81] A house was licensed for worship in 1771, a barn in 1800, and a shop in 1820.[82]

The first chapel in the parish was built by the Wesleyan Methodists in 1799 on the east side of Garth Ends, now Chapel Street.[83] A new chapel was erected on the opposite side of the street in 1889, and the old one converted into the Liberal Hall.[84] The new chapel is a large ornate building with an angle-turret, built of yellow brick with red-brick and stone dressings. It fell out of use in 1965[85] but still stood in 1969.

The Primitive Methodists built a chapel in 1821, on the corner of Carter Lane and Chapel Street.[86] It was replaced by a new chapel in 1874.[87] The latter is a large red-brick building of three storeys, with yellow-brick and stone dressings, and has an elaborate front elevation containing a recessed arcaded entrance on the first floor. In 1889 there were said to be 127 members.[88] Services were still held there in 1969.

In 1865 the proportion of dissenters was estimated to be about two thirds of the population of the parish. The incumbent reported in 1868 that dissent was the main impediment to his work, as 'most of the people that profess anything at all go to the meeting-houses', and this complaint was reiterated in 1884.[89]

EDUCATION. There seems to have been a school in Flamborough throughout the 17th and 18th centuries, for schoolmasters are recorded in 1604-5, 1662, 1709, 1723-4, and 1781.[90] In the later 18th century the churchwardens were responsible for the upkeep of the school-house, first mentioned in 1756 when it was repaired.[91] In 1795 a brick floor was laid there and other work was done at intervals up to 1806-7.[92] By 1811 the school was being held at the east end of the north chancel aisle of the church, and in that year a faculty was granted to enlarge the schoolroom there.[93] Children continued to be taught in the church until 1845.[94]

In 1819 there were said to be three dame schools in the parish with a total of 70 children.[95] By 1835 there were four such schools, with a total attendance of 110 boys and girls, who were taught at their parents' expense.[96] There were still three dame

---

[63] *Y.A.J.* xxix. 172; Brearley, *Parish Ch.* 30.
[64] *Y.A.J.* xxix. 170.
[65] Morris, *E.R. Yorks.* 163; Brearley, *Parish Ch.* 36, 38-41.
[66] *Gent. Mag. Libr. Eng. Topog.* xiv. 223; Morris, *E.R. Yorks.* 163-4. In 1620 it was described as 'a tomb with a picture of death thereon': *Dodsworth's Ch. Notes* (Y.A.S. Rec. Ser. xxxiv), 183.
[67] *Inventories of Ch. Goods*, 21. [68] E.R.R.O., PR. 2355.
[69] B.I.H.R., TER. J. Flamborough 1857; *Inventories of Ch. Goods*, 20.
[70] B.I.H.R., TER. J. Flamborough 1865; Churches index. [71] Boulter, 'Ch. Bells', 216; see above, p. 74.
[72] Brearley, *Parish Ch.* 53.
[73] Ibid. 54-5.
[74] *Yorks. Ch. Plate*, i. 249.
[75] E.R.R.O.
[76] York Dioc. Regy., Sentences of consecration; B.I.H.R., CD. 446.
[77] H. Aveling, *Post Reformation Catholicism in E. Yorks. 1558-1790* (E. Yorks. Loc. Hist. Ser. xi), 59.
[78] *Baptists of Yorks.* (1912), 64.
[79] *Herring's Visit.* i. 218.
[80] B.I.H.R., Bp. V. 1764/Ret. 190.
[81] E.R.R.O., MRP/1/7.

[82] B.I.H.R., DMP. 1771/29; G.R.O. Worship Returns, Vol. v, nos. 1563, 3414.
[83] H.O. 129/24/524; O.S. Map 6" (1854).
[84] Date on building; see p. 153.
[85] Ex inf. Counc. T. Woodhouse, Flamborough, 1969.
[86] G.R.O. Worship Rets., Vol. v, no. 3596; H.O. 129/24/524; O.S. Map 6" (1854).
[87] Bulmer, *Dir. N. & E.R. Yorks.* (1892), 190. See plate facing p. 129.
[88] H. Woodcock, *Sketches of Prim. Meth. on Yorks. Wolds*, 67.
[89] B.I.H.R., V. 1865/Ret. 186; V. 1868/Ret. 171; Bp. V. 1884/Ret.
[90] B.I.H.R., Schools index; E. Mellor, 'Flamborough' (TS. in Bridlington Pub. Libr.), 7-9.
[91] Mellor, 'Flamborough', 7.
[92] E.R.R.O., PR. 2355.
[93] F. Brearley, *Hist. Flamborough*, 133. There is no evidence for the suggestion that the school was held in the church as early as 1793: *Flamborough: Village and Headland*, ed. R. Fisher, 19.
[94] J. Lawson, *Primary Educ. in E. Yorks. 1560-1902* (E. Yorks. Loc. Hist. Ser. x), 16.
[95] *Rets. on Educ. of Poor, 1819*, 1080.
[96] *Educ. Enquiry Abstract, 1835*, 1084.

schools in 1865, with a total attendance of 60–65 children, mainly under six years old.[97] By 1868 one of these schools had closed.[98] In 1871 there was a private day-school, attended by 15 boys and 15 girls.[99]

A National school was built in 1845 on land given by Walter Strickland on the corner of School Lane and South Sea Lane,[1] and an extension for infants was made by the Revd. J. F. Ogle between 1850 and 1855.[2] Attendance at the school about 1854 was 80 boys, 50 girls, and 30 infants. The annual income was about £24 from school pence, £10 from private subscriptions, and £6 from the Church of England Education Society.[3] By 1857–8 the school was also in receipt of an annual government grant.[4] In 1858 it was said that the school might be better attended if a better schoolmaster were engaged.[5] Total attendance was 184 in 1908, and until 1927 it varied only between 150 and 201. It declined in the 1930s and in 1938 it was only 114.[6] From about 1948, when the children from Sewerby school were sent to Flamborough,[7] until about 1960 some classes were held in the Wesleyan Methodist Church schoolroom.[8] Although a new infants' school was proposed in 1951, and land for it later acquired,[9] it had not been built by 1969. The average number on the roll in 1969 was 133.[10]

A night school is said to have been held by the vicar about 1850,[11] and an adult evening school, begun in 1865, met thrice weekly with an attendance of about 20.[12] In 1877 it was reported that evening schools had been unsuccessful.[13]

CHARITIES FOR THE POOR. In 1674 Sir Thomas Strickland left money to the poor of Flamborough.[14] In 1810 the endowment was said to consist of about £766, producing £20 a year.[15] By a Scheme of 1891 the income was used for money payments, to provide help and goods for the sick, and to make subscriptions or donations to hospitals or friendly societies. The endowment then amounted to £1,223, producing nearly £34 a year.[16] In 1933 the income of about £30 a year was used to provide each of 178 people with a stone of flour, each of 75 people with a cwt. of coal, and a donation of £5 to the Lloyd Hospital, Bridlington. In 1966 the income of about £31 was used to provide two families with 28 cwt. of coal each.[17]

Melchior Gibbon, by will proved in 1726, left a rent-charge of £1, to be distributed each Christmas Eve to the poor.[18] By 1823 the money was given to poor widows.[19] Francis Walmsley, by will proved in 1782, left £1 4s. a year to be given in penny loaves each month to the poor. This, together with a similar bequest to the poor of Bempton,[20] was charged on two houses in Bridlington in 1822, when the proceeds were distributed in cash.[21] Between 1866 and 1890 the money was distributed in bread.[22] By 1935 Gibbon's and Walmsley's charities were administered jointly and 44 people each received 1s. Between 1962 and 1969 the income was distributed among 12–20 people each year.[23] In 1971 only about £1 was received and no distribution was made.[24]

C. H. Childers, by will proved in 1881, left £1,000, the interest to be distributed each 21 December among the poor of the parish, without regard to their religious persuasion or their receipt of parochial relief.[25] In 1897 the income amounted to £27 and in 1937 to £25.[26] In 1963–9 the income of £25–£30 was distributed among 60–78 people each year[27] and in 1971 to 52 people.[28]

FOLKTON

FOLKTON lies on the northern edge of the wolds, about 10 miles north-west of Bridlington. The parish, which includes the townships of Flixton and Flotmanby, stretches for 3 miles from the high wolds in the south, across the chalk escarpment, and into the low ground of the Vale of Pickering in the north.[1] Folkton and Flixton may have been Anglian settlements and Flotmanby was probably of Scandinavian origin.[2] The villages of Flixton and Folkton and the site of the depopulated village of Flotmanby lie on the spring-line at the foot of the escarpment. On the wolds the parish boundary makes little use of marked natural features. A short section of the southern boundary, however, follows the bottom of a dry valley, and much of the eastern boundary with Hunmanby also uses dry valleys, although part of this boundary was described as new in 1807 and was probably straightened at the inclosure of that year.[3] Barrows were used for the alignment of sections of the southern parish boundary and the internal boundary between Folkton and Flotmanby; part of the boundary between Folkton and Flixton follows a prehistoric earthwork. On the low ground the boundaries mostly follow

[97] B.I.H.R., V. 1865/Ret. 186.
[98] Ibid. V. 1868/Ret. 171.
[99] Rets. rel. Elem. Educ. 1871, 474.
[1] Ed. 7/135; E.R.R.O., DDCV/parcel 22.
[2] Flamborough, ed. Fisher, 92.
[3] Ed. 7/135.
[4] Mins. of Educ. Cttee. of Council, 1857–8 [2380], H.C., p. 196 (1857–8), xlv.
[5] W. White, A Month in Yorks. 84.
[6] Bd. of Educ. List 21 (H.M.S.O.).
[7] See p. 100.
[8] E.R. Educ. Cttee. Mins. 1950–1, 210; ex inf. Counc. T. Woodhouse, Flamborough, 1969.
[9] E.R. Educ. Cttee. Mins. 1952–3, 54; ex inf. Counc. Woodhouse.
[10] Ex inf. Chief Educ. Officer, County Hall, Beverley.
[11] Flamborough, ed. Fisher, 92.
[12] B.I.H.R., V. 1865/Ret. 186.
[13] Ibid. V. 1877/Ret.

[14] Flamborough: Village and Headland, ed. R. Fisher, 171.
[15] E.R.R.O., DDX/31/5.
[16] Flamborough, ed. Fisher, 171–2.
[17] Char. Com. files.
[18] Flamborough, ed. Fisher, 172.
[19] 9th Rep. Char. Com. 734.
[20] See p. 16.
[21] 9th Rep. Char. Com. 734.
[22] Flamborough, ed. Fisher, 172.
[23] Char. Com. files.
[24] Ex inf. Counc. T. Woodhouse, Flamborough, 1971.
[25] Flamborough, ed. Fisher, 173.
[26] Kelly's Dir. N. & E.R. Yorks. (1897), 459; (1937), 461.
[27] Char. Com. files.
[28] Ex inf. Counc. Woodhouse.
[1] This article was written in 1971.
[2] P.N.E.R.Yorks. (E.P.N.S.), 115–16.
[3] Registry of Deeds, Beverley, Folkton inclosure map.

watercourses, notably Spital beck in the west. The irregular northern parish boundary, which is also the wapentake and riding boundary, is formed by the old course of the river Hertford, part of which is now called the Little Hertford river. The area of the parish is 5,498 a., of which Flixton accounts for 2,561 a., Folkton for about 1,970 a., and Flotmanby for about 960 a.[4]

The most prominent feature of the landscape is the steep wolds escarpment, which crosses the parish from west to east, rising sharply from about 150 ft. above sea-level near the villages at its foot to over 475 ft. at Flixton and Folkton brows and to about 400 ft. at Flotmanby brow. The parish comprises three markedly different areas, the flat, low-lying, and peat-covered carr-land of the vale in the north, the escarpment, the lower slopes of which are covered by a broad belt of sand and gravel, and the typically open wold-land in the south.

In the north much of the ground lies at less than 100 ft. It is crossed by many small streams and dikes flowing into the river Hertford, the straight embanked course of which is a result of the early-19th-century drainage of the area, before which much of the land was marsh and carr.[5] South of the escarpment the ground continues to rise, although more gently, to over 500 ft. around Sharp Howes and to over 550 ft. at the western parish boundary. The wolds are dissected by numerous steep-sided dry valleys, including Merry, Lang, and Duntze Dales in the west, and Camp and Stocking Dales in the east. A smaller valley was known in the later 12th century as Dedhill Dale, its name probably deriving from the finding of a corpse there,[6] and the name survives as Deedle hill. Raven and Bording Dales were also mentioned in the 12th century. The former may take its name from a Scandinavian personal name and the latter derives from 'Baldwinesdale'.[7]

Numerous prehistoric embankments and barrows formerly existed on the wolds in the parish. One of the most prominent of those that remain is the speech-mound, called Spell Howe, which may have been the meeting-place of Turbar hundred.[8] One of the Folkton barrows has yielded the well known ritual 'drums' or cylinders of chalk.[9] There is also much evidence of early settlement on the low ground below the escarpment, and a site in Flixton ings has produced both Romano-British and Anglian pottery.[10]

Camp Dale, lying doubtless as its name implies below the crest of a hill,[11] is first mentioned c. 1160, when Rievaulx abbey had a grange there.[12] In 1563 Camp Grange barn stood in the south of Folkton township near the Hunmanby boundary,[13] but no building apparently remained in 1807.[14] Earthworks in Camp Dale near its junction with Stocking Dale, known since at least 1850 as the Camp,[15] presumably mark the site of the former grange. They chiefly comprise two rectangular enclosures, and Camp well lies between them.

The amount of woodland in the parish has been much reduced since the mid 19th century[16] and only a few small plantations remain. The pattern of large regular fields in Flixton and Folkton townships is a result of the early-19th-century inclosures, and the irregular field-pattern around the site of Flotmanby village may reflect the inclosure of that area in the Middle Ages.[17]

The Malton–Filey road crosses the parish below the escarpment, forming the main village street of Flixton, referred to as 'town gate' in 1563.[18] Before its course was altered it also formed the main street of Folkton village. It continues through Flotmanby township and into Muston as Flotmanby Lane. There are few other roads in the parish. Flixton Carr Lane, which leads from Flixton village northwards into the former carr-lands, was set out by the inclosure commissioners in 1806;[19] it is carried over the river Hertford by a modern bridge and becomes a field-road thereafter. Carr Lane, running northwards from Folkton village into Cayton (Yorks. N.R.), was also set out at inclosure.[20] The road formerly continued southwards beyond the Malton–Filey road, linking up with the road to Hunmanby, which still climbs the wolds escarpment as White Gate Hill. The main road from Staxton towards Scarborough follows the course of Spital beck along the western parish boundary.

Near Folkton village changes occurred in the courses of both the Hunmanby and the Filey roads, probably in the early 19th century. In 1770 the Filey road still ran through the village but by 1807, and probably at the inclosure of that year, its course was altered. A section 1½ mile long to the east of the village was stopped-up and a new road was built from the west end of the village street on the present, more direct, line; it rejoins the old line near West Flotmanby Farm. There is an old uninscribed milestone on the new section of road. At the same time that section of the Hunmanby road lying between the old and new roads to Filey was also stopped-up.[21]

The small village of Folkton is consequently by-passed by the modern Malton–Filey road. Manor Farm, at the west end, has an 18th- or early 19th-century two-storeyed farm-house, built of chalk with red-brick gables, quoins, and dressings; the farmyard is surrounded by a group of contemporary buildings, including a barn next to the house, which are constructed of similar materials.[22] Several prominent farm buildings of chalk and brick, belonging to Grange Farm, stand on the opposite side of the road near the church. Church Farm is also probably of the 18th century, with later alterations, and there are several mainly chalk-built cottages of one or two storeys of the same period. Later buildings include four Council houses. A

---

[4] Ibid. CI/254/19; O.S. Map 6" (1854).
[5] See p. 172.
[6] *P.N.E.R. Yorks.* 116; *Rievaulx Charty.* (Sur. Soc. lxxxiii), 116.
[7] *P.N.E.R. Yorks.* 116; *Rievaulx Charty.* 49, 298-9.
[8] *P.N.E.R. Yorks.* 116; see above, p. 3.
[9] *V.C.H. Yorks.* i. 382-3; *Y.A.J.* xix. 448-9; illus. in S. Thomas, *Pre-Roman Brit.* pl. 155.
[10] *Y.A.J.* xxxix. 193, 221; Mary Kitson Clark, *Gaz. of Roman Remains in E. Yorks.* 84.
[11] *P.N.E.R. Yorks.* 115-16.
[12] *Rievaulx Charty.* 50, 115 n., 116 n.; *E.Y.C.* ii, p. 516.
[13] Castle Howard MS., Box 24, Survey of Estates, 1563.
[14] Regy. of Deeds, Folkton incl. map.
[15] O.S. Map 6" (1854).
[16] Ibid.
[17] See p. 172.
[18] Castle Howard MS., Box 24, Survey of Estates, 1563.
[19] Regy. of Deeds, CI/69/4.
[20] Ibid. /254/19.
[21] Regy. of Deeds, Folkton incl. map; T. Jefferys, *Map of Yorks.* 1772; J. Cary, *Map of E.R. Yorks.* 1789, 1793; C. Greenwood, *Map of Yorks.* 1834.
[22] See plate facing p. 273.

public house, generally known as the Bell but in the 1870s as the Tate's Arms, existed from at least the early 19th century until c. 1930.[23] Manor House and the former Rectory both stand in their own grounds on the Filey road to the east and west of the village respectively.

The larger and more closely built-up village of Flixton lies 1½ mile west of Folkton. Most of the buildings stand in the main street, formed by the Malton–Filey road, and in North Street, which continues beyond the village as Flixton Carr Lane. At the end of North Street several springs feed a stream flowing into the carrs. Back Lane, south of the main street, is first mentioned in 1717;[24] an old uninscribed mile-stone near its west end may indicate that it was at some time used as the main route for through-traffic. Limekiln Lane leads southwards from the main street, continuing beyond Back Lane as a short green cul-de-sac.

One of the more noteworthy houses in the village is Flixton House, in North Street, known in the mid 19th century as Spring Hall.[25] It has a long, early-19th-century, two-storeyed front, faced with stucco, and two single-storeyed flanking wings with raked parapets. A more humble one-and-a-half storey chalk-built house, probably of the late 18th century, stands back from North Street and was derelict in 1971; its barn is also of chalk, with red-brick quoins and eaves courses. Danby House, in North Street, a mainly chalk-built double-fronted house with a brick gable and dentil eaves cornice, is dated 1811. A brick house near the junction of the main street and North Street has tie-rod ends shaped to form the date 1819. Other 18th- and early-19th-century houses in the main street, including Welbourn Farm, are largely of chalk. Along the street there are also numerous farm buildings of chalk and brick.

There are two inns. For much of the 19th century there was only one, the New Inn, in North Street; by 1971 the name had become the Old House. The increase in tourist traffic to Filey after the Second World War probably led to the enlargement c. 1965 of the Foxhound inn, which has stood in the main street since at least the 1890s.[26]

Much 20th-century development has taken place on the road between the two villages and many private houses and bungalows, as well as about twenty-five Council houses, have been built there. Bungalows and chalets and two caravan sites have also appeared, mainly since the Second World War, along the Malton road west of Flixton village and the Scarborough road.

The former hamlet of Flotmanby probably stood between East and West Flotmanby Farms; some earthworks remain near the latter farm, but most of the site was destroyed in 1955.[27] A fishpond, dry in 1971, lay near West Flotmanby Farm. The main street of the hamlet may have been formed by the old course of the Filey road, one stretch of which had apparently been diverted further south to its present course by 1808,[28] perhaps when the small park near West Flotmanby Farm was created. In the mid 19th century the old course of the road apparently still existed,[29] but by 1971 only a short section remained. The Filey road was straightened near the entrance to West Flotmanby Farm c. 1966. The large red-brick farm-house is of 18th-century origin, with front rooms added along the west side in the early 19th century. A further addition was made in the 20th century, when the front door was moved to the south end. The extensive outbuildings are mainly of 19th-century date, several being of Filey brick, but an altered barn, which incorporates stone from the North Riding, is of the previous century. Standing east of the farmyard is an early-18th-century dovecot, a small rectangular red-brick building with stone quoins, plinth, and eaves cornice.

Most of the other isolated farm-houses in the parish originated after the early-19th-century inclosures. An exception is Flixton Carr House Farm in the north-east of the parish, a one-and-a-half-storeyed chalk building, of 18th- or early-19th-century date but with an altered front. Its site, however, may have been in constant habitation since the Middle Ages. In the early 1950s much medieval pottery was discovered in a ditch south of the house and stones, probably from a building, were found near by.[30] There was a small hospital at Flixton in the Middle Ages[31] and it has been suggested that it lay at the north end of the village, near the present Flixton House.[32] The location of this and of another hospital in Staxton probably indicates the early importance of the road which crosses the Vale of Pickering at this point.[33]

In 1377 Folkton had 71 poll-tax payers and Flotmanby 22.[34] In 1674 33 households in Folkton and Flotmanby together were recorded in the hearth-tax assessment, of which 10 were discharged for poverty; of the 23 that were taxed, 18 had only one hearth, 4 had 2, and one had nine.[35] Flixton was a little larger. In 1377 it had 80 poll-tax payers[36] and in 1670 33 households were recorded in the hearth-tax assessment, including 6 discharged for poverty. Discharged households were not recorded in 1674 but of the 26 that were taxed 25 had only one hearth and one had two.[37] There were about 64 families in the whole parish in 1743[38] and about 55 in 1764.[39] In 1801 the population was 266. It rose steadily to a peak of 580 in 1841 before declining to 439 in 1901.[40] It fell to 419 in 1921, rose to 497 in 1951, and stood at 477 in 1961.[41]

MANORS AND OTHER ESTATES. In 1086 there was a single estate, of 9 carucates, in Folkton township. It had been held as two manors by Carle and Otre before the Conquest, but in 1086 it was in the king's hands.[42] It later passed to the Gant fee

---

[23] Directories; local inf.
[24] Regy. of Deeds, F/77/162.
[25] O.S. Map 6" (1854).
[26] Local inf. The Foxhound inn is not mentioned in directories but it may have been the premises of the beer-seller mentioned in 1872 and later.
[27] Med. Archaeol. i. 166; Y.A.J. xxxviii. 61.
[28] J. Cary, Map of E.R.Yorks. 1808.
[29] O.S. Map 6" (1854).
[30] T. C. M. Brewster, Two Med. Habitation Sites in Vale of Pickering (Yorks. Mus.), 13.

[31] See p. 170.
[32] Ex inf. Mr. T. C. M. Brewster, 1971.
[33] See p. 336.
[34] E 179/202/62 mm. 32–3.
[35] E 179/205/521.
[36] E 179/202/62 m. 26.
[37] E 179/205/514, 521.
[38] Herring's Visit. i. 215.
[39] B.I.H.R., Bp. V. 1764/Ret. 193.
[40] V.C.H.Yorks. iii. 489.
[41] Census.
[42] V.C.H.Yorks. ii. 204, 323.

and the overlordship descended in the Gant and Tattershall families, passing to the Tattershall heir Joan of Driby on the division of the fee in 1309.[43] The Tattershall lordship is last mentioned in 1428.[44]

A mesne lordship was held by the Greystock family in the Middle Ages and later. Early members of that family, Walter son of Ives and his son Ranulph (fl. 1166), granted land in Folkton to Rievaulx abbey in the mid 12th century.[45] In 1284–5 4 carucates were held by the Greystocks under the Gants.[46] The lordship descended, like Butterwick manor, in the Greystock and Howard families[47] and is last mentioned in the early 17th century.[48]

A family which took its name from the village probably held the tenancy in demesne in the later 12th century. Henry of Folkton was mentioned in 1208[49] and in 1246 his son Walter made an exchange of land with Walter's son Ranulph.[50] In 1254 Ranulph of Folkton held 3 carucates.[51] The manor of *FOLKTON* passed soon after to the Lacys. Richard de Lacy married Gillian, the daughter of Ranulph of Folkton,[52] and in 1268 they accused Ranulph of breaking an agreement with them concerning the manor.[53] Ranulph's widow Alice held part of it in dower in 1278–9[54] but by 1303 all 6 carucates of the Tattershall fee were in the hands of Richard de Lacy.[55] In 1346 of the 3½ carucates which that fee was then said to contain in Folkton, Edmund, Thomas, and John Lacy held 1½ carucate, 5½ bovates, and a bovate respectively,[56] and in 1428 Thomas and William Lacy held 8 and 4 bovates respectively.[57] In 1525 Thomas Lacy died seised of the manor, which then contained 27 bovates in Folkton and 3 in Flixton.[58] The estate descended to his grandson Robert Lacy, who died in 1588 leaving a son and two daughters as heirs. The son, John, died in 1604–5, still a minor, and the manor was divided between his sisters Mary, wife of William St. Quintin, and Everild, wife of William's brother Herbert.[59] Herbert St. Quintin died in 1634 leaving his brother William as his heir[60] and the manor descended in the St. Quintin family[61] until 1787, when it was sold by Sir William St. Quintin to Mark Bell.[62]

By will dated 1789 Bell devised his property to trustees for the life of his son James, who had become insane that year. In the event of James dying without issue Folkton manor was to pass to one of the trustees, William Tate, a great-nephew of Mark Bell.[63] At inclosure in 1807 James Bell was awarded 998 a. as lord of the manor.[64] He apparently died *c.* 1814 and soon afterwards the manor passed to James Bell Tate, nephew of William Tate.[65] It was retained by the Tates until the earlier 20th century,[66] comprising 1,138 a. in 1910.[67] Emily Tate died in 1931[68] and the following year the estate was vested in Gladys Hume,[69] who in 1945–6 sold 761 a. in various lots, including Manor House and 41 a. to J. G. Edwards.[70] In 1957 Edwards sold the property to G. M. Harrod,[71] who has since retained it. Gladys Hume sold the remaining 348 a. of the estate in 1953.[72]

The present Manor House is a gabled, later-19th-century, red-brick building standing in its own grounds near the Filey road east of the village.

Several religious houses held estates in Folkton. In the later 12th century Rievaulx abbey had a grange called 'Kamp',[73] which probably included land in Folkton, Flotmanby, and Hunmanby.[74] In 1158 Walter son of Ives granted Rievaulx ½ carucate in Folkton.[75] His son Ranulph confirmed the gift in 1162–75 and added a 'tillage' called Ravensdale, apparently of 9 a., and pasturage for 1,000 sheep and the plough-beasts used for the tillage.[76] In 1162–7 William son of Tibbald granted the abbey 16 a. in Folkton[77] and probably in the early 13th century William of Hunmanby gave a plot of 30 a.[78] Other grants to Rievaulx included 60 a. of wold land by Kirkham priory.[79] In 1271 the abbey also had land which it had been granted by Alice, widow of Henry of Folkton.[80]

Camp grange was retained by Rievaulx until the Dissolution.[81] It passed soon after to the Babthorpe family; in 1557 William Babthorpe held the 'manor or grange' of Flotmanby[82] and in the late 16th century Camp grange was in the hands of Ralph Babthorpe.[83] Lands in 'Camp', Flotmanby, and Folkton were sold by Ralph and his son William Babthorpe to William St. Quintin in 1611,[84] and they subsequently descended with Folkton manor.[85]

Bridlington priory was granted 2 bovates in Folkton before 1175 by Tibbald son of Reinfrid,[86] and in the late 12th or early 13th century Henry

---

[43] *Feud. Aids*, vi. 27, 141, 225; *Yorks. Inq.* iv. 36; *Cal. Close*, 1307–13, 102; *Cal. Inq. p.m.* vii, p. 470; see below, p. 231.
[44] *Feud. Aids*, vi. 266.
[45] *E.Y.C.* ii, p. 430 n.; see below.
[46] *Feud. Aids*, vi. 27.
[47] C.P. 40/892 m. 362d.; C 142/44/152; C 142/109/44; C 142/222/13; Castle Howard MSS., Box 24, Surveys of Estates, 1537, 1563; *Yorks. Inq.* iii. 139; iv. 36; *Yorks. Inq. Hen. IV–V*, 32, 144; *Cal. Inq. p.m.* vi, pp. 30, 307; vii, p. 470; xiv, pp. 30–2; *Yorks. Fines, 1347–77*, 217; iii. 67; 1603–14, 73, 91; *Cal. Close*, 1360–4, 500; 1402–5, 202; see below, p. 193.
[48] *Yorks. Fines, 1614–25*, 33, 183.
[49] *Yorks. Fines, John* (Sur. Soc. xciv), 120.
[50] *Yorks. Fines, 1232–46*, 127–8.
[51] *Yorks. Inq.* i. 37.
[52] *Visit. Yorks. 1584–5 and 1612*, ed. J. Foster, 160.
[53] J.I. 1/1050 m. 47.
[54] *Rievaulx Charty.* (Sur. Soc. lxxxiii), 404.
[55] *Yorks. Inq.* iv. 36.
[56] *Feud. Aids*, vi. 225.
[57] Ibid. 266.
[58] C 142/44/152.
[59] *Visit. Yorks. 1584–5 and 1612*, 160, 163; G.E.C. *Baronetage*, ii. 161.
[60] C 142/735/85.
[61] E.R.R.O., DDSY/68/58, 60; see below, p. 224.

[62] Registry of Deeds, Beverley, BM/146/228.
[63] Ibid. BO/515/797; C 211/3/B. 174.
[64] Regy. of Deeds, CI/254/19.
[65] Ibid. CK/544/890; HF/150/209; E.R.R.O., Land Tax; Burke, *Land. Gent.* (1879), s.v. Tate of Cheam Hall; White, *Dir. E. & N.R. Yorks.* (1840), 385.
[66] Directories.
[67] Regy. of Deeds, 122/84/77.
[68] Ibid. 452/119/101.
[69] Ibid. /123/102.
[70] Ibid. 688/471/391; 691/405/340; 692/329/281; 703/120/102; 725/280/234.
[71] Ibid. 1079/24/16.
[72] Ibid. 936/419/373.
[73] *Rievaulx Charty.* 115 n.
[74] See pp. 165, 169.
[75] *E.Y.C.* ii, p. 506.
[76] Ibid. 514, 517; *Rievaulx Charty.* 238.
[77] *E.Y.C.* ii, p. 516.
[78] *Rievaulx Charty.* 238, 397.
[79] Ibid. 238, 250, 298–300.
[80] *Cal. Close*, 1272–9, 491.
[81] S.C. 6/Hen. VIII/4553, 4556.
[82] E.R.R.O., DDGD/Box 1.
[83] B.M. Add. MS. 26718, f. 36.
[84] *Yorks. Fines, 1603–14*, 164.
[85] See above.
[86] *E.Y.C.* ii, pp. 517–8.

Wolf gave 2 more.[87] In the later 13th century Richard de Lacy granted the priory 50 cart-loads of turf a year from his marsh in Folkton and pasturage 'in the field' for 300 sheep.[88] In 1535 Bridlington's estate there was worth 12s. a year,[89] and in 1557 2 bovates and a garth of that value, said to be the only property of the former priory in Folkton, were granted to Thomas Wood.[90] In 1251 the Knights Templars held a toft and a bovate in Folkton[91] which presumably passed to the Knights Hospitallers. The latter held property in the township in 1539–40 and this was restored to them when the order was briefly revived in 1558.[92]

About 1276 Richard de Lacy encroached on the marshes of neighbouring North Riding townships,[93] and for this land, said in the 14th century to consist of 280 a. in Folkton marsh, succeeding lords of the manor paid 5s. a year to the honor of Pickering.[94] The rent is last mentioned in 1661, when it was said to be for 180 a. in the marsh.[95]

In 1086 6 carucates in Flotmanby were soke of Hunmanby. One bovate was held by the college of St. John, Beverley, of the archbishop of York and the remaining 5 carucates and 7 bovates by Gilbert de Gant.[96] By 1284–5 all 6 carucates were in the Gant fee.[97] The overlordship descended, like that of Folkton, in the Gant and Tattershall families.[98] A mesne lordship was held by the Greystocks and later the Howards from at least 1166[99] and is last mentioned in 1589.[1]

The Scrope family held the manor of FLOTMANBY in the later 12th century, when Robert Scrope granted 2 bovates there to Bridlington priory.[2] In 1205 his granddaughters Maud and Alice granted a carucate and the service from 2 bovates there to their uncle Simon Scrope.[3] He gave 6 tofts and 13 a. to Bridlington priory[4] and his son Henry, sometimes called Henry Wolf, made further grants to the priory, including all his demesne in Flotmanby.[5] Thornton abbey granted Bridlington 2 bovates in Flotmanby, which it had been given by Walter Scrope.[6] Later in the 13th century Agnes daughter of Ancelin Scrope granted to Richard de Berneville her chief lordship (*capitale dominium*) in Flotmanby, together with 5 tofts and 9 bovates there. Berneville granted the property to Bridlington priory.[7] No later reference to the Scropes in Flotmanby has been found.

Bridlington acquired other land in the township in the 13th century. In 1240 William son of Robert granted the priory 2 bovates and Godfrey of Butterwick confirmed Andrew of Killingholme's gift of another.[8] In 1251 Stephen of Cottam confirmed his father Alan's gift of a capital messuage and 11 bovates,[9] and other grants included 2 bovates by William of Haterbergh and 4 bovates by Walter of Buckton, the latter in exchange for property elsewhere.[10] By 1303 the priory held 4 carucates in Flotmanby[11] and the prior was returned as one of the lords of the township in 1316.[12] Bridlington retained the manor until the Dissolution.[13] In 1535 it was worth £6 7s. a year.[14]

In 1543 the manor, consisting of 33 bovates, was granted by the Crown to William Babthorpe.[15] It descended in the Babthorpe family[16] until 1637, when Ralph Babthorpe sold it to John Buck.[17] In 1674 Robert Buck was assessed for a house of nine hearths.[18] The manor was apparently divided into three parts c. 1700. A third seems to have passed to each of Robert Buck's daughters Anne Lutton and Mary Buck, with whom their father made a settlement in 1699–1700,[19] and the other third to Robert's son John (d. by 1725). In 1725 Mary Buck devised her share to Anne Lutton,[20] whose estate later passed to the Roberts family. In 1737 John Roberts and his daughter Anne held a third part of the manor[21] and by 1749 two thirds were held by Edward Dowsett, whose wife was Anne's sister Elizabeth.[22] In 1787–8 Dowsett's trustees sold two thirds of WEST FLOTMANBY manor to Elizabeth Woodall[23] and in 1804 John Woodall owned the estate.[24] John Buck's third part apparently passed to a son Robert, whose daughter Elizabeth Buck sold it in 1763 to F. W. Osbaldeston.[25] In 1804 Humphrey Osbaldeston owned a third of the manor.[26] It descended like the capital manor of Hunmanby, and in 1856 West Flotmanby manor was reunited when Admiral Mitford sold his third to W. E. Woodall.[27] On the death of J. W. Woodall in 1905 the estate passed to his executor C. H. Dent,[28] who sold it in 1935, then amounting to 655 a., to R. N. Goodall.[29] He sold the 201-acre West Flotmanby Wold farm in 1945[30] and the 454-acre West Flotmanby farm in 1952.[31]

---

[87] *Bridlington Charty.* 82.
[88] Ibid. 9, 89; *Yorks. Inq.* iii. 139.
[89] *Valor Eccl.* (Rec. Com.), v. 120.
[90] E 318/2165; *Cal. Pat.* 1555–7, 393–5.
[91] *Yorks. Fines, 1246–72,* 23.
[92] *Miscellanea,* iv (Y.A.S. Rec. Ser. xciv), 91; *Cal. Pat.* 1557–8, 319.
[93] *Rot. Hund.* (Rec. Com.), i. 107.
[94] *Yorks. Inq.* iii. 74; *Cal. Inq. p.m.* xi, p. 99; *Honour and Forest of Pickering,* i (N.R. Rec. Ser. N.S. i), 15, 52; ii (N.R. Rec. Ser. N.S. ii), 18, 173; iii (N.R. Rec. Ser. N.S. iii), 17; iv (N.R. Rec. Ser. N.S. iv), 62, 199, 214, 245.
[95] *Hon. and For. of Pickering,* i. 103.
[96] *V.C.H. Yorks.* ii. 215, 272, 323.
[97] *Feud. Aids,* vi. 27.
[98] Ibid. 141, 225, 266; *Cal. Inq. p.m.* iv, p. 107; vii, p. 470; see above, p. 167.
[99] C 142/44/152; C 142/109/44; C 142/189/55; Castle Howard MSS., Box 24, Surveys of Estates, 1537, 1563; *E.Y.C.* ii, p. 430 n.; *Cal. Inq. p.m.* iv, p. 107; vii, p. 470; *Yorks. Inq. Hen. IV–V,* 32.
[1] C 142/222/13.
[2] *Bridlington Charty.* 80; for pedigree of the Scropes see J. Foster, *Pedigrees of . . . Yorks.* iii, s.v. Scrope of Bolton.
[3] *E.Y.C.* ii, p. 490; *Bridlington Charty.* 81.
[4] *Bridlington Charty.* 87.
[5] Ibid. 9, 82.
[6] Ibid. 84; *Yorks. Fines, 1232–46,* 57.
[7] *E.Y.C.* ii, p. 491; *Bridlington Charty.* 84–5.
[8] *Bridlington Charty.* 83, 86; *Yorks. Fines, 1232–46,* 71–2.
[9] *Bridlington Charty.* 82–3.
[10] Ibid. 4, 85, 88, 91.
[11] *Yorks. Inq.* iv. 36.
[12] *Feud. Aids,* vi. 170.
[13] *Bridlington Charty.* 88–9; *Cal. Inq. p.m.* vi, p. 30; *Cal. Chart. R. 1427–1516,* 67, 120.
[14] *Valor Eccl.* v. 120.
[15] E 318/63; *L. & P. Hen. VIII,* xviii (2), p. 60.
[16] C 142/102/62; C 142/367/20; B.M. Add. MS. 26718, ff. 59, 104; *Yorks. Fines, 1603–14,* 147, 164; *1614–25,* 204–5.
[17] C.P. 25(2)/523/13 Chas. I Mich. pt. 2, no. 41; C.P. 43/298 rot. 151; E.R.R.O., DC/10/219.
[18] E 179/205/521.
[19] C.P. 25(2)/896/11 Wm. III Hil. no. 25.
[20] Regy. of Deeds, I/153/342.
[21] Ibid. P/344/883.
[22] Ibid. U/70/137.
[23] Ibid. BN/94/137; /96/139; /97/140.
[24] E.R.R.O., DDCB/12/6.
[25] E.R.R.O., AE/44/95; /45/96.
[26] E.R.R.O., DDCB/12/6.
[27] Regy. of Deeds, HR/346/422.
[28] Ibid. 79/3/3 (1905); 86/497/467 (1906).
[29] Ibid. 519/284/225.
[30] Ibid. 707/251/211.
[31] Ibid. 926/320/269.

Another estate in Flotmanby was held in the 13th century by the Constable family of Frismarsh and later of Catfoss.[32] In 1227 Simon Constable held 2 carucates in Flotmanby[33] and in 1278 Fulk Constable agreed with Bridlington priory on the boundaries of their respective estates there.[34] The holding descended to Stephen Constable,[35] who sold it in 1527–8 to Robert Lacy.[36] He died seised of *EAST FLOTMANBY* manor in 1556.[37] It subsequently descended with Folkton manor to Sir William St. Quintin,[38] who sold it in 1786, then known as 'Flotmanby Grange otherwise East Flotmanby' and comprising 347 a., to Mark Bell.[39] Under Bell's will, dated 1789,[40] it passed to Francis Tate, who held it in 1815,[41] and it was sold in 1848 by his devisees to T. W. Rivis.[42] By 1872 it had apparently passed to W. P. Herrick (d. 1876)[43] and it descended in the Herrick family until 1947, when A. P. Curzon-Howe-Herrick sold it to Minnie Taylor.[44] She sold it in 1948 to Arthur Smith[45] who, in 1952, sold 100 a. to A. Heath.[46] In 1954 the whole 312 a. was bought by W. Brooksbank.[47]

Rievaulx abbey held property in Flotmanby, which was probably incorporated in Camp grange.[48] In the late 12th or early 13th century Simon Scrope granted the abbey 50 a. 'above Waldike' and other land,[49] and Walter Schankes gave pasture for 40 sheep and about 3 a. of arable, some of which lay 'in the valley below Camp near the boundary of Folkton'.[50]

There were two estates in Flixton in 1086: one of 10 carucates, which had been held as two manors by Carle and Otre before the Conquest, and the other of 4 carucates, which was soke of Bridlington. Both were held by the king in 1086.[51]

The overlordship of the larger estate probably passed to the Greystocks before 1166, when Ranulph son of Walter held land in Flixton.[52] Certainly by 1242–3 the estate, then said to be of 8 carucates, was in the Greystock fee[53] and the overlordship descended, like Folkton manor, in the Greystock and later the Howard families;[54] it is last mentioned in the early 17th century.[55]

An early demesne tenant was a family which took its name from the township. Amfrid of Flixton and Ace his son witnessed several charters in the late 12th or early 13th century[56] and c. 1225 Ace of Flixton held 20 bovates in Flixton.[57] In 1242–3 he or another Ace was chief tenant there of the Greystocks.[58] In 1305 another Ace of Flixton granted the reversion of his estate, including 20 tofts, 24 bovates, and 30 a. in Flixton, to Tibbald of Brigham,[59] whose son William was returned as one of the lords of the township in 1316.[60] In 1317, however, Tibbald held 4½ carucates there.[61]

The estate, referred to as *FLIXTON* manor in 1336,[62] descended in the Brigham family[63] to George Brigham, who sold it in 1549 to Richard Shippabottom.[64] He died in 1565 seised of 3 closes, 15 bovates, and 15 a. of meadow.[65] His son Robert died in 1579 leaving four sisters as heirs.[66] In 1580 the manor was apparently settled by three of the sisters on the fourth, Anne, wife of Edward Elrington.[67] Anne Elrington died seised of it in 1600[68] and in 1604 her son Ralph sold it to William Hustler,[69] who in 1638 conveyed it to eight people, including William Dent and Thomas Coundon.[70] In 1682 William Dent is said to have sold 'the manor', presumably his share of it, to Mary Towry.[71] The estate apparently descended, however, in the Coundon (or Condon) family[72] to Thomas Condon, who sold it in 1716, then consisting of 4 closes and 14 bovates, to Samuel Minithorpe.[73] In 1756 Jane Minithorpe, apparently Samuel's daughter, sold the manor to William Minithorpe,[74] who already held a large estate in the township, the origin of which is not known.

In 1802 the Revd. John Minithorpe sold his estate, then comprising 39 a. of old-inclosed land and 62 bovates, to R. C. Broadley.[75] At inclosure in 1806 Broadley was awarded 1,007 a.[76] He sold the estate in 1812 to W. J. Denison[77] and it was retained by the Denisons, later earls of Londesborough, until the early 20th century. In 1912–13 the 2nd earl of Londesborough sold 831 a., including 674 a. to W. K. Triffitt.[78] In 1920 the 4th earl sold 420 a. to Walter Dawson,[79] who in 1921 acquired the 630-

---

[32] For pedigree of the Constables, of Catfoss, see J. Foster, *Pedigrees of . . . Yorks.* iii.
[33] *Yorks. Fines, 1218–31*, 74.
[34] *Bridlington Charty.* 88–9.
[35] *Feud. Aids*, vi. 225, 266; *Yorks. Inq.* iv. 36; *Cal. Inq. p.m.* vi, p. 30; *Hen. VII*, iii, pp. 305–6; *L. & P. Hen. VIII*, i (1), p. 164.
[36] Sta. Cha. 2/27/54; *Yorks. Fines*, i. 50.
[37] C 142/109/44.
[38] C 142/189/55; C 142/222/13; E.R.R.O., DDSY/68/58, 60, 68; *Yorks. Fines, 1614–25*, 30.
[39] Regy. of Deeds, BM/28/54.
[40] Ibid. BO/515/797; Francis was the brother of William Tate, to whom Bell granted the reversion of Folkton manor: see above, p. 167.
[41] Regy. of Deeds, CY/275/409.
[42] Ibid. GO/345/393.
[43] Ibid. 153/479/416; 760/518/417.
[44] Ibid. 760/518/417.
[45] Ibid. 779/213/166.
[46] Ibid. 923/360/311.
[47] Ibid. 968/150/139; 979/63/59.
[48] See p. 167.
[49] *Rievaulx Charty.* 239.
[50] Ibid. 300; *E.Y.C.* ii, p. 472.
[51] *V.C.H. Yorks.* ii. 197–8, 204, 322.
[52] *E.Y.C.* ii, pp. 430 n., 513–14.
[53] *Bk. of Fees*, ii. 1100.
[54] Castle Howard MSS., Box 24, Surveys of Estates, 1537, 1563; C 142/189/55; C 142/222/13; C 142/224/23; *Feud. Aids*, vi. 27, 142, 226, 266; *Yorks. Inq.* i. 37; *Cal. Inq. p.m.* vi, p. 29; viii, p. 498; xiv, pp. 30–2; *Yorks. Fines*, i. 300; iii. 67; *1603–14*, 73, 91; see below, p. 193.
[55] *Yorks. Fines, 1614–25*, 33, 183.
[56] *Bridlington Charty.* 25, 80, 135, 292 etc.
[57] *Reg. Gray* (Sur. Soc. lvi), 6.
[58] *Bk. of Fees*, ii. 1100.
[59] *Yorks. Fines, 1300–14*, 51.
[60] *Feud. Aids*, vi. 169; *Yorks. Fines, 1327–47*, 103. The other lord in 1316 was Eleanor de Percy, but there is no other reference to the Percy interest in Flixton.
[61] *Cal. Inq. p.m.* vi, p. 29.
[62] *Yorks. Fines, 1327–47*, 103.
[63] C 142/69/190; *Yorks. Fines, 1327–47*, 103; *1347–77*, 22; *Cal. Pat. 1408–13*, 3.
[64] C.P. 40/153 m. 52d.; *Yorks. Fines*, i. 142.
[65] C 142/142/120.
[66] C 142/185/58; Robert's sisters are given as Agnes, Dorothy, Elizabeth, and Margaret, but Agnes appears to be a mistake for Anne.
[67] *Yorks. Fines*, ii. 156, 159.
[68] C 142/279/416.
[69] *Yorks. Fines, 1603–14*, 25.
[70] C.P. 25(2)/523/13 Chas. I East. pt. 2, no. 19.
[71] E.R.R.O., DAR. TD/92.
[72] Ibid. DDGR/29/2.
[73] Regy. of Deeds, E/361/633.
[74] Ibid. W/151/320; Z/105/234.
[75] Ibid. CD/453/706.
[76] Ibid. CI/69/4.
[77] E.R.R.O., DDHB/11/1.
[78] Regy. of Deeds, 146/217/194; /260/233; 156/285/234.
[79] Ibid. 223/106/88.

acre Manor House farm from J. W. Triffitt.[80] Alan Dawson sold much of the estate in separate lots between 1946 and 1965,[81] including in the latter year the 318-acre Manor Farm to R. H. Mason,[82] who has since retained it.

The Argam family held land in Flixton under the Greystocks in the Middle Ages. Between 1162 and c. 1175 Ranulph son of Walter confirmed to Malger of Argam the turbary in Flixton marsh which the Argams had long held of Ranulph's ancestors.[83] In 1254 William of Argam held a plot in the marsh[84] and in 1303 he or another William bought property in Flixton from John of Hunmanby.[85] In 1317 William of Argam held 4 bovates and a turbary[86] and in 1346 he or another William held 15 bovates of the Greystock fee.[87] The holding descended with Argam manor to the Constables, of Flamborough,[88] and the manor of FLIXTON was forfeited to the Crown on the attainder of Robert Constable in 1537; it then included a close and 14 bovates.[89] In 1563 part of the estate was granted to Thomas Wood and William Frankland.[90] About 1695 another Thomas Wood died seised of property in Flixton,[91] but its further descent has not been traced. In the later 16th century the Crown let other land of the former Constable estate. In 1565, 1584, and 1597 6 bovates were let to William and James Jordan and Robert Moyser respectively and in 1580 and 1592 8 bovates were let to William Lacy and Robert Topping respectively.[92] Nothing more is known of these holdings.

In 1208 Robert of Boythorpe unsuccessfully claimed a carucate in Flixton from Walter son of Ives.[93] In 1254 Isabel of Boythorpe held 2 bovates of the Greystocks,[94] one of which apparently passed later to William Bard, who granted it to Bridlington priory.[95]

The overlordship of the 4 carucates in Flixton which in 1086 were soke of Bridlington[96] passed to the Gants, and later the Tattershalls, and a mesne lordship was held of them by the Greystocks in the 13th and 14th centuries.[97]

The demesne tenancy passed to the Nevilles in the early 12th century and descended like Muston to the heirs of Maud Malbis and Hawise of Lowthorpe.[98] In 1317 the heirs of John Malbis held 4½ carucates of the Gant fee[99] and in 1346, when the family is mentioned for the last time in Flixton, William Malbis held 10 bovates of the Greystock fee.[1] The holding may have descended to the Beverley family, the descent of whose estate is traced below.[2] The share of Hawise of Lowthorpe descended to the Heslertons. In 1371 Simon Heslerton held an estate in Flixton which probably passed soon after, together with his Fordon holding, to Bridlington priory.[3]

In 1537 William Beverley held an estate in Flixton.[4] Property there was sold by John Beverley to Peter Paulin in 1545 and by Paulin to Michael Farthing in 1559.[5] In 1577 Farthing sold the holding to Henry Haggett and he, in 1602, sold it to John and Ralph Harrison,[6] whose family already held property in the township, Anthony Harrison having died seised of 11 bovates in 1596.[7] In 1606 Robert Harrison sold property there to Denis Garford.[8]

The holding may have passed to the Nesfields, who apparently held land in Flixton from at least 1638.[9] The estate descended in that family[10] to Theophilus Nesfield, who was awarded 212 a. at inclosure in 1806.[11] In 1838 his grandson Nesfield Cook sold the estate to W. J. Denison[12] and it subsequently descended with Flixton manor.[13]

Several religious houses held estates in Flixton. The hospital of St. Mary and St. Andrew, Flixton, sometimes called Carmanspital or Hertford hospital, held ½ bovate of the Greystock fee in 1317.[14] In 1563 property called the Spital was held by Lord Dacre of Gillesland and Greystock; it comprised several closes and 2 bovates.[15] It descended, like Butterwick manor, to William Howard, who died seised of it in 1644.[16] Its further descent has not been traced. Bridlington priory was granted property by William Bard and probably also by Simon Heslerton,[17] and at the Dissolution its estate was worth about £2.[18] In 1589 part, at least, was in the hands of Anne Elrington[19] and probably subsequently descended with the manor. Wykeham priory was granted 2 bovates in Flixton by Juette Monceaux.[20] They were let by the Crown after the Dissolution to Brian and William Lacy and Robert Moyser in 1564, 1580, and 1597 respectively.[21] Nun Monkton priory held land in Flixton worth, together with its Binnington estate, £3 6s. at the Dissolution.[22] The estate was granted in 1538 to John Neville, Lord Latimer,[23]

---

[80] Regy. of Deeds, 236/386/314.
[81] Ibid. 790/458/382; 794/9/8; 966/530/475; 1359/146/128 etc.
[82] Ibid. 1408/55/44; /178/150.
[83] E.Y.C. ii, pp. 513–4.
[84] Yorks. Inq. i. 37.
[85] Yorks. Fines, 1300–14, 33.
[86] Cal. Inq. p.m. vi, p. 29.
[87] Feud. Aids, vi. 226.
[88] Ibid. 266; Cal. Close, 1360–4, 500; Yorks. Fines, i. 44, 125; see above, p. 6.
[89] S.C. 6/Hen. VIII/4324.
[90] E 318/2567.
[91] E.R.R.O., DDBM/35/6.
[92] E 310/27/159 no. 7; E 310/28/168 no. 11; E 310/32/191 no. 20; E 310/32/194 no. 84; E 310/33/202 no. 60.
[93] Yorks. Fines, John, 142.
[94] Yorks. Inq. i. 37.
[95] Cal. Pat. 1307–13, 144; Bridlington Charty. 91.
[96] V.C.H.Yorks. ii. 197, 322.
[97] Feud. Aids, vi. 27, 141, 266; Cal. Close, 1307–13, 102; Cal. Inq. p.m. vi, p. 30; vii, p. 470.
[98] B.M. Add. MS. 26737, f. 66; see below, p. 279.
[99] C 133/109/40; Cal. Inq. p.m. vi, p. 29.
[1] Feud. Aids, vi. 226.
[2] See below.
[3] See below and p. 235.
[4] Castle Howard MS., Box 24, Survey of Estates, 1537.
[5] Yorks. Fines, i. 113, 228.
[6] Ibid. ii. 105; iv. 181.
[7] C 142/245/11.
[8] Yorks. Fines, 1603–14, 49.
[9] C.P. 25(2)/523/13 Chas. I East. pt. 2, no. 19.
[10] E 179/205/521; Regy. of Deeds, E/227/396; /247/436; F/76/161; K/612/1305; E.R.R.O., Land Tax.
[11] Regy. of Deeds, CI/69/4.
[12] Ibid. HI/155/128.
[13] See p. 169.
[14] Cal. Inq. p.m. vi, pp. 29, 308; E.Y.C. ii, p. 495; V.C.H. Yorks. iii. 307.
[15] Castle Howard MS., Box 24, Survey of Estates, 1563.
[16] C 142/774/15; see above, p. 193.
[17] See above.
[18] Valor Eccl. v. 120.
[19] E 112/63/619.
[20] J. Burton, Mon. Ebor. 256.
[21] E 310/27/159 no. 7; E 310/28/168 no. 79; E 310/32/191 no. 20.
[22] Valor Eccl. v. 255.
[23] L. & P. Hen. VIII, xiii (1), p. 136.

whose son John died seised of it in 1577 leaving four daughters as heirs.[24] It apparently descended with the Binnington property to the Wrights[25] and in 1600 John and Christopher Wright sold it to Richard Darley.[26] Its further descent is not known.

ECONOMIC HISTORY. In 1086 the four estates in Folkton, Flotmanby, and Flixton were probably waste. Before the Conquest the king's estate in Folkton had land for 4 ploughs and was worth £1 10s., while the larger estate in Flixton had land for 15 ploughs and was worth £2 10s.[27]

The open-field area of Folkton township may have been divided from an early date into four fields. About 1162–7 a sixteen-acre holding in 'the field' there lay in 'Whitefield', 'Aldefield', 'Sternekeld', and 'Camb'.[28] The fields probably lay mostly on the wolds and on the slopes below the scarp. Camb, later Camp, for instance, was situated in the south of Folkton township[29] and in the later 12th or early 13th century 60 a. of arable on Folkton Wold were mentioned. At the same period other arable areas on the wolds included a plot called Ravensdale and 10 a. near Lang Camp and Dedhill Dale.[30] In the late 17th century open-field land below the escarpment is described as extending as far north as the carrs. The four fields were then known as West, Camp, Cloven How, and Old fields.[31] At inclosure in 1807 the 'fields' on the lower scarp slopes were distinguished from the 'wold' to the south,[32] which was probably only irregularly cultivated. Allotments were made simply from 'the open fields'.[33]

Flotmanby had its own open-field system in the Middle Ages. In the late 12th or early 13th century 5 bovates lay dispersed regularly throughout 'the whole field', and East field was also mentioned. At about the same period 8 a. of a nine-acre holding lay equally divided between two parts of 'the field', and 1 a. lay in Holm, north of the village.[34] A strip of arable at 'Westclif' was mentioned in the late 12th or early 13th century. A group of lynchets still visible in 1971 suggests that there was some cultivation of strips on the escarpment. From an early date the arable land apparently extended on to the lower ground in the north of the township. Thus Henry Scrope's 6 bovates of demesne in the early 13th century lay between 'Waldike' and the marsh.[35] The full extent of the open-field area is not known but c. 1543 the former Bridlington priory estate there included 33 bovates.[36]

The open fields of Flixton were named in 1563 as East, West, Middle, North, and South fields. Much of the open-field area then lay on the wolds.[37] In the late 17th century only East, West, and Middle fields were recorded.[38] The full extent of the fields was first revealed in 1718, when there were 100 bovates.[39] The inclosure Act of 1802 mentions Wold field, Wold Brow, Low field, and Low Sands,[40] but in the award of 1809, apart from 310 a. from West field, allotments were made simply from 'the fields' or 'the wold'.[41]

The low ground in the north of the parish provided meadow for all three townships. In 1246 there was reference to 12 a. of meadow in Folkton[42] and probably also in the 13th century John of Folkton gave Rievaulx abbey 8 a. of his demesne meadow there.[43] In 1557 three areas that were probably common meadow in Folkton were Nether ing, West ing, and West carr,[44] and in the late 17th century the rector held 10 a. of meadow land in the ings.[45] In 1807 the ings lay in the north-west of the township and at inclosure 27 a. were allotted from the East and 36 a. from the West ings.[46]

In the 13th century a meadow called the 'Red' was mentioned in Flotmanby[47] and Simon Scrope granted to Rievaulx abbey all his meadow in 'Nok' or 'Hoc' and Horseholm there.[48] In 1557 a close called the Holmes lay in West Flotmanby[49] and in the mid 19th century the area north of West Flotmanby Farm was known as Great Holme.[50] In the late 17th century 22 'gads' of the rector's meadow land in Flotmanby lay dispersed within two closes.[51] In 1774 the 346-acre St. Quintin estate in East Flotmanby contained 53 a. of meadow land.[52] Common meadow in Flixton was mentioned in 1713 and the Holmes, referred to in 1716, may have been part of it.[53] Allotments were made from the ings at inclosure.[54]

There were extensive commons and pastures in all the townships in the Middle Ages and later, and large numbers of sheep were kept, probably mainly on the wolds. In 1158 Rievaulx abbey was granted pasture in Folkton for 1,000 sheep[55] and in 1277 Bridlington priory received a similar grant for 300 sheep in 'the field' there.[56] In 1563 15 a. of 'good grass ground' lay in the south of the township near the Hunmanby boundary.[57] The open fields also provided pasture for sheep and in the late 17th century the stint at Folkton was 10 sheep-gates in the fields for each house and 12 for each bovate.[58] In 1774 Folkton manor contained nearly twice as much pasture, about 1,000 a., as arable.[59] In 1807 the common lay on the low ground in the north-east of the township and the moor on the wolds in the south-east.[60]

In 1299 Bridlington priory was pasturing 500 sheep from Flotmanby and Burton Fleming at

[24] C 142/177/62.
[25] See p. 335.
[26] Yorks. Fines, iv. 142.
[27] V.C.H. Yorks. ii. 198, 204, 272, 322–3.
[28] E.Y.C. ii, p. 516.
[29] O.S. Map 6" (1854).
[30] Ibid.; Rievaulx Charty. (Sur. Soc. lxxxiii), 49, 238.
[31] B.I.H.R., TER. J. Folkton n.d.
[32] Registry of Deeds, Beverley, Folkton inclosure map.
[33] Ibid. CI/254/19.
[34] Bridlington Charty. 84–5, 87.
[35] Ibid. 82, 88.
[36] E 318/63.
[37] Castle Howard MS., Box 24, Survey of Estates, 1563.
[38] B.I.H.R., TER. J. Folkton n.d.
[39] E.R.R.O., DDHU/5/14.
[40] 42 Geo. III, c. 107 (Local and Personal).
[41] Regy. of Deeds, CI/69/4.
[42] Yorks. Fines, 1232–46, 127.
[43] Rievaulx Charty. 250.
[44] E.R.R.O., DDGD/Box 1.
[45] B.I.H.R., TER. J. Folkton n.d.
[46] Regy. of Deeds, CI/254/19; Folkton incl. map.
[47] Bridlington Charty. 85.
[48] Rievaulx Charty. 239, 300.
[49] E.R.R.O., DDGD/Box 1.
[50] O.S. Map 6" (1854).
[51] B.I.H.R., TER. J. Folkton n.d.
[52] Regy. of Deeds, AS/389/642.
[53] Ibid. E/227/396; F/118/253.
[54] Ibid. CI/69/4.
[55] E.Y.C. ii, p. 514.
[56] Bridlington Charty. 9, 89; Yorks. Inq. iii. 139.
[57] Castle Howard MS., Box 24, Survey of Estates, 1563.
[58] B.I.H.R., TER. J. Folkton n.d.
[59] Regy. of Deeds, AS/389/642.
[60] Ibid. Folkton incl. map.

Hunmanby,[61] and in the early 16th century the priory had a 'sheep-master' at Flotmanby.[62] In 1787 West Flotmanby manor contained two closes, totalling 159 a., called Sheep Walk.[63]

In 1563 the tenant of a two-bovate holding in Flixton had common rights for 300 sheep in the fields.[64] In the late 17th century sheep-pasturage in the fields was said to be unstinted[65] but in 1731 a cottager had ten sheep-gates there.[66] In 1748 there were still gates in the fields but common rights for sheep on the high wold were unstinted.[67] The moor was mentioned in the inclosure Act of 1802[68] but was not referred to in the award.

The low-lying marshes and carrs in the north of the parish along the river Hertford provided rough pasture, turbaries, and fisheries until the early-19th-century drainage. All the townships had a marsh in the Middle Ages. About 1276 Richard de Lacy encroached on the marshes of neighbouring North Riding townships and added about 280 a. to Folkton marsh,[69] and in 1277 he granted to Bridlington priory 50 cart-loads of turf a year from his marsh and turbary in Folkton.[70] Two Folkton turf-diggers were mentioned in 1363.[71] The marsh had probably become known as the Common carr by the late 17th century, when each house and each bovate had two beast-gates in it. Hall carr was mentioned at the same date.[72] At inclosure in 1807 allotments totalling 125 a. were made from Folkton carr, 92 a. from East carr, 57 a. from the Lord's carr, and 21 a. from Turf Grafts.[73]

In the late 12th and 13th centuries Flotmanby marsh also contained turbaries and fisheries[74] and two fishermen were mentioned.[75] In 1278 Fulk Constable and Bridlington priory agreed on the boundaries of their marsh and pasture in Flotmanby, Fulk being assigned land in the east up to the Muston boundary and the priory in the west. Common rights over their respective portions were extinguished and they were entitled to inclose their land 'in any way they choose'.[76] In 1390 the Constable estate contained a 200-acre moor called the Ling carr.[77] In 1538 two of the former priory's carrs in Flotmanby, the Prior's and the Sheep-master's carrs, were let by the Crown to William Babthorpe,[78] who in 1557 exchanged with Brian Lacy his right of turbary in Flotmanby 'every year or every third year' for other property in the township.[79] In 1787 closes in West Flotmanby included eleven carrs totalling 187 a.[80]

A turbary in Flixton marsh is mentioned between 1162 and c. 1175[81] and again in 1317.[82] In 1446–7 it was stated that Flixton hospital was endowed with two strips (*seliones*) of moor and pasture in the township, together with common pasture for 24 cows and a bull 'in a place called the Forthside'. Accommodation at the hospital was said to save travellers by night from the dangers of 'water, marshes, and swamps' in the area.[83] In 1563 two turbaries formerly belonging to the Constable family were let by the Crown[84] and in the same year the Greystock holding included a turbary called Turfgrave and common rights for ten cows and a bull in Flixton carr.[85] In the late 17th century the rector's 4 bovates carried 16 gates in the carr[86] and in 1711 a one-bovate holding had 6 gates there.[87] In 1716 a holding included two flats 'each going directly through the Common carr . . . in a place called Spittle Grafts', together with 12 beast-gates and one bull-gate in the carr,[88] and a one-bovate holding had 3 cow-gates and turbary rights there.[89] In 1748 the carr was also known as the Summer pasture.[90] At inclosure in 1806 allotments totalling 580 a. were made from the carr, in addition to about 3 a. from the Ling carr.[91]

In 1773 there were 341 a. in Folkton, 320 a. in Flotmanby, and 922 a. in Flixton of the fenny ground, of small value, which bordered the upper reaches of the Derwent and Hertford.[92] In 1800 a drainage Act was passed for the three townships and many others[93] and in 1809 it was reported that 291 a. in Folkton, 275 a. in Flotmanby, and 661 a. in Flixton had actually been improved by the drainage scheme.[94]

There was some early inclosure in all three townships. In Folkton a demesne meadow called 'Ovenamhenge', mentioned in the late 12th or 13th century,[95] and a meadow close called Ownams, referred to in the late 17th century, suggest intakes from the waste. At the latter date New close and Camp closes were also mentioned[96] and in 1807 there were 123 a. of old inclosure.[97] An ovenam was also mentioned in Flotmanby in the late 12th or 13th century[98] and following the agreement of 1278 much of the low ground in the north may have been inclosed by Bridlington priory and the Constable family.[99] Flotmanby apparently suffered severely from the Black Death, its tax assessment being reduced by 100 per cent for two successive years in 1353–4. It was last separately taxed in 1452, when its assessment was the smallest in the wapentake.[1] There was presumably little uninclosed ground after the depopulation of the village. In the late 17th century 'Mr. Buck's new close' was mentioned[2] and

---

[61] *Bridlington Charty.* 73; see below, p. 237.
[62] E 318/63.   [63] Regy. of Deeds, BN/94/137.
[64] Castle Howard MS., Box 24, Survey of Estates, 1563.
[65] B.I.H.R., TER. J. Folkton n.d.
[66] Regy. of Deeds, M/262/422.
[67] Ibid. S/516/1259.
[68] 42 Geo. III, *c.* 107 (Local and Personal).
[69] *Rot. Hund.* (Rec. Com.), i. 107; *Honour and Forest of Pickering*, ii (N.R. Rec. Ser. N.S. ii), 173; see above, p. 168.
[70] *Bridlington Charty.* 9; *Yorks. Inq.* iii. 139.
[71] *Yorks. Sessions of the Peace* (Y.A.S. Rec. Ser. c), 53.
[72] B.I.H.R., TER. J. Folkton n.d.
[73] Regy. of Deeds, CI/254/19.
[74] *Bridlington Charty.* 85; *Rievaulx Charty.* 300.
[75] *Bridlington Charty.* 84, 88.
[76] Ibid. 88–9.
[77] C.P. 40/519 m. 459.
[78] E 318/63.
[79] E.R.R.O., DDGD/Box 1.
[80] Regy. of Deeds, BN/94/137.   [81] *E.Y.C.* ii, pp. 513-14.
[82] *Cal. Inq. p.m.* vi, p. 29.
[83] *E.Y.C.* ii, pp. 468-9, 469 n.   [84] E 318/2567.
[85] Castle Howard MS., Box 24, Survey of Estates, 1563.
[86] B.I.H.R., TER. J. Folkton n.d.
[87] Regy. of Deeds, D/19/27.
[88] Ibid. E/363/637.
[89] Ibid. G/21/51.
[90] Ibid. S/516/1259.
[91] Ibid. CI/69/4.
[92] E.R.R.O., DDSY/11/2–5.
[93] 40 Geo. III, c. 118 (Local and Personal); see below, p. 280.
[94] E.R.R.O., PR. 2775.
[95] *Rievaulx Charty.* 250.
[96] B.I.H.R., TER. J. Folkton n.d.
[97] Regy. of Deeds, CI/254/19.
[98] *Bridlington Charty.* 84.
[99] Ibid. 88–9; see above, p. 169.
[1] E 179/202/127; *Y.A.J.* xxxviii. 61.
[2] B.I.H.R., TER. J. Folkton n.d.

since at least 1718 there have been only two farms in the township.³ In 1787 West Flotmanby manor lay entirely in closes⁴ and nothing remained to be dealt with at inclosure in 1807.⁵ In 1563 the former Constable estate at Flixton included Brigman close⁶ and in the late 17th century a furlong was known as 'Upper Ownams'. Spittle close, mentioned at the same date, was probably inclosed by the former hospital.⁷ In 1718 Rasin close and Widow Nesfield's close were mentioned.⁸ In 1722 a proposal to inclose 100 a. on the north side of the Flixton–Folkton road was made by certain Flixton freeholders⁹ but it is not known if the scheme was carried out. In 1802 the manorial estate alone contained 39 a. of old inclosure.¹⁰

Inclosure of the remaining open-field area of Folkton township occurred in 1807,¹¹ under an Act of 1802,¹² and dealt with 1,715 a. James Bell, as lord of the manor, was awarded 998 a. The rector received 570 a. for tithes and glebe and the vicar 146 a. for tithes. The only other allotment was of 1 a. The commonable land in Flixton, amounting to 2,441 a., was inclosed in 1806,¹³ under an Act of 1802.¹⁴ R. C. Broadley, as lord of the manor, was allotted 1,007 a., the rector received 501 a. for tithes and glebe, and the vicar got 90 a. for tithes. Theophilus Nesfield was awarded 212 a., John Woodall 186 a., Humphrey Osbaldeston 124 a., and Charles Ringrose 117 a. There was one allotment of 62 a. and 16 of under 10 a. each.

In 1801 811 a. in the parish were under crops, mainly barley (305 a.), turnips or rape (193 a.), and oats (185 a.).¹⁵ Seeds and clover were being sown in Flixton in the early 19th century.¹⁶ The amount of land under arable increased during the 19th century as the former carr-lands in the north and the pasture on the high wolds were brought into cultivation; in East Flotmanby in 1838 there were 253 a. of arable and only 80 a. of meadow and pasture¹⁷ and in 1905 the whole parish contained 3,616 a. of arable, 1,728 a. of meadow and pasture, and 102 a. of woodland.¹⁸ Most of the grassland lay on the low ground and the scarp slopes in 1971.

There have been from 3 to 6 farmers at Folkton in the 19th and 20th centuries; in 1937 4 farms had acreages of 150 or over. Since the early 18th century there have been 2 farmers at Flotmanby and since the early 19th century there have usually been from 8 to 13 at Flixton, where 3 farms in 1937 had acreages of 150 or over.¹⁹

A mason was mentioned at Folkton in 1225²⁰ and in 1731 there was a weaver in Flixton who had a hemp garth.²¹ Market-gardeners were recorded in the parish between 1892 and 1929, and in 1937 there were refreshment rooms at Flixton.²² There was a chalk quarry still being worked near the Fordon road in 1971.

A mill at Folkton was mentioned for the first and only time in 1246.²³ There were apparently two windmills at Flotmanby in the 13th century, one held by the Scropes²⁴ and the other given by Kirkham priory to Rievaulx abbey.²⁵ Nothing more is known of them. A mill in Flixton was mentioned in 1225 and 1305²⁶ and a miller there in 1596²⁷ and 1817.²⁸ A water-mill is said to have existed at the north end of the village in the early 19th century.²⁹

LOCAL GOVERNMENT. There is a court roll for the Constable manor in Flixton for 1525.³⁰ The assize of bread was claimed by John de Greystock in all three townships in the late 13th century.³¹ No parochial records before 1835 are known. In 1837 Folkton joined the Scarborough union.³²

CHURCH. The rector of Folkton was mentioned between 1162 and c. 1175.³³ In 1225, when a rector was instituted, an existing vicarage was held by a 'chaplain'.³⁴ The sinecure rectory and the vicarage continued as separate livings until 1856, when they were united as a rectory with cure of souls.³⁵ A chapel at Flotmanby, presumably dependent on Folkton church, was granted in the later 13th century by Agnes Scrope to Richard de Berneville and by him to Bridlington priory.³⁶ No other reference to it has been found.

The advowson of the rectory descended, like Butterwick manor, in the Greystock and Howard families³⁷ to Charles, earl of Carlisle, who sold it in 1694 to a trustee acting for the Revd. John Gibson.³⁸ In 1728 Gibson's nephew John Stainton sold it to William Osbaldeston³⁹ and it descended, with Hunmanby manor, in the Osbaldeston, later the Osbaldeston-Mitford, family⁴⁰ until 1920. It was then sold to Sir Henry Readett Bayley;⁴¹ he sold it to Harrogate College in 1925⁴² and it passed to the Martyrs' Memorial Trust in 1952.⁴³

The advowson of the vicarage descended with that of the rectory until 1786, when the rector himself

---

³ E.R.R.O., DDHU/5/14; O.S. Map 6″ (1854).
⁴ Regy. of Deeds, BN/94/137.
⁵ Ibid. CI/254/19; Folkton incl. map.
⁶ E 318/2567.
⁷ B.I.H.R., TER. J. Folkton n.d.
⁸ E.R.R.O., DDHU/5/14.
⁹ Ibid. /16.
¹⁰ Ibid. DDLO/Box 1 (b).
¹¹ Regy. of Deeds, CI/254/19.
¹² 42 Geo. III, c. 111 (Priv. Act).
¹³ Regy. of Deeds, CI/69/4.
¹⁴ 42 Geo. III, c. 107 (Local and Personal).
¹⁵ 1801 Crop Returns.
¹⁶ E.R.R.O., DDX/202/41.
¹⁷ B.I.H.R., TA. 221S.
¹⁸ Acreage Returns, 1905.
¹⁹ Directories.
²⁰ *Reg. Gray* (Sur. Soc. lvi), 4–5.
²¹ Regy. of Deeds, M/262/422.
²² Directories.
²³ *Yorks. Fines, 1232–46*, 127.
²⁴ *Bridlington Charty.* 80.
²⁵ *Rievaulx Charty.* 299.
²⁶ *Reg. Gray*, 6; *Yorks. Fines, 1300–14*, 51.
²⁷ B.I.H.R., Prob. Reg. xxvi, f. 356.
²⁸ E.R.R.O., PR. 2771.
²⁹ Local inf.
³⁰ S.C. 2/211/40.
³¹ J.I. 1/1110 m. 148.
³² *3rd Rep. Poor Law Com.* 174.
³³ *E.Y.C.* ii, p. 514.
³⁴ *Reg. Gray* (Sur. Soc. lvi), 4–5.
³⁵ *Lond. Gaz.* 8 Aug. 1856, p. 2739.
³⁶ *Bridlington Charty.* 84–5.
³⁷ Castle Howard MS., Box 24, Survey of Estates, 1537; C 142/774/15; *Cal. Inq. p.m.* i, p. 83; vi, p. 30; xiv, p. 32; *Yorks. Inq. Hen. IV–V*, 32, 144; *Yorks. Fines, 1614–25*, 33, 183; see below, p. 193.
³⁸ E.R.R.O., DDHU/5/5–7, 9–10.
³⁹ Ibid. /20–1; Registry of Deeds, Beverley, K/405/844.
⁴⁰ P.R.O. Inst. Bks.; E.R.R.O., DDHU/5/2, 24, 27, 30; /17/21.
⁴¹ Regy. of Deeds, 209/184/157.
⁴² Ibid. 318/410/342.
⁴³ *York Dioc. Cal.*

presented the vicar, possibly without the consent of the Osbaldestons. In 1796 and 1820 the rector again presented, in the latter year Herbert Phillips presenting himself; he continued to hold both livings until they were united.[44] In 1837 Humphrey Osbaldeston sought a decision whether he or the rector was patron,[45] and in 1852 an opinion was given that it was the rector.[46]

In 1291 the rectory was valued at £26 13s. 4d.[47] It was worth £13 6s. 8d. in 1363,[48] £16 in 1525–6,[49] and £15 net in 1535.[50] In 1650 it was valued at £105,[51] in 1692 at about £108,[52] and in 1718 at about £124.[53] In 1829–31 the average net income of the rectory and vicarage together was £874 a year[54] and c. 1850 they were valued at £1,236.[55] In 1856 the consolidated rectory was worth £550 a year.[56]

In 1225 the rector let his Flixton corn tithes to William the clerk for life.[57] In 1692 corn and hay tithes accounted for the greater part of the rector's income.[58] At the inclosure of Flixton in 1806 the rector was allotted 501 a. for tithes,[59] and when Folkton was inclosed in 1807 he received 210 a. for tithes in Folkton and 77 a. for tithes in East Flotmanby. He was also awarded 199 a. of recently-inclosed land in Flixton belonging to Humphrey Osbaldeston and John Woodall for the tithes which they owed him in West Flotmanby.[60] Certain tithes in East Flotmanby, however, were not commuted at that time and in 1838, when they were owned by J. B. Tate, they were commuted for £40.[61]

Half a carucate of rectorial glebe is mentioned in 1225, when it was let along with the Flixton corn tithes, and by 1284–5 the church was also endowed with a carucate in Folkton.[62] In 1692 the Folkton glebe included 6 houses and 8 bovates and there were still 4 bovates at Flixton. At the inclosure of Flixton in 1806 the rector was allotted 43 a. for glebe, and in 1807 he was similarly allotted 283 a. for glebe at Folkton.[63]

In 1856, when the rectory and vicarage were merged, the glebe of both livings, amounting to 1,794 a., was reapportioned. Folkton rectory retained 712 a., subject to a payment of £100 a year to Muston vicarage, Hunmanby vicarage was allotted 979 a., subject to a payment of £50 a year to Muston, and 102 a. in Octon were transferred to Burton Fleming vicarage.[64] Folkton's land was sold in 1920.[65]

The parsonage house at Folkton was in disrepair in 1591 and 'in great decay' in 1623.[66] In the late 17th century it adjoined the churchyard,[67] and in 1692 it was let with the glebe.[68] In 1809 it was described as built of brick and stone (perhaps chalk), with a tiled roof, and as containing three ground-floor rooms and two chambers.[69] A new Rectory, of red-brick and stone, was built in 1859 on the Filey road west of Folkton village.[70] It was sold c. 1950[71] and in 1971 was known as Folkton House.

In 1225 the vicar had the usual small tithes and offerings, except for the hay tithes, which were retained by the archbishop of York.[72] The vicarage was worth £6 13s. 4d. in 1291,[73] £9 3s. 6d. in 1525–6,[74] and £8 11s. 10d. net in 1535.[75] By 1650 it was worth £28[76] and in 1694 £30.[77] It was sequestrated in 1696,[78] probably on account of the poverty of the living. In 1716 it was stated that £5 a year had been paid 'of good will only' by the rector to recent vicars,[79] and the vicarage was augmented in 1718 with £200 from Queen Anne's Bounty and a total of £200 from the rector and the archbishop of York.[80]

Tithes represented the whole value of the vicarage in 1535.[81] At the inclosure of Flixton in 1806 the vicar was allotted 90 a. for tithes[82] and in 1807, when Folkton was inclosed, he received 146 a. for the tithes of Folkton and 35 a. for those of East Flotmanby. He was also awarded 86 a. in Flixton for his tithes in West Flotmanby.[83]

In 1243 the vicar claimed from Kirkham priory 60 a. in Folkton which the previous vicar had held of the rector.[84] The priory, however, evidently upheld its right and later gave the land to Rievaulx abbey.[85] In 1723 Bounty and other money was used to buy 10 bovates of glebe at Octon[86] and in 1742 to buy 4½ a. at Middleton (Yorks. N.R.).[87]

The vicar had two tofts in 1225,[88] and in the late 17th century he had a house near the parsonage house.[89] The vicarage house was said in 1764 to be brick-built and thatched, and to contain two rooms and two chambers.[90] By 1817 the roof was of tiles.[91] It stood opposite the church in 1850 but had apparently been demolished by 1889.[92]

In 1315 the rector was permitted to have an oratory in his 'manor' at Folkton.[93] In 1447 it was stated that the vicar had long celebrated mass every

---

[44] E.R.R.O., DDHU/5/2, 24, 31.
[45] Ibid. /24.
[46] Ibid. /27.
[47] *Tax. Eccl.* (Rec. Com.), 303, 326.
[48] *Cal. Close,* 1360–4, 501.
[49] *Y.A.J.* xxiv. 65.
[50] *Valor Eccl.* (Rec. Com.), v. 123, 146.
[51] *T.E.R.A.S.* ii. 56–7.
[52] E.R.R.O., DDHU/5/4.
[53] Ibid. /14.
[54] *Rep. Com. Eccl. Revenues,* 934–5.
[55] E.R.R.O., DDHU/5/28.
[56] Ibid. /29, 30; *Lond. Gaz.* 8 Aug. 1856, p. 2739.
[57] *Reg. Gray,* 6.
[58] E.R.R.O., DDHU/5/4.
[59] Regy. of Deeds, CI/69/4.
[60] Ibid. /254/19.
[61] B.I.H.R., TA. 221S.
[62] *Reg. Gray,* 6; *Feud. Aids,* vi. 27.
[63] See p. 173.
[64] E.R.R.O., DDHU/5/29, 30; *Lond. Gaz.* 8 Aug. 1856, pp. 2739–42.
[65] E.R.R.O., DDHU/17/22.
[66] B.I.H.R., Churches index.
[67] Ibid. TER. J. Folkton n.d.
[68] E.R.R.O., DDHU/5/4.
[69] B.I.H.R., TER. J. Folkton 1809.
[70] Ibid. 1861.
[71] Local inf.
[72] *Reg. Gray,* 4–5.
[73] *Tax. Eccl.* 303, 326.
[74] *Y.A.J.* xxiv. 65.
[75] *Valor Eccl.* v. 123.
[76] *T.E.R.A.S.* ii. 56–7.
[77] E.R.R.O., DDHU/5/5.
[78] Ibid. /10–11.
[79] B.I.H.R., TER. J. Folkton 1716.
[80] Ibid. 1726; Hodgson, *Q.A.B.* 440.
[81] *Valor Eccl.* v. 123.
[82] Regy. of Deeds, CI/69/4.
[83] Ibid. /254/19.
[84] *Monastic Notes,* i (Y.A.S. Rec. Ser. xvii), 101.
[85] See p. 167.
[86] B.I.H.R., TER. J. Folkton 1726; E.R.R.O., DDHU/5/17.
[87] B.I.H.R., TER. J. Folkton 1743.
[88] *Reg. Gray,* 4–5.
[89] B.I.H.R., TER. J. Folkton n.d.
[90] Ibid. 1764.
[91] Ibid. 1817.
[92] O.S. Map 6" (1854, 1893).
[93] *Fasti Parochiales,* iii. 24.

year on St. Andrew's Day in the chapel of the hospital of St. Mary and St. Andrew, Flixton.[94] There were three chaplains at Folkton in 1525–6, each receiving a stipend of £4.[95]

Several vicars were non-resident and held other livings. In 1743 the vicar held the curacies of Filey, Speeton, and Muston, as well as Hunmanby, where he lived. He employed an assistant curate at Folkton.[96] In 1764 the assistant curate also had charge of Filey.[97] An assistant was employed from 1813 to 1829[98] but for the rest of the 19th and in the earlier 20th centuries the incumbent apparently held no other livings, employed no curates, and usually resided, although in 1884 he lived at Ganton.[99] In 1967–8 the rector also held the vicarage of Willerby, where he lived.[1]

The rectory was sequestrated in 1824–48 because of the Revd. Herbert Phillips's debts. On his death in 1856 the glebe and buildings were 'in a very dilapidated state' and 'a large sum' of money was needed for their repair.[2]

In 1743 and 1746 a service was held each week and communion was administered four times a year; in 1743 about eighty and in 1764 sixty people were said to have received the previous Easter.[3] By 1865 there were two services each week and communion was held monthly with about six communicants.[4] In 1936 there were three celebrations of communion each month,[5] and in 1971 there was one service each week.

The church of ST. JOHN THE EVANGELIST, Folkton, is built of stone and consists of chancel, aisleless nave, and west tower. Of the Norman church there remain a blocked round-headed north doorway and the jambs of the chancel arch; each jamb consists of three shafts with scallop and volute capitals, one of which is carved with a rabbit's head. The tub-shaped font, which is encircled by two cable mouldings, is also Norman. The lower two stages of the tower, although much repaired, and the tower arch date from the 13th century. There is a lancet window, widely-splayed inside, in the west face of the tower and another in the second stage of the south face. A string-course runs between the first and second stages and there is one angle and one clasping buttress. On the east face of the tower an earlier roof-line of the nave is visible, higher than the present roof and with its apex further north. Also of 13th-century date is a trefoil-headed lancet window in the north wall of the nave, near its east end. The chancel was probably rebuilt in the 13th century; there is another lancet, now blocked, in its north wall and the chancel arch appears to be of the same period. The latter, of two chamfered orders, evidently replaced the original 12th-century arch and does not fit the earlier jambs which support it. Probably in the 15th century a large square-headed Perpendicular window was inserted in the north wall of the nave, cutting the stone band which runs along the outside of the wall. Similar windows in the north and south walls of the chancel were probably inserted at the same period; both are now blocked, as are a smaller window and a square-headed priest's door in the south wall.

In 1771 the church was in such decay that it needed partly rebuilding and a faculty was obtained in that year to reduce the width of the nave by about 10 ft.[6] The plan of the church before these alterations is not clear, but the present off-centre position of the chancel arch and the evidence of the earlier roof-line of the nave both suggest that there may formerly have been a south aisle. If so, the aisle must have been destroyed when the nave was narrowed. In 1772 a faculty was obtained to repair the chancel and shorten it by about half.[7] The quoins and much of the masonry of the east wall date from that period. Repairs to the church were again carried out in the 1850s.[8] The present south wall of the nave, with its south doorway and two square-headed windows, copies of the Perpendicular windows in the north wall, may have been remodelled at that time or later in the 19th century. The pointed three-light east window of the chancel and the small trefoil window above it were inserted in 1854.[9] Extensive repairs to the tower were carried out between 1877 and 1881[10] and the top stage, with a two-light round-headed belfry window in each face, was added. The church was restored and repewed and 'the old gallery' removed in 1894,[11] and the nave was reroofed in 1906.[12]

There are wall monuments to the Revd. William Minithorpe (d. 1774) and to the Revd. John Minithorpe (d. 1816) and his son Edwin (d. 1821). On the sill of the west window is part of the shaft of an Anglo-Danish cross, ornamented with a 'dragonesque' design. Part of a similar cross-shaft from Folkton was given in the 19th century to York Museum.[13] The north window of the nave contains fragments of medieval painted glass, including representations of a bishop, three faces, and the arms of Greystock and Ferrers.[14]

There were three bells in 1552[15] and 1764.[16] Two of the three surviving bells, dated 1675 and 1727, were made by Samuel Smith, the elder and younger, of York, respectively.[17] The plate consists of a silver cup made by Gurney & Co. of London in 1751 and apparently given by Richard Osbaldeston when bishop of Carlisle (1747–62), and a silver paten and flagon given by Admiral Mitford in 1859.[18] The registers begin in 1665 and are complete, apart from several gaps between 1669 and 1716.[19]

A burial ground, midway between Folkton and Flixton, was consecrated in 1922.[20]

NONCONFORMITY. In the 1570s Brian Lacy and between 1600 and 1633 members of the

---

[94] *E.Y.C.* ii, p. 469 n.
[95] *Y.A.J.* xxiv. 78.
[96] *Herring's Visit.* i, pp. xiii, 215.
[97] B.I.H.R., Bp. V. 1764/Ret. 193.
[98] E.R.R.O., PR. 2771.
[99] B.I.H.R., Bp. V. 1884/Ret.
[1] *Crockford.*
[2] E.R.R.O., DDHU/5/31; B.I.H.R., Seq. 1824.
[3] B.I.H.R., Bp. V. 1764/Ret. 193; *Herring's Visit.* i. 215.
[4] B.I.H.R., V. 1865/Ret. 188.
[5] Ibid. Bp. V. 1936/Ret. 278.
[6] Ibid. FAC 1771/3.
[7] Ibid. 1772/1.
[8] E.R.R.O., PR. 2777.
[9] Sheahan and Whellan, *Hist. York & E.R.* ii. 472.
[10] B.I.H.R., Churches index; E.R.R.O., PR. 2777.
[11] *Kelly's Dir. N. & E.R. Yorks.* (1897), 460.
[12] Ibid. (1913), 533.
[13] Morris, *E. Yorks.* 167; *V.C.H. Yorks.* ii. 117, 131; *Y.A.J.* xx. 151, 194; xxi. 259; xxiii. 276.
[14] *Y.A.J.* xxv. 79.
[15] *Inventories of Ch. Goods*, 25.
[16] B.I.H.R., TER. J. Folkton 1764.
[17] Boulter, 'Ch. Bells', 216.
[18] *Yorks. Ch. Plate*, i. 249–50.
[19] Barley, *Par. Docs. E.R.* 49–50. The earlier registers are in E.R.R.O.
[20] York. Dioc. Regy., Sentence of consecration.

Babthorpe family were reported to be recusants. In 1640 there were ten Roman Catholics in the parish.[21] In 1743 an Anabaptist was reported,[22] but there were said to be no dissenters in 1764.[23] Houses in Flixton were licensed for worship in 1811 and 1819.[24] The first chapel was built there in 1821 by the Primitive Methodists;[25] it is said to have been a brick building at the north end of the village used as a cottage in 1971.[26] It was replaced in 1841 by a new chapel[27] and in 1889 there were 22 members in Flixton and 5 in Folkton.[28] The small plain red-brick building with square-headed windows stands in the east of the village and was still used in 1971.

A red-brick Wesleyan chapel, with a round-headed doorway and windows, was built at the east end of Flixton village in 1841.[29] It ceased to be used c. 1939[30] but still stood in 1971.

EDUCATION. There was a schoolmaster in Folkton in 1700 and 1713[31] but no school was reported in the parish in 1743.[32] A National school was built midway between Flixton and Folkton villages in 1832. In 1835 it was attended by 55 boys and girls and was financed by voluntary contributions and school pence.[33] It first received an annual government grant in 1878.[34] In 1871 42 children were in attendance.[35] From 1908 to 1932 attendance varied only between 52 and 70. The small red-brick school was enlarged in the 20th century, probably in 1935. In 1938 the attendance was 42,[36] and the average number of children on the roll in 1971 was 46.[37]

There was a dame school in 1865 with an attendance of about 20 infants. In that year the vicar also reported that an evening school had recently been held, but without success.[38]

CHARITIES FOR THE POOR. Sir William St. Quintin, by will proved in 1651, left £4 to the poor of Folkton, the interest to be distributed annually by the overseers.[39] Nothing more is known of it.

FOSTON ON THE WOLDS

THE large and irregularly shaped parish of Foston lies some 4 miles south-east of Great Driffield, in the upper part of the valley of the river Hull.[1] Foston may originally have been an Anglian settlement. Despite its suffix, the village is 3 miles south of the lowest slopes of the wolds; this late addition to the name, perhaps made in the 16th century, was presumably intended to distinguish the village from Foston in the North Riding. The parish stretches for nearly 5 miles from north to south, including the townships of Great Kelk, Gembling, and Brigham. Kelk and Brigham are also Anglian, the former perhaps named from the presence of chalk in the generally clayey soil and the latter being the 'homestead near the bridge',[2] perhaps a reference to a predecessor of the later Frodingham bridge.

Most of the land is low-lying and for the most part the parish boundaries are formed by watercourses: the river Hull in the south-west, Frodingham beck and Old Howe in the south-east, Foston or Kelk beck in the north-west, and various smaller streams and drains. In Great Kelk the boundary diverges significantly from Kelk beck at one point, where the area known as Lynesykes lies beyond it; the watercourse around Lynesykes was probably connected with Great Kelk water-mill, which stood near by.[3] The internal township boundaries in part follow watercourses too, and Foston itself is divided from Brigham by Foston beck. The total area of the ancient parish was 4,898 a., Great Kelk accounting for 1,173 a., Gembling 1,235 a., Foston 1,108 a., and Brigham 1,382 a.[4] The only recorded boundary change was made in 1884, when a small and uninhabited detached portion of Nafferton was transferred to Brigham.[5] In 1935 Great Kelk was combined with Little Kelk (formerly extra-parochial) as Kelk civil parish, Foston with Brigham as Foston civil parish, and Gembling with Beeford as Beeford civil parish.[6] In 1953, however, Gembling was transferred to Foston.[7]

The flat landscape of the parish is relieved only by several small 'islands' of sand and gravel, rising above the undulating boulder clay that covers most of the area. Most striking is the steep-sided hill on which Brigham village stands. Others are Barf hill, in Great Kelk township, crowned by one of the few pieces of woodland in the parish, and Cruckley hill, in Brigham. The islands exceed 50 ft. above sea-level; so does a larger hummock around Foston village, though this is not composed of sand and gravel. The boulder-clay land is for the most part more than 25 ft. above sea-level, but some of it is lower and so are the areas of alluvium along the streams. Much of Brigham township is in fact below 25 ft., emphasizing the prominence of Brigham hill. Over much of the parish the regular field

---

[21] H. Aveling, *Post Reformation Catholicism in E. Yorks. 1558–1790* (E. Yorks. Loc. Hist. Ser. xi), 17, 36, 58.
[22] *Herring's Visit.* i. 215.
[23] B.I.H.R., Bp. V. 1764/Ret. 193.
[24] G.R.O. Worship Returns, Vol. v, nos. 2492, 3264.
[25] White, *Dir. N. & E.R.Yorks.* (1840), 386.
[26] Local inf.
[27] H.O. 129/24/525; O.S. Map 6" (1854).
[28] H. Woodcock, *Sketches of Prim. Meth. on Yorks. Wolds*, 154.
[29] H.O. 129/24/525.
[30] Local inf.
[31] B.I.H.R., Schools index.
[32] *Herring's Visit.* i. 215.
[33] *Educ. Enquiry Abstract, 1835*, 1084; O.S. Map 6" (1854).
[34] *Rep. of Educ. Cttee. of Council, 1878–9* [C. 2342–I], p. 1033, H.C. (1878–9), xxiii.
[35] *Rets. rel. Elem. Educ. 1871*, 476.
[36] *Bd. of Educ. List 21* (H.M.S.O.).
[37] Ex inf. Chief Educ. Officer, County Hall, Beverley, 1971.
[38] B.I.H.R., V. 1865/Ret. 188.
[39] *Abstracts of Yorks. Wills, 1665–6* (Y.A.S. Rec. Ser. ix), 40.
[1] This article was written in 1968.
[2] *P.N.E.R. Yorks.* (E.P.N.S.), 91–2.
[3] See p. 186.
[4] O.S. Map 6" (1854).
[5] *Census*, 1891. It was part of land called Eastholmes.
[6] *Census*, 1931.
[7] Ibid. 1961.

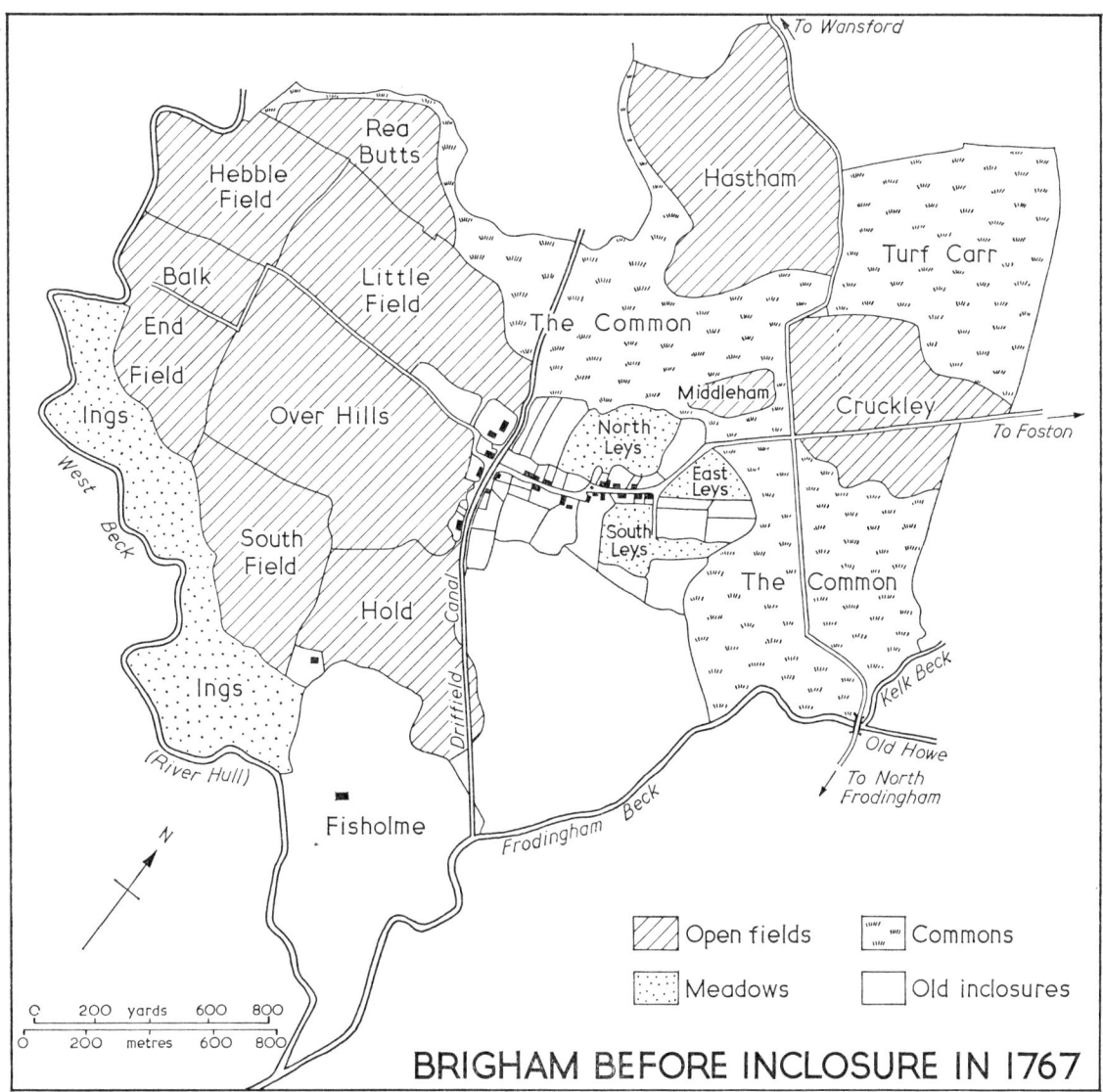

BRIGHAM BEFORE INCLOSURE IN 1767

pattern reflects the late inclosure of open fields and commons. At Gembling, however, there are some markedly long and narrow closes belonging to cottagers who had common rights on the village green. In Great Kelk the modern field pattern has a predominantly east-west alignment, perpetuating the unusually uniform lay-out of the former open fields.[8] A noteworthy feature of the landscape in Brigham is the Driffield canal, opened in 1770,[9] a large section of which was used by two sailing clubs in 1968.

The road pattern in Foston is uncomplicated. One winding road follows the spine of the parish and leads northwards to Lowthorpe. Great Kelk and Foston villages lie along the road and Brigham is at its southern end. Gembling village, around a long triangular green, is on an offshoot from the spine road. Few other roads enter the parish. One from Gransmoor leads to Kelk, another from Beeford leads to Foston, and the road from North Frodingham to Wansford crosses the parish in Brigham.

Several of the roads and field lanes have distinguishing names. Thus in Gembling township Criftings Lane, Cockerell Lane, and Out Gate leave the three corners of the green; two stretches of the spine road are called Gembling Lane and Long Lane, and Old Howe Lane leads to Beeford. In Foston itself the main road leads towards Brigham as Sheepdike Lane and Cowslams Lane. In Brigham township the spine road is called Brigham Lane and Cruckley Lane. In Kelk there are Folly Balk and Newsome Lane, and also High Street. The last name is applied not to the spine road but to part of what has become a field lane; it perhaps suggests that the through road in Kelk once ran west of the present line.[10]

The parish church lies midway along the straggling mile-long village of Foston. With one exception the farm-houses all stand by the village street: only Carr House lies out in the fields. The houses and cottages, all of brick, are of the 18th century and later, and few possess noteworthy features. Some single-storeyed 18th-century cottages near the former Vicarage have, like others in the district, a projecting course at the eaves and a string-course. More noteworthy are four large early-19th-century

[8] See p. 184.
[9] B. F. Duckham, *Inland Waterways of E. Yorks. 1700–1900* (E. Yorks. Loc. Hist. Ser. xxix), 20.
[10] O.S. Map 6" (1854). See map on p. 178.

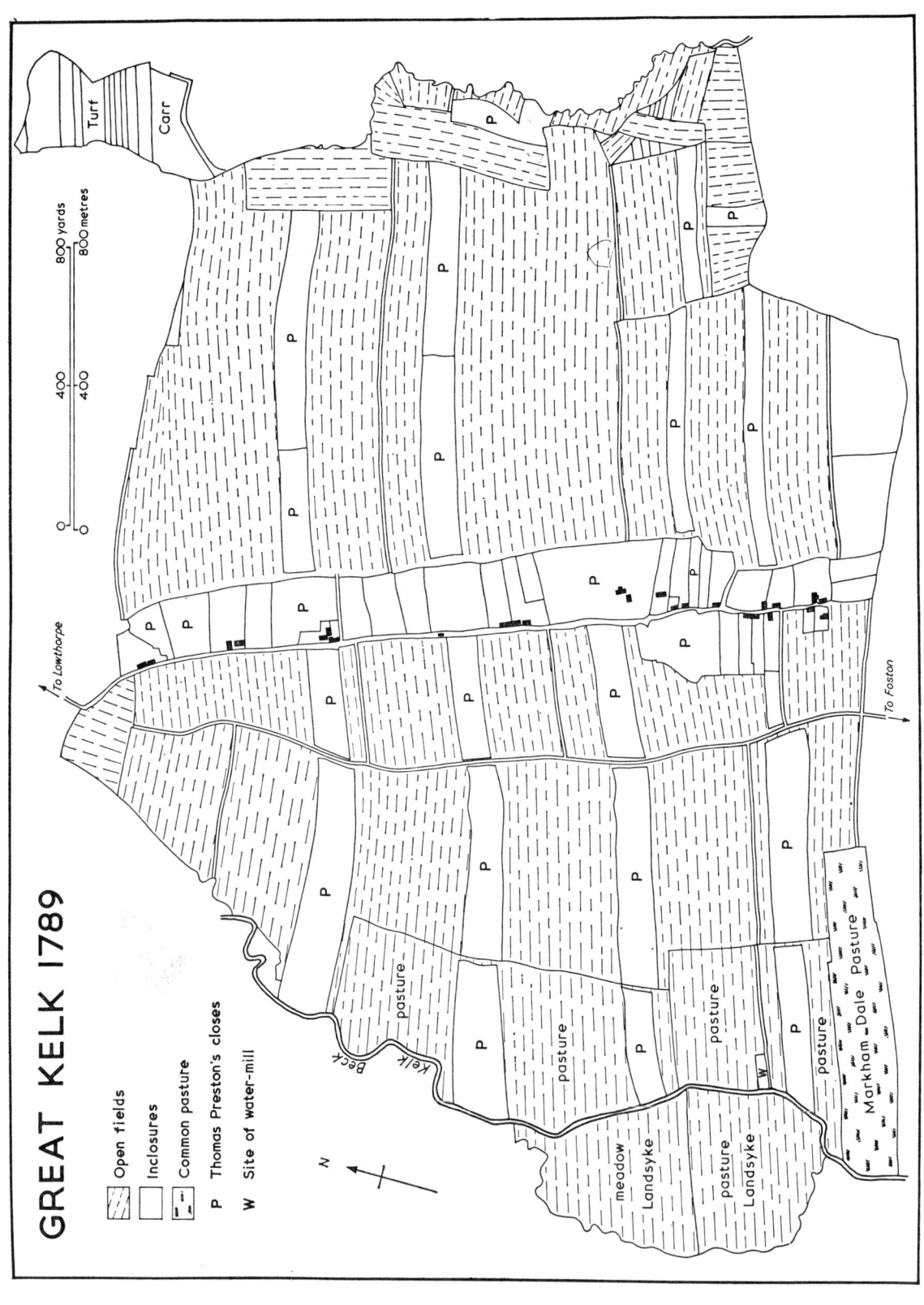

houses of three bays close to the site of the water-mill, and six late-19th-century 'picturesque' cottages near by with ornamental bargeboards. The former Cross Keys inn, which was mentioned as early as 1796,[11] apparently closed during the First World War and became a dwelling-house. The Plough inn had appeared by 1933.[12] Other buildings in Foston include eight Council houses and a village hall, opened in 1952.[13]

Brigham village, 1½ mile south-east of Foston, contains few buildings of note. There are four large 19th-century farm-houses, one of them called Manor House and another, out of the village, known as Little Brigham. There are two Council houses. The former Brigham Arms stands at the bottom of the village, facing the canal; it was open until the early 20th century, having replaced the Board between 1823 and 1840.[14] Near by an old swing bridge carries the road over the canal. Away from the village, in the low-lying fields near the river Hull, are farm buildings known as Fisholme Barn which bear the name of a medieval manor; there is a moated house-site near by and other earthworks suggesting the site of a small hamlet.[15] At Frodingham bridge a farm-house stands near the sites of the Blue Ball public house, mentioned in 1823,[16] and a landing-place,[17] on the Brigham bank of the navigable Frodingham beck.

The few houses of Gembling village, nearly a mile north-east of Foston, are not remarkable, though an outbuilding of cobbles reflects the nearness of the coast. There are two noteworthy farm-houses side-by-side on the green, one of the 18th century with three bays and a porch, the other of c. 1840 and more imposing in appearance. Close by there are some massive farm buildings, and Gembling Lane End Farm has a notable wagon shed. Gembling House is an early-19th-century farm-house. There are two Council houses. The village green covers 14 a. and is said to have been used to rear large flocks of geese, for which Gembling was noted in the 19th century; it was still common land in 1968.[18]

Great Kelk village is over a mile north of Foston. Except at the southern end all the buildings lie on the east side of the main road; the houses are scattered, with intervening crofts and ancient closes, and the village stretches for a mile along the road. All the farm-houses in the township are in the village itself. In 1849 there were 10 and more houses, 8 'homesteads', 20 cottages, and more than 10 garths and 'old garths' in the village; it is noticeable that fifteen of the cottages were concentrated at the extreme northern end of the village.[19] Most of the houses are of brick, but this is the part of the parish nearest to the wolds and two houses contain chalk. The Chestnut Horse, which replaced the Board public house between 1858 and 1872,[20] bears the date 1793. There are four Council houses.

In 1377 there were 118 poll-tax payers in Foston itself, 92 in Brigham, 76 in Great Kelk, and 58 in Gembling.[21] The villages were still of modest size in 1670, when there were 44 households in Foston, 38 in Brigham, and 42 in 'Kelk' (perhaps including Little Kelk) and Gembling together. In 1674 11 households in Foston were discharged from the hearth tax; of those that were taxed, 20 had one hearth each, 5 had 2, and one had three. In Brigham 6 were discharged; 26 had one hearth, 3 had 2, and 3 had 3 to five. In 'Kelk' and Gembling 8 were discharged; 26 had one hearth, 4 had 2, 3 had 3 or 4, and one had six.[22] By 1743 there were said to be about 87 families in the whole parish, and by 1764 about 60.[23]

The population of the parish in 1801 was 377. It rose to a peak of 792 in 1841, and then dropped steadily to 480 in 1901. The trend in the individual townships was much the same. In Foston there were 175 inhabitants in 1801, 344 in 1841, and 195 in 1901; in Brigham there were 80 in 1801, 151 in 1831, and 58 in 1901; and in Great Kelk there were 61 in 1801, 211 in 1861, and 122 in 1901. Gembling's population, however, showed several fluctuations during the century. It was 61 in 1801, at a maximum of 123 in 1861, and 105 in 1901.[24] In the 20th century the population of the parish rose to 551 in 1921 and then dropped to 465 in 1931. Even with Little Kelk included, as it was from 1951, there were only 480 people in Foston and Kelk civil parishes in 1961.[25]

MANORS AND OTHER ESTATES. Foston and its townships were divided into numerous estates at the time of the Domesday Survey. Foston itself comprised a single estate in 1086, held of William de Percy by Hugh. Before the Conquest its 5 carucates had been held by Carle.[26] The overlordship descended with the manor of Nafferton in the Percy family.[27]

Under the Percies the manor of *FOSTON* formed part of the Arundel fee. It was probably held by William of Arundel in 1166,[28] and later by Roger of Arundel.[29] Roger died before 1213 and by 1221 his lands had been divided between John of Belvoir, Nicholas of Anstey, Thomas of Hotham, William the Constable, and Thomas of Birkin,[30] who were either the husbands or descendants of coheirs. The last-named does not appear to have been assigned any part of Foston.

John of Belvoir surrendered his share of the manor, which consisted of 9 bovates, to the overlords,[31] and Henry de Percy seems to have given it to Robert le Boteler. It had passed to John le Gras

---

[11] Y.A.S. MSS., MS. 709b.
[12] *Kelly's Dir. N. & E.R. Yorks.* (1913), 534; (1921), 519; (1933), 471.
[13] Local inf.
[14] Baines, *Hist. Yorks.* (1823), ii. 182; White, *Dir. E. & N.R. Yorks.* (1840), 387; *Kelly's Dir. N. & E.R. Yorks.* (1905), 502; (1909), 514.
[15] See pp. 182, 187. [16] Baines, *Hist. Yorks.* (1823), ii. 182.
[17] E.R.R.O., DDSY/6/13, 23.
[18] Directories; L. D. Stamp and W. G. Hoskins, *Common Lands of Eng. & Wales*, 337.
[19] E.R.R.O., DDLG/15/20.
[20] White, *Dir. Hull & York* (1858), 440; *Kelly's Dir. N. & E.R. Yorks.* (1872), 365.

[21] E 179/202/62 mm. 17, 29, 38, 39.
[22] E 179/205/514, 521.
[23] B.I.H.R., Bp. V. 1764/Ret. 195; *Herring's Visit.* i. 213.
[24] *V.C.H. Yorks.* iii. 489.
[25] *Census.*
[26] *V.C.H. Yorks.* ii. 263.
[27] See p. 285.
[28] *Red Bk. Exch.* (Rolls Ser.), 425.
[29] C.P. 40/299 m. 229d; *Percy Charty.* (Sur. Soc. cxvii), 5.
[30] *Rot. de Ob. et Fin.* (Rec. Com.), 491; *Ex. e Rot. Fin.* (Rec. Com.), i. 66; *Percy Charty.* 135.
[31] *Percy Charty.* 111, 115.

by 1251[32] and he held 12¾ bovates in Foston in 1315.[33] Before his death c. 1331[34] John had let the estate to William de la Pole, but the lease was given up in 1343 to John's daughter Isabel and her husband Thomas of Burn.[35] After Thomas's death, before 1348, Isabel married Hugh of Clitheroe[36] and the estate passed by 1355 to their daughter Isabel, wife of Sir Richard Tempest.[37] The Tempests held it until it passed, some time before 1451, to John Norton and Denise Mallory, relatives of the Tempest family.[38] John Norton held Foston at his death in 1489,[39] but in 1524-5 his son John sold it to Robert Creyke of Marton.[40] The estate subsequently descended with Marton.[41] Ralph Creyke was allotted 470 a. in Foston at inclosure in 1780,[42] and the Creykes retained the land until 1873, when it was sold to Thomas Jessopp. Thomas sold it to William Jessopp in 1878, and he conveyed it to Marmaduke Sellers in 1904. It has since remained in the Sellers family.[43]

The second shareholder of Roger of Arundel, Nicholas of Anstey, died c. 1225,[44] leaving a daughter Denise who married in turn Walter Langton, Warin de Munchensy, and, apparently, Robert le Boteler.[45] Denise lived until 1304 when 3 bovates in Foston passed to her granddaughter Denise, wife of Hugh de Vere.[46] Hugh and Denise granted the estate in 1308 to Gerard Salvin, in exchange for a rent from it.[47] The rent passed from Denise de Vere (d. 1314) to her cousin Aymer de Valence, earl of Pembroke (d. 1323),[48] and from him to his niece Joan, wife of David de Strabolgi, earl of Atholl.[49] At the death of Joan's grandson, another David, in 1375[50] the rent seems to have been assigned to his daughter Elizabeth.[51] Her son Sir Henry Percy of Atholl died in 1432 and the rent passed to his daughter Elizabeth, wife of Thomas Burgh.[52] The land at Foston seems to have reverted to her son Thomas, created lord Burgh, before 1475.[53] His great-grandson William sold it in 1559 to John Palmer,[54] whose grandson Dudley died without issue in 1666 when administration of his goods was granted to his cousin Edward Digges.[55] In 1728 the land belonged to Sir Rowland Alston, Bt., Christopher Digges being a party to a conveyance then made.[56] Sir Rowland was succeeded in 1774 by his son Thomas, who was allotted 60 a. in Foston at inclosure in 1780.[57] The Alstons retained the estate until 1833, when it was sold to J. M. Hall.[58] In 1878 it was acquired by William Jessopp, and in 1904 he sold it to T. R. Stork.[59] After Stork's death in 1936 the estate was in 1942 vested in Constance Holton, and in the same year she made a gift of it to T. G. Rymer; it was then still referred to as Foston manor.[60] Rymer sold it to J. H. Holtby in 1952.[61]

The third shareholder, Thomas of Hotham, died before 1223.[62] His son Robert granted 9¾ bovates in Foston to the college of St. John, Beverley,[63] and 5 bovates to John of Driffield, who seems to have held it under the college.[64] Another John of Driffield gave the holding shortly after 1285 to Robert Ughtred, rector of Foston.[65] In 1310 the Ughtred holding comprised 7 bovates.[66] At the death of another Robert Ughtred c. 1590 the so-called manor was taken into Crown custody on behalf of a creditor of Ughtred's, William Patten. Dorothy Constable, daughter and heir of Robert Ughtred, claimed the land in 1591 under a lease from Patten.[67]

No more is known of this share of the manor, but it may perhaps be identified with the 107-acre estate which was allotted at inclosure in 1780 to John Rickaby.[68] The Rickaby family held the estate until 1861, when another John Rickaby's trustees sold it to Robert Easby.[69] G. R. Easby sold it to P. A. Crawford in 1912, Crawford to J. A. Shouler in 1919, Shouler to J. A. Sellers in 1924, and Elizabeth and William Sellars to T. R. Stork in 1933.[70] Like Stork's other share of the manor, but in 1937, the estate was given to T. G. Rymer. Rymer sold it to P. N. Tennant in 1960.[71]

The remaining shareholder, William the Constable of Flamborough, was assigned a quarter of the advowson of Foston church. If the Constables received any land as well, it may have passed to William the marshal, who held ½ carucate in Foston in 1314.[72] This holding is perhaps to be identified with the land later held by the Monceaux family. Thomas Monceaux (probably d. 1345)[73] had a house and 4 bovates there, which descended with his other estates to Sir Martin del See.[74] At the latter's death in 1494 Foston was assigned to his daughter Margaret, widow of Sir Henry Boynton.[75] She died

---

[32] K.B. 27/88 m. 8; J.I. 1/1044 m. 1d.; /1046 m. 1; *Percy Charty.* 95.
[33] *Cal. Inq. p.m.* v, p. 319.
[34] *Cal. Close,* 1341–3, 423.
[35] *Cal. Inq. Misc.* ii, p. 443; *Yorks. Fines, 1327–47,* 166.
[36] *Cal. Close,* 1346–9, 605; W. Flower, *Visit. Yorks.* (Harl. Soc. xvi), 238.
[37] *Yorks. Fines, 1347–77,* 49; J. Foster, *Pedigrees . . . of Yorks.* i, *sub* Tempest of Tong.
[38] C.P. 25(1)/293/72 no. 369.
[39] *Cal. Inq. p.m. Hen. VII,* i, pp. 225–6.
[40] C.P. 40/1046.   [41] See p. 96.
[42] Registry of Deeds, Beverley, BB/212/25.
[43] Ibid. LC/367/477; MM/412/645; 69/203/186 (1904); 848/10/9; 854/298/241.
[44] *Rot. Litt. Claus.* (Rec. Com.), ii. 57.
[45] *Cal. Close,* 1231–4, 508; *Ex. e Rot. Fin.* i. 268; ii. 213; Turner and Coxe, *Cal. Charters and Rolls in Bodl.* 672.
[46] *Abbrev. Plac.* (Rec. Com.), 252; *Cal. Fine R. 1272–1307,* 245, 498.
[47] *Yorks. Fines, 1300–14,* 67; *Cal. Inq. p.m.* vi, p. 274.
[48] *Cal. Inq. p.m.* v, p. 268; vi, p. 328.
[49] Ibid. vi, pp. 328, 480; C.P. 40/299 m. 229d; *Cal. Close,* 1323–7, 446.
[50] *Complete Peerage,* i. 182.
[51] C.P. 25(1)/278/146 no. 12; *Yorks. Inq. Hen. IV–V,* 20–1.
[52] C 139/58/37; C 139/162/16.
[53] C 142/19/155.
[54] C 54/561 no. 24; *Complete Peerage,* ii. 76–7; *Yorks. Fines,* i. 228.
[55] P.C.C. 1666, f. 179; W. Musgrave, *Obituary,* iv, ed. G. J. Armytage (Harl. Soc. xlvii), 346.
[56] C.P. 43/583 m. 229. See *V.C.H. Yorks. N.R.* ii. 7.
[57] Regy. of Deeds, BB/212/25.
[58] Ibid. ES/197/246.
[59] Ibid. MP/116/156; 71/417/392 (1904).
[60] Ibid. 555/266/207; 651/487/411.
[61] Ibid. 908/545/458.
[62] K.B. 26/84 m. 10.   [63] B.M. Lansd. Ch. 394.
[64] C.P. 40/87 m. 70; /98 m. 39; /299 m. 229d.; *Yorks. Lay Subsidy, 1297* (Y.A.S. Rec. Ser. xvi), 155.
[65] C.P. 40/60 m. 121; /98 m. 39; *Reg. Romeyn,* i (Sur. Soc. cxxiii), 197; *Bridlington Charty.* 171.
[66] *Cal. Inq. p.m.* v, p. 106.
[67] C 3/236/5.
[68] Regy. of Deeds, BB/212/25.
[69] Ibid. IE/61/91.
[70] Ibid. 140/385/347; 194/160/131; 284/523/450; 474/449/350.
[71] Ibid. 576/234/182; 1177/78/67.
[72] *Cal. Inq. p.m.* v, p. 319; *Cal. Close,* 1313–18, 149.
[73] *Cal. Inq. p.m.* viii, p. 409.
[74] B.M. Harl. MS. 2117, f. 316.
[75] *Test. Ebor.* iv. 100; Foster, *Pedigrees of . . . Yorks.* iii, *sub* Boynton.

in 1536 and 6 bovates at Foston passed to her grandson Matthew.[76] Before 1581 Thomas Boynton sold the land to Silvester Hildyard,[77] and it passed that year to his daughter Joan, wife of James Harwood.[78] The land is not mentioned again until 1758, when it was in the possession of the St. Quintins; it subsequently followed the same descent as Harpham manor.[79] Only 1 a. was allotted at inclosure in 1780 to Sir William St. Quintin,[80] but the St. Quintins subsequently secured several other small allotments made in that year. The estate, consisting of about 80 a., was sold in separate lots in 1921.[81]

In the township of Brigham in 1086 there were three estates: two, of half a carucate and a carucate, belonged to the king, while the third, of 3½ carucates, belonged to the count of Mortain.

The half-carucate estate was held by the Crown as a berewick of Great Driffield manor.[82] The land was subsequently given by Henry I to the Frismarsh family,[83] and Osbert of Frismarsh later gave a bovate of land at Brigham to Bridlington priory.[84] By 1207 the land of Osbert's nephew, another Osbert, in Brigham was in the hands of the Crown by escheat;[85] in 1225 it was granted to Roger of Hales, and c. 1230 to Peter Grimbaud at a rent of £1 12s.[86] Driffield manor was in 1236 granted to Joan, queen of Scots, for life,[87] and 1½ carucate at Brigham was thereafter held with that manor[88] until 1566. The estate, or part of it, was then sold by Sir Christopher Danby to Christopher Estoft.[89] The latter's nephew and heir Thomas Estoft died seised of the estate in 1568,[90] and Thomas's son John conveyed it in 1598 to Thomas Bainton.[91]

William Bainton was one of the leading inhabitants of Brigham in 1670.[92] At his death his estate was divided among his daughters and coheirs, one of whom was Anne, wife of William Stephenson. Their son, another William, sold the property to William Wilkinson in 1724, when it included 3 bovates.[93] In 1763 James and William Wilkinson sold 6 bovates, all of which were said to have formerly been part of Bainton's estate, to Richard Mosey.[94] At inclosure in 1767 Mosey was allotted 111 a.[95] He was succeeded after 1776 by his nieces Bessy and Frances Mosey, and by 1821 the whole holding of about 120 a. was in the possession of William Hought, who had married Bessy.[96] Part of the property belonged to the Houghts until 1883, when 69 a. became part of the Sykes estate.[97]

Part of the first Crown estate of 1086, amounting to 4 bovates, was held under the lords of Driffield by the Sewerby family from some time before 1314.[98] It descended, like Sewerby manor, from William of Sewerby to the Pigots soon after 1450.[99] Sir Ranulph Pigot was succeeded in 1503 by the three daughters of his brother Thomas, and Foston was apparently divided between Margaret[1] and Elizabeth. No more is known of Margaret's share. Elizabeth's part descended like her share of Sewerby, eventually being acquired by Ralph Creyke in 1588.[2] A later Ralph Creyke was allotted 25 a. in Brigham at inclosure in 1767.[3] This land descended, like the Creykes' Foston estate, to William Jessopp, whose trustees sold it in 1906 to T. R. Stork; in 1937 it passed to G. A. Johnson.[4]

The second Crown estate in Brigham was soke of Bridlington manor in 1086.[5] The fee afterwards passed to the Gants and Tattershalls and was held with Hunmanby manor.[6] By 1302 the estate was held in demesne by Theobald of Brigham,[7] and it subsequently descended with the Brigham family's manor there.[8]

The count of Mortain's estate of 3½ carucates had been held in 1066 by Guneware, and in 1086 it was probably held by Richard de Surdeval.[9] By 1106 Richard's son-in-law Ralph Paynel had succeeded him.[10] Brigham was part of the Paynels' estates which were later granted to the archbishop of Canterbury,[11] and it was held under the archbishops as overlords until at least 1542.[12] Under the Paynels Brigham was held from at least 1166 by the Meynell family. The heir of John de Meynell, his granddaughter Alice, conveyed her estates to Sir Henry Percy in 1376.[13] Subsequently some confusion seems to have arisen as to the overlordship of the manor.[14]

The demesne lords of *BRIGHAM* may have been members of the Frismarsh or Brigham family by the 12th century.[15] The manor descended in the Brigham family[16] until 1794, when William Brigham sold it to Sir Christopher Sykes.[17] William

---

[76] B.M. Add. MS. 26723, f. 17d.
[77] C 142/198/42(1); /204/92.
[78] C 60/423 no. 42.
[79] C 54/6183 no. 7; see below, p. 224.
[80] Regy. of Deeds, BB/212/25.
[81] Ibid. 228/76/62; /243/194; etc.
[82] V.C.H. Yorks. ii. 197, 226, 323.
[83] Pipe R. 26 Hen. II (P.R.S. xxix), 62; E.Y.C. iii, p. 112.
[84] Bridlington Charty. 310.
[85] Pipe R. 9 John (P.R.S. N.S. xxii), 81; Ex. e Rot. Fin. i. 135.
[86] J.I. 1/1043 m. 9d.; Ex. e Rot. Fin. i. 135; Bk. of Fees, i. 356; ii. 1354; Testa de Nevill (Rec. Com.), 368.
[87] Cal. Pat. 1232-47, 158.
[88] B.M. Add. MS. 26725, f. 85; Cal. Close, 1413-19, 229, 251; Rot. Hund. (Rec. Com.), i. 114; Cal. Doc. Scot. ii. 99; Feud. Aids, vi. 31; Yorks. Inq. i. 109; ii. 95-6; Hen. IV-V, 55, 118; Cal. Chart. R. 1300-26, 406; Cal. Inq. Misc. vii, p. 288; see below, p. 253.
[89] C 142/60/17; Yorks. Fines, i. 327.
[90] C 142/151/48.
[91] Yorks. Fines, iv. 113.
[92] E.R.R.O., CSR/20/77.
[93] Regy. of Deeds, I/39/85.
[94] Ibid. AE/1/1.
[95] Ibid. AK/164/9.
[96] Ibid. AW/306/525; DM/129/146.
[97] Ibid. NR/118/162.
[98] B.M. Add. MS. 26722, f. 370; 26725, f. 85; Cal. Chart. R. 1300-26, 239.
[99] C 66/450 m. 31; C 1/220/4; Cal. Inq. p.m. vii, p. 402; Test. Ebor. i. 67; ii. 136-7; iv. 6, 214; Yorks. Fines, ii. 115; see above, p. 95.
[1] C 142/56/53.
[2] C 142/673/3; Yorks. Fines, iii. 106.
[3] Regy. of Deeds, AK/164/9.
[4] Ibid. 84/250/243 (1906); 569/488/399.
[5] V.C.H. Yorks. ii. 197: it was there described as lying in 'Elestolf'.
[6] C 60/456 no. 32; B.M. Harl. MS. 805, f. 87; Feud. Aids, vi. 31; Cal. Inq. p.m. iv, pp. 108, 265; Cal. Close, 1307-13, 100-1.
[7] Cal. Inq. p.m. iv, p. 108.
[8] See below.
[9] V.C.H. Yorks. ii. 154-5, 226.
[10] Ibid. 155.
[11] K.B. 26/71 m. 7.
[12] B.M. Add. MS. 26719, f. 23; 26731, f. 49; C 142/69/190; C 145/313/11; E 179/202/5, 44; Feud. Aids, vi. 31, 169.
[13] C 145/313/11; Red Bk. Exch. 430; Cal. Inq. p.m. iii, pp. 428-9; ix, p. 317; Yorks. Fines, 1347-77, 190.
[14] C 142/173/41; /258/16.
[15] B.M. Harl. MS. 6070, f. 341d.
[16] For pedigree see Burke, Land. Gent. (1855), 130-1.
[17] E.R.R.O., DDSY/6/16.

Brigham's son William repurchased a small farm on the estate in 1823,[18] but the remainder rested with the Sykeses until 1920, when the whole estate was sold in separate lots.[19]

In 1349 land in Brigham belonged to Thomas, Lord Wake, and was attached to Cottingham manor.[20] The fee descended with Cottingham,[21] but by 1597 the tenancy had passed to the Brigham family[22] and this land was presumably held thereafter with their manor.

In the mid 14th century William Brigham made a gift of a plot of land near his manor of 'Fiskeholme',[23] and in 1494 another William Brigham bequeathed all his goods at Fisholme to his widow.[24] It therefore appears that in the Middle Ages the manor of Brigham included land, and perhaps a manor-house, known as Fisholme. In 1571 *FISHOLME* was sold by George Brigham to Thomas Wilberforce[25] and it became a separate manor, sometimes known as *LADY FISHOLME*, perhaps from the chapel of Our Lady there.[26] The Wilberforce family retained it until 1836, when the trustees of William Wilberforce, the philanthropist, sold it to Sir Tatton Sykes.[27] Thereafter it descended with the other Sykes property in Brigham.

In the township of Great Kelk there was a single estate in 1086. Together with its berewicks at Gembling and Reighton, it had been held in 1066 by Ulviet. By 1086 it was said to comprise 5 carucates, and was held by St. John's college, Beverley, under the archbishop of York.[28] The overlordship remained with the college, passing to the Crown at the Dissolution.[29]

Under the provosts of Beverley the manor of *GREAT KELK* was held by the Kelk family, perhaps as early as the 12th century.[30] They retained it until 1573, when Christopher Kelk sold it to Silvester Hildyard.[31] Silvester's daughter and heir Joan Harwood obtained possession of the manor in 1596.[32] The Harwoods sold it in 1617 to Roger and Edmund Wingate, and Edmund sold it in 1628 to John Norton.[33] Land in Kelk was devised in 1657 by Samuel Norton to his nephews.[34] The manor was again mentioned in 1675 when Timothy Johnson conveyed it to James Johnson.[35] Timothy Johnson described himself as lord of Great Kelk in 1669 and 1681.[36] The St. Quintins later became lords of the manor, perhaps in right of the house and bovate which Sir William St. Quintin acquired from Richard and Mallory Pearson in 1720.[37] The estate descended with Foston in the St. Quintin family[38] until 1957, when 17 a. in Great Kelk were sold as part of Turtle Hill farm, in Harpham.[39]

The St. Quintin estate in Great Kelk was thus a small one, and at inclosure in 1849 William St. Quintin was allotted only 19 a.; he also had several houses and cottages in the village.[40] The rest of the old manorial estate seems to have been split up, and land at Kelk frequently changed hands in the late 16th and early 17th centuries.[41] Some of it, a bovate and some closes in 1719 for example, eventually became part of the estate of John Grimston.[42] Some was acquired by the Greames. Five bovates of land passed from the Wingates to Ralph Porter in 1622[43] and to John Greame in 1710. Another 4 bovates, which had belonged to Samuel Norton, were bought by Greame in 1679. About 70 a. were added to the estate in 1847, and in 1849 the Lloyd Greames had 367 a. in Kelk. Another 50 a. were added in 1850–1.[44] The estate subsequently remained in the Lloyd Greame family.[45] In 1969 about 380 a. were held by the trustees of Yarburgh Lloyd Greame (d. 1965).[46]

A second estate in Great Kelk, held under the provosts of Beverley,[47] consisted of 1½ bovate of land shortly after 1276, when it was sold by William of Sunderlandwick to Amand of Routh.[48] The estate then descended with Routh manor[49] in the Routh and Cutt families[50] until 1549, when Sir John Cutt sold Routh to John and Richard Michelbourne.[51] The land at Kelk then descended, like Routh, in moieties held by two branches of the Michelbourne family, until the moieties were reunited in 1614 in the possession of Sir Richard Michelbourne.[52] In 1618 Sir Richard sold property there to Ralph Porter and Edmund Wingate, and in the following year Porter conveyed it to Robert Langdale.[53] Sir Richard Michelbourne was selling other property in Kelk in 1610.[54]

The former Michelbourne property may have later become the nucleus of John Grimston's estate at Great Kelk. Grimston was acquiring land there in the early 18th century, some of it from Thomas Langdale.[55] By the late 18th century the Grimstons had 10 bovates.[56] In 1785 Robert Grimston sold his

---

[18] Sheahan and Whellan, *Hist. York & E.R.* ii. 473.
[19] Regy. of Deeds, 192/147/135; 222/39/37; 223/332/275; 224/7/5; /295/257; 225/159/128.
[20] *Cal. Inq. p.m.* ix, p. 206.
[21] C 139/24/36; *Cal. Inq. p.m.* x, p. 49; *Yorks. Inq. Hen. IV–V*, 126.
[22] C 60/456 no. 32.
[23] B.M. Harl. MS. 6070, f. 341.
[24] G. Poulson, *Holderness*, ii. 269.
[25] C.P. 40/1295.
[26] See p. 187.
[27] Regy. of Deeds, FB/302/328. For pedigree see Burke, *Hist. Commoners*, iv. 722.
[28] *V.C.H. Yorks.* ii. 215, 323.
[29] C 142/26/10; /40/71; /113/45; /204/92; C 143/198/2; /285/9; *Yorks. Lay Subsidy, 1297,* 153.
[30] For pedigree see *Lincs. Ped.* ii (Harl. Soc. li), 556; *Gen.* iv. 186.
[31] C.P. 40/1321; *Yorks. Fines,* ii. 39.
[32] C 60/423 no. 42.
[33] *Yorks. Fines, 1614–25,* 98; *Visit. Yorks. 1584–5 and 1612,* ed. J. Foster, 528; C 54/2748 no. 19; C 5/402/59.
[34] *Abstracts Yorks. Wills* (Y.A.S. Rec. Ser. ix), 117.
[35] C 5/473/22; C.P. 25(2)/756/27 Chas. II Trin. no. 29.
[36] C 5/507/68, 70.

[37] Regy. of Deeds, G/398/876.
[38] See p. 181.
[39] Regy. of Deeds, 1082/489/443.
[40] E.R.R.O., DDLG/15/20.
[41] *Yorks. Fines, passim.*
[42] Regy. of Deeds, G/272/607. See below.
[43] *Yorks. Fines, 1614–25,* 207.
[44] E.R.R.O., DDLG/15/20, 33, 47, 89, 90; Regy. of Deeds, GG/126/147.
[45] See p. 95.
[46] Regy. of Deeds, 324/443/374; 387/107/93; 1552/321/290.
[47] J.I. 1/1485 m. 1d.; B.M. Add. MS. 26718, ff. 13, 75; 26722, ff. 223d., 290; G. Poulson, *Beverlac,* 589.
[48] J.I. 1/1067 m. 37d.
[49] B.M. Add. MS. 26722, f. 223d.
[50] C 1/9/440; B.M. Add. MS. 26722, ff. 223d., 290; *Yorks. Fines, 1300–14,* 57; *1347–77,* 202; *Cal. Chart. R. 1341–1417,* 301; Poulson, *Beverlac,* 589.
[51] *Yorks. Fines,* ii. 140.
[52] Ibid. *1614–25,* 11.
[53] Ibid. 109, 136.
[54] Ibid. *1603–14,* 144.
[55] Regy. of Deeds, N/8/13.
[56] E.R.R.O., DDLG/15/49.

estate, then comprising 423 a., to Thomas Preston.[57] Henry Preston acquired another 94 a. in 1829 and in 1849 he had 523 a.[58] The Preston family retained the estate until 1940, when 520 a. were sold by Beatrice Preston to the Ainsty Trust Co. The property was subsequently split up, the company selling 378 a. of it to E. C. Bousfield and J. D. Spofforth in 1962.[59]

Two bovates of the fee of the provosts of Beverley were sold in the early 13th century by Robert of Kelk to Hugh de Capella and his wife Joan.[60] Later this land was given by Joan to Bridlington priory.[61] At the Dissolution the land was valued at 5s. and then comprised half a bovate and half a close.[62] In 1557 it was rated for John Goodale,[63] but in 1571–2 it was let by the Crown to Roger Allen and in 1590 it was granted to Edward Wingate.[64] The Wingate family's lands later became part of the Greame and Grimston estates.

In the township of Gembling in 1086 there were 5 carucates which formed a berewick of Great Kelk, and like it they belonged to St. John's college, Beverley.

By at least 1229 the demesne lords of the manor of *GEMBLING* were probably members of the Gras family. The archbishop then confirmed a grant to John le Gras to have a chaplain at Gembling.[65] In 1348 John of Gembling held an estate there of the prior of Bridlington,[66] and in 1392 John son of John of Gembling, the prior of Bridlington, and John Monceaux all apparently held land in the township.[67]

The principal estate in Gembling appears to have descended from John Monceaux to Sir Martin del See,[68] and to have been assigned on Sir Martin's death to his daughter Joan Hildyard. She died in 1527 seised of 10 houses and 16 bovates of land.[69] The Hildyards, who acquired more land in the parish in 1555 from Thomas Foston,[70] held the manor until the 18th century. In 1737 Sir Robert Hildyard sold it to the Revd. Thomas Wakefield,[71] but by 1765 it belonged to William St. Quintin,[72] and it subsequently descended with Foston.

Though the St. Quintins acquired the manorial rights in the 18th century they owned little land in Gembling. In 1783 Sir Robert Hildyard had at least 713 a. and in 1819 at least 860 a.,[73] and much of this passed to the Dents and the Harrisons. In 1837 570 a. of the Hildyard estate were sold to Joseph Dent[74] and in 1831 300 a. of it went to Richard Harrison.[75] Until the early 20th century the Bainton family also had an estate in Gembling.[76] The Dents remained the chief landowners until 1935 when J. W. Dent sold nearly 560 a. to S. R. Tennant.[77] The Harrisons retained their estate until late in the 19th century, but in 1906 288 a. of it were acquired by Sir Joseph Rymer and 82 a. by T. R. Stork.[78] The former land was sold by Walter Rymer's widow to W. J. Gilliatt in 1952, and the latter passed like Stork's Foston estate to J. H. Holtby in 1952.[79]

The Knights Hospitallers of Beverley had property in Foston in 1539–40,[80] and it was restored to them, with their other possessions, when the order was briefly revived in 1558.[81]

The rectory was let in 1424 by the Carthusians of Hull, its appropriators since 1380.[82] Succeeding lessees were John and Janet Grindall in 1527–8,[83] John Brigham,[84] Richard Venables from 1546,[85] Arthur Dakyns from 1582, and William Wright, Christopher Simpson, and John Thompson from 1588. In 1599 the rectory was granted in fee to John Flint and William Jenkinson in trust for Elizabeth, countess of Shrewsbury.[86] At her death in 1607 it passed to her son William Cavendish,[87] later earl of Devonshire.

The value of the tithes to the earl of Devonshire in 1650 was £146.[88] At the death of William, duke of Devonshire, in 1729 the rectory passed to his son Lord James Cavendish, and from him it was bought by Charles, earl of Portmore, in 1731.[89] At the inclosure of Brigham in 1767 the earl of Portmore was allotted 55 a. in lieu of tithes and dues, together with a rent-charge of £70 from the other landowners. When Foston was inclosed in 1780 the earl received 137 a. in lieu of tithes and dues, 99 a. in lieu of his 4 bovates of glebe and common rights, and 5s. a year from some anciently-inclosed lands.[90] Henry Dawkins bought the rectory from the earl in 1783[91] and the property then consisted of 55 a. and £70 a year in Brigham; 247 a. and 5s. a year in Foston; 25 a. and tithes worth c. £60 a year, together with some whins, in Kelk; and about £27 in lieu of the tithes in Gembling, which it was thought had been commuted at inclosure. The whole estate was then held on lease by Francis Danby at £320 a year. Dawkins subsequently reached agreement with the occupiers of land in Gembling whereby the old composition was replaced in 1792 by rent-charges totalling £130. In that year Danby's rent was increased to £440.[92] In 1806 Dawkins sold the rectory to Thomas Parkin. Most of it was bought in 1820 by John Greame, but the tithes of land in Kelk called Markham Dale were not acquired until 1830. Greame also bought in 1830 the tithes of 20 a. of

[57] Regy. of Deeds, BI/163/263.
[58] Ibid. EG/88/105; E.R.R.O., DDLG/15/20.
[59] Regy. of Deeds, 638/428/353; 1260/60/57.
[60] *Bridlington Charty.* 163.
[61] Ibid. 8.
[62] *Valor Eccl.* (Rec. Com.), v. 120; *Miscellanea,* iii (Y.A.S. Rec. Ser. lxxx), 17.
[63] B.M. Harl. MS. 607, f. 93b.
[64] E 318/Box 42/2263; C 66/1351 m. 25.
[65] *Reg. Gray* (Sur. Soc. lvi), 29.
[66] C.P. 40/353 m. 212.
[67] C.P. 40/527 m. 201d.
[68] C.P. 25(1)/281/163 no. 6.
[69] C 142/48/90.
[70] *Yorks. Fines,* ii. 187.
[71] Regy. of Deeds, O/422/1042.
[72] C.P. 43/729 m. 343.
[73] E.R.R.O., DX/116; DDX/24/21.
[74] Regy. of Deeds, EE/293/287; EZ/220/208.
[75] Ibid. EO/21/22; /80/94; B.I.H.R., TA. 112S.
[76] Regy. of Deeds, 189/249/219.
[77] Ibid. 532/322/245.
[78] Ibid. 9/176/165 (1886); 89/254/246; /255/247 (1906).
[79] Ibid. 908/545/458; 923/357/309.
[80] *Miscellanea,* iv (Y.A.S. Rec. Ser. xciv), 97.
[81] *Cal. Pat.* 1557–8, 321.
[82] *Cal. Papal Reg.* vii. 513; see below, p. 187.
[83] E 315/32/82.
[84] *Miscellanea,* iii (Y.A.S. Rec. Ser. lxxx), 136.
[85] *L. & P. Hen. VIII,* xxi (2), p. 440.
[86] C 66/1317 m. 4; C 66/1494 mm. 3, 11; E.R.R.O., DDLG/15/50.
[87] C 142/312/137.
[88] *T.E.R.A.S.* ii. 52.
[89] E.R.R.O., DDLG/15/51.
[90] Regy. of Deeds, AK/164/9; BB/212/25.
[91] E.R.R.O., DDLG/15/114.
[92] Ibid. DX/116.

land and some cottages in Gembling,[93] so becoming the sole impropriator.

The tithes of Markham Dale were merged in 1840, but those of most of the township of Great Kelk were commuted in 1842 for a rent-charge of £205 payable to John Greame.[94] The tithes that still remained in Gembling were commuted in 1843. Those from 221 a. were replaced by rent-charges totalling £52 15s. payable to the owners of the land, and those on 21 a. were replaced by rents of £4 19s. payable to Yarburgh Greame.[95]

ECONOMIC HISTORY. In 1086 there was reckoned to be land for three ploughs in Foston, but Hugh had only one and two villeins had another. Foston's value had fallen from £2 in 1066 to 15s. in 1086. There was also a water-mill. No comparable information exists for the townships.[96]

The open fields of Foston township were, in 1780, East, West, Mill, and Little fields. East field occupied practically all the ground between the village street and the south-eastern parish boundary, and its area was then 358 a. West field lay to the north-west of the village street, stretching out to the pastures and carrs, and its area was about 200 a. The other fields were much smaller: Mill field, lying between Foston beck and the road to Brigham, comprised about 60 a. and Little field, adjoining the carrs north of the Brigham road, was apparently even smaller.[97]

In 1789 the open fields of Great Kelk covered most of the township. East and West fields lay on either side of the village street and together contained 35 flats or furlongs. The 'grain' of the furlongs was remarkably regular. In West field all the strips, with the exception of those in one small furlong, ran from east to west. The pattern was similar in East field, only the small furlongs occupying the uneven ground in the extreme east having different alignments. Ley farming was apparently practised at that time: alongside Kelk beck, five furlongs in West field were described as pasture, and beyond the beck the area then known as Landsyke consisted of one furlong of meadow and one of pasture.[98] At inclosure in 1849 there were about 800 a. in the open fields.[99]

Common rights for cattle and sheep in the open fields were maintained until the 19th century. In 1847 the Greames made a claim to the inclosure commissioners for $67\frac{3}{4}$ gates in the the fields, $78\frac{1}{2}$ average gates, and 96 sheep-gates.[1] The St. Quintin claim comprised a cow-gate in West field in summer (perhaps in the furlongs described as pasture in 1789), 2 average gates in each field, and 6 winter sheep-gates in each field.[2] In 1806 the rector enjoyed a cow-gate in 'Mill pasture', which was one of the pasture furlongs in West field, a quarter cow-gate (or a 'foot') in the fallow field, used for a calf, and average gates for two cows and a calf in the fields from about a fortnight before Martinmas until Lady Day.[3]

The practice of laying down part of the open fields to meadow and pasture may have been of long standing in Kelk. In 1679 and 1681 Timothy Johnson, as lord of the manor, alleged breaches by his neighbours of several customs of husbandry in the township. He referred to the open fields as the 'faugh' fields and named East field. Of the open-field land he said that 'part whereof are yearly ploughed, and other part being meadow is usually mowed by the respective owners thereof, and other part thereof is some years laid down and casted for pasture'.[4]

The open-field pattern of Brigham at the time of inclosure in 1767[5] was in marked contrast to the simple layout of fields in Foston and Great Kelk. The open-field areas were known as Little field, Rea Butts, Hebble field, Over Hills, Balk End field, and South field, all lying south-west of the village towards the river Hull, and Middleham, Cruckley, and Hastham, beyond the common to the north of the village. The southerly group probably also included an area called Hold. The open-field acreage cannot be accurately determined from the award, but together with the meadows and pastures there were said to be $48\frac{1}{2}$ bovates. The arrangement of the open-field land in ten areas, each of limited extent, suggests the use of a course of husbandry different from that usually associated with two or three large open fields. In 1724, when 3 bovates in Brigham changed hands, one was said to be called 'Hastam' and the others to lie in 'the infield'.[6] It is possible, therefore, that some of the 'fields' of Brigham were irregularly cultivated as an outfield, while others were more intensively used.

Though there are references to open-field holdings in Gembling in the Middle Ages,[7] the layout of the fields there is not known. In 1783 it was said that the oldest unhabitants had a tradition that the township formerly consisted of $39\frac{3}{4}$ bovates.[8]

The common meadows and pastures of Foston township were mainly in the north-west, on the low-lying ground around Foston beck and the dikes. Turker pasture, lying east of the beck, contained about 120 a. in 1780, and Great, Little, Calem, and Liege carrs and Cowslams, all west of the beck, comprised altogether nearly 200 a. In the south, around the confluence of Foston beck and Old Howe, there were about 20 a. in Thredham carr and 16 a. of meadow in Scurves, the narrow strip between the two streams.[9] Little is known of the use of these grounds, but in 1712 there is mention of five and a half pasture gates in 'the carr'.[10]

In Great Kelk, apart from the furlongs in West field already mentioned, the only common pasture was that provided by Markham Dale and Turf carr. Markham Dale contained about 25 a. in the south-west corner of the township. At inclosure William St. Quintin laid claim to it as lord of the manor and alleged that he and other freeholders had rights to pasturage and whins there. He gave up his claim, however, to a rival claim by John Greame so that the inclosure might go ahead.[11] Turf carr lay in the

---

[93] E.R.R.O., DDLG/15/5, 52–3, 72.
[94] B.I.H.R., TA. 177L.   [95] Ibid., TA. 112S.
[96] V.C.H. Yorks. ii. 263. The combined entry for Kelk and Gembling also includes Reighton.
[97] Registry of Deeds, Beverley, BB/212/25.
[98] E.R.R.O., DX/125.   [99] Ibid. DDLG/15/20.
[1] Ibid. /10.   [2] Ibid. DDSQ (2)/Box 1.
[3] Ibid. DDLG/15/52.   [4] C 5/507/69, 70.
[5] Regy. of Deeds, AK/164/9.   [6] Ibid. I/39/85.
[7] Turner and Coxe, Cal. of Charters and Rolls in Bodl. 607–8 (references of 1413, 1437).
[8] E.R.R.O., DX/116.   [9] Regy. of Deeds, BB/212/25.
[10] E.R.R.O., DDRI/22/168.
[11] Ibid. DDLG/15/10; DDSQ (2)/Box 1.

north-east, on the far side of the stream dividing Kelk from Gransmoor, and contained 24 a. at inclosure. It lay in strips, and St. Quintin claimed the right to dig turf there and to pasture cattle from his farm at Turtle Hill in Harpham.[12]

There were extensive common meadows and pastures in Brigham. Meadow called the ings lay alongside the river Hull, and on the slopes of the hill on which the village stood were three pastures, North, South, and East leys. The common, comprising a dozen named grounds, lay across the width of the township north of the village. Finally, in the extreme north, lay Turf carr, containing some 100 a. in 1767. At inclosure there were 38 common rights in the common and the carr, 29 of them belonging to William Brigham as lord of the manor.[13]

Whatever commons there may have been in Gembling were inclosed at an early date, but in 1819 cottages on the village green had a right of stray for cattle there,[14] and the green was still used as a common in 1968.

The low-lying ground which comprised most of the meadows and commons in the parish was in constant need of drainage to prevent flooding. The danger was especially great in Brigham, through which much water flowed from Wansford, Nafferton, Lowthorpe, and elsewhere on its way to the river Hull. Frequent efforts to maintain and improve the drains were made in the late 17th and early 18th centuries.[15] In the late 18th century a 'wind engine' was in use in Brigham.[16]

The most extensive early inclosure in the parish was that which took place at an uncertain date in Gembling. In 1607 the payment of hay tithes from the 'ancient oxgang' and the 'new pasture' was in dispute.[17] In 1639 it was recalled that 'Mr. Hildyard' had inclosed the commons[18] and in 1783 it was said locally that inclosure had occurred more than 200 years earlier.[19] There was little early inclosure in Foston township and in 1780 the ancient inclosures consisted mainly of crofts and garths along the village street.[20] At Brigham, in addition to the village crofts, there were in 1783 235 a. of old inclosures which represented the Wilberforce estate of Fisholme manor.[21] Some of this land may have been inclosed as early as the 13th century, for in 1229–30 Hugh and Theobald of Brigham had been accused of making purprestures in the township.[22]

At Great Kelk some open-field land had been inclosed by 1719, when John Grimston bought 8 closes in West field and 7 in East field.[23] These closes, lying in regular bands across the open fields, are clearly shown on a map of 1789, by which time they belonged to Thomas Preston.[24] In 1849 the ancient inclosures totalled 273 a.; 206 a. of these belonged to Preston and his closes in the open fields accounted for about 160 a.[25] Inclosure of the rest of the open fields at Kelk was recommended in vain in the 1780s, with conversion of the two fields to three as an alternative means of improvement: it was said that the land was 'only what may be called half land being only one crop and one fallow, and there is a great deal of land in the pastures covered with whins'.[26]

The remaining open fields and commons of Brigham, Foston, and Great Kelk were inclosed in the late 18th and 19th centuries. Brigham was inclosed in 1767[27] under an Act of the previous year.[28] The commissioners found that there were 1,019 a. of commonable grounds and the allotments made totalled 1,002 a. The lord of the manor, William Brigham, died while the inclosure was in progress and his devisees were allotted 677 a. Richard Mosey received 111 a. and William Wilberforce, the elder, 62 a. The impropriator of the rectory was allotted 55 a., as well as a rent-charge. There were only six other allotments, ranging from 5 a. to 25 a.

Foston township was inclosed in 1780[29] under an Act of 1776.[30] The commonable grounds totalled 1,000 a., and 994 a. were allotted. William St. Quintin received only 1 a. as lord of the manor, and the impropriator 236 a. The largest allotment was the 470 a. given to Ralph Creyke; other substantial allotments went to John Rickaby (107 a.), Thomas Alston (60 a.), William Warner (43 a.), and the devisees of two men who had shared a holding (35 a.). There were twelve other allotments, ranging from under 1 a. to 16 a.

Great Kelk was inclosed as late as 1849,[31] under the general Inclosure Acts, and 886 a. were involved. The lord of the manor, William St. Quintin, was allotted only 19 a. The two outstanding allotments were the 342 a. made to Yarburgh Greame, of Sewerby, and the 317 a. to Henry Preston. The Revd. J. F. Ogle received 96 a., and Rosamond Dixon 55 a. The other six allotments were all small, ranging from 1 a. to 11 a.

There continued to be an appreciable acreage of pasture after inclosure. The rectorial estate, for example, included in 1783 173 a. of arable and 143 a. of meadow and pasture in the parish.[32] In Gembling township in 1789 there were 362 a. of arable, 273 a. of meadow, and 432 a. of pasture, but by 1843 the balance was changing; there were then 700 a. of arable and 517 a. of meadow and pasture.[33] The chief crop at Gembling in 1789 was wheat, accounting for 124 a. out of 259 a. under crops.[34] In 1801, when there were 1,394 a. under crops in Foston (clearly referring to a larger area than the township), wheat was grown on 507 a., oats on 456 a., and barley on 237 a. Out of 439 a. under crops in Brigham, however, there was virtually no wheat and 320 a. was under oats.[35] Of a farm at Great Kelk in

---

[12] Ibid. DDSQ (2)/Box 1.
[13] Regy. of Deeds, AK/164/9.
[14] E.R.R.O., DDX/24/21.
[15] Ibid. CSR/4/12, 57; /12/51; /19/8, 73; /20/25, 77.
[16] Ibid. DDRI/6/2; DDSY/6/10, 16.
[17] B.I.H.R., C.P., H. 390.
[18] E.R.R.O., DDKG/142/c.
[19] Ibid. DX/116.
[20] Regy. of Deeds, BB/212/25.
[21] E.R.R.O., DX/116.
[22] Memoranda Roll, 14 Hen. III (P.R.S. n.s. xi), 58.
[23] Regy. of Deeds, G/272/607.
[24] E.R.R.O., DX/125.
[25] Ibid. DDLG/15/20.
[26] Ibid. /3.
[27] Regy. of Deeds, AK/164/9.
[28] 6 Geo. III, c. 54 (Priv. Act).
[29] Regy. of Deeds, BB/212/25.
[30] 16 Geo. III, c. 107 (Priv. Act).
[31] E.R.R.O., DDLG/15/20 (including map).
[32] Ibid. DX/116.
[33] Ibid.; B.I.H.R., TA. 112S.
[34] E.R.R.O., DX/116.
[35] 1801 Crop Returns.

1851 it was said that 'the tillage appears to have been impoverished by the occupiers previous to the inclosure' but that it was 'useful land ... strong and rather wet, suitable for corn but not for ... turnips'.[36]

In 1789 1,067 a. in Gembling were divided among fifteen farmers, but there were only four large farms of 100 a. to 300 a.[37] In the 19th and 20th centuries there have usually been about ten farmers in Foston, though there were only 5 in 1872; 6 to 8 in Brigham; 7 or 8 in Great Kelk; and 5 to 8 in Gembling, though there, too, there was a reduction by half in 1872.[38]

Several non-agricultural occupations in Foston were fostered by the navigation established on the river Hull in the late 18th century, for Foston beck was navigable up to the corn-mill at Foston. There was a tannery near by in the early 19th century, but in 1839 it was converted to a brewery which remained until the 1880s.[39] The buildings were in 1968 used as a farm. There was also a brewery in Brigham, next to the navigation at Frodingham bridge, in the mid 19th century.[40] Sand and gravel were formerly quarried on Brigham and Cruckley hills.

A water-mill at Foston was recorded in 1086.[41] It has been suggested that the course of Foston beck was changed, during the period of Danish settlement, so that it ran across the higher boulder clay land and provided a strong head of water for the mill as it dropped towards the stream later known as Old Howe.[42] The mill was often mentioned in the Middle Ages, apparently as appurtenant to Foston manor.[43] In 1565 and 1578 John Normanvill sold parts of 'three fulling mills and a water-mill' to Seth Holme, who in 1594 conveyed a water-mill to William Harrison.[44] The Harrisons held the mills until the mid 17th century.[45] A corn-mill and two fulling mills in Foston belonged to Edward Habbersham in 1726, but by 1737 the fulling mills were disused. The corn-mill was rebuilt by William Warner in or soon after 1747, and in 1792 it was sold by John Hanchett to William St. Quintin. Extensive repairs were carried out in 1792–6.[46] In 1796 it was described as having two water-wheels, and there were a mill-house and six cottages for men employed about the mill.[47] By 1850 the mill was powered by steam as well as water[48] and it so continued until it was burnt down in 1892.[49] Millers in Foston were again mentioned in the 1920s,[50] and it was presumably then that a small building was erected on part of the site to house a turbine. This building, long since disused, and the foundations of the earlier mill remained in 1968. There was also a windmill at Foston, a short distance from the water-mill, which existed by 1850.[51] The stump of the tower was left in 1968.

A water-mill at Great Kelk was mentioned in 1544,[52] and in 1578 it was granted by Ralph Ellerker to William Strickland; Strickland still had it in 1611.[53] After frequently changing hands in the 17th and 18th centuries, it was acquired in 1764 by William St. Quintin.[54] It had ceased to be used by 1842, when it was described as 'old mill'; it stood on Kelk beck near the ground later known as Lynesykes.[55]

In 1609 an occupant of a dwelling and 'firehouse' in Kelk disputed the payment of tithes on his kiln to the farmer of the rectory, although it was stated that every inhabitant with a kiln had long been accustomed to pay such tithes.[56] There is no indication of the use to which the kilns were put.

LOCAL GOVERNMENT. The overlordship of Foston descended with Nafferton and in the late 16th century the court of Nafferton Lenox manor swore a jury and appointed a constable, 2 aletasters, and a pinder for Foston.[57] In the late 18th century a jury was sworn at the St. Quintin's manor of Ruston Parva to serve for Kelk and Gembling; 2 bylawmen, a constable, and a pinder were appointed for Kelk and a constable and a pinder for Gembling. During the 18th and early 19th centuries the St. Quintins held separate courts for Foston, Great Kelk, and Gembling. A pinder and a constable were often appointed for each place, and 2 bylawmen were still chosen for Kelk in the early 19th century.[58]

Surviving parochial records include churchwardens' accounts beginning in 1782, surveyors' accounts and rate-books for 1774–1800 and later periods, and overseers' accounts for 1848–67.[59] Foston joined the Driffield union in 1836 and the former parish poorhouse, adjoining the churchyard, was disposed of in 1841.[60]

CHURCH. There was a church at Foston in 1086[61] and in the Middle Ages there were chapels in at least two of the dependent townships.[62] The advowson originally belonged to the lords of Foston manor. Thus William of Arundel presented in King John's reign.[63] The advowson was in dispute in 1290–1 between four of the shareholders of Roger of Arundel, namely Denise de Munchensy, William the Constable, Robert Ughtred, and John le Gras.[64]

---

[36] E.R.R.O., DDLG/15/23.
[37] Ibid. DX/116.   [38] Directories.
[39] Baines, *Hist. Yorks.* (1823), ii. 207; White, *Dir. E. & N.R. Yorks.* (1840), 386; Sheahan and Whellan, *Hist. York & E.R.* ii. 473; *Kelly's Dir. N. & E.R. Yorks.* (1889), 389.
[40] White, *Dir. E. & N.R. Yorks.* (1840), 387; O.S. Map 6" (1854).
[41] *V.C.H. Yorks.* ii. 263.
[42] June A. Sheppard, 'A Danish River-diversion', *Y.A.J.* xxxix. 58–66.
[43] e.g. *Cur. Reg. R.* xi. 472; xii. 185; *Rolls of Justices in Eyre for Yorks. 1218–19* (Selden Soc. lvi), 354; *Cal. Inq. p.m.* vi, p. 274.
[44] *Yorks. Fines,* i. 305; ii. 132; iv. 7.
[45] L.R. 2/230 f. 133; C 66/1967 m. 1; C 142/494/11.
[46] E.R.R.O., DDSQ(2)/Box 1.
[47] Y.A.S. MSS., MS. 709b.
[48] O.S. Map 6" (1854).   [49] *Filey Post,* 10 Dec. 1892.
[50] *Kelly's Dir. N. & E.R. Yorks.* (1925), 540; (1929), 500.
[51] O.S. Map 6" (1854).
[52] B.M. Add. MS. 26723, ff. 178 9.
[53] E.R.R.O., DDRI/7/4, 7; *Yorks. Fines,* ii. 114.
[54] E.R.R.O., DDSQ (2)/Box 1.
[55] B.I.H.R., TA. 177L. It is not shown on O.S. Map 6" (1854).
[56] B.I.H.R., C.P., H. 457.   [57] *Y.A.J.* x. 77, 79, 80.
[58] Y.A.S. MSS., DD. 89 (call rolls and jury papers).
[59] Barley, *Par. Docs. E.R.* 50; access to these records could not be obtained in 1970.
[60] Char. Com. files; *3rd Rep. Poor Law Com.* 168.
[61] *V.C.H. Yorks.* ii. 263.   [62] See p. 187.
[63] Presentations to 'Foston' as part of the Forest of Knaresborough refer not to Foston on the Wolds (as stated in *Fasti Parochiales,* iii. 31) but to Fewston (Yorks. W.R.).
[64] *Reg. Romeyn,* i (Sur. Soc. cxxiii), 214, 218; *E.Y.C.* xi, pp. 198–9; xii, p. 148.

Each shareholder and his successors appears to have enjoyed a quarter of the advowson.

By 1323 William the Constable's share had been acquired by Aymer de Valence, who was entitled to present for two turns, while Thomas Ughtred and John le Gras had the next two.[65] By 1334, however, the whole of the advowson had been secured by Sir William de la Pole,[66] and he presented that year.[67] William was licensed in 1365 to give the advowson to a hospital he proposed to found at Hull, but he died before this could be done and eventually, in 1378, his son Sir Michael gave the advowson as part of the foundation endowment of the Carthusian priory there.[68] The rectory, which had been valued at £33 6s. 8d. in 1291,[69] was appropriated in 1380 and a vicarage ordained in 1381.[70]

The priory retained the advowson until the Dissolution. A presentation was made in 1540 by Isabel and Brian Tunstall, by virtue of a grant from the priory.[71] A grant of the advowson to the archbishop of York in 1558[72] presumably lapsed on the accession of Elizabeth I. Presentations were made by the Crown until 1635.[73] In 1706 the patron was the duke of Devonshire and in 1788 Henry Dawkins,[74] both of whom owned the rectory. In 1806 Dawkins sold the advowson to Thomas Parkin, from whom it passed in the same year to William Wright.[75] By 1835 it had passed to the Revd. Ralph Otterburn.[76] In 1861–2 it was acquired by Miss E. Bayles[77] and in 1876 it was given by Sarah Bayles to the archbishop of York.[78] The archbishops have since remained the patrons.

When the vicarage was ordained in 1381 the vicar was awarded a stipend of £16 to be paid out of the rectory.[79] This remained the value in 1535.[80] The stipend was paid by the impropriators in the 17th, 18th, and 19th centuries,[81] and doubtless in the 16th.[82] The living was augmented by £200 from Queen Anne's Bounty in both 1782 and 1792, and by a parliamentary grant of £1,200 in 1824.[83] In 1818 its value was £36,[84] and in 1829–31 the average net income was £102.[85] In 1884 the net income was £144.[86]

In 1780 1 a. of glebe land was allotted to the vicar at the inclosure of Foston, in lieu of a horse-gate in the carr. The close lay on the south side of Vicarage garth.[87] In 1786 7 a. at Bewholme were bought with Bounty money, and by 1849 the vicarage had also acquired 5 a. at Great Driffield.[88]

At ordination in 1381 the Carthusians were enjoined to build a parsonage house at a place called Everardcot.[89] In the late 16th century an alehouse was found to be kept there,[90] but by 1685 the building had been demolished; its site was a small close opposite the church, known as Vicarage garth.[91] There was subsequently no vicarage house for a long period; in 1865 the vicar was living in a house 'at one extremity of the township of Foston',[92] and c. 1900 the mill-house was used by the vicar after the destruction of the water-mill.[93] A Vicarage was built c. 1907–9,[94] on the land allotted in 1780.

The chapel of St. Margaret at Great Kelk existed in 1328, when an inquiry into the foundation of a chantry there was ordered.[95] In 1347 William of Kelk was licensed to give a house, 4 bovates of land, and 9 a. of pasture in Great Kelk and Sigglesthorne to the chaplain.[96] In 1535 the chantry-priest received £1 8s. from property at Sigglesthorne and a stipend of £2 13s. 4d. from Hull priory.[97] The chapel may not have survived the suppression of the chantry, and in 1560 the Sigglesthorne possessions of the chantry, then described as dedicated to St. Catherine, were granted to Thomas Wood and Thomas Fale.[98] The Kelk lands of the chantry were in 1571 let to John Burthall.[99] The endowments were in 1600 granted to Henry Best and John Halliwell, and in 1607–8 to Lady Drummond.[1] Brigham chapel existed in 1354, when John and Elizabeth Hay gave a house and 4 bovates of land to found a chantry in it,[2] and there may have been a second chapel at Fisholme manor. In 1400 permission was given for services to be held in the chapels of Brigham and Fisholme, dedicated to St. Mary the Virgin.[3] The chapel of Brigham or its chaplain were mentioned in several 15th-century wills.[4] In 1535 the chantry had property, including 6 bovates of land, worth £4.[5] In 1553 its possessions were granted to Christopher Estoft and Thomas Doweman, and in 1584–5 Anthony Collins and Lawrence Woodnett were granted the chapel and land in Fisholme, where a statue called 'the lady of Fisholme' stood.[6] One or other of the chapels in the townships was referred to in 1566 when Francis Barker and Thomas Blackway were granted land in Foston 'in which there was a chapel, now destroyed'; they were also granted a kitchen in Foston which had belonged to a guild.[7]

For a period in the early 14th century a statue of the Virgin, which had been at Fraisthorpe,[8] was in

---

[65] *Cal. Inq. p.m.* vi, p. 337.
[66] C.P. 40/299 m. 229d.; /423 m. 357.
[67] *Fasti Parochiales*, iii. 33. [68] *V.C.H. Yorks.* iii. 190–1.
[69] *Tax. Eccl.* (Rec. Com.), 304.
[70] *Cal. Pat.* 1377–81, 318; *Fasti Parochiales*, iii. 30.
[71] *Fasti Parochiales*, iii. 34–5.
[72] *Cal. Pat.* 1557–8, 420. [73] *Fasti Parochiales*, iii. 35.
[74] P.R.O. Inst. Bks.; B.I.H.R., Sharp MS. 3, p. 201.
[75] C.P. 43/893 m. 5; E.R.R.O., DDLG/15/52–6.
[76] *Rep. Com. Eccl. Revenues*, 934–5.
[77] *Clergy List*, 1860, 1861.
[78] *Lond. Gaz.* 30 May 1876, p. 3240.
[79] *Fasti Parochiales*, iii. 30.
[80] *Valor Eccl.* (Rec. Com.), v. 122; *Miscellanea*, iii (Y.A.S. Rec. Ser. lxxx), 131.
[81] B.I.H.R., TER. J. Foston 1716 etc.; *T.E.R.A.S.* ii. 52.
[82] *Cal. Pat.* 1558–60, 426. This lease seems to have been ineffective.
[83] Hodgson, *Q.A.B.* 440.
[84] Lawton, *Rer. Eccles. Dioc. Ebor.* 298.
[85] *Rep. Com. Eccl. Revenues*, 934–5.
[86] B.I.H.R., Bp. V. 1884/Ret.
[87] Regy. of Deeds, BB/212/25; B.I.H.R., TER. J. Foston 1716, 1770.
[88] B.I.H.R., TER. J. Foston 1809, 1849.
[89] *Fasti Parochiales*, iii. 30.
[90] B.I.H.R., Churches index.
[91] Ibid. TER. J. Foston 1685. [92] Ibid. V. 1865/Ret. 191.
[93] *Dalesman*, July 1961.
[94] Plans of these dates among the par. rec.
[95] *Fasti Parochiales*, iii. 31. [96] *Cal. Pat.* 1345–8, 299.
[97] *Valor Eccl.* v. 122; see also *Monastic Suppression Papers* (Y.A.S. Rec. Ser. xlviii), 120; *Miscellanea*, iii. 131; *Y.A.J.* xxiv. 77.
[98] E 318/Box 48/2566; *Cal. Pat.* 1558–60, 455–6.
[99] *Cal. Pat.* 1569–72, 266.
[1] C 66/1539 m. 28; C 66/1740 m. 18.
[2] *Cal. Pat.* 1354–8, 83; *Yorks. Fines, 1347–77*, 47.
[3] *Cal. Papal Letters*, v. 277.
[4] B.I.H.R., Prob. Reg. ii, ff. 498, 626; *Test. Ebor.* iv. 7–8.
[5] *Valor Eccl.* v. 125. The 'Foston chantries' mentioned in the *Valor* were presumably those of Great Kelk and Brigham: ibid. 126. The chaplain who received £4 net at 'Foston' chapel in 1525–6 was presumably at Brigham: *Y.A.J.* xxiv. 77.
[6] C 66/1263 m. 2; E 318/Box 28/1599; *Cal. Pat*, 1553, 258.
[7] *Cal. Pat.* 1563–6, 475. [8] See p. 207.

Foston church. The rector of Foston, Robert the Constable, brought a suit against the prior of Bridlington in 1313 for the theft of the statue, and in 1314 the rector was given leave of absence for two years to prosecute the business of his church, perhaps in connexion with this matter. The prior succeeded, however, in retaining the statue.[9] Constable also held another benefice, and John of Chesterfield was given a canonry at Beverley in 1353, while he was rector.[10]

Richard Hunter, vicar in 1635, had been removed by 1650 but was restored in 1660.[11] In the 18th century the vicar held other livings and resided at Nafferton;[12] the vicar in 1825 was also non-resident, and in 1835 the incumbent held another living and employed an assistant curate.[13]

In 1665 the incumbent was accused of neglecting to hold services and conduct baptisms and burials. He claimed, however, that after his institution the previous year he had held services three weeks out of four, and later once a fortnight.[14] Services were held once a fortnight in winter and twice every three weeks in summer in 1743; communion was then administered four times a year and was received by about seventy people.[15] By 1764 services were fortnightly all the year, but there were only 20–25 communicants.[16] Two services were held each Sunday in 1851,[17] and in 1864 communion was administered eight times a year, with only five communicants.[18] In 1871 only the vicar and his family took communion.[19] By 1877 three services were held each Sunday, as well as communion,[20] but the latter was administered only fortnightly by 1936.[21] In 1968 there were two services each Sunday.

The church of ST. ANDREW is built of stone and brick, but much of it is covered with pebble-dash. It consists of chancel, nave, north aisle, west tower, and south porch.[22] Of the early Norman fabric there remain two small round-headed windows in the south wall of the nave, and there is a plain Norman tub font. The four-bay aisle was added in the later 13th century and has pointed arches, with round pillars and simple moulded capitals. The chancel, and probably also the chancel arch, were built or remodelled about the same time. The most westerly windows in both side walls, which contain primitive plate tracery, are of the same date, as are two sedilia; a third was mutilated when windows were inserted in the south chancel wall in the 15th century. In the 14th century the aisle may have been widened and rebuilt with square-headed windows. The east window, a large window in the south wall of the nave, the three-stage tower, and the brick clerestory are all of the 15th century; both the tower and clerestory have battlements. Some of this work may have benefited from an indulgence in 1427 to those who gave alms to the church; the vicar had submitted that the building was ruinous, lacking a tower, and that the parishioners lacked the means to carry out the work.[23]

Repairs were in progress in 1663, but the chancel was out of repair in 1694. Orders were given in 1721 for the screen to be removed and the walls whitewashed. A faculty was granted in 1824 for the church to be repaired, and there were said to be square box pews in 1865.[24] A west gallery was erected in 1825,[25] but is has since been removed. The church was reseated by Sir Tatton Sykes in 1886 and the interior was restored in 1896.[26]

The only tomb is one bearing the recumbent effigy of a knight which has been suggested to represent William of Brigham (d. c. 1278).[27] A window in the nave contains the arms of Greystock and Neville, perhaps of the 14th century,[28] and there is also a fragment of medieval glass in the east window. There is a Royal Arms in the chancel.

There were three bells in 1552,[29] but by 1764 only two.[30] In 1827 three new bells were cast, one at least by James Harrison of Barton.[31] The plate consists of a silver cup and cover, made in London in 1618, a chalice and paten of 1874, and a flagon and paten of pewter.[32] The registers begin in 1653 and are complete except for a gap between 1773 and 1784 for baptisms and burials.[33]

The base of a cross stands in the churchyard. A new burial ground opposite the church, in the former Vicarage garth, was consecrated in 1892.[34]

NONCONFORMITY. A single non-communicant was recorded in the parish, in Brigham township, on several occasions between 1590 and 1706. In the 1630s and 1660s the offender was Mary, wife of Ralph Wilberforce.[35]

In 1676 sixteen dissenters were recorded in Foston.[36] There were reported to be no dissenters or meeting-places in the parish in 1764,[37] but houses in Great Kelk were licensed for worship in 1788 and 1810, and another in Foston in 1823.[38] The Methodists had some twenty members at Kelk in 1787–91.[39]

The first chapel in the parish was built in Foston township in 1802 by the Wesleyan Methodists.[40] It

---

[9] *Cal. Pat.* 1313–17, 60, 148, 245; *Reg. Greenfield*, iii (Sur. Soc. cli), 217; *Cal. Inq. Misc.* i, p. 358.
[10] *Cal. Papal Letters*, ii. 52; iii. 479.
[11] *Walker Revised*, ed. A. G. Matthews, 394.
[12] E.R.R.O., DX/116; B.I.H.R., Bp. V. 1764/Ret. 195; *Herring's Visit.* i. 213.
[13] B.I.H.R., TER. J. Foston 1825; *Rep. Com. Eccl. Revenues*, 934–5.
[14] B.I.H.R., C.P., H. 2744.
[15] *Herring's Visit.* i. 213.
[16] B.I.H.R., Bp. V. 1764/Ret. 195.
[17] H.O. 129/24/523.
[18] B.I.H.R., V. 1865/Ret. 191.
[19] Ibid., V. 1871/Ret. 174.
[20] Ibid., V. 1877/Ret.
[21] Ibid., Bp. V. 1936/Ret. 16.
[22] Morris, *E. Yorks.* 168.
[23] *Cal. Papal Letters*, vii. 522.
[24] B.I.H.R., Churches index.
[25] White, *Dir. E. & N.R. Yorks.* (1840), 386.
[26] *Kelly's Dir. N. & E.R. Yorks.* (1893), 425; (1897), 460. The seats were said to have been brought from Garton on the Wolds church c. 1880: Bulmer, *Dir. E. Yorks.* (1892), 195.
[27] *Y.A.J.* xxviii. 367–8.
[28] Ibid. xxv. 80.
[29] *Inventories of Ch. Goods*, 26.
[30] B.I.H.R., TER. J. Foston 1764.
[31] Boulter, 'Ch. Bells', 217.
[32] *Yorks. Ch. Plate*, i. 251.
[33] Barley, *Par. Docs. E.R.* 50.
[34] York Dioc. Regy., Declaration of consecration. A plan of the ground as proposed in 1880 is among the par. recs.
[35] H. Aveling, *Post Reformation Catholicism in E. Yorks. 1558–1790* (E. Yorks. Loc. Hist. Ser. xi), 59.
[36] Bodl. MS. Tanner 150, ff. 27 sqq.
[37] B.I.H.R., Bp. V. 1764/Ret. 195.
[38] G.R.O. Worship Returns, Vol. v, nos. 714, 2359, 3855; B.I.H.R., DMH. 1788/14; DMH. Reg. 1, p. 443.
[39] E.R.R.O., MRP/1/7.
[40] H.O. 129/24/523.

was replaced by a new chapel near by in 1879 and this was used until 1967.[41] The later chapel, designed by Joseph Earnshaw, is built of red and white brick, with stone and terracotta dressings; it has an ornate front with a Venetian window and a blind balustrade at roof level. The earlier building was bought by public subscription and renovated in 1923–4 for use as a village hall and reading room,[42] but it has since been demolished. The second chapel in Foston was built by Samuel Stables for the Independents in 1814, and in 1851 it was said to be connected with the chapel at North Frodingham.[43] The congregation does not appear to have survived much later, for the chapel was closed by 1865.[44] The shell of the chapel remained, near the mill at the west end of the village, in 1968.

In Great Kelk the Wesleyans built a chapel in 1814 and it still stands.[45] It was replaced by a new building on an adjacent site in 1894,[46] built of red and white brick with stone dressings. Services were still held there in 1968.

A Wesleyan chapel in Brigham was built in 1819[47] and remained in use until the 1950s.[48] It still stood in 1968.

In Gembling a chapel was built, on the south side of the green, by the Primitive Methodists in 1845.[49] There were fourteen members in 1889.[50] The chapel was disused before 1954[51] and had been demolished by 1968.

Although there is no known Friends' meeting-house in the township, Kelk gave its name to a Monthly Meeting attended by Quakers in the area in the late 17th and early 18th centuries. The meetings were held sometimes at Kelk, sometimes at other villages, including Haisthorpe, Harpham, and Carnaby. During the 18th century Bridlington became the main meeting-place.[52]

EDUCATION. A school was being kept in Kelk in 1305, when Stephen of Garton, presumably the master, was warned by St. John's college, Beverley, that it was prejudicial to the college's grammar school at Beverley.[53] There were schoolmasters at Gembling in 1662, Brigham in 1682, and Foston in 1713.[54] In 1794 it was said that a house in Brigham, lately built by the overseers of the poor, was used as a school-house.[55] By 1835 there were three schools in the parish. Two were in Foston township, one having 28 boys and the other 4 boys and 12 girls, and the third in Great Kelk, with 9 boys and 8 girls;

all the children were taught at their parents' expense.[56] A new school was erected, perhaps in 1844, when plans were submitted for a government building grant.[57] It stood near the Plough inn,[58] but it is not known how long it survived. By 1865 there was only a dame school in the village, said to be attended by 20–50 children, and in 1868 there was in addition a school taught by a man 'who could do nothing else'.[59] By 1871 all the children in the parish attended schools in neighbouring villages.[60]

In 1872 an undenominational school was built midway between Foston and Gembling to serve those townships and Kelk. It was supported by voluntary contributions and by fees, paid in 1873 by 35 boys, 24 girls, and 12 infants.[61] The first annual government grant was received in 1873.[62] In 1889 the average attendance was 90[63] and in 1908 62.[64] The school was transferred to the county council in 1907 and the building was altered and enlarged in 1908–9.[65] The average attendance was as high as 71 in 1912 but fell subsequently and in 1938 was only 44.[66] The average number on the roll in 1969 was 39.[67]

An evening school was held in Foston in the 1860s and 1870s, but with little success.[68]

CHARITIES FOR THE POOR. Anne Walker, of Beverley, by will proved in 1707, devised four cottages to Robert Walker, one of them being already divided into three rooms for poor widows of Foston. She left the widows a rent-charge of £1 10s., on condition that the township kept the alms-houses in repair. The terms of the will were still being observed in 1822.[69] The alms-houses were allotted 1 a. at inclosure in 1780[70] and this was producing £5 rent in the later 19th century.[71]

The alms-houses are said to have been rebuilt in 1887,[72] still with accommodation for three persons. Subsequently they were often wholly or partially unoccupied, but in 1930 the cottages and land still produced £6 rent and there was £73 in hand. A Scheme of that year provided that if no widows were available the rooms might be let to other occupants. Several widows later lived there, but in 1937 three old men were renting the houses. The Charity Commissioners failed in 1938 to enforce the payment of the rent-charge, judgement being given that Anne Walker's intentions applied only to the original alms-house. The later building, a

---

[41] G.R.O. Worship Reg. no. 24800.
[42] Char. Com. files; *Kelly's Dir. N. & E.R. Yorks.* (1925), 540; 'Annals of Bridlington', vol. 31, p. 70.
[43] H.O. 129/24/523; Sheahan and Whellan, *Hist. York & E.R.* ii. 473.
[44] B.I.H.R., V. 1865/Ret. 191.
[45] H.O. 129/24/523.
[46] G.R.O. Worship Reg. no. 34551.
[47] H.O. 129/24/523; G.R.O. Worship Reg. no. 2858.
[48] Local inf.
[49] H.O. 129/24/523.
[50] H. Woodcock, *Sketches of Prim. Meth. on Yorks. Wolds*, 145.
[51] G.R.O. Worship Reg. no. 5137.
[52] E.R.R.O., DDQR/12–16, Mins. etc. of the Kelk (later Bridlington) Monthly Meeting. Two inhabitants of Great Kelk were described as Quakers in 1679: C 5/507/69.
[53] *Bev. Chap. Act Bk.* i (Sur. Soc. xcviii), 48.
[54] B.I.H.R., Schools index.
[55] E.R.R.O., DDSY/6/16.
[56] *Educ. Enquiry Abstract, 1835*, 1085.
[57] E.R.R.O., SGP 25.
[58] O.S. Map 6" (1854).
[59] B.I.H.R., V. 1865/Ret. 191; V. 1868/Ret. 175.
[60] *Rets. rel. Elem. Educ. 1871*, 472–5.
[61] E.R.R.O., SGP 26; Ed. 7/135.
[62] *Rep. of Educ. Cttee. of Council, 1873* [C. 1019–I] H.C., p. 436 (1874), xviii.
[63] *Kelly's Dir. N. & E.R. Yorks.* (1889), 389.
[64] *Bd. of Educ. List 21* (H.M.S.O.).
[65] E.R. Educ. Cttee. *Mins.* 1907–8, 304; 1908–9, 53; 1909–10, 146, 236.
[66] *Bd. of Educ. List 21*.
[67] Ex inf. Chief Educ. Officer, County Hall, Beverley, 1969.
[68] B.I.H.R., V. 1865/Ret. 191; V. 1868/Ret. 175; V. 1877/Ret.
[69] *9th Rep. Char. Com.* 734, which wrongly dates the will to 1717; Char. Com. files; B.I.H.R., Bp. V. 1764/Ret. 195.
[70] Registry of Deeds, Beverley, BB/212/24.
[71] Char. Com. files.
[72] *Kelly's Dir. N. & E.R. Yorks* (1889), 389.

simple single-storey brick structure, was derelict in 1968 and no alternative arrangements had been made for the use of the charity money.[73]

In 1822 the Poor's Money consisted of £18, held at interest by several inhabitants of Foston; the income was distributed by the overseers. Another £2 had already been lost by that time, and no more is known of the charity.[74]

By 1786 there were two other small benefactions: of £5 for the poor of Gembling and £1 for those of Kelk. Interest on the former was being distributed by the overseers in 1822, but the latter was then said to have been used about twenty years earlier to repair the poorhouse.[75] No record has been found of either gift after 1822.

Kelk civil parish benefits from the charity of Alice Gray, which also applies to Nafferton and Lowthorpe.[76]

FOXHOLES

FOXHOLES lies on the wolds about 10 miles north-west of Bridlington, and the parish, which includes the townships of Butterwick and Boythorpe, extends from east to west for about 3 miles.[1] Foxholes and Butterwick were probably Anglian villages and Boythorpe may have been a subsidiary Scandinavian settlement.[2] The villages of Foxholes and Butterwick and the two remaining farms at Boythorpe lie in the valley of the Gypsey Race but most of the parish occupies the adjoining wold slopes. Several sections of the parish boundary follow the bottoms of dry valleys or are aligned upon the highest points of the wolds on both sides of the valley. The internal township boundaries appear to make little use of prominent natural features. Part of the southern boundary with Thwing and Weaverthorpe follows a prehistoric earthwork. The area of the ancient parish is 4,306 a., of which 1,635 a. lie in Foxholes, 891 a. in Boythorpe, and 1,779 a. in Butterwick. In 1935 all three townships were combined as Foxholes civil parish.[3]

In the valley of the Gypsey Race much of the ground is less than 200 ft. above sea-level. Foxholes village lies mainly at a height of 200 ft.–250 ft. in the Dale, which runs northwards from the main valley. The wold slopes rise steeply to 450 ft. and more in both the north and the south of the parish. Several prominent dry valleys dissect the wolds, especially in the west of the parish, where they include the steep-sided Old Dale in Butterwick. The wold slopes were largely occupied by open-field land in the Middle Ages and the regular field pattern throughout the parish reflects the various inclosures of the 18th and early 19th centuries.[4] Most of the land was under arable in 1970, although there was some pasture in the valley, and the landscape presents a typically open appearance, broken only by a few small plantations in Butterwick, probably the result of the planting activities of the earls of Carlisle in the late 18th and early 19th centuries.

The Gypsey Race, known in Butterwick as the Lord's beck in the 16th and the Lord's river in the 18th and 19th centuries,[5] flows eastwards across the parish, but much of it is beneath the ground, particularly in the summer. Ditches mark its course where it is not visible on the surface. As early as 1622 it was described as falling 'into the earth' between Butterwick and Boythorpe.[6] In the 16th century the inhabitants of Boythorpe paid a free rent of 2s. to the lord of Butterwick manor to have a watercourse (*cursum aque*),[7] probably meaning the free use of the Race, and as late as 1837 this payment was still made 'for the privilege of the water'. In the 1820s misuse of the Race, even outside Butterwick, was dealt with at the manorial court there.[8] In 1669 the inhabitants of Boythorpe alleged that the Race was 'all grown up and the current stopped'.[9] The Butterwick inclosure Act empowered the commissioners to alter the course of the Race, so long as the interests of other villages were not prejudiced.[10] The inclosure award, however, merely stipulated that the lord of the manor should scour and cleanse the Race up to the point where it was accustomed to be cleansed by the inhabitants of Boythorpe.[11]

Butterwick village lies around the junction of the Sherburn–Langtoft road, which runs from north to south across the wolds, and the Weaverthorpe to Wold Newton road, along the valley bottom. Boythorpe also stands on the latter road. The main street of Foxholes is formed by the Driffield–Scarborough road, sections of which, within the village, were formerly known as High End Lane and Low End Lane.[12] From the village centre Church Lane leads north-westwards towards Ganton, and other minor roads lead to Octon Grange and to Sherburn. In the late 18th century a road apparently ran north-eastwards from Foxholes into Wold Newton parish, where it was known as North Cotes Road.[13] Between 1772 and 1839, however, it seems to have been diverted to join the Scarborough road north of the village.[14] Another road formerly ran south-eastwards from Foxholes to Thwing. The section between the village and the Wold Newton road was stopped up between 1772 and 1839[15] and the remainder, up to and beyond the parish boundary, was similarly closed in the latter year in connexion with the impending inclosure of Foxholes. In its place a new road was made leading south from the Wold Newton road on the line of the parish boundary and continuing into Thwing.[16]

---

[73] Char. Com. files. [74] *9th Rep. Char. Com.* 734.
[75] Ibid. 734–5.
[76] See p. 297.
[1] This article was written in 1970.
[2] *P.N.E.R. Yorks.* (E.P.N.S.), 114–15.
[3] *Census*, 1931.
[4] See p. 195.
[5] Castle Howard MS., Box 24, Survey of Estates, 1563; 11 Geo. III, c. 95 (Priv. Act); O.S. Map 6" (1854). The first reference to the Lord's beck was in 1563 when Lord Dacre of Gillesland and Greystock was lord of the manor.
[6] *Dodsworth's Ch. Notes* (Y.A.S. Rec. Ser. xxxiv), 220.
[7] Castle Howard MSS., Box 24, Surveys of Estates, 1537, 1563.
[8] N.R.R.O., ZDS/Manorial: Wykeham, call rolls and court papers of Butterwick manor, 1751–1850; see below, p. 196.
[9] E.R.R.O., CSR/4/37. [10] 11 Geo. III, c. 95 (Priv. Act).
[11] Registry of Deeds, Beverley, AT/79/10.
[12] E.R.R.O., PR. 15 (Foxholes inclosure award and map).
[13] T. Jefferys, *Map of Yorks.* (1772); see below, p. 298.
[14] E.R.R.O., TA. Foxholes.
[15] Ibid.; Jefferys, *Map of Yorks.* (1772).
[16] E.R.R.O., HD. 45.

Changes have also occurred in the course of the east–west valley road, which in the late 18th century divided just east of Butterwick, one branch running north-eastwards through Boythorpe to Foxholes village and the other taking a more southerly course along the valley bottom to Wold Newton. Between 1772 and 1839 a road was built to link the two branches and to replace a short stretch of the northern road. The rest of the northern road was shifted southwards to run along the valley bottom to Wold Newton and the southern road was stopped up.[17]

The small village of Foxholes consists mostly of modest houses and cottages dating from the 18th to the 20th century. Although the main material is brick, much chalk remains and several of the earlier buildings are entirely of this material. The most noteworthy building is the former Rectory, now called Foxholes Manor.[18] Near by stands a pair of derelict two-storeyed chalk cottages, of the 18th or early 19th century. The 19th-century buildings include Cottage and Manor Farms, in the centre of the village, and two terraces each containing five brick cottages. Extensive 20th-century buildings have replaced the workshops of a former foundry in the north of the village,[19] an abbatoir has been established by a meat company in the south, and twelve Council houses have been built in Well Lane. The Ship inn was open from at least 1823 to 1850.[20]

The hamlet of Boythorpe, about a mile to the south-west of Foxholes, may never have recovered from an apparently severe visitation of the Black Death, and certainly after the mid 14th century it was never separately taxed.[21] In 1772 and later there were only two farm-houses on the site.[22] The present houses are early-19th-century brick buildings, but both have end walls of chalk. Around both farms is an area of small regular fields which may formerly have been the crofts and garths, and the area immediately to the north was known as Garth Heads in the mid 19th century.[23] In a field beside the road are prominent, if indeterminate, earthworks, including what appears to a be former roadway.

About ½ mile further west is the small village of Butterwick, with a pond at its centre. Manor House Farm, two storeys high and three bays long, is built mainly of chalk and has 18th- and 19th-century features. Rectory Farm is a one-and-a-half storeyed building, mainly of chalk, probably dating from the 18th century. Also in the village are Grange Farm, dated 1851, and East End Farm, perhaps of slightly earlier date; the latter has a dentil course under the eaves. There are six Council houses. Several earthworks in the village, notably in a field south of Manor House Farm, suggest the sites of former crofts and garths. The only isolated farm in the parish is the late-19th-century Wilson's Wold Farm,

north of Butterwick. Falconer's Hall, first mentioned in 1805,[24] stood in the north of the parish near the Foxholes to Sherburn road. It was the home in the late 18th and early 19th centuries of Thomas Thornton (1757–1823), lord of the manor, who revived the sport of falconry.[25] The house was demolished before 1850, but its foundations were still visible in 1970.

In 1377 Foxholes, perhaps including Butterwick and Boythorpe, had 57 poll-tax payers.[26] In 1670 21 households, 8 of which were discharged for poverty, were recorded in the hearth-tax assessment for Foxholes alone. Four years later the number of discharged households is not recorded but of the 11 which paid, 9 had only one hearth each and 2 had three.[27] In 1743 about 20 families were reported in Foxholes and Boythorpe, and in 1764 there were 13 families in Foxholes and 2 in Boythorpe.[28] The population of Foxholes increased steadily from 130 in 1801 to 177 in 1831. It then rose sharply to 249 in 1841 and more slowly to a peak of 335 in 1871. It had fallen to 212 in 1901,[29] but increased to 247 in 1911 before again declining to 201 in 1931. Even after Butterwick was included in the civil parish the population was only 237 in both 1951 and 1961.[30]

Butterwick, together with Boythorpe, had 24 households in 1670, 5 of them too poor to pay the hearth tax. In 1674, of the chargeable households, 11 had one hearth each, 2 had 2, and one had three.[31] In 1743 there were 9 families in Butterwick and in 1764 eight.[32] In 1801 the population was 85 and until 1901 it varied only between 82 and 109.[33] It declined to 71 by 1921 and stood at 77 in 1931.[34]

MANORS AND OTHER ESTATES. In 1086 there were two estates in Foxholes, of 2 and 5 carucates respectively, both belonging to the king; the smaller one was soke of Bridlington manor.[35]

The larger estate was given to Robert de Brus soon after 1086[36] and the overlordship descended in the Brus, Thwing, and Lumley families, like that of Thwing manor.[37] It was last mentioned in 1431–2.[38] In 1166 a mesne lordship was probably held of Adam de Brus by Godfrey of Harpham and in 1243 Anselm of Harpham held land of the fee.[39] The mesne lordship was last mentioned in 1284–5.[40]

The manor of FOXHOLES was held of the Harphams c. 1280 by Robert of Acklam,[41] and in 1316 he was returned as lord of the township.[42] In 1346 William and Marmaduke of Acklam held 17 bovates there.[43] The manor apparently passed to Thomas Barry, whose widow in 1392 granted it to Thomas Walworth,[44] and by 1428 part of the estate had passed to Thomas Nicholson, the largest tenant of the Brus fee with 8 bovates.[45] William Nicholson was said to have sold 9 bovates about 1527 to a Scot

---

[17] Ibid.; TA. Foxholes; Jefferys, *Map of Yorks.* (1772).
[18] See p. 197.
[19] See p. 195.
[20] Baines, *Hist. Yorks.* (1823), ii. 207; O.S. Map 6″ (1854).
[21] E 179/202/53.
[22] Jefferys, *Map of Yorks.* (1772).
[23] O.S. Map 6″ (1854).
[24] Regy. of Deeds, CK/241/415.
[25] *D.N.B.*
[26] E 179/202/62 m. 4.
[27] E 179/205/514, 521.
[28] B.I.H.R., Bp. V. 1764/Ret. 196; *Herring's Visit.* i. 214.
[29] *V.C.H. Yorks.* iii. 489.
[30] Census.
[31] E 179/205/521.
[32] B.I.H.R., Bp. V. 1764/Ret. 196; *Herring's Visit.* i. 114.
[33] *V.C.H. Yorks.* iii. 489.
[34] Census.
[35] *V.C.H. Yorks.* ii. 197, 204, 291.
[36] Ibid. 291.
[37] *Bk. of Fees*, ii. 1098; *Feud. Aids*, vi. 141, 225, 266; see below, p. 326.
[38] C 139/55/42.
[39] *E.Y.C.* ii, p. 14.
[40] *Feud. Aids*, vi. 28.
[41] *Plac. de Quo Warr.* (Rec. Com.), 194.
[42] *Feud. Aids*, vi. 169.
[43] Ibid. 225.
[44] *Yorks. Deeds*, x. 78–9.
[45] *Feud. Aids*, vi. 266.

without the king's licence,[46] and the property was consequently forfeited. It was granted by the Crown in 1531 to Edward Goldsborough,[47] who in 1533 sold it to James Vavasour.[48] Its descent has not been traced further, and when a manorial estate was subsequently built up by the Osbaldeston family it included land from both the Brus and the Gant fees.

The manor of Foxholes belonged to Richard Osbaldeston in 1686.[49] The estate was increased by the purchase of 8 bovates from Francis Taylor in 1709, 14½ bovates from Thomas Condon in 1721, and 5 bovates from John Towse in 1737.[50] At inclosure in 1840 Bertram Osbaldeston-Mitford was awarded 927 a.[51] The Osbaldeston-Mitfords held the estate until 1920, when all 950 a. were sold to Sir Henry Readett Bayley.[52] It was disposed of in separate lots in 1921 and 1923.[53]

The 2-carucate Domesday estate was subsequently given to the Gants and the overlordship later passed to the Tattershalls.[54] The estate descended like Hunmanby manor to the earls of Northumberland in the 15th century and to the Crown in 1537.[55]

Walter of Bubwith, who held 10 bovates, was the largest demesne tenant of the Gant fee in 1284–5.[56] The holding is last mentioned in 1346, when Richard of Bubwith had one carucate in Foxholes.[57] By 1428 the largest tenant was William Wilsthorpe, with 13 bovates.[58] Land from this fee later contributed to the Osbaldeston manor.

Of the smaller estates in the township, that of the Browne family probably originated in 1614 in the purchase by Richard Browne of property from Thomas and George Etherington.[59] In 1831 John Browne sold 4 bovates to Charles Ringrose,[60] and about the same time Richard Browne's devisees sold 9½ bovates to David Taylor.[61] At inclosure in 1840 Ringrose was awarded 108 a. and Taylor 265 a.[62] Taylor died in 1847 and his estate passed to Brian Taylor Harland,[63] and in 1862 Thomas Harland sold it to Sir Francis Legard.[64] In 1911 Sir Algernon Legard sold it to Harold Wrigley and in 1961 E. W. Wrigley conveyed it to Kathleen Megginson.[65]

In 1539–40 the Knights Hospitallers held property in Foxholes, including a cottage called Cross Place,[66] and it was restored to them when the order was temporarily revived in 1558.[67] In 1570–1 it was let by the Crown to Marmaduke Langdale.[68]

In 1086 Boythorpe was a berewick of Burton Agnes and contained 5 carucates. It had been held by Morcar before the Conquest but in 1086 it was held of the king by a rent-payer.[69] The overlordship had passed to the Brus family before 1233[70] and in 1281 it was assigned to Walter Fauconberg,[71] whose wife Agnes was a sister and coheir of Peter de Brus (d. 1272).[72] Before 1422 it passed to the Neville family on the marriage of Joan the daughter of Thomas, Lord Fauconberg (d. 1407), to William Neville, later earl of Kent.[73] Their daughter Alice married Sir John Conyers[74] and in 1531, the last time it is mentioned, the overlordship was held by Christopher, Lord Conyers.[75]

A family which took its name from the township were demesne tenants in the mid 12th century.[76] Isabel, possibly the daughter and heir of Robert of Boythorpe, married Robert of Killingholme, who held land of the Brus fee in 1243.[77] Their son Andrew of Boythorpe[78] had been succeeded before 1279 by his son John of Killingholme,[79] who in 1284–5 held 4 of the 6 carucates then said to be in the township.[80] In 1316 the lords of the township were returned as Walter of Fauconberg and Ralph son of William.[81] In 1328 the Boythorpe holding, including 25 bovates, was confirmed to Ralph Bulmer, subject to the life interest of Ralph of Boythorpe in 6 bovates.[82]

The manor of *BOYTHORPE* was held by the Bulmer family until 1537,[83] when it was forfeited to the Crown following Sir John Bulmer's participation in the Pilgrimage of Grace.[84] The estate later seems to have been restored to Sir John's son Sir Ralph Bulmer, who died in 1558 leaving it to his three daughters Joan, wife of Francis Cholmeley, Frances, who later married Marmaduke Constable of Cliffe, and Millicent, later wife of Thomas Grey.[85] They apparently shared the manor about 1564 with five illegitimate daughters of Sir Ralph Bulmer[86] and it was divided into eight portions. In 1565 an eighth part was sold by Francis Cholmeley to John Ellerton, who had bought other property in the township from Marmaduke Lacy in 1560.[87] Another eighth part was sold in 1566 by Ralph Williamson to Sir George Bowes and Thomas Grimston. Bowes and Edmund Smithson bought property in Boythorpe from Sampson Norton and Reynold Farley in 1570 and a further eighth part of the manor in 1574 from Thomas Clarke.[88] In 1583 Ralph Grey sold an eighth part to Thomas Peirson and Robert Baitson.[89] In 1594 five eighths of the manor were sold by Thomas Lademan to Christopher Ellerton. Most

---

[46] E 150/232/14.
[47] *L. & P. Hen. VIII*, v, p. 237.
[48] E.R.R.O., DC/53/736.
[49] Ibid. DDHU/10/1 (75).
[50] Registry of Deeds, Beverley, A/115/163; H/204/426; P/43/105.
[51] E.R.R.O., DDHU/7/1.
[52] Regy. of Deeds, 209/184/157.
[53] Ibid. 227/180/149; /183/152; /482/401; 229/220/200; 267/17/15.
[54] *Feud. Aids*, vi. 28, 141.
[55] B.M. Add. MS. 26718, ff. 40d., 43, 60; see below, p. 231.
[56] *Feud. Aids*, vi. 28.
[57] Ibid. 226.
[58] Ibid. 266.
[59] *Yorks. Fines, 1614–25*, 19.
[60] Regy. of Deeds, EO/208/220.
[61] Ibid. /367/354; ES/32/41.
[62] E.R.R.O., DDHU/7/1.
[63] Regy. of Deeds, GG/354/42.
[64] Ibid. IG/389/534; IH/296/376.
[65] Ibid. 134/290/265; 1240/343/310.
[66] *Miscellanea*, iv (Y.A.S. Rec. Ser. xciv), 90.
[67] *Cal. Pat.* 1557–8, 319.
[68] E 310/31/186 f. 110.
[69] *V.C.H. Yorks.* ii. 198, 323.
[70] B. M. Add. Chart. 20550.
[71] *Cal. Close*, 1279–88, 106.
[72] C 132/41/13.
[73] C 138/58/42; *Cal. Close*, 1419–22, 243; *Complete Peerage*, v. 281–2.
[74] *Complete Peerage*, v. 286.
[75] C 142/52/23.
[76] *Whitby Charty.* i (Sur. Soc. lxix), 90.
[77] *E.Y.C.* ii, p. 228; *Bk. of Fees*, ii. 1098.
[78] *Bridlington Charty.* 131.
[79] J.I. 1/1058 m. 1d.
[80] *Feud. Aids*, vi. 28.
[81] Ibid. 168. The head of the Boythorpe family may have been a minor at that time.
[82] *Yorks. Fines, 1327–47*, 6.
[83] *Cal. Inq. p.m.* xv, p. 83; *Yorks. Inq. Hen. IV–V*, 51, 173; *Test. Ebor.* v. 306–19. In 1428 Edmund, Lord Hastings, held the estate, then comprising 20 bovates. He was the second husband of Agnes, former wife of Sir Ralph Bulmer: C 139/82/45; *Feud. Aids*, vi. 266.
[84] E 150/237/28; S.C. 6/Hen. VIII/4335, 4336.
[85] C 142/116/78; W. Flower, *Visit. Yorks.* (Harl. Soc. xvi), 44.
[86] *Collectanea, Topographica et Genealogica*, viii. 71.
[87] *Yorks. Fines*, i. 234, 312.
[88] Ibid. 328, 371; ii. 51.
[89] Ibid. iii. 10.

St. Mary's Church, Bridlington, c. 1853

Flamborough Church: the rood screen and loft

St. Mary's Church, Bridlington: north side of nave

St. Mary's Church, Bridlington: capital from cloisters

Reighton Church: the Norman font

if not all of the manor thus seems to have been acquired by the Ellertons.

The manor was sold in 1616 by John Ellerton to Zachariah Steward[90] and in 1662 another Zachariah Steward sold it to William Lutton.[91] In 1713 John Headlam, whose wife Anne was the daughter of Ralph Lutton, sold it, then consisting of a manor-house and 25 bovates, to Samuel Moor.[92] Moor acquired other property, including 9 bovates from Thomas Condon in 1721[93] and 9 bovates from the devisees of John Mainforth in 1756-7.[94] Moor, by will proved in 1761, devised the manorial estate to David Beilby,[95] who sold it in 1794, then consisting of about 790 a. of closes and 'flats', to Thomas Thornton.[96] His descendant, Edward Thornton Wodehouse, held 694 a. in 1838[97] and the estate was held by that family until the death of Albert Thornton Wodehouse in 1914. It was settled by his trustees in 1949 on C. E. C. Thornton,[98] who sold it in 1958 to G. D. Rivis.[99]

The origin of an estate held by Francis Browne in 1673[1] is not known. In 1769, when it was vested in another Francis Browne, it consisted of 12 bovates, in addition to 70 a. of grassland and 10 a. of arable.[2] It was sold by Francis Browne to Joseph Sykes of West Ella in 1787,[3] and in 1838 Richard Sykes held about 180 a. in Boythorpe, together with 98 a. in Foxholes.[4] The estate, then known as Boythorpe Cottage farm, was sold in 1913 by C. A. V. Sykes to G. H. Burton,[5] in whose family it has since remained.

The Knights Hospitallers held a furlong of land in Boythorpe in 1539-40[6] and this was briefly restored to them in 1558.[7] It was let by the Crown in 1570-1 to Marmaduke Langdale,[8] in 1581 to Henry Harding,[9] and in 1596 to Robert Smith.[10] Nothing further is known of it.

In 1086 there was one estate at Butterwick containing 12 carucates, held by the count of Mortain.[11] The overlordship had passed by the earlier 12th century to the Fossard family.[12] On the marriage of the granddaughter of William Fossard to Peter Mauley, probably in the earlier 13th century,[13] it passed to the Mauleys and is last mentioned in 1517.[14]

Early demesne tenants of this fee were a family which took their name from the township. Durand of Butterwick granted land to Whitby abbey c. 1120-35.[15] In 1255 Ellen, daughter-in-law of Robert of Butterwick, gave him in exchange for land elsewhere a third of the manor of *BUTTERWICK*, except for ½ carucate, which he had probably given as dower on her marriage to his son Thomas.[16] In 1259 Peter de Mauley claimed the custody of Eustace, son and heir of Robert of Butterwick, from William son of Ralph and others.[17] By 1279, however, the manor was held by Ralph son of William,[18] who in 1284-5 had all 12 carucates in Butterwick. He was returned as lord of the township in 1316.[19] In 1346, on the death of Elizabeth, widow of Robert son of Ralph, the estate passed to William, Lord Greystock, Robert's grandson.[20] In 1428 John, Lord Greystock, held 10 carucates in Butterwick.[21] The manor was held by the Greystock family until the death of Lord Greystock in 1487. He was succeeded by his granddaughter Elizabeth who married Lord Dacre of Gillesland.[22]

In 1569 George, Lord Dacre of Gillesland and Greystock, was succeeded by his three sisters.[23] His property was divided in 1586, Butterwick manor passing to Elizabeth, wife of William, Lord Howard.[24] The manor descended in the Howard family until the early 19th century. Charles Howard was made earl of Carlisle in 1661[25] and Frederick, earl of Carlisle, was awarded 1,007 a. in Butterwick at the inclosure of 1774; he also had 49 a. of old inclosures.[26] In 1808 he sold the estate, consisting of 1,079 a., to William Beverley,[27] who sold it in 1820 to Dorothy Langley.[28] On the death of Marmaduke Langley in 1851 the estate passed to his nephew W. H. Dawnay, 7th Viscount Downe.[29] In 1892 Sir Hugh Dawnay, the 8th viscount, gave 898 a. in Butterwick to his son Eustace Dawnay,[30] who sold it in 1901 to C. E. Fox.[31] Fox died in 1919[32] and the following year his executors sold the estate in separate lots, including Manor House farm, of 556 a., to J. W. Bannister.[33] The remainder of the Downe estate was given by Sir Hugh Dawnay in 1909 to his eldest son John Dawnay,[34] who sold it in 1920 as a 513-acre farm to Christopher Jackson.[35]

The Bard family held an estate in Butterwick from at least the late 13th century.[36] At the death of Durand Bard in 1376 his coheirs were his sisters Isabel and Alice.[37] Isabel married Robert Martin and in 1411 they obtained the Butterwick estate by agreement with Alice and her husband John

---

[90] *Yorks. Fines, 1614-25*, 56.
[91] C.P. 25(2)/752/14 Chas. II. Trin. no. 39.
[92] Regy. of Deeds, E/177/306.
[93] Ibid. H/206/431.
[94] Ibid. Z/7/14; /222/508; /231/532; /432/991; AB/37/82.
[95] Ibid. AD/93/232.
[96] Ibid. BS/499/710; see below, p. 195.
[97] E.R.R.O., TA. Foxholes.
[98] Regy. of Deeds, 1118/140/129.
[99] Ibid. /143/130.
[1] B.I.H.R., C.P., H. 2905.
[2] Regy. of Deeds, AM/175/289; /176/290.
[3] Ibid. BM/266/439.
[4] E.R.R.O., TA. Foxholes.
[5] Regy. of Deeds, 151/340/280.
[6] *Miscellanea*, iv. 90.
[7] *Cal. Pat.* 1557-8, 319.
[8] E 310/31/186 no. 110.
[9] E 310/27/163 no. 71.
[10] E 310/27/159 no. 100.
[11] *V.C.H. Yorks.* ii. 226.
[12] *E.Y.C.* ii, pp. 331, 359, 378.
[13] J. W. Clay, *Ext. & Dorm. Peerages of N. Counties*, 133.
[14] C 142/32/7.
[15] *E.Y.C.* ii, p. 378.
[16] *Yorks. Fines, 1246-72*, 194.
[17] K.B. 26/162 m. 14d.
[18] *Cal. Inq. p.m.* ii, p. 172; *Plac. de Quo Warr.* 191.
[19] *Feud. Aids*, vi. 28, 168.
[20] C 134/82/2; *Cal. Close*, 1313-18, 489; *Complete Peerage*, vi. 192.
[21] *Feud. Aids*, vi. 267.
[22] *Cal. Inq. p.m.* x, p. 421; xiv, p. 30; *Cal. Close*, 1402-5, 202; Burke, *Dorm. & Ext. Peerages*, 254.
[23] Burke, *Dorm. & Ext. Peerages*, 254.
[24] *Household Bks. of Lord William Howard* (Sur. Soc. lxviii), 396.
[25] *Complete Peerage*, iii. 34.
[26] Regy. of Deeds, AT/79/10.
[27] Ibid. CO/63/105.
[28] Ibid. DH/184/216.
[29] J. T. Ward, *E. Yorks. Landed Estates in the 19th Cent.* (E. Yorks. Loc. Hist. Ser. xxiii), 28.
[30] Regy. of Deeds, 54/400/364 (1892); Burke, *Peerage* (1963), 755.
[31] Regy. of Deeds, 35/465/439 (1901).
[32] Ibid. 203/319/280.
[33] Ibid. 207/252/223; /290/258.
[34] Ibid. 111/107/97.
[35] Ibid. 213/470/404.
[36] *Yorks. Fines, 1272-1300*, 30.
[37] C 136/35/8.

Houghton.[38] In 1428 Robert Martin held 20 bovates in Butterwick.[39] The further descent of this estate is not known but it may be identifiable with that of 17 bovates sold in 1682 by Michael Wharton to Thomas Condon.[40] In 1721 he or another Thomas Condon sold 21½ bovates to Thomas Boreman,[41] whose estate passed between 1740 and 1770 to William Simpson.[42] By 1774 it had passed to William Ness, who received 326 a. at inclosure that year.[43] In 1814 Ness sold the estate to the Revd. Francis Blackburne,[44] who sold it in 1820 to Dorothy Langley.[45] It subsequently descended with Butterwick manor.[46]

Durand of Butterwick gave a carucate of the Fossard fee in Butterwick to Whitby abbey c. 1120–35.[47] In 1227 the abbot granted this land to Robert of Butterwick[48] and it seems to have subsequently descended with Butterwick manor.[49] Durand of Butterwick also gave ½ carucate in Butterwick to St. Mary's abbey, York, between 1122 and c. 1137.[50] Nothing more is known of this land but it may be that which later formed the endowment of the church.[51] Two tofts and pasture for 60 sheep, 3 cows, a horse, and 6 swine in Butterwick were given to St. Peter's, later St. Leonard's, hospital, York,[52] between 1160 and 1175 by Durand of Butterwick.[53] The property was granted by the Crown in 1568 to Percival Bowes and John Moyser.[54] In 1539–40 the Knights Hospitallers held property in Butterwick called St. John Croft.[55] It was briefly restored to them in 1558,[56] and was let by the Crown to Marmaduke Langdale in 1570–1.[57]

ECONOMIC HISTORY. There is scanty information about medieval tenants and their holdings in any of the townships, but more is known for the 16th century. In 1531 Boythorpe manor comprised 4 bovates held freely, 2 held by tenants-at-will, and 26 of demesne, which were let out.[58] There were also two free tenants in 1537 who held land in Boythorpe of Butterwick manor. Butterwick then comprised 18 bovates held by free tenants, 24 of demesne held at lease, and 49 held by 8 tenants-at-will.[59] In 1563 there were 5 freeholders at Butterwick, one of whom held 16 bovates, 2 held one bovate each, and 2 held only cottages and crofts. Nine tenants-at-will then held 74 bovates, one man having the manor-house, some closes, and 26 bovates of demesne. Of the others one man held 14 bovates, one held 13, one held 8, 2 held 6 each, and 2 had cottages and crofts. The rents of the tenants-at-will amounted to about £20, nearly the whole value of the manor.[60] At Foxholes the smaller tenants included grassmen in the 17th century. One was mentioned in 1630,[61] and 'grass people' were forbidden to carry away whins from the open fields in 1669.[62]

In 1669 by-laws dealt with the management of the 'cornfield' of Foxholes township,[63] and in the late 17th century at least some of the open-field strips there still seem to have been regularly dispersed. In 1685 the vicarial glebe lay 'all over and in every fall throughout the fields'.[64] South field is mentioned in 1716[65] and East field in 1720.[66] In 1850, after inclosure, areas of the parish were known as South, East, and Whin fields, the last-named in the north-east.[67] The size of the open fields is first revealed in 1777, when there were 44 bovates of tithable land and 4 of glebe.[68] Each of the 29 bovates of the Osbaldeston estate in 1835 contained 31 a.[69]

At Butterwick in 1563 there were two fields, North and South, containing together 100 bovates, each of about 7 a. The fields each contained about 350 a. and most tenants' holdings were divided equally between the two.[70] In 1716 the glebe lay dispersed regularly in every furlong throughout the fields.[71] At inclosure in 1774 allotments totalling 842 a. were made from North field and 794 a. from South field.[72] In 1563 it was said that the soil of the township was good for corn, which the inhabitants sold to near-by towns.[73] At Boythorpe in the early 13th century 2 bovates lay 'towards the sun' and another lay near 'Selandes'.[74] The town field was mentioned in 1721.[75] By 1787, when the township was already partly inclosed,[76] there were two fields called Low and North fields.[77]

Several of the by-laws made in 1669 and 1688 concern pasturage in the open fields and commons of Foxholes. The stint for each house was one beast-gate in the 'pasture' and for each bovate one beast-gate, 20 sheep-gates, and either one horse- or 2 beast-gates in the Horse pasture. Each cottager had a beast-gate and 10 sheep-gates. Whins, forbidden to 'grass people', were allowed without limit to those receiving parochial relief.[78] On several occasions in the 1690s shepherds from neighbouring parishes were fined for trespassing in the Beast pasture.[79] In 1720 a strip in the open field, described as a 'rood-broadland', probably situated in the north-east of the township, was said to be 'old swarth'.[80] In 1840 a holding of 27½ bovates had 30 beast-gates and 665 sheep-gates, one of 9½ bovates had 9½ beast- and 260 sheep-gates, one of 3 bovates had 3 beast- and 108 sheep-gates, and one of ½ acre had ½ beast- and 20 sheep-gates.[81] In 1850 the name Beast pasture was

---

[38] C.P. 25(1)/279/152 no. 40.
[39] *Feud. Aids*, vi. 267.
[40] E.R.R.O., DDGR/29/2.
[41] Regy. of Deeds, H/301/631.
[42] Ibid. R/50/118; AO/88/84.
[43] Ibid. AT/79/10; AU/340/548; /342/550.
[44] Ibid. CX/358/442.
[45] Ibid. DK/47/57.   [46] See p. 193.
[47] *E.Y.C.* ii, p. 378; *Whitby Charty.* i. 5, 64.
[48] *Whitby Charty.* i. 668.   [49] See p. 193.
[50] *E.Y.C.* ii, p. 379.   [51] See p. 196.
[52] *V.C.H.Yorks.* iii. 336.
[53] *E.Y.C.* ii, p. 380.
[54] *Cal. Pat.* 1566–9, 281.
[55] *Miscellanea*, iv. 94.
[56] *Cal. Pat.* 1557–8, 319.
[57] E 310/31/186 no. 110.
[58] S.C. 6/Hen. VIII/4335.
[59] Castle Howard MS., Box 24, Survey of Estates, 1537.
[60] Ibid. 1563.
[61] B.I.H.R., Prob. Reg. xli, f. 330.
[62] E.R.R.O., DDHU/10/78.
[63] Ibid.
[64] B.I.H.R., TER. J. Foxholes 1685.
[65] Ibid. 1716.
[66] Registry of Deeds, Beverley, G/425/922.
[67] O.S. Map 6" (1854).
[68] E.R.R.O., DDHB/57/157.
[69] Ibid. DDHU/17/13.
[70] Castle Howard MS., Box 24, Survey of Estates, 1563.
[71] B.I.H.R., TER. J. Foxholes 1716.
[72] Regy. of Deeds, AT/79/10.
[73] Castle Howard MS., Box 24, Survey of Estates, 1563.
[74] B.M. Add. Chart. 20550.
[75] Regy. of Deeds, H/206/431.   [76] See p. 195.
[77] Regy. of Deeds, BM/266/439.
[78] E.R.R.O., DDHU/10/1 (80), 78.
[79] Ibid. /1 (92), 19, 31, 44.
[80] Regy. of Deeds, G/425/922.
[81] E.R.R.O., DDHU/7/1.

given to the area north of the village near the parish boundary.[82]

A holding in Butterwick between 1160 and c. 1175 included pasturage for 60 sheep, 3 cows, a horse, and 6 swine.[83] There seems to have been little permanent grassland in the township, however, before inclosure. In 1563 the inhabitants were said to have no other pasture 'but as they cut off a corner of their field of their arable land'. They had no 'sheep pasture or common moors or heaths but only the common arable land fields . . . as they lay them'. The soil of the township was said to be unsuitable for pasture and meadow and the inhabitants bought most of their hay.[84] About 1770 there were 6 houses and 14 cottages with common rights in Butterwick. The stint was 20 sheep and 2 beasts for each house, 10 sheep and one beast for each cottage, and 10 sheep and one beast for each bovate. Horses were pastured in South field until 1 August and afterwards in North field.[85]

There is some evidence of early inclosure in the parish. In 1376 John of Middleton had enough inclosed land at Foxholes to provide pasture for 6 horses, 12 cows, 12 swine, and 200 sheep.[86] In 1531 Edward Goldsborough held three closes there, containing 10 a. of pasture.[87] In Butterwick in 1563 four demesne closes contained 14 a.[88] and in 1774 there were 68 a. of old inclosure in the township.[89] Although by the later 18th century Boythorpe was owned by only two proprietors, much of their land remained uninclosed. Some inclosure had taken place by 1769, when the Browne estate included, in addition to open-field land, 4 pasture closes, a 70-acre field called the intake, and 10 a. of arable called Cold Mebb.[90] There was still uninclosed land in the township in 1787, but by 1794 the manorial estate consisted of 790 a. of closes and 'flats', the latter being groups of consolidated strips in the fields. By 1805 the 790 a. were said to lie entirely in closes.[91]

The remaining open-field area of Foxholes was inclosed in 1840,[92] under the general Inclosure Act of 1836.[93] In all 1,540 a. were allotted. Bertram Osbaldeston-Mitford, lord of the manor, received 927 a., and the rector was allotted 115 a. for his glebe. Three other men received substantial allotments: David Taylor 265 a., Charles Ringrose 108 a., and Richard Sykes 98 a. There were five allotments of 10 a. or under. The open fields of Butterwick were inclosed in 1774,[94] under an Act of 1771,[95] and 1,636 a. were allotted. The earl of Carlisle, lord of the manor, received 1,007 a., the rector of Foxholes 287 a. for glebe and tithes and 15 a. for his freehold, William Ness 326 a., and there was an allotment of an acre.

In 1794 the earl of Carlisle's South farm in Butterwick contained 320 a. of sheep-walk and whins, on which were kept 300–360 sheep, and only 140 a. of arable.[96] In 1801 564 a. in the parish were under crops, mainly oats (197 a.), rape or turnips (124 a.), and barley (118 a.).[97] The amount of land under arable may have increased by 1838, when 2,364 a. were cultivated in Foxholes and Boythorpe alone. There were then only 75 a. of permanent grass and 10 a. of woodland.[98] In 1850 a large area of whins lay in the valley bottoms in the north and south of the township.[99] In 1905 there were 2,093 a. of arable and 188 a. of grassland in Foxholes and Boythorpe, and 1,422 a. of arable, 225 a. of grassland, and 59 a. of woodland in Butterwick.[1] There have been from 3 to 5 farmers in Foxholes in the 19th and 20th centuries, always 2 in Boythorpe, and usually 4 in Butterwick.[2] Many of the farms were large. In 1795, for example, two owned by the earl of Carlisle in Butterwick were of 576 a. and 475 a.[3] and two in Foxholes sold by Robert Osbaldeston-Mitford in 1920 were of over 400 a.[4] In 1937 only one farm in the parish had an acreage of less than 150.[5]

There was a firm of machine-makers and wheelwrights in Foxholes by 1840,[6] presumably occupying the iron foundry which stood at the north end of the village in 1850.[7] Three cast-iron grave slabs in the churchyard, two dated 1847 and one 1862, were probably made at the foundry.[8] Later in the century it was described as an iron and brass foundry and a machine manufactory. It was owned by Robert Hall at least from 1872 to 1893, but by 1897 it had been taken over by John Scruton and named Providence foundry;[9] the Scrutons have owned it ever since. At the beginning of the 20th century it produced waggons and carts, in addition to agricultural machinery, and it remained in use until c. 1942. Blacksmith's and joiner's shops were attached to the foundry. About 1942 these, together with the furnace and castings shop and the moulder's shop, were demolished and new workshops, show-rooms, and offices were built on the site for the agricultural engineering business which replaced the foundry.[10] A house and one workshop, dating from the later 19th century, were all that remained of the earlier buildings in 1970.

A mill is first recorded in Foxholes in 1302[11] and there was a windmill in 1614.[12] Mill hill is mentioned in 1716.[13] Butterwick manor had a dilapidated windmill in 1359.[14] The windmill there in 1563 was said to stand in North field.[15] A mill is first recorded in Boythorpe in 1328 and there was a windmill in 1616.[16] In 1713 the manor included a windmill hill, with multure and toll.[17]

[82] O.S. Map 6" (1854.)
[83] E.Y.C. ii, p. 380.
[84] Castle Howard MS., Box 24, Survey of Estates, 1563.
[85] Information kindly provided by Dr. A. Harris, citing Castle Howard MS., Box 11, Parcel 95, Butterwick inclosure papers.
[86] Cal. Pat. 1374–77, 414.
[87] L. & P. Hen. VIII, v, p. 237.
[88] Castle Howard MS., Box 24, Survey of Estates, 1563.
[89] Regy. of Deeds, AT/79/10.
[90] Ibid. AM/175/289.
[91] Ibid. BM/266/439; BS/499/710; CK/241/415.
[92] E.R.R.O., PR 15 (award and map).
[93] 6 & 7 Wm. IV, c. 115.
[94] Regy. of Deeds, AT/79/10.
[95] 11 Geo. III, c. 95 (Priv. Act).
[96] E.R.R.O., DDHB/57/192; A. Harris, Rural Landscape of E.R. Yorks. 87.
[97] 1801 Crop Returns.
[98] E.R.R.O., TA. Foxholes.
[99] O.S. Map 6" (1854).
[1] Acreage Returns, 1905.
[2] Directories.
[3] E.R.R.O., DDHB/57/199.
[4] Regy. of Deeds, 209/184/157.
[5] Kelly's Dir. N. & E.R. Yorks. (1937), 436, 464.
[6] White, Dir. E. & N.R. Yorks. (1840), 387.
[7] O.S. Map 6" (1854).
[8] Two of these were removed in 1971.
[9] Directories.
[10] Ex inf. Mr. K. Scruton, Foxholes, 1970.
[11] Yorks. Fines, 1300–14, 19.
[12] Ibid. 1614–25, 19.
[13] B.I.H.R., TER. J. Foxholes 1716.
[14] Cal. Inq. p.m. x, p. 421.
[15] Castle Howard MS., Box 24, Survey of Estates, 1563.
[16] Yorks. Fines, 1327–47, 6; 1614–25, 56.
[17] Regy. of Deeds, E/177/306.

LOCAL GOVERNMENT. There are surviving court records of the Osbaldeston manor in Foxholes for several years between 1669 and 1694[18] and for the period 1792–1847.[19] Matters dealt with in the 17th century include the usual agricultural offences and minor affrays. In 1694 2 bylawmen and 2 surveyors of highways were appointed, and in the late 18th and early 19th centuries the officers sworn were usually 2 affeerors, 2 bylawmen, a pinder, and a constable. After 1818 no bylawmen were appointed. until they briefly reappeared in 1828 and 1829. A constable continued to be appointed until 1842 and the pinder and affeerors until 1847. No presentments were made by the jury in the late 18th and early 19th centuries.

A manorial court at Butterwick is first mentioned in 1365.[20] In 1359 a common oven belonging to the manor was in the hands of the tenants,[21] perhaps as a result of disruption caused by the Black Death. By 1563 the tenants' obligation to use it seems to have been commuted to an 'oven farm', which was worth a total of about 5s. a year. The tenants-at-will each paid between 2d. and 4d. a year and two freeholders paid 7d. and 2s.[22]

Records of the earl of Carlisle's court at Butterwick survive for the period 1744–1849.[23] A constable was appointed regularly until 1841 and a deputy constable as well from 1837 to 1841. Two bylawmen were appointed in 1766, 1770, and 1817, and 2 affeerors from 1831 to 1836. A pinder was appointed from 1817 to 1846. In most years the jury had nothing to present. In 1821 the surveyors of highways of Helperthorpe, East and West Lutton, and Duggleby were fined at the court for diverting the Gypsey Race through the streets of their villages and permitting its pollution. Similar cases were presented in 1826. Encroachments on waste land were also dealt with in the 1820s and 1830s.

No parochial records before 1835 are known. In 1836 Foxholes joined the Driffield union.[24]

CHURCHES. Foxholes church was mentioned c. 1100–15, when it was given by Geoffrey Bainard, together with Burton Agnes church on which it was then dependent, to St. Mary's abbey, York.[25] There is no later reference to its dependence on Burton Agnes. Later evidence shows that whatever Bainard's gift may originally have implied it came in practice to be limited to the advowson and a pension of £8. The benefice income was further abated by the gift before 1170 by Henry of Boythorpe's father of two-thirds of the corn tithes on the Boythorpe demesne.[26] The rest of the tithe belonged to the rector. The living was always treated as a rectory and no vicarage was ordained. The chapel of Butterwick, traceable from between 1122 and c. 1137, was for long dependent on Foxholes.[27]

The advowson of Foxholes was held by St. Mary's abbey until the Dissolution.[28] It was granted by the Crown in 1595 to John Wells and Henry Best[29] and by 1596 it had passed to Sir Thomas Crompton, who sold it that year to his brother-in-law Sir William Gee.[30] It was held by the Gee family until 1768, when Roger Gee sold it to the Revd. Henry Foord.[31] It was sold c. 1782 by Barnard Foord to Joseph Sykes of West Ella, who presented in 1783.[32] In 1894 C. P. Sykes sold it to the Revd. Joseph Chapelow and he the following year to the Revd. William Roberts.[33] Roberts died in 1933 and in 1935 it was vested in Keble College, Oxford,[34] the patron in 1967–8.[35]

The tithes of Foxholes and Butterwick were let by St. Mary's abbey between 1161 and 1184 to William son of Richard.[36] The rectory was worth £26 13s. 4d. in 1291, reduced to £18 in the new taxation; outgoings were £8 to St. Mary's abbey and £1 to Whitby abbey.[37] In 1309 the rectory was said to be worth £28,[38] and in 1535 its value was about £22 net; £8 was still paid to St. Mary's.[39] In 1650 the rectory, including Butterwick, was worth £120 a year[40] and in 1777 £430.[41] In 1829–31 the average net income, excluding Butterwick, was £531 a year.[42]

The tithes on the Boythorpe demesne, which were confirmed to Whitby abbey before 1170,[43] were in 1264 let by Whitby to Bridlington priory. They were worth £1 in 1308,[44] and in 1535 the rector paid 12s. to the priory in lieu of them.[45] That rent was granted by the Crown in 1549 to Edward Pease and James Wilson.[46] The remainder of the tithes belonged to the rector. In 1774 those in Butterwick were commuted at inclosure for 237 a.,[47] and in 1838 those in Foxholes and Boythorpe were commuted for a rent-charge of £410.[48]

In 1685 the rector had 4 bovates of glebe in both Foxholes and Butterwick.[49] He was allotted 50 a. in Butterwick in 1774 and 115 a. at the inclosure of Foxholes in 1840.[50] In 1942 297 a. of glebe in Butterwick were sold to Keble College, Oxford, and in 1950 121 a. in Foxholes were sold to George Wadsworth.[51]

The first reference to a rectory house at Foxholes is in 1685.[52] It was said to have been rebuilt c. 1716,[53]

---

[18] E.R.R.O., DDHU/10/1 (75, 86, 92), 19, 20, 25, 27, 31, 34, 37, 41, 44, 78.
[19] Ibid. /66.
[20] Cal. Pat. 1364–7, 137.
[21] Cal. Inq. p.m. x, p. 421.
[22] Castle Howard MS., Box 24, Survey of Estates, 1563.
[23] N.R.R.O., ZDS/Manorial: Wykeham, call rolls and court papers of Butterwick manor, 1751–1850.
[24] 3rd Rep. Poor Law Com. 168.
[25] E.Y.C. i, p. 273; ii, p. 33.
[26] Whitby Charty. i (Sur. Soc. lxix), 4, 90.
[27] See p. 197.
[28] Fasti Parochiales, iii. 35–7.
[29] E.R.R.O., DDKE/5/1.
[30] Ibid. DDCB/4/91; J. Foster, Pedigrees of . . . Yorks. iii, sub Gee, of Bishop Burton. See also Yorks. Fines, 1603–14, 43.
[31] E.R.R.O., DDKE/5/12.
[32] Ibid. /21–22.
[33] Registry of Deeds, Beverley, 71/192/183; 72/443/42 (1895).
[34] Ibid. 495/616/480; 523/414/327.
[35] Crockford.
[36] B.M. Stowe Ch. 444.
[37] Tax. Eccl. (Rec. Com.), 304, 326.
[38] Cal. Papal Regs. ii. 59.
[39] Valor Eccl. (Rec. Com.), v. 126.
[40] T.E.R.A.S. ii. 57.
[41] E.R.R.O., DDHB/57/157.
[42] Rep. Com. Eccl. Revenues, 934–5.
[43] See above.
[44] Whitby Charty. ii (Sur. Soc. lxxii), 472, 628.
[45] Valor Eccl. v. 126.
[46] Cal. Pat. 1549–51, 45.
[47] Regy. of Deeds, AT/79/10.
[48] E.R.R.O., TA. Foxholes.
[49] B.I.H.R., TER. J. Foxholes 1685.
[50] E.R.R.O., DDHU/7/1; Regy. of Deeds, AT/79/10.
[51] Regy. of Deeds, 652/521/446; 849/406/338.
[52] B.I.H.R., TER. J. Foxholes 1685. A late-13th-cent. reference to 'hostium ecclesiae de Butterwick', meaning the church door, is wrongly translated in Yorks. Deeds, x. 38, as 'the house of the church'.
[53] Lawton, Rer. Eccles. Dioc. Ebor. 299.

and in 1764 it contained two rooms 'on a floor' and was thatched. By 1770 the house was tiled, and in 1781 it was said to consist of two parlours, a kitchen, and a back kitchen. It was thus a single-storeyed building. By 1819, after having been 'greatly added to and improved by the late rector', the Rectory contained three ground-floor rooms, in addition to the kitchen, and eight bedrooms with garrets above.[54] The house, which stands near the church, was sold by the rector in 1946 to George Wadsworth,[55] who renamed it Foxholes Manor.[56] It is of red brick and three storeys high, and the principal front is five bays long with a central porch.

A church at Butterwick was probably granted to St. Mary's abbey, along with that at Foxholes, but the first certain reference is between 1122 and c. 1137, when it was described as a chapel belonging to Foxholes church.[57] There is mention of the churchyard in 1563[58] and from the late 17th century at least it also had marriage rights,[59] but Butterwick remained a chapelry of Foxholes until 1858, when it was made a separate ecclesiastical parish and deemed a vicarage.[60] In 1947 the parishes of Foxholes and Butterwick were united.[61]

In 1184–9 Robert son of Durand of Butterwick confirmed his father's gift to St. Mary's abbey of the advowson of Butterwick.[62] It was presumably retained by the abbey until the Dissolution, and subsequently passed into the possession of the rector of Foxholes. Certainly by 1823 the rector was patron[63] and the advowson thereafter descended like that of Foxholes.

In 1525–6 the chaplain at Butterwick received a stipend of £4.[64] The chapelry was awarded £200 from Queen Anne's Bounty in each of the years 1790, 1791, 1811, 1812, and 1813 and a parliamentary grant of the same amount in 1810.[65] In 1829–31 the average net income of the chapelry was £47, out of which the curate received a stipend of £20.[66] The net value in 1884 was £58.[67]

Between 1817 and 1825 Bounty money was used to buy 10 a. of glebe in Beverley.[68] In 1685 a vacant house-plot belonged to Butterwick chapelry. Between 1781 and 1786 a chalk cottage with a thatched roof was erected by the rector. It still stood in 1825[69] but in 1835 there was said to be no glebe house at Butterwick[70] and there is no later evidence of one.

Land in Boythorpe, which had been given for a lamp in Foxholes church, and land in Foxholes, given to support an obit, was granted by the Crown in 1571 to Francis Barker and Thomas Browne.[71]

Several medieval rectors were pluralists and were non-resident. In 1295 the rector also held the living of Kirkby in Cleveland (Yorks. N.R.),[72] and in 1309 another rector was permitted to hold two other benefices and to be non-resident for three years while in the king's service.[73] The succeeding rector was licensed to be absent on several occasions between 1328 and 1340, and in 1340 he was licensed to farm the church during his absence. His successor was given leave of absence in 1357 and 1360.[74] In 1527 the rector also held Slingsby (Yorks. N.R.), in 1535 the sub-treasurership of York Minster, and in 1546 the prebend of Apesthorpe in the minster. He retained all three, together with Foxholes, until his death in 1553.[75]

Between 1122 and c. 1137 St. Mary's abbey, in recognition of ½ carucate of land given by Durand of Butterwick, agreed that a priest should perpetually celebrate in Butterwick chapel.[76] In 1525–6 there was a chaplain at Butterwick.[77]

In 1742 the rector of Foxholes received permission to hold the vicarage of Weaverthorpe, and he also held the curacy of Butterwick.[78] Both before and after it was made a separate living in 1858, however, Butterwick was usually held separately from Foxholes.[79] In 1835 the rector was also vicar of Seamer (Yorks. N.R.),[80] but later rectors seem to have been resident and to have held no other livings. In 1835 the curate of Butterwick also held the curacy of North Dalton[81] and in 1871 the vicar of Butterwick was also the assistant chaplain at Scarborough gaol. He was non-resident in 1877,[82] and in 1884 and 1892 he lived at Weaverthorpe, where he held the vicarage.[83] In 1894 it was said of Butterwick that 'for all practical and parochial purposes this parish is linked with Weaverthorpe'.[84] Since 1896, however, the livings of Foxholes and Butterwick have been held together.[85] In 1970 the rector was also vicar of, and resident at, Ganton.

In the course of a tithe dispute in 1678 the defendant referred to Caleb Wilkinson, the rector, as a 'presbyterian rascal'.[86]

A service was held at Foxholes each Sunday in 1743 and communion was administered four times a year. Between 20 and 30 people had received the previous Easter.[87] By 1865 two services were held each Sunday and communion was administered six times a year to 14–15 people.[88] By 1871 communion was received monthly by about 18 people[89] and by 1884 twice a month by 12–14 people.[90] At Butterwick a service was held each Sunday in 1743 and communion was administered four times a year.[91] In 1865, when no services were being held, it was

---

[54] B.I.H.R., TER. J. Foxholes 1764, 1770, 1781, 1819.
[55] Regy. of Deeds, 734/17/15.
[56] Local inf.
[57] E.Y.C. ii, p. 379.
[58] Castle Howard MS., Box 24, Survey of Estates, 1563.
[59] B.I.H.R., TER. J. Butterwick 1685 etc.
[60] Bulmer, Dir. E. Yorks. (1892), 158.
[61] York Dioc. Regy., Orders in Council 690.
[62] E.Y.C. ii, p. 381.
[63] Baines, Hist. Yorks. (1823), ii. 185.
[64] Y.A.J. xxiv. 65.
[65] Hodgson, Q.A.B. 436.
[66] Rep. Com. Eccl. Revenues, 924–5.
[67] B.I.H.R., Bp. V. 1884/Ret.
[68] Ibid., TER. J. Butterwick 1825.
[69] Ibid. Butterwick 1685, 1825; Foxholes 1781, 1786.
[70] Rep. Com. Eccl. Revenues, 924–5.
[71] Cal. Pat. 1569–72, 237.
[72] Fasti Parochiales, iii. 36.
[73] Cal. Papal Regs. ii. 59.
[74] Fasti Parochiales, iii. 37.
[75] Y.A.J. xxxvi. 247.
[76] E.Y.C. ii, p. 379.
[77] Y.A.J. xxiv. 78.
[78] Herring's Visit. i. 215.
[79] B.I.H.R., V. 1865/Ret. 98, 192; V. 1871/Ret. 94, 175; V. 1877/Ret.; Bp. V. 1884/Ret.; Baines, Hist. Yorks. (1823), ii. 185; Sheahan and Whellan, Hist. York & E.R. ii. 475.
[80] Rep. Com. Eccl. Revenues, 934–5.
[81] Ibid. 924–5.
[82] B.I.H.R., V. 1871/Ret. 94; V. 1877/Ret.
[83] Ibid., Bp. V. 1884/Ret.; Bulmer, Dir. E. Yorks. (1892), 158.
[84] B.I.H.R., Bp. V. 1894/Ret.
[85] Kelly's Dir. N. & E.R. Yorks. (1897), 434 and later directories.
[86] B.I.H.R., C.P., H. 3332.
[87] Herring's Visit. i. 215.
[88] B.I.H.R., V. 1865/Ret. 192.
[89] Ibid., V. 1871/Ret. 175.
[90] Ibid., Bp. V. 1884/Ret.
[91] Herring's Visit. i. 114.

reported that the living had been vacant since *c.* 1861 and that the service had been taken in the mean time by the curate of Langtoft.[92] By 1871 there was again a weekly service and communion was received about five times a year by six people.[93] By 1884 communion was administered monthly.[94] In 1970 a service was held each week at Foxholes and fortnightly at Butterwick.

The church of ST. MARY, Foxholes, was completely rebuilt in 1866[95] and consists of nave, apsidal chancel, north aisle, south porch, and south-west bell-turret. Its predecessor, described in 1856 as a 'small ancient building', consisted of nave and chancel separated by 'a fine Norman arch' and had a west door and a small bell-turret.[96] It had been extensively restored in 1785.[97] The new building of 1866 was designed in the Norman style by G. Fowler Jones.[98] It is mainly of sandstone, with limestone dressings. The aisle arcade consists of three round arches on round pillars of Mansfield stone. Before 1877 a dado of glazed Minton tiles was inserted in the chancel.[99] The four chancel windows contain coloured glass by Capronnier of Brussels.[1] The three aisle windows were inserted in 1916, 1917, and 1919, the earliest as a memorial to a 'hostile air raid'. There are three earlier-19th-century monuments to the Sykes and Foord families.

In 1552 the church contained two bells[2] and there were still two before the rebuilding in 1866.[3] Two new bells were cast in that year by J. Taylor & Co. of Loughborough. One of the old bells, made in 1710 by E. Seller of York, was also retained.[4] The plate includes a cup, made in London in 1720 by William Gamble and given by the rector in 1768, and a chalice, paten, and flagon, all made in London in 1866 and given by the rector in that year.[5] The registers of baptisms and burials begin in 1654 and that of marriages in 1655. With the exception of entries of baptisms in 1686-8 and of marriages in 1685-8, they are complete.[6]

The church of ST. NICHOLAS, Butterwick, is a small plain building of stone and consists of structurally undivided nave and chancel, with a south porch and a west bellcot. Little remains of the Norman church. A break in the masonry of both the north and south walls occurs about 30 ft. from the west end, to the west of which the walls are apparently Norman work. Some of the external masonry in the west wall, however, may have been renewed in the 14th century. The Norman font stands on its original circular base and is ornamented with arcading and a cable-moulding. Traces of a Norman chancel arch were revealed during the late-19th-century restoration and several carved stones and corbels of Norman date were found beneath the floor, many of them remaining in the church in 1970. A stone with chevron ornamentation is built into a short buttress in the middle of the west wall; the buttress was described in 1882 as 'modern'.[7]

The church was partly rebuilt probably in the 14th century and there are two much restored windows of that date in the south wall, together with a blocked lancet at a lower level. There are no windows in the north or west walls. In the chancel are a plain piscina and an aumbry and there is a low wide round-headed tomb recess in the north wall. The church had a 'steeple' in 1552[8] and also in 1786, when it was wooden,[9] but it was replaced in the late 18th or early 19th century by a small brick bellcot.

The church was thoroughly restored by G. Fowler Jones in 1882,[10] when the east end was largely rebuilt. A square-headed three-light east window was inserted and a south doorway and porch were built, all in the Perpendicular style. The mullions and tracery of the nave windows were renewed, the bellcot was repaired, and the church was newly floored, plastered, and pewed.

During the restoration the recumbent effigy of a knight was discovered beneath the floor. The figure, which probably represents Robert FitzRalph, Lord Grimthorpe and Greystock (d. 1317), is dressed in a long surcoat and carries a shield on which faint traces of the arms of Grimthorpe were formerly discernible. The legs are crossed and the feet rest on a dog and an angel. The monument, which is attributed to a Lincoln workshop, may have originally lain in the tomb recess. In her will of 1346 Elizabeth of Greystock, wife of Robert FitzRalph, asked to be buried in the church.[11] There is also an elaborate late-13th-century coffin-lid with a dogtooth border and a sword, shield, and vines carved in relief.[12]

There were two bells in 1552[13] and later.[14] The plate includes a silver cup and cover made in 1662 by William Waite of York.[15] Until the late 18th century Butterwick entries were included in the Foxholes parish registers. Separate registers begin in 1796 for baptisms, 1799 for marriages, and 1801 for burials.[16]

NONCONFORMITY. There were two protestant dissenters in Foxholes in 1676[17] but none was reported in the parish in 1743.[18] Houses were licensed for nonconformist worship at Foxholes in 1811, 1816, 1818, and 1828 and at Butterwick in 1765 and 1817 (two).[19] A chapel was built in Foxholes by the Wesleyan Methodists in 1820[20] and rebuilt,

---

[92] B.I.H.R., V. 1865/Ret. 98. [93] Ibid., V. 1871/Ret. 94.
[94] Ibid., Bp. V. 1884/Ret.
[95] Ibid., V. 1868/Ret.; Churches index.
[96] Sheahan and Whellan, *Hist. York & E.R.* ii. 475.
[97] B.I.H.R., FAC. 1777/3.
[98] Ibid., V. 1868/Ret.; Churches index.
[99] Ibid., V. 1877/Ret.
[1] Par. rec. in church, Revd. W. Roberts, 'Notes on Hist. of Foxholes with Boythorpe and Butterwick'.
[2] *Inventories of Ch. Goods*, 22.
[3] B.I.H.R., Churches index.
[4] Boulter, 'Ch. Bells', 217. [5] *Yorks. Ch. Plate*, i. 251–2.
[6] Barley, *Par. Docs. E.R.* 51. In 1970 the earlier registers were in E.R.R.O., PR. 2736–9; the later registers remain in the church.
[7] Par. rec. in church, newspaper cutting in register of baptisms, 1796–1812.
[8] *Inventories of Ch. Goods*, 25.
[9] B.I.H.R., TER. J. Foxholes 1786.
[10] Par. rec. in church, newspaper cutting in reg. of baptisms, 1796–1812.
[11] Morris, *E. Yorks.* 131; *Y.A.J.* xxv. 76.
[12] *Y.A.J.* xlii. 341.
[13] *Inventories of Ch. Goods*, 25.
[14] B.I.H.R., TER. J. Foxholes 1786; Boulter, 'Ch. Bells', 216.
[15] *Yorks. Ch. Plate*, i. 233.
[16] Barley, *Par. Docs. E.R.* 28. The reg. of marriages, 1814–37, is in E.R.R.O.
[17] Bodl. MS. Tanner 150, ff. 27 sqq.
[18] *Herring's Visit.* i. 114, 214.
[19] G.R.O. Worship Returns, Vol. v, nos. 241, 2484, 2935, 3077, 3139, 3232, 4146; Worship Reg. no. 12618.
[20] H.O. 129/24/523.

on the same site in the main street, in 1872.[21] It is a red-brick building with Gothic windows and stone and blue-brick dressings. In 1865 many people were said to attend both church and chapel.[22] No chapel was built in Butterwick but a building was licensed for worship by the Primitive Methodists in 1861.[23] In 1889 they had 24 members there and were reported to hold services in a loft, having formerly used a cottage.[24] Their meeting-place ceased to be used in 1906.[25]

EDUCATION. In 1662 Edward Smith was licensed to teach at a school in Foxholes.[26] In 1824 the 'school house' was mentioned[27] and by 1835 there was a 'daily school', with 10 boys and 4 girls, financed by subscriptions and school pence.[28] A new school was built in the main street in 1852 and in 1865 the average attendance was 45. The income was then £40 from voluntary subscriptions and about £20 from school pence.[29] The school first received an annual government grant in 1868.[30] By 1871 it had accommodation for 68 children.[31]

A new school was built on the same site for juniors and infants in 1887.[32] The average attendance was 48 in 1908 and until 1936 it varied only between 42 and 56. It fell to 25 in 1938.[33] In 1920 the building was reported to be unsuitable for school use. Improvements were made to the building in 1923–4 and in the latter year it was said to be satisfactory.[34] The school was closed in 1949 and the children transferred to Wold Newton.[35] The building was used as a village hall in 1970.

There is no record of a school in Butterwick. In 1889 the children were said to attend schools at Foxholes and Weaverthorpe[36] and in 1894 at Weaverthorpe only.[37]

An evening school was held at Foxholes in 1865, with an attendance of about 35. It still existed in 1877 but was said to have only 'very moderate' success.[38]

CHARITIES FOR THE POOR. None known.

FRAISTHORPE

THE compact parish of Fraisthorpe, which includes the site of the deserted village of Auburn, lies on the coast about 4 miles south of Bridlington.[1] It is situated entirely on the Plain of Holderness. Fraisthorpe was probably a Scandinavian settlement, but Auburn, near the 'eel stream', may have been Anglian.[2] Part of the site of Auburn village, where only one farm-house now remains, still lies beside Auburn beck, but much of it is now covered by the sea. Both Fraisthorpe and Auburn were originally chapelries of Carnaby, but they gained a substantial degree of ecclesiastical independence and are therefore treated separately here.[3] Although the whole township is included in this article, that part of Auburn to the north of Auburn beck, amounting to about 75 a.[4] or well over a third of the township, lay in Bridlington parish.

The parish boundary largely follows watercourses, the most noteworthy being the Earl's Dike, which forms the southern boundary with Barmston for about 2 miles and is also the wapentake boundary. The western boundary is also formed for its whole length by a watercourse, and Auburn beck forms part of the northern boundary. The Earl's Dike took its name from the counts of Aumale, lords of adjoining Holderness.[5] The total area of the parish in 1850 was 1,987 a., of which Auburn accounted for 204 a.[6] Until 1935 for civil purposes Fraisthorpe included both Auburn and the neighbouring township of Wilsthorpe; in that year, however, Fraisthorpe and Auburn were combined with Barmston as Barmston civil parish.[7]

The landscape of the parish is low-lying and open. Around Brackendale Farm and Fraisthorpe village itself the land reaches a height of over 40 ft. above sea-level. Elsewhere it is little over 25 ft., falling below this along the streams bounding the parish and along Carr Dike, which flows southwards into the Earl's Dike. The especially low-lying grounds were formerly used largely as carr, moor, and meadow land. Much of the remaining land was pasture and the open fields were relatively small.[8] In modern times the proportion of arable has probably increased but a large amount of land in the parish is still used for pasture.

Most of the parish is covered by boulder clay, with alluvium along the streams. The low cliffs along the sea-shore thus consist largely of clay and the sea has made considerable encroachments into the parish. The site of Auburn village has largely been lost. The process had begun by 1570, when the sea caused the collapse of a house there.[9] In 1636 there were ten houses in Auburn and by about 1716 there were seven houses and a chapel.[10] In 1731 only three houses remained, and the chapel was demolished in the same year.[11] By 1823 there was

---

[21] G.R.O. Worship Reg. no. 20988.
[22] B.I.H.R., V. 1865/Ret. 192.
[23] G.R.O. Worship Reg. no. 12618.
[24] H. Woodcock, *Sketches of Prim. Meth. on Yorks. Wolds*, 140.
[25] G.R.O. Worship Reg. no. 12618.
[26] B.I.H.R., Schools index.
[27] Registry of Deeds, Beverley, DT/165/181.
[28] *Educ. Enquiry Abstract, 1835*, 1085.   [29] Ed. 7/135.
[30] *Rep. of Educ. Cttee. of Council, 1868–9* [4139], H.C., p. 625 (1868), xx.
[31] *Rets. rel. Elem. Educ. 1871*, 474.
[32] *Kelly's Dir. N. & E.R.Yorks.* (1889), 389.
[33] *Bd. of Educ. List 21* (H.M.S.O.).
[34] E.R. Educ. Cttee. *Mins.* 1920–1, 45; 1923–4, 164, 211; 1924–5, 169.

[35] Ex inf. Chief Educ. Officer, County Hall, Beverley, 1970.
[36] *Kelly's Dir. N. & E.R.Yorks.* (1889), 363.
[37] B.I.H.R., Bp. V. 1894/Ret.
[38] Ibid., V. 1865/Ret. 192; V. 1877/Ret.
[1] This article was written in 1968.
[2] *P.N.E.R.Yorks.* (E.P.N.S.), pp. xxii, 87.
[3] See p. 206.
[4] *Kelly's Dir. N. & E.R.Yorks.* (1879), 372–3.
[5] *P.N.E.R.Yorks.* 3.   [6] O.S. Map 6″ (1854).
[7] *Census*, 1931.   [8] See p. 205.   [9] *Y.A.J.* xlii. 14.
[10] C 142/553/45; E.R.R.O., DDX/17/138. The latter, a map and survey of Sir William Strickland's manor, is undated but on it is written in pencil 'surveyed by Mr. Dowding about 1716'.
[11] *Y.A.J.* xxxviii. 58; *Herring's Visit.* i. 39.

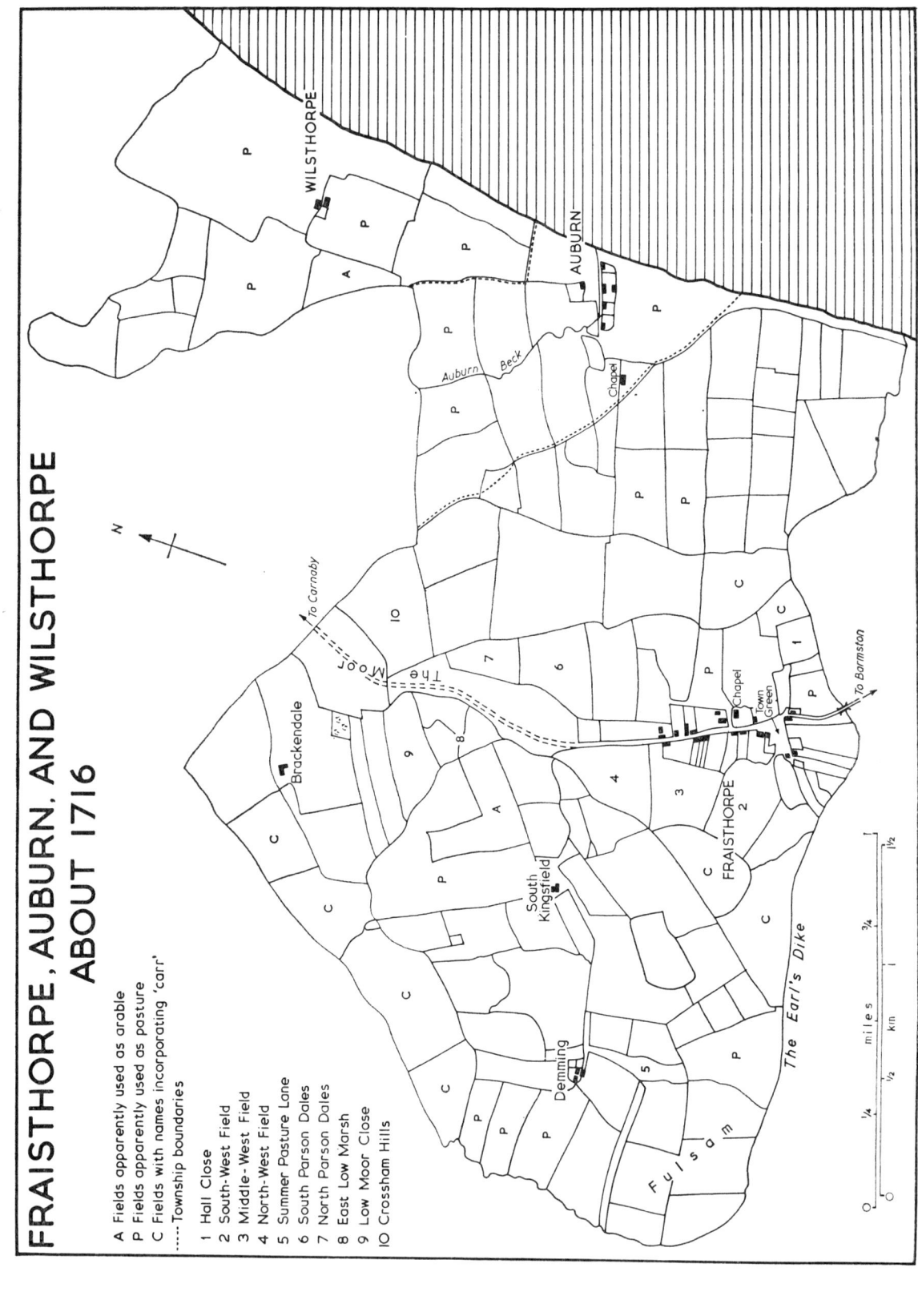

only one occupied farm-house, along with a small cottage, in the township.[12] A local tradition has it that the sea washing over the village ruins produces a distinctive sound, and this has given rise to the saying that 'Auburn Dolly is sobbering'.[13] The shore-line has apparently retreated about 200 yds.–300 yds. since the early 18th century.[14] Most of the encroachment took place before 1850.[15] In 1968 there was only one house, Auburn House Farm, which stands about 200 yds. from the shore. It is an 18th-century building of cobbles, with outbuildings of the same material surrounding a fold-yard in front of the house. Old Auburn House, which was already very near the cliff edge in 1850, was demolished in 1941,[16] but its foundations were still visible on the edge of the cliff immediately south of the beck in 1968. Earthworks in a field adjoining the cliff, south of the beck, mark part of the site of the village, and the site of the chapel is indicated by a small mound about 150 yds. south-west of Auburn House. There was a lime-kiln near by in the late 19th century.[17]

In 1588 there were three beacons in Fraisthorpe, about a mile from the sea, which took light from Bridlington and passed it to Holderness.[18] They still existed in 1756.[19] The right to take a payment for the groundage of ships driven ashore in Fraisthorpe was said in 1722 to have long belonged to the Stricklands of Boynton.[20]

Throughout the 18th and early 19th centuries the main Beverley–Bridlington road ran close to the sea through Fraisthorpe and Auburn.[21] In 1761 that part of the road from Beverley to White Cross was turnpiked and in 1767 a trust was formed to turnpike the remainder as far as Bridlington. The latter trust, however, was not renewed, possibly because of the dangerous nature of the road due to erosion.[22] In 1789 the inhabitants of Auburn were presented for the non-repair of part of the road.[23] In 1850 the road still existed,[24] but most had been washed away by 1912, when part of it and a milestone were uncovered by the shifting of a sand dune.[25]

The old road was replaced between 1832 and 1850 as the main Beverley–Bridlington road by another further inland running through Fraisthorpe village.[26] In 1924 its circuitous course in Barmston and Fraisthorpe was straightened, bypassing Fraisthorpe village,[27] and Fraisthorpe New Bridge, over the Earl's Dike, dates from that improvement. There was a bridge in Fraisthorpe as early as 1461, when money was left for its repair.[28]

The nine-acre 'town green' formerly adjoined the road to the south of Fraisthorpe village, with houses on each side.[29] The remaining cottages and farmhouses are mainly of the 18th century onwards. At the north end of the village is Manor Farm, a **T**-shaped red-brick building of two storeys. It is of 17th-century origin but its front was altered in the 18th century and a kitchen wing was added at the rear in the 19th century. The attic windows, one now blocked, in the gable-ends have moulded brick pediments, and a blocked first-floor window in the north end has a brick hood-mould. The main front has a dentil brick eaves course and a dentil band between the storeys, and these continue around the house as plain brick string-courses. A large 19th-century brick farm-house has patches of cobbles incorporated in the walls, and at Manor Farm and at the south end of the village there are low ranges of cobble-stone outbuildings. The large 19th-century Manor House Farm stands at the south end of the village. There are four outlying farm-houses, all situated in the western half of the parish: Demming, first mentioned in 1521,[30] South Kingsfield and Brackendale, both in existence by *c.* 1716,[31] and North Kingsfield, in existence by 1789.[32] The present buildings are of brick, with some outbuildings of cobbles, and all date from the 19th century or later. The road giving access to North and South Kingsfield and Demming continues beyond Fraisthorpe and formerly led into Haisthorpe village. These isolated farms are presumably the result of early inclosure.[33]

Fraisthorpe had 60 poll-tax payers in 1377 and Auburn 32.[34] The decline of Auburn may have begun with the Black Death, for its tax quota was reduced by 55 per cent in 1354; it was called a 'very beggarly village' in 1571.[35] By 1674 there were 35 households in Fraisthorpe and Auburn together, of which 12 were discharged from the hearth tax; of the 23 that were taxed, 16 had only one hearth each, 3 had 2, 3 had 5, and one, that of Nicholas Woodhouse, the impropriator, had eight.[36] By 1743 there were only 15 families in the parish,[37] and in 1764 there were twelve.[38] The population of Fraisthorpe and Auburn together was 87 in 1801 and 103 in 1831. Fraisthorpe alone had a population of 92 in 1841; the number subsequently varied between 82 and 104, and was again 92 in 1901. There were 12 inhabitants in Auburn in 1841, a peak of 21 ten years later, and only 6 in 1901.[39] In 1911 the joint population was 100, and even with Wilsthorpe included it was only 102 in 1921 and 120 in 1931.[40]

MANORS AND OTHER ESTATES. Fraisthorpe comprised three estates in 1086; two of them each consisted of a carucate, one being a berewick of Sherburn, and the third contained 7 carucates. The largest estate had been held before the Conquest by

---

[12] Baines, *Hist. Yorks.* (1823), ii. 151.
[13] Ex inf. the rector, Barmston, 1970; *T.E.R.A.S.* xxv. 8–9.
[14] E.R.R.O., DDX/17/138; O.S. Map 2½″ (1953).
[15] O.S. Map 6″ (1854).
[16] Ibid.; ex inf. Mr. H. Smith, Auburn, 1969.
[17] O.S. Map 6″ (1854, 1892).
[18] J. Nicholson, *Beacons of E. Yorks.* 8.
[19] E.R.R.O., QSF. East. 1756, D.12.
[20] E 134/8 & 9 Geo. I Trin./6.
[21] J. Tuke, *Map of Yorks.* (1787); J. Cary, *Map of E.R. Yorks. with Ainsty Liberty* (1789, 1805, 1818); *Map of Turnpike Roads of Yorks.* (1810); C. Greenwood, *Map of E.R. Yorks.* (1834).
[22] K. A. MacMahon, *Roads and Turnpike Trusts in E. Yorks.* (E. Yorks. Loc. Hist. Ser. xviii), 27, 38–9, 70.
[23] E.R.R.O., QSF. Mich. 1789, B.2.
[24] O.S. Map 6″ (1854).
[25] T. Sheppard, *Lost Towns of Yorks. Coast*, 197.
[26] Greenwood, *Map of E.R. Yorks.* (1834); O.S. Map 6″ (1854).
[27] E.R.C.C. Mins. 1924–5, 130, 192, 240, 342.
[28] B.I.H.R., Prob. Reg. ii, f. 456 v.
[29] E.R.R.O., DDX/17/138.
[30] *Miscellanea*, iii (Y.A.S. Rec. Ser. lxxx), 8.
[31] E.R.R.O., DDX/17/138.
[32] Cary, *Map of E.R. with Ainsty* (1789).
[33] See p. 205.
[34] E 179/202/62 mm. 28, 30.
[35] *Y.A.J.* xlii. 14.
[36] E 179/205/521.
[37] *Herring's Visit.* i. 216–17.
[38] B.I.H.R., Bp. V. 1764/Ret. 197.
[39] *V.C.H. Yorks.* iii. 489.
[40] *Census*.

Ligulf, and in 1086 it belonged to the count of Mortain[41] and was probably held by Richard de Surdeval.[42] Like the Mortain estate at Boynton, it passed into the Paynel fee and later to the archbishop of Canterbury.[43] The overlordship subsequently descended with the archbishops and was last mentioned in 1428.[44] The Meynell family had a mesne tenancy of the estate,[45] and in 1636 Hedon's manor was still said to be part of the Meynell fee.[46]

By the mid 12th century the demesne lord of the capital manor of *FRAISTHORPE* was Erenburg of Burton, who held at least 6 carucates there. She married first Ulbert the Constable and secondly Gilbert de Alost, who already had four sons, Thomas, Ralph, Stephen, and Hugh. Before her second marriage Erenburg granted a carucate to Swine priory.[47]

Erenburg's son and heir Robert the Constable seems to have divided his property in Fraisthorpe between three of his half-brothers. Thomas de Alost received the manor-house and 2 carucates, Ralph got 2 carucates, and Stephen one.[48] At various times Thomas made grants to Bridlington priory, including the manor-house, ½ carucate, and 6 bovates. He also gave a bovate to his nephew Simon de Alost.[49] Stephen de Alost granted 6 bovates to Bridlington priory[50] and added 2 bovates to his mother's gift to Swine priory.[51] About 1240 the prioress of Swine granted all this land to Bridlington priory.[52] Ralph de Alost granted a bovate of his share to his son Simon, who gave it, along with the bovate from Thomas de Alost, to Bridlington.[53] Other of Ralph's lands may have passed by the early 13th century to Erenburg, wife of Oliver of Croom, who released to Bridlington their rights in 3 bovates in Fraisthorpe.[54] Other land obtained by Bridlington included 3⅓ bovates from Henry of Pocklington[55] and 2 bovates from Gregory of Flamborough.[56] In 1299 the priory held altogether 6 carucates of the Meynell fee in Fraisthorpe.[57]

The Domesday estate which was a berewick of Sherburn was held by Game in 1066 and by Hugh son of Baldric in 1086.[58] It later passed to the Mowbray fee and in 1285 it was held by the Vescy family under the Mowbrays.[59] In 1316 the joint lord of Fraisthorpe, with Nicholas Meynell, was John de Crepping,[60] who was Roger de Mowbray's executor.[61] The whole carucate was granted to Bridlington priory before 1153 by Roger de Mowbray.[62] It was held of the priory at farm by Henry Silver until 1182,[63] when the canons granted it to Thomas de Alost in exchange for his quitclaiming to them the township of Speeton.[64] Thomas later granted half of his carucate to the priory and half to Henry of Carthorpe.[65] The latter ½ carucate was probably that which Asketin of Bempton at the end of the 12th century granted to William of Buckton, and which Arnald of Buckton, in the 13th century, granted to the priory.[66]

The third estate belonged to the Crown and was held in 1066 by Carle and in 1086 by Uctred.[67] It was subsequently included in the Gant fee, which later passed to the Tattershalls, and it was held of them by Bridlington priory.[68]

Thus by the early 14th century Bridlington priory held the greater part of Fraisthorpe and the manor remained in the possession of the priory until the Dissolution. Demming House, pasturage, and a stock of cattle were let *c.* 1537 by the Crown to William Newsted, who had previously been the priory's tenant.[69] The estate was afterwards let successively to John Goldwell,[70] Richard and Robert Atkinson,[71] and, without the house, to Anthony Jackson.[72] The rest of the lands of the manor were let during the later 16th and early 17th centuries in various holdings.[73] In 1605 the whole manor, including Demming House, was granted to Prince Charles,[74] but it was resumed by the Crown in 1613.[75] In 1616 it was granted to George Villiers, later duke of Buckingham.[76] The estate was sold in 1647 to Sir William Strickland,[77] who was already in possession of Hedon's manor, with which the capital manor subsequently descended.

Earthworks in a field called Hall closes, south-east of the village, may mark the site of a manor-house. In the mid 16th century a close was mentioned which had formerly belonged to the priory and was called Hall garth.[78]

A holding formed from the largest Domesday estate was in the hands of the Hedon family for much of the 15th and 16th centuries. Its origin seems to have been in land held by the Meaux family of the Meynell fee in the 13th century. In 1225 Thomas of Meaux held 11 bovates in Fraisthorpe and in 1225–6 he quitclaimed some small parcels to Bridlington priory.[79] His son John of Meaux (or Dringhoe) succeeded to the land, and it seems to have passed in the late 13th century to Thomas de Poynton,[80] who in 1299 was said to hold 5 bovates in Fraisthorpe.[81] In the early 14th century Thomas's son John held 2 carucates there of the Meynell fee.[82] Another John Poynton held

---

[41] *V.C.H.Yorks.* ii. 226, 277, 287, 322.
[42] Ibid. 154–5, 226; *E.Y.C.* ii, p. 136.
[43] See p. 22.
[44] *Feud. Aids*, vi. 32, 141, 265.
[45] Ibid. 32; *Yorks. Inq.* iii. 118.
[46] C 142/553/45; *Cal. Inq. p.m.* iii, p. 49.
[47] *E.Y.C.* iii, pp. 76–7.
[48] *Bridlington Charty.* 194–5, 200.
[49] Ibid. 195–8, 200.
[50] Ibid. 200.
[51] J. Burton, *Mon. Ebor.* 253.
[52] *Bridlington Charty.* 201.
[53] Ibid. 198–9.
[54] Ibid. 196, 207–8.
[55] Ibid. 202.
[56] Ibid. 203–4.
[57] *Cal. Inq. p.m.* iii, p. 429.
[58] *V.C.H.Yorks.* ii. 277, 322.
[59] *Feud. Aids*, vi. 32.
[60] Ibid. 169.
[61] *Cal. Close*, 1307–13, 133.
[62] *Bridlington Charty.* 206.
[63] Ibid. 14, 208.
[64] *E.Y.C.* ii, p. 494.
[65] *Bridlington Charty.* 206–7.
[66] Ibid. 203. The half carucate was of the Mowbray fee.
[67] *V.C.H.Yorks.* ii. 287, 322.
[68] *Feud. Aids*, vi. 32; *Cal. Inq. p.m.* iv, p. 265; vii, pp. 469–70.
[69] E 315/408 ff. 5, 6; *Miscellanea*, iii (Y.A.S. Rec. Ser. lxxx), 8.
[70] *Cal. Pat.* 1566–9, 291.
[71] C 66/1177 m. 7.
[72] E 310/29/170 no. 12.
[73] e.g. E 309/Box 4/15 Eliz. no. 24; E 310/30/181 no. 79.
[74] C 66/1674 m. [24].
[75] C 66/1993 m. 8.
[76] C 66/2090 m. 7.
[77] C 54/3373 m. 1.
[78] E 318/Box 25/1421.
[79] *Bridlington Charty.* 205–6.
[80] A Thomas de Poynton had confirmed a grant made by Thomas of Meaux in 1226: ibid. 206.
[81] *Yorks. Inq.* iii. 118.
[82] B.M. Add. MS. 26731, ff. 47–8.

land in Fraisthorpe in 1397,[83] but the family were not mentioned again. The estate may have passed by 1428 to John Hedon, who was then said to hold 12 bovates in Fraisthorpe of the Canterbury fee.[84] In 1535 Elizabeth, widow of John Hedon, attorned all her property in Fraisthorpe to Sir John Constable, Walter and William Grimston, John Thorp, Edward Roos, and Peter Frodingham.[85] The date at which the estate passed to William Strickland is uncertain, but in 1575–6 he bought six houses and cottages with lands in Fraisthorpe from Brian Heydon (presumably Hedon).[86] At any rate, at his death in 1598 Strickland was in possession of HEDON'S MANOR.[87]

In 1754 Demming Farm, with 263 a. of land, was conveyed by Sir George Strickland to Francis Boynton.[88] It passed in 1782 to Robert Appleton,[89] after whose death it was divided into two parts in 1836. The farm was reunited with the main estate in 1893 when both parts were sold to Sir Charles Strickland.[90] In 1949 the Revd. J. E. Strickland sold North Kingsfield, South Kingsfield, Brackendale, and Demming farms, comprising altogether about 900 a., to the tenants.[91] The remainder of the estate, containing 750 a. in Fraisthorpe and 287 a. in Auburn, was sold by Robert Strickland in 1968.[92]

An estate in Fraisthorpe was held by the Grimstons in the 17th century. It may have originated as the dowry of Grace, daughter of William Strickland, on her marriage with John Grimston, possibly c. 1600. Josiah Grimston or his son Robert was the last of the family to live at Fraisthorpe. The latter was baptized in Auburn chapel in 1673.[93] By 1716 the estate had passed to Sir William Strickland, who then held all the land in the parish.[94]

In the late 12th century the Knights Hospitallers held a toft in Fraisthorpe.[95] In 1539–40 their property consisted of a cottage, and a toft and croft.[96] It was restored to them when the order was briefly revived in 1558.[97] The cottage was sold in 1598 by Henry Griffith to Ralph and Henry Vicarman.[98]

In 1185–95 Thomas de Alost granted to St. Giles's hospital, Beverley, 4 bovates and other property.[99] In 1299 Warter priory, to which the hospital had been annexed in 1277,[1] held ½ carucate in Fraisthorpe of the Meynell fee.[2] After the Dissolution the Fraisthorpe property was granted to Thomas, earl of Rutland.[3] His son Henry sold it in 1557 to Christopher Estoft[4] but it is not mentioned in the inquisition taken after Estoft's death c. 1565.[5] It may have passed by then to William Strickland, whose family by 1605 was certainly in possession of the former Warter lands in Auburn.[6] It subsequently descended with the Strickland estate.

Auburn consisted in 1086 of two estates, the larger of which contained one carucate and belonged to Chilbert's manor of Carnaby.[7] This estate passed soon after the Conquest to the Percy fee[8] and the overlordship subsequently descended in the Percy family: it is last mentioned in 1636.[9] The second estate became part of the Meynell fee and there was later some confusion as to the fee in which certain holdings lay.

By the early 12th century part at least of the Percy lands in Auburn was held by the Arundels,[10] and in 1166 William of Arundel had land there.[11] William's land probably passed to Roger of Arundel, who died before 1213,[12] and was subsequently divided between five coheirs.[13] In the early 14th century Denise de Munchensy, the descendant of one of them, Nicholas of Anstey, held 3 bovates of the Percy fee in Auburn.[14] On her death in 1304 this land passed to her granddaughter Denise and her husband Hugh de Vere.[15] They granted the estate in 1308 to Gerard Salvin, in exchange for a yearly rent from it.[16] Salvin also acquired other land of the Percy fee about this time. In 1310 John of Brompton, whose wife Beatrice was probably the coheir of Sir William of Preston, who held 2 bovates in Auburn in the early 14th century, sold his lands there to Salvin.[17] In 1316 Gerard Salvin was recorded as one of the three lords of Auburn.[18] His son George in 1333 bought houses and lands in Auburn from William de la Chambre.[19] In 1428, however, George Salvin was said to hold 2 bovates of the Canterbury fee, while the lands in Auburn of the Percy fee were held by John Palmer and John Frost.[20] The Salvins still held land in Auburn in 1563[21] but there is no further mention of them. It is possible that their lands passed soon after to the Constables.

In the early 14th century John of Sewerby held one bovate and John le Gras 2 bovates in Auburn of the Percy fee, the latter holding having descended from another coheir of Roger of Arundel, John of Belvoir.[22] It is possible that the Gras holding passed to the Constables of Flamborough. Richard Constable held land in Auburn of the Percy fee in the late 13th century[23] and Marmaduke Constable in 1368.[24] This land, however, was said to be held of the Canterbury fee in 1428, when it comprised 2 bovates.[25] The Constable holding was still 2 bovates in 1488[26] but after the attainder of Robert Constable

---

[83] B.M. Cott. MS. Vitell. C vi, f. 215.
[84] *Feud. Aids*, vi. 265.
[85] E.R.R.O., DDX/29/4.
[86] *Yorks. Fines*, ii. 78.
[87] C 142/273/84.
[88] Registry of Deeds, Beverley, AZ/368/604.
[89] Ibid. FA/288/317.
[90] Ibid. 58/310/294 (1893).
[91] Ibid. 809/520/425; 810/432/353; 812/169/135; /170/136.
[92] Ibid. 1581/214/165.
[93] J. Foster, *Pedigrees of . . . Yorks*. iii.
[94] E.R.R.O., DDX/17/138.
[95] *Bridlington Charty*. 198.
[96] *Miscellanea*, iv (Y.A.S. Rec. Ser. xciv), 98.
[97] *Cal. Pat.* 1557–8, 319.
[98] *Yorks. Fines*, iv. 94.
[99] *E.Y.C.* ii, pp. 153–5.
[1] *V.C.H. Yorks*. iii. 301.
[2] *Cal. Inq. p.m.* iii, p. 429.
[3] E.R.R.O., DDEV/50/13; *Monastic Suppression Papers*, (Y.A.S. Rec. Ser. xlviii), 165.
[4] *Yorks. Fines*, i. 199; *Cal. Pat.* 1555–7, 329.
[5] C 142/144/153.
[6] E 134/3 Jas. I Hil./13.
[7] *V.C.H. Yorks*. ii. 287, 322.
[8] *E.Y.C.* xi, p. 14.
[9] C 142/553/45.
[10] *E.Y.C.* ii, p. 201.
[11] Ibid. xi, pp. 196–7.
[12] *Percy Charty*. (Sur. Soc. cxvii), 5.
[13] See p. 179.
[14] *Percy Charty*. 471.
[15] *Yorks. Inq*. iv. 69.
[16] *Yorks. Fines, 1300–14*, 67; see above, p. 180.
[17] *Yorks. Fines, 1300–14*, 80.
[18] *Feud. Aids*, vi. 169.
[19] *Yorks. Fines, 1327–47*, 55.
[20] *Feud. Aids*, vi. 266.
[21] *Y.A.J.* x. 72–3.
[22] *Percy Charty*. 471.
[23] *Cal. Inq. Misc*. i, pp. 286–7.
[24] C 135/202/1.
[25] *Feud. Aids*, vi. 265.
[26] C 142/3/116.

his holding in Auburn was said in 1537 to be only about ½ bovate.[27] The rest of his lands may have passed earlier to the Constables of Frismarsh and Catfoss.[28] In 1563 the heirs of Stephen Constable of Catfoss held land in Auburn.[29] In 1591 Christopher Constable sold his land there to William Strickland.[30] The Constable lands which passed to the Crown after Robert Constable's attainder seem to have passed by 1563 to Matthew, earl of Lennox, who was then described as lord of the manor of *AUBURN*,[31] but nothing more is known of them.

Other land of the Percy fee in Auburn was part of Barmston manor, the descent of which it followed until the death of Sir Martin del See in 1497,[32] when it passed to his daughter Joan Hildyard. In 1527 Joan held 46 a. of land in Auburn.[33] In 1557 Christopher Hildyard sold the property to Thomas Taylor[34] and in 1611 John Taylor sold it to William Strickland.[35]

A toft in Auburn was given to the hospital of St. Giles, Beverley, by Peter de Percy in the 13th century. It was later granted by the hospital to Bridlington priory, to support a chaplain in Auburn chapel.[36] Other land seems to have been granted to the priory and in 1316 the prior of Bridlington was named as one of the three lords of Auburn.[37] The property was held by the priory until the Dissolution. In 1550 a house and 4 bovates, described as 'chantry premises' formerly in the possession of the priory, were let to William Lutton.[38] By 1598, however, all the former priory lands in Auburn were apparently held by William Strickland.[39] Either St. Giles's hospital or Warter priory[40] was probably granted other land in Auburn, for in 1368 Warter held land there of Henry Percy.[41] After the Dissolution it was granted to Thomas, earl of Rutland,[42] and it subsequently descended like the Warter lands in Fraisthorpe.

In 1086 the smaller estate in Auburn, consisting of ½ carucate, was held of the king by Carle.[43] It later belonged to the Meynells and the archbishops of Canterbury.[44] In 1428 4 bovates in Auburn were said to be of the Canterbury fee.[45] The overlordship is last mentioned in 1603.[46]

These lands were held of the Meynells in the 13th century by the Lowthorpe family, and by 1300 they had been divided between the two Lowthorpe heirs, Margery of Heslerton and Cecily of Heslerton.[47] In 1316 John of Heslerton was returned as one of the three lords of Auburn.[48] The moieties seem to have been reunited by 1371, when Simon Heslerton granted the reversion of 4 bovates in Auburn, held by Euphemia Heslerton for her life, to John Lawrence, of Buckton, John of Gisburn, Thomas of Hedon, and Simon Swanne.[49] In 1381 Henry, earl of Northumberland, licensed Bridlington priory to acquire the reversion of the property from them.[50] The priory seems to have succeeded to the land, which it held until the Dissolution.

By 1598 the whole manor of Auburn was in the possession of William Strickland.[51] In 1635 Walter Strickland had all 13½ bovates there,[52] and the land subsequently descended with the Strickland estate in Fraisthorpe.

The tithes of Fraisthorpe and Auburn belonged to Bridlington priory from the mid 12th century.[53] After the Dissolution some of the tithes in Fraisthorpe were let by the Crown successively to Ralph Constable in 1537–8,[54] Thomas Wentworth in 1555,[55] Thomas Newenham in 1567,[55] William Strickland in 1578,[56] and William Wilson in 1601.[57] Other Fraisthorpe tithes were granted in 1550 to John Bellow and William Fuller,[58] and by 1560 they belonged to Robert Vicarman.[59] In 1650 the Fraisthorpe tithes were worth £46 and belonged to Robert Vicarman's heirs,[60] Anne Carlisle, Everell Welfit, and Frances Langthorne.[61] Nicholas Woodhouse was described as impropriator between 1663 and 1685.[62] In the early 18th century William Strickland bought the tithes in three parts, one from Elizabeth Carlisle, Lawrence Buck, and Anne Welfit,[63] another from Henry Langthorne and Edmund Walters,[64] and the third from Gabriel Ibbitson.[65] In 1754 Sir George Strickland sold the tithes of the Demming farm estate to Francis Boynton and in 1848 they were merged.[66]

The Auburn tithes had earlier descended differently from those at Fraisthorpe. The fish tithes were let along with Bridlington rectory in 1538 and later.[67] In 1592 the Auburn tithes were granted to William Tipper and Robert Dawe[68] and by 1598 they belonged to William Strickland.[69] In 1650 they were worth £15.[70]

ECONOMIC HISTORY. In 1086 Hugh son of Baldric's estate of one carucate was said to contain land for half a plough, but in 1086 it was waste. Uctred's estate, also of one carucate, had one plough,

---

[27] E 150/237/29.
[28] Foster, *Pedigrees of . . . Yorks.* iii.
[29] *Y.A.J.* x. 72–3.
[30] *Yorks. Fines,* iii. 155.
[31] *Y.A.J.* x. 72–3.
[32] E 179/202/104; C.P. 25(1)/281/163 no. 6; G. Poulson, *Holderness,* i. 185.
[33] C 142/48/90.
[34] *Yorks. Fines,* i. 212.
[35] Ibid. *1603–14,* 156.
[36] *Bridlington Charty.* 176.
[37] *Feud. Aids,* vi. 169.
[38] E 310/32/190 no. 37.
[39] See below.
[40] See p. 203.
[41] C 135/202/1.
[42] C 66/669 m. 12; C 66/698 m. 31; *L. & P. Hen. VIII,* xvi, p. 325.
[43] *V.C.H. Yorks.* ii. 204, 322.
[44] *Cal. Inq. p.m.* iii, pp. 428–9; v, p. 54; *Feud. Aids,* vi. 32, 141, 211.
[45] *Feud. Aids,* vi. 265.
[46] C 142/273/84.
[47] See p. 273.
[48] *Feud. Aids,* vi. 169.
[49] *Yorks. Fines, 1347–77,* 154.
[50] *Bridlington Charty.* 454.
[51] C 142/273/84.
[52] C 142/553/45.
[53] See p. 206.
[54] *L. & P. Hen. VIII,* xiii (1), p. 138.
[55] *Cal. Pat.* 1554–5, 180; 1566–9, 1.
[56] E 310/33/199 no. 28.
[57] E 310/28/167 no. 45.
[58] E 318/Box 25/1421; *Cal. Pat.* 1549–51, 253.
[59] C 142/184/38.
[60] *T.E.R.A.S.* ii. 55.
[61] E.R.R.O., DDLG/14/3; /17/1.
[62] Ibid. DPX/58, Fraisthorpe, p. 14; B.I.H.R., TER. J. Fraisthorpe 1685.
[63] C.P. 25(2)/983/2 Anne Hil. pt. 4, no. 21.
[64] C.P. 25(2)/983/3 Anne Hil. no. 39.
[65] C.P. 25(2)/1085/11 Geo. I Hil. no. 74.
[66] Regy. of Deeds, GK/330/327; LT/314/479.
[67] See p. 44.
[68] Grove, *Alienated Tithes,* p. cxxxiii.
[69] C 142/273/84.
[70] *T.E.R.A.S.* ii. 55.

although there was said to be land for only half a plough. The estate was worth 5s.[71] No such information is given for the other estates.

About 1240 the holdings of four 'nativi' in Fraisthorpe were given by Swine priory to Bridlington priory.[72] The labour services of tenants-at-will of Bridlington in 1434 included digging and drying 40 cart-loads of turf, and making, drying, and stacking 20 cart-loads of hay and thatch.[73] In 1538–9 the rents of customary tenants at Fraisthorpe amounted to over £7 and those of tenants-at-will to over £4, and all the former priory's tenants in Auburn held their land at will.[74] On the Lennox manor in Auburn in 1563 there were 2 free tenants and 26 customary tenants.[75] By 1609 all the tenants on at least the capital manor of Fraisthorpe were leaseholders: one had 15 bovates, one had 7, one had 6, 2 had 5, one had 4, and one had one. All except the last-mentioned also had 3 gates in the common. Two tenants held stocked pasture farms of 54 a. and 36 a. respectively and 3 cottagers each held a garth and 2 gates.[76]

Because of the low-lying and heavy nature of the land, much of the parish was from early times used for pasture and meadow, and the economy of the parish has always been predominantly pastoral. At the end of the 12th century Thomas de Alost included in a gift to St Giles's hospital, Beverley, pasturage in Fraisthorpe for 300 sheep, 16 oxen, 3 horses, 10 cows, and a bull. He provided that the offspring of the livestock might remain with their mothers until they were one year old, after which they must be moved to the common pasture. Thomas included in his gift 10 a. at Crosholm, the modern Crossham in the north of the parish, for the construction of a sheepfold, with permission to inclose it with a ditch.[77] Many field names of the 12th and 13th centuries reveal their pastoral nature: e.g. Crosholm, Fuelesholm, Fulsic, Little Sandholm, Kerdales, Brigesic, and Horeholm.[78] Bridlington priory, which by the early 14th century held the largest manor in Fraisthorpe, had a sheepfold there by 1226.[79] In the 16th century the former priory's lands were predominantly meadow and pasture.[80]

Thomas de Alost in the late 12th century had a marsh in Fraisthorpe which provided 20 cart-loads of turf a year for St. Giles's hospital.[81] It was said to be 'beyond Fuelesholm', an area covering nearly 100 low-lying acres in the south-west of the parish, adjoining the Earl's Dike, in 1716, when it was known as 'Fulsam'.[82] In 1307 the marsh was in the possession of Bridlington priory, which was then licensed by the lord of Burton Agnes to inclose it with a ditch on the west side. This ditch may be what is now called Demming Drain. The marsh was still being used to provide turves for the priory in 1434.[83]

Meadow land lay mainly along the streams. In the 12th century 'Fuelesholm' was meadow land, and 'the meadow which is called Fulsic' was said to be in the eastern part of the parish.[84] In addition about a third of the open fields probably consisted of meadow land in 1609.[85] The 'common pasture' of Fraisthorpe was mentioned in 1185–95[86] and 'common on the moor' in 1609.[87] After final inclosure, in the 17th or early 18th century, two closes described as Fraisthorpe moor and consisting of 65 a. lay to the north of the village, on either side of the Carnaby road. Adjoining closes of pasture, called East Low moor, Low moor close, Crossham hills, and South and North Parson Dales, together containing 106 a., may have previously formed part of the moor.[88] Until 1439, when the prior renounced his rights, Bridlington's lands in Fraisthorpe also carried rights of common pasture 'in the moor and marsh' of Burton Agnes.[89]

Bridlington priory apparently played a large part in the early inclosure of pasture land. In 1278, following a dispute, John of Dringhoe acknowledged that the priory might without hindrance hold the capital manor 'with all closes towards the sea, and on every side inclosed'.[90] Between 1488 and 1517 the prior inclosed and converted 40 a. of arable to pasture.[91] Demming House, a farm belonging to the priory, had pasture closes in the West field of Fraisthorpe in the 16th century. This farm was let both before and after the Dissolution together with a stock of animals, which in 1568 consisted of 46 cows and 8 bulls.[92] To judge from the field names of c. 1716, after inclosure, there was or had been carr, pasture, and meadow near the streams along the whole of the western and almost the whole of the southern parish boundaries. In Auburn the eastern side of the township adjoining the sea was then pasture.[93]

There was nevertheless some open-field land from early times. The fields of Fraisthorpe were mentioned in the late 12th century;[94] 2 bovates were said to lie 'through all the field' in the early 13th century;[95] and selions and butts were mentioned in 1225.[96] Auburn apparently had its own fields, as a bovate was said to lie 'through the whole field' there in 1448.[97] In 1609 there were apparently two open fields in Fraisthorpe, East field and 'North and West fields'. A survey of that year gives details of the holdings of 11 out of 16 tenants of the Crown manor. Six of them held open-field land totalling 168 a., divided equally between the two fields. About two-thirds of this acreage consisted of arable and the rest meadow.[98]

---

[71] *V.C.H. Yorks.* ii. 226, 277, 287, 322.
[72] *Bridlington Charty.* 201.
[73] *Monastic Chancery Proc.* (Y.A.S. Rec. Ser. lxxxviii), 18.
[74] Dugdale, *Mon.* vi. 290.
[75] *Y.A.J.* x. 72–3.
[76] E.R.R.O., DPX/58, Fraisthorpe, pp. 5–7. Eleven holdings are fully described, one only partially.
[77] *E.Y.C.* ii, pp. 154–5.
[78] Ibid. 153–4; *Bridlington Charty.* 205–7, 210.
[79] *Bridlington Charty.* 206.
[80] E 310/33/199 no. 28.
[81] *E.Y.C.* ii, pp. 154–5.
[82] E.R.R.O., DDX/17/138.
[83] *Mon. Chanc. Proc.* 18.
[84] *E.Y.C.* ii, pp. 154–5.
[85] E.R.R.O., DPX/58, Fraisthorpe, pp. 5–7.
[86] *E.Y.C.* ii, pp. 154–5.
[87] E.R.R.O., DPX/58, Fraisthorpe, p. 5.
[88] Ibid. DDX/17/138.
[89] Ibid. DDWB/5/45.
[90] *Bridlington Charty.* 205.
[91] *T.R.H.S.* N.S. vii. 248.
[92] E 310/29/170 nos. 12, 18; *Miscellanea*, iii (Y.A.S. Rec. Ser. lxxx), 8.
[93] E.R.R.O., DDX/17/138.
[94] *E.Y.C.* ii, pp. 153–4; *Bridlington Charty.* 194, 200.
[95] *Bridlington Charty.* 207.
[96] Ibid. 205–6.
[97] Ibid. 176.
[98] E.R.R.O., DPX/58, Fraisthorpe, pp. 5–7. The arable holdings were always referred to as lying in 'North and West field', but the meadow holdings were said to be in 'West field' alone.

The two fields lay broadly to the east and west of the village. By *c.* 1716 62 a. of land just west of the village had been divided into closes called Southwest, Middle-west, and North-west fields. Further west the area now occupied by North and South Kingsfield and Demming farms has an irregular field-pattern suggesting early inclosure,[99] and in 1577 the inclosed lands belonging to Demming House were said to be in the West field of Fraisthorpe.[1] Thus it seems that West field was largely inclosed in the Middle Ages, probably by Bridlington priory, and only a small part remained to be inclosed in the 17th or early 18th century. The land to the east of the village and in Auburn township exhibits a more regular field pattern and probably until the early 18th century consisted largely of open fields and common pasture. The early inclosure of Fraisthorpe, whether in the Middle Ages or in the 17th or early 18th century, is probably reflected in the relatively small size of the closes *c.* 1716. Most were under 20 a., about a third were between 20 a. and 40 a., and only four closes were over 40 a.[2]

By *c.* 1716 the whole parish had been inclosed, and there were then 13 holdings in Fraisthorpe and one in Auburn. Two holdings were of over 200 a., those of Robert Grimston, who held most of Auburn, and Leonard Meeke, tenant of Brackendale farm in Fraisthorpe. One was between 150 a. and 200 a., 2 were between 100 a. and 150 a., 4 were between 50 a. and 100 a., and 5 were under 50 a.[3] Since inclosure the proportion of arable land in the parish has probably increased. In 1801 there were 457 a. of land under crops, notably oats (202 a.).[4]

In 1841 there were six farmers and four cottagers in Fraisthorpe, and one farmer and one cottager in Auburn.[5] The number of farmers in each township has subsequently changed little. Throughout the 19th and 20th centuries there have usually been 5–7 farmers in Fraisthorpe, and always one in Auburn.[6] In 1921 all seven farms in Fraisthorpe and that in Auburn were of 150 a. or over.[7]

There was a weaver at Fraisthorpe in 1614,[8] and fishing was carried on at Auburn, at least in the 16th and early 17th centuries.[9] By 1851 and until at least 1905 there was a gravel-dealer at Auburn,[10] and a brickmaker was recorded in 1905 also.[11] A windmill was mentioned at Fraisthorpe in the late 12th century and a miller in the 13th.[12]

LOCAL GOVERNMENT. No manorial records and no parochial records before 1835 are known. In 1836 Fraisthorpe joined the Bridlington union.[13]

CHURCHES. Chapels at Fraisthorpe[14] and Auburn were mentioned in the 12th century and seem originally to have been dependent on the mother-church at Carnaby. A mediety of Auburn chapel was granted to Bridlington priory before 1140[15] and the other mediety, together with Fraisthorpe chapel, was presumably included in the grant of Carnaby church to the priory between 1148 and 1153.[16] Although a vicarage was ordained at Carnaby by 1268,[17] the priory presumably supplied the two chapels with chaplains, perhaps using the tithes of the townships to reward them; the tithes of Auburn were said in 1605 to have been long so used.[18] Fraisthorpe and part of Auburn buried at Carnaby in the 16th and early 17th centuries, and the rest of Auburn at Bridlington,[19] and they have never had burial rights. Fraisthorpe and Auburn remained separate curacies until 1731 when, following the demolition of Auburn chapel, they were combined.[20] By 1851 the curacy had been united with the vicarage of Carnaby[21] and it so remained until 1929, when it was transferred to Barmston.[22]

After the Dissolution curates were nominated by the lay rectors and paid out of the rectorial tithes. Thus the nomination to Auburn was acquired by the Stricklands in 1603,[23] and in 1650 Sir William Strickland was also said to have the nomination at Fraisthorpe,[24] though it was only later that the Stricklands acquired the tithes there. They subsequently retained the nomination and were also patrons of the combined living until 1929; the patronage of Barmston belongs to the Wickham-Boynton family.[25]

In 1525–6 the curates' stipends were £4 each.[26] The curate at Fraisthorpe received £2 a year in 1685 and £3 in 1716 and 1726,[27] and at Auburn £2 13s. 4d. in 1650 and subsequently.[28] In 1658 it was ordered that augmentations should be settled on ministers to preach weekly at the two chapels.[29] In 1743, after Auburn and Fraisthorpe had been united, the curate received £5 13s. 4d.,[30] and that stipend continued to be paid throughout the 18th and 19th centuries.[31] The living was augmented by £200 from Queen Anne's Bounty in 1737, 1767, and 1787, and by a parliamentary grant of £600 in 1824.[32] The value of the living was about £10 in 1764, £17 in 1781, £28 in 1817, and £40 in 1825.[33] The average net income in 1829–31 was £38 a year.[34]

In 1767 Bounty money was used to buy about 7 a. of glebe in Dringhoe, and in 1770 6 a. was acquired in Bonwick.[35] The glebe was all sold in 1921.[36]

The curate of Fraisthorpe seems never to have had a residence. In the Middle Ages the curate of

---

[99] E.R.R.O., DDX/17/138; DDCV/parcel 115.
[1] E 310/29/170 no. 12.
[2] E.R.R.O., DDX/17/138.
[3] Ibid.
[4] 1801 Crop Returns.
[5] E.R.R.O., DDX/3/3.
[6] Directories.
[7] *Kelly's Dir. N. & E.R. Yorks.* (1921), 520.
[8] B.I.H.R., Prob. Reg. xxxiii, f. 98.
[9] E 134/3 Jas. I Hil./13; *L. & P. Hen. VIII*, xiii (1), p. 134.
[10] H.O. 107/2367; directories.
[11] *Kelly's Dir. N. & E.R. Yorks.* (1905), 472.
[12] *Bridlington Charty.* 206, 209.
[13] *3rd Rep. Poor Law Com.* 167.
[14] *Bridlington Charty*, 197, 200.
[15] *E.Y.C.* ii, p. 446.
[16] Ibid. xi, p. 115.
[17] See p. 129.
[18] E 134/3 Jas. I Hil./13.
[19] Ibid.
[20] *Herring's Visit.* i. 39.
[21] H.O. 129/24/524.
[22] York Dioc. Regy., Orders in council 593.
[23] C 142/273/84.
[24] *T.E.R.A.S.* ii. 55.
[25] *Crockford.*
[26] *Y.A.J.* xxiv. 77–8.
[27] B.I.H.R., TER. J. Fraisthorpe 1685, 1716, 1726.
[28] Ibid. 1685, 1716; *T.E.R.A.S.* ii. 55.
[29] *Cal. S.P. Dom.* 1657–8, 374.
[30] B.I.H.R., TER. J. Fraisthorpe 1743.
[31] Ibid. Auburn 1781, 1786; Fraisthorpe 1764, 1861; Bp. V. 1900/Ret. 74.
[32] Hodgson, *Q.A.B.* 433, 440.
[33] B.I.H.R., TER. J. Auburn 1764; Fraisthorpe 1764, 1781, 1817, 1825.
[34] *Rep. Com. Eccl. Revenues*, 934.
[35] B.I.H.R., TER. J. Fraisthorpe 1770, 1777.
[36] Regy. of Deeds, Beverley, 229/485/427.

Auburn may have lived on the toft given for his use in the 13th century by St. Giles's hospital, Beverley, to Bridlington priory.[37] There was a residence at Auburn in 1582[38] and in 1605,[39] but it had gone by 1743, when the curate of Fraisthorpe with Auburn lived at Boynton, where he was vicar.[40]

A guild-house was mentioned in Fraisthorpe in 1556,[41] and a former chantry in Auburn, dedicated to St. Nicholas, was recorded in the late 16th century.[42]

In the late 13th century Thomas de Poynton bought a statue of the Virgin in Scotland and put it in Fraisthorpe chapel, where it stood for five years until his death in 1299. During that time the image became widely venerated and attracted offerings. The ambiguous status of Fraisthorpe chapel in relation to Carnaby is reflected in a claim to the offerings by the prior of Bridlington as rector of Carnaby, to which Fraisthorpe chapel was said to be 'annexed', and a counter-claim by the vicar of Carnaby. A compromise was reached whereby the prior received two-thirds of the offerings, and the vicar the rest. After Thomas de Poynton's death his widow Joan sold the statue to Robert the Constable, rector of Foston, who set it up in his church. The prior, however, claimed it as his property and in 1313 regained possession by force.[43] He seems to have returned it to Fraisthorpe, but by 1315 it had been forcibly removed by the Grimstons, one of whom was vicar of Cottam. The prior was still trying to recover it from them in 1331.[44]

Throughout the Middle Ages and later Fraisthorpe curacy was often held with Carnaby. In 1310 William de Bolom was described as vicar of Carnaby and of its chapel of Fraisthorpe.[45] In 1368, 1380, 1552, and 1663–81 the vicar of Carnaby also held Fraisthorpe.[46] In 1526, however, the two livings were held separately.[47]

Auburn chapel seems to have been held independently of Carnaby and Fraisthorpe until the 17th century. In 1620–36 one man was curate of both Fraisthorpe and Auburn,[48] and between 1682 and 1691 one man similarly held both of them, having been curate of Auburn since 1673. In 1715 the curate of Fraisthorpe since 1699 and of Flamborough since 1710 also became curate of Auburn. In 1693–7 the curate of Fraisthorpe also held the vicarage of Rudston, and in 1691 the vicar of Carnaby held the curacy of Auburn.[49] From 1739 until the livings were united the vicars of Carnaby also held Fraisthorpe with Auburn, and lived at Boynton.[50] For most of the later 19th century there was an assistant curate at Fraisthorpe, and in 1894 he was said to be paid by Sir Charles Strickland.[51] There was an assistant curate in 1900, but not in 1936,[52] by which time Fraisthorpe with Auburn had been transferred to Barmston.

Two curates in the 17th century were Puritans, Thomas Clark (1620–36) and Enoch Sinclair (1638–40).[53]

In 1743 a service was held at Fraisthorpe once a month and the curate said that 'it has never been performed oftener'. Communion was administered three times a year and was received by about fourteen people.[54] By 1764 there was a service only once every six weeks; communion was still administered three times a year.[55] By 1868 there was a service each Sunday and about three people received communion every six weeks.[56] In 1936 communion was administered monthly and in 1968 there was still a service each Sunday.[57]

The small church of ST. EDMUND, Fraisthorpe, dates largely from the 19th century and consists of a structurally undivided nave and chancel. It is built mainly of cobble-stones, with ashlar and brick quoins and openings. It stands on a prominent mound which may be artificial. The only features that remain of the earlier church are the plain circular font and part of a 12th- or 13th-century round pier surmounted by a capital, which has been incorporated in the south wall. In 1720–1 the chancel was ordered to be repaired,[58] and the brick quoins at the exterior angles of the chancel walls probably date from then, although some of the bricks appear to be older than others. The church was substantially rebuilt in 1893 to commemorate Mary Simpson and her work among farm servants.[59] The rebuilding was financed by countrywide offerings and the architects were Smith and Brodrick of Hull. The triple-lancet east window, the single-lancet west and side windows, the doorway, the roof, and the bellcot, containing one small bell, are all of that date.[60] During the rebuilding the pre-Reformation altar stone was embedded 'underneath the place where it formerly stood' because of its mutilated condition.[61]

The church of ST. NICHOLAS, Auburn, was taken down about 1590 because it stood very near the sea and was rebuilt further inland on Auburn common. In 1605 it was said to be in need of repair as 'the end of the chapel where the bells ring is under-propped'.[62] In 1720 it again needed restoration[63] but repair was neglected so that in 1731 it was 'scarce fit for public use', this state of affairs being attributed to depopulation.[64] Consequently, under a licence from the archbishop, it was demolished the same year.[65] A mound and the foundations of walls mark the site. The Norman tub font, with chevron ornamentation, was transferred to Wragby church (Yorks. W.R.).[66]

There were two bells at Fraisthorpe in 1552[67] but

[37] *Bridlington Charty.* 176.
[38] B.I.H.R., Churches index.
[39] E 134/3 Jas. I Hil./13.
[40] *Herring's Visit.* i. 39.
[41] E.R.R.O., DDCC/139/65.
[42] *Y.A.J.* xx. 258.
[43] *Bridlington Charty.* 448; *Cal. Inq. Misc.* i, pp. 358–9. The latter is dated '8 Edward' and is wrongly attributed to 1280. See above, p. 187.
[44] *Cal. Pat.* 1330–4, 203.
[45] *Bridlington Charty.* 448.
[46] *Fasti Parochiales*, iii. 18; *Inventories of Ch. Goods*, 27; E.R.R.O., DPX/58, Fraisthorpe, p. 15.
[47] *Fasti Parochiales*, iii. 5, 19.
[48] R. A. Marchant, *Puritans and Ch. Courts in Dioc. York*, 239.
[49] E.R.R.O., DPX/57, Auburn, p. 5; /58, Fraisthorpe, p. 15.
[50] See p. 129.
[51] B.I.H.R., Bp. V. 1894/Ret.
[52] Ibid. Bp. V. 1900/Ret. 74; Bp. V. 1936/Ret. 261.
[53] Marchant, *Puritans and Ch. Courts in Dioc. York*, 239, 279, 319.
[54] *Herring's Visit.* i. 216–17.
[55] B.I.H.R., Bp. V. 1764/Ret. 197.
[56] Ibid. V. 1868/Ret. 100.
[57] Ibid. Bp. V. 1936/Ret. 261; ex inf. the rector, Barmston, 1969.
[58] B.I.H.R., Churches index.
[59] Plaque in church; see p. 29.
[60] B.I.H.R., FAC. 1892/20; Bridlington Pub. Libr., plan chest, bottom drawer.
[61] Plaque in church.
[62] E 134/3 Jas. I Hil./13.
[63] B.I.H.R., Churches index.
[64] *P.N.E.R. Yorks.* (E.P.N.S.), 87.
[65] *Herring's Visit.* i. 39.
[66] E.R.R.O., DPX/57, Auburn, p. 7.
[67] *Inventories of Ch. Goods*, 28.

by 1764 only one.[68] In 1968 there was one small bell. The plate includes a silver cup, made in Sheffield in 1865, and a modern plated chalice and paten.[69] In 1552 Auburn chapel had two bells in the 'steeple'[70] and these may have been used in the new building c. 1590. On the demolition of the chapel in 1731 the two bells were preserved. Sir William Strickland removed one to Boynton, where it still hangs in the courtyard of the hall, and the other was given by his son Sir George Strickland to Sir Rowland Winn, of Nostell Priory.[71]

The register of baptisms for 1599–1717, burials for 1595–1706, and marriages for 1596–1713 is bound in the front of the first Carnaby register (1653–1769). Fraisthorpe entries appear in the Carnaby registers from the late 17th century until 1929,[72] thereafter in the Barmston registers. Fraisthorpe has had a separate baptismal register since 1965.[73]

NONCONFORMITY. Thomas England and Robert Milner were presented in 1679 for allowing conventicles to be held in their houses.[74] In 1731 6 out of 15 people in Auburn[75] and in 1743 2 families out of 15 in the whole parish were Quakers.[76] There were said to be no dissenters in the parish in 1764[77] but in 1795 a house was licensed as a meeting-place.[78] In 1868 and 1889 the Primitive Methodists used a house in Fraisthorpe for their meetings and in the latter year were said to have seven members.[79]

EDUCATION. There is no known provision for the education of Fraisthorpe children until 1871, when a new school was built at Carnaby. It was for the use of Fraisthorpe and Boynton parishes as well as Carnaby.[80]

CHARITIES FOR THE POOR. In 1803 Lady Strickland bequeathed £20 for the poor, and in 1822 it was producing interest of £1 a year which was distributed among unrelieved widows and others.[81] From at least 1880 until 1903 the charity was administered with the Strickland Charity in Boynton and Carnaby and the income, 12s. a year in 1903, was distributed among the poor of all three parishes. In 1903 the incumbent was directed to administer the Fraisthorpe charity separately.[82]

GANTON

GANTON lies about 13 miles north-west of Bridlington and the parish, roughly rectangular in shape, stretches for 4 miles from the high wold ground in the south, across the wolds escarpment, to the low-lying ground of the Vale of Pickering in the north.[1] The township of Potter Brompton occupies the western part of the parish. Both Ganton and Potter Brompton were probably Anglian settlements. The prefix Potter, first recorded in the late 13th century, is derived from the potteries which existed then and later.[2] The village of Ganton and the hamlet of Potter Brompton, about ¾ mile to the west, lie on the spring-line at the foot of the escarpment. On the wolds a short section of the eastern parish boundary follows a prehistoric earthwork and several sections run along the bottoms or sides of small dry valleys. Other sections, particularly of the western boundary, which is also the wapentake boundary, seem to be aligned upon the highest points of the wolds. On the low ground the boundaries largely follow watercourses, notably Windle beck in the east. The irregular northern boundary, which is also the wapentake and riding boundary, follows the old course of the river Derwent, part of which is now called Head Dike. The internal boundary between Ganton and Potter Brompton is not known, but on the wolds it may have followed a prehistoric earthwork, a section of which remains, which ran southwards from the scarp across the parish and into Foxholes. The area of the parish is 3,982 a.[3]

Ganton is divided by the escarpment of the wolds, which runs across the parish from south-west to north-east. The landscape varies between three markedly different areas: the flat and low-lying Vale of Pickering, composed of alluvial sands, clays, and gravels; the steep and well-wooded escarpment; and the undulating and open wold-land in the south. On the wolds there were formerly many pre-historic embankments and barrows, and early Anglian settlement is suggested by the discovery in one barrow of a burial dating from c. 550.[4] The slopes below the escarpment were also the scene of early settlement, and both Romano-British pottery and an Anglian cemetery have been found near Windle Beck Farm.[5]

Much of the low ground, which was formerly largely marsh and carr, is less than 75 ft. above sea-level. Several streams and dikes flow into the rivers Derwent and Hertford, which meet near Hay bridge. The Hertford, and the Derwent downstream from their confluence, both flow in straight embanked courses which were made during the drainage of the area in the early 19th century. In the Middle Ages the Derwent apparently flowed in two courses,[6] one of them, later abandoned, on the line of the parish boundary and the other perhaps near the line of the

---

[68] B.I.H.R., TER. J. Fraisthorpe 1764.
[69] *Yorks. Ch. Plate*, i. 252; ex inf. the rector, 1970. A plated paten, which was in the church in 1912, is now missing.
[70] *Inventories of Ch. Goods*, 27.
[71] E.R.R.O., DPX/57, Auburn, pp. 6–7.
[72] E.R.R.O.
[73] Ex inf. the rector, 1969.
[74] B.I.H.R., ER. V/CB. 5.
[75] *Kirkby's Inquest*, 59 n.
[76] *Herring's Visit.* i. 216–17.
[77] B.I.H.R., Bp. V. 1764/Ret. 197.
[78] Ibid., DMH. 1795/64.
[79] Ibid., V. 1868/Ret. 100; H. Woodcock, *Sketches of Prim. Meth. on Yorks. Wolds*, 83.
[80] See p. 131.
[81] *9th Rep. Char. Com.* 735.
[82] Char. Com. files; see above, p. 29.
[1] This article was written in 1970. Use has been made of material compiled by Mrs. Margaret Craig.
[2] *P.N.E.R. Yorks.* (E.P.N.S.), 118–19; *Y.A.J.* xxxix. 445; see below, p. 213.
[3] O.S. Map 6" (1854).
[4] *V.C.H. Yorks.* ii. 93.
[5] Ex inf. Mr. T. C. M. Brewster, 1971.
[6] *Bridlington Charty.* 137–8; see below, p. 213.

GARTON ON THE WOLDS:
the Sykes monument

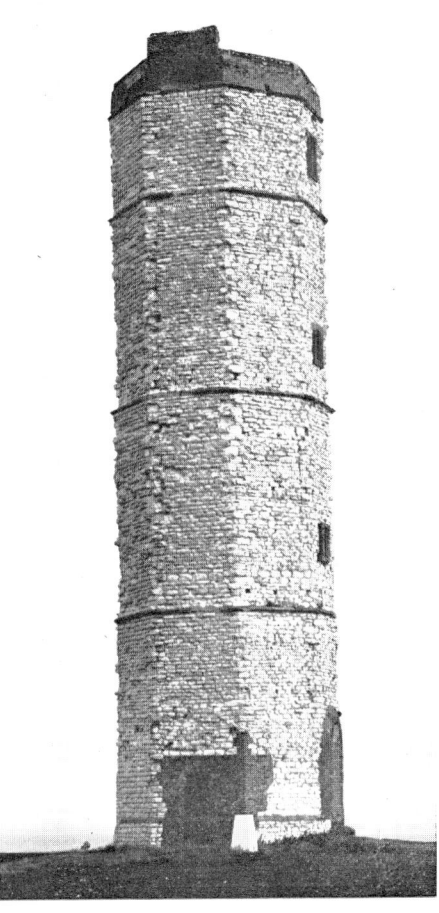

FLAMBOROUGH:
the old lighthouse

FLAMBOROUGH HEAD: the cliffs and lighthouse, *c.* 1928

THORPE HALL, RUDSTON: the dairy

GARTON ON THE WOLDS CHURCH: decoration in the nave

present river. There are several large plantations on the low ground.

The ground rises gently at first at the foot of the escarpment and the villages lie mainly at between 125 ft. and 175 ft. There are several springs below the escarpment, including one between Ganton and Potter Brompton which has formed a pond called Winter Beck Hole. Ganton Hall, which stands on the rising ground south of the village, is surrounded by a well-wooded park of nearly 200 a.[7] extending from the Malton–Scarborough road southwards to include part of the escarpment. The ground rises steeply south of the villages to 550 ft. at Ganton and Potter Brompton brows. The former is referred to as 'Pekesbru' in the later 12th century.[8] The shallow valley in which Ganton village and the site of the old hall lie continues southwards to cut a steep-sided gash obliquely into the face of the escarpment. The escarpment presents a markedly wooded appearance, owing largely to the planting activities of Sir Digby Legard in the later 18th century.[9] On the wolds south of the escarpment the ground falls to as little as 300 ft. at the southern parish boundary. Two prominent dry valleys, Ganton Dale and Warren Slack, together with several small side valleys, dissect the wold slopes. There is little woodland, apart from a shelter-belt around Warren House Farm. The wolds and slopes below the escarpment were largely in open-field cultivation in the Middle Ages and the pattern of large regular fields results from the inclosure of 1804.[10] Arable farming is now predominant, though there is still some pasture on the low ground and the escarpment.

The main Malton–Scarborough road crosses the parish below the escarpment but there are few other roads in the parish. A road running over the wolds from Foxholes crosses the Scarborough road near Ganton village. The section north of the village leading into Wykeham (Yorks. N.R.) was set out as a private road by the inclosure commissioners in 1804.[11] It later became a public road giving access to the railway station. Beyond the railway it becomes a farm road and is carried over the river Derwent by Hay bridge. The bridge was repaired with stone in 1778, widened with bricks in 1780, and again repaired in 1795.[12] By 1970 the earlier bridge had been replaced by a modern structure. The road north of the bridge is called Green Lane.

The main street of Ganton, probably that referred to as the Town Gate in 1558,[13] runs southwards from the Scarborough road and joins the Foxholes road at the south end of the village. North of the Scarborough road the village street continues as a short cul-de-sac. The single street of Potter Brompton leads southwards from the Scarborough road and ends at the foot of the escarpment. Ganton and Potter Brompton villages were formerly linked by Church Balk, which has probably always been a footpath, and Coach Balk, probably formerly for wheeled traffic. A short section of Coach Balk remains at the Potter Brompton end as a green lane. Two field-roads, one known as Ings Causeway, give access to the low ground in Potter Brompton. In the later 18th century a road led southwards from Potter Brompton village over the wolds to Weaverthorpe,[14] but it had disappeared by 1850.[15] On the wolds a minor road runs eastwards from Ganton Wold Farm into Willerby parish. The York–Scarborough railway line, which runs from west to east across the north of the parish, was opened in 1845.[16] Ganton station was closed for passengers in 1930 and for goods in 1964,[17] and it had been demolished by 1970. A warehouse still stands near the site.

Most of the houses in Ganton stand along each side of the village street, between the Scarborough road and the church. A stream runs beside the street, which is bordered by wide grass verges. The cottages, built of brick or chalk, are mostly white-washed and several are of a storey and a half. The older ones date from the 18th century, but a blocked mullioned window in a cottage opposite the Vicarage may indicate an earlier origin. Some of the 19th-century houses were altered or enlarged by Harold Wrigley in 1937–8.[18] A row of three houses was built by Wrigley in 1920, and there are six Council houses. A chalk-built early-19th-century public house, the Greyhound, stands on the Scarborough road. There has been a public house in the village since at least 1823, when it was called the Red Lion,[19] but the Greyhound was in existence by 1872.[20] Several substantial houses on the road leading towards the Derwent apparently owe their existence to the attraction of the golf course. This, one of Yorkshire's leading courses, covers about 150 a. to the north-west of the village and was opened in 1893.[21] The club-house and three large houses opposite are designed in the gabled domestic style of *c.* 1900.

There are few buildings of note in Potter Brompton. One much-altered house, mainly of chalk, is dated 1751. Four Council houses are dated 1926, and a 19th-century house was altered by Harold Wrigley in 1938.[22] Beside the Scarborough road a little to the west of the hamlet is a monument inscribed 'W.H.F.' and dated 1874; it commemorates the death while hunting of a member of the Foulis family of Heslerton.[23]

There are several outlying farms in the parish, none apparently dating from before the early-19th-century inclosure. They include on the low ground Bog Hall, which was rebuilt in 1913 by Harold Wrigley,[24] Hay Bridge House, and Windle Beck Farm. All have similar barns, built of chalk with decorative brick dressings. On the wolds the farms include Brompton Wold, Ganton Wold, Warren House, and Cat Babbleton Farms. Ganton Dale House, in the south-east of the parish, was an inn from at least 1804 to the 1820s.[25] It now stands beside the Driffield–Scarborough road, which here skirts the parish boundary, but it is said to owe its existence to a coach road which formerly ran along

---

[7] Registry of Deeds, Beverley, 134/290/265.
[8] *Bridlington Charty.* 137–8.
[9] A. Young, *A Six Months Tour through the North of Eng.* ii. 23–6.
[10] Regy. of Deeds, CA/320/43.   [11] Ibid.
[12] E.R.R.O., PR. 2762.   [13] Y.A.S. MSS., DD 15/22.
[14] T. Jefferys, *Map of Yorks.* (1772).
[15] O.S. Map 6" (1854).
[16] W. W. Tomlinson, *The North-Eastern Railway*, 461.
[17] Ex inf. Brit. Rail (E.R.), Doncaster, 1971.
[18] Inscriptions on buildings.
[19] Baines, *Hist. Yorks.* (1823), ii. 209.
[20] *Kelly's Dir. N. & E.R. Yorks.* (1872), 368.
[21] Regy. of Deeds, 957/197/172; *Kelly's Dir. N. & E.R. Yorks.* (1897), 464.
[22] Inscription on building.
[23] Ex inf. Mr. Brewster, 1971.
[24] Inscription on building.
[25] Regy. of Deeds, CA/320/43; Baines, *Hist. Yorks.* (1823), ii. 209.

the valley bottom;[26] this explains its position at right-angles to the modern road. It is a large 18th- or early-19th-century building, with a three-storeyed front of chalk ashlar and large stone kneelers in the gables; there are lower side wings with raked parapets.

The number of Ganton's poll-tax payers in 1377 is not known but Potter Brompton had 22.[27] In 1674 48 households in Ganton and Potter Brompton together were recorded in the hearth-tax assessment, of which 25 were discharged; of the 23 that were taxed 20 had only one hearth, and one each had 5, 10, and 13, the last being Ganton Hall.[28] In 1743 about 30 families were reported[29] and in 1764 32.[30] In 1801 the population was 223. It rose steadily to 275 by 1831 and sharply to a peak of 428 in 1841, before declining to 339 in 1881. It then increased to 393 in 1901,[31] before again declining in the 20th century. In 1951 the population was 305 and in 1961 240.[32]

MANORS AND OTHER ESTATES. In 1086 there was one estate in Ganton, consisting of 8 carucates, which was soke of Bridlington manor. Before the Conquest it had been held by Morcar but in 1086 it was in the king's hands.[33] It subsequently passed to the Gants and later the Tattershalls.[34] On the division of the Tattershall fee in 1306 it passed to Thomas de Cailly[35] and the overlordship apparently lapsed soon after.

The Acklams were demesne tenants of the estate. Roger of Acklam died before 1231 leaving as coheirs his daughters Joan and Agnes.[36] The estate apparently passed to Agnes, for in 1250 her heir Nicholas of Acklam held it.[37] In 1284–5 Robert of Acklam held 5 carucates.[38] The estate descended to Thomas Acklam in the late 14th century and in 1392 his widow Elizabeth granted it to Robert Acklam, together with another estate in Ganton which had been held by her father Robert Bossall.[39] Thereafter the manor of *GANTON* descended as a single holding of 8 carucates.

Robert Acklam was last mentioned in 1409,[40] and by 1428 the manor was held by William Willesthorpe.[41] In 1493 his property, or that of another William Willesthorpe, was divided between his daughters, Isabel and Agnes Bennet, and Brian Palmes, who had married another daughter Anastasia, then dead.[42] Apparently the manor passed to Isabel, who later married Robert Creyke. In 1546 their son Walter[43] died in possession of it,[44] and his son Ralph had livery in 1551.[45] The manor was subsequently acquired by Marmaduke Lacy, who held it at his death in 1578,[46] and his son Marmaduke sold it in 1586 to John Legard.[47] It subsequently descended in the Legard family[48] until 1911, when it was sold by Sir Algernon Legard to Harold Wrigley. It then consisted of 3,518 a. lying in both Ganton and Potter Brompton townships.[49] Two years later Wrigley bought the 263-acre Glebe farm.[50] Apart from 143 a. sold to Ganton Golf Club in 1953[51] the estate has since been retained by the Wrigleys.

In 1586 the manor-house on John Legard's newly-purchased estate at Ganton was described as 'new builded, the walls of chalk-stone and covered with slate'.[52] It occupied a site at the foot of the escarpment, about 300 yds. south-east of the church. In 1674 it contained thirteen hearths.[53] An early-18th-century view shows a steep-roofed Elizabethan building of two storeys and attics with gabled projections, perhaps containing staircases, on the south front;[54] the base of one of these may have served as an entrance porch with a doorway at the side, as at Burton Agnes Hall.[55] Between the two projections was a five-bay façade, surmounted by three small gables. The windows were mullioned and transomed, some with hood-moulds. At the east end of the house a third gabled wing may have been part of a late-17th-century addition which included a new staircase. The house was evidently extended and partly rebuilt in the late 18th or early 19th century, when the entrance range was three storeys high under a hipped roof.[56] In 1886–8 the present Ganton Hall was built on higher ground to the south and the old house was demolished.[57] The new building is in the Jacobean style, of red brick with stone dressings, and contains two storeys with attics. The main north-facing elevation has a recessed centre with projecting side-wings, and there are shaped gables on this and the end elevations. The central entrance has a large stone portico.

Extensive stables and outbuildings, enclosing a courtyard, stand on the lower ground to the north, near the site of the former house. At least two ranges, dated 1832, served that house. They are single-storeyed and rough-cast, with pedimented central features and round-headed openings. A chalk-built cottage block on the east side of the court is dated 1903, with the initials A.W.L.

A mesne lordship in 3 carucates of the Gant fee was held by the Percy family, probably from the time of the marriage of Emme, daughter of Gilbert de Gant, and Alan de Percy in the early 12th century.[58] In 1176 the estate of William de Percy was divided and Joscelin of Louvain, husband of William's daughter Agnes, received the Ganton

---

[26] Ex inf. Mr. Brewster, 1971.
[27] E 179/202/62 m. 35.
[28] E 179/205/521.
[29] *Herring's Visit.* ii. 15.
[30] B.I.H.R., Bp. V. 1764/Ret. 205.
[31] *V.C.H. Yorks.* iii. 489.
[32] Census.
[33] *V.C.H. Yorks.* ii. 197 & n. Only 7 carucates were recorded in the main entry but 8 in the summary.
[34] *Feud. Aids*, vi. 27, 141; *E.Y.C.* ii, p. 432.
[35] *Cal. Close*, 1307–13, 99.
[36] J.I. 1/1042 m. 9d; *E.Y.C.* ii, p. 52.
[37] K.B. 26/141 m. 11d.
[38] *Feud. Aids*, vi. 27.
[39] *Yorks. Deeds*, x. 78–9; see below, p. 211.
[40] *Yorks. Deeds*, x. 79.
[41] *Feud. Aids*, vi. 266; see below, p. 335.
[42] C.P. 40/924 m. 316; C.P. 40/926 m. 415.
[43] C 142/52/18.
[44] C 142/74/57.
[45] *Cal. Pat.* 1553, 368.
[46] C 142/117/14; C 142/185/68.
[47] *Yorks. Fines*, iii. 50.
[48] *Visit. Yorks. 1584–5 and 1612*, ed. J. Foster, 54; G.E.C. *Baronetage*, iii. 147.
[49] Regy. of Deeds, 134/290/265.
[50] Ibid. 156/11/11.
[51] Ibid. 957/197/172.
[52] J. D. Legard, *The Legards of Anlaby and Ganton*, 161.
[53] E 179/205/521.
[54] B. M. Lansd. MS. 914 f. 199d., reproduced in Legard, *The Legards*, facing p. 162.
[55] See p. 108.
[56] Drawings at Ganton Hall.
[57] Legard, *The Legards*, 162.
[58] *E.Y.C.* ii, p. 483; *Feud. Aids*, vi. 27.

holding.[59] He was succeeded in 1190 by his eldest son Henry, who took his mother's name,[60] and the lordship continued to be held by the Percies until at least the later 14th century.[61]

Early demesne tenants of this holding were the Ganton family. Richard of Ganton held 3 carucates in 1176.[62] The estate passed to the Bossalls *c.* 1200 on the marriage of Henry of Ganton's daughter Maud and Richard of Bossall, who was in possession from at least 1206.[63] In 1284–5 John of Bossall held 3 carucates of the Percies.[64] The Bossalls retained the holding until the marriage before 1392 of Elizabeth, daughter of Robert Bossall (fl. 1369), and Thomas of Acklam.[65] It subsequently followed the descent of the manorial estate.[66]

An estate in Ganton of ½ carucate passed to Robert de Brus soon after 1086.[67] In 1166 it was held of Brus by Ricolf of Ganton[68] and later by his son Roger, who exchanged the holding, or part of it, for land elsewhere.[69] Its further descent is uncertain but this may have been the 4 bovates given to Guisborough priory by Agnes wife of Henry FitzRalph at an unspecified date.[70]

Land in Ganton was granted to Bridlington priory in the late 12th century by Nicholas of Ganton. William of Ganton gave some near-by land *c.* 1170–1212[71] and about the same time land was also given by William of Bossall. In 1192 3 bovates were confirmed to the priory by William son of Roger.[72] In 1535 the priory's land was worth 16*s.*[73] In 1250 the Knights Templars held two tofts in Ganton of Henry son of Ralph and in the following year they were said to hold two tofts, possibly the same ones, of Joscelin of Ganton.[74] Small holdings of both the Templars and Knights Hospitallers were mentioned in 1252.[75] The Templars' property probably passed to the Hospitallers. In 1539–40 the latter held property in Ganton worth 4*s.* a year[76] and it was restored to them when the order was briefly revived in 1558.[77] A toft and croft in Ganton held of the Percies were granted to St. Leonard's hospital, York, by Maud of Ganton and her son Richard in the early 13th century.[78] Nothing more is known of these holdings.

In 1086 there was one estate in Potter Brompton, consisting of 3 carucates, which was soke of the manor of Burton Agnes. Before the Conquest it had been held by Morcar but in 1086 it was in the hands of the king.[79] Soon after 1086 14 bovates were given to Robert de Brus.[80] The overlordship later passed to Hugh Bigod, possibly after the death of Adam de Brus in 1143, when Adam his son was a minor. In 1166 6 carucates in the township were held of Bigod by William of Aumale as a mesne lordship.[81] In 1278 the overlordship passed to John of Eston[82] but after his death in 1301 it was apparently regained by Roger Bigod.[83] In 1284–5 a mesne lordship in this estate was held by Robert of Everingham.[84] He was succeeded by Adam of Everingham, who died in possession in 1341 and whose heir was his son Adam.[85]

The demesne tenants in the 12th century were the Brompton family. Rayner of Brompton was succeeded by his son Rayner, who was living in the later 12th century,[86] and by his grandson Richard Brito,[87] probably the Richard le Bret who was living in 1236.[88] In 1268 John, son of Thomas le Bret, held an estate in Potter Brompton[89] and John Bret was returned as lord of the township in 1316.[90] The estate descended to Robert Bret, who died before 1423.[91]

Nothing is known of the subsequent descent of the manor of *POTTER BROMPTON* until 1493, when, like Ganton manor, it was part of the estate which was divided between the heirs of William Willesthorpe.[92] The manor may have passed to Brian Palmes, who in 1519 had a life interest in it. In that year, however, it was held by Isabel Willesthorpe and her second husband Thomas Wentworth.[93] In 1551 Ralph Creyke, Isabel's grandson by her first marriage, held the manor subject to a life interest of the Wentworths,[94] and he sold it to Ralph Thwing in 1558.[95] In 1566 the manor passed to Ralph Thwing's daughter Ursula,[96] who later married Cuthbert Dawnay, and then to her son John Dawnay.[97] In 1630 Mary, John Dawnay's daughter and heir, married John Legard, and the estate subsequently descended with Ganton manor.[98]

Dawnay Lodge, a large farm-house at the south end of the hamlet, was built in 1889, supposedly on the site of a former manor-house of the Dawnays.[99] The foundations of a 16th-century house have been found near by.[1]

A carucate in Potter Brompton, with extensive sheep pastures on the wold, was given by Rayner of Brompton to Bridlington priory in the 12th century.

---

[59] *Percy Charty.* (Sur. Soc. cxvii), 461–3.
[60] *Complete Peerage,* x. 448.
[61] *Feud. Aids,* vi. 27; *Cal. Inq. p.m.* xii, p. 226.
[62] *Percy Charty.* 463.
[63] Ibid. 108; *Yorks. Fines, John* (Sur. Soc. xciv), 102.
[64] *Feud. Aids,* vi. 27.
[65] *E.Y.C.* ix, p. 176; *Reg. Gray* (Sur. Soc. lvi), 81, 94; *Cal. Close,* 1272–9, 371; *Cal. Fine R.* 1273–1307, 168; *Cal. Inq. p.m.* ii, p. 486; v, p. 319; x, p. 27; xii, p. 226; *Yorks. Fines, 1347–77,* 191; *Yorks. Deeds,* x. 78–9.
[66] See p. 210.
[67] *V.C.H. Yorks.* ii. 292.
[68] *E.Y.C.* ii, pp. 13–14.
[69] *Guisborough Charty.* i (Sur. Soc. lxxxv), 210.
[70] Ibid. 196; J. Burton, *Mon. Ebor.* 344.
[71] *Bridlington Charty.* 137.
[72] Ibid.
[73] *Valor Eccl.* (Rec. Com.), v. 120.
[74] K.B. 26/143 m. 14d; K.B. 26/142 m. 6d; J.I. 1/1046 m. 28d.
[75] J.I. 1/1047 m. 6d.
[76] *Miscellanea,* iv (Y.A.S. Rec. Ser. cxiv), 92, 94.
[77] *Cal. Pat.* 1557–8, 319.
[78] *Guisborough Charty.* ii (Sur. Soc. lxxxix), 302 n.
[79] *V.C.H. Yorks.* ii. 198.
[80] Ibid. 292.
[81] *E.Y.C.* i, pp. 490–1.
[82] *Cal. Chart. R.* 1257–1300, 208–9; *Cal. Close,* 1272–9, 466; *Complete Peerage,* i. 356–7.
[83] *Cal. Close,* 1288–96, 370; *Cal. Inq. p.m.* iv, pp. 3–4; *Yorks. Deeds,* i. 170.
[84] *Feud. Aids,* vi. 27.
[85] *Cal. Inq. p.m.* viii, p. 226.
[86] *E.Y.C.* iii, pp. 60–61, 70.
[87] *Bridlington Charty.* 139–40.
[88] Ibid. 107.
[89] Ibid. 143; *Yorks. Fines, 1246–72,* 139.
[90] *Feud. Aids,* vi. 169.
[91] *Cal. Chart. R.* 1327–41, 271; *Yorks. Deeds,* ix. 152–3; x. 79, 168.
[92] C.P. 40/924 m. 316; C.P. 40/926 m. 415; see p. 210.
[93] *Yorks. Fines,* i. 33.
[94] Ibid. 157.
[95] Y.A.S. MSS., DD 15/18, 20.
[96] C 142/129/85; C 60/382 no. 45.
[97] C 142/523/168; *Visit. Yorks. 1584–5 and 1612,* ed. J. Foster, 80; Legard, *The Legards,* 163–4.
[98] C 142/564/155; G.E.C. *Baronetage,* iii. 147; Legard, *The Legards,* 163; see above, p. 210.
[99] Bulmer, *Dir. E. Yorks.* (1892), 203; O.S. Map 6" (1854).
[1] Ex inf. Mr. T. C. M. Brewster, 1971.

The estate was held of the priory by the Willerby family in the 12th and 13th centuries, when further grants were made.[2] At the Dissolution the priory held property in Potter Brompton worth £2 17s. 4d.[3] In 1557 former priory lands there, including pasturage for 400 sheep, were let by the Crown to Francis Aslaby and in 1570 to Alexander Morley.[4] It is likely that the property passed to the Legards by the early 17th century.[5]

The Knights Templars held property in Potter Brompton in 1252[6] and in 1539–40 the Hospitallers held 2 houses and 2 bovates there, worth about 4s.,[7] which were temporarily restored to them in 1558.[8] In 1563 former property of the Hospitallers was granted by the Crown to Thomas Wood and William Frankland.[9]

In 1291 the rectory, which had long since been given to Bridlington priory,[10] was worth £10, reduced to £5 6s. 8d. in the new taxation; it was valued at the latter amount in 1428.[11] After the Dissolution it was let to Adam Bardisey in 1539,[12] Marmaduke Lacy in 1561 and 1575,[13] and John Legard in 1586,[14] before being granted in fee to Edmund Downing and Roger Rante in 1592.[15] The hay tithes of Ganton and Potter Brompton were let in 1570 to Alexander Morley.[16] The rectory had passed to the Legards by 1643[17] and thereafter descended in that family.[18] In 1650 the tithes were worth £50 a year.[19] At inclosure in 1804 Sir John Legard's rectorial allotment was combined with that for his manorial lands.[20]

ECONOMIC HISTORY. In 1086 Potter Brompton was certainly and Ganton probably waste.[21] A grant, probably of the late 12th or 13th century, records 4 *nativi* in Ganton, holding altogether 4 tofts and 4 bovates.[22] Grassmen were mentioned in the parish in the 16th century,[23] in 1573, for example, when a Ganton woman bequeathed 4d. to every grassman in the village and 2d. to every husbandman.[24] The size of tenants' holdings is first recorded in 1558 when, in Potter Brompton, one tenant held 6 bovates, 2 held 5 each, one held 4, 2 held 2 each, and one held one bovate; 3 others had only cottages and garths.[25] In 1551 there were 8 houses and 4 cottages in Potter Brompton[26] and in 1645 16 houses and 12 cottages in Ganton.[27]

There were apparently two open fields in Ganton in the Middle Ages. A grant, probably of the late 12th century, refers to selions and bovates lying in the East and West fields,[28] and these fields were again mentioned in 1558.[29] The fields probably lay mainly on the lower slopes of the escarpment. Thus the 12th- or 13th-century furlongs included 'Canunclifdale' and 'Estclifdale', both in West field, the latter extending from 'Clifdike as far as Pekesbru'.[30] In 1645 the open fields of Ganton contained 64 bovates[31] and at inclosure in 1804 716 a. were said to lie in 'Ganton fields and wold'. Nothing is known of the names or situation of the open fields of Potter Brompton. In 1804 an allotment of 912 a. was made from the 'fields, common and wold' of the township.[32]

There were extensive commons and pastures in the parish in the Middle Ages and later, and much of the high wold south of the escarpment seems to have been devoted to sheep pasture until the late-18th- and 19th-century improvements.[33] In the later 12th century Bridlington priory was granted pasture for 800 sheep in 'the field', referred to in a later confirmation as 'the pasture', of Potter Brompton. Another grant to the priory was of pasture for 300 sheep on the wold there, where the priory had a sheepfold. A 70-acre pasture called Wildholme was mentioned about the same time.[34] In 1552, when Ganton sheep pasture was mentioned, over 500 sheep were kept in the township by the lords of Ganton and Potter Brompton manors.[35] In 1557 land formerly held by Bridlington priory in Potter Brompton included pasture for 400 sheep and 30 a. of pasture on the 'Browe'.[36] John Legard's manorial estate included pasturage at Ganton for 400 sheep in 1587[37] and for 500 in 1645.[38] Many inhabitants of the parish bequeathed ten or more sheep in the 16th and 17th centuries.[39]

In the late 18th century Sir Digby Legard said of his estate at Ganton that it was usual to stock the open wold land with sheep and cultivate only a small area because of the distance from the farm-houses and the difficulty of conveying manure. He added, however, that because of 'the rage of ploughing' in recent years a form of outfield cultivation had been practised on the high wold. The farmers ploughed sections of their sheep-walk 'to take a crop or two' and then let it lie fallow for 15–20 years before taking another crop.[40]

A manorial rabbit-warren lay 'in the fields of Ganton' in 1587 and 1645,[41] possibly in the area now covered by the golf course, part of which is known as Warren hill.[42] In 1634 John Dawnay, lord of Potter Brompton, claimed the right to keep rabbits on the commons there.[43] In the mid 19th century an area on the high wold south of the township was known as Potter Brompton warren.[44]

The low-lying and, until the early 19th century,

---

[2] *Bridlington Charty.* 107, 139–42.
[3] Dugdale, *Mon.* vi (1), 290.
[4] Legard, *The Legards,* 155; *Cal. Pat.* 1569–72, 251.
[5] C 142/564/155.   [6] J. I. 1/1047 m. 6d.
[7] *Miscellanea,* iv. 92, 94.   [8] *Cal. Pat.* 1557–8, 319.
[9] Ibid. 1560–3, 576.   [10] See p. 214.
[11] *Tax. Eccl.* (Rec. Com.), 326; *Feud. Aids,* vi. 326.
[12] *L. & P. Hen. VIII,* xiv (1), p. 309.
[13] C 66/1134 m. 31; *Cal. Pat.* 1560–3, 182.
[14] C 66/1276 m. 11.   [15] C 66/1390 m. 22.
[16] *Cal. Pat.* 1569–72, 251.   [17] C 142/774/6.
[18] Regy. of Deeds, CA/320/43; *T.E.R.A.S.* ii. 57.
[19] *T.E.R.A.S.* ii. 57.   [20] See p. 213.
[21] *V.C.H. Yorks.* ii. 197–8, 323.
[22] *Guisborough Charty.* i (Sur. Soc. lxxxvi), 196.
[23] B.I.H.R., Prob. Reg. xix, ff. 439, 582; R. I. 30, f. 181.
[24] Ibid. Prob. Reg. xix, f. 582.
[25] Y.A.S. MSS., DD 15/20.
[26] *Yorks. Fines,* i. 157.
[27] C 142/774/6.   [28] *Bridlington Charty.* 137–8.
[29] Y.A.S. MSS., DD 15/22.
[30] *Bridlington Charty.* 137–8; see above, p. 208.
[31] C 142/774/6.
[32] Registry of Deeds, Beverley, CA/320/43.
[33] See p. 213.
[34] *Bridlington Charty.* 108, 140, 143.
[35] E.R.R.O., DDPA/4/2; Y.A.S. MSS., DD 15/14.
[36] J. D. Legard, *The Legards of Anlaby and Ganton,* 155.
[37] Ibid. 90.
[38] C 142/774/6.
[39] B.I.H.R., Prob. Reg. x, f. 52; xxi, f. 130; xxiii, f. 739; xliv, f. 177; lviii, f. 249; R. I. 29, f. 79.
[40] A. Young, *A Six Months Tour Through the North of Eng.* ii. 16–17.
[41] C 142/774/6; Legard, *The Legards,* 90.
[42] O.S. Map. 6" (1854, 1958).
[43] Legard, *The Legards,* 215.
[44] O.S. Map 6" (1854).

ill-drained ground in the north of the parish along the river Derwent provided some meadow land from an early date. Land in Ganton granted by William of Bossall to Bridlington priory, probably in the later 12th century, included 7½ a. in his 'demesne meadow called Middledale. . . extending from Derwent as far as the water of the other Derwent'. In exchange the priory granted William land in the meadows of Ganton.[45] Some land was being improved in the late 12th century, when 'the new meadow' in the marsh of Potter Brompton was mentioned.[46] In Ganton meadow called the Main ings was referred to in 1552[47] and Ganton ings, near the Derwent, in 1804.[48] A meadow called Brompton Parks was mentioned in 1558.[49]

The marshes and carrs of the low ground also included large areas often referred to as waste or moor. In 1335 the lord of Potter Brompton was said to have taken into cultivation land in the waste[50] and later reclamation is suggested by a reference in 1716 to a piece of 'the low grounds called Roundabouts', which in 1743 was said to lie 'in the intake'.[51] A large area of marsh and moorland was recorded in Potter Brompton in 1551[52] and the Common carr in Ganton in 1803.[53]

The waste and moor also provided turf and whins. A turbary in the marsh of Potter Brompton is mentioned in 1392 and 1551.[54] In the later 16th century the lord of the manor accused Catherine Thwing of unlawfully cutting whins on Ganton moor or common. She claimed, however, that tenants had the right to take whins to sell, making a total payment of 3s. 4d. a year to the lord of the manor for the privilege.[55] In 1634, during a dispute over the commons of Potter Brompton, John Dawnay, then lord of the manor, claimed the right to cut whins for sale.[56] In the 18th century the vicar was entitled to cut whins in Potter Brompton[57] and in 1804 a 25-acre close in the north-west of the parish was known as Lord's Whins. At inclosure allotments totalling 272 a. were made from Ganton common and 142 a. from Potter Brompton common.[58]

The low-lying lands in the north of the parish were always liable to flooding and proposals were made in the 1770s to drain them. In 1773 there were said to be 427 a. in Ganton and 243 a. in Potter Brompton of the typically fenny ground, of small value, which bordered the upper reaches of the Derwent and Hertford.[59] In 1800 a drainage Act was passed for Ganton, Potter Brompton, and many other townships.[60] The work was to be financed and maintained by an annual assessment on all land-owners benefiting from it, and in 1804 the commissioners for the Act were already making such an assessment.[61]

There seems to have been a substantial amount of early inclosure in the parish. In 1493 several closes were recorded in Ganton, including New close, 'Aldegarth', and 'Gebongarth'.[62] In 1634 Francis Constable was prevented from inclosing part of Potter Brompton common by the lord of the manor. In reply Constable caused a 'piece of old grass' in the common called 'Marflatt' to be ploughed up.[63] In 1645 there were five demesne closes in Ganton[64] and in 1685 more were recorded, including Fishpond, Well, and Beck closes and Mill Crofts, the last-mentioned lying in the ings.[65] One method by which Sir Digby Legard improved his estate in the late 18th century was by making closes of at least 40 a. He also introduced grasses, sainfoin, and clover.[66] In 1804 there were over 1,500 a. not involved in the final inclosure. The allotments included one of about 250 a. which lay entirely in closes, including Warren hill (34 a.), Carr lands (24 a.), Snipe carr (42 a.), and Horse pasture (22 a.).[67]

The remaining open-field area of Ganton and Potter Brompton was inclosed in 1804[68] under an Act of 1803.[69] Sir John Legard, as lord of the manor and impropriator, received 2,041 a. and the vicar was allotted 247 a. for tithes. There were no other allotments.

In 1801 there were only 523 a. under crops in Ganton, mainly wheat (220 a.) and oats (191 a.).[70] The amount of land under arable probably increased during the 19th century and in 1905 there were 2,689 a. of arable, 995 a. of grassland, and 376 a. of woodland,[71] the latter reflecting the planting activities of the Legards, particularly Sir Digby, in the late 18th and early 19th centuries.[72] A plantation, now cleared, in the south of the parish was named after Sir Digby.[73] In the 19th and 20th centuries there have been 5–9 farmers in Ganton and 3–4 in Potter Brompton.[74]

From the early 13th century until about the later 14th century there were potteries at Potter Brompton, producing coarse unglazed ware. In 1953–4 six simple pit kilns, which had been fired by peat, were excavated near Potter Hill Farm and many potsherds were found.[75] In 1552 a house in Ganton contained a kiln[76] and a testator in 1583 left the 'use and occupation' of his kiln for a year, but the purpose of such kilns is not known.[77] A weaver was recorded in Potter Brompton in 1589[78] and there were weavers in the parish throughout the 18th and early 19th centuries.[79] In 1823 a 'machine maker' was recorded.[80]

[45] *Bridlington Charty.* 137–8; see above, p. 208.
[46] Ibid. 107.
[47] E.R.R.O., DDPA/4/2.
[48] Regy. of Deeds, CA/320/43.
[49] Y.A.S. MSS., DD 15/20.
[50] *Bridlington Charty.* 144.
[51] B.I.H.R., TER. J. Ganton 1716, 1743.
[52] C.P. 40/1147 m. 228d.
[53] E.R.R.O., DDCV/Parcel 22.
[54] C.P. 40/1147 m. 228d.; *Yorks. Deeds*, x. 78–9.
[55] C 3/117/14.
[56] Legard, *The Legards*, 215.
[57] B.I.H.R., TER. J. Ganton 1743.
[58] Regy. of Deeds, CA/320/43; O.S. Map 6" (1854).
[59] E.R.R.O., DDSY/11/2–5.
[60] 40 Geo. III, c. 118 (Local and Personal); see below, p. 280.
[61] E.R.R.O., DDCB/12/6. The assessment for 1874 is in ibid. DDSY/103/10.
[62] C.P. 40/926 m. 415.
[63] Legard, *The Legards*, 215.
[64] C 142/774/6.
[65] B.I.H.R., TER. J. Ganton 1685.
[66] Young, *Six Months Tour*, ii. 22, 25–6.
[67] Regy. of Deeds, CA/320/43.
[68] Ibid.
[69] 43 Geo. III, c. 89 (Priv. Act, not printed).
[70] 1801 Crop Returns.
[71] Acreage Returns, 1905.
[72] Young, *Six Months Tour*, ii. 23–6.
[73] O.S. Map 6" (1854).
[74] Directories.
[75] *Y.A.J.* xxxix. 445; see below, p. 337.
[76] Y.A.S. MSS., DD 15/14.
[77] B.I.H.R., Prob. Reg. xxii, f. 439.
[78] Ibid. xxiv, f. 115.
[79] E.R.R.O., PR. 2746, 2748.
[80] Baines, *Hist. Yorks.* (1823), ii. 209.

The only evidence of corn-milling is the existence of a manorial windmill at Ganton in 1586.[81]

LOCAL GOVERNMENT. No manorial records are known. The only surviving parochial records are surveyors' accounts for 1774–1838.[82] They show that those officers maintained gates, ditches, Hay bridge, and the village pond, and banked the river. Until 1800 work on the roads was done by statute labour or by workmen hired with composition money. From 1812 a rate was levied, usually of between 2d. and 6d. in the pound; in 1820–1 a rate of 9d. raised about £64.

In 1837 Ganton joined the Scarborough union.[83]

CHURCH. Ganton church is said to have originally been a chapelry,[84] possibly belonging to Willerby church since both were given by Adelard the hunter to Bridlington priory in the early 12th century. Ganton had, however, become parochial by 1125–30,[85] about which time its church was dedicated by the archbishop.[86] A vicarage had apparently been ordained by 1230, when a vicar is first mentioned.[87] The church income was divided between rector and vicar in the proportion of two to one, and this arrangement was confirmed in 1367.[88]

The advowson was retained by the priory until the Dissolution.[89] A grant of it to the archbishop of York in 1558[90] presumably lapsed on the accession of Elizabeth I. It generally passed with the rectory and so was let to Marmaduke Lacy in 1561 and 1575[91] and to Edmund Downing and Roger Rante in 1592.[92] By 1634 it was held by John Legard[93] and it subsequently descended with the capital manor. In 1970 the patron was Michael Wrigley.[94]

In 1291 the vicarage was valued at £5 6s. 8d., reduced to £3 6s. 8d. in the new taxation,[95] and it was again valued at the lower figure in 1428.[96] The net value in 1535 was £5 2s. 6d.[97] and in 1650 £25 a year.[98] In 1829–31 the average value of the living was £131 net[99] and in 1884 the net value was £180.[1]

Tithes provided most of the income until inclosure. There was no glebe, but in 1546 the vicar held land on lease and kept a flock of about forty sheep.[2] In 1743 he had common rights for six cows[3] and in 1764, in addition, 30 sheep-gates in the fields.[4] At inclosure in 1804 the vicar was awarded 247 a. in lieu of tithes.[5] In 1913 263 a. of glebe were sold.[6] In 1929 J. F. Pearson left by will proved in that year £1,071 to be invested for the augmentation of the vicar's stipend or, on the failure of this, for the benefit of the poor of Ganton. In 1970 the interest, known as the Bainbridge Bequest, was paid half-yearly to the vicar.[7]

A vicarage house is first mentioned in 1309, when the priory was charged with failing to provide sufficient buildings for it.[8] The house is again recorded in 1535 and from 1685 onwards.[9] It was rebuilt in 1738 with three rooms 'on a floor' and a back kitchen.[10] The present large red-brick Vicarage was built south of the church in 1868.[11]

William of Bossall was permitted, probably in the later 13th century, to hold services in an oratory which he had built in the parish, in a marshy place called St. Francis's isle.[12] A chaplain served in Ganton church, with an income of £2 net, in 1525.[13] At least two vicars in the 18th century held other livings, in 1743 Willerby and in 1764 Wykeham (Yorks. N.R.).[14] In the early 19th century the vicar also held Lund and Sherburn.[15] In 1835 there was an assistant curate.[16] In 1970 the vicar was also rector of Foxholes with Butterwick.

William Langdale (vicar 1574–1621) apparently had puritan sympathies and in 1590 he was cited for not wearing a surplice and not using a cross in baptism.[17] He was succeeded by his son Ambrose, who made an agreement in 1655 with John Legard, the patron, that 'being of great age and not sufficient to discharge the office of vicar', he should resign the vicarage to Legard in return for an annuity of £13 6s. 8d. and a rent-free house for life.[18] About 1660, however, the vicarage was in dispute between Langdale and James Colquhoun, who seems to have been instituted to Ganton at that time. The latter was ejected in 1662.[19]

There was a service each Sunday in 1743 and communion was celebrated four times a year. About sixty people were said to have received the previous Easter.[20] There was still a weekly service in 1764.[21] In 1865 there were two Sunday services; communion was then administered about eight times a year, but by 1869 it was celebrated fortnightly, with 16–17 communicants.[22] By 1871 it was celebrated every Sunday, with about eight communicants. In both 1877 and 1884, however, it was celebrated only monthly.[23] In 1970 there was a service each Sunday.

The church of ST. NICHOLAS, Ganton, is wholly of stone and consists of chancel, nave, north

---

[81] *Yorks. Fines*, iii. 50.
[82] E.R.R.O., PR. 2762.
[83] *3rd. Rep. Poor Law Com.* 174.
[84] *Bridlington Charty.* 137.
[85] *E.Y.C.* ii, p. 427.
[86] *Bridlington Charty.* 137.
[87] J.I. 1/1043 f. 1d.
[88] B.I.H.R., Churches index; *Yorks. Deeds*, x. 77–8.
[89] *Fasti Parochiales*, iii. 40–1.
[90] *Cal. Pat.* 1557–8, 420.
[91] Ibid. 1560–3, 182; C 66/1134 m. 31.
[92] C 66/1390 m. 22.
[93] C 142/774/6.
[94] Ex inf. the vicar, 1970.
[95] *Tax. Eccl.* (Rec. Com.), 326.
[96] *Feud. Aids*, vi. 326.
[97] *Valor Eccl.* (Rec. Com.), v. 125.
[98] *T.E.R.A.S.* ii. 57.
[99] *Rep. Com. Eccl. Revenues*, 936–7.
[1] B.I.H.R., Bp. V. 1884/Ret.
[2] Ibid., Reg. 19, f. 79.
[3] Ibid., TER. J. Ganton 1743.
[4] Ibid. 1764.
[5] Registry of Deeds, Beverley, CA/320/43.
[6] Ibid. 156/11/11; see above, p. 210.
[7] Char. Com. files; ex inf. the vicar, 1970.
[8] *Reg. Greenfield*, v (Sur. Soc. cliii), 234.
[9] B.I.H.R., TER. J. Ganton 1685, 1716; *Valor Eccl.* v. 125.
[10] B.I.H.R., TER. J. Ganton 1743; Lawton, *Rer. Eccles. Dioc. Ebor.* 300.
[11] Bulmer, *Dir. E. Yorks.* (1892), 203.
[12] *Bridlington Charty.* 138–9; *V.C.H. Yorks.* iii. 204. An area beyond the parish boundary is still called Francis's ings.
[13] *Y.A.J.* xxiv. 78.
[14] B.I.H.R., Bp. V. 1764/Ret. 205; *Herring's Visit.* ii. 15.
[15] J. D. Legard, *The Legards of Anlaby and Ganton*, 109.
[16] *Rep. Com. Eccl. Revenues*, 936–7.
[17] R. A. Marchant, *Puritans and Ch. Courts in Dioc. York, 1560–1642*, 259.
[18] B.I.H.R., Clergy index; C.P., H. 2678.
[19] Ibid., C.P., H. 5085; B. Dale, *Yorks. Puritanism and Early Nonconformity*, 42–3; *Calamy Revised*, ed. A. G. Matthews, 126.
[20] *Herring's Visit.* ii. 15.
[21] B.I.H.R., Bp. V. 1764/Ret. 205.
[22] Ibid., V. 1865/Ret. 201; V. 1868/Ret. 183.
[23] Ibid., V. 1871/Ret. 182; V. 1877/Ret.; Bp. V. 1884/Ret.

aisle, south transept, south porch, and west tower with spire.[24] Although there was a church at Ganton in the 12th century, the earliest part of the existing fabric dates only from the late 14th century, when the rebuilding of the whole church seems to have started. Features of the nave and chancel which are probably of that date include blocked windows in the south chancel wall and a two-light window with geometrical tracery at the west end of the north aisle. Carved stops on the nave arcade, representing female heads, appear to have 14th-century head-dresses. The enriched hood-mould over the south doorway has a similar head-stop; the other wears a crown. The north doorway is blocked. Most of the windows in the church have panelled tracery of early Perpendicular design, suggesting that rebuilding was completed near the beginning of the 15th century. The south porch, which is roofed with heavy stone slabs above a ribbed vault, carries over the entrance the arms of Willesthorpe, impaling Acklam quartering Percy of Kildale. The arms suggest a date in the early 15th century.[25] The west tower is probably of the same date as the porch. It has diagonal buttresses and a three-light window with panel tracery in the west wall. There are similar two-light windows at the belfry stage and an octagonal stone spire rises from behind an embattled parapet. Two stair turrets are visible internally on the west wall of the nave; they are corbelled out at a high level at either side of the tower arch.

The north aisle, of four bays, projects eastwards beyond the nave so that the fourth bay forms a chapel north of the chancel. At its east end are two ogee-headed niches; one, placed across the angle, is supported on a carved figure and has a crocketed canopy with a finial. Near by are an aumbry, a piscina, and a partially blocked squint. The north arcade has wide pointed arches and octagonal piers, the moulded capitals adorned with rosettes. The church contains a plain circular font.

The south transept has, since the late 17th century, served as a mortuary chapel for the Legard family. The lower part is bricked up to form a burial vault, shut off from the nave by a wooden screen. The east end of the chancel was completely rebuilt in 1843. A new east window was inserted, with geometric tracery and stained glass by Wailes of Newcastle.[26]

Four of the vaults in the mortuary chapel bear inscriptions to members of the Legard family, who died in 1848, 1852, 1853, and 1854. There are monuments in the chapel to John (d. 1678) and another John (d. 1738). In the chancel and aisle are monuments by the Fishers of York to Sir Digby (d. 1773), Frances (d. 1777), George (d. 1796), and Sir Digby (d. 1822); and by Skelton of York to the Revd. W. Legard (d. 1826), and Sir Thomas (d. 1830). There is also a monument by Deare of Rome to William Wilson (d. 1792), 'a man who adorned the garden' of the Legards.

There were three bells in 1552[27] and later.[28] One was made by Samuel Smith, the elder, of York in 1682 and another by J. Warner & Sons of London in 1864. The third is uninscribed.[29] The plate includes a silver chalice and paten, described in 1912 as 'quite modern'.[30] The registers of burials begin in 1553, of baptisms in 1556, and of marriages in 1653, and they are complete except for several small gaps in the 16th and 17th centuries.[31]

NONCONFORMITY. In the 16th and 17th centuries members of the Dawnay family, of Potter Brompton, were recusants.[32] No dissenters were reported in the parish in 1743 or 1764,[33] but a house at Ganton was licensed for nonconformist worship in 1773[34] and one at Potter Brompton in 1788.[35] The Methodists were holding a Sunday school in the parish in 1833[36] and in 1869 the vicar reported that Methodism had some influence in the parish; there was, however, no dissenting place of worship and there were said to be no avowed dissenters.[37] In 1877 the Methodists used a room in Ganton as a classroom and for prayer meetings,[38] possibly in a cottage in the main street, which was used as a Wesleyan chapel from at least 1892 until 1970, when it closed.[39]

EDUCATION. In 1835 there were two schools in Ganton. One, with 20 girls, had begun in 1829 and was supported entirely by fees. The second, with 16 boys and 8 girls, was financed by school pence and a subscription of £5 a year from Sir T. D. Legard.[40] In 1871 a new school, with accommodation for 52 juniors and infants, was built in the north of the village. In 1872, when the average attendance was 54, its income was £43 from subscriptions and £16 from school pence.[41] From 1875 it also received an annual government grant.[42] The building was enlarged in 1887 to accommodate 90 children, and a library, containing about 400 books, was added.[43] The school was further enlarged in 1912 to accommodate 112 children.[44] The average attendance declined from 76 in 1908 to 39 in 1936.[45] In 1970 the average number on the roll was seventeen.[46]

An evening school held in the 1860s and 1870s was poorly supported. In 1883, however, an evening school held in the winter was said to be successful, with an attendance of about twenty.[47]

CHARITIES FOR THE POOR. In 1616 John Legard was said to have 'lately founded and erected' an alms-house in Ganton for four poor people,

---

[24] See plate facing p. 257.
[25] Y.A.J. xxv. 80–1; see above, p. 210.
[26] E.R.R.O., PR. 2749.   [27] Inventories of Ch. Goods, 22.
[28] B.I.H.R., TER. J. Ganton 1770.
[29] Boulter, 'Ch. Bells', 217; V.C.H. Yorks. ii. 452.
[30] Yorks. Ch. Plate, i. 253.   [31] E.R.R.O.
[32] H. Aveling, Post Reformation Catholicism in E. Yorks. 1558–1790 (E. Yorks. Loc. Hist. Ser. xi), 58; J. D. Legard, The Legards of Anlaby and Ganton, 165.
[33] B.I.H.R., Bp. V. 1764/Ret. 205; Herring's Visit. ii. 15.
[34] G.R.O. Worship Returns, Vol. v, no. 387.
[35] B.I.H.R., DMH. 1773/10.
[36] Educ. Enquiry Abstract, 1835, 1085.
[37] B.I.H.R., V. 1868/Ret. 183. This return is dated 1869.
[38] Ibid., V. 1877/Ret.
[39] O.S. Map 6" (1892); local inf.
[40] Educ. Enquiry Abstract, 1835, 1085.
[41] Ed. 7/135; Rets. Rel. Elem. Educ. 1871, 476.
[42] Rep. of Educ. Cttee. of Council, 1875 [C. 1513–I], H.C., p. 659 (1876), xxiii.
[43] Inscription on building; Kelly's Dir. N. & E.R. Yorks. (1889), 392.
[44] E.R. Educ. Cttee. Mins. 1912–13, 244, 323.
[45] Bd. of Educ. List 21 (H.M.S.O.).
[46] Ex inf. Chief Educ. Officer, County Hall, Beverley, 1970.
[47] B.I.H.R., V. 1865/Ret. 201; V. 1868/Ret. 183; V. 1877/Ret.; Bp. V. 1884/Ret.

which he endowed with land and tithes in Willerby parish worth about £140. Three of the inmates, who had to be Anglicans over 50 years of age, were to come from Ganton and one from Staxton. After the death of Legard and his wife the inmates were to be chosen by the incumbents of Ganton and Willerby and their churchwardens.[48] Nothing more is known of the charity.

GARTON ON THE WOLDS

THE large parish of Garton, roughly square in shape, lies on the southern edge of the wolds about 2 miles north-west of Great Driffield.[1] The village was probably an Anglian settlement.[2] Most of the parish is occupied by south-facing slopes which rise from the boulder clay and gravel of the low ground in the south and south-west of the parish to the high chalk wold land in the north. The eastern parish boundary with Elmswell is formed by a green lane known as Garton Balk, and the southern boundary follows another green lane, which may be a prehistoric trackway. The more westerly section of the northern boundary with Sledmere follows a Roman road, which is elsewhere called Wold Gate,[3] and further east it runs along the line of a prehistoric earthwork for about a mile before following the valley in Garton Bottom. The area of the ancient parish is 4,147 a. In 1935 Garton civil parish was enlarged by the transference of 1,466 a. from Elmswell and Little Driffield civil parish.[4]

There is a marked contrast in the landscape of the parish north and south of the village. In the south a large area lies at between 100 ft. and 150 ft., falling below 100 ft. in the extreme south-east. Much of this lower-lying ground was formerly used as pasture, but in modern times arable farming has been predominant. North of the village the wold slopes rise to over 475 ft. in the north-west of the parish, and a large area of Garton Wold is above 300 ft. Three valleys dissect the wold land: in the west Garton Slack and in the north and north-east, beyond Garton Wold, Garton Bottom and Warren Dale. The wold slopes are now almost totally under arable cultivation. The only areas of woodland in the parish are shelter-belts around three farms on the wolds.

There is reason to believe that there may have been continuous settlement in Garton from prehistoric times. The valley known as Garton Slack has yielded considerable evidence of occupation from the Neolithic to the Romano-British periods. Outstanding among the Iron-Age discoveries was a chariot burial excavated in 1971. A Romano-British house and inclosure date from the 2nd and 3rd centuries.[5] Romano-British and Anglian burials have been found in the area of the brickyard, and other Anglian burials, along with coins of the 7th and 8th centuries, have been excavated in a prehistoric earthwork near the Sykes monument.[6] A large Anglian cemetery discovered in the south-east of the parish, between the railway line and the parish boundary, consisted of two groups of graves, one apparently pagan and the other Christian.[7]

The village lies mainly along the Driffield–York road. Until the late 18th century, however, this road led from Driffield through the village and north-westwards over Garton Wold to Sledmere. Near the east end of Garton another road diverged from the first, skirted the southern margins of the village, and ran on westwards towards Wetwang and York. At inclosure in 1771 the more southerly road was abandoned and the Wetwang road diverted to a straight course, joining the Sledmere road west of the village.[8] Part of the village, including the church, lies south of the Driffield–York road, where there was formerly a network of small lanes stretching as far as the old Wetwang road. Several of these lanes have ceased to be used but parts of both them and the old Wetwang road may be traced as hollow ways, still visible in 1969. Earthworks in the southern part of the village and others near the west end may mark the sites of former houses. Just beyond the western extremity of the village there are embankments indicating the irregular outline of Moss close,[9] which was apparently an early inclosure.

The green lanes which now mark the eastern, southern, and north-western boundaries of the parish were all designated as public roads at inclosure, together with the road that still follows the boundary in Garton Bottom. The green lane on the southern boundary was part of a road from Pocklington to Driffield, and a former wood beside it was known as Coach Road plantation.[10] The Kirkburn road, running south from the main village street, was also laid out at inclosure. It became Station Road after the Malton–Driffield railway line was built across the parish and opened in 1853. The line was closed for passenger traffic in 1950 and for goods in 1958;[11] the track has since been lifted but the station remained in 1969.

Most of the village houses lie along the York–Driffield road, which forms High Street, with a few on the remaining small lanes to the south. In the early 18th century two of the village streets were called King Street and Priest Lane.[12] A pond called the Mere lies in the middle of the village on the north side of what may have been a village green, a triangular area enclosed by High Street and the lanes. Until c. 1830 the stocks stood there. By 1895, however, the 'green' had been made into gardens.[13] Although it contains some modern buildings, the village has not been extended at either end during

[48] W. K. Jordan, *The Charities of Rural Eng. 1480–1660*, 270; J. D. Legard, *The Legards of Anlaby and Ganton*, 93–4.
[1] This article was written in 1969, with some later additions.
[2] *P.N.E.R. Yorks.* (E.P.N.S.), 58, 96.
[3] Mary Kitson Clark, *Gaz. of Roman Remains in E. Yorks.* 45.
[4] *Census*, 1931. [5] *Antiquity*, xlv. 289–92.
[6] J. R. Mortimer, *Forty Years' Researches in Burial Mounds*, 237–8, 246, 376–7.

[7] Ibid. 247–57.
[8] Regy. of Deeds, Beverley, AT/243/27; T. Jefferys, *Map of Yorks.* (1772); C. Greenwood, *Map of Yorks.* (1817).
[9] O.S. Map 6" (1855).
[10] Ibid.
[11] K. Hoole, *Regional Hist. of Rlys. of Gt. Brit.* iv (*The North-East*), 57.
[12] B.I.H.R., TER. J. Garton 1726, 1743.
[13] T.E.R.A.S. iii. 47.

the last century. The houses and cottages date from the 18th to the 20th century and are mainly built of brick; very little chalk remains, though one barn is of that material.

In Station Road the small so-called Manor House is built of brick and stone and dates largely from the 19th century. The houses and cottages along the north side of High Street form harmonious groups of dark red brick. They are mainly of 18th- and early-19th-century date, some of the cottages being of a storey and a half and the village shop having two bowed windows to the front. The most distinguished frontage is that of Manor Farm, which is two storeys high and seven bays wide, the windows alternating with blank panels. The house, which was probably built in the mid 18th century, has a pantile roof, a moulded eaves cornice, and a central doorway with dentil cornice and eared architrave.[14] The brick barn and outbuildings are of similar date. Other farmhouses in the village, all dating from the 19th century, include East End, Railtons, Cedar House, and West End Farms. Manor House, formerly High Field Farm, is a grey-brick building, five bays long with a pedimented porch. Several early-19th-century brick cottages in the village were being demolished in 1969: these were a row of seven in Station Road, another row of seven in High Street, and behind the latter a group of twelve others. Modern buildings include fourteen Council houses, as well as a small estate of bungalows and houses near the church.[15]

There were two inns in Garton in 1823, the Three Tuns and the Chase. By 1840 there were three, the Cross Keys, the Star, and the Oak.[16] By 1858 the Oak had disappeared but it had returned as the Green Tree by 1872.[17] From 1889 to 1901 the Cross Keys was the only inn recorded and from 1905 to 1929 there was none, although a beer-seller lived in the village.[18] By 1933 the Oak Tree had reappeared[19] and was still in existence, as the Oak, in 1969.

There are four outlying farms in the parish, Garton Field, Garton Grange, and High Field, formerly Crust's, Farms on the wold slopes north of the village and Low (formerly Sheep Walk) Farm on the lower ground in the south-west. All date from after the inclosure of 1775. At High Field and Garton Field Farms the late-18th-century farmhouses adjoin their larger 19th-century successors. The Sykes monument, a 120-foot-high look-out tower built in 1865 in memory of Sir Tatton Sykes (1772–1863), stands at the highest point near the boundary with Sledmere and forms a landmark for miles around. It was designed by John Gibbs of Oxford in a Venetian Gothic style and is built of grey stone, with contrasting bands and ornament in red and black stone. There are sculptured bas-reliefs, by Forsyth, on the south and east sides of the base, the former representing agricultural implements and the latter Sir Tatton Sykes on horseback. Above the base is an inscription to Sykes from 'those who loved him as a friend and honoured him as a landlord'.[20]

In 1377 Garton had 202 poll-tax payers.[21] By the late 17th century the population had apparently declined and in 1670 only 41 households, including 12 exempted, were listed in the hearth-tax assessment. In 1674 the exempted households are omitted but of the 30 chargeable 18 had only one hearth each, 8 had 2, 2 had 3, and 2 had six.[22] In 1743 there were said to be 42 families in the parish[23] and in 1764 46.[24] In 1801 the population was 288. It rose steadily during the 19th century to a peak of 572 in 1861 and thereafter declined to 440 in 1901.[25] In the 20th century it has continued to fall and in 1951 there were 371 inhabitants.[26]

MANORS AND OTHER ESTATES. In 1086 there were two estates in Garton. One, of 19 carucates, was held by the count of Mortain, and the other, of 9 carucates, by the archbishop of York.[27]

The count's estate consisted of three separate holdings in 1086. One, held in demesne, contained 8 carucates; another, of 7 carucates, had been held in 1066 by Mule, Orm, Sonulf, and Torchil; and the third, of 4 carucates, had been held as a manor by Asulf.[28] William, count of Mortain, was attainted in 1106 and his lands passed to the Crown.[29] His Garton estate had probably passed by the 1130s to Walter Espec,[30] whose property was divided after his death between the children of his three sisters, Garton passing in 1157–8 to Robert Ros, son of Adelina.[31] The manor of GARTON was held in chief as part of the barony of Helmsley or Ros until 1539.[32]

The family of Ros or Roos held the manor, consisting of 17 carucates in 1284–5, 1346, and 1428,[33] until the death of Edmund, Lord Ros, in 1508.[34] It later passed to George Manners, son of Edmund's sister Eleanor and her husband Robert Manners.[35] In 1539 it was sold by Thomas Manners, Lord Ros, created earl of Rutland in 1525, to Sir William Holles,[36] whose son's widow Catherine married John Hugford.[37] The reversion after Catherine's death had passed by 1573 to John Payne, who in that year settled it on his son William.[38] In 1576 John and Catherine Hugford sold the manor to the trustees of William Payne.[39] In 1634 another William Payne sold it to William Hustler[40] who, shortly before his

---

[14] See plate facing p. 321.
[15] Baines, *Hist. Yorks.* (1823), ii. 209.
[16] White, *Dir. E. & N.R. Yorks.* (1840), 388.
[17] White, *Dir. Hull & York* (1858), 441; *Kelly's Dir. N. & E.R. Yorks.* (1872), 369.
[18] Directories.
[19] *Kelly's Dir. N. & E.R. Yorks.* (1933), 475.
[20] J. F. Blakeborough, *Sykes of Sledmere*, 132; *The Builder*, 8 Apr. 1865, pp. 244–5; ex inf. Sir Nikolaus Pevsner. See plate facing p. 208.
[21] E 179/202/62 m. 11.
[22] E 179/205/514, 521.
[23] *Herring's Visit.* ii. 16–17.
[24] B.I.H.R., Bp. V. 1764/Ret. 209.
[25] *V.C.H. Yorks.* iii. 489.
[26] *Census.*
[27] *V.C.H. Yorks.* ii. 215, 226, 323. In the summary 25 carucates are assigned to the count.

[28] Ibid. 226.
[29] *Complete Peerage*, ii. 360.
[30] *Rievaulx Charty.* (Sur. Soc. lxxxiii), p. xxiii; *V.C.H. Yorks. N.R.* i. 491.
[31] Dugdale, *Mon.* vi. 209; *Y.A.J.* xxiv. 328; *Pipe R. 1156–8* (Rec. Com.), 146.
[32] Burke, *Dormant and Extinct Peerages*, 460.
[33] *Feud. Aids*, vi. 30, 211, 268.
[34] Burke, *Dorm. and Ext. Peerages*, 460. The property lay under attainder in 1461–85.
[35] *Complete Peerage*, xi. 107.
[36] *Yorks. Fines*, ii. 86.
[37] *Lincs. Pedigrees* (Harl. Soc. li), 483, 508.
[38] *N. Country Wills*, ii (Sur. Soc. cxxi), 224–5.
[39] *Yorks. Fines*, ii. 88, 90.
[40] C 54/3043 m. 3.

death in 1644, settled his estates on his wife Ellen, with the remainder to his son William.[41] In 1651 the latter disputed the validity of this settlement, which deprived him of maintenance and which he claimed to have been obtained from his father by duress.[42]

By 1660 the manor was in the possession of William Hustler, who conveyed it in that year to James Edwards.[43] In 1681 Edwards sold it to Richard Graham,[44] who seems to have been acting for Reginald Graham of Nunnington (Yorks. N.R.).[45] Reginald died in 1685 and the manor passed to his nephew Sir Richard Graham, created Viscount Preston in 1681.[46] He was attainted in 1689[47] and four years later the reversion after the death of Reginald's widow was granted to Charles Howard, earl of Carlisle, and Sir George Fletcher for 99 years.[48] Richard Graham was later pardoned[49] and by 1703 again held the manor.[50] It passed after the death of Charles Graham in 1738 to his aunt Lady (Catherine) Widdrington.[51] By her will, proved in 1757, she devised the manor to Thomas Howard for life, with remainder successively to Charles Graham, William Graham, and Sir Bellingham Graham of Norton Conyers (Yorks. N.R.).[52]

Thomas Howard held the manor until at least 1780.[53] In 1769 William Graham sold his reversion to Charles Graham,[54] who sold his interest in 1773 to Sir Bellingham Graham.[55] In the same year the latter leased the manor from Thomas Howard[56] and at inclosure in 1775 he was awarded a total of 1,915 a., of which he received 1,706 a. as lessee of the manor.[57] By 1785 he had succeeded to the manor[58] and in 1792, after his death, his trustees sold his Garton estate, with a total area of 1,984 a., to Sir Christopher Sykes.[59] Between 1792 and 1848 the Sykes family acquired other land in Garton[60] and after buying about 70 a. from Elizabeth Boyes in 1848[61] Sir Tatton Sykes's estate there amounted to over 3,700 a. The estate was still held by the Sykes family in 1970. In the 20th century several small plots, mainly in the village, have been sold,[62] and in 1964–7 75 a. in Garton Slack were sold for sand and gravel workings.[63]

The 9 carucates belonging in 1086 to the archbishop of York had been held at the Conquest as two manors by Ulviet and St. John's college, Beverley. The whole estate was held by the college in 1086.[64] By 1284–5 only 2 carucates were held by the college; another belonged to St. Mary's abbey, York, and 6 had apparently passed to the Montagu fee.[65]

It was presumably land of St. John's college which was given by the provost of Beverley to St. Catherine's chantry in Beverley minster in 1450.[66] After the Dissolution 8 bovates formerly belonging to the chantry were granted by the Crown to Francis Morrice and Francis Philips, who sold them in 1611–12 to William Towse.[67]

The largest tenant of the Montagu fee in the early 14th century was Thomas of Ardern with 13 bovates.[68] In 1428 20 bovates belonged to the Arderns,[69] and in 1529 Joan Rokeby, daughter of Anthony Ardern and widow of Thomas Creyke of Marton, died seised of 20 bovates in Garton.[70] The estate seems to have descended in the Creyke family until at least 1645,[71] but it has not been traced further.

In 1284–5 an estate of 6 carucates lay in the Mowbray fee.[72] It is possible that this land represents the 6 carucates of the Mortain fee which were not included in the text of the Domesday Survey.[73] The largest tenant of the fee in the early 14th century was Thomas of Grindale with 10 bovates,[74] but no more is known of the holding.

Several substantial estates were built up with land from two or more of the fees in Garton. A family taking its name from the village may have had land there since the mid 12th century,[75] and in 1279 John of Garton held more than 21 bovates.[76] By 1346 members of the family held all 6 carucates of the Mowbray fee, 7 bovates of the Montagu fee, and one carucate of the Ros fee.[77] The family was apparently last mentioned in 1388, when 7 bovates belonging to Robert of Garton were taken into the king's hands for debt.[78]

In 1428 20 bovates of the Mowbray fee belonged to Thomas Newport.[79] The estate seems to have passed in the 16th century to Thomas Thwaite, who bought Newport land elsewhere, and in 1559 Thwaite settled land in Garton on William and Henry Kirkby.[80] In 1567 the Kirkbys sold it to William Beverley and he in the same year to Thomas Beverley; it then included over 21 bovates.[81] In 1579 it was bought by George Cresswell,[82] who already owned part of the Bulmer manor in Garton. Sir William Bulmer bought 30 bovates from Edward Gower in 1527[83] and at his death in 1531 he held 24 bovates described as the manor of

---

[41] C 142/774/4.
[42] C 5/12/15.
[43] C.P. 25(2)/752/12 Chas. II Mich. no. 52.
[44] C 54/4569 m. 9.
[45] In 1693–4 Susanna Graham, wife of Reginald, held the manor for life: H. F. Waters, *Genealogical Gleanings in Eng.* i. 557.
[46] *V.C.H. Yorks. N.R.* i. 546; *Descent of Lands on the Wolds* (n.d., c. 1860), 39.
[47] *V.C.H. Yorks. N.R.* i. 546.
[48] C 66/3374 m. 7.
[49] *Complete Peerage*, vi. 302.
[50] E.R.R.O., DDSY/24/1.
[51] Ibid./23/269; *Descent of Lands on the Wolds*, 34.
[52] E.R.R.O., DDSY/23/269.
[53] Ibid./24/5, 6.
[54] Ibid./23/269.
[55] Ibid.; Registry of Deeds, Beverley, AR/419/806; *Descent of Lands on the Wolds*, 39.
[56] Regy. of Deeds, AS/63/105; E.R.R.O., DDSY/23/269.
[57] E.R.R.O., DDSY/23/46.
[58] Regy. of Deeds, BH/567/972.
[59] Ibid. BQ/454/706.
[60] See p. 219.
[61] E.R.R.O., DDSY/23/249, 252, 262.

[62] Regy. of Deeds, 373/427/355; 410/331/259; /334/201; /335/262; 411/128/98, etc.
[63] Ibid. 1390/317/284; 1455/520/453; 1496/506/440.
[64] *V.C.H. Yorks.* ii. 215.
[65] *Feud. Aids*, vi. 30.
[66] *Beverley Chapter Act Bk.* ii (Sur. Soc. cviii), p. lxxxviii; *Cal. Pat.* 1446–52, 312.
[67] E.R.R.O., DDSY/23/2, 3; DDDA/3/7; *Descent of Lands on the Wolds*.
[68] B.M. Add. MS. 26729, f. 114.
[69] *Feud. Aids*, vi. 268.
[70] C 142/80/100; *Test. Ebor.* ii. 195; iv. 35 n.
[71] *Royalist Composition Papers*, i (Y.A.S. Rec. Ser. xv), 17–18.
[72] *Feud. Aids*, vi. 30.
[73] See p. 217 n.
[74] B.M. Add. MS. 26729, f. 114.
[75] *Red Bk. Exch.* (Rolls Ser.), 433.
[76] *Yorks. Inq.* i. 187.
[77] *Feud. Aids*, vi. 211.
[78] C 131/36/4.
[79] *Feud. Aids*, vi. 268.
[80] *Yorks. Fines*, i. 229.
[81] Ibid. 335–6; C 54/774 m. 9.
[82] C 54/1057 m. [2].
[83] *Yorks. Fines*, i. 49.

GARTON.[84] The estate was divided between the eight daughters of Sir Ralph Bulmer (d. 1558) but by 1585 at least seven of the shares had been acquired by George Cresswell.[85] The descent of Cresswell's land has not been traced but the estate may have passed to the Towse family.

The Towses were buying land in Garton in the later 16th and early 17th centuries[86] and it descended in several branches of the family. In 1643 William Towse settled 20 bovates on his son Brian (d. 1680)[87] and at inclosure in 1775 Jane Cooke, daughter of another Brian Towse, received 99 a. in lieu of them.[88] This land subsequently descended with the rectorial estate.[89] Land belonging to William Towse, brother of Brian (d. 1680), passed in 1692 to his daughter Jane, wife of Timothy Overend.[90] In 1715 Overend had 24 bovates.[91] He sold his estate in 1742 to Mark Kirkby, and after Kirkby's death in 1748 it passed to his nephew Richard Sykes.[92] At inclosure in 1775 Christopher Sykes was awarded 282 a.[93] which later descended with the capital manor. Another member of the family, Jeremiah Towse, sold 12 bovates and a house called Butler's Hall to Francis Leppington in 1709.[94] Leppington bought other land, and in 1775 he was allotted 138 a.[95] He sold it to Sir Christopher Sykes in 1786.[96] Jeremiah's brother Timothy Towse had 5 bovates in 1741,[97] some of which passed to Thomas Barmby in 1757. The Barmbys already had 15 bovates in Garton, said to have been acquired from John Towse in the late 17th century.[98] In 1774 Thomas Barmby sold all 20 bovates to Sir Bellingham Graham, for which he was allotted 209 a. in 1775.[99] It was sold to Sir Christopher Sykes in 1792, along with the capital manor.[1]

About 1200 William of Garton quitclaimed to Ellerton priory 5 bovates which he had previously held as tenant of the priory.[2] In the early 14th century Thomas *nepos capellani* held 3 bovates of the priory.[3] At the Dissolution Ellerton's land was worth £1 4s.[4] In 1536–7 Thomas Toox, possibly a member of the Towse family, had a lease of 6 bovates of the priory's land.[5] In 1322 land in Garton was confirmed to Watton priory.[6] After the Dissolution the land was granted to the archbishop of York.[7] The Knights Templars held land in Garton by the 13th century[8] and the Knights Hospitallers of Beverley had 17 bovates there in 1539–40.[9]

The rectory, which was given to Kirkham priory in the 12th century,[10] was worth £20 in 1291, reduced to £12 in the new taxation;[11] it was still valued at £12 in 1428.[12] By 1336 the glebe amounted to 16 bovates.[13] In 1535 the rectory was worth about £25.[14] It was let to William Rawghton in 1526[15] and to Ralph Lathere before 1535.[16] After the Dissolution leases were granted to James Simpson and William Savage in 1544,[17] Thomas Wood in 1561,[18] Philip Constable in 1575,[19] Ralph Bourchier in 1583 and 1596,[20] and John Turner, Thomas Wilson, and Elizabeth Atkinson in 1600.[21] The rectory was granted in fee in 1609 to Francis Morrice and Francis Philips, and they sold it in 1616 to John Turner.[22] In 1650 it was worth £140.[23] Christopher Turner's daughter Christiana married Benjamin Ashton and in 1715 the rectory was sold by the Ashtons to Brian Towse.[24] Towse's daughter Jane Cooke[25] was awarded 1,269 a. for tithes and glebe at inclosure in 1775.[26] In 1779 she devised her estate to Robert Lakeland, whose widow Elizabeth sold it in 1792 to Edward Topham[27] and he in 1800 to Sir Christopher Sykes.[28] It subsequently descended with the capital manor.

ECONOMIC HISTORY. In 1066 the archbishop's estate was worth £2 5s. and there was land for five ploughs, but in 1086 the land was waste. The seven-carucate holding of the count of Mortain's estate had land for ten ploughs but it, too, was waste in 1086. The count's manor, with 4 carucates, was said to have land for two ploughs but in 1086 the count had one plough and four sokemen and two villeins had three more.[29]

Cottars on the estate of John of Garton in 1279 paid a total of £1 6s. 8d. rent,[30] and in 1285 there were 17 cottages worth £1 10s. a year on the Ros estate, which also included 2 bovates held in bondage.[31] About 1537 all 24 bovates of the Bulmer manor were held by tenants-at-will.[32] In 1703 there were 25 manorial tenants[33] and in 1879 about fifty cottagers paid a total of £177 rent.[34] There were probably never many free tenants in Garton, only one on the Ros estate in 1285, for example.[35]

There is no indication of the size or position of the open fields before the 18th century. Wandale is mentioned in the 12th century and later,[36] and part

---

[84] B.M. Add. MS. 26722, f. 401; *Test. Ebor.* v. 310–12.
[85] B.M. Add. MS. 26726, f. 57; 26728, f. 5; 26731, f. 7; C 142/116/78; C 54/939 m. 1; C 54/1004 m. [42 from end]; C 66/1096 m. 33; *Yorks. Fines*, i. 328, 371; ii. 51, 79, 110, 117; iii. 43.
[86] *Yorks. Fines*, ii. 46; iii. 126; *1603–14*, 109; *1614–25*, 145–6; see above, p. 218.
[87] E.R.R.O., DDSY/23/10, 157.
[88] Ibid. /46; Regy. of Deeds, AT/243/27.
[89] See below.
[90] *Descent of Lands on the Wolds*, 37. For a pedigree of the Towses see ibid. 40.
[91] E.R.R.O., DDSY/24/4.
[92] Ibid. /23/227; /108/3.
[93] Ibid. /23/46.   [94] Ibid. /60.
[95] Ibid. /46, 61.   [96] Ibid. /80.
[97] Ibid. /41.
[98] Ibid. /24/4; *Descent of Lands on the Wolds*, 38.
[99] E.R.R.O., DDSY/23/41, 46.
[1] See p. 218.   [2] *E.Y.C.* x, p. 151.
[3] B.M. Add. MS. 26729, f. 114.
[4] *Valor Eccl.* (Rec. Com.), v. 128.
[5] E 303/22/Yorks./191.
[6] B.M. Harl. Chart. 55E, 23.
[7] *Cal. Pat.* 1550–3, 117–18.
[8] *Y.A.J.* xxix. 382; *Yorks. Inq.* i. 187.
[9] *Miscellanea*, iv (Y.A.S. Rec. Ser. xciv), 92.
[10] See p. 221.
[11] *Tax. Eccl.* (Rec. Com.), 304, 326.
[12] *Feud. Aids*, vi. 327, where 'vicaria' seems to mean the rectory.
[13] *Cal. Chart. R.* 1327–41, 363.
[14] *Valor Eccl.* v. 103.
[15] *Monastic Chancery Proc.* (Y.A.S. Rec. Ser. lxxxviii), 72–3.
[16] C 1/561/40.
[17] *L. & P. Hen. VIII*, xix (1), p. 648.
[18] *Cal. Pat.* 1560–3, 28.   [19] E 310/31/184 no. 17.
[20] E 310/32/192 no. 43; C 66/1449 m. 20.
[21] E 310/28/167 no. 52; C 66/1556 m. 28.
[22] E.R.R.O., DDSY/23/157.   [23] *T.E.R.A.S.* ii. 53.
[24] E.R.R.O., DDSY/23/157.   [25] Ibid.
[26] Ibid. /46; Regy. of Deeds, AT/243/27.
[27] E.R.R.O., DDSY/23/157.
[28] Ibid. /174.   [29] *V.C.H. Yorks.* ii. 215, 226.
[30] *Yorks. Inq.* i. 187.   [31] *Cal. Inq. p.m.* ii, p. 345.
[32] S.C. 6/Hen. VIII/4335.   [33] E.R.R.O., DDSY/24/1.
[34] Ibid. /107/15.   [35] *Yorks. Inq.* ii. 33.
[36] E.R.R.O., DDHV/9/21; DDCV/parcel 104; B.I.H.R., TER. J. Garton 1749; *P.N.E.R. Yorks.* (E.P.N.S.), 96.

of the open fields lay waste in 1350 'through the pestilence'.[37] The town field is mentioned in 1625.[38] At inclosure in 1775 there were three fields: South field covered about 1,200 a., West field about 1,050 a. between the York and Sledmere roads, and North field 1,513 a., practically the whole of the area north of the village street and east of the Sledmere road.[39]

In the 18th century an infield-outfield system of cultivation was used. In 1732 lands in the 'out fields' are mentioned,[40] and a survey of two farms in 1798, after inclosure, distinguished between infield and outfield land. On one farm infield land comprised 176 a. and outfield land 417 a., and on the other 310 a. and 488 a. respectively.[41] The outfield land was presumably cultivated periodically and used for grazing in the intervening years.[42] In 1798 it included areas called the Great Sheep Walk, Hill Top, Hill Side, and 'the great piece at Northside'.[43] In 1715 the horse and cow pastures were mentioned,[44] and in 1766 the town pasture contained 81 a. and the sheep walk 700 a.[45] The last may have been in the south-west of the parish, where Sheepwalk Farm and plantation were situated in 1851.[46] Water Holme, mentioned in 1768, may have been meadow land.[47] Pastures and meadows were presumably reckoned with the open fields at inclosure in 1775.

There is some evidence of early inclosure. William Beverley's estate in 1567 included six closes,[48] and in 1643 five meadow closes were held by Brian Towse.[49] More inclosure occurred in the 18th century; a pre-1775 survey of a farm included 9 a. of 'new inclosed ground in the Bayle'.[50]

The remaining open-field land was inclosed in 1775[51] under an Act of 1774.[52] The commonable grounds totalled 3,895 a., and 3,837 a. were actually allotted. Sir Bellingham Graham, lessee of the manor, received 1,915 a., and Jane Cooke, the impropriator, 1,368 a. Three other men received substantial allotments: Christopher Sykes got 282 a., Edward Leppington 138 a., and William Severs 71 a. In addition the vicar received 41 a. for glebe and tithes and there were eighteen allotments of 4 a. or under.

By 1851 over 200 a. of land, mainly in the west of the parish, were under plantations[53] as a result of the activities of the Sykes family, particularly Sir Christopher (1749–1801) and Sir Tatton (1772–1863), in the late 18th and early 19th centuries.[54] By 1905, however, the area of woodland had been reduced to about 50 a.[55] Garton has been predominantly in arable cultivation in the 19th and 20th centuries. In 1801 1,473 a., or over a third of the total area of the parish, were under crops, chiefly wheat, barley, and rape or turnips, which were each grown on between 370 a. and 400 a.[56] In 1882 a farm of 779 a. had 614 a. of arable,[57] and in 1905 3,245 a. of the parish were arable and only 658 a. were under permanent grass.[58] There have usually been from 10 to 13 farms in the 19th and 20th centuries,[59] several of them very large. In 1882 2 farms were over 700 a., one was of 500 a.–700 a., 3 were of 300 a.–500 a., one was of 100 a.–300 a., and 3 were under 100 a.[60] In 1937 6 farms had acreages of 150 or over and 5 were smaller.[61]

A brickyard, owned by the Sykes family, was in operation for much of the 19th and early 20th centuries.[62] It may have begun production in 1812, when it was reported to Sir Mark Sykes that a first clamp of 40,000 bricks had been fired.[63] From 1879 to 1881 over 1½ million bricks were sold, and in the latter year 90,000 and 40,000 bricks were produced in two successive fortnights.[64] By 1909, however, only about 10,000 bricks were made each fortnight,[65] and the yard probably ceased production after 1914. A kiln and a much-altered row of brickworkers' cottages still stood in 1969.

There were weavers in the village in 1778, 1783, and 1816,[66] and a rope- and net-maker in 1840.[67] The only reference to a mill is in 1285.[68] Sand and gravel have been quarried commercially in Garton Slack since 1964.[69]

LOCAL GOVERNMENT. There are surviving manorial court rolls for 1609–26.[70] They show that the lord enjoyed the assize of bread and ale. The court dealt with its infringement, with the removal of boundary stones between Garton and Wetwang, but mainly with agrarian offences. In 1625–6 four affeerors were appointed. Other court records survive for the years 1712–30 and 1768–81,[71] when the court met once a year. In 1712 a constable, 2 bylawmen, and a pinder were appointed, and in 1717 in addition 3 affeerors. In 1722 and later a deputy constable was often appointed. From 1768 no affeerors and from 1776 no bylawmen were appointed. Matters dealt with were again mainly agricultural but in most years from 1768 to 1780 no offences were presented.

There are no known parochial records before 1835. Garton joined the Driffield union in 1836.[72]

CHURCH. There was a church at Garton in 1086.[73]

[37] *Cal. Inq. p.m.* ix, p. 372.
[38] E.R.R.O., DDCV/parcel 104.
[39] Ibid. DDSY/23/46; Registry of Deeds, Beverley, AT/243/27.
[40] E.R.R.O., DDHV/14/1.
[41] Ibid. DDSY/23/161.
[42] A. Harris, *Rural Landscape of E.R. Yorks.* 24–5.
[43] E.R.R.O., DDSY/23/161.
[44] Ibid. DDCV/parcel 104.
[45] Ibid. DDSY/23/266.
[46] O.S. Map 6" (1855).
[47] E.R.R.O., DDSY/23/189.
[48] C 54/774 m. 9.
[49] E.R.R.O., DDSY/23/10.
[50] Ibid. /34/45.
[51] Ibid. /23/46; Regy. of Deeds, AT/243/27.
[52] 14 Geo. III, c. 71 (Priv. Act).
[53] O.S. Map 6" (1855).
[54] J. T. Ward, *E. Yorks. Landed Estates in the 19th Cent.* (E. Yorks. Loc. Hist. Ser. xxiii), 13.
[55] Acreage Returns, 1905.
[56] 1801 Crop Returns.
[57] E.R.R.O., DDSY/97/37.
[58] Acreage Returns, 1905.
[59] Directories.
[60] E.R.R.O., DDSY/97/37.
[61] *Kelly's Dir. N. & E.R. Yorks.* (1937), 468.
[62] E.R.R.O., DDSY/101/74; /98/54, 86.
[63] Ibid. /101/74.
[64] Ibid. /98/86.
[65] Ibid. /54.
[66] Ibid. PR. 1033–4
[67] White, *Dir. E. & N.R. Yorks.* (1840), 388.
[68] *Yorks. Inq.* ii. 33.
[69] Regy. of Deeds, 1390/317/284; 1455/520/453; 1496/506/640.
[70] E.R.R.O., DDCV/Parcel 104.
[71] Ibid.; DDSY/24/6.
[72] *3rd Rep. Poor Law Com.* 168.
[73] *V.C.H. Yorks.* ii. 226.

About 1133–9 Walter Espec gave it, together with a carucate and land called 'St.Michael's flat', to Kirkham priory, which he had founded about 1122, supposedly on the advice of his uncle William Espec, then rector of Garton.[74] A vicarage was ordained, possibly c. 1294.[75]

The advowson was retained by the priory until the Dissolution.[76] A grant of it to the archbishop of York in 1558[77] presumably lapsed on the accession of Elizabeth I and it has remained with the Crown.

At ordination the vicar was assigned a house and 2 bovates, together with small tithes and rents.[78] In 1535 the net value of the vicarage was £5 6s. 8d.[79] and in 1650 £13 6s. 8d.[80] By 1663 it was only £4.[81] In 1716 the vicar reported that he received £6 10s. a year from Benjamin Ashton, but this payment was only for his own life. The vicarage was valued at £16 10s. in 1764.[82] The living was augmented with £200 from Queen Anne's Bounty in each of the years 1769, 1787, and 1792,[83] and in 1797 there ended a long period of sequestration,[84] presumably for poverty. The average net income in 1829–31 was £125.[85] The gross value was said in 1883 to have recently fallen to £147.[86]

At inclosure in 1775 the vicar received 41 a. in lieu of glebe and all except personal tithes,[87] which still formed part of the income of the living in 1865.[88] Between 1770 and 1777 about 9 a. were bought in Nafferton,[89] in 1787 9 a. in Bempton, and in 1821 a further 4 a. in Nafferton, all with Bounty money.

A vicarage house was recorded in 1535.[90] In 1685 it was said that the house had been demolished 'in the time of . . . Oliver Cromwell',[91] although the one-acre close on which it had stood, known as Vicarage garth, was retained by the vicars until at least 1865. There was subsequently no Vicarage until 1862 when one was built on the Driffield road near the eastern parish boundary.[92] It is a gabled red-brick building with blue- and yellow-brick ornament.

In the mid 13th century John le Romeyn gave rents of 10s. from land in Garton to support an obit in the church.[93]

There seems to have been a chapel dedicated to St. Agnes in the parish, and in 1563, together with a garden, it was granted to William Strowbridge.[94] In 1681 a close called Chapel garth was mentioned,[95] and in 1851 a small field of that name lay to the west of the village.[96]

In 1306 the vicar also held the living of Kirby Grindalythe.[97] From the mid 17th century to 1862 the incumbents were non-resident and they usually held other livings. John Dobson (vicar 1679–1722) was also vicar of Kirby Grindalythe.[98] In 1743 the vicar also held the livings of Watton, Skerne, and Hutton Cranswick, where he lived,[99] and in 1835 he also held the curacies of Lowthorpe with Ruston Parva and Skerne.[1] By 1865, however, he held no other benefice.[2] The only reference to an assistant curate is in 1884.[3] Two noteworthy vicars were John Eddowes (1852–7), author of *The Agricultural Labourer as he really is*, and James Cooper (1857–61), who wrote *The Claims of the Unendowed Churches*.[4]

A service was held only every fortnight in 1743 and also in 1764, when the vicar pleaded poverty as the reason; communion was administered four times a year and was received by about fifty people in 1743 and thirty in 1764.[5] By 1851 one[6] and by 1865 two services were held each Sunday and in the latter year communion was administered each month, with 12–15 communicants.[7] The average number of communicants had risen to 25 by 1884.[8] By 1936 communion was administered fortnightly. In 1969 there were two services each Sunday.

The large church of *ST. MICHAEL* consists of chancel, aisleless nave, and west tower. It is of late Norman origin but owes much of its present form and the remarkable decoration of its interior to 19th-century restorations.

The west tower and south wall of the nave have survived from the 12th-century church. The massive tower is of four stages, with flat clasping buttresses. The fine west doorway has a semicircular arch of four orders with chevron and billet ornament, supported on jamb shafts with scalloped capitals. Above the door is a much-decayed carving of St. Michael and the dragon, with an angel on either side. A round-headed window at a higher level is flanked by shafts with volute capitals.[9] The top stage of the tower, which has two-light belfry windows and a parapet, is a Perpendicular addition. Internally the 12th-century responds of the tower arch, with cable and scalloped decoration to the capitals, were raised in height to support a later pointed arch. The south wall of the nave is divided externally into 3 bays by pilaster buttresses. It retains two small Norman windows and a third window of the 14th century with flowing tracery. Some of the carved corbels have been preserved from the 12th-century corbel tables on both the north and south sides of the church.

The chancel was said to be out of repair on several occasions between 1679 and 1714 and in the latter year part was reported to have fallen down. In 1721 and 1723 restoration was called for. In the former year the north door in the nave was to be walled up, the windows at the west end and in the 'steeple'

---

[74] B.M. Add. MS. 26731, f. 105v.; Dugdale, *Mon.* vi. 208; *Cal. Chart. R.* 1327–41, 360–1; F. Ross, *Celebrities of Yorks. Wolds*, 190.
[75] *Fasti Parochiales*, iii. 42.
[76] Ibid. 43–5.
[77] *Cal. Pat.* 1557–8, 420. 'Garton' in this grant may possibly be Garton in Holderness.
[78] *Fasti Parochiales*, iii. 42–3.
[79] *Valor Eccl.* (Rec. Com.), v. 125.
[80] *T.E.R.A.S.* ii. 53.
[81] B.I.H.R., TER. J. Garton 1663.
[82] Ibid. 1685, 1749.
[83] Hodgson, *Q.A.B.* 440.
[84] Lawton, *Rec. Eccles. Dioc. Ebor.* 300.
[85] *Rep. Com. Eccl. Revenues*, 936–7.
[86] B.I.H.R., Bp. V. 1884/Ret.
[87] E.R.R.O., DDSY/23/46.
[88] B.I.H.R., TER. J. Garton 1865.
[89] Ibid. 1764, 1770, 1817, 1825.
[90] *Valor Eccl.* v. 125.
[91] B.I.H.R., TER. J. Garton 1685.
[92] Ibid. 1865.
[93] *Reg. Romeyn*, ii (Sur. Soc. cxxviii), pp. iii n., viii.
[94] C 66/999 m. 17.
[95] C 54/4569 m. 9.
[96] O.S. Map 6" (1855).
[97] *Fasti Parochiales*, iii. 43.
[98] *Y.A.J.* xxv. 63 n.
[99] *Herring's Visit.* ii. 16–17.
[1] *Rep. Com. Eccl. Revenues*, 936–7.
[2] B.I.H.R., V. 1865/Ret. 203.
[3] Ibid. Bp. V. 1884/Ret.
[4] Ross, *Celebrities of Yorks. Wolds*, 52–3.
[5] B.I.H.R., Bp. V. 1764/Ret. 209; *Herring's Visit.* ii. 16–17.
[6] H.O. 129/24/523.
[7] B.I.H.R., V. 1865/Ret. 203.
[8] Ibid. Bp. V. 1884/Ret.
[9] See plate facing p. 129.

'pulled down' and reglazed, and the church whitewashed. In 1723 a new south door was to be built, several windows in the tower and the west end reopened and glazed, the floor and the chancel leads relaid, and the north door of the chancel walled up.[10] About 1770 the chancel floor was relaid.[11]

A major restoration took place in 1856 to the designs of J. L. Pearson, at the cost of Sir Tatton Sykes (d. 1863) and the parishioners.[12] It has been suggested that Sir Tatton Sykes (d. 1913), who was subsequently responsible for restoring or rebuilding more than a dozen churches in the area, had much to do with such work even in his father's lifetime.[13] In all cases some of the foremost church architects of the day were employed. Pearson's restoration at Garton appears to have included the rebuilding of the nave, except for the south wall, and of the chancel, all in the Norman style. He also added a vestry and repaired the tower. A new 'Norman' south doorway is of four orders, richly decorated with chevrons and scallops. The triple east window, which has a circular window above it, is similarly decorated, and internally there is an open arcade of three arches above the chancel arch.

Between 1872 and 1880 a further restoration was carried out, under the direction of G. E. Street, which seems to have been largely concerned with the adornment of the interior.[14] A 4-foot-high dado of coloured encaustic tiles was inserted, and all the walls, except those under the tower, were covered with mural paintings by Clayton and Bell. The roof timbers were also richly painted and the floors relaid with coloured mosaics. The marble font with a wooden cover and the alabaster reredos also date from this period. Stained glass was inserted in all the windows which had not been so treated at the earlier restoration. As before most of the cost was borne by Sir Tatton Sykes.[15] Finally, in 1899 the church was fitted with oak pews to the design of Temple Moore.[16]

There are two mutilated recumbent figures, one of a woman with her head beneath a canopy, and the other of a cross-legged man. In the churchyard are two grave-slabs, possibly of the 13th century, one of which bears a foliated cross in relief and the other, 'a curious semi-effigial monument',[17] shows a woman's head and hands appearing in a quatrefoil at the top and her feet emerging at the base.

In 1552 there were three bells[18] and there were still three in 1969, one dated 1593, another 1617, and the third, by Taylor & Son of Loughborough, of 1857.[19] The plate consists of silver cup, paten, flagon, and alms-dish. The cup was made in York in 1662 and the paten by Richard Bayley of London in 1716. The flagon and alms-dish, which were given in 1856 by Mary, wife of Sir Tatton Sykes (d. 1863), were made in London the same year.[20] The registers begin in 1653 and are complete.[21]

Additions to the churchyard were made in 1881 and 1936.[22]

Sir Tatton Sykes, by will proved in 1913, left £550 in trust for the maintenance of the church and churchyard,[23] and payments have subsequently been made by the trustees as needed.[24] Jane Cooke, by will dated 1779, left £240, the interest to be given to the vicar for preaching a sermon each Sunday instead of only fortnightly. If he failed to do so the money was to be employed in repairing the church. After her death, however, the bequest was challenged and the legacy was never paid.[25]

NONCONFORMITY. In 1676 there were six protestant dissenters in Garton.[26] In 1711 the house of Timothy Towse was licensed for Quaker worship[27] and in 1720 Towse, described as 'an eminent Quaker speaker', was prosecuted for not paying tithes.[28] In 1743 there were said to be no dissenters in the parish,[29] but a Quaker was again reported in 1764.[30] The Methodists had 44 members at Garton in 1787 and 1789 and about 36 in 1790–1.[31] Houses were licensed for worship in 1769[32] and 1821.[33]

The first chapel in the parish was built by the Wesleyans in 1786 and rebuilt in 1809.[34] It was replaced by a new chapel in 1854[35] and that in its turn in 1894.[36] The present building is Gothic, built of red brick with stone and blue-brick dressings. Services were still held in 1969.

The Primitive Methodists built a chapel in 1824,[37] replaced in 1871.[38] The new chapel is of red brick with yellow-brick and stone dressings, and has round-headed windows. It had ceased to be used by 1954,[39] but still stood in 1969.

EDUCATION. In 1743 Thomas Pearson, a Cambridge graduate, taught reading, writing, and the principles of Christianity to about 14 children in Garton. It was then said that 'his meat from house to house is most he gets for his instruction', for he received very small wages.[40] In 1764 there was said to be 'a young man who has of late taught some small children'.[41] A schoolmaster was mentioned in 1775.[42] Jane Cooke, by will dated 1779, left £120 to the schoolmaster to teach reading and writing.[43] By 1791

---

[10] B.I.H.R., Churches index.
[11] Ibid. TER. J. Garton 1764.
[12] *Building News*, v (1859), 1175; *Assoc. Archit. Socs.* vi (1862), p. cxii.
[13] *Country Life*, 26 Sept. 1968, 770.
[14] See plate facing p. 209.
[15] B.I.H.R., Ch. Ret. 1.
[16] *Kelly's Dir. N. & E.R. Yorks.* (1913), 538; *Country Life*, 26 Sept. 1968, 770.
[17] Morris, *E.R. Yorks.* 173; *Y.A.J.* xlii. 337–8.
[18] *Inventories of Ch. Goods*, 23–4.
[19] Boulter, 'Ch. Bells', 217.
[20] *Yorks. Ch. Plate*, i. 254.
[21] E.R.R.O.
[22] York Dioc. Regy., Sentences of consecration.
[23] Char. Com. files.
[24] Ex inf. the vicar, 1972.
[25] 11th Rep. Char. Com., H.C. 433, p. 720 (1824), xiv.
[26] Bodl. MS. Tanner 150, ff. 27 sqq.
[27] E.R.R.O., Quarter Sess. Order Bk. A, p. 27.
[28] B.I.H.R., Bp. 26/4.
[29] *Herring's Visit.* ii. 16–17.
[30] B.I.H.R., Bp. V. 1764/Ret. 209.
[31] E.R.R.O., MRP/1/7.
[32] B.I.H.R., DMH. 1769/11.
[33] Ibid. DMH. Reg. 1, pp. 262–3.
[34] H.O. 129/24/523.
[35] G.R.O. Worship Reg. no. 2860.
[36] Date on building.
[37] H.O. 129/24/523.
[38] H. Woodcock, *Sketches of Prim. Meth. on Yorks. Wolds*, 127.
[39] G.R.O. Worship Reg. no. 13817.
[40] *Herring's Visit.* ii. 16–17; J. Lawson, *Primary Educ. in E. Yorks. 1560–1902* (E. Yorks. Loc. Hist. Ser. x), 6.
[41] B.I.H.R., Bp. V. 1764/Ret. 209.
[42] E.R.R.O., DDSY/23/46.
[43] 11th Rep. Char. Com. 720.

there was a school-house,[44] and a new school was apparently built in the early 19th century.[45] In 1819 the schoolmaster taught about 50 children, who paid fees, and in 1824 £5 to £7 was said to be received each year from Cooke's charity.[46] There were two schools by 1835. The older one was attended by 37 boys and 5 girls and its income from the Cooke endowment was then £6 a year.[47] The schoolmaster was chosen by the villagers. No child was taught free, but the poor paid lower fees.[48] A second school was attended by 10 boys and 30 girls and was supported by a subscription of £5 5s. a year and by fees.[49]

The present red-brick school was built in 1843 opposite the church on land leased from Sir Tatton Sykes.[50] It first received an annual government grant in 1868–9.[51] The attendance was then 75 children over 6 years old and 30 infants.[52] By 1871 the school was associated with the National Society.[53] It was rebuilt by Sir Tatton Sykes with accommodation for 150 in 1891.[54] In 1908 the income from Cooke's charity was about £4 10s. a year. A Scheme of that year directed that it should thenceforward be used to provide maintenance grants for children receiving secondary education or for students training to be teachers who had attended an elementary school at Garton for at least two years, and to provide books and fittings for a school library at Garton.[55] In 1908 the average attendance at the school was 80 and until 1913 there was little variation. It then gradually declined and was only 54 in 1938.[56] In 1969 the average number on the roll was 57.[57] The income from Cooke's charity was about £8 in 1972.[58]

In 1868 the vicar reported that a night school was held during winter but without much success.[59]

CHARITIES FOR THE POOR. In 1743 it was reported that Robert Taylor had bequeathed £1 a year to be divided equally between the vicar and poor widows of the parish.[60] It was later said that the vicar's share was for preaching an annual sermon. Taylor's executor withheld payment and no more is heard of the charity after 1764.[61]

The Poor's Fund, amounting to £7, was used in the early 19th century to build a new school.[62]

John Lamplough, by will proved in 1896, left £100, the interest to be distributed at Christmas among the poor of Garton at the vicar's discretion.[63] In 1931 the income of about £2 was distributed among 11 people. In 1964 the income was still about £2.[64]

HARPHAM

HARPHAM lies at the southern edge of the wolds, 5 miles from Great Driffield.[1] It may be a settlement of Scandinavian origin.[2] It has always been a chapelry of neighbouring Burton Agnes,[3] but it came to be regarded as a distinct parish and is therefore described separately here. Northwards the township, which is roughly rectangular in shape, extends as far as the ancient road called Wold Gate[4] and almost touches the eastern end of Kilham village. In the south Harpham extends into the Plain of Holderness, where its boundaries mostly follow streams and dykes. There is no prominent natural boundary with Burton Agnes on the east, but on the west Lowthorpe beck separates Harpham from Kilham and Lowthorpe. The boundaries have undergone little change, but Moorhouse field, comprising about 100 a., was transferred to the township from Burton Agnes in 1884.[5] As a result the area of Harpham was increased to 2,258 a. Since 1935 the civil parish of Harpham has included the former civil parishes of Lowthorpe and Ruston Parva.[6]

The landscape of Harpham exhibits the same twofold character as that of Burton Agnes: north of the village large arable fields extend up the bare wold slopes, which reach a height of 150 ft.–250 ft. above sea-level at Wold Gate; south of the village plantations and pasture fields give more variety to the low-lying area on the plain, much of it only 25 ft.–50 ft. in height. The wold slopes were occupied by the open fields of the township until inclosure in the later 18th century, and much of the low-lying ground was common moor and carr. The plantations which have appeared since inclosure lie mostly along the western margin of the parish, stretching for 1½ mile alongside Lowthorpe beck. The remains of a Roman villa have been excavated on the wold slopes.[7]

The village itself lies south of the Bridlington–Driffield road, at the very foot of the wold slope, the main street closely following the 50-foot contour. Other houses lie along the road that runs from the west end of the village towards Lowthorpe, and along a road extending southwards from the main street to the churchyard. Near the church is the site of the manor-house of the St. Quintin family, together

---

[44] E.R.R.O., DDSY/23/286.
[45] See below.
[46] 11th Rep. Char. Com. 720; Rets. on Educ. of Poor, 1819, 1081.
[47] Educ. Enquiry Abstract, 1835, 1085.
[48] Lawton, Rer. Eccles. Dioc. Ebor. 301.
[49] Educ. Enquiry Abstract, 1835, 1085.
[50] Bulmer, Dir. E. Yorks. (1892), 204.
[51] Rep. of Educ. Cttee. of Council, 1868–9 [4139], H.C., p. 625 (1868–9), xx.
[52] B.I.H.R., V. 1868/Ret. 185.
[53] Rets. rel. Elem. Educ. 1871, 474.
[54] Kelly's Dir. N. & E.R. Yorks. (1897), 465.
[55] Char. Com. files.
[56] Bd. of Educ. List 21 (H.M.S.O.).
[57] Ex inf. Chief Educ. Officer, County Hall, Beverley, 1969.
[58] Ex inf. Dept. of Educ. and Science.
[59] B.I.H.R., V. 1868/Ret. 185.
[60] Herring's Visit. ii. 16–17.
[61] B.I.H.R., Bp. V. 1764/Ret. 209.
[62] 11th Rep. Char. Com. 720.
[63] Bempton par. rec., extract from will (in Bempton Vicarage).
[64] Char. Com. files.
[1] This article was written in 1967.
[2] P.N.E.R. Yorks. (E.P.N.S.), 30, 90.
[3] See p. 226.
[4] See p. 1.
[5] Census, 1891.
[6] Ibid. 1931.
[7] T.E.R.A.S. xiii. 141–52; Hull Mus. Publ. xxiii, passim; Y.A.J. xxxviii. 117–18. A pavement is on display in the City Hall, Hull.

with the Drummer's well into which, according to tradition, a drummer boy was pushed by one of the St. Quintins.[8] A second well, at the eastern end of the village, takes its name from St. John of Beverley, who is traditionally said to have created it. It is covered by a stone cupola which bears the inscription 'St. John's Well Rebuilt 1856'.[9] Harpham is reckoned to be the birthplace of St. John of Beverley,[10] though there is no contemporary evidence for this.

The older houses of the village are mostly undistinguished buildings of either red, or mottled pink and yellow, brick, but a few are built of chalk and these include the St. Quintin Arms. All appear to date from the 18th and 19th centuries and two carry the dates 1775 and 1793. Later houses include three with the inscription 'W.H. St. Q. 1911', and eight Council houses. With the exception of Turtle Hill, in the extreme south-east of the parish, and Harpham Grange, on the wold slope, all the farmhouses are in the village itself. Six of them date from the late 18th or earlier 19th century and their farms were probably the chief ones created after the inclosure of 1776.[11] The most substantial houses are Manor Farm and Sykes Farm. The former is said to have been rebuilt in 1824; it has a pedimented doorway in the centre of a symmetrical five-bay front.[12] The farm buildings include a typical 18th-century barn at Sykes Farm and an early-19th-century barn at Westend Farm which has an arched end elevation with decorative brickwork. A village hall for Harpham and Lowthorpe is dated 1933.

Several of the roads radiating from the village have distinctive names. Sykes Balk and Butt Balk lead northwards from the village street, becoming Harpham Lane and Sandy Lane after crossing the Driffield–Bridlington road. The road towards Lowthorpe was formerly called London Road and, further from the village, Carr Lane, but it has come to be known as Station Road: it leads to Lowthorpe railway station. From the neighbourhood of the church Daggett Lane leads into the fields to the south-east; and the village street is continued eastwards as Out Gates, a road in part unfenced which formerly led around Moorhouse field on its way to Harpham moor. Finally the main Driffield–Bridlington road is known as 'Street' in its course across Harpham.[13] At the western township boundary Bracey bridge until recent years carried this road over Lowthorpe beck.[14]

Close to the bridge is Bracey garth plantation, which may mark the site of St. Helen's hospital, Braceford. The small hospital was attached to St. Mary's chantry in Burton Agnes church, and the chantry had a piece of land called Braceford garth.[15]

A noteworthy feature of the social life of the village was the St. Quintin Lodge of the Independent Order of Druids. It existed from at least 1846 until the Second World War,[16] and latterly met in the St. Quintin Arms.[17]

Judging from the number of poll-tax payers in 1377, 153,[18] Harpham was then not much smaller than Burton Agnes itself. It was assessed together with Gransmoor for the hearth tax, but in 1743 there were reported to be 30 families there.[19] In 1801 there were 172 inhabitants and, although the number increased to 274 in 1861, there were still only 193 in 1901.[20] In 1931 the population was 200.[21]

MANOR AND OTHER ESTATES. In 1086 4 carucates at Harpham formed a berewick of Burton Agnes and were held by the king. A further 8 carucates were held by Ernuin the priest, who had also been the pre-Conquest tenant.[22] Ernuin's estate was later given to Robert de Brus,[23] and Brus probably acquired the Crown estate too, for in 1284–5 he had 12 carucates and 8 bovates in Harpham.[24] The overlordship subsequently descended like that of Burton Agnes.[25]

The immediate lord of HARPHAM, as of Burton Agnes, in the 12th century was evidently Roger de Stutville. At the death of his son Anselm before 1199, however, Harpham passed to his sister Agnes, wife of Herbert de St. Quintin,[26] and so was separated from Burton Agnes. The eldest coheir Alice and her descendants subsequently held the mesne lordship of Harpham, between the St. Quintins and the overlords.[27] Harpham subsequently descended in the St. Quintin family,[28] and it was the chief seat of the family until the 17th century. Earthworks near the church mark the site of the manor-house. Private oratories were permitted there in 1314 and 1443.[29] The date of the St. Quintins' removal to Scampston is not certainly known,[30] but there was no outstanding house in Harpham when the hearth tax was assessed in the 1670s. On the death of Sir William St. Quintin without issue in 1795 Harpham was inherited by his nephew W. T. Darby, who assumed the surname St. Quintin.[31] Harpham remained in the St. Quintin family until the death in 1943 of Violet H. St. Quintin, widow of W. H. St. Quintin (d. 1933); it then passed to their daughter Margery Violet, who had married Lt. Col. E. G. S. L'Estrange Malone.[32] In 1957 the 118-acre Turtle Hill farm was sold,[33] but the rest of the estate, about 1,750 a. besides plantations, was in 1959 vested in L'Estrange Malone's daughter Lady Legard, wife of Sir Thomas Legard, the present owner.[34]

By 1265 a small estate in Harpham was

---

[8] W. Smith, *Ancient Springs and Streams of E.R. Yorks.* 60–7.
[9] Ibid. 122–30.
[10] Leland, *Collectanea*, ed. T. Hearne (1774), iv. 100.
[11] See p. 226.
[12] Sheahan and Whellan, *Hist. York & E.R.* ii. 477.
[13] O.S. Map 6" (various edns.).
[14] See p. 320.
[15] E.R.R.O., DDSQ/5/18; DDWB/20/4; *Monastic Notes*, i (Y.A.S. Rec. Ser. xvii), 17.
[16] Its records are in E.R.R.O., DDX/61.
[17] Ex inf. Mr. H. S. Welburn, Harpham, 1967.
[18] E 179/202/62 m. 13.
[19] *Herring's Visit.* ii. 91.
[20] *V.C.H. Yorks.* iii. 489.
[21] Census.
[22] *V.C.H. Yorks.* ii. 198, 287.
[23] Ibid. 291–2.
[24] *Feud. Aids*, vi. 31.
[25] See p. 117.
[26] *Pipe R. 1 John* (P.R.S. N.S. x), 53; *Abbrev. Plac.* (Rec. Com.), 76, 222; *E.Y.C.* ix. 29–30.
[27] e.g. *Cal. Inq. p.m.* i, p. 200; vi, pp. 30, 307.
[28] For lineage see *Visit. Yorks. 1584–5 and 1612*, ed. J. Foster, 162; *G.E.C. Baronetage*, ii. 161. The St. Quintin baronetcy was created in 1642.
[29] *Reg. Greenfield*, iii (Sur. Soc. cli), 220; *T.E.R.A.S.* xxi. 38.
[30] *Country Life*, 1 Apr. 1954.
[31] *G.E.C. Baronetage*, ii. 162.
[32] Registry of Deeds, Beverley, 533/40/34; 676/589/476; 719/547/456.
[33] Ibid. 1082/489/443.
[34] Ibid. 1129/159/139; Burke, *Peerage* (1967), 1474.

held by Thomas of Lowthorpe,[35] and shortly after it passed to the Heslerton family. In 1308 Robert of Heslerton held 4 tofts and 2 bovates there[36] as a moiety of the estate, which subsequently descended with the manor of Lowthorpe in two branches of the family.[37]

The college of Lowthorpe in 1373 acquired the reversion of two houses and 2 bovates in Harpham from Simon Heslerton, then held by his widow for life.[38] In the same year St. Leonard's hospital, York, was given three houses and 2 bovates in Harpham, to say mass for the parents of Thomas Heslerton.[39] After the Dissolution they were let in 1554 to James Cokeson and others.[40]

Braceford hospital, in Harpham, had 10 tofts and 4 bovates in the township in the 1330s.[41] The hospital was attached to the chantry of St. Mary in Burton Agnes church, and a house, a close, and 4 bovates in Harpham were regularly recorded as belonging to the chantry.[42]

Other land in Harpham belonged to the chantry of St. Leonard in Speeton chapel. Thus a cottage and a croft, formerly belonging to the chantry, were in 1611 granted by the Crown to Francis Morrice and Francis Philips,[43] who in 1612 sold them to William St. Quintin.[44] Another part of the chantry's possessions in Harpham, comprising a house, 5 bovates and 4 closes, was let to James Cokeson and others in 1554[45] and was sold to Henry St. Quintin by George Northend in 1613.[46] A chantry in Gransmoor chapel also had land in Harpham.[47]

ECONOMIC HISTORY. In the Middle Ages free tenants were apparently few and most of the land no doubt belonged, as it did in later centuries, to the St. Quintins and the church. A glimpse of the customary tenants is given in 1330, when Sir Geoffrey de St. Quintin's widow held a third of the manor in dower. She had the services of 13 tenants, 8 of whom were in bondage; the average size of their holdings was nearly 2 bovates.[48]

The open fields of Harpham extended from the village northwards up the wold slopes. In 1685 the four fields were known as Middle, West, East, and South fields,[49] but by the later 18th century there were only Middle, East, and West fields, and the last-named was alternatively called Beck field.[50] There are few indications of the total area of arable land, but the manor contained 84 bovates in 1613 and 1,276 a. of arable in 1714.[51] The inclosure Act of 1773[52] referred to 108 bovates, containing about 1,400 a.

There was no doubt always meadow land along the west side of the open-field area, near Lowthorpe beck. How Mill meadow is mentioned in 1330, for example, and Bracey garth was described as meadow or pasture; Sleight ings, mentioned in 1613,[53] may also have been in this part of the township. In 1716 several 'low grounds' beyond the beck were said to be 'made by the cut for the use of the mill and by the continual alteration of its course'; the grounds were called Little Ruston Mill Holme, Field Holme, Nete Holme, Knaws Holme, Whiting Holme, and Gabriel Holme, and all were 'referred to common use and customs'.[54] By 1773 West field was reckoned to include the meadow and carr; a large part of it was then called the Neatholmes,[55] and this has since remained its name.[56]

The common pastures lay in the south of the township, on the low-lying ground. Immediately south of the village and stretching to the parish boundary was an area described in 1509 as 'common moor' and known as South carr.[57] The carr may have consisted of two distinct parts, for East carr is mentioned as early as 1246[58] and East and West carrs were inclosed in 1776. In addition the south-east part of Harpham was occupied by Harpham moor, a continuation of the extensive tract of moor that extended across Burton Agnes. When Sir William de St. Quintin granted the prior of Bridlington the right to use a road and droveway over Burton Agnes moor in 1299, the prior granted St. Quintin a similar road over the moor between Gransmoor and Harpham.[59] The whole stretch of moor was shared by the inhabitants of Burton Agnes and Harpham.[60] In 1773 Harpham moor and East and West carrs were said to contain altogether about 600 a.; the inclosure award gives no further details beyond a reference to Kelk carr in Harpham.[61] Part of the moor was known as Brunton hill, and in 1666 it was 'stored with conies' and used, along with ground in neighbouring Little Kelk, as a rabbit warren.[62]

A little early inclosure is recorded in the township. A small area of open-field land was inclosed by William St. Quintin in 1633–4, but his action was not considered to be contrary to law, 'the township being in want of grazing'.[63] There were the usual crofts and garths around the village and there was also some inclosure from the moor and carr. In 1714 the manor contained 283 a. of inclosed ground in Harpham, mostly in small garths and closes but also including 40 a. in East carr and 102 a. in West carr.[64] In 1724 eight pieces of newly-improved land, of unspecified extent, were described as 'part of a moor lately inclosed', and there were also two closes called the Little intack (12 a.) and the Old intack (14 a.).[65] By 1770 the vicarial glebe included a close of 13 a. on the moor and another of 2 a. in the carr.[66]

---

[35] *Yorks. Inq.* i. 102; *Cal. Inq. p.m.* i, p. 200.
[36] *Cal. Inq. p.m.* v, p. 54.
[37] *Yorks. Fines, 1327–47*, 140. See below, p. 273.
[38] *Cal. Pat.* 1340–7, 161, 259; *Abbrev. Rot. Orig.* (Rec. Com.), ii. 327; *Yorks. Fines, 1347–77*, 166; *T.E.R.A.S.* xxiv. 36.
[39] *Cal. Pat.* 1370–4, 409; *Abbrev. Rot. Orig.* ii. 333.
[40] *Cal. Pat.* 1553–4, 294.
[41] E.R.R.O., DDWB/20/4.
[42] See p. 115.
[43] E.R.R.O., DDDA/3/7.
[44] Ibid. DDSQ/5/9.
[45] *Cal. Pat.* 1553–4, 294.
[46] E.R.R.O., DDSQ/5/10.
[47] See p. 115.
[48] *T.E.R.A.S.* xxi. 32–4.
[49] B.I.H.R., TER. J. Harpham 1685.
[50] Ibid. Burton Agnes 1770; 13 Geo. III, c. 69 (Priv. Act).
[51] C 142/670/72; E.R.R.O., DDSQ uncalendared.
[52] 13 Geo. III, c. 69.
[53] C 142/670/72; T.E.R.A.S. xxi. 33; *Abstracts of Yorks. Wills* (Y.A.S. Rec. Ser. ix), 39.
[54] B.I.H.R., TER. J. Burton Agnes 1716.
[55] 13 Geo. III, c. 69.
[56] O.S. Map 6″ (1854 and subsequent edns.).
[57] E.R.R.O., DDSQ/5/5.
[58] *P.N.E.R. Yorks.* (E.P.N.S.), 90.
[59] *Bridlington Charty.* 171.
[60] E.R.R.O., DDSQ/5/7; DDWB/18/11; see p. 112.
[61] Registry of Deeds, Beverley, AT/296/31; 13 Geo. III, c. 69.
[62] Univ. of London Libr., Fuller Collection, indenture of 1666.
[63] P.C. 2/43 p. 301; /44 pp. 40, 50; *Cal. S.P. Dom.* 1634–5, 56.
[64] E.R.R.O., DDSQ uncalendared.
[65] Regy. of Deeds, H/707/1444.
[66] B.I.H.R., TER. J. Burton Agnes 1770.

The closes were probably enjoyed in lieu of the vicar's common rights there, for he was said in 1773 to have already had 'compensation' for those rights.[67]

The remaining open-field and other common land was inclosed in 1776 under an Act of 1773.[68] Of the 1,879 a. dealt with Sir William St. Quintin was allotted 1,603 a. and the whole of the Kelk carr; in addition, as lessee from the archbishop of York of the rectorial glebe and tithes, St. Quintin received a further 126 a. Most of the remaining land went to the vicar of Burton Agnes, who was allotted 90 a. in lieu of glebe, tithes, and other profits. The only other landowner received 2 a.[69]

After inclosure most of the St. Quintin land was held by a few substantial tenant farmers. In 1796, for example, 1,758 a. out of a total of 1,909 a. lay in seven farms, each containing 200 a.–300 a.[70] Six of these farms had houses on the sites of the six principal farm-houses in the village in 1967; the seventh farm was at Turtle Hill.[71] There were nearly 30 smaller holdings in 1796, half of them consisting of an acre or less. Three areas in Harpham were apparently still used in common in the 1790s: the sheepwalk, in the extreme north near Wold Gate, was shared by the six chief farms, as was ground called North and South Lingholme, and several of the smaller tenants had shares of the 'cottagers' pasture'. Turtle Hill, on the former Harpham moor, had by far the lowest rented value of any of the farms; the moor was, indeed, described in 1796 as rough pasture and furze which needed to be broken up and laid down alternately as the only means of bringing it into a regular course of husbandry.

The number of principal farms has subsequently changed little. In 1829 there were eight farm-houses: the six in the village, Turtle Hill, and the rectorial farm-house, which had land in both Burton Agnes and Harpham. This last farm was later known as Field House Farm or Harpham Grange.[72] In the later 19th and 20th centuries there have been 9–12 farmers.[73]

At least from the 13th to the 18th centuries there were millers in the township. Up to three or four water-mills appear to have existed together in Harpham, presumably on the beck separating it from Lowthorpe. How, Acre, Hall, and New mills are all mentioned in 1330;[74] Hall Mill had been recorded in 1297, and How Mill in 1299,[75] and later references include those to Acre, Holme, and Ros mills in 1460, How Mill in 1547, and Acre and Yait mills in 1567.[76] The manor still had three water-mills in 1613.[77] Though no doubt chiefly for corn, one of the water-mills was described as a fulling mill in 1476.[78] One water-mill still existed in 1716;[79] its site may have been close to Burnt Mill bridge, south-west of the village.[80]

LOCAL GOVERNMENT. In the late 13th century the St. Quintins claimed the assize of bread and ale at Harpham.[81] Surviving manorial court papers[82] show that 2 bylawmen, 2 constables, and a pinder were being appointed in the late 18th and early 19th centuries. The pinder continued to be appointed throughout the 19th century and the bylawmen still in 1914.

There are surviving churchwardens' accounts for 1799–1869.[83] In 1836 Harpham joined the Driffield union.[84]

CHURCH. A church at Harpham is first mentioned c. 1100–15, when it was given, along with Burton Agnes church, to St. Mary's abbey, York.[85] Harpham has always been a chapelry of Burton Agnes, but its chapel is large and it eventually came to be regarded as a parish church. Already in 1650 Harpham was described as 'fit to be made a parish',[86] and in the earlier 19th century the chapel was said to be accounted a parish church.[87] It had long enjoyed burial and other rights.[88] Presentation has always been made to Harpham as a curacy held with Burton Agnes, and the chapelry contributed to the income and property of the mother-church.[89]

A chantry of St. Mary at Harpham was founded in 1340 by William de St. Quintin, who endowed it with a house and 4 bovates of land in Harpham.[90] It was valued at £2 13s. 4d. in 1535.[91] The chantry property, lately held by William St. Quintin, was let in 1563 to Walter Griffith[92] and in 1580 to George St. Quintin.[93] A priest's cottage and close in Harpham, granted in 1571 to Francis Barker and Thomas Browne,[94] were probably part of the chantry property, of which no more is known. Obits were founded in the church by Anthony St. Quintin in 1444 and John St. Quintin in 1515.[95] In 1525–6 there were, surprisingly, as many as five chaplains at Harpham, with net incomes varying from £2 to £4 13s. 4d., as well as a chantry-priest, who also had £4 13s. 4d.[96]

The chapelry was normally served by a curate resident at Harpham.[97] He may have lived in a small house which in the 17th and 18th centuries belonged to the vicarage,[98] but in the early 20th century a house was built, perhaps expressly for the purpose, in which the curate subsequently lodged.[99]

---

[67] 13 Geo. III, c. 69.
[68] Ibid.
[69] Regy. of Deeds, AT/296/31.
[70] Y.A.S. MSS., MS. 709b.
[71] E.R.R.O., DDSQ(2), Box 1 (A): an undated rental similar to that of 1796, but with plans of the farms.
[72] Ibid. IA; Sheahan and Whellan, *Hist. York & E.R.* ii. 477. See also church-rates: E.R.R.O., PR. 1878.
[73] Directories.
[74] *T.E.R.A.S.* xxi. 33.
[75] E.R.R.O., DDSQ/5/1; *Bridlington Charty.* 171.
[76] E.R.R.O., DDSQ/5/4; DDWB/20/35; *T.E.R.A.S.* xxi. 52.
[77] C 142/670/72.
[78] *T.E.R.A.S.* xxi. 40.
[79] B.I.H.R., TER. J. Burton Agnes 1770.
[80] O.S. Map 6" (1854).
[81] J.I. 1/1110 m. 84.
[82] Call rolls and jury papers, 1789–1914: Y.A.S. MSS., DD. 89.
[83] E.R.R.O., PR. 1878.
[84] *3rd Rep. Poor Law Com.* 168.
[85] *E.Y.C.* ii, p. 33.
[86] *T.E.R.A.S.* ii. 57.
[87] Lawton, *Rer. Eccles. Dioc. Ebor.* 292.
[88] B.I.H.R., wills.
[89] See pp. 114–15.
[90] *Cal. Pat.* 1338–40, 454; *Cal. Close,* 1349–54, 319.
[91] *Valor Eccl.* (Rec. Com.), v. 124.
[92] *Cal. Pat.* 1563–6, 46.
[93] C 66/1189 m. 10.
[94] C 66/1074 m. 34.
[95] *Test. Ebor.* ii. 95–6; v. 54–5. See also B.I.H.R., Prob. Reg. xi, ff. 17, 224, 598.
[96] *Y.A.J.* xxiv. 69, 77.
[97] e.g. *Inventories of Ch. Goods,* 32; *Rep. Com. Eccl. Revenues,* 922–3. See above, p. 116.
[98] B.I.H.R., TER. J. Harpham 1685; Burton Agnes 1716, 1770.
[99] Ex inf. Mr. H. S. Welburn, Harpham, 1967.

In 1743 it was said to be the 'ancient custom' for a service to be held in the church only once a fortnight because many inhabitants frequently went to the parish church; the then vicar reported, however, that he himself had always preached there every Sunday. Communion was at that time administered four times a year and was received by about twenty people.[1] One Sunday service was still being held in 1764[2] and in 1851.[3] By 1865 there were two, but in 1868 and in the 1870s and 1880s again only one.[4] In 1894, however, there were three Sunday services. Communion was received monthly in 1865, and in 1868 there were about sixteen communicants at these services. By 1884 it was held twice monthly with an average at most seasons of fifteen communicants.[5] In 1967 there was one service each Sunday.

The church of ST. JOHN OF BEVERLEY is built largely of stone and consists of chancel, nave, north chapel, south porch, and west tower. Of the Norman church the only feature which remains is a small round-headed window, widely splayed internally, on the south side of the nave. Norman masonry, however, is still visible in the external walls of both nave and chancel. The church was remodelled in the 14th century, when the chapel and tower were added. The latter, which is unusually tall and massive, was presumably the work of Joan, widow of William St. Quintin, who was licensed in 1374 to crenellate a bell-tower which she proposed to build in the churchyard.[6] Both tower and chapel are good and almost unaltered examples of 14th-century work. Extensive repairs were probably carried out soon after 'great damage' had been done to the church during a storm in 1715, and the chancel needed a new roof in 1722.[7] The east wall of the chancel, which is of red brick, was probably rebuilt in 1833–4, when the pews were also extensively altered.[8] It may have been at the same period that the roof of the nave was raised, brick being used to add height to the walls and to build, or rebuild, the south porch. The chancel and tower were restored in 1909–14 by William St. Quintin, under the direction of T. L. Moore. A restoration of the nave and tower, by W. H. St. Quintin and his mother, was completed in 1935, under the direction of Milner and Craze.[9]

The outstanding feature of the interior of the building is the north chapel with its tombs and monuments, chiefly of the St. Quintin family. It contains two stone coffins and, in a recess, the stone effigy of a woman. The earliest monument which can be identified is the alabaster chest tomb of William St. Quintin (d. 1349), which lies beneath a cusped and crocketed ogee arch between the chapel and the chancel. The sides of the tomb are panelled in quatrefoils, each with a shield, and on the top is an alabaster slab incised with the figures of William and his wife.[10] On the floor of the chapel is a brass of Thomas St. Quintin and his wife (d. 1418), with their figures placed under an elaborate double canopy. Near by is the brass of Thomas St. Quintin (d. 1445).[11] Other St. Quintin memorials include wall monuments to Sir William (d. 1649), by E. C. Falsgrave;[12] Sir William (d. 1723), the Hull M.P., erected in 1768; John (d. 1746); Sir William (d. 1770); Matthew (d. 1785); and Matthew (d. 1876). There is also a monument to Mary Darby (d. 1773), by John Fisher of York. The 14th-century windows in the chapel contain heraldic glass by William Peckitt of York, and similar glass in a south window of the nave is signed by him and dated 1771.

There are two monuments in the chancel: one, with allegorical figures and relief portraits, is to Charlotte St. Quintin (d. 1762), by J. Wilton, the other to William St. Quintin (d. 1805). The altar rails were installed in or after 1961, replacing those of 1726, and the glass of the east window was inserted in 1935, apparently replacing a window dating from the restoration of 1909–14.[13] The nave contains a west gallery, box pews, and the Royal Arms of William IV, all probably of 1833–4.

In 1552 there were two 'small bells'.[14] There are now three bells, one dated 1610, another 1617, and the third, which was made by T. Mears of London, 1812.[15] The plate consists of a silver chalice and paten, hallmarked 1895, and a plated salver.[16] The registers date from 1720 and are complete.[17]

The old churchyard lay on the north and south sides of the church, but an extension to the west was made in 1889.[18]

NONCONFORMITY. In the late 16th century Gabriel St. Quintin was reported as a recusant.[19] Two houses were licensed for dissenters' worship in 1788 and a third in 1808.[20] In the late 19th century, before a chapel was built, the Wesleyan Methodists are said to have used a shed behind a house in the main village street.[21] The chapel was built in 1893;[22] it is of white and red brick with stone dressings, and in the Gothic style. Services were still held there in 1967.

EDUCATION. A petty school in Harpham, without endowment, is first mentioned in 1743, when it was attended by about 15 children.[23] A school was attended by 20 pupils in 1819.[24] In 1866 the children paid fees of between 1d. and 6d. to the mistress, whose salary of £35 was met by Mrs. St.

---

[1] *Herring's Visit.* i. 37.
[2] B.I.H.R., Bp. V. 1764/Ret. 103.
[3] H.O. 129/24/523.
[4] B.I.H.R., V. 1865/Ret. 93; V. 1868/Ret. 90; V. 1871/Ret. 90; V. 1877/Ret.; Bp. V. 1884/Ret.; Bp. V. 1894/Ret.
[5] Ibid. V. 1865/Ret. 93; V. 1868/Ret. 90; Bp. V. 1884/Ret.
[6] *Cal. Pat.* 1370–4, 407.
[7] B.I.H.R., ER. V/Ch. P. 1722.
[8] Morris, *E.R. Yorks.* 185 suggests 1827, but money was spent on bricks and labour in 1833–4: E.R.R.O., PR. 1878.
[9] Inscriptions in church.
[10] *T.E.R.A.S.* x. 25–6, with illus.
[11] *Y.A.J.* xii. 211–16, with illus.; xiv. 509.
[12] By his will he left £20 for a monument 'after the best fashion according to my degree': *Abstracts of Yorks. Wills* (Y.A.S. Rec. Ser. ix), 39.
[13] Morris, *E.R. Yorks.* 185; inscriptions.
[14] *Inventories of Ch. Goods*, 32.
[15] Boulter, 'Ch. Bells', 217.
[16] *Yorks. Ch. Plate*, i. 258.
[17] E.R.R.O.
[18] Plan in church; York Dioc. Regy., Declaration of consecration.
[19] H. Aveling, *Post Reformation Catholicism in E. Yorks. 1558–1790* (E. Yorks. Loc. Hist. Ser. xi), 58; *Y.A.J.* xxxv. 163–4.
[20] B.I.H.R., DMH. 1788/15; G.R.O. Worship Returns, Vol. v, nos. 716, 738, 2187.
[21] Ex inf. Mr. H. S. Welburn, Harpham, 1967.
[22] *Kelly's Dir. N. & E.R. Yorks.* (1897), 467.
[23] *Herring's Visit.* ii. 91.
[24] *Rets. on Educ. of Poor, 1819*, 1082.

Quintin.[25] The first annual parliamentary grant was received in 1867.[26] The school was united with the National Society. The average attendance was 65 in 1866 and 56 in 1871,[27] and it varied little thereafter; in 1938 it was still 59.[28] Harpham school was closed in 1967 and the pupils transferred to Burton Agnes.[29] The building consists of a low section, apparently of two periods and perhaps dating from the early 19th century, and a higher section added later in the century.

CHARITIES FOR THE POOR. In 1649 Sir William St. Quintin left £4 to be held by the overseers 'for the yearly maintenance of the poor'.[30] No more is known of it.

HUNMANBY

THE extensive and irregularly shaped parish of Hunmanby lies next to Filey Bay, 8 miles north-west of Bridlington.[1] The village has always been large and might well be described, as it was by John Wesley in 1784, as 'a little town'.[2] The life of Hunmanby was for long dominated by the Osbaldeston and Osbaldeston-Mitford families from the hall and park which overlook the village. Its character of an 'estate village' has, however, been largely lost since the sale of the former Osbaldeston estate in the 1920s, and in the 20th century it has been given a new aspect by summer visitors to the village itself as well as to the holiday camp, chalets, and caravans which have appeared by the sea.

The parish stretches over 6 miles inland to include the chapelry of Fordon, where there was also, in 1086, the now-lost hamlet of 'Ledemare'. Hunmanby township itself included two hamlets depopulated in the Middle Ages: Bartindale, at the southern extremity of the parish, and Fowthorpe, near the sea. Hunmanby, Fowthorpe, and Bartindale may all have been of Scandinavian origin but Fordon was certainly Anglian.[3] The parish boundaries often run along dry valleys on the wolds, and sections of the southern boundary with Burton Fleming follow prehistoric earthworks. Towards the sea the boundaries partly follow streams, notably Reighton gill in the south-east. The total area of the ancient parish was 8,452 a., of which Fordon accounted for 1,464 a.[4] In 1935 932 a. towards the sea were transferred to Filey urban district. Fordon was as early as 1858 transferred to Burton Fleming for ecclesiastical purposes,[5] but it remained in the civil parish of Hunmanby until 1935, when it was transferred to Wold Newton civil parish.[6] The entire history of Fordon is nevertheless dealt with in this article.

Hunmanby is physically divided by the escarpment of the wolds, which runs from north-west to south-east across the township and goes on to reach the sea at Speeton. The hall and park lie on the escarpment and Hunmanby village is largely at the foot of the slope. To the west and south the landscape is typical of the wolds. Much of the land there lies at more than 300 ft. above sea-level, exceeding 400 ft. in the extreme west; there are numerous prominent dry valleys, among them Fleming, Cans, South, Hunmanby, Bartin, and Wan Dales. Fordon hamlet lies at the junction of four deep valleys, including East, West, and North Dales, and the land rises from 200 ft.–300 ft. in the valley bottoms to 500 ft. and more on the wolds. There are few plantations, save in the shelter belts around the wolds farms, and the pattern of large regular fields in both Hunmanby and Fordon is mainly the result of the inclosure of 1809.

The wolds escarpment is less marked in Hunmanby than in the parishes to the west, where it faces the Vale of Pickering, or indeed in Reighton and Speeton to the east. The landscape to the north and east of the escarpment is, however, very different from that of the wolds. The gently undulating ground towards the sea is largely composed of boulder clay and much of it is only 100 ft.–150 ft. above sea-level. Numerous streams cross this area, several of them joining to flow northwards through Muston to the river Hertford. The land along this north-flowing stream has long been called the Dams. It may have been one of the branches of this stream which in 1327 was called the river Burlyn;[7] the name Burlyn was also applied in the early 14th century to a close and to 'a messuage outside the vill',[8] and in 1600 there were closes and meadows called 'Burlingdam'.[9]

Other streams on the low-lying ground produce small but pronounced valleys as they approach the sea. The most notable are Long Whins gill, flowing down Primrose Valley to the sea at Mile Haven; Reighton gill, reaching the sea at Hunmanby Gap; and Flat Cliff gill, flowing to Butcher Haven. The unstable boulder clay cliffs exceed 100 ft. in height but fall gently to the shore over a distance of some 200 ft. Much of the wet clay land was formerly occupied by Hunmanby moor and part of this, too, was inclosed in 1809. Some of the low-lying land was, however, inclosed at earlier periods and this may be reflected in the pattern of small and irregular fields east of Hunmanby village.

The beach and rights on the foreshore belonged to the lords of the manor of Hunmanby from early times. About 1280 Gilbert de Gant upheld his claim to take whales washed up at Hunmanby, the heads and tails reserved to the Crown.[10] The limit of manorial fishing rights in Filey Bay, from Reighton Gap to Filey Brigg, was traditionally established by

---

[25] Ed. 7/135; *Educ. Enquiry Abstract, 1835*, 1086.
[26] *Mins. of Educ. Cttee. of Council, 1867* [4051], H.C., p. 729 (1867–8), xxv.
[27] Ed. 7/135; *Rets. rel. Elem. Educ. 1871*, 474.
[28] Directories; *Bd. of Educ. List 21* (H.M.S.O.).
[29] E.R. Educ. Cttee. *Mins.* 1963–4, 96–7; ex inf. Chief Educ. Officer, County Hall, Beverley, 1967.
[30] *Abstracts of Yorks. Wills* (Y.A.S. Rec. Ser. ix), 40.
[1] This article was written in 1970.

[2] *Jnl. of John Wesley*, ed. N. Curnock, vi. 518–9.
[3] *P.N.E.R. Yorks.* (E.P.N.S.), 108–10.
[4] O.S. Map 6" (1854). [5] See p. 241.
[6] *Census*, 1931.
[7] *Cal. Inq. p.m.* vii, p. 14.
[8] *Yorks. Inq.* iv. 34, 54; vi. 19.
[9] E.R.R.O., DDHU/9/32, pp. 18 sqq.; C 142/598/70.
[10] E.R.R.O., DDHU/9/1; *Plac. de Quo Warr.* (Rec. Com.), 200.

a man riding into the sea at low tide with a pair of horses and then throwing a javelin seawards. Fish were caught with a drag net, pulled by horses. The ceremony was last performed in 1928.[11] The beach belonged to the lords of the manor until 1926 and in the following year it was acquired by Filey urban district council.[12] Large amounts of gravel and cobbles had formerly been taken from the shore for road works in the district, as much as 1,500 tons a year being used in the 1860s.[13]

Hunmanby village stands at the centre of a network of roads. Running across the wolds are roads to Folkton to the north-west, Wold Newton and Burton Fleming to the south-west, and Rudston to the south. Others follow approximately the line of the escarpment northwards to Muston and south-eastwards to Reighton. Two minor roads lead to the sea at Mile Haven and the Gap and a third gave access to North moor. To the east of the village the main Bridlington–Filey road crosses Hunmanby; its course has several times been improved and straightened, most notably in 1969–70. An old uninscribed mile-stone stands beside the Folkton road and another on the Burton Fleming road. There are similar stones, of unknown date, in near-by parishes. In Fordon four roads converge on the hamlet, from Flixton, Willerby, Wold Newton, and Burton Fleming. The last of these provided only a circuitous route to Hunmanby and for some purposes Fordon has long had closer links with Wold Newton than with its mother village.[14] Hunmanby has also had rail communications since 1847, when the Bridlington–Filey line was opened.

In the middle of Hunmanby village, between the church and the entrance to the hall and park, lies the triangular market-place known as Cross Hill. The chief village street, leading southwards from the church, was known until the 18th century as Southgate[15] but by the early 19th century had acquired the alternative name of Bridlington Street.[16] Southgate is mentioned in 1373.[17] North of the church Bridlington Street is joined by Stonegate, Northgate, and Castle Hill, the last formerly known as Ratten Row.[18] Stonegate, which is mentioned as early as 1376,[19] and Bridlington Street are connected by Hungate Lane, which is mentioned in 1544.[20] Bowling Green Lane leads off Stonegate and Garton Lane is a cul-de-sac on the west side of Bridlington Street. Garton Lane formerly continued, however, as the road to Rudston, and another lane also led into it from Bridlington Street. These lanes were stopped up by Humphrey Osbaldeston in 1826–7 and New Road, along the south side of his extended park, was made in their place.[21] A public road ran at that time only half way along the back, or west side, of the park, but in the early 20th century it was extended for the whole distance.[22]

The hall grounds and park cover 56 a.,[23] extending along the hillside behind the village for more than ½ mile from Castle Hill at the northern end to New Road. An entrance to the park from the south end of Bridlington Street is marked by a tall pointed archway with the appearance of a Gothic ruin; it is said to have been built in 1829 by Humphrey Osbaldeston with stone from Filey Brigg.[24] The street called Castle Hill takes its name from the adjoining motte which is all that remains of Gilbert de Gant's castle.[25] The Osbaldeston mansion, a little to the south of Castle Hill, looks over the village towards the sea.[26] The hall and park were in 1928 acquired for use as a Methodist girls' boarding school and extensive new buildings have since been erected in the grounds, together with a vast new Methodist church next to Cross Hill.[27]

On Cross Hill the medieval market cross, a tall square shaft with steps around it, still stood in 1970. The stocks, which stood near by,[28] were accidentally burnt c. 1860.[29] Around the market-place nearly all the houses date from the 18th and early 19th centuries. They include Osgodby House, built early in the 18th century, and Denmark House, a later-18th-century building with a five-bay frontage. Both these fronts have large stone panels carved with a spurious heraldic crest, placed there by the Readett Bayleys.[30] The White Swan is a long whitewashed brick building apparently dating from the early 19th century. Bridlington Street, Stonegate, and the southern end of Northgate are all closely built-up with houses, mostly of the 18th century and later, built of brick or rough chalk blocks. The Old Manor House, or Low Hall, in Sheep Dike Lane dates from the 17th century[31] and another early house is a two-storeyed chalk building in Northgate bearing the date 1694. More than twenty one-and-a-half storeyed cottages, some of chalk, dating from the 18th and 19th centuries still remain scattered through the village. The 18th- and 19th-century houses are not generally noteworthy, with the exception of Wrangham House, the former Vicarage.[32] There are several three-bay houses in Northgate, some of them built of chalk. Mill Farm in Bridlington Street, near Cross Hill, has a late-18th-century front of chalk ashlar with brick dressings, and further south in that street are several brick farm-houses with chalk outbuildings. The 19th-century buildings include Telford House in Bridlington Street, dated 1829, a brick dovecot in the same street, dated 1897, and Batworth, a large red-brick house on the Muston road.

The 20th-century expansion of the village has taken place in all directions and was continuing in 1970. Council houses include 18 in Stonegate, 27 on the Folkton road, and 64 in Northgate, about fifty of these houses having been built before the Second World War.[33] There are many private houses in those roads, in Bridlington Street, and on the

---

[11] *N. & Q.* 9th ser. vii. 362; N.E. Sea Fisheries Cttee. *Mins.* 1896–7, Executive Cttee., p. 13; Lucy M. Owston, *Hunmanby, E. Yorks., a Story of Ten Centuries*, 68; *Hunmanby 1874–1965* (Hun. Par. Counc.), 26.
[12] Registry of Deeds, Beverley, 334/539/415; 343/23/18.
[13] E.R.R.O., DDHU/9/84. [14] See e.g. p. 244.
[15] E.R.R.O., DDGD/box 4; DDHU/9/267.
[16] Y.A.S. MSS., MD. 116/1.
[17] E.R.R.O., DDHU/9/368.
[18] O.S. Map 6" (1854).
[19] B.M. Cott. MS. Vesp. E. xx, f. 288b.
[20] S.C. 2/21/63.
[21] E.R.R.O., HD/30. [22] O.S. Map 6" (1913, 1929).
[23] Regy. of Deeds, 263/189/153.
[24] Owston, *Hunmanby*, 63.
[25] *V.C.H. Yorks.* ii. 45.
[26] See p. 232.
[27] See p. 243.
[28] O.S. Map 6" (1854).
[29] Owston, *Hunmanby*, 68–70; *Kelly's Dir. N. & E.R. Yorks.* (1901), 509.
[30] Ex inf. Miss Owston.
[31] See p. 234. [32] See p. 242.
[33] *Hunmanby 1874–1965*, 15.

Muston road. At the south end of the village, near the railway station, there has also been some industrial development.[34]

The public buildings in the village include, in Low Stonegate, the former pinfold and lock-up. The latter, sometimes called the 'Black Hole',[35] is a small rectangular brick building, without windows. It has separate sections for men and women, entered by twin doorways with gratings above them; a central tablet bears the date 1834. The adjoining pinfold is built of cobbles. By 1823 there were three public houses in the village: the White Swan, the Buck, and the Black Horse. The last ceased to exist some time after 1858, as did the Royal Oak,[36] which had been built on the Bridlington–Filey road in 1839.[37] In addition the Railway Tavern was in existence by 1909[38] and others remaining in 1970 were the Horseshoe and the Veterinary Arms.

By 1850 there were about twenty farm-houses outside the village,[39] most of them no doubt originating after the inclosure of 1809. The farm known as Graffitoe was for a time renamed Lind House, after a visit to it by Jenny Lind in 1848 while she was staying at Filey.[40] The isolated house known as Long Whins was the only one standing near Primrose Valley until late in the century. By 1909, however, there were several others there, including Southcliffe and the Rotherham and District Children's Convalescent Home, the latter opened in 1904.[41] Southcliffe was used as a private school at least from 1906 until the 1930s.[42] For a few years after 1910 there was an airfield near the cliffs.[43] Houses, bungalows, and chalets in the area have steadily increased in number; by 1970 there was also a caravan camp there, and another at Low Field Farm. Since c. 1900 land on the north side of Primrose Valley has formed part of Filey golf course.[44] At Hunmanby Gap bungalows began to be built in the 1930s. A holiday camp was opened by Butlins Ltd. in 1946[45] and covers an extensive site between the Bridlington–Filey road and the sea; it has its own railway station with a branch from the main line. Not far from the camp are the disused reservoirs of Filey waterworks, constructed in 1858 and 1886.[46]

Of the two former hamlets in Hunmanby, there is no trace of the site of Fowthorpe. Its land lay on either side of Primrose Valley and the hamlet may have stood near the Filey–Bridlington road, where the name Chapel Hill, mentioned in 1566,[47] has survived. The site of Bartindale is clearly marked by earthworks around Bartindale Farm.[48] At Fordon three bungalows have recently been added to the hamlet, which had previously consisted of only two 19th-century houses, Low Fordon Farm, and the chapel. All lie near a prominent pond, which was dry in 1970. Low Fordon is an 18th-century chalk-built house with extensive chalk outbuildings.[49]

A large population resulted in a wide range of social activities in the village from the late 18th century onwards, often encouraged by the paternal interest of the owners of the Hunmanby estate. The Hunmanby Amicable Society was founded in 1778[50] and the Hunmanby Association for the Prosecution of Felons in 1793.[51] Another friendly society was referred to as the 'New Club' in 1827,[52] and the Cow Club, which provided compensation when members lost their animals, was in existence from c. 1807 until 1952.[53] A lodge of shepherds was started c. 1840, providing benefit for its members and holding an annual feast day, and continued until the early 20th century.[54] The Hunmanby Nursing Fund was started in 1896.[55] Francis Wrangham, vicar from 1795 to 1840, was concerned in the establishment of several of the early societies, as well as in the formation of a free dispensary for the poor of the village in 1819, a savings bank, and a free library housed in the vestry c. 1807.[56] The library later passed to the Literary Institute, founded in 1849.[57] A men's reading room and club, later called the Institute, was established in 1907 in a former infants' school in Stonegate. In 1925 it moved to a former brewery in Bridlington Street and in 1945 was taken over by the newly-formed Hunmanby Social Development Committee; the building has since been demolished.[58] The Lushington Band, later known as the Widow Singers, was formed c. 1840 and continued to raise funds for the poor until after the First World War.[59] A village band continued, however, until 1961.[60] Finally, the first of a long series of annual exhibitions and shows was held in the village in 1853 by the Floral, Horticultural, Poultry, Foal, and Lamb Society. This was succeeded by the Fanciers' Society, which held its first show in 1904, and the 'Hunmanby Show' continued until the Second World War. The earlier shows were held in the Temperance Hall in Stonegate, but later a field near Park House Farm was used.[61] Another feature of Hunmanby unusual in the villages of the area was the provision of a gasworks. It was established in 1854 and improved plant was installed in Garton Lane in 1863. The gas was used almost exclusively for house lighting and the works were last mentioned in 1897.[62]

The hamlet of Fordon was assessed separately for taxation until the 15th century, but thereafter was

---

[34] See p. 239.
[35] O.S. Map 6" (1854). See plate facing p. 273.
[36] White, *Dir. Hull & York* (1858), 444.
[37] Sheahan and Whellan, *Hist. York & E.R.* ii. 479. It was sold in 1865: E.R.R.O., DDHU/9/245, 248–9.
[38] O.S. Map 6" (1913).
[39] Ibid. (1854).
[40] Sheahan and Whellan, op. cit. 480.
[41] O.S. Map 6" (1983, 1913); *Filey Post*, 4 June 1904.
[42] O.S. Map 6" (1929); *Kelly's Dir. N. & E.R. Yorks.* (1933), 495; *Filey Post*, 2 June 1906.
[43] *Filey Post*, 30 July 1910; 15 Nov. 1913.
[44] See p. 145.
[45] J.A.R. Pimlott, *The Englishman's Holiday*, 248.
[46] See p. 145.
[47] Y.A.S. MSS., MD. 116/14.
[48] The farm is described in W. G. Hoskins, *Hist. from the Farm*, 79–84.
[49] See plate facing p. 32.
[50] E.R.R.O., QDC/2/19.
[51] Ibid. DDHU/9/78.
[52] Hunmanby Par. Counc. Rec., Overseers' Acct. Bk. 1784–1829.
[53] E.R.R.O., PR. 768 (Cow Club Min. Bk.); M. Sadler, *Archdeacon Francis Wrangham*, 24.
[54] Owston, *Hunmanby*, 71–2.
[55] Hun. Par. Counc. Rec., scrapbk. p. 68.
[56] Owston, *Hunmanby*, 64; Sadler, *Wrangham*, 23–5.
[57] Sheahan and Whellan, *Hist. York & E.R.* ii. 480.
[58] E.R.R.O., PR. 770 (Institute Min. Bk.); Hun. Par. Counc. Rec., scrapbk. pp. 102–3, 143.
[59] Owston, *Hunmanby*, 70–1.
[60] *Hunmanby 1874–1965*, 12–13.
[61] Hun. Par. Counc. Rec., scrapbk. pp. 58–9; Owston, *Hunmanby*, 60; *Hunmanby 1874–1965*, 17.
[62] Sheahan and Whellan, *Hist. York & E.R.* ii. 480; Bulmer, *Dir. E. Yorks.* (1892), 213; *Kelly's Dir. N. & E.R. Yorks.* (1897), 487.

included with Wold Newton.[63] Bartindale was assessed separately in 1297, when there were only four taxpayers, and thereafter with Argam; Fowthorpe does not appear in taxation records at all. In 1377 there were 293 poll-tax payers in Hunmanby.[64] There were 97 deaths from the plague at Hunmanby in 1605.[65] In 1674 55 households were discharged from the hearth tax; of the 107 that were taxed, 77 had only one hearth each, 20 had 2, 7 had 3, and one each had 5, 6, and eleven.[66] There were 120 families in Hunmanby and 5 in Fordon in 1743,[67] and about 145 in the whole parish in 1764.[68] The population of Hunmanby in 1801 was 757 and that of Fordon in 1821, when it was first separately enumerated in the census, was 48.[69]

Hunmanby's population increased substantially in the 19th century, to 903 in 1811, 1,018 in 1821, 1,214 in 1841, and a maximum of 1,387 in 1861. It was 1,289 in 1901.[70] By 1921 there had been a further rapid growth, to 1,501. Of the population of 1,414 in 1931, 163 were in the area shortly to be transferred to Filey urban district. Hunmanby's population continued to increase and was 1,512 in 1961.[71] The population of Fordon rose to 63 in 1841, fell to 38 in 1861, recovered to 60 in 1871, and fell once more to 38 in 1891–1901.[72] It remained at about 40 in the early 20th century.[73]

MANORS AND OTHER ESTATES. There were two estates in Hunmanby in 1086: one of 23 carucates, which had been held by Carle in 1066, and the other of one carucate, which had been held by Chilbert. The larger estate was held in 1086 by Gilbert de Gant;[74] it became the centre of a small local honor, which descended like the principal manor and is recorded until the late 14th century.

The Gants retained HUNMANBY until 1294, when another Gilbert de Gant was obliged to surrender it to Robert of Tattershall, who claimed it by inheritance from Philip of Tattershall.[75] Philip's father Robert had married a niece of Gilbert de Gant, who was a widow in 1185, and in 1199 Philip gave the king £6 13s. 4d. to secure lands given to him by his uncle Roger who held them by grant from Robert de Gant.[76] At the death of another Robert of Tatershall in 1306,[77] a third of the manor was assigned in dower to his mother Joan of Tattershall (d. 1335).[78] The rest passed to Robert's heirs Thomas de Cailly, son of Emma sister of Robert of Tattershall (d. 1298), and Emma's sisters Joan of Driby and Isabel of Orby. Their shares were finally assigned in 1309.[79] The widow and heirs of Gilbert de Gant (d. 1298) unsuccessfully laid claims to the manor for several years.[80]

John of Orby was assigned a share of Joan of Tattershall's dower in 1336.[81] The Orbys held their share of the manor until 1369, when, on the death of John's widow Margaret, it passed to their granddaughter Mary Percy.[82] Before 1382 Mary married John Roos; he died in 1393 and she in 1394 without issue. The rights in remainder of her share of the manor were quitclaimed in 1395 to feoffees.[83] Those feoffees seem also to have acquired the Cailly portion[84] and in 1405 they gave seisin in two-thirds of the manor to Sir Henry Percy.[85]

Thomas de Cailly, who inherited part of the manor in 1306, died in 1316 and the property passed to his nephew Adam of Clifton.[86] In 1336 Adam was assigned a share of Joan of Tattershall's dower.[87] After the death of Constantine of Clifton in 1395 the holding was apparently acquired before 1398 by the feoffees who held the Orby portion of the manor.[88]

Thus two-thirds of the manor descended in the Percy family until Henry Percy, 6th earl of Northumberland, conveyed them to the Crown, with his other northern estates, in 1537.[89] The manor was in 1544 granted to Matthew, earl of Lennox, and his wife,[90] and it was later sometimes known as the Lennox manor.[91] It passed back to the Crown on the accession of the Lennoxes' grandson James I. A grant of the manor to John, Lord Digby, in 1620[92] was apparently ineffective, for in 1629 Hunmanby was assigned to trustees for the City of London in return for loans to the Crown.[93] In the same year the manor was sold to John Pearson of Harpham, reserving a rent to the City.[94] Members of the Leppington family were tenants of part of the manor[95] and they apparently successfully claimed ownership of it, for in 1649 Pearson sold it to Robert Leppington in pursuance of a decree in Chancery.[96] In 1665 Leppington conveyed it to William Osbaldeston.[97]

The manor was held by the Osbaldestons until the death of F. W. Osbaldeston in 1770, when Hunmanby passed to his great-nephew Humphrey Brooke, who then assumed the surname Osbaldeston.[98] Humphrey subsequently added to the estate[99] and for these additional lands, which he held in fee

---

[63] Its poll-tax certificate is mutilated: E 179/202/62 m. 45.
[64] Ibid. m. 8.
[65] E.R.R.O., PR. 1146.
[66] E 179/205/521.
[67] Herring's Visit. i. 218; ii. 90.
[68] B.I.H.R., Bp. V. 1764/Ret. 61.
[69] V.C.H. Yorks. iii. 489.
[70] Ibid.
[71] Census.
[72] V.C.H. Yorks. iii. 489.
[73] Census.
[74] V.C.H. Yorks. ii. 271.
[75] K.B. 27/141 m. 4; Cal. Inq. p.m. viii, p. 22.
[76] Rot. de Dominabus (P.R.S. xxxv), 3; Rot. de Ob. et Fin. (Rec. Com.), 19; Complete Peerage, xii(1), 646–7.
[77] Cal. Fine R. 1272–1307, 547.
[78] Cal. Inq. p.m. vii, p. 469.
[79] Cal. Close, 1307–13, 99–102.
[80] C.P. 40/171 m. 105;/173 m. 421;/179 m. 424;/183 m. 240;/192 m. 188;/198 m. 92;/199 m. 184 d.;/216 m. 187.
[81] Cal. Inq. p.m. viii, p. 47.
[82] Ibid. x, p. 94; xv, p. 230; Cal. Close, 1354–60, 17; Cal. Pat. 1343–5, 226.

[83] C 136/258/123; C.P. 25(1)/290/57 no. 281; Cal. Close, 1392–6, 493–5; Cal. Inq. p.m. xv, p. 230.
[84] See below.
[85] J. W. Clay, Ext. & Dorm. Peerages of N. Cos. 162; Cal. Pat. 1405–8, 51.
[86] Cal. Inq. p.m. vi, p. 19; viii, p. 22.
[87] Ibid. viii, p. 47.
[88] Complete Peerage, iii. 308; Cal. Pat. 1396–9, 334.
[89] See p. 285.
[90] L. & P. Hen. VIII, xix(1), p. 628.
[91] e.g. E.R.R.O., DDHU/9/74.
[92] C 66/2220 m. 6.
[93] C 66/2505 m. 17; E.R.R.O., DDKG/142(c); DDGR/13/5; P. E. Jones and R. Smith, Guide to the Records at Guildhall, London, 55.
[94] E.R.R.O., DDHU/9/55.
[95] Ibid. DDKG/142(c); E 134/11 Chas. I Mich./50; C 142/598/70.
[96] E.R.R.O., DDHU/9/60.
[97] Ibid. /62–7.
[98] Burke, Land. Gent. (1898), i. 518.
[99] e.g. Registry of Deeds, Beverley, AO/193/224; AP/174/253; AR/395/756.

simple, he was allotted 272 a. at inclosure in 1809; his total allotment, mostly representing the entailed manorial estate and tithes, amounted to about 3,300 a., excluding both Bartindale and Fordon.[1] Further additions were made to the estate after inclosure.

At Humphrey Osbaldeston's death in 1835 the entailed estate passed, by a settlement under F. W. Osbaldeston's will, to a relative, Bertram Mitford, who adopted the additional surname Osbaldeston.[2] The Osbaldeston-Mitfords retained the manor until 1920, when it was sold to Sir Henry Readett Bayley. By that time the enlarged estate comprised nearly 5,000 a., again excluding Bartindale and Fordon.[3] The estate was split up and sold in separate lots in the 1920s.

The land which Humphrey Osbaldeston held in fee simple passed in 1835 to his daughter Theodosia, who assumed her paternal surname Brooke and died in 1850. It then passed to her niece Jane, whose husband R. S. Robson assumed the name Brooke. At Jane's death in 1871 she was succeeded by Humphrey Brooke Firman, who was a distant relative of Sir Richard Osbaldeston (d. 1728).[4] This holding amounted to 489 a. in 1867.[5] Part was the farm called Long Whins, which Firman sold in 1900;[6] the rest was sold in separate lots, mainly in 1919.[7]

After the death of Admiral Robert Mitford in 1870 Hunmanby Hall was occupied by a succession of tenants, including J. R. Pease of Hull and Lord William Cecil.[8] Sir Henry Readett Bayley, however, lived at the hall until 1923, when it was sold to C. H. W. Wilson, Baron Nunburnholme. In 1928 it was acquired as a Methodist girls' boarding school.[9]

Hunmanby Hall is a large brick building of which the original shape and extent have been obscured by later alterations, more particularly after it became a school. The early house was of two storeys and attics and had an H-shaped plan. It consisted of a central range and two cross-wings, a service wing on the north and a 'parlour' wing on the south. The core of this house dates from the early 17th century, when the Osbaldestons were beginning to build up their estate in Hunmanby, but whether or not it stood on the site of a medieval manor-house is not known. The oldest surviving features, a stone fire-place with a four-centred arch, an altered staircase, and panelling of the earlier 17th century, occur in the back or west half of the central range.[10] The side wings, if not there originally, were certainly in existence before the end of the 17th century.[11] A room in the south wing is lined with bolection-moulded oak panelling, which, if *in situ*, suggests a later-17th-century date; a fireback there is dated 1663.

About 1700–20 the eastern half of the central range was added or remodelled as a tall three-storeyed structure with cellars below. It was given a handsome 'Queen Anne' façade to the east, overlooking a forecourt still framed by the earlier wings. The front was built of red brick with lavish stone dressings, the storeys separated by moulded string-courses and the whole surmounted by a balustrade. It was five bays wide, the three central bays breaking slightly forward and having stone quoins. The windows above the central doorway were emphasised by stone surrounds, the top one with a segmental pediment. A domed lantern, which has now disappeared, was set centrally behind the balustrade.[12] Internally a fine early-18th-century staircase has survived. The most easterly room in the south wing was refitted in the middle of the 18th century and there are signs of alterations to both wings and to the back of the house at that time.

The west end of the south wing was altered by Admiral Mitford in the 19th century, reputedly to resemble the bridge of a ship. In the 1920s the rear elevation of the central range was embellished by the Nunburnholmes with somewhat fanciful Renaissance features. Also in the 20th century the courtyard at the rear was enclosed by a covered way joining the ends of the two wings. Little change was made to the east front before 1928, although at some period, perhaps in the later 18th century, a pediment had been added above the doorway.[13] After 1928, however, a single-storeyed school dining-hall was built out over the forecourt, its front projecting beyond the old side wings. The ground floor of the Queen Anne façade was taken down, and this was partly reproduced at the front of the new dining-hall, some of the original material being re-used. The two upper storeys of the old façade have remained in position.

North of the house an 18th-century brick outbuilding, probably a former stable block, has recessed arcading to its front. Since 1928 extensive new school buildings have been erected in the grounds north-west of the house.

In the early 17th century various grants of land were made by the Crown out of the Lennox manor, and this was apparently the origin of several of the small holdings later existing in Hunmanby. In the years around 1800 a substantial estate was built up by John Hall and William Drinkrow by the purchase of such holdings,[14] and at inclosure in 1809 they were allotted 605 a. in lieu of about 30 bovates.[15] The Halls retained the land, known as Howe Farm, until it was amalgamated with the Osbaldeston estate in 1856.[16]

Joan of Driby, the third coheir of Robert of Tattershall in 1306, granted her share of the manor in 1323 to James Roos, who in 1336 obtained his share of Joan of Tattershall's dower.[17] At the death of Sir Robert Roos in 1441 his heirs were his daughters Margery Wittilbury and Eleanor.[18]

---

[1] e.g. Registry of Deeds, Beverley, CQ/1/1.
[2] Burke, *Land. Gent.* (1937), 1607–8.
[3] Regy. of Deeds, 209/184/157.
[4] Burke, *Land. Gent.* (1898), i. 517–18.
[5] Regy. of Deeds, KC/353/454. [6] See p. 233.
[7] Regy. of Deeds, 198/421/358; 199/30/24; /42/35; /43/36; /257/221; /373/326. [8] Directories.
[9] Regy. of Deeds, 263/189/153; 366/549/447.
[10] Miss B. M. Bray, headmistress, kindly allowed the hall to be examined in 1970 and 1971.
[11] They are shown on a drawing of the east front c. 1720: B.M. Lansd. 914, f. 216. The house already had 11 hearths in 1674: E 179/205/104.
[12] B.M. Lansd. 914, f. 216.
[13] A triangular pediment is shown on a photograph of c. 1870 (*penes* Miss L. M. Owston), a segmental pediment in the early 20th century (Hun. Par. Counc. Rec., scrapbk. pp. 3, 52–3), and none at all in 1926 (ibid. p. 147).
[14] Regy. of Deeds, BO/141/209; CD/154/227; /351/539; CE/560/851; CM/434/677.
[15] Ibid. CQ/1/1.
[16] Ibid. HM/37/36.
[17] C 143/157/13; *Cal. Pat.* 1321–4, 303; *Cal. Inq. p.m.* vii, p. 470; viii, p. 47.
[18] C 139/106/24; *Cal. Fine R.* 1437–45, 272; *Cal. Close*, 1447–54, 86–7.

Margery seems to have died without issue and the estate later passed to Eleanor's husband John Paulet.[19] In 1525 it was described as the manor of *HUNMANBY*.[20] Sir William Paulet in 1539 granted it to Sir James Strangways[21] (d. 1541). Sir James's heirs were his sister Joan Mauleverer and his nephew Robert Roos;[22] they were in dispute with William, Lord Dacre, on whom lands had been settled by Sir James Strangways, and in 1544 Hunmanby was assigned in dower to Sir James's widow Elizabeth (d. 1580), who later successively married Francis Neville and Charles Brandon, with reversion to Robert Roos.[23]

In 1581 Robert Roos conveyed the manor to Edward, earl of Rutland, and it passed in 1587 to his daughter Elizabeth, *suo jure* Lady Roos and later the wife of Lord Burghley.[24] Her son William, Lord Roos, sold it to William Leppington and Robert Ringrose in 1612, and Ringrose assigned his right to Leppington the same year.[25] The so-called Roos manor was in 1664 sold by Joseph Leppington to William Osbaldeston,[26] who soon after acquired the capital manor with which this estate was then united.

Certain property in Hunmanby, some of it in Fowthorpe, did not pass with the manor from the Gants to the Tattershalls in 1294, having been previously granted by Gilbert de Gant to his brother Adam and his wife Agnes.[27] Adam and Agnes had no issue and half of the holding, including 15½ bovates of land, reverted to Roger of Kerdiston (d. c. 1337), a coheir of Gilbert de Gant.[28] It was taken into the king's hands in 1353–4,[29] and the Kerdistons' title was not acknowledged until 1373.[30] William Kerdiston alienated the estate to feoffees in 1376 and in 1379 they assigned it to John Paulin and John Acome; the latter released his interest in 1382.[31] William Paulin died seised of the property in 1460.[32] The Paulins were recorded in Hunmanby at later dates but there is no evidence for the subsequent descent of this property.

The other half of Adam de Gant's holding reverted to Peter Mauley (IV), another coheir of Gilbert de Gant.[33] It was granted by Mauley to William of Hastings the younger, who transferred it to William of Hastings the elder. In 1349 it reverted to Peter Mauley (V).[34] At the death of Peter Mauley (VIII) in 1415 the estate was inherited by his sisters Constance Bigot and Elizabeth Salvin.[35] Constance Bigot and John Salvin held it in equal portions in 1438,[36] but Constance applied for a division of the Mauley inheritance in 1439[37] and she was assigned the manor of *HUNMANBY*.[38] When Sir Francis Bigot was attainted in 1537[39] the property passed to the Crown.

Various leases of the property were made, but by 1600 10½ bovates of former Bigot land had passed to John Legard,[40] who also acquired other land in Hunmanby.[41] Most of the Legard estate lay in Fowthorpe,[42] and in 1799 it comprised 118 a. and a farm-house called Long Whins.[43] It then passed to John Weldon and in 1830 to H. B. Osbaldeston.[44] At the latter's death in 1835 the property descended with Osbaldeston's personal estate to the Brookes and Firmans.[45] H. B. Firman sold it to R. W. Smith in 1900,[46] and many small lots had been sold for holiday development in Primrose Valley before Smith died in 1946.[47]

Several substantial estates in Hunmanby were held under the chief lords. By the mid 13th century, for example, the Marmion family held 2 carucates from the Gants,[48] and they retained their estate until the mid 14th century. By 1360 dower was held in the reputed manor of *HUNMANBY* by Maud, widow of Robert Marmion (fl. 1338).[49] Robert's coheirs were his sisters Joan and Avice. In 1360 a moiety of the manor was held by Joan and her husband Sir John de Folvill,[50] but at her death in 1362 Joan was succeeded by Maud, a daughter by a previous marriage.[51] In 1401 Maud sued Henry FitzHugh and his wife Elizabeth, granddaughter of Avice Marmion, for a moiety of Robert Marmion's Yorkshire lands.[52] In 1418, however, the manor was conveyed by the FitzHughs to John Laton.[53]

The manor apparently passed to Sir Robert Constable and was forfeited to the Crown in 1537.[54] Various leases of it were made during the rest of the century.[55] Edward Wingate (d. 1597) obtained a grant of it in 1590,[56] and it passed to his nephew George (d. 1604).[57] Its later descent has not been traced.

Four carucates of land were held from the Marmions by Lora de Gant in 1304, and at her death in 1309 they reverted to the coheirs of her husband Gilbert.[58] The share of Julian de Gant was acquired in 1315 by Adam de Gant,[59] and he held 10 bovates in 1323.[60] It presumably descended with his other lands in Hunmanby.[61]

---

[19] C 142/8/70.
[20] C 139/43/56.
[21] L. & P. Hen. VIII, xiv(2), p. 223.
[22] C 142/67/81.
[23] Ibid.; C 142/194/19; L. & P. Hen. VIII, xvi, p. 176; xix(1), p. 14; Yorks. Fines, i. 91, 264.
[24] C 142/218/52; C 142/239/101; Yorks. Fines, ii. 177.
[25] E.R.R.O., DDHU/9/45(a), (b).
[26] Ibid. (c).
[27] K.B. 27/141 m. 4; Cal. Close, 1318–23, 660.
[28] C 135/51/10.
[29] Cal. Inq. Misc. iii, p. 337.
[30] Cal. Pat. 1370–4, 358; Cal. Inq. p.m. xi, pp. 72–3.
[31] Cal. Pat. 1377–81, 352; 1381–5, 203–4; Yorks. Deeds, ix. 106.
[32] C 139/178/52.
[33] Abbrev. Plac. (Rec. Com.), 296.
[34] C 143/260/19; Cal. Pat. 1340–3, 563; Cal. Inq. p.m. ix, p. 438.
[35] Yorks. Inq. Hen. IV–V, 115; Cal. Fine R. 1413–22, 124–5.
[36] C 139/93/48.
[37] C.P. 40/714 m. 485.
[38] C 139/143/28.
[39] S.C. 6/Hen.VIII/4420; T.E.R.A.S. xvii. 17–18, 22.
[40] E.R.R.O., DDHU/9/32; Y.A.S. MSS., MD. 116/16–19.
[41] See p. 234.
[42] E.R.R.O., DDHU/20/5.
[43] Regy. of Deeds, BZ/591/925.
[44] Ibid. EL/93/111.
[45] See p. 232.
[46] Regy. of Deeds, 23/353/324 (1900).
[47] Ibid. 737/288/186.
[48] J.I. 1/1179 m. 10; Yorks. Assize R. (Y.A.S. Rec. Ser. xliv), 87; Cal. Close, 1307–13, 102.
[49] C.P. 40/561 m. 111.
[50] Yorks. Fines, 1347–77, 75.
[51] C 135/158/81.
[52] C.P. 40/561, m. 111.
[53] C.P. 25(1)/280/153 no. 40.
[54] S.C. 6/Hen.VIII/4324.
[55] Ibid. /4333; C 66/1351 m. 25; Cal. Pat. 1560–3, 360.
[56] C 66/1351 m. 25; C 142/255/176.
[57] C 142/288/126.
[58] Yorks. Inq. iv. 36; Cal. Fine R. 1307–19, 39; Cal. Close, 1307–13, 170.
[59] C.P. 25(1)/270/88 no. 19.
[60] Cal. Close, 1318–23, 660.
[61] See above.

Another estate established by the mid 14th century was that of the Zouche family. It included two thirds of a mill in Hunmanby, held by Roger la Zouche in right of his wife in 1353.[62] Part of the property apparently descended to the Ellerkers,[63] and at his death in 1539 Sir Ralph Ellerker held a reputed manor of *HUNMANBY*.[64] In 1569 Edward Ellerker conveyed 6 bovates of land there to Thomas Shipton (d. 1577), who devised them to his son George.[65] Also in 1569 Ellerker sold other property to Marmaduke Lacy, and in 1586 the Lacys conveyed it to John Legard.[66]

Some of the Zouche land was held by Sir Thomas Sewerby in the 1350s, including a windmill and manor-house in Fowthorpe.[67] In the 15th century William Sewerby gave 8 bovates in Fowthorpe and a plot in Hunmanby, held of the earl of Northumberland, to Sir Geoffrey Pigot and his wife, who was William's daughter.[68] By c. 1520 the estate had passed to Thomas Pigot's three coheirs, Margaret Metcalf, Joan Hussey, and Elizabeth Strangways.[69] The Metcalfs still had their share in 1547 when, at the partition of estates, the manor of *HUNMANBY*, together with Fowthorpe field, was allotted to Christopher Metcalf.[70] In 1600 2 bovates called 'Pigot lands' belonged to John Legard.[71] The Pigot and Lacy lands may have subsequently descended with Legard's other property in Hunmanby.[72]

An estate of 4 carucates was granted by Gilbert de Gant to the Stane family, probably in the early 13th century, and was held of them by Vivian de Rossale in 1286.[73] It was held by Beatrice, widow of Sir Walter Rossale, before the death of their son John in 1403.[74] In 1408 Beatrice and her husband Sir John Prendergast released their right in the reputed manor of *HUNMANBY* to Sir Walter's daughter Eleanor Dagworth, who was coheir with her sister Alice Ingilfeld.[75] In 1416, after Alice's death, her husband agreed that the manor should be assigned to Eleanor, then the wife of Sir John Mortimer.[76]

In 1451 the property was granted to Sir Richard Hamerton and others to the use of James Hamerton,[77] and it is later referred to as the Hamerton manor.[78] The family held it until 1596, when Paul Hamerton conveyed it to Ralph Westrop.[79] The manor passed to Thomas Westrop in 1622,[80] and in the following year he sold it to Sir Richard Osbaldeston.[81] It later descended with the capital manor.

It was apparently from the Hamerton manor, with small contributions from other holdings, that the Stutville estate in Hunmanby was built up. In 1621 Charles Stutville was said to hold 12½ bovates of Thomas Westrop and in 1637 his son, another Charles, held them of Sir Richard Osbaldeston.[82] Of this land 11½ bovates apparently passed by sale and exchange c. 1700 from another Charles Stutville to Sir Richard Osbaldeston[83] and the remainder passed, like the Stutville estate in Fordon,[84] to the Grimstons. In 1783 Thomas Grimston conveyed about 90 a. in Hunmanby to Richard Clark, who sold them in separate lots the same year.[85]

It was perhaps the Stutvilles who built the Old Manor House, or Low Hall, in Sheep Dike Lane as their 'manor-house', for in 1783 Richard Clark sold the house 'commonly called the Old Hall' to Humphrey Osbaldeston;[86] two years later it was put to use as the parish workhouse.[87] The Stutvilles had occupied a five-hearth house in 1674, the only large house in the parish apart from those of the Osbaldestons and the vicar,[88] and their house had six principal rooms, besides 'garrets', in 1694.[89] Low Hall is an early- or mid-17th-century house of two storeys and attics, built of chalk with stone quoins. It is T-shaped, the cross-wing being at the north end. The stem of the T, which may have been shortened at some period, retains stone mullioned windows on its west side, facing the road. There are similar windows at the west gable-end of the wing, those to the ground and first floors being of four lights. At the opposite end of the wing is a massive stone chimney and, in the north wall, a stone doorway with a four-centred head. Internally there are signs of 18th-century alterations and there was formerly a spiral stair against the north wall.

One carucate in Hunmanby was held by Andrew Grimston in 1298, apparently in right of his wife Joan by inheritance from her father Roger of Hunmanby (d. by 1276).[90] Roger Grimston held it in 1304.[91] Part of this holding, comprising 2 bovates in 1428,[92] descended to Marmaduke Grimston in 1586.[93] Marmaduke sold property in Hunmanby to Francis Capleman in 1589.[94]

Twelve bovates were held in 1294 by Arnald of Buckton.[95] Two of these bovates were apparently in Fordon and they descended with Buckton manor in the 14th century.[96] A holding described as 4 bovates in 1529,[97] and afterwards called the manor of *HUNMANBY*, also descended with Buckton[98] and last appears in an inquiry on the estates of George Pockley in 1698.[99]

One carucate was held in the early 14th century by Robert of Boynton[1] and it descended in the Boynton family at least until the end of that century.[2]

Several small estates were held by religious houses.

[62] C 131/9/8.
[63] C 140/71/57.
[64] C 142/61/57; Yorks. Sta. Cha. Proc. i (Y.A.S. Rec. Ser. xli), 35.
[65] Y.A.S. MSS., MD 116/11; C 142/275/323; Yorks. Fines, i. 368.
[66] Yorks. Fines, i. 368; iii. 50.
[67] C 131/9/8; Yorks. Deeds, v. 131.
[68] C 1/546/39; C 142/2/75.
[69] C 1/546/39.
[70] Y.A.J. iii. 65.
[71] DDHU/9/32.
[72] See p. 233.
[73] Abbrev. Plac. 210; Cur. Reg. R. 1203–5, 191; Yorks. Deeds, viii. 75–6.
[74] C 137/42/23.
[75] Cal. Close, 1405–9, 387.
[76] Ibid. 1413–19, 356.
[77] E.R.R.O., DDHU/9/13.
[78] e.g. ibid. /74.
[79] Yorks. Fines, iv. 46.
[80] C.P. 43/158/59.
[81] E.R.R.O., DDHU/9/50.
[82] C 142/389/120; C 142/553/43.
[83] E.R.R.O., DDGR/13/11; C 5/136/58; C 5/361/11. These transactions were part of an agreement reached after a dispute about inclosure: see p. 238.
[84] See p. 235.
[85] Regy. of Deeds, BF/270/466; BH/39/68; etc.
[86] Ibid. BH/39/67.
[87] See p. 241.
[88] E 179/205/521.
[89] B.I.H.R., C.P., H. 4722.
[90] C 133/85/4; Cal. Pat. 1272–81, 133.
[91] Cal. Inq. p.m. iv, p. 108.
[92] E 179/202/104.
[93] C 142/210/124.
[94] Yorks. Fines, iii. 107.
[95] K.B. 27/141 m. 4.
[96] Cal. Inq. p.m. vii, p. 403; see above, p. 83.
[97] C 142/50/142.
[98] C 142/254/20; C 142/453/83; C 142/459/54; S.C. 2/211/63; E 179/202/44; B.M. Add. MS. 26718, f. 117.
[99] E 134/10 Wm. III East./24.
[1] C 133/85/4; Cal. Inq. p.m. iv, p. 108.
[2] C 135/49/20; C 143/161/16; Cal. Close, 1327–30, 37; Abbrev. Rot. Orig. (Rec. Com.), i. 284; ii. 13.

In the mid 12th century 2 bovates were granted by Gilbert de Gant to Rievaulx abbey.³ Before the Dissolution lands in Hunmanby called Twyndall, or Twilling, were let by Rievaulx to Bridlington priory, and in 1545 they were granted by the Crown to John Broxholme and John Bellow.⁴ Anthony Harrison held them at his death in 1596 and they passed with Reighton manor to Thomas Harrison in 1635.⁵ Bridlington also received a gift of one bovate, as well as a grant of pasturage by Gilbert de Gant.⁶

The lazar house (*maladeria*) in Hunmanby is mentioned in the 12th century⁷ and it held a carucate of land in 1308.⁸ A toft belonging to the Templars is mentioned in the 12th century;⁹ the Knights Hospitallers of Beverley had property in Hunmanby in 1539–40,¹⁰ and it was restored to them when the order was briefly revived in 1558.¹¹ These lands were granted in 1563 to Thomas Wood and William Frankland.¹²

The one-carucate estate recorded in Hunmanby in 1086 was perhaps that later known as the manor of *BARTINDALE*. The overlordship belonged to the Tattershalls in the early 14th century¹³ and the land was apparently held from them in 1304 by John son of John of Hunmanby. John had granted reversionary rights in land in Hunmanby to William of Argam in 1303¹⁴ and Bartindale subsequently descended like Argam.¹⁵ After the attainder of Sir Robert Constable in 1537, Bartindale was let by the Crown to John Bell.¹⁶ It was later acquired by Ralph Hansbie, who in 1600 conveyed it to Robert Ellis.¹⁷ Like part of Argam Bartindale passed from the Ellises to Elizabeth and John Greenhill; in 1767 they conveyed it to Richard Jordan, and in the same year Jordan sold it to F. W. Osbaldeston.¹⁸ At inclosure in 1809 nearly 350 a. in Bartindale were allotted to the Osbaldestons,¹⁹ and 375 a. there passed to the Bayleys in 1920.²⁰ The land was subsequently sold with the rest of the estate.

In 1086 an estate of 5 carucates in Fordon belonged to the king, having been held in 1066 by Carle.²¹ The overlordship subsequently descended in the Gant and Tattershall families.²² The estate was held under them by the Nevilles and was divided between the daughters and coheirs of Roger de Neville. The Malbis family, representing the elder daughter, retained a mesne lordship there in the later 13th and 14th centuries.²³ The manor of *FORDON* descended like Muston²⁴ to the heirs of Maud Malbis and Hawise of Lowthorpe.

In the later 13th century William Malbis granted at least 12 bovates in Fordon to Bridlington priory, which already had a carucate there by the gift of Walter de Gant.²⁵ The share of Hawise of Lowthorpe descended to John and Robert of Heslerton, who each had a carucate in Fordon.²⁶ In 1377 the reversion of Robert's share was granted to the priory,²⁷ and at the Dissolution the priory's land in Fordon was worth £4 12s.²⁸

Some of the former priory land was apparently granted for the maintenance of Fordon chapel. In 1591 the site of the chapel and land called Chapel Flats were granted by the Crown to Sir Edward Stanley,²⁹ and in 1609 Robert Rank conveyed the land, comprising 5 bovates, to Charles Stutville.³⁰ It was later described as late of Fordon chapel and formerly of Bridlington priory.³¹ Other priory land, amounting to 3½ bovates, was granted in 1591 to John Welles and Charles Best, who conveyed it in 1595 to Stutville.³² More priory property apparently went to the Constable family. In 1587 Christopher Constable sold 8 bovates to John Harrison, who conveyed it in 1590 to Stutville.³³

John of Heslerton's land in Fordon passed to his son Walter³⁴ and apparently descended like Carnaby manor³⁵ to the Hiltons³⁶ and the Stricklands, passing at some time in the 17th century to the Osbaldestons.³⁷ A further 2 bovates, which had belonged to the Condons since at least 1682, were acquired by the Osbaldestons in 1721.³⁸ At inclosure in 1809 the Osbaldestons were allotted 673 a. in Fordon, and another 177 a. for tithes.³⁹ In 1920 873 a. there passed to the Bayleys⁴⁰ and were subsequently sold in separate lots.

One carucate of land in 'Ledemare', in Fordon, was held by Carle in 1066 and belonged to the king in 1086.⁴¹ It formed part of the Neville fee and was granted in 1232 by Maud of Ganton to Whitby abbey.⁴² At the Dissolution the abbey had property in Fordon worth £1 4s.⁴³ In 1590 8 bovates of former Whitby land was granted by the Crown to John Rant and Thomas Hutton, and they sold it the same year to Charles Stutville.⁴⁴

The Stutville estate in Fordon had thus been built up from various sources in the late 16th and early 17th centuries. When Charles Stutville died in 1621 he had 19½ bovates in the township.⁴⁵ Like that in Argam the Stutville estate in Fordon passed to the

---

³ *Rievaulx Charty.* (Sur. Soc. lxxxiii), 47, 115, 186, 260.
⁴ *L. & P. Hen. VIII,* xx(2), p. 537.
⁵ C 142/245/11.
⁶ *Bridlington Charty.* 73; see below, p. 237.
⁷ *E.Y.C.* ii, p. 474.
⁸ *Cal. Inq. p.m.* iv, p. 261.
⁹ *E.Y.C.* ii, p. 474.
¹⁰ *Miscellanea,* iv (Y.A.S. Rec. Ser. xciv), 90.
¹¹ *Cal. Pat.* 1557–8, 319.
¹² Ibid. 1560–3, 576.
¹³ *Cal. Inq. p.m.* iv, p. 108; *Feud. Aids,* vi. 141.
¹⁴ *Cal. Inq. p.m.* iv, p. 108; *Yorks. Fines, 1300–14,* 33.
¹⁵ See p. 6.
¹⁶ *L. & P. Hen. VIII,* xiii(1), p. 140.
¹⁷ *Yorks. Fines,* iv. 157; *Royalist Composition Papers,* iii (Y.A.S. Rec. Ser. xx), 70.
¹⁸ Regy. of Deeds, AI/139/285; /421/830.
¹⁹ Ibid. CQ/1/1.
²⁰ Ibid. 209/184/157.
²¹ *V.C.H. Yorks.* ii. 204.
²² E 179/202/104; *Cal. Inq. p.m.* iv, p. 107; *Feud. Aids,* vi. 28, 141.
²³ *Feud. Aids,* vi. 28.
²⁴ See p. 279.
²⁵ *Bridlington Charty.* 2, 75–6; *Feud. Aids,* vi. 28; *Cal. Pat.* 1307–13, 443.
²⁶ B.M. Add. MS. 26729, f. 113; *Cal. Inq. p.m.* v, p. 54; see below, p. 273.
²⁷ C 143/391/3; *Cal. Pat.* 1377–81, 8.
²⁸ *Valor Eccl.* (Rec. Com.), v. 120.
²⁹ C 66/1377 m. 1.
³⁰ E.R.R.O., DDGR/9/10.
³¹ C 142/389/120.
³² E.R.R.O., DDGR/9/1.
³³ Ibid. /1, 5.
³⁴ *Parl. Rep. Yorks.* i (Y.A.S. Rec. Ser. xci), 107.
³⁵ See p. 126.   ³⁶ C 3/82/33.
³⁷ Regy. of Deeds, L/411/756.
³⁸ Ibid. H/204/426; E.R.R.O., DDGR/29/2.
³⁹ Regy. of Deeds, CQ/1/1.
⁴⁰ Ibid. 209/184/157.
⁴¹ *V.C.H. Yorks.* ii. 204, 323.
⁴² *Whitby Charty.* i (Sur. Soc. lxix), 140; ii (ibid. lxxii), 536; *Cal. Chart. R.* 1327–41, 293.
⁴³ *Valor Eccl.* v. 82.
⁴⁴ E.R.R.O., DDGR/9/4.
⁴⁵ C 142/389/120; C 142/553/43.

Grimstons in the 18th century, to John Farthing in 1804, and to Franky Hopkinson in 1822.[46] It comprised old closes, totalling 12 a., and 19¾ bovates, for which 461 a. were allotted at inclosure in 1809.[47] In 1853 James Hopkinson sold it to Benjamin Hemsworth.[48] It appears to have been conveyed in 1891 from Benjamin and J. D. Hemsworth to R. B. Parker,[49] but by 1895 Beatrice, Lady Inglefield (later Baroness von Haugwitz) had an interest in it.[50] In 1928 it was conveyed to the administrator of German property, under the Treaty of Peace Order, 1924, and sold by him the same year to Robert and Harold Gatenby.[51] The latter became the sole proprietor in 1946.[52]

The rectory belonged to Bardney abbey from 1115.[53] It was valued at £100 in 1291.[54] In 1297 Bardney was licensed to sell the tithes before tithing took place,[55] and the rectory was several times let by the abbey in the 14th century.[56] The right to thraves in Hunmanby was the subject of dispute between Bardney and Bridlington priory. These alms, represented by two thraves or 2d. from each plough, belonged to St. John's college, Beverley, but those arising in Hunmanby were granted between 1130 and 1140 to Bridlington.[57] The method of taking thraves from the tithes of Hunmanby was settled between Bardney and Bridlington between 1187 and c. 1197.[58] After further dispute, however, a settlement was reached in 1299 whereby Bridlington was to have the tithes of its demesnes in Burton Fleming, while Bardney was to have the thraves of Hunmanby parish.[59] Bardney also had glebe land in Hunmanby. Besides the carucate given by Gilbert de Gant, various small parcels of land were granted to the abbey,[60] and in 1360 there were 9 bovates in all.[61] In 1535 the rectory was worth £64.[62]

Bardney had let the rectory in 1528 to Robert Lutton, and after the Dissolution the Crown let the reversion of Lutton's lease to Sir Henry Gate in 1566 and 1575.[63] Lutton was involved in a dispute over the payment of tithes in 1543–4.[64] The rectory was granted by the Crown to Edmund Downing and Roger Rante in 1592 and it thenceforth descended with the advowson.[65] In 1650 it was worth £180;[66] there were still 4 bovates attached to it in 1625.[67] The payment of mortuaries and tithes to Richard Osbaldeston was disputed by Charles Stutville in 1694.[68] At inclosure in 1809 Humphrey Osbaldeston was allotted 926 a. for tithes in Hunmanby and 177 a. for those in Fordon.[69]

ECONOMIC HISTORY. By 1086 Hunmanby was the centre of extensive estates, with berewicks at Wold Newton and at 'Ricstorp', in Muston, and with soke at Muston and Flotmanby, and at 'Scolfstona', perhaps also in Muston. Bartindale was a separate estate, as was Fordon with its berewick of 'Ledemare'; Fowthorpe is not mentioned in the Domesday Survey. Gilbert de Gant's estate at Hunmanby had land for thirteen ploughs; in 1086 Gilbert actually had 3 ploughs, and 8 villeins and 6 bordars had 4 more. This estate also had meadow land, one league long and half a league wide. Together with its berewicks and soke Hunmanby had fallen in value from £12 before the Conquest to £3 in 1086. The estate which probably comprised Bartindale had land for half a plough; it had been worth 4s. but was waste in 1086. Fordon and 'Ledemare' together had land for three ploughs and were worth £1 before the Conquest.[70]

There were extensive demesnes in the early 14th century, including 20 bovates of arable land, as well as some meadow and pasture. The rents of customary and free tenants, however, made a large contribution to the manorial income. In 1298 27 free tenants held more than 68 bovates and paid rents of over £12. There were 50 free tenants named in 1302 and 25 in 1303, besides the holders of fees.[71] By 1539–40 free tenants' rents were valued at only about £2.[72] There were at least 19 freeholders on the Lennox manor in 1600.[73]

Customary tenants were numerous. In 1298 25 tofts and 25 bovates of land were held in bondage, 8 bovates were let at the will of the lord, and there were 35 cottages, the total rental of these holdings being nearly £16. The number of cottages was reduced to 11 in 1302 and 10 in 1303 and 1306, but this is apparently to be explained by the inclusion of some cottagers with the free tenants in 1302 and by the appearance in 1303 and 1306 of 21 tofts let at will; the number of bovates held in bondage remained unchanged. The services of the bond tenants and cottagers are recorded in 1303. The former were required, for each bovate, to do 9 days' work in autumn, reaping, and one day with a cart, carrying corn; one day's work at hay-time with a cart; and 2 days' work in winter with a horse, harrowing or ploughing. The cottagers did 7 days' work in autumn, reaping.[74] The rents of unfree tenants were worth about £39 in 1539–40[75] and there were about twenty such tenants on the Lennox manor in 1600.[76]

The most complete account of tenant holdings is that given in 1600, when the former Lennox manor was surveyed, together with the former Bigod lands and the Roos and Hamerton manors. The Lennox demesnes and unfree tenant land were then held by 23 tenants, of whom 4 had 6–7 bovates, 4 had 3½–4½,

---

[46] See p. 7.   [47] Regy. of Deeds, CG/290/40; CQ/1/1.
[48] Ibid. HA/96/100.   [49] Ibid. 42/203/186 (1891).
[50] Ibid. 76/289/276 (1895); 92/317/283 (1897).
[51] Ibid. 365/240/200; 378/167/137.
[52] Ibid. 720/95/77.   [53] See p. 241.
[54] Tax. Eccl. (Rec. Com.), 326.
[55] Reg. Romeyn, ii (Sur. Soc. cxxviii), 205–6.
[56] Reg. Greenfield, iii (Sur. Soc. cli), 213; v (ibid. cliii), 270; Cal. Inq. Misc. ii, p. 86; Cal. Pat. 1350–4, 293; 1360–4, 74.
[57] E.Y.C. i, p. 97.   [58] Ibid. ii, p. 478.
[59] Bridlington Charty. 66–7; Reg. Romeyn, ii. 225, 227–8, 231.
[60] B.M. Cott. MS. Vesp. E. xx, ff. 183–93; Cal. Chart. R. 1327–41, 255–7.
[61] Cal. Close, 1360–4, 74.
[62] Valor Eccl. (Rec. Com.), iv. 81.
[63] C 66/1130 m. 38; Cal. Pat. 1563–6, 437.
[64] Select Tithe Causes (Y.A.S. Rec. Ser. xciv), 16–17.
[65] See p. 241.
[66] T.E.R.A.S. ii. 58.   [67] E.R.R.O., DDHU/9/53.
[68] B.I.H.R., C.P., H. 4337, 4722.
[69] Regy. of Deeds, CQ/1/1.
[70] V.C.H. Yorks. ii. 204, 271–2.
[71] Yorks. Inq. iii. 67; iv. 35, 54.
[72] S.C. 6/Hen. VIII/4283.
[73] E.R.R.O., DDHU/9/32, p. 6.
[74] Yorks. Inq. iii. 67; iv. 35, 54, 126. In 1306 the bondmen's hay-time works were replaced by a day's work in autumn, carting dung.
[75] S.C. 6/Hen. VIII/4283.
[76] E.R.R.O., DDHU/9/32, pp. 4–5.

7 had 3, and 8 had one to 2½ bovates. Of the 19 freeholdings on the Lennox manor, the largest comprised 10½ bovates, 6 were of 5–9 bovates, 6 of 2, and 6 of one or 1½ bovate. The 6 tenants of the Roos lands had one to 3½ bovates each.[77] The holdings of Bigod and Hamerton land are not specified in 1600, but in 1624 17 tenants held the Hamerton property; the largest holding comprised 7 bovates and 10 were of only one bovate each.[78] In Fordon, after the Dissolution, there were only 6 tenants on the former Bridlington priory land, one having 8 bovates, 4 about 6 bovates each, and one 3½ bovates.[79]

The open fields of Hunmanby are first named in 1600, when they were called East, South, and West North West fields, one of which was said to lie fallow each year.[80] By that time the open-field land lay mostly on the wolds, though it extended on to the lower ground in the south-east of the township. It included the territory of Bartindale, which was already depopulated but which may have had its own open fields in the Middle Ages. The hamlet of Fowthorpe had been depopulated, too, but Fowthorpe field, presumably the former open-field land, was by 1600 used as pasture;[81] it was situated entirely on the low-lying ground below the wolds escarpment. The total amount of open-field land in Hunmanby was at least 120 bovates in 1298;[82] in 1600 there were 205 bovates and 54 a. of odd lands, and each bovate was reckoned at 16 a.[83] During the 17th and 18th centuries parts of the open fields were, as will be seen later, used as pasture leys, and in 1783 a six-course rotation was introduced into the fields. The three earlier field names thus lost their significance and at inclosure in 1809 allotments were made from numerous named areas of open-field land. In all about 4,600 a. were allotted from areas which had probably been open-field arable and leys.[84]

The open fields at Fordon were named in both the 13th century and in 1609 as East and West fields.[85] At the former date there was an intake, or 'ovenham', in each field. The extent of the open fields in the Middle Ages is not known, but after the Dissolution the former Bridlington priory land there amounted to 36 bovates.[86] The fields contained about 450 a. in 1597, but the land was described as 'very bad, barren and stony'. Half was sown each year with barley and oats and half left fallow, but the ground had 'so much taken out of the same' that the villagers had to sow 20 qr. of peas each year to make up their requirements.[87] The inclosure award of 1809 does not distinguish the different areas from which allotments were made in Fordon.

There were three areas of common meadow in Hunmanby in 1600, in which 20 tenants, 19 freeholders, and the proprietors of the former Bigod lands and the Roos and Hamerton manors all had rights. Each bovate to which a share of the meadows was attached carried the right to half a day's mowing in the ings, and a quarter of a day in each of North Twillings and Ing Barf.[88]

Common pasturage rights in the open fields are first recorded *c.* 1150, when pasture for 500 sheep in the field of Hunmanby was granted to Bridlington priory by Gilbert de Gant, and between 1160 and 1175 a similar grant was made to Rievaulx abbey.[89] In 1299 Bridlington was using the pasture for its sheep from Flotmanby and Burton Fleming.[90]

The chief area of common pasture in Hunmanby was the moor, stretching across the low ground towards the sea. A piece of moor ground is mentioned between 1156 and 1184,[91] and Gilbert de Gant appears to have deprived Avice Marmion of common in a three-acre parcel of moor in the mid 13th century.[92] He or another Gilbert de Gant is traditionally said to have given the moor to maintain the poor and 'Sir Richard' (Osbaldeston) to have taken it from them again.[93] There are frequent references in 16th- and 17th-century court rolls to animals trespassing on the moor.[94] In 1600 it was said to be used by husbandmen and cottagers without stint but apportioned among them according to the value of their tenements.[95] Leases granted by the Crown in the early 17th century out of the Lennox manor show that tenant's rights of common in fact took the form of an acreage equivalent: thus a holding might have 'common of pasture in the moor at the rate of 4 a.'[96] The outgangs, or outgates, gave access to the moor from the village and themselves provided pasturage, rights which William Leppington was disputing with Charles Stutville and other inhabitants in 1635.[97]

In 1713 about thirty inhabitants, headed by another Charles Stutville, alleged that Sir Richard Osbaldeston deprived them of common by keeping a rabbit warren on the moor. Witnesses stated that freeholders had been accustomed to put their animals on the moor and to cut whins there unhindered; one gave the stint on the outgangs as two horse-gates from 18 August[98] 'for all the year', and described common on the moor as being for cows, young beasts, and steers from 18 August to 11 November and for sheep, horses, and all cattle from 11 November to 25 March. Sir Richard was said to have recently built a lodge on the moor and to have a warrener, and the rabbits ran there 'like flocks of sheep'.[99] Agreement was reached between William Osbaldeston, the vicar, and the freeholders in 1738 whereby the rabbits were to be cleared from the moor, with the exception of an area on the north side which was to be inclosed for Osbaldeston's warren.[1] Much of the moor remained as common until 1809, when about 330 a. were allotted at inclosure, as well as some 30 a. in the Outgates.[2]

The stint of sheep allowed on the commons and open fields was carefully regulated in the 18th

---

[77] Ibid. pp. 4–6.
[78] Ibid. /10/1(51).
[79] S.C. 12/10/35.
[80] E.R.R.O., DDHU/9/32, pp. 3, 4.
[81] See p. 238.
[82] *Yorks. Inq.* iii. 67.
[83] E.R.R.O., DDHU/9/32.
[84] Regy. of Deeds, CQ/1/1.
[85] E.R.R.O., DDGR/9/10; *Bridlington Charty.* 75.
[86] S.C. 12/10/35.
[87] E 178/2778.
[88] E.R.R.O., DDHU/9/32, pp. 4, 8, 9.
[89] *E.Y.C.* ii, pp. 471, 473.
[90] *Bridlington Charty.* 73.
[91] *E.Y.C.* ii, p. 474.
[92] J.I. 1/1179 m. 10; *Yorks. Assize R.* (Y.A.S. Rec. Ser. xliv), 87.
[93] Lucy M. Owston, *Hunmanby, E. Yorks., a Story of Ten Centuries*, 67.
[94] See p. 240.
[95] E.R.R.O., DDHU/9/32, pp. 4, 9.
[96] e.g. E 310/30/178 no. 13; E.R.R.O., DDHU/9/31.
[97] E 134/11 Chas. I Mich. /53.
[98] Perhaps 23 Apr., the Feast of St. Helen of Udine.
[99] E 134/12 Anne Trin./9.
[1] 12 Geo. II, c. 10 (Priv. Act).
[2] Regy. of Deeds, CQ/1/1.

century. It was fixed at 20 animals for each house or cottage in 1761, but altered to 5 for a house and 15 for each bovate of land in 1782. The number allowed for a bovate was reduced to 10 in 1791, and no Scottish or moor sheep, 'commonly called Jock sheep', were to be kept. In the following year the stint of sheep allowed between 29 September and 2 February was fixed at 6 for a house and 16 for a bovate.[3]

In Fordon a pasture called Hallcliff is mentioned in the 13th century,[4] and in 1597 the common pastures were said to be limited to 'some high and great hills', too steep and stony to be ploughed. The chief source of common pasture was the fallow openfield land; this had been surcharged by several inhabitants and orders were laid down for its use in 1597. Not more than five cows were to be pastured for each house and 6 bovates of land from 3 May to 11 November, though at harvest-time as many oxen might be kept as were needed for harvesting and for carting manure. Each cottager was to have only one cow on the pastures. Sheep were limited to 24 for each bovate and 10 for each cottage. The grounds were to be laid on 25 March each year to give grass time to grow on the thin soils. There were in addition 40 a. of poor land which, though they would not yield a load of hay to an acre, were kept for hay and for pasturing horses. This was apparently the horse pasture known as the Firth.[5]

Inclosed pasture, held in severalty, existed in Hunmanby by at least the late 13th century. Such closes, all apparently on the low-lying ground, contributed £1 to £2 to the value of the manor in 1302–6 and included North moor, Damside, and Holmes.[6] By 1600 there were closes totalling over 200 a., many of them held by tenants; they included North moor (30 a.), Oak (22 a.), and Rosemore closes, and Turf Dam and Damland Side.[7]

The pasture held in severalty and the commons were apparently insufficient to meet the inhabitants' needs in the 17th and 18th centuries, and parts of the open fields were laid to pasture. In 1672, by a bylaw made in the Osbaldestons' manor court, seven open-field areas — Ing Barf, Twillings, Rosedale, Harboras, the ings, the demesnes, and Lady Dale — were inclosed for use as summer pasture by the owners or occupiers of land lying within them. The following year it was agreed that the land should remain as pasture for 21 years and that tithes should be paid by composition. The by-law was confirmed in 1693, but Charles Stutville and others were alleged to have ploughed within the pasture, denying the court's power to authorise conversion to pasture. The dispute lasted until 1697, when the Osbaldestons' rights were upheld.[8] The manor court dealt with several cases of surcharging the Low Field pasture,[9] as this area was called; most of it lay on the boulder clay, between the village and the moor.[10] In 1697 regulations for the Low Field pasture were included in the pains. It was to be used from 3 May to 11 November, and stinted: certain bovates within it were to carry the right to 1¼ beast-gate, but the 4 bovates in Flemingdale Fall were to have only one gate each and the 16½ bovates in Lady Dale Fall only 12 gates in all. These two furlongs were said to be part of the pasture, although the former at least was on the wolds far removed from the other areas.[11] The same pains included regulations for a separate horse pasture, to be used in the summer of 1697. Ten furlongs and other pieces of land were involved, at least four of them, including Cansdale, lying on the wolds in the west corner of Hunmanby township.[12] The setting aside of pasture for horses was apparently not a new departure in 1697, for there had been numerous cases of surcharging the horse pasture in 1688.[13]

Regulations for the various pastures were also included in the pains drawn up in 1732; no one was to have more animals in the horse pasture than he had bovates in the fields, and common bulls were to be provided for Rosedale pasture.[14] Ground at Caddy Barf, on the wolds in the south-east of Hunmanby, 'lately' inclosed for a horse pasture in 1773 was ordered to be used, as appointed by the bylawmen, for horses until corn harvest, then for sheep, and afterwards to be unstocked during the winter; only those with land in it were to use it.[15]

In the case of Fowthorpe field conversion to pasture took place much earlier. An enquiry made in 1598–9 revealed that the Crown had 4½ bovates of pasture there formerly belonging to the Bigods, and 1½ formerly of the earl of Lennox; John Legard had 9½, Ralph Westrop 1½, and John and George Walker 4; 16½ of these 21 bovates of pasture had some meadow attached to them as well. The field was measured and found to contain 351 a. of pasture and 27 a. of meadow, with 6 a. of marsh in the Fen carr.[16] Tithe compositions were paid for gates in the field in the late 16th century.[17]

The laying down of sections of the open fields for pasture was accompanied by other attempts to improve the husbandry of the village, especially by introducing new crops. Robert Stutville, for example, had 20 a. under rape in 1695,[18] and the Osbaldestons were said in 1812 to have introduced sainfoin into the East Riding about 70 or 80 years earlier.[19] Clover was introduced in or soon after 1754, when 35 owners and occupiers agreed that certain parts of the open fields, then being cropped with barley, should be sown with clover and afterwards with wheat. Any of the 35 participants might, however, keep to the 'usual course of husbandry', provided that animals were not allowed to graze on the clover.[20]

The most ambitious improvement was a 'plan of management' introduced by Isaac Leatham, then Humphrey Osbaldeston's agent, in 1783. By it he claimed that each open field was used 'in as beneficial a manner as if it were inclosed'. A six-course rotation was followed: (1) turnips, (2) barley, (3) grass seeds, (4) grass seeds, (5) wheat, and (6)

---

[3] E.R.R.O., DDHU/10/81.
[4] *Bridlington Charty.* 6, 75. [5] E 178/2778.
[6] *Yorks. Inq.* ii. 67; iv. 34, 54, 126.
[7] E.R.R.O., DDHU/9/32, pp. 16 sqq.
[8] Ibid. DDGR/34/7; C 5/129/28; C 5/136/6, 58; C 5/177/63; C 5/361/11; C 5/622/33.
[9] E.R.R.O., DDHU/10/1 (82, 90, 91 etc.); /22.
[10] O.S. Map 6″ (1854).
[11] E.R.R.O., DDHU/10/80. Elsewhere, accts. of tithe compositions paid for gates show 18 bovates in the Demesnes with 22½ gates (i.e. 1¼ gate to each bovate) and 16 bovates in Lady Dale with 12 gates: ibid. /9/76.
[12] Ibid. /10/80. [13] Ibid. /1 (82).
[14] Ibid. /81, nos. 18, 63–7, 91, 104.
[15] Ibid. no. 112.
[16] E 178/2791.
[17] E.R.R.O., DDHU/9/26.
[18] B.I.H.R., C.P., H. 4722.
[19] H. E. Strickland, *Gen. View of Agric. E.R. Yorks.* 145.
[20] E.R.R.O., DDHU/10/80.

oats, peas, or beans. Leatham had wanted three consecutive years of seeds but the farmers had insisted on an additional corn crop (i.e. the sixth course). The turnips and grass were to be fed off with sheep according to each man's proportion of land sown.[21] It is not known for how long this plan was followed, but men were punished for having animals in the turnips in 1789 and 1793,[22] and a by-law was introduced in 1799 to prevent the grazing of animals in the turnip field or among the turnips.[23]

It was not long, however, before the remaining open fields and commons were inclosed. The inclosure was carried out in 1809[24] under an Act of 1800[25] and dealt with 5,005 a. in Hunmanby and 1,411 a. in Fordon; allotments made totalled about 4,950 a. and 1,400 a. respectively. Humphrey Osbaldeston received altogether 3,367 a., of which 673 a. lay in Fordon, together with 926 a. in lieu of tithes in Hunmanby and 177 a. for tithes in Fordon. The vicar received, for tithes, 270 a. in Hunmanby and 82 a. in Fordon. Other large allotments were of 461 a. in Fordon to John Farthing, 605 a. in Hunmanby to John Hall and William Drinkrow, and 113 a. in Hunmanby to John Clarkson, the elder. The remaining allotments, all in Hunmanby, were 6 of between 20 a. and 50 a., 6 of between 10 a. and 19 a., and 19 of under 10 a.

In the rest of the 19th and in the 20th centuries the number of farmers and smallholders in Hunmanby has usually been over thirty; in Fordon there were usually three, increasing to five in the 1920s and 1930s. In the 20th century there have also been one or two market-gardeners in Hunmanby.[26] The importance of dairy farming was stressed in 1914, when over 100 cows were kept in the parish.[27] Some of these animals no doubt belonged to the small-scale farmers who were members of the Cow Club[28] and to those who used the Cottage pasture. In 1836 this pasture comprised 40 a., let by the lords of the manor to sixteen people.[29] By 1854, when rules were made for stocking the pasture, the old field had been replaced by two others comprising 32 a.; six people were then each keeping a cow there.[30] A locally celebrated stud of hackneys had its home at the White Swan in the 1890s.[31]

There was little non-agricultural employment in the village before the 19th century, though two Hunmanby weavers were found in 1399 to be infringing the rights of weavers in the city of York,[32] and an occasional weaver, skinner, glover, and mariner is mentioned in the 16th, 17th, and 18th centuries.[33]

A mill in Hunmanby, presumably a water-mill, was first mentioned in 1125, when Walter de Gant gave the tithes of it to Bardney abbey;[34] in the 1140s Gilbert de Gant gave the mill to St. Peter's hospital, York, but it was later exchanged for other property in Hunmanby.[35] A windmill was recorded as part of the capital manor in 1298,[36] and by 1600 the manor included two windmills, a horse-mill, and a malt-mill.[37] In 1635 William Leppington, then the owner of the windmills, which were called Old mill and Gardiner mill, was attempting to enforce suit of mill upon Charles Stutville and other inhabitants.[38] Provisions for the proper conduct of the mills were included in the pains in 1732.[39] By the early 19th century there was a single windmill, standing west of the village near the Folkton road, but a second mill was built on the Bartindale road in or just before 1830.[40] Two millers were mentioned in 1858[41] but the newer mill had apparently gone out of use by 1872.[42] The other fell out of use shortly before 1909[43] and no trace of either mill remained in 1970.

With the opening of the railway in 1847 much corn was despatched from Hunmanby by train and a corn, seed, and flour depot was later established near the station.[44] Large amounts of butter were also sent to market from the village after the establishment of a creamery in the former brewery in Bridlington Street c. 1890.[45] By 1914 the chief product was milk, sent especially to Scarborough.[46] The creamery was last mentioned in 1921.[47]

Brick-making was carried on as early as 1713, when clay was taken for that purpose from pits in the outgangs.[48] In 1783 Brick Kiln close, to the north of the village, was mentioned.[49] There were brickyards on either side of Northgate by 1850[50] and they were run for much of the century by the Hutchinson family;[51] they apparently became disused in the early 20th century.[52] In the 1890s a brickyard was opened near the railway station and was worked by the Parkers until 1940, and another brickyard, adjoining the Parkers', closed in 1939.[53] F. W. Parker was already described as an engineer and brickmaker in 1897[54] and the engineering works continued after the demise of the brickyard. In 1970 there were two engineering, a plastics, and a precast concrete works on the site. Chalk was being burnt for lime at the Vicarage quarry, on the Reighton road, by 1850,[55] and there was later a quarry and lime-works on the Bartindale road, with five kilns in 1926.[56] The quarries have since ceased to be used.

Two roperies in Stonegate were in operation in

---

[21] Ibid.; I. Leatham, *Gen. View of Agric. E.R. Yorks.* (1794), 45–7.
[22] E.R.R.O., DDHU/10/2 (64).
[23] Ibid. /80.
[24] Regy. of Deeds, CQ/1/1.
[25] 39 & 40 Geo. III, c. 81.
[26] Directories.
[27] *Hull Times*, 2 May 1914.
[28] See p. 230.
[29] E.R.R.O., DDHU/17/16.
[30] Hun. Par. Counc. Rec., scrapbk. p. 83.
[31] Owston, *Hunmanby*, 58.
[32] *Cal. Inq. Misc.* vi, pp. 246–7.
[33] B.I.H.R., Prob. Reg. xxix, ff. 251, 703; xxxv, f. 10; xliii, f. 455; xlvi, f. 155; E.R.R.O., DDHU/9/134, 138, 142; /10/1 (29).
[34] B.M.Cott. MS. Vesp. E. xx, f. 55b.
[35] *E.Y.C.* ii, pp. 469, 472.
[36] *Yorks. Inq.* iii. 67.
[37] E.R.R.O., DDHU/9/32, pp. 22, 38.
[38] E 134/11 Chas. I Mich. /53.
[39] E.R.R.O., DDHU/10/81, nos. 4–7.
[40] Ibid. /9/285.
[41] White, *Dir. Hull & York* (1858), 445.
[42] *Kelly's Dir. N. & E.R. Yorks.* (1872), 509; O.S. Map 6" (1893).
[43] *Kelly's Dir. N. & E.R. Yorks.* (1905), 530; (1909), 541; O.S. Map 6" (1909).
[44] *Kelly's Dir. N. & E.R. Yorks.* (1872), 509.
[45] Bulmer, *Dir. E. Yorks.* (1892), 213.
[46] *Hull Times*, 2 May 1914.
[47] *Kelly's Dir. N. & E.R. Yorks.* (1921), 546.
[48] E 134/12 Anne Trin. /9.
[49] E.R.R.O., DDHU/9/230.
[50] O.S. Map 6" (1854).
[51] E.R.R.O., DDHU/9/168, 171; directories.
[52] O.S. Map 6" (1913); directories.
[53] Directories; ex inf. Miss Owston.
[54] *Kelly's Dir. N. & E.R. Yorks.* (1897), 486.
[55] O.S. Map 6" (1854).
[56] Hunmanby Par. Counc. Rec., scrapbk. p. 142.

1850, one of them at Low Hall,[57] and by 1872 there were three. There were still three in 1892, but they were then in Bridlington Street, on Cross Hill, and in Northgate. The last-mentioned is said to have been founded in 1877[58] and it was the longest-lived, continuing until the 1920s. A maltster at Hunmanby was mentioned in 1823, and a brewery and malting in Bridlington Street survived until about 1890.[59]

By the early 20th century, when half-a-dozen people were keeping apartments,[60] holiday-making was beginning to provide some employment in Hunmanby. Many holiday facilities have been introduced into the area since the Second World War. Butlin's holiday camp employs a number of Hunmanby people, and many cottages in the village are let as holiday accommodation.

MARKETS AND FAIRS. A market at Hunmanby existed by 1231, when Gilbert de Gant complained that it was prejudiced by another established at Filey, and in 1240–1 it was agreed that Gilbert should have half the profits at Filey in right of his Hunmanby market.[61] In the early 14th century the market was held on Wednesdays and was worth £6 13s. 4d.,[62] but in 1361 it was described as a poor market.[63] The former Northumberland share of the tolls and stallage at both Hunmanby and Filey was valued at only 13s. 4d. in 1539–40.[64] In 1618 William Leppington, then lord of the Roos manor, was granted a Tuesday market and fairs on 25 April and 18 October.[65] A fair on St. Luke's Day is mentioned in 1641,[66] and in 1790 there were fairs on 6 May and 2 October.[67] No market was recorded in 1792 and in 1856 it was said to have been long discontinued.[68] Fairs on 6 May and 29 October were, however, recorded in 1792. Cattle, sheep, and horses, as well as toys, pedlary, and other goods, were sold there, but by at least the early 20th century the fairs were pleasure fairs as well.[69] An October pleasure fair was still held, on Cross Hill, in 1970. A fortnightly cattle market is said to have been established in 1855[70] but it is not known how long it survived. Hirings on the first Tuesday after 23 November were still held into the 20th century.[71]

LOCAL GOVERNMENT. There are surviving court rolls for 1544,[72] 1564, and 1572,[73] when the capital manor in Hunmanby was held by the earl of Lennox, and for several years between 1609 and 1628,[74] when the same manor was in the hands of the Crown. They show that the lords enjoyed the assize of bread and ale. Other matters dealt with included the usual agricultural offences, and actions for debt and trespass. Constables were mentioned in 1572 and bylawmen in 1614. Courts had been held three-weekly in the early 14th century[75] but in 1539–40 and in the late 17th century they were said to be held twice a year.[76]

The Marmions were in 1253 granted the right to hold a court for their tenants by Gilbert de Gant.[77] Courts were still held after the Constables succeeded to the property.[78]

For the Hamerton manor a long series of court rolls exists from 1451, when the Hamertons acquired the manor, extending through the period of the Westrops' ownership (1596–1623) into that of the Osbaldestons; the last roll dates from 1639.[79] There are also some estreats of amercements, jury presentments, and rentals for the same period, and a charge to the jury of 1545.[80] The courts were much concerned with the usual agricultural and domestic offences, and sometimes also with details of tenancies, with the timber needed for repairs to tenants' houses,[81] and with the putting out of the poor's stock money.[82]

By 1665 the Osbaldestons held the former Lennox, Roos, and Hamerton manors and thereafter they held a combined manorial court for Hunmanby. Court rolls survive for 1666 and 1674–5,[83] and there are estreats, jury presentments, verdicts, and lists, call rolls, and rentals from the period 1675–1847.[84] There are pains drawn up in 1697 and a book of 105 pains laid in 1732, with amendments to 1811.[85] Agricultural and domestic matters bulk large in these papers, and the appointment of officers is also recorded. In the late 17th century there were 2 constables, 6 bylawmen, 2 surveyors of highways, 2 ale-tasters, 2 leather searchers, 2 market searchers, and a pinder.[86] A century later 2 constables, 6 bylawmen, 2 affeerors, and a pinder were being appointed. Bylawmen are last mentioned in 1801, just before the final inclosure of open fields and commons, but constables, affeerors, and a pinder were still being appointed in the 1840s.[87] From the 13th century onwards the lords of the capital manor enjoyed stranded whales and other rights on the foreshore.[88]

The work of the vestry is illustrated by surviving vestry minutes beginning in 1822 and by overseers' accounts of 1784–1836.[89] A churchwardens' account survives for 1662.[90] A select vestry, consisting of at least seven members, was formed in 1822. The officers appointed were 2 overseers of the poor, 4

[57] O.S. Map 6" (1854).
[58] Owston, Hunmanby, 58.
[59] Directories.
[60] Kelly's Dir. N. & E.R. Yorks. (1905), 530; (1909), 541.
[61] Bracton's Note Bk. ed. Maitland, p. 386; Cur. Reg. R. xiv. 224.
[62] Yorks. Inq. iii. 67; iv. 34, 54, 126.
[63] Cal. Inq. p.m. xi, p. 165.
[64] S.C. 6/Hen. VIII/4283.
[65] C 66/2150 no. 10.
[66] Farming Bk. of Hen. Best of Elmswell (Sur. Soc. xxxiii), 114.
[67] E.R.R.O., QSF Mich. 1790, E.9.
[68] 1st Rep. Royal Com. on Market Rights [C.5550], p. 219, H.C. (1888), liii; Sheahan and Whellan, Hist. York & E.R. ii. 479.
[69] 1st Rep. Royal Com. Mkt. Rights, p. 219; Sheahan and Whellan, op. cit. ii. 479; Hun. Par. Counc. Rec., scrapbk. p. 63; Owston, Hunmanby, 57, 72–3.
[70] Sheahan and Whellan, op. cit. ii. 479.

[71] Directories.
[72] S.C. 2/211/63–6.
[73] Y.A.J. x. 69–71, 81–2.
[74] S.C. 2/211/64–7.
[75] Yorks. Inq. iv. 34.
[76] C 5/177/63; S.C. 6/Hen. VIII/4283.
[77] J.I. 1/1179 m. 10.
[78] S.C. 6/Hen. VIII/4324.
[79] E.R.R.O., DDHU/10/1 (1–68), 2, 3.
[80] Ibid. /1 (70–4), 17, 47–59, 69, 70, 73.
[81] For such repairs see e.g. ibid. /1 (2, 3, 5, 11, 18, 40).
[82] See p. 245.
[83] E.R.R.O., DDHU/10/1 (69), 4, 5.
[84] Ibid. /1 (79–116), 6–16, 21–3, 28, 35, 39, 46, 60–4.
[85] Ibid. /80, 81.
[86] Ibid. /1 (82, 83, 88, 111–12).
[87] Ibid. /64.
[88] See p. 228.
[89] Hunmanby Par. Counc. Rec.
[90] B.I.H.R., C.P., H. 4838.

surveyors of highways, and 2 or more constables. From 1822 the assistant overseer was salaried. The vestry, or 'committee', generally met at the Buck, the White Swan, or the Black Horse until the 1890s, when the National schoolroom became the regular meeting-place. Little other business is recorded in the minutes, but in 1869 it was decided to let the herbage of the lanes.

The overseers levied a rate of 4d. in the pound in 1784, producing £35, and they held and loaned the town stock. A workhouse was established in 1785 and two fivepenny rates were levied that year. In the 1790s the rate increased and was as high as 1s. 2d. in 1798; it varied between 2d. and 8d. in the first decade of the 19th century, but rose to 1s. 2d. in the second and was usually 1s. 8d. in the 1820s and 1830s. The giving of out-relief and the payment of cottage rents were supplemented by relief in the workhouse,[91] kept in Low Hall, in Stonegate, which the overseers rented from Humphrey Osbaldeston. The workhouse was used by other townships as well, and at various times Bessingby, Buckton, Burton Fleming, Butterwick, Filey, Firby, Flamborough, Folkton, Fordon, Foxholes, Gransmoor, Muston, Osgodby (Yorks. N.R.), Reighton, Rudston, Skipsea, and Speeton made payments to the Hunmanby overseers. It was agreed in 1810 that the 'rent' of such townships should be £2 2s. a year and that they should make additional payments for their own paupers housed there. The overseers occasionally paid for the teaching of poor children in the house. The workhouse was closed in 1836 when Hunmanby joined the Bridlington union.[92]

CHURCH. Hunmanby church is first mentioned in 1086.[93] It was given by Walter de Gant to Bardney abbey (Lincs.) in 1115, together with its dependent chapels of Bartindale, Burton Fleming, Fordon, Fowthorpe, Muston, Reighton, and Wold Newton, and a carucate at Argam.[94] Walter's father Gilbert de Gant had refounded the abbey in 1086–7.[95] A vicarage was ordained at Hunmanby in 1269.[96] Burton Fleming, Muston, Reighton, and Wold Newton all later became separate parishes.[97] Fordon chapelry was transferred to Burton Fleming only in 1858[98] and it is treated in the present article. The hamlets of Bartindale and Fowthorpe were subsequently depopulated and the chapels have long ceased to exist.

The advowson belonged to Bardney abbey until the Dissolution.[99] Grants of it to Thomas, earl of Northumberland, in 1557 and to the archbishop of York in 1558[1] presumably lapsed on the accession of Elizabeth I, and the Crown still presented in 1588.[2] In 1592 the advowson was granted to Edmund Downing and Roger Rante,[3] and in the same year they conveyed it to Ralph Westrop.[4] The Crown presented in 1616, during the minority of Westrop's nephew Ralph, and Cuthbert Bradley presented for one turn in 1619. Ralph was succeeded by his brother Thomas Westrop, and he presented in 1621.[5] In 1623 Westrop conveyed the patronage to Richard Osbaldeston[6] and, after a presentation for one turn by Sir Thomas Widdrington, William Tindall, and Richard Elmhirst in 1644,[7] it subsequently descended with the capital manor in the Osbaldeston family. It passed to the Readett Bayleys in 1920[8] and was sold to Harrogate College in 1925.[9] It was acquired by the Martyrs' Memorial Trust in 1952.[10]

At ordination in 1269 the vicar was assigned a toft and a third of the tithes of Hunmanby, including Fordon, Bartindale, and Fowthorpe, excepting those from the Gant demesne; he was to pay Bardney abbey 6s. 8d. a year.[11] The vicarage was worth £13 6s. 8d. in 1291,[12] £12 in 1525–6,[13] and about £20 net in 1535.[14] By 1650 it was said to be worth £70.[15] In 1829–31 the average net income was £350 a year.[16]

Tithes represented almost the whole value of the vicarage in 1535. At inclosure in 1809 the vicar was allotted 270 a. for tithes in Hunmanby and 82 a. for those in Fordon.[17] The only glebe land mentioned in the 17th and 18th centuries was less than an acre in the open fields.[18] In 1856 Hunmanby was allotted 979 a. formerly belonging to Folkton rectory, subject to a payment of £50 a year to Muston vicarage. Hunmanby was to retain 27 a. in Fordon, but the other 55 a. there were transferred with the chapelry to Burton Fleming.[19] There were thus 1,276 a. of glebe belonging to Hunmanby. The land in Folkton and Fordon was sold in 1921, and most of that in Hunmanby in 1920 and 1929.[20]

The vicar had a toft in 1269 and he received the profits of a house in 1535,[21] but there is no definite evidence of a Vicarage until 1596. Then and in 1623 it was said to be in great decay.[22] It stood next to the churchyard and is recorded with its dovecot from 1685 onwards;[23] it had six hearths in 1674.[24] In 1764 it was described as built of brick and tile and as containing 2 rooms, 2 chambers, and 4 closets, with a back kitchen and outbuildings of stone (presumably chalk) and thatch.[25] This house, evidently a mid-18th-century building, still stood in 1970, when it

---

[91] A house in Northgate in 1662 had adjoining it a 'little house...formerly called the workhouse': E.R.R.O., DDHU/9/133. This may refer to a parish poorhouse.
[92] 3rd Rep. Poor Law Com. 167.
[93] V.C.H. Yorks. ii. 271.
[94] B.M. Cott. MS. Vesp. E. xx, f. 55b; Dugdale, Mon. i. 628–9. Chapels at 'Geldston' and 'Straxton' were also mentioned in 1115, but not in Walter's confirmation of the gift in 1125: Mon. i. 630.
[95] Dugdale, Mon. i. 628–9; V.C.H. Lincs. ii. 97.
[96] Reg. Giffard (Sur. Soc. cix), 55.
[97] See pp. 123, 281, 301, 308.
[98] York Dioc. Regy., Orders in Council 157.
[99] Fasti Parochiales, iii. 47.
[1] Cal. Pat. 1557–8, 188, 420.
[2] Fasti Parochiales, iii. 48–9; Cal. Pat. 1553–4, 150; 1558–60, 256; 1566–9, 328; 1569–72, 74.
[3] C 66/1390 m. 22.
[4] E.R.R.O., DDHU/9/110.
[5] Inst. Bks.; Fasti Parochiales, iii. 49; see above, p. 234.
[6] E.R.R.O., DDHU/9/50.
[7] Inst. Bks.
[8] Registry of Deeds, Beverley, 209/184/157.
[9] Ibid. 318/410/342.
[10] York Dioc. Cal.
[11] Reg. Giffard, 55–6.
[12] Tax. Eccl. 304; it is given as £16 in ibid. 326.
[13] Y.A.J. xxiv. 65.
[14] Valor Eccl. v. 125.
[15] T.E.R.A.S. ii. 58.
[16] Rep. Com. Eccl. Revenues, 944–5.
[17] Regy. of Deeds, CQ/1/1.
[18] B.I.H.R., TER. J. Hunmanby 1685 etc.
[19] Lond. Gaz. 8 Aug. 1856, pp. 2739–42.
[20] Regy. of Deeds, 205/436/380; 230/365/307; 236/224/182; /225/183; 238/123/103.
[21] Reg. Giffard, 55–6; Valor Eccl. v. 125.
[22] B.I.H.R., Churches index.
[23] Ibid. TER. J. Hunmanby 1685 etc.
[24] E 179/205/521.
[25] B.I.H.R., TER. J. Hunmanby 1764.

was known as Wrangham House. It is five bays long and two storeys high with attics; a moulded string-course runs between the storeys and the main façade has a modillion eaves cornice. The central doorcase has fluted pilasters and a dentilled pediment enclosing a semicircular fanlight. The house was extended in 1803 by Francis Wrangham by the addition of a rear wing to house his library.[26] There is an early-19th-century coachhouse. In 1957 a house in Northgate was acquired for a Vicarage, and the old building was subsequently used as business premises.[27]

A house was given to Bardney abbey to support a lamp in the church[28] and the image of Our Lady of Pity is mentioned in 1515.[29] The lamp and image may have been maintained by St. Mary's guild, which is mentioned in 1483.[30] In 1538 the alderman and two 'greves' of the guild let a house belonging to them, and there are subsequent references to a house called the guildhall and to land formerly belonging to the guild.[31]

Hunmanby's dependent chapels at Bartindale and Fowthorpe were mentioned in 1360,[32] but there is no subsequent reference to them. The name 'Chapel Hill' is applied to land near the site of Fowthorpe village.[33] It is possible that the chapel at Fordon ceased to be used in the 16th century, perhaps being suppressed as if it were a chantry chapel.[34] A house and 10 a. of land were granted to Bardney in respect of the chapel before 1331.[35] In 1591 a Crown grant was made of the site of the 'late' chapel, together with land belonging to it;[36] then and in the early 17th century[37] the property was said to have belonged to Fordon chapel and formerly to Bridlington priory.

Several vicars of Hunmanby held other livings but few seem to have been non-resident; assistant curates were sometimes employed. Both the vicar and a chaplain were named in 1299,[38] and in 1525–6 a chaplain had a stipend of £4 a year.[39] In 1582 the vicar was non-resident.[40] The vicar in 1743, Richard Osbaldeston, was also rector of Folkton and of Hinderwell (Yorks. N.R.), as well as dean of York, where he lived. His assistant curate was resident, but he also had charge of Filey, Folkton, Muston, and Speeton.[41] The vicar in 1835, Francis Wrangham, was rector of Dodleston (Ches.), a prebendary in York and Chester, and archdeacon of the East Riding.[42] Vicars appear to have resided in the later 18th and 19th centuries and there was an assistant curate in 1884.[43]

Richard Chapman (vicar 1621–34) had Puritan sympathies and in 1632 was presented for not wearing a surplice and not reading services.[44] Thomas Rose was probably a nonjuror; he was presented in 1692 for refusing to read special forms of prayers and thanksgiving.[45] The most noteworthy incumbent in modern times was Francis Wrangham (vicar 1795–1840). He took an active part in village affairs, helping to found a free dispensary for the poor; setting up a savings bank, the 'Cow Club', and a free library, housed in the vestry; and interesting himself in the Lancasterian school. He was a writer and bibliophile, and collected an extensive library.[46]

There was one service each Sunday at Hunmanby in 1743 but at Fordon services were held only on Good Friday and St. Stephen's Day. Communion was celebrated monthly at Hunmanby, with about forty recipients, and twice a year at Fordon, with about twenty.[47] By 1851 there were two Sunday services at Hunmanby[48] and by 1884 a service on Wednesdays as well; in the latter year communion was celebrated twice a month and was received by 25 people. By 1936 communion was once-monthly.[49] At Fordon there was a monthly service in 1851.[50] The chapel was transferred to Burton Fleming parish in 1858, and in 1865 a service was held every fortnight; communion was then received three times a year by six or seven people.[51] In 1970 two services were held each Sunday at Hunmanby, and only one a year at Fordon.

The church of *ALL SAINTS*, Hunmanby, consists of nave, chancel, north aisle, west tower, and south porch, and is largely of stone, with some cobbles and chalk.[52] Both nave and chancel belonged to a large early Norman church of the late 11th or early 12th century. The nave was then without aisles and the long chancel retains Norman buttresses at its east end and some visible Norman masonry. The responds of the semicircular chancel arch have single shafts with scalloped capitals. The south doorway, with a Maltese cross in the tympanum, and the west door, now an archway leading to the tower, are of the same period. The plain round Norman font is no longer in use. The unbuttressed tower was probably added later in the 12th century; its lower stages contain five 'slit' windows and two small round openings, and in the second stage there is a two-light window with a central shaft.

The north aisle was added in the 13th or 14th century. The arcade of five bays has pointed arches supported on two circular and two octagonal piers. The two-light windows in the aisle are of 14th-century design but are not ancient. In the south wall of the nave are four large pointed windows with Decorated tracery which, in their present form, date from 1844. The most westerly is set in its original opening and all may be copies of former 14th-century work. The belfry stage of the tower, with its two-light windows, embattled parapet, and angle pinnacles, is an addition of the 15th century, and the south porch may be of the same period.

The chancel was said to be in great decay in the

[26] Tablet on house; Lucy M. Owston, *Hunmanby, E. Yorks., a Story of Ten Cents.* 3–4.
[27] Regy. of Deeds, 1075/31/29; 1108/130/121.
[28] B.M. Cott. MS. Vesp. E. xx, f. 288b.
[29] *Test. Ebor.* v. 62–3.
[30] B.I.H.R., Prob. Reg. v, f. 78.
[31] B.M. Lansd. Chart. 458; Add. MS. 26718, f. 66; C 142/389/120; *Cal. Pat.* 1569–72, 38.
[32] *Cal. Pat.* 1360–4, 74.
[33] O.S. Map 6" (1854 etc.).
[34] E.R.R.O., DDCC/139/65.
[35] *Cal. Chart. R.* 1324–41, 256.
[36] C 66/1377 m. 1.
[37] C 142/389/120.
[38] *Reg. Romeyn*, ii. 215, 277.
[39] *Y.A.J.* xxiv. 78.
[40] B.I.H.R., Churches index.
[41] *Herring's Visit.* ii. 90–1.
[42] *Rep. Com. Eccl. Revenues*, 944–5.
[43] B.I.H.R., Bp. V. 1884/Ret.
[44] R. A. Marchant, *Puritans and Ch. Courts in Dioc. Ebor.* 238.
[45] B.I.H.R., C.P., H. 4591.
[46] Owston, *Hunmanby*, 63–5; his works are listed in M. Sadler, *Archdeacon Francis Wrangham*, 61 sqq.
[47] *Herring's Visit.* i. 219; ii. 90–1.
[48] H.O. 129/24/524.
[49] B.I.H.R., Bp. V. 1884/Ret.; Bp. V. 1936/Ret. 288.
[50] H.O. 129/24/524.
[51] B.I.H.R., V. 1865/Ret. 189.
[52] Morris, *E. Yorks.* 223–4.

late 16th and early 17th centuries,[53] and its north wall was rebuilt in the 18th century.[54] The porch was authorized to be lowered in 1811 and it was perhaps then that it was divided into two.[55] The east window and the windows in the south walls of the chancel and nave are part of a thorough restoration of 1844–5; the interior was restored at the same time.[56] The stone archway above the churchyard gate was erected in memory of Admiral Mitford in 1870.[57] A further restoration of the church, during which the nave and tower walls were refaced, took place in 1903–4.[58]

Fragments of crosses and an Anglian cross-head[59] are built into the exterior of the aisle wall. In the church are a broken stone coffin and a slab bearing a cross fleury, a chalice, and a paten.[60] There is a 14th-century tomb niche below one of the windows in the south nave wall. Seventeenth-century monuments are a brass plate to Christopher Littell, vicar (d. 1682), and a stone to John Osbaldeston (d. 1694). The most noteworthy later monuments are one to members of the Staveley family (d. 1742–71), with relief carving and portrait medallions, and another to several of the Osbaldestons (d. 1707–70). The latter is by the Fishers of York and has a mourning female figure with an urn. The Osbaldeston vault lies under the chancel.[61]

The altar rails, which have an unusual bowed projection at the centre, are of the 17th century. A loft at the west end was erected under a faculty of 1784.[62] The present gallery, which contains the organ, appears to belong to the restoration of 1844–5. Other fittings of that date include pews, choir stalls, pulpit, and desk, giving the whole interior a period flavour which is enhanced by the wealth of furnishings on the walls. Besides commandment and psalm boards, they include six hatchments to members of the Osbaldeston and Mitford families, a Royal Arms dated 1745, and a charity board of 1825. High on the walls all round the nave are seventeen shields of various manorial lords; they were originally painted on the walls but they have been restored from time to time and are now painted on sheets of iron.[63] Painting done on the chancel arch in 1844 has since been removed; the font also dates from 1844.[64] The church contains its original chained Bible of 1541.

There were three bells in the church in 1552.[65] Four are recorded in 1764 and later,[66] but one of these may have been the clock bell. One of the three surviving bells was made in 1619 and the others in 1663.[67] A silver chalice was said in 1552 to have been sold to repair the church.[68] The plate comprises a silver cup, made in York in 1639; a silver paten, with London hallmark for 1679; a silver flagon, made in London in 1753 and bearing the arms of Richard Osbaldeston (bishop of Carlisle 1747–62); a silver box, made in London in 1898; and a pewter flagon, of 1668.[69] The registers of baptisms and burials begin in 1584 and of marriages in 1583; they are complete except for baptisms in 1726, burials in 1645–50 and 1654–1726, and marriages in 1585–6, 1644–50, and 1652.[70]

Of the original chapelries in Hunmanby parish Reighton already had right of burial by 1685; the others buried at Hunmanby and all, including Reighton, paid fees to the vicar there. The chapelries also contributed towards the repair of the mother church.[71] An additional burial ground, at the south end of the village, was consecrated in 1892,[72] and the churchyard was enlarged in 1960.[73]

The chapel of ST. JAMES, Fordon, is a tiny building of stone patched with brick, consisting simply of a nave and a sanctuary.[74] Norman masonry is visible in the south wall. Part of the south door, which has a segmental tympanum, and two shafts with scalloped capitals, which may have belonged to the original chancel arch, are of Norman date. The font has inverted stiff-leaf foliage of the 13th century on its base. The partly legible inscription '168–' on a stone over the doorway suggests a restoration date and may indicate the period at which the 'churchwarden Gothic' windows were inserted in the south and west walls. There was a thorough restoration in 1876, when the present chancel arch was built.[75] The Geometrical east window and the very small brick vestry on the north are probably of the same date. The brick bellcot contains one bell. The plate comprises a silver cup bought in 1661 and electroplated paten, flagon, and plate dated 1876.[76]

NONCONFORMITY. A few recusants were reported in Hunmanby in the later 16th century and sometimes about ten in the 17th.[77] In 1676 there were also three protestant dissenters[78] and in 1743 one family of Anabaptists.[79] Houses or barns were licensed for worship in 1780, 1787, 1788, and 1799.[80]

A Wesleyan Methodist chapel in Stonegate was licensed in 1816,[81] though it is said to have been built before 1800.[82] It was replaced by a chapel built in Bridlington Street in 1871 and was subsequently used as the Temperance Hall;[83] the large plain brick building still stood in 1970. The new chapel was of red brick with stone dressings and in the Gothic style. It remained in use until 1958; the small tower was subsequently removed but the chapel still stood, housing a shop and a branch County library, in 1970. Cross Hill Methodist Church, overlooking the

---

[53] B.I.H.R., Churches index.
[54] Conjectural plan in church.
[55] Ibid.; B.I.H.R., Churches index.
[56] E.R.R.O., PR. 1147, p. 26; tablet in church.
[57] Inscription on arch.
[58] *Kelly's Dir. N. & E.R. Yorks.* (1905), 529.
[59] *Y.A.J.* xxi. 259–60.
[60] Ibid. xlii. 334, fig.
[61] A plan of it is in E.R.R.O., PR. 1147, pp. 23–5.
[62] Lawton, *Rer. Eccles. Dioc. Ebor.* 302–3.
[63] They are described in *All Saints' Ch.* (2nd edn. 1963) (duplicated booklet); *Y.A.J.* xxv. 86.
[64] E.R.R.O., PR. 1147, p. 26.
[65] *Inventories of Ch. Goods*, 21.
[66] B.I.H.R., TER. J. Hunmanby 1764 etc.
[67] Boulter, 'Ch. Bells', 217.
[68] *Invent. Ch. Goods*, 21.
[69] *Yorks. Ch. Plate*, i. 275–6.
[70] E.R.R.O.
[71] B.I.H.R., TER. J. Hunmanby 1685 etc.
[72] Ibid. CD. 515.
[73] York Dioc. Regy., Sentence of consecration.
[74] Morris, *E. Yorks.* 168.
[75] B.I.H.R., V. 1877/Ret.; date on chancel arch.
[76] *Yorks. Ch. Plate*, i. 250.
[77] H. Aveling, *Post Reformation Catholicism in E. Yorks. 1558–1790* (E. Yorks. Loc. Hist. Ser. xi), 58.
[78] Bodl. MS. Tanner 150, ff. 27 sqq.
[79] *Herring's Visit.* ii. 90.
[80] B.I.H.R., DMH. 1780/20; 1787/16; 1788/2; 1799/42; G.R.O. Worship Returns, Vol. v, nos. 578, 697, 700, 1502.
[81] B.I.H.R., DMH. Reg. 1, p. 10; G.R.O. Worship Rets., Vol. v, no. 3030; O.S. Map 6" (1854).
[82] H.O. 129/24/524.
[83] Bulmer, *Dir. E. Yorks.* (1892), 213.

market-place and adjoining the grounds of Hunmanby Hall School, was registered for worship in 1958.[84] It is a huge brick building, designed by B. W. Blanchard, intended for both public and school use.[85]

The Particular Baptists built a chapel in 1816 in Hungate Lane.[86] A lending library was attached to their Sunday school by 1835.[87] The chapel seems to have gone out of use in the 1870s[88] and was subsequently used as a Wesleyan Sunday school.[89] The brick building, with stone dressings, still stood in 1970. The chapel had its own burial ground.[90]

A Primitive Methodist chapel was built in Hungate Lane in 1841.[91] There were 36 members in 1889.[92] The chapel was last used in 1964[93] and has since been demolished. The Plymouth Brethren were said in 1894 to meet in a hall in Hunmanby.[94]

There has never been a nonconformist chapel in Fordon, and in 1865 three Wesleyans living in the hamlet worshipped at Wold Newton.[95]

EDUCATION. Masters of petty schools in Hunmanby are recorded in 1563, 1636–7, 1698–9, and in the early 18th century. In 1636–7 the school was held in the church.[96] A school run on Lancasterian principles was established in 1810 by Humphrey Osbaldeston,[97] but by 1816 the schoolmaster was receiving advice from the National Society.[98] It was still supported by Osbaldeston in 1819, when there were 71 pupils; four other schools then had 133 pupils.[99] In 1835 the National school, supported by Osbaldeston and by school pence, was attended by 44 boys and 44 girls, and a lending library was attached to it. By this time there were five other schools, one of them established in 1830, with altogether 45 boys and 67 girls, taught at their parents' expense.[1] In 1854 the National school received £55 in voluntary contributions and £10 in school pence, paid by 36 children;[2] the contributions included £40 a year from Admiral Mitford.[3] By 1856–7 the school also received an annual parliamentary grant.[4] In 1871 130 children were in attendance.[5] The school was situated on the north side of the churchyard, behind Stonegate.[6] It was replaced in 1905 and was used as a church hall in 1970.

An infants' school was opened in 1875 in a building on the corner of Stonegate and Hungate Lane which had previously been used as the Wesleyan Sunday school; it began with 37 pupils,[7] and in 1877 there were about 70.[8] After 1907 the building was used as a village institute and reading room[9] but it no longer stood in 1970.

A large new school was built in Stonegate in 1905.[10] The attendance was about 210–230 between 1908 and 1914, but it fell to about 170–190 between the world wars.[11] The average number of children on the roll in 1970 was 129.[12]

A night school was held in Hunmanby in the 1860s and was said to be well attended.[13]

Fordon children have generally attended school at Wold Newton.[14]

CHARITIES FOR THE POOR. Henry Cowton, by will dated 1696, left two-fifths of his residuary estate to the poor of Hunmanby.[15] Of the proceeds in 1823 £5 5s. was used for a free dispensary in the parish, £6 6s. was spent on coal for the alms-houses (see below), and £40 was distributed in cash to 60–70 people, with preference to members of the Church of England.[16] The income was £40 in 1971 and 26 people were given money.[17] Cowton also gave a rent-charge of £3, which was used for the alms-women in 1823.[18]

The alms-houses, later known as the Widows' Hospital, were said in 1743 to have been founded by the ancestors of William Osbaldeston.[19] In 1810 there were six rooms, on the north side of the churchyard, but two were subsequently removed and the school-house built on the site.[20] In 1823 the building consisted of three tenements, seldom occupied by more than four widows, and the Osbaldestons maintained it. Each widow at that time received a peck of barley each month from Humphrey Osbaldeston, £3 a year from him as the owner of a field charged by Henry Cowton (see above), and £4 a year as a dole which was supposed to come from the same estate as the £3.[21] In 1932 there were only two tenements; they were sold in 1958 and only the shell of one of them remained in 1970. In 1960 there was a stock of £120 deriving from the sale of the alms-houses and the field, and in 1964 the income was £3; since the sale of the alms-houses the money has been given to needy people in the village.[22]

Robert Mitford, by will proved in 1870, bequeathed sufficient money to provide an annual

---

[84] G.R.O. Worship Reg. no. 66839.
[85] Inscription in church; ex inf. Miss Owston.
[86] B.I.H.R., DMH. Reg. 1, pp. 7–8; G.R.O. Worship Rets., Vol. v, no. 3020; H.O. 129/24/524.
[87] Educ. Enquiry Abstract, 1835, 1088.
[88] B.I.H.R., V. 1868/Ret. 244; V. 1877/Ret.; *Kelly's Dir. N. & E.R. Yorks.* (1872), 508; (1879), 609.
[89] Bulmer, *Dir. E. Yorks.* (1892), 213; O.S. Map 6" (1913).
[90] Gravestones were lying in an adjoining garden in 1970: ex inf. Miss Owston.
[91] Sheahan and Whellan, *Hist. York & E.R.* ii. 480.
[92] H. Woodcock, *Sketches of Prim. Meth. on Yorks. Wolds*, 154.
[93] Ex inf. Miss Owston. There is a photograph of the chapel in Hun. Par. Counc. Rec., scrapbk. p. 108.
[94] B.I.H.R., Bp. V. 1894/Ret.
[95] Ibid. V. 1865/Ret. 189.
[96] Ibid. Schools index.
[97] Baines, *Hist. Yorks.* (1823), ii. 357.
[98] J. Lawson, *Primary Educ. in E. Yorks. 1560–1902* (E. Yorks. Loc. Hist. Ser. x), 15.
[99] *Rets. on Educ. of Poor, 1819*, 1084.
[1] *Educ. Enquiry Abstract, 1835*, 1088.
[2] Ed. 7/135.
[3] Sheahan and Whellan, *Hist. York & E.R.* ii. 480.
[4] *Mins. of Educ. Cttee. of Counc. 1856–7* [2237], H.C., p. 187 (1857 Sess. 2), xxxiii.
[5] *Rets. rel. Elem. Educ. 1871*, 476.
[6] O.S. Map 6" (1854).
[7] Bulmer, *Dir. E. Yorks.* (1892), 213; *Hunmanby, 1874–1965*, 8.
[8] B.I.H.R., V. 1877/Ret.
[9] See p. 230.
[10] Date on building.
[11] Bd. of Educ. List 21 (H.M.S.O.).
[12] Ex inf. Chief Educ. Officer, County Hall, Beverley, 1970.
[13] B.I.H.R., V. 1865/Ret. 275; V. 1868/Ret. 244.
[14] Ibid. V. 1865/Ret. 189; *Rets. rel. Elem. Educ. 1871*, 474; see below, p. 302.
[15] For the rest of his charity see p. 81.
[16] *10th Rep. Char. Com.*, H.C. 103, p. 653 (1824), xiii.
[17] Ex inf. the vicar, 1972.
[18] *10th Rep. Char. Com.* 653.
[19] *Herring's Visit.* ii. 90.
[20] Lucy M. Owston, *Hunmanby, E. Yorks., a Story of Ten Centuries*, 68.
[21] *10th Rep. Char. Com.* 654.
[22] Char. Com. files.

income of £20, of which £15 was to be used to buy coal and the rest was to go to the Hunmanby clothing club. In 1939 the charity had stock worth £667 and 39 people were given 10s. each.[23] The income in 1971 was £21 and 11 people were given coal.[24]

The poor's stock, which is mentioned as early as 1596, rose from £6 in 1601 to £12 in 1625 and £14 in 1632. Its administration was accounted to the court of the Hamerton manor. The money was put out at interest and the poor of the manor received 3s. 2d. in 1625 and 2s. 11d. in 1632.[25] No more is known of it.

LITTLE KELK

THOUGH it was apparently regarded as a chapelry in the parish of Foston on the Wolds in the 13th century,[1] Little Kelk was long styled an extra-parochial district. For ecclesiastical purposes it was united with Lowthorpe in 1929,[2] and in 1935 Little and Great Kelk were combined to form the civil parish of Kelk.[3] There is now neither chapel nor village, and the area of the compact township is only 727 a.[4]

Little Kelk lies 4 miles east-north-east of Great Driffield on the Plain of Holderness. It adjoins Great Kelk to the south, and on the north the villages of Lowthorpe and Harpham are only ½ mile distant. Most of the township lies at between 25 ft. and 50 ft. above sea-level and is covered with boulder clay and alluvium, but at a few points, notably Kelk hill, the ground exceeds 50 ft. in height and is composed of sand and gravel. Much of the township boundary is formed by streams and dikes, including Kelk beck on the west. The ground known as Arden hills, however, lies beyond the beck as far as a dike which may mark a change in the course of the main stream, or the site of a watermill. There are extensive plantations in the northwest of the township, adjoining Harpham, and a large sand and gravel quarry on Kelk hill.

Any village of Little Kelk which may have existed in the Middle Ages probably stood near the centre of the township, around the junction of roads leading to Lowthorpe, Burton Agnes, and Great Kelk. A causeway crossing the Great Kelk road was in 1850 described as the track of a paved road, and there are other earthworks to the west, in Ash garths.[5] These features, forming no coherent pattern, may mark the site of the grange which Bridlington priory established here, rather than the village site. Nunnery hill, which also lies in Ash garths, appears to be a tumulus.[6]

Half-a-dozen scattered houses now comprise Little Kelk. One, together with the Methodist chapel, is close to the most northerly houses of Great Kelk village. The chief farms are Whitehall and Little Kelk Farms, the latter a large later-19th-century house of yellow brick. The Hull–Scarborough railway line, opened in 1846, crosses the township, and Lowthorpe station is in Little Kelk.

Little Kelk is not separately mentioned in either tax records or visitation returns, and there is no indication of its population until the 19th century. In 1801 there were 21 inhabitants and by 1821 51. Marked fluctuations occurred later in the century, the number increasing from 42 in 1871 to 91 in 1881, and then falling to 60 by 1901.[7] There was little change up to 1931.[8]

MANOR AND OTHER ESTATES. In 1086 the whole of Little Kelk lay in a single estate of 2 carucates, belonging to the king. It had been held in 1066 by Uctred.[9] The land later became part of the fee of the lords of Holderness.[10] In the late 12th century it was held by Anselm de Stutville, who died by 1199 leaving five sisters as coheirs.[11] They apparently transferred their interest in Little Kelk to the Friboys family. Sir John de Friboys held it about 1235–49, and his estates passed to his daughters Joan, wife of John of Hollym, and Philippa, wife of Robert son of Hugh.[12] About 1271 Joan gave up her rights as mesne lord to Bridlington priory.[13] The share of Philippa and Robert son of Hugh (d. c. 1265) passed, apparently through their daughter Elizabeth by marriage, to William de Chestrunt, who was holding Little Kelk in 1284–5.[14] In 1316 it was returned as belonging to Hugh de Mora.[15] Nothing more is known of this mesne lordship and in 1322 Bridlington priory was said to hold the estate directly of the Crown.[16]

An area of land, marsh, and wood in Little Kelk was given by Anselm de Stutville to Robert Talun, and in the early 13th century Talun acquired another 14 a. from Alice of Swanthorpe.[17] Some of this land was subsequently given by Talun to Bridlington priory, and some was given, probably by Talun's grandson, another Robert, to Stephen of Kilham; Stephen's son Alan later gave it to the priory.[18] Robert Talun the grandson also gave a bovate of land to John of Cottam, who sold it to Walter son of Ranulf son of Mayolf, by whom it was given to the priory.[19] By 1240 the remainder of the estate had passed to Joan Talun, wife of Hugh de Capella,[20] and in 1252 the prior of Bridlington gave most of his property there to Hugh.[21] Joan later

---

[23] Ibid. [24] Ex inf. the vicar, 1972.
[25] E.R.R.O., DDHU/10/1 (41, 43, 46–7, 52, 54), 2 (74).
[1] See p. 247.
[2] York Dioc. Regy., Orders in Council 1/597.
[3] *Census*, 1931.
[4] O.S. Map 6" (1854). [5] Ibid.
[6] *V.C.H. Yorks.* ii. 70.
[7] Ibid. iii. 489.
[8] *Census*.
[9] *V.C.H. Yorks.* ii. 204, 323.
[10] B.M. Add. MSS. 26718, ff. 1, 86; 26731, f. 86d.; *Cal. Inq. p.m.* iv, p. 353; *Cal. Pat.* 1281–92, 174; *Cal. Close*, 1318–23, 618; G. Poulson, *Holderness*, i. 71; *Kirkby's Inq.* 377.
[11] *E.Y.C.* ix, p. 29; *Abbrev. Plac.* (Rec. Com.), 76.
[12] B.M. Cott. MS. Vit. C vi, f. 11; *Chron. de Melsa* (Rolls Ser.), ii. 28; *Bridlington Charty.* 169; *Kirkby's Inq.* 377.
[13] *Bridlington Charty.* 169–70.
[14] B.M. Cott. MS. Vit. C vi, f. 11; *Feud. Aids*, vi. 41; *Cal. Inq. p.m.* iv, p. 353.
[15] *Feud. Aids*, vi. 162.
[16] *Cal. Close*, 1318–23, 618; *Cal. Inq. Misc.* ii, p. 175.
[17] *Bridlington Charty.* 162, 164.
[18] Ibid. 164–7. [19] Ibid. 170–2.
[20] K.B. 26/141 m. 13d.; *Bridlington Charty.* 168; *Yorks. Fines*, 1232–46, 75.
[21] *Bridlington Charty.* 167–8.

married William de Boyville, and in 1271 they gave the whole manor of *LITTLE KELK* to the priory.[22]

Bridlington priory retained the manor until the Dissolution, when it was worth £20.[23] In the late 15th and early 16th centuries the priory let it to the lords of Burton Agnes.[24] In 1541 Little Kelk was sold by the Crown to Sir Anthony Knyvett;[25] it passed in 1544 to John Allen and later the same year he sold it to Sibyl Martin.[26] In 1549, however, Sibyl conveyed it to Sir George Griffith,[27] and it descended with Burton Agnes.[28]

Part of the estate was sold in the 17th century. Both Margaret Salvin and Henry Corbett, by wills proved in 1654 and 1671 respectively, referred to land there which they had bought from Sir Henry Griffith.[29] It was apparently from the lands disposed of by the Griffiths that the St. Quintin family built up its estate in Little Kelk. A close of 133 a. called Kelk leys belonged to Robert Crompton in 1685, and this passed to the St. Quintins in the same way as the Crompton lands in Ruston Parva.[30] Sir William St. Quintin bought the 34-acre Arden close in 1762;[31] at least 80 a., including closes called High Lingham and Ash close, in 1769;[32] and the 48-acre Fatbeasts closes, which had been Henry Corbett's in 1671, in 1772.[33] By 1779 the St. Quintins had at least 378 a. in Little Kelk, in 1796 451 a.,[34] and they held manorial courts for Little Kelk in the 19th century.[35] The estate descended in the family like Harpham,[36] and in 1959 Lady Legard had 360 a. of land, besides plantations, in Little Kelk.[37]

The remaining Griffith lands, not sold in the 17th century, descended like Burton Agnes to the Boyntons, and they still had the manor of Little Kelk in the earlier 18th century.[38] The Boynton property included the 63-acre Thorn close.[39] It may have passed to the Hebdens, for in the 1730s they had land there called Lady closes or Thorn closes, which comprised a farm known as Little Kelk or Kelk Gembling.[40] James Hebden sold it in 1744 to Anne Cottrell (d. 1761). Still referred to as the manor of Little Kelk, the farm passed to Anne's daughter Elizabeth, and then to Elizabeth's son Samuel Powell.[41] In 1873 the Revd. Richmond Powell sold the farm, then consisting of 183 a., to Vickerman Coultas (d. 1887).[42] Its descent has not been traced further.

The tithes belonged to the rector of Foston on the Wolds and were leased in the 13th century by Bridlington priory.[43] Bridlington still leased them in 1535, by which time Foston rectory belonged to the Carthusian priory, Hull. They were then worth £8 13s. 4d.[44] In 1556–8 the tithes were let by the Crown to George Griffith for £8 13s. 4d. a year,[45] and in 1583–4 to Henry Griffith.[46] In 1585 they were granted to Sir Christopher Hatton.[47] In 1625, however, they were said to be worth £1 to the Griffiths.[48] The tithes subsequently belonged to the lords of the manor and other landowners, including John Pearson in 1665.[49] A rent-charge of £36 for the tithes of 180 a. belonging to Henry Powell was merged in 1847,[50] and in 1896 it was said that the tithes of 470 a. had been merged and that others worth £48 9s. remained.[51]

ECONOMIC HISTORY. It seems that as early as the 13th century some of the land here was held in severalty. Much of the low-lying ground was used as meadow, and there are references to Godefrayholme, Stevenholme, and Alaynholme. Robert Talun's grant of Godefrayholme and other land to Stephen of Kilham was made on condition that Stephen should make two breaches in the ditch with which he had surrounded the land, so that Robert might have pasture there until the month of March. Lands called Brundon and Arden were also part of the property granted to Bridlington priory.[52] Robert Talun's grant to the priory included a road through his ploughland (*cultura*), as well as 'Brachenhil', the near-by marsh, arable land in the marsh, and common of pasture in the marsh and the common field.[53]

In the early 14th century sales of corn earned nearly half the cash receipts of the priory's grange, and produced from twice to four times as much as livestock. The corn, grown on 83 a. of land in 1324, comprised barley, dredge, peas, and oats. In 1324 the quantity of dredge grown surpassed that of the other three crops together, but in 1348, when the total yield was higher, the quantities were more even. The demesne stock included up to 17 horses; there were also cattle, pigs in large numbers, poultry, and a few sheep.[54]

Inclosure may have been completed by the priory, and substantial acreages of inclosed ground are mentioned in the 17th and 18th centuries. Such are Fatbeasts or Fatby's closes (48 a.) in 1671 and later;[55] closes called the Summer grounds and Thorn close in 1690;[56] Turf close (18 a.) in 1731;[57] Lingham closes (about 70 a.), Calf close, and Stock Mill Holme in 1744;[58] Ash close (30 a.) in 1717;[59] Kelk leys (133 a.) in 1685;[60] and Arden close (34 a.)

---

[22] J.I. 1/1050 m. 58; *Yorks. Fines, 1246–72*, 178; *Bridlington Charty.* 169.
[23] *Valor Eccl.* (Rec. Com.), v. 120.
[24] Univ. of London Libr., Fuller Collection, deeds of 1467–1515; *T.E.R.A.S.* xix. 1–3; *Miscellanea*, iii (Y.A.S. Rec. Ser. lxxx), 11.
[25] *L. & P. Hen. VIII*, xvi, p. 239.
[26] Ibid. xix (1), p. 641; *Yorks. Fines*, i. 111.
[27] *Yorks. Fines*, i. 140; *Cal. Pat. 1547–8*, 204. See also Univ. of London Libr., MSS. 476/3–4. [28] See p. 108.
[29] B.I.H.R., Prob. Reg. lii, f. 283; Univ. of London Libr., Fuller Collection, MS. of 1656; *Abstracts of Yorks. Wills* (Y.A.S. Rec. Ser. ix), 84.
[30] E.R.R.O., DDSY/62/64; Registry of Deeds, Beverley, H/624/1263; /705/1443; N/285/638. See below, p. 321.
[31] Regy. of Deeds, AD/311/638; /312/639–40.
[32] Ibid. AM/340/553. [33] Ibid. AP/324/571.
[34] Ibid. BC/40/57; Y.A.S. MSS., MS. 709b.
[35] See p. 247. [36] See p. 224.
[37] Regy. of Deeds, 1129/159/136.
[38] E.R.R.O., DDWB/20/56, 67, 70. [39] Ibid. /60–1.
[40] Regy. of Deeds, M/141/228; O/295/742.
[41] Ibid. S/121/279; AD/60/148; HA/112/114.
[42] Ibid. LE/418/560; 21/63/60 (1887). [43] See p. 247.
[44] *Valor Eccl.* v. 120; *Miscellanea*, iii. 24, 134; see below, p. 187.
[45] Univ. of London Libr., Fuller Collection.
[46] E 309/Box 8/26 Eliz./7.
[47] H. Grove, *Alienated Tithes*, p. cxxxiii.
[48] E.R.R.O., DDWB/20/44.
[49] B.I.H.R., Prob. Reg. xlvii, f. 369v.
[50] Registry of Deeds, Beverley, HA/113/115.
[51] Grove, *Alienated Tithes*, 454, 518.
[52] *Bridlington Charty.* 164–70.
[53] E.R.R.O., DDWB/12/1; *T.E.R.A.S.* xix. 5.
[54] Univ. of London Libr., Fuller Collection, Kelk accts.
[55] B.I.H.R., Prob. Reg. lii, f. 283; Registry of Deeds, Beverley, Z/458/1051.
[56] E.R.R.O., DDWB/20/60; Regy. of Deeds, O/295/742.
[57] Regy. of Deeds, M/127/201.
[58] Ibid. S/77/186. [59] Ibid. G/96/220.
[60] E.R.R.O., DDSY/62/64.

in 1717.[61] Pasture ground called Kelk Out Leyes was used in 1666 for a rabbit warren, along with ground in neighbouring Harpham.[62]

In 1796 the 451-acre estate of the St. Quintin family was let to nine men, but there was only one large farm, of 261 a.[63] There have been two or three farmers in the 19th and 20th centuries.[64]

In the 13th century Bridlington priory had a water-mill at Little Kelk called Twagrind, consisting of two mills under one roof. When he gave the mill to the priory, Robert Talun undertook not to build another mill between the prior's and his own, and the prior's mill was subsequently moved to a new site.[65] Talun's mill is not mentioned again. The priory mill descended with the manor. It was described as two fulling mills in 1544.[66] Probably in 1654 Sir Henry Griffith sold the mill, then described as a water-corn-mill called Lingham mill, to Richard Ash or Esh.[67] Lingham mill was one of the mills which was taking custom from Nafferton water-mill in 1632.[68] It appears to have been sold to William St. Quintin in 1695.[69] By 1744 Lingham or Saunders Wife mill had fallen down or been demolished,[70] and there is no later reference to a mill in Little Kelk.

LOCAL GOVERNMENT. Rolls of Bridlington priory's manorial court survive for several years in the earlier 14th and earlier 15th centuries. An aletaster is mentioned in the former period, and a constable, two affeerors, and two carrgraves in the latter.[71] In the early 19th century a constable and a pinder were appointed for Little Kelk at courts held by the St. Quintins. Later in the century the officers were normally a bailiff and a pinder, and their appointment continued until 1914.[72]

In 1836 Little Kelk joined the Driffield union.[73]

CHURCH. A chapel at Little Kelk is mentioned in 1275, when the rector of Foston let the tithes there to Bridlington priory for £8 13s. 4d.[74] In 1291 the chapel was worth £6 13s. 4d.[75] The priory paid a chaplain to celebrate in the chapel in 1323–4 and 1347–8.[76] A chantry is referred to in 1320,[77] and one of the chaplains at 'Kelk' in 1525–6 may have served it; its net value was then £4.[78] There is no other certain reference to the chapel. Little Kelk remained extra-parochial until it was united with Lowthorpe for ecclesiastical purposes in 1929.[79]

NONCONFORMITY. A Primitive Methodist chapel was built in 1861.[80] There was 'a good vigorous society' with 39 members in 1889.[81] The chapel ceased to be used in 1962,[82] but the simple stuccoed building with round-headed windows still stood in 1968.

EDUCATION. No evidence.

CHARITIES FOR THE POOR. None known.

KILHAM

THE extensive and irregularly shaped parish of Kilham lies on the wolds about 7 miles west of Bridlington.[1] During the Middle Ages Kilham was both a market and, in the 14th century at least, an administrative centre. Sessions of the peace were held there in 1363 and 1391–2,[2] and the sheriff's tourn in 1369.[3] Kilham's importance as a market centre was longer-lasting. It was based on the grant of a market and fair in the early 13th century, and the situation of the village, between the high wolds to the north and west and the lowlands to the south, favoured the development of a more than purely local market. By 1778, however, it was dismissed as 'a market town... but of little note'.[4] The cutting of the Driffield canal in 1770 quickened its decline, and during the 19th century Kilham became little more than a large country village, while Driffield took over its former role as the main regional market centre.[5]

The parish stretches for about 5½ miles from east to west and about 4 miles from north to south, including in the north the territory of the deserted village of Swaythorpe. Kilham is probably of Anglian origin, and Swaythorpe a subsidiary Scandinavian settlement.[6] Several sections of the parish boundary follow dry valley bottoms and others make use of prehistoric earthworks. The southern boundary, for example, runs for over a mile along an embankment west of Gallows hill, and further east it follows a now ploughed-out section of the same earthwork. The boundary east of Swaythorpe is apparently aligned upon a barrow. In the north and east the boundary follows the Roman roads known as High Street and Wold Gate, and Lowthorpe beck forms the boundary in the south-east. The total area of the parish is 8,173 a., of which Swaythorpe accounts for 790 a.[7]

[61] Regy. of Deeds, F/108/231.
[62] Univ. of London Libr., Fuller Collection, indenture of 1666.
[63] Y.A.S. MSS., MS. 709b.   [64] Directories.
[65] Bridlington Charty. 164–8.   [66] Yorks. Fines, i. 111.
[67] B.M. Add. MS. 26728, f. 26; C 3/434/109.
[68] See p. 291.   [69] C.P. 25(2)/895/7 Wm. III Trin. no. 29.
[70] Regy. of Deeds, S/77/186.
[71] Univ. of London Libr., Fuller Collection.
[72] Y.A.S. MSS., DD. 89: call rolls and jury papers, 1807–1914.
[73] 3rd Rep. Poor Law Com. 168.
[74] Bridlington Charty. 127; T.E.R.A.S. xviii. 110.
[75] Tax. Eccl. (Rec. Com.), 304.
[76] Univ. of London Libr., Fuller Collection, Kelk accts.
[77] Fasti Parochiales, iii. 31.   [78] Y.A.J. xxiv. 77.
[79] York Dioc. Regy., Orders in Council 1/597.
[80] Date on building.
[81] H. Woodcock, Sketches of Prim. Meth. on Yorks. Wolds, 145.
[82] Local information.
[1] This article was written in 1971.
[2] Yorks. Sessions of the Peace (Y.A.S. Rec. Ser. c), 68; B. H. Putnam, Procs. before J.P.s, Ed. III to Ric. III (Ames Found.), 435, 437, 439, 455–6.
[3] Public Works in Med. Law, ii (Selden Soc. xl), 310.
[4] D. Defoe, Tour Through Gt. Brit. (1778 edn.), iii. 210.
[5] F. Ross, Hist. Driffield, 30; see below, p. 258.
[6] P.N.E.R. Yorks. (E.P.N.S.), 97–8.
[7] O.S. Map 6" (1854).

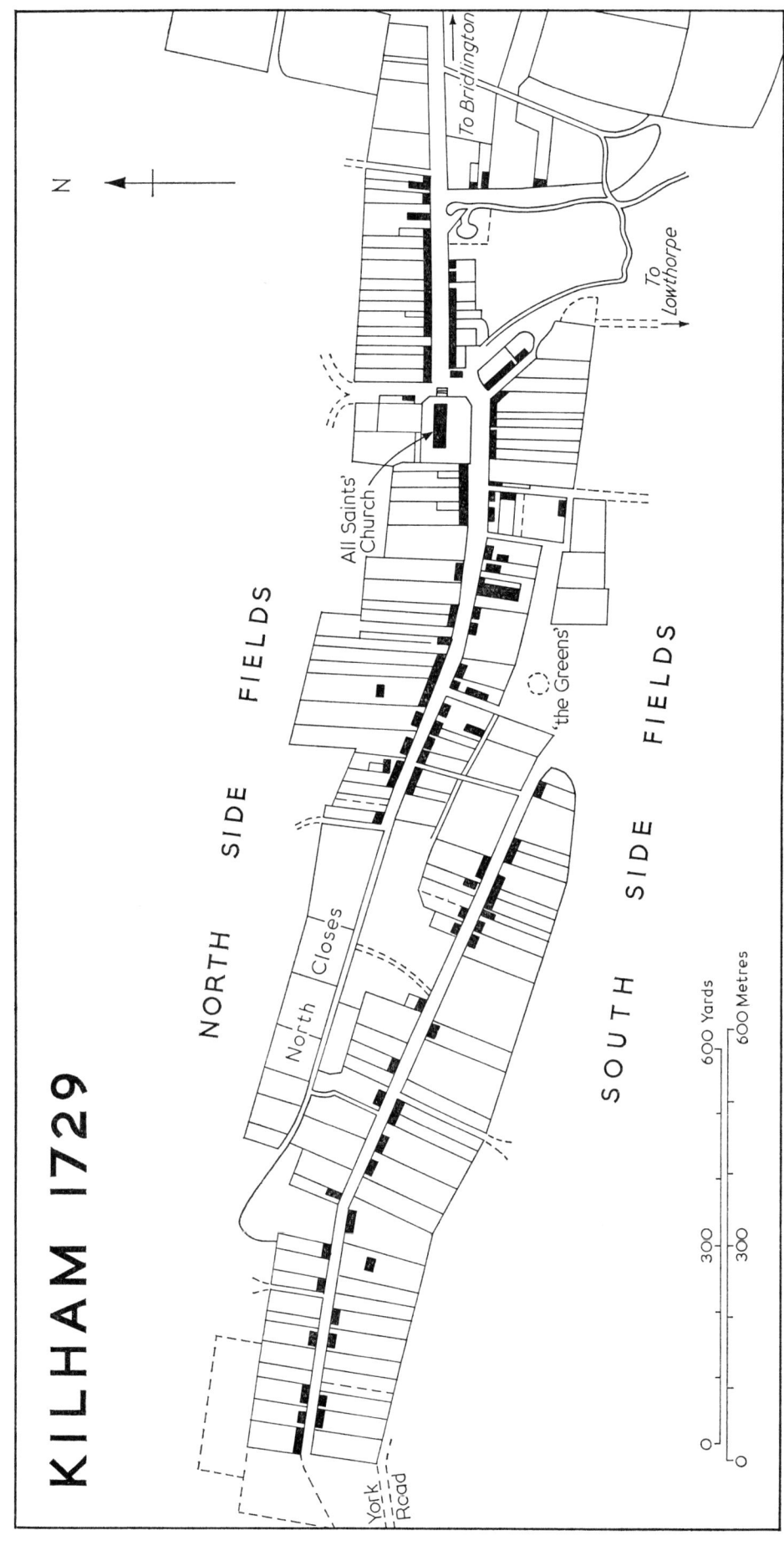

Kilham lies at the junction of two streams forming the headwaters of Lowthorpe beck, which flows southwards on its way to the river Hull. The village stands mostly in the valley of the more westerly stream, and the valley continues—dry beyond the limits of the village—as Middle Dale, leading into Langtoft. The other valley contains the Old Gypsey and it runs north and then west from the village, eventually forming another prominent dry valley known at different points as Barton, Broach, and Tog Dales. The rest of the parish occupies the rolling wold slopes between and beyond these main valleys. Swaythorpe village lay on the slopes of one of the many smaller dry valleys.

The wolds rise steeply from the main valleys in the north and west of the parish, much more gently in the east. Large areas of the wolds exceed 300 ft. above sea-level, reaching 425 ft.–475 ft. in places near the northern and western boundaries and over 500 ft. in the extreme north-west, in Swaythorpe. In the east the wolds reach a maximum of 275 ft. on the ridge that runs from Kilham village towards Bridlington. The village stands at only 75 ft.–125 ft. above sea-level, and much of the valley bottom along Lowthorpe beck is below 75 ft. The pattern of large regular fields in Kilham results from the inclosure of 1773, before which the wold area was largely open-field land. Swaythorpe exhibits a similar field-pattern, probably the result of later subdivision of a large farm created after the depopulation of the village.[8]

There was settlement near Kilham village in prehistoric, Roman, and early Anglian times. Prehistoric remains include a large Iron-Age cemetery north of the village.[9] Two east–west Roman roads cross the parish, one in Swaythorpe and the other through Kilham village. The latter road, running from the east as Wold Gate, apparently forms the main village street. Westwards from the village York Road is thought to lie on the line of the Roman road,[10] but a causeway described as 'ancient road'[11] which descends the wolds a little further north may alternatively represent that stretch of the Roman route. A pagan Anglian cemetery has been found north-east of Kilham[12] and a Christian one south-west of the village.[13]

Several other roads converge on Kilham. One runs north-westwards to Langtoft, and from it another road formerly led northwards to Swaythorpe;[14] the latter was presumably the 'lane which extends towards Swaythorpe' mentioned in the 12th or 13th century.[15] It is now merely a footpath and field track, but it is still known as Swaythorpe Road. Two roads lead northwards from the village, to Thwing and Burton Fleming respectively, and a branch from the latter runs north-eastwards to Rudston. Three roads lead southwards, one to Pockthorpe, another, known as Driffield Lane, to Ruston Parva, and the third to Harpham. In the earlier 18th century an additional road ran southwards from near the church to Lowthorpe.[16] It had been stopped up by 1772[17] and its course is now marked by a footpath. North of the village Sheep Rake Lane is one of several field roads on the wolds.

The street pattern within the village is complex. The main street, closely built up, runs along the north side of the valley, its various sections known as East, Church, and Middle Streets; East Street is presumably the East Gate mentioned in 1317,[18] and Middle Street may have been the North Gate mentioned in 1620.[19] To the east the main street is continued as Wold Gate, but at its western end it terminates with a right-angled bend leading into a narrow side lane. The street formerly continued further west, however, eventually joining up with the Langtoft road, but this section apparently came to be disused during the 18th century. It was all open in 1729 but part had been stopped up by 1772.[20] Part of its course was still visible in 1971 as a hollow way, but part had apparently become the bed of the stream flowing along the valley bottom. The wetness of the low-lying ground suggests a reason for the abandonment of this part of the street.

A second street, much less closely built up than the first, runs along the south side of the valley. It may have been the South Gate mentioned in 1620.[21] It was later called West Street and that part of the village is known as West End. The different alignment and character of the two streets suggests that West End may have been a later extension of the original village, perhaps connected with its prosperity as a market centre. Eighteenth-century maps[22] indicate a rectangular open space, lying south of the main street and near the end of West Street, which may possibly have been used as a fairground. The space was probably 'the Greens', where the early grammar school and a poorhouse were built.[23] A common gravel pit which occupied the school site in 1822 was probably that awarded by the inclosure commissioners in 1773, and what may have been a pit is indicated on the same spot in 1729.[24] Several small lanes ran into the open space; one of them, significantly called Green Lane, still connects the two parts of the village, but the others no longer exist.

On the north and south sides of the village there were, in 1772, continuous back lanes running beyond the crofts and garths. They existed at least in part in 1729. By 1850, however, part of the south back lane was disused;[25] the remainder is known as Mill Back Side. Several side lanes off the village streets include Hotham and Church Lanes, the latter mentioned in 1664,[26] and the Ruston road leaves the main street as Baptist Street.

Lowthorpe beck, sometimes known within the parish as Kilham beck,[27] originates at springs from

---

[8] See p. 256.
[9] Ex inf. Mr. T. C. M. Brewster, 1971.
[10] Mary Kitson Clark, *Gaz. of Roman Remains in E. Yorks.* 45.
[11] O.S. Map 6" (1854).
[12] J. R. Mortimer, *Forty Years' Researches in Burial Mounds*, 344; *V.C.H. Yorks.* ii. 87–8; O.S. Map 6" (1854, 1956).
[13] Ex inf. Mr. Brewster, 1971.
[14] E.R.R.O., DDDU/12/53.
[15] *Bridlington Charty.* 145.
[16] E.R.R.O., DDDU/12/53.
[17] Ibid. /11/277.
[18] Ibid. DDCC/55/3.
[19] Ibid. DDDU/12/3.
[20] Ibid. /11/277; /12/53; O.S. Map 6" (1854).
[21] E.R.R.O., DDDU/12/3.
[22] Ibid. /11/277; /12/53.
[23] See pp. 259, 262.
[24] E.R.R.O., DDDU/11/12, 277; /12/53; *9th Rep. Char. Com.* 736.
[25] E.R.R.O., DDDU/11/277; /12/53; O.S. Map 6" (1854).
[26] E.R.R.O., DDDU/12/3.
[27] Ibid. /54.

which the village may take its name.[28] One spring feeds two ponds at Beck Head, at the end of East Street. Another, at Tancred Pit Hole, about a mile north of the village, supplies the Old Gypsey, which joins Lowthorpe beck south of Beck Head. Tancred Pit Hole and the Old Gypsey are first named in 1793.[29] A third spring, at the west of the village near Back Lane, has been known as Frost Pit or Frost Pit Well since at least the early 17th century.[30] Near by stands a 19th-century pump with a cast-iron platform, and there is a similar one in the village near the church. From the spring a stream flows eastwards a little to the south of the main street before turning north and entering a culvert under the road. It may formerly have flowed in a channel along Church Street, for in 1718 'the Bow bridge' was situated near the churchyard[31] and in 1809 'the bridge in the street' was mentioned.[32] By 1850 the stream had been culverted.[33] It reappears further east and eventually joins Lowthorpe beck south of Beck Head. Several by-laws of the 17th and 18th centuries relate to the use and cleansing of the various springs and streams.[34]

Among several springs in the now dry valleys is that at Hen Pit Hole, near the Langtoft road about 1½ mile from the village. In the 19th century water was said to flow from it with great force.[35] In 1809 the spring ran copiously for 20 days, flooding the main village street.[36] By 1923 the amount of water from the spring was reported to be much reduced[37] and in 1971 it was dry. At inclosure in 1773 a common watering place was allotted at the head of the Old Gypsey east of the Burton Fleming road.[38]

The large village extends for about 1¼ mile from east to west but, as already noted, since at least the early 18th century only the eastern part has been closely built up. In West End the buildings are widely dispersed and there are many vacant garths and crofts, in addition to earthworks which may indicate the sites of former houses. Shrinkage at West End seems to have taken place both before and after 1729, when some of the garths were already empty. The former westward extension of the main village street is similarly flanked by earthworks, and other empty garths and house-sites lie on either side of Middle Street. The latter include the site of a house which was the largest in Kilham in 1729, when it belonged to Jonas Thompson.[39] The wide part of Church Street may have been used as a market-place. It is possible that the street there was even wider before 1717–18, when a wall was built around the churchyard.[40] At the side of the road is a so-called 'bull-ring', an iron ring set into a large block of stone, which was placed in its present position c. 1890.[41] A lock-up stood on the other side of Church Street but had gone by 1895.[42]

The houses and cottages in the village are mostly of brick, much of it probably from the local brickyard.[43] Most of them date from the 18th and early 19th centuries, and later-19th-century buildings include one or two substantial houses of yellow brick. Little work in chalk is evident apart from boundary walls and outbuildings. Few 18th-century cottages survive; a former example was that of a saddler who, in 1745, lived in a one-storeyed house of two rooms, the 'foreroom' and the parlour, and a shop.[44] East, Church, and Middle Streets contain a number of farm-houses and tradesmen's dwellings of which the frontages are more sophisticated architecturally than those found in most of the wold villages. The most ambitious front is that of Hall Farm, in East Street, which bears the date 1716. The house was owned in 1729 by a member of the Thompson family.[45] The front, of red brick with stone dressings, is three storeys high and five bays wide, the central bay projecting and having a moulded string and flanking pilasters. The raked parapet which forms a pediment above the façade has probably been altered, as has a lunette window in the tympanum. There is a central round-headed doorway. The house is only one room deep, but a service wing on the west side has recently been demolished and there may originally have been a corresponding wing to the east. The early-18th-century staircase occupies a central projecting bay at the rear, lighted by a round-headed and lunette window; an enriched 18th-century fire-place survives on the ground floor.

Clackna Farm, also on the south side of East Street, is a mid-18th-century house having a two-storeyed symmetrical stuccoed front and a wide pilastered and pedimented doorway. 'Five Pennies', dating from the late 18th century, has a three-bay plan of which one bay is entered by a subsidiary doorway and may therefore have been self-contained. The north side of East Street is continuously built up and contains several double-fronted early-19th-century houses; the most impressive is the stucco-fronted Eastgate House, which has a central doorway with pediment, fluted columns, paterae, and fan-light. A pair of brown-brick cottages is dated 1800. The former brewery has a road frontage pierced by an archway, now blocked; the adjacent double-fronted house dates from c. 1840.[46] Earlier houses in this row are the present post office, a low 18th-century building, and a house of a storey and a half at the corner of Church Lane which has a double-bowed window, formerly a shop-front.[47] At the east end of the street the older part of Manor Farm is an 18th-century chalk-built house with stone quoins, set at right-angles to the road.

A group of houses on the south side of Church Street includes Church View, a two-storeyed 18th-century building of dark red brick with stone quoins and keystones; the front, originally of five bays, has been altered at one end as part of a separate

---

[28] *P.N.E.R. Yorks.* 97n.
[29] E.R.R.O., DDDU/12/5.
[30] Ibid. /3; O.S. Map 6″ (1854).
[31] E.R.R.O., PR. 2014. In 1772 the stream is shown as originating towards the west end of, and flowing along, Middle Street, turning south near the church: T. Jefferys, *Map of Yorks.* 1772.
[32] E.R.R.O., PR. 2017.
[33] O.S. Map 6″ (1854).
[34] E.R.R.O., DDDU/12/3–5.
[35] Directories; W. Smith, *Anc. Springs and Streams of E.R. Yorks.* 25–6.
[36] E.R.R.O., PR. 2017.
[37] Smith, op. cit. 26.
[38] E.R.R.O., DDDU/11/12, 277.
[39] Ibid. /12/53.
[40] E.R.R.O., PR. 2014.
[41] *T.E.R.A.S.* iii. 45.
[42] Ibid.; O.S. Map 6″ (1854); Sheahan and Whellan, *Hist. York & E.R.* ii. 482.
[43] See p. 258.
[44] B.I.H.R., R. AS. 14B/93.
[45] E.R.R.O., DDDU/12/53.
[46] See p. 258.
[47] See plate facing p. 128.

dwelling. Rutland House, opposite the churchyard, has a three-bay plan and an off-centre doorway with its keystone dated 1764. A second doorway, perhaps original, gives access to a self-contained single-bay section of the house with a separate staircase. Further east is the Saddlers, a two-storeyed double-fronted house of red brick dating from the 18th century; two ground-floor bay windows of early-19th-century design have been added to the front with, between them, entrance steps flanked by cast-iron balustrades.

In Middle Street are several detached double-fronted houses of the earlier 19th century with Georgian doorways, some of the frontages being of variegated brick. They include the Elms farm-house, Belgrave Lodge, and Manor Cottage. High Farm, near the west end of the street, is of whitewashed brick and of slightly earlier date. Several terraces of late-19th-century brick cottages remain in Middle Street, in Back Lane, and at the east end of the village. Twentieth-century development has occurred mainly in the east of the village, where several bungalows and houses have been built in Back Lane and a dozen in Driffield Lane; modern infilling has taken place in Middle Street. There are twelve Council houses in Green Lane and fourteen in Mill Back Side.

An inn, built of chalk, is recorded as early as 1420–1,[48] and in 1721 the Green Dragon stood near the market cross.[49] The latter may later have been rebuilt as the Star, first mentioned in the early 19th century,[50] which still stands opposite the church. The Black Bull is first mentioned in 1818[51] and the Plough and the Royal Oak in 1823.[52] By 1840 the Royal Oak had been replaced by the Blacksmith's Arms.[53] The Plough ceased to exist during the 1870s and the Black Bull between 1879 and 1889, but by 1892 the Bay Horse had made its appearance[54] on the site of the Plough.[55] The Blacksmith's Arms closed in 1970.[56]

A friendly society, known as the Kilham Unanimous Society, was established in 1780 and monthly meetings were held at the Black Bull in 1818.[57] The Kilham Union Society was founded in 1808 and met at the Star.[58] The Temperance Hall, which has a yellow-brick front with red-brick dressings, was built on the site of the grammar school in Church Lane in 1880; a reading room was attached.[59] By 1909 it had become the Foresters' Hall[60] and a friendly society still met there in 1915.[61] It was used as a village hall in 1971.

A house on the north side of East Gate was used as a private lunatic asylum, known as Kilham Retreat, between at least 1858 and 1864, when it closed. Accommodation was provided for six women but in 1863–4 there were only three or four. The proprietors were successively John Atkinson and his sister Emily.[62]

By 1850 there were about a dozen farm-houses outside the village, all apparently dating from after the inclosure of 1773. Most of them are 19th-century buildings. Old Dotterill Farm, however, lying north of the village, is a late-18th-century house, later converted into two cottages; it is mainly chalk-built but with red-brick gables, window and door openings, and dentil eaves course. Behind it is a well and the horse-operated machinery for raising water still remained in 1971, when the house was derelict. It was perhaps replaced by Dotterill Park, a white-brick house which was built in 1854 about ½ mile further north.[63]

The site of the former village of Swaythorpe is clearly marked by extensive and prominent earthworks north of Swaythorpe Farm. House-sites and a street can be distinguished. A small pond in the north of the site was known as Chapel Well in the mid 19th century and west of it lies the possible site of the chapel. Earth banks there mark the foundations of a small rectangular building, aligned east to west, with a rounded east end. A circular mound near the centre of the site was described in 1850 as the site of a windmill, but an earthwork to the north-west, described as an embankment cross,[64] is perhaps the site of a post mill; the 'cross' is now ploughed-out. Swaythorpe Farm is a large mid-19th-century house.

Kilham has always been one of the largest villages in the wapentake, and judged by its tax assessments it was also the wealthiest in the Middle Ages. Swaythorpe, until its depopulation, was only a small hamlet but there is no reliable indication of its size. In 1377 there were 363 poll-tax payers in Kilham[65] and in 1670 131 households were recorded in the hearth-tax assessment. In 1674 39 households were discharged from the tax; of the 76 that were taxed 44 had only one hearth, 14 had 2, 11 had 3, 5 had 4, and one each had 6 and seven.[66] In 1743 there were about 100 families in the parish[67] and in 1764 97, including '7 or 8 undersettlers or single persons'.[68] In 1801 there were 588 inhabitants.

Kilham's population increased rapidly in the early 19th century to 789 in 1811 and 971 in 1821. It subsequently rose more slowly to a peak of 1,252 in 1861, before falling to 946 in 1901.[69] The steady decline has continued in the 20th century, to 853 in 1921, 771 in 1951, and 737 in 1961.[70]

Robert Gardener (d. 1798), a native of Kilham, is said to have invented c. 1775 a type of artificial dew-pond, which was widely used on the wolds.[71]

MANORS AND OTHER ESTATES. In 1086 there were four estates in Kilham. One, comprising 3 carucates and 2 bovates, had been held in 1066 by four thegns, but in 1086 it was in the king's hands. The largest Domesday estate, consisting of 30 carucates, was held both before and after the

---

[48] B.M. Harl. Roll H.12.
[49] Regy. of Deeds, H/107/225.
[50] E.R.R.O., QDC/2/22.
[51] Ibid. /21.
[52] Baines, *Hist. Yorks.* ii. 360.
[53] White, *Dir. E. & N.R. Yorks.* (1840), 392.
[54] Directories.
[55] O.S. Map 6" (1854).
[56] Local inf.
[57] E.R.R.O., QDC/2/21.
[58] Ibid. /22.
[59] Bulmer, *Dir. E. Yorks.* (1892), 220.
[60] *Kelly's Dir. N. & E.R. Yorks.* (1909), 544 etc.
[61] *Hull Times*, 2 Jan. 1915.
[62] E.R.R.O., QAL/3/36; Regy. of Deeds, KS/294/388.
[63] Sheahan and Whellan, *Hist. York & E.R.* ii. 481.
[64] O.S. Map 6" (1854, 1956).
[65] E 179/202/62 m. 36.
[66] E 179/205/514, 521.
[67] *Herring's Visit.* ii. 138.
[68] B.I.H.R., Bp. V. 1764/Ret. 85.
[69] *V.C.H. Yorks.* iii. 489.
[70] *Census.*
[71] H. E. Strickland, *Gen. View Agric. E.R.* (1812), 217.

Conquest by a king's thegn, Ernuin the priest,[72] and it apparently passed to the king soon after the completion of the Survey. These two estates formed the royal manor of *KILHAM*, half of which was granted by the king to the archbishop of Rouen in 1154–8. The other half had been granted previously to the chapter of Rouen.[73] In 1284–5 the Rouen estate comprised 38 carucates and in 1316 the archbishop was returned as lord of the township.[74] Rouen's tenure of the manor was interrupted by deprivation on several occasions, usually because of the French wars. King John took it into his hands[75] and in 1205 Richard de Belhus, the archbishop's tenant, gave two saddle-horses to have possession of it.[76] About 1321 the manor, which had recently been taken into the king's hands, was redelivered to the archbishop.[77] In 1324 it was again confiscated and custody of it was granted to Peter de Galicien,[78] described as its keeper in 1326.[79] In 1330 the custody of half the manor was granted to Thomas of Garton for as long as it should remain in the king's hands by voidance of the see.[80] In 1334 the archbishop and chapter of Rouen granted the manor to William of Melton, archbishop of York.[81] In 1340 the archbishop had royal licence to enfeoff two men who would transfer the manor to William son of Henry of Melton and his wife Joan. William son of Henry, who was the archbishop's heir, completed the transaction in 1341, after the latter's death.[82]

The manor, which comprised 249 bovates in 1362,[83] was retained by the Meltons until the early 16th century.[84] In 1511 Sir John Melton settled it on his daughter Dorothy, who later married George D'Arcy,[85] and D'Arcy was lord in 1530.[86] John, Lord D'Arcy, died without surviving heirs in 1635[87] and the manor passed to his widow; she later married Sir Francis Fane, who was in possession by 1639.[88] Fane died in 1680[89] and by 1689 the manor had passed to William Savile, grandson of John, Lord D'Arcy's sister Anne. Savile's father, another William, had been granted the reversion of the manor by Lord D'Arcy in 1633.[90]

On the death of William Savile in 1692 the manor was divided between his daughters Mary, Anne, and Dorothy. Mary Savile married William Mawde and they had issue, Major, Mary, and Rosamond. Mary married Darcy Preston, to whom in 1730 Major and Rosamond sold their interest in the manor. Anne Savile married John Smithson and her third of the manor passed in 1702 to John's mother Eleanor. In 1711 Eleanor devised her estate to her son-in-law William Iveson and in 1730 his daughter-in-law Elizabeth sold it to Darcy Preston. Savile's other daughter Dorothy married John Ricard, on whose death in 1724 her third of the manor was divided between their children Elizabeth, Arthur, Catherine, and Essex. Elizabeth sold her interest in the manor to Darcy Preston in 1726, Catherine in 1738, and Arthur in 1742. Essex married Henry More and after her death he sold his interest to Preston in 1747.[91] At inclosure in 1773 Darcy's son John Preston was awarded 1,175 a.[92]

In 1792 Preston sold the manor, then comprising 1,231 a., to Sir Christopher Sykes,[93] and in 1813 Sir Mark Sykes sold the estate in separate lots.[94] The purchaser of the manor and the largest holding, about 800 a., was Thomas Duesbery.[95] In 1877 W. H. T. Duesbery sold 765 a. to W. H. Denison, Lord Londesborough,[96] and the estate was split up and sold by W. F. H. Denison, earl of Londesborough, in 1906–7. The 264-acre Grange farm passed to Harry Middlewood, the 264-acre Kilham Field farm to Richard Standy, and the 239-acre Manor farm to John Johnson.[97] Johnson died in 1920[98] and three years later the estate was acquired by R. D. Kirk,[99] who sold it in 1927 to G. H. Thompson.[1] The Thompsons have since retained it.

In 1816 Sir Mark Sykes sold 212 a. in Kilham to J. B. La Marche.[2] By 1872 the holding had passed to Thomas Holden, who sold it that year to W. H. Harrison-Broadley.[3] The 206-acre Westfield farm was sold in 1956 by Doris Harrison-Broadley to L. J. Marr.[4]

In the early 13th century the Thwing family held an estate in Kilham of the archbishop and chapter of Rouen. About 1227 Marmaduke of Thwing gave to William the Constable, of Holderness, on his marriage with Marmaduke's daughter Cecily, one bovate in demesne and a mesne lordship in 6 carucates in Kilham, for which William and Cecily were to render service to Rouen.[5] Part, at least, of the estate descended to Sir John Constable (d. 1587), who sold property in Kilham to Thomas Dalton in 1568.[6] The descent of this estate has not been traced further.

---

[72] *V.C.H. Yorks.* ii. 197, 204, 282, 287.
[73] *Cal. Doc. France*, ed. Round, pp. 4, 5; *E.Y.C.* i, pp. 338–41.
[74] *Feud. Aids*, vi. 26, 168.
[75] *Yorks. Assize R. John* (Y.A.S. Rec. Ser. xliv), 27.
[76] *Rot. de Ob. et Fin.* (Rec. Com.), 335.
[77] *Cal. Fine R. 1319–27*, 66–7; *Abbrev. Rot. Orig.* i (Rec. Com.), 259.
[78] *Abbrev. Rot. Orig.* i. 284; *Cal. Fine. R. 1319–27*, 324.
[79] *Cal. Mem. R. 1326–7*, 272.
[80] *Cal. Pat. 1330–4*, 54.
[81] *Yorks. Fines, 1327–47*, 70.
[82] Ibid. 150; *Cal. Pat. 1338–40*, 413; *1340–3*, 164; *Cal. Inq. p.m.* viii, p. 198.
[83] *Cal. Inq. p.m.* xi, p. 285.
[84] C 140/58/47; C 142/25/121; *Cal. Close, 1360–4*, 358; *Abbrev. Rot. Orig.* ii (Rec. Com.), 302; *Test. Ebor.* i. 246; *Cal. Pat. 1408–13*, 280. For pedigrees of the Melton family see W. Flower, *Visit. Yorks.* (Harl. Soc. xvi), 202; G. Poulson, *Holderness*, ii. 199.
[85] C 142/70/60.
[86] E.R.R.O., DDDU/12/48.
[87] J. Foster, *Pedigrees of... Yorks.* iii, *sub* Preston, of Askham Bryan. The D'Arcy barony, which had been forfeited when Thomas, Lord D'Arcy, was executed for treason in 1536, was restored to his son George in 1548: J. W. Clay, *Ext. & Dorm. Peerages of N. Cos.* 43; *Complete Peerage*, iii. 20.
[88] E.R.R.O., DDDU/12/3.
[89] *Royalist Composition Papers*, i (Y.A.S. Rec. Ser. xv), 215, 217; *Complete Peerage*, iv. 78.
[90] E.R.R.O., DDDU/11/39, 96; Foster, *Pedigrees of... Yorks.* iii, *sub* Preston, of Askham Bryan.
[91] E.R.R.O., DDDU/11/39.
[92] Ibid. /12.
[93] Ibid. /39, 221.
[94] Ibid. /18, 202.   [95] Ibid. /202, 231; /22/4.
[96] Registry of Deeds, Beverley, MH/343/509.
[97] Ibid. 91/153/142 (1906); 94/388/350; /407/368 (1907).
[98] Ibid. 226/465/384.
[99] Ibid. 259/249/209.
[1] Ibid. 343/425/362.
[2] Ibid. CZ/424/647.
[3] Ibid. DDHB/7/40–2, 44.
[4] Regy. of Deeds, 1040/372/330.
[5] J.I. 1/1046 m. 51; *Yorks. Deeds*, i. 101; *E.Y.C.* xi, pp. 204–5.
[6] *Yorks. Fines*, i. 358.

Other Constable land, however, apparently descended in another branch of the family to Marmaduke and Roger Constable, who held property in the parish in 1542.[7] Some of it was sold in 1568 to Walter Story.[8] In 1577 Story sold an estate there to George Mainprise,[9] who had previously acquired other land in the parish.[10] In 1591 Mainprise died seised of 48½ bovates in Kilham, leaving 9 bovates, together with lands in Thwing,[11] in trust for his three younger daughters, then minors, 13½ bovates to his son Richard, and 26 bovates to his eldest daughter Ellice.[12] It was subsequently further divided.

Another part of the Thwing estate in Kilham descended in the Thwing and Lumley families with Thwing manor[13] and was sold with it in 1579 by John, Lord Lumley, to Sir Thomas Heneage.[14] In 1588 Heneage exchanged the property for certain Crown lands elsewhere.[15]

The Thompson family, who leased the rectory from the earlier 17th to the earlier 19th century,[16] also acquired a large freehold estate during the 17th century. In 1641 Thomas Drinkrowe sold property in the parish to Richard Thompson (d. 1653),[17] and in 1720 12 bovates of Gustavus Thompson's estate was known as Drinkrowe's farm.[18] In 1645 Richard Thompson held, in addition to the rectory, lands in Kilham said to have been worth about £35 a year before the Civil War.[19] After his death in 1653 his estate was apparently divided between his sons Jonas and Richard (d. 1713),[20] and thereafter two branches of the family held estates in Kilham. Both branches evidently bought additional property during the later 17th and early 18th centuries.

Jonas's estate descended to his grandson, another Jonas Thompson (d. 1739), who was Lord Mayor of York in 1731.[21] In 1717 his estate included 82½ bovates in the parish,[22] and in 1734 he bought a further 9 bovates from Christopher Beale.[23] At inclosure in 1773 Jonas's son Richard Thompson was awarded 1,490 a. for his freehold estate, in addition to 579 a. for rectorial tithes and glebe.[24] The estate descended in the Thompson family until 1918, when it was sold as five farms, including the 802-acre West Field farm, by the trustees of Anne Thompson (d. 1913).[25]

The estate of Richard Thompson (d. 1713) passed to his grandson Gustavus,[26] whose widow in 1758 sold 56½ bovates to Joshua Wilson. She retained a further 12 bovates,[27] for which her devisees were awarded 164 a. at inclosure in 1773. Joshua Wilson then received 762 a. for his freehold estate, in addition to 459 a. for rectorial tithes and glebe.[28] The estate, which consisted of 1,000 a. in 1909, has subsequently descended in the Wilson family.[29] H. C. B. Wilson sold the 228-acre High farm in 1927 to the county council.[30]

An estate belonging to the Ewbank family may be traced at least from 1573, when Christopher Ewbank bought property in Kilham.[31] On the death of Richard Ewbank in 1634 his estate, then comprising 20 bovates, passed to his daughters Isabel, who later married Brian Towse, and Catherine, later wife of George Sinclair.[32] The Kilham property apparently descended in the Sinclair family as there is no further reference to the Towses in the parish. On the death of John Sinclair in 1764[33] the estate was divided between his daughters Anne, who married John England, and Elizabeth, wife of Benjamin Glossop. In 1768 Anne and John England sold their share of the estate to Francis Owston[34] who, in 1769, sold 8 bovates and in 1771 a further 5 bovates to John Outram.[35] Elizabeth and Benjamin Glossop sold their share of the estate, 7 bovates, to Outram in 1770.[36] Outram bought a further 8½ bovates in 1769, 19 bovates in 1770, and about 60 a. in 1772.[37] At inclosure in 1773 he was awarded 684 a.[38] In 1786 his devisees sold 220 a. to Ralph Creyke[39] and in 1792 his son Benjamin Outram sold 223 a. to Sir Christopher Sykes.[40] The remainder of the estate descended in the Outram family until it was sold by Sir Francis Outram in 1927 in three lots totalling 187 a.[41]

In 1086 6 carucates in Kilham held by the king were soke of Great Driffield manor.[42] In 1241 Driffield, together with its soke in Kilham, was granted by the king to Christine, wife of William, count of Aumale, in exchange for other property.[43] The estate later passed to Christine's sister Dervorguilla, wife of John de Balliol, and in both 1268 and 1290 the Kilham lands comprised one bovate held in demesne and 5 carucates and 7 bovates held by under-tenants.[44] In 1296 the Balliol estate, including Driffield manor and its soke in

---

[7] C 142/65/79.
[8] *Yorks. Fines*, i. 354.
[9] Ibid. ii. 99.
[10] *Yorks. Fines*, i. 323, 365–7; ii. 38.
[11] See p. 327.
[12] C 142/232/65.
[13] E.R.R.O., DDCC/55/3, 4; *Yorks. Fines, 1347–77*, 14; i. 30; *Cal. Inq. p.m.* xiv, pp. 55–6, 74–5; *Cal. Inq. Misc.* vii, p. 41; *Cal. Pat.* 1553–4, 157–9; see below, p. 326.
[14] *Yorks. Fines*, ii. 138.
[15] Ibid. iii. 93.
[16] See p. 255. For a pedigree of the Thompson family see Foster, *Pedigrees of ... Yorks.* iii, sub Thompson, of Humbleton and Kilham, and of Kirby Hall, Sheriff Hutton, etc. See also J. T. Ward, *E. Yorks. Landed Estates in the 19th Cent.* (E. Yorks. Loc. Hist. Ser. xxiii), 65.
[17] E.R.R.O., DC/10/195.
[18] Regy. of Deeds, G/368/814; see below.
[19] *Roy. Comp. Pap.* i. 10.
[20] Foster, op. cit., sub Thompson.
[21] Ibid.
[22] Regy. of Deeds, G/200/452; *Y.A.J.* i. 315.
[23] Regy. of Deeds, O/61/130.
[24] E.R.R.O., DDDU/11/12; see p. 255.
[25] Regy. of Deeds, 160/189/164; /190/165; 183/280/242; /282/244; /283/245; /300/260; 186/120/102.
[26] Ibid. E/156/269. Gustavus's father was Robert Thompson (fl. 1715) and not Richard, as stated by Foster, op. cit., sub Thompson.
[27] Regy. of Deeds, AA/66/130.
[28] E.R.R.O., DDDU/11/12; see p. 255.
[29] Directories; Regy. of Deeds, 117/194/170.
[30] Regy. of Deeds, 343/576/480.
[31] *Yorks. Fines*, ii. 29.
[32] C 142/528/65; C 3/464/28.
[33] Regy. of Deeds, AB/426/767.
[34] Ibid. AL/74/134.
[35] Ibid. AM/163/268, 269; AP/99/159.
[36] Ibid. AM/545/561.
[37] E.R.R.O., DDSY/36/2.
[38] Ibid. DDDU/11/12.
[39] Regy. of Deeds, BI/582/902; see below, p. 254.
[40] Ibid. BQ/301/461; E.R.R.O., DDSY/36/2.
[41] Regy. of Deeds, 350/292/239; 354/176/143; 356/423/346.
[42] *V.C.H. Yorks.* ii. 197.
[43] *Cal. Chart. R. 1226–57*, 262; *Plac. de Quo Warr.* (Rec. Com.), 210.
[44] *Yorks. Inq.* i. 109; ii. 96; *Rot. Hund.* i (Rec. Com.), 114.

Kilham, was forfeited to the king, who in 1306 granted it to John of Brittany, earl of Richmond.[45] He still retained it in 1320[46] but it probably reverted to the Crown in 1341.[47] By the late 14th century the manor of Driffield and its soke had passed to the Scrope family.[48] The Kilham estate is last mentioned as appurtenant to Driffield manor in 1455, when Sir John Scrope died in possession.[49]

A family which took its name from the township was apparently an early demesne tenant of this fee. In 1218–19 Stephen of Kilham held one carucate, some of which, at least, was appurtenant to Driffield manor.[50] John of Kilham granted 2 bovates which were soke of Driffield, probably in the late 12th or 13th century, to Robert Burser. The latter granted them to his sister Isabel and she to Robert Wiles, by whom they were given to Bridlington priory before 1290.[51] In 1288 Richard of Kilham granted to Edmund of Kilham 7 bovates and the reversion of 2 more.[52] The estate may have descended to John of Kilham, whose daughter and heir Agnes married Thomas Mountford (d. 1489) of Hornby (Yorks. N.R.).[53] It is likely that Thomas and Agnes endowed a chantry in Hornby church with the Kilham estate.[54] In 1320 the Kilham estate of Gerard Salvin, the descent of which is traced below,[55] included 6 bovates which were soke of Driffield manor.[56]

Soke land of Driffield also belonged to the Creyke family. Thomas Creyke, by will dated 1488, left land in Kilham called 'Driffield fee'.[57] His son Robert died in 1539 seised of twelve houses and cottages and 30 bovates, held of Kilham manor.[58] The estate subsequently descended with Marton manor in the Creyke family.[59] At inclosure in 1773 Ralph Creyke was awarded 655 a.[60] and he increased his estate by the purchase of 220 a. from the devisees of John Outram in 1786.[61] The estate, then comprising about 850 a., was sold in 1873–4 by Ralph Creyke in separate lots.[62] The largest, the Dotterill Park estate, consisting of about 400 a., was bought by Thomas Oddy[63] and it was retained by the Oddys until the death of J. H. Oddy in 1929.[64] It was subsequently sold to Charles Burdass and the Burdass family have since retained it.[65]

In 1066 7 carucates in Kilham were held as two manors by Forne and Game. In 1086 the estate was held by Otes Arblaster.[66] In 1200 Robert Arblaster brought a lawsuit against Gilbert of Fangfoss concerning 14 bovates in Kilham.[67] In 1284–5 3 carucates of the estate were held by Richard de Gorun and 3 carucates of the Chauncy fee.[68] Nothing more is known of Gorun's estate, but it may have been part of the Chauncy fee. In 1302–3 and 1346 the Chauncy lands were said to consist of 2½ carucates,[69] but another 14th-century survey attributed 5 carucates and 6 bovates to the fee.[70] In 1356 Thomas Chauncy granted his Kilham estate to William of Melton,[71] who died in 1362 seised of 6 carucates said to have been formerly part of the Chauncy fee.[72] The overlordship thereafter descended with Kilham manor.[73]

In 1259–60 Walter of Thirkleby, who held Kilham manor at farm in 1250,[74] secured possession of various small holdings in Kilham which were probably held of the Chauncy fee.[75] Walter's widow Lettice married Nicholas Wake and their heir Sybil married Robert Salvin. In 1289 Sybil, then a widow, granted the reversion of her Kilham estate to her son Gerard.[76] In 1302 Gerard Salvin obtained a quitclaim of a small estate in Kilham.[77] At his death in 1320 his estate comprised 19 bovates held of William Chauncy, 5 bovates of the archbishop of Rouen, 6 bovates of the earl of Richmond, and nearly 4 bovates of Richard Thorny,[78] the last-mentioned possibly holding a mesne lordship under the Chauncys. In 1428 another Gerard Salvin was returned as holding 8 bovates of the Chauncy fee in Kilham.[79] The estate was apparently dispersed during the 16th century. In the 1590s Ralph Salvin sold property there to Thomas Milner and to Bartholomew Williamson and John Cawood.[80] The descent of the estate has not been traced further, but it is likely that part, at least, passed during the 17th century to the Thompson family.[81]

In 1308 Gerard Salvin was granted property in various townships by Hugh de Vere and his wife Denise in exchange for a rent from it and from his other estates, including that at Kilham.[82] The rent descended as in Foston to Sir Henry Percy's daughter Elizabeth, wife of Thomas Burgh,[83] and it has not thereafter been traced.

Several religious houses and chantries held estates in Kilham. The largest holding was the 18 bovates of the chantry of the Virgin in Hornby church (Yorks. N.R.).[84] It is likely that this land was given to the chantry by Thomas Mountford (d. 1489) and his

---

[45] V.C.H. Hunts. ii. 9; T. Rymer, Foedera, i. 1002; Cal. Chart. R. 1300–26, 406.
[46] Cal. Inq. p.m. vi, p. 133.
[47] V.C.H. Hunts. ii. 9.
[48] C 136/78/28; Cal. Close, 1405–9, 30; 1413–19, 229, 251; Cal. Inq. Misc. vii, p. 288.
[49] C 139/161/14.
[50] Rolls of Justices in Eyre for Yorks. 1218–19 (Selden Soc. lvi), 49, 59.
[51] Bridlington Charty. 145–6; see below, p. 255.
[52] Yorks. Fines, 1272–1300, 86.
[53] Y.A.J. xvii. 286.
[54] See below.
[55] See below.
[56] Cal. Inq. p.m. vi, p. 133.
[57] Test. Ebor. iv. 37–8.
[58] C 142/61/53.
[59] C 142/84/57; /138/45; Yorks. Fines, 1614–25, 218; Roy. Comp. Pap. i. 17–18; see above, p. 96.
[60] E.R.R.O., DDDU/11/12.
[61] Regy. of Deeds, BI/582/902; see above, p. 253.
[62] Ibid. LG/283/372; /284/373; /342/460; LH/254/337; /256/339; LI/183/226; LN/90/109; /228/292.
[63] The estate comprised 605 a. in Kilham and Rudston: ibid. LG/274/362; see below, p. 312.
[64] Ibid. 394/77/67; /78/68.
[65] Ibid. 644/132/115; local inf.
[66] V.C.H. Yorks. ii. 282, 323.
[67] Rot. de Ob. et Fin. 54.
[68] Feud. Aids, vi. 31; the 'barony' may refer to Skirpenbeck, the seat of the Chauncy family.
[69] Ibid. 142, 211.
[70] B.M. Add. MS. 26729, f. 115d.
[71] E 151/317/17; Cal. Pat. 1354–8, 341; Abbrev. Rot. Orig. ii. 242, 302.
[72] Cal. Inq. p.m. xi, p. 285.
[73] C.P. 40/482 m. 434d; E 179/202/84; C 136/103/33; C 139/157/22.
[74] K.B. 26/142 m. 27d; /143 m.3.
[75] K.B. 26/168 m. 1; 176 m. 27d; Rot. Hund. i. 114.
[76] K.B. 26/176 m. 27d; Yorks. Fines, 1272–1300, 89.
[77] Yorks. Fines, 1300–14, 21.
[78] Cal. Inq. p.m. vi, p. 133.
[79] Feud. Aids, vi. 267.
[80] Yorks. Fines, iii. 143; iv. 70, 99.
[81] See p. 253.
[82] Yorks. Fines, 1300–14, 67; see above, p. 180.
[83] E.R.R.O., DDHU/17/6; C 139/162/16; Cal. Close, 1318–23, 659; Cal. Inq. p.m. vi, p. 480; vii, pp. 289–92; Yorks. Inq. Hen. IV–V, 20.
[84] E 310/31/188 no. 69; Valor Eccl. (Rec. Com.), v. 248.

wife Agnes, daughter of John of Kilham.[85] The land was let by the Crown to Robert Thorpe in 1569 and to Thomas Scudamore in 1585.[86] It was still in the Crown's hands in 1602, when it was in the occupation of Thomas and Edward Johnson.[87] Its further descent has not been traced.

Bridlington priory held a small estate. In 1277 Henry of Bolton gave it 2 bovates[88] and, probably also during the 13th century, Christine Buzenant and Robert Wiles each granted 2 bovates.[89] After the Dissolution the estate, then comprising 5 bovates, was let by the Crown to Thomas Scudamore in 1568–9 and to Thomas Brandsby in 1576.[90] The priory of Arden (Yorks. N.R.) was granted 1⅛ bovate by Geoffrey de Thorny in 1252.[91] After the Dissolution the holding, comprising 2¾ bovates, was let to Martin Garret in 1563, Thomas Scudamore in 1568–9, and Thomas Johnson in 1585.[92] In 1585 land in Kilham formerly belonging to St. William's college, York, was let to Thomas Johnson.[93]

In 1086 9 carucates in Swaythorpe, held before the Conquest by Forne, were in the hands of Otes Arblaster.[94] Probably as early as 1115–18,[95] and certainly by 1166, the estate formed part of the Chauncy fee.[96] The overlordship passed from Thomas Chauncy to William of Melton in 1356 and thereafter descended with Kilham manor.[97]

Early demesne tenants included Jordan Foliothe, who gave land in Swaythorpe to St. Peter's hospital, York, in 1160–70,[98] and Walter of Warter, who gave a toft to the hospital in 1190–1210.[99] The Thwing family is first referred to in the township in 1289, when Marmaduke of Thwing was confirmed in possession of a third part of SWAYTHORPE manor.[1] The estate descended with the Thwing land in Kilham[2] and passed with it from Sir Thomas Heneage to the Crown in 1588.[3] Its further descent has not been traced but it presumably passed to the Griffith family.

Sir Walter Griffith held 4 bovates in Swaythorpe at his death in 1481,[4] and more land was later acquired by the Griffiths.[5] The estate, known as Swaythorpe manor, descended with Burton Agnes[6] to Sir Henry Griffith, who sold it in 1653, when it apparently comprised virtually the whole township, to John Anlaby. In 1653 or 1654 Anlaby sold it to Durand Hotham[7] and it descended in the Hotham family[8] until between 1856 and 1862, when it passed to Sir Charles Legard; it then consisted of 777 a.[9]

Sir Algernon Legard sold the estate in 1911 to Harold Wrigley,[10] and the Wrigleys have since retained it.

About 1225 Robert de Meynell granted to Walter of Thirkleby 2 carucates in Swaythorpe,[11] and together with the Thirkleby estate in Kilham the property passed to the Salvins.[12] By 1345 the estate comprised 20 bovates.[13] Part, at least, descended to William Salvin, who in 1533 sold property in Swaythorpe to Marmaduke Constable, of Wassand.[14] Its descent has not been traced further.

The rectory was appropriated by the dean of York in the 13th century[15] and let by him in 1532 to Bartholomew Thwing, in 1542 to Thomas Ledes, in 1596 to Timothy Hutton,[16] in 1617 to Sir Timothy Hutton, and in 1629 and 1638 to Francis Thompson.[17] The Thompson family remained lessees until the early 19th century. In 1645 the rectory was said to have been worth £160 a year before the Civil War; the lessee then paid an annuity of £50 to Henry Thompson, a York alderman.[18] In 1650 the gross value was £250, and the rent was paid to the Commonwealth.[19] In 1692 the rectory was said to be worth about £300[20] and in 1728 tithes were worth £268 and 8 bovates of glebe £18.[21]

In 1760 Richard Thompson sold half of his lease to Joshua Wilson[22] and at inclosure in 1773 Thompson was allotted 532 a. and a rent-charge of £102 10s. for tithes in Kilham, and Wilson 418 a. and £102 10s. They also received 47 a. and 41 a. respectively in lieu of the glebe, then known as 'Proctor lands'. The Swaythorpe tithes were not commuted at that time,[23] and from at least 1796 until 1844 they were let to the Hotham family.[24] In the latter year they were commuted for £256 7s. 6d.[25]

The Thompsons continued as lessees of half the rectory until 1835, when it was let to John Singleton.[26] Joshua Wilson's lease of the other half was renewed in 1796, but in 1814 and 1817 the property was let to the trustees of the Revd. Francis Drake.[27] In 1844 the rectory was transferred to the Ecclesiastical Commissioners,[28] and they have since retained it.

ECONOMIC HISTORY. In 1086 at least three of the four estates in Kilham were waste, namely those held by the king as soke of Driffield manor, by Otes Arblaster, and by Ernuin. Otes's estate had been worth £1 in 1066. The king's estate of 3 carucates

---

[85] V.C.H. Yorks. N.R. i. 320; see above, p. 254.
[86] E 310/31/188 no. 69; E 310/33/202 no. 58.
[87] E 134/45 Eliz. Hil./16.
[88] Yorks. Fines, 1272–1300, 10; Bridlington Charty. 147–8.
[89] Bridlington Charty. 7, 145–6, 149; see above, p. 254.
[90] E 310/30/181 no. 75; E 310/32/196 no. 42.
[91] Cal. Chart. R. 1226–59, 382.
[92] E 310/28/164 no. 9; /32/196 no. 42; /33/202 no. 58.
[93] E 310/33/202 no. 58.
[94] V.C.H. Yorks. ii. 282, 323.
[95] Ibid. 183.
[96] E.Y.C. ii, p. 175.
[97] C 143/317/17; Cal. Pat. 1354–8, 341; see above, p. 252.
[98] E.Y.C. ii, p. 189.
[99] Ibid. pp. 189–90.
[1] Yorks. Fines, 1272–1300, 87.
[2] See p. 253.
[3] Yorks. Fines, iii, 93.
[4] C 140/80/43.
[5] E.R.R.O., DDWB/17/1; Yorks. Fines, i. 101.
[6] See p. 108.
[7] E.R.R.O., DDHO/38/2; /70/8.
[8] Ibid. /21/23; /37/3; /70/15, 22, 37; /71/5.
[9] Regy. of Deeds, KT/328/449; 134/290/265; Sheahan and Whellan, Hist. York & E.R. ii. 482.
[10] Regy. of Deeds, 134/290/265.
[11] Hist. MSS. Com. lxix, Middleton, p. 60.
[12] See p. 254.
[13] C.P. 40/337 m. 74.
[14] Yorks. Fines, i. 66.
[15] See p. 259.
[16] D. & C. York, Torre MS. 'York Minster'.
[17] Ibid. S 3 (5) b, pp. 17, 101; S 1 (1) f.
[18] Royalist Composition Papers, i (Y.A.S. Rec. Ser. xv), 10.
[19] T.E.R.A.S. ii. 56.
[20] C 5/197/25.
[21] D. & C. York, S 3 (5) a, p. 11.
[22] Ibid. S 3 (5) c, p. 48d.
[23] E.R.R.O., DDDU/11/12.
[24] D. & C. York, S 1 (1) e, p. 44; B.I.H.R., TA. 543S.
[25] B.I.H.R., TA. 543S.
[26] D. & C. York, S 1 (1) e, p. 43; E.R.R.O., DDDU/11/217; Registry of Deeds, Beverley, EX/275/311; /276/313.
[27] D. & C. York, S 1 (1) e, p. 44.
[28] Lond. Gaz. 19 July 1844, pp. 2499–2505.

and 2 bovates had land for three ploughs and was worth £2 before the Conquest. Ernuin's 30-carucate estate, together with 10 carucates in Harpham and Gransmoor, contained land for 20 ploughs and had been worth £15 in 1066. At Swaythorpe, Otes Arblaster's estate had land for nine ploughs and had been worth £1 before the Conquest, but in 1086 it, too, was waste.[29]

Customary tenants were numerous on the capital manor in the 14th and 15th centuries. In 1362, for example, 22 tenants held 220 bovates and paid £22 rent, as well as performing 80 autumn works and other boon-works worth £4 a year, and in 1420–1 the rents of tenants-at-will amounted to about £14. In both years the demesne lands, mills, and tolls were let at farm, producing about £11 in 1420–1.[30] In 1530 32 tenants-at-will paid about £44;[31] in 1718 22 customary tenants paid about £200 and in 1752 16 paid about £300.[32] These tenants held meadow and pasture, the mills, and 60–70 bovates of arable land, including the demesne. There were about 10 landless cottagers and a few tenants held only pasture or meadow. The largest open-field holding contained 12½ bovates in 1530 and 20½ in 1752, and the average size of a holding was respectively 4 and 11 bovates in those years.

From the 15th to the 18th century free rents on the capital manor amounted to about £20–£25. There were 44 free tenants in 1530, about 25 in the earlier 18th century, and about 20 in the 19th century.[33]

After the Dissolution tenants of the former Bridlington priory estate in Kilham held by copy of court roll and were still obliged to carry stone for the repair of the piers at Bridlington.[34]

The open-field area of Kilham was apparently divided from an early date into two large fields, lying on the wold slopes north and south of the village. They are first named in the early 14th century, North field c. 1317 and South field in 1320.[35] They were later subdivided and known from at least the early 17th century as the North Side and the South Side fields.[36] The East and West fields, mentioned in 1608,[37] were apparently part of the North and South Side fields.[38] In 1362 there were at least 249 bovates of open-field land in Kilham.[39] At inclosure in 1773 3,960 a. were allotted from the North Side and 2,995 a. from the South Side fields.[40]

In 1729 there were 29 'fields' or furlongs in the North Side fields and 18 in the South Side. A rotation of crops, based on groups of furlongs, was practised in each of the Sides.[41] In 1639 the number of bylawmen was apparently increased and thenceforward there were to be six, three responsible for each Side,[42] and they regulated the cropping of groups of furlongs each year. Because not all farmers held equal amounts of land in both Sides, a field of a particular crop assigned on one Side had to be duplicated on the other.[43]

It is possible that part of the open fields was not regularly cultivated and that, in the 18th century at least, an infield-outfield system was practised. In 1740 an inhabitant was fined for trespassing in 'the South Side outfield',[44] and in the mid 19th century areas in the north-east and north-west of Kilham were known as Out field.[45]

Swaythorpe apparently had its own open fields in the Middle Ages. The 'common field' there is mentioned in 1421, when two waste tenements and 1½ bovate were delimited.[46] The township probably suffered severely from the Black Death,[47] but a yeoman still had a plough there in 1437[48] and a toft, croft, and 4 bovates were recorded in 1482.[49] The township may have been finally depopulated by the Griffith family in the late 15th or 16th century.[50] In 1545 a ruined house and four tofts were mentioned, together with 12 bovates,[51] but by the early 17th century the whole township had apparently been converted to pasture. In 1621 'a sheep pasture called Swaythorpe' was held by Henry Griffith.[52] From at least the early 18th century the township was cultivated as one farm,[53] and it was subdivided into closes by the mid 19th century.[54]

Meadow land lay mainly in the valleys. In 1362 8 a. of demesne meadow was recorded,[55] and in 1530 the demesne included meadow called Mill leys and Bridlington leys.[56] In 1620 the occupiers of Mill leys were required to provide gates for the passage of carts; it lay south-east of the village, beside Lowthorpe beck.[57] In 1771 Mill leys was commonable each year from 10 October to 5 April.[58] Hall ings, also part of the demesne in 1530, lay west of the village near the Langtoft road.[59] Meadow or pasture called the Crofts was recorded in 1675.[60]

Much of the pasture in Kilham probably lay on the higher wold slopes on the periphery of the township. In 1293 200 a. of pasture belonged to the manor.[61] In 1340 a manorial rabbit warren was mentioned[62] and in 1362 the demesne included a warren and a pasture called Burrow.[63] In 1420–1 a demesne pasture called 'Birhowe' lay in the west 'between the fields of Kilham and Langtoft'.[64] The warren and the Burrow were also recorded in 1455[65] and 1530,[66] and the Burrow is referred to until the early 17th century.[67]

Areas called the Cow pastures lay within both the

---

[29] V.C.H. Yorks. ii. 197, 204, 282, 287.
[30] B.M. Harl. Roll H. 12; Cal. Inq. p.m. xi, p. 285.
[31] E.R.R.O., DDDU/12/48.
[32] Ibid. /50.
[33] Ibid. /48, 50–1; B.M. Harl. Roll H. 12.
[34] E 310/28/164 no. 9.
[35] E.R.R.O., DDCC/55/4, 5.
[36] Ibid. /3; DDDU/11/59.
[37] L.R. 2/229 f. 258.
[38] E.R.R.O., DDDU/11/12; /12/53; an area in the west of the parish was known as Kilham West field in the mid 19th century: O.S. Map 6" (1854).
[39] Cal. Inq. p.m. xi, p. 285.
[40] E.R.R.O., DDDU/11/12.
[41] Ibid. /12/54; A. Harris, Open Fields of E. Yorks. (E. Yorks. Loc. Hist. Ser. ix), 7–8.
[42] E.R.R.O., DDDU/12/3.
[43] Ibid.; Harris, op. cit. 7.
[44] E.R.R.O., DDDU/12/2; Harris, op. cit. 7.
[45] O.S. Map 6" (1854).
[46] T.E.R.A.S. xix. 20.
[47] E 179/202/53.
[48] Monastic Notes, i (Y.A.S. Rec. Ser. xvii), 250.
[49] C 140/80/43.
[50] See p. 255.
[51] E.R.R.O., DDWB/17/1.
[52] Hull Univ. Libr. MS. DWB/9/1.
[53] E.R.R.O., DDHO/14/16–46, 53–4.
[54] O.S. Map 6" (1854).
[55] Cal. Inq. p.m. xi, p. 285.
[56] E.R.R.O., DDDU/12/48.
[57] Ibid. /3, 53.
[58] 11 Geo. III, c. 44 (Priv. Act).
[59] E.R.R.O., DDDU/12/3, 48.
[60] Ibid. DDSY/36/2.
[61] Plac. de Quo Warr. (Rec. Com.), 213.
[62] Cal. Pat. 1338–40, 494.
[63] Cal. Inq. p.m. xi, p. 285.
[64] B.M. Harl. Roll H. 12.
[65] C 139/157/22.
[66] E.R.R.O., DDDU/12/48.
[67] Ibid. DC/53/3451, 3461; C 142/273/82; Yorks. Fines, iii. 98; 1614–25, 55.

BRIDLINGTON: the Alexandra Hotel

FILEY: the Crescent

GANTON CHURCH

LANGTOFT CHURCH: the sedilia

North and South Side fields in 1620 and the bylawmen were responsible for regulating them. Each inhabitant had common rights on whichever pasture lay within the Side containing most of his land.[68] The Horse pasture was mentioned in 1721, when it was stipulated that only draft oxen were to be pastured there.[69] In 1814, after inclosure, about 200 a. were said to have been 'lately called the Sheep pasture'[70] and in the mid 19th century an area in the west of the parish between York Road and the Langtoft road was known as the Sheepwalk.[71] Enroachments on the commons are recorded in 1631 and 1633, when men were ordered to restore grassland which they had ploughed from 'the lord's waste' and from balks between furlongs. In 1620 whins growing in the West field should have been taken only with the lord's permission.[72]

The inhabitants had pasture rights on all the commons and on the open fields after harvest. In 1620 the stint was one beast or horse and 10 sheep for each bovate, 10 sheep for each house, and 5 sheep for each cottage. As early as 1620 the large number of cottagers with common rights was causing concern, and inhabitants of cottages built since 1591 were then denied such rights. The stint for cattle was reduced in 1721 to one beast or two young animals for every 3 bovates. Provision was made in 1734 for the letting of unused gates.[73]

There was apparently little early inclosure of commonable land. The demesne in 1530 included Hall garth, Great close, and Stroms, and there were then also seven closes in the hands of tenants-at-will.[74] All these closes were, however, confined to the area of crofts and garths around the village.[75]

Proposals for a partial inclosure of the open fields were made c. 1770, by which some land would have remained uninclosed but in consolidated 'flats'.[76] A full inclosure was nevertheless decided upon and an Act secured in 1771.[77] Despite the hostility of the vicar,[78] inclosure took place in 1773.[79] Commonable land to be inclosed amounted to 7,107 a., and 7,003 a. were actually allotted. John Preston, as lord of the manor, was awarded 1,175 a. Richard Thompson received 1,490 a., as well as 579 a. for tithes and glebe, and Joshua Wilson received 762 a., together with 459 a. for tithes and glebe. Thompson and Wilson were each directed to build a farm-house on their rectorial allotments to replace buildings on the glebe. The vicar received 82 a. in lieu of tithes. There were three other large allotments: John Outram got 684 a., Ralph Creyke 655 a., and Foord Newton 291 a. There were also 3 allotments of 100 a.–200 a., 3 of 50 a.–100 a., 3 of 10 a.–50 a., and 21 of under 10 a. each.

In 1801 2,421 a. in Kilham were under crops, mainly barley (767 a.), oats (607 a.), wheat (517 a.), and turnips or rape (413 a.).[80] Cinquefoil and grass seeds were sown on Thomas Duesbery's estate c. 1813. About 200 a. of Duesbery's land in the north-east of the parish were still in one large allotment, although under arable cultivation; subdivision took place soon after.[81] It was reported c. 1830 that the introduction of bone manure and turnips within the previous 15–20 years had greatly improved farming at Kilham.[82] In 1905 about 6,500 a. there were under arable, 1,000 a. were grassland, and 89 a. woodland.[83]

The number of farmers in the parish in the 19th and 20th centuries has varied between 22 and 33. Some farms were very large: Swaythorpe farm, for example, has comprised about 770 a. since at least the earlier 18th century, and Kilham West Field farm covered 802 a. in 1913.[84] In 1921 14 farms had acreages of 150 or over and 11 were smaller; in 1937 there were 11 large farms and 22 smaller.[85] Swaythorpe farm was nominated the best-managed farm in Yorkshire in 1839 by the Yorkshire Central Agricultural Society.[86] In 1844 it comprised 586 a. of arable, 171 a. of grassland, and 6 a. of woodland.[87]

A 237-acre farm was bought by the county council in 1910 and divided into eighteen smallholdings, mostly between 7 a. and 20 a. each.[88] In 1937 there were nine smallholders in Kilham.[89] In 1823 a gardener and seedsman and in the 1840s two cattle-dealers and a horse-dealer were recorded.[90] A market-gardener was first mentioned in 1872 and in the later 19th and 20th centuries there have usually been from 2 to 5 of them.[91] There was a large turkey farm in 1970.

As a market centre Kilham no doubt had tradesmen and shopkeepers who served the surrounding countryside. In 1420–1 the lord of the manor owned several shops, including four newly-built in the east part of the village,[92] and a shop was held by St. Lawrence's chantry in 1535.[93] There are several references to shops during the 17th century;[94] mercers were recorded in 1619 and 1641, and grocers in 1671.[95] One grocer, Robert Gibson, issued a trade token in 1667.[96] In the 18th century, in addition to the usual village craftsmen and tradesmen, an apothecary, a glazier, a mantua-maker, several weavers, a brick-layer, and a 'mechanic' were recorded.[97] In 1764 a large section of the population was said to consist of 'poor handicrafts'.[98] Glovers, a fellmonger, a book-seller, surgeons, a druggist, a tinner, a watch-maker, a veterinary surgeon, and a builder were all mentioned in the 19th century. A cycle-maker, mentioned in 1909,

---

[68] E.R.R.O., DDDU/12/3.
[69] Ibid. /4.
[70] Ibid. /11/21.
[71] O.S. Map 6" (1854).
[72] E.R.R.O., DDDU/12/3.
[73] Ibid. /3, 4.
[74] Ibid. /48.
[75] Ibid. /3, 53.
[76] Ibid. DDX/40/190.
[77] 11 Geo. III, c. 44 (Priv. Act).
[78] Olga Wilkinson, *Agric. Revolution in E.R. Yorks.* (E. Yorks. Loc. Hist. Ser. v), 8–9.
[79] E.R.R.O., DDDU/11/12.
[80] 1801 Crop Returns.
[81] E.R.R.O., DDDU/11/255; A. Harris, *Rural Landscape of E.R. Yorks.* 67–8.
[82] E.R.R.O., DDDU/11/218.
[83] Acreage Returns, 1905.
[84] E.R.R.O., DDHO/14/16–46, 53–4; Registry of Deeds, Beverley, 160/190/165.
[85] Directories.
[86] Sheahan and Whellan, *Hist. York & E.R.* ii. 482.
[87] B.I.H.R., TA. 543S.
[88] E.R.C.C. *Mins.* 1910–11, 69, 399, 401.
[89] *Kelly's Dir. N. & E.R. Yorks.* (1937), 490–1.
[90] Baines, *Hist. Yorks.* (1823), ii. 360; White, *Dir. E. & N.R. Yorks.* (1840), 392; (1846), 445–6.
[91] Directories.
[92] B.M. Harl. Roll H. 12.
[93] *Valor Eccl.* (Rec. Com.), v. 120; see below, p. 260.
[94] E.R.R.O., DDDU/11/80; /12/3.
[95] Ibid. /11/59, 63; DC/10/195.
[96] P. Whitting, *Coins, Tokens and Medals of E.R. Yorks.* (E. Yorks. Loc. Hist. Ser. xxv), 26.
[97] E.R.R.O., PR. 2015.
[98] B.I.H.R., Bp. V. 1764/Ret. 85.

had become an engineer by 1913, and the business survived until c. 1930. A carter and wagonette proprietor, recorded from 1909 to 1921, gave way to a haulage contractor in the late 1920s and 1930s.[99] In 1971 there was a firm of agricultural engineers and also a coal merchant.

Several individual occupations are especially noteworthy. The first evidence of rope-making in the parish is in 1739.[1] A ropery was established c. 1825[2] and by 1840 there were two rope-makers.[3] In the mid 19th century one ropery lay in East Street and another south of the village in Driffield Lane.[4] One apparently ceased to exist between 1879 and 1889.[5] The other, in East Street and adjoining the Burton Fleming road, was owned by the Kilham Rope Company in the 1890s and 1900s, and was run from the 1920s by the Harrison family.[6] It ceased to exist in the late 1930s or early 1940s.[7]

Brick-making was first recorded in 1743, when a Kilham man paid the lord of the manor for the privilege.[8] A brick- and tile-maker was recorded in 1823[9] and ten years later a brickyard.[10] In the mid 19th century the yard was situated south of the Rudston road, east of the village,[11] and bricks, draining tiles, and pantiles were all made.[12] It apparently ceased to be used in the early 20th century.[13]

Malting is first explicitly mentioned in 1758, when a former malt-kiln was used as a barn,[14] but kilns recorded from the 16th century onwards may have been for drying corn or malt.[15] A malt-kiln, worth £7 a year, was mentioned in 1863.[16] A steam brewery was established in 1840 and it survived as a combined brewery and malting until at least 1897. The buildings, including the stump of the chimney, still stood in East Street in 1971. A smaller brewery was established in 1852 and apparently survived until the 1890s.[17]

A mill in Kilham is first mentioned in 1200.[18] By 1293 the archbishop of Rouen held two mills,[19] and a windmill and a water-mill belonged to the manor in 1362.[20] The bylaws of 1620 included an obligation on the lessees of the water-mill to maintain paths and bridges leading to it.[21] There were still both water- and windmills in 1694[22] but the former is not mentioned again. It stood on Lowthorpe beck, south of Beck Head. By the mid 19th century a windmill stood in the south of the village, in Mill Back Side,[23] and a miller was recorded throughout the 19th and early 20th centuries. By 1889 wind was supplemented by steam power and by 1937 the mill was powered solely by oil.[24] It became disused soon after;[25] the miller's house and the brick tower still stood in 1971.

MARKET AND FAIRS. From the 13th to the 19th century Kilham filled the role of a regional market centre. A Tuesday market and an annual fair on 9 and 10 August were granted to the chapter of Rouen in 1227.[26] In 1334, however, William of Melton received a grant of a Saturday market and two annual fairs, one lasting from 9 to 11 August and the other from 29 October to 3 November.[27] Only the market and the three-day fair were mentioned in 1362.[28] In 1455, however, both fairs were recorded, though the second was then held from 31 October to 1 November.[29] Between 1723 and 1790 the dates of the fairs were changed to 21 August and 12 November[30] and by 1770 the market-day was Thursday.[31] From at least the earlier 17th until the mid 19th century the November fair was also a statute fair for the hiring of servants.[32] A market was apparently still held in 1792,[33] but by 1823 it was said to have 'long declined' and to be 'wholly disused'.[34] Both fairs still survived in 1872[35] but by 1888 they had ceased to exist.[36]

Tolls from the market and fairs were received by the lord of the manor.[37] During the 18th century the manorial officers usually included two market-searchers,[38] and stall-gear was kept in a toll-house. The tolls are first specified in the early 18th century[39] and the rates were the same in 1814, when inhabitants of Kilham were exempt from tolls on livestock, though not from stallage.[40] Open stalls were used at the August fair but in November the stalls were covered. Between 1719 and 1725 the tolls were let for £10 a year, but thereafter they steadily decreased[41] and by 1833 they were worth only £5.[42] Accounts of fair tolls survive for 1814–16.[43]

Panniermen sold fish at the market in 1620.[44] Henry Best of Elmswell noted in 1641 that the November fair at Kilham was the last of the year in the area and consequently the prices of produce and livestock were 'a rule for the country until the next

---

[99] Directories.
[1] E.R.R.O., PR. 2015.
[2] Sheahan and Whellan, *Hist. York & E.R.* ii. 481.
[3] White, *Dir. E. & N.R. Yorks.* (1840), 392.
[4] O.S. Map 6″ (1854).
[5] *Kelly's Dir. N. & E.R. Yorks.* (1879), 612; (1889), 415.
[6] Directories; O.S. Map 25″ (1910).
[7] Local inf.
[8] E.R.R.O., DDDU/12/50.
[9] Baines, *Hist. Yorks.* ii. 360.
[10] E.R.R.O., PR. 2029.
[11] O.S. Map 6″ (1854).
[12] Sheahan and Whellan, *Hist. York & E.R.* ii. 481.
[13] Directories; O.S. Map 6″ (1892, 1911).
[14] Regy. of Deeds, AA/66/130.
[15] Ibid. G/200/452; E.R.R.O., DDDU/12/48; E 301/66 no. 156; L.R. 2/229 f. 255; C 142/667/176.
[16] E.R.R.O., PR. 2029.
[17] Sheahan and Whellan, *Hist. York & E.R.* ii. 481; directories.
[18] *Cur. Reg. R.* i. 215; *Rot. de Ob. et Fin.* (Rec. Com.), 54.
[19] *Plac. de Quo Warr.* 213.
[20] *Cal. Inq. p.m.* xi, p. 285; for later references see C 136/103/33; B.M. Harl. Roll H. 12; E.R.R.O., DDDU/12/48.
[21] E.R.R.O., DDDU/12/3.
[22] Ibid. /11/80.
[23] O.S. Map 6″ (1854).
[24] *Kelly's Dir. N. & E.R. Yorks.* (1889), 415–6; (1937), 49.
[25] Local inf.
[26] *Cal. Chart. R.* 1226–57, 46; *Rot. Litt. Claus.* ii (Rec. Com.), 191.
[27] *Cal. Chart. R.* 1327–41, 310.
[28] *Cal. Inq. p.m.* xi, p. 285.
[29] C 139/157/22.
[30] E.R.R.O., DDDU/12/50; QSF. Mich. 1790, E.9.
[31] *Yorks. Fairs and Mkts.* (Thoresby Soc. xxxix), 175.
[32] *Farming Bk. of Hen. Best of Elmswell* (Sur. Soc. xxxiii), 135; Sheahan and Whellan, *Hist. York & E.R.* ii. 481.
[33] *1st Rep. Royal Com. Mkt. Rights and Tolls*, Vol. i, [C.5550], p. 218, H.C. (1888), liii.
[34] Baines, *Hist. Yorks.* ii. 359.
[35] *Kelly's Dir. N. & E.R. Yorks.* (1872), 511.
[36] *1st Rep. Royal Com. Mkt. Rights and Tolls*, i. 218.
[37] C 136/103/33.
[38] E.R.R.O., DDDU/12/52.
[39] Ibid. /50.
[40] Ibid. /11/211.
[41] Ibid. /12/50.
[42] Ibid. PR. 2029.
[43] Ibid. DDDU/11/236.
[44] Ibid. /12/3.

spring'. At that fair he sold foals, old horses, and all sorts of sheep. Kilham's situation 'betwixt Holderness and the Wolds' increased its importance as a sheep market, for lowland farmers acquired stock there.[45] The main livestock fair in the early 19th century was still apparently that held in November. At the August fair in 1816 there were no sheep, 'and seldom are any at this fair', and no horses.[46] In 1840, however, both fairs were said to be 'well supplied with all kinds of cattle'.[47] In the early 19th century tradesmen from Kilham and elsewhere had stalls at the fairs. At the August fair in 1814 shoemakers had eighteen stalls and there were also hardware, cheese, and cap stalls.[48]

The site of the markets and fairs is not certainly known. There may have been a fairground south of the main street,[49] but both the markets and the fairs may have been held in the wide part of Church Street south and east of the church. A by-law of 1620 obliged householders and shopkeepers in East Gate to cleanse the street in front of their premises before a fair, and stalls were prohibited in the streets without licence. The 'market-place' is also mentioned in 1620.[50] A market cross stood in Kilham in 1721[51] but had apparently been removed by the mid 19th century.[52] A cross now in Lowthorpe churchyard is said to be from Kilham market-place.[53]

LOCAL GOVERNMENT. As lord of Kilham the archbishop of Rouen claimed various franchises, including infangtheof, gallows, tumbril, and the assize of bread and ale.[54] In 1303 there was a prison, presumably franchisal, in the village.[55] Gallows hill, a barrow south-west of the village, may have been the place of execution. When excavated it was found to have been disturbed at the centre, perhaps when a gallows was erected, and there were some shallow burials upon it, possibly medieval.[56]

There are surviving rolls of pains and by-laws 'anciently made' by the manorial court and enrolled in 1620, with additions and amendments to 1734; another roll records pains between 1793 and 1811.[57] There is also a 17th-century list of articles of inquiry to be made by the court jury.[58] The by-laws concern the usual agricultural and domestic matters and also deal with the appointment and functions of officers, infringements of the assize, the exclusion of strangers liable to become a burden on the parish, and the administration of the market and fairs. It was stipulated that every occupier of land should carry a cart-load of stone for each bovate held, under the direction of the surveyors of highways, for the repair of the roads. Other officers mentioned include the bylawmen. In 1639 it was laid down that there should be six of them, three to regulate the North Side and three the South Side fields. They were to be chosen from among inhabitants whose land lay wholly or mainly within the fields for which they were to be responsible.[59] Meetings of the bylawmen were to be convened by the pinder. Constables were to render an annual list of the parish armour, in addition to their own accounts. The parish neat-herd was also mentioned.

There are surviving court records, mainly estreats of amercements, jury papers, and call rolls, for the periods 1703–1813 and 1852–66.[60] The court dealt mainly with agricultural offences and petty misdemeanors. After inclosure in 1773 there were fewer presentments and in many years none at all. Throughout the 18th century the officers generally appointed were 2 constables, 6 bylawmen, 2 market-searchers, and a pinder. In the earlier 18th century there were also occasional references to 2 water-searchers, 2 affeerors, and a swine-herd. Bylawmen were last mentioned in 1771, just before inclosure. The other officers continued to be appointed until at least 1813.

Churchwardens' accounts and vestry minutes survive for the period 1833–1902.[61] There were always two churchwardens. In the 18th and early 19th centuries there were also two overseers of the poor.[62] There were poorhouses in the churchyard by 1702,[63] and in 1764 a poorhouse there was described as an old thatched building of brick and mud, divided into three one-roomed tenements, which had been built by the parish about ten years earlier.[64] It was presumably another poorhouse which was said in 1783 to have been recently built on 'the Greens'.[65] It was reported in 1822 that money left by Robert and Jonas Thompson had been used to buy a poorhouse, and in that year a poorhouse was still being maintained by the parish.[66] In 1836 Kilham joined the Driffield union.[67]

CHURCH. Between 1100 and 1108 Kilham church was granted to the see of York by the king, who between *c.* 1119 and 1129 directed that it should be enjoyed by the dean. It was confirmed to the dean by the archbishop[68] and it remained a peculiar of the deanery until 1844, when it was vested in the Ecclesiastical Commissioners.[69] A vicarage was ordained in 1252.[70] A chapel at Swaythorpe, dedicated to St. Leonard, was mentioned for the first time in 1348 and for the last in 1388.[71]

The advowson of Kilham belonged to the dean of York[72] until 1868, when it was transferred to the

---

[45] *Farming Bk. of Hen. Best of Elmswell*, 30, 114; Harris, *Rural Landscape*, 33.
[46] E.R.R.O., DDDU/11/236.
[47] White, *Dir. E. & N.R. Yorks.* (1840), 392.
[48] E.R.R.O., DDDU/11/236.
[49] See p. 249.
[50] E.R.R.O., DDDU/12/3.
[51] Regy. of Deeds, H/107/225.
[52] O.S. Map 6" (1854).
[53] *T.E.R.A.S.* iv. 2 n.; see below, p. 277.
[54] J.I. 1/1110 m. 78.
[55] *Cal. Pat.* 1301–7, 177.
[56] Ex inf. Mr. T. C. M. Brewster, 1971.
[57] E.R.R.O., DDDU/12/3–5.
[58] Ibid. /55.
[59] See p. 256.
[60] E.R.R.O., DDDU/12/1, 2, 6–47, 52.
[61] Ibid., PR. 2029.
[62] Ibid. DDDU/11/16; /12/51.
[63] Ibid., PR. 2017.
[64] B.I.H.R., Bp. V. 1764/Ret. 85.
[65] E.R.R.O., DDDU/11/16; see above, p. 249.
[66] *9th Rep. Char. Com.* 736; see below, p. 263.
[67] *3rd Rep. Poor Law Com.* 168.
[68] *E.Y.C.* i, pp. 333–7.
[69] *Lond. Gaz.* 19 July 1844, pp. 2499–2505.
[70] *Reg. Gray* (Sur. Soc. lvi), 211, 213.
[71] *Yorks. Fines, 1347–77*, 14; *Cal. Inq. p.m.* xiv, pp. 56–8; *Cal. Pat.* 1385–9, 445.
[72] C 5/197/25; D. & C. York, S 1 (1) e, pp. 43–4; E.R.R.O., DDDU/11/217; *Fasti Parochiales*, iii. 50–1. In 1388 Roger of Fulthorpe gave his son Thomas the advowson of Kilham: *Cal. Inq. Misc.* v, p. 14; it was presumably held by grant from the dean.

Crown,[73] which still held it in 1971.[74] The advowson of Swaythorpe chapel was held by Thomas Thwing from at least 1348 until his death in 1374.[75]

At ordination in 1252 the vicar was assigned the usual small tithes and oblations, except wool and lamb tithes, the three main oblations, the tithe of mills, flax, and hemp, and mortuaries in livestock.[76] In 1535 the vicarage was worth £6 net.[77] In 1645 the impropriator paid the vicar about £20 a year[78] and four years later the vicarage was augmented, though apparently only temporarily, with £50 a year out of Burton Agnes rectory.[79] In 1650 the vicarage was worth £15 8s. net.[80] In 1692 and throughout the 18th and much of the 19th centuries the impropriator paid the vicar £10 a year.[81] The vicarage was worth £35 in 1716.[82] The average net income in 1829–31 was £145[83] and in 1850 the living was worth £240.[84] It was endowed out of the common fund in 1863 with £84 a year[85] and in 1884 its net value was £243.[86]

In 1535 the income came wholly from tithes.[87] In 1716 it also included the rent of a close.[88] At inclosure in 1773 the vicar was awarded 82 a. and a rent-charge of 6s. 4d. a year for his Kilham tithes.[89] On the commutation of the Swaythorpe tithes in 1844 he received a rent-charge of £11.[90] The glebe was still held in 1971.

A vicarage house is first mentioned in 1571, when the vicar was accused of allowing an ale-house to be kept in it.[91] In 1578 it was in decay. It was again said to be in disrepair in 1663,[92] and c. 1700 the vicar planted trees in the close 'where the old house stood'.[93] In 1743 there was said to have been no vicarage house within living memory and the vicar rented a house.[94] In 1764 the vicar reported that he had built himself a house near the church.[95] There was no Vicarage, however, until one was built in 1860 in Driffield Lane.[96] The large red-brick house with yellow-brick bands and dressings was sold in 1959.[97]

A chantry certainly existed at Kilham, though there was some confusion as to its foundation and its location. In 1351 Alan Kilham was licensed to grant a house, £1 rent, and 6 bovates of land in Kilham to a chaplain to celebrate at the altar of St. Mary in the church of St. Lawrence.[98] The chantry is generally regarded as having been in the parish church of All Saints, and it was usually called St. Lawrence's chantry. When suppressed c. 1547, however, it was said to lie 1,000 ft. from the parish church, and it was thought to have been founded by the ancestors of the then lord of the manor.[99]

The chantry was worth £4 in 1525–6,[1] £3 6s. 8d. in 1535, when its property included 5 bovates of land,[2] and £3 17s. 4d. net in 1547.[3] Grants of its former property after the suppression include a 'guildhall' in 1563 and a close called Spittle garth in 1590.[4] The latter may at one time have belonged to or been the site of a hospital, mentioned in 1297 and 1333–4.[5] Spittle garth lay west of the village, beside the Langtoft road.[6] Four bovates of former chantry land were let to Martin Garret in 1563, and 5 bovates were let to Thomas Brandsby in 1576 and 1585[7] before being granted in fee to Richard Young and Thomas Lake in 1590.[8] By 1608 the land had been acquired by William Burtham[9] and in 1619 it passed to his son Nicholas.[10]

It was stipulated on the ordination of the vicarage in 1252 that the vicar should 'keep one chaplain always with him',[11] and in 1525–6 a chaplain had a stipend of £4 6s. 8d. a year.[12]

In 1662 the vicar also held the livings of Boynton and Carnaby.[13] In 1743 he lived at Thwing and served as curate there and at Rudston during the absence of the incumbents.[14] Between 1742 and 1764 he was also master of the grammar school.[15] An assistant curate was employed in 1774, when he was also usher of the school,[16] and in 1835.[17] In 1871 and 1884 the vicar, E.F.B.B. Fellowes, was non-resident and employed a curate;[18] his debts led to the sequestration of the church between 1871 and 1883.[19] In 1971 the vicar also held the livings of Lowthorpe and Ruston Parva,[20] and he lived at Lowthorpe.

In 1743 a service was usually held twice a week, although recently only one had been held because the vicar had also been serving Rudston church. Communion was administered five times a year and about 125 people had received the previous Easter.[21] In 1764 at least one service was held weekly. About thirty people usually communicated.[22] By 1865 there were regularly two services each week and communion was held every month with about fifteen communicants.[23] In 1884 communion was sometimes administered twice a month in summer,

---

[73] *Lond. Gaz.* 15 Sept. 1868, p. 4978.
[74] *Crockford.*
[75] *Yorks. Fines, 1347–77*, 14; *Cal. Inq. p.m.* xiv, pp. 53–8.
[76] *Reg. Gray*, 213.
[77] *Valor Eccl.* (Rec. Com.), v. 123.
[78] *Roy. Comp. Pap.* i. 10.
[79] *Cal. Cttee. for Compounding*, 162.
[80] *T.E.R.A.S.* ii. 56.
[81] C 5/197/25; B.I.H.R., TER. J. Kilham 1716 etc.
[82] B.I.H.R., TER. J. Kilham 1716.
[83] *Rep. Com. Eccl. Revenues*, 946–7.
[84] H.O. 129/24/523.
[85] *Lond. Gaz.* 28 July 1863, pp. 3735–6.
[86] B.I.H.R., Bp. V. 1884/Ret.
[87] *Valor Eccl.* v. 120.
[88] B.I.H.R., TER. J. Kilham 1716.
[89] E.R.R.O., DDDU/11/12.
[90] B.I.H.R., TA. 543S.
[91] J. S. Purvis, *Tudor Par. Docs. of Dioc. York*, 195.
[92] B.I.H.R., Churches index.
[93] E.R.R.O., PR. 2013.   [94] *Herring's Visit.* ii. 138–9.
[95] B.I.H.R., Bp. V. 1764/Ret. 85.
[96] Ibid. TER. J. Kilham 1861; *Rep. Com. Eccl. Revenues*, 946–7.
[97] Regy. of Deeds, 1157/242/222.
[98] C 143/304/4; *Cal. Pat.* 1350–4, 133.

[99] *Chantry Surv.* i (Sur. Soc. xci), 139; *Yorks. Deeds*, ix. 111.
[1] *Y.A.J.* xxiv. 69.   [2] *Valor Eccl.* v. 123.
[3] E 301/66 no. 56.
[4] C 66/1348 m. 5; *Cal. Pat.* 1563–6, 52.
[5] *Yorks. Lay Subsidy, 1297* (Y.A.S. Rec. Ser. xvi), 138; *Y.A.J.* xv. 205.
[6] E.R.R.O., DDDU/12/54.
[7] E 310/28/164 no. 9; E 310/30/181 no. 75; E 310/33/202 no. 6.
[8] C 66/1348 m. 5.   [9] L.R. 2/229 f. 254.
[10] C 142/670/103.
[11] *Reg. Gray*, 213.
[12] *Y.A.J.* xxiv. 69.
[13] *Fasti Parochiales*, iii. 51.
[14] *Herring's Visit.* iii. 173; see below, p. 329.
[15] B.I.H.R., Bp. V. 1764/Ret. 85; Schools index; see below, p. 262.
[16] D. & C. York, S 3 (5) d.
[17] *Rep. Com. Eccl. Revenues*, 946–7.
[18] B.I.H.R., V. 1871/Ret. 263; Bp. V. 1884/Ret.
[19] Ibid. Seq. 1871–83.
[20] *Crockford.*
[21] *Herring's Visit.* ii. 138–9.
[22] B.I.H.R., Bp. V. 1764/Ret. 85.
[23] Ibid. V. 1865/Ret. 289.

usually to about thirty people.[24] In 1936 a communion service was held every Sunday[25] and in 1971 there were two, sometimes three, services each Sunday.

The large church of ALL SAINTS is built of stone and consists of chancel, aisleless nave, west tower, and south porch. The wide nave is Norman and has an external corbel table on both sides, with several original corbels remaining. There are pilaster buttresses on the south side only. The windows are later insertions. The Norman south doorway, round-arched and of six orders, is one of the most notable features of the church. The outer orders and the enriched gable-shaped tympanum above the arch project forward from the nave wall, an arrangement which is obscured by the later addition of a porch. The tympanum is decorated with an all-over pattern of fluted herring-bone ornament and sunk lozenge-shaped panels, now incomplete. The orders of the arch all have chevron enrichment; some of the supporting shafts are missing but their capitals survive, carved with scallops, volutes, and, in one case, a human figure. Internally the nave is tall and spacious but retains no Norman features. Many stones with chevron carving, however, have been incorporated in the inner walls of the later tower. The circular font, said to have been rescued from a garden,[26] is also Norman, although apparently retooled; it is ornamented with incised arcading and, at the rim, with a half cable moulding.

The chancel was entirely rebuilt in the late 13th or early 14th century. It is as wide as the nave, austere and lofty. Prominent stepped buttresses support the walls externally. The east window and the three large windows on each side contain intersecting tracery. On the south side is a cinquefoil-headed piscina and three sedilia, all with 13th-century type mouldings, together with a priest's door. The wide chancel arch has shafted jambs with foliage capitals of fully-developed Decorated character. The shafts bear marks of the insertion of a rood screen.

The tall west tower probably dates from the early 15th century. It has an embattled parapet and is supported by diagonal buttresses. In the west wall is a pointed doorway with a hood-mould and a Perpendicular window. Above the window is a shield, surmounted by an ogee-canopied niche containing what is apparently a bishop's mitre. The arms on the shield may be those of William Grey (dean of York, 1421–5), who in 1425 became bishop of London.[27] The tall tower arch is of two chamfered orders, the chamfers being carried down the jambs without capitals. Flanking the arch the two western angles of the nave are cut off by diagonal walls behind which staircases are housed; an ogee-headed doorway at the north-west corner gives access to one of them. High up in the south wall near the east end of the nave is a small blocked window, perhaps intended to light the rood. The large south porch, the building of which damaged the Norman doorway, may have originated in the 15th century. In the later 19th century is was described as 'partly of stone, part of wood'.[28] It is now extensively patched with brick and exhibits no medieval features.

In 1568 the glass in the nave windows was broken and two years later the church was 'in some decay'. In 1592 both chancel and porch were in disrepair, and during the next ten years complaints were often made about the ruinous state of the church.[29] In 1818 the church was repewed and a west gallery erected.[30] It may have been then or a few years later that it underwent a 'thorough repair'.[31] Early-19th-century work includes the wood-framed nave windows, large and pointed with 'Gothic' glazing-bars. Each side wall has two windows, while near the west end are shorter windows, one above the other, the upper ones designed to light the gallery. The round-headed south door within the Norman opening is also of the early 19th century. The church was again restored in 1865–6, when the nave and tower were reroofed,[32] and in 1898 the church was repewed.[33] The chancel was again restored in 1927.[34] None of the later restorations appears to have been drastic, so that in spite of the removal of the gallery the late-Georgian aspect of the nave has largely survived.

There is a Royal Arms. Tablets to members of the Thompson, Outram, and Prickett families include one to Marmaduke Prickett (d. 1765) and his wife Anne (d. 1789). The east window contains 20th-century stained glass by Kempe and Tower.[35] In the churchyard an upright stone coffin bears a sundial dated 1799.

There were three bells in 1552[36] and 1764.[37] Two of the three surviving bells are dated 1608, one of them cast by Henry Oldfield. The third is dated 1663 and was made by Samuel Smith, the elder, of York.[38] A gold and silver chalice was bequeathed to the church by William Wade in 1497.[39] It was perhaps the 'old communion cup' which was sold in the late 19th century. The plate consists of a silver cup, made in Birmingham in 1868 by 'T P & S', and two plated patens and a flagon.[40] The registers of baptisms and marriages begin in 1653 and those of burials in 1656. They are complete.[41]

A burial ground, on the Burton Fleming road, was consecrated in 1957.[42]

NONCONFORMITY. A Roman Catholic family was reported in Kilham in 1764.[43] There is evidence of Quakerism in the parish in the early 18th century. Between 1705 and 1709 two Kilham people and two from outside the parish were buried in 'the Quakers' burying place', sometimes referred to as the Quaker garth.[44] The burial ground is again mentioned in 1809.[45] In 1764 a family of Anabaptists was reported

---

[24] Ibid. Bp. V. 1884/Ret.
[25] Ibid. Bp. V. 1936/Ret. 25.
[26] Y.A.J. xxvi. 289.
[27] Ibid. xxv. 87.
[28] Ibid. xxvi. 289.
[29] Ibid. xviii. 207, 212, 216, 223, 229, 323, 328, 336, 340.
[30] Lawton, Rer. Eccles. Dioc. Ebor. 303.
[31] T. Allen, Hist. Yorks. (1831), ii. 322.
[32] B.I.H.R., Ch. Ret. 2; V. 1865/Ret. 289; plaque in tower.
[33] Kelly's Dir. N. & E.R. Yorks. (1901), 513.
[34] Ibid. (1929), 525.
[35] Ex inf. Sir Nikolaus Pevsner, 1971.
[36] Inventories of Ch. Goods, 24.
[37] B.I.H.R., TER. J. Kilham 1764.
[38] Boulter, 'Ch. Bells', 217; Y.A.J. ii. 193; V.C.H. Yorks. ii. 452.
[39] Test. Ebor. iv. 114–15.
[40] Yorks. Ch. Plate, i. 278.
[41] E.R.R.O.
[42] York Dioc. Regy., Sentence of consecration.
[43] B.I.H.R., Bp. V. 1764/Ret. 85.
[44] E.R.R.O., PR. 2014.
[45] B.I.H.R., TER. J. Kilham 1809.

in the parish.[46] The Methodists had 17 members in Kilham in 1787 and the number increased to between 31 and 42 in 1788–91.[47] A house and a shop were licensed for worship in 1777 and 1821 respectively.[48]

The Methodists registered the first chapel in the parish in 1789[49] and it was replaced by a new one, in Middle Street, in 1815.[50] It was rebuilt on the same site in 1907[51] and the chapel, a red-brick building with stone dressings, was still used in 1971. The Wesleyan Sunday school, which existed in 1835,[52] was housed in a schoolroom in Middle Street by 1850,[53] and the building was used by the Methodists until 1969.[54] A Primitive Methodist chapel was built at the west end of Middle Street in 1824.[55] It was replaced by a new chapel in Baptist Street in 1860,[56] and there were 77 members in 1889.[57] It ceased to be used in 1946[58] and has since been demolished.

The Baptists built a chapel in 1819 in the road leading to Ruston Parva, which later became known as Baptist Street.[59] In 1821 there were ten members.[60] Their Sunday school, established in 1830, had a lending library attached to it by 1835.[61] The church gradually declined after the 1880s and by 1912 there were only six members.[62] The chapel finally closed *c.* 1920 and was used as a reading room until after the Second World War; it has since been demolished.[63] The Temperance Hall was registered by the Salvation Army in 1882, but by 1896 it was no longer so used.[64]

In 1868 the majority of parishoners were said to be dissenters, although many attended church.[65] In 1884 the vicar again complained about dissent and in 1900 it was said that 'the neglect of church work in past years' had given dissent a strong hold. In 1936 the vicar reported that the Methodists were strong but that relations with them were very cordial.[66]

EDUCATION. A free grammar school was founded at Kilham in 1633 by John, Lord D'Arcy. He built a school-house on 'the Greens' and endowed it with a rent-charge of £30 a year from the manor, £20 for the master's stipend and £10 for the usher's.[67] Masters and ushers were regularly recorded from the 1660s,[68] and the patronage descended in the heirs of Lord D'Arcy.[69] In 1764 about 30 boys and girls received free instruction in English, writing, and accounts, but there were rarely more than two or three boys learning Latin.[70] About 1797 the master claimed that by the terms of the endowment he was obliged to teach only grammar, and not reading, writing, or arithmetic. Sir Christopher Sykes, as lord of the manor, consequently withheld the annuity. The master's claim was upheld by a lawyer's opinion, and it was reported that in the past parents had paid for their children to be taught writing and accounts.[71]

In 1819 the number of pupils was 50–70 and the master received quarterly fees for teaching reading, writing, and accounts.[72] By 1822 there were generally 90–100 pupils in winter and 80–90 in summer, the master taking 'as many. . . as the school will accommodate'. The total included 10–12 boarders and about the same number of day-pupils from neighbouring parishes. Only about a dozen pupils were taught Latin, still without charge. Fees paid for instruction in English, reading, writing, and arithmetic were reported to have been agreed between the parishioners and the previous master. Additional fees were charged to wealthier parents. The whole of the rent-charge was then received by the master, there being no usher, and the school was held in a house belonging to the master and built at his expense.[73] This was perhaps the school-house which stood in Church Lane in 1850.[74]

The school contained 80 boys and girls in 1835[75] but by 1865 it had declined to about 30 boys.[76] In 1884 it was reorganized as a secondary school under a Charity Commissioners' Scheme. Free instruction was abolished and scholarships, open to boys who had spent three years in any public elementary school in Kilham and district, were established.[77] By 1892 the school was being held in a recently-built yellow-brick house called Laurel Banks, in Wold Gate.[78] The Scheme, however, proved a failure and by 1896 the school was in abeyance. In 1902 the endowment was converted into two scholarships, known as D'Arcy Exhibitions, each worth £15 a year and tenable at Bridlington Grammar School and Bridlington Girls' High School.[79]

In 1835 there were five other schools in Kilham, one of them established in 1828. They had a total attendance of 83 pupils, taught at their parents' expense.[80] The National school was built at the corner of Mill Back Side and Driffield Lane in 1847. In 1862 the average attendance was 60 boys and 30 girls. It then received £25 in voluntary contributions, £5 from endowments, and £10 10s. from school

---

[46] B.I.H.R., Bp. V. 1764/Ret. 85.
[47] E.R.R.O., MRP/1/7.
[48] B.I.H.R., DMH. 1777/19; DMH. Reg. 1, p. 374.
[49] Ibid. DMH. 1789/16; G.R.O. Worship Returns, Vol. v, nos. 759, 771.
[50] H.O. 129/24/523; O.S. Map 6" (1854).
[51] G.R.O. Worship Reg. nos. 2865, 42577.
[52] *Educ. Enquiry Abstract, 1835*, 1089.
[53] O.S. Map 6" (1854).
[54] Local inf.
[55] H.O. 129/24/523; G.R.O. Worship Rets., Vol. v, no. 3950; O.S. Map 6" (1854).
[56] G.R.O. Worship Reg. nos. 5135, 9346. The original chapel was not deregistered until 1875.
[57] H. Woodcock, *Sketches of Prim. Meth. on Yorks. Wolds*, 141.
[58] G.R.O. Worship Reg. no. 9346.
[59] H.O. 129/24/523; O.S. Map 6" (1956).
[60] *Baptists of Yorks.*, ed. C. E. Shipley, 207.
[61] *Educ. Enquiry Abstract, 1835*, 1089.
[62] *Baptists of Yorks.* 207.
[63] Directories; local inf.
[64] G.R.O. Worship Reg. no. 26571.
[65] B.I.H.R., V. 1868/Ret. 258.
[66] Ibid., Bp. V. 1884/Ret.; Bp. V. 1900/Ret. 204; Bp. V. 1936/Ret. 25.
[67] E.R.R.O., DDDU/11/96, 208; *V.C.H. Yorks.* i. 483.
[68] B.I.H.R., Schools index.
[69] *Complete Peerage*, iv. 70–2, 75–8.
[70] B.I.H.R., Bp. V. 1764/Ret. 85.
[71] E.R.R.O., DDSY/36/10.
[72] *Rets. on Educ. of Poor, 1819*, 1085.
[73] *9th Rep. Char. Com.* 735.
[74] O.S. Map 6" (1854). There was an unnamed building on the site as early as 1729: E.R.R.O., DDDU/12/53.
[75] *Educ. Enquiry Abstract, 1835*, 1088–9.
[76] B.I.H.R., V. 1865/Ret. 289.
[77] *V.C.H. Yorks.* i. 483; *Kelly's Dir. N. & E.R. Yorks.* (1889), 415.
[78] Bulmer, *Dir. E. Yorks.* (1892), 220; local inf.
[79] E.R.R.O., DDX/25/9; *V.C.H. Yorks.* i. 483; *Kelly's Dir. N. & E.R. Yorks.* (1897), 489; (1909), 544.
[80] *Educ. Enquiry Abstract, 1835*, 1089.

pence.⁸¹ It received an annual parliamentary grant by 1850.⁸² In 1871 85 children were in attendance.⁸³ From 1908 to 1914 the attendance varied only between 158 and 170, but it fell to about 120–140 between the World Wars.⁸⁴ It was an all-age school until 1952, when senior pupils were transferred to the Bridlington secondary schools.⁸⁵ The average number of children on the roll in 1971 was 54.⁸⁶

In 1865 the vicar reported that an evening school had been held in Kilham and in 1884 that another had been held in the winter months, both with little success.⁸⁷

CHARITIES FOR THE POOR. From the time when Kilham church was assigned to the deanery of York,⁸⁸ the revenues of the benefice were charged with providing 50 poor persons of Kilham, Pocklington, and Pickering (Yorks. N.R.) with food daily and with clothing in winter. The alms are said to have been paid until the deanship of Robert of Scarborough (1279 to c. 1291) but not afterwards.⁸⁹

Robert Thompson (d. 1736) and Jonas Thompson (d. 1739) left £20 and £10 respectively to the poor of Kilham. In 1822 it was reported that both endowments had been used to buy a poorhouse and no money had apparently ever been distributed to the poor. It was then recommended that payments should be made in accordance with the donors' intentions,⁹⁰ but no more is known of them.

Elizabeth Thompson, by will dated 1745, left £5 in trust, the interest to be distributed annually among poor widows of the parish. The endowment was apparently administered by the Prickett family⁹¹ until 1866, when it was assigned to the vicar and another inhabitant.⁹² In 1931 the income of 5s. a year was distributed to five widows.⁹³

Edward Watson, probably in the late 18th century, left £5 a year to the poor out of land in Kilham. In 1822 the money was distributed among poor widows.⁹⁴ No more is known of it.

Poor widows also benefited from a bequest of £1 10s. to the churchwardens by one Drinkrow in the 18th century. In 1822 the interest was regularly distributed.⁹⁵ No more is known of it.

Elizabeth Knowsley, by will dated 1800, left £50 in trust, the interest to be distributed among the poor of Kilham. In 1803 the principal was invested in stock and in 1822 it was reported that the dividends had been regularly used to subsidize the poor-rate. Thenceforth the money was to be used for the poor.⁹⁶ In 1971 the income of about £2 from £85 stock was distributed among eleven people.⁹⁷

LANGTOFT

THE large parish of Langtoft, irregular in shape, lies on the wolds about 6 miles north of Great Driffield.¹ Its situation is high; only in valley bottoms does it include any land lower than 200 ft. above sea-level. Including the depopulated township of Cottam, which lay on the wold slopes about 1½ mile south-west of Langtoft village, it extends for about 5 miles from north-east to south-west across hills and dry valleys. The parish boundaries often run in the valley bottoms. Much of the northern boundary, however, follows High Street, on the line of a Roman road,² and another part of this boundary seems to have been aligned on a Bronze-Age barrow near Octon cross-roads.³ A short section of the southern boundary follows a prehistoric earthwork. The total area of the ancient parish is 6,168 a., of which 2,586 a. lie in Cottam.⁴ In 1935 Cottam township was combined with Cowlam to form the new civil parish of Cottam.⁵

The landscape of the parish is typical of the high wolds. The exposed slopes are dissected by many steep-sided dry valleys, the most prominent being that in which Langtoft village lies and which may be the 'long piece of ground' of the place-name. Others include Tog Dale, Crake Dale, West Dale, and Crooked Dale in Langtoft, and Bortree Dale, Lambert Dale, Cottam Well Dale, and Phillips' Slack in Cottam. Lambert Dale is first mentioned, as Lamcotedale, in the 12th century.⁶ There is little woodland apart from shelter-belts around the wolds farms. The pattern of large regular fields mainly results from the inclosures of 1805 in Langtoft and 1851 in Cottam, before which much of the wold ground lay in the open fields. Most of the parish is now under arable, although since about 1939 an airfield, now disused, has covered a large area in the centre of Cottam township.⁷

Most of the land in the parish is more than 300 ft. above sea-level. The valley in which Langtoft village lies is mainly at 200 ft.–250 ft. The ground rises steadily from the village to over 525 ft. at the northern and over 500 ft. at the western boundary. To the north-east it rises to over 450 ft. before falling again in Tog Dale to under 350 ft. The situation of the village in a valley surrounded on three sides by steep hills has made it especially liable to flooding after heavy rain. A marble slab in the wall of a cottage records the occurrence of a 'great flood'

---

⁸¹ Ed. 7/135.
⁸² *Mins. of Educ. Cttee. of Council, 1849–50* [1215], p. 497, H.C. (1850), xliii.
⁸³ *Rets. rel. Elem. Educ. 1871*, 474.
⁸⁴ *Bd. of Educ. List 21* (H.M.S.O.).
⁸⁵ E.R. Educ. Cttee. *Mins.* 1951–2, 225; 1952–3, 69.
⁸⁶ Ex inf. Chief Educ. Officer, County Hall, Beverley, 1971.
⁸⁷ B.I.H.R., V. 1865/Ret. 289; Bp. V. 1884/Ret.
⁸⁸ See p. 259.
⁸⁹ *Cal. Inq. Misc.* ii, pp. 2–3 (inq. of 1308). For the dean's dates see *York Minster Fasti*, i. 8–9.
⁹⁰ *9th Rep. Char. Com.* 736. A memorandum in the par. reg. of 1794–1812 (E.R.R.O., PR. 2017) states that Robert left £5 and Jonas £20.

⁹¹ *9th Rep. Char. Com.* 736.
⁹² E.R.R.O., PR. 2017.
⁹³ Char. Com. files.
⁹⁴ Ibid.; *9th Rep. Char. Com.* 736.
⁹⁵ E.R.R.O., PR. 2017; *9th Rep. Char. Com.* 736.
⁹⁶ Plaque in church; *9th Rep. Char. Com.* 736.
⁹⁷ Ex inf. Mrs. V. A. Fincher, Kilham, 1972.
¹ This article was written in 1970.
² See p. 247.
³ W. Greenwell, *British Barrows*, 204; *Excavations Annual Report, 1966* (H.M.S.O.).
⁴ O.S. Map 6" (1854).
⁵ *Census*, 1931.
⁶ *P.N.E.R. Yorks.* (E.P.N.S.), 96–7.
⁷ See p. 266.

in 1657,[8] and there were serious floods in 1888 and 1892. On the last occasion the centre of the village was flooded to a depth of 7 ft., several cottages were destroyed, and over 60 buildings suffered damage.[9] Cottam village lay on the slopes at the head of Cottam Well Dale at 425 ft.–475 ft. To the south a broad belt of land, much of it now covered by the airfield, lies at over 475 ft. The ground then falls away to under 150 ft. at the southern boundary.

Langtoft village lies mainly along the Driffield–Foxholes road, which is known as Tire Ewe Hill south of the village, Main Street within it, and Scarborough Gate to the north. Minor roads converging on the village include Cottam Lane and the Kilham road. The so-called Occupation Road existed by 1772 and formerly led north-westwards to High Street. Finally a road known as West Gate within the village and Malton Gate beyond runs westwards and until at least 1772 led to West Lutton.[10] It now leads only as far as the Weaverthorpe–Cottam road beyond the parish boundary. A fifth road formerly led into the village from Butterwick. Between 1772 and 1817 it was joined to Scarborough Gate about a mile north of the village by a short connecting road, now known as Mill Lane, and its southern section was blocked.[11] A field road now marks part of its former course. In the earlier 19th century much money was spent on keeping the roads open in winter and on repairing their surfaces.[12]

Most of the houses in the village lie along or close to Main Street. Back Street forms a loop on the east side of Main Street, and Church Street gives access to the church from West Gate. Connecting roads include Green Lane, Chapel Lane, and Rattan Row. The valley side south of Cottam Lane has long been known as Bunker's Hill. There were formerly two ponds in the village: Low Mere, at the junction of Main and Back Streets, and a smaller one at the junction of West Gate and Main Street. They were drained c. 1960.[13] A stone village cross in a late Gothic style, apparently erected in the early 20th century, and said to have been given by Sir Tatton Sykes,[14] stands near the site of Low Mere. It is raised on three octagonal steps and the shaft, which has a carved base, carries a niche with a carved figure.

Most of the buildings in the village are undistinguished houses and cottages dating from the 18th to the 20th century. It was reported in 1901 that the cottages were in general 'neither suitable nor commodious enough for labourers'.[15] Many of the older buildings are of chalk, although most have been patched or altered in brick, possibly a result of repairs to flood damage in the late 19th century. A row of twelve, probably 19th-century, chalk cottages, with brick footings and quoins, stands in West Gate. Slightly larger houses include Cattle Bank House and Manor Farm, formerly Manor House.[16] There are 24 Council houses. An innkeeper was mentioned in 1729[17] and by 1823 there were two public houses, the Nelson and the George and Dragon.[18] The former had become the Ship by 1840.[19] The George and Dragon was closed c. 1960.[20]

Away from the village the stump of a 19th-century windmill, together with the miller's house, still stands in Mill Lane. There were seven outlying farm-houses in the township by 1850,[21] all probably built after the early-19th-century inclosure. They include Field House, Westfield House, Langtoft Grange, Togdale Farm, and Maiden's Cottage. The last-mentioned is a large house of two storeys, with a lower range of two labourers' cottages at one end.

The road pattern in Cottam has undergone several changes. Cottam Lane formerly continued southwards through the township to Driffield, but a half-mile section south of Cottam House was probably closed when the airfield was built c. 1939 and another section was only a field-road in 1970. In the late 18th century a road led from Cottam Lane near the village site north-westwards to West Lutton, but by 1817 its course had been altered beyond the parish boundary to lead to Weaverthorpe. The road which mainly forms the internal boundary between Langtoft and Cottam and links the Weaverthorpe road with the Langtoft–Driffield road was made between 1817 and 1850. It replaced a section of the Weaverthorpe road, which was a field-road in 1970. The Roman road known elsewhere as Wold Gate formerly crossed the southern part of the township in a north-easterly direction and was known as York Road;[22] in 1970 part of its former course was marked by field boundaries.

The site of the deserted village of Cottam, among the finest in the East Riding, is marked by prominent earthworks, including house-sites and hollow ways. The disused church stands in the north of the site; near by is a small pond, dry in 1970. Cottam House stands near the village site.[23] The other buildings in the township are all isolated farms. They include Cottam Grange, a two-storeyed double-fronted house of chalk, partly rendered, with contrasting painted quoins and a central porch; it dates from the 18th or early 19th century. Cottam Warren House Farm was built c. 1849 following the destruction of the rabbit warren.[24] About a mile east of the village is Cottam Well, in the dry valley to which it has given its name; the hand-pump also had an engine-driven pumping mechanism which still remained in 1970.

Cottam is associated with one of the miracles of St. John of Beverley, who is said to have cured two inhabitants.[25] Peter of Langtoft, the celebrated chronicler and canon of Bridlington priory, who wrote a chronicle of England in French verse, was probably born at Langtoft in the late 13th century.[26]

In 1377 there were 100 poll-tax payers in Langtoft and 50 in Cottam.[27] In 1638 Langtoft was 'very sore

---

[8] This slab apparently replaces an inscribed chalk block: J. D. Hood, *Waterspouts on Yorks. Wolds*, 19; Sheahan and Whellan, *Hist. York & E.R.* ii. 483.
[9] For an acct. of the floods see Hood, op. cit. *passim*.
[10] T. Jefferys, *Map of Yorks.* (1772).
[11] Ibid.; C. Greenwood, *Map of Yorks.* (1817).
[12] See p. 269. [13] Local inf.
[14] Ex inf. the vicar, 1971.
[15] *Hull News*, 24 Aug. 1901.
[16] O.S. Map 6" (1854, 1958).
[17] E.R.R.O., PR. 1176.
[18] Baines, *Hist. Yorks.* (1823), ii. 361–2.
[19] White, *Dir. E. & N.R. Yorks.* (1840), 393.
[20] Local inf.
[21] O.S. Map 6" (1854).
[22] Jefferys, *Map of Yorks.* (1772); Greenwood, *Map of Yorks.* (1817); O.S. Map 6" (1854 and later edns.).
[23] See p. 266. [24] See p. 268.
[25] *Y.A.J.* iii. 278.
[26] F. Ross, *Celebrities of Yorks. Wolds*, 96; *The Chronicle of Pierre de Langtoft in French Verse. From the Earliest Period to the Death of King Edw. I*, ed. T. Wright (Rolls Ser.).
[27] E 179/202/62 mm. 6, 37.

infected' with the plague.[28] In 1670 47 households were included in the hearth-tax assessment in Langtoft and Cottam together, and of these 9 were exempt for poverty. Four years later, of the 36 households which were taxed 30 had only one hearth each, 3 had 2, 2 had 3, and one had four.[29] In 1743 there were said to be about 50 families in Langtoft and only one in Cottam.[30] In 1764 there were 42 families.[31] In 1801 the population of Langtoft was 276 and of Cottam 16. At Langtoft the average intercensal increase was about 50 from 1801 to 1861, when the population was 688.[32] It subsequently declined steadily until 1931, when it was 465. It increased to 486 in 1951 but 10 years later it had fallen to 460. The population of Cottam had increased only to 25 by 1831 but it grew rapidly thereafter, particularly following the creation of Warren Farm c. 1849, to a peak of 116 in 1871. It, too, declined steadily thereafter and in 1931 it was 63.[33]

MANORS AND OTHER ESTATES. By 1086 an estate of 9 carucates in Langtoft, which had been held in 1066 by Ulf, and another of 9 carucates in Cottam had both been assigned by the archbishop of York to the chapter.[34] In 1284–5 the chapter were said to have 21½ carucates in Langtoft and 12 in Cottam,[35] and in 1316 they were described as lords of both places.[36] Cottam was retained by the chapter for the benefit of the common fund (*communia*), but land at Langtoft was set aside for the support of particular prebends. Three of the prebends, Langtoft, Stillington, and Strensall, were founded by or in the 12th century, but the fourth, Bishop Wilton, was not established until 1242.[37]

The estate of Langtoft prebend was later known as the manor of LANGTOFT. Between 1164 and 1170 the archbishop condemned as 'extremely prejudicial' the alienation of small parcels of the prebendal lands and forbade such grants for the future; the alienees simultaneously restored the property.[38] The manor consisted of 59 bovates in 1295.[39] It was sold by the Commonwealth in 1649 to Robert Holborne[40] but recovered at the Restoration. It descended with the prebend until it came to be vested in the Ecclesiastical Commissioners in 1841 upon a voidance of the prebend.[41] Over 700 a. were held of the manor in 1805, about 500 a. of it by copyhold,[42] and between 1894 and 1906 about 400 a. of copyhold land were enfranchised by the commissioners.[43] The Broadley family acquired several holdings of land in this manor during the 19th century,[44] and of the enfranchised land about 280 a. belonged to the Broadleys in 1904.[45] It subsequently descended with their manor of West Hall.[46]

Bishop Wilton prebend at its establishment in 1242 was annexed to the treasurership of York minster.[47] It had 37 bovates in Langtoft.[48] The treasurership and with it the prebend were abolished in 1547[49] and the former prebendal lands were later granted to Edward, duke of Somerset. They subsequently descended with the manor of Bishop Wilton, which passed to Sir William Hildyard (d. 1632) and later to his son-in-law William Norton.[50] It was sold c. 1768 to Matthew Smith[51] and in 1786 to Sir Christopher Sykes.[52] The former prebendal land in Langtoft, however, was all held by freeholders. The largest freehold estate was known in 1712 as the manor of WEST HALL, comprising 20 bovates; it was then sold by Michael Barstow to Susannah Gunby.[53] Her executor sold it in 1727 to Henry Jarratt[54] and it passed to Henry Broadley in 1774 on his marriage with John Jarratt's daughter Betty.[55] At inclosure in 1805 Betty Broadley was allotted 226 a.[56] The Broadleys, later the Harrison-Broadleys, acquired other land in Langtoft and the estate amounted to nearly 1,200 a. in 1895. J. B. Harrison-Broadley sold 161 a. in 1921[57] and the estate was finally split up in 1947–8, when Doris Harrison-Broadley sold 1,016 a. in separate lots.[58]

Another freehold estate held of Bishop Wilton manor was that of 14 bovates belonging to Richard Holtby in 1710.[59] It was sold by John Holtby to Robert Grimston in 1751[60] and by him in 1768 to the Revd. Mark Sykes.[61] At inclosure in 1805 Sir M. M. Sykes was awarded 190 a.,[62] which descended in the Sykes family until it was sold after the death of Sir Mark Sykes in 1919.[63]

The prebend of Strensall's estate comprised 32 bovates in the Middle Ages.[64] It descended with Strensall manor[65] until 1841, when it came to be vested in the Ecclesiastical Commissioners upon a voidance of the prebend.[66] The estate comprised about 350 a. in 1805.[67] It included several small freehold estates and some copyhold land which was enfranchised in the 1890s.[68] About 70 a. of former Strensall land were acquired by Sophia Broadley in 1859[69] and subsequently descended with the Broadley manor.

Stillington prebend had 32 bovates in Langtoft in 1295.[70] It descended with Stillington manor, which was let to Christopher Croft in 1625 and sold to him

---

[28] Hull Corp. Rec., Bench Bk. no. 5, p. 495.
[29] E 179/205/514, 521.
[30] *Herring's Visit.* i. 161; ii. 165.
[31] B.I.H.R., Bp. V. 1764/Ret. 112.
[32] *V.C.H. Yorks.* iii. 489.
[33] Ibid.; *Census*.
[34] *V.C.H. Yorks.* ii. 211–12.
[35] *Feud. Aids*, vi. 30, 32.
[36] Ibid. 205.
[37] *York Minster Fasti*, ii (Y.A.S. Rec. Ser. cxxiv), 46, 68, 70, 86.
[38] *E.Y.C.* i, pp. 130, 137–8.
[39] *Miscellanea*, iv (Y.A.S. Rec. Ser. xciv), 36–7.
[40] C 54/3512 no. 37.
[41] *Lond. Gaz.* 25 Sept. 1855, p. 3551.
[42] Registry of Deeds, Beverley, CI/14/2.
[43] Ibid. 70/92/90 (1894); 72/416/394 (1895); 87/465/415 (1906); 101/295/271.
[44] Ibid. CF/70/109; CI/14/2; MP/287/416; E.R.R.O., DDHB/24/1, 2.
[45] Regy. of Deeds, 67/162/154 (1904).
[46] See below.
[47] *York Minster Fasti*, ii. 86.
[48] D. & C. York, Torre MS. 'Peculiars', 647.
[49] *V.C.H. Yorks.* iii. 380.
[50] E.R.R.O., DDSY/4/145–8, 150, 158, 164, 166.
[51] Ibid. /102; Regy. of Deeds, AL/102/177; AN/334/24.
[52] Regy. of Deeds, AN/334/24; BL/578/919.
[53] Ibid. A/665/947.
[54] Ibid. K/433/912.
[55] E.R.R.O., DDX/31/540, 543.
[56] Regy. of Deeds, CI/14/2.
[57] Ibid. 236/57/49.
[58] Ibid. 770/2/2; 774/177/158.
[59] Ibid. A/322/459.
[60] Ibid. U/417/789.
[61] Ibid. AL/251/448.
[62] Ibid. CI/14/2 and inclosure map.
[63] Ex inf. Estate Office, Sledmere, 1970.
[64] D. & C. York, Torre MS. 'Peculiars', 647.
[65] See *V.C.H. Yorks. N.R.* ii. 193–4.
[66] B.I.H.R., Inst. AB. 20, pp. 376–7; *Lond. Gaz.* 5 Nov. 1852, p. 2898.
[67] Regy. of Deeds, CI/14/2.
[68] Ibid. 68/136/124 (1894); 94/169/163 (1897).
[69] E.R.R.O., DDHB/24/1, 2.
[70] *Miscellanea*, iv. 30.

by the Commonwealth in 1649,[71] but recovered at the Restoration. In 1805 the estate comprised about 370 a., and 218 a. of it were held on lease by Stephen Croft.[72] In 1808 Croft's lease was acquired by R. C. Broadley.[73] The land descended with the prebend until 1865, when upon a voidance of the prebend it was sold by the Ecclesiastical Commissioners to W. H. Harrison-Broadley.[74] The Broadleys and Harrison-Broadleys also acquired several smaller holdings of former Stillington land.[75] It subsequently descended with the Broadley manor.

Two other Domesday estates in Langtoft belonged to the Crown, each consisting of 3 carucates; one had been held in 1066 by Otre, and the other was in 1086 soke of Burton Agnes manor.[76] By 1284–5 one of these estates belonged to the archbishop and was held under him by Reynold Fitz Piers.[77] Land of this fee, amounting to 2 carucates in 1286, was held by the Salvins and was granted by Gerard Salvin to William Maheu in 1300.[78] It was perhaps the manor of *LANGTOFT* held by John Mowbray in 1465–6[79] and by Sir William Bulmer in 1531.[80] It was forfeited to the Crown in 1537, when it consisted of 24 bovates, on the attainder of John Bulmer, but was restored to his son Ralph[81] and by 1564 had passed with Boythorpe manor[82] to Ralph's eight daughters. Anne Bulmer and her husband Anthony Welbury sold five sixths of the manor in 1575 to Robert Baitson[83] and the remaining sixth was sold by Ralph Grey in 1583 to Baitson and Thomas Peirson.[84] The estate had apparently passed to the Hellards by 1700,[85] and in 1731 Samuel Hellard's property included 18 bovates.[86] George Hellard sold it to William Osbaldeston in 1758,[87] and at inclosure in 1805 Humphrey Osbaldeston was allotted 270 a.[88] The estate was sold by J. P. Osbaldeston-Mitford to W. H. Harrison-Broadley in 1875; it then consisted of 277 a. known as Langtoft farm.[89] It subsequently descended with the Broadley manor.[90]

The chapter's manor of *COTTAM*, which was leased by members of the Knowsley family in the 18th and early 19th centuries,[91] comprised 92 bovates in 1698[92] and 2,220 a. at inclosure in 1851.[93] The chapter sold 1,420 a. to J. T. Foord in 1851 and this was confirmed by the Ecclesiastical Commissioners in 1853.[94] In 1858 the commissioners sold Foord a further 810 a. known as Warren farm.[95] The estate, consisting of 2,316 a. in Cottam and 235 a. in Langtoft, was sold in 1894 by the Revd. R. H. Foord to G. S. Robson.[96] The Langtoft land, known as Westfield farm, was sold in 1912 by Robson's trustees to George Groundrill and J. C. Wharram,[97] and the 859-acre Warren farm in Cottam to J. W. Nettleton in the same year.[98] The remainder of the estate, comprising two farms totalling 1,465 a., was sold by the trustees in 1917 to P. H. Booth.[99] His daughter Julia Stead sold 273 a. of Cottam House farm in 1938[1] and the remainder of the farm, 649 a., in 1949 to the Air Ministry.[2] Her trustees conveyed the remainder of the estate, consisting of the 567-acre Cottam Grange farm, to C. D. H. Stead in 1969.[3] The Air Ministry sold its land in Cottam in 1960 in separate lots.[4]

On the south side of the village site is Cottam House, now a farm-house but built as a substantial residence, probably by Richard Knowsley (d. 1774) about the middle of the 18th century. Part of the garden is still enclosed by a high brick wall and an 18th-century stable range stands to the south. A coach-house, now demolished, is said to have been dated 1763.[5] The house originally consisted of a three-storeyed block to which lower side wings were later added. The main approach was then from the west and the entrance front of the 18th-century house faced in that direction. It is of red brick, five bays wide, with sash windows and an altered central doorway. Internally an elegant staircase of *c.* 1760 survives.

The rectorial tithes belonged to the prebend of Langtoft from at least the later 13th century.[6] They were let in the 16th and 17th centuries to the Spencer family[7] and in 1650 the rectory was worth £140, including £40 for the tithes of Cottam.[8] In the 18th and early 19th centuries the lessees were the Knowsleys.[9] In 1794 there were 'sundry oxgangs' of glebe[10] and at the inclosure of Langtoft in 1805 the lessee was awarded 229 a. for glebe and 483 a. for tithes.[11] The Cottam tithes were commuted in 1843 and the prebendary was awarded a rent-charge of £210 11s. 6d.; the lessee received £4 8s. 6d. for the tithes of the glebe.[12] For much of the rest of the 19th century the lessees of the rectorial estate were the Gibbons family,[13] who also had a small freehold estate in Cottam.[14] In 1921 380 a. of the rectorial estate were sold to G. R. Shipley.[15]

ECONOMIC HISTORY. The chapter estates in both Langtoft and Cottam both contained land for five ploughs in 1066, when they were worth £2 each.

In 1086 both were waste. The royal estate which was soke of Burton Agnes was also waste. The second royal estate was worth 10s. in 1066 and had land for two ploughs.[16]

Most of the tenants on the prebend of Langtoft's estate were bondmen in 1295, 25 of them holding 42 bovates. Of these, one held 4 bovates, 5 held 3 each, 5 held 2, 13 held one, and one had only a toft. In addition 14 cottars each held a toft and an acre of land. Each cottar either paid 4d. for an autumn boon-work or helped to carry corn 'to the prebendary's table', and he also rendered hens and eggs at Christmas.[17] On the prebend of Stillington's estate in the same year 16 bovates were held by tenants-at-will, and seven cottars and one villein each held a toft.[18] Undated surveys, probably of the later 14th century, show that there was waste on the estates of all four prebends. On the Langtoft estate 21 tenants held the same number of bovates as in 1295, but there were sixteen waste holdings. On the Stillington estate there were eleven waste holdings. On the Bishop Wilton estate fifteen tenants held 43 bovates; of these, one had 19 bovates, one had 4, 3 had 3 each, 4 had 2, 3 had one, and 3 had only tofts and crofts. There were two waste holdings. On the Strensall estate fourteen tenants held 31 bovates; of these, one had 8 bovates, one had 7, one had 3, 6 had 2 each, and one had one. Another tenant held a sheepfold and a 'waste place', 3 had waste holdings, and the prebendary was said to have 'many holdings now waste'.[19]

By the 17th century there were many copyholders on the Langtoft prebendal estate. They paid a total of about £7 rent in 1638[20] and again in 1777, when there were 29 of them.[21] The chapter estate at Cottam was held by eight leaseholders in 1638,[22] but by only one in 1698.[23]

Freeholders numbered only three and four respectively on the Langtoft and Stillington estates in 1295 and in the later 14th century.[24] Later there were many small freeholders in the township: 32 in 1783 and 40 in 1830.[25]

The open fields of Langtoft lay on the wolds to the east and west of the valley in which the village is situated. There were probably always two fields, called at inclosure in 1805 East and West fields.[26] An area in the north-west of the parish was known as the Out field in 1850,[27] suggesting that an infield-outfield system may have been followed before inclosure. Cottam's fields are first referred to in 1569, but not named.[28] The inclosure award of 1851 suggests an earlier division into East and West fields.[29]

The extent of the open fields in Langtoft is first revealed in 1794, when there were 192 bovates.[30] At inclosure in 1805 allotments totalling 1,543 a. were made from East field and 1,666 a. from West field, with 173 a. said to lie in both.[31] The size of a bovate on the manor of Langtoft in 1295 was 16 a.[32] In 1743 the strips comprising the 6 bovates of vicarial glebe were dispersed regularly in every furlong in the fields.[33] In 1760–1 the Sykes estate of 16 bovates included 2 consisting of 'balks implowed', one recently.[34]

In 1698 there were 92 bovates in Cottam[35] and in 1851 each bovate there contained 27 a.[36] The lessee of the manor increased the value of the estate during the 18th century by laying down a rabbit warren before 1732 on formerly arable land and sowing sainfoin in the 1760s.[37]

There is no evidence of any permanent meadow land in Langtoft before inclosure. In Cottam in 1843 250 a. of meadow and pasture lay mainly in Cottam Well Dale and Garton Bottom.[38] There seems to have been little permanent pasture in Langtoft before 1805, and no areas of common or pasture were recorded in the inclosure award of that year, but land in the open fields was probably laid down to grass from time to time.[39] As in Cottam, what permanent pasture there was doubtless lay along the valleys, where ploughing was difficult. The steep valley side east of the village has been known as Cattle Bank since at least the mid 19th century.[40] Sheep were certainly being kept in the 16th century[41] and in the early 18th century sheep from out of the parish were pastured there in summer.[42] The pressure on Langtoft's pasturage was probably increasing during the 18th century. In 1764 common rights were unstinted, but by 1781 they had been stinted. Every bovate then carried rights of one beast- or horse-gate and 7 sheep-gates.[43] The large number of sheep kept in the open fields was mentioned during discussions about inclosure.[44]

Cottam was last taxed separately in the mid 15th century[45] and it may have been reduced in size in the late Middle Ages. In 1706 there was still a small village, with nine houses and cottages and extensive open fields. The tenants were then said to be poor and their houses costly to repair owing to the scarcity of timber in the area. In 1719 the chapter authorized the lessee of the manor to maintain only four houses and to demolish the rest 'as soon as conveniently may be'. In 1726 there were still six houses but by 1732 a warren had been made on the former arable fields in the south of the township.[46] In 1843 the warren and 'rough pasture' covered 843 a.[47] but the warren was reconverted to arable shortly afterwards.[48]

In 1623 Henry Best, lord of Elmswell manor, claimed that he and his predecessors had im-memorially enjoyed common rights for 300 sheep at all times of the year on a 'great close or field' of

---

[16] V.C.H. Yorks. ii. 198, 204, 211–12.
[17] Miscellanea, iv (Y.A.S. Rec. Ser. xciv), 36–8.
[18] Ibid. 30.
[19] D. & C. York, M 2(2) c, ff. 31, 41, 45d., 46d.
[20] Ibid. S 1(1) f.   [21] E.R.R.O., DDX/40/77.
[22] D. & C. York, S 1(1) f.   [23] Ibid. a.
[24] Ibid. M 2(2) c, ff. 31, 41, 45d., 46d.; Miscellanea, iv. 30, 36–8.
[25] E.R.R.O., Land Tax.
[26] Registry of Deeds, Beverley, CI/14/2.
[27] O.S. Map 6" (1854).
[28] Select 16th-Cent. Causes in Tithe (Y.A.S. Rec. Ser. cxiv), 111–14.
[29] E.R.R.O., IA. Cottam, 1851.
[30] Ibid. DDX/40/195.   [31] Regy. of Deeds, CI/14/2.
[32] Miscellanea, iv. 36.
[33] B.I.H.R., TER. J. Langtoft 1743; Y.A.J. xxxvii. 337.
[34] E.R.R.O., DDSY/98/66.
[35] D. & C. York, S 1(1) a.
[36] E.R.R.O., IA. Cottam, 1851.
[37] D. & C. York, S 1(1) a, c.
[38] A. Harris, Rural Landscape of E.R. Yorks. 101.
[39] Ibid. 28.   [40] O.S. Map 6" (1854).
[41] E.R.R.O., DDWB/25/7.
[42] B.I.H.R., TER. J. Langtoft 1716.
[43] Ibid. 1764, 1781.   [44] See p. 268.
[45] E 179/202/127.   [46] D. & C. York, S 1(1) a.
[47] B.I.H.R., TA. 48S.
[48] E.R.R.O., DDGD/Box 1/3; Harris, Rural Landscape, 100–101.

500 a. in Cottam known as Monkleys. This field, in which several people had strips, was probably the area which later became Cottam warren. It was divided by a road and the custom was said to be that when half was sown with corn the rest was left as sheep pasture. One of the proprietors of Cottam, who also had common rights for 200 sheep on Monkleys, disputed Best's right[49] but apparently without success. In 1735 'a sheep walk called Cottam Walks' was let with land in Elmswell,[50] and in 1849–50 W. J. Denison, lord of Elmswell, claimed the right to pasture 400 sheep on 318 a. of the former Cottam warren during the day, before driving them to Elmswell at night. It was stated that the three proprietors of land in Cottam also had pasture rights for sheep both day and night on the same part of the warren. At the inclosure of Cottam in 1851 Lord Londesborough, Denison's heir, was awarded 70 a. in lieu of his right of stray.[51] The area in the north of the township west of Cottam House was known as Horse pasture in the mid 19th century.[52]

There is no evidence of early inclosure at Langtoft, and at Cottam, in 1706, there were only 'small pieces of inclosure about the town'.[53] The inclosure of the remaining open-field land in Langtoft was first mooted in 1774 and there were meetings of proprietors in 1776, 1783, and 1794. It was said in 1794 that the objections of Richard Knowsley, the lessee of the prebend, had prevented the proposed inclosure. After Knowsley's death, however, terms for the inclosure were agreed in 1800[54] and an Act was passed in 1801.[55] At one stage it had been suggested that a partial inclosure, together with consolidation of open-field holdings, would be preferable to a complete inclosure because so many sheep were kept that 'the fences . . . can never be got up'.[56]

The inclosure finally took place in 1805.[57] There were said to be 3,434 a. to be dealt with and 3,382 a. were actually allotted. Robert Knowsley, as lessee of the prebendary of Langtoft, received 712 a. for rectorial glebe and tithes, as well as 89 a. for 4 copyhold bovates. The vicar was awarded 297 a. for glebe and tithes. Six other people received large allotments: R. C. Broadley got 579 a., Humphrey Osbaldeston 270 a., Betty Broadley 229 a., Sir Mark Sykes 196 a., Joseph Vickerman 173 a., and William Paul 153 a. There were 3 allotments of 100 a.–150 a., 2 of 50 a.–100 a., 5 of 10 a.–50 a., and 20 of under 10 a. It was stipulated that copyholders were to be admitted by the lords of their manors without payment of fines and on the same terms as before, and freeholders were to hold of their lords subject to the same free rents as previously.

The remaining open-field land of Cottam was inclosed in 1851[58] under the general Inclosure Act of 1846.[59] In all, 2,553 a. were allotted. The chapter, as lords of the manor, received 2,220 a., and the vicar was awarded 30 a. for glebe. The trustees of Sir John Gibbons received 144 a. and J. T. Foord 46 a., and Lord Londesborough got 70 a. for his right of stray.

In 1801 1,138 a. were under crops in Langtoft and Cottam together, about a fifth of the total area of the parish. Oats were then growing on 502 a., barley on 290 a., and turnips or rape on 240 a.[60] Both townships have remained predominantly arable in the 19th and 20th centuries. In 1843 about 1,400 a. out of about 2,500 a. in Cottam were arable,[61] and soon afterwards 843 a. were converted from warren and rough pasture to arable.[62] In 1905 nearly 3,000 a. in Langtoft were arable; about 300 a. were under permanent grass and there were 50 a. of woodland.[63]

There have usually been from 12 to 14 farms in Langtoft in the 19th and 20th centuries, although there were 19 in 1846 and 17 in 1858.[64] In 1921 7 out of 13 farms had acreages of 150 or over[65] but by 1937 there were 10 larger and only 4 smaller farms.[66] Since c. 1850, when Warren Farm was built,[67] there have usually been three farms in Cottam. In 1893 their acreages were 889, 860, and 567.[68]

A weaver was recorded at Langtoft in 1732.[69] There were chalk quarries and at least one lime-kiln in the 19th century.[70] A maker of cattle medicine was mentioned in the 1870s.[71] There was a mill at Langtoft in 1300[72] but no further evidence of one until a windmill was mentioned in 1712.[73] In 1854 a mill stood about ¾ mile north of the village by the Butterwick road.[74] It was described in 1856 as an old post mill,[75] but this was subsequently replaced by a brick tower mill. A miller was last mentioned in 1925.[76] The stump of the tower remained in 1970.

LOCAL GOVERNMENT. In 1295 the profits of the prebend of Langtoft's manorial court were said to be infrequent and worth little.[77] There are surviving court records, mainly call rolls, accounts of fines and fees, and minutes, of the same manor from 1770 to 1917.[78] Two affeerors were the only officers mentioned in the 18th century, but in 1857 a bailiff and a pinder were sworn. Most of the business concerned admissions and surrenders of property. In 1876 it was reported that courts were formerly held at intervals of a few years 'as business required', but no general court had then been held for thirteen years.

Churchwardens' accounts survive for 1767–1856, constables' accounts for 1794–1846, and surveyors'

---

[49] C 2/Jas. I/B22/13.
[50] E.R.R.O., DDHV/9/2.
[51] Ibid. IA. Cottam, 1851.
[52] O.S. Map 6" (1854).
[53] D. & C. York, S 1(1) a. In 1569 Ralph Conyers had 168 a. of closes in 'Cottam': E 164/38/250d.–251. This has been identified with Cottam in Langtoft: *Ag. H.R.* vi. 97. It was, however, West Coatham (in Kirkleatham) (Yorks. N.R.): *P.N.N.R. Yorks.* (E.P.N.S.), 156; *Cal. Pat.* 1569–72, 341; and see C 142/55/94.
[54] E.R.R.O., DDX/40/191.
[55] 41 Geo. III, c. 93 (Priv. Act).
[56] Harris, *Rural Landscape*, 65.
[57] Regy. of Deeds, CI/14/2.
[58] E.R.R.O., IA. Cottam, 1851.
[59] Ibid. DDGD/Box 1/3.
[60] 1801 Crop Returns.
[61] E.R.R.O., DDX/40/167.
[62] Ibid. DDGD/Box 1/3; Harris, *Rural Landscape*, 100–101.
[63] Acreage Returns, 1905.
[64] Directories.
[65] *Kelly's Dir. N. & E.R. Yorks.* (1921), 553.
[66] Ibid. (1937), 495.
[67] E.R.R.O., DDGD/Box 1/3a.
[68] Ibid. DDCV/Parcel 21/17.
[69] Ibid. PR. 1176.
[70] O.S. Map 6" (1854).
[71] Directories.
[72] *Yorks. Fines, 1272–1300*, 140.
[73] Regy. of Deeds, A/665/947.
[74] O.S. Map 6" (1854).
[75] Sheahan and Whellan, *Hist. York & E.R.* ii. 483.
[76] *Kelly's Dir. N. & E.R. Yorks.* (1926), 575.
[77] *Miscellanea*, iv (Y.A.S. Rec. Ser. xciv), 38.
[78] E.R.R.O., DDX/40/43–67, 73–81, 89–145, 165, 168, 172–3, 178.

accounts for 1808–30.[79] There were two churchwardens. The single constable was responsible for repairing the well, the pinfold, and the stocks. There were two surveyors of highways. In both 1814 and 1815 over £9 was spent on 'snow cutting' and high rates were sometimes needed to pay for road repairs: in 1825, for example, a rate of 1s. 5d. in the pound raised £92, of which £52 was spent on 'covering' the Malton road. There were two overseers of the poor in the earlier 19th century and in 1833 they rented a building, perhaps for a poorhouse, standing on waste land at Langtoft.[80] In 1836 Langtoft joined the Driffield union.[81]

CHURCH. A church at Langtoft and a chapel at Cottam may have existed in the Norman period,[82] but they are both first mentioned only in 1274, when the church was appropriated to the prebend of Langtoft and a vicarage ordained.[83] The parish remained a peculiar of the prebend with contentious jurisdiction reserved to the chapter.[84] Cottam has subsequently remained a chapelry of Langtoft, although it was described in 1650 as 'fit to be a parish'.[85]

The advowson belonged to the prebendary of Langtoft until 1840,[86] when it was transferred to the archbishop of York,[87] the patron in 1970.[88]

At ordination in 1274 the chapter assigned to the vicar the small tithes 'outside the limits of the gardens and crofts'.[89] In 1302 the vicar was given a toft by the prebendary of Langtoft.[90] The vicarage was worth £6 13s. 4d. in both 1291 and 1428.[91] In 1481 it was said to be insufficiently endowed, being worth scarcely £4 13s. 4d. a year.[92] In 1535 it was worth £8 net.[93] In 1650 the impropriator paid £25 13s. 4d. a year to the Commonwealth out of the rectory, doubtless for the vicar's stipend.[94] In 1716, as well as his income from his glebe and tithes, the vicar received a rent of £12 3s. 4d. a year from Sir William Strickland's estate at Carnaby, the result of an augmentation made 'many years since' by a prebendary of Langtoft. Dr. William Stainforth, also the prebendary, by will proved in 1714, left £80 to the vicarage to buy land worth £4 a year.[95] In 1716, however, the land bought was said to be worth only £3 10s. a year.[96] The net annual value of the vicarage was said in 1763 to be £31 9s. 8d.[97] The average net income in 1829–31 was £354[98] and in 1850 the living was worth about £440.[99]

The valuation of 1535 included, besides tithes, £1 for 6 bovates of glebe in Langtoft.[1] By 1664 the vicarage also had two small closes in Langtoft and two closes and several furlongs in Cottam then called Church flats, but in the 18th and 19th centuries Priest flats,[2] which carried the same common rights as 4 bovates of land.[3] At the inclosure of Langtoft in 1805 the vicar received 76 a. for glebe and 221 a. for tithes.[4] In 1843, when the tithes of Cottam were commuted, the vicar received a rent-charge of £108[5] and at the inclosure of Cottam in 1851 he was awarded 30 a. for glebe there.[6] In 1921 153 a. of glebe were sold[7] and in 1953 a further 153 a.[8]

A house near the churchyard was provided at the ordination of the vicarage in 1274.[9] In 1663 repairs to the vicarage house were ordered[10] but in 1716 the vicar stated that there had been no house 'this 50 years and more', although there was a 'vicarage yard' adjoining the churchyard.[11] There was subsequently no Vicarage[12] until a large red-brick house was built near the church in 1887.[13]

A condition attached to the ordination of the vicarage in 1274 was that the vicar should support a chantry with two chaplains in both the church and the chapel.[14] In 1525–6, in addition to the vicar, there was a parochial chaplain at Langtoft, whose stipend was £4 a year.[15] A guild dedicated to St. Catherine existed in the church in 1528[16] but nothing more is known of it. About 1450 Hawise Aske left two torches to the church and two to Cottam chapel.[17]

In 1375 the vicar was presented for immorality,[18] and about 1600 the vicar's immorality was alleged by the impropriator.[19] The vicar lived at Langtoft in 1743,[20] although there was no vicarage house. In 1764 his successor gave the lack of a house as the reason for his non-residence.[21] In 1835 and from at least 1865 to 1877 the vicar also held the living of North Grimston, where he resided.[22] Later incumbents seem to have been resident and to have held no other livings. In 1764 the vicar employed an assistant curate,[23] and there was an assistant curate from 1865 to 1877.[24]

A service was held at Langtoft twice a week in 1743, except for one Sunday each month, when a service was held in Cottam chapel. Communion was then administered four times a year at Langtoft, when about ten people received, and three times a year at Cottam, generally to four or five communicants.[25] The services were the same in 1764 except that communion was administered only three times a year at Langtoft, with 40 communicants the previous Easter. No communion service seems to have been held at Cottam then or subsequently.[26] By 1865 a service was held each Sunday at Langtoft

---

[79] Ibid., PR. 1186–8.
[80] Ibid. DDX/40/66.
[81] 3rd Rep. Poor Law Com. 168.
[82] See p. 270.
[83] Fasti Parochiales, iii. 51.
[84] V.C.H. Yorks. iii. 85.
[85] T.E.R.A.S. ii. 53.
[86] Fasti Parochiales, iii. 51–3; Rep. Com. Eccl. Revenues, 948–9.
[87] Under 3 & 4 Vic., c. 113.
[88] Crockford.
[89] Fasti Parochiales, iii. 51.
[90] Lawton, Rer. Eccles. Dioc. Ebor. 304.
[91] Tax. Eccl. (Rec. Com.), 297; Feud. Aids, vi. 333.
[92] York Fabric Rolls (Sur. Soc. xxxv), 260.
[93] Valor Eccl. (Rec. Com.), v. 122.
[94] T.E.R.A.S. ii. 53.
[95] Y.A.J. i. 276.
[96] B.I.H.R., TER. J. Langtoft 1716.
[97] J. Ecton, Thesaurus, 534.
[98] Rep. Com. Eccl. Revenues, 948–9.
[99] H.O. 129/24/524.
[1] Valor Eccl. v. 122.
[2] B.I.H.R., TER. J. Langtoft 1726 etc.
[3] D. & C. York, K 1/LAN 1.
[4] Regy. of Deeds, CI/14/2.
[5] E.R.R.O., DDX/40/167.
[6] Ibid. IA. Cottam, 1851.
[7] Regy. of Deeds, 229/380/334; 230/266/227; 231/262/214.
[8] Ibid. 931/322/284.
[9] Fasti Parochiales, iii. 51.
[10] B.I.H.R., Churches index.
[11] Ibid. TER. J. Langtoft 1716.
[12] Ibid. 1726 etc.
[13] Bulmer, Dir. E. Yorks. (1892), 231.
[14] Fasti Parochiales, iii. 51.
[15] Y.A.J. xxiv. 78.
[16] Test. Ebor. v. 132–3.
[17] Ibid. ii. 142.
[18] Fasti Parochiales, iii. 52.
[19] B.I.H.R., C.P., H. 2314.
[20] Herring's Visit. ii. 165.
[21] B.I.H.R., Bp. V. 1764/Ret. 112.
[22] Ibid. V. 1865/Ret. 316; V. 1868/Ret. 285; V. 1877/Ret.; Rep. Com. Eccl. Revenues, 948–9.
[23] B.I.H.R., Bp. V. 1764/Ret. 112.
[24] Ibid. V. 1865/Ret. 316; V. 1868/Ret. 285; V. 1877/Ret.
[25] Herring's Visit. i. 162; ii. 165.
[26] B.I.H.R., Bp. V. 1764/Ret. 112.

and once a month at Cottam, and communion was administered six times a year to 10–12 people.[27] By 1877 two services were held each Sunday at Langtoft and one at Cottam, and communion was administered monthly to about fourteen people.[28] A service continued to be held weekly at Cottam until *c*. 1900, when it again became monthly. Soon afterwards a service was held only once a year, at harvest thanksgiving, and that was discontinued during the First World War.[29] The chapel has since been disused. At Langtoft in 1900 the vicar reported that litany was said every alternate Sunday in order to shorten the service as the farm meal-time was noon.[30] In 1936 communion was administered weekly,[31] and in 1970 there were two services each Sunday.

The church of *ST. PETER*, Langtoft, built of limestone, consists of chancel, nave with north and south aisles, west tower, south porch, and north vestry. Much of the fabric was renewed in 1903 when both aisles and the vestry were built. Although no Norman work survives, the fact that there was a Norman font at Cottam suggests that the mother church at Langtoft was also in existence at that period. The west tower dates from the early 13th century, when it may have been added to an older church. It has clasping buttresses at the west corners, single lancet windows in the south and north faces, and a double-lancet window in the top stage of the south face. A corbel table runs along each face below the restored parapet. Internally the tower arch is supported on corbels. There are indications of three or four former roof levels against the east wall of the tower inside the nave.

The medieval church possessed a south aisle, probably built early in the 13th century and later extended eastwards. It is not known when the aisle was demolished but it had disappeared before 1903, when the present one was added.[32] The original aisle windows had apparently been reset in the south wall of the nave; they consisted of two 13th-century lancets and, further east, two traceried windows of the 14th century. A plain porch of brick and stone had been built outside the south door, its character suggesting that demolition had already taken place before the early 19th century. Parts of the south arcade evidently survived, perhaps incorporated in the nave wall. Traces of the east end of the medieval aisle and of the springing of its window arch are still visible beyond the modern east wall.

In the mid 14th century the early chancel was evidently pulled down and the nave and south aisle was extended eastwards. The new 14th-century chancel was higher than the nave and survives in much its original form. In the south wall it has a priest's doorway, surmounted externally by an ogee canopy, and three windows with curvilinear tracery; there are two similar windows on the north side. The east window and east buttresses appear to date from the 20th century but elsewhere the uniform gabled buttresses are original. Internally the chancel contains a fine set of three sedilia, all trefoil-headed under crocketed ogee canopies with richly-carved finials. The 12th-century font, large and round, was once at Cottam. The subjects of its six carved panels include Adam and Eve and the martyrdoms of St. Andrew and St. Lawrence.[33]

In 1472 it was reported that the stalls in the chancel were in disrepair and that the glass in the windows was broken. Nine years later there were said to be no stalls, the windows were still broken, and the chancel roof was in disrepair.[34] In 1521 the vicar bequeathed 20 lambs for mending the roof.[35] The chancel was again mended in the early 17th century, the nave was reroofed and the tower repaired in 1832,[36] and the church was also restored in 1862.[37]

A major restoration and partial rebuilding of the church was carried out in 1900–3 at the expense of Sir Tatton Sykes. The architect was C. Hodgson Fowler,[38] who was evidently sympathetic towards the medieval fabric, copying many of its features and preserving others. The north aisle was added with a north vestry beyond it; two 14th-century windows from the former north wall of the nave were set in the aisle and a late Perpendicular window in the vestry. A new south aisle and south porch were built and the south arcade was reconstructed, partly with surviving material. It is of six bays and has three early-13th-century circular piers of which the 'water-holding' bases and parts of the shafts are ancient. A fragment of the westernmost arch is original, as is the 14th-century base of one of the two octagonal piers further east. A trefoil-headed lancet window was reset near the west end of the south wall but the other aisle windows are new. At the same time the chancel walls were strengthened, the tower was repaired and its parapet rebuilt, and the church was reroofed.[39]

A 13th-century grave slab to 'Alina de Val . . .' in the north aisle has an incised 'bracelet-type' cross and a pair of shears.[40] There are monuments to Richard Knowsley (d. 1774) and his children, and to Elizabeth (d. 1800), wife of Robert Knowsley. The windows in the chancel are by Kempe and Tower, *c.* 1903.[41]

There were three bells at Langtoft in 1552,[42] but only two in 1764[43] and 1970. One is dated 1620 and the other, made by 'W.O.' of York, 1641.[44] The plate includes a silver cup, made in York in 1634 by James Plummer, and two pewter plates.[45] The registers of baptisms, burials, and marriages begin in 1587 and are complete.[46]

An addition was made to the churchyard in 1899.[47] Sir Tatton Sykes, by will proved in 1913, left £550 in trust for the maintenance of the church and churchyard.[48]

The chapel of the *HOLY TRINITY*, Cottam, is a small late-19th-century red-brick building, which stands alone on the former village site. It consists of

[27] B.I.H.R., V. 1865/Ret. 316.   [28] Ibid. V. 1877/Ret.
[29] *Hull Daily Mail*, 13 Sept. 1950.
[30] B.I.H.R., Bp. V. 1900/Ret. 222.
[31] Ibid. Bp. V. 1936/Ret. 29.
[32] Morris, *E.R. Yorks.* 136–7; *Y.A.J.* xxxvi. 6; *T.E.R.A.S.* x. 115.
[33] The font was moved to Langtoft in 1950: ex inf. the vicar, 1971.
[34] *York Fabric Rolls*, 256, 260.   [35] *Test. Ebor.* v. 132.
[36] E.R.R.O., PR. 1176, 1186; B.I.H.R., Prob. Reg. D/C v, f. 246v.   [37] B.I.H.R., Ch. Ret. 2.

[38] *Country Life*, 26 Sept. 1968, 770, 772.
[39] Morris, *E.R. Yorks.* 258; *Kelly's Dir. N. & E.R.Yorks.* (1905), 537; N.M.R., photo. of ch. from S.W. before restoration.   [40] *Y.A.J.* xlii. 341.
[41] Ex inf. Sir Nikolaus Pevsner, 1971.
[42] *Inventories of Ch. Goods*, 25.
[43] B.I.H.R., TER. J. Langtoft 1764.
[44] Boulter, 'Ch. Bells', 218.
[45] *Yorks. Ch. Plate*, i. 282.   [46] In E.R.R.O.
[47] York Dioc. Regy., Sentence of consecration.
[48] Char. Com. files; see p. 222.

chancel and nave with west bell-turret. Little is known of the earlier chapel, although the font, now at Langtoft,[49] proves its existence in the 12th century. In 1840 the chapel contained only one pew and a reading desk[50] and in 1856 it was described as 'a small, plain, ancient, building'.[51] About 1890 it was completely rebuilt, with lancet windows, at the expense of the Revd. Richard Foord.[52] After the discontinuance of services[53] it gradually decayed, and in 1970 it was in ruins.

In 1552 there were two 'little' bells at Cottam.[54] In 1970 there was no bell. The church plate in 1912 included a silver cup made in York by Francis Tempest in 1609 and a silver paten given by the vicar in 1881;[55] they are now in Langtoft church. A marriage register exists for 1837–93.[56]

NONCONFORMITY. Houses were licensed for worship by dissenters in 1776, 1802, and 1833.[57] The Methodists had ten members in Langtoft in 1788–91.[58] The first chapel was licensed by the Wesleyan Methodists in 1808.[59] It stands in Back Street[60] and has been used as a Sunday school since 1876.[61] It was replaced by a new chapel near by in 1874;[62] this is a red-brick building with white- and blue-brick dressings and it was still used for worship in 1970.

The Primitive Methodists built a chapel in Cottam in 1839[63] and a school-room was added in 1848.[64] They comprise together a plain red-brick building. There were 36 members in 1889.[65] The chapel ceased to be used c. 1950[66] but still stood in 1970.

The vicar reported in 1868 that the strength of dissent in the parish was his greatest impediment[67] and in 1889 it was said that the Wesleyans had always been strong, although the Primitives were 'relatively feeble'.[68]

EDUCATION. Michael Dickinson, to whom the churchwardens allowed 3s. in 1780 for 'a house for scholars',[69] may have been the first schoolmaster in the parish. A schoolmaster is mentioned in 1801[70] and by 1819 there were two schools, in which 40 children were taught.[71] By 1835 there were three schools, in which 60 boys and girls were taught at their parents' expense.[72] A Church of England National school was built in 1845[73] near the church. In 1871 it had accommodation for 64 pupils but 80 children were in fact taught there. There were then also two private day-schools, attended by a total of 24 girls.[74] The National school was enlarged in 1873 and two years later school pence were paid by 51 boys, 51 girls, and 50 infants, although the average attendance was only 81. Other sources of income were subscriptions and voluntary rates.[75] A government grant was first received in 1875–6.[76] The school was in financial difficulties in 1894, however, because of the failure of several people to pay the voluntary rate.[77]

In 1898 it was reported that increased accommodation was needed. Plans for enlarging the school to provide places for 122 boys and girls and 34 infants were approved in 1902[78] and the work was carried out in 1905–6.[79] Between 1908 and 1914 attendance varied only between 107 and 120 but from 1919 to 1938 it was only once over 100, in 1932; in other years it varied between 71 and 96.[80] In 1970 the average number on the roll was 39.[81]

There has never been a school at Cottam and children from the township have attended that at Langtoft in the 19th and 20th centuries. In 1897 it was decided that the township should contribute to the school's finances in proportion to the number of of its children attending, then 15[82] out of an average total of 122.[83] Cottam also contributed towards the cost of rebuilding the school in 1905–6.[84]

CHARITIES FOR THE POOR. John Lamplough, by will proved in 1896, bequeathed £100 for the benefit of the poor of Langtoft.[85] The income in 1971 was nearly £2 and payments of 5s. to 10s. each were made to widows.[86]

LOWTHORPE

LOWTHORPE lies 4 miles east of Great Driffield and is one of the string of villages situated at the southern edge of the wolds, between Driffield and Bridlington.[1] The village was probably of Scandinavian origin.[2] Like its neighbour Harpham, Lowthorpe village lies off the main road to Bridlington and, indeed, the whole of its territory is south of that road. Lowthorpe's southerly situation may be explained by the presence of Ruston Parva to the north-west, in a small valley cut into the wold

---

[49] See p. 270.
[50] White, Dir. E. & N.R. Yorks. (1840), 393.
[51] Sheahan and Whellan, Hist. York & E.R. ii. 484.
[52] Kelly's Dir. N. & E.R. Yorks. (1897), 494; J. T. Ward, E. Yorks. Landed Estates in 19th Cent. (E. Yorks. Loc. Hist. Ser. xxiii), 64. [53] See p. 270.
[54] Inventories of Ch. Goods, 25.
[55] Yorks. Ch. Plate, i. 235–6.
[56] Barley, Par. Docs. E.R. 34. Its whereabouts were unknown in 1971: ex inf. the vicar.
[57] G.R.O. Worship Returns, Vol. v, nos. 446, 1726, 4310; B.I.H.R., DMH. Reg. 1, p. 689. [58] E.R.R.O., MRP/1/7.
[59] G.R.O. Worship Rets., Vol. v, no. 2193.
[60] O.S. Map 6″ (1854). [61] Char. Com. files.
[62] Date on building.
[63] H.O. 129/24/523; date on building.
[64] Date on building.
[65] H. Woodcock, Sketches of Prim. Meth. on Yorks. Wolds, 142.
[66] G.R.O. Worship Reg. no. 11002; local inf.
[67] B.I.H.R., V. 1868/Ret. 285.

[68] Woodcock, Prim. Meth. on Wolds, 142.
[69] E.R.R.O., PR. 1186. [70] Ibid. 1187.
[71] Rets. on Educ. of Poor, 1819, 1085.
[72] Educ. Enquiry Abstract, 1835, 1091. [73] Ed. 7/135.
[74] Rets. rel. Elem. Educ. 1871, 474. [75] Ed. 7/135.
[76] Rep. of Educ. Cttee. of Council, 1875–6 [C. 1513–I], H.C., p. 663 (1876), xxiii.
[77] B.I.H.R., Bp. V. 1894/Ret.
[78] E.R.R.O., SBM. Langtoft Sch. Bd. Min. Bk. 1896–1903.
[79] E.R. Educ. Cttee. Mins. 1905–6, 297; 1906–7, 55, 147.
[80] Bd. of Educ. List 21 (H.M.S.O.).
[81] Ex inf. Chief Educ. Officer, County Hall, Beverley, 1970.
[82] E.R.R.O., Min. Bk. 1896–1903.
[83] Kelly's Dir. N. & E.R. Yorks. (1897), 494.
[84] E.R. Educ. Cttee. Mins. 1906–7, 156, 232.
[85] Char. Com. files; ex inf. the vicar, 1972.
[86] Ex inf. Mr. J. W. Harland, Langtoft, 1972.
[1] This article was written in 1967–8.
[2] P.N.E.R. Yorks. (E.P.N.S.), 93.

slopes: Ruston occupies the higher ground which normally belongs to the wold-edge villages. In compensation the elongated parish of Lowthorpe stretches southwards nearly 3 miles across the Plain of Holderness. On the plain the parish boundary almost everywhere follows watercourses: White dike separates Lowthorpe from Nafferton to the west, and Lowthorpe beck (becoming Kelk beck as it flows south) divides it from the Kelks and Foston on the east. At two points the boundary diverges from the beck along minor watercourses, which may mark changes in the course of the main stream or the sites of water-mills. In the north-east Lowthorpe beck forms the boundary with Harpham. The straight north-western boundary, on the wold slopes, is aligned upon Fox hill, a prominent barrow on the highest ground in the parish, and the boundary runs around the base of the mound. The area of the parish is 1,969 a. Since 1935 Lowthorpe has been combined with Harpham and Ruston Parva in the civil parish of Harpham.[3]

The level and open landscape of the plain dominates much of the parish. South of the village a large area lies at between 25 ft. and 50 ft. above sea-level; further south still much of the land is below 25 ft. in height, with an 'island' of slightly higher ground known as Cattleholmes. These low-lying grounds were formerly used to a large extent as moor, carr, and meadow land, but in modern times arable farming has been predominant. North and west of the village the rising wold ground provided a limited area for the open fields of Lowthorpe. In the west this ground rises to little more than 75 ft. above sea-level, but in the north it rises more steeply to exceed 100 ft. near the Fox hill barrow. This again is now largely arable land. Along the eastern margin of the parish there are pastures skirting Lowthorpe beck, and near the village some variety is given to the landscape by the parkland of Lowthorpe Lodge. The only noteworthy area of woodland is a large plantation known as Church wood, which partly surrounds the church.

The village occupies a low-lying site near Lowthorpe beck, around the junctions of roads to Ruston, Nafferton, and Kelk. A stretch of road near the beck is called Mill Lane and a back lane Water Lane.[4] In the Middle Ages roads in the village were known as Little Gate, mentioned as early as 1190, and Nethergate.[5] The road to Kelk crosses the beck and a by-pass channel of the former water-mill by two small bridges, said to have been built in the late 1830s and to have been the first bridges placed there.[6] The beck is also bridged by the Hull–Scarborough railway line, opened in 1846, but Lowthorpe station is situated in Little Kelk.

Lowthorpe Lodge is a large brick house built by the St. Quintin family c. 1840, and said to replace an 'ancient mansion' demolished in 1826.[7] The latter may have been a house built by the St. Quintins after they acquired their Lowthorpe estate in the 18th century, or possibly the house of the Pearson family.[8] In the late 19th century the St. Quintins used Lowthorpe Lodge mainly as a shooting lodge; they were determined game-preservers and the beck was, and remains, an excellent trout stream.[9] Church wood is also traditionally the site of a 'hall',[10] and there are indeterminate earthworks in the parkland near the church; if a house ever existed in this locality it may have been the rectory house used by the priests of Lowthorpe college.[11] There were also at least two cottages near the churchyard in 1642.[12] There is no record of a medieval manor-house in Lowthorpe, though the Salvin family may have had a large house in the village: a toft of Dame Mary Salvin's called 'Lekeplace' is mentioned in 1372 and later.[13]

The house and cottages in the village vary widely in date and style. Two simple red-brick houses bear the dates 1771 and 1776 respectively, and the water-mill, now demolished, is said to have been built in 1777.[14] There are two pairs of mid-19th-century houses with pointed windows and diagonal glazing bars, another pair bearing the initials of W. H. St. Quintin and the date 1905, and four Council houses. The farm-houses in the village are the former mill house, Bathclose Farm, and Wellclose Farm, the last a large 19th-century house. Several scattered houses stand away from the village. To the north, on the Ruston road, is the Elms, a large late-19th-century house of yellow brick, formerly occupied by the bailiff of the St. Quintin estate.[15] In the west, near the Nafferton boundary, is Sleights Farm, formerly known as Lowthorpe Field. On the Nafferton road, south of the village, are Outgates Farm, bearing the date 1789, and a house with the initials of W. H. St. Quintin and the date 1913; the former is a typical 18th-century house with steep roof and dormers. Millingdale House is a large 19th-century building standing on a slight rise in the low-lying ground a mile south of the village. Finally, a further mile to the south, is a small group of houses at Cattleholmes. This includes two late-18th-century houses, one a large building with three end gables and 19th-century bay windows.

Lowthorpe had 146 poll-tax payers in 1377.[16] In 1674 there were 29 households, 8 of them discharged from the hearth tax. Of those taxed 15 had only one hearth each, 5 had 2, and one had fifteen.[17] Only 14 families were reported in 1743 and about 10 in 1764.[18] The population was 159 in 1801 and 139 in 1851, but by 1901 had increased to 189.[19] There were 159 inhabitants in 1931.[20]

MANOR AND OTHER ESTATES. At the Conquest there were three estates in Lowthorpe. Two of them, assessed at 4 carucates and 1½ carucate, belonged to the king; the third, of 1½ carucate, was held by the archbishop of York.[21]

The Crown estates subsequently formed part of

[3] *Census*, 1931. [4] O.S. Map 6" (1854).
[5] *T.E.R.A.S.* xxi. 45, 47, 50, 51, 53.
[6] E.R.R.O., QAB/1/9.
[7] Sheahan and Whellan, *Hist. York & E.R.* ii. 484; White, *Dir. E. and N.R. Yorks.* (1840), 394.
[8] See p. 273.
[9] *Kelly's Dir. N. and E.R. Yorks.* (1879), 620; J. T. Ward, *E. Yorks. Landed Estates in the 19th Cent.* (E. Yorks. Loc. Hist. Ser. xxiii), 31.
[10] O.S. Map 6" (1854).
[11] See p. 275. [12] Y.A.S. MSS., MS. 709a.
[13] *T.E.R.A.S.* xxi. 47, 50, 52.
[14] Sheahan and Whellan, *Hist. York & E.R.* ii. 484; see below, p. 275.
[15] Directories. [16] E 179/202/62 m. 7.
[17] E 179/205/521.
[18] B.I.H.R., Bp. V. 1764/Ret. 132; *Herring's Visit.* ii. 164.
[19] *V.C.H. Yorks.* iii. 489.
[20] *Census*.
[21] *V.C.H. Yorks.* ii. 204, 215, 287, 323.

NAFFERTON: the malting and corn-mill

RUSTON PARVA: Bracey Bridge water-mill

Folkton: a barn at Manor Farm

Hunmanby: the lock-up and the pinfold

Bessingby: the dovecot

Carnaby: the wagon shed at Carnaby House

the fee of the Meynells, who held them of the archbishop of Canterbury, and he of the king.[22] The larger of the two had been held before the Conquest by Norman and Asa; in 1086 it was in the hands of Game, although claim was laid to it by Richard de Surdeval. The second Crown estate had been held by Egfrid in 1066.[23] It seems likely that in the 12th century all the Crown land in Lowthorpe came into the tenancy of the family that took its name from the village. Walter of Lowthorpe certainly held 2 bovates there in 1234.[24] The last of the family to hold the estate was Thomas, who was in possession in 1270;[25] by 1279 he was dead, leaving his daughters Cecily and Margery as heirs.[26]

By 1290–1 Cecily and Margery had married respectively Robert and John of Heslerton,[27] each of whom held $2\frac{1}{2}$ carucates there in right of his wife.[28] The manor of LOWTHORPE was held in two moieties by the Heslertons[29] until both parts were granted to Lowthorpe college in the later 14th century. In 1364 Thomas, grandson of John Heslerton, was licensed to grant his moiety of the manor to the college,[30] and in 1372 Simon Heslerton obtained licence to grant the reversion of the other moiety, a transaction which was completed the following year.[31]

The college retained the manor until its dissolution in 1548.[32] In that year Thomas Haynes obtained a lease of the college and its lands from the Crown,[33] and a further lease was granted in 1565.[34] Haynes's widow obtained another lease in 1584 and devised it to Robert Man, who conveyed the manor-house to Henry, earl of Huntingdon. In 1586 Sir Edward Hastings conveyed this interest to Ralph Westrop, and he granted it the following year to Marmaduke Langdale.[35] The manor and other college lands were in 1609 granted in fee to Hugh Jones and John Shepherd,[36] and later that year they conveyed the manor to Henry Osborne.[37] John Suckling obtained a grant of it in 1612 from Osborne.[38] At his death in 1627 Sir John Suckling directed that his Yorkshire lands should be sold,[39] and in 1630 his executors sold the manor of Lowthorpe to Thomas and John Pearson.[40]

By 1583 property in Lowthorpe was already in the possession of the Pearson family of Harpham,[41] and after acquiring the manor John Pearson lived at Lowthorpe.[42] Sir Matthew Pearson in 1674 had a house there with fifteen hearths.[43] The Pearsons sold the manor to Sir William St. Quintin in 1720,[44] and the property subsequently followed the descent of Harpham.[45] In 1947 the 417-acre Millingdale farm and in 1948 the 207-acre Sleights farm were sold to Leonard Smith and William Martinson respectively.[46] The rest of the estate, comprising 997 a. as well as plantations in 1959,[47] still belonged to Lady Legard in 1968.

The estate of the archbishop of York had been in the liberty of St. John of Beverley at the Conquest and in 1086.[48] It apparently remained within the liberty until the Dissolution,[49] but little is known of the demesne tenants during that time, although part of the estate at least was held by the Salvins.[50] After the Dissolution much of it eventually came into the hands of the Fox family. It was presumably former liberty land which Anthony Madyson granted to William Angevyn in 1562, and Angevyn to Richard Fox in 1563.[51] When George Fox died in 1586 he had 8 bovates of land and other property in Lowthorpe which was said to be held of the queen, as of her manor of Ruston Parva, and to have formerly belonged to the provost of Beverley.[52] The family still had property in Lowthorpe in the earlier 17th century.[53] The estate may have been acquired by the Tancreds of Whixley (Yorks. W.R.), for when Sir Richard Tancred was fined for delinquency in 1645 he had property in Lowthorpe which was claimed to be worth £60 and out of which a rent was payable to the manor of Ruston.[54]

The holding of the Salvin family in Lowthorpe consisted at least in part of land of the liberty of Beverley. It is first recorded in 1303, when Gerard Salvin received a grant of free warren in his demesne lands there,[55] and Lowthorpe was among the properties on which he charged a yearly rent, payable to Hugh de Vere and his wife, in 1308.[56] Like the Salvins' Kilham estate the Lowthorpe holding had belonged to the Thirkleby family which in 1260 had 9 bovates of land, 59 a. of pasture, and other property there.[57] The likelihood that this land was that of the liberty of Beverley is strengthened by the allegation of Gerard Salvin in 1312–13 that the church of Lowthorpe belonged to the liberty and that the advowson therefore belonged to him, and not to the Heslertons.[58] At his death in 1320 Gerard Salvin had 18 a. of meadow in Lowthorpe, held of the Heslertons, and land called the 'Devises', held of the provost of Beverley.[59] In 1344 another Gerard was

---

[22] *E.Y.C.* ii, pp. 134–6; *Feud. Aids*, vi. 31, 141; *Cur. Reg. R.* xiii. 67; *Cal. Inq. p.m.* iii, p. 428; v, p. 54. For the 'Canterbury fee' held by the Meynells in Yorks. see *V.C.H. Yorks. N.R.* ii. 311.
[23] *V.C.H. Yorks.* ii. 204, 287, 293.
[24] *Yorks. Fines, 1232–46*, 19.
[25] *Reg. Giffard* (Sur. Soc. cix), 55, 61, 286.
[26] C.P. 40/17 m. 41.
[27] *T.E.R.A.S.* xxiv. 30.
[28] *Cal. Inq. p.m.* iii, p. 428.
[29] *Cal. Chart. R. 1300–26*, 39; *Yorks. Fines, 1327–47*, 162; *Cal. Inq. p.m.* v, p. 54.
[30] *Cal. Pat. 1361–4*, 435.
[31] Ibid. *1370–4*, 161, 259; *Yorks. Fines, 1347–77*, 166; *Abbrev. Rot. Orig.* (Rec. Com.), ii. 327.
[32] E 315/116 ff. 78–9; E 321/25 no. 86; E 321/31 no. 63.
[33] E 321/31 no. 1.
[34] *Cal. Pat. 1563–6*, 366.
[35] E 134/37 & 38 Eliz. Mich./15.
[36] C 66/1802 no. 15; *Cal. S.P. Dom. 1603–10*, 533.
[37] Y.A.S. MSS., MS. 709a.
[38] *Yorks. Fines, 1603–14*, 184.
[39] C 142/446/87.
[40] Y.A.S. MSS., MS. 709a.
[41] C 142/310/77; *Yorks. Fines*, iii. 10; iv. 134.
[42] Y.A.S. MSS., MS. 709a; *Dugdale's Visit. Yorks.* (Sur. Soc. xxxvi), 76.
[43] E 179/205/521.
[44] Registry of Deeds, Beverley, G/398/876.
[45] See p. 224.
[46] Regy. of Deeds, 775/409/347; 782/379/327.
[47] Ibid. 1129/159/136.
[48] *V.C.H. Yorks.* ii. 215.
[49] *Bev. Chapter Act Bk.* ii (Sur. Soc. cviii), 322; G. Poulson, *Beverlac*, 641.
[50] B.M. Lansd. MS. 896, f. 126; *Cal. Inq. p.m.* vi, p. 133; see below.
[51] *Yorks. Fines*, i. 259, 276.
[52] C 142/276/563.
[53] E 179/204/424; E 179/205/478; E 179/261/2, 3; C 142/277/53; C 142/245/79.
[54] *Royalist Composition Papers*, i (Y.A.S. Rec. Ser. xv), 65–70.
[55] *Cal. Chart. R. 1300–26*, 37.
[56] *Yorks. Fines, 1300–14*, 67; see above, pp. 180, 254.
[57] K.B. 26/169 m. 10d.; *Year Bks. 6 Edw. II* (Selden Soc. xxxiv), 48 sqq.
[58] *Year Bks. 6 Edw. II*, 48 sqq.
[59] *Cal. Inq. p.m.* vi, p. 133.

claiming a large estate in Lowthorpe from Sir George Salvin, including 8 bovates of land.[60] In 1429 the Salvins still had 8 bovates in Lowthorpe, said to be held as part of the archbishop of Canterbury's fee,[61] and they had the same amount of land in 1494.[62] The Salvins were disposing of property in Lowthorpe in the 16th century: to Marmaduke Constable and others in 1533, to Adam Smalewood and Christopher Ellerton in 1578, and to Bartholomew Williamson and John Cawood in 1597.[63]

Several holdings, at various dates, were composed of land in Cattleholmes. The Hothams had a quarter of a pasture there in 1224, and soon after that date Robert of Hotham granted his right in Cattleholmes to the liberty of Beverley.[64] In 1304 Denise de Munchensy held a pasture or turbary in Cattleholmes of Robert of Heslerton,[65] and in 1310 Robert Ughtred died possessed of a pasture called Cattleholmes, held of John of Heslerton.[66] A quarter part of 400 a. of moor in Cattleholmes was included in Simon Heslerton's grant of his share of Lowthorpe manor to Lowthorpe college in 1373.[67] The Constables had 40 a. in Cattleholmes in 1496,[68] and their property there was worth £10 in 1536–7.[69] Cattleholmes was perhaps among the lands Marmaduke Constable exchanged with the Crown in 1546–7. In 1558 the Crown granted to William Etherington (or Edrington) and Edward Beseley a manor-house called Cattleholmes, formerly Marmaduke Constable's, and a quarter part of land there, formerly of Lowthorpe college; Etherington was then already tenant of both properties.[70] A dispute over the payment of tithes from Cattleholmes in 1595–6 reveals that the Constables had, in fact, owned three-quarters of the land and the college one quarter.[71] The Etheringtons sold land in Lowthorpe and Cattleholmes in 1564 to John Nettleton and Richard Thurley, in 1600 to Thomas Sylvester, and in 1611 to William Spinke.[72] They retained some of the estate, however, until at least 1627.[73] A farm called Cattleholmes which belonged to Anne Jegon of Wansford in 1674 may have been part of the former Etherington estate.[74]

Several other religious houses had property in Lowthorpe. Bridlington priory had a small estate there by the early 14th century, when gifts of 2 bovates and other land were confirmed by the Crown.[75] In the early 16th century the priory had 3 bovates there, worth 3s. a year.[76] After the Dissolution some of this property was in the hands of John Goodale in 1557,[77] and a grant of other former priory lands was made in 1563 to Thomas Wood and William Frankland.[78] The Knights Hospitallers of Beverley had a cottage in Lowthorpe in 1539–40,[79] and this was restored to them, with their other property, when the order was briefly revived in 1558.[80] Nunkeeling priory was given a water-mill in Lowthorpe at an unknown date,[81] and in 1536 the priory had a parcel of land there.[82]

After the dissolution of Lowthorpe college the tithes were leased, along with the manor, by Thomas Haynes.[83] John Hotham was in dispute about them with Haynes's widow in 1582.[84] A Crown grant of the 'free chapel or college' of Lowthorpe was in 1590 made to William Tipper and Robert Dawe,[85] but Elizabeth Haynes's lease of the property nevertheless passed, with the manor, to Marmaduke Langdale; thus in 1595 Langdale was engaged in a lawsuit about tithes due to him from Cattleholmes.[86] When the manor was granted to Jones and Shepherd in 1609[87] the tithes were separately granted to Francis Philips and Richard More.[88] In 1610 John Suckling conveyed them to Edmund Cooke[89] but Suckling was still in possession at his death in 1627.[90]

The tithes of Lowthorpe were acquired, with the manor, by Thomas and John Pearson in 1630.[91] Those of Cattleholmes, however, were separated from the rest and in 1627 Sir George Throckmorton and Richard Etherington conveyed them to Robert Crompton.[92] In 1650 the tithes of Lowthorpe, then worth £80 a year, belonged to John Pearson, and those of Cattleholmes, worth £10, to a Mr. Crompton and a Mr. Spink.[93] In 1720 the tithes passed to Sir William St. Quintin[94] and subsequently descended with the manor.

ECONOMIC HISTORY. In 1086 the Crown estate of 1½ carucate had land for one plough and was worth 10s. On the king's four-carucate estate there was land for two ploughs but the six villeins there had only one plough and the estate was worth only 8s. The archbishop of York's estate was largely waste in 1086.[95]

The low-lying ground in the southern part of the parish was from early times occupied by meadow, pasture, and carr. In the 13th and 14th centuries part of the area appears to have been used as common pasture and for digging turves.[96] The most southerly part of Lowthorpe comprised the pasture known as Cattleholmes; the name first occurs in the

---

[60] C.P. 40/337 m. 74.
[61] E 179/202/104.
[62] Cal. Inq. p.m. Hen. VII, i, p. 406.
[63] Yorks. Fines, i. 66; ii. 129; iv. 70.
[64] B.M. Lansd. Ch. 394; Cur. Reg. R. xi. 472.
[65] Abbrev. Plac. (Rec. Com.), 252; Yorks. Inq. iv. 70; Cal. Close, 1302–7, 177.
[66] Cal. Inq. p.m. v, p. 106. Ughtred may have succeeded to the Hotham holding: see above, p. 180.
[67] See p. 273.
[68] Cal. Close, 1485–1500, 259–60.
[69] S.C. 6/Hen. VIII/4334.
[70] Cal. Pat. 1557–8, 390.
[71] E 134/37 Eliz. East./30; E 134/38 Eliz. East./2; E 134/38 Eliz. Hil./19.
[72] Yorks. Fines, i. 289; iv. 154; 1603–14, 154.
[73] C 142/259/33; C 60/463 no. 44; C 60/504 no. 18; Yorks. Fines, iv. 172, 179; 1614–25, 27.
[74] E.R.R.O., DDSY/68/23.
[75] Bridlington Charty. 8, 157–9.
[76] Miscellanea, iii (Y.A.S. Rec. Ser. lxxx), 17.
[77] B.M. Harl. MS. 607, f. 93b.
[78] Cal. Pat. 1560–3, 576.
[79] Miscellanea, iv (Y.A.S. Rec. Ser. xciv), 87.
[80] Cal. Pat. 1557–8, 319.
[81] B.M. Cott. MS. Otho C. viii, f. 88.
[82] E 315/401 f. 134; Valor Eccl. (Rec. Com.), v. 115.
[83] See p. 273.
[84] E 134/24 Eliz. East./9.
[85] C 66/1340 mm. (I) 40, (II) 30.
[86] E 134/37 Eliz. East./30; E 134/37 & 38 Eliz. Mich./45; E 134/38 Eliz. Hil./19; E 134/38 Eliz. East./2; B.I.H.R., R. As. 8/13, 15, 18; 19/56, 72–6.
[87] See p. 273.
[88] C 66/1757 m. 7.
[89] Yorks. Fines, 1603–14, 123.
[90] C 142/446/87.
[91] Y.A.S. MSS., MS. 709a.
[92] C.P. 25(2)/518/3 Chas. I East. pt. 3, no. 1.
[93] T.E.R.A.S. ii. 52.
[94] Regy. of Deeds, G/398/876.
[95] V.C.H. Yorks. ii. 204, 215, 287.
[96] K.B. 26/165 m. 9; J.I. 1/1044 m. 1d.; Bridlington Charty. 159; Cal. Pat. 1313–17, 63; T.E.R.A.S. xxi. 49.

late 12th century and it perhaps denotes an island of higher ground where cattle collected.[97] It may have occupied about 400 a.[98] Just north of Cattleholmes, where Millingdale House stood in 1968, was an area of pasture referred to in 1586 as the 'Mettindales'.[99] There were apparently still common rights in this land in 1724, when a cattle-gate in 'Mettendale' is mentioned,[1] and in 1738.[2] Nearer the village, and along the beck in the north-east, there was much meadow land.[3]

The location and extent of the open fields of Lowthorpe are not known. There are early references to open-field land, and North field was mentioned in the early 14th century.[4] In the 19th century lands north and west of the village were known respectively as North fields and Lowthorpe field,[5] and this was no doubt where the open fields lay, on the wold slopes. The open fields still existed in 1642, when, in addition to the manor-house and water-mill, John Pearson had 12 bovates of demesne land, 6 other bovates, meadow in Lady Mill ings, pasture in the Mettendales, and turf 'grafts' and common rights in the common carr. Tenants held 8 houses, 19 cottages, 20 bovates of land, 12 closes, pasture in the Mettendales, and turf and pasture rights in the carr.[6]

Inclosure of at least part of the open fields apparently took place in the early 18th century, for in 1724 three closes, containing altogether 16 a., were described as formerly part of North field and Lady Mill ings, 'lately inclosed'.[7] An account of lands belonging to the manor in the same year mentions a number of closes, but it is not clear whether all the lands listed were inclosed; the names North field and West field were both used.[8]

Drainage of the low-lying parts of the parish still presented difficulties in the 18th and 19th centuries, and there were disputes with Nafferton about responsibility for the cleansing of Scarfe dike:[9] this was perhaps an earlier, or an alternative, name for White dike, which forms the boundary between the two parishes. Extensive work was apparently being done to improve the drainage in Lowthorpe in the 1840s.[10] Much of the low-lying part of the parish probably remained under pasture in these centuries, and in 1801 the area under crops in Lowthorpe was only 518 a.,[11] i.e. about a quarter of the total acreage.

A relatively small number of tenants has farmed the St. Quintin estates in modern times. In 1783 there were ten occupiers,[12] and in 1796 only ten of the 23 tenants who held the St. Quintins' 1,616 a. were in possession of farms. Only six of the farms of 1796 were over 100 a., the largest comprising 316 a.[13] In the 19th and 20th centuries there have been about eight farmers, one of them also being the miller. The St. Quintin estate has also provided employment for several men not directly concerned with farming, such as land agent, gamekeepers, water-bailiff, and woodman.[14] In addition to preservation, the estate has been noted for the pioneer improvement of livestock.[15] In 1968 there was a large turkey farm at the Elms.

There has been little other non-agricultural employment in Lowthorpe, and a Friday market and fair on 10–12 November, granted to John of Heslerton in 1304,[16] were not recorded again. A brickyard near the Nafferton boundary was in use in 1850.[17] There was a water-mill in Lowthorpe as early as 1327, when reference is made to the dam of 'Wathemyln'.[18] Wath Mill was close to the village[19] and was probably on the site occupied by the modern mill. It was perhaps the same mill that was described as a fulling mill in 1565.[20] The latest building on the site is said to have been built in 1777,[21] and it remained in full working order until a few years before its demolition in 1959.[22]

LOCAL GOVERNMENT. Court papers of the St. Quintins show that two bylawmen, a constable, and a pinder were frequently appointed in the early 19th century. A pinder was still appointed in 1914. In 1738 and in the 1770s pains for Lowthorpe were laid at the court at Harpham. Most of them were concerned with sewers, roads, and bridges, and the poorhouses were mentioned in 1776.[23]

No parochial records before 1835 are known. In 1836 Lowthorpe joined the Driffield union.[24]

CHURCH. A church at Lowthorpe is first mentioned in 1086, when it lay within the larger of the two Crown estates.[25] The neighbouring village of Ruston Parva was a chapelry of Lowthorpe throughout the Middle Ages, later being regarded as a separate cure.[26] Lowthorpe church was made collegiate in 1333. The rector and John of Heslerton, as patron, in that year placed the church at the disposal of the archbishop of York, and he ordained that there should be a rector, alternatively called master or warden, who was to celebrate mass at least thrice weekly, and six chantry priests in the church. A seventh chantry was added in 1364. All the priests were to live in the rectory house and to receive stipends.[27] After the dissolution of the college in 1548 the church continued to serve the parish. Institutions were made in 1557 and 1579,[28] on the

[97] P.N.E.R. Yorks. (E.P.N.S.), 93.
[98] See p. 274.
[99] C 142/563/276.
[1] Registry of Deeds, Beverley, H/711/1445.
[2] Y.A.S. MSS., DD. 89.
[3] Regy. of Deeds, H/711/1445; C 142/563/276; E 310/172/70; T.E.R.A.S. xxi. 45 sqq.
[4] T.E.R.A.S. xxi. 45, 54.
[5] O.S. Map 6" (1854).
[6] Y.A.S. MSS., MS. 709a.
[7] Regy. of Deeds, H/705/1443.
[8] Ibid. /711/1445.
[9] E.R.R.O., CSR/14/89; /31/129; DDSQ (2)/Box 1/E.
[10] Ibid. DDSQ (2)/Box 1/E.
[11] 1801 Crop Returns.
[12] E.R.R.O., Land Tax, 1783.
[13] Y.A.S. MSS., MS. 709b.
[14] Directories.

[15] J. T. Ward, E. Yorks. Landed Estates in the 19th Cent. (E. Yorks. Loc. Hist. Ser. xxiii), 31.
[16] Cal. Chart. R. 1300–26, 39.
[17] O.S. Map 6" (1854).
[18] T.E.R.A.S. xxi. 46.
[19] Ibid. 51; Public Works in Med. Law, ii (Selden Soc. xl), 310.
[20] E 310/29/172 no. 70.
[21] Sheahan and Whellan, Hist. York & E.R. ii. 484.
[22] Ex inf. Mr. H. S. Welburn, Harpham.
[23] Call rolls and jury papers, 1789–1914: Y.A.S. MSS., DD. 89.
[24] 3rd Rep. Poor Law Com. 168.
[25] V.C.H. Yorks. ii. 287.
[26] See p. 323.
[27] V.C.H. Yorks. iii. 365. For presentations to the chantries see Fasti Parochiales, iii. 102–10.
[28] See p. 276.

former occasion Thomas Fugall being presented. Fugall had been described as curate of Lowthorpe in 1552. Joseph Somers in 1743 was also described as curate.[29] The two perpetual curacies of Lowthorpe and Ruston Parva were united in 1852[30] and the living was later styled a vicarage. The extra-parochial district of Little Kelk was united with Lowthorpe for ecclesiastical purposes in 1929.[31]

The advowson of the church belonged to the lords of the manor in the 13th and 14th centuries: presentations were made in right of the heir of Walter of Lowthorpe in 1226, by Thomas of Lowthorpe in 1270, and in right of another Lowthorpe heir in 1281.[32] Robert of Heslerton presented in 1329 and the Heslertons retained the patronage until 1372, when they made their final presentation.[33] Their right was in dispute in 1312 and the archbishop presented in that year.[34] The advowson is said to have passed to the Hotham family by the marriage of Agnes, daughter of John Heslerton, to Sir John Hotham (d. 1370).[35] Sir John Hotham first presented in 1393,[36] and his family enjoyed the advowson until 1536, when a presentation was made in right of Francis Hotham.[37]

At the dissolution of the college the advowson passed to the Crown, which in 1557 allowed a nomination to be made by three men to whom Francis Hotham had previously granted his next right of presentation.[38] A grant of the advowson by the Crown to the archbishop of York in 1558[39] presumably lapsed on the accession of Elizabeth I. John Hotham presented in 1579.[40] The advowson was granted, with the rectory, to Francis Philips and Richard More in 1608–9,[41] and in 1720 the Pearsons sold it to Sir William St. Quintin.[42] It subsequently descended with the manor.[43]

In 1291 the church was worth £16, reduced to £10 13s. 4d. in the new taxation.[44] When, after the Dissolution, the property of the college was granted to Thomas Haynes, the Crown assumed the responsibility of providing for ministers at both Lowthorpe and its chapelry of Ruston.[45] In 1650 the minister of Lowthorpe had a stipend of £10 from the Exchequer, together with £20 paid out of the tithes of Lowthorpe and Ruston.[46] The Crown stipend remained part of the income,[47] which was augmented three times from Queen Anne's Bounty in the 18th century: £200 was given in 1749 and again in 1766, and in 1780 a further £200 was given to meet benefactions of £100 from Sir William St. Quintin and £100 from the minister of Lowthorpe.[48] In 1829–31 the average net income of Lowthorpe was £64.[49] The net income of Lowthorpe with Ruston Parva was £148 in 1884.[50]

Glebe land was acquired in the 18th century. By 1770 the first two augmentations of £200 had been used, together with money belonging to Ruston, to buy 16 a. in Cottingham: two thirds of the land was reckoned to belong to Lowthorpe. By 1781 the Bounty money received in the previous year had been used to buy 20 a. in Nafferton.[51] There was no vicarage house for the living until 1893,[52] when a large house was built near the church.

In the mid 16th century the living of Lowthorpe was held together with Hessle and Hull by the notorious Thomas Fugall, who was deprived of Hull in 1561 for a variety of offences.[53] Lowthorpe was held with Kilham in the late 17th century. In the 18th century the curate lived at Nafferton, and he also held that living as well as Ruston and Foston on the Wolds.[54] The living was subsequently held with Rillington and Thorpe Bassett, and in the early 19th century with Ruston and Garton on the Wolds.[55]

In 1743 and 1764 a service was held in the church only once a fortnight; communion was administered three times a year and was received by 20–30 people.[56] By 1851 one service was held each week,[57] and in 1864 communion was received six times a year by about eight people.[58] In 1884 the incumbent held two weekly services, apparently one at Lowthorpe and one at Ruston.[59] In 1900 communion was administered whenever a morning service was held, and in 1936 it was administered once a week.[60] In 1968 there was one service each Sunday.

The church of *ST. MARTIN*, built largely of stone, consists of ruined chancel, nave, south porch, and west tower. Great changes were evidently made to the church after it became collegiate in 1333. The lofty chancel, now roofless and disused, certainly dates from the mid 14th century and the continuation of its moulded plinth around the walls of the nave and tower suggests that there may have been a complete rebuilding at this period. The chancel is of two bays, the north wall having external buttresses and containing two large three-light windows with reticulated tracery. The south wall, which has been partly rebuilt, has a similar window in its western bay and a small doorway further east. There is evidence that the chancel was originally longer, for the buttresses which support its east end are formed from the walls of an additional bay; the buttresses incorporate parts of the jambs and sills of another pair of windows. The structure was probably reduced in length after the dissolution of the

---

[29] *Inventories of Ch. Goods*, 22–3; *Herring's Visit*. ii. 164.
[30] York Dioc. Regy., Orders in Council 1/94.
[31] Ibid. 1/597.
[32] *Reg. Gray* (Sur Soc. lvi), 14; *Reg. Giffard* (Sur. Soc. cix), 55, 61, 286; *Reg. Wickwane* (Sur. Soc. cxiv), 114.
[33] *Yorks. Fines, 1327–47*, 60; *Fasti Parochiales*, iii. 55–6.
[34] *Reg. Greenfield*, i (Sur. Soc. cxlv), 83; iii (Sur. Soc. cli), 206–7.
[35] *Fasti Parochiales*, iii. 53.
[36] Ibid.; *Yorks. Inq. Hen. IV–V*, 101.
[37] C 142/51/82; C 142/84/46; *Fasti Parochiales*, iii. 56–8; *L. & P. Hen. VIII*, iv (3), p. 2856.
[38] *Cal. Pat.* 1555–7, 504.   [39] Ibid. 1557–8, 401.
[40] *Fasti Parochiales*, iii. 58.
[41] C 66/1757 m. 7.
[42] Registry of Deeds, Beverley, G/398/876.
[43] York Dioc. Regy., Orders in Council 1/94, 597; J. Ecton, *Thesaurus Rer. Eccles.* (1788 edn.), 24; *Rep. Com. Eccl. Revenues*, 952–3; Lawton, *Rer. Eccles. Dioc. Ebor.* 305; *Crockford*.

[44] *Tax. Eccl.* (Rec. Com.), 303, 326.
[45] *Cal. Pat.* 1563–6, 366.
[46] *T.E.R.A.S.* ii. 52.
[47] B.I.H.R., TER. J. Lowthorpe n.d. etc.
[48] Ibid. 1781; Hodgson, *Q.A.B.* 446.
[49] *Rep. Com. Eccl. Revenues*, 952–3.
[50] B.I.H.R., Bp. V. 1884/Ret.
[51] B.I.H.R., TER. J. Lowthorpe 1770, 1781.
[52] *Kelly's Dir. N. & E.R. Yorks.* (1893), 459.
[53] H. Aveling, *Post Reformation Catholicism in E. Yorks. 1558–1790* (E. Yorks. Loc. Hist. Ser. xi), 11; *V.C.H. Yorks. E.R.* i. 289.
[54] B.I.H.R., Bp. V. 1764/Ret. 132; *Herring's Visit*. ii. 164.
[55] E.R.R.O., DPX/58, Lowthorpe, p. 5; *Rep. Com. Eccl. Revenues*, 952–3.
[56] B.I.H.R., Bp. V. 1764/Ret. 132; *Herring's Visit*. ii. 164.
[57] H.O. 129/24/523.   [58] B.I.H.R., V. 1865/Ret. 335.
[59] Ibid. Bp. V. 1884/Ret.
[60] Ibid. Bp. V. 1900/Ret. 235; Bp. V. 1936/Ret. 289.

college when such an imposing chancel may have been considered unnecessary or undesirable. The present east wall, perhaps of reused medieval masonry, contains a square-headed mullioned and transomed window of post-Reformation date. A trefoil-headed piscina in this wall may have been moved from its original position in the demolished eastern bay.

The shortened chancel was probably abandoned in the later 18th century. An inscribed stone in the nave wall, which has now disappeared, is said to have recorded that the church roof was repaired in 1776 and that the building was repaved and repewed and the chancel 'contracted' in 1777.[61] Certainly the chancel was still in use in 1712, when Sir Matthew Pearson and his brother John were buried there 'under the great stone'.[62] A broken floor slab with an inscription to the brothers is still partly *in situ*. It was probably in 1777 that a small brick extension to the nave, projecting into the disused chancel, was built behind the chancel arch to accommodate the altar. Other brickwork which may be of the same date includes the belfry stage of the tower and the blocking of all the windows in the former chancel.

A drawing of the church made in 1859 is described as showing the building 'as it appeared prior to the restoration now in progress'.[63] The nave is shown with one south window similar to the 14th-century windows in the former chancel; there is a doorway without a porch and a small window further west. The nave then had an embattled parapet concealing the roof and its walls were of the same height as those of the chancel. The restoration of the nave involved a new high-pitched roof with lower eaves, the insertion of new windows throughout, and the addition of a south porch. Internally the chancel arch, which has crudely-carved capitals and may be of 16th-century date, has survived in an altered form. The medieval font has been retained.

The west tower almost certainly formed part of the 14th-century church, but a west window in its lower stage appears to be a 16th-century insertion. The upper stage, a mean brick structure with wooden Gothic-style windows and angle pinnacles, probably dates from the later 18th century.

The chief monument is a tomb bearing the figures of a man and woman with the branches of a tree spreading over their bodies, from which it springs; the heads of twelve children appear at the ends of the branches as if fruit from the tree. This monument was formerly in the chancel. It has been suggested that it is the tomb of John of Heslerton, who founded the college in 1333,[64] or of Thomas of Heslerton (d. 1355–6).[65] There is also a tradition that the tomb came from Ruston.[66] A brass of a knight, attributed to *c.* 1420, was once in the chancel.[67] It may commemorate George Salvin (d. 1417) and his wife.[68] The remains of a chest tomb in the chancel formerly bore a brass to John Pearson (d. 1665), made by Thomas Mann of York.[69] The chancel was evidently used as a burial place for members of the Pearson family in the 18th century. Besides the floor slab of 1712, already mentioned, there is another to William Pearson (d. 1717).

The church contains a Royal Arms of William IV. Part of a carved cross-head, dug up in the churchyard, is said to be pre-Norman.[70] Outside, near the east end of the church, stands a cross which is traditionally believed to have come from the market-place at Kilham.

There were three bells in the tower in 1552,[71] but there are now only two, made in 1786 and 1787.[72] The plate includes a silver cup and paten, a stoneware flagon with silver mountings, and a wooden mazer bowl with a silver ring; all were presented to the church in 1723 by Frances Rokeby, daughter of John Pearson, of Lowthorpe. There is also a gold ring, given by her in 1711.[73] The cup and paten have the London hallmark of 1700, the mountings of the flagon have the London mark for 1573, and the mazer is perhaps of the mid 15th century. It is possible that the mazer had belonged to the college, which at the Dissolution had 'a mazer with a band', as well as 'a great horn garnished with silver'.[74] The registers begin in 1546 and are complete.[75]

The churchyard was enlarged in 1902.[76]

NONCONFORMITY. In 1676 two dissenters were reported in Lowthorpe,[77] but there is no other record of nonconformist activity in the parish until the licensing of a house for worship in 1788.[78] In 1864 the vicar claimed that 'nearly all the people are Methodist in both my villages'.[79] There has never been a chapel of any denomination in Lowthorpe, however, and the Methodists used the chapels at Ruston and Harpham.

EDUCATION. There was a schoolmaster at Lowthorpe in 1563 and again in 1706–7,[80] but at no time since has there been a school in the parish. It was reported in 1818 that £1 had been bequeathed 'a few years since' towards the teaching of children in Lowthorpe, Ruston Parva, and Harpham, but it was not known whether the money was used.[81]

CHARITIES FOR THE POOR. The poor of Lowthorpe shared with those of Nafferton and Kelk the proceeds of Gray's charity.[82]

---

[61] Bulmer, *Dir. E. Yorks.* (1892), 237.
[62] Hull Univ. MSS., DP/135.
[63] Hanging in church.
[64] Ex inf. Sir Nikolaus Pevsner, who ascribes the tomb to the early 14th century on stylistic grounds. Sir John had seven surviving children in 1333–4: *Yorks. Fines, 1327–47*, 60.
[65] *T.E.R.A.S.* xxiv. 41; *Parl. Rep. Yorks.* i (Y.A.S. Rec. Ser. xci), 106.
[66] Bulmer, *Dir. E. Yorks.* 236.
[67] *Y.A.J.* xiv. 510, with illus.
[68] *Yorks. Ch. Notes* (Y.A.S. Rec. Ser. xxxiv), 219.
[69] *Y.A.J.* xii. 222.
[70] *Y.A.J.* xxxi. 4.
[71] *Inventories of Ch. Goods*, 22–3.
[72] Boulter, 'Ch. Bells', 218.
[73] The gifts are recorded in the first register of baptisms etc.
[74] *Yorks. Ch. Plate*, i. 287–8, including illus. of the flagon; *Invent. Ch. Goods*, 85.
[75] E.R.R.O. The post-1812 registers are still at Lowthorpe.
[76] York. Dioc. Regy., Sentence of consecration.
[77] Bodl. MS. Tanner 150, ff. 27 sqq.
[78] B.I.H.R., DMH. 1788/16; G.R.O. Worship Returns, Vol. v, no. 713.
[79] B.I.H.R., V. 1865/Ret. 335.
[80] B.I.H.R., Schools index.
[81] *Rets. on Educ. of Poor, 1819*, 1086.
[82] See p. 297.

MUSTON

MUSTON lies about a mile south-west of Filey, the irregularly shaped parish stretching from the sea in the east, across the wolds escarpment, and up to the high wold ground in the west.[1] The low-lying part of the parish includes former carr land in the Vale of Pickering. Much of the parish boundary follows watercourses on the low ground, and for ½ mile it runs along the sea-shore, but on the wold slopes it follows no prominent natural features. The area of the ancient parish was 2,293 a.,[2] but in 1935 327 a. were transferred to Filey urban district.[3]

In the north of the parish much of the peat-covered carr land is less than 100 ft. above sea-level, and the boulder-clay land towards the sea mostly lies at 100 ft. to 150 ft. A ridge of slightly higher ground, exceeding 175 ft. and including Beacon and Mill hills, lies between Muston and Filey, and Muston Bottoms, lying alongside one of the headwaters of the river Hertford, separates the ridge from the wold slopes. The wolds escarpment turns southwards in Muston parish to run towards the sea and it rises only gradually here, in contrast to the steep 'brows' in Folkton to the west. From about 125 ft. at Muston village the ground rises to over 400 ft. on Muston Wold; most of the wold land is covered with boulder clay, though the chalk is exposed at a few points, notably around a quarry south-west of the village. The only woodland is in small plantations on the wolds, including that at Green Cliff, on the escarpment.

The main village street is formed by a road running from Folkton, following the foot of the escarpment; Hunmanby Road leads southwards from the main street and continues up the escarpment as High Lane. At the east end of the village the main street joins the Bridlington–Scarborough road and continues beyond it towards Filey. The only other road in the parish is Carr Lane, leading northwards from the village to farms in the former carrs. On High Lane is an old uninscribed milestone, similar to those in near-by parishes.[4] The Bridlington–Filey railway line, opened in 1847, crosses the parish in the east.

The village lies chiefly to the west of the stream which flows in Muston Bottoms, where a small green adjoins the road. Both the main street, part of which is called West Street, and Hunmanby Road are closely built-up; the three-step base of a medieval cross stands at the road junction. The remainder of the village lies east of the stream, along the Filey road. Most of the houses date from the 18th and 19th centuries and are variously built of local brick and chalk, and of stone brought from the area north of Filey. The older buildings include cottages of a storey and a half near the east end of the village and six houses bearing 18th-century dates, several of the date-stones having moulded borders and arched heads with key blocks. Among these houses are a two-storeyed cottage (1724); a house in West Street (1752); a two-storeyed building of stone and brick, formerly the Cross Keys inn (1755); and three houses in Hunmanby Road (1736, 1738, and 1776). The least altered example is that in Hunmanby Road dated 1738. It has a two-storeyed front, four bays wide; the walls are of stone and brick, faced with stucco, and there are quoins, a string-course, and a modillion eaves cornice of moulded brick. The three-room plan shows the persistence well into the 18th century of a traditional 17th-century plan: the doorway and entrance passage are off-centre, having the kitchen on one side and the 'hall', with the parlour beyond, on the other.[5] Several other 18th-century houses in Muston are similarly planned. Late-18th-century or early-19th-century buildings include Muston Hall[6] and Muston Lodge, and among the 20th-century buildings are sixteen Council houses. There is one public house, the Ship. In 1823 there was also a second inn, the Cross Keys,[7] which continued in use until the 1960s.[8]

Apart from several farm-houses, the only outlying buildings are a row of early-20th-century houses known as Seadale Terrace, apparently built as lodging-houses;[9] they are situated in the area transferred to Filey in 1935. Near by, around Muston Grange, there were caravan camps in 1970. The stump of a windmill stands on Mill hill. A short distance north-west of the mill, on Beacon hill, a beacon still stood until c. 1809. Three beacons at Muston took light from Reighton in 1588 and gave it to Staxton.[10] Payments for repairing and supervising the beacon were made in 1755–6.[11]

In 1377 there were 66 poll-tax payers.[12] In 1672 57 householders were charged to or exempt from the hearth tax. Of the 47 households that were chargeable in 1674, 36 had only one hearth each, 7 had 2, and 4 had from 3 to five.[13] There were said to be about 40 families in Muston in 1743[14] and 1764.[15] The population in 1801 was 236; it rose to a maximum of 417 in 1841, remained at just below 400 in 1851–81, and then fell to about 340 in 1891–1900.[16] It was 348 in 1931, including 35 people in the area which was to be transferred to Filey in 1935, and by 1961 there were only 300 people in Muston.[17]

MANORS AND OTHER ESTATES. In 1086 4 carucates in 'Ricstorp', in Muston, comprised a berewick of Hunmanby manor, and 3 carucates in 'Scloftone', perhaps also in Muston, and 4 carucates in Muston itself were soke of Hunmanby. All three estates were held by Gilbert de Gant. A fourth estate, consisting of 2 carucates in Muston, belonged to the king.[18]

Like that of Hunmanby the overlordship of Muston passed from the Gants to the Tattershalls late in the 13th century.[19] Under the Gants the

[1] This article was written in 1970.
[2] O.S. Map 6" (1854).
[3] Census, 1931.
[4] See p. 229.
[5] See plate facing p. 321.
[6] See p. 279.
[7] Baines, *Hist. Yorks.* (1823), ii. 370.
[8] Local inf.
[9] Directories.
[10] J. Nicholson, *Beacons of E. Yorks.* 8, 45.
[11] E.R.R.O., QSF Mich. 1755, D.8; East. 1756, D.12.
[12] E 179/202/62 m. 44.
[13] E 179/205/504, 521.
[14] *Herring's Visit.* ii. 196.
[15] B.I.H.R., Bp. V. 1764/Ret. 164.
[16] *V.C.H. Yorks.* iii. 489.
[17] *Census*.
[18] *V.C.H. Yorks.* ii. 204, 272.
[19] See p. 231.

Cockfield family apparently had a substantial interest in Muston, Filey, and Reighton in the mid 13th century. Maud Escrop claimed dower in 18 bovates in Muston from Simon of Cockfield in 1240, and Simon made a small gift there to Bardney abbey.[20] At Filey Simon joined Ralph de Neville in consenting to an agreement about tithes in 1231,[21] presumably the Ralph de Neville whom Walter de Gant enfeoffed in 7 carucates and 6 bovates in Muston.[22] This estate was held by the Nevilles until the death of Roger de Neville, when it was divided between his daughters Maud Malbis and Hawise of Lowthorpe.[23] The Malbis family retained its share until 1384, when the manor of *MUSTON* was assigned to Elizabeth Malbis, wife of Adam Beckwith.[24] The manor was held by the Beckwiths until 1579, when William and Roger Beckwith sold it to Christopher Maltby.[25] At the death of Maltby's son, another Christopher, in 1618 Muston was divided between his daughters Catherine, Everild, and Frances.[26]

Catherine Maltby later married Michael Warton.[27] Frances and her husband Thomas Tankard conveyed their share of the manor to Everild and her husband Sir George Wentworth in 1631,[28] and these two shares were in 1635 conveyed to Michael Warton.[29] The manor descended in the Warton family until the death of another Michael Warton in 1725, leaving his estates in undivided shares to his sisters and heirs Mary Pennyman, Elizabeth Pelham, and Susanna Newton. In 1775, however, the estates were divided and Muston fell to the share of Michael Newton: he received 906 a. there, together with common rights.[30]

In 1813–14 trustees for the sale of Newton's estates disposed of Muston in several lots, the largest being those bought by Christopher Russell (288 a.), Thomas Broadley (286 a.), John Hall (196 a.), and William Darley (111 a.).[31] In 1887 112 a. of the Russell holding, including Muston Hall, were acquired by William Cooper.[32] They passed to Irene and J. A. Shaw in 1948–9,[33] and the Shaws sold the hall to James Henderson in 1955 and the land to Eric Barker in 1956.[34]

Muston Hall is a stuccoed, two-storeyed, building consisting of an early-19th-century main block with a hipped roof, flanked by later side wings. At both back and front are central entrance porches surmounted by cast-iron balustrades which form first-floor balconies. The doorways have fanlights and the central first-floor window at the front is round-headed. Some of these features may have been added in the 20th century, when the house was evidently modernised.

The Broadleys and later the Harrison-Broadleys held their land in Muston until 1919, when Pilmoor farm was sold to Henry Prodham.[35] The Prodhams have since retained it.

John Hall sold his land, with a house called Muston Grange and an additional 30 a. and a windmill, to Humphrey Osbaldeston in 1826.[36] At Osbaldeston's death in 1835 this estate passed, like his estate held in fee simple at Hunmanby, to Theodosia Brooke[37] and in 1838 she had 302 a. in Muston.[38] In 1871 it passed to H. B. Firman, who sold Muston Grange farm, with 180 a., to Edwin Martin in 1891,[39] Mill farm in 1899, and Fox Hill farm in 1919.[40] Grange farm passed to Smithson Young in 1920 and to Frank Sillito in 1946.[41]

William Darley's share of the Newton estates was added to the Darley's existing holding in Muston,[42] and they also acquired in 1814 111 a. which had belonged to the Hills.[43] Emma Darley held 243 a. in 1838[44] and the Darley trustees kept the estate until it was split up soon after 1900; Muston Lodge, Carr House farm, and Mount Pleasant farm were among the lots then sold.[45]

The share of the manor which passed from the Nevilles to Hawise of Lowthorpe descended to John and Robert of Heslerton.[46] Robert had 10½ bovates in Muston at his death in 1309[47] and the Heslertons still had land there in 1346.[48] It seems likely that at least some of this property passed to the St. Quintins, who had land in Muston by 1366[49] and 6 bovates in 1428.[50] Various houses and lands were sold by the St. Quintins in the 1560s, the recipients including John Consett,[51] and a third of the so-called 'manor' was sold to Robert and William Lowson in 1575.[52] Francis Consett in 1600 conveyed property in Muston to William Tate and Thomas Atkinson.[53] Part of the Lowson's holding may have passed in the 17th century to the Greames of Sewerby.[54]

Although most of the Gant lands in Muston thu descended differently from the manor of Hunmanby the Hunmanby connexion was nevertheless maintained. In the 16th and 17th centuries the lords of Hunmanby held courts for Muston[55] and in the 19th and early 20th centuries the Mitfords and Osbaldeston-Mitfords were regarded as lords of Muston manor.[56] Some land at Muston may also have followed the descent of Hunmanby. In addition to land acquired in 1768 and 1826, which passed to the Brookes in 1835,[57] the Osbaldestons also had a

---

[20] *Yorks. Fines, 1232–46*, 79; see below, p. 281.
[21] *Bridlington Charty.* 78.
[22] B.M. Add. MS. 26737, f. 66; *E.Y.C.* ii, p. 461.
[23] *Plac. de Quo Warr.* (Rec. Com.), 207.
[24] C.P. 25(1)/278/143 no. 1; see also *V.C.H. Yorks. N.R.* i. 555.
[25] *Yorks. Fines*, ii. 144.
[26] C 142/373/41; *Visit. Yorks. 1584–5 and 1612*, ed. J. Foster, 551.
[27] *Dugdale's Visit. Yorks.* (Sur. Soc. xxxvi), 331.
[28] E.R.R.O., DDHU/17/27.
[29] C.P. 25(2)/522/11 Chas. I East. pt. 2, no. 1.
[30] 15 Geo. III, c. 49 (Priv. Act).
[31] Registry of Deeds, Beverley, CX/343/420; /491/640; CY/17/24; /72/112; E.R.R.O., DDHU/3/6 (map).
[32] Regy. of Deeds, 16/207/200 (1887).
[33] Ibid. 797/48/40; 813/603/472.
[34] Ibid. 996/153/140; 1031/400/340.
[35] Ibid. 201/228/184.
[36] Ibid. DY/113/139.
[37] See p. 232.
[38] B.I.H.R., TA. 490L.
[39] Regy. of Deeds, 42/424/394 (1891).
[40] Ibid. 16/534/494 (1899); 199/258/222.
[41] Ibid. 222/251/221; 740/81/65.
[42] E.R.R.O., Land Tax, 1783 etc.
[43] Regy. of Deeds, CW/487/672.
[44] B.I.H.R., TA. 490L.
[45] Regy of Deeds, 51/44/41 (1903); 53/49/49 (1903); 83/409/383 (1906).
[46] *E.Y.C.* ii, p. 465; see above, p. 273.
[47] *Cal. Inq. p.m.* v, p. 54.
[48] *Feud. Aids*, vi. 228–9.
[49] *Yorks. Fines, 1347–77*, 118.
[50] *Feud. Aids*. vi. 265–6.
[51] *Yorks. Fines.* i. 275, 289, 295, 315–6.
[52] Ibid. ii. 67.
[53] Ibid. iv. 141.
[54] E.R.R.O., DDLG/24/2 sqq.
[55] See p. 281.
[56] Directories.
[57] See above and p. 280.

family estate of longer standing in Muston; in the 1830s this amounted to about 80 a.[58] and comprised Crake House farm. The house and 54 a. later passed to Frances Hurt, who sold them to Alfred Arkwright in 1876.[59] They subsequently passed to J. D. Legard in 1883, Edwin Martin in 1890, R. A. Savile in 1911, M. G. Lumb in 1921, and E. B. Marris in 1958.[60]

The Crown estate of 2 carucates in 1086 had been held before the Conquest by Alden.[61] By 1284–5 it was part of the Gant fee[62] and a mesne tenancy under the Tattershalls was held by the Raygate family in the 14th century.[63] This manor of *MUSTON* was held in demesne by the Bucktons from at least 1284–5,[64] Gilbert de Gant, it is said, having enfeoffed Walter of Buckton in the reign of Henry III.[65] By the early 16th century the manor may have passed to the Constables.[66] John Constable sold property here to John Pawling in 1579 and he conveyed it to Christopher Maltby the next year; and Christopher Constable sold other property to Maltby in 1581.[67] Maltby was found in 1585 to hold certain lands which had belonged to Walter Buckton.[68] The property may subsequently have descended with the capital manor.[69]

Some land in Muston remained with the Constables in the 16th and 17th centuries. Thus Christopher Constable had a quarter of the manor in 1622.[70] It was presumably part of this property which Sir Robert Constable sold in 1713–14, the chief conveyance being of eleven small closes to Simon Grindall in 1713.[71] Grindall's grandson sold most of these closes to F. W. Osbaldeston in 1768, and in 1772 they were transferred to Humphrey Osbaldeston.[72] This was apparently part of the estate which passed to Theodosia Brooke in 1835.[73]

The rectory of Hunmanby, with the tithes of Muston, was given to Bardney abbey in 1115.[74] The church was valued with the mother-church at Hunmanby in 1291 and 1535, and after the Dissolution the estate descended with the rectory of Hunmanby.[75] The Muston tithes were worth £36 in 1625[76] and 1650.[77] In 1835–6 the Osbaldestons received £117 from rectorial tithes,[78] but when they were commuted in 1838 rent-charges totalling £255 were allotted to Bertram Osbaldeston-Mitford, and £6 more was allotted to him in 1841.[79]

ECONOMIC HISTORY. By 1086 most of Muston was dependent, as berewick or soke, upon Hunmanby manor. The berewick of 'Ricstorp' then had land for 3 ploughs, and 5 villeins and 2 bordars had 2 ploughs on it. Details concerning the soke land are combined with those for Flotmanby, which was also soke of Hunmanby; thus Muston, 'Scloftone', and Flotmanby had land for 7 ploughs, on which 16 villeins and 4 bordars had 4 ploughs. The small Crown estate had land for one plough and was worth £1.[80] Little is known of the two early hamlets which apparently lay in Muston. 'Sleeton' is mentioned in 1160–76[81] and 'Slocton' in 1201,[82] but there is no evidence for the location of either it or 'Ricstorp'.

The open-field land in Muston probably lay mainly on the wold slopes, on the gently rising ground below the escarpment, and on the ridge of higher ground towards Filey. North and South fields are mentioned in 1603–4 and Beacon field in 1640.[83] On the low ground to the north were the carrs, which may at certain periods have been divided into two or more common pastures. In 1685, for example, the vicar had six gates in the 'tenants' carr'[84] and in 1775 Michael Newton had four cattle-gates in the 'husbandmen's carr' and nineteen described simply as 'in the carrs'.[85] Gates in the Winter carr are mentioned in 1684.[86] There may also have been common pasture in the high wold ground known as Pilmoor, which covered 241 a. in 1838.[87]

An inclosure by agreement appears to have been carried out at Muston in the late 16th or early 17th century. In 1603 there is mention of land lying 'throughout the fields', but at the same time 18 bovates were described as being in a newly-inclosed close adjoining North field and 11 bovates in another close.[88] The most explicit reference to an inclosure comes from 1637, when a quitclaim was granted of lands given in exchange 'at the late division of the lordship of Muston and the freeholders severed from the lords'.[89] Subsequently in the 17th century there are many references to closes, including Beaconfield close. 'Beacon hedge' in Beacon field is also mentioned as the boundary of certain closes.[90] Some of the closes were in the more low-lying parts of the parish, and Beacon field was almost certainly inclosed at this time; but the wolds lands were presumably involved, too, for there is no reference to a later inclosure of open fields.

The wet carr lands, however, were not inclosed until the early 19th century. Proposals to drain them were made in the 1770s and in 1773 there were said to be 85 a. in Muston which were typical of the fenny ground, of small value, along the upper reaches of the Derwent and Hertford.[91] An engineer's report was printed in 1800,[92] and in the same year a drainage Act was passed for Muston and many

---

[58] E.R.R.O., DDHU/17/13; B.I.H.R., TA. 490L.
[59] Regy. of Deeds, MC/385/589.
[60] Ibid. NU/278/410; 36/376/350 (1890); 136/176/145; 230/210/181; 1108/422/386.
[61] *V.C.H. Yorks.* ii. 204.
[62] *Feud. Aids*, vi. 27.
[63] C 260/132/no. 10; *Cal. Inq. p.m.* vi, p. 210; vii, p. 403; viii, p. 223.
[64] *Feud. Aids*, vi. 27.
[65] C 145/174/10.
[66] *Yorks. Fines*, i. 44.
[67] Ibid. ii. 135, 160, 175.
[68] B.M. Add. MS. 26718, f. 44.
[69] See p. 279.
[70] C 142/269/20; /524/23; *Abstracts of Yorks. Wills, 1665–6* (Y.A.S. Rec. Ser. ix), 158.
[71] Regy. of Deeds, D/121/196; E/162/277; E/175/303.
[72] Ibid. AL/121/213; AR/69/130.
[73] See p. 279.
[74] See p. 281.
[75] See p. 236.
[76] E.R.R.O., DDHU/11/3, 4.
[77] *T.E.R.A.S.* ii. 59.
[78] E.R.R.O., DDHU/17/14.
[79] B.I.H.R., TA. 490L.
[80] *V.C.H. Yorks.* ii. 204, 272.
[81] *E.Y.C.* ii, p. 461.
[82] *Cur. Reg. R.* ii. 12.
[83] Hull Univ. MSS., DRA 340–1, 354.
[84] B.I.H.R., TER. J. Muston 1685.
[85] E.R.R.O., DDEF/21/132.
[86] Hull Univ. MSS., DRA 397.
[87] B.I.H.R., TA. 490L; Pilmoor Farm perpetuates the name.
[88] Hull Univ. MSS., DRA. 340.
[89] Ibid. 351.
[90] Ibid. 353 sqq.
[91] E.R.R.O., DDSY/11/2–5.
[92] Ibid. /10.

other townships.[93] An annual assessment was to be raised to construct and maintain the drainage works, and by 1804 the commissioners for the Act were already assessing landowners in the various townships.[94] Even after being drained at least part of the carrs was still used in common: in 1814, for example, William Darley acquired 92 a. of the carrs in which eight people had 56 cattle-gates.[95]

Only 369 a. were returned as being under crops in 1801,[96] but in the later 19th and 20th centuries arable farming has been predominant in the parish, with some permanent pasture on the low ground and on the wolds escarpment. In 1838 1,448 a. were arable and 724 a. meadow and pasture[97] and in 1904–18 only 22 a. of the 280-acre Pilmoor farm, on the wolds, were under grass.[98] In the 19th and early 20th centuries there were usually 12–15 farmers in the parish, one of whom was also a miller, as well as one or two market-gardeners. There was a slight increase in the 1920s and 1930s, with 16–17 farmers and 3–4 smallholders.[99]

A tanner was mentioned in 1823.[1] Apartment houses were first recorded at Seadale Terrace, near Filey and the sea, in 1905.[2] A windmill was mentioned in 1341[3] and later.[4] In 1826 it was a post mill.[5] A miller is last recorded in 1913[6] and only the stump of the brick tower mill remained in 1970.

LOCAL GOVERNMENT. Courts held for the manor of Hunmanby in the 16th and 17th centuries also had jurisdiction in Muston. One undated court roll, probably of the 16th century, records the election of a constable and two aletasters for Muston,[7] and a constable is also mentioned in 1662.[8] In the later 17th, 18th, and early 19th centuries many of the Osbaldestons' estreats, jury presentments, and verdicts include Muston.[9]

No parochial records before 1835 are known. In 1837 Muston joined the Scarborough union.[10]

CHURCH. In 1115 Walter de Gant gave the church of Hunmanby, with Muston and its other dependent chapels, to Bardney abbey.[11] Simon of Cockfield also gave two tofts in Muston to Bardney.[12] A vicarage was ordained at Muston, apparently in 1269. The vicar was to have a toft, a third of the tithes of corn and lambs, and all the wool tithes, small tithes, and offerings, except the first choice of moveables; he was to pay a pension of £1 10s. a year to Bardney.[13]

Bardney regularly presented to the living until the Dissolution and thereafter the advowson descended like that of Hunmanby, the Crown presenting in the later 16th century, Thomas Westrop in 1619, and William Osbaldeston in 1661.[14] The patronage passed from the Osbaldestons to the Readett Bayleys in 1920,[15] was sold to Harrogate College in 1925,[16] and in 1952 passed to the Martyrs' Memorial Trust.[17]

The vicarage was worth £6 10s. in 1535[18] and £25 in 1650.[19] In 1829–31 the average net income was £153[20] but it was substantially increased in 1856 when payments of £50 each were awarded from Folkton rectory and Hunmanby vicarage.[21] The gross value was about £250 in 1884.[22]

Tithes provided much of the vicarial income. In 1835–6 the vicar received £59[23] and at commutation in 1838 he was allotted rent-charges of £127.[24] There were only 4 a. of glebe in 1535[25] and only 6 a., together with 6 beast-gates, in 1685,[26] and no additional land was subsequently acquired. The glebe was sold in 1927.[27] The toft mentioned in 1269 was retained and there was a parsonage house on it in 1535 and later.[28] In 1764 the house was described as built of chalk and thatch, and it had only two ground-floor rooms and a chamber above.[29] In the 19th century it was unfit for the vicar's residence[30] and a large new house, of red brick with blue-brick and stone dressings, was built on the site in 1873.[31]

The church benefits from the charity of the Revd. William Green, who by will proved in 1870 bequeathed £200, the interest to be used to maintain his gravestone and for church expenses. In 1947 and later the whole of the income was used for the upkeep of the church.[32]

Several ministers at Muston in the 18th and 19th centuries held other livings and resided elsewhere. In 1743 the curate of Hunmanby served Muston,[33] as did the vicar of Hunmanby in 1835, though he had a curate at Muston.[34] In 1868 the vicar lived at Filey, but other incumbents in the late 19th century were resident at Muston.[35] In 1970 the vicar of Hunmanby was curate-in-charge at Muston.

In 1537 the parishioners alleged before the Council in the North that the vicar, John Dobson, had failed to pray for the king, had spoken against him in the church porch and in the alehouse, and had supported Rome; Dobson was found guilty and was executed.[36]

There was one service each Sunday in 1743 and communion was celebrated four times a year, about sixty people receiving it the previous Easter.[37] By

---

[93] 40 Geo. III, c. 118 (Local and Personal Act).
[94] E.R.R.O., DDCB/12/6. The assessment for 1874 is in ibid. DDSY/103/10.
[95] Registry of Deeds, Beverley, CY/72/112.
[96] 1801 Crop Returns. [97] B.I.H.R., TA. 490L.
[98] E.R.R.O., DDX/202/9. [99] Directories.
[1] Baines, *Hist. Yorks.* (1823) ii. 370.
[2] *Kelly's Dir. N. & E.R. Yorks.* (1905), 548.
[3] *Cal. Inq. p.m.* viii, p. 223.
[4] B.M. Add. MS. 26718, f. 36d.; *Cal. Pat.* 1553–4, 85–6; *Yorks. Fines, 1614–25*, 122.
[5] Regy. of Deeds, DY/113/139.
[6] *Kelly's Dir. N. & E.R. Yorks.* (1913), 580.
[7] S.C. 2/211/64–6; *Y.A.J.* x. 69.
[8] *Cal. S.P. Dom.* Add. 1660–85, 66. [9] See p. 240.
[10] *3rd Rep. Poor Law Com.* 174.
[11] Dugdale, *Mon.* i. 628–9.
[12] B.M. Cott. MS. Vesp. E. xx, f. 197.
[13] *Reg. Giffard* (Sur. Soc. cix), 56–7.
[14] *Fasti Parochiales*, iii. 59–60; see above, p. 241.
[15] Registry of Deeds, Beverley, 209/184/157.
[16] Ibid. 318/410/342. [17] *York Dioc. Cal.*
[18] *Valor Eccl.* (Rec. Com.), v. 124. [19] *T.E.R.A.S.* ii. 59.
[20] *Rep. Com. Eccl. Revenues*, 956–7.
[21] *Lond. Gaz.* 8 Aug. 1856, pp. 2739–42.
[22] B.I.H.R., Bp. V. 1884/Ret.
[23] E.R.R.O., DDHU/17/14. [24] B.I.H.R., TA. 490L.
[26] B.I.H.R., TER. J. Muston 1685. [25] *Valor Eccl.* v. 124.
[27] Regy. of Deeds, 340/315/244.
[28] B.I.H.R., TER. J. Muston 1685; *Valor Eccl.* v. 124.
[29] B.I.H.R., TER. J. Muston 1764.
[30] Ibid. 1861; Lawton, *Rer. Eccles Dioc. Ebor.* ii. 305.
[31] *Kelly's Dir. N. & E.R. Yorks.* (1879), 624.
[32] Char. Com. files. [33] *Herring's Visit.* ii. 196.
[34] *Rep. Com. Eccl. Revenues*, 956–7.
[35] B.I.H.R., V. 1868/Ret. 326; V. 1871/Ret. 329; V. 1877/Ret.; Bp. V. 1884/Ret.
[36] *Y.A.J.* xxxiv. 379–80; *L. & P. Hen. VIII*, xii (2), pp. 426–8.
[37] *Herring's Visit.* ii. 196.

1865 there were two weekly services, though in 1868 there was still only one in winter. Communion was celebrated eight times a year in 1871 and monthly by 1877; it was received by 7–14 people in the later 19th century.[38] There was one service each week in 1970.

The church of ALL SAINTS was reopened in 1864 after a complete rebuilding.[39] The chancel of the earlier building was in great decay in 1596 and later,[40] and the church, which consisted of nave, chancel, south porch, and wooden bell-turret, was described as small and mean in 1856.[41] The new building, in the Early English style, consists of nave, chancel, north and south aisles, south porch, and west bell-turret. Preserved from the old church are a pillar piscina, an altar slab, and a roughly square stone bowl, probably a holy water stoup. A plain round font may be of the 12th century and there are two small carved heads in the porch. The east window was inserted in 1882.[42]

There were two bells in the church in 1552.[43] They are said to have been dated 1410 and to have been recast at the rebuilding of the church.[44] The 'new' bells, bearing the date 1863, are by Warner & Sons of London.[45] The plate consists of a silver cup, given by Richard Osbaldeston and made in London in 1751, and silver paten and flagon, given by Admiral Mitford in 1864.[46] The earliest register covers the period 1541–1730, with some gaps in the 1650s and 1690s. There are also marriage registers from 1754 onwards, but no others for baptisms and burials before 1813.[47]

Muston continued to bury at the mother-church at Hunmanby until a churchyard was consecrated at Muston in 1828.[48] A dispute about the relationship between the churches in 1584 shows that burial fees were paid to Hunmanby and that Muston also contributed to the repair of Hunmanby church.[49] A contribution towards repairs was made in 1662,[50] and fees for burials were still payable in the early 18th century.[51]

NONCONFORMITY. In 1743 there was one family of papists in Muston[52] but there is no further record of dissent until the early 19th century. The Congregationalists built Providence Chapel, in the main village street, it is said in 1815;[53] Hannah Tate provided it,[54] and it may have been the 'newly-erected building' which was registered in 1818.[55] The chapel was closed c. 1872,[56] but the plain brick building, formerly having a stuccoed front, still stood in 1970.

In 1821 a barn was registered for worship and in 1824 a Primitive Methodist chapel was built in Hunmanby Road.[57] The Primitive Methodists had 30 members in 1889.[58] A Wesleyan chapel, a wooden building moved from Scarborough, was put up in 1886[59] in the main street. The latter had been removed by 1970, when the former Primitive chapel was still in use.

It was reported in 1865 and 1877 that the dissenters in the village also attended the parish church, but the incumbent in 1884 said that dissent hindered his work.[60]

EDUCATION. There were two day-schools at Muston in 1835, one with 14 boys and 6 girls and the other, begun in 1832, with 12 girls; all the children were taught at their parents' expense.[61] A National school was built in 1855 on a site given by Admiral Mitford, and in 1857 the school was supported by voluntary contributions and school pence, the latter paid by 38 boys and 32 girls.[62] An annual government grant was received by 1873–4,[63] and there were about 50 pupils in 1877.[64] The school was enlarged in 1894.[65] The average attendance was 58 in 1908; it fell below 50 during and after the First World War and below 40 in the later 1930s.[66] The school was closed in 1964 and the pupils transferred to schools in Filey.[67] The red-brick building, with stone dressings, still stood in 1970.

An evening school was held five days a week in winter in 1857,[68] and it it was said in 1884 that a night school had been tried with only partial success.[69]

CHARITIES FOR THE POOR. By will dated 1697 Elisha Trott, of Scarborough, bequeathed a rent-charge of £1 a year to the poor of Muston out of a house and farm at Flotmanby.[70] The money was distributed to eight people in 1930 and four in 1967.[71]

Nothing is known of the nature of the 'poor houses' which the trustees for the sale of Michael Newton's estates sold to Christopher Hutchinson in 1813.[72] They stood near the church in 1850[73] but have since been demolished. The quarter-acre poor's land in Muston had by the early 19th century become appropriated to Filey.[74]

---

[38] B.I.H.R., V. 1865/Ret. 368; V. 1868/Ret. 326; V. 1871/Ret. 329; V. 1877/Ret.; Bp. V. 1884/Ret.
[39] Ibid. V. 1865/Ret. 368.
[40] Ibid. V. 1595–6/CB. 3; V. 1615/CB.
[41] Sheahan and Whellan, Hist. York & E.R. ii. 484; G. A. Poole and J. W. Hugall, Churches of Scarborough, Filey, and Neighbourhood (1848), 121.
[42] Bulmer, Dir. E. Yorks. (1892), 243.
[43] Inventories of Ch. Goods, 24.
[44] Bulmer, Dir. E. Yorks. 243.
[45] Boulter, 'Ch. Bells', 218.
[46] Yorks. Ch. Plate, i. 292–3.
[47] E.R.R.O.
[48] B.I.H.R., CD. 147.
[49] Ibid. C.P., G. 2153. See also E 134/42 & 43 Eliz. Mich./29.
[50] B.I.H.R., C.P., H. 4838.
[51] Ibid. TER. J. Muston 1716, 1726.
[52] Herring's Visit. ii. 196.
[53] B.I.H.R., V. 1865/Ret. 368; J. G. Miall, Congregationalism in Yorks. 324. In 1851 the date of erection was given as 1817: H.O. 129/24/525.
[54] Baines, Hist. Yorks. (1823), ii. 370.
[55] B.I.H.R., DMH. Reg. 1, p. 73; G.R.O. Worship Returns, Vol. v, no. 3225.
[56] B.I.H.R., V. 1877/Ret.
[57] Ibid. DMH. Reg. 1, pp. 305, 477; G.R.O. Worship Rets., Vol. v, nos. 3610, 3927; date on chapel.
[58] H. Woodcock, Sketches of Prim. Meth. on Yorks. Wolds, 154.
[59] Kelly's Dir. N. & E.R. Yorks. (1889), 429; (1897), 504.
[60] B.I.H.R., V. 1865/Ret. 368; V. 1877/Ret.; Bp. V. 1884/Ret.
[61] Educ. Enquiry Abstract, 1835, 1092.
[62] Ed. 7/135.
[63] Rep. of Educ. Cttee. of Counc. 1873–4 [C. 1019–I], p. 442, H.C. (1874), xviii.
[64] B.I.H.R., V. 1877/Ret.
[65] Kelly's Dir. N. & E.R. Yorks. (1901), 528.
[66] Bd. of Educ. List 21 (H.M.S.O.).
[67] E.R.C.C. Mins. 1964–5, 6.
[68] Ed. 7/135.
[69] B.I.H.R., Bp. V. 1884/Ret.
[70] 9th Rep. Char. Com. (1823), 733.
[71] Char. Com. files.
[72] Registry of Deeds, Beverley, CU/451/524.
[73] O.S. Map 6" (1854).
[74] See p. 151.

NAFFERTON

NAFFERTON is one of the largest parishes and most populous villages in the wapentake.[1] It lies only 2 miles from Great Driffield and is the most westerly of the villages situated at the southern edge of the wolds, between Driffield and Bridlington. It was presumably an Anglian settlement but the first element in the name is a Scandinavian personal name; a pre-Conquest cemetery has been found a short distance north of the church.[2] The village itself stretches for a mile southwards from the main Driffield–Bridlington road, while the elongated parish extends 3 miles across the wolds on the north and 3 miles across the Plain of Holderness on the south. In the Middle Ages there were two chapelries in the parish, but the hamlet of Pockthorpe, on the wolds, has long been depopulated; it was probably a subsidiary Scandinavian settlement. Wansford, at the southern extremity of Nafferton, was perhaps Anglian in origin, taking its name from 'Wandel's ford' across the river Hull. In the early Middle Ages there was apparently also a small hamlet on the wold slopes, where the field name Windersome recalls the former existence of a group of houses buffeted by the winds. Other Scandinavian names in the parish are Houndale and Thornholme, the latter an area of meadows near the river Hull.[3] The total area of the parish is 5,821 a., of which Wansford accounts for 922 a.[4] and Pockthorpe for about 700 a.[5]

The boundary with Kilham to the north runs along a prehistoric earthwork for much of its length, and another earthwork, Green Dikes, formed part of the internal boundary between Nafferton and Pockthorpe; the name Green Dikes is recorded as early as the 13th century.[6] On the lower wold slopes a small valley and stream known as Nafferton Slack divide Nafferton from Driffield to the west. The parish boundary on the plain partly follows watercourses, as does the internal boundary between Nafferton and Wansford. The most noteworthy of these watercourses is White dike, which for 3 miles forms the boundary with Lowthorpe to the east. On the south Nafferton is divided from Skerne by the river Hull, sometimes known here as West beck or Westwater. No boundary changes are known until 1884, when two small and uninhabited detached portions of Nafferton were transferred, one to Wansford and the other to the neighbouring township of Brigham.[7] Greater changes were made in 1935, when the civil parish of Nafferton was increased by the transference of 2,774 a. from Great Driffield, and when Wansford was merged with the civil parish of Skerne.[8]

The landscape of the parish exhibits the marked contrasts of the wolds and the plain. From a height of 50 ft. above sea-level at the centre of the village the ground rises steadily to over 300 ft. on the top of Nafferton Wold; still further north it falls to under 125 ft. in a dry valley known as Slatterdale before rising again to nearly 300 ft. at the northern parish boundary. Much of Slatterdale and all the ground beyond it formed the territory of Pockthorpe. The open character of the wolds is modified by several windbreaks and plantations, notably around Wold House, and similar plantations are a prominent feature of the Pockthorpe estate. Much of the wold ground lay within the open fields until inclosure. South of Nafferton village a broad belt of land lies below 50 ft. above sea-level, though in the west there is a small area of slightly higher ground which as early as the 13th century was known as 'Hyap', from the Old English *heap*, a hill.[9] In the south-east of the parish the ground is lower still, below 25 ft., and an extensive tract comprised Nafferton carrs until inclosure. The hamlet of Wansford itself lies around the 25-foot contour. The regular field-pattern of both wolds and plain is the result of the inclosure of 1772, and many straight dikes on the plain reflect the continuing problems of drainage in more recent times. Arable farming predominates now throughout the parish.

At the centre of Nafferton village is a large pond, fed by springs, which was artifically created, or at least enlarged, to serve the adjoining water-mill. From the pond Nafferton beck, straightened for much of its length, flows south to meet the river Hull at Wansford. Just south of Nafferton, Spittle beck joins Nafferton beck; its name, and that of Spittle fields, derives from a small hospital which existed in the early 14th century.[10] At Wansford Nafferton beck drove a second water-mill. The river Hull forms the parish boundary, but the fishing rights in it belonged to Wansford manor and its waters provided power for another mill in Wansford. The river has long been noted as a trout stream. In the 1790s Sir Christopher Sykes's water-bailiff reported that many local 'gentlemen' fished there, as well as others from as far afield as Hull, York, Doncaster, Bradford, Manchester, Liverpool, and London.[11] In 1856 the Trout inn was still patronised by anglers of 'high degree'.[12] On the north side of the river Hull the Driffield canal was opened in 1770.

The village of Nafferton stands in the centre of the parish at the junction of several roads. The main street continues northwards, as Hag Lane, towards Pockthorpe, and southwards towards Wansford. A second street branches from it and runs south-eastwards, as Carr Lane, towards Lowthorpe. Two roads, leading to Driffield and Bridlington, join the main street at the north end of the village. With the growing importance of the Driffield–Bridlington road this double junction presented difficulties, and in 1927 a bypass was constructed to avoid the village.[13] Other roads lead from the village into the fields: to the west Markman Lane and Houndale Lane, and to the east Brickfield Lane, leading to the former brickworks in Lowthorpe parish. Various sections of the long main street and several of the

---

[1] This article was written in 1968.
[2] J. R. Mortimer, *Forty Years' Researches in Burial Mounds*, pp. lxxxiii, 343–4.
[3] *P.N.E.R. Yorks.* (E.P.N.S.), 94.
[4] O.S. Map 6" (1854).
[5] See p. 286.
[6] *P.N.E.R. Yorks.* 94.
[7] *Census*, 1891. These portions were respectively part of Snakeholmes and part of Eastholmes.
[8] Ibid. 1931.
[9] *P.N.E.R. Yorks.* 94.
[10] *Percy Charty.* (Sur. Soc. cxvii), 68.
[11] E.R.R.O., DDSY/68/89.
[12] Sheahan and Whellan, *Hist. York & E.R.* ii. 487.
[13] *Hull Times*, 26 July 1913; E.R.C.C. *Mins.* 1926–7, 367; 1927–8, 261.

side streets have long borne distinctive names, about a dozen in all.[14] Among the oldest of these names are Howe Lane, which appears as 'the road of Scalhau' c. 1300,[15] and Priest Gate, mentioned as 'Prestlane' in 1308.[16] Others are North, Copper, West, and Nether Gates; High, Middle, Main, and Railway Streets; Commercial Row; and Coulson Hill.

The church dominates the village centre, where four streets meet, and close by were the lock-up, the stocks, and the pinfold.[17] The closely-built streets contain no buildings earlier in date than the 18th century, and little work in chalk is evident apart from boundary walls and outbuildings. Of the 18th-century houses nine carry inscribed stones: two of these are not fully legible, but the others date from 1748, 1756, 1772, 1776, 1777, 1781, and 1799. It is clear that the rebuilding and enlargement of the village went on throughout the 19th century, and the red-brick houses and cottages are of all styles and periods. Most are modest, but some more pretentious houses of the late 18th and early 19th centuries, often three bays wide, are to be found in various parts of the village; especially noteworthy is a group around the junction of High Street and Commercial Row. Nafferton Hall, standing back from High Street, dates from c. 1800; it has a semicircular classical portico and various Victorian embellishments.

The north end continued to be the most highly-favoured 'residential' part of the village throughout the 19th century, and it was here that several large detached houses were built for local landowners. Nafferton Lodge, for example, was occupied by Jacob Laybourne by 1840,[18] and later in the century it was rebuilt and renamed Filbert Grove.[19] The Villa (now Westwood Close) and Elm House were both built in the second half of the century. By the later 19th century the village was probably also proving attractive as a place of residence for people from Driffield, and new houses of this period include three semi-detached pairs in the Driffield road. Much 20th-century building, both before and after the Second World War, has also taken place in this area, and a new public house, the Star, has been provided. The most recent development has been the erection in the 1960s of an estate of houses in the former grounds of Nafferton Hall.

Apart from Nether Hall, a large Victorian grey-brick house, most of the 19th- and 20th-century building at the south end of the village is more modest. Some of the housing there was no doubt provided for workmen at the railway, coal depot, and flour mills. The railway station was probably built by 1846, when the Hull–Bridlington line was opened. The large mill and malting, of five and six storeys, near the pond was built in 1840.[20] Associated stables and other buildings surround a large courtyard near by. Station Mills were rebuilt in 1878,[21] but a row of four houses next to them is dated 1861 and these are no doubt the cottages described in that year, along with the mill itself, as 'lately built'.[22] On the east side of the village there are about fifty Council houses.

Nafferton has had a variety of public buildings befitting a village of its size. For long there have been four inns; in 1840 they were the Board, the Cross Keys, the King's Head, and the White Horse, the first of these being replaced by the Bluebell by 1850.[23] The White Horse closed in the 1920s,[24] but the Star opened in the 1930s.[25] There are several meeting-rooms in the village. A hall in High Street has served various purposes, among them Salvation Army meeting-place, Temperance Hall, Village Institute, and Conservative Club.[26] The Jubilee Parish Rooms, in West Gate, were provided in 1904. The Village Hall, in Main Street, was presented by Mr. C. Longbottom in 1946;[27] it had been built in 1861 by the Loyal Order of Ancient Shepherds, a society which was said to have a branch membership of about 400 working men in the 1890s and which maintained its Nafferton branch until the Second World War.[28] The Conservative and Liberal Clubs were both formed in 1885.[29] One institution which probably drew its inmates from beyond the village itself was a girls' boarding school, housed in Nafferton Hall in 1856 and still existing in the 1870s.[30]

A sewerage scheme was instituted at Nafferton as early as 1890.[31] From near the end of the 19th century the village also had the uncommon distinction of being well-lit, as a result of the work of the Nafferton Lighting Committee. In 1897 a balance of £17 was available from a Diamond Jubilee Fund and it was used to provide thirteen street oil lamps, a number which was later more than doubled. The committee was supported by voluntary subscription and by an annual grant from the Town Trust,[32] and it continued in operation until 1931,[33] when electricity was supplied to the village.[34]

In 1850 there were 10 outlying farms, 4 on the low-lying ground south of the village, one to the west, and 5 on the wolds.[35] The wold houses include the Grange and Wold House, the latter said to have been built for John Dickson in 1854.[36] To the east of Wold House are the fields called Windersome, and there lies the grave of Richard Laybourne (d. 1820), who asked to be buried on his own land rather than in the church.[37] Further north is a farm known as Nafferton Kesters, a name which occurs at least as early as the late 16th century.[38]

Little remains of the deserted hamlet of Pockthorpe, though its site is still marked by prominent

---

[14] O.S. Map 6″ (1854 and later edns.).
[15] *Bridlington Charty.* 151.
[16] *Percy Charty.* 85.   [17] O.S. Map 6″ (1854).
[18] White, *Dir. E. & N.R. Yorks.* (1840), 395.
[19] *Kelly's Dir. N. & E.R. Yorks.* (1893), 466.
[20] See plates facing pp. 272, 320.   [21] See p. 291.
[22] Registry of Deeds, Beverley, IC/255/319.
[23] White, *Dir. E. & N.R. Yorks.* (1840), 395; O.S. Map 6″ (1854).
[24] *Kelly's Dir. N. & E.R. Yorks.* (1925), 587; (1929), 541.
[25] Ibid. (1933), 514.
[26] *Hull Times*, 26 July 1913.
[27] Inscriptions on buildings.
[28] *Kelly's Dir. N. & E.R. Yorks.* (1893), 465; and subsequent edns.
[29] Ibid. (1893), 465.
[30] Sheahan and Whellan, *Hist. York & E.R.* ii. 486; *Kelly's Dir. N. & E.R. Yorks.* (1872), 525; (1879), 626.
[31] Ex inf. Clerk to the Council, Driffield R.D.C., 1968.
[32] See p. 296.
[33] E.R.R.O., DDX/158/1–4.
[34] Ex inf. District Manager, Yorks. Elect. Bd., Bridlington, 1968.
[35] O.S. Map 6″ (1854).
[36] Sheahan and Whellan, *Hist. York & E.R.* ii. 486.
[37] Mortimer, *Forty Years' Researches*, 343.
[38] Req. 2/55/84. It is possible that the land called Kirestoft in the early Middle Ages (*Bridlington Charty.* 151) and Nafferton Christofts in 1609 (L.R. 2/230 f. 110) is to be identified with Nafferton Kesters.

earthworks.[39] An 18th-century farm-house close by was demolished in 1969, but Pockthorpe Hall remains.

The houses of Wansford are mostly strung out along the Nafferton–Foston road where it approaches the river Hull. At the north end of the hamlet are the church, parsonage house, and school, all built by Sir Tatton Sykes, and at the south end stands the Trout inn. The oldest houses are of the 18th century; one of them bears the date 1776 and another is called the Manor House. Most of the cottages that were built for workers at the carpet manufactory c. 1790[40] still stand, some, near the canal, called the Row, others, further north, called Ireland Square.[41] Part of the Row was, however, demolished in 1969. There are also a dozen Council houses in the hamlet. Two outlying farms are the Grange, on the Foston road, and Thornham Farm, near the river Hull.

Though the canal itself is a prominent part of the landscape, there are few ancillary features associated with it. Wansford landing, on the west side of the Row, is now overgrown, and the landing-place allotted in 1772 to Nafferton,[42] near the junction of the canal and Nafferton beck,[43] is no longer recognizable as such. In 1817 some inhabitants of Nafferton were said to have gone to Wansford and claimed ground near the factory as a landing-place.[44] One late-19th-century building on the canal bank near the site of the factory has the appearance of a warehouse, and it may have been associated with the flour-milling and merchanting business that was conducted there after the factory closed.[45] There are two single locks and one pair on the stretch of the canal lying in Wansford. A swing bridge still exists over the pair of locks, at Snakeholme, and another such bridge, now replaced by an immovable structure, formerly carried the Skerne road across the canal. Another bridge carries the road over the river Hull, presumably on the site of the ford from which the hamlet was named. The present brick and stone bridge may date from soon after 1812, when an agreement for building a bridge was made between the lords of Wansford and Skerne.[46]

In 1377 there were 240 poll-tax payers in Nafferton, 40 in Wansford, and 18 in Pockthorpe.[47] By 1670 there were 101 households in Nafferton and Pockthorpe together, and 42 in Wansford. Four years later 22 households in Nafferton were discharged from the hearth tax; of the 74 that were taxed, 61 had only one hearth each, 8 had 2, 2 had 3, one had 6, and 2 had seven. In Wansford 8 households were discharged; 22 had one hearth each, 2 had 2, one had 3, and 2 had four.[48] In 1743 there were said to be about 100 families in the whole parish and in 1764 about 120.[49] The population of Nafferton in 1801 was 721 and of Wansford 378.[50]

Significant changes in the population of both places occurred in the 19th century. At Nafferton the average inter-censal increase was almost 100 from 1801 until 1861, when the population was 1,311. The figure remained at between 1,200 and 1,300 for the rest of the century and beyond. In 1931 it was slightly under 1,200; a comparable figure is not available thereafter because of the enlargement of the civil parish, but there was certainly some increase between 1951 and 1961. The population of Wansford dropped a little in the first two decades of the 19th century, and then fell sharply from 344 in 1821 to 152 in 1831: it seems likely that the closure of the carpet factory was the cause. A partial recovery followed, but numbers remained at around 200–250 for the rest of the century. By 1931 there were only 142 inhabitants.[51]

MANORS AND OTHER ESTATES. In 1086 there were 3 estates in Nafferton. William de Percy had 23 carucates and 2 bovates in Nafferton, which had been held in 1066 by Carle, and the soke of 5 carucates in Pockthorpe. The count of Mortain had one carucate in Pockthorpe. And the king had 6 bovates in Nafferton, which had been held in 1066 by Barch. The hamlet of Wansford was not mentioned separately in the Survey.[52] The Mortain estate later passed to the Percies,[53] and they also appear to have acquired the Crown estate.

Disputes between William and Richard de Percy in the early 13th century show that they then held the manors of Nafferton, comprising 18 carucates, and Wansford, comprising 2 carucates and 6 bovates.[54] In 1284–5 the Percy holding consisted of 14 carucates and 2 bovates in Nafferton, 6 carucates in Pockthorpe, and 2 carucates and 6 bovates in Wansford.[55] Pockthorpe is first referred to as a manor in 1401.[56] The whole of Nafferton remained in the possession of the Percies until Henry Percy, earl of Northumberland, conveyed it to the Crown, with his other northern estates, in 1537.[57]

Nafferton manor was granted by the Crown in 1544 to Matthew, earl of Lennox, and his wife,[58] and it was later sometimes known as *NAFFERTON LENNOX*, to distinguish it from the Constable manor.[59] It passed back to the Crown on the accession of the Lennoxes' grandson James I. Much of the manor was subsequently leased from the Crown by tenants, and in 1609 the manor-house itself and the demesne lands were held by Marmaduke Langdale; he had acquired the lease from William Wilberfoss, who had originally obtained it from the earl of Northumberland.[60] In 1617 the manor was granted by James I to Prince Charles for 99 years,[61] and it was later assigned to trustees for the City of London in return for loans to the Crown. The City still had it

---

[39] An air photograph is in *Y.A.J.* xxxviii, facing p. 66.
[40] See p. 292.
[41] Perhaps named after Francis Ireland, who owned land in the parish in 1783: E.R.R.O., Land Tax 1783.
[42] Regy. of Deeds, AQ/97/13.
[43] E.R.R.O., DDSY/68/119.
[44] Ibid. /94.   [45] See p. 292.
[46] E.R.R.O., QAB/1/4.
[47] E 179/202/62 mm. 2, 3, 1 respectively.
[48] E 179/205/514, 521.
[49] B.I.H.R., Bp. V. 1764/Ret. 166; *Herring's Visit.* ii. 204.
[50] *V.C.H. Yorks.* iii. 489.   [51] Ibid.; *Census.*
[52] *V.C.H. Yorks.* ii. 204, 226, 263.

[53] *E.Y.C.* xi, p. 15.
[54] *Percy Charty.* (Sur. Soc. cxvii), 6, 8; *Yorks. Fines, 1218–31,* i, 108–11; *Cur. Reg. R.* xiii. 271–2.
[55] *Feud. Aids,* vi. 30, 142, 230, 266–7.
[56] *Yorks. Inq. Hen. IV–V,* 16.
[57] *Yorks. Fines,* i. 77; J. M. W. Bean, *Estates of the Percy Family, 1416–1537,* 154. For pedigrees of the Percies see *Complete Peerage; Visit. Yorks. 1563 and 1564,* ed. C. B. Norcliffe, 241–4.
[58] *L. & P. Hen. VIII,* xix (1), p. 628. And see E 178/2538.
[59] For the Constable estate see p. 287.
[60] L.R. 2/230 f. 114. And see C 1/1263/58–61.
[61] C 66/2099 no. 3; C 66/2109 no. 2.

in 1639.[62] The manor was let in 1633 to John Pearson and others for two lives.[63] Despite being let in 1661 to William Stanley, Sir John Monson, and Henry Wilkinson for 21 years,[64] it was in 1665 still held by John Pearson.[65] In 1720 it was acquired from the Pearsons by Sir William St. Quintin,[66] and it thereafter descended like Harpham in the St. Quintin family.[67] The house known as Manor House, in Railway Street (formerly Priestgate), was sold by Lady Legard to R. E. Wiles in 1948, and the land, 25 a., was sold to William Martinson the same year.[68]

The manor of *WANSFORD* was also granted by the Crown in 1544 to Matthew, earl of Lennox, and his wife,[69] returning to the Crown at the accession of James I, and in 1604 it was granted to John Suckling.[70] He later added to the estate, acquiring ten cottages and 4½ bovates of land from William Beverley in 1620 and a three-acre close from Robert Johnson in 1622.[71] Before his death in 1627 Sir John Suckling directed that his Yorkshire estates should be sold,[72] and in 1630 his executors sold Wansford to Ralph Metcalf.[73] Ralph was succeeded by his son William, whose widow Anne married Arthur Jegon, and by 1665 the manor belonged to the Jegons.[74] Arthur Jegon also acquired two houses and 10 a. of land in Wansford from John Pearson in 1665.[75] The manor was sold in 1719 to Sir William St. Quintin and he made several small additions to the estate.[76] In 1787 it passed to Sir Christopher Sykes, the estate then comprising 681 a. and two water-mills in Wansford and 61 a. in Nafferton.[77] The Sykeses made some small additions in 1792, from Christopher Bainton, in 1817, from the Revd. George Ion, and in 1818, from John Boyes.[78] The estate was retained by the Sykes family until 1920 when it was sold in separate lots.[79] The house known as Manor House is of the late 18th century and has a porch with fluted Tuscan columns, besides Victorian embellishments.

The Leeds family had property in Nafferton and Pockthorpe as early as 1559[80] and from 1612 onwards they were described as holding the manor of *POCKTHORPE*.[81] In 1717 Francis Place and Robert Leeds granted the manor to Thomas Wilson.[82] From Wilson it passed to Anthony Nicholson in 1734, and Nicholson sold it to Joseph Hudson the same year.[83] In 1769 John Hudson sold Pockthorpe to Robert McFarland,[84] who added a bovate to the estate that year, and at inclosure in 1772 he was allotted the whole hamlet, said to comprise 682 a., together with 39 a. in Nafferton.[85] After McFarland's death in 1786 his trustees sold the manor to John Watts (d. 1818), and he devised it to William Hall. In 1826 the estate was more accurately computed to contain 738 a. Hall died in 1840 and three years later his trustees sold the manor to W. H. Harrison.[86] The Harrisons, later the Harrison-Broadleys, held the estate until 1956, when Doris Harrison-Broadley and June Malet sold Pockthorpe Hall and 786 a. to L. J. Marr. Stella and A. L. Marr owned it in 1968.[87] Part of the hall is said to have been pulled down in 1849,[88] and the present house probably dates from that time; it is of three storeys, stuccoed, with bay windows on the ground and first floors. In the grounds is a small brick building with crow-stepped gables and ball finials, perhaps of the early 18th century.

There were numerous subordinate holdings under the Percies in the Middle Ages. Several of these estates were large and their ownership may be traced over a long period; and a few were occasionally known as manors. Three of the more noteworthy were those of the Salvins, the Thornholmes, and the Constables.

Gerard Salvin was acquiring property in Nafferton and Pockthorpe at least as early as 1303 and 1310,[89] and in 1314 he held 4½ bovates under the Percies.[90] Nafferton was among the properties on which Salvin charged a yearly rent, payable to Hugh de Vere and his wife, in 1308.[91] By 1428 the Salvin holding was described as of 8 bovates.[92] The family's land was apparently dispersed in the 16th century. In 1502 Ralph Salvin granted his reputed manor of *NAFFERTON* to Sir Ralph Bygod, and others;[93] in 1533 William Salvin granted property in Pockthorpe to Marmaduke Constable, and in 1535 he granted rents from his property there to Richard Leeds;[94] and Ralph Salvin sold houses and land in Nafferton to Thomas Pearson and John Harrison in 1578.[95]

Hugh of Thornholme was acquiring property in Wansford in 1310–11,[96] and in 1314 he held a bovate from the Percies.[97] By 1428 the holding was described as of 2 bovates,[98] and in 1359 and 1430 as *THORNHOLME* manor;[99] in 1433 Thomas Thornholme let his manor-house there.[1] By 1497 the property was known as Thornholme Garth, and in 1506 it consisted of the house and 200 a. of adjoining closes.[2] The estate was held by the family until

---

[62] E.R.R.O., DDKG/142/(c); P. E. Jones and R. Smith, *Guide to the Records at Guildhall, London*, 55.
[63] C.P. 25(2)/521/9 Chas. I Hil. no. 54. It thus came to be held by the Pearsons, of Lowthorpe: see Y.A.S. MSS., MS. 709a.
[64] C 66/2965 no. 3.
[65] B.I.H.R., Prob. Reg. xlvii, f. 369v.
[66] Registry of Deeds, Beverley, G/398/876.
[67] See p. 224.
[68] Regy. of Deeds, 778/214/191; 782/379/327.
[69] *L. & P. Hen. VIII*, xix (1), p. 628.
[70] C 66/1634 m. 11; *Cal. S.P. Dom.* 1603–10, 162.
[71] E.R.R.O., DDSY/68/2, 3.
[72] C 142/446/87.
[73] E.R.R.O., DDSY/68/6.
[74] Ibid. /16; C 142/496/24.
[75] E.R.R.O., DDSY/68/19.
[76] Ibid. /44, 46, 49, 51, 56, 66.
[77] Ibid. /71.
[78] Ibid. /81, 127, 138.
[79] Regy. of Deeds, 192/147/135; 218/201/177, etc.
[80] L.R. 2/230 f. 107; *Yorks. Fines*, i. 226, 357; iii. 128; 1603–14, 134.
[81] E.R.R.O., DDHB/30/1, 4, 6, 12; *Yorks. Fines, 1603–14*, 193; *1614–25*, 171. For the Leeds family see C 3/364/14; *Dugdale's Visit. Yorks.* (Sur. Soc. xxxvi), 286.
[82] E.R.R.O., DDHB/30/17.
[83] Ibid. /18, 31a.
[84] Ibid. /23.
[85] Ibid. /24; Regy. of Deeds, AQ/97/13.
[86] E.R.R.O., DDHB/30/59, 60.
[87] Regy. of Deeds, 1040/372/330; 1536/67/57.
[88] Directories.
[89] *Yorks. Fines, 1300–14*, 30, 80.
[90] *Cal. Inq. p.m.* v, p. 320.
[91] *Yorks. Fines, 1300–14*, 67.
[92] *Feud. Aids*, vi. 266–7.
[93] C.P. 40/961 m. 430 d.
[94] E.R.R.O., DDWB/20/33; *Yorks. Fines*, i. 66.
[95] *Yorks. Fines*, ii. 123.
[96] *T.E.R.A.S.* xix. 24–5; *Yorks. Deeds*, x. 183.
[97] *Cal. Inq. p.m.* v, p. 318.
[98] *Feud. Aids*, vi. 266–7.
[99] E.R.R.O., DDWB/18/6; *Yorks. Deeds*, x. 185.
[1] E.R.R.O., DDWB/20/26.
[2] *Cal. Inq. p.m. Hen. VII*, ii, pp. 38–9; iii, pp. 87–8.

the death of John Thornholme in 1599.³ By 1611 it had passed to Richard Levens, who sold it that year to Robert Salvin and Walter Calvert.⁴ In 1616 the latter sold it to Darcy Wentworth and Charles Hutton.⁵ It had been acquired by the Wilberforce family by 1783⁶ and probably much earlier. It was sold in 1835, then consisting of 114 a., by William Wilberforce to Richard Arkwright and in 1852 the executors of Charles Arkwright (d. *c.* 1851) sold it to Albert Denison, Lord Londesborough.⁷ William, Lord Londesborough, sold it, then known as Thornham farm, to Ivy A. Hanson in 1910 and in 1944 she sold it to H. L. Shouler. It then consisted of 120 a.⁸ In 1945 Shouler sold it to Eva Crawford, from whom he repurchased it in 1963.⁹

The Constable family's interest in Nafferton may date from the early 13th century, for William the Constable, of Flamborough, was one of the heirs of Roger of Arundel (d. 1210). The Arundels held land in Nafferton¹⁰ from the Percies and part of it apparently passed to the Constables.¹¹ By the 1260s Robert and Richard Constable both had land in Nafferton,¹² and in 1314 Robert Constable held 2 carucates there from the Percies.¹³ The Constable estate lay in Pockthorpe and Wansford, as well as Nafferton itself,¹⁴ and at least by the early 16th century it was regarded as a manor. In 1546 Sir Marmaduke Constable granted the manor of *NAFFERTON CONSTABLE* to the Crown¹⁵ and it was subsequently held by a succession of lessees. Constable had let it in 1538 to William Burwell, who assigned the lease to Henry Snell, and in 1557 the Crown renewed the lease to Snell.¹⁶ In 1565 the manor was let to Anne Laybourne, in 1573–4 and 1582 again to Snell, and in 1590 to Henry Noell.¹⁷ There were thirteen leaseholders of former Constable land in 1609, all holding under the lease of 1590; the manor-house and most of the land were in the hands of Thomas Burton, the younger.¹⁸ In 1612 the manor was granted in fee by the Crown to Martin Freeman,¹⁹ and in 1658 it was sold by Elizabeth Frank to John Pearson.²⁰ The Pearsons kept it until 1720, when it was conveyed to Sir William St. Quintin.²¹

The Constable manor-house was known as Nether Hall and it occupied a large moated site towards the south end of the village, in Nether Gate²². The Victorian Nether Hall stands close by. Near the moats is an area known as the Parks; it belonged to the manor-house and was called Park Close in 1609 and the Parks in 1642.²³

The fragmentation of Nafferton among many owners is reflected in the large number of fines levied in the 16th and 17th centuries, and in the complexity of the inclosure award of 1772.²⁴ The manor of Nafferton Lennox itself apparently consisted of only three houses, 5 bovates of land, and some pasture when the Pearsons held it in the 17th century.²⁵ In 1796 the St. Quintins had only a cottage and 30 a. of land,²⁶ and in the 19th and 20th centuries there were half a dozen 'chief landowners', while a St. Quintin was merely 'lord of the manor'.²⁷ The largest landowner in Nafferton before inclosure was James Moyser, who was allotted 934 a. in 1772. He had acquired part of his estate in 1718, when William Pearson's widow sold him 40 bovates and various closes.²⁸ In the 19th century John Dickson (d. 1899) came to be the largest landowner. In addition to acquiring 632 a. of the rectorial estate in 1843,²⁹ he bought 603 a. from E. D. Conyers in 1856.³⁰

Several religious houses had small estates in Nafferton. Meaux abbey was given two houses in Wansford in 1182–97 and it held them, of the Percies, until the Dissolution.³¹ The property was held in 1586 by Robert Johnson.³² In 1595, described as the manor of Wansford, it was given by the Crown to Edmund Downing and Roger Rante, together with Skerne manor, which had also belonged to Meaux.³³ The Wansford property apparently subsequently descended with Skerne. Bridlington priory was given at least 4 bovates of land and several tofts in Nafferton in the 13th century,³⁴ and at the Dissolution it had property there worth about £4 and more in Wansford worth 5s.³⁵ The property was held on lease from the Crown in 1609, when Gregory Bransby had 2 houses, 5 bovates, and 2 closes of former priory possessions.³⁶ Lastly the Knights Hospitallers of Beverley had 3 houses and 14 a. of land in Nafferton and Pockthorpe in 1539–40,³⁷ and it was restored to them when the order was briefly revived in 1558.³⁸

The tithes belonged to Meaux abbey from the late 13th century.³⁹ The value of the church was reduced to £33 6s. 8d. in the new taxation.⁴⁰ In 1535 the gross value to Meaux was £46 4s. 6d., the net value nearly £21.⁴¹ The tithes due to the church were first mentioned *c.* 1090–6 when two thirds of the tithes of his demesne lands were given by William de Percy to Whitby abbey.⁴² In 1235–49 these tithes were worth £4; the pension paid by

---

³ E.R.R.O., DDWB/23/16, 17.
⁴ *Yorks. Fines, 1603–14*, 161. ⁵ Ibid. *1614–25*, 61.
⁶ E.R.R.O., Land Tax.
⁷ Regy. of Deeds, FB/136/159; GX/322/387.
⁸ Ibid. 121/8/8; 670/377/323.
⁹ Ibid. 709/380/331; 1329/243/218.
¹⁰ Nafferton was said to belong to Roger of Arundel in 1201, when a supposed miracle occurred there: *Chron. Roger de Howden* (Rolls Ser.), iv. 170.
¹¹ *E.Y.C.* xi, pp. 197–200.
¹² *Cal. Inq. Misc.* i, pp. 286–7.
¹³ *Cal. Inq. p.m.* v, p. 320.
¹⁴ C 139/103/28; C 142/11/49; *Cal. Close, 1485–1500*, 259–60.
¹⁵ *Yorks. Fines*, i. 125. And see ibid. ii. 27, 188.
¹⁶ *Cal. Pat.* 1557–8, 2.
¹⁷ Ibid. 1563–6, 158; C 66/1117 m. 21; C 66/1344 m. 21.
¹⁸ L.R. 2/230 ff. 129–31.   ¹⁹ C 66/1931 no. 4.
²⁰ Y.A.S. MSS., MS. 709a. See also *Abstracts Yorks. Wills* (Y.A.S. Rec. Ser. ix), 93.
²¹ Regy. of Deeds, G/398/876. ²² O.S. Map 6″ (1854).
²³ L.R. 2/230 f. 129; Y.A.S. MSS., MS. 709a.
²⁴ See p. 290.   ²⁵ Y.A.S. MSS., MS. 709a.
²⁶ Ibid. 709b.   ²⁷ Directories.
²⁸ Regy. of Deeds, G/133/302.   ²⁹ See p. 288.
³⁰ Regy. of Deeds, HM/214/240.
³¹ B.M. Cott. MS. Vit. C. vi, ff. 40, 193, 215; *Chron. de Melsa* (Rolls Ser.), i. 230; ii. 173, 229.
³² B.M. Add. MS. 26718, f. 44.
³³ C 66/1426 m. 14.
³⁴ *Bridlington Charty.* 149–53; *Cal. Pat. 1307–13*, 444–5.
³⁵ *Valor Eccl.* (Rec. Com.), v. 120; *Miscellanea*, iii (Y.A.S. Rec. Ser. lxxx), 17.
³⁶ L.R. 2/230 f. 132.
³⁷ *Miscellanea*, iv (Y.A.S. Rec. Ser. xciv), 87.
³⁸ *Cal. Pat.* 1557–8, 319.
³⁹ See p. 293.
⁴⁰ *Tax. Eccl.* (Rec. Com.), 326.
⁴¹ *Valor Eccl.* v. 108.
⁴² *E.Y.C.* ii, pp. 200–1, 212, 228; *Whitby Charty.* (Sur. Soc. lxix, lxxii), 3, 29, 57, 119, 223, 363.

Meaux to Whitby, in respect of the tithes, was £1 10s. in 1291 and £2 in 1535.[43] Certain tithes in Nafferton were sold by Meaux in 1315.[44] The total value of tithes, great and small, was just over £40 in 1535; there were then also 7 bovates of glebe, worth over £4, and 6 houses and 2 closes belonging to the church, worth nearly £2.[45] After the Dissolution the rectory was granted by the Crown to the archbishop of York in 1544,[46] and two years later the archbishop was granted the tithes which had been enjoyed by Whitby.[47]

The rectory was farmed out by the archbishops in the 16th and 17th centuries. In 1556, for example, the archbishop let the tithes to Humphrey Conysbye.[48] Peter Acklam was the farmer in 1614, 1618, and 1621, when he was involved in disputes over the payment of tithes.[49] In 1647, after the confiscation of archiepiscopal property, it was reported that Sir Miles Sands had earlier taken a lease from the archbishops and that he had assigned it to a Mr. Luckins; the latter was described as the lessee in 1650. The total value of the rectory in 1647 was £254, of which the tithes accounted for £231 and the glebe for £19. In 1650 the value of the rectory was put at £260, and the tithes of Wansford were said to contribute £40 of that sum.[50] Late in 1650 the rectory was sold by Sir John Wollaston and others to James Methorpe.[51] In 1665 it was in the possession of John Pearson.[52] Later in the century, after the restoration of the property of the see, the archbishop's farmer at Nafferton was Anne Jegon, who was involved in several disputes about tithe payment in the 1670s and 1680s.[53]

The rectory was held by the St. Quintins in 1758,[54] and at the time of inclosure in 1772 the archbishop's lessee was Sir William St. Quintin. In lieu of half of his tithes St. Quintin was awarded rents totalling about £230: £184 in Nafferton, £26 6s. in Wansford, and £19 10s. in Pockthorpe. For the other half he was allotted land: 421 a. for tithes in Nafferton, 56 a. for those in Wansford, and 63 a. for those in Pockthorpe. Furthermore he received 93 a. in lieu of glebe land and common rights belonging to the rectory.[55] In 1786 St. Quintin conveyed the rectorial estate to Richard Lovel. It passed to Fenwick Brown in 1828 and to John Dickson in 1843.[56] By 1877 both the rent-charge of £19 10s. and the allotment of 63 a. had been added to the Harrison-Broadley estate.[57] Dickson, however, retained much of the rectorial estate until his death in 1899.[58] It was subsequently sold in separate lots by A. J. Wise and F. N. Preston,[59] by whom it was held under the terms of Dickson's will.

ECONOMIC HISTORY. In 1086 there was reckoned to be land for 15 ploughs on the Percy estate in Nafferton and for $2\frac{1}{2}$ in Pockthorpe; in fact, William de Percy had only 3 ploughs in Nafferton and 13 villeins had 3 more. There was also a water-mill there, and there was meadow land 2 leagues long and $\frac{1}{2}$ league broad. The value of Nafferton had fallen from £8 in 1066 to £2 10s.[60]

The hamlet of Wansford was always small, and a Thursday market and a fair on 21–22 July, granted to Henry de Percy in 1304,[61] seem to have done little to enhance its status. The market, with tolls from goods carried on the river Hull (*cum tolneto aque*), brought in only 13s. 4d. in 1314,[62] and it was not mentioned again. Pockthorpe was even smaller and little is known about its topography and economy. The names of various sections of open-field land there were recorded in the early Middle Ages, and there are also references to tofts. A cross may have stood in the hamlet, for land was described as 'at the cross of Pockthorpe' (*apud crucem*).[63] In 1609 land in Nafferton was described as 'at the north end of the town nigh the cross'.[64] There were also references to houses in Windersome in the early 14th century;[65] in 1314, for example, 3 tofts and a carucate and 2 bovates of land there belonged to the manor.[66] By the 17th century there were apparently no houses there and the ground was used as pasture.[67]

The value of the Percy manor, when first recorded in 1258–9, was about £33, but the survey then made is apparently incomplete and it was made at a time when the lands were uncultivated and the houses, mill, and ponds were overwhelmed (*obruta*).[68] In 1314 the manor was worth about £76.[69] In later valuations Nafferton and Wansford were recorded separately. Nafferton was worth between £80 and £100 from the mid 15th to the early 17th century, and Wansford about £18–£20.[70] The Constable manor was valued at £15–£16 in the 1530s[71] and in 1609.[72]

At least in the 14th century the demesnes of the capital manor were kept in hand by the Percies. In 1314, for example, the demesnes included 19 bovates of arable, 86 a. of meadow, and 2 pastures and a turbary; together with the manor-house and the water-mill, they were valued at about £28, over a third of the total value of the manor.[73] The demesnes were still in hand, at least in part, in 1352 and 1405,

---

[43] *Whitby Charty.* 713; *Tax. Eccl.* 335; *Valor Eccl.* v. 82.
[44] *Reg. Greenfield*, i (Sur. Soc. cxlv), 151, 160.
[45] *Valor Eccl.* v. 108.
[46] *L. & P. Hen. VIII*, xx (1), pp. 215–16.
[47] Ibid. xxi (2), p. 163. The Crown had previously let the Whitby tithes: E 321/5/96; E 321/24/87; E 303/25/Yorks./933.
[48] C 1/1442/20.
[49] B.I.H.R., C.P., H. 1068, 1335, 1462.
[50] Lambeth MS. 918, xvii, ff. 12–13; *T.E.R.A.S.* ii. 52–3.
[51] C 54/3629 m. 14.
[52] B.I.H.R., Prob. Reg. xlvii, f. 369v.
[53] Ibid. C.P., H. 3348, 3447, 3504, 3552, 3614, 3812, 4116, 4399, 4400, 4415u, 4877, 4890.
[54] E.R.R.O., DDWB/24/31.
[55] Registry of Deeds, Beverley, AQ/97/13.
[56] Ibid. BM/62/115; DO/251/271; EF/83/113; FU/315/352.
[57] E.R.R.O., DDHB/30/32, 33, 38, 43, 47; see above, p. 286.
[58] Regy. of Deeds, 16/33/31 (1899).
[59] Ibid. 16/516/476 (1899); 227/452/381, etc.
[60] *V.C.H. Yorks.* ii. 263.
[61] *Cal. Chart. R.* 1300–26, 39.
[62] C 134/41/1.
[63] *Yorks. Deeds*, x. 129–30; *Percy Charty.* (Sur. Soc. cxvii), 96.
[64] L.R. 2/230 f. 112.
[65] *Yorks. Fines, 1300–14*, 33; *Percy Charty.* 85.
[66] C 134/41/1.
[67] L.R. 2/230 ff. 110, 120, 122–4, 126, 129; Y.A.S. MSS., MS. 709a.
[68] C 132/23/7; *Yorks. Inq.* i. 71.
[69] C 134/41/1.
[70] S.C. 6/Hen. VIII/4483; S.C. 11/959; J. M. W. Bean, *Estates of the Percy Family, 1416–1537*, 38, 47, 60.
[71] S.C. 6/Hen. VIII/4234–6; S.C. 12/27/34; E 315/288 f. 1.
[72] L.R. 2/230 ff. 106–36.
[73] C 134/41/1.

but they were being farmed out by 1525–6, when William Worm took a lease of them.[74] Henry Wedall paid a rent of £20 for the manor-house and demesnes in 1539.[75] The rent was the same in 1609, when the demesne lands included 24 bovates of arable and 160 a. of meadow and pasture.[76] On the Constable manor, a tenant paid about £5 for the 'head house', called Nether Hall, and its 6 bovates of arable in the 1530s,[77] and the rent for the house, 9 bovates of arable, and 50 a. of meadow and pasture in 1609 was £7-odd.[78]

Much land in Nafferton was held freely of the Percies in the Middle Ages. There were numerous under-tenants, often holding their land by knight service. In 1314, for example, there were 4 in Wansford, 3 in Pockthorpe, and 13 in Nafferton.[79] In 1346 there were 10 and in 1428 nine.[80] In addition freeholders in 1258–9 paid 15s. in rents and in 1314 about £5.[81] By 1609 there were 17 free tenants on the Lennox manor, none on the Constable; their property included 8 houses, 16 cottages, and 19 bovates of land.[82]

The Percy manor in 1258–9 included 32 bovates held in bondage, and 48 bovates were similarly held in 1314. In the former year there were also 19 cottars in Nafferton, each with a toft and a small amount of land, 15½ a. in all; other cottars in Wansford had only their tofts.[83] The services of the Percy tenants are not recorded, but those of the tenants of Meaux abbey in 1397 are known. Four tenants each held a house and 2 a. of land; each was obliged to mow a bovate of grass belonging to the rectory, to reap a bovate of grass and 13 sheaves of corn, to do at least 6 boon works in autumn, and to render 2 hens at Christmas and 20 eggs at Easter. Three other tenants performed no services, while a fourth only rendered hens and eggs.[84] It was at about this time that Meaux was said to have commuted the services of its tenants at Nafferton.[85] The former existence of boon works on the Percy manor is reflected in money payments made by 27 tenants of Nafferton Lennox in lieu of 'boons' in 1609.[86]

Of the eleven or twelve tenants of the Constable manor in 1536–7 and 1609, excluding the demesne tenant, only three had open-field holdings, comprising 2, 3, and 4 bovates. Several men also had odd parcels of land, but three or four had none at all. All but one tenant in 1609 had rights in the commons. On the Lennox manor in 1609 there were 64 leaseholders, in addition to the tenants of the manor-house and water-mill; 30 of them had open-field bovates, 3 holdings being of ½ bovate, 5 of one bovate, 4 of 2, one of 2½, 6 of 3, 2 of 3½, 4 of 4, one of 4½, 2 of 5, one of 6, and one of 7½ bovates. Nineteen cottagers had neither bovates nor any other land, but each of the 64 tenants had rights in the commons.[87]

Much of the open-field land lay on the wolds in Nafferton and Pockthorpe, but an extensive area of the ground called Heap, rising a little above the generally low-lying land in both Nafferton and Wansford, was also in open-field cultivation. References to arable land in the latter area occur from the 13th century onwards.[88] There is no evidence to show whether Pockthorpe and Wansford had separate field systems, though the 'fields' of Pockthorpe are mentioned in the early Middle Ages[89] and in the 17th century there was a South field in Wansford.[90] The number of open fields in Nafferton is also uncertain. By the 17th century there are references to holdings being dispersed between numerous sections of the fields, including East, West, Navy, and Heap fields. One bovate lay 'through the East wold', and another 'through the West Headlands'.[91] 'The 6 fields of Nafferton' are referred to, without names, in the early 18th century,[92] but in the inclosure award of 1772 only four fields are named. Allotments totalling 662 a. were made in 1772 from East field, 545 a. from West field, 361 a. from Heap field, and 113 a. from Navy field. A further 653 a. were allotted from the Wold, and if this was also arable, as seems likely, the open-field area distinguishable in the award is more than 2,300 a. Other allotments did not lie wholly in any one area.[93] The 700-odd acres of Pockthorpe also remained uninclosed until 1772, but it is unlikely that the arable land there had continued in common cultivation after the depopulation of the hamlet.

The extent of the open fields at an earlier date than 1772 is apparently never fully revealed in surveys of the manor. Thus in 1258–9 only 46 bovates were mentioned,[94] and in 1314 82.[95] In 1609 a survey which included the Lennox and Constable manors, but excluded Wansford and probably Pockthorpe too, referred to 168 bovates, besides over 100 a. of arable in small parcels.[96] In the 17th century the size of most bovates was 11 a.; a few were of 6 a.–10 a.[97] By that time the glebe at least had been to some extent consolidated: certain flats or furlongs in various parts of the fields were wholly glebe land, one strip in each flat being vicarial glebe and the remaining eight rectorial.[98]

Meadow land lay on the low ground in the southern half of Nafferton, and near the river Hull in Wansford. Meadows mentioned in the 13th century, all in the south of the parish, include 'Kantrayenges', 'Comuneng', 'Pokethorpeng', and 'Goseholm'.[99] In 1609 meadow in Canter ings, West ing, Snakeholme, Owseholme, and Gooseholme formed part of Nafferton Lennox manor,[1] and in 1688 Wansford manor had meadow in Hall ings, West ings, and Snakeholme.[2] The total area of meadow land is uncertain. In 1258–9 40 a. of demesne meadow were

---

[74] Bean, op. cit. 12–13, 55.
[75] S.C. 6/Hen. VIII/4283.
[76] L.R. 2/230 f. 114.
[77] S.C. 12/27/34.
[78] L.R. 2/230 f. 129.
[79] Cal. Inq. p.m. v, pp. 314, 318–20.
[80] Feud. Aids, vi. 230, 266–7.
[81] C 132/23/7; C 134/41/1.
[82] L.R. 2/230 ff. 107–8.
[83] C 132/23/7; C 134/41/1.
[84] B.M. Cott. MS. Vit. C vi, f. 217v.
[85] Chron. de Melsa (Rolls Ser.), iii. 228.
[86] L.R. 2/230 ff. 115–28.
[87] S.C. 6/Hen. VIII/4324; S.C. 12/27/34; L.R. 2/230 ff. 114–31.
[88] C 3/453/129; Bridlington Charty. 151, 154; Percy Charty. 121.
[89] Yorks. Deeds, x. 129–30.
[90] E.R.R.O., DDSY/68/19; Y.A.S. MSS., MS. 709a.
[91] Lambeth MS. 918, xvii, f. 12; Y.A.S. MSS., MS. 709a.
[92] E.R.R.O., DDHB/30/16, 20.
[93] Registry of Deeds, Beverley, AQ/97/13.
[94] C 132/23/7.
[95] C 134/41/1.
[96] L.R. 2/230 ff. 106–36.
[97] Ibid.; Lambeth MS. 918, xvii, f. 12; E.R.R.O., DDHB/30/2.
[98] B.I.H.R., TER. J. Nafferton n.d. to 1764.
[99] Percy Charty. 68, 77, 97.
[1] L.R. 2/230 ff. 110, 114, 118, 124.
[2] E.R.R.O., DDSY/68/29.

mentioned and in 1314 86 a.[3] The acreage of the common meadows inclosed in 1772 cannot be determined, but the meadows involved were Nun ings, Snakeholmes, Canter ings, and West ings.[4]

Until at least the 17th century the pastures and commons of Nafferton included a sheep pasture on the wolds, belonging to the manor. This was probably the place called 'the thorns' (*spineta*) in the late 13th century, when Henry de Percy enjoyed rights of warren in it.[5] In 1314 the manor had a pasture called Nafferton Thorns.[6] In 1609 Nafferton Lennox manor had 36 a. of sheep pasture,[7] and in 1658 the manor had a sheep pasture called the Hag, or the Thorns.[8] The name 'Thorns Nook' still survives, and the road running from Nafferton towards Pockthorpe is called Hag Lane. Other sheep pasturage was presumably available in 1609 in Sheep close, where a tenant of land belonging to the Constable manor had three gates.[9] The 100 sheep-gates belonging to the rectory in 1647[10] may, however, have been on the open fields or on the low-lying 'common moors'. There was apparently also a common cow pasture in the 17th century, for the Constable manor had cow-gates in 'Shape'.[11] At inclosure in 1772 36 a. were allotted in 'Shaps' besides other land not separately described;[12] ground still called Shap lies immediately south of the village, near Nafferton beck.[13]

The moors in the south-east of Nafferton comprised largely marsh and carr, and they provided turf grounds as well as pasture. Both turbary and pasture rights are recorded as early as the 13th century.[14] In 1314 the manor had a pasture called West carr, as well as a turbary where animals could be agisted.[15] All tenants enjoyed rights in these commons. When in 1344 Henry de Percy gave permission for five new tofts to be built, he specified that each occupant should have the same rights of pasture and turbary as other cottagers in Nafferton.[16] In 1609 there were beast-gates in the marsh ground, including West carr, and turf 'grafts' in the carrs, and nearly 100 men had pasture rights in the common moors. The pasture rights were expressed as an acreage-equivalent of each man's share, and they totalled about 520 a.; about 2 a. were enjoyed in respect of a house or cottage, and about 3 a. for a bovate of land. The largest shares were the 40 a. belonging to Nafferton Lennox demesne farm and the 35 a. of the Constable manor demesne.[17] There are references in 1620 to the Broad carr and the Little carr, and in 1650 to Broad carr ley.[18] In Wansford a cottager asserted that he paid the St. Quintins 8*d.* a year as an acknowledgement for his right of common and for a cottage which he had built on the waste about 1726.[19]

At inclosure in 1772 allotments of about 970 a., and others which are not separately described, were made in 'the Common'. Other allotments lay in West Cow moor.[20]

Effective drainage of the carrs depended upon co-operation with the inhabitants of Brigham, for much water passed that way before reaching the river Hull.[21] There were disputes, too, with Lowthorpe about responsibility for various stretches of Scurfe dike (apparently later known as White dike), which divided the two parishes.[22] Carr-water also drained into Mill beck, which needed constant attention in both Nafferton and Wansford.[23]

At the inclosure of 1772 nearly 1,000 a. of the parish were not accounted for, and some extensive early inclosure seems to have taken place. The Thornholme family's estate in Wansford was inclosed by the 16th century: in 1506 it was said to consist of about 200 a. of meadow, pasture, and marsh in closes lying around Thornholme Garth.[24] In 1753 the estate included the Great Summer pasture, an unnamed close, Calf close (10 a.), Thornholme ings (70 a.), and marsh ground (20 a.).[25] In the 17th century the manor of Wansford also contained some inclosed ground, and in 1688 at least fifteen closes were named.[26] At Pockthorpe the depopulation of the hamlet had not involved extensive inclosure. In 1768 the manor included only 40 a. of inclosed land,[27] and when the 682 a. of the hamlet were allotted to Robert McFarland in 1772 he was simply required to ring-fence the land where necessary to separate it from other allotments.[28]

In Nafferton itself individual closes were mentioned in the 17th and 18th centuries,[29] and land allotted in 1772 was described as abutting upon old inclosures. The Crown apparently contemplated an inclosure in the early 17th century, for several leases prepared in 1601 included a proviso that the tenants should agree to any inclosure made by Crown commissioners,[30] but it is not clear whether anything was done. In 1609 about thirty-five closes are recorded in the Lennox and Constable manors, but they were small and their total acreage was only about eighty.[31] The inclosure award of 1772 dealt with land in several named closes which were presumably being re-allotted.

The greater part of the open-field and other common land in Nafferton was inclosed in 1772[32] under an Act of 1769.[33] In all 4,863 a. were allotted. Sir William St. Quintin, as lord of the manors of Nafferton Lennox and Wansford, received 605 a. As lay rector, for tithes and glebe he was allotted a further 633 a., in addition to rents. The heirs of James Moyser received 934 a., and the whole

[3] C 132/23/7; C 134/41/1.
[4] Regy. of Deeds, AQ/97/13.
[5] *Rot. Hund.* (Rec. Com.), i. 114; *Percy Charty.* 96; *Yorks. Sess. Peace* (Y.A.S. Rec. Ser. c), 24; *Cal. Pat.* 1374–7, 59.
[6] C 134/41/1.
[7] L.R. 2/230 f. 114.
[8] Y.A.S. MSS., MS. 709a.
[9] L.R. 2/230 f. 129.
[10] Lambeth MS. 918, xvii, f. 12.
[11] Y.A.S. MSS., MS. 709a.
[12] Regy. of Deeds, AQ/97/13.
[13] The name is recorded as early as the 13th cent.: *Percy Charty.* 77.
[14] B.M. Cott. MS. Vit. C vi, f. 40; *Cur. Reg. R.* xi. 482–3.
[15] C 134/41/1.
[16] *Percy Charty.* 193.
[17] L.R. 2/230 ff. 110–32.
[18] C 3/453/129; C 142/709/179.
[19] E.R.R.O., DDSY/68/87.
[20] Regy. of Deeds, AQ/97/13.
[21] E.R.R.O., CSR/4/12; /19/8.
[22] Ibid. /4/33; /12/35; /20/77.
[23] Ibid. /9/39.
[24] Ibid. DDWB/23/16.
[25] Ibid. DDSY/6/40.
[26] Ibid. /68/3, 20, 29.
[27] Ibid. DDHB/30/22.
[28] A. Harris, 'The Lost Village and the Landscape of the Yorks. Wolds', *Ag. H.R.* vi. 97.
[29] E.R.R.O., DDHB/30/3, 20; L.R. 2/230 ff. 110–32.
[30] E 310/28/166 nos. 25, 31, 51, 56.
[31] L.R. 2/230 ff. 110–32.
[32] Regy. of Deeds, AQ/97/13.
[33] 8 & 9 Geo. III, sess. 2, c. 31 (Priv. Act).

hamlet of Pockthorpe, and some adjoining land in Nafferton, in all 721 a., went to Robert McFarland. Eight other men received substantial allotments: William Paul, the younger, got 290 a., his father 192 a., Robert Forge 167 a., Christopher Laybourne, the younger, 163 a., William Laybourne 141 a., Robert Laybourne 117 a., Richard Laybourne 110 a., and Richard Esh 107 a. For the rest, there were 3 allotments of 50 a.–100 a., 5 of 20 a.–50 a., 15 of 10 a.–20 a., and 30 of under 10 a. The trustees of the town got 8 a. and the trustees for the poor 9 a.

Most of the wold part of the parish has remained predominantly arable since inclosure. Already c. 1840 the manor of Pockthorpe had 590 a. of arable, with only 100 a. under grass and 95 a. of plantations,[34] and in 1801 the acreage under crops in Nafferton was 1,688.[35] Even the low-lying areas in the south were largely given over to arable farming as drainage improved.[36] The inclosure commissioners had made many provisions for drainage in the award of 1772 and they ordered that an overseer of drains should be appointed. The responsibility for Scurfe dike was still being disputed with Lowthorpe in the 1780s, and much attention had to be given to Nafferton beck in the 19th century.[37] The fragmented pattern of landownership seen at inclosure was maintained in the 19th and 20th centuries, and there have usually been between 20 and 30 farmers in Nafferton and 5 to 10 in Wansford.[38] In the present century there have also been a few men engaged in poultry-rearing and market-gardening.[39]

In 1840 about fifty people followed a craft or trade that was not directly concerned with agriculture, and a similar number has been so employed ever since.[40] Milling and malting will call for separate treatment. Brickmaking, mentioned in 1840, continued until the early 20th century at a brickworks north-west of the village. The house has the word 'Pottery' picked out in coloured tiles on the roof. Whiting manufacture and limeburning continued until the First World War; three chalk pits on Nafferton Wold all contained lime-kilns in 1850,[41] and one of the quarries was still worked in 1968, though lime was no longer burnt. The village trades of blacksmith and wheelwright developed in the late 19th century into engineer, and in the 20th into motor mechanic and 'auto-wrecker'. There were agricultural-machine proprietors and haulage contractors, and in the years before the First World War a manufacturer of portable buildings, who sent poultry-houses and sheds all over the country.[42]

The river Hull or West beck and the Driffield canal increased the local importance of Nafferton and Wansford. In the late 13th and 14th centuries Wansford was a collecting centre for corn from a wide area of the wolds, which was sent down-river to Hull, before export to supply the king's armies in Scotland and elsewhere.[43] In the early 17th century the river at Wansford was 'navigable for great boats which sail and carry barley'.[44] The canal was opened in 1770, and in 1786 Wansford manor included a wharf, a warehouse, and granaries on the banks of the canal.[45] The canal was subsequently used to carry the products of the carpet factory and corn-mill in Wansford. It was probably of little consequence to the parish long before it went out of use during the Second World War.

Nafferton water-mill was first recorded in 1086,[46] and frequently thereafter.[47] In 1602 the mill was let by the Crown to Thomas Johnson, together with the multure and soke of all tenants in Nafferton,[48] and a similar lease was taken by Edmund Cooke in 1607.[49] In 1609 the mill was held by Sir John Suckling,[50] but in 1610 it was granted by the Crown to Edward Ferrers and Francis Philips;[51] in 1617 Ferrers sold it to Suckling, whose executors sold it in 1630 to Thomas and John Pearson.[52] In 1632 and again in 1679 the Pearsons were engaged in lawsuits with tenants of the manor and with the farmer of the rectory about their withdrawal of soke. The evidence given reveals that in 1632 the miller ground only malt on one day each week, and that c. 1640 the Pearsons converted the mill into two, one for corn, the other for shelling oats and grinding malt.[53] A large new building was erected in 1840 as a combined corn-mill and malting,[54] and it was still so described in the 1890s. In the 20th century it became solely a malting and remained in operation until 1966.[55] Steam power was added in the 19th century, and subsequently electric power, but the water-wheel still survived in 1968.

There was also a windmill in Nafferton, mentioned in 1632.[56] A windmill on the Bridlington road was built in 1829 and steam power was added in 1840.[57] It was described as 'old windmill' by 1892,[58] but the disused tower still stood in 1968.

The end of corn-milling at the water-mill may have been connected with the erection by Mathias Nornabell of a large new steam mill near the railway station in 1878. Nornabell had bought the existing steam mill there in 1861, when it was described as 'lately built'.[59] The new mill was at first a malting as well. In 1890 grinding by rollers was introduced, and the mill was still producing flour in 1968; since 1904 it has belonged to Thirsk & Sons.[60]

Other water-mills were part of Wansford manor. By 1688 there were two mills: the manor then included 'Read House', with a water corn-mill, and White House, with a fulling mill.[61] The former was on Nafferton beck and the latter on the river Hull.

[34] E.R.R.O., DDHB/30/60.
[35] 1801 Crop Returns.
[36] E.R.R.O., DDSY/97/37, 38.
[37] Ibid. CSR/14/89; /31/400–401.
[38] Ibid. DDSY/68/154–9, 161–72, 174; /97/37–38; directories.
[39] Directories.
[40] This paragraph is mainly based on directories.
[41] O.S. Map 6" (1854).
[42] Hull Times, 26 July 1913.
[43] Y.A.J. xlii. 140–1. For river tolls see above, p. 288.
[44] Dodsworth's Ch. Notes (Y.A.S. Rec. Ser. xxxiv), 164. See also Farming Bk. of Hen. Best of Elmswell (Sur. Soc. xxxiii), 112.
[45] E.R.R.O., DDSY/68/119; see above, p. 177.
[46] V.C.H. Yorks. ii. 263.
[47] e.g. S.C. 6/Hen. VIII/4283; Abbrev. Plac. (Rec. Com.), 252; Cur. Reg. R. xii. 185; Percy Charty. 42, 461–2.
[48] C 66/1576 m. 8.
[49] C 66/1736 m. 21.
[50] L.R. 2/230 f. 123.
[51] C 66/1821 no. 1.
[52] Y.A.S. MSS., MS. 709a.
[53] E 134/8 Chas. I East./1; E 134/31 Chas. II Mich./20.
[54] H. D. Watts, 'Industrial Geog. of Rural E. Yorks.' (unpubl. M.A. thesis, Univ. of Hull, 1964), 92; date on building. See above, plate facing p. 272.
[55] Ex inf. Mr. P. M. Hurrell, Nether Hall, Nafferton, 1968.
[56] E 134/8 Chas. I East./1.
[57] Sheahan and Whellan, Hist. York & E.R. ii. 486.
[58] O.S. Map 6" (1892).
[59] Regy. of Deeds, IC/255/319.
[60] Kelly's Dir. N. & E.R. Yorks. (1879), 625; Watts, thesis cit. 79, 92; Regy. of Deeds, 70/362/344 (1904).
[61] E.R.R.O., DDSY/68/29.

The fulling mill was presumably used for locally-woven cloth, but there is little evidence of cloth-making in the parish. A Wansford weaver was found in 1399 to be infringing the rights of the weavers of York,[62] and there were references to two weavers and a shearman in the early 17th century.[63] Members of the Bainton family were dyers in the earlier 18th century,[64] and when the mills were sold to Sir Christopher Sykes in 1787 the fulling mill had a dyehouse and bleaching ground near by.[65]

In 1788 Sykes agreed to let the fulling mill for 31 years to Thomas and Christopher Bainton and John Boyes, the elder (d. 1790), so that they might carry on a factory there, and he licensed them to build fourteen cottages for workmen.[66] Work was in progress the same year, and in 1790 Sykes gave permission for the buildings to be insured and two more cottages built; besides the old dyehouse, there were a cotton and worsted mill, a counting-house, and combing and weaving shops.[67] In 1792 the Baintons and John Boyes, the younger, a Hull grocer, took two other men into partnership, and in 1792–3 worsted yarn was being spun and made into carpeting.[68] The Driffield canal had no doubt provided an incentive to the venture, and in 1793 Christopher Bainton had two sloops and a lighter.[69]

From the outset the factory was handicapped by lack of capital and by the need for more power to work the machinery. It ran at a loss in 1792–6, but annual gains were then made until 1804, when the installation of cotton machinery caused a heavy loss. The water supply to the mill had been improved in 1795.[70] Under John Boyes's management[71] the factory ran at a profit from 1805 to 1815,[72] but it nevertheless failed when Boyes became bankrupt in 1816. There were then 26 carpet looms. Arrangements were made in 1817 for the Sykeses to finance Boyes's continued operation of the factory, and it was still at work in 1823.[73] Further efforts were made to improve the water supply to the mill in these last years.[74]

The mill was perhaps converted to corn-milling in 1833, when Sykes let it to Thomas Bainton, miller, of Foston.[75] The Baintons were working it as a corn- and bone-mill in 1856, by which time the water-wheel had been supplemented by a steam engine.[76] By 1872 the mill was operated by Mathias Nornabell, trading as a corn, seed, cake, coal, manure, and bone merchant, and it continued to be so used after Nornabell moved to Nafferton in 1878.[77] In the 1890s the mill closed[78] and little trace of it remains. It had been a prominent feature of the landscape: the mill-race and reservoir had stretched for nearly a mile alongside the canal, and the factory had been a substantial building.[79]

The mill on Nafferton beck had meanwhile continued as a corn-mill, and in the 19th century it was also used as a malting.[80] It was occupied by a 'farmer and miller' until it ceased to be used c. 1920.[81] The mill and miller's house still stood in 1968.

LOCAL GOVERNMENT. There are surviving court records for Nafferton Lennox manor in 1572–3,[82] 1609–11, and 1627–8[83] and for Wansford in 1572–3. Separate juries were sworn for Nafferton and Wansford at the courts held in 1572–3, and there were constables for each place. The officers appointed in 1572 were 2 constables, 2 ale-tasters, and a pinder. The matters dealt with included pleas of debt, agricultural offences, and infringements of the assize of bread and ale. Most of the business in 1609–11 and 1627–8 concerned agricultural offences, and the bylawmen were mentioned in 1611.

Courts were still being held by the St. Quintins for Nafferton Lennox manor in modern times, call rolls and jury papers surviving for 1803–1914. Either one or two constables and a pinder were being appointed throughout this period. Pains and by-laws recorded in 1775 and 1832 were concerned with such matters as straying animals, sewers, streets, and bridges.[84]

Some light is thrown on parish government in Wansford by the difficulties which arose after John Boyes's bankruptcy at the carpet factory.[85] The poor-rate in Wansford averaged 3s. 11d. in the pound in the six years 1816–21. Employment at the factory supported 20 men, 19 wives, and 73 children who lived in the township, and in 1820–1 they received £159 out of total payments for poor-relief in Wansford of £228. It was estimated that employment at the factory nevertheless saved £463 in relief. The highway rates averaged 1s. 6½d. in the pound in the five years 1816–20. The factory was not assessed, but Boyes, as its tenant, repaired about half the length of the roads in Wansford. The constable's assessment at that time raised about £20 a year.[86]

There are surviving vestry minutes of 1822 onwards[87] and churchwardens' accounts of 1632[88] and 1812–47.[89] The vestry was a select one in 1822, chosen in accordance with the second Sturges Bourne Act of 1819.[90] Churchwardens, overseers of the poor (usually two in number), and surveyors of highways (usually 2–5) were elected at vestry meetings during the rest of the century. In the earlier years poor-relief was the main business transacted, and there was a parish workhouse, the master of which received £5 5s. a year in 1822. A paid officer to assist the overseers and surveyors was appointed from 1842 onwards and in 1889 the office of 'assistant overseer' was formally created.

In 1849 the vestry adopted the Lighting and

---

[62] *Cal. Inq. Misc.* vi, p. 246.
[63] *Wills in the York Regy. 1603–11* (Y.A.S. Rec. Ser. xxvi), 91; *1627–36* (Y.A.S. Rec. Ser. xxxv), 50.
[64] E.R.R.O., DDSY/68/74, 76, 80.
[65] Ibid. /119.
[66] Ibid. /120.
[67] Ibid. /99, 144.
[68] Ibid. /100, 146.
[69] Ibid. /147.
[70] Ibid. /89, 93, 107, 148.
[71] i.e. John Boyes, the younger; he was joined as a partner by his son, another John, in 1810: ibid. /107.
[72] Ibid. /93.
[73] Ibid. /94–96, 111, 115; Baines, *Hist. Yorks.* (1823), ii. 397.
[74] E.R.R.O., DDSY/68/106–10.
[75] Ibid. 139.
[76] Sheahan and Whellan, *Hist. York & E.R.* ii. 487.
[77] *Kelly's Dir. N. & E.R. Yorks.* (1872), 525; (1879), 626.
[78] Ibid. (1893), 466; (1897), 505.
[79] E.R.R.O., DDSY/68/153 (map of 1805); O.S. Map 6" (1854).
[80] Watts, 'Industrial Geog. of Rural E. Yorks.', 92; *Kelly's Dir. N. & E.R. Yorks.* (1872), 525.
[81] Directories; local inf.
[82] *Y.A.J.* x. 63–80.
[83] S.C. 2/211/89–90.
[84] Y.A.S. MSS., DD. 89.
[85] See above.
[86] E.R.R.O., DDSY/68/111.
[87] Ibid. PR. 1827.
[88] B.I.H.R., C.P., H. 1960.
[89] E.R.R.O., PR. 1828.
[90] 59 Geo. III, c. 12.

Watching Act of 1833[91] so far as it concerned the watching of the village. In 1854 and 1855 subscriptions were collected to buy flour and a committee was appointed to sell it to the poor at two thirds of the cost price. During the earlier 19th century Wansford, instead of being rated along with Nafferton, usually contributed a quarter or a fifth of the churchwardens' expenses; from 1850 onwards, however, Wansford was included in the parish rate. In 1836 Nafferton and Wansford joined the Driffield union.[92]

CHURCHES. A church at Nafferton was first mentioned in 1232, when it belonged to the Percies.[93] Between 1286 and 1291, however, the church was acquired by Meaux abbey.[94] A vicarage was ordained in 1303.[95] In the Middle Ages there were chapels in the hamlets of both Pockthorpe and Wansford, the latter briefly having rights of burial before they were removed, at the instance of Meaux abbey, in 1354.[96] It seems that neither chapel survived the dissolution of the chantries. Wansford was said in 1650 to be 'fit to be a parish',[97] but it was not until 1868 that a new chapel was built there. In 1907 a separate parish was created.[98] In 1925, however, Wansford was united with Skerne, and in 1955 it was transferred to Nafferton.[99]

The advowson belonged to the Percies[1] until 1302 when it was granted to Meaux;[2] the abbey presented the last rector in 1303,[3] shortly before the ordination of the vicarage. Thereafter the vicarage was in the gift of the archbishop of York.[4] Sir Tatton Sykes became the patron of the new living at Wansford in 1907. When Wansford was united with Skerne the Sykes family was to have two turns out of three and after 1955 the patrons of Nafferton and Wansford were to present alternately.[5] In 1960, however, the archbishop became the sole patron.[6]

The church was worth £60 in 1291.[7] When the vicarage was ordained in 1303 the vicar was awarded a stipend of £13 6s. 8d. to be paid out of the rectory, together with a bovate of land, common of pasture, and the site for a parsonage house to be built by Meaux abbey.[8] In 1535 the gross value of the vicarage was £13 18s. 8d.[9] The stipend continued to be paid in the 17th, 18th, and 19th centuries.[10] The living was twice augmented with £200 from Queen Anne's Bounty, in 1780 and 1802, and also with a parliamentary grant of £1,200 in 1814.[11] In 1818 its value was about £98,[12] and in 1829-31 the average net income was £139.[13] The new chapel at Wansford was endowed by Sir Tatton Sykes and grants were made to it by the Ecclesiastical Commissioners.[14] The net income of Nafferton with Wansford was £296 in 1884.[15]

At inclosure in 1772 the vicar was allotted 13 a. in lieu of the bovate of glebe.[16] By 1825 a nine-acre close at Bewholme had been bought with Bounty money, and by 1868 a further 17 a. had been acquired in Nafferton.[17] In 1962 16 a. in Nafferton were sold.[18]

The parsonage house provided for in 1303 was duly built, and in 1372-96 Meaux was repairing it and adding new buildings there.[19] A new house was provided by Archbishop Lamplugh (1688-91), consisting of two ground-floor rooms, two chambers, and garrets, and built of brick and tile; to this Archbishop Sharp (1691-1714) added a shed for a back kitchen.[20] It was no doubt a later house which in 1959 was replaced by a new Vicarage,[21] on the same site in Main Street.

When the parish of Wansford was created in 1907 a large Vicarage was built near Wansford church by Sir Tatton Sykes.[22] After 1925 it was used by the incumbent of Skerne with Wansford,[23] and after 1955 it was sold.

Wansford chapel, dedicated to St. Nicholas, was in existence before 1330, when it was refounded by Ellis of Wansford; he endowed it with 2 houses in York and £5 rent.[24] The inhabitants were ordered to repair the chapel roof and the advowson was given to York corporation. Ellis presented in 1330 and 1331, and no presentation by York is known.[25] John of Thornholme left land in 1383 for a chaplain to celebrate in the chapel for six years,[26] and in 1392 Richard Brown was licensed to grant 3 houses and 6 bovates and 26 a. of land in Nafferton and Wansford to a chaplain celebrating services there.[27] Richard presented in 1399 and after his death the advowson passed to the Percies, who last presented in 1523. John Potter was presented by the Crown in 1539.[28]

The chantry chapel was valued at £4 6s. 8d. in 1535, when its possessions comprised a house and a bovate of land in Wansford, and 3 bovates and other land in Nafferton.[29] In 1552, after the dissolution of the chantry, there were said to be two bells, but the lead and plate had been removed.[30] In the following year the Crown granted 'the chantry house' and 2 a. of meadow, then in the occupation of John Potter, to Christopher Estofte and Thomas Doweman.[31]

---

[91] 3 & 4 Wm. IV, c. 90.   [92] *3rd Rep. Poor Law Com.* 168.
[93] *Reg. Gray* (Sur. Soc. lvi), 54.
[94] *Chron. de Melsa* (Rolls Ser.), ii. 229; *Tax. Eccl.* (Rec. Com.), 303. In 1320 Meaux was pardoned for acquiring the church in mortmain without licence: *Cal. Pat.* 1317-21, 521, 524.
[95] *Reg. Corbridge*, i (Sur. Soc. cxxxviii), 190.
[96] Lawton, *Rer. Eccles. Dioc. Ebor.* 306-7.
[97] *T.E.R.A.S.* ii. 53.
[98] *Lond. Gaz.* 23 Aug. 1907, p. 5777.
[99] Ibid. 26 May 1925, p. 3541; 1 Nov. 1955, p. 6149.
[1] *Reg. Gray*, 54; *Reg. Corbridge*, i. 184; *Cal. Pat.* 1232-47, 496; *Cur. Reg. R.* xii. 292.
[2] *Cal. Pat.* 1301-7, 100.   [3] *Chron. de Melsa*, ii. 229.
[4] *Reg. Corbridge*, i. 191, 193; *Cal. Pat.* 1385-9, 431; *Fasti Parochiales*, iii. 63-5; Inst. Bks.
[5] *Lond. Gaz.* 23 Aug. 1907; 26 May 1925; 1 Nov. 1955.
[6] York Dioc. Regy., Orders in Council 1/759.
[7] *Tax. Eccl.* 326.
[8] *Reg. Corbridge*, i. 190-1.   [9] *Valor Eccl.* v. 124.
[10] B.I.H.R., TER. J. Nafferton n.d. to 1868.
[11] Hodgson, *Q.A.B.* 449.
[12] Lawton, *Rer. Eccles. Dioc. Ebor.* 306.
[13] *Rep. Com. Eccl. Revenues*, 956-7.
[14] E.R.R.O., DDSY/101/35; /104/148; B.I.H.R., TER. J. Nafferton 1868.
[15] B.I.H.R., Bp. V. 1884/Ret.
[16] Regy. of Deeds, AQ/97/13.
[17] B.I.H.R., TER. J. Nafferton 1825, 1868.
[18] Regy of Deeds, 1279/237/214.
[19] *Chron. de Melsa*, ii. 226-7.
[20] B.I.H.R., TER. J. Nafferton 1726.
[21] Ex inf. the vicar, 1968.
[22] Tablet in Wansford church.
[23] *Lond. Gaz.* 26 May 1925, p. 3541.
[24] *Chron. de Melsa*, ii. 306-7. It had earlier been dedicated to SS. Mary and Nicholas: *Y.A.J.* ii. 189.
[25] *Fasti Parochiales*, iii. 117.
[26] E.R.R.O., DDWB/25/1.   [27] *Cal. Pat.* 1391-6, 153.
[28] *Fasti Parochiales*, iii. 117-18.
[29] *Valor Eccl.* v. 126.   [30] *Inventories of Ch. Goods*, 53.
[31] *Cal. Pat.* 1553, 257.

Five years later, however, this property, together with the 'chapel yard', was granted to Sir George Howard.[32] In 1566 the chapel and a garth were granted to Thomas Blackway and Francis Barker, and in 1564 chantry lands in Nafferton were let to Anne Laybourne.[33] In 1607 a grant was made to George Ward and Robert Morgan of the chantry property, including 3 houses, 7 bovates, and 27 a.[34] Robert Laybourne and Agnes Harrison each held a house and 4 bovates of chantry land from the Crown in fee farm in 1609.[35]

The chapel of St. Edmund the King at Pockthorpe was mentioned in 1328, when Walter of Pockthorpe was licensed to grant lands there to a celebrant chaplain.[36] A small gift for the support of the chapel was made in 1445.[37] In 1556 it was recalled that bells and lead had been removed from the chapel after the dissolution of the chantry.[38]

The incumbent of Nafferton had no assistant curate in the 18th century, but by 1864 an assistant had charge of the services at Wansford. In 1900 there were two assistants, but by 1936 none.[39] In 1743 the vicar held the livings of Foston, Lowthorpe, and Ruston Parva, as well as Nafferton where he lived.[40]

Philip Pecket, who was the incumbent at Nafferton in 1652–3, moved to Lastingham (Yorks. N.R.) in 1656 and was ejected in 1660.[41] Francis Morris, the naturalist, was vicar from 1844 to 1854.[42]

Only one service was held each Sunday in 1743; communion was administered four times a year and was received by about eighty people.[43] In 1764 the incumbent again pleaded poverty as the reason for only one service being held. There were then 40–50 communicants.[44] By 1851 there were two services each week at Nafferton and one at Wansford, where the schoolroom was used for worship.[45] In 1864 communion was received monthly by about twenty people at Nafferton and fewer than ten at Wansford.[46] Four years later there were two Sunday services at Wansford also.[47] By 1936 communion was administered weekly.[48] In 1968 two services were held each Sunday at Nafferton and one at Wansford.

The large church of *ALL SAINTS*, Nafferton, is built of stone and consists of chancel, nave, north and south aisles, south porch, and west tower.[49] Successive restorations in the 19th century have obscured many of its original features. The earliest work is of the 12th century, but all that remains of this date is the chancel arch, the font, and some masonry, probably re-used, in the external walls. The arch responds have Norman capitals and plain chamfered abaci, but the arch itself is pointed and slightly four-centred, suggesting that it may have been rebuilt. The surface of the circular font is covered with intricate interlacing ornament surmounted by a cable moulding. The church was altered and enlarged from the 14th century onwards, the chancel being rebuilt first. To the south of the chancel arch is a partly-blocked squint with a shouldered head. The south and north aisles are additions of the 14th and 15th centuries respectively. The embattled west tower and the clerestory were probably built in the 15th century, but a large Perpendicular window in the west wall of the tower and the doorway below it may be still later insertions.

An example of 17th-century maintenance work is that done in 1632, when money was spent on the windows, timber, brickwork, paving, stalls, bells, and porch.[50] The first of several restorations in the 19th century was undertaken in 1828 and included the provision of new pews.[51] Further work in 1846 is said to have included the reconstruction and raising of the roof.[52] About 1870 the clerestory and other windows were reglazed, a new window was put in the south wall of the chancel, and a new organ and vestry provided.[53] And in 1883 work was done on the chancel, including the roof, and the tower roof was renewed and a new clock installed.[54]

There is a large tomb niche in the wall of the south aisle; in the north aisle is a small figure, once recumbent, which has been built into the wall. A much-worn stone slab is carved with two life-sized effigies, probably of the 14th century; foliage carving is spread over their bodies and above their heads are mutilated canopies.[55] Wall tablets commemorate Christopher Paul (d. 1737), Thomas Smith (d. 1856), parish clerk for 36 and schoolmaster for 58 years, and Robert Worrall (d. 1657).

There are 19th-century memorial windows to members of the Dickson family. In 1895 Richard Laybourne gave £50 stock for the maintenance of a window to Jacob Laybourne (d. 1862), of the family tomb in the churchyard, and of Richard Laybourne's grave in the fields at Windersome.[56]

There were four bells in 1552[57] but by 1764 only three.[58] Between 1781 and 1825 one bell was removed,[59] and it was not until 1882 that a third bell was again provided, given by R. Holtby.[60] The plate includes a cup, paten, and flagon, all with London hall-marks for 1865, and a silver box, made in London in 1903.[61] The registers begin in 1653, those of burials having a gap from 1757 to 1769.[62]

A new burial ground, next to the churchyard, was consecrated in 1896.[63]

The Revd. James Davidson, by will proved in 1906, left £100 for the upkeep of a window in the

---

[32] *Cal. Pat.* 1557–8, 413.
[33] Ibid. 1563–6, 158, 475.
[34] C 66/1747 m. [29].
[35] L.R. 2/230 f. 132.
[36] *Cal. Pat.* 1327–30, 242; *Percy Charty.* 160.
[37] *Yorks. Deeds,* iii. 8–9.
[38] E.R.R.O., DDCC/139/65.
[39] B.I.H.R., Bp. V. 1764/Ret. 166; V. 1865/Ret. 371; *Herring's Visit.* ii. 205.
[40] *Herring's Visit.* ii. 205.
[41] *Calamy Revised,* ed. A. G. Matthews, 385.
[42] *D.N.B.*
[43] *Herring's Visit.* ii. 205.
[44] B.I.H.R., Bp. V. 1764/Ret. 166.
[45] H.O. 129/24/523.
[46] B.I.H.R., V. 1865/Ret. 371.
[47] Ibid. V. 1868/Ret. 329.
[48] Ibid. Bp. V. 1936/Ret. 36.

[49] Morris, *E.R. Yorks.* 275–6.
[50] B.I.H.R., C.P., H. 1960.
[51] White, *Dir. E. & N.R. Yorks.* (1840), 394. A plan of the seating, made in 1829, is in the Vicarage.
[52] *Kelly's Dir. N. & E.R. Yorks.* (1872), 524.
[53] Ibid.; B.I.H.R., V. 1871/Ret. 332.
[54] B.I.H.R., Bp. V. 1884/Ret.; *Kelly's Dir. N. & E.R. Yorks.* (1893), 465.
[55] For somewhat similar carving see p. 277.
[56] Tablet under window. See p. 284.
[57] *Inventories of Ch. Goods,* 30.
[58] B.I.H.R., TER. J. Nafferton 1764.
[59] Ibid. 1781, 1825.
[60] Ibid. FAC. 1881/11; Boulter, 'Ch. Bells', 218; Bulmer, *Dir. E. Yorks.* (1892), 245.
[61] *Yorks. Ch. Plate,* i. 294.
[62] E.R.R.O.
[63] B.I.H.R., CD. 552.

north aisle of the church and for the upkeep of certain graves, including his own. The income was £3 a year in 1929–31. He also left £200 for the Sunday school and for the bell-ringers. An income of £3 a year was distributed among the ringers in 1929–31.[64]

The church of ST. MARY, Wansford, was built in 1868 at the cost of Sir Tatton Sykes, and was designed by G. E. Street, in a mainly late-13th-century style.[65] It consists of chancel, nave, south porch, and west bell-turret. The screen and pulpit are of coloured marble. Sykes bequeathed £500 to the church at his death in 1913.[66]

NONCONFORMITY. In 1676 five dissenters were recorded at Nafferton,[67] and in 1764 about six were said to attend the Anabaptists' meeting at Bridlington.[68] There was then no meeting-place in Nafferton, but houses and other buildings were licensed for worship in 1778, 1780, 1788, 1796 (two), 1802, 1808, and 1817.[69]

The Methodists had about twenty members at Nafferton in 1787–91.[70] The first chapel in the parish was licensed by the Wesleyan Methodists in 1801,[71] though it may have been built a few years earlier.[72] It has twice been rebuilt, in 1839[73] and in 1907,[74] and services were still held there in 1969. The present building is of grey brick and stone, in the Gothic style,[75] and the chapel site has apparently always been in Main Street. An Independent chapel was licensed in 1817[76] but it ceased to be used c. 1860.[77] The building, in West Gate, appears to have been demolished. The third chapel to be built was the Primitive Methodists', in Priestgate, licensed in 1826.[78] A new chapel was built in Coppergate, of mottled and grey brick and stone, in 1858,[79] and in 1889 there were 91 members belonging to the Primitive Methodist congregation.[80] The chapel fell out of use in 1964[81] but it still stands.

The Salvation Army registered a hall in High Street in 1885, but had ceased to use it by 1896,[82] and the Shepherd's Hall during 1924.[83] The Four Square Gospel Church registered the High Street hall in 1946, ceasing to use it by 1954.[84]

At Wansford the Methodists had 10 members in 1790 and 20 in 1791,[85] a development probably reflecting the opening of the carpet factory. A Wesleyan chapel was built c. 1809[86] and remained in use until c. 1960.[87] The Primitive Methodists licensed a meeting-place in 1861[88] and this was replaced by a chapel, of red and yellow brick, built in 1864.[89] There were eight members in the Primitives' congregation in 1889[90] and their chapel was used until 1906.[91] Its closure is said to have been due to the closing-down of the large flour mill a few years earlier. The chapel was subsequently used as a reading room[92] and meeting-hall, and both it and the former Wesleyan chapel still stood in 1967.

The vicar reported in 1864 that his work was impeded by dissent, and in particular by the results of the action of the lessee of the rectory who, 40 years earlier, had built a school on church property and appropriated it to the dissenters.[93] This complaint was made again in 1877 when it was said that the leading dissenters in Nafferton had been brought up in the school.[94] In 1868 the incumbent estimated that there were about 700 dissenters in the parish.[95]

EDUCATION. Masters at the 'free' school in Nafferton are recorded in 1685 and throughout the 18th century.[96] The school was endowed in 1709 by John Baron, who bequeathed £5 a year to it from a house in Bridlington. It was said in 1823 that the stipend was intended to encourage the master to live at Nafferton and that he was not obliged to teach any children free of charge.[97] In 1819 there was, in fact, one free scholar but 40 other children paid fees;[98] 25–30 children were taught in 1823, all paying fees.[99]

There was also a petty school in Nafferton in the 18th century at which the Revd. Joseph Somers taught.[1] In 1819 there were three dame schools, attended by 30–40 children all told.[2] By 1835 four such schools, started between 1820 and 1832, were attended by 44 boys and 36 girls, whereas only 12 boys and 3 girls were at the 'free' school.[3] In the mid century there were still two dame schools.[4]

The 'free' school, which was united with the National Society, stood in High Street. It was built, or rebuilt, in 1815[5] and again in 1845,[6] and by 1849 it was in receipt of an annual government grant.[7]

---

[64] Char. Com. files.
[65] Tablet in church.
[66] Char. Com. files.
[67] Bodl. MS. Tanner 150, ff. 27 sqq.
[68] B.I.H.R., Bp. V. 1764/Ret. 166.
[69] Ibid. DMH. 1778/9; 1780/2; 1788/18; 1796/130, 136; DMH. Reg. 1, p. 9; G.R.O. Worship Returns, Vol. v, nos. 502, 559, 717, 1256, 1262, 1746, 2186, 3027.
[70] E.R.R.O., MRP/1/7.
[71] G.R.O. Worship Rets., Vol. v, no. 1679.
[72] The date of building is given as 1785 in H.O. 129/24/523, and 1792 in Sheahan and Whellan, *Hist. York & E.R.* ii. 486.
[73] White, *Dir. E. & N.R. Yorks.* (1840), 394.
[74] *Kelly's Dir. N. & E.R. Yorks.* (1909), 560.
[75] Nafferton successfully applied for a bequest made by John Hatfield, of Manchester, for the building of a Wesleyan chapel in a village of 1,000–2,000 inhabitants: *Hull Times*, 26 July 1913.
[76] G.R.O. Worship Rets., Vol. v, no. 3120; B.I.H.R., DMH. Reg. 1, p. 38.
[77] It was said to be no longer used in 1856 (Sheahan and Whellan, *Hist. York & E.R.* ii. 486), but the parish incumbent reported it as existing in 1864 (B.I.H.R., V. 1865/Ret. 371.)
[78] B.I.H.R., DMH. Reg. 1, p. 38; G.R.O., Worship Rets., Vol. v, no. 4013. It was said in 1851 to have been built in 1824: H.O. 129/24/523.
[79] Date on building.
[80] H. Woodcock, *Sketches of Prim. Meth. on Yorks. Wolds*, 142.
[81] G.R.O. Worship Reg. no. 8940.
[82] Ibid. no. 28664.
[83] Ibid. no. 49256.
[84] Ibid. no. 61496.
[85] E.R.R.O., MRP/1/7.
[86] H.O. 129/24/523.
[87] Local inf. It was deregistered, already disused, in 1964: G.R.O. Worship Reg. no. 2416.
[88] Ibid. no. 12621.
[89] Date on building.
[90] Woodcock, *Prim. Meth. on Wolds*, 144.
[91] G.R.O. Worship Reg. no. 16850.
[92] *Hull Times*, 21 Mar. 1914.
[93] B.I.H.R., V. 1865/Ret. 371.
[94] Ibid. V. 1877/Ret.
[95] Ibid. V. 1868/Ret. 329.
[96] B.I.H.R., Schools index.
[97] *9th Rep. Char. Com.* 738.
[98] *Rets. on Educ. of Poor, 1819*, 1087.
[99] *9th Rep. Char. Com.* 738.
[1] B.I.H.R., Schools index.
[2] *Rets. on Educ. of Poor, 1819*, 1087.
[3] *Educ. Enquiry Abstract, 1835*, 1092.
[4] M. C. F. Morris, *The British Workman*, 6–7.
[5] Date on building.
[6] Ed. 7/135; Bulmer, *Dir. E. Yorks.* (1892), 245.
[7] *Mins. of Educ. Cttee. of Counc. 1849* [1215], H.C., p. 499 (1850), xliii.

The 1815 building was in 1854-5 fitted up as a separate infants' school, with an average attendance of 50 in 1859.[8] The attendance at the two schools in 1864 was 76 boys and girls and 50 infants.[9] A new building was erected for the infants in 1880.[10] The Wesleyans had built a day-school behind their chapel in 1847[11] and this also had a government grant by 1849. The Church and Wesleyan schools together had accommodation for 270 children in 1871 and were attended by 111 boys and 83 girls.[12]

The two schools were about the same size in 1908, when the average attendance was 109 at the Church school and 103 at the Wesleyan. By 1912, however, the respective figures were 129 and 69.[13] By this time the Church infants' school and the Wesleyan school were both considered unfit for further use, and a new county school was built in West Gate in 1913-14. The Church mixed school was improved, but the Wesleyan school was closed in 1914, though the building still stood in 1968.[14] The average attendance in 1919 was 121 at the county school and 88 at the Church school, and in 1938 85 and 73 respectively.[15]

The Church school was eventually closed in 1958 and the pupils transferred to the county school, but the premises in High Street continued to be used for infants.[16] Pupils from Wansford also attended the county school after 1966, and the average number of pupils enrolled at Nafferton in 1967 was about 130.[17] The £5 income of Baron's charity was still received in 1968, having previously been divided between Nafferton and Wansford schools.[18]

At Wansford there was a separate school by 1819, when there were 20 pupils;[19] there were only 8 boys and 4 girls at the school in 1835.[20] A new building was erected by Sir Tatton Sykes in 1849,[21] and by 1851 the school had an annual government grant.[22] The average attendance in 1851 was about 70,[23] and in 1871 28 boys and 40 girls.[24] By the 1850s there was also a separate department for infants.[25] A new school, designed by G. E. Street, was built by Sir Tatton Sykes in 1877[26] and enlarged in 1903,[27] and children from Brigham attended it until 1913.[28] The attendance was 55 in 1908, but gradually declined and was only 25 in 1938.[29] The school was closed in 1966 and the children transferred to Nafferton county school.[30] Both the early-19th-century school and the later school still stand.

An adult evening school at Nafferton was held for a month in 1864, but it was badly attended. In 1877 it was reported that a reading room had been provided, and that a mechanics' institute and an evening school had been tried 'only with temporary success'.[31] A reading room at Wansford was opened in 1910.[32]

CHARITIES FOR THE POOR. By will dated 1698 Thomas Robinson devised a house and a croft in West Gate, the rent to be distributed to the poor of Nafferton. The premises had been conveyed to trustees for the purposes of the charity by 1735. Also before 1735 Thomas Moore gave a cottage, 2 a. of land, and common of pasture to the poor. In 1823 the combined Poor's Estate property comprised the West Gate croft and a nine-acre allotment made at inclosure in 1772. The houses no longer stood and the parish poorhouse had been built on the site of one of them. The rents totalled £25 10s. in 1823 and were distributed to the poor twice a year.[33] In 1857 the income was £46; about this time some twenty widows and forty families benefited twice a year.[34]

The charity was regulated by Schemes of 1870 and 1890, when this, the Town Land, and Baron's educational charity[35] were all brought together. It was laid down in 1890 that a third of the income of the Poor's Estate should be used for education and the rest to aid the poor in various ways. The income was then £34 in rents from 11 a. of land and three houses in Priestgate. The endowments were increased by £200 stock, provided under the terms of the Revd. James Davidson's will, proved in 1906.

In 1935 the income was £35 in rents, together with £6 interest on £233 stock. Doles totalling £14 were paid to 43 poor people, and £12 was used for clothing and coal. The income in 1962 included £78 rents and £4 from Davidson's endowment, and the total income had risen to £94 by 1966.[36] Repairs to the charity property have taken up much of the income in recent years.[37] Two cottages in Priestgate with the inscription 'Feoffee Cottages restored 1898' probably belong to this charity.

It is not known how the property known as the Town Land was acquired, but it was probably represented by the cottage, 2 a. of land, and common of pasture tenanted by 'the town' in 1609.[38] The profits were already used for the common expenses of the village in 1737, and in 1823 they were used for such purposes as money payments to the poor, the provision of corn, the teaching and apprenticing of poor children, and the repair of highways. The property consisted in 1823 of two crofts and an eight-acre allotment made at inclosure, and the total rents were £36.[39] In 1857 the income was £47 and expenditure included the payment of £5 each to the National and Wesleyan schools.[40]

The income of the Town Land charity was £48

[8] Ed. 7/135.
[9] B.I.H.R., V. 1865/Ret. 371.
[10] *Kelly's Dir. N. & E.R. Yorks.* (1893), 466.
[11] Sheahan and Whellan, *Hist. York & E.R.* ii. 486.
[12] *Rets. rel. Elem. Educ. 1871*, 474-5.
[13] *Bd. of Educ. List 21* (H.M.S.O.).
[14] E.R. Educ. Cttee. *Mins.* 1910-11, p. 58; 1911-12, pp. 53, 249, 319; 1913-14, p. 323; 1914-15, p. 74.
[15] *Bd. of Educ. List 21.*
[16] E.R. Educ. Cttee. *Mins.* 1957-8, p. 66; ex inf. Chief Educ. Officer, County Hall, Beverley, 1968.
[17] Ex inf. Chief Educ. Officer.
[18] Char. Com. files; ex inf. Mr. H. Foster, Nafferton, 1972.
[19] *Rets. on Educ. of Poor, 1819*, 1087.
[20] *Educ. Enquiry Abstract, 1835*, 1092.
[21] Sheahan and Whellan, *Hist. York & E.R.* ii. 487.
[22] *Mins. of Educ. Cttee. of Counc. 1851* [1479], H.C., p. 559 (1852), xxxix.
[23] Ed. 7/135.
[24] *Rets. rel. Elem. Educ. 1871*, 474.
[25] Sheahan and Whellan, *Hist. York & E.R.* ii. 487.
[26] E.R.R.O., DDSY/98/84; inscription in Wansford church; Bulmer, *Dir. E. Yorks.* (1892), 246.
[27] *Kelly's Dir. N. & E.R. Yorks.* (1913), 623.
[28] E.R. Educ. Cttee. *Mins.* 1913-14, 247.
[29] *Bd. of Educ. List 21.*
[30] E.R. Educ. Cttee. *Mins.* 1963-4, 146; ex inf. Chief Educ. Officer.
[31] B.I.H.R., V. 1865/Ret. 371; V. 1877/Ret.
[32] *Kelly's Dir. N. & E.R. Yorks.* (1913), 623.
[33] *9th Rep. Char. Com.* 737.
[34] Accts. in vestry minutes, 1822-91: E.R.R.O., PR. 1827.
[35] See p. 295.
[36] Char. Com. files.
[37] Ex inf. Mr. H. Foster, Nafferton, 1972.
[38] L.R. 2/230, f. 127.
[39] *9th Rep. Char. Com.* 738.
[40] Accts. in vestry mins. 1822-91.

in 1878, when it was largely used for the schools, the church clock, and the cleansing of Nafferton beck. The charity was regulated by the Scheme of 1890, which provided for the income to be used for the improvement of the village and for education. The income was then £33 rent from 11 a. of land and four houses in Priestgate. Rents of £32 were received in 1935 and expenditure then included £12 to the various schools in Nafferton and Wansford, £3 for the reading room, £6 for footpaths, and £6 to clubs and societies in the village. The income was £59 in 1962, rising to £92 in 1966.[41] In recent years money has been used for the village hall, recreation club, playground, and churchyard.[42]

George Hodgson, by will proved in 1874, left £200, the income to be distributed at Christmas to the 6 oldest and most deserving poor in Nafferton.[43] In 1890[44] and in 1929–31 about 17s. each was being given. The income in 1965 was £5 from £206 stock.[45]

Thomas Jefferson in 1932 settled in trust an eight-acre close called the Parks. The income was to be used in part to buy 6 tons of coal for distribution at Christmas to needy inhabitants of the parish who had lived there for at least two years. The remaining income was to be divided between the parish church and the two Methodist chapels.[46] In 1970 the rent from the Parks was £40 and £52 was spent that year in giving 2 cwt. of coal to each of 40 people.[47]

Alice Gray, by will proved in 1950, left the residue of her estate to be used for the benefit of the inhabitants of the civil parishes of Nafferton and Kelk, and the township of Lowthorpe. She recommended that cottages might be built for the aged poor, but this was subsequently considered to be impracticable. A Scheme of 1953 laid down that the income should be used to provide goods, money, and domestic help for the sick poor. In 1965 the income was £202 from £7,761 stock; £130 was divided among 35 inhabitants of Nafferton and £74 was distributed in Kelk and Lowthorpe.[48]

The Revd. James Davidson, by will proved in 1906, left £200 for the Poor's Estate and £300 for various church purposes.[49]

In 1823 £13 a year was received from several old benefactions in Wansford. The interest was distributed by the overseer of the poor to widows in the township.[50] This charity may have supported almshouses later in the century. There were 'Orphans Houses' in Wansford in 1850,[51] and in 1892 it was said that there had formerly been alms-houses for three widows, who received 16s. a year from a bequest made by a St. Quintin.[52] The vicar of Nafferton alleged in 1897 that three houses for the poor in Wansford had been pulled down 'some years' before by Sir Tatton Sykes and rebuilt as one house, no longer occupied by the poor.[53] No more is known of this charity.

WOLD NEWTON

WOLD NEWTON lies 8 miles north-west of Bridlington in the valley of the Gypsey Race.[1] The parish, roughly rectangular in shape, stretches from the valley bottom for over a mile northwards up the wold slopes, ending at one of the prominent dry valleys cut into the high wolds. The village was probably an Anglian settlement; 'Wold' occurs as a suffix or prefix from the 12th century onwards. From the late 12th century the village was also sometimes called Newton Rochford, from the manorial family of that name.[2] The parish boundary in the north follows the side of the dry valley, and part of the southern boundary follows the Gypsey Race. The area of the ancient parish is 2,028 a.[3] In 1935 the civil parish was enlarged by the transfer of Fordon township from Hunmanby civil parish.[4]

From about 150 ft. above sea-level in the valley bottom in the south, the ground rises to over 450 ft. on the wold before falling sharply to 350 ft. on the side of the dry valley along the northern boundary. The open fields had occupied the whole of the wold slopes and an extensive common pasture lay on the highest ground in the north; the valley bottom was meadow land. The regular field pattern over the entire parish is a result of the inclosure of 1776.

Most of the parish is now arable, though there is some pasture in the valley. Several small plantations and shelter belts lie on the wold slopes and on the steep side of the dry valley.

The Gypsey Race may have followed an ill-defined course in the valley bottom before inclosure, but a clear-cut channel was apparently made on the commissioners' instructions in 1776. The Mere, at the southern end of the village, was chiefly fed by the Race;[5] it was first expressly mentioned in 1721.[6] The Mere and wells provided the village with its water; new wells were sunk in each street in 1804 and pumps were installed for them c. 1844.[7]

The village lies on the lower wold slopes, reaching to within 200 yds. of the Gypsey Race. Ancient inclosures known as Ramsbrough, later Rainsbrough,[8] continue the pattern of crofts and garths down to the stream and beyond, suggesting that the village may have formerly extended further south. The houses lie along Front and Back Streets, which meet near both ends of the village. At the southern end of the village Laking and Butt Lanes run into a small village green, beside which are two prehistoric barrows mistakenly known as Butt Hills.[9] Another prominent barrow stands near Bridge Farm. Other

---

[41] Char. Com. files.
[42] Ex inf. Mr. Foster.
[43] Char. Com. files.
[44] Vestry mins. 1822–91.
[45] Char. Com. files.
[46] Ibid.
[47] Ex inf. Mr. W. A. Watson, Nafferton, 1972.
[48] Char. Com. files.
[49] See pp. 294, 296.
[50] *9th Rep. Char. Com.* 739.
[51] O.S. Map 6" (1854).
[52] Bulmer, *Dir. E. Yorks.* (1892), 246.

[53] Char. Com. files.
[1] This article was written in 1960, with some revision in 1970. Use has been made of material compiled by Miss Celia B. Clarke.
[2] *P.N.E.R. Yorks.* (E.P.N.S.), 114.
[3] O.S. Map 6" (1854).
[4] *Census*, 1931.
[5] e.g. T. Allen, *Hist. Yorks.* iv. 96.
[6] Par. Recs., Register (at Thwing Rectory).
[7] Ibid. Register and Vestry min. bk. 1843–94.
[8] See p. 300.
[9] Ex inf. Mr. T. C. M. Brewster, 1971.

streets in the village were Green Lane, an access way from Butt Lane to the Gypsey Race; Stafford Lane, leading from Front Street into West field; Folly Lane, the northern section of Back Street; and Shoemaker Lane, which links Front and Back Streets.[10]

The pattern of roads around the village is a simple one. Front Street continues northwards over the wold to Fordon and was mentioned c. 1300.[11] From east to west along the wold top runs North Cotes Road, set out by the inclosure commissioners approximately on the line of an earlier road leading from Foxholes towards Hunmanby. A short stretch of road apparently linked the Hunmanby road with the village in the 18th century.[12] Southwards Front Street leads to Thwing and successive stretches of it were known as Outgates, Long Lane, and Rainsbrough Lane. The other chief road in the parish runs east–west along the valley bottom, linking Wold Newton with Foxholes and Burton Fleming. In 1772 this road still followed a course alongside the Gypsey Race, crossing the Thwing road on the south bank of the stream and linking up with a similar waterside road in Burton Fleming. It was apparently at inclosure in 1776 that the road was moved to a drier course further north, which also had the advantage of running through the village.[13]

The chief building of note in the village is Wold Newton Hall, standing between Front and Back Streets south of the church. It was built in 1797-1809[14] by William Hutchinson of Wold Newton, who in 1795 had married Katherine, daughter of Humphrey Osbaldeston, lord of the manor.[15] From at least 1844[16] the hall was owned by the Cadmans, who sold it in 1907 to James Calder. Calder had let it by 1913 and sold it in 1920.[17] The brick and slate building is of two and three storeys. In the centre of the south front is a three-sided bay window rising through three floors. There is a service wing to the east and later alterations include the addition of a west wing; after 1948 the building was converted into flats.[18]

Most of the houses and cottages in the village are of brick and date from the 18th to the 20th century. Several houses, however, incorporate some chalk walling and there are numerous farm buildings of this material. The 19th-century work includes two terraces, one of five and one of nine houses, and there are about 20 Council houses. The Anvil Arms is an 18th- and 19th-century building. As the Blacksmith's Arms it was in existence by 1867;[19] in the earlier years of the century the village inn had been the Plough.[20]

After inclosure in 1776 several outlying farmhouses were built. By 1818 there were three: one was on the rectorial estate and was later known as the Grange.[21] By 1850 there were two other isolated farm-houses, Westfield House and Westfield Farm.[22] Six other allotments in 1776 were so laid out that they reached into the village and these continued after 1850 to be farmed from there.[23]

Poor agricultural labourers and their families were assisted by a clothing society, founded in the village in 1854 and continuing at least until 1896. Each year 20–30 people made monthly payments and 6–12 others were 'honorary subscribers'; they raised, all told, about £20–£30 a year and clothing was given to about thirty poor families.[24]

In 1674 37 households were included in the hearth-tax assessment for Wold Newton and Fordon, 9 of them discharged from the tax; of those that were charged 24 had only one hearth, one had 2, and 3 had three.[25] In 1743 there were 16 families in the parish[26] and in 1764 eighteen.[27] The population in 1801, again including Fordon, was 106 and in 1821, without it, 177. The number of inhabitants in Wold Newton alone showed marked variations later in the century; it rose from 245 in 1841 to 351 in 1861, before falling steadily to 274 in 1901.[28] In 1931 it was 265; even after Fordon had been included in the civil parish the population was only 289 in 1951, falling to 247 in 1961.[29]

MANOR AND OTHER ESTATES. In 1086 7 carucates of land in Wold Newton formed a berewick of Hunmanby manor and were held with it by Gilbert de Gant.[30] Four more carucates were held by the king, of which 3 had been held in 1066 by Chilbert and one by Ligulf; these were later added to the Gant fee and the whole reckoned at 12 carucates.[31] The overlordship of Wold Newton followed that of Hunmanby until the early 14th century, passing to Robert of Tattershall in 1294 and to Thomas de Cailly upon the division of the Tattershall fee in 1306.[32] At his death in 1316 Thomas de Cailly's heir was his nephew, Adam of Clifton,[33] but the overlordship had by then apparently lapsed.

Wold Newton was included in the dowry bestowed on his daughter Emme by Gilbert de Gant (I) on her marriage with Alan de Percy about the beginning of the 12th century,[34] and the mesne lordship thus created was held by the Percy family until the mid 15th century at latest, though details of its tenure there are lacking.[35]

---

[10] Registry of Deeds, Beverley, AT/354/37 and inclosure map; T. Jefferys, *Map of Yorks.* (1772); O.S. Map 6″ (1854). [11] B. M. Cott. MS. Vesp. E. xx, ff. 196–196v.
[12] Regy. of Deeds, AT/354/37 and map.
[13] Ibid.; Jefferys, *Map of Yorks.* (1772).
[14] *Gent. Mag.* 1809, lxxix (1), 87; and ex inf. Capt. D. W. Foxon, Wold Newton Hall, 1960.
[15] *Gent. Mag.* 1795, lxv (1), 437; Burke, *Land. Gent.* (1937), 788, *sub* Firman.   [16] *Gent. Mag.* 1844, cxv (2), 311.
[17] Regy. of Deeds, 93/209/202 (1907); 213/536/452; *Kelly's Dir. N. & E.R. Yorks.* (1913), 636.
[18] Ex inf. Capt. Foxon.
[19] Par. Recs., Vestry min. bk., 1843–94, *sub* 1867; *Kelly's Dir. N. & E.R. Yorks.* (1872), 562.
[20] Baines, *Hist. Yorks.* (1823), ii. 402; White, *Dir. E. & N.R. Yorks.* (1840), 398.
[21] C. Greenwood, *Map of Yorks.* (1818).
[22] O.S. Map 6″ (1854).
[23] See M. B. Gleave, 'Dispersed and Nucleated Settlement in the Yorks. Wolds, 1770–1850', Inst. Brit. Geographers, *Trans. & Papers*, xxx. 114–15.
[24] Subscription bk., at Thwing Rectory, 1970.
[25] E 179/205/521.   [26] *Herring's Visit.* ii. 221.
[27] B.I.H.R., Bp. V. 1764/Ret. 141.
[28] *V.C.H. Yorks.* iii. 489 n., 490.   [29] *Census.*
[30] *V.C.H. Yorks.* ii. 204, 272, 323.   [31] *Feud. Aids,* vi. 28.
[32] *Cal. Inq. p.m.* ii, p. 373; iv, pp. 105, 107–8, 257–8, 265; *Cal. Close,* 1307–13, 100; *Complete Peerage,* ii. 470; xii (1), 650–3; see above, p. 231.
[33] *Cal. Inq. p.m.* vi, p. 19; vii, pp. 133–4. For pedigree of Clifton see *Complete Peerage,* ii. 307–38.
[34] *Bridlington Charty.* 72; *Whitby Charty.* i (Sur. Soc. lxix), 29; ii (Sur. Soc. lxxii), 688, 690; *E.Y.C.* ii, pp. 482–3. For discussion of Emme's parentage see *Complete Peerage,* x. 439–40.
[35] C 139/162/22; *Cal. Inq. p.m.* v, pp. 318–19; *Cal. Close,* 1313–18, 149; *Cal. Chanc. R. Var.* 1277–1326, 126; *Percy Charty.* (Sur. Soc. cxvii), 177–8.

By the end of the 12th century the demesne lords of *WOLD NEWTON* were the Rochford family, from whom the parish derived its alternative name. In 1187 Simon of Rochford was probably holding the manor.[36] The Rochfords continued to hold it until 1381, when Joan Rogerson, probably the daughter of a 'Sir Walbran de Rocheford', and her husband sold it to Sir Ralph Hastings.[37]

Wold Newton remained in the possession of the Hastings family[38] until in 1463 it formed part of an exchange of lands in Leicestershire and Yorkshire made by Sir Ralph's great-grandson William, Lord Hastings, with Sir John Lovel (d. 1465).[39] Following the attainder in 1485 of Sir John's son Francis, Viscount Lovel,[40] the king granted the manor in 1487 to Sir Edmund Bedingfield (d. 1496).[41] Wold Newton descended in the Bedingfield family[42] to Sir Edmund's grandson Sir Henry Bedingfield,[43] who, in exchange for other lands, surrendered it to the Crown in 1556.[44]

In 1610 a grant of the manor was made to Christopher Sotherton and John Wotton,[45] who were dealing in it in 1613.[46] It is not known when the manor came into the hands of the Osbaldeston family, who by the mid 17th century held the capital manor of Hunmanby.[47] Humphrey Osbaldeston was lord of the manor at inclosure in 1776, when he was allotted 78 a.[48] The estate remained in the Osbaldeston and Osbaldeston-Mitford families until 1907, when it was sold to James Calder.[49] In the same year Calder also acquired the Cadman estate in the parish, comprising 612 a.[50] William Cadman had come into the possession of nearly 600 a. in 1857, after the death of Abraham Rhodes;[51] the latter had bought it in 1833, much of it having belonged previously to the Hutchinsons and, after 1826, to John Thorpe.[52] The Calder estate was sold in separate lots, much of it in 1920, including the 73-acre Manor farm.[53]

In the 12th century, Emme, wife of Alan de Percy,[54] gave a carucate of land in Wold Newton to Bridlington priory,[55] and other small grants were made to the priory during the Middle Ages.[56] At the Dissolution Bridlington had property there worth £1 12s.[57] In 1608 John Bossall held a house and 8 bovates of former priory land;[58] this had apparently passed before 1632 to Samuel Buck of Carnaby, who in that year died holding a house, 8 bovates, and 4 closes in Wold Newton, all the former property of the priory.[59]

Whitby abbey also held land in the parish. Walter de Percy gave 2 carucates of land to the abbey,[60] and in 1290 it was granted a further 10 bovates.[61] Whitby retained its property until the Dissolution. By the end of the 16th century the abbey's former holding was in the possession of the Wingate family. From Edward Wingate (d. 1597)[62] the holding passed to his nephew George (d. 1604),[63] who settled it during his lifetime on his second son Edward.[64] The descent has not been traced further. Meaux abbey held a tenement in Wold Newton and in 1539–40 the Crown received from it a rent of 5s.[65] Like the former lands of Bridlington priory, this was held by Samuel Buck in 1632.[66]

The Tyrwhitt family held property in the parish from the 14th to the 16th century. In 1385 the family acquired 6 tofts, 16 bovates, and 2 a. of meadow there from Thomas Ryse,[67] and Sir William Tyrwhitt held 8 bovates in 1428.[68] A member of his family was holding land there in 1590,[69] but by 1608 'Turwhit land' was held by the vicar[70] and its subsequent descent is not known.

The rectorial tithes belonged to Bardney abbey from 1115.[71] They were let to Richard Lutton in 1528 and after the Dissolution were included in a Crown lease of Hunmanby rectory made in 1566 to Sir Henry Gate from the expiry of Lutton's lease.[72] They were conveyed with Hunmanby rectory to the Westrops in 1592 and to the Osbaldestons in 1623.[73] They were separated from that rectory in 1637 and granted with the advowson to Edward Hutchinson.[74] Thenceforth they descended with the advowson.[75]

---

[36] *E.Y.C.* ii, p. 483.
[37] B.M. Add. MS. 26736, f. 120; *Cal. Inq. p.m.* ix, p. 27; *Feud. Aids*, vi. 28, 169, 225; *Yorks. Deeds*, ix. 129; Hist. MSS. Com. *Hastings, I*, 195; *Yorks. Fines, 1327–47*, 29; *Cal. Close, 1381–5*, 124. Sir Ralph Hastings was a member of a cadet branch of the family of Hastings, later earls of Pembroke, and he already held an annual rent of £20 out of the manor by a grant of 1379: Hist. MSS. Com. *Hastings, I*, 195.
[38] C 139/162/22; Hist. MSS. Com. *Hastings, I*, 195–6; *Cal. Close, 1396–9*, 195–6; J. Nichols, *Leics.* iii (2), 566 n. For a pedigree of the Hastings family see Nichols, op. cit. 607.
[39] B.M. Harl. MS. 3881, f. 15; C.P. 25(1)/281/162/13; Hist. MSS. Com. *Hastings, I*, 296.
[40] C 140/13/27; C 140/19/20; *Rot. Parl.* (Rec. Com.), vi. 276, 502–3.
[41] *Cal. Pat. 1485–94*, 189; F. Blomefield, *Norf.* vi. 177.
[42] *Cal. Inq. p.m. Hen. VII*, ii, p. 63; *L. & P. Hen. VIII*, i (1), p. 387; xiv (2), p. 224; xvi, p. 499. For pedigree see Burke, *Peerage* (1959), 191, *sub* Paston-Bedingfield, and Blomefield, *Norf.* vi. 177–8 and between 178 and 179.
[43] *D.N.B.*
[44] *Cal. Pat. 1555–7*, 76; *Yorks. Fines*, i. 195; Hist. MSS. Com. *Var. Colls. VIII*, 7.
[45] C 66/1895 nos. 7–10.
[46] *Yorks. Fines, 1603–14*, 196.
[47] C 142/610/94; see p. 231.
[48] 12 Geo. III, c. 98 (Priv. Act); Regy. of Deeds, AT/354/37.
[49] Regy. of Deeds, 98/530/494 (1907).
[50] Ibid. 93/209/202 (1907).
[51] Ibid. HQ/7/7–8.
[52] Ibid. DX/338/395; EQ/311/356; /355/401; /361/402; see p. 300.
[53] e.g. ibid. 212/492/415; /495/418; /576/482; 213/373/314.
[54] Both d. probably before Dec. 1135: *Complete Peerage*, x. 440 and n.
[55] *E.Y.C.* ii, p. 482. The gift was made free of all service except the king's geld called 'Tenementale'.
[56] *Bridlington Charty.* 72, 173; *Cal. Pat. 1388–92*, 8.
[57] *Valor Eccl.* (Rec. Com.), v. 120.
[58] L.R. 2/229 f. 248.
[59] C 142/726/100.
[60] *Whitby Charty.* i. 4, 122; ii. 364, 754; *E.Y.C.* ii, p. 228; *Feud. Aids*, vi. 28, 265.
[61] C 143/10/15; *Rot. Parl.* i. 63; *Cal. Pat. 1281–92*, 364; *Whitby Charty.* ii. 552–3.
[62] C 142/255/176.
[63] C 142/288/126.
[64] Ibid.; *Yorks. Fines, 1603–14*, 20.
[65] Dugdale, *Mon.* v. 398.
[66] C 142/726/100.
[67] C.P. 25(1)/278/143/41.
[68] *Feud. Aids*, vi. 265.
[69] P.C.C. 91 Sainberde.
[70] L.R. 2/229 f. 248. This may have been the land on which the vicar was assessed in 1599 and 1600: E 179/204/335, 357.
[71] See p. 301.
[72] C 66/1024/22; all advowsons were excepted from this lease.
[73] See p. 236.
[74] See p. 301.
[75] *Cal. Cttee. for Compounding*, 2018; *T.E.R.A.S.* ii. 59; *V.C.H. Yorks. N.R.* ii. 427, 499–500. For a Hutchinson pedigree see *Dugdale's Visit. Yorks.* ed. J. W. Clay, ii. 439–41.

The tithes were valued at £37 in 1650,[76] and at inclosure in 1776 they were converted into 225 a. and an annuity of £6.[77] E. H. Dawnay, the patron, sold the estate in 1901 to James Varley, and it passed to James Wilson in 1918 and to Charles Grace in 1942.[78]

ECONOMIC HISTORY. In 1086 the holding in Wold Newton of 7 carucates, which was a berewick of Hunmanby, had land for four ploughs; the king's 3 carucates were valued at 10s. and provided land for a plough and a half, and his holding of one carucate had land for four oxen.[79]

In 1397 the lord of the manor was said to have the services of freeholders and neifs, and the chattels of neifs and all that went with them.[80] In 1455 the manor consisted of a manor-house site not built upon, 12 houses, 30 bovates of land held by tenants-at-will, 6 a. of meadow, 4 crofts, and 4s. rent a year from free tenants. The total value was £8 6s. a year.[81] Ten years later the manor was worth about £5.[82] There were 14 tenants in 1597.[83] The earliest evidence for the size and nature of tenant holdings comes from 1608. Three freeholders then had 25 bovates or 200 a. Eleven leaseholders held in all 56½ bovates, or about 450 a., of open-field land, about 120 a. of meadow and pasture, and about 20 a. in closes, as well as 12 houses, a cottage, 17 barns, and, a kiln. The largest holding by lease included 7 bovates and 16½ a. of pasture, the smallest 4 bovates and 8 a. of pasture.[84]

Two of the holdings of 1608 were described as equally divided between East and West fields. The fields lay on the wold slopes north of the Gypsey Race, but in 1628 they were said to extend southwards as far as the fields of Thwing and Octon.[85] At inclosure in 1776 there were over 1,120 a. in the two open fields, allotments made wholly from East field totalling 539 a. and from West field 500 a. The 39 a. in Oxlands may also have been common arable land.[86] North of the open fields, on the highest wold ground, lay an extensive area of common pasture. In 1716 and 1770 the East and West pastures were mentioned, and East and West Nescotes in 1743.[87] In 1772 it was described as a 'large pasture called the Wold'.[88] It was called North Coats in 1776, when allotments totalling 382 a. were made from it. The common meadows lay in the south, near the Gypsey Race. In 1776 they apparently comprised the ings, containing 93 a., East Swarth, of 58 a., and West Swarth, of about 110 a.[89] In addition there was some meadow and pasture within the open-field area, and in 1608 about 120 a. of such land was described as 'lands' ends'.[90]

There were numerous small inclosures around the village in 1597, amounting to about 63 a. They included Milnedams, the east and west crofts, a close 'beyond the dovecot', the well garth, Ramsbrough, Buttcroft, and Howland. Butland was then described as 'lately inclosed'.[91]

The open fields and other common lands were inclosed in 1776,[92] under an Act of 1772.[93] Allotments were made totalling 1,822 a. Humphrey Osbaldeston, as lord of the manor, was alloted 78 a., Richard Langley, as impropriator, 225 a., and the vicar 176 a. There were nine other allotments, one of only 6 a. but the others all substantial: William Rickinson got 144 a., William Hutchinson 173 a., Richard Brown 274 a., Robert Hutchinson, the elder and the younger, 168 a. and 141 a., respectively, Richard Coulson 177 a., William Coulson 100 a., and John Wilson 150 a. Each of the eleven chief allotments included land which lay north of 'the balk above the middle flat'. This land, which covered parts of the former East and West fields and the whole of North Coats, amounted to 791 a. and the commissioners directed that it should all, with the exception of 111 a. allotted to Richard Brown, remain open, to be used as sheepwalk or otherwise as the proprietors thought fit. In 1801 only 549 a. were reported as under crops in Wold Newton,[94] but the parish subsequently became largely arable. During the 19th and 20th centuries the number of farmers and smallholders increased from six in 1823 to a dozen in the 1930s.[95]

There was apparently a water-mill at Wold Newton in 1218–19,[96] and a miller is mentioned in the early 14th century.[97] No more is known of a water-mill, though the field name Milnedams, or 'the dam', occurs c. 1600.[98] One tenant had a horse-mill in 1620.[99] By 1819 there was a windmill in the north-west of the parish, high on the wold slopes.[1] A miller is last mentioned in 1893[2] and the disused mill still stood in 1910;[3] it has since been demolished.

LOCAL GOVERNMENT. The surviving church-rate book for 1739–1878 shows that there was one churchwarden until the 1820s and thenceforth two.[4] There are also surviving overseers' rate books and accounts for 1755–1805 and 1820–36.[5] A 'hospital' existed in 1720[6] and this may have been the 'town's house' which was repaired in 1794 and later. It was perhaps rebuilt or extended in 1802, when £13 10s. was spent in 'building a poorhouse', and the town's house was repaired on several occasions up to at least 1816. There were usually two overseers and most of the relief given was in kind rather than in regular money payments. The rate varied considerably. In 1756 a rate of 2d. in the pound raised £2 from 15 householders, and in 1764 a rate of 10d.

---

[76] T.E.R.A.S. ii. 59.
[77] Registry of Deeds, Beverley, AT/354/37.
[78] Ibid. 37/330/318; /331/319 (1901); 190/285/246; 651/290/246.
[79] V.C.H. Yorks. ii. 204, 272.
[80] Cal. Close, 1396–9, 195.
[81] C 139/162/22.
[82] C 140/13/27; C 140/19/20.
[83] E 310/30/179 no. 15.
[84] L.R. 2/229 ff. 248–53.
[85] B.I.H.R., Prob. Reg. xli, f. 50.
[86] Registry of Deeds, Beverley, AT/354/37.
[87] B.I.H.R., TER. J. Wold Newton 1716, 1743, 1770.
[88] C.J. xxxiii. 504a.
[89] Regy. of Deeds, AT/354/37.
[90] L.R. 2/229 ff. 248–53.
[91] E 310/27/159 no. 52.
[92] Regy. of Deeds, AT/354/37; the map, dated 1772, in E.R.R.O.
[93] 12 Geo. III, c. 98 (Priv. Act).
[94] 1801 Crop Returns.
[95] Directories.
[96] Rolls of Justices in Eyre for Yorks. (Selden Soc. lvi), 352.
[97] Percy Charty. (Sur. Soc. cxvii), 177.
[98] C 66/1895 no. 7; E 310/27/159 no. 52; L.R. 2/229 ff. 250–2.
[99] B.I.H.R., Prob. Reg. xxxvi, f. 11.
[1] E.R.R.O., DDHU/14/3, 6.
[2] Kelly's Dir. N. & E.R. Yorks. (1893), 510.
[3] Regy. of Deeds, 127/473/428.
[4] There are also records of vestry business for 1839–1924 in a separate book. All at Thwing Rectory, 1970.
[5] At Thwing Rectory, 1970.
[6] B.I.H.R., ER. V/Ch. P. 1720.

raised £9 from the same number. The rate was greatly increased in the 1820s and 1830s. It was 1s. 6d. in 1820, 2s. 2d. in 1824, and 2s. 9½d. in 1832, when it raised £91 from 18 people. The town stock was occasionally mentioned; when on loan in 1756 it realized 1s. 4d. interest and in 1794 and 1816 £3. A payment was made to Rillington poorhouse in 1827 and later, and Wold Newton was evidently one of the townships which sent paupers there;[7] in 1836 Wold Newton joined the Bridlington union.[8]

CHURCH. In 1115 Walter de Gant gave Hunmanby church, with Wold Newton and its other dependent chapels, to Bardney abbey.[9] A vicarage was ordained at Wold Newton, apparently in 1269. The vicar was to have a toft and 2 bovates of land, a third of the corn and lamb tithes, and the whole tithe of wool; he was to pay a pension of £1 10s. a year to Bardney.[10]

The abbey retained the advowon until the Dissolution.[11] Five presentations were then made by the Crown between 1543 and 1561.[12] The advowson was probably included in the grant of the rectory of Hunmanby to the Westrops,[13] and 'Westrope Laycoke' presented in 1621.[14] After passing to the Osbaldestons in 1623, Wold Newton was granted, like Reighton,[15] to Edward Hutchinson in 1637. His son presented in 1690.[16] The advowson subsequently descended with the manor of Wykeham (Yorks. N.R.). Richard Hutchinson (d. c. 1755) assumed the name Langley. His grandson Richard Langley (d. 1817) devised his estates to his cousin Marmaduke Dawnay (d. 1851), who in 1824 assumed the name Langley. The advowson then descended in the Dawnay family to William Henry Dawnay, Viscount Downe (d. 1857),[17] whose widow held it until her death in 1900, whereupon it passed to her son E. H. Dawnay.[18] It was transferred to the archbishop of York in 1927.[19]

The vicarage was valued at £6 13s. 4d. in 1291,[20] and at nearly £7 in 1535.[21] In 1650 it was worth £30[22] and in the 18th century £27 net.[23] In 1829–31 the average value of the living was £113 net.[24]

The vicarial glebe consisted of 2 bovates in 1685, including ⅓ bovate in the ings.[25] At inclosure in 1776 the vicar was allotted about 26 a. for glebe, about 150 a. for tithes, and a modus of nearly £6 for tithes of old inclosures.[26] Ninety acres of glebe were sold in 1945 and 86 a. in 1964.[27] The parsonage house in 1685 was chalk-built and in 1749 it comprised kitchen, parlour, buttery, and two bedrooms.[28] In the early 19th century it was unfit for residence[29] and it is said to have been replaced in 1839 by a house containing four main rooms on each floor, cellars, and attics.[30] This large brick and slate building has been known as the Hollies since 1928, when vicars ceased to reside. The earlier house, a single-storey building of chalk, was used as a church-room in 1936[31] and still stood in 1970.

From at least the 18th century onwards several vicars held the living in plurality. One incumbent, instituted in 1742, resided at Reighton but served both cures himself.[32] Another had already been rector of Thwing since 1767 when instituted to Wold Newton in 1785 and thenceforth held both livings until his death in 1802.[33] The vicar from 1829 to 1860[34] also held the living of Wykeham (Yorks. N.R.), and employed a curate at Wold Newton, at least during a period when the Vicarage was described as unfit for residence.[35] In 1872 a curate lived at the Vicarage in the vicar's absence.[36] Since 1928 the living has been held with that of Thwing and vicars have resided at Thwing Rectory.[37]

In 1567 it was alleged that the vicar did not say the services distinctly and made a six-year old boy say them with him,[38] and in 1575 no sermons were preached.[39] There was a service each Sunday in 1743 and Holy Communion was celebrated four times a year, with about twenty communicants.[40] There was still one service each week in 1851,[41] but by 1865 there were three Sunday services and communion was celebrated each week, with 10–12 communicants.[42] By 1894 there were only two Sunday services.[43] In 1970 there was one service, sometimes two, each Sunday.

The church of ALL SAINTS[44] is a stone building consisting of nave, chancel, north aisle, south porch, and west bell-turret. Norman masonry can be recognized in the south and west walls of the nave. The only architectural features to survive from the original church are a small round-headed window high up in the south nave wall near its east end, the south doorway, and the remains of jamb shafts belonging to a former chancel arch. The south doorway appears to date from the earlier 12th century. The tympanum is carved with chequer-work ornament and has, in the centre, a cross enclosed in a circle; there is a ring in one of the top quadrants and three circles in the other.[45] The capitals of the jamb shafts are carved with a wheel pattern on the

[7] N. Mitchelson, *Old Poor Law in E. Yorks.* (E. Yorks. Loc. Hist. Ser. ii), 13.
[8] *3rd Rep. Poor Law Com.* 167.
[9] Dugdale, *Mon.* i. 628–9.
[10] *Reg. Giffard* (Sur. Soc. cix), 56; *V.C.H. Yorks.* iii. 29.
[11] *Fasti Parochiales*, iii. 94–5.
[12] *Cal. Pat.* 1553–4, 359; 1560–3, 85; *Fasti Parochiales*, iii. 95.
[13] See p. 236.
[14] *Fasti Parochiales*, iii. 95.
[15] C.P. 25(2)/523/12 Chas. I Hil. pt. 3, no. 17.
[16] P.R.O., Inst. Bks.
[17] Ibid.; White, *Dir. E. & N.R. Yorks.* (1840), 398; Lawton, *Rer. Eccles. Dioc. Ebor.* 315; *V.C.H. Yorks. N.R.* ii. 500.
[18] *Kelly's Dir. N. & E.R. Yorks.* (1901), 581.
[19] York Dioc. Regy., Orders in Council 582.
[20] *Tax. Eccl.* (Rec. Com), 304; *Miscellanea*, i (Y.A.S. Rec. Ser. lxi), 143; *Feud. Aids*, vi. 327.
[21] *Valor Eccl.* (Rec. Com.), v. 122.
[22] *T.E.R.A.S.* ii. 59.
[23] Ecton, *Thesaurus*, 535; Bacon, *Liber Regis*, 1132.
[24] *Rep. Com. Eccl. Revenues*, 980.
[25] B.I.H.R., TER. J. Wold Newton 1685.
[26] Ibid. 1770; Regy. of Deeds, AT/354/37.
[27] Regy. of Deeds, 698/398/344; 1357/445/398.
[28] B.I.H.R., TER. J. Wold Newton 1685, 1749.
[29] *Rep. Com. Eccl. Revenues*, 980.
[30] B.I.H.R., TER. J. Wold Newton 1861; Sheahan and Whellan, *Hist. York & E.R.* ii. 492.
[31] B.I.H.R., Bp. V. 1884/Ret.; Bp. V. 1936/Ret. 310.
[32] *Herring's Visit.* iii. 221.
[33] J. A. Venn, *Alum. Cantab.*
[34] *Gent. Mag.* 1860, ccix(2), 210.
[35] *Rep. Com. Eccl. Revenues*, 980.
[36] *Kelly's Dir. N. & E.R. Yorks.* (1872), 562.
[37] *Crockford.*
[38] J. S. Purvis, *Tudor Par. Docs. of Dioc. York*, 126–7.
[39] B.I.H.R., V. 1575/CB. 1, f. 88.
[40] *Herring's Visit.* iii. 221.   [41] H.O. 129/24/524.
[42] B.I.H.R., V. 1865/Ret. 601   [43] Ibid. Bp. V. 1894/Ret.
[44] The dedication was established as All Saints in 1828: York Dioc. Regy., Sentence of consecration. Variant forms were referred to subsequently: e.g. *Crockford* and directories.
[45] *T.E.R.A.S.* x. 111.

east side and a goose-like bird on the west. The circular font is probably of the later 12th century; the top of the bowl is decorated with a cable-moulding and a continuous pattern of leaves enclosed by triangles.[46]

The square weather-boarded bell-turret is comparatively modern, together with the timbers inside the nave which support it. The masonry at the west gable-end, however, is carried up to form the west face of the turret, suggesting that there was always some provision for a bell at the west end of the church. In the south wall of the nave is a late-14th-century three-light window with a square head, and, further west, a 15th-century window. The three-light east window in the chancel has been renewed but may also have been of 15th-century origin.

In 1575 the church was said to be in a bad state of repair.[47] Some repairs were carried out in 1833-4 and in 1838-9, at which latter date the church was said to be dilapidated, and services were held in the schoolroom.[48] In 1850-1 the chancel was rebuilt by Marmaduke Langley, the patron; it carries the date 1850 on its east wall. The north aisle, which is separated from the nave by four pointed arches resting on cylindrical piers, was added in 1857, replacing a former aisle.[49] During renovations carried out in 1899, at which date a new pulpit was installed, tablets inscribed with the Lord's Prayer, the Creed, and the Commandments were uncovered on the south wall; in 1970 they were hanging at the back of the nave.[50] There are also Royal Arms of 1713 and 1839. A west gallery to seat 40 children was built in 1833-4.[51] The accommodation was said in 1835 to be sufficient[52] but the repairs of 1839 included the re-pewing of the church.[53]

There are two bells, one of which is dated 1694.[54] In 1552 there was a silver chalice,[55] and a silver chalice and a pewter flagon and plate were mentioned in terriers of 1777 and 1786.[56] A fresh set of plate, all bearing the Dawnay arms, was presented by the patron, Lady Downe, in 1860.[57]

The registers of burials begin in 1708 and are complete except for the years 1786-1828; those of baptisms begin in 1723 and are complete, those of marriages in 1725, with a gap in 1836-7.[58]

Wold Newton retained some dependence on the mother-church at Hunmanby and contributed towards its repair in 1662, for example.[59] A 'hamlet fee' continued to be paid to Hunmanby for repairs and other expenses until at least the 1850s,[60] although in 1839 Wold Newton was already resisting the payment.[61] Wold Newton was also dependent on Hunmanby for its burial ground until 1828, when its own churchyard was consecrated.[62]

NONCONFORMITY. In 1788 a house in Wold Newton was licensed as a meeting-place for Protestant dissenters.[63] In 1839 ground was acquired on the east side of the 'high road'[64] (i.e. Front Street) for a Wesleyan chapel which was built the same year.[65] The building is of brick with pointed Gothic windows, and it included a Sunday schoolroom underneath the chapel. A Sunday school extension was opened in 1954.[66]

In 1851 there was also a Primitive Methodist meeting-place in Wold Newton, built since 1841 but not used exclusively as a place of worship.[67] In 1865 the Primitive Methodists were said to use the schoolroom and a cottage,[68] but a chapel was built between 1868 and 1877.[69] There were twelve members in 1889.[70] The chapel was still used in the early 20th century[71] but has since been demolished.

EDUCATION. In 1764 there was a petty school in the village where a master taught English, writing, and accounts, and some gave religious instruction.[72] In 1832 a school was built in Front Street by Abraham Rhodes[73] and supported after his death by an annual allowance of £20 from his executors and subscriptions from other landowners.[74] From 1863 it also received an annual parliamentary grant.[75] In 1861 voluntary contributions amounted to £28 and school pence brought in about £15; the average attendance was then 39.[76] In 1871 there were 48 children in attendance.[77] A new two-roomed school was built close by in 1872; William Cadman, of Wold Newton Hall, provided the site and payment for a mistress.[78] The old school, a single-storey chalk building, was occupied as a cottage in 1970.

A school board for Wold Newton and Fordon was formed in 1879; it bought the school and enlarged it to accommodate 90 children.[79] The average attendance in 1880 was 49.[80] The school was further enlarged in 1899 and 1908 and average attendance at that period was 80-85.[81] Numbers fell to 40-50 after the First World War and to about 30 in the 1930s.[82] A new school was built in Back Street in

---

[46] For another carved tympanum see p. 330.
[47] B.I.H.R., V. 1575/CB. 1, f. 88.
[48] Par. rec., Vestry min. bk., 1839-1924.
[49] Sheahan and Whellan, *Hist. York & E.R.* ii. 492.
[50] *Kelly's Dir. N. & E.R. Yorks.* (1901), 581.
[51] Par. rec., Vestry min. bk., 1839-1924.
[52] *Rep. Com. Eccl. Revenues*, 980.
[53] Par. rec., Vestry min. bk., 1839-1924.
[54] Boulter, 'Ch. Bells', 219.
[55] *Inventories of Ch. Goods*, 24.
[56] *Yorks. Ch. Plate*, i. 337.
[57] Ibid. 336-7; *Y.A.J.* xxv. 90.
[58] Barley, *Par. Docs. E.R.* 108. They are at Thwing Rectory.
[59] B.I.H.R., C.P., H. 4838; see also E 134/42 & 43 Eliz. Mich./29.
[60] Sheahan and Whellan, *Hist. York & E.R.* ii. 492.
[61] Par. rec., Vestry min. bk. (at Thwing Rectory).
[62] B.I.H.R., CD. 146.
[63] G.R.O. Worship Returns, Vol. v, no. 731.
[64] C 54/12162 nos. 10, 11.
[65] H.O. 129/24/524; date on building.
[66] Ex inf. Revd. W. H. Pittam, Wesley Manse, Sherburn, 1960.
[67] H.O. 129/24/524.
[68] B.I.H.R., V. 1865/Ret. 601.
[69] Ibid. V. 1868/Ret. 558; V. 1877/Ret.
[70] H. Woodcock, *Sketches of Prim. Meth. on Yorks. Wolds*, 79.
[71] *Kelly's Dir. N. & E.R. Yorks.* (1909), 615.
[72] B.I.H.R., Bp. V. 1764/Ret. 141.
[73] Sheahan and Whellan, *Hist. York & E.R.* ii. 493.
[74] Ibid.; *Kelly's Dir. N. & E.R. Yorks.* (1872), 562.
[75] *Rep. Educ. Cttee. of Counc.* [3171], p. 577, H.C.(1863), xlvii.
[76] Ed. 7/135.
[77] *Rets. rel. Elem. Educ. 1871*, 476.
[78] Par. rec., Vestry min. bk., 1843-94, *sub* 1871 etc.; E.R.R.O., Sch. bd. mins. and accts. 1879-1903.
[79] Ibid.; *Lond. Gaz.* 20 June 1879 (p. 4027); 13 Aug. 1880 (p. 4461).
[80] Ed. 7/135.
[81] *Kelly's Dir. N. & E.R. Yorks.* (1901), 582; (1909), 615.
[82] *Bd. of Educ. List 21* (H.M.S.O.).

1967 for children from Wold Newton and Thwing,[83] and in 1969 the average number on the roll was 64.[84] The 1872 building was unused in 1970.

There was a lending library at the school in 1856, and in 1872 it contained over 300 books.[85] A reading room was built in 1894 to house it and was used until at least 1937.[86]

CHARITIES FOR THE POOR. None known.

REIGHTON

REIGHTON lies by the sea 6 miles north-west of Bridlington, the compact parish stretching 2 miles inland across the chalk escarpment and into the wolds.[1] The Anglian settlement of Reighton was probably named after the strip or ridge (*ric*) of ground, formed by the escarpment, on which the village stands.[2] In the 12th century the name *Strop'* occurs, apparently referring to Reighton, and it may allude to the same strap or band of ground.[3] The village for long consisted of two groups of houses, one along the top of the escarpment and the other near its foot, though modern building has partially linked them together. North of the escarpment lies a wide belt of lower ground, and on the cliff tops beyond there has been a considerable development of holiday facilities. Towards the sea a long stretch of the western parish boundary follows Reighton gill. The boundary follows no marked natural features across the high wold slopes, but towards Speeton and Grindale in the south it makes use of two prominent dry valleys, Maiden's Grave Slack and Bell Slack. The prehistoric earthwork known as Argam Dikes formed another stretch of the boundary on the wolds. The area of the ancient parish is 1,818 a.[4] The civil parish was enlarged to include Speeton in 1935.[5]

The chalk escarpment in Reighton, especially to the east of the village, is prominent and steep, rising from about 200 ft. above sea-level to over 400 ft. in a distance of 500 yds. These slopes are known as Reighton hills and they were probably called 'the Hills' by at least the 17th century.[6] To the west of the village the escarpment is less steep and rises to only about 350 ft. A small valley, cut obliquely into the hills, separates the two contrasting stretches of the escarpment. The valley provided the site for the lower part of the village, and a series of banks raised along and across it, known as Pond hills, suggests that at some time there were fishponds there. Below the escarpment a stream flows eastwards from this valley towards the sea in Speeton.

The low ground, also dissected by several other small streams, varies in height from about 200 ft. to 100 ft. at the sea. As in Hunmanby and Speeton, the boulder clay cliffs are characterized by numerous land-slips and present no very steep face to the sands. Both Reighton gill and another stream called the Gill have eroded steep-sided valleys back from the cliffs. In the south of the parish the ground falls steadily from 425 ft. above the escarpment to only 200 ft.–250 ft. in the dry valleys that are cut into the wolds. The large regular fields over much of the parish result from the inclosure of open fields on the wolds, and common moors and meadows on the low ground, in 1820. The open landscape is rarely broken by trees and plantations, except for some few around the village itself and near Reighton Hall.

The road which links the two parts of the village, climbing steeply up the escarpment, is now part of the main Bridlington–Filey road. Until modern times, however, the main road may have lain to the south of the village, keeping to the high ground and leading to Filey via Hunmanby. An old mile-stone stands by this road. Other roads on the wolds lead eastwards to Speeton and southwards to Burton Fleming and Grindale. Two roads connect the village with the low ground; one, known as Oxtrope Lane in 1850 and later as Watson's Lane, formerly gave access to the Meadow ings and the Cow pasture,[7] and the other, Sands Road, leads to the sea. The Bridlington–Filey railway line, opened in 1847, crosses the south of the parish.

The crofts and garths of the village mostly lie around the lower village street, known as St. Helen's Lane, and the upper street, now Church Hill. The upper street formerly continued eastwards to and beyond the site of Reighton Hall, with garths all the way. To the west of Church Hill there are pronounced earthworks marking the boundaries of several old crofts. Beyond these earthworks is a deep double ditch, continuing the line of a small lane which leads down to the lower village; it may be prehistoric. North of St. Helen's Lane are other banks, marking the boundary between the village garths and the Common moor.[8]

The village still contains many houses and outbuildings built wholly or partly of chalk, as well as much 18th- and 19th-century brick. In the lower part of the village, Manor House is an altered 18th-century house of chalk, with brick dressings, and has extensive farm buildings of chalk, brick, and cobbles. Near by is a one-and-a-half storeyed cottage, and a similar chalk and brick cottage stands further down Watson's Lane. Johnson's Farm is not far from Manor House and has similar outbuildings. The farm-house is a long red-brick structure with its upper floor partly in the roof and an early three-bay plan. It was probably built or remodelled early in the 18th century. In 1850 it was known as Johnson Villa[9] and adjoining it is an early-19th-century double-fronted annexe with chequered brick walls. In the upper part of the village the most noteworthy

---

[83] E.R. Educ. Cttee. *Mins.* 1967–8, 80, 92, 118, 205.
[84] Ex inf. Chief Educ. Officer, County Hall, Beverley, 1969.
[85] Sheahan and Whellan, *Hist. York & E.R.* ii. 493; *Kelly's Dir. N. & E.R. Yorks.* (1872), 562.
[86] *Kelly's Dir. N. & E.R. Yorks.* (1897), 556; (1937), 552.
[1] This article was written in 1970.
[2] *P.N.E.R. Yorks.* (E.P.N.S.), 107.
[3] Ibid.; *Rievaulx Charty.* (Sur. Soc. lxxxiii), 48–9.
[4] O.S. Map 6" (1854).
[5] *Census*, 1931.
[6] E.R.R.O., DDHU/12/2–3; see p. 307.
[7] O.S. Map 6" (1854, 1958). Oxtrope Lane was perhaps named from a close in the vicinity called Oxthorpe: Registry of Deeds, Beverley, inclosure award not enrolled and map.
[8] Regy. of Deeds, incl. map.
[9] O.S. Map 6" (1854). See plate facing p. 321.

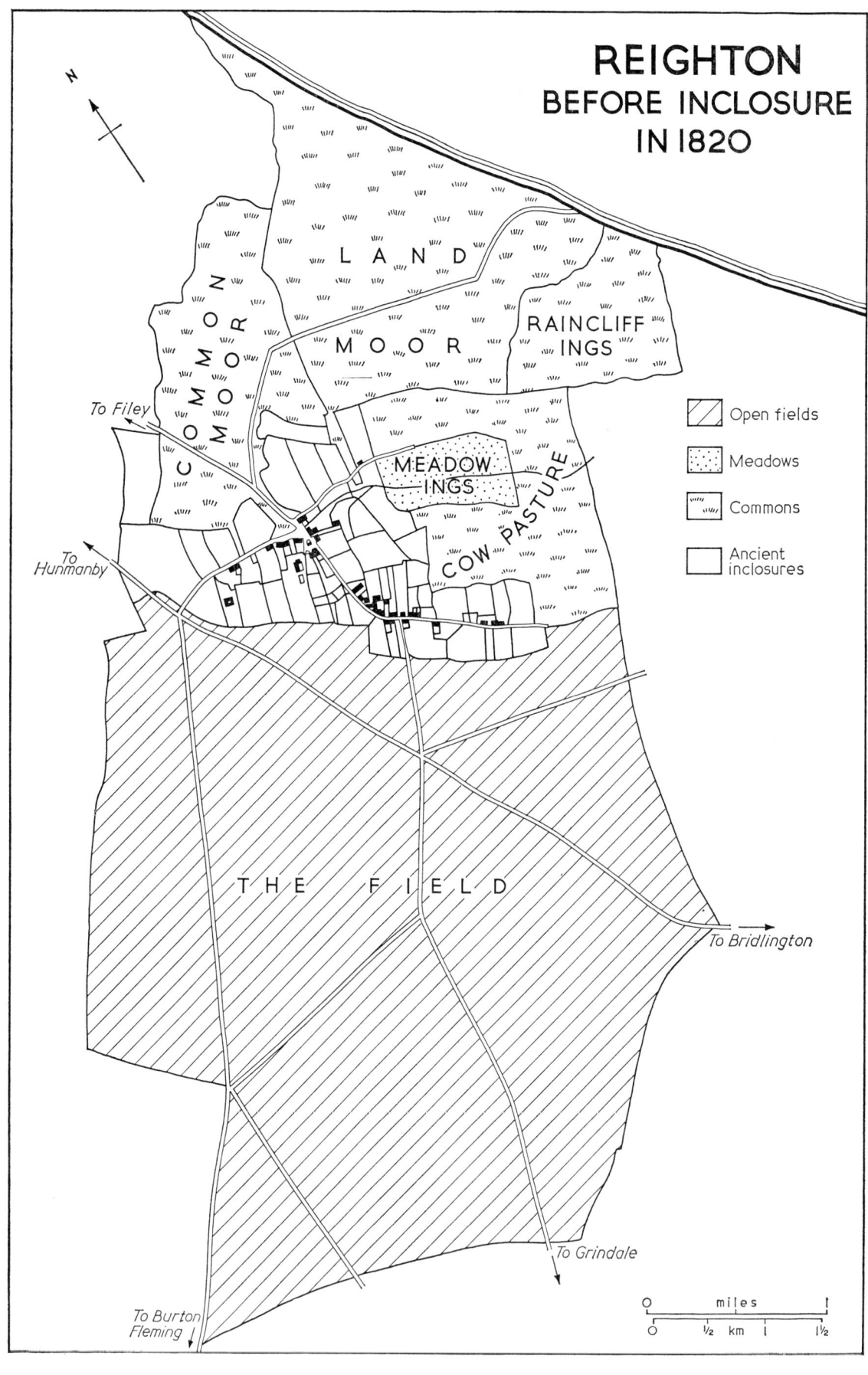

houses are Reighton Hall,[10] the former Vicarage,[11] and Reighton House, the last-named a large farmhouse built, like its outbuildings, of chalk as well as brick. Throughout the village there are many 19th- and 20th-century houses, including twelve Council houses in St. Helen's Lane.

There are few outlying farm-houses in the parish, including only one, Moor House Farm, which was built before 1850. The Dotterel inn, on the Bridlington road south of the village, was built in the early 1820s,[12] and near by are six Council houses. The building of chalets and bungalows on the cliff top around Sands Road began before the Second World War and continued after it, and there has been extensive development on the south side of the Gill.

Both parts of the village — the lower in the small valley on the slopes of the escarpment, and the upper on a patch of sand and gravel above it — had supplies of water from springs and wells, and a pond, now dry, lay in the lower section. St. Helen's well, in the valley, is mentioned as a spring called 'Elnewelle' in the 13th century.[13] High on the escarpment is Knox well,[14] and it may have been in this vicinity, rather than by the sea, that two men were drowned in 1390 in a well at 'Reighton cliff'.[15]

In 1674 38 households were recorded at Reighton, 9 of which were discharged from the hearth tax. Of those that were charged 19 had only one hearth each, 8 had 2, and 2 had three.[16] There were said to be 30 families in 1743[17] and 42 in 1764.[18] The population in 1801 was 149. Apart from a small drop in 1831–41, it steadily increased to a peak of 254 in 1881, before falling to 219 in 1901.[19] In 1931 Reighton had 194 inhabitants.[20]

MANORS AND OTHER ESTATES. There were three estates at Reighton in 1086. One, of 6 carucates, was soke of Berenger de Todeni's manor of Buckton. A second, of 5 carucates, had previously been held by Tof and Gam and after the Conquest belonged to the Crown. The third, of 3 carucates, belonged to the archbishop of York. It had been held by Ulviet in 1066 and had passed to the liberty of St. John, Beverley, by 1086, when it was regarded as a berewick of Kelk.[21]

Berenger de Todeni's land subsequently passed under the overlordship of the Gants and later the Tattershalls. In the early 12th century part of it was already in the tenancy of the Argam family,[22] and this manor of Reighton followed the descent of Argam manor[23] until the attainder of Sir Robert Constable in 1537.[24] It was sometimes known as the *ARGAM FEE*.

The manor was eventually granted by the Crown to Edward Wingate in 1590,[25] and in 1608 Wingate's grandson, another Edward, conveyed it to Robert Harrison.[26] Also in 1608 Wingate sold other property to William Jordan and this may have been the origin of part of the Jordans' holding in this fee.[27] In 1639 property was settled on John Harrison, the elder and younger.[28] By 1681 the manor was in the hands of Henry and Dorothy Ball, Dorothy perhaps being the Harrisons' heir, and they in that year sold it to James Cockerell.[29] In 1744 Robert Cockerell sold it to William Osbaldeston.[30]

The Osbaldestons were allotted 207 a. at inclosure in 1820[31] and had 245 a. in 1835.[32] Reighton then descended with Hunmanby[33] until 1870, when it passed, under the will of Robert Mitford, to his daughter Margaret, wife of W. A. T. Amherst, created Baron Amherst in 1892.[34] Their daughter Mary, Baroness Amherst, who married Lord William Cecil, sold the Manor House and the land in 1918 to B. H. Bradshaw[35] and the Bradshaws have since retained it. B. H. Bradshaw also obtained, in 1959, a farm of 95 a. which in the 19th century had belonged to Robert Crowe and later to the Cranswicks.[36]

A separate estate was created from the Argam Fee in 1219, when William of Argam granted 2 carucates to Simon of Hales.[37] Geoffrey of Cockfield unsuccessfully laid claim to land occupied by Nicholas and Robert of Hales in 1242.[38] A member of the Hales family still held the estate in 1346.[39]

Like land in Muston[40] another part of the Gant estate in Reighton was held by the Nevilles. It was described as the manor of *REIGHTON* in 1201.[41] Again like Muston it passed to the Malbis family, which still held it in 1309,[42] and some of it may have descended to the Whartons in the 17th century. When the former Wharton estates were divided in 1775 there were 36 a. in Reighton, and these fell to the share of Michael Newton.[43] In 1813 the Newton trustees sold 23 a. to H. E. Strickland,[44] brother of Sir William Strickland. After buying other land, much of it from G. J. Jordan, H. E. Strickland was allotted 140 a. at inclosure in 1820.[45] About 110 a. of this land later passed successively to John Hesp and William Graburn, before apparently being merged with the main Strickland estate in Reighton.[46]

The estate held by the Crown in 1086 later

---

[10] See p. 306.
[11] See p. 309.
[12] Regy. of Deeds, incl. map; ibid. DW/11/12 (calling it 'recently' built in 1825); Baines, *Hist. Yorks.* (1823), ii. 381.
[13] *P.N.E.R. Yorks.* 108.
[14] Knock well in 1850: O.S. Map 6" (1854, 1958).
[15] *Select Coroners' Rolls* (Selden Soc. ix), 126.
[16] E 179/205/521.
[17] *Herring's Visit.* iii. 37.
[18] B.I.H.R., Bp. V. 1764/Ret. 209.
[19] *V.C.H. Yorks.* iii. 490.
[20] *Census.*
[21] *V.C.H. Yorks.* ii. 204, 215, 322, 324 n.
[22] B.M. Cott. MS. Aug. ii. 56; *Bridlington Charty.* 45.
[23] See p. 6.
[24] S.C. 6/Hen. VIII/4334; *Cal. Inq. p.m.* iv, p. 108; *Feud. Aids*, vi. 228.
[25] C 66/1351 mm. 26–7.
[26] *Yorks. Fines, 1603–14*, 90.
[27] Ibid. 87.
[28] C.P. 25(2)/524/15 Chas. I Trin. no. 29.
[29] C.P. 25(2)/759/33 Chas. II Mich. no. 38; *Dugdale's Visit. Yorks.* (Sur. Soc. xxxvi), 172.
[30] Registry of Deeds, Beverley, R/269/648.
[31] Regy. of Deeds, award not enrolled.
[32] E.R.R.O., DDHU/17/13.
[33] See p. 232.
[34] E.R.R.O., DDX/74/3; *Complete Peerage.*
[35] Regy. of Deeds, 190/274/239; *Complete Peerage.*
[36] Ibid. 35/270/261 (1890); 860/54/35; 1126/496/426.
[37] *Yorks. Fines, 1218–31*, 23.
[38] J.I. 1/1047 m. 57; *Yorks. Assize Rolls* (Y.A.S. Rec. Ser. xliv), 70.
[39] *Cal. Close, 1307–13*, 101; *Feud. Aids*, vi. 228; *Yorks. Deeds*, ix. 140–1.
[40] See p. 279.
[41] *Abbrev. Plac.* (Rec. Com.), 32.
[42] C 133/124/1; *Cal. Close, 1307–13*, 101.
[43] E.R.R.O., DDEV/21/132
[44] Regy. of Deeds, CX/224/284.
[45] Ibid., award not enrolled.
[46] Ibid. GD/115/121; HQ/372/447; KD/363/483; LU/250/366.

belonged to the counts of Aumale and may have been given before 1127 to Alan de Mounceaux.[47] The 5 carucates were still held by the Mounceaux family in 1284–5,[48] but in 1298 Peter de Mounceaux granted them to Gerard Salvin.[49] The Mounceaux apparently retained a mesne lordship in the estate.[50] The manor was held by the Salvins until the early 16th century and was sometimes known as the *SALVIN FEE*. At least part of it was sold by George Salvin to George Swillington in 1537.[51] In 1632 part of the fee belonged to Sir Matthew Boynton.[52]

Some land in this fee was acquired by the Jordan family. In 1606 William Jordan had a manor-house called Uphall and 13 bovates described as of the Aumale fee, of which 11 bovates were Swillington land.[53] In 1760 4 bovates of the former Salvin Fee were sold by William Jordan to Matthew Smith and became part of Smith's large estate.[54]

The Domesday estate of the liberty of Beverley, which was sometimes known as the *FRANCHISE FEE*, seems to have been split up during the Middle Ages. Thus 3 bovates and a share of 2 others were held by the heirs of William of Argam *c.* 1400,[55] and Sir Robert Constable had 2 bovates in 1441;[56] both these holdings probably descended with the Argam Fee.

One of the principal holdings apparently derived from the Franchise Fee was acquired by the Jordan family. Robert Beaveshire had held 7 bovates of the fee *c.* 1400,[57] and these may have passed to Robert Jordan, who held 7 bovates of the provost of Beverley in 1639.[58]

The Jordan family's estate in Reighton was extensive and it included land from all three fees. William Jordan, Robert's father, at his death in 1623, had 13 bovates of the Salvin Fee, as already mentioned, 2 bovates called 'Flamborough Lands', which had presumably been the Constable holding in the Franchise Fee, and 14 other bovates.[59] The Jordans' estate was subsequently divided. Some of it passed to Matthew Smith, the elder, perhaps in 1705 when Francis and William Jordan and others conveyed land in Reighton and elsewhere to Smith and others who may have been his trustees.[60]

Matthew Smith, the younger, had an estate including 27 bovates *c.* 1770[61] and his trustees were by far the largest landowners in Reighton in 1783.[62] The estate was sold in 1789 to Sir George Strickland and then included 4 bovates of the Salvin Fee, 17¼ of the Argam Fee, 10 of the Franchise Fee, 11 of both the Argam and Franchise Fees, and 2 of 'Abbey Land'.[63] The estate also included a reputed manor of Reighton which Smith had bought from William St. Quintin in 1775, and which was said to be parcel of St. Quintin's manor of Ruston Parva.[64]

Sir William Strickland also bought land in all three fees from Samuel Jordan (in 1801), Matthew Wood, Francis Wardell (1789), Luke Walmsley (1790), and John Allison (1789). Those purchases accounted for 433 a. of the 938 a. which Strickland was allotted at inclosure in 1820.[65] The estate descended like Burton Fleming in the Strickland and Strickland-Constable families[66] until it was broken up and sold in the 1920s; the lots included 356 a. sold to Tom Bayes in 1920 and 382 a. to the East Riding county council in 1929.[67] The hall and its grounds were sold in 1919 to W. H. Willatt and passed to George Brocklehurst in 1949, Doris Jessup in 1951, and F. F. Johnson in 1967.[68]

Reighton Hall stands apart from the village, its grounds occupying the sites of crofts and garths along the former extension of the upper village street. It was built in the early 18th century and substantially rebuilt *c.* 1810.[69] The house is of two storeys and attics, with rendered brick walls and a frontage of six bays. Much of the interior, as well as the elegant semicircular porch, are of the date of rebuilding. There are also several fittings brought from elsewhere in 1967, including three chimney-pieces by Henry Cheere from Kilnwick Hall.[70] The outbuildings include an 18th-century octagonal brick dovecot and a stable range of chalk and brick. The rebuilding of the house was probably carried out by Henry E. Strickland, author of *Agriculture of the East Riding of Yorkshire* (1812). His son Hugh E. Strickland, the naturalist, was born there in 1811.[71]

Bridlington priory was one of several religious houses with estates in Reighton. Mauger of Argam gave 4 bovates to the priory in the early 12th century and a Mauger of Reighton subsequently gave 2 more bovates. William of Ganton added 7 bovates which Mauger of Reighton had once held, Hawise of Etton gave 1⅓ bovate, and *c.* 1250 Geoffrey of Cockfield gave a further bovate.[72] These gifts may all have been from the Argam Fee. At the Dissolution the priory had lands in Reighton worth £1 7s.[73] The property perhaps passed in the 16th century to Thomas Portington, who in 1586 conveyed a reputed manor of Reighton to Michael Wharton.[74] In 1590 Wharton was said to hold it of Bridlington manor.[75] It may have descended with the Wharton's share of the Argam Fee.

In 1148–56 Ralph de Neville gave a carucate of land in Reighton to Rievaulx abbey and Gilbert de Gant gave a further 2 bovates.[76] The land was let shortly before the Dissolution to William Jordan[77] and it probably formed part of the Jordan estate in the 17th century, subsequently descending with it.[78] Bardney abbey (Lincs.) received several gifts from Mauger of Reighton in the early 12th century,

---

[47] *Bridlington Charty.* 182, 300.
[48] *Feud. Aids*, vi. 28.
[49] K.B. 27/155 m. 25; *Abbrev. Plac.* 238.
[50] C 135/76/16.
[51] *Yorks. Fines*, i. 79.
[52] E 134/8 & 9 Chas. I Hil./15.
[53] C 142/504/53; /678/47.
[54] Regy. of Deeds, AD/190/422; see below.
[55] B.M. Lansd. MS. 896, f. 125.
[56] C 139/103/28.
[57] B.M. Lansd. MS. 896, f. 125.
[58] C 142/754/54.
[59] C 142/678/47.
[60] C.P. 25(2)/983/3 Anne Hil. no. 42.
[61] E.R.R.O., DDSY/4/105, 107.
[62] Ibid. Land Tax.
[63] Regy. of Deeds, BP/60/93.
[64] Ibid. AW/97/150.
[65] Ibid. BN/395/607–8, 611; BO/435/669; CD/423/651; inclosure award not enrolled; E.R.R.O., DDGD/Box 1 (schedule of deeds of Strickland estate at Reighton).
[66] See p. 121.
[67] Regy. of Deeds, 228/291/239; 398/337/273.
[68] Ibid. 196/97/86; 831/326/272; 892/66/53; 1508/140/134.
[69] Bulmer, *Dir. E. Yorks.* (1892), 255.
[70] Ex inf. Mr. F. F. Johnson, 1971.
[71] *D.N.B.*
[72] B.M. Cott. MS. Aug. ii. 56; *Bridlington Charty.* 45–7.
[73] *Valor Eccl.* (Rec. Com.), v. 120.
[74] *Yorks. Fines*, iii. 52.
[75] C 142/224/31.
[76] *E.Y.C.* ii, pp. 471, 485; *Rievaulx Charty.* (Sur. Soc. lxxxiii), 48–9.
[77] *Rievaulx Charty.* 317, 352.
[78] See above.

including 3 bovates of land.[79] In 1376 2 bovates were let to farm and a house was held by William Baxter, who may have been the vicar of Reighton.[80] In 1536 the 2 bovates were certainly held by the vicar.[81] After the Dissolution they apparently descended with the rectory.[82] The Knights Hospitallers of Beverley had property in Reighton in 1539–40,[83] and it was restored to them when the order was briefly revived in 1558.[84]

The great tithes were appropriated by Bardney abbey in 1115.[85] After the Dissolution they descended with the rectory of Hunmanby[86] until 1637, when Richard Osbaldeston granted them, along with the advowson, to Edward Hutchinson.[87] They were worth £42 in 1650.[88] By 1737 they had passed from Hutchinson's son, another Edward, to the latter's brother and heir Richard Langley; in that year Langley conveyed them to Matthew Smith.[89] In or about 1774 the corn tithes were paid by a modus of £1 a bovate, bringing in £88 all told, and other tithes were worth £30.[90] The tithes passed, with Smith's estate and the advowson, to Sir George Strickland in 1789,[91] and at inclosure in 1820 Sir William Strickland was awarded 166 a. in lieu of them.[92] Tithes on a three-acre close were still paid until 1844, when they were commuted for a payment of 14s. to Strickland.[93] The tithe allotment became part of the Strickland estate in the parish.

ECONOMIC HISTORY. There is little indication of the state of the village in 1086, though the Crown estate had land for two ploughs and was worth 16s.[94] Early evidence of the lay-out of the open-field land in Reighton is lacking. The number of the fields and their names are not recorded, though 'the up field above the town' is mentioned in 1726.[95] Corn tithes were collected from 88 bovates of land in the late 18th century[96] and at inclosure in 1820 allotments totalling just over 1,000 a. were made from 'the field'.[97] In 1820 the open-field land lay entirely on the wolds, and there is no definite evidence that it had ever extended to the area below the escarpment. In 1632, however, part of the Land moor was said to lie in ridge and furrow.[98]

The common meadow land may by 1820 have been confined to the Meadow ings, an area of about 30 a. around the small stream running below the chalk escarpment. Adjoining the sea were Raincliff ings, but by at least the 18th century these were apparently used as common pasture. Several landowners were described as having 'bovates' or acres there in the 18th century as a means of expressing their share of the pasturage; thus one man had '3 a. being 3 gates'.[99] About 1774 Matthew Smith's estate included 20 beast-gates in Raincliff ings,[1] and all 64 a. of Raincliff ings were allotted at inclosure.[2]

The chief areas of common pasture were those called the Common moor and the Land moor at inclosure, when they amounted to about 120 a. and 240 a. respectively.[3] In the late 17th century the Land moor contained 228 a., divided between the three fees: 128 a. in Argam Fee, 43 a. in Franchise Fee, and 57 a. in Salvin Fee.[4] The Common moor was said in 1632 to be used for cows for part of the year and for other animals for the rest.[5] It was still used in common in the 18th century: Michael Newton had $\frac{1}{4}$ gate there in 1775,[6] for example, and the vicar had $2\frac{1}{2}$ beast-gates in 'the moor'.[7] The Land moor was also used in common in 1632, but it may have been inclosed later that century. Though it was divided into several large allotments in 1820 it is possible that the commissioners were re-allotting numerous early inclosures.[8]

The Cow pasture lay south-east of the village, astride the escarpment and around the Meadow ings, and it contained about 100 a. in 1820.[9] A pasture called the Hill, where beast-gates were enjoyed,[10] was perhaps part of it. The steepest section of the escarpment was apparently overgrown with whins, which enroached into the pasture and meadow. Whins taken there and on the moors are frequently mentioned as a perquisite of cottagers and landowners in Reighton.[11] A by-law made in 1726 obliged the inhabitants to root up whins in 'the Hills', starting near 'the Ing dike' and clearing 30 yds. a year until they reached the foot of the hills. Finally, there was the usual common pasture in the open fields; it was presumably both fields and moors which were stinted in 1726 at four sheep for each bovate or cottage from 25 March to 29 September and eight for the rest of the year.[12] The vicar had five sheep-gates attached to each of two cottages in 1764.[13]

Small closes in Reighton are frequently mentioned from the 16th century onwards and no doubt were mostly within the large area of ancient inclosures which surrounded the village in 1820.[14] A close made 'de novo' to the inconvenience of Robert Constable was ordered, at his court held in 1531, to be removed.[15] Several small closes were at some time taken from the open fields immediately west of the village, where traces of ridge and furrow were visible in 1970. More significant, if problematical,

[79] B.M. Cott. MS. Vesp. E. xx, ff. 193–4.
[80] Ibid. 288; Lansd. MS. 896, f. 125.
[81] Valor Eccl. v. 123.
[82] E.R.R.O., DDGD/Box 1 (deeds of 1737).
[83] Miscellanea, iv (Y.A.S. Rec. Ser. xciv), 90.
[84] Cal. Pat. 1557–8, 319.
[85] See p. 308.
[86] See p. 236.
[87] C.P. 25(2)/523/12 Chas. I Hil. pt. 3, no. 17.
[88] T.E.R.A.S. ii. 58.
[89] E.R.R.O., DDGD/Box 1.
[90] Ibid. DDSY/4/105, 107.
[91] Regy. of Deeds, BP/60/93.
[92] Ibid. award not enrolled.
[93] B.I.H.R., TA. 296S.
[94] V.C.H. Yorks. ii. 204.
[95] E.R.R.O., PR. 2317.
[96] Ibid. DDSY/4/105.
[97] 966 a. were allotted solely from the Field and about 55 a. were in an allotment made jointly from several areas: Registry of Deeds, Beverley, inclosure award not enrolled and map.
[98] E 134/8 & 9 Chas. I Hil./15.
[99] e.g. Regy. of Deeds, N/411/881; AZ/138/206; BN/395/611; CS/594/807.
[1] E.R.R.O., DDSY/4/105, 107.
[2] Regy. of Deeds, award and map.
[3] 86 a. and 197 a. respectively were allotted solely from the moors; the remaining acreages lay in joint allotments from more than one area.
[4] E.R.R.O., DDHU/12/27.
[5] E 134/8 & 9 Chas. I Hil./15.
[6] E.R.R.O., DDEV/21/132.
[7] B.I.H.R., TER. J. Reighton 1764.
[8] See p. 308.
[9] Regy. of Deeds, award and map.
[10] Ibid. BM/178/282; CD/423/651.
[11] e.g. ibid. M/394/621; incl. award; B.I.H.R., TER. J. Reighton 1716; E.R.R.O., DDHU/12/1–9, 25.
[12] E.R.R.O., PR. 2317.
[13] B.I.H.R., TER. J. Reighton 1764.
[14] Regy. of Deeds, inclosure award.
[15] S.C. 2/211/38.

is the 'flatting and inclosing' of the Land moor in the late 17th century. Nineteen freeholders, who were described as having 136 'bovates' in the moor, were allotted 25 closes, totalling 211 a. Most of the closes were small, varying between 2 a. and 14 a., but two of them contained 31 a. and 34 a. Each allottee was ordered to maintain the fences on one or two sides of each close.[16] This inclosure appears to have been an accomplished deed rather than a proposal. Common rights may later have been restored to the Land moor or the early closes may, as already suggested, have been re-allotted in 1820.

The open fields and common pastures and meadows were finally inclosed in 1820[17] under an Act of 1811;[18] 1,593 a. were dealt with and allotments made totalling 1,568 a., while exchanges were arranged involving 28 a. of old inclosures. Sir William Strickland received 1,114 a., including 166 a. in lieu of rectorial tithes, Humphrey Osbaldeston 207 a., and Henry E. Strickland 140 a. The vicar was allotted 63 a. in lieu of tithes and there were three other allotments, of 59 a., 12 a., and one acre. Since inclosure there have usually been 5–8 farmers in Reighton, increasing to 10 or 11 in the 1930s.[19]

A mill at Reighton is mentioned in 1241[20] and a water-mill was described as newly-built in 1348.[21] A windmill is mentioned in 1635[22] and as late as 1713.[23] Some employment was provided in the late 19th century at a brickyard at the north end of the village and a quarry near Burton Fleming Lane, both said to have been unsuccessful ventures of the vicar, William Rowley.[24] There had been a lime-kiln near the Grindale road as early as 1850.[25]

LOCAL GOVERNMENT. There are many surviving court papers for the Argam Fee, the earliest dating from 1531 and 1536 and relating to various manors held by Robert Constable.[26] Isolated records survive of courts held in 1649, 1665, and 1666 for the Harrisons,[27] and in several years in the earlier 18th century for the Cockerells.[28] Long, though broken, series of estreats, call rolls, and jury lists and verdicts cover much of the 18th and earlier 19th centuries, courts being held after 1744 by the Osbaldeston family.[29] There are also by-laws, made at a court held in 1726 and confirmed in 1734.[30]

In 1632 it was said that although tenants of the other fees did suit at the court of the Argam Fee they also owed suit elsewhere: those of the Salvin Fee to Sir Matthew Boynton's court at Barmston and those of the Franchise Fee to the Crompton's court at Ruston Parva.[31]

In 1665–6 4 bylawmen, a constable, a pinder, and 2 ale tasters were sworn at the courts, which dealt with routine agricultural offences, the neglect of common day works, and the pollution of St. Helen's well. Four bylawmen, 2 constables, a pinder, and 2 affeerors were usually appointed in the 18th century and still in the 1830s and 1840s, with the exception of the bylawmen who are last recorded about 1810.

There are no surviving parish records before 1835. In 1836 Reighton joined the Bridlington union.[32]

CHURCH. In 1115 Walter de Gant gave the church of Hunmanby, with Reighton and its other dependent chapels, to Bardney abbey.[33] A vicarage was ordained at Reighton, apparently in 1269. The vicar was to have a third of the tithes of corn and lambs and all small tithes and tithes of wool, together with all offerings except the first choice of moveables; he was to pay a pension of £1 10s. 8d. to Bardney.[34] In 1919 the curacy of Speeton was united with the living.[35]

Soon after Gant's gift had been made his undertenant, Mauger of Argam, extinguished by quitclaim any right in the advowson he may have had,[36] and the abbey regularly presented until the Dissolution. The advowson then at first descended like Hunmanby rectory.[37] William Lutton presented in 1559, the Crown in 1579, and Thomas Westrop in 1620.[38] After passing to the Osbaldestons in 1623, however, Reighton was separated from Hunmanby. In 1637 Richard Osbaldeston granted the advowson to Edward Hutchinson, who was to marry Frances Osbaldeston,[39] and their son, another Edward, presented in 1683 and 1690.[40] The patronage apparently passed with the tithes to Richard Langley and in 1737 to Matthew Smith,[41] for Smith presented several times up to 1768.[42] Two turns in three were in 1789 conveyed by Smith's trustees to Sir George Strickland,[43] who in 1794 obtained the third turn, which Smith's widow had held as dower.[44] The advowson has since been held by the Stricklands and the Strickland-Constables, who have had three turns in four as a result of the union of Reighton and Speeton in 1919; the fourth turn has been held by the earls of Londesborough and since 1929 by the archbishop of York.[45]

The vicarage was valued at £9 10s. 4d. in 1535[46] and was said to be worth £30 in 1650.[47] The living was augmented by £200 from Queen Anne's Bounty in 1803[48] and by a parliamentary grant of £900, given in 1826 to meet a benefaction of property worth £600 by Sir William Strickland.[49] By 1829–31 the average annual income was £177 net.[50] In 1884 the net income was £216.[51]

---

[16] E.R.R.O., DDHU/12/26–7 (undated), including map.
[17] Regy. of Deeds, award and map.
[18] 51 Geo. III, c. 21.
[19] Directories.
[20] C.P. 25(1)/264/35 no. 2.
[21] *Yorks. Deeds*, ix. 140–1.
[22] E 134/11 Chas. I Mich./53.
[23] Regy. of Deeds, E/167/286.
[24] Ibid. 303/380/318; G. Alcock, *Hist. Notes of Reighton*, 26.
[25] O.S. Map 6" (1854).
[26] S.C. 2/211/38.
[27] E.R.R.O., DDHU/12/1–3.
[28] Ibid. /4–8.
[29] Ibid. /9–25, 31.
[30] E.R.R.O., PR. 2317, printed in *Miscellanea*, iii (Y.A.S. Rec. Ser. lxxiv), 100–3.
[31] E 134/8 & 9 Chas. I Hil./15.
[32] *3rd Rep. Poor Law Com.* 167.
[33] Dugdale, *Mon.* i. 628–9.
[34] *Reg. Giffard* (Sur. Soc. cix), 56.
[35] York Dioc. Regy., Orders in Council 524.
[36] B.M. Cott. MS. Vesp. E. xx, f. 194.
[37] See p. 236.
[38] *Fasti Parochiales*, iii. 66–7.
[39] C.P. 25(2)/523/12 Chas. I Hil. pt. 3, no. 17.
[40] Inst. Bks.
[41] See p. 307.
[42] Inst. Bks.
[43] Registry of Deeds, Beverley, BP/60/93.
[44] Ibid. BU/45/71.
[45] York Dioc. Cal. 1930; *Crockford*, 1967–8; see above, p. 103.
[46] *Valor Eccl.* (Rec. Com.), v. 123.
[47] *T.E.R.A.S.* ii. 58.
[48] Hodgson, *Q.A.B.* 451.
[49] Lawton, *Rer. Eccles. Dioc. Ebor.* ii. 307; see below.
[50] *Rep. Com. Eccl. Revenues*, 960–1.
[51] B.I.H.R., Bp. V. 1884/Ret.

At inclosure in 1820 the vicar was awarded 63 a. of land and rents of £55 in lieu of tithes.[52] The tithes on a three-acre close were commuted in 1844 for a payment of 7s. to the vicar.[53] There were 2 bovates of glebe land in 1535 which in the 18th century were reckoned to contain about 16 a.–18 a.[54] The 77 a. of glebe were sold in 1925.[55]

A house, perhaps a parsonage house, belonged to the vicarage from at least 1535 onwards. It was out of repair in 1680. In 1716 it was said to contain four bays of building and in 1764 it was chalk-built and thatched, with two ground-floor rooms and two chambers.[56] In the early 19th century the Vicarage was described as a 'small dilapidated cottage' and it stood just to the south of the churchyard. Sir William Strickland was then proposing to give the vicar a larger house and some land near by, presumably the gift which had occasioned the parliamentary grant of 1826. The new house was a brick building of two storeys, three bays long, with parlour, 'house', kitchen, and dairy on the ground floor.[57] It still stood in 1970, having been used as the Vicarage[58] until 1962, when a new house was built opposite the church.[59]

The living was usually held in plurality in the 18th and 19th centuries. The vicar was resident in 1743, but also held Wold Newton. In 1764 he lived at Welton, near Hull, and employed a curate who himself lived at Langtoft.[60] In 1835, and in the 1860s and 1870s, the vicar was resident but also held the curacy of Bessingby.[61]

One service was held each week in 1743 and 1764, and communion was administered three times a year to about thirty people.[62] By 1865 communion was held twice-yearly, with about five recipients, and by 1884 monthly, with about a dozen. There were two services each Sunday by 1884,[63] and this was still the case in 1970.

The church of ST. PETER is built of stone and consists of nave, chancel, north aisle, west tower, and south porch.[64] The tower and much of the nave were rebuilt between 1890 and 1905. Of the aisleless Norman church there remain the jambs of the south doorway, the chancel arch, and the font. The low but massive chancel arch is semicircular and of three orders, supported on jamb shafts with scalloped capitals. The unusual square font has a cable ornament round the top, an attached shaft at each corner with a moulded base and scalloped capital, and a different geometrical pattern covering each of the four faces.[65] At the end of the 12th century a north aisle was added to the nave and the chancel was apparently rebuilt. There are small lancet windows in the south and east walls of the chancel and at the east end of the aisle. In the north wall of the chancel is an opening, not thought to be a 'squint',[66] which may survive from the 12th-century chancel. The three-bay arcade to the aisle, dating from c. 1170–1200, has semicircular arches of two chamfered orders. The piers are circular with nail-head ornament to the capitals and 'water-holding' bases.

The church was in poor repair in the late 16th century and it suffered storm damage in 1714. Work ordered in 1720–1 included the removal of the porch,[67] but if this was done a new porch, apparently of chalk and brick, was subsequently put up. The church was also given a small brick tower, perhaps in the 17th or 18th century. The chancel was restored in 1831 and the south side of the nave refaced with brick about the same period; the north side was refaced with cobbles 'a few years' before 1892.[68]

By the late 19th century the porch and tower, and indeed the whole west end of the church, were ruinous and before 1897 both were demolished. The nave was restored during the last 20 years of the century, tiles replacing cobbles on the floor, box pews being removed, and walls being renovated or perhaps rebuilt. By 1901 the porch had been rebuilt, too, and the raising of a new tower had begun, and by 1905 the tower was completed. The old chancel remained, but its brick floor was tiled in 1912.[69] The tower retains a cobbled floor, either preserved or replaced.

There were two bells in the tower in 1552.[70] Of the present bells, one is dated 1675 and was made by Samuel Smith, the elder, of York, and both were recast in 1908.[71] The plate includes a silver-plated cup and pewter paten,[72] as well as a set given to the church in 1891.[73] The registers begin in 1559 and are complete.[74]

Reighton retained some dependence on the mother-church at Hunmanby and contributed towards its repair, for example, in 1662.[75] Burials at Reighton were subject to the payment of a 'skin-penny' to the vicar of Hunmanby until at least the early 18th century. The payment was apparently made reluctantly in 1720 and may have ceased soon after.[76] Reighton churchyard was extended in 1924.[77]

NONCONFORMITY. There is no record of dissent in Reighton until the registration for worship of a house in 1811.[78] A Wesleyan Methodist chapel, in the main village street, was built in 1818[79] and enlarged in 1857.[80] It was replaced in 1925 by a new pebble-dashed chapel close by,[81] and the old

---

[52] Regy. of Deeds, award not enrolled.
[53] B.I.H.R., TA. 296S.
[54] Ibid. TER. J. Reighton 1685 etc.; *Valor Eccl.* v. 123.
[55] Regy. of Deeds, 303/380/318.
[56] B.I.H.R., TER. J. Reighton 1716, 1764; ER. V/CB. 5; *Valor Eccl.* v. 123.
[57] E.R.R.O., DDGD/Box 1 (survey of glebe with drawings of Vicarage).
[58] e.g. O.S. Map 6" (1854).   [59] Ex inf. the vicar, 1971.
[60] B.I.H.R., Bp. V. 1764/Ret. 209; *Herring's Visit.* iii. 37.
[61] B.I.H.R., V. 1865/Ret. 422; V. 1868/Ret. 374; V. 1871/Ret. 379; *Rep. Com. Eccl. Revenues*, 960–1.
[62] B.I.H.R., Bp. V. 1764/Ret. 209; *Herring's Visit.* iii. 37.
[63] B.I.H.R., V. 1865/Ret. 422; Bp. V. 1884/Ret.
[64] Morris, *E. Yorks.* 294.
[65] *T.E.R.A.S.* x. 110. See plate facing p. 193.
[66] G. Alcock, *Hist. Notes of Reighton*, 9.
[67] B.I.H.R., Churches index.
[68] Bulmer, *Dir. E. Yorks.* 254.
[69] Photographs in church, mostly dated 1886–1905; Alcock, *Reighton*, 10–11.
[70] *Inventories of Ch. Goods*, 33.
[71] Boulter, 'Ch. Bells', 218; Alcock, *Reighton*, 11; *V.C.H. Yorks.* ii. 452.
[72] *Yorks. Ch. Plate*, i. 301–2.
[73] E.R.R.O., PR. 2275, note at front.   [74] E.R.R.O.
[75] B.I.H.R., C.P., H. 4838; see also E 134/42 & 43 Eliz. Mich./29.
[76] E.R.R.O., PR. 2275 (entries for 1706 and 1720).
[77] York Dioc. Regy., Sentence of consecration.
[78] G.R.O. Worship Returns, Vol. v, no. 2443.
[79] H.O. 129/24/524; stone in chapel-yard; O.S. Map 6" (1854).
[80] Bulmer, *Dir. E. Yorks.* (1892), 254.
[81] G.R.O. Worship Reg. no. 50098; Registry of Deeds, Beverley, 339/136/114.

building was subsequently demolished. The Primitive Methodists were holding services in 1851[82] and they are said to have converted a cottage for use as a chapel in 1870.[83] They had eleven members in Reighton in 1889.[84]

The vicar of Reighton stated in 1868 that nearly half the population attended the Wesleyan chapel, but that many of them went to church as well.[85]

EDUCATION. The vicar, Richard Leadbeater, was keeping a school in Reighton in 1563.[86] There was a dame school in 1835, attended by 15–20 children, and still in 1851.[87] Children went to schools in Grindale and Hunmanby in 1871,[88] but in 1875 a school board was formed for Reighton and Speeton and a school built in Speeton township.[89]

CHARITY FOR THE POOR. In 1634 John Jordan bequeathed £1 to the poor of Reighton,[90] but no more is heard of it.

RUDSTON

THE large parish of Rudston lies on the wolds about 5 miles west of Bridlington.[1] It stretches about 3 miles from north to south and over 4 miles from east to west, including the township of Thorpe and about two thirds of Caythorpe. The rest of Caythorpe has long been regarded as part of Boynton parish[2] but the whole township is dealt with here. Rudston is a settlement of Anglian origin, deriving its name from a 'rood' in the churchyard, in fact a Bronze-Age monolith. Thorpe and Caythorpe, depopulated villages lying in the valley east of Rudston, may have been subsidiary Scandinavian settlements.[3] Rudston village lies in the valley of Grindalythe at a point where the Gypsey Race changes course from south to east. The southern parish boundary with Burton Agnes and Carnaby is formed by Wold Gate. Elsewhere the boundary follows no prominent natural features. The comparatively late eastern boundary with Boynton is undefined for much of its length.[4] The area of the ancient parish is 5,551 a., of which that part of Caythorpe within the parish accounted for 1,334 a.[5]

The landscape of much of the parish exhibits the typical wold characteristics of undulating open slopes intersected by shallow dry valleys. The tree-planting activities of the Bosville family during the 19th century, however, created a large area of woodland in the valley and on the lower wold slopes south of Thorpe Hall. There were 145 a. of woodland on the Thorpe estate in 1955.[6] Apart from windbreaks and shelter-belts around the isolated farms, the only plantations on the wolds are Fox Cover in the south and North wood in the east of the parish.

The village lies in the valley mostly at a height of less than 100 ft. above sea-level, although part of it runs up a spur of the wolds and the church stands at over 125 ft. Much of the land in the valley east of the village, including the sites of the former villages of Thorpe and Caythorpe, also lies below 100 ft. The wolds rise steeply west of the village to over 375 ft. in the north-west of the parish and to the south they reach over 275 ft. at Rudston Beacon and at the barrow called South Side Mount. North of the village a broad belt of land lies at between 100 ft. and 150 ft. on each side of the Gypsey Race, but further east the land again rises to over 275 ft. The pattern of large regular fields in Rudston township results from the inclosure of 1777, before which much of the wold area was open-field land. The fields south of Thorpe Hall and Low Caythorpe Farm, however, probably reflect in their greater irregularity the early inclosure there.[7] Most of the parish is now under arable cultivation.

There is much evidence to suggest that there may have been continuity of settlement near Rudston from prehistoric times onwards. There may have been a religious centre in the area from the late Neolithic or early Bronze Age until the Iron Age: thus, in addition to the monolith in the churchyard, a henge monument was situated near by in Burton Fleming,[8] and the embankments known as Argam Dikes and at least three *cursus* are all centred on the valley at Rudston.[9] Several Neolithic and Bronze-Age barrows stand on the wolds and two Iron-Age cemeteries have been found in the valley north of the village.[10] A Roman villa dating from the 3rd and 4th centuries stood about ½ mile south-west of the village on the site of several huts of immediately pre-Roman date.[11] Anglian burials of the pagan period have also been found.[12]

The main road through the village is that from Sledmere to Bridlington, known in the mid 19th century as Bridlington Gate and in modern times as High Street.[13] It runs east–west across the parish forming the northern side of a triangle of roads around which the village lies. The western side is formed by a road formerly known as Burton Agnes Balk,[14] which runs southwards to Burton Agnes. The section of this road within the village is called Long Street. It may be the 'west street' mentioned

---

[82] H.O. 129/24/524.
[83] Bulmer, *Dir. E. Yorks.* 254.
[84] H. Woodcock, *Sketches of Prim. Meth. on Yorks. Wolds*, 154.
[85] B.I.H.R., V. 1868/Ret. 374.
[86] Ibid., Schools index.
[87] H.O. 129/24/524; *Educ. Enquiry Abstract, 1835*, 1093.
[88] *Rets. rel. Elem. Educ. 1871*, 476.
[89] See p. 104.   [90] E.R.R.O., PR. 2275.
[1] This article was written in 1970.
[2] See p. 21.
[3] *P.N.E.R. Yorks.* (E.P.N.S.), 98–9.
[4] See p. 21.
[5] O.S. Map 6" (1854).
[6] Registry of Deeds, Beverley, 1002/377/325.

[7] See pp. 315–16.
[8] See p. 119.
[9] See p. 6; *Y.A.J.* xlii. 9.
[10] I. M. Stead, *La Tène Cultures of E. Yorks.* 3, 111; *Y.A.J.* xlii. 110, 240.
[11] *Y.A.J.* xxxi. 366–76; xxxii. 214–20; xxxiii. 81–6, 320–38; xxxiv. 102–3; xxxviii. 259; xli. 10, 173, 329, 562; xlii. 7; I. A. Richmond, *Roman Pavements from Rudston, E. Yorks.* (Hull Mus. Publ. ccxv); *Excavations Annual Report 1963–6* (H.M.S.O.). Three pavements from the villa are on display in Hull Museums.
[12] F. and H. W. Elgee, *Archaeol. of Yorks.* 183; *Y.A.J.* i. 180–1.
[13] O.S. Map 6" (1854 and later edns.).
[14] Ibid. (various edns.).

in 1312.[15] The south-eastern side of the triangle is formed by East Gate, which continues south-westwards as Kilham Lane. It formerly joined the Bridlington road east of the village,[16] but the last third of a mile is now a field road and footpath. East Gate is first mentioned in 1397.[17] One other road leaves the village, running north to Burton Fleming. Other roads, all in the west of the parish, run from High Street to Kilham, Burton Fleming, and Thwing.

The village area is large and the houses dispersed, suggesting that the settlement may formerly have been more densely built up. Most of the buildings have probably always been sited away from the banks of the Gypsey Race, as they were in 1970, because of the danger of flooding.[18] It was the Race, however, together with a spring at the foot of the hill on which the church stands, which provided Rudston's water supply. The spring may have been that (*scaturiginem fontium*) referred to in the 12th or early 13th century.[19] There are several back lanes and connecting roads within the village. One, now a field road, connects High Street with Kilham Lane west of the village. Water Lane, so called from its proximity to the Race, is now a footpath. Others are Church Lane and Marton Lane. Back Side Lane runs south of the village from Burton Agnes Balk into the fields south of Thorpe Hall; it, too, is now largely a field road.

Most of the buildings in the village are undistinguished cottages and houses dating from the 18th to the 20th century. The main material is brick, although some buildings, chiefly barns and outbuildings, are of chalk and many incorporate patches of it. An altered cottage on the south side of High Street bears a reset date tablet of 1739. Other cottages, of a storey and a half and built mainly of chalk, probably date in part from the 18th century. In Long Street, in its own grounds, is Rudston House, the birthplace of the writer Winifred Holtby.[20] It is an earlier-19th-century white-brick building with a front of three bays and two storeys and a central Doric porch. Modern buildings include eighteen Council houses.

By at least 1892 a reading room housing a parish library of about 700 volumes, and supported by an endowment of £600 bequeathed by Dudley Beaumont, stood near the infants' school in Church Lane. The building was damaged by a bomb in 1943 and in the following year Sir Godfrey Bosville Macdonald sought permission to use the endowment for adapting and maintaining the former Wesleyan chapel as a village hall.[21] The village hall was opened in 1945 and was still in use in 1971. An inn, standing in High Street in the west of the village, was known from at least 1823 to 1854 as the Red Lion,[22] but since at least 1872 it has been the Bosville Arms.[23]

The present inn is a mid-19th-century building of white brick. The bridge which carries East Gate over the Gypsey Race is a 19th-century brick structure of three arches. In the mid 19th century there was a ford and a footbridge on High Street,[24] but the Race there is now culverted.

Thorpe Hall has long been the only house on the site of the former village of Thorpe, about ½ mile east of Rudston. The hall stands in 57 a. of gardens and park-land south of the Bridlington road.[25] Similarly, since at least 1762 Low Caythorpe farmhouse has been the only building on the site of the former village of Caythorpe, ½ mile further east.[26] The present building is a large brown-brick house apparently dating from the 19th century. The site of the village to the east and west of the house is marked by earthworks, including several rectangular house-sites. None of the isolated farm-houses in the parish dates from before the later 18th century. Springdale Farm includes two houses, both of whitewashed brick, one an 18th- and the other a 19th-century building.

There were beacons in 1573 at 'Many Howes in Rudston Field', presumably on the hill by the southern parish boundary, near several barrows, on which a later beacon certainly stood. Several parishes were responsible for maintaining the beacons.[27] In 1588 there were two beacons, which took light from Flamborough and Reighton and passed it on to Ruston Parva.[28] The later beacon was probably taken down c. 1830.[29]

Rudston had, together with Thorpe, 198 poll-tax payers in 1377, and Caythorpe a further 40.[30] In 1670, together with both its by then depopulated townships, Rudston had 58 households included in the hearth-tax assessment, 35 of them exempt for poverty. The exempt were not recorded in 1674, but of the 35 chargeable households 26 had only one hearth each, 3 had 2, 3 had 3, 2 had 8, and one had nine.[31] In 1743 there were said to be 50 families in the parish[32] and in 1764 42.[33] In 1801 the population was 296. It rose quickly to 518 in 1831 and to a peak of 605 in 1861, before declining to 552 in 1901.[34] It has continued to fall steadily in the 20th century and in 1961 there were 401 inhabitants.[35]

MANORS AND OTHER ESTATES. In 1086 there were three estates in Rudston, each comprising 8 carucates. One was held in 1066 by Guneware and in 1086 by Richard Surdeval of the count of Mortain.[36] It passed, probably following the count's rebellion in 1088, to William Peverell,[37] who granted it to St. Mary's abbey, York, between 1100 and 1122.[38]

The manor of RUDSTON, consisting of 37 bovates, was held by the abbey at the Dissolution

---

[15] E.R.R.O., DDWB/15/30.
[16] O.S. Map 6″ (1854).
[17] E.R.R.O., DDWB/15/53.
[18] See p. 316.
[19] W. Smith, *Springs and Streams of E.R.* 5; *Bridlington Charty.* 194.
[20] Plaque in church.
[21] Char. Com. files; Bulmer, *Dir. E. Yorks.* (1892), 259.
[22] Baines, *Hist. Yorks.* (1823), ii. 384; White, *Dir. E. & N.R. Yorks.* (1840), 396; O.S. Map 6″ (1854).
[23] Directories.
[24] O.S. Map 6″ (1854).
[25] See p. 314.
[26] E.R.R.O., DDBV/10/1.

[27] P. Royston, *Rudston: Sketch of its Hist. and Antiq.* 38–9.
[28] J. Nicholson, *Beacons of E. Yorks.* 8.
[29] Ibid. 49–51.
[30] E 179/211/35 mm. 3, 30.
[31] E 179/205/514, 521.
[32] *Herring's Visit.* iii. 36.
[33] B.I.H.R., Bp. V. 1764/Ret. 223.
[34] *V.C.H. Yorks.* iii. 490.
[35] *Census.*
[36] *V.C.H. Yorks.* ii. 226.
[37] It is wrongly stated in *V.C.H. Yorks.* ii. 185 that this manor was that held in 1066 by Ligulf and in 1086 by Uctred.
[38] *E.Y.C.* i, p. 350; *Cal. Chart. 1300–26*, 119.

and was subsequently let by the Crown. In 1552 14 bovates were let to Thomas Swinton and the whole estate in 1569 to John Harrison,[39] in 1584 to Richard Mulcaster, and in 1595 to John Palmer.[40] In 1600 it was granted in fee to Rowland Wandesford and Ralph Harrison,[41] who sold it soon after to Francis Boynton of Barmston. In 1602 he sold 18 bovates and other land to John Harrison,[42] the descent of whose estate is traced below.[43] The remainder of the manorial estate[44] descended in the Boynton family of Barmston and later of Burton Agnes.[45] At inclosure in 1777 Sir Griffith Boynton received 641 a. as lord of the manor.[46] In 1801 he sold 382 a. to Ralph Creyke of Marton,[47] but the rest was retained until 1920, when Cycely M. Wickham-Boynton sold it, then known as Manor House farm and consisting of 283 a., to Thomas Brompton.[48] In 1941 A. and H. Brompton sold it to M. E. Thompson, who still held it in 1970, except for 46 a. sold in 1950.[49] In 1874 Ralph Creyke sold about 191 a. to Walter Norton, and a year later Norton sold it to James W. Macdonald,[50] apparently a trustee of Alexander Bosville Macdonald of Thorpe Hall, a minor.[51] The land has subsequently descended with the estate of that family.[52] In 1873 Ralph Creyke had sold unspecified land in Rudston, perhaps the rest of his estate there, along with land in Kilham to Thomas Oddy.[53]

In 1473 William Scargill held 12 bovates in Rudston[54] which had apparently been subinfeudated by the abbey. In 1519 the estate was described as the manor of *RUDSTON*.[55] It descended to Margaret Scargill, wife of Sir John Gascoigne, who sold it in 1563 to Edward Gilberd.[56] He conveyed it in the following year to John Wood[57] and in 1604 Barnay Wood sold it, still described as a manor, to Robert Ellis,[58] who increased the estate by the purchase of 2 bovates from Robert Knowsley in 1614.[59] In 1653 another Robert Ellis compounded for his father's delinquency.[60] He or another Robert Ellis died apparently in 1712[61] and the estate subsequently descended through his three daughters.[62] In 1767 the manor was held by J. R. Greenhill and his wife Elizabeth, granddaughter of Robert Ellis.[63] Greenhill sold it in 1777 to John Farthing,[64] who had earlier acquired other land in Rudston.[65] At inclosure in 1777 Farthing was awarded 599 a.[66] He or another John Farthing (d. c. 1822) vested the estate in his daughter Franky, wife of James Hopkinson.[67] In 1822 the latter sold the estate, then known as Springdale and comprising 638 a., to Joseph Hopkinson.[68] C. N. and C. R. Hopkinson sold it in 1875 to J. W. Macdonald,[69] and it has since descended in the Bosville Macdonald family.[70]

Other land in Rudston formerly held by undertenants of the abbey was acquired in the later 16th century by John Harrison, whose family had held land in the parish in the reign of Henry VIII.[71] Harrison bought land in 1555 from Elizabeth Brandon, in 1566 from John Thornholme, in 1571 from Edward Warcop, in 1582 from Judith Archer, and in 1591 from the heirs of Margaret Tyndale.[72] Harrison and his son William also acquired land of other fees in the late 16th and early 17th centuries[73] and on the latter's death in 1632 he held, in addition to the land bought from Francis Boynton,[74] a capital messuage, 30 bovates, various closes, and other land.[75] In 1681 Henry Ball and his wife Dorothy, the only daughter of John Harrison, sold 13 bovates to James Cockerill.[76] In 1766 another James Cockerill sold it to John Farthing.[77] The remainder of the Harrison estate was sold before 1683 by John Harrison and after his death by his widow Anne to Sir John Buck. The estate then comprised 65 bovates and many closes. In 1752 it was sold by Sir Charles Buck to Benjamin Hudson,[78] and at inclosure in 1777 Harrington Hudson was awarded 895 a.,[79] most of which was in lieu of the former Harrison estate. In 1826 another Harrington Hudson sold his Rudston estate, then comprising 919 a., to W. J. Denison.[80] It descended in the Denison family[81] until 1906, when W. F. H. Denison, earl of Londesborough, sold it to David Holtby.[82] In 1919 Holtby sold it as two farms: Rudston House farm, of 532 a., was acquired by Ernest Dawson, and Denby House farm, of 406 a., by Arthur Falkingham.[83]

The second Domesday estate had been held in 1066 by Merlesuain and belonged in 1086 to Ralph Paynel.[84] The overlordship passed from the Paynels to the Gants in the 12th century[85] and to the Lutterells in 1230.[86] It is last mentioned in 1428.[87]

Early under-tenants of this fee were the family which took their name from the township. In the

---

[39] E 310/29/170 no. 69.
[40] E 310/30/179 no. 63.
[41] C 66/1537 m. 16.
[42] E.R.R.O., DDWB/15/84.
[43] See below.
[44] C 142/367/59.
[45] See p. 108.
[46] Registry of Deeds, Beverley, BB/18/7.
[47] Ibid. CC/570/857.
[48] Ibid. 212/464/394.
[49] Ibid. 644/539/448; 855/87/75.
[50] Ibid. LN/412/543; LU/339/499.
[51] J. T. Ward, *E. Yorks. Landed Estates in the 19th Cent.* (E. Yorks. Loc. Hist. Ser. xxiii), 60.
[52] See p. 314.
[53] Regy. of Deeds, LG/274/362; see above, p. 254.
[54] C.P. 40/848 m. 469.
[55] C 142/34/23.
[56] *Yorks. Fines*, i. 278.
[57] E.R.R.O., DDBM/19/24, 25.
[58] Ibid. /26; *Yorks. Fines, 1603–14*, 14.
[59] E.R.R.O., DDBM/19/30.
[60] *Royalist Composition Papers*, iii (Y.A.S. Rec. Ser. xx), 70–2.
[61] Regy. of Deeds, A/659/939.
[62] Ibid. Z/448/1030; see above, p. 7.
[63] Regy. of Deeds, AI/140/286; /282/568.
[64] Ibid. AS/98/161.
[65] See below.
[66] Regy. of Deeds, BB/18/7.
[67] Ibid. DM/393/470; /240/281.
[68] Ibid. /240/281.
[69] Ibid. LU/339/499.
[70] See p. 314.
[71] S.C. 12/4/18.
[72] *Yorks. Deeds*, iv. 128–31.
[73] *Yorks. Fines*, ii. 110, 137; iii. 12, 159; *1603–14*, 49.
[74] See above.
[75] C 142/727/130.
[76] E.R.R.O., DDBM/19/37, 38.
[77] Regy. of Deeds, AI/167/342.
[78] Ibid. W/183/394.
[79] Ibid. BB/18/7.
[80] Ibid. DY/210/256.
[81] Albert Denison was created Baron Londesborough in 1850 and W. H. Denison earl of Londesborough in 1887: Ward, *E. Yorks. Landed Estates*, 17–18.
[82] Regy. of Deeds, 91/4/3 (1906).
[83] Ibid. 193/483/417; /490/424.
[84] *V.C.H. Yorks.* ii. 270.
[85] *Red Bk. Exch.* (Rolls Ser.), 433.
[86] *E.Y.C.* vi, p. 140.
[87] *Feud. Aids*, vi. 268.

mid 12th century Malger son of Turold of Rudston gave one carucate in Rudston to Bridlington priory.[88] In 1166 Malger's brother Robert held land in Rudston of the Gant fee.[89] The estate had descended by *c.* 1227 to Robert's granddaughter Avice and her husband Geoffrey of Tournai.[90] In 1284–5 Richard of Tournai held 8 carucates of the Lutterell fee, of which 4 carucates were held of him by Bridlington priory.[91] In 1331 John Tournay received a grant of free warren on his Rudston estate,[92] but by 1346 the 8 carucates of this fee had passed to Thomas of Follifoot.[93] The estate subsequently became much divided.

The third Domesday estate had been held in 1066 by Ligulf and in 1086 it belonged to Uctred, a king's thegn.[94] It passed soon after 1086 to Robert de Brus and the overlordship later descended, like Burton Agnes,[95] in the Thwing and Lumley families. A mesne lordship was held of the Brus fee in Rudston by the Merlay family in 1284–5.[96] Again like Burton Agnes, this descended in the 14th century to the Greystock and Somerville families and later to the Griffiths of Burton Agnes.[97]

The demesne tenants of the Brus fee in the 13th century were members of the Rudston family. In 1284–5 the heirs of William of Rudston held 8 carucates of the Brus fee and another William of Rudston was returned as one of the lords of Rudston in 1316.[98] In 1352 3 bovates were held of William of Rudston,[99] the last reference to the family. By 1428 six under-tenants held a total of 47 bovates of the Brus fee, the largest holding being the 16 bovates held by Richard Fairfax.[1] Sir Thomas Fairfax died in 1505 seised of the manor of RUDSTON.[2] Sir William Fairfax sold it in 1578 to John Wright[3] and he in 1596 to William Constable of Caythorpe and Thomas Pearson.[4] It was subsequently split up.

Several religious houses, besides St. Mary's abbey, held land in Rudston in the Middle Ages. The largest estate was that of Bridlington priory. In the mid 12th century Malger of Rudston gave the priory one carucate and by the early 14th century other grants, many by members of the Rudston family, had increased the priory's estate to over 20 bovates.[5] The value of the property in 1535 was nearly £6.[6] In 1562 the lands of the former priory, amounting to over 32 bovates, were let to John Fisher.[7] The Crown subsequently let the estate in holdings of various sizes, the last lease, of 9 bovates, being in 1591.[8] No grant of the estate has been found but it is likely that it passed to the Boynton family.[9]

St. Mary's abbey granted 4 bovates in 1254 to Meaux abbey[10] and in 1535 Meaux's estate was worth 16s.[11] It was granted in 1610 to Edward Bates and Henry Elwes and they sold it to Sir Francis Boynton the same year.[12]

In the mid 13th century William of Haisthorpe granted a rent of 10s. from land in Rudston to Swine priory.[13] The priory held land there in the mid 15th century,[14] and in 1535 its estate was worth 3s.[15] The property, amounting to one bovate, was let in 1567 to Thomas Scothorpe.[16] Property in Rudston formerly held by Warter priory was granted in 1541 to Thomas Manners, earl of Rutland.[17] In 1539–40 the Knights Hospitallers received rents from property in Rudston,[18] and it was restored to them when the order was briefly revived in 1558.[19]

In 1086 there were three estates at Caythorpe. The largest, consisting of 5 carucates, had been held as two manors in 1066 by Egfrid and Chilbert and in 1086 it was held by the king. Another, of 4 carucates, was held in both 1066 and 1086 as part of St. Peter's liberty, York, by the archbishop of York. The third estate comprised 3 carucates and was held in 1086 by the count of Mortain.[20] The overlordship of St. Peter's was last mentioned in 1542.[21] The count's estate was granted between *c.* 1100 and 1115, when it consisted of 4 carucates, to St. Mary's abbey, York, by Niel Fossard,[22] who seems to have been the count's tenant in 1086 or soon after. The overlordship of St. Mary's was also last mentioned in 1542.[23]

The manor of CAYTHORPE was formed mainly out of the archbishop's and the Mortain estates. It may have originated in the grant of 4 carucates by St. Mary's abbey between 1122 and *c.* 1137 to Siward of Caythorpe. A further ½ carucate was granted by the abbey between *c.* 1137 and 1161 to Siward's son William.[24] William of Caythorpe died in 1296 seised of 4 carucates held of St. Mary's and 4 more held of St. Peter's.[25] In 1346 John of Caythorpe also held 4 bovates of the Aumale fee.[26] The manor descended in the Caythorpe family until 1434, when it was settled on Eustachia, daughter of John Caythorpe and widow of Richard Fairfax.[27] It descended in the Fairfax family until 1513, when Thomas Fairfax sold his property in Caythorpe and Rudston to William Constable,[28] son of Sir Robert Constable of Flamborough[29] and the first member of the family of Constable of Caythorpe. The manor and the Rudston lands[30] descended in this family

---

[88] *E.Y.C.* ii, p. 487; *Bridlington Charty.* 191–2; see below.
[89] *E.Y.C.* ii, p. 488 n. [90] Ibid. vi, p. 140.
[91] *Feud. Aids*, vi. 30.
[92] *Cal. Chart. R.* 1327–41, 229. [93] *Feud. Aids*, vi. 212.
[94] *V.C.H. Yorks.* ii. 287.
[95] See p. 107. [96] *Feud. Aids*, vi. 30.
[97] *Cal. Inq. p.m.* vi, pp. 30, 307; viii, p. 88.
[98] *Feud. Aids*, vi. 30, 168.
[99] *Cal. Inq. p.m.* ix, p. 459.
[1] *Feud. Aids*, vi. 266.
[2] *Cal. Inq. p.m. Hen. VII*, ii, pp. 582–3.
[3] *Yorks. Fines*, ii. 115.
[4] Ibid. iv. 48. Sir William was still said to have been seised of the manor on his death in 1598 (C 142/255/127) but it was not held by Thomas, Viscount Fairfax, on his death in 1637 (C 142/554/74).
[5] E.R.R.O., DDWB/15/1, 6, 10; *Bridlington Charty.* 7, 185, 188–90, 193.
[6] *Valor Eccl.* (Rec. Com.), v. 120.
[7] E 310/33/197 no. 58.
[8] E 310/29/175 no. 41; /30/177 no. 43; /31/183 no. 22; /32/194 no. 129; /33/202 no. 115.
[9] See p. 312. [10] *Yorks. Fines, 1246–72*, 96.
[11] *Valor Eccl.* v. 108.
[12] E.R.R.O., DDWB/15/64. [13] Ibid. /26.
[14] *Cal. Pat.* 1446–52, 306.
[15] *Valor Eccl.* v. 114. [16] E 310/31/183 no. 22.
[17] E.R.R.O., DDEV/50/13.
[18] *Miscellanea*, iv (Y.A.S. Rec. Ser. xciv), 93.
[19] *Cal. Pat.* 1557–8, 319.
[20] *V.C.H. Yorks.* ii. 204, 211, 226, 323.
[21] C 142/65/79.
[22] *E.Y.C.* ii, p. 325.
[23] C 142/65/79.
[24] *E.Y.C.* ii, p. 372.
[25] *Yorks. Inq.* iii. 34.
[26] *Feud. Aids*, vi. 228.
[27] C.P. 25(1)/280/157 no. 17; *T.E.R.A.S.* vii. 7.
[28] C 142/48/91.
[29] W. Flower, *Visit. Yorks.* (Harl. Soc. xvi), 65.
[30] See above.

until 1709, when John Constable sold them to John Hudson.[31] Caythorpe manor was held by the Hudson family until after the death of Harrington Hudson c. 1827.[32] In 1831 the property was sold by Hudson's trustees to the trustees of William Bosville of Thorpe,[33] and it has since descended with Thorpe manor.[34]

The king's Domesday estate had passed by 1284–5 to the earl of Aumale's fee of Holderness. The Aumale overlordship is last mentioned in 1428. A mesne lordship in Caythorpe was held of the earl by Ingram de Mounceaux in 1284–5[35] and it descended in the Mounceaux family until 1419, when John de Mounceaux granted it to Brian del See.[36] In 1497 it was settled on Margaret Boynton, daughter of Sir Martin del See,[37] and she still held it in 1521.[38] The estate was divided among several under-tenants.[39]

In 1086 there was one estate of 3 carucates at Thorpe held by the count of Mortain.[40] After the count's forfeiture it probably passed to the archbishop of Canterbury, the overlord in 1284–5, and his overlordship is last mentioned in 1428. The Meynell family held a mesne lordship under the archbishops by 1284–5[41] and it was last referred to in 1528.[42]

An early demesne tenant of this fee seems to have been the family of Thorpe, a member of which is first recorded in the late 12th century.[43] In 1299, however, Robert of Boynton held all 3 carucates in Thorpe of Nicholas de Meynell, possibly as a second mesne lordship.[44] In 1305 he granted to Robert of Thorpe a toft and a bovate in Thorpe,[45] and in 1316 the latter was returned as lord of the township.[46] In 1379 Robert of Thorpe held 9 bovates there.[47] The Thorpe family are last referred to in 1396[48] and the 14 bovates at Thorpe in 1428 were held by three under-tenants.[49]

By the earlier 16th century the manor of THORPE had passed to Thomas Newport, who sold it in 1548 to Thomas Thwaite.[50] In 1557 Thwaite sold the manor to John Wood.[51] He increased the estate by purchases from Francis Constable of Caythorpe in 1561, and from John Wright in 1588.[52] He also bought land in Rudston from Thomas Smith in 1560.[53] The manorial estate descended in the Wood family until c. 1695, when Thomas Wood devised it, then consisting of pasture closes and 24 bovates, to his relative Thomas Hassell.[54] Another Thomas Hassell died in 1773[55] and two years later the estate was sold by Giles Earle of Beningbrough and members of the Bourchier family, presumably Hassell's devisees or trustees, to Godfrey Bosville.[56]

Bosville's daughter Elizabeth had married Sir Alexander Macdonald in 1768 and in the early 19th century their son Godfrey assumed the additional name of Bosville.[57] The estate has since descended in the Bosville Macdonald family. In 1955 it comprised over 4,000 a. in Rudston, Thorpe, and Caythorpe[58] and in 1970 it was owned by Sir Ian G. Bosville Macdonald, Bt., of Sleat.

Thorpe Hall, the seat of the Bosville Macdonald family, is an extensive house of brick, mostly covered with rough-cast, with stone or plaster quoins and slate roofs concealed behind parapets. It dates largely from the 18th and 19th centuries. The original house forms a square three-storeyed block near the east end of the present building. Much of the walling and two stone-mullioned basement windows on the south front may date from the late 17th or early 18th century, but the house was probably extensively remodelled, externally and internally, in the middle of the 18th century.[59] The entrance front, facing north, is of five bays and has liberal stone dressings. The central bay breaks slightly forward and, like the ends of the elevation, has bold rusticated quoins. The central entrance, with a 19th-century Tuscan doorcase, is contained in a prominent enclosed porch of the same date, which also has rusticated quoins. Above the entrance, the round-headed first-floor window and the second-floor window both have painted plaster surrounds. The parapet over the central bay is raised into a high centre-piece decorated with a single shell motif. The south front, now rough-cast to match the later parts of the building, is also of five bays. There are quoins to the central projecting bay and, between the ground and first floors, a central Venetian window to light the staircase. The interior of the original house contains some mid-18th-century features but most date from the Regency period and later.

At each end of this original house a projecting cross-wing was built, perhaps in the late 18th century. The gallery contained in one of the wings is said to have been added in 1779.[60] They both, however, bear signs of an extensive remodelling in the early 19th century and contain no interior features earlier than the Regency period. The east wing contains a large Regency ground-floor window on the east elevation with a blocked window on each side. Both wings also have large ground-floor windows on both north and south elevations. The wings, which are of two storeys but are nearly as high as the original three-storeyed block, have parapets and plaster quoins to match the stone ones on the older house, but there is also a band between the storeys. At the west end of the house a long two-storeyed range, ending in another cross-wing, was added, it is said, in 1886.[61] This addition, which was built in a similar style to that of the earlier wings, nearly doubled the size of the house.

[31] Regy. of Deeds, A/172/236.
[32] Ibid. DZ/340/389.
[33] E.R.R.O., DDBM/5/4.
[34] See below.
[35] Feud. Aids, vi. 30, 267.
[36] E.R.R.O., DDWB/20/22.
[37] Ibid. DDCC/3/22.
[38] Ibid. /141/66.
[39] Feud. Aids, vi. 211, 267.
[40] V.C.H. Yorks. ii. 226, 323.
[41] Feud. Aids, vi. 30, 265.
[42] C 142/48/91.
[43] Bridlington Charty. 191–2.
[44] Cal. Inq. p.m. iii, p. 428.
[45] E.R.R.O., DDCC/90/1.
[46] Feud. Aids, vi. 169.
[47] Cal. Inq. p.m. xv, p. 31.
[48] Cal. Close, 1392–6, 501.
[49] Feud. Aids, vi. 265.
[50] E.R.R.O., DDBM/19/22; Yorks. Fines, i. 136, 165.
[51] E.R.R.O., DDBM/19/1, 22.
[52] Ibid. /4, 22.
[53] Yorks. Fines, i. 241.
[54] E.R.R.O., DDBM/19/15, 22; /35/6.
[55] Regy. of Deeds, AS/90/150.
[56] Ibid. AW/78/125.
[57] Ward, E. Yorks. Landed Estates, 59; for pedigree see Burke, Peerage (1963), 1549.
[58] Regy. of Deeds, 1002/377/325.
[59] Ex inf. Dr. I. Hall, 1970; the house is illus. in G. B. Wood, Historic Homes of Yorks. pl. 41.
[60] Wood, Hist. Homes of Yorks. 124.
[61] Ibid. 125.

Near the house are several outbuildings dating from the early 19th century. They include an orangery, an octagonal timber-built game larder, and a dairy.[62] The dairy, also octagonal, has projecting eaves supported on cast-iron columns to form a verandah; some of the two-light round-headed windows contain stained glass roundels, and internally there are marble tables in the centre and round the walls.[63] Further from the house is a long red-brick stable block, with a central pediment and a modillion cornice, probably dating from the later 18th century. Near by are kennels and a dovecot. The hexagonal dovecot, probably of the early 19th century, is built of timber and supported on high brick pillars; a central cupola contains entrance holes.[64]

The gardens and park, together containing 57 a.,[65] lie south and east of the house. They incorporate two lakes, formed by the construction of weirs across the Gypsey Race. The upper lake is said to have been made in 1815, to provide employment during the agricultural depression, and the other a few years later. Near the stables the Race is spanned by a three-arched bridge, faced with sea-worn stone from Filey Brigg.[66]

The rectorial tithes of Rudston belonged to St. Mary's abbey, York, from the mid 14th century.[67] In 1540–1 they were worth nearly £22.[68] The rectory was let by the abbey and was held by Anthony Fenton in 1532[69] and Christopher Fenton in 1540–1.[70] After the Dissolution it was let by the Crown to Michael Green in 1551 and 1567,[71] William Green in 1582,[72] and William Langford in 1590.[73] In 1600 it was granted in fee to Rowland Wandesford and Ralph Harrison,[74] and they sold it soon after to Francis Boynton, who died seised of it in 1617.[75] The rectory was worth £140 in 1650.[76] At inclosure in 1777 Sir Griffith Boynton was awarded 236 a. in lieu of half the corn tithes in Rudston, 21 a. for half those in that part of Caythorpe township within Rudston parish, and 14 a. for half those in Thorpe. He received rent-charges for the other half of the tithes: £111 in Rudston, £15 in Caythorpe, and £10 in Thorpe.[77] The rectorial estate descended with the capital manor[78] until 1920, when Cycely M. Wickham-Boynton sold it, then known as Hinds House farm and consisting of 273 a., to Albert and Henry Robson.[79] It was still held by the Robson family, as Breeze farm, in 1970.

When the church was appropriated to the abbey in 1354 the archbishop of York reserved to himself as indemnity a pension of £1 10s., and another of 10s. to the chapter of York.[80] These were still paid out of Sir Francis Boynton's rectorial estate in 1816, although the archbishop's pension had decreased to £1.[81] In 1920 the rectorial estate paid a yearly pension of 10s. 8d. to the Ecclesiastical Commissioners.[82]

ECONOMIC HISTORY. In 1086 the estates of the count of Mortain and Ralph Paynel in Rudston were waste. Paynel's estate contained land for four ploughs and had been worth £3 in 1066. The third estate, held by Uctred, also had land for four ploughs, although in 1086 there were only two, one held by Uctred himself and the other by five villeins.[83] Of the three estates in Caythorpe in 1086, that held by the king contained land for three ploughs and was worth £1. The archbishop of York's estate had land for two ploughs and had decreased in value from 10s. in 1066 to 8s.[84] No economic information is given about the third Domesday estate in Caythorpe or that in Thorpe.

Information about the open-field system of Rudston is scanty. A late-12th- or early-13th-century grant refers to a bovate of land lying regularly throughout 'the whole field of Rudston',[85] and 2 bovates were similarly described in 1312.[86] Four bovates lay waste in 1352.[87] There were presumably two or more fields, although a reference in 1331 to South field[88] is the only indication of a name. All the land allotted at inclosure in 1777 was simply said to lie in 'the fields of Rudston'.[89] The open fields lay upon the wold slopes to the west, north, and south of the village. Grain-bearing land (*terram granosam*) in 1520 lay on 'Speteykes',[90] and Spittecks was the name of a bovate in 1616.[91] Spithooks is the modern name of the area south of the village and east of the Kilham road.[92] In 1663 7 bovates known as Long Lands lay between the village and Burton Fleming.[93] Corn from Rudston was supplied to the king in the late 13th and early 14th centuries. In 1298 wheat was sent to Wansford and thence to Hull, and in 1304 corn from Rudston was again sent to Hull.[94] In 1316 corn from the manor was sent to St. Mary's abbey, York.[95]

The village of Caythorpe was partially inclosed and probably wholly depopulated before 1517 by Sir Thomas Fairfax, who converted 300 a. of arable to pasture, evicted 20 people, and destroyed five houses.[96] Any open-field land which remained was probably never again cultivated in common. In 1540 Jane Constable had a flock of 400 sheep in Caythorpe field.[97] By 1762 the whole township was inclosed. South of the Sledmere–Bridlington road the closes are irregular and may represent the late-15th- or early-16th-century inclosure. The more

---

[62] The orangery and dairy are said to be of 1821: ibid.
[63] See plate facing p. 209.
[64] Illus. Wood, *Hist. Homes of Yorks.* pl. 42.
[65] Regy. of Deeds, 1002/377/325.
[66] Wood, *Hist. Homes of Yorks.* 126.
[67] See p. 317.
[68] S.C. 6/Hen. VIII/4595.
[69] *L. & P. Hen. VIII,* v, p. 522.
[70] S.C. 6/Hen. VIII/4595.
[71] E.R.R.O., DDWB/15/71; E 310/29/172 no. 12; *Cal. Pat.* 1566–9, 65.
[72] E.R.R.O., DDWB/15/62.
[73] C 66/1345 m. 13.
[74] C 66/1537 m. 16; E.R.R.O., DDWB/15/82a.
[75] C 142/367/59.
[76] *T.E.R.A.S.* ii. 56.
[77] Registry of Deeds, Beverley, BB/18/7.
[78] See p. 312.
[79] Regy. of Deeds, 207/337/302.
[80] *Fasti Parochiales,* iii. 69.
[81] E.R.R.O., DDWB/23/38.
[82] Regy. of Deeds, 207/337/302.
[83] *V.C.H. Yorks.* ii. 226, 270, 287.
[84] Ibid. 204, 211.
[85] *Bridlington Charty.* 85–6.
[86] E.R.R.O., DDWB/15/30.
[87] *Cal. Inq. p.m.* ix, p. 459.
[88] E.R.R.O., DDWB/15/37.
[89] Registry of Deeds, Beverley, BB/18/7.
[90] *Test. Ebor.* v. 116–17.
[91] B.I.H.R., C.P., H. 1183.
[92] O.S. Map 2½" (1953).
[93] B.I.H.R., TER. J. Rudston n.d.
[94] *Y.A.J.* xlii. 141; see above, p. 291.
[95] *Cal. Pat.* 1313–17, 555.
[96] *Trans. R.H.S.* n.s. vii. 247; *Y.A.J.* xxxviii. 59.
[97] *Test. Ebor.* vi. 106–7.

regular fields to the north were perhaps the result of later inclosure by the Constable or Hudson families. Two large closes on the lower slopes north of the road were called the 'east and west sides of the Tillage field'. North of these lay the two sides of Chemidale field.[98] The boundary between Tillage and Chemidale fields was described in 1800 as the division between 'swarth' and tillage.[99]

Thorpe probably had its own field system, though it is not known how long a village community survived there.[1] In 1688 and 1775 24 bovates in North and South fields belonged to the manor,[2] but it is unlikely that the open-field area was cultivated in common after the depopulation of the village. A reference in 1775 to the 'arable part of Thorpe North field'[3] suggests that another part of the field was then either permanent pasture or used as leys. The whole township was divided into closes by 1850.[4]

The low-lying ground beside the Gypsey Race presumably provided meadow land for all three townships from an early date. In 1762 three closes bordering the stream in Caythorpe were called Long Holmes and Carr, Middle Holmes, and Holmes,[5] and in 1850 South ings lay south of the stream in Rudston.[6] In 1279–80 the rector of Rudston was given common rights for himself and his successors in 24 a. of meadow, for all animals except pigs, from hay-making to 11 November.[7]

Permanent pasture land, together with common rights in the open fields, seems to have supported many sheep in the parish. In 1466, for example, a tenant of Martin del See owned 240 sheep,[8] and Jane Constable had 400 at Caythorpe in 1540.[9] The upper wold slopes were probably the main areas of pasture. In 1762 the 'swarth' area in the north of Caythorpe included closes called North Whins and Old Leys, and on the slopes south of the Bridlington road lay Hord and Rayle pastures.[10] In Thorpe the Cow pasture is mentioned in 1688 and North ings in 1775.[11] In 1850 there were three areas in Rudston known as 'the Sheepwalk', one in the far west of the parish, another in the south around Rudston Beacon, and the third on the slopes north of Thorpe Hall. The Great pasture lay in the south of Thorpe and Caythorpe.[12] In the later 16th century pasture on certain common balks which were called Rudston St. Mary's was parcelled out among the poorer villagers at small rents.[13] In 1772 a cottage in Rudston had one beast-gate and five sheep-gates.[14] During an outbreak of 'distemper' among horned cattle in 1748–9, nearly 250 beasts died in Rudston.[15]

It is not clear how much early inclosure took place in Rudston, but some ancient inclosed lands, including Gare closes, are recorded. The remaining open-field area was inclosed in 1777,[16] under an Act of 1774,[17] when 3,665 a. were allotted. Sir Griffith Boynton, as lord of the manor, received 641 a., as well as 271 a. for tithes, and the vicar was allotted 254 a. for glebe and tithes. Three other men received large allotments: Godfrey Bosville got 997 a., Harrington Hudson 895 a., and John Farthing 599 a. There was also one allotment of 2 a. and 6 of 1 a.

On the lower-lying grounds near the Gypsey Race there was a constant danger of flooding,[18] and in 1809 many people were forced to leave their homes.[19] In the earlier 18th century responsibility for cleansing the Race was put into the pains, but in 1740 Benjamin Hudson and other landowners asked that it should be removed as 'scouring it only makes the water sink into the ground'. In the same year, however, other inhabitants asked that it should be continued in pain 'otherwise Rudston will suffer damage from flooding'. It seems to have been removed, for in 1761 owners and occupiers of land adjoining the Race petitioned that it should again be put in pain to be scoured. At inclosure in 1777 provision was made for that part of the Race from the Burton Fleming boundary to the main street of Rudston to be kept clean at public expense.[20]

Sainfoin was grown in Rudston in the later 18th century.[21] In 1801 816 a. were under crops, mainly barley (280 a.), rape or turnips (200 a.), and oats (190 a.),[22] and in 1905 about six times as much land was under arable as pasture.[23] A mixed farming economy supported large flocks of Leicester sheep in the parish in the later 19th century.[24] There have usually been from 9 to 12 farms in the parish in the 19th and 20th centuries, although in the 1930s the number increased to between 13 and fifteen.[25] Several of them were large. In 1775 two farms owned by Godfrey Bosville were of 463 a. and 465 a.,[26] and of the twelve owned by the Bosville Macdonald family in 1955 one, Low Caythorpe, was over 800 a., one was over 500 a., and three were between 400 a. and 500 a.[27]

There was probably a brickworks in the parish from at least the early 17th to the later 18th century. A kiln was owned by William Harrison in 1618[28] and Harrington Hudson, the owner of the former Harrison estate,[29] was directed to make a brickyard near the Kilham road on land allotted to him at inclosure in 1777.[30] He was required to dig within six years enough clay to make 300,000 bricks on land 'adjoining upon that part . . . from whence bricks have heretofore been made'. If the brickyard was duly made, it is not known when it closed. Brick Kiln close was sold by Harrington Hudson to W. J. Denison in 1826,[31] but there was no brickyard in the parish in 1850.[32]

A mill is first recorded in Rudston in 1227.[33] In

[98] E.R.R.O., DDBV/10/1.
[99] Ibid. DDBM/5/1.
[1] Y.A.J. xxxviii. 69.
[2] E.R.R.O., DDBM/19/15; Regy. of Deeds, AW/78/125.
[3] E.R.R.O., DDBM/19/5.
[4] O.S. Map 6" (1854).
[5] E.R.R.O., DDBV/10/1.
[6] O.S. Map 6" (1854).
[7] J.I. 1/1056 m. 26.
[8] T.E.R.A.S. xix. 74.
[9] Test. Ebor. vi. 106–7.
[10] E.R.R.O., DDBV/10/1.
[11] Ibid. DDBM/19/6, 15.
[12] O.S. Map 6" (1854).
[13] T.E.R.A.S. xix. 77.
[14] Regy. of Deeds, R/58/135.
[15] P. Royston, Rudston: Sketch of its Hist. & Antiq. 35–6.
[16] Regy. of Deeds, BB/18/7.
[17] 14 Geo. III, c. 79 (Priv. Act).
[18] E.R.R.O., CSR/4/358; /12/97; /19/76; /20/35; /27/30; /31/357, 396.
[19] Royston, Rudston, 36.
[20] Regy. of Deeds, BB/18/7.
[21] E.R.R.O., DDBM/19/6.
[22] 1801 Crop Returns.
[23] Acreage Returns, 1905.
[24] Royston, Rudston, 55.
[25] Directories.
[26] E.R.R.O., DDBM/19/5, 6.
[27] Regy. of Deeds, 1002/377/325.
[28] Yorks. Fines, 1614–25, 114.
[29] See p. 312.
[30] Regy. of Deeds, BB/18/7.
[31] Ibid. DY/210/256.
[32] O.S. Map 6" (1854).

1296 William of Caythorpe held a water-mill and a windmill in Caythorpe,[34] and three years later a water-mill was mentioned in Rudston.[35] There was a manorial windmill in Thorpe in 1584[36] and a windmill belonged to the Harrison estate in Rudston in 1620.[37] There is no later reference to mills, but Mill close adjoined Low Caythorpe farm-house in 1762.[38]

LOCAL GOVERNMENT. The assize of ale was a franchise of Rudston manor. Infringements of it were still prosecuted in 1652, when the court also dealt with affrays and enforced parish labour.[39] In 1666 all the court's business concerned agrarian offences.[40] In 1610 there was a pinder.[41]

Churchwardens' accounts survive for 1747–1894.[42] There were always two churchwardens. Money was regularly spent at the beating of the bounds. In 1822 four cottages belonging to the parish were occupied by paupers.[43] In 1836 Rudston joined the Bridlington union.[44]

CHURCH. There was a church at Rudston between 1100 and 1122, when the advowson was given by William Peverell to St. Mary's abbey, York.[45] The church was appropriated to the abbey in 1354 and a vicarage ordained the same year.[46] In 1958 Grindale and Argam and in 1963 Boynton were united with the benefice,[47] but in 1970 Grindale and Argam were detached from it.[48] A chapel at Caythorpe was mentioned for the first and only time in 1556.[49]

The abbey's patronage was unsuccessfully disputed by certain tenants of the Lutterell fee from the late 12th to the 14th century.[50] Although the Crown often presented incumbents during vacancies,[51] the advowson of the vicarage was retained by the abbey until the Dissolution. A grant of it to the archbishop of York in 1558[52] presumably lapsed on the accession of Elizabeth I. The Crown presented in 1571 and 1603, and the archbishop collated by cession in 1612, but by 1661 the patronage had passed to Sir Francis Boynton.[53] Since at least 1717 the advowson has belonged to the archbishop.[54]

The church was worth £40 in 1291, reduced to £26 13s. 4d. in the new taxation. By 1291 it was charged with a portion of £4 and a pension of £1 10s., payable to St. Mary's abbey.[55] By 1305 a pension was also paid to St. John's college, Beverley.[56] The rector claimed in 1280–1 that his predecessor had been granted a free tenement, carrying right of common in 24 a. of meadow, by William Bolle. The gift was confirmed to the church that year.[57]

At the ordination of 1354 the vicar was awarded a house, the small tithes and oblations, and 3 bovates of land from the rectorial glebe, worth altogether £16 8s. 9d. The abbey was to be responsible for the upkeep of the chancel and all other burdens. In 1357, however, the ordination was altered; the vicar was awarded 7 bovates, with the provision that he was to bear all burdens ordinarily incumbent on the church, together with a third of the extraordinary ones except the upkeep of the chancel.[58] In 1525–6 the vicarage was valued at £8,[59] in 1535 at £9 13s. 6d. net,[60] and in 1650 at £45.[61] In 1829–31 the average net income of the living was £236.[62] The net income in 1884 was £300, having recently diminished by nearly £100.[63] The new living of Argam and Grindale was allotted £100 from the income of Rudston in 1970.[64]

Tithes accounted for most of the income in 1535.[65] Between 1535 and 1685 the hay tithe of Caythorpe was commuted to a yearly payment of 6s. 8d.[66] At inclosure in 1777 the vicar received 63 a. for half his tithes in Rudston, 17 a. for half those in Thorpe, and 13 a. for half those in that part of Caythorpe within Rudston. For the other half he received rent-charges of £24 10s. in Rudston, £10 10s. in Thorpe, and £7 10s. in Caythorpe.[67] There were 7 bovates of glebe in 1535[68] and at inclosure the vicar received 161 a. for them.[69] Glebe farm, consisting of 259 a., was sold in 1949 to Sir Godfrey M. Bosville Macdonald.[70]

A parsonage house was awarded at the ordination of 1354, but it was not mentioned again until 1663.[71] It was in disrepair in 1701 and 1706,[72] and in 1710, during a sequestration of the vicarage, the vicarial tithes were ordered to be used to pay for its repair.[73] A new house was apparently built soon after, for in 1716 the Vicarage was said to have been given by the then vicar.[74] In 1764 the house was described as chalk-built and thatched, and it contained three ground-floor rooms, two chambers, and garrets. There were also chalk-built barn and stable. By 1777 the house had been repaired with brick and had a tiled roof.[75] Between 1818 and 1835 it fell into disrepair.[76] A new house was provided by A. W. M.

---

[33] *Yorks. Fines, 1218–31*, 102.
[34] *Cal. Inq. p.m.* iii, p. 200.
[35] B.M. Add. MS. 26737, f. 58.
[36] *Yorks. Fines*, iii. 19.
[37] C 2/Jas.I /D 1/31.
[38] E.R.R.O., DDBV/10/1.
[39] Ibid. /86.
[40] Ibid. /87.
[41] *T.E.R.A.S.* xix. 78.
[42] Par. rec. in vestry.
[43] Registry of Deeds, Beverley, DM/240/281.
[44] *3rd Rep. Poor Law Com.* 167.
[45] *E.Y.C.* i, p. 350.
[46] *Fasti Parochiales*, iii. 69.
[47] York Dioc. Regy., Orders in Council 747, 781.
[48] Ex inf. Revd. Dr. W. B. Johnston, Burton Fleming, 1970.
[49] E.R.R.O., DDCC/139/65.
[50] *E.Y.C.* i, pp. 351–2; *Rolls of Justices in Eyre for Yorks.* (Selden Soc. lvi), 102–5; *Yorks. Fines, 1218–31*, 46; *Cal. Cur. Reg. R.* x. 330, 344; xi. 29–30; xii. 32; *Monastic Notes*, ii (Y.A.S. Rec. Ser. lxxxi), 55, 57, 65; *Cal. Pat.* 1348–50, 212.
[51] *Fasti Parochiales*, iii. 72; *Cal. Pat.* 1396–9, 277, 286, 354.
[52] *Cal. Pat.* 1557–8, 420.
[53] *Fasti Parochiales*, iii. 73.
[54] Inst. Bks. (1717–1823); *Rep. Com. Eccl. Revenues*, 962–3; *Crockford*, 1967–8.
[55] *Tax. Eccl.* (Rec. Com.), 304.
[56] *Beverley Chapter Act Bk.* (Sur. Soc. xcviii), 82.
[57] J.I. 1/1056 m. 26; /1067 m. 59d., 60; /1076 m. 28d.
[58] *Fasti Parochiales*, iii. 69.
[59] *Y.A.J.* xxiv. 65.
[60] *Valor Eccl.* (Rec. Com), v. 123.
[61] *T.E.R.A.S.* ii. 56.
[62] *Rep. Com. Eccl. Revenues*, 962–3.
[63] B.I.H.R., Bp. V. 1884/Ret.
[64] Ex inf. Revd. Dr. Johnston.
[65] *Valor Eccl.* v. 123.
[66] B.I.H.R., TER. J. Rudston 1663.
[67] Regy. of Deeds, BB/18/7.
[68] *Valor Eccl.* v. 123.
[69] Regy. of Deeds, BB/18/7.
[70] Ibid. 816/470/376.
[71] B.I.H.R., TER. J. Rudston n.d.
[72] Ibid. Churches index.
[73] Ibid. Bp. 3/54–5.
[74] Ibid. Bp. 5/225; TER. J. Rudston 1716.
[75] Ibid. TER. J. Rudston 1764, 1777.
[76] Lawton, *Rer. Eccles. Dioc. Ebor.* 307; *Rep. Com. Eccl. Revenues*, 962–3.

Bosville Macdonald in 1888 and was subsequently enlarged by subscription.[77] It was replaced by a new Vicarage in 1964,[78] built on a different site near the church.

There was a guild in the church before the Dissolution, apparently dedicated to the Virgin. In 1548 a cottage called 'the guild-house', which had belonged to it, was granted to Sir Michael Stanhope and John Bellow.[79] Other grants of the house were, however, made to Francis Barker and Thomas Brown in 1571 and to Francis Morrice and Francis Philips in 1611.[80]

In 1255 Wichard *transmontanus* was replaced as rector of Rudston under a papal constitution for the removal of non-resident foreigners.[81] There are numerous instances of plurality and non-residence by incumbents in the Middle Ages and later. In 1300 John of Snainton was licensed to celebrate for one year in an oratory in his uncle's manor of Snainton (Yorks. N.R.),[82] and about fourteen years later he was a canon of Howden and archbishop's clerk as well as rector of Rudston. John of Nassington, the next rector, was a canon of York and the archbishop's official and vicar-general.[83] The rector was licensed to be absent for two years in both 1331 and 1337,[84] and in 1414 he was permitted to farm the revenues of the vicarage and his other benefices during ten years absence.[85] The vicar was non-resident and held other livings in 1567, and he did not employ a curate.[86] The vicar in 1743 was also vicar of Burton Fleming and of Hayton with Bielby, as well as assistant curate of Givendale with Millington. He then lived at Pocklington and the vicar of Kilham had recently been taking the services at Rudston.[87] In 1764 the vicar was non-resident but had an assistant curate.[88] In 1835 the incumbent was also rector of Holy Trinity, York, and a vicar-choral at York Minster, and he employed an assistant curate at Rudston.[89] From at least 1865 to 1871 the vicar was minister of a proprietary chapel in London, where he lived, and he employed a curate at Rudston.[90] Later vicars have been resident. Nathanial Grantham (vicar 1612–61)[91] refused to pay the clerical subsidy in 1632 and 1634.[92]

In 1743 a service was held every Sunday and communion was administered four times a year, usually to about fifty people.[93] In 1846 the vicar, Robert Dallin, was suspended for drunkenness,[94] and the relative smallness of the congregation was attributed by the curate in 1865 to 'the great neglect of past years'. By 1865 there were two services each Sunday and communion was received every month by about fourteen people. By 1871 communicants were said to have increased to about twenty[95] and by 1884 to have decreased to twelve. In 1936 communion was administered weekly,[96] and in 1970 there were two services each Sunday, three every fourth week.

The church of *ALL SAINTS*, built wholly of stone, consists of chancel, nave with north and south aisles, west tower, and south porch. Of the Norman building all that remains externally is the lower part of the tower, below the belfry stage, where Norman masonry can still be seen. It is unbuttressed and contains a plain blocked round-headed west doorway into which has been set a trefoil-headed lancet window. There are small round-headed windows in the north, south, and west faces. The tower was heightened during the restoration of 1861[97] and the whole belfry stage appears to be of that date. It is surmounted by an embattled parapet and on each face is a round-headed opening of two lights, divided by a mid-wall shaft. Inside the church the plain round-headed tower arch and the round font, decorated with a curious diaper pattern, are also Norman.

The three-bay aisles, probably dating from c. 1300, have pointed arches supported on circular piers. The east windows in the aisles are pointed and contain reticulated tracery. The remaining aisle windows are square-headed. All are in the style of the later 14th century but date from the 1861 restoration.[98] There are piscinae at the east end of both aisles and a rectangular partially blocked opening, which may have been a squint, in the north aisle. The chancel was built or remodelled in the 14th century and has prominent buttresses, with gables and finials, of that period. The windows contain geometrical tracery: except for the two most westerly, which are original, they are later-19th-century facsimiles.[99] There is a large trefoiled piscina and three trefoiled sedilia, with richly crocketed gables, in the south wall, together with a priest's door.

In 1540 Jane Constable left £1 to repair 'the body of the church'.[1] The chancel needed repair in 1676 and the whole church in 1706.[2] A gallery was built, probably at the west end, in 1748.[3] The church was thoroughly repaired in 1829.[4] A major restoration was carried out by G. Fowler Jones in 1861. The aisles and south porch were rebuilt, the chancel screen removed, the church reroofed, and the tower heightened.[5] The church was decorated in 1869 by 'Mr. Collman of London', and the reredos of Ancaster stone, with marble shafts to the arcading and panels filled with Minton tiles, dates from then.[6] A wooden choir vestry was constructed in 1938 at the west end of the north aisle in memory of Alice E. Bosville Macdonald.[7]

There is a 14th-century coffin lid with an elabor-

---

[77] Bulmer, *Dir. E. Yorks.* (1892), 259.
[78] Ex inf. the vicar, 1970.
[79] *Cal. Pat.* 1548–9, 38.
[80] Ibid. 1569–72, 237; E.R.R.O., DDDA/3/7.
[81] *Reg. Gray* (Sur. Soc. lvi), 120.
[82] *Reg. Corbridge*, i (Sur. Soc. cxxxviii), 121.
[83] *Reg. Greenfield*, v (Sur. Soc. cliii), 361.
[84] *Fasti Parochiales*, iii. 71.
[85] *Cal. Papal Reg.* vi. 439.
[86] B.I.H.R., Churches index.
[87] *Herring's Visit.* i. 111, 121; ii. 19, 138; iii. 36.
[88] B.I.H.R., Bp. V. 1764/Ret. 223.
[89] *Rep. Com. Eccl. Revenues*, 962–3.
[90] B.I.H.R., V. 1865/Ret. 438; V. 1868/Ret. 387; V. 1871/Ret. 392.
[91] *Fasti Parochiales*, iii. 73.
[92] *Y.A.J.* xxi. 160.
[93] *Herring's Visit.* ii. 138; iii. 37.
[94] B.I.H.R., Seq. 1846.
[95] Ibid. V. 1865/Ret. 438; V. 1871/Ret. 392.
[96] Ibid. Bp. V. 1884/Ret.; Bp. V. 1936/Ret. 295.
[97] E.R.R.O., DDEL/13/1.
[98] Ibid.; *Kelly's Dir. N. & E.R. Yorks.* (1872), 538.
[99] P. Royston, *Rudston: Sketch of its Hist. & Antiq.* 25–6; *Kelly's Dir. N. & E.R. Yorks.* (1872), 538.
[1] *Test. Ebor.* vi. 106–7.
[2] B.I.H.R., Churches index.
[3] Par. rec. in vestry, churchwardens' accts. 1747–1894.
[4] Sheahan and Whellan, *Hist. York & E.R.* ii. 489.
[5] B.I.H.R., Churches index; E.R.R.O., DDEL/13/1; Royston, *Rudston*, 16–17, 23.
[6] Royston, *Rudston*, 16, 28–30.
[7] Plaque in church.

ately carved cross,[8] and a stone bowl with angle shafts which may have been a holy water stoup. Brasses commemorate Sir William Constable of Caythorpe (d. 1527) and his wife Jane (d. c. 1540),[9] and Catherine (d. 1677), wife of John Constable. The second is by Thomas Mann of York. There are several 19th-century monuments to the Bosville Macdonald family. That to Richard Beaumont (d. 1877) and his wife Susan, daughter of Godfrey Bosville Macdonald, contains portrait medallions supported by mourning angels. There is a memorial to Winifred Holtby (1898–1935), who is buried in the churchyard.

There was a parish orchestra in the early 19th century; in 1809 a teacher of 'psalmery' was engaged.[10] There were three bells in 1552.[11] Of the three surviving bells one is dated 1590 and the others, made by Samuel Smith, the elder and younger, of York, are dated 1663 and 1720 respectively.[12] The churchwardens were presented in 1663 for having defective bells[13] and the bell bearing that date may have been cast as a result. The plate includes a cup, paten, and flagon, all presented by Julia, wife of Henry Willoughby, Baron Middleton, in 1861.[14] The registers begin in 1550 and are complete.[15]

An addition was made to the churchyard in 1927.[16] The Bronze-Age monolith stands close to the church, the position of which it presumably determined. The 'rood' element in the village name suggests that a cross-head may have been affixed to the stone in an attempt to Christianize an already venerated site.[17] In 1449 the wapentake court met at 'le stane' of Rudston.[18] Near by, in the corner of the churchyard, is a double-cist which was placed there in 1871 after being excavated from a barrow near Wold Gate.[19]

NONCONFORMITY. In 1558 Anthony Maxwell (vicar 1535–71) was referred to as a recusant.[20] The Constables of Caythorpe were Roman Catholics from the late 16th to the 18th century. Two members of the family entered religious orders in the early 17th century[21] and in 1607 others lived in Lincolnshire in an attempt to avoid persecution.[22]

Houses in the village were licensed for worship in 1777, 1804, and 1823.[23] The Methodists had five members at Rudston in 1791.[24] The first chapel in the parish was built by the Wesleyans in 1811.[25] A new chapel was built in Marton Lane in 1879. It has round-headed windows and is of red brick with yellow-brick dressings.[26] It ceased to be used for worship in 1939[27] and in 1970 was used as the village hall.

The Primitive Methodists built a chapel in 1830.[28] It was described some ten years later as a 'tumble-down sort of place' and the membership was 'small, poor, excitable and very demonstrative'.[29] A new chapel was built in East Gate in 1877, when there were 20 members.[30] It is a plain red-brick building with a rendered front and was still used for services in 1970.

In 1865 the vicar reported that most of his parishioners were dissenters.[31] In 1877 the Wesleyans were said to be few and well-disposed to the church but the Primitive Methodists were strong.[32]

EDUCATION. There was a school in Rudston during most of the 17th century. The parishioners agreed c. 1620 that yearly payments should be made to the parish clerk both for his wages as clerk and for his 'pains in teaching school'. Each parishioner was to pay 6d., later 2d., for every bovate held, 8d. for a house, and 4d. for a cottage. The parents of poor children were to pay nothing more but extra payments were to be made by wealthier parents. The parish clerks continued to hold a school on this basis until c. 1674, when John Ellard refused to do so, claiming that the customary payments were the parish clerk's wages only. During the ensuing lawsuit several deponents stated that for many years all parents of children over 10 years old had paid, besides the customary payments, 1s. to 1s. 6d. a quarter for teaching.[33] The 'school-house' was mentioned in 1709.[34]

There was no school in 1743 and 1764.[35] Richard Harrison (d. 1840) started teaching in Rudston c. 1780[36] and by 1819 there were two schools in which about 60 children were taught.[37] There were still two in 1835, one with an attendance of 25 boys and girls, and the other, said to have begun in 1825, with 22 boys and girls. The poorest children were then taught freely, 'at the expense of those who are charitably inclined', and the rest at their parents' expense.[38]

An infants' school was built c. 1840 at the west end of Church Lane. In 1871 it had an attendance of 24. The income was mainly from school pence.[39] The attendance varied only between 25 and 31 from 1908 to 1914. It then declined and in 1921, when the school closed, it was only eighteen.[40] The school, a one-storeyed brick building, still stood in 1970.

A National school was built opposite the church

---

[8] Y.A.J. xlii. 341.
[9] The date of her death is left blank.
[10] Par. rec., chwdns. accts.
[11] Inventories of Ch. Goods, 31.
[12] Boulter, 'Ch. Bells', 218; V.C.H. Yorks. ii. 452.
[13] E.R.R.O., DPX/58, Rudston, p. 5.
[14] Yorks. Ch. Plate, i. 306; Burke's Peerage (1970), 1808.
[15] Barley, Par. Docs. E.R. 122.
[16] York. Dioc. Regy., Sentence of consecration.
[17] Information relating to the monolith has kindly been supplied by the staff of the Royal Commission on Historical Monuments, York. See above, plate facing p. 33.
[18] Cal. Pat. 1446–52, 306; see above, p. 5.
[19] Y.A.J. xlii. 254–8.   [20] Fasti Parochiales, iii. 73.
[21] H. Aveling, Post Reformation Catholicism in E. Yorks. 1558–1790 (E. Yorks. Loc. Hist. Ser. xi), 17, 37, 58.
[22] J. T. Cliffe, Yorks. Gentry, 176.
[23] B.I.H.R., DMH. Reg. 1, pp. 402–3; G.R.O. Worship Returns, Vol. v, nos. 481, 2303.
[24] E.R.R.O., MRP/1/7.   [25] H.O. 129/24/524.
[26] Bulmer, Dir. E. Yorks. (1892), 259.
[27] G.R.O. Worship Reg. no. 2387.
[28] H.O. 129/24/524; G.R.O. Worship Rets., Vol. v, no. 4105; E.R.R.O., DDBM/19/42.
[29] H. Woodcock, Sketches of Prim. Meth. on Yorks. Wolds, 68.
[30] Ibid. 70; G.R.O. Worship Reg. no. 23736.
[31] B.I.H.R., V. 1865/Ret. 438.
[32] Ibid. V. 1877/Ret.
[33] B.I.H.R., C.P., H. 3211, 3226, 3273, 3310, 3375, 3423, 3436, 4396–8.
[34] Registry of Deeds, Beverley, A/264/376.
[35] B.I.H.R., Bp. V. 1764/Ret. 223; Herring's Visit. iii. 36.
[36] J. Lawson, Primary Educ. in E. Yorks. 1560–1902 (E. Yorks. Loc. Hist. Ser. x), 23.
[37] Rets. on Educ. of Poor, 1819, 1089.
[38] Educ. Enquiry Abstract, 1835, 1094.
[39] Ed. 7/135.   [40] Bd. of Educ. List 21 (H.M.S.O.).

in 1859. Its income consisted of voluntary contributions and school pence paid by 30 boys and 15 girls.[41] An annual government grant was first received in 1860–1.[42] The total attendance was 104 in 1871[43] and from 1908 to 1938 it varied between 48 and 71.[44] The school closed in 1966 and the children were transferred to Boynton.[45] The building, of red brick with white-brick dressings, still stood in 1970.

In 1859 an evening school was held thrice weekly in winter.[46] It still existed in 1856[47] but ceased soon after.[48]

CHARITIES FOR THE POOR. In 1607 John Harrison gave the poor of Rudston a rent-charge of £1 a year out of land in the parish, and confirmed the gift in his will of the same year. In 1823 no record was found of any payments and the property liable to the charge was not known.[49]

RUSTON PARVA

RUSTON PARVA lies in a small but prominent valley cut into the lower slopes of the wolds.[1] It is nearly 4 miles from Driffield, and the village stands ½ mile north of the main Driffield–Bridlington road. Ruston was presumably an Anglian settlement but the first element in the name is a Scandinavian personal name. By the early 14th century it was called Little Ruston to distinguish it from Long Riston in Holderness.[2] Ruston was in the Middle Ages a chapelry of Lowthorpe but it later came to be regarded as a separate parish.[3] The parish is roughly triangular in shape and most of its 972 acres occupy wold ground on the valley sides. On the west a section of the parish boundary with Nafferton appears to follow a continuation of a prehistoric earthwork known as Green Dikes,[4] and a barrow stands close to the boundary line.[5] Similarly, part of the boundary with Kilham to the north follows a prehistoric earthwork and a green lane which continues the line of the earthwork. On the south the boundary with Lowthorpe is apparently aligned upon another barrow.[6] Lowthorpe beck forms a natural boundary in the east, where Ruston parish extends beyond the confines of its valley and abuts upon Harpham. The winding course of the beck here was straightened by the inclosure commissioners in 1805.[7] Bracey bridge, over the beck, was in Ruston, and a small southwards extension of the boundary took the near-by watermill into Ruston too. Since 1935 Ruston Parva has been combined with Harpham and Lowthorpe in the civil parish of Harpham.[8]

Ruston village is hemmed in by the steep slopes of the wolds which rise to over 200 ft. above sea-level in the west and north, and to over 125 ft. in the east. Most of this ground was formerly occupied by the open fields of Ruston, and the regular pattern of the modern fields, largely in arable cultivation, is the result of the inclosure of 1805. Only the valley bottom is used as pasture. A small diked stream occupies part of the valley below the village, but above it the valley is largely dry. Behind the village the eastern valley sides are broken by mounds and hollows marking old chalk quarries, and south of the village an extensive quarry is still worked.

In the valley bottom the road through Ruston runs directly south-eastwards to Lowthorpe and north-westwards to the site of Pockthorpe deserted village. The latter stretch of the road is known as Shepherdton Mere. Two roads ascend the valley sides. One leads north to Kilham, the other, New Road, runs south-westwards to join Beacon Lane and the main Driffield road. New Road is probably a creation of the inclosure of 1805, but Beacon Lane is of some antiquity. The latter ran for only about ¼ mile northwards from the Driffield road, providing access to the beacon that once stood on the barrow near the Nafferton boundary. Ruston beacon was in existence in 1588 and survived into the 19th century; it took its light from Rudston beacon and passed it to Bainton beacon.[9]

The main Driffield–Bridlington road runs obliquely across the parish, dipping sharply into the valley where it forms a cross-roads with the Ruston–Lowthorpe road. At the eastern parish boundary Bracey bridge formerly carried the main road over Lowthorpe beck. In 1965, however, the course of the road was straightened and the bridge bypassed.[10] The name 'Brayceford' occurs c. 1340 but by 1369 the ford had been replaced by 'Brayceforthbrig'.[11] The repair of the bridge was said in 1369 to be the responsibility of St. John's college, Beverley,[12] which owned the manorial estate, and in the early 15th century the bridge was repaired with stone by the college.[13]

The village street and two back lanes form a figure-of-eight around which most of the houses are situated. At the centre is a tiny green and the pedestal of a cross[14] still stands at the roadside. The church stands on the hillside above the village, approached by a sunken pathway from near the green. The names Town Street, Church Lane, and 'Lowdlane' are all recorded in 1733,[15] and King Street in 1763.[16] The map prepared in 1801 at the

---

[41] Ed. 7/135.
[42] Rep. of Educ. Cttee. of Council, 1860–1 [2828], H.C., p. 757 (1861), xlix.
[43] Rets. rel. Elem. Educ. 1871, 476.
[44] Bd. of Educ. List 21.
[45] Par. rec. in Vicarage, Managers' min. bk. 1946–68; E.R. Educ. Cttee. Mins. 1966–7, 88.
[46] Ed. 7/135.
[47] B.I.H.R., V. 1865/Ret. 438.
[48] Ibid. V. 1868/Ret. 387.
[49] 9th Rep. Char. Com. 739.
[1] This article was written in 1967–8.
[2] P.N.E.R. Yorks. (E.P.N.S.), 93–4.
[3] See p. 323.
[4] See p. 283.
[5] V.C.H. Yorks. ii. 70.
[6] See p. 272.
[7] Registry of Deeds, Beverley, CI/1/1.
[8] Census, 1931.
[9] J. Nicholson, Beacons of E. Yorks. 8, 52–3; E.R.R.O., LT/9/54.
[10] E.R.C.C. Mins. 1964–5, 256; 1965–6, 138.
[11] P.N.E.R. Yorks. 90.
[12] Public Works in Med. Law, ii (Selden Soc. xl), 310.
[13] Sheffield City Libr., Lindsay Coll. 69 (undated MS.).
[14] See T.E.R.A.S. iv. 10 for its measurements.
[15] Regy. of Deeds, N/285/638.
[16] E.R.R.O., DDDU/11/137.

Nafferton Railway Station

The Old Town, Bridlington: No. 46 High Street

Farm-house at Muston, built in 1738

Manor Farm, Garton on the Wolds

A cottage at Bessingby

Johnson's Farm, Reighton

time of inclosure[17] shows 26 crofts and garths in the village, with houses standing in fifteen of them. Several of these garths, on the east side of the village, have since been abandoned but their boundaries are still marked by banks on the hillside near the old chalk quarries.

Most of the village houses are undistinguished buildings of the late 18th and 19th centuries, one of them bearing the date 1782. Most are of red brick, but one of the earlier cottages is built entirely of chalk, and the demolition of adjacent buildings reveals that chalk was used for the party walls of several others. One row of cottages was apparently built at the same time as the adjoining Methodist chapel in the early 19th century. A farm at the north end of the village and another near the church both date from the 18th century, but Manor Farm was built on the St. Quintin estate after inclosure and two other farm-houses were built outside the village in the 19th century. The water-mill near Bracey bridge is said to have been built in 1807,[18] but the adjoining miller's house dates from the 18th century. The mill is now disused but the water-wheel, gearing, and stones still remained *in situ* in 1967. One other isolated house is that standing at the cross-roads south of the village; it was a public house, the New Inn, in 1850[19] but was apprently not so used for long.[20]

There were 85 poll-tax payers at Ruston in 1377,[21] and 32 households were assessed to or discharged from the hearth tax in 1670. The number of households in 1674 was 29, 9 of which were discharged from the tax; of the rest one had 8 hearths, one had 4, 3 had 3 each, one had 2, and 14 had only one.[22] There were said to be about 17 families in 1743.[23] In 1801 there were only 94 inhabitants, but after a continuous increase the population reached a maximum of 185 in 1851. Thereafter it declined and, after a drop of 56 in the previous decade, it was only 84 in 1901.[24] It stood at the same figure in 1931.[25]

MANOR AND OTHER ESTATES. In 1086 there were two estates in Ruston: 9 carucates were held by the archbishop of York as a berewick of Lowthorpe, and 3 carucates belonged to the king.[26]

At the Conquest the archbishop's estate had formed part of the liberty of St. John of Beverley,[27] and it remained so until the Dissolution.[28] Demesne tenants under the provost of Beverley included William of Caythorpe, who in 1296 held 6 bovates.[29]

In 1584 the manor of *RUSTON*, which was said to have lately been held by Thomas Hellard, was granted by the Crown to Thomas and Christopher Hellard for life; in 1588, however, it was granted to Edmund Downing and Miles Dodding.[30] In the 17th century the manor belonged to the Crompton family. Robert Crompton suffered a recovery of it in 1663,[31] and in 1674 he occupied the largest house in Ruston, with eight hearths.[32] The manorial estate was subsequently split up for a short period. The greater part of it, together with the manor-house and manorial rights, remained with the Cromptons and was granted by John Crompton to Sir John Thompson in 1723.[33] In the following year Thompson conveyed it to Sir William St. Quintin.[34] The smaller part of the estate was sold by the Cromptons to Edward Dry; he left it to his widow in 1722 and she had sold it to Sir William St. Quintin by 1733. St. Quintin was also said in 1733 to have 'lately' acquired other property in Ruston from Christopher Megson.[35] The manor was reconveyed to Thompson by St. Quintin in 1733,[36] but some time between 1748 and 1755 it was returned to St. Quintin.[37] The estate subsequently followed the descent of Harpham.[38] At inclosure in 1805 467 a. were allotted to the St. Quintins, besides 56 a. for tithes, and Lady Legard had about 540 a. of land, as well as some plantations, in 1959.[39]

The manor-house no longer remains, but a drawing of c. 1720 shows a two-storeyed building with attics. The main front was of seven bays, the central three recessed, and the door surround and angle-quoins were rusticated.[40]

The Crown estate in Ruston had been held in 1066 by Egfrid.[41] By the beginning of the 13th century it formed part of the Percy fee[42] and it was later held under the lords of that fee by the Tournay family. The Tournays seem to have inherited it from the Rudstons family, of Rudston.[43] In 1219 Geoffrey Tournay, who was married to the heir of one branch of the Rudstons, had the custody of land in Ruston belonging to a second branch of the Rudstons.[44] Geoffrey Tournay's grandson is recorded as having property in Ruston in 1319–20.[45] The estate remained in the family and passed to John Tournay (d. 1404).[46] The last known reference to the family's possession of it was in 1575, when Anthony Tournay died seised of it.[47]

Several small estates were subsequently formed out of this land and eventually acquired by the Greame family. A manor-house called Upper House and 16 bovates of land were in 1675 sold by John

---

[17] Regy. of Deeds.
[18] Sheahan and Whellan, *Hist. York & E.R.* ii. 489.
[19] O.S. Map 6" (1854).
[20] There was a victualler at Ruston in 1840 (White, *Dir. E. & N.R. Yorks.* 397) and in 1872 (*Kelly's Dir. N. & E.R. Yorks.* 539).
[21] E 179/202/62 m. 31.
[22] E 179/205/514, 521.
[23] *Herring's Visit.* iii. 38.
[24] *V.C.H. Yorks.* iii. 490.
[25] Census.
[26] *V.C.H. Yorks.* ii. 204, 215, 323.
[27] Ibid. 215.
[28] B.M. Lansd. MS. 896, f. 125; *Cal. Chart. R. 1300–26*, 241; *Test. Ebor.* ii. 141; *Beverley Chapter Act Bk.* i (Sur. Soc. xcviii), 117; ii (Sur. Soc. cviii), 322, 339; G. Poulson, *Beverlac*, 618, 641.
[29] *Cal. Inq. p.m.* iii, p. 200.
[30] C 66/1318 m. 17.
[31] C.P. 43/324 m. 29.
[32] E 179/205/521.
[33] Registry of Deeds, Beverley, H/624/1263.
[34] Ibid. H/705/1443.
[35] Ibid. N/285/638; see below, p. 322. For the Dry family see also C 5/11/23; C 5/398/29.
[36] Regy. of Deeds, N/285/638.
[37] Y.A.S. MSS., DD. 89.
[38] See p. 224.
[39] Regy. of Deeds, CI/1/1; 1129/159/136.
[40] B.M. Lansd. MS. 914, f. 258.
[41] *V.C.H. Yorks.* ii. 204.
[42] K.B. 26/88 m. 26; E 179/202/44, 104; *Percy Charty.* (Sur. Soc. xcvii), 9, 55; *Feud. Aids*, vi. 32; *Cal. Close, 1313–18*, 150; *Yorks. Fines, 1218–31*, 108–11.
[43] See p. 313.
[44] *Percy Charty.* 55.
[45] C.P. 40/233 m. 122d.
[46] C.P. 40/547 m. 337; J.I. 1/1490 m. 3; K.B. 27/562 m. 67; B.M. Lansd. MS. 207(c), f. 577; *Lincs. Pedigrees* (Harl. Soc. lii), 1002.
[47] C 142/171/69.

Gibbon to Melchior Hicks, and in 1699 Hicks conveyed them to Robert Greame.[48] At inclosure in 1805 101 a. were allotted to John Greame.[49] In 1748 11 bovates were acquired from John Sinclair by John Mason, and in 1794 another John Mason sold them to Robert Cross. At inclosure 69 a. were allotted to Matthew Cowton, who had married Cross's daughter Sybil, and in 1815 Cowton sold them to John Greame.[50] Also in 1815 Greame acquired from Cowton 26 a. which had been John Bell's tithe allotment in 1805.[51] The estate descended in the Greame and Lloyd Greame families until 1935, when Yarburgh Lloyd Greame sold 208 a. to R. J. Jefferson.[52]

The manor-house of this estate may have stood at the south end of the village, in a garth which belonged to John Greame in 1801.[53] Traces of a moated site could still be seen there in 1968.

The tithes of Ruston belonged to Lowthorpe college.[54] After the Dissolution the chapel at Ruston was included in the lease of the Lowthorpe tithes to Thomas Haynes.[55] By 1650 the impropriators at Ruston were John Pearson, Christopher Margison, and William Dry, and the estate was then worth £80 a year.[56] The Dry family apparently still had a share of the tithes in the early 18th century.[57] The Bell and Boyes families had acquired an interest in the tithes by the 1780s,[58] and in 1801 there were three impropriators. These were William St. Quintin, who had the tithes of hay in the old inclosures and all the tithes from 27 bovates, John Boyes, who had the tithes of 54 bovates, and John Bell, who had those of 15 bovates.[59] Under the inclosure award of 1805 the St. Quintins received 56 a., Boyes 112 a., and Bell 26 a.[60] Bell's allotment soon passed to the Greames and Boyes's to the Brewins and the Olivers.[61] John Dickson, of Nafferton, later held some of this land.[62]

ECONOMIC HISTORY. The chief estate in Ruston in 1086 was described as a berewick of the archbishop of York's manor at neighbouring Lowthorpe, though it much exceeded it in size.[63] Little is known about the village in the Middle Ages, but an undated account, probably of *c.* 1420, throws some light on the organization of the manorial estate.[64] St. John's college then had 15 bovates of demesne land, let to various tenants, and 15 bovates held in bondage. Other rents were received from seven cottages, a plot called 'lathplace', a croft called Kirk croft, and from the water-mill with its adjoining meadow. About 11*s.* was paid by tenants in lieu of works: for autumn works, for works called 'Rustonlades', and for carrying thraves from Reighton to Ruston; these tenants were, moreover, excused payment of £1 10*s.* for further works. A payment of 1*s.* was made for a custom called 'Yholstoth', and 42 hens were given by tenants at Christmas.

The open fields occupied the greater part of the parish before inclosure, no doubt with some land under grass in the valley. In 1675, for example, there were two closes of meadow or pasture, called Ing closes, at the east end of the village.[65] When John Crompton sold the manor in 1723 it included seven closes, one of them called Ancient Holme, and there was also meadow land called the Holme.[66] The open fields contained 96 bovates in all in 1687, 81 of them being freehold and the rest copyhold. The largest owner was Robert Crompton, who as lord of the manor had 43 freehold bovates, 15 of them comprising his demesne lands; Sir Matthew Pearson of Lowthorpe had 6 freehold bovates.[67] The St. Quintin estate consisted in 1796 of 568 a., held by nine tenants, with as much as 542 a., or 58 bovates, lying in three large farms.[68]

The open fields of Ruston were inclosed in 1805[69] under an Act of 1801.[70] The award dealt with 908 a. altogether, the greater part of the area of the parish. The St. Quintins, as lords of the manor, were allotted 467 a., including a few perches in lieu of an annual rent of 3*s.* 4*d.* called 'the Green rent'; in addition, for their share of the tithes they were allotted 56 a. John Greame received 101 a.; John Boyes 162 a., including 112 a. for tithes; Sybil Cowton 69 a.; and John Bell 26 a. for tithes. There were two other allotments, both of 1 a., made in respect of cottages which were to continue to be in copyhold tenure.

The continued predominance of arable farming after inclosure is illustrated by a farm of 203 a. let by John Greame in 1822: as many as 176 a. were then arable.[71] In 1840 there were four farmers in Ruston, and this was the usual number in the late 19th and early 20th centuries, one of them also being the miller.[72] There was a large poultry farm in 1967.

The most noteworthy of the non-agricultural occupations found in the village were milling and lime-burning. There was reference to a mill near 'Brayceford' *c.* 1340,[73] and the water-mill is subsequently frequently mentioned as part of the manorial estate. In 1530 a lease of the mill contributed to the liberty of Beverley's income from the manor.[74] After the Dissolution the mill was for a time separated from the rest of the estate, for in 1567 it was let by the Crown to Robert Raunson,[75] but it subsequently belonged to the Cromptons and succeeding lords of the manor. It was described in 1796 as an old mill, much out of repair,[76] and it is

---

[48] E.R.R.O., DDLG/23/37–8.
[49] Regy. of Deeds, CI/1/1.
[50] E.R.R.O., DDLG/23/1–4, 17, 47.
[51] Ibid. /43, 48.
[52] Regy. of Deeds, 525/357/274; see above, p. 95.
[53] Regy. of Deeds, inclosure map.
[54] See p. 323.
[55] See p. 274.
[56] *T.E.R.A.S.* ii. 52.
[57] E.R.R.O., DDSY/108/31.
[58] Ibid. DDLG/23/41; DDMC/Deeds 736a.
[59] 41 Geo. III, c. 92 (Private and Personal, not printed).
[60] Registry of Deeds, Beverley, CI/1/1.
[61] *Rep. Com. Eccl. Revenues*, 962–3; Lawton, *Rer. Eccles. Dioc. Ebor.* 308; Boyes conveyed his share to John Brewin in 1802, before the inclosure award was made: Regy. of Deeds, CE/430/629; see above.
[62] J. T. Ward, *E. Yorks. Landed Estates in the 19th Cent.* (E. Yorks. Loc. Hist. Ser. xxiii), 63; Bulmer, *Dir. E. Yorks.* (1892), 260.
[63] *V.C.H. Yorks.* ii. 215.
[64] Sheffield City Libr., Lindsey Coll. 69.
[65] E.R.R.O., DDLG/23/37.
[66] Registry of Deeds, Beverley, H/624/1263.
[67] Y.A.S. MSS., MS. 709a.   [68] Ibid. 709b.
[69] Regy. of Deeds, CI/1/1.
[70] 41 Geo. III, c. 92 (Private and Personal, not printed).
[71] E.R.R.O., DDLG/23/29.
[72] Directories.
[73] *P.N.E.R. Yorks.* (E.P.N.S.), 90.
[74] G. Poulson, *Beverlac*, 618.
[75] *Cal. Pat.* 1566–9, 139.
[76] Y.A.S. MSS., MS. 709b.

said to have been rebuilt in 1807.[77] It continued in use until c. 1942.[78]

Chalk quarried at Ruston was already being burnt for lime in 1723, when a lime-kiln was part of the manorial estate.[79] In 1801 the St. Quintins had a quarry and lime-kiln, apparently in the same position as the present quarry.[80] There were eight kilns in the quarry in 1850[81] and a lime-burner was among the inhabitants of the village throughout the 19th century and until about 1930. By 1933 the Ruston Parva Lime Co. was in existence,[82] and it still worked the quarry in 1967, though lime had ceased to be burnt several years earlier.[83]

LOCAL GOVERNMENT. Manorial courts were mentioned c. 1420, when four were held by St. John's college.[84] Something of the working of the manorial court in the 18th century is seen in court papers of Sir John Thompson and Sir William St. Quintin.[85] The officers appointed were 2 bylawmen, 2 affeerors, a constable, and a pinder. The St. Quintins' court still appointed a constable in the early 19th century and two bylawmen in the mid century, and a pinder was still appointed in 1914.

No parochial records before 1835 are known. In 1836 Ruston joined the Driffield union.[86]

CHURCH. In the Middle Ages Ruston was a chapelry of Lowthorpe. It was so described in 1312,[87] and soon after it was appropriated to Lowthorpe college together with its mother-church.[88] In 1358 the archbishop licensed the rector of Lowthorpe to have Ruston chapel served by one of the chaplains of the college.[89] The Pope granted an indult to the same effect in 1415, after the chaplains had stated that services at Ruston were celebrated by a priest at their expense; they were to govern the chapel themselves, despite their obligation of continual residence at Lowthorpe.[90] After the dissolution of the college Ruston eventually came to be regarded as a separate cure, the Crown paying by 1565 the curate's stipend, as at Lowthorpe.[91] In 1650 the 'preaching minister', though he was also the minister at Lowthorpe, had a separate stipend from the Crown for serving Ruston.[92] In the early 19th century Ruston and Lowthorpe were regarded as separate perpetual curacies.[93] They were united in 1852.[94]

The advowson, like that of Lowthorpe, belonged to the St. Quintins in the earlier 19th century.[95]

The living had an income of £5 6s. 8d. in 1650, by way of the stipend paid by the Crown.[96] This continued to be part of the income,[97] which was augmented by £200 from Queen Anne's Bounty in each of the years 1741, 1763, 1787, 1817, 1824, and 1832.[98] The average net income in 1829–31 was £51.[99] By 1770 Bounty money had been used to buy glebe land at Cottingham: 16 a. were acquired jointly with Lowthorpe and a third of the land belonged to Ruston. By 1781 8½ a. in Nafferton had been bought, in 1821 8 a. there were added, and 4 a. more in Nafferton were subsequently acquired.[1]

The curacy seems always to have been held in conjunction with Lowthorpe[2] and there is no record of the employment of an assistant curate. In 1743 and 1764 a service was held once a fortnight at Ruston; communion was administered three times a year and was received by 25–35 people.[3] By 1851 there was a weekly service,[4] and in 1864 communion was celebrated six times a year, with six communicants.[5] In 1884 there was apparently still only one service.[6] Communion was administered once a month in 1900.[7] One service was held each Sunday in 1968.

Nothing is known of the earlier chapel of ST. NICHOLAS,[8] though the circular Norman font in the present church presumably came from it. The church as rebuilt in 1832[9] is a small, simple, building of grey brick and sandstone, consisting of chancel, nave, and bell-turret. It contains box pews and a two-decker pulpit.

There are two bells.[10] The plate consists of a silver cup with a London hallmark of 1578, and a paten and flagon, both of 1891.[11] The registers begin in 1572 and are complete.[12]

The churchyard was extended in 1931.[13]

NONCONFORMITY. There is no record of dissent in Ruston until the licensing for worship of a house in 1788; a second house was licensed in 1807 and a chapel in 1811.[14] The Methodists had nine members at Ruston in 1787 and about fifteen at Ruston and Harpham together in 1788–91.[15] The early chapel was presumably that, not far from the parish church, which was used by the Wesleyan Methodists in 1850.[16] The Wesleyans continued to use the chapel until 1906.[17] The Primitive Methodists met in a cottage in 1868; they were

[77] Sheahan and Whellan, Hist. York & E.R. ii. 489. The date 1803 is inscribed on an old mill-stone, set into the ground outside the mill.
[78] Ex inf. occupier, 1967. See p. 321.
[79] Regy. of Deeds, H/624/1263.
[80] Ibid. CI/1/1; 41 Geo. III, c. 92.
[81] O.S. Map 6" (1854).
[82] Directories.
[83] Local inf.
[84] Sheffield City Libr., Lindsey Coll. 69.
[85] Court rolls and other papers, c. 1730 onwards; call rolls and jury papers, 1793–1914: Y.A.S. MSS., DD. 89.
[86] 3rd Rep. Poor Law Com. 168.
[87] Reg. Greenfield, iii (Sur. Soc. cli), 203.
[88] See p. 275.
[89] Fasti Parochiales, iii. 54.
[90] Cal. Papal Regs. vi. 511.
[91] Cal. Pat. 1563–6, 366.
[92] T.E.R.A.S. ii. 52.
[93] Lawton, Rer. Eccles. Dioc. Ebor. 308.
[94] York Dioc. Regy., Orders in Council 1/94.
[95] Ibid.; Lawton, loc. cit.; Rep. Com. Eccl. Revenues, 962–3.
[96] T.E.R.A.S. ii. 52.
[97] B.I.H.R., TER. J. Ruston n.d., 1743, etc.
[98] Hodgson, Q.A.B. 451–2; Lawton, Rer. Eccles. Dioc. Ebor. 308.
[99] Rep. Com. Eccl. Revenues, 962–3.
[1] B.I.H.R., TER. J. Ruston 1770, 1781, 1825, 1865; Lowthorpe 1861.
[2] See p. 276.
[3] B.I.H.R., Bp. V. 1764/Ret. 132; Herring's Visit. iii. 38.
[4] H.O. 129/24/523.
[5] B.I.H.R., V. 1865/Ret. 335.
[6] Ibid. Bp. V. 1884/Ret.
[7] Ibid. Bp. V. 1900/Ret. 235.
[8] Dedication recorded in 1415: Cal. Papal Regs. vi. 511.
[9] Date on building.
[10] Y.A.J. ii. 218.
[11] Yorks. Ch. Plate, i. 306–7.
[12] The first register (1572–1719) is in E.R.R.O., the second is at Lowthorpe.
[13] York Dioc. Regy., Sentence of consecration.
[14] B.I.H.R., DMH. 1788/17; G.R.O. Worship Returns, Vol. v, nos. 715, 2064, 2522. In 1851 it was said that the chapel had been built in 1810: H.O. 129/24/524.
[15] E.R.R.O., MRP/1/7.
[16] O.S. Map 6" (1854).
[17] G.R.O. Worship Reg. no. 2866.

still holding meetings in 1877, and in 1894 they shared the Wesleyan chapel.[18] In 1889 they had sixteen members.[19] The chapel was apparently brought back into use, by the Primitives, in the 1920s[20] and finally ceased to be used in 1961.[21] The building of 1811 seems to have served throughout, and it still stood in 1968.

EDUCATION. There may have been a school in Ruston in the late 18th century, for the daughter of a schoolmaster was baptized there in 1788.[22] In 1818 eight children were taught at a school in Ruston and a few others went to neighbouring parishes.[23] By 1833 the only school was that held on Sundays by the Wesleyans,[24] and there is no later record of a day-school.

CHARITIES FOR THE POOR. None known.

THWING

THWING lies on the wolds about 8 miles west of Bridlington and the village has the highest situation of any in the wapentake.[1] It formerly had two hamlets, Octon, which was an Anglian settlement, and the lost 'Fornetorp', which was probably Scandinavian.[2] From west to east the elongated parish stretches for up to 4 miles across hills and dry valleys, and only in the north, where it extends into the valley of the Gypsey Race, does it include any low ground. Two sections of the northern parish boundary run along the modern course of the Race, and part of the southern boundary follows High Street, on the line of a Roman road.[3] For a short distance in the south-west the boundary lies along a prehistoric earthwork, and the eastern boundary, running straight down the wold slope, is apparently aligned upon a barrow known as Willy Howe. The internal boundary between Thwing and Octon partly follows the bottom of a dry valley called Syn Dale. The total area of the parish is 4,024 a., of which 1,808 a. lie in Octon.[4]

Much of the ground is more than 300 ft. above sea-level; it exceeds 400 ft. in the south, and a small area in the extreme south-west is between 500 ft. and 540 ft. The slopes in the northern part of the parish are dissected by a dozen dry valleys, the most prominent being Syn Dale in the centre and Old Dale, in Octon to the west. In the extreme north the ground falls to 150 ft.–175 ft. in the valley of the Gypsey Race. The land is now largely under arable, and there are only a few windbreaks and plantations. The pattern of large regular fields is mainly that created at the inclosure of the open fields in 1769.

Six comparatively minor roads converge on the village of Thwing. Three of them run northwards to Burton Fleming, Wold Newton, and Foxholes, in the valley of the Gypsey Race. Two others lead southwards to join High Street, which itself mostly runs beyond the parish boundary, in Kilham; the two roads then lead on to Rudston and Kilham. The sixth road connects Thwing with Octon to the west. In addition the road along which Octon itself lies is connected to High Street in the south and continues northwards to Foxholes. Finally the Foxholes–Langtoft road cuts across the south-west corner of Thwing parish. Few of these roads are named, but the road to Kilham leaves Thwing village as Butt Lane and the Foxholes road is called Skipper Lane in the north of the parish.[5]

The village of Thwing lies at 300 ft.–350 ft. above sea-level at the uppermost end of Syn Dale, close to a ridge of high ground which may be the 'strip of land' from which the village is named. Springs and a string of ponds, mostly in the dale, include the Mere and the Keld. At inclosure in 1769 the former was set aside for the supply of water to the village, and the 'common watering place' then known as West Keld was included in the rector's allotment.[6] Earthworks probably marking the sites of buildings may be seen at several points, those near Manor Farm perhaps being the remains of the manor-house. The mostly brick-built houses and cottages in the village date from the 18th to the 20th century, but chalk appears in a few houses and in many out-buildings. The most notable farm-house, at the north side of the village, is a three-bay house of the 18th century. Part of a dovecot, of 18th- or 19th-century date, remained at Rectory Farm in 1970. Later buildings include a terrace of double-fronted houses and a dozen Council houses. There is one public house in the village, the Raincliffe Arms, which is first recorded in 1893. In 1879 and 1889 there had been a Rampant Horse, and the Bottle and Glass is mentioned between 1823 and 1872.[7]

A mile west of Thwing, on the side of another dry valley, lay the hamlet of Octon. Until the 15th century Octon was assessed for taxes separately from Thwing and was apparently little diminished at that date; it subsequently declined and most of the former hamlet, including its chapel, is now marked by a series of prominent earthworks. The remaining houses in 1970 included a one-and-a-half-storey cottage of brick and chalk, a large yellow-brick farm-house of the 19th century, and four Council houses. The cottage, which consists of three bays and externally appears to be of the 18th century, retains two internal cruck trusses of much earlier date. Survival of this form of construction is extremely

---

[18] B.I.H.R., V. 1868/Ret. 298; V. 1877/Ret.; Bp. V. 1894/Ret.
[19] H. Woodcock, *Sketches of Prim. Meth. on Yorks. Wolds*, 140.
[20] *Kelly's Dir. N. & E.R. Yorks.* (1929), 559. The name stone, with date obliterated, lay on the ground near the building in 1967.
[21] Ex inf. Revd. D. H. Prescott, Nafferton, 1970.
[22] Hull Univ. Libr. DP/135, notes from par. rec.
[23] *Rets. on Educ. of Poor, 1819*, 1089.
[24] *Educ. Enquiry Abstract, 1835*, 1094.

[1] This article was written in 1961, with some amendment to 1970. Use has been made of material compiled by Mrs. Mary E. Dymond.
[2] *P.N.E.R. Yorks.* (E.P.N.S.), 112–14.
[3] Mary Kitson Clark, *Gaz. of Roman Remains in E. Yorks.* 44; I. Margary, *Roman Roads in Brit.* ii. 153.
[4] O.S. Map 6" (1854).   [5] Ibid.
[6] Registry of Deeds, Beverley, AK/376/29.
[7] Baines, *Hist. Yorks.* (1823), ii. 395; *Kelly's Dir. N. & E.R. Yorks.* (1872), 554; (1879), 658; (1889), 465; (1893), 499.

rare in the East Riding. The trusses, which divide the bays, have saddles below the ridge, collars, and roughly-shaped blades. There were doubtless similar trusses at the two ends of the building before the exterior was remodelled.

A mile to the north-west of Octon lies Octon Grange, now consisting of two 19th-century farmhouses. Earthworks near by mark the site of the former grange which Meaux abbey established at Octon.[8] Apart from those at Octon Grange, the chief scattered farms in the parish are Low Barn and Wold Cottage, neither of them far from the Gypsey Race, and Octon Lodge, high in the south-west of the parish. The author Edward Topham retired to Wold Cottage and in 1799 he erected a monument to mark the place where a meteorite fell in 1795.[9]

Thwing had 134 poll-tax payers in 1377.[10] Octon was always a small hamlet, but there is no reliable indication of its size.[11] In 1670 47 households at Thwing were included in the hearth-tax return, of which 11 were discharged from payment. Four years later 35 households were chargeable; of these, 26 had only one hearth, 5 had 2, 2 had 3, and one each had 6 and seven.[12] There were 40 families in the parish in 1743[13] and 34 in 1764.[14] There were about 20 crofts along the street of Octon in 1769, but only 8 of them contained houses.[15] The population in 1801 was 217. It rose steadily to 350 in 1831 and rapidly to 452 in 1841, but numbers fell during most of the later 19th century and in 1901 there were 326 inhabitants.[16] After a rise to 339 in 1911, the population has steadily fallen to 244 in 1961.[17]

MANORS AND OTHER ESTATES. In the main body of the text of the Domesday Survey only two holdings in Thwing are recorded. The first consisted of 8 carucates, which lay in the soke of the king's manor of Burton Agnes,[18] and the second comprised 2 carucates and 2 bovates. The holding in the soke of Burton Agnes was given to Robert de Brus immediately after the Survey was made and is recorded in an account of his fee appended to the main body of the text; a further holding of 10 carucates is similarly recorded.[19] In the Domesday summary, however, the king is recorded as holding 17 carucates and 2 bovates in Thwing.[20] It seems likely, since the account of the Brus fee is probably the latest document, that the holdings in the vill had been consolidated in that fee. The consolidated assessment of 17¼ carucates mentioned in the summary survives, however, at least until 1284–5.[21] At that date there were three holdings in Thwing: one of 6 carucates and another of 3 carucates and 2 bovates were both said to be held of the Brus family immediately; in the third holding of 8 carucates a mesne lordship had been created and this was held of Brus by the family of Percy of Kildale. It seems likely that the Percy mesne holding was created here as it was in Kirkleatham (Yorks. N.R.) by the marriage of Isabel, daughter of Adam de Brus, to Henry Percy in the later 12th century.[22] The Percies of Kildale descended from Walter, a grandson of this Henry.[23]

The ascription of the overlordship to Brus in 1284–5 is, however, difficult to interpret for Peter de Brus (III) died in 1272 leaving his four sisters as coheirs.[24] In some later documents Thwing is still said to be of the fee of Brus.[25] Generally speaking the descent of the overlordship of the three holdings was much confused.[26] The 8 carucates of the Percy mesne tenancy often seem to have been considered as held in chief and several documents between 1314 and 1510 mention no mesne lordship.[27] In 1484, moreover, when the manor was in dispute, it was said that John Percy, formerly 'chief lord of the fee', had renounced his rights to the Crown.[28] One piece of evidence suggests, nevertheless, that the Brus overlordship was maintained, for in 1344 John Percy was said to hold of the heir of Nicholas de Meynell.[29] Meynell was the illegitimate son of a union between Lucy (granddaughter of Lucy de Brus and Marmaduke of Thwing) and Nicholas de Meynell. To her bastard son Lucy must have assigned her Brus inheritance and the overlordship passed, through his daughter Elizabeth, to the family of Darcy and successively to the Conyers and Bellasis families.[30] It is for this reason that a document of 1619 speaks of property held of Henry Bellasis, of his fee of Thwing.[31]

About the 6-carucate holding there was probably similar confusion. It seems possible that the overlordship had been assigned to the tenant, Marmaduke of Thwing, who had married Lucy de Brus before the death of Peter de Brus in 1272.[32] On the grounds mentioned above, the overlordship would have descended via Nicholas Meynell to the Bellasis family. It seems, however, that the overlordship was generally deemed to lie with the Thwings and their successors the Lumleys.[33] In 1400 the manor was confiscated by the Crown[34] and upon its return to the Lumleys was said to be held in chief by them.[35]

Of the fate of the overlordship of the remaining 3 carucates and 2 bovates nothing is known. It had been held of Brus by the Harphams, whose chief holding lay in Octon, and it was perhaps to that family that the overlordship passed after 1272.[36]

Although nothing certain is known of the demesne

---

[8] C. Platt, *Monastic Grange in Med. Eng.* 225.
[9] Sheahan and Whellan, *Hist. York & E.R.* ii. 490–1; *D.N.B.*
[10] E 179/202/62 m. 9.
[11] It was combined with Swaythorpe in the poll-tax return.
[12] E 179/205/514, 521.   [13] *Herring's Visit.* iii. 173.
[14] B.I.H.R., Bp. V. 1764/Ret. 91.
[15] E.R.R.O., IA. Thwing, inclosure award map.
[16] *V.C.H. Yorks.* iii. 490.   [17] *Census.*
[18] *V.C.H. Yorks.* ii. 198, 204.   [19] Ibid. 291.
[20] Ibid. 323.   [21] *Feud. Aids*, vi. 30.
[22] *Cal. Pat.* 1429–36, 532, where the marriage is wrongly said to have taken place temp. Edw. I; *Percy Charty.* (Sur. Soc. cvii), 131–2; *V.C.H. Yorks. N.R.* ii. 258.
[23] G. Brenan, *Hist. of House of Percy*, i. 6.
[24] *Yorks. Inq.* i. 147.

[25] e.g. E 179/202/104; *Feud. Aids*, vi. 141.
[26] Thwing is not mentioned in the division of the Brus fee in 1272 in *Yorks. Inq.* i. 147; *Cal. Close*, 1272–9, 39–40; 1279–88, 90, 105–7.
[27] *Cal. Inq. p.m.* v, p. 319; vi, p. 239; viii, p. 369; xiv, pp. 55, 74–5.
[28] C.P. 40/887 m. 204.   [29] C 143/272/1.
[30] *V.C.H. Yorks. N.R.* ii. 322.
[31] C 142/668/200.   [32] *Yorks. Inq.* i. 147.
[33] Between 1377 and 1383 the overlordship may have belonged to Wm. of Botreaux and his wife Eliz., one of the coheirs of Thos. of Thwing: *Cal. Close*, 1374–7, 499; 1396–9, 49.
[34] *Cal. Inq. Misc.* vii, p. 41.   [35] *Feud. Aids*, vi. 260.
[36] See p. 327; it may have been part of the share of Marg. de Roos, a coheir of Peter de Brus: *Cal. Close*, 1279–88, 106; *Feud. Aids*, vi. 30.

lordship of *THWING* until the 13th century, it has been reasonably conjectured that Robert son of Robert of Thwing held ½ knight's fee there of Adam de Brus in 1166.[37] The Thwing family's name was presumably derived from the place-name and this suggests an early connexion with the vill.[38] By the early 13th century the family was well established there.[39] By 1284–5 both the 6- and the 8-carucate holdings of the Brus fee were in the lordship of the Thwings.[40] The manor remained in the family until the death of Thomas, Lord Thwing, in 1374.[41]

The manor then passed to the Lumleys by the marriage of Lucy, sister of Thomas Thwing, to Robert Lumley.[42] On Thomas's death Robert Lumley's grandson, another Robert, succeeded to the manor under a previous agreement. The Lumleys' subsequent tenure of it was interrupted on several occasions. In 1399–1400 Ralph, Lord Lumley, was executed for treason and his lands were granted to the earl of Somerset, but in 1405 Sir John Lumley was restored to his father's inheritance.[43] In the 1480s the manor was apparently assigned to the use of John Wilkinson and his wife, and in 1516 it was claimed by John, Lord Lumley (d. 1544), from John Glyn and his wife Joan, relict of John Wilkinson.[44] The Lumleys certainly had full possession by 1524.[45] John Lumley's son George was executed in 1537 but his relict, who later married John Knottisford, held the manor until her death at an unknown date, when it was confiscated by the Crown. In 1554 her son John, Lord Lumley (d. 1609), after the reversal of his father's attainder, inherited the manor,[46] which he sold in 1579 to Sir Thomas Heneage.[47]

In 1588 Sir Thomas exchanged the manor for other lands with the Crown.[48] In 1650 it was sold by Crown commissioners to John Saunderson,[49] but the sale was nullified at the Restoration and in 1665 the manor was granted to Queen Katherine.[50] In 1696 Thwing was given by the Crown to William Bentinck, earl of Portland,[51] whose grandson sold it in 1735 to John Grimston.[52] At inclosure in 1769 Robert Grimston was allotted 1,489 a.,[53] and in 1777 he sold the manor with 1,557 a. of land to R. C. Broadley.[54] In 1803 Broadley conveyed it to Robert Prickett,[55] and after the latter's death in 1844 it was sold to George Hudson.[56] Albert Denison, Lord Londesborough, bought it from Hudson in 1849.[57] The estate was held by the earls of Londesborough until the early 20th century. In 1907 180 a. were sold to J. C. Wharram[58] and in 1909 the manor of Thwing, with 816 a. in Thwing and 1,615 a. in Octon, was sold to James Calder.[59] The Calders retained it until it was sold in separate lots in 1920–1, 1924, and 1936;[60] Manor Farm, with 338 a., went to Albert Conner in 1920.[61]

It is possible that the 2 carucates and 2 bovates of land in Thwing held by Chilbert and Grinchel before the Conquest[62] corresponded to the holding of 3 carucates and 2 bovates held by William of Harpham in 1284–5 in the Brus fee.[63] The lands owned by the Harphams in Thwing are several times mentioned earlier in the 13th century.[64] No further record has been found of the Harpham holding, but it may correspond to the land held by William of Argam in 1307.[65] It descended with Argam to Sir Robert Constable of Flamborough,[66] and was confiscated with his other estates in 1537.[67] The land may have been restored to the Constables,[68] but its later descent has not been traced. It had apparently been split up by 1616.[69]

In 1086 Octon was assessed at 14 carucates, held of the king by the count of Mortain.[70] A further two holdings were royal demesne: one carucate in 'Fornetorp',[71] which had been held by Torulf before the Conquest, and 3 carucates in 'Fornetorp' and Octon, which formed a berewick of Thwing.[72]

The Mortain manor apparently passed in 1088 to Niel Fossard[73] and from the Fossards to Peter Mauley, upon his marriage about 1214 to the Fossard heir, Isabel of Turnham.[74] Mauley is described as holding in chief 12 carucates in Octon in the late 13th century, the remaining 2 carucates having been split off to form the serjeanty described below.[75] The Mauley overlordship descended with that of Butterwick.[76]

The family which took its name from the place

---

[37] *E.Y.C.* ii, p. 14. [38] *Complete Peerage.*
[39] *Rolls of Just. for Yorks.* (Selden Soc. lvi), 394; *Rot. Litt. Claus.* (Rec. Com.), ii. 138; *Cal. Close,* 1227–31, 371; *V.C.H. Yorks.* iii. 24; *Complete Peerage.*
[40] *Feud. Aids,* vi. 30.
[41] *Cal. Inq. p.m.* vi, p. 239.
[42] *Yorks. Fines, 1347–77,* 14–15; *Cal. Inq. p.m.* xiv, pp. 53–9; *Complete Peerage.*
[43] *Yorks. Inq. Hen. IV–V,* 38–9; *Cal. Pat.* 1399–1401, 173; 1408–13, 351; *Feud. Aids,* vi. 260; *Complete Peerage.*
[44] C.P. 40/887 mm. 204, 272d.; C 1/313/40.
[45] *Cal. Pat.* 1553–4, 157–9; the Lumleys retained the manor throughout the period of its disputed use: *Cal. Pat.* 1485–94, 127; *Cal. Inq. p.m. Hen. VII,* iii, p. 263; *L. & P. Hen. VIII,* ii (1), p. 193.
[46] *Cal. Pat.* 1553–4, 157–9. [47] *Yorks. Fines,* ii. 138.
[48] C 66/1319 m. 38; E 178/2703.
[49] C 66/2351 no. 14; E 317/Yorks./57; C 54/3520 no. 33.
[50] C 66/3080 no. 1.
[51] C 54/4810 no. 11. Rob. Stafford died in 1671 (*Y.A.J.* xx. 316) and all rights belonging to his heirs in respect of a lease of the manor were included in this grant, as was another lease of 1650 of messuages and lands in Thwing: *Cal. S.P. Dom.* 1660–1, 367.
[52] Registry of Deeds, Beverley, O/174/423.
[53] Ibid. AK/376/29.
[54] Ibid. AT/388/40; AY/80/137. [55] Ibid. CA/265/34.
[56] Ibid. GA/81/102; /131/168.
[57] Ibid. GQ/145/164. [58] Ibid. 93/354/335 (1907).
[59] Ibid. 114/144/137.

[60] Ibid. 212/27/26; /498/421; 215/9/8; 219/331/281; 232/400/335; 278/29/25; 552/24/22.
[61] Ibid. 211/216/189.
[62] *V.C.H. Yorks.* ii. 204.
[63] *Feud. Aids,* vi. 30.
[64] *Pipe R.* 1176 (P.R.S. xxv), 117; *Cur. Reg. R.* xii. 398, 525; *Bridlington Charty.* 172; *Yorks. Fines, 1246–72,* 149–50; see below, p. 328.
[65] C 143/68/13; in 1537 Robt. Constable, heir of the Argam property, held 3 carucates and 7 bovates in Thwing: S.C. 6/Hen. VIII/4324.
[66] S.C. 2/211/38; *Cal. Close,* 1313–18, 485; *Cal. Inq. p.m.* vii, p. 403; viii, p. 223; *Cal. Inq. p.m. Hen. VII,* i, p. 152; see above, p. 6.
[67] S.C. 6/Hen. VIII/4324; *V.C.H. Yorks.* iii. 414.
[68] About 1580 Robt. Constable petitioned the Crown for his grandfather's estates, including lands in Thwing: E.R.R.O., DDHA/18/52. See p. 154.
[69] C 2/Jas. I/C 3/75.
[70] *V.C.H. Yorks.* ii. 323; it is recorded only in the summary.
[71] The name 'Fornetorp' does not occur again.
[72] *V.C.H. Yorks.* ii. 204, 323.
[73] Ibid. 155; *E.Y.C.* ii, p. 326 n.
[74] *E.Y.C.* ii, pp. 326 n., 327, 374 n.; *Complete Peerage.*
[75] *Feud. Aids,* vi. 30.
[76] Ibid. 142, 211, 267; *Cal. Pat.* 1330–4, 369; *Cal. Inq. p.m.* viii, p. 201; xv, p. 321; by 1302 the holding had been reassessed at 8 carucates and throughout the period was held with Boynton and Butterwick.

held land in Octon from at least the mid 12th century.[77] In 1260 John of Octon was granted free warren in his demesne lands there.[78] It was probably his son, another John, who in 1280 granted 15 bovates to Hugelin of Thwing for life.[79] By 1289 Marmaduke of Thwing was holding OCTON manor and in that year he agreed to pay an annuity to John of Octon's widow for life, in settlement of her claim to land in dower in Octon and elsewhere.[80] The manor thus passed to the Thwing family and in 1292 Marmaduke obtained a grant of free warren in Octon.[81] This holding thenceforth descended with Thwing and seems to have lost its identity as a separate manor. It was included in the transfer to Sir Thomas Heneage in 1579,[82] and appears to have been split up in 1584, when Heneage granted a portion of it to George Mainprise and a smaller holding to John Bossall, rector of the 'east' mediety of Thwing church.[83] In 1591 Mainprise died seised of 35 bovates in Octon, which he left in trust for the use of his 3 younger daughters;[84] his holding cannot be identified thereafter.

Several religious houses held small amounts of land in Octon during the Middle Ages — the Knights Hospitallers in the 12th century, the nuns of Wykeham (Yorks. N.R.) and St. Leonard's hospital, York, from the 12th to the 15th centuries, and Kirkstall abbey (Yorks. W.R.) in the 13th century. Former land of Nunkeeling priory, which was first mentioned at the Dissolution, was valued at 5s. in 1563.[85]

Two carucates of the Fossard fee formed by 1226 a tenancy in serjeanty held by William of Mowthorpe for the service of one archer.[86] The holder in 1231 was Anketin Mallore, William's son-in-law, to whom the king had granted it as a marriage settlement. At that date the serjeanty was held for the service of one archer for the defence of York castle for 40 days.[87] By 1250 the land was divided among five tenants, including John of Octon, under Anketin Mallore, who rendered £1 a year to the Crown for this alienation.[88] In the early 14th century part or all of the land was held directly from the Crown by John of Octon, probably grandson of the John named as a tenant in 1250. The serjeanty is last mentioned in 1333, when an enquiry was ordered to determine whether Geoffrey Hacun, parson of North Cave, and John of Warter had been unjustly distrained by the Exchequer for arrears of rent owed on the holding by the late John of Octon.[89]

It seems likely that the Crown holdings of 1086 together formed the Harpham fee, from which grants were made to Meaux abbey to form what later came to be known as Octon grange. In the mid 12th century 2½ carucates and a site for the grange were granted by Henry of Octon; Godfrey of Harpham confirmed the grant of 2 of the carucates, which were held of him, and himself granted a further carucate.[90] Godfrey later quitclaimed to the abbey a ditch and wall on the western side of the grange and the monks' sheepfolds outside the gate on the southern side.[91] Meaux retained the grange until the Dissolution, when it was worth £5;[92] it was at farm to Robert Hogeson and John Watford in 1540.[93] Crown grants of former abbey land at Octon were made to William Edrington and Edward Beseley in 1558[94] and to Edward Wingate in 1590.[95] It was perhaps the latter's estate which was held by the Tancreds in the 17th century.[96] Some of the former Meaux land was acquired by the Omblers in the 18th century.[97]

By the time of inclosure in 1769 the largest holdings in Octon, apart from that belonging to Thwing manor, were those of 391 a. allotted to Charles Roper and 231 a. allotted to Thomas Ombler.[98] These were acquired by R. C. Broadley in 1785 and 1791, respectively,[99] and thereafter descended with Thwing manor. When the Calders split up the estate in the 20th century, one farm at Octon Grange was sold in 1924 to R. E. Copeland; it passed to Walter Coates in 1945 and to Peter Armstrong in 1949.[1] A second farm there was sold to Condie Assets Ltd. in 1936; it passed to Wilfrid Hood in 1942 and to George Atkinson later the same year.[2] A farm at Octon was sold by the Calders to W. J. Burdass in 1920. J. C. Burdass had acquired, in 1910, the Octon land of the Osbaldeston–Mitfords, which had amounted to 171 a. at inclosure in 1769.[3] The Burdasses have since retained their Octon estate.

ECONOMIC HISTORY. In 1086 the king's estate at Thwing, which was soke of Burton Agnes, was waste. Of the other holdings, that of 2 carucates and 2 bovates had land for two ploughs, and the carucate in 'Fornetorp' land for half a plough.[4]

The apparent prosperity of Thwing up to the late 14th century may reflect the presence of the Thwing family,[5] one of whom, Marmaduke (III), obtained a grant of a market on Wednesdays and a fair on 6–8 July.[6] There is some evidence of poverty among the villagers in the 14th century. Waste tenements are referred to in 1361[7] and the profits of the manor court, despite an increase from 10s. a year in 1344 to £2 13s. 4d. in 1374, were said to be no more in the latter year because of the poverty of the tenants.[8] The manor-house, with demesne of 25 bovates and some closes, was worth about £19 in 1588, and

[77] See below.
[78] Cal. Chart. R. 1257–1300, 29.
[79] Yorks. Fines, 1272–1300, 59.
[80] Ibid. 87.
[81] Cal. Chart. R. 1257–1300, 428.
[82] Yorks Fines, ii. 138. .
[83] Ibid. iii. 21, 23; B.I.H.R., C.P., H. 2873.
[84] C 142/232/65.
[85] Chron. de Melsa (Rolls Ser.), i. 103; E.Y.C. i, p. 157; ii, pp. 101, 373–6; Feud. Aids, vi. 267; Cal. Pat. 1553, 104; 1560–3, 576; Valor Eccl. (Rec. Com.), v. 115; Yorks. Fines, 1218–31, 68.
[86] Bk. of Fees, i. 358.
[87] Ibid. ii. 1354. Stipulation was also made for a serjeant to lead the king's treasure through the county.
[88] Ibid. 1201.
[89] Cal. Close, 1333–7, 58.
[90] Chron. de Melsa, i. 102–3.
[91] E.Y.C. ii, pp. 372–3.
[92] Valor Eccl. v. 108.
[93] S.C. 6/Hen. VIII/4612.
[94] Cal. Pat. 1557–8, 390.
[95] C 66/1351 m. 25.
[96] Royalist Composition Papers, i. 65–6; Cal. S.P. Dom. Addenda, 1660–85, 67.
[97] Regy. of Deeds, H/286/604; BP/361/597.
[98] Ibid. AK/376/29.
[99] Ibid. AW/439/746; BI/8/17; BP/361/597.
[1] Ibid. 278/29/25; 691/327/276; 814/67/55.
[2] Ibid. 552/24/22; 652/389/333; /391/334.
[3] Ibid. AK/376/29; 129/23/20; 215/9/8.
[4] V.C.H. Yorks. ii. 198, 204.
[5] See p. 326.
[6] Cal. Chart. R. 1226–57, 472.
[7] Cal. Inq. p.m. xi, p. 259.
[8] Ibid. viii, p. 369; xiv, p. 56.

tenants' land was valued at £31.[9] In 1650 the manor-house, closes, and 250 a. of demesne were worth £29; tenants' land was valued at £48 and the profits of the court were nearly £7.[10]

Of the 11 tenants of the manor in 1588 2 had 9 bovates, and one each had 8, 7, 4, 2, one, and ½ bovates. Two others had only a cottage and garth, and another held the smithy.[11] There were also 11 tenants in 1650 and their holdings were of much the same size as in 1588. Each bovate in 1650 was said to comprise 10 a., and holdings were also measured by the number of 'lands or ridges' they contained: there were generally 12 or 13 lands to the bovate.[12]

There is some evidence that Thwing and Octon had separate open fields, for Thwing field and Octon field are mentioned in the 16th and 17th centuries. The subdivision of this land in Octon is not known, but East and West fields are sometimes distinguished in Thwing.[13] By at least the 18th century the open fields of both townships were regulated in the manorial court of Thwing.[14] At inclosure in 1769 Thwing and Octon fields accounted for all the commonable land; allotments totalling 1,837 a. were made in Thwing field, 1,213 a. in Octon field, and 683 a. were allotted indistinguishably from both fields.[15]

Of common meadow or pasture there is little indication at any period. Even Meaux abbey's grange at Octon seems to have been largely arable, with sheep-rearing dependent upon common rights over open-field land or pasturage in arable closes when they were fallow or harvested. In the 12th century Meaux had common of pasture for 500 sheep, but in the early 13th century, after a dispute, John of Octon granted the abbey instead common rights appurtenant to the 30 bovates which it held in Octon.[16] The grange was let by the abbey in both 1298 and 1396.[17] An undated document, probably of the 15th century, shows that Meaux had 410 a. of arable and 25 a. of pasture at Octon, and it seems likely that some of this was inclosed.[18] In 1769 there were a dozen small closes around the site of the grange; their area is not stated but was hardly more than 60 a.[19] There was also apparently a pasture set aside for horses and cows at Octon in the 18th century; in 1750 it was stated that it was 'bounded out' by the bylawmen on or before 10 April each year. In the same year the stint for sheep in the parish was 8 for each bovate and 6 for a house, and for beasts 2 for every 3 bovates and one for a house.[20]

Apart from any inclosures thus made by Meaux there were several closes belonging to the manor of Thwing. These totalled 15 a. in 1650 and included Wipeham, adjoining Wold Newton.[21] A close called Wipholm is mentioned as early as 1344[22] and the name may eventually have been corrupted to the Wykeham close of 1769.[23] The rest of the parish was inclosed in 1769[24] under an Act of the same year.[25] A total of 3,763 a. were dealt with and allotments of 3,733 a. all told were made. The lord of the manor, Robert Grimston, received 1,489 a. and the rector 557 a. for tithes and glebe. Substantial allotments also went to Charles Roper, with 391 a., and Thomas Ombler, with 231 a., both described as of Octon Grange. Richard Newton received 191 a., Stephen Bennison 175 a., Humphrey Osbaldeston 171 a., Francis Matson 149 a., and Robert Vickerman and Mary Raper 119 a. each. Two other allotments were of between 20 a. and 50 a., 3 of between 10 a. and 20 a., and 4 of under 10 a. Farming in Thwing remained predominantly arable after inclosure, and in 1801 1,422 a. were under crops.[26] There have been between 10 and 15 farmers in the 19th and 20th centuries.[27]

A miller is mentioned as early as 1297[28] and there was a windmill at Octon in 1323.[29] A windmill is recorded in the late 16th century, and in 1685 a windmill and a horse-mill paid tithe.[30] A mill is not mentioned again, but Mill closes lay near the south end of Octon hamlet in 1769.[31]

LOCAL GOVERNMENT. The assize of bread and ale was a franchise of the lords of Thwing in the late 13th century.[32] There are surviving jury verdicts and other papers covering the years 1722–76 and 1805–63.[33] The officers commonly appointed in the 18th century were an affeeror, bylawmen, constables, and a pinder, and the court was largely concerned with agricultural matters. Regulations drawn up in 1750 dealt with open fields and pasturage, but others made in 1805 were adjusted to the new routine of the inclosed parish.[34]

Overseers of the poor are mentioned in 1630, when money was left for them to distribute.[35] There were two small unendowed alms-houses in 1720.[36] No parochial records before 1835 are known. In 1836 Thwing joined the Bridlington union.[37]

CHURCH. The benefice of Thwing was a rectory of medieties. It is first mentioned in an undated charter of the 13th century when John of Harpham granted the advowson of one mediety to Bridlington priory.[38] The priory presented to this mediety in 1233 and, although the archbishop collated by lapse in 1280 or 1281, it retained the advowson until the Dissolution, when it passed to the Crown.[39] The

---

[9] E 178/2703.
[10] E 317/Yorks./57.
[11] E 178/2703.
[12] E 317/Yorks./57.
[13] B.I.H.R., TER. J. Thwing 1663, 1685; Registry of Deeds, Beverley, AK/376/29.
[14] E.R.R.O., DDLO/26/1, 2.
[15] Regy. of Deeds, AK/376/29.
[16] Chron. de Melsa (Rolls Ser.), i. 103, 430.
[17] C. Platt, Monastic Grange in Med. Eng 103, 225.
[18] B.M. Cott. MS. Vit. C. vi, f. 218; E.H.R. li. 197.
[19] E.R.R.O., IA. Thwing. It has been suggested that the tithe-free land around Octon Grange, amounting to 543 a. in 1839, represents the consolidated medieval grange: Platt, Monastic Grange, 61–2. Most of this land was, however, still uninclosed in 1769.
[20] Ibid. DDLO/26/1.
[21] E 317/Yorks./57.
[22] Cal. Inq. p.m. viii, p. 368.
[23] E.R.R.O., IA. Thwing.
[24] Regy. of Deeds, AK/376/29; map in E.R.R.O., IA. Thwing.
[25] 8 & 9 Geo. III, sess. 2, c. 32 (Priv. Act).
[26] 1801 Crop Returns.
[27] Directories.
[28] Lay Subsidy, 1297 (Y.A.S. Rec. Ser. xvi), 141.
[29] Cal. Inq. p.m. vi, p. 239.
[30] B.I.H.R., TER. J. Thwing 1685; Yorks. Fines, ii. 129.
[31] E.R.R.O., IA. Thwing.
[32] J.I. 1/1110 m. 81.
[33] E.R.R.O., DDLO/26/1–7.
[34] Ibid. /1, 6.
[35] B.I.H.R., Prob. Reg. xli, f. 150.
[36] Ibid. ER. V/Ch.P. 1720, f. 152.
[37] 3rd Rep. Poor Law Com. 167.
[38] Bridlington Charty. 172.
[39] Ibid. 3; Reg. Gray (Sur. Soc. lvi), 59, 75–6, 108; Reg. Wickwane (Sur. Soc. cxiv), 96, 108.

first reference to the advowson of the other mediety occurs in 1301, when its custody, after sequestration, had been assigned to Geoffrey Maucovenant, who presented in that year.[40] He again presented in 1312, but in 1335 the advowson was in dispute between William of Thwing and Geoffrey de Stutville.[41] William of Thwing held the advowson at his death in 1340;[42] thereafter it followed the descent of the manor and was included in the exchange of 1588 when it passed to the Crown. The Crown retained both medieties and from the later 17th century it became customary for one rector to be presented to both.[43] In 1748, at the request of the then rector and with the consent of the Crown, the archbishop consolidated the medieties.[44] The patronage has remained in the hands of the Crown.

In 1292 the value of each mediety was £20, but this was reduced to £12 in the new taxation.[45] In 1525 each mediety was valued at £6 13s. 4d.[46] and in 1535 at £8 11s. 11d. net. The gross income of each mediety in the latter year was subject to outgoings of 8s. 5d., of which a rent of thraves and corn worth 2s. 8d. was paid to the provost of Beverley.[47] In 1650 the total valuation for both medieties was £127.[48] In 1829–31 the average net income was £520 a year[49] and in 1884 £700.[50]

In 1535 tithes accounted for most of the income.[51] In 1769, at inclosure, the tithe of one mediety was commuted for a rent-charge of £102 10s., and that of the other for 479 a. of land.[52] In the 18th century land formerly belonging to Octon Grange was exempt from the payment of tithe;[53] it amounted to 543 a. in 1839, when tithes on it were commuted for a rent-charge of £53 a year.[54] The glebe is mentioned in 1317, when a house appurtenant to it was in dispute,[55] but nothing is known of its size until 1535, when each mediety had 3 bovates.[56] In 1769 it comprised 78 a., including a stone-pit.[57] This, together with the 479 a. awarded in lieu of tithes, remained to the rectory until 1920, when it was sold for £20,824, which was invested.[58] In 1923 £3,333 of this sum were transferred to the poorly-endowed benefice of Sculcoates.[59]

The parsonage house and grounds were probably enlarged in 1344, when a licence was granted to the lord of the manor to alienate a toft and 1½ a. of land to the rector of an unspecified mediety for that purpose.[60] In 1535 each rector had a house.[61] By the 17th century the two houses were known as the east and west parsonages. The west was better-provided than the east,[62] possibly because the lords of the manor owned the advowson of the mediety to which it belonged.[63] In 1674 it had six hearths,[64] and in 1685 it comprised at least nine rooms, with outbuildings, a dovecot, and several closes and garths, in addition to glebe land in the open fields.[65] The last reference to a separate east parsonage occurs in 1743[66] but it must have been in a ruinous condition at that date since in 1721 it was said to have been down several years.[67] It was presumably the west parsonage which was occupied after the late 17th century when it became customary for one rector to be appointed to both medieties. No trace of either house remained in 1970. The modern Rectory, in an isolated position at the west end of the village, is a large brick and slate house built in 1870–1.[68]

The advowson of a chantry dedicated to St. Thomas the Apostle was held by Thomas of Thwing in 1348 and at his death in 1374;[69] the foundation has been attributed to him.[70] The advowson descended with the manor and was held by John Lumley at his death in 1421.[71] In 1387 there was a guild dedicated to the Holy Trinity, but nothing further is known of it.[72] In the earlier 15th century small bequests to the Virgin and John the Baptist probably refer to lights or altars in the church.[73]

There are several instances of absentee rectors, and of others holding their living in plurality. Two had leave of absence to study in the 13th and early 14th centuries, and in 1257, 1349, and 1476 the rectors obtained permission to hold their mediety in plurality with another benefice.[74] In 1743 the rector of the two medieties was serving as chaplain on board the warship *Prince Frederick*, and in 1764 he lived at Scarborough, employing a curate who himself lived at Rudston.[75] The incumbent in 1835 was also rector of St. Nicholas, Nottingham;[76] in 1868 he lived near London,[77] and in 1871 the rector, a different man, also had a chaplaincy at Lincoln's Inn;[78] all three men employed a curate at Thwing.

In 1650 the parliamentary commissioners reported that the parish was served by Edward Fowler, who had been rector of a mediety in 1640 and was not deprived.[79] In 1668, in the course of a dispute, it was disclosed that the lessee of the manor-house had taken over and much altered the reading place and seat on the south side of the church reserved for the rector of the 'east' mediety. It was also shown that the rectors of the medieties had always had a place reserved for them, one on each side of the church; in the settlement of the dispute the then rector of the two medieties was granted the right to both pews.[80]

---

[40] *Reg. Corbridge*, i (Sur. Soc. cxxxviii), 169.
[41] *Reg. Greenfield*, iii (Sur. Soc. cli), 203; *Yorks. Fines, 1327–47*, 80.
[42] *Cal. Inq. p.m.* viii, p. 202.
[43] B.I.H.R., Adm. 1662, 1747. In 1667 the rectors of both medieties died about the same time and Robt. Constable was appointed to both: ibid., Reg. 6, p. 70.
[44] Ibid. Bp. 3/88; Lawton, *Rer. Eccles. Dioc. Ebor.* 314.
[45] *Tax. Eccl.* (Rec. Com.), 304, 326; *Cal. Pat. 1338–40*, 253.
[46] *Y.A.J.* xxiv. 65.
[47] *Valor Eccl.* (Rec. Com.), v. 124.
[48] *T.E.R.A.S.* ii. 58.
[49] *Rep. Com. Eccl. Revenues*, 974–5.
[50] B.I.H.R., Bp. V. 1884/Ret.
[51] *Valor Eccl.* v. 124.
[52] Registry of Deeds, Beverley, AK/376/29.
[53] B.I.H.R., TER. J. Thwing 1726, 1749.
[54] Ibid. TA. 108S.
[55] C.P. 40/217 m. 75.
[56] *Valor Eccl.* v. 124.
[57] Regy. of Deeds, AK/376/29.
[58] Ibid. 220/353/307; ex inf. the rector, 1961.
[59] York Dioc. Regy., Orders in Council 625.
[60] *Abbrev. Rot. Orig.* (Rec. Com.), 170; *Cal. Pat. 1343–5*, 331.
[61] *Valor Eccl.* v. 124.
[62] B.I.H.R., TER. J. Thwing 1685 to 1743.
[63] E 178/2703.
[64] E 179/205/521.
[65] B.I.H.R., TER. J. Thwing 1685.
[66] Ibid. 1743.
[67] Ibid. ER. V/CB. 15, f. 43.
[68] Ex inf. the rector, 1961.
[69] B.I.H.R., Reg. 10, f. 192; *Cal. Inq. p.m.* xiv, pp. 53–9.
[70] Lawton, *Rer. Eccles. Dioc. Ebor.* 314.
[71] C 139/55/42.
[72] B.I.H.R., Reg. 14, f. 16.
[73] Ibid. Prob. Reg. ix, f. 211; xi, f. 187.
[74] *Cal. Papal Regs.* i. 351; xiii (2), 498; *Cal. Papal Pets.* i. 183.
[75] B.I.H.R., Bp. V. 1764/Ret. 91; *Herring's Visit.* iii. 173–4.
[76] *Rep. Com. Eccl. Revenues*, 974–5.
[77] B.I.H.R., V. 1868/Ret. 502.
[78] Ibid., V. 1871/Ret. 508.
[79] B.I.H.R., V. 1640/Exh. Bk.; Reg. 6, p. 70; *T.E.R.A.S.* ii. 58.
[80] B.I.H.R., C.P., H. 2873.

In 1743 one service was held in the church every Sunday and Holy Communion was celebrated four times a year. Communion was received by 40–50 people in the 18th century.[81] By 1851 the services had been increased to two on Sundays[82] and by the end of the century communion was celebrated at least once every month. There were only 10–20 communicants at this period.[83] In 1936 communion was celebrated twice on Sundays and once on Wednesdays.[84] In 1970 there were two, sometimes three, services each Sunday.

The church of ALL SAINTS consists of chancel, nave with north aisle, west tower, and north and south doorways, the latter with a porch. The prevailing style of architecture is that of the 13th and 14th centuries,[85] but many of the features, including the present tower, date from a restoration of 1900. There are, however, some remains of a 12th-century church. The south doorway is of that period, having shafts with spiral ornamentation and carved capitals, and a tympanum with a crudely-carved *Agnus Dei* below a 'zig-zag' arch.[86] The chancel arch is also of the 12th century; it has three orders with two roll-mouldings, flanked by plain shafts with carved and scalloped capitals. A small restored lancet window near the west end of the south nave wall may replace one of the 13th century. The north aisle was added to the nave in the late 13th or early 14th century, when the arcade of four pointed arches resting on octagonal piers was built. The east end of the aisle was altered or extended rather later in the 14th century to accommodate the chantry dedicated to St. Thomas. Between aisle and chapel is an arch supported on corbel brackets. On the east wall of the chapel is a small relief of a figure kneeling at an altar. There is a projecting piscina with trefoiled head on the south side and, above it, a very long 'squint' towards the chancel. The aisle windows, except for one which is apparently of the 17th century, date from the restoration of 1900. An original three-light 14th-century window with reticulated tracery in the south nave wall has a tomb recess below it. Another three-light window was inserted in the same wall in the 15th century. The present chancel does not appear to be ancient and the east window, of five lights, probably dates from 1836. The other windows are even later insertions.[87] Before the restoration of 1900 the west tower appears to have stood partly within the area of the present nave. Its date is not known but the belfry stage had no medieval features.[88]

Bequests for the upkeep of the fabric were made in the 15th and 16th centuries.[89] Externally above the north doorway is a tablet of 1686 perhaps recording repairs at that date. Over the window to the west of the doorway a stone is inscribed 'Thos. Ebor 1691', suggesting that the window may have been inserted in memory of Thomas Lamplugh (1615–91), archbishop, born in Thwing. In 1738 the choir was in need of repair.[90] A faculty was granted in 1803 to rebuild the chancel,[91] and in 1814 the church was repewed at the expense of the parishioners. In 1836 Robert Prickett, lord of the manor, thoroughly repaired the church and gave the glass in the five lights of the east window.[92]

An extensive restoration took place in 1900 under the direction of Temple Moore.[93] The tower was demolished and a small new one was built beyond the west end of the nave. It has plain square-headed belfry windows, but in its south wall an original trefoil-headed lancet of the later 13th century has been reset. The south porch was erected as a memorial to Archbishop Lamplugh.[94] The porch contains what may be a 14th-century stoup with a traceried head; several ancient fragments, including the head of a foliated cross, are built into the walls. During the restoration two galleries of the 18th or early 19th century were removed from the north aisle.[95] The 12th-century font was installed in the church at the turn of the 19th century. It is said to have come from Sewerby and has lozenge-pattern decoration similar to that on the font at Flamborough.[96]

The monuments include the recumbent effigy of a priest in eucharistic garments, thought to represent a 14th-century member of the Thwing family.[97] There are several monuments to the Lowish family.

There are two bells; that of 1720 was made by Samuel Smith, the younger, and that of 1762 by E. Seller, both of York.[98] The plate comprises a silver-gilt chalice, salver, and dish, dated 1689, the gift of Archbishop Lamplugh. A pewter flagon, dating from at least 1764, has been lost.[99] The registers begin in 1691 and are largely complete, except for the years 1727–35.[1] An addition was made to the churchyard in 1900.[2]

Between 1180 and 1210 Adam, rector of Thwing, granted John of Octon the right to have services celebrated in the chapel of St. Michael at Octon by a chaplain. This grant was in accordance with the terms of an earlier gift of 2 bovates and a toft to Thwing church, made at an unknown date by an ancestor of John of Octon to obtain similar rights.[3] In 1328 the archbishop stipulated that the rectors of Thwing should pay £1 6s. 8d. a year for a chaplain to serve the chapel from Martinmas to Whitsun, attendance at the church of Thwing by Octon inhabitants being obligatory on specified days.[4] The patronage of the chapel was held by the Thwing family and descended with the manor to the Lumleys. In 1327 William of Thwing endowed a chantry in the chapel with 4 bovates and 3 a. of land and rents of £1 6s. 8d. for a chaplain to celebrate daily for the soul of his father Marmaduke.[5] Nothing further is known of this chantry except that the

---

[81] B.I.H.R., Bp. V. 1764/Ret. 91; *Herring's Visit.* iii. 173–4.
[82] H.O. 129/24/524.
[83] B.I.H.R., V. 1877/Ret.; Bp. V. 1884/Ret.; Bp. V. 1894/Ret.
[84] Ibid., Bp. V. 1936/Ret. 309.
[85] Morris, *E.R. Yorks.* 313–15.
[86] For a similar tympanum see p. 302.
[87] Before the 1900 restoration the south wall of the chancel had no windows: photo. in church.
[88] Photos. in church.
[89] B.I.H.R., Prob. Reg. ii, f. 492; viii, f. 16; ix, f. 210; *Test. Ebor.* iv. 38; vi. 212.
[90] B.I.H.R., ER. V/Ch.P. 1738.
[91] Ibid. FAC. 1803/3.
[92] *Kelly's Dir. N. & E.R. Yorks.* (1872), 554.
[93] *Guide* in church; *D.N.B.*
[94] Tablet in porch.
[95] Photo. in church.
[96] *T.E.R.A.S.* x. 108–9.
[97] *Guide*; *D.N.B.*
[98] Boulter, 'Ch. Bells', 218; *V.C.H. Yorks.* ii. 452.
[99] B.I.H.R., TER. J. Thwing 1764; Bp. V. 1764/Ret. 91; *Yorks. Ch. Plate*, i. 326.
[1] Barley, *Par. Docs. E.R.* 145.
[2] York Dioc. Regy., Sentence of consecration.
[3] *E.Y.C.* ii, p. 376.
[4] Lawton, *Rer. Eccles. Dioc. Ebor.* 314.
[5] C 143/192/8; *Cal. Pat.* 1327–30, 145.

advowson remained with the lords of Thwing manor until the 15th century.

Octon chapel is last mentioned in 1400, when the advowson was in the king's hands owing to the forfeiture of Ralph Lumley.[6] Earthworks still mark its supposed site.

NONCONFORMITY. In 1663 a Quaker at Thwing was presented for failing to pay the church assessment,[7] and eight dissenters were reported in 1676.[8] There was one dissenting family in 1720.[9] Houses were registered for worship in 1789, 1802, and 1831.[10] A Wesleyan Methodist chapel was built at the west end of the village about 1810,[11] and it was presumably that which was registered for worship in 1814.[12] It was rebuilt and enlarged in 1839[13] and completely rebuilt in 1906.[14] A Primitive Methodist chapel was built at the east end of the village in 1840.[15] There were only six members in 1889.[16] The chapel was still standing in the early 20th century but was demolished after 1937.[17]

The rector of the parish church commented in 1868 that most of his parishioners were nonconformist. By 1884 it was said that all except two or three families were dissenters, and a similar complaint was made at the end of the century.[18]

EDUCATION. In 1682 an unlicensed schoolmaster was teaching in Thwing,[19] and in 1764 a master taught English in the village.[20] By 1819 there was an unendowed school with 25 pupils, but farm labourers could not afford to send their children there.[21] In 1833 there were two day-schools, one each for boys and girls, each with an attendance of about 25 children. Fees were paid but an annual gift from the rector and the lord of the manor enabled a number of poor children to attend without payment.[22] In 1835 the same lord of the manor, Robert Prickett, built a school and school-house.[23] The school, which was of brick and slate and stood south of the church on the site of the earlier girls' school,[24] was in 1844 transferred to trustees. In 1863 there were about 30 children in attendance; a rival school with about 15 pupils was said to be held in the church.[25] The school was united with the National Society by 1868 and an annual government grant was first received that year.[26] By 1871, when it was the only school in the village, it had accommodation for 49 and an average attendance of 34.[27]

In 1881 a school board was formed at the request of the ratepayers. It proposed to take over the National school, where the accommodation was said to be inadequate,[28] but the trustees would not agree to the transfer. In 1884 a government loan was granted and a new school, with accommodation for 70 children, was built on the Foxholes road on a site given by W. H. F. Denison, earl of Londesborough.[29] By 1894 the National school was used as a parish room[30] and this remained in use in 1970.

The board always had difficulty in retaining teachers and as early as 1886 the inspector reported unsatisfactorily on the condition of the school.[31] The average attendance was 47 in 1893.[32] The school was reported to be inefficient in 1897 and withdrawal of the annual grant was threatened, but by 1901 an improvement was noted.[33] The accommodation was increased to 90 in 1909. The average attendance was 58 in 1908 and remained at between 60 and 70 until the 1930s; in 1938 it was 47.[34] Senior pupils were transferred to Filey in 1953.[35] The school was closed in 1967 and the children transferred to Wold Newton.[36]

A night school was held during the winter of 1868.[37] Special classes were held at the Rectory in 1877 for girls who had left day-school, and it was said that some young farm workers were also having special instruction.[38]

CHARITIES FOR THE POOR. Mary Austin, in a codicil to her will dated 1770, bequeathed £100, the interest to be divided among six poor widows in the parish; by another codicil a further £100 was added.[39] In 1896 the income was £5 10s., in 1907 £5,[40] and in 1961 £5 5s.[41]

John Stephenson, by will of 1717, left £1 for the poor, and Thomas Vickerman similarly left £5 at his death in 1776. In 1926 the joint income of these charities was 7s. and the capital was then £2 10s. and £12 11s. respectively. About 1857 M. Deane bequeathed about £57 for the upkeep of two graves.[42] Income of nearly £2, apparently from this bequest, was in 1961 used along with the income from Stephenson's and Vickerman's charities.[43]

---

[6] See p. 326.
[7] B.I.H.R., V. 1662-3/CB. 1.
[8] Bodl. MS. Tanner 150, ff. 27 sqq.
[9] B.I.H.R., ER. V/Ch.P. 1720.
[10] G.R.O. Worship Returns, Vol. v, nos. 753, 1686, 4262.
[11] H.O. 129/24/524.
[12] G.R.O. Worship Returns, Vol. v, no. 2952.
[13] H.O. 129/24/524. There appear to have been 2 returns for the same chapel.
[14] Ex inf. the rector, 1961.
[15] H.O. 129/24/524.
[16] H. Woodcock, *Sketches of Prim. Meth. on Yorks. Wolds*, 78.
[17] Directories.
[18] B.I.H.R., V. 1877/Ret.; Bp. V. 1884/Ret.; Bp. V. 1894/Ret.; Bp. V. 1900/Ret. 391.
[19] B.I.H.R., V. 1682/CB.
[20] Ibid. Bp. V. 1764/Ret. 91.
[21] *Rets. on Educ. of Poor, 1819*, 1095.
[22] *Educ. Enquiry Abstract, 1835*, 1097.
[23] Ed. 7/135; Sheahan and Whellan, *Hist. York & E.R.* ii. 490; *Kelly's Dir. N. & E.R. Yorks.* (1889), 465.
[24] O.S. Map 6" (1854); ex inf. the rector, 1961.
[25] Ed. 7/135.
[26] *Rep. of Educ. Cttee. of Counc. 1868* [4139], p. 633, H.C. (1868–9), xx.
[27] *Rets. rel. Elem. Educ. 1871*, 476.
[28] E.R.R.O., Sch. Bd. Min. Bk., 10 Mar. and 14 June 1881.
[29] Ibid. 1881–2, *passim*; *Kelly's Dir. N. & E.R. Yorks.* (1889), 465; O.S. Map 6" (1892).
[30] B.I.H.R., Bp. V. 1894/Ret.
[31] E.R.R.O., Sch. Bd. Min. Bk., *passim*.
[32] *Ret. of Schs. 1893* [C. 7529], pp. 744–5, H.C. (1894), lxv.
[33] E.R.R.O., Sch. Bd. Min. Bk., 4 Aug. 1897; 5 July 1901.
[34] *Bd. of Educ. List 21* (H.M.S.O.).
[35] E.R. Educ. Cttee. *Mins.* 1953–4, 75, 144.
[36] Ibid. 1967–8, 80, 92, 118.
[37] B.I.H.R., V. 1868/Ret. 502.
[38] Ibid. V. 1877/Ret.
[39] *9th Rep. Char. Com.* 739.
[40] Char. Com. files.
[41] Ex inf. the rector, 1961.
[42] Char. Com. files.
[43] Ex inf. the rector, 1961.

WILLERBY

THE parish of Willerby, roughly rectangular in shape, lies on the northern edge of the wolds, 12 miles north-west of Bridlington.[1] It includes the townships of Binnington and Staxton, the former only a small hamlet but Staxton a much larger village than Willerby itself. The three settlements are of mixed Anglian and Scandinavian origin: Binnington may be purely Anglian, but the other names contain elements from both periods.[2] There is a long history of settlement in the area, for at a site just to the east of Staxton village evidence has been found of occupation during the early Bronze Age, the early Iron Age, and the Romano–British periods. Sixth-century material was also found and near by there was an Anglian cemetery. The same site yielded the remains of a 13th-century house, but the centre of settlement was by then presumably on the site of the modern village.[3]

The parish stretches for 4 miles from north to south, from the rivers Derwent and Hertford, which form the wapentake and riding boundary, across the low ground of the vale, over the chalk escarpment, and up to the high wolds. Parts of the parish boundary on the low ground follow watercourses, notably Spital beck in the east, and on the wolds use is made of several prehistoric earthworks and dry-valley bottoms. The total area of the ancient parish is 4,567 a., of which 1,686 a. lie in Willerby, 1,576 a. in Staxton, and 1,305 a. in Binnington.[4]

South of the escarpment much of the wold ground in the parish exceeds 500 ft. above sea-level and reaches a maximum of 585 ft. just behind Staxton brow. The wolds are, however, deeply dissected by several steep-sided dry valleys, the most prominent being Well Slack and Cotton Dale which together run almost the full width of the parish. South of these lay Prior Moor, an area used by the flocks of Bridlington priory in the Middle Ages, and beyond that another valley, Ness Slack. Between Ness Slack and the southern parish boundary is an area known as Binnington Ness, which forms a projection of Binnington into Willerby township. The characteristic open landscape of the wolds includes several long shelter-belts, and there are plantations on some of the steeper valley sides, but the amount of woodland has been much reduced since the mid 19th century.[5] Most of the woodland had no doubt been planted after the inclosures of Staxton in 1803 and Binnington in 1804, when the open fields and sheep-walks gave way to a pattern of large regular fields.

Binnington, Willerby, and Staxton brows form one of the highest and steepest stretches of the north-facing wolds escarpment and were known in the Middle Ages as the Cliff.[6] South of Staxton village, for example, the ground rises nearly 400 ft. in little more than a quarter of a mile. There are several plantations on these slopes. Below the escarpment the chalk gives way to a broad belt of sand and gravel, at first between 100 ft. and 200 ft. above sea-level but further north much of it below 100 ft. The higher parts of the sands were formerly used as open-field land and meadow, the lower formed the ill-drained carrs which also extended across the alluvium bordering the rivers in the extreme north of the parish. The low lands were included in the inclosures of 1803–4 and it was at that time that the waterlogged ground was being drained, as in neighbouring parishes, under the Muston Drainage Act of 1800.[7] Drainage work included the cutting of a new straight channel for the river Hertford, which crosses the parish to the south of the winding courses of the old Derwent and Hertford, the latter subsequently known as the Little Hertford river. The flat open landscape of these areas is relieved by a number of plantations in Willerby and Binnington townships.

All three villages lie close to the Malton–Filey road, which runs west–east below the escarpment. From this road at Spital Corner the road to Seamer, in the North Riding, runs along the eastern boundary of Willerby parish and apparently represents an ancient route across the vale. It formerly crossed the river at the 'goat ford' which by the 12th century had given its name to the river Hertford.[8] From Staxton village, ¾ mile west of Spital Corner, another road climbs the wold escarpment and runs southwards towards Great Driffield and, eventually, Beverley. It is mentioned in the 13th century[9] and is frequently called Beverley Gate. The Beverley, Malton, and Seamer roads now form part of the trunk roads from Hull and Leeds to Scarborough, and various improvements have been made to them in the 20th century. The medieval 'road of Langeslac'[10] was probably another way up to the wolds, and in modern times field roads from all three villages have led up the escarpment. In the south of the parish other minor roads lead to Fordon and to Ganton.

The villages all lie a short distance to the north of the Malton–Filey road. The village street of Staxton runs parallel to the main road to which it is joined by East and West Townend Roads and by a small lane near the centre of the village. The street continues westwards to Willerby as Wain's Lane and beyond Willerby it formerly continued to Binnington.[11] The latter road was probably the Kirkegate or Kirkesti of the Middle Ages.[12] Several lanes lead from the villages northwards into the ings and carrs. The York–Scarborough railway line, opened in 1845,[13] crosses the north of the parish.

Until the 20th century the parish church and Manor and Grange Farms were all that remained of Willerby village. The grass fields around them, still unfenced from the former village street, contain extensive earthworks, some of which may mark the sites of crofts and garths, others the position of

---

[1] This article was written in 1961 and revised in 1971. Use has been made of material compiled by Mrs. Mary E. Dymond.
[2] *P.N.E.R. Yorks.* (E.P.N.S.), 117–18.
[3] *Y.A.J.* xxxix. 193–223; T. C. M. Brewster, *Two Med. Habitation Sites in Vale of Pickering* (Yorks. Mus.), 7, 12, 41.
[4] O.S. Map 6" (1854).
[5] Ibid. (1854 and later edns.).
[6] *Bridlington Charty.* 96, 117.
[7] See p. 337.
[8] *P.N.E.R. Yorks.* 6, 118.
[9] *Bridlington Charty.* 114, 117, 127.
[10] Ibid. 127.
[11] T. Jefferys, *Map of Yorks.* (1772); O.S. Map 6" (1854).
[12] *Bridlington Charty.* 122, 125.
[13] K. A. MacMahon, *Beginnings of E. Yorks. Rlys.* (E. Yorks. Loc. Hist. Ser. iii), 11.

Bridlington priory's grange.[14] Manor Farm comprises two distinct parts forming a large house with a double-gabled roof: a 19th-century brick range, two storeys high and three bays long, has been added to the front of a slightly lower 18th-century chalk-built house, again of two storeys. The extensive chalk farm buildings were partly derelict in 1971. Grange Farm includes an older chalk house but the present brick farm-house is a later-19th-century building. Several 20th-century houses and bungalows have been built at and near the village site; they include a group on the main Malton road and, towards Staxton, 34 Council houses near the village hall, which was opened in 1938.[15]

The hamlet of Binnington, ¾ mile west of Willerby, consists of two farm-houses and several cottages, mostly of the 19th century, with some slight traces of earthworks which may indicate the sites of former houses.

The large village of Staxton contains few houses apparently earlier than the 18th century, though the date 1649 appears on a much-altered cottage, now the Stirrup (formerly the Board) inn.[16] Many of the farm-houses and cottages are of chalk; of the later brick buildings several are in the striped and mottled brick common at Filey.[17] The only other dated house, of 1721, is May Farm, a two-storeyed cement-rendered chalk building with a three-bay plan and off-centre doorway more typical of the 17th than of the 18th century. Another 18th-century house with a similar early plan was standing empty and semi-derelict at the east end of the village in 1971. It is of a storey and a half, built of chalk but much repaired with brick, and has stone dressings, a dentil eaves course, and a pedimented doorcase. Several chalk barns in the village have brick or stone plinths, quoins, and eaves courses. Houses on the main road include the much-altered Hare and Hounds, an inn which has existed since at least the early 19th century,[18] and two square 19th-century brick farm-houses, one of them with stone quoins, both of which have symmetrical fronts and classical doorcases. Twentieth-century buildings in Staxton include 22 Council houses.

About ¼ mile east of Staxton is Spital House, standing near the banks and hollows which mark the site of the medieval hospital of St. Mary.[19] Excavations near by have yielded 13th- or 14th-century pottery.[20] The farm-house is of 18th-century origin but has been much altered. It consists of a three-bay section, of one storey with attics, to which a slightly higher one-bay section, also of one storey and attics, has been added at the end. The two parts, both of which are of chalk, are not on the same alignment. The room over the smaller section is said to have been the 'men's end'.[21] Other outlying buildings in the parish, all apparently of the 19th century, include Willerby Wold House, a large and imposing farm-house.

Staxton beacon was in existence in 1588, taking its signal from Muston and passing it on to Cowlam.[22] It stood on a barrow on a hill behind the escarpment. The discovery of 4th-century pottery on the hill-top suggests that there may have been a Roman signal station there.[23] On the same site in 1971 the Ministry of Defence had an early-warning radar station, opened in 1938.[24]

In 1377 there were 81 poll-tax payers in Willerby, 36 in Binnington, and 71 in Staxton.[25] In 1670 the number of households assessed to or discharged from the hearth tax was 21 in Willerby, 19 in Binnington, and 25 in Staxton. Four years later, when 29 households in the whole parish were discharged, 11 of the chargeable households in Willerby had one hearth each, one had 2, and one had 7; 6 of those in Binnington had one hearth and one had 2; and 17 of those in Staxton had one hearth and one had two.[26] In 1743 there were said to be 'about 32' families in the parish[27] and in 1764 27.[28] The decline since the 1670s indicated by these figures was principally felt in Willerby township.

The *Census* reports do not give separate figures for each township. The population of the whole parish was 192 in 1801. It rose to a peak of 468 in 1861, declined to 413 in 1871, recovered to 446 in 1891, and stood at 365 in 1901.[29] The enumerator's return of 1851 shows that there were by then only 7 houses and 63 inhabitants at Willerby but still 14 houses and 85 people at Binnington; Staxton had 61 houses and 274 inhabitants.[30] In the 20th century the population slowly increased and there were 407 people in the parish in 1961.[31]

MANORS AND OTHER ESTATES. In 1086 there was a single estate, of 5 carucates, at Willerby, which was soke of the king's manor of Bridlington.[32] It later formed part of the Gant fee and the overlordship passed from the Gants to the Tattershalls.[33] The manor was still said to be in the Tattershall fee in the early 15th century,[34] but it is not known to whom it passed on the division of that fee in 1309.[35]

In 1284–5 4½ of the 6 carucates in Willerby were subject to a mesne tenancy of the Wake family.[36] This interest may have arisen through the marriage of Gunnore, widow of Robert de Gant, and Nicholas de Stutville. The Wakes inherited the Stutville fee[37] and held land in Willerby at least until the death in 1425 of Joan, widow of John Grey, a remote descendant of the Wakes.[38]

The demesne tenants of *WILLERBY* manor in the 12th century were the family which took its name

---

[14] *Bridlington Charty.* 120, 125, 127, 129; C. Platt, *Monastic Grange in Med. Eng.* 244.
[15] Local inf.
[16] Local inf. These were presumably the premises of the 'beer retailer' mentioned in 1872 and later: directories.
[17] See p. 136.
[18] Directories.
[19] *V.C.H. Yorks.* iii. 332.
[20] *Archaeological Newsletter*, vol. iv (4), 62–3.
[21] Ex inf. occupant, 1971.
[22] J. Nicholson, *Beacons of E. Yorks.* 8, 54.
[23] Ex inf. Mr. T. C. M. Brewster, 1971.
[24] Ex inf. Ministry of Defence, 1971.
[25] E 179/202/62 mm. 22, 23, 27.
[26] E 179/205/514, 521.
[27] *Herring's Visit.* iii. 220–1.
[28] B.I.H.R., Bp. V. 1764/Ret. 135.
[29] *V.C.H. Yorks.* iii. 490.
[30] H.O. 107/2368.
[31] *Census.*
[32] *V.C.H. Yorks.* ii. 198.
[33] *Bridlington Charty.* 100; *Cal. Inq. p.m.* iv, p. 108; *Feud. Aids*, vi. 141.
[34] *Feud. Aids*, vi. 226, 266.
[35] *Cal. Close*, 1307–13, 99–102; Willerby may have been assigned to Thos. de Cailly, whose portion included land in Staxton.
[36] *Feud. Aids*, vi. 27.
[37] *E.Y.C.* ii, p. 433; ix, pp. 15–22.
[38] C 139/24/36.

from the village. Adelard the hunter held it of Walter de Gant about 1136,[39] and he gave the church and ½ carucate of land there to Bridlington priory.[40] Further gifts were made by Adelard's son Henry of Willerby and by other members of the family.[41] As a result of these and other gifts the priory held 4½ carucates in Willerby in 1284–5.[42]

The priory held the manor until the Dissolution, when it was worth about £5 15s.[43] It was let to George Burton in 1528 and he still held it in 1537.[44] It subsequently remained in the hands of the Crown until 1602, subject to leases of the manor-house and other lands to John Carvell in 1561, William Weston in 1571, and George Appleby in 1590.[45] In 1602 the manor, including a windmill and other property mentioned in the leases, was granted to Thomas Coundon.[46] It was held by the Coundons or Condons until the death of another Thomas in 1779.[47] In 1780 Elizabeth Condon and Thomas Condon Mellish assigned the estate to trustees who sold it in 1786 to R. C. Broadley,[48] and in 1799 Broadley sold it, comprising 1,780 a., to Joseph Denison.[49]

The Denisons, later earls of Londesborough, retained the estate until it was broken up in the early 20th century. In 1912 644 a. were sold to Henry Prodham, about 120 a. to Arthur Kitching and L. J. Simpson, and 701 a. to Walter Dawson.[50] Six years later a further 262 a., comprising Manor House farm, were sold to J. M. Rayner.[51] Dawson acquired Prodham's farm in 1919 and the Dawsons still held a large part of their estate in 1970.[52] Kitching and Simpson sold their land to Rayner in 1920 and the Rayners have since retained their estate.[53]

The Knights Templars had ½ carucate in Willerby in 1284–5.[54] In 1539–40 the Knights Hospitallers of Beverley had property in all three townships; it was restored to them when the order was briefly revived in 1558, but grants of it were made in 1560 to Thomas Fale and Thomas Wood and in 1571 to Francis Barker and Thomas Brown.[55] Rievaulx abbey had land and pasture in Willerby, acquired from Henry of Willerby in 1152; it was passed on to Bridlington priory in 1175.[56]

Binnington consisted of a 6-carucate estate in 1086 forming part of the count of Mortain's fee; before the Conquest it had belonged to Chilbert.[57] The overlordship passed to the Fossard family and to the Mauleys.[58] A mesne lordship was held in 1242 by the Nevilles.[59]

By the 13th century the Cornburgh family apparently had the largest holding in BINNINGTON manor. In 1225 the prioress of Nun Monkton was confirmed in land granted to her house by William of Cornburgh,[60] and other members of the family also held land in the township.[61] In 1250 Osbert of Cornburgh enfeoffed Walter Gower in all except 2 bovates of his two-carucate holding in Binnington, and Walter's son William, having been accorded possession after a lawsuit, later enfeoffed William Bergh.[62] In 1284–5 Marmaduke of Thwing was returned as lord of the manor, but in 1313 his lordship was disputed and in 1316 William Bergh was returned as lord.[63] The Thwings retained some interest in Binnington, however, which descended to their successors the Lumleys.[64]

In 1328 William Bergh's son Alexander granted a house, 6 bovates and other land, and the service of his freeholders in Binnington to Eleanor Percy.[65] The manor was held by the Percies[66] until the death of Henry Percy, earl of Northumberland, in 1537, when it was granted to the Crown with their other Yorkshire estates.[67] The manor was let by the Crown to Richard Sharpe in 1555, but later the same year it was granted in fee to Henry Gate.[68] In 1557 Thomas, earl of Northumberland, was granted the reversion of some of the former Percy lands, including Binnington.[69] Gate's son Edward nevertheless conveyed the manor in 1599 to Richard Darley, his son-in-law,[70] who in 1634 sold it to Thomas Coundon.[71] It remained in the Coundon family until 1716, when it was sold to Sir John Legard.[72] At inclosure in 1804 the Legards were the only allottees, receiving 1,052 a.,[73] and they kept Binnington until 1911, when Sir Algernon Legard sold the 1,139-acre estate to Harold Wrigley.[74] The Wrigleys still held it in 1970.

Nun Monkton priory held land in Binnington from at least the early 13th century, when gifts of 10 bovates and a house were confirmed.[75] At the Dissolution its property in Binnington and Flixton was worth £3 6s.[76] The Binnington lands were in 1538 granted to John Neville, Lord Latimer,[77] whose son John died seised of them in 1577 leaving four daughters as heirs.[78] The subsequent descent of the estate is obscure. In 1543 John Neville had devised certain rents in Binnington to his cousin John Constable, with reversion to the younger John Neville,[79] and it was perhaps as a result of this that the Constables obtained a share of the land. In 1579

---

[39] *E.Y.C.* ii, p. 428. [40] *Bridlington Charty.* 100.
[41] Ibid. 100–36, *passim*; *E.Y.C.* ii, p. 497 n.
[42] *Bridlington Charty.* 103–36, *passim*; *Feud. Aids*, vi. 27.
[43] *Valor Eccl.* (Rec. Com.), v. 120.
[44] S.C. 6/Hen. VIII/4430.
[45] *Cal. Pat.* 1560–3, 126; 1569–72, 294; *Cal. S.P. Dom.* 1581–90, 676. [46] Y.A.S. MSS., MD. 58.
[47] Registry of Deeds, Beverley, AZ/544/868.
[48] Ibid. BD/17/27; BL/502/787.
[49] Ibid. BZ/295/476.
[50] Ibid. 146/331/277; 147/344/306; /379/335.
[51] Ibid. 185/393/327.
[52] Ibid. 193/391/340; 1656/469/378.
[53] Ibid. 217/413/369; 1508/472/429; /473/430.
[54] *Feud. Aids*, vi. 27; *Rot. Hund.* (Rec. Com.) i. 114; *Bridlington Charty.* 103, 127, 139.
[55] *Miscellanea*, iv (Y.A.S. Rec. Ser. xciv), 91, 94; *Cal. Pat.* 1557–8, 319; 1558–60, 455–6; 1569–72, 237.
[56] *Bridlington Charty.* 114–16; *Y.A.J.* xl. 478 sqq.
[57] *V.C.H. Yorks.* ii. 226, 323.
[58] *Feud. Aids*, vi. 27, 142, 225, 267; *Cal. Pat.* 1330–4, 369; see above, p. 326.

[59] *Feud. Aids*, vi. 27; *Bk. of Fees*, ii. 1100.
[60] *Cal. Papal Regs.* i. 102.
[61] J.I. 1/1040 m. 11; /1042 m. 10; *Close R.* 1227–31, 107.
[62] K.B. 26/135 m. 2; *Percy Charty.* (Sur. Soc. cxvii) 164–6.
[63] *Feud. Aids*, vi. 27, 169; *Percy Charty.* 164–6.
[64] E 179/202/103; *Cal. Inq. p.m.* xiv, p. 56; *Cal. Close,* 1396–9, 49; see above, p. 326.
[65] *Percy Charty.* 158–9.
[66] Ibid. 377; *Cal. Close*, 1349–54, 422; 1364–8, 140.
[67] J. M. W. Bean, *Estates of the Percy Family, 1416–1537,* 61.
[68] *Cal. Pat.* 1554–5, 124. [69] Ibid. 1557–8, 184.
[70] Y.A.S. MSS., DD. 15/5B; *Visit. Yorks. 1584–5 and 1612,* ed. J. Foster, 60, 87; *V.C.H. Yorks. N.R.* ii. 93.
[71] Y.A.S. MSS., DD. 15/14B.
[72] Ibid. /23; Regy. of Deeds, E/375/656; J. D. Legard, *Legards of Anlaby and Ganton,* 163.
[73] Regy. of Deeds, CA/320/43. [74] Ibid. 134/290/265.
[75] *Cal. Papal Regs.* i. 102. [76] *Valor Eccl.* v. 255.
[77] *L. & P. Hen. VIII*, xiii(1), p. 136.
[78] C 142/177/62. [79] *Test. Ebor.* vi. 162–3.

John Constable conveyed half of the reputed manor of Binnington to Robert Wright.[80] The land later passed to the Legards, probably in 1716 when the Coundons sold them 8 bovates in addition to the land which had come from the Darleys.[81]

Bridlington priory had 4 bovates in Binnington worth £1 at the Dissolution.[82] Grants of it were made to Henry Gate, along with Binnington manor, in 1555, and to Francis Barker and Thomas Brown in 1571.[83] The Knights Hospitallers also had property in Binnington.[84]

In 1086 there were two estates in Staxton, one of 5 carucates, which had been held before the Conquest by Carle and Torfin, the other of one carucate, which was soke of Morcar's manor of Bridlington. Both were in the king's hands in 1086.[85] They later became part of the Gant fee, subsequently passed to the Tattershalls,[86] and in 1309 were assigned to the portion of Thomas de Cailly.[87] Staxton was still described as part of the Tattershall fee in the 15th century.[88] As in Willerby, the Wake family had a mesne tenancy.[89]

In the mid 12th century William Percy, a grandson of Gilbert de Gant, was lord of *STAXTON*,[90] and in 1284–5 6 of the 7 carucates in the township lay in the Percy fee. Eleanor Percy was lord of Staxton in 1316[91] and Henry Percy held land there at his death in 1368.[92] There is no further reference to the Percy holding.

Under the Percy family land was held in the late 12th century by the Gantons.[93] It passed to the Bossalls, probably on the marriage of Maud of Ganton and Richard Bossall,[94] and in 1257 William Bossall was granted free warren at Staxton.[95] The Bossalls retained the estate until the mid 14th century.[96] In 1357 Robert Bossall and his wife held a life interest in the manor, with remainder to Richard of Bolton and his wife Elizabeth.[97] This Elizabeth may have been Bossall's daughter, who later married Thomas of Acklam and whose son Robert inherited the lands of Robert Bossall.[98]

In 1517 it was said that William Willesthorpe had died seised of the manor of Staxton[99] and it is likely that the Willesthorpes obtained the holding from the Acklams in the early 15th century, when Bossall manor was certainly conveyed to them.[1] On the death of William Willesthorpe his lands were divided among three coheirs and Staxton passed to Brian Palmes, who had married Anastasia Willesthorpe. Staxton apparently reverted after Palmes's death to the heirs of Isabel Willesthorpe, another of the coheirs, whose son Walter Creyke died seised of a house and 6 bovates there in 1546.[2] In 1615 the manor was conveyed by Robert Lakin to Richard Huntley.[3]

It was perhaps the same estate, no longer called a manor, which had passed to the Coundons by the early 18th century. In 1716 Thomas Coundon conveyed a manor-house and 6 bovates of land belonging to it, together with one other bovate, to John Williamson.[4] The same estate was sold by Williamson's son to Joshua Reeve in 1751, and by Reeve's grandson to R. C. Broadley in 1795.[5]

Broadley was acquiring other land about this time. In 1796 he bought 2 bovates from William Mosey[6] and in 1801 16 bovates from William Nesfield, 4 of which had formerly belonged to the earls of Carlisle[7] and 11 others had been acquired by Theophilus Nesfield from Thomas Coundon in 1721.[8] Thus by 1801 Broadley had 25 bovates in the township and at inclosure in 1803 he was allotted 527 a., besides 9 a. for tithes.[9] After Broadley's death in 1812 his estate was sold to W. J. Denison and in 1917 the Denisons sold it to Walter Dawson.[10] Most of it still belonged to the Dawsons in 1970.

Several estates in Staxton belonged to religious houses in the Middle Ages. Many grants of land were made by the Ganton, Staxton, and Bossall families, among others, to Bridlington priory,[11] which had property there worth £1 6s. at the Dissolution.[12] The Staxton land was subsequently included in the leases and grants of the priory's property in Willerby.[13] The Knights Hospitallers also had land in Staxton.[14] Matthew Stokesley died seised of one bovate of former Hospitallers' land in 1624.[15]

The priory of Handale (Yorks. N.R.) held land in Staxton from its foundation in 1133.[16] Its holding amounted to one carucate in 1346[17] and at the Dissolution was valued at 12s.[18] It may have been from the former Handale lands that an estate in Staxton was acquired by the Dacre family, which had 4 bovates there in 1563.[19] The property apparently passed in 1607 from Francis Dacre to William, Lord Howard,[20] and it was held by the Howards (from 1661 the earls of Carlisle) until the mid 18th century.[21] After the death of Henry, earl of Carlisle, in 1758 the land was conveyed by his trustees in 1768 to Theophilus Nesfield,[22] and in 1801 William Nesfield sold these 4 bovates to R. C. Broadley.[23]

---

[80] C.P. 40/1363 m. 139.
[81] Regy. of Deeds, E/375/656.
[82] S.C. 6/4430; *Valor Eccl.* v. 120.
[83] *Cal. Pat.* 1554–5, 124; 1569–72, 237.
[84] See p. 334.
[85] *V.C.H. Yorks.* ii. 197, 204, 322.
[86] *Feud. Aids*, vi. 27, 141.
[87] *Cal. Close*, 1307–13, 100; see above, p. 333.
[88] *Feud. Aids*, vi. 225, 230, 266.
[89] C 139/24/36; *Cal. Inq. p.m.* ix, p. 206; x, p. 49.
[90] *E.Y.C.* ii, pp. 228–9; *Complete Peerage.*
[91] *Feud. Aids*, vi. 27, 169.
[92] *Cal. Inq. p.m.* xii, p. 226.
[93] *Bridlington Charty.* 92–3.
[94] Ibid. 94; *E.Y.C.* ix, pp. 175–6 n.
[95] *Cal. Chart. R.* 1226–57, 471.
[96] *Percy Charty.* 470; *Cal. Inq. p.m.* v, p. 319; xii, p. 226; *Feud. Aids*, vi. 225, 230.
[97] E.R.R.O., DDX/56/2.
[98] *Yorks. Deeds*, x. 78–9; see above, p. 211.
[99] Y.A.S. MSS., DD. 15/7.

[1] *Feud. Aids*, vi. 266; W. J. Belt, *Story of Bossall Hall and Manor*, 55.
[2] Y.A.S. MSS., DD. 15/7, 12; see p. 210.
[3] *Yorks. Fines*, 1614–25, 42.
[4] Regy. of Deeds, E/360/632.
[5] Ibid. U/471/898; BU/574/872.
[6] Ibid. BW/490/693.   [7] See below.
[8] Regy. of Deeds, H/207/432; CD/104/143.
[9] Ibid. CA/235/32; E.R.R.O., DDDV/10/p. 12.
[10] Regy. of Deeds, CS/519/726; CU/197/191.
[11] *Bridlington Charty.* 92–9.
[12] *Valor Eccl.* v. 120.   [13] See p. 334.
[14] See p. 334.   [15] C 142/667/169.
[16] *E.Y.C.* ii, p. 240; *V.C.H. Yorks.* ii. 165.
[17] *Feud. Aids*, vi. 225.   [18] *Valor Eccl.* v. 87.
[19] Castle Howard MS., Box 24, Survey of Estates, 1563.
[20] *Yorks. Fines*, 1603–14, 73.
[21] C 142/774/15; Regy. of Deeds, S/129/300; /130/301; *Yorks. Fines*, 1603–14, 91.
[22] Y.A.S. MSS., MD. 58; Regy. of Deeds, AM/116/193.
[23] Regy. of Deeds, CD/104/142; /105/143.

The hospital of St. Mary held a carucate of land in Staxton in 1284–5 which had been given to it by Gilbert de Gant.[24] The hospital belonged to Bridlington priory, which had property at 'Spittell' worth 4s. at the Dissolution.[25] The estate later passed to the Gates, who acquired land in Binnington in 1555,[26] and in 1616 Edward Gate died seised of the manor-house of 'Spittles'.[27] The estate later passed to the Coundons, and in 1721 Thomas Coundon sold the house, various ancient closes, and 10 bovates of land to Stephen Bennison.[28] In 1732 Bennison conveyed the property to James Boyes, the elder, and in 1761 the assignees of Boyes's son James sold it to Robert Duesbery.[29] It then passed, in 1781, to Duesbery's daughter Catherine,[30] who died in 1798 and devised the Staxton and Spittles property to her nephew Thomas Thornton.[31] At inclosure in 1803 Thornton was allotted 201 a.;[32] the ancient closes amounted to 17 a. In 1826 Thornton sold the estate to W. J. Denison and the Denisons in 1917 to Walter Dawson. Spital House Farm, with part of the land, was sold in 1970.[33]

The rectory, which had been appropriated by Bridlington priory in the early 12th century,[34] was valued at £6 13s. 4d. in 1291 and at £5 in the new taxation.[35] In the Middle Ages most of the tithes belonged to the priory. At Staxton, however, two-thirds of the grain tithes of the demesnes were given to Whitby abbey by Richard Percy, and the gift was confirmed in 1161–4.[36] In 1264 Whitby let these tithes to Bridlington for 20 qr. of barley a year,[37] and at the Dissolution a pension due to the abbey from Bridlington[38] may represent that rent. Marmaduke of Thwing was described as rector of Willerby in 1306,[39] but this may refer to the rectorial tithes of Binnington alone, where Marmaduke held the manor.[40] In the early 16th century the rectorial tithes and glebe were leased from the priory by George Burton for £12.[41]

After the Dissolution the former Whitby abbey tithes in Staxton were let to William Proctor in 1539–40[42] and granted in fee to Edward Pease and James Wilson in 1549.[43] The remaining tithes in Staxton and all those in Willerby were granted in 1553 to Thomas Sidney and Nicholas Halswell.[44] The Binnington tithes may have descended with the manor. The rectory was thus much divided in the 16th century, but in the early 17th century the tithes came into the possession of the Coundons and the Legards[45] and in 1650 they were worth £60.[46]

In Willerby and Binnington the tithes descended with the manorial estates, which comprised most if not all of those townships, and so came to be merged. In Staxton, where land ownership was more fragmented, Sir John Legard sold the grain tithes in several lots in 1783.[47] By 1801 they were in the hands of the various landowners, except that Thomas Thornton enjoyed the tithes from 7 bovates of R. C. Broadley's land.[48] At inclosure in 1803 Thornton was consequently awarded a rent-charge of £10 13s. 9d. The wool and lamb tithes in Staxton descended from the Coundons to R. C. Broadley, and in lieu of them he received 9 a. in 1803, the only tithe allotment made.[49]

ECONOMIC HISTORY. In 1086 the estate of Carle and Torfin at Staxton had land for three ploughs, and the soke of Bridlington, which included Willerby and part of Staxton, was described as much wasted.[50] Apart from the three villages beneath the escarpment, there may have been a few cottages on the wold at 'Cotedail', a name which occurs in the late 12th and 13th centuries.[51]

The open fields of all the townships apparently lay not only on the gentle slopes below the wold escarpment but also on the high wolds. 'Cotedail', for example, was 'the strips or plots of land near the cottages'.[52] Some of the high field land may have been only irregularly cultivated. Thus when Adelard of Willerby confirmed his father's grant of pasturage to Bridlington he undertook to plough no more land than his father had done and to provide the priory with access to their sheepfold unimpeded by his ploughed land, wherever that land might be.[53] One culture was called Ovenam in the 13th century,[54] perhaps indicating an intake from the waste. East and West fields at Staxton, which are mentioned in the Middle Ages, certainly included wold ground and may have extended to the slopes below the escarpment.[55] The 4 bovates of the Dacre estate in 1563 comprised lands in East, Middle, and West fields 'under the hill', and in East, Middle, and West fields 'on the wold'.[56] By the time of inclosure in 1803 the slopes below the wolds were known as Low field, but it is not clear how much of the wold ground was then permanently arable, though it included areas known as Wold field and, in the extreme south, Moor field.[57]

The arrangement of the fields in Binnington and Willerby is more uncertain. The high ground included Binnington Ness, protruding into the township of Willerby, and some land here was irregularly cultivated in the 17th and 18th centuries.[58] Only 'Binnington field' is referred to at inclosure in

[24] Feud. Aids, vi. 27; V.C.H. Yorks. iii. 332.
[25] Valor Eccl. v. 120.
[26] See p. 334.
[27] C 2/Jas. I/D.13/11.
[28] Regy. of Deeds, H/205/427.
[29] Ibid. N/182/406; AD/294/608.
[30] E.R.R.O., DDDU/23/5. Her second husband was the Revd. Robt. Young.
[31] Ibid. /21/49; Land Tax 1798–9.
[32] Regy. of Deeds, CA/235/32.
[33] Ibid. DY/120/143; 206/316/272; 1649/270/252.
[34] See p. 338.
[35] Tax. Eccl. (Rec. Com.), 326.
[36] E.Y.C. ii, pp. 201 n., 228–9.
[37] Bridlington Charty. 98; Monastic Notes, i (Y.A.S. Rec. Ser. xvii), pp. 23–4.
[38] Valor Eccl. v. 82.
[39] Reg. Greenfield, iii (Sur. Soc. cli), 124.
[40] See p. 334.
[41] Miscellanea, iii (Y.A.S. Rec. Ser. lxxx), 21.
[42] L. & P. Hen. VIII, xv, p. 566.
[43] Cal. Pat. 1549–51, 45.
[44] Ibid. 1553, 56.
[45] Y.A.S. MSS., DD. 15/7, 24; MD. 58, 119; Yorks. Fines, iii. 9; iv. 187; 1603–14, 59, 75, 185.
[46] T.E.R.A.S. ii. 57.
[47] Registry of Deeds, Beverley, BF/228/387; /229/388–9; /230/390–1; BL/45/40; BR/532/862.
[48] E.R.R.O., DDDV/10/p. 12.
[49] Regy. of Deeds, CA/235/32.
[50] V.C.H. Yorks. ii. 197–8, 204.
[51] P.N.E.R. Yorks. (E.P.N.S.), 118; Bridlington Charty. 94.
[52] P.N.E.R. Yorks. 118.
[53] Bridlington Charty. 102.
[54] Ibid. 94.
[55] Ibid. 96.
[56] Castle Howard MS., Box 24, Survey of Estates, 1563.
[57] Registry of Deeds, Beverley, CA/235/32 and map.
[58] B.I.H.R., TER. J. Willerby 1749; Ganton 1685.

1804.[59] The West field of Willerby is mentioned in the Middle Ages.[60]

The extent of the open fields is also uncertain. At the Dissolution Bridlington priory had at least 43 bovates in the parish, 34 of them in Willerby where the demesnes alone included 19 bovates.[61] In 1794 there were 1,032 a. of field land at Staxton, 872 a. of it on the wold, 130 a. below the escarpment, and 30 a. to the east and west of the village.[62] At Binnington 701 a. of field land and wold were inclosed in 1804.[63] The wold ground was probably sheepwalk that was only intermittently broken up for crops.

On the high wolds there were extensive sheep pastures belonging to Bridlington priory. In the mid 12th century the priory had pasture for 500 sheep in Willerby, acquired sufficient for 300 more from Rievaulx abbey, and hired enough for a further 160 sheep at 2s. a year. Richard of Ganton gave the priory pasture for 400 sheep in Staxton field, as well as land for a sheepfold near by. There were other sheepfolds in Willerby.[64] The whole of this area of sheep pasture was known as Prior's moor in 1536–7 and later.[65] In 1599 pasture for 400 sheep on East Ness belonged to Binnington manor,[66] and in the 17th and 18th centuries the Ness was at different times ploughed, grazed, or laid for hay.[67]

The carrs and meadows in the north of the parish provided grazing, hay, and turf in the Middle Ages.[68] Landholders enjoyed rights there and at least two men quitclaimed their right of turbary to Bridlington priory, receiving in return 20 cart-loads and 9,000 turves respectively.[69] In 1563 the common rights enjoyed by one tenant in Staxton entitled him to keep, for each bovate, one ox or horse in 'the ox pasture called the horse carr' and cows without stint in 'the neat pasture called the carr', and for each bovate and for his house 20 sheep. He also had several parcels of the Land ings.[70] In 1794 there were said to be 316 a. in the Common carr, 92 a. in the Horse carr, and — nearer Staxton village — 60 a. in the ings.[71] At Binnington 240 a. of ings and 110 a. of carr were inclosed in 1804.[72]

The taking-in of meadow land from the waste, as of arable land on the wold, is indicated by a meadow called Ovenam lying in the marsh of Willerby in the 12th century.[73] Banks and ditches were used to identify and demarcate parcels of common land, both on the wold and on the low ground,[74] and they may not be an indication of the inclosure of common arable or meadow. Some of the banks on the wold, which include 'Twameredike' and 'Clifdich', were probably prehistoric earthworks. At least one piece of carr ground was temporarily withdrawn from the commons to provide hay: in 1306 the commoners agreed that 'Newenge' should be inclosed as meadow from March to Michaelmas each year, and used as common for the rest of the year.[75]

Several closes around the village of Staxton, most of them near Spittles, were mentioned in the 17th and 18th centuries,[76] and New close, 'lately' taken from the ings, was referred to in 1729.[77] In 1794 the old inclosures in Staxton amounted to 60 a. and they chiefly comprised the area around Spittles and a block of former ings ground north-west of the village.[78]

It is not known when the final inclosure of Willerby took place, and it was apparently achieved without a formal agreement or Act of Parliament. The ring-fencing of large tracts on the wolds, held by tenants under the Coundons and under R. C. Broadley, may have preceded division into smaller fields. One of Broadley's tenants in 1789 had c. 620 a., including 65 a. of tillage on the wolds, 65 a. in Prior moor, 80 a. of tillage below the wolds, 320 a. of sheepwalk, and nearly 80 a. in four closes. His crops included turnips and clover.[79]

Binnington was inclosed in 1804,[80] under an Act of 1803,[81] and Staxton in 1803,[82] under an Act of 1801.[83] All 1,051 a. inclosed at Binnington were awarded to Sir John Legard. At Staxton the commissioners found 1,557 a. remaining to be inclosed and made allotments totalling 1,449 a. R. C. Broadley received 536 a., Samuel Clarkson 265 a., Thomas Thornton 201 a., Hugh Marsden 200 a., and the vicar 189 a., together with a share in 23 a. more. The remaining eight allotments, each of 5 a. or less, were made to cottagers who had possessed only common rights in the carrs.

The drainage of the low-lying northern parts of the townships went hand in hand with their inclosure. There were said in 1773 to be 434 a. of fenny ground, of little value, in Willerby, 381 a. in Binnington, and 372 a. in Staxton,[84] and the parish was among those to benefit from work done under the Muston Drainage Act of 1800.[85] In the 19th and 20th centuries there have usually been 3 farms in Willerby, one or 2 in Binnington, and 5 or 6 in Staxton.[86]

There was a mill at Willerby in the early Middle Ages[87] and a windmill existed until at least 1602.[88] The foundations of a post-mill, with 13th- and 14th-century pottery, have been found near Staxton village. In the 13th and 14th centuries Staxton, along with Potter Brompton[89] and perhaps other villages near by, was the scene of intensive pottery manufacture, and pottery found in excavations over a wide area is known to archaeologists as 'Staxton ware'. Half-a-dozen kilns, using the Speeton Clay outcrop below the chalk escarpment, have been

---

[59] Regy. of Deeds, CA/43/320.
[60] *Bridlington Charty.* 121, 129.
[61] S.C. 6/Hen. VIII/4430.
[62] E.R.R.O., DDDU/10/7, p. 3.
[63] Regy. of Deeds, CA/320/43.
[64] *Bridlington Charty.* 93, 100, 102, 115, 117, 126.
[65] S.C. 6/Hen. VIII/4430; O.S. Map 6" (1854).
[66] Y.A.S. MSS., DD. 15/5B.
[67] B.I.H.R., TER. J. Willerby 1749; Ganton 1685.
[68] *Bridlington Charty.* 99–100, 102.
[69] Ibid. 99, 130–1, 133.
[70] Castle Howard MS., Box 24, Survey of Estates, 1563.
[71] E.R.R.O., DDDU/10/7, p. 3.
[72] Regy. of Deeds, CA/320/43.
[73] *Bridlington Charty.* 110, 117, 124.
[74] Ibid. 113–14, 117, 125–6, 129, 135.
[75] Ibid. 99–100.
[76] B.I.H.R., TER. J. Willerby 1716 to 1781; Ganton 1685.
[77] Regy. of Deeds, K/683/1461.
[78] Ibid. inclosure map; E.R.R.O., DDDU/10/7, p. 3.
[79] E.R.R.O., DDHB/57/177.
[80] Regy. of Deeds, CA/320/43.
[81] 43 Geo. III, c. 89 (Priv. Act, not printed).
[82] Regy. of Deeds, CA/235/32 and map. The comrs.' notebk. is in E.R.R.O., DDDU/10/7. The inclosure is discussed in *Ag. H.R.* xiii(2), 106–15.
[83] 41 Geo. III, c. 115 (Priv. Act, not printed).
[84] E.R.R.O., DDSY/11/2. [85] See p. 280.
[86] Directories. [87] *Bridlington Charty.* 123.
[88] Y.A.S. MSS., MD. 58; *Cal. Pat.* 1560–3, 126.
[89] See p. 213.

found.[90] There have been few other noteworthy non-agricultural occupations in the parish. In the 1920s and 1930s Staxton's position on main roads to the coast led to the establishment of several garages and refreshment rooms,[91] and there were four garages in 1971.

LOCAL GOVERNMENT. Little is known of manorial administration in the parish. A Binnington man was acting as a constable in 1719,[92] and a constable and pinder were still being appointed for the Denisons' manor of Willerby in the earlier 19th century.[93]

Overseers were mentioned in 1661, when money bequeathed to the poor was to be distributed by them and the churchwardens.[94] Churchwardens' accounts of 1838–98 show that in the mid 19th century there was a churchwarden for each township, but that by the 1870s only two were appointed.[95]

In 1837 Willerby joined the Scarborough union.[96]

CHURCH. In the early 12th century Adelard the hunter granted the church of Willerby to Bridlington priory, together with ½ carucate of land. His son Henry of Willerby gave a further ½ carucate.[97] By 1246 the living was deemed to be a vicarage.[98]

The advowson was held by the priory until the Dissolution.[99] In 1566 James Milner presented by virtue of a grant from the priory.[1] Thereafter presentations were made by the Crown until 1856,[2] with the exception of 1691, when Thomas Coundon presented.[3] By 1866 the patronage belonged to the Revd. E. Day, the incumbent,[4] and it was still held by the Days in 1967–8.[5]

At the Dissolution the vicar enjoyed a third of the profits of Bridlington priory's share of the rectory,[6] and this arrangement may have long been customary. In 1291 the vicarage was worth £5 and in 1318 £3 6s. 8d.[7] The net value was £8 in 1525 and £9 in 1535, when tithes constituted the whole of the income.[8] In 1650 the value was £24.[9] The average net income in 1829–31 was £116 a year.[10]

Various tithes in all three townships were received by the vicar in the 17th and 18th centuries.[11] At the inclosure of Staxton in 1803 the vicar was allotted 185 a. in lieu of his tithe in the whole parish, together with a rent-charge of nearly £28 on Sir John Legard's land in Binnington.[12] The allotment was said to be worth £125 in 1851.[13] Only one or two small parcels of glebe land belonged to the vicarage in the 17th and 18th centuries but these may have given rise to the allotment of 4 a. to the vicar as a freeholder in 1803. He and another man were also allotted 23 a. in lieu of common rights, but this land was soon sold.[14] No other glebe was acquired and most of the land allotted for tithes in 1803 was sold in 1919.[15]

A house belonging to the priest of Willerby is mentioned in the Middle Ages[16] and there was a parsonage house in the early 16th century.[17] The house was ruinous in 1670 and 1693,[18] and in 1726 the vicar had a 'frontstead',[19] perhaps the site of the parsonage house. In 1818 there was said to be a small farm-house, unfit for residence by the vicar, and there was no house in 1835.[20] The present Vicarage, a large house of yellow and red brick, was built at the west end of Staxton village between 1876 and 1879.[21]

In the late 12th century Richard of Ganton gave land and pasture to Bridlington priory to endow a chantry in the chapel of St. Giles, at Staxton.[22] In 1295 Nicholas Bossall, whose family had succeeded the Gantons as lords of Staxton, quitclaimed to the priory his right to have a chantry in the chapel.[23] Besides the vicar there was a second priest at Willerby in 1525, with a living worth £4, who may have served the chapel.[24] The former property of Bridlington's 'free chapel of Willerby and Staxton' was mentioned in 1634.[25] Chapel close or garth, recorded in the 18th century,[26] may have been the site of the building. In the mid 12th century Adelard the hunter gave land to provide for lights before the high altar in Willerby church, and a bequest was made to the light of the Virgin in 1467.[27] Land given for lamps and an obit were granted away by the Crown in 1570–1.[28]

During the 18th and 19th centuries most of the incumbents of Willerby were non-resident and held other livings. A curate served on behalf of the non-resident vicar in 1726, but in 1743 the vicar served Willerby himself, though he lived at Ganton, which he also held.[29] Similarly, the vicar served the cure himself in 1764, though he lived at Folkton, which he also served along with Filey. In 1835 the vicar was also incumbent of Salton and Sinnington (Yorks. N.R.). In 1865 he lived at Norton, holding that benefice, and his curate at Willerby was also vicar of Ganton; the curate in 1868 and 1871 was also

---

[90] Y.A.J. xxxix. 446; Med. Archaeol. ii. 213; ix. 218.
[91] Directories.
[92] E.R.R.O., QSF Mich. 1719 B.10.
[93] Ibid. DDLO/29/2.
[94] B.I.H.R., Prob. Reg. xliii, f. 692.
[95] E.R.R.O., PR. 2776.
[96] 3rd Rep. Poor Law Com. 174.
[97] Bridlington Charty. 100; E.Y.C. ii, p. 427.
[98] Fasti Parochiales, iii. 91. The 'rector' was mentioned in 1306 and 1315: ibid.
[99] Ibid. 92–3.
[1] Ibid. 93.
[2] P.R.O. Inst. Bks. 1721–1830; Rep. Com. Eccl. Revenues, 978–9; Sheahan and Whellan, Hist. York & E.R. ii. 491.
[3] Inst. Bk.
[4] York Dioc. Cal. 1866, p. 108.
[5] Crockford.
[6] Miscellanea, iii (Y.A.S. Rec. Ser. lxxx), 21.
[7] Tax. Eccl. (Rec. Com.), 326.
[8] Y.A.J. xxiv. 65; Valor Eccl. (Rec. Com.), v. 122.
[9] T.E.R.A.S. ii. 57.
[10] Rep. Com. Eccl. Revenues, 978–9.
[11] B.I.H.R., TER. J. Willerby n.d. to 1781.
[12] Regy. of Deeds, CA/235/32.
[13] H.O. 129/24/525.
[14] Regy. of Deeds, CK/551/897.
[15] Ibid. 199/318/278.
[16] Bridlington Charty. 133.
[17] C 1/609/46.
[18] B.I.H.R., Churches index.
[19] Ibid., TER. J. Willerby 1716.
[20] Lawton, Rer. Eccles. Dioc. Ebor. 315; Rep. Com. Eccl. Revenues, 978–9.
[21] Regy. of Deeds, LZ/164/246; Kelly's Dir. N. & E.R. Yorks. (1879), 665.
[22] Bridlington Charty. 92–3, 104.
[23] Ibid. 99.
[24] Y.A.J. xxiv. 78.
[25] Y.A.S. MSS., MD. 58.
[26] B.I.H.R., TER. J. Willerby 1716; Ganton 1685; etc.
[27] Ibid., Prob. Reg. iv, f. 246; Bridlington Charty. 117.
[28] Cal. Pat. 1569–72, 38, 237.
[29] B.I.H.R., ER. V/Ch. P. 1726; Herring's Visit. iii. 220–1.

vicar of Butterwick.[30] In 1967-8 the vicar also held the rectory of Folkton.[31]

In 1743 a service was held once each Sunday and Holy Communion was celebrated four times a year, with about 65 regular communicants.[32] In the 1860s and 1870s there were sometimes said to be two Sunday services, sometimes only one, but two apparently became usual later. By 1877 communion was celebrated monthly, with four or five communicants.[33] The Sunday schoolroom was licensed for worship during the church restoration of 1881-2, and thereafter certain services were held there.[34] There were alternately one and two services at the church each Sunday in 1971.

The church of ST. PETER consists of structurally undivided chancel and nave, with a north aisle, west tower, and south porch.[35] It is built entirely of stone. There are no remains of the 12th-century church and the present building is of 13th-century origin, partly rebuilt in the 18th and 19th centuries. The narrow north aisle, of five-and-a-half bays, stretches the whole length of the church and retains its 13th-century arcade supported on one octagonal and four round piers. It has pointed arches of two chamfered orders, their hood-moulds terminating in stops of heads and stiff-leaf foliage. The capitals are carved with fleuron and nail-head ornament and, in one case, with what appear to be limpet shells. The tower, of the same date or a little later, cuts off half a bay at the west end of the arcade. It is of two stages, with set-back buttresses to the lower stage, a prominent square stair-turret, and a west window of three lancet-shaped lights. The tower arch matches those of the arcade.

The chancel was in 'great decay' in the late 16th century, and still so in 1615 when the windows were open to the weather and one side of the church was propped up. The north walls were ordered to be repaired in 1721 and faculties were obtained in 1783 to alter the north wall and in 1793 to rebuild the chancel on a smaller scale.[36] It was presumably in the late 18th century, therefore, that the chancel was shortened and the aisle rebuilt on a narrower plan. A thorough restoration in 1881-2[37] appears to have obliterated any 18th-century features. Lancet windows in the aisle and chancel are of 19th-century date, together with the three-light east window with Decorated tracery. Two square-headed windows in the south wall of the nave have also been renewed, their style suggesting that the originals may have been of the 16th or early 17th century. The font comprises a simple octagonal bowl on a similar stem. Over the porch doorway is a carving of St. Peter with his keys.

There were three bells in 1552 and still three in the 20th century, one of them dated 1638 and another 1676.[38] The plate includes a cup made in London in 1764 and a paten of 1879.[39] The registers begin in 1653 and are complete.[40] The churchyard was extended in 1955.[41]

NONCONFORMITY. Houses in Staxton were registered for worship in 1800 and 1811.[42] A Wesleyan Methodist chapel was built at the west end of Staxton in 1813[43] and a Primitive Methodist chapel at the other end of the village in 1847.[44] In 1865 the Wesleyans in the parish were said to be numerous, but in 1877 neither chapel was well attended.[45] The Primitives had 20 members in 1889.[46] Both buildings were still standing in 1971 and the former primitive chapel was still in use.

EDUCATION. The assistant curate was said in 1726 to teach children in the church.[47] In 1819 about 20 pupils attended a private school, which enjoyed a benefaction of £3 3s. a year.[48] Two schools were started in 1826, one a Sunday school where free instruction was to be had, the other a fee-paying school which in 1835 was attended by 26 girls and 44 boys.[49] It may have been the latter school which stood on the south side of Staxton village street near the junction with Carr Lane in 1850, and which was described as a National school in 1856.[50] There were 26 pupils in 1871.[51] A dame school for infants also existed in 1865.[52]

A board school, built on a site at the west end of Staxton village, was opened in 1878.[53] The building accommodated boys, girls, and infants, and about 50 children attended in 1878; school pence supplemented income from rates.[54] An annual parliamentary grant was first received in 1879.[55] The average attendance increased to 78 in 1899[56] and the school was enlarged in 1901 to give accommodation for 111 children.[57] Average attendance up to the Second World War was usually between 70 and 80; it fell to 64 in 1922 and was 60 in 1938.[58] In 1963 the village hall was being rented to provide additional accommodation.[59] There were 20 children on the roll in 1971.[60]

CHARITIES FOR THE POOR. None known.

[30] Ibid., Bp. V. 1764/Ret. 135; V. 1865/Ret. 595; V. 1868/Ret. 552; V. 1871/Ret. 556; V. 1877/Ret.; *Rep. Com. Eccl. Revenues*, 978-9.   [31] *Crockford*.
[32] B.I.H.R., Bp. V. 1764/Ret. 135; *Herring's Visit*. iii. 220-1.
[33] B.I.H.R., V. 1865/Ret. 595; V. 1868/Ret. 552; V. 1871/Ret. 556; V. 1877/Ret.; Bp. V. 1884/Ret.
[34] Ibid. Bp. V. 1894/Ret.   [35] Morris, *E. Yorks*. 349.
[36] B.I.H.R., Churches index; Lawton, *Rer. Eccles. Dioc. Ebor*. 315.
[37] E.R.R.O., PR. 2776; *Kelly's Dir. N. & E.R. Yorks*. (1889), 472.
[38] *Inventories of Ch. Goods*, 29; Boulter, 'Ch. Bells', 219.
[39] *Yorks. Ch. Plate*, i. 334.
[40] E.R.R.O., PR. 2778-9, 2782.
[41] York Dioc. Regy., Sentence of consecration.
[42] G.R.O. Worship Returns, Vol. v, nos. 1583, 2491.
[43] Char. Com. files.
[44] H.O. 129/24/525; O.S. Map 6" (1854).
[45] B.I.H.R., V. 1865/Ret. 595; V. 1877/Ret.

[46] H. Woodcock, *Sketches of Prim. Meth. on Yorks. Wolds*, 154.
[47] B.I.H.R., ER. V/Ch. P. 1726.
[48] *Rets. on Educ. of Poor, 1819*, 1097.
[49] *Educ. Enquiry Abstract, 1835*, 1099.
[50] O.S. Map 6" (1854); Sheahan and Whellan, *Hist. York & E.R*. ii. 492.
[51] *Rets. rel. Elem. Educ. 1871*, 476.
[52] B.I.H.R., V. 1865/Ret. 595.
[53] E.R.R.O., SB. Sch. Bd. Mins., p. 50.   [54] Ed. 7/135.
[55] *Rep. of Educ. Cttee. of Counc. 1879* [C. 2562-I], H.C., p. 741 (1880), xxiii.
[56] *Ret. of Schs. 1899* [Cd. 315], H.C., p. 398 (1900), lxv (2).
[57] *Public Elem. Schs. 1905* [Cd. 3182], H.C., p. 697 (1906), lxxxvi; stone on building.
[58] *Bd. of Educ. List 21* (H.M.S.O.).
[59] E.R. Educ. Cttee. *Mins*. 1963-4, 60.
[60] Ex inf. Chief Educ. Officer, County Hall, Beverley, 1971.

INDEX

NOTE. An italic page-number denotes an illustration on that page or facing it.

Among the abbreviations used in the index the following may need elucidation: abp., archbishop; Alex., Alexander; Alf., Alfred; And., Andrew; Ant., Anthony; Art., Arthur; b., born; bp., bishop; Bart., Bartholomew; Benj., Benjamin; Cath., Cathedral or Catherine; chap., chapel; char., charity; Chas., Charles; Chris., Christopher; ch., church; coll., college; Cuth., Cuthbert; dau., daughter; Dav., David; d., died; econ. hist., economic history; Edm., Edmund; educ., education; Edw., Edward; Eliz., Elizabeth; Ern., Ernest; fam., family; fl., flourished; Fred., Frederick; Geof., Geoffrey; Geo., George; Gilb., Gilbert; Greg., Gregory; Hen., Henry; Herb., Herbert; hosp., hospital; ho., house; Humph., Humphrey; Jas., James; Kath., Katherine; Lawr., Lawrence; Leon., Leonard; loc. govt., local government; man., manor; mkt., market; Marg., Margaret; Marm., Marmaduke; m., married; Mat., Matthew; Mic., Michael; Nath., Nathaniel; Nic., Nicholas; nonconf., nonconformity; Pet., Peter; Phil., Philip; Reg., Reginald; Ric., Richard; riv., river; Rob., Robert; Rog., Roger; Rom. Cath., Roman Catholicism; Sam., Samuel; Sim., Simon; sis., sister; s., son; Steph., Stephen; Thos., Thomas; Tim., Timothy; Vct., Viscount; w., wife; Wal., Walter; Wm., William.

Abbott, Bart., 6, 8
Acklam:
    Agnes, dau. of Rog., 210
    Eliz., see Bossall
    Joan, dau. of Rog., 210
    John, 12
    Leon., 12
    Marm. of, 191
    Nic. of, 210
    Pet., 288
    Rob. (fl. c. 1300), 191, 210
    Rob. (fl. c. 1400), 210, 335
    Rog., 210
    Thos. (d. by 1392), 210–11, 335
    Thos. (fl. 1581), 12
    Wm. of, 191
    fam., 12, 210, 215, 335
Adam, rector of Thwing, 330
Adelard the hunter, see Willerby
Admiralty, 160
Agars, Geo., 77
Ainsty Trust Co., 183
Air Ministry, 110, 127, 266
airfields, 106, 110, 125, 230, 263–4
Albert, Prince Consort, 60
Aldbrough, 14
Alden, 280
Alexander III, King of Scotland, 72 n
Allen:
    John, 246
    Rog., 183
Allison, John, 306
Allured, Mat., 88
alms-houses, see Bridlington; Burton Agnes; Foston on the Wolds; Ganton; Hunmanby; Nafferton
Alost:
    Erenburg, see Burton
    Gilb. de, 202
    Hugh de, 202
    Ralph de, 202
    Sim. de, 202
    Steph. de, 202
    Thos. de, 101, 202–3, 205
Alston:
    Sir Rowland, 180
    Thos., 180, 185
    fam., 180
America, North, 54
America, United States of, 32
Amherst:
    Marg., see Mitford
    Mary, Baroness, m. Lord Wm. Cecil, 305
    W. A. T., Baron, 305
Ampleforth (Yorks. N.R.), 149
Ancaster stone, 318
Anderson, Bart., 35, 92
Angevyn, Wm., 273
Anglian remains, 21, 92, 165, 208, 216, 249, 283, 310, 332
Anlaby, John, 255
Anne, Queen, 73
Anstey:
    Denise, m. 1 Wal. Langton, 2 Warin de Munchensy, 3 Rob. le Boteler, 180, 186, 203, 274
    Nic. of, 179–80, 203
Apesthorpe, prebend of, see York, Cath. ch. of St. Peter
Appleby, Geo., 334
Appleton, Rob., 203
Appleton, Nun, priory (Yorks. W.R.), 25
Arblaster:
    Otes, 254–6
    Rob., 254
Archer, Judith, 312
Arches:
    Maud, m. Wm. de Cauntelo, 12
    Osbert de, 12
Archil (fl. 1066), 24
architects, see Bakewell; Barry, John; Beale, R. J.; Bilson; Blanchard; Botterill; Brierley; Brodrick; Brodrick, Lowther, and Walker; Burlington; Carr; Craze; Cundy; Earnshaw; Fowler, C. H.; Freeman, Wm.; Frith; Gibbs; Hawes; Johnson, F. F. and Thos.; Jones, G. F.; Kent, Wm.; Lockwood; Lowther; Matson, John; Milner and Craze; Moore, T. L.; Musgrave; Newton, P. M.; Pearson, J. L.; Pritchard; Scott; Scott and Moffatt; Sharpe, Edm.; Sheperdson; Smith, Alf. and R. G.; Smith and Brodrick; Smith, Brodrick, and Lowther; Smythson; Stewart, W. B.; Street; Tilney; Truelove; Walker; Worth; Wright, Jos.
Arden (Ardern):
    Ant., 96, 218
    Joan, m. 1 —— Rokeby, 2 Thos. Creyke, 96, 218
    Thos. of, 218
    fam., 218
Arden priory (Yorks. N.R.), 255
Argam:
    Gillian, m. John of Aske, 6
    Malger of (two of this name), 6–7, 170
    Mauger of, 306, 308
    Sybil, m. —— Cumberworth, 6
    Thos. of, rector of Argam, 7
    Wm. of (fl. 1180–90), rector of Argam, 7
    Wm. of (fl. 13th cent.) (? two of this name), 6–7, 12, 170, 305
    Sir Wm. of (fl. 14th cent.), 170, 235, 326
    Sir Wm. of (d. c. 1403), 6, 306
    fam., 8, 11, 170, 305
Argam, 3, 6–8, *32*, 87, 231, 241
    ch., 7–8, 89, 100, 116, 317
    econ. hist., 7
    loc. govt., 7
    man. and other estates, 6–7, 12, 121, 155, 170, 235, 305, 326
    rectors, 7; *and see* Dade, Thos.
    windmill, 7
Argam Dikes, 4, 6, 303, 310
Arkwright:
    Alf., 280
    Chas., 287
    Ric., 287
Armstrong, Pet., 327
Arnett, M., 163
Arundel:
    Anne, countess of, see Dacre
    Eleanor, m. Hen. de Percy (d. 1314), 169 n, 334–5
    Rog. of, 179–80, 186, 203, 287
    Wm. of, 179, 186, 203
    fam., 203, 287
Asa (fl. 1066), 273
Ash (Esh):
    Ric. (fl. 1654), 247
    Ric. (fl. 1772), 291
Ashton:
    Benj., 219, 221
    Christiana, see Turner
Aske:
    Gillian, see Argam
    Hawise, 269
    John of, 6, 8
Aslaby, Francis, 212
Aston, see Ayton
Asulf, 217
Atholl, earl of, see Strabolgi, Dav. de
Atkinson:
    Eliz., 219
    Emily, sis. of John, 251
    Geo., 327
    John, 251
    Ric., 202
    Rob., 202
    Thos., 279
Aubigny:
    Gunnore de, m. 1 Rob. de Gant, 2 Nic. de Stutville, 333
Auburn (in Fraisthorpe), 3, 20, 30, 69, 125–6, 129, 199, *200*, 201, 203–8
Aumale:
    Agnes of, m. Adam de Brus (fl. later 12th cent.), 106
    Steph., count of, 26
    counts of, 24–5, 105, 199, 306, 313–314; *and see* Forz; Gros
Austin, Mary, 331
Avery, John, 44
Ayton (Aston, Eston):
    John of, 139, 211
    Wm. of, 139
    fam., 139

Babthorpe:
    Ralph, 167–8
    Wm. (fl. c. 1550), 167–8, 172
    Wm. (fl. 1611), 167
    fam., 167–8, 176
Bagot, Mary, m. W. H. Dawnay, 301–302
Bailey, Rob., 35
Bainard:
    Agnes, m. Rob. de Brus, 107 n
    Geof., 107, 114, 196
Bainton:
    Anne, m. Wm. Stephenson, 181

INDEX

Chris., 292
Thos. (fl. 1598), 181
Thos. (fl. 1788), 292
Thos. (fl. 1833), 292
Wm., 181
fam., 183, 292
Bainton, 320
Baitson, Rob., 192, 266
Bakewell, Wm., 37
Baldric, Hugh s. of, 202, 204
Ball:
  Dorothy, see Harrison
  Hen., 305, 312
Balliol:
  Dervorguilla, w. of John de, 253
  John de, 253
Baltic Sea, 53–4
Banaster, John, 25, 92
Bannister, J. W., 193
Baptists, 16, 75–6, 90, 117, 124, 163, 176, 243–4, 261–2, 295
Barber, John, 12
Barber and Whitwell, plate-makers, 28
Barch (fl. 1066), 285
Bard:
  Alice, m. John Houghton, 193
  Durand, 193
  Isabel, m. Rob. Martin, 193
  John, 139
  Wm., 170
  fam., 193
Bardisey, Adam, 212
Bardney abbey (Lincs.), 7, 122–3, 236, 239, 241–2, 279–81, 299, 301, 306–8
  abbot of, see Stainfield
Barker:
  Alf., 62
  Ann, 82
  Eric, 279
  Francis, 85, 149, 187, 196, 226, 294, 318, 334–5
Barmby:
  Hen., 107
  Rob., 88
  Thos., 219
  fam., 219
Barmston, 53, 199
  ch., 8, 71, 116, 206–8
  inhabitants of, 24, 44, 108–9, 312
  man., 129, 204, 308
Barnes:
  Capt. E., 67
  Miles, 45
Barnes-Lawrence, A. L., vicar of Bridlington, 74
Barnshaw:
  Francis, 12
  Martin, 12
Baron:
  Chris., 76
  Geo., 76
  John, 295–6
Barr, Mark, 35, 59
Barrow upon Humber (Lincs.), 74
Barry:
  John, 135
  Thos., 191
Barstow, Mic., 265
Bartindale (in Hunmanby), 5, 7, 228, 230–2, 235–7, 241–2
Barton upon Humber (Lincs.), 188
Barugh:
  Jas., 121
  Thos., 121, 123
Bates, Edw., 313
Bateson, G. N. de Yarburgh, 136
Bathyanny, Count, 49
Battle, Wal., 37, 39
Battom, Wm., 141
Baxter, Wm., 307
Bayes, Tom, 306
Bayles:
  Miss E., 187
  Sarah, 187

Bayley, Ric., 222; and see Readett Bayley
beacons, 10, 32, 101, 153, 201, 278, 311, 320, 333
Bealby:
  Chas., 83
  fam., 83
Beale:
  Chris., 253
  R. J., 67
Beaucock:
  Dr. Edw., 35
  Eleanor, see Hustler
Beaufort, John, earl of Somerset, 326
Beaumont:
  Dudley, 311
  Ric., 319
  Susan, see Bosville Macdonald
Beauvais:
  Hudson, 63
  Rob., 35
Beaveshire, Rob., 306
Beckett, Wm., 121
Beckwith:
  Adam, 279
  Eliz., see Malbis
  Rob., 21
  Rog., 279
  Thos., 142
  Wm., 279
  fam., 279
Bedingfield:
  Sir Edm., 299
  Sir Hen., 299
  fam., 299
Bee, Edw., 97
Beeford, 14, 20, 71, 161, 176
Beilby, Dav., 193
Belet, Mic., parish priest of Burton Agnes, 114
Belgium, see Brussels; Tournai
Belhus, Ric. de, 252
Bell:
  Jas., 167, 173
  John (fl. c. 1800), 6, 322
  John (fl. 1538), 6, 105, 235
  Mark, 167, 169
  Ric., 6
  Thos., 90
  fam., 6–7, 322
  and see Clayton and Bell
bell-founders, see Conyers, John (fl. 1630); Harrington and Latham; Harrison, Jas.; Mears; Mears and Stainbank; Naylor Vickers & Co.; Oldfield; Seller; Smith, Sam., jr. and sr.; Taylor & Son; Warner, J. & Sons
Bellasis:
  Hen., 325
  fam., 325
Bellow, John, 71, 204, 235, 318
Belvoir, John of, 179, 203
Belwood, Wm., 83
Bempton:
  Ankerin of, 12
  Asketin of, 202
Bempton, 3, 5, **8–16**, 82, 85, 92, 221
  chars., 9, 12, 16, 83, 164
  ch., 14–15, 70, 90, 103–4, 161
  econ. hist., 13–14
  educ., 16, 85
  mans. and other estates, 10–13, 83–4
  nonconf., 15–16
  perpetual curate, see Burrow
  windmills, 10, 14
  and see Newsham
Beningbrough (in Newton upon Ouse) (Yorks. N.R.), 314
Bennet, Agnes, see Willesthorpe
Bennison, Steph., 328, 336
Benson:
  J., 77
  John, 77

Bentinck, Wm., earl of Portland, 326
Bentley:
  Hen., 134, 143
  fam., 144
Bergh:
  Alex., 334
  Wm., 334
Beriot, Geof., 120
Berneville, Ric. de, 168, 173
Beruake:
  Joan, see Marmion
  Maud, dau. of Joan, 233
Beseley, Edw., 274, 327
Bessingby, 3, 5, **17–21**, 30, 32, 75, 91, 125, 127, 241, *273*, *321*
  ch., 20–1, 27, 129, 309
  econ. hist., 19–20
  educ., 21, 80, 131
  extension of Bridlington into, 17–18, 20–1, 37, 40, 57, 69, 79
  Hall, 18
  loc. govt., 20
  man. and other estates, 18–19, 91, 105
  mills, 20
  nonconf., 21
  perpetual curate, see Bradley, Chris.
Best:
  Chas., 235
  Hen., author of the 'farming book', 258, 267–8
  Hen. (another), 44, 102, 105, 187, 196
Beswick:
  Geo. (fl. 16th cent.), 139
  Geo. (fl. 1787), 140
  Geo. (d. 1829), 149
  Geo. (fl. 1847), 140
  W. M. B., 149
  fam., 139, 149
Beverley:
  John, 170
  Thos., 218
  Wm. (fl. 16th cent.), 170, 218, 220
  Wm. (fl. 1620), 286
  Wm. (fl. 19th cent.), 193
  fam., 170
Beverley, 51
  communications with, 67, 125, 201
  corporation, 47, 71
  inhabitants of, 58, 96, 189
  Knights Hospitallers of, 121, 183, 219, 235, 274, 287, 307, 334
  land at, 103, 197
  Minster, 73, 218
  St. Giles's hosp., 203–5, 207
  St. John's coll., 3, 110, 168, 180, 182–3, 188–9, 218, 236, 273–4, 305–6, 317, 320–3, 329
  and see John, Saint
Bevrère, Drew de, 105
Bewholme, 103, 187, 293
Bielby (in Hayton), 124, 318
Bigod (Bigot, Bygod):
  Constance, see Mauley
  Sir Francis, 233
  Hugh, 211
  Sir Ralph, 286
  Sir Rog. (fl. 1234), 139
  Rog. (fl. 1301), 211
  fam., 237–8
Bilson, John, 28, 79–80
Binnington (in Willerby), 4, 170–1, 332–8
Bird, Thos., 97
Birdsall, 79
Birkhead, Jas., vicar of Burton Agnes, 116
Birkin, Thos. of, 179
Birmingham, 134, 146, 261
Black Death, 26, 86, 88, 92, 105, 172, 191, 196, 201, 220, 256
Blackburn:
  W. H., 81–2
  Wm., 148
Blackburn (Lancs.), 65

Blackburne, Revd. Francis, 194
Blackway, Thos., 149, 187, 294
Blake, Hen., 82
Blakelock:
  Edw., 97
  Ralph, 97
  Rob., 97
  fam., 97
Blakiston, Sir Thos., 10, 83
Blanchard, B. W., 244
Blancher, Wm., 55
Bolle, Wm., 317
Bolom, Wm. de, vicar of Carnaby and perpetual curate of Fraisthorpe, 207
Bolton:
  Alice, see Meynell
  Eliz., see Bossall
  Hen. of, 255
  Ric. of, 335
  Rob. of, 23
Bolton Percy (Yorks. W.R.), 126
Bonwick (in Skipsea), 71, 90, 161, 206
Booth:
  Julia, m. —— Stead, 266
  P. H., 266
Bossall:
  Eliz., m. 1 Ric. of Bolton, 2 Thos. of Acklam, 210–11, 335
  John of (fl. 1284), 211
  John (fl. c. 1600), 299, 327
  Maud, see Ganton
  Nic., 338
  Ric. of, 211, 335
  Rob., 210–11, 335
  Wm. of (fl. 12th cent.), 211, 213
  Wm. of (fl. 13th cent.), 214, 335
  fam., 211, 335, 338
Bossall (Yorks. N.R.), 335
Bosville:
  Eliz., m. Sir Alex. Macdonald, 314
  Godfrey, 314, 316
  Wm., 314
  fam., 310
  and see Bosville Macdonald
Bosville Macdonald of Sleat:
  Sir Alex. W., 312, 317–18
  Alice E., 318
  Sir Godfrey (d. 1832), see Macdonald
  Sir Godfrey M. (d. 1951), 311, 317
  Sir Ian G., 314
  Susan, m. Ric. Beaumont, 319
  fam., 121, 312, 314, 316, 319
  and see Bosville; Macdonald
Boteler:
  Denise, see Anstey
  Rob. le, 179–80
Botreaux:
  Eliz., see Thwing
  Wm. of, *325 n*
Botterill, Wm., 76
Bottomley, Wm., 140
Bouch:
  Jeffrey, 121
  John, 121
  fam., 121
Boulton, R. G. H., 154–6
Bound:
  John, 105
  Thos., 105
Bourchier:
  Jas., 25, 92
  Ralph, 219
  fam., 314
Bousfield, E. C., 183
Bower:
  Edw., 53
  John (fl. 17th cent.), 32, 35, 53, 122
  John (fl. 1754), 121–2
  Leon., 44–5, 121–2
  Wm. (d. 1671), 44, 73, 79
  Wm. (fl. 1705), 121
  fam., 53
Bowes:
  Sir Geo., 12, 192
  Percival, 194
Boyes:
  Eliz., 218
  Jas. (fl. 1732), 336
  Jas. (fl. 1761), 336
  John (I) (d. 1790), 292
  John (II), 286, 292
  John (III), 292 n
  John (fl. 1801), 322
  fam., 322
Boyle, Ric., earl of Burlington, 23
Boynton:
  Alice of, 25
  Cycely, m. T. L. Wickham, 108, 312, 315
  Eliz. (fl. 15th cent.), m. Thos. Newport, 25
  Eliz. (d. 1708), w. of Wm. (d. 1689), 119
  Frances, see Griffith
  Sir Francis (d. 1617), 44, 312–13, 315
  Sir Francis (d. 1695), 19, 108, 111, 317
  Sir Francis (b. 1718), 23–4, 203–4
  Sir Francis (d. 1832), 315
  Sir Griffith (d. 1731), 106, 109, 112–13, 117, 119
  Sir Griffith (d. 1761), 23–4, 110, 113, 117
  Sir Griffith (d. 1778), 117–18, 312, 315–16
  Sir Hen. (d. by 1497), 24, 180
  Sir Hen. (d. 1854), 42, 113, 117
  Sir Hen. (d. 1869), 106–7
  Sir Hen. S. (d. 1899), 108, 116, 118
  Ingram of, 10, 24
  John of, 25–7
  Marg., see See
  Mary, 113
  Mat. (d. 1540), 32, 44, 181
  Sir Mat. (d. 1647), 44, 71, 306, 308
  Sir Rob. of (fl. early 14th cent.), 25, 234, 314
  Sir Rob. (fl. 1377), 86
  Rob. (fl. 15th cent.), 25
  Rog., 25–6
  Sir Thos., 23–4, 181
  Wal. of (fl. 12th cent.), 12
  Sir Wal. (fl. 14th cent.), 24
  Wm. of (fl. c. 1200), 24
  Wm. (d. 1689), 119
  fam., 24–5, 44, 106, 108–10, 117, 154, 234, 246, 312–13
Boynton, 3, **21–9**, 32, 85, 91, 93, 105, 124–5, 201, 310
  chars., 29, 131, 208
  ch., 7, 20, 26–8, *49*, 89, 129–30, 207, 260, 317
  econ. hist., 25–6
  educ., 28–9, 90, 131, 208, 320
  Hall, 22–4, *48–9*, 208
  loc. govt., 26
  man. and other estates, 10, 22–5, 44, 83, 95, 126, 202, 326 n
  mills, 26
  nonconf., 28
  vicars, 27; and see Kenyon
Boythorpe:
  And. of, 192
  Hen. of, 196
  Isabel of, m. Rob. of Killingholme, 170, 192
  Rob. of, 170, 192
  fam., 192
Boythorpe (in Foxholes), 4, 107, 190–197, 266
Boyville:
  Joan de, see Talun
  Wm. de, 246
Braceford, see Harpham; Ruston Parva
Bracey bridge, see Ruston Parva
Bradford (Yorks. W.R.), 283
Bradley:
  Chris., perpetual curate of Bessingby, 20–1
  Cuth., 241
  Thos., 56
  fam., 56 n
Bradshaw:
  B. H., 305
  fam., 305
Brafferton (Yorks. N.R.), 115
Braganza, see Katherine
Braithwaite, Geo., 75
Brandon:
  Chas., duke of Suffolk (d. 1545), 114
  Sir Chas. (fl. later 16th cent.), 95, 139, 233
  Eliz., see Pigot
Brandsby, Thos., 255, 260
Bransby, Greg., 287
Bratoft, Thos., 158
Bret (Brito):
  John le, 211
  Ric. le, 211
  Rob., 211
  Thos. le, 211
Brewin:
  John, 322 n
  fam., 322
Brewster:
  Rob., 127
  Thos., 127
brick-making, 20, 40, 99, 113, 128, 143, 160, 206, 220, 239, 258, 275, 291, 308, 316
Bridlington (Burlington), including the Old Town and the Quay, 1, 3, 16, **29–106**, 120, 135, 153, 161, 164, 201, 295
  agriculture, 46–7
  Albert Town, 37, 39, 91
  Alexandra Hotel, 35, 43, 59, *256*
  alms-houses, 67
  Avenue (house), 41, 66, 79
  batteries, 32–3
  Bay, 29, 32, 54, 60, 153, 159
  Bayle, 33, 45–6, 62–3, 65–9, 77–9, *113*
  Beaconsfield estate, 35, 43, 59–60, 65
  Belvedere estate, 39, 61
  borough, corporation, council, 30, 33, 49, 55, 61–2, 64–7, 69–70, 78, 80, 91–2, 95–6, 104–5, 151–2, 155
    arms, 70
    insignia, 70
    town hall, 70
  boundaries, 17, 30–1, *31*, 90–2, 104, 151
  Burlington Ho., 67, 82
  Castleburn, 31–2
  chars., 80–2, 93
  Church (Low) Green, 33, 40, 55
  chs., 70–5, 199
    Emmanuel, 75, 92, 106
    Christ Ch., 35, 65, 74–5, 78, 80, 92, 100, 106, 163
    Holy Trinity, 35, 37, 74–5, 100
    St. Anne, 67
    St. Hilda, 37, 74, 77, 80
    St. Mary's (Priory Ch.), 14–15, 20, 32, 39–40, 45, 65–6, 70–8, 81–2, 90, 92, 104, 161, *192–3*
  convalescent homes, 66
    St. Anne's, 35
  corn exchange, 55, 69, 79
  domestic buildings, 40–4, *320*
  Dominican convent, 41, 75
  educ., 37, 70, 74–5, 78–80, 263
    Girls' High Sch., 16, 41, 78, 80, 262
    Grammar Sch., 18, 78–80, 161, 262
    Knitting Sch., 73, 78–9
  Field Ho. and estate, 35, 42
  fishing, 2, 33, 35, 49, 50–1, 54, 141–2, 159

INDEX

Bridlington (*cont.*)
  fort, 32–3
  Fort Hall and estate, 35, 59–60
  growth of, 18, 20–1, 30, 33–40, *34*, 90, 92, 95
  harbour, 19, 30–2, 39, 47–50, 53, 56, 59–61, 64–5, 68–9, 77, 91, 98, *128*, 132, 256
  High Green, 33, 40, 42, 55
  hosps., 66, 164
  industry, 33, 49, 53–4, 56–8, 75
    industrial estate, 18, 57–8
  inns, 41–2, 55, 58, 62, 67, 73, 75
  life-boats, 49–50, 66
  loc. govt., 68–70
  loc. govt. board, 17, 30, 33, 35, 37, 39, 59–60, 62, 64–6, 69–70, 90, 92
  lords feoffees, 17, 32–3, 44–6, 55, 62, 64–6, 68–9, 79
  Low Green, *see* Church Green
  man. and other estates, 4, 18, 22, 32–3, 40, 44–6, 68–9, 95, 101, 169, 181, 191, 204, 210, 333, 335–6
  mkts. and fairs, 2, 32–3, 37, 54–6, 68, 79; *and see* corn exchange
  Masonic Hall, 37
  mills, 33, 56–7
  nonconf., *see* protestant nonconf.; Rom. Cath.
  perpetual curates, 71; *and see* Rickaby, Cornelius
  places of entertainment:
    baths, 42, 58–60, 62, 77
    cinemas, 62
    museums and art gallery, 59, 61–3
    parks, 41, 60–1
    People's Palace, 60–2
    Royal Prince's Parade, *frontispiece*, 59–62, 64, 70
    Spa, 39, 60–2, 64, 70
    theatres and halls, 58, 60–2, 75
    Victoria Rooms, *frontispiece*, 59–60, 62, 69–70, 75
  poor-law union, 7, 14, 20, 26, 67, 69, 99, 114, 123, 129, 160, 206, 241, 301, 308, 317, 328
  population, 30–1, 91, 95
  Postill estate, 39
  priory, 23, 30, 32–3, 44–5, 89, 132
    canons, 149; *and see* Charder; Langtoft
    ch. and conventual buildings, 33, 40, 45–6, 72–4, 163
    priors, *see* Burstwick; Hampton; Thwing, John; Wood, Wm.
    property of, 12–14, 17–20, 24–7, 44, 46–7, 51, 56, 68, 70, 84–6, 88, 91–2, 95, 97–9, 101–2, 105, 109–12, 114, 120, 122, 126–9, 138–40, 143, 147, 152, 156–8, 160–1, 167–73, 181, 183, 188, 196, 202, 204–7, 211–14, 235–237, 242, 245–7, 254–6, 274, 287, 299, 306, 312–13, 328, 332–8
    school, 78
    sub-prior, *see* Hardy
  protestant nonconf., 16, 28, 62–3, 67, 71–2, 75–8, 80, 163, 189, 295
  public services:
    cemetery, 66
    electricity supply, 37, 57, 64
    fire precaution, 37, 65
    gas supply, 35, 64, 70
    police, 37, 65
    postal, telegraph, and telephone services, 66–7
    sewerage, 65, 69–70
    street cleansing, etc., 65, 70
    water supply, 64
  regatta, 49, 60
  resort, 2, 28, 33, 35, 57–62, 68, 70, 74, 92, 100, 137, 145

Rom. Cath., 35, 75; *and see* Dominican convent
rural district council, 64
sea defences, 30, 35, 37, 39, 56, 59–61, 69–70
shipping and trade, 2, 33, 48–9, 51–55, 142
social institutions, 62–4
  libraries, 58, 62–3
  newspapers, 58, 63–4
  Sailors' and Working Men's Club, 50, 63, 66
  societies, 62–3
  temperance halls, 35, 62, 77
South Burlington estate, 37
steward of, 32
street plan, *36*, *38*; *and see* growth of
transport, 67–8, 125, 201; *and see* railways
urban district council, 55, 60, 69–70
vicar, *see* Barnes-Lawrence
Wellington Rd. estate, 35, 43
workhouse, 67, 69
and see Buckton; Easton; Grindale; Hilderthorpe; Marton; Sewerby; Speeton; Thwing, John of; Wilsthorpe
Bridlington and District Nursing Assoc., 82
Bridlington and Quay Water Co., 64
Bridlington County Institution, 67
Bridlington Gas Co., *see* Burlington
Bridlington Hydropathic Ltd. 60
Brierley, W. H., 137
Brierley and Holt, engineers, 65
Brigg, Thos., 115
Brigham (or Frismarsh):
  Geo., 169, 182
  Hugh of, 185
  John, 183
  Osbert of (fl. 12th cent.), 181
  Osbert of (fl. 1207), 181
  Ralph, 127
  Theobald of (fl. 1229), 185
  Theobald (Tibbald) of (fl. *c.* 1300), 169, 181
  Thos., 127, 140
  Wm. of (fl. *c.* 1300), 169, 188
  Wm. (fl. mid 14th cent.), 182
  Wm. (fl. 1494), 182
  Wm. (d. 1815), 181, 185
  Wm. (b. 1792), 182
  fam., 169, 181–2
Brigham (in Foston on the Wolds), 3, 55, 176–7, *177*, 179, 181–9, 283, 290, 296
British Soc., 125
Brito, *see* Bret
Brittany, John of, earl of Richmond, 254
Broadley:
  Betty, *see* Jarratt
  Hen. (d. 1797), 11, 265
  Hen. (d. 1851), 15
  John, 11
  R. C., 13, 169, 173, 266, 268, 326–7, 334–7
  Sophia, 265
  Thos., 279
  fam., 11–12, 14, 265–6, 279
  and see Harrison-Broadley
Brocklehurst, Geo., 306
Brodrick, *see* Smith
Brodrick, Lowther, and Walker, architects, 75
Brompton:
  A., 312
  Beatrice, *see* Preston
  H., 312
  John of, 203
  Rayner of (earlier 12th cent.), 211
  Rayner of (later 12th cent.), 211
  Thos., 312
  fam., 211

Brompton, Potter (in Ganton), 4, 107, 208–13, 215, 337
Brontë, Charlotte, 58, 86, 143–4
Bronze-Age remains, 119, 151, 165, 216, 263, 310, 332
Brooke:
  Hen., 139
  Humph., later H. B. Osbaldeston, 138, 140–1, 147, 168, 173–4, 229, 231–4, 236–7, 239, 241, 244, 266, 268, 279–80, 298–300, 308, 328
  R. S., *see* Robson
  Rob., 139
  Theodosia, *see* Osbaldeston
  fam., 147
Brooksbank, W., 169
Broughton (Yorks. N.R.), 78
Brown (Browne):
  Sir Ant., 87
  Fenwick, 288
  Francis (fl. 1673), 193
  Francis (fl. 1769), 193
  John, 192
  Ric. (fl. 1392), 293
  Ric. (fl. 1614), 192
  Ric. (fl. 1776), 300
  Ric. (fl. 19th cent.), 63
  Thos., 85, 196, 226, 318, 334–5
  fam., 192, 195
Broxholme, John, 235
Brus:
  Adam de (d. 1143), 211
  Adam de (fl. later 12th cent.), 106–107, 191, 211, 325–6
  Agnes de, w. of Adam de, *see* Aumale
  Agnes de, w. of Rob. de, *see* Bainard
  Agnes de, m. Wal. Fauconberg, 192
  Isabel, m. Hen. de Percy (d. by 1196), 325
  Lucy de, m. Marm. of Thwing, 107, 325
  Pet. de, 107, 192, 325
  Rob. de, 107, 109–10, 191, 211, 224, 313, 325
  fam., 10–11, 84, 107, 109–10, 191–192, 325–6
Brussels, 198
Bubwith:
  Ric. of, 192
  Wal. of, 192
Buc, *see* Buck
Buchan, earl of, *see* Erskine
Buck (Buc):
  Anne (fl. *c.* 1700), m. —— Lutton, 168
  Anne (fl. 19th cent.), m. Sir F. L. Wood, 71, 127
  Cath., m. Revd. Alex. Cooke, 71, 127
  Sir Chas., 312
  Eliz., *see* Green
  Eliz. (fl. 1763), dau. of Rob. (fl. 18th cent.), 140, 168
  Gocelin, 86
  Sir John (fl. 1630s), 105, 127, 140, 168
  John (fl. 1650s), 92, 105
  Sir John (d. by 1725), 168, 312
  Lawr., 204
  Mary, dau. of Rob. (fl. 17th cent.), 168
  Revd. Mat., 71
  Ralph, 86
  Rob. (fl. 17th cent.), 168
  Rob. (fl. 18th cent.), 168
  Sam. (d. 1632), 19, 127, 299
  Sam. (d. 1806), 19, 71, 127–8
  fam., 127, 140, 172
Buckingham, duke of, *see* Villiers
Buckton:
  Arnold of, 10, 83, 85, 120, 234
  Asketil of, 12
  Ernald of, 83, 202

Buckton (*cont.*)
John of (fl. 13th cent.), 84
John of (fl. 14th cent.), 85-6
Malger of, 84
Pet., 10
Rob. of, 84
Ursula, m. John Collingwood, 10, 83
Wal. of (fl. 13th cent.), 10, 24, 120, 168, 280
Wal. of (fl. 14th cent.), 10, 85
Wm. of (fl. earlier 13th cent.), 10, 83, 202
Wm. of (fl. 1284-1316), 10, 83-4, 86
Wm. (d. 1530), 10, 83, 138
fam., 10, 83, 85-6, 138, 280
Buckton (in Bridlington), 3, 5, 8, 10, 14, 16, 30, 69, **82-5**, 204, 241
chap., 70, 85
chars., 16, 83
econ. hist., 85
educ., 85
Hall, 83, *84*
mans. and other estates, 10-12, 83-84, 234, 305
nonconf., 85
windmills, 83, 85
Buckton (in Settrington), 83
Bugthorpe, prebend of, *see* York, Cath. ch. of St. Peter
Bulmer:
Agnes, later m. Edm., Lord Hastings, 192 *n*
Anne, m. Ant. Welbury, 266
Frances, m. Marm. Constable, 192
Joan, m. Francis Cholmeley, 192
Sir John, 192, 266
Millicent, m. Thos. Grey, 192
Ralph (fl. 1328), 192
Sir Ralph (fl. 15th cent.), 192 *n*
Sir Ralph (d. 1558), 192, 219, 266
Sir Wm., 218, 266
fam., 192, 219
Burdass:
Chas., 254
J. C., 327
W. J., 327
fam., 254, 327
Burdett:
Gertrude, 45
John, 84
Burgh:
Eliz., *see* Percy
Thos. (fl. 1432), 180, 254
Thos., Lord (fl. 1475), 180
Wm., 180
Burghley, Lord, *see* Cecil
Burghope, Geo., vicar of Burton Agnes, 117, 119
Burghwallis (Yorks. W.R.), 129
Burlington, earl of, *see* Boyle
Burlington, *see* Bridlington
Burlington (later Bridlington) Gas Light (later Gas) Co., 64
Burn:
Isabel, *see* Gras
Thos. of, 180
Burrow, E. J., perpetual curate of Bempton, 15
Burser:
Isabel, sis. of Rob., 254
Rob., 254
Burstwick, Rob., prior of Bridlington, 73
Burthall, John, 187
Burtham:
Nic., 260
Wm., 260
Burton:
Erenburg of, m. 1 Ulbert the Constable, 2 Gilb. de Alost, 202
G. H., 193
Geo., 334, 336
Rob., 13-14
Thos., 287
Wm., 13
Burton, Agnes, 4-5, 24, 64, **106-19**, 154, 223-5, 312-13
alms-houses, 107, 119
chars., 116-19
ch., 8, 27, 71, 113-17, 196, 224-6, 260
econ. hist., 111-13
educ., 111, 116, 118, 131, 228
Hall, 106, 108, *112*, 210
loc. govt., 113-14
mans. and other estates, 4, 106-15, *113*, 192, 205, 211, 224, 246, 255, 266-7, 313, 325, 327
mills, 113
nonconf., 117-18
vicars and parish priests, 116; *and see* Belet; Burghope *and see* Gransmoor; Haisthorpe; Thornholme
Burton Fleming (North Burton), 3-4, 7, 27, 85, 99, **119-25**, 171, 237, 241
chars., 125
ch., 8, 89-90, 123-4, 174, 228, 241-2, 318
econ. hist., 122-3
educ., 125
loc. govt., 123
Maiden's Grave, 4, 119, 310
man. and other estates, 7, 120-2, 236, 306
nonconf., 124-5
windmills, 120, 123
Burton hundred, 3-4
Burwell, Wm., 287
Buscel, Rob., 91
Bushell:
Chas., 110
Francis, 110
Sir Hen. (d. 1602), 117
Hen. (fl. mid 17th cent.), 110
Butlin's holiday camp, 145-6, 230, 240
Butterwick:
Durand of, 193-4, 197
Ellen, dau.-in-law of Rob. of, 193
Eustace of, 193
Godfrey of, 168
John of, 155
Rob. of, 193-4, 197
Thos. of, 193
Butterwick (in Foxholes), 4, 167, 170, 173, 190-1, 193-9, 214, 241, 326, 339
Buzenant, Christine, 255
Byass, John, 121
Bygod, *see* Bigod

Cadman:
Wm., 299, 302
fam., 298-9
Caen (Calvados, France), 73
Cailly:
Emma de, *see* Tattershall
Thos. de, 86, 210, 231, 298, 333, 335
Caine, Andie, *see* Taylor, Ern.
Calder:
Jas., 298-9, 326
fam., 299, 326-7
Callis, Thos., 116
Calverley:
Cath., *see* Thornholme
John, 44
Sir Wm. (d. by 1599), 110
Wm. (fl. 1611), 110
Calvert:
Jas., vicar of Boynton, 27
Thos., vicar of Burton Agnes, 116
Wal., 287
canal, *see* Driffield
Cambridge, duchess of, *see* Fairbrother
Cambridge, University, 78, 222
Cammish:
Florence, 151
Wm., 142
Camplesham, Wm., vicar of Boynton, 27
Cancellor, Jas., 18
Canterbury, abp. of, 6, 10, 12-13, 22-3, 25, 44, 83-4, 95, 181, 202-4, 273-4, 314
Capella:
Hugh de, 183, 245
Joan, *see* Talun
Capleman, Francis, 234
Capronnier, glass painter, 198
Cardell, John, 156
Cardoyl, Hugh de, 86
Carle, 6, 44, 95, 120, 166, 169, 179, 202, 204, 231, 235, 285, 335-6
Carleton, John of, 120
Carliell (Carlile):
Anne, 204
Eliz., 93, 95, 204
Hen., 84, 95
John, 19, 95, 127
Randall, 84, 98
Rob., 84
Thos., 19
Tristram, 84
Wm., 99
fam., 84, 93, 95-6
Carlisle, bp of, *see* Osbaldeston, Ric.
Carlisle, earls of, *see* Howard
Carnaby:
Beatrice, w. of Durand of, 127
Durand of, 127
John, 127
Norman of, 128
Roncanus, 127
Carnaby, 4, 17, 21, 104, 106-7, **125-131**, 189, *273*, 299
chars., 29, 131, 208
ch., 20-1, 27-8, 129-30, 199, 206-8, 260
econ. hist., 127-8
educ., 21, 29, 118, 131, 208
loc. govt., 128-9
mans. and other estates, 126-7, 203, 235, 269
mills, 128
nonconf., 130
Temple, 24, 126
vicars, 129; *and see* Bolom; Simpson, Francis
Carr, John, 24, 28
Carrick:
John, 7
Rob., 7, 121
Carthorpe, Hen. of, 202
Carvell, John, 334
Castleburn, *see* Bridlington
Catfoss (in Sigglesthorne), 169, 204
Cattleholmes, *see* Lowthorpe
Cauntelo:
Maud, *see* Arches
Wm. de, 12, 44
Cave, North, 327
Cave, South, 8
Cavendish:
Lord Jas., 183
Wm., earl of Devonshire (d. 1626), 183
Wm., duke of Devonshire (d. 1707), 187
Wm., duke of Devonshire (d. 1729), 183
Cawood:
John, 254, 274
Marm., 109
Wal., 109
Wm., 109
fam., 109-10
Cayley:
Ann, *see* Williamson
Wm., vicar of Burton Agnes, 116-117

INDEX

Caythorpe:
  Eustachia, m. Ric. Fairfax, 313
  John of (fl. 1346), 313
  John of (fl. 1434), 313
  Siward of, 313
  Thos. of (fl. 13th cent.), 24
  Thos. of (fl. 1346), 105
  Wm. of (fl. *c.* 1150), 313
  Wm. of (d. 1296), 313, 321
  fam., 313
Caythorpe (in Rudston), 4–6, 11, 21, 27, 310–11, 313–17, 319
Cayton:
  Hen. of (d. by 1206), 139
  Hen. s. of Hen. of, 139
  Wm. of, 139
Cayton (Yorks. N.R.), 151
Cecil:
  Eliz., *see* Manners
  Mary, *see* Amherst
  Sir Wm., Lord Burghley (d. 1598), 233
  Lord Wm. (d. 1943), 232, 305
Chaloner, *see* Chawney
Chamberlain, Leon., 77
Chambre, Wm. de la, 203
Champion:
  Anne, *see* Coverley
  Maud, 11
  fam., 11–12
chantries, 14, 27, 85, 103, 120, 115–116, 160–1, 187, 224–6, 247, 257, 260, 269, 275, 293–4, 329–30, 338
Chapelow, Revd. Jos., 196
Chapman, Ric., vicar of Hunmanby, 242
Charder, Rob., canon of Bridlington, 73
Charity Commissioners, 81, 189, 262
Charles I (Prince Charles), 18, 120, 202, 285
Chauncy:
  Thos., 254–5
  Wm., 254
  fam., 254–5
Chawney (Chaloner, Chawner), Humph., 32
Cheere, Hen., 306
Chenut (fl. 1066), 24
Cheshire, *see* Chester; Dodleston
Chester, earl of, *see* Hugh
Chester:
  constable of, *see* Constable (Niel; Wm.)
  honor of, 10, 154, 160
  prebend of, 242
Chesterfield, John of, 188
Chestrunt, Wm. de, 245
  his w., *see* Elizabeth
Chilbert (fl. 1066), 120, 126–7, 203, 231, 298, 313, 326, 334
Childers, C. H., 164
Cholmeley (Cholmley):
  Francis, 192
  Sir Geo., 131
  Joan, *see* Bulmer
Church of England Education Soc., 164
Civil War, 32
Clapton, Wm., 12
Clark (Clarke, Clerke):
  Elinor, 136, 148
  G. W., 155
  Pet., vicar of Carnaby, 129
  Ric., 234
  Thos. (fl. 1574), 12, 192
  Thos. (fl. 1620–36), perpetual curate of Fraisthorpe, 207
  Wm., 97
Clarkson:
  John, 239
  Sam., 337
Clay:
  A. T., 135
  Rob., 40

Clayton, Sir John, 153
Clayton and Bell, painters, 222
Cleeton (in Skipsea), 105
Clerke, *see* Clark
Clibert (fl. 1066), 91, 95, 98, 155
Cliff, J. T. T., 109
Cliffe, North (in Sancton), 192
Clifton:
  Adam of, 231, 298
  Constantine of, 86, 231
Clinton:
  Lord Chas., 58
  Lord Rob., 58
Clitheroe:
  Hugh of, 180
  Isabel (fl. 1340s), *see* Gras
  Isabel (fl. 1355), m. Sir Ric. Tempest, 180
Clixby (Lincs.), 8
Close:
  Jane (fl. 1722), *see* Stutville
  Jane, dau. of last, m. Thos. Grimston, 7
  John, 7
coastal erosion, 30–1, 33, 67, 91, 104–105, 144, 201; *and see* Bridlington; Filey; s.v. sea defences
coastguards, 66, 101, 132, 153
Coates:
  E. F. (Sir Edw.), 114–15
  Wal., 327
  Wm., 155
Coatham, W. (in Kirkleatham) (Yorks. N.R.), 268 *n*
Cockerell (Cockerill):
  Jas. (fl. 1681), 305, 312
  Jas. (fl. 1766), 312
  Rob., 305
  fam., 308
Cockfield:
  Geof. of, 305–6
  Sim. of, 142, 279, 281
  fam., 138, 279
Cokeson, *see* Cookeson
Cokethorpe Park (in Ducklington) (Oxon.), 154 *n*
Colbatch, Revd. Geo., 110
Collingwood:
  Sir Cuth., 10
  John, 10, 83
  Rob., 10, 83
  Ursula, *see* Buckton
Collins, Ant., 7, 187
Collinson, Rob., 71
Collman, Mr., 318
Colquhoun, Jas., vicar of Ganton, 214
Colson, fam., 57
Colyear, Chas., earl of Portmore, 183
Condie Assets Ltd., 327
Condon, *see* Coundon
Congregationalists, 76–7, 282
Conner, Albert, 326
Consett:
  Francis, 279
  John, 279
Constable:
  Cath., w. of John (fl. *c.* 1700), 319
  Cecily, *see* Thwing
  Chas., 121
  Chris., 84, 138, 204, 235, 280
  Dorothy, *see* Ughtred
  Erenburg, *see* Burton
  Frances, *see* Bulmer
  Francis (? two of this name), 213, 314
  Fulk, 169, 172
  Jane, w. of Sir Wm. (d. 1527), 315–316, 318–19
  Sir John (d. 1542), 11, 203
  Sir John (d. 1587), 10, 252, 280, 334–5
  John (fl. *c.* 1700), 314, 319
  Lettice, m. Thos. de Houton, 97
  Sir Marm. (d. 1377), 155, 157, 161, 203
  Sir Marm. (d. 1520), 8, 10, 154, 163

  Marm. (d. 1558), 111, 255
  Sir Marm. (d. 1560), 32, 156, 161, 253, 274, 286–7
  Marm. (fl. later 16th cent.), 192
  Mary, m. Sir Geo. Strickland, 121
  Maud, *see* Hatfield
  Niel, constable of Chester, 154
  Phil., 108, 219
  Ralph, 204
  Ric., 203, 287
  Rob. the (fl. mid 12th cent.), 154, 202
  Rob. the (d. by 1208), 156
  Rob. the (d. *c.* 1270), 91, 97, 155, 158, 161, 287
  Rob. the (fl. 14th cent.), rector of Foston on the Wolds, 188, 207
  Rob. the (fl. 14th cent.), 157, 287
  Rob. (d. 1400–1), 158
  Rob. (d. 1441), 12, 155, 306
  Sir Rob. (d. 1488), 6, 12
  Sir Rob. (d. 1537), 6, 11–12, 27, 154–5, 158, 170, 203–4, 233, 235, 305, 307–8, 313, 326
  Rob. (d. *c.* 1590), 6, 154, 160–1, 326 *n*
  Rob. (fl. 1667), rector of Thwing, 329 *n*
  Sir Rob. (d. 1720), 138, 280
  Rog., 253
  Sim., 169
  Steph., 169, 204
  Wm., constable of Chester (d. 1125–30), 154, 160
  Wm., constable of Chester (d. 1130–9), 154
  Wm. the (fl. early 13th cent.), 156, 179–80, 252, 287
  Wm. the (d. 1319), 155–7, 186–7
  Sir Wm. (d. 1527), 313, 319
  Wm. (fl. mid 16th cent.), 10–11
  Wm. (d. 1601), 10, 138, 313
  Wm. (d. 1655), 11, 154
  Ulbert the, 202
  fam., 8, 12, 84–5, 97, 108, 122, 138, 154–5, 169–70, 172–3, 203, 235, 240, 253, 274, 280, 286–290, 313, 316, 319, 326, 334
Conyers:
  Alice, *see* Neville
  Chris., Lord, 192
  E. D., 287
  Sir John (fl. 15th cent.), 23
  John (fl. 1630), 130
  Margery, *see* D'Arcy
  Ralph, 268 *n*
  fam., 325
Conyngham, Lord Albert, later Lord Albert Denison, Baron Londesborough, 102–3, 287, 312 *n*, 326
Conysbye, Humph., 288
Cook:
  Nesfield, 170
  W. S., 23
Cooke:
  Revd. Alex., 71, 127
  Cath., *see* Buck
  Edm., 274, 291
  Isaac, 12
  Jane, *see* Towse
  John, 97
  P. D., 138
Cookeson (Cokeson), Jas., 18–19, 225
Cooper:
  A. N., vicar of Filey, 148
  Jas., vicar of Garton on the Wolds, 221
  Wm., 279
Cootes, Edm., 139
Copeland (Coopland, Coupland):
  R. E., 327
  R. W., 156, 161
  W. W., 63
Corbett, Hen., 246
Cordell, Wm., 56

345

corn-milling, 56–7, 62, *272*; *and see under places*, s.vv. mills, watermills, windmills
Cornburgh:
  Osbert of, 334
  Wm. of, 334
  fam., 334
Cottam:
  Alan of, 168
  John of, 245
  Steph. of, 168
Cottam (in Langtoft), 4–5, 207, 263–271
Cottingham, 182, 276, 323
Cotton, Geo., 127
Cottrell:
  Anne, 246
  Eliz., m. —— Powell, 246
Cottrell-Dormer:
  Chas., 154
  Frances, *see* Strickland
  Clement, 154
Coulson:
  Chris., 139
  Fairlie (Farley), 139, 149
  Ric., 300
  Rob., 139
  Wm., 300
Coultas, Vickerman, 246
Council in the North, 281
Coundon (Condon):
  Eliz., 334
  Thos. (fl. early 17th cent.), 169, 334
  Thos. (fl. late 17th cent.), 194, 338
  Thos. (fl. early 18th cent.), 169, 192–4, 335–6
  Thos. (d. 1779), 334
  fam., 169, 235, 335–7
Counsell, Hugh, 14, 20
Coupland, *see* Copeland
Courtney, John, 58
Coventry (Warws.), 74
Coverley:
  Anne, m. —— Champion, 11
  John, 13
  Sam., 11–13
  fam., 12
Cowart:
  Chas., 86
  Geo., 86
Cowlam, 263, 333
Cowton:
  Hen., 37, 71, 79, 81, 93, 244
  Mat., 322
  Sybil, *see* Cross
Cox, Rob., 77
Cranswick, fam., 305
Crashaw (Crashawe), Wm., perpetual curate of Bridlington and vicar of Burton Agnes, 71, 116
Crawford:
  Eva, 287
  P. A., 180
Craze, *see* Milner
Crepping (? Cressinges)
  John de, 110, 202
  Rob. de, 110
Cresswell, Geo., 218
Cressy, Dame Cath., 12, 155
Creyke:
  Agnes, *see* Heslerton
  Greg., 97
  Isabel, *see* Willesthorpe
  Joan, *see* Arden
  Ralph (fl. 1551), 210–11
  Ralph (fl. 1588), 95, 181
  Ralph (d. 1826), 97, 99, 180–1, 185, 253–4, 157, 312
  Ralph (fl. 1870s), 254, 312
  Rob., s. of Thos., 96
  Rob. (d. 1539), 180, 210, 254
  Thos., 96, 218, 254
  Wal., 210, 335
  Wm., 96
  Mrs., 153
  fam., 92–3, 95–7, 180, 218, 254

Croft:
  Chris., 265
  Sir Jas., 115–16
  Steph., 266
Crompton:
  John, 321–2
  Rob. (fl. 1627), 274
  Rob. (fl. late 17th cent.), 246, 321–2
  Sir Thos., 196
  Mr., 274
  fam., 308, 321–2
Cromwell, Thos., 46
Croom:
  Erenburg, w. of Oliver of, 202
  Oliver of, 139, 202
  Thos. of, 139
Cross:
  Rob., 322
  Sybil, m. Mat. Cowton, 322
Cross Bone Fertilisers Ltd., 54, 57
Crosyer, Pet., 18
Crowe, Rob., 305
Cumberland, *see* Kirkbride
Cumberworth:
  Sybil, *see* Argam
  Sir Thos., 6, 8
Cundy, Thos., 18
Curzon-Howe-Herrick, A. P., 169
Cutt:
  Sir John, 182
  fam., 182

Dacre:
  Anne, countess of Arundel, 11
  Eliz. (fl. 1487), *see* Greystoke
  Eliz. (fl. 1586), m. Wm., Lord Howard, 193
  Francis, 11, 335–6
  Geo., Lord Greystoke and Lord Dacre of Gilsland, 193
  Wm., Lord Greystoke and Lord Dacre of Gilsland, 11, 23, 170, 190 *n*, 233
  fam., 335–6
Dade:
  Thos., vicar of Burton Agnes and rector of Argam, 116–17
  Wm., 116
Dagworth, Eleanor, *see* Rossale
Dailes, Hen., 76
Dakyns, Art., 183
Dale:
  Mary, 81
  Thos., 81
Dales, Wm., 115
Dallin, Rob., vicar of Rudston, 318
Dalton:
  N., 197
  Thos., 252
Damer, Geo., Vct. Milton, 58
Danby:
  Sir Chris., 181
  Francis, 183
Danelaw, 2
Danes' Dyke, *see* Flamborough
Darby:
  Mary, 227
  W. T., later W. T. D. St. Quintin, 224, 227, 322
D'Arcy (Darcy):
  Anne, m. —— Savile, 252
  Dorothy, *see* Melton
  Eliz. (fl. 1352), *see* Meynell
  Eliz. (fl. 1418), m. Sir Jas. Strangeways, 23
  Geo., 252
  John (fl. 1532), 23
  John, Lord (d. 1635), 252, 262
  Margery, m. Sir John Conyers, 23
  Phil., 23
  Thos., Lord, 252
  fam., 325
Darewski, Herman, 62
Darley:
  Emma, 279

  Geo., 98–9
  Ric., 171, 334
  Wm., 279–80
  fam., 279, 335
Davidson, Jas., vicar of Nafferton, 294, 296–7
Dawe, Rob., 204, 274
Dawkins, Hen., 183, 187
Dawnay:
  Cuth., 211
  E. H., 300–1
  Eustace, 193
  Sir Hugh, Vct. Downe, 193
  John (fl. 17th cent.), 211–13
  John (d. 1931), 193
  Marm., later Marm. Langley, 193, 301–2
  Mary (fl. 1630), m. John Legard, 211
  Mary, Lady Downe (d. 1900), *see* Bagot
  W. H., Vct. Downe, 193, 301
  Ursula, *see* Thwing
  fam., 211, 215, 301–2
Dawson:
  Alan, 170
  Ern., 312
  John (fl. 1690s), 98
  John (fl. 1813), 11
  Wal., 169, 334–6
  fam., 334–5
Day:
  E., vicar of Willerby, 338
  fam., 338
Deane, M., 331
Deare, ——, 215
Denison:
  Lord Albert, *see* Conyngham
  Jos., 334
  Wm. F. H., earl of Londesborough (d. 1917), 169, 252, 287, 312
  Wm. H. F., earl of Londesborough (d. 1900), 252, 312 *n*, 331
  Wm. J., 102–3, 169–70, 268, 312, 316, 335–6
  fam., 169, 308, 312, 334–6, 338
Denmark, 51
Denney:
  J. H., 114
  John, vicar of Burton Agnes, 114, 116
Dent:
  C. H., 168
  J. W., 183
  Jos., 183
  Marg., *see* Ellis
  Wm. (fl. 17th cent.), 169
  Wm. (fl. 1735), 7
  fam., 183
depopulated villages, 1; *and see* Argam; Auburn; Bartindale; Binnington; Boythorpe; Caythorpe; Cottam; Easton; Flotmanby; Fowthorpe; Hilderthorpe; Kelk, Lit.; Marton; Newbiggin; Newsham; Octon; Pockthorpe; Ricstorp; Rodebestorp; Scagetorp; Swaythorpe; Thorpe; Willesthorpe
Derwent, riv. (Yorks.), 172, 208–9, 213–14, 280, 332
Despenser:
  Alex., 84
  Geof., 26
Devonshire, earl and duke of, *see* Cavendish
Dickinson:
  Mic., 271
  Wm., 140
Dickleburgh (Norf.), 124
Dickson:
  John, 284, 287–8, 322
  fam., 294
Digby, John, Lord, 231
Digges:
  Chris., 180

INDEX

Edw., 180
Diocesan Church Extension Soc., 161
Dixon:
  John, 6
  Rosamond, 185
Dobson:
  John (fl. 1537), vicar of Muston, 281
  John (fl. c. 1700), vicar of Ganton on the Wolds, 221
Dodding, Miles, 321
Dodleston (Ches.), 242
Dogger Bank, 141
Doncaster (Yorks. W.R.), 283
Dowding, Mr., 199 n
Dowman (Doweman):
  John, 25
  Thos., 187, 293
Downe, Vct., see Dawnay, Hugh and W. H.
Downing, Edm., 212, 214, 236, 241, 287, 321
Dowsett:
  Edw., 140, 160
  Eliz., see Roberts
Drake, Revd. Francis, 255
Driby, Joan of, see Tattershall
Driffield:
  John of, 180
  John, s. of John of, 180
Driffield, Gt., 23, 64, 67, 145, 247, 283–4
  land at, 187
  man., 3, 181, 253–5
  poor-law union, 186, 196, 226, 247, 259, 269, 275, 293, 323
  see also Driffield, Lit.; Elmswell
Driffield, Lit. (in Gt. Driffield), 216
Driffield canal, 177, 179, 247, 283, 285, 291–2
Driffield hundred, 3
Dringhoe, John of, see Meaux
Dringhoe (in Skipsea), 124, 206
Drinkrow (Drinkrowe):
  Thos., 253
  Wm., 232, 239
  ——, 263
Drummond, Lady, 187
Dry:
  Edw., 321
  Wm., 322
  fam., 321 n, 322
Ducklington (Oxon.), see Cokethorpe
Duckmanton, Florence, 82
Duesbery:
  Revd. C. L. T., 109
  Cath., later m. Revd. Rob. Young, 336
  Rob., 336
  Thos., 109, 252, 257
  W. H. T., 252
  Wm. D. T., see Thornton
Duggleby, 196
Dukes:
  Geo., 60
  Moses, 56
Duncombe, Revd. Augustus, 114
Durham, co., see Frosterley; Sunderland
Dyneley (Dynely):
  Hen., 105, 127
  Wm., 105

Earle:
  Giles, 314
  fam., 73
Earl's Dike, 68, 199–201, 205
Earnshaw, Jos., 35, 37, 39, 43, 60, 62, 67, 76–7, 189
Easby:
  G. R., 180
  Rob., 180
East, Far and Middle, 53
East Anglia, 51; and see Dickleburgh; Romford; Yarmouth

East Yorkshire Motor Services Ltd., 67
East Yorkshire (Wolds Area) Water Board, 64, 146
Easton, Ric., 86
Easton (in Bridlington), 3, 17–18, 21–2, 30, 69, 80, **85–6**
  econ. hist., 86
  estates, 86
  mill, 86
Ecclesiastical Commissioners, 14, 161, 255, 259, 265–6, 293, 315
Eddowes, John, vicar of Garton on the Wolds, 221
Edrington, see Etherington
Edwards:
  J. G., 167
  Jas., 218
Edwyn, Wm., 6
Egfrid (fl. 1066), 273, 313, 321
egg-collecting, 9, 82, 101, 152
Eglesfield, John, 6
Elaf (fl. 1066), 86
Eleanor, queen of Henry III, 72
Electric and International Telegraph Co., 66
Elestolf (in Foston on the Wolds), 3, 181
Elgin Marbles, 15
Elizabeth I, Queen, 109
Elizabeth, dau. of Robert s. of Hugh, m. Wm. de Chestrunt, 245
Ella, Kirk (including West Ella), 118, 193, 196
Ellard, John, 319
Ellerker:
  Edw., 234
  Sir Ralph (d. 1539), 11, 234
  Ralph (fl. 1578), 186
  fam., 234
Ellerton:
  Chris., 192, 274
  John (fl. 1565), 192
  John (fl. 1616), 193
  fam., 193
Ellerton priory, 219
Ellis:
  Eliz., m. Mat. Noble, 7
  Marg., m. Wm. Dent, 7
  Mary, m. Rob. Fulthorpe, 7
  Isabel, see Knowsley
  Ric., 92
  Rob. (d. 1622), 6, 8, 235, 312
  Rob. (d. 1644), 6, 120
  Rob. (fl. c. 1650), 6–7, 312
  Rob. (d. 1712), 6–7, 312
  fam., 235
Elmhirst, Ric., 241
Elmswell (in Gt. Driffield), 3, 53, 216, 258, 267–8
Elrington:
  Anne, see Shippabotham
  Edw., 127, 169
  Ralph, 169
Elwas, Hen., 313
Emden (Germany), 53
Emerson, Geo., 158
Emmotland (in N. Frodingham), 29
England:
  Anne, see Sinclair
  John, 253
  Thos., 208
Ernuin the priest, 109, 224, 252, 255–256
Erskine:
  Dav., earl of Buchan, 44
  Frances, see Fairfax
Escrop, Maud, 279
Esh, see Ash
Espec:
  Adelina, m. —— Ros., 217
  Wal., 217, 221
  Wm., 221
Essex, see Romford
Estoft (Estofte):
  Chris., 181, 187, 203

John, 181
Thos., 181
Eston, see Ayton
Eterstorp (in Filey), 138
Etherington (Edrington):
  Geo., 192
  Ric., 274
  Thos., 192
  W., vicar of Boynton, 27
  Wm., 274, 327
  fam., 274
Etton, Hawise of, 306
Europe, 53; and see Brussels; Denmark; France; Germany; Holland; Ireland; Lisbon; Low Countries; Norway; Rome; Sweden; Switzerland; Tournai
Everingham:
  Adam of, 211
  Adam, s. of Adam of, 211
  Rob. of, 211
Ewbank:
  Cath., m. Geo. Sinclair, 253
  Chris., 253
  Isabel, m. Brian Towse, 253
  Ric., 253
  fam., 253

Fairbrother, Sarah, duchess of Cambridge, 144
Fairfax:
  Eustachia, see Caythorpe
  Frances, m. Dav., earl of Buchan, 44
  Hen., 44
  Ric., 313
  Sir Thos. (d. 1505), 11, 313, 315
  Thos. (fl. 1513), 313
  Thos., Vct. (d. 1637), 313 n
  Sir Wm., 95, 313
  fam., 313
fairs, see markets
Fale, Thos., 105, 187, 334
Falkingham, Art., 312
Falsgrave, E. C., 227
Falsgrave (Yorks. N.R.), 138
Fane, Sir Francis, 252
Fangfoss, Gilb. of, 254
Farley:
  Barbara, 140
  Humph., 140
  Reynold, 140, 192
  Tristram, 140
Farlington (Yorks. N.R.), 8
Farthing:
  Franky, m. Jas. Hopkinson, 7, 121, 236, 312
  John, 7, 121, 236, 239, 312, 316
  Mic., 170
Fauconberg:
  Agnes, see Brus
  Joan, m. Wm. Neville, 192
  Thos., 192
  Wal., 192
Featherston, Tom, 121
Fell, M. H., 136
Fellowes, E. F. B. B., vicar of Kilham, 260
Fenton:
  Ant., 315
  Chris., 315
Fenwick, Mic., 154
Ferrers:
  Edw., 291
  fam., 175
Ferriby, North, priory, 109
Fewston (Yorks. W.R.), 186
Field, see Walker
Fiennes, Celia, 106
Filey, 1, 4–5, 55, **131–51**, *133*, 230, 241, 279, 280
  agriculture, 140–1
  Bay, 131–2, 141–2, 228
  Brigg, 131–2, 141, 144–5, 229, 315
  chars., 151, 282

Filey (cont.)
  chs., 135, 147–9, 175, 242, 338
  domestic buildings, 136–8, *256*
  educ., 141, 150–1, 282, 331
  fishing and shipping, 2, 50, 132, 134, 137, 140–2, 150–1
  growth of, 131, 134–6
  industry, 143
  life-boats, 142
  loc. govt., 146–7
  loc. govt. board, 131, 144, 147
  mans. and other estates, 138–40, 142, 146
  mkt. and fairs, 134, 142–3, 240
  mills, 143
  prot. nonconf., 149–50
  public services, 145–6, 230
  resort, 2, 134, 142–5, 230, 240
  Rom. Cath., 147, 149
  sea defences, 132, 144–5, 147
  shipping, *see* fishing
  social institutions, 145
  urban district council, 131, 136–7, 140, 142, 145–7, 228–9, 231, 278
    arms, *147*
  vicar, *see* Cooper, A. N.
  and see Eterstorp; Gristhorpe; Lebberston; Newbiggin; Rodebestorp; Scagetorp
Filey Estate Brick Co., 143
Filey Gas Co., 146
Filey Waterworks Co., 145–6
Firby (in Westow), 241
Firman:
  H. B., 140, 232–3, 279
  fam., 140, 147, 233
Fisher:
  Gideon, 102
  John (fl. 1562), 313
  John (fl. 1773), 227
  Wm., 102
  fam., 73, 102, 215, 243
Fisherton Anger (Wilts.), 59
fishing, 2, 99, 206, 228–9, 272, 283; *and see* Bridlington; Filey; Flamborough; Scarborough
Fisholme (Lady Fisholme) (in Foston on the Wolds), 55, 179, 182, 185, 187
FitzHugh:
  Eliz., w. of Hen., 233
  Hen., 233
  Rob., *see* Tattershall
  Rog., *see* Tattershall
FitzNiel, Wm., 18
FitzRalph:
  Agnes w. of Hen., 211
  Hugh, 120
  Rob., Lord Grimthorpe and Greystoke, 108, 193, 198
  Sir Wm., 193
  fam., 198
FitzRobert, *see* Tattershall, Phil.
FitzWilliam (Fitzwilliam):
  Charlotte, Countess, *see* Ponsonby
  Sir Ralph, 192–3
  William, Earl Fitzwilliam, 58
FitzWilliam, Lords, *see* Greystoke, John, Ralph, and William
Flamborough:
  Greg. of, 155, 202
  Lawr. of, 155
  Niel of, 155
  Otes of, 155
  Theobald of, 155
  Vivian of, 155
  Wm. of, 97
  fam., 97
Flamborough, 3, 5, 30–2, 61, 64, **151–64**, 241, 311
  chars., 16, 164
  ch., 15, 74, 90, 103, 156, 160–3, *192*, 207
  Danes' Dyke, 8, *33*, 68, 93, 151–3, 157
  econ. hist., 156–60
  educ., 100, 163–4
  fishing, 2, 50, 142, 152–4, 156, 158–9
  Head, 1, 9, 29, 32, 53, 82, 92–3, 101, 151, 153, 155, 159, *208*
  inhabitants of, 6, 10–12, 180, 203, 287, 313, 326
  life-boats, 153
  loc. govt., 160
  man. and other estates, 6, 95, 97, 152, 154–8, 160
  mills, 158
  nonconf., *129*, 163
  perpetual curates, *see* Marvell; Ogle, J. F.
  resort, 151, 159–60
Fletcher:
  Sir Geo., 218
  J. T. T., 23, 86
  Jas., 7
  John, 8
Flint, John, 183
Flixton:
  Ace of (fl. c. 1200), 169
  Ace of (fl. 1305), 169
  Amfrid of, 169
Flixton (in Folkton), 3, 8, 164–7, 169–176, 334
Flotmanby (in Folkton), 3, 140, 151, 164–9, 171–4, 236–7, 280, 282
Foliath, Jordan, 255
Folkingham:
  Joan, *see* Pigot
  Sir Thos., 139
Folkton:
  Alice, w. of Ranulph of, 167
  Alice, w. of Hen. of, 167
  Gillian, m. Ric. de Lacy, 167
  Hen. of, 139, 167
  John of, 171
  Ranulph of, 167
  Wal. of, 167
  fam., 139
Folkton, 3, 64, **164–76**, 241, *273*, 278
  chars., 176
  ch., 124, 148, 173–5, 241–2, 281, 338–9
  econ. hist., 171–3
  educ., 176
  hosp. of St. Mary and St. And., 170, 172–3, 175
  loc. govt., 173
  mans. and other estates, 166–71
  mills, 173
  nonconf., 175–6
  rector and vicar, *see* Phillips (Herb.)
  and see Flixton; Flotmanby
Follifoot, Thos. of, 313
Folvill:
  Joan, *see* Marmion
  Sir John de, 233
Foord:
  Barnard, 196
  Revd. Hen., 196
  J. T., 266, 268
  Revd. R. H., 266, 271
  fam., 198
Fordon (in Hunmanby), 3, 5, *32*, 123–124, 170, 228–32, 234–9, 241–4, 297–8, 302
Forge, Rob., 291
Forne (fl. 1066), 254–5
Fornetorp (in Thwing), 4, 324, 326–7
Forno (fl. 12th cent.), 18
Forster:
  C. E., 64
  Chas., 64
  Wm., 64
  Mrs., 64
Forsyth, Jas., 217
Forth, Wm., 63
Forz:
  Christine, w. of Wm. de (d. 1260), 253
  Wm. de, count of Aumale (d. 1241), 139
  Wm. de, count of Aumale (d. 1260), 253
Fossard:
  Niel, 313, 326
  Wm., 193
  fam., 193–4, 326–7, 334
Foster:
  Chris., 141
  Leon., 139
  Ric., 156, 161
  Rob., 139
Foston (Yorks. N.R.), 176
Foston on the Wolds, 3, 55, **176–90**, 254, 292
  alms-houses, 189–90
  chars., 189–90
  ch., 186–8, 207, 245–7, 276, 294
  econ. hist., 184–6
  educ., 189
  loc. govt., 186
  mans. and other estates, 179–86
  mills, 176, 179, 184, 186–7
  nonconf., 188–9
  rectors and vicars, 188; *and see* Somers
  and see Brigham; Elestolf; Fisholme; Gembling; Kelk, Gt.
Foulis:
  Hannah, *see* Robinson
  J. R., 83
  Mark R., 10, 83–5
  fam., 10, 85, 209
Fowler:
  C. H., 162, 270
  Edw., rector of Thwing, 329
Fowthorpe (in Hunmanby), 228, 230–231, 233–4, 236–8, 241–2
Fox:
  C. E., 193
  Geo., 273
  Ric., 273
  fam., 273
Foxholes, 3, **190–9**, 241
  chs., 196–8, 214
  econ. hist., 194–5
  educ., 199
  loc. govt., 196
  mans. and other estates, 191–4
  mills, 195
  nonconf., 198–9
  rector, *see* Wilkinson, Caleb
  and see Boythorpe; Butterwick
Fraisthorpe, 3, 30, 32, 104, **199–208**, *200*
  chars., 29, 208
  chs., 20, 125, 129, 187–8, 206–8
  econ. hist., 204–6
  educ., 29, 131, 208
  loc. govt., 206
  mans. and other estates, 102, 112, 201–4
  nonconf., 208
  perpetual curates, 207
  windmill, 206
  and see Auburn
France, 32, 51, 53, 153, 252; *and see* Caen; Rouen
Frank, Eliz., 287
Frankland, Wm., 170, 212, 235, 274
Freeman (Freman):
  Martin, 287
  Wal., 111
  Wm., 76–7
Friboys:
  Isabel de, 121
  Joan, m. John of Hollym, 245
  Sir John de, 121, 245
  Pet. de, 120
  Philippa, m. Rob. s. of Hugh, 245
Friends, Society of (Quakers), 75–6, 149–50, 189, 208, 222, 261, 331
Frismarsh (fam.), *see* Brigham
Frismarsh (? in Patrington), 169, 204
Frith, *see* Worth

INDEX

Frodingham, Pet., 203
Frodingham, North, 176, 179, 186, 189; *and see* Emmotland
Frost, John, 203
Frosterley (co. Dur.), 73
Fugall, Thos., perpetual curate of Lowthorpe, 276
Fuller, Wm., 204
fulling mills, 186, 226, 247, 291–2; *and see* woollen mills
Fulthorpe:
  Mary, *see* Ellis
  Rob., 7
  Rog. of, 259 *n*
  Thos. of, 259 *n*
Furby:
  Geo., 63
  J. W., 63
  John, 63
  Wm., 63–4

Galicien, Pet. de, 252
Gam, *see* Game
Gamage:
  Ant., 87
  John, 141
  Wm., 87
Gamble, Wm., 198
Game (Gam) (fl. 1066), 202, 254, 273, 305
Gane:
  Florence, 97
  fam., 97
Gant:
  Adam de, 233
  Agnes, w. of Adam de, 233
  Alice de, 96
  Emme de, m. Alan de Percy, 210, 298–9
  Gilb. de (d. *c.* 1095), 18, 168, 210, 229, 231, 235–6, 241, 278, 298
  Gilb. de (d. 1156), 18, 91, 101–2, 105, 120, 138, 237, 239, 306
  Gilb. de (d. 1241), 142–3, 234, 240
  Gilb. de (d. 1274), 237, 240, 280
  Gilb. de (d. 1298), 142, 228, 231, 233
  Gilb. de (? which one), 336
  Gunnore, *see* Aubigny
  Julian de, 233
  Lora de, w. of Gilb. de (d. 1298), 233
  Rob. de, 231, 333
  Wal. de, 7, 18, 32, 44, 70, 73, 84, 86, 91, 96, 147, 235, 239, 241, 279, 281, 301, 308, 334
  fam., 6, 10–11, 24, 32, 44, 47, 83–4, 86–7, 91, 96, 101–2, 105, 109, 119–20, 138, 166–8, 170, 181, 192, 202, 210, 231, 233, 235, 278–80, 305, 312–13, 333, 335
Ganton:
  Hen. of, 211
  Joscelin of, 211
  Maud of, m. Ric. of Bossall, 211, 235, 335
  Nic. of, 211
  Ric. of (fl. 1176), 211
  Ric. of (fl. 13th cent.), 211, 337–8
  Ricolf of, 211
  Rog. of, 211
  Wm. of (? two of this name), 211, 306
  fam., 211, 335, 338
Ganton, 4, 144, 175, **208–16**
  alms-houses, 215–16
  chars., 215–16
  ch., 197, 214–15, *257*, 338
  econ. hist., 212–14
  educ., 215
  Hall, 209–10
  loc. govt., 214
  mans. and other estates, 210–12
  nonconf., 215
  vicars, 214

windmill, 214
and see Brompton
Gardener, Rob., 251
Garford, Denis, 170
Garforth, John, 92
Garrett (Garret), Martin, 12, 255, 260
Garthwaite, Jeremiah, vicar of Carnaby, 129
Garton:
  John of, 218–19
  Rob. of, 218
  Steph. of, 189
  Thos. of, 252
  Wm. of, 219
Garton (in Holderness), 221
Garton on the Wolds, 3, **216–23**, *321*
  chars., 223
  ch., *129*, 188, *209*, 220–2, 276
  econ. hist., 219–20
  educ., 222–3
  loc. govt., 220
  mans. and other estates, 217–19
  mill, 220
  nonconf., 222
  vicars, 221
Gascoigne:
  Sir John, 311
  Marg., *see* Scargill
Gate:
  Edw., 334, 336
  Sir Hen., 236, 299, 334–5
  fam., 336
Gatenby:
  Harold, 236
  Rob., 236
Gee:
  Rog., 196
  Sir Wm., 196
  fam., 196
Geldston, 241 *n*
Gembling:
  John of (fl. 1348), 183
  John s. of John of (fl. 1392), 183
Gembling (in Foston on the Wolds), 3, 176–7, 179, 182–6, 189–90
Germany, 130; *and see* Emden
Gibbon:
  John, 322
  Melchior, 44, 155, 164
  fam., 155
Gibbons:
  Sir John, 268
  fam., 266
Gibbs, John, 217
Gibson:
  Revd. John, 173
  Rob., 257
  Wm., 56
Gilberd, Edw., 312
Gilbert union, *see* Hunmanby; Rillington
Gill, Mark, 130
Gilliatt, W. J., 183
Gisburn, John of, 204
Givendale, 318
glass-painters, *see* Capronnier; Kempe and Tower; Peckitt, Wm.; Wailes
Glossop:
  Benj., 253
  Eliz., *see* Sinclair
Glyn:
  Joan, *see* Wilkinson
  John, 326
Godolgham, Wm., 25, 92
Goldsborough, Edw., 192, 195
Goldwell, John, 202
golf courses, 61, 91, 145, 160, 209–10, 230
Goodale, John, 183, 274
Goodall, R. N., 168
Goodrick, Sim., 48
Goro (fl. 12th cent.), 84
Gorun, Ric. de, 254
Goulton:
  Chris., 18, 21
  Thos., 18

Gower:
  Sir Edw., 87, 218
  Wal., 87, 334
  Wm., 334
Graburn, Wm., 135, 147, 305
Grace, Chas., 300
Grace, Pilgrimage of, 32, 192
Graham:
  Sir Bellingham, 218–20
  Chas. (d. 1738), 218
  Chas. (fl. 1757), 218
  Reg., 218
  Ric. (fl. 1681), 218
  Sir Ric., Vct. Preston (d. 1689), 218
  Susanna, w. of Reg., 218 *n*
  Wm., 218
Gransmoor (in Burton Agnes), 4–5, 55, 106–7, 109–19, 224–5, 241, 256
Grant:
  Dorothy, *see* Mirfield
  Thos., 92
  fam., 92
Grantham, Nath., vicar of Rudston, 318
Gras:
  Agnes, m. —— of Rotsea, 95
  Isabel, m. 1 Thos. of Burn, 2 Hugh of Clitheroe, 180
  John le (fl. 1229), 183
  John le (d. *c.* 1331), 179–80, 186–7, 203
  Wm. le, 95
  fam., 95, 183
Gray:
  Alice, 190, 277, 297
  Thos., 74
  Wal., abp. of York, 72
  and see Grey
Graystoke, *see* Greystoke
Greame:
  Alicia, m. Geo. Lloyd, 95
  John (d. 1746), 93, 95–6, 182
  John (d. 1798), 18–19, 73, 87–9, 96–8
  John (d. 1841), 7, 73, 90, 95–100, 183–4, 322
  Rob., 87, 322
  Thos., 100
  Wm., 97
  Yarburgh, later Yarburgh Yarburgh, 73, 82, 87–9, 95–6, 99–100, 184–5
  fam., 7, 73, 87–9, 92–3, 95–7, 99, 183–4, 279, 321–2
  and see Lloyd Greame
Green:
  Eliz., m. Sir John Buck, 105, 127, 140
  John, 118
  Mic., 315
  Ric., vicar of Burton Agnes, 116, 118
  Wm. (fl. 1595), 105, 127, 315
  Wm. (d. 1600), vicar of Burton Agnes, 116, 118
  Wm. (d. 1605), 105, 140
  Wm. (d. 1870), vicar of Muston, 281
Green & Son, 64
Greenham, Francis, 161
Greenhill:
  Eliz., *see* Noble
  John R., 7, 235, 312
Gregory, John, 8
Grey:
  Joan, w. of John, 333
  John, 333
  Millicent, *see* Bulmer
  Ralph, 192, 266
  Rob., 13
  Thos., 192
  Wm., dean of York and bp. of London, 261
  and see Gray
Greystoke (Graystoke, Greystock)
  Eliz., m. Thos. Dacre, 193

Greystoke (cont.)
　John de (d. 1306), 108, 173
　John de, Lord Greystoke and Lord FitzWilliam (d. 1436), 193
　Mary, see Mauley
　Ralph de, Lord Greystoke and Lord FitzWilliam (d. 1323), 108
　Ralph de, Lord Greystoke and Lord FitzWilliam (d. 1418), 84
　Ralph de, Lord Greystoke and Lord FitzWilliam (d. 1487), 193
　Wm. de (fl. 13th cent.), 11, 84, 107–8, 110
　Wm. de, Lord Greystoke and Lord FitzWilliam (d. 1359), 193
　fam., 108–11, 167–70, 172–3, 175, 188, 193, 313
　and see Ranulph s. of Walter; Walter s. of Ives
Greystoke, Lords, see Dacre, Geo. and Wm.; FitzRalph, Rob.; Greystoke, John, Ralph, and Wm.
Griffith:
　Frances, m. Sir Mat. Boynton, 108
　Sir Geo., 246
　Sir Hen. (d. 1620), 108–10, 115, 117, 203, 246
　Sir Hen. (d. 1654), 108, 110–11, 115, 117–19, 154, 246–7, 255–6
　Joan, see Somerville
　Rhys ap, 108
　Sir Wal. (d. 1481), 108, 112, 117, 255
　Sir Wal. (d. 1531), 109, 115, 117
　Wal. (fl. 1560s), 111, 115–16, 226
　fam., 106, 108–10, 115, 117, 246, 255–6, 313
Grimbaud, Pet., 181
Grimsby (Lincs.), 141
Grimston:
　And., 234
　Grace, see Strickland
　Jane, see Close
　Joan, see Hunmanby
　John (fl. c. 1600), 203
　John (fl. 18th cent.), 155, 182, 185, 326
　Josiah, 203
　Sir Marm., 234
　Rob. (fl. earlier 18th cent.), 83, 203, 206, 265
　Rob. (d. 1790), 18–19, 155, 157–8, 182, 326, 328
　Rog., 234
　Thos. (fl. 1566), 192
　Thos. (d. 1821), 7–8, 234
　Wal., 203
　Wm., 203
　fam., 7–8, 19, 105, 182–3, 203, 207, 234, 236
Grimston, North, 269
Gimthorpe, Lord, see FitzRalph, Rob.
Grinchel (fl. 1066), 326
Grindale (Grindall):
　Janet, 183
　John, 183
　Marm., 12–13, 25
　Ralph of, 88
　Sim., 280
　Thos. of, 218
　Wal. of, 87–8
　fam., 11, 24, 87, 138
Grindale (in Bridlington), 3, 6, 30, **87–90**
　ch., 7–8, 15, 69–70, 89–90, 100, 161, 317
　econ. hist., 88–9
　educ., 90, 310
　loc. govt., 89
　man. and other estates, 87–8
　nonconf., 90
　prebend of, see York, Cath. ch. of St. Peter
　windmill, 89
Grindalythe, see Gypsey Race
Gristhorpe:
　Rog. s. of Uctred of, 139
　Uctred of, 139
Gristhorpe (in Filey), 4, 131–2, 134, 137–41, 146–7, 149–51
Gros, Wm. le, count of Aumale, 211
Groundrill, Geo., 266
guilds (religious), 14, 20, 71, 115, 129, 161, 207, 242, 269, 318, 329
Guisborough priory (Yorks. N.R.), 211
Gunby, Susannah, 265
Guneware (fl. 1066), 181, 311
Gunson, Percival, 7
Gurney & Co., 175
Gypsey Race, stream and valley of (Grindalythe), 1, 6, 17, 19, 21–2, 24–6, 29–31, 33, 37, 47, 56, 65, 68, 85, 91, 119–20, 123, 125, 190, 196, 297–8, 310–11, 315–16, 324

Habbersham, Edw., 186
Hacun, Geof., 327
Haggett, Hen., 170
Haisthorpe:
　John of, 110
　Wm. of (fl. 13th cent.), 313
　Wm. of (fl. 14th cent.), 110
　fam., 110
Haisthorpe (in Burton Agnes), 4–5, 106–7, 109–19, 125, 189
Hales (Hale):
　Nic. of, 305
　Rob. of, 305
　Rog. of, 181
　Sim. of, 83, 139, 305
　Thos. of, 83
　fam., 305
Halifax, Vct., see Lindley
Hall:
　J. M., 180
　John, 138, 232, 239, 279
　Rob., 195
　Wm., 286
　fam., 232
Halliday, A., 145
Halliwell, John, 187
Halswell, Nic., 336
Hamerton:
　Jas., 234
　Paul, 234
　Sir Ric., 234
　fam., 236–7, 240, 244
Hampton, John, prior of Bridlington, 73
Hanby, Phil., 51
Hanchett, John, 186
Handale priory (Yorks. N.R.), 335
Hansbie, Ralph, 235
Hanson, Ivy A., 287
Harcourt, Laura, 75
Hardcastle, Ric., 53, 56, 76
Harding, Hen., 193
Hardwick, Thos., 11
Hardy, Pet., sub-prior of Bridlington, 73
Harker, Mary, 155
Harland:
　B. T., 192
　Marg., 45
　Thos., 35, 192
Harold (fl. 1066), 105
Harold, Earl, 154
Harpham:
　Anselm of, 191
　Godfrey of, 191, 327
　John of, 328
　Wal. of, 115
　Wm. of, 326
　fam., 191, 325–7
Harpham, 4–5, 103, 107, 115, 182, 185, **223–8**, 247, 272, 320
　chars., 228
　ch., 106, 116, 226
　econ. hist., 225–6
　educ., 118, 227–8, 277
　inhabitants of, 55, 109, 112, 139, 231, 273
　loc. govt., 113, 226
　man. and other estates, 181, 224–5, 246, 256, 273, 275, 286, 321
　nonconf., 189, 227, 277, 323
　St. Helen's hosp., Braceford, 115, 224–5
　water-mills, 225–6
Harrington and Latham, bellfounders, 74
Harrison:
　Agnes, 294
　Anne, w. of John (fl. later 17th cent.), 312
　Ant., 170, 235
　Dorothy, m. Hen. Ball, 305, 312
　Geo., 81–2
　Jas. (? two of this name), 74, 188
　John (fl. later 16th cent. and earlier 17th cent.; more than one of this name), 170, 235, 286, 305, 312, 320
　John (fl. later 17th cent.), 312
　Jos., 121
　Ralph, 170, 312, 315
　Ric., 183, 319
　Rob., 170, 305
　Thos. (fl. 1635), 235
　Thos. (fl. 1942), 121
　W. H., later Harrison-Broadley, 252, 266, 286
　Wm., 186, 312, 316
　fam., 121, 183, 186, 258, 286, 308, 316–17
Harrison-Broadley:
　Doris, 14, 252, 265, 286
　Miss L. I., 163
　J. B., 265
　W. H., see Harrison
　fam., 14, 265–6, 279, 286, 288
Harrod, G. M., 167
Harrogate College, 123, 173, 241, 281
Harthill wapentake, 3
Harvey, Gen., 140
Harwood:
　Jas., 181
　Joan, see Hildyard
Hassell:
　Thos. (fl. 1695), 314
　Thos. (d. 1773), 314
Hastings:
　Agnes, see Bulmer
　Edm., Lord, 192
　Sir Edw., 273
　Hen., earl of Huntingdon, 273
　Sir Ralph, 299
　Wm., sr. (fl. early 14th cent.), 233
　Wm., jr. (fl. early 14th cent.), 233
　Wm., Lord (fl. 1463), 299
　fam., earls of Pembroke, 299
Haterbergh, Wm. of, 168
Hatfield:
　John (fl. 16th cent.), 10
　John (fl. c. 1900), 295 n
　Maud, m. Wm. Constable, 10
　Rob., 10
　fam., 10, 84
Hatfield (in Mappleton), 10
Hatton, Sir Chris., 246
Haugwitz, Baroness von, see Inglefield
Hawes, J. C., 75
Haworth (Yorks. W.R.), 58
Hay:
　Eliz., 187
　John, 187
Haynes:
　Eliz., w. of Thos., 273–4
　Thos., 273–4, 276, 322
Hayton, 124, 318; and see Bielby
Headlam:
　Anne, see Lutton
　John, 193

INDEX

Heath, A., 169
Hebblethwaite:
  Harriet, 45
  Jas., 44–5, 47, 73
  fam., 41, 45
Hebden:
  Jas., 139, 246
  fam., 246
Hedon (Heydon):
  Brian, 203
  Eliz., w. of John (fl. 1530), 203
  John (fl. 1428), 203
  John (fl. c. 1530), 203
  Thos. of, 204
  fam., 202
Hellard:
  Chris., 321
  Geo., 266
  Rob., 23
  Sam., 266
  Thos., 321
  fam., 266
Hellercar, John, 87
Helmsley (or Ros), barony, 217
Helperthorpe, 196
Hemsworth:
  Benj., 236
  J. D., 236
Henderson, Jas., 279
Heneage, Sir Thos., 253, 255, 326–7
Henrietta Maria, queen of Charles II, 32, 120
Henry I, King, 68, 181
Henry III, King, 72
Henry V, King, 32
Henry s. of Ralph, 211
Herrick:
  W. P., 169
  fam., 169
  and see Curzon-Howe-Herrick
Hertford, riv., 131, 165, 172, 208, 213, 228, 278, 280, 332
Heslerton:
  Agnes (fl. 14th cent.), m. Sir John Hotham, 276
  Agnes (? fl. 16th cent.), m. Wm. Creyke, 96
  Cecily, see Lowthorpe
  Euphemia, w. of Wal. (fl. earlier 14th cent.), 126, 204
  Eustacia, see Percy
  John (fl. 14th cent.), 12, 96, 204, 235, 273–5, 277, 279
  John (? fl. 16th cent.), 96
  Margery, see Lowthorpe
  Rob. (d. 1309), 96, 138, 225, 235, 273–4, 276, 279
  Rob. (fl. 1346), 138, 276
  Sim., 170, 204, 225, 273–4
  Thos., 12, 225, 273, 277
  Wal. (fl. earlier 14th cent.), 126, 235
  Wal. (d. by 1368), 127
  fam., 138, 170, 225, 273, 276, 279
Heslerton, 209
Heslington, 82
Hesp, John, 305
Hessle, 276
Hickman, Dixy, 13
Hicks, Melchior, 322
Hickson, Rachel, 63
High Street (Roman road), 247, 263, 310–11, 324
Hilderthorpe, John s. of Arundel of, 91
Hilderthorpe (in Bridlington), 3, 5, 50, **90–2**, 105
  char., 82
  ch., 69, 74–5, 92
  econ. hist., 92
  educ., 74, 80
  estates, 44, 86, 91–2, 105
  growth of Bridlington into, 30, 37, 39–40, 43–4, 65, 67–70
Hildyard:
  Chris., 204
  Joan (d. 1527), see See

Joan (fl. 1581), m. Jas. Harwood, 181–2
Pet., 91, 105
Sir Rob. (fl. 1737), 183
Sir Rob. (fl. c. 1800), 183
Silvester, 181–2
Sir Wm., 265
Mr., 185
fam., 183
Hill:
  Ric., 25
  fam., 279
Hilton:
  Sir Wm. (fl. 1428), 126
  Wm. (fl. 1573), 126
  fam., 126, 235
Hinderwell (Yorks. N.R.), 242
Hirst:
  John, 87
  Ric., 87
Hobson, Sarah, 74
Hodgson:
  Geo., 297
  Jane, see Tymperton
  Phineas, 13
  Rob., 91
  Wm., 13
  fam., 13
Hogeson, Rob., 327
Holborne, Rob., 265
Holden, Thos., 252
Holderness, 201, 252, 320
  lordship of, 3, 105, 199, 245, 314
  Plain of, 1, 17, 29, 106, 125, 199, 223, 245, 272, 283
  wapentake, 3
Holiday, Mary, 74
Holland, Rob., 44, 102, 105
Holland, 32; and see Rotterdam
Holles:
  Cath., m. John Hugford, 217
  Sir Wm., 217
Hollym:
  Joan, see Friboys
  John of, 245
Holme, Seth, 186
Holme upon Spalding Moor, 158
Holt, see Brierley
Holtby:
  Dav., 6, 312
  J. H., 180, 183
  John, 265
  R., 294
  Ric. (fl. 1710), 265
  Ric. (d. 1896), 7
  Rob., 6
  Winifred, 311, 319
Holton, Constance, 180
Hood, Wilfred, 327
Hopkinson:
  C. N., 312
  C. R., 312
  Franky, see Farthing
  Jas., 7, 121, 236, 312
  Jos., 312
Hopper, Alice, 82
Hornby (Yorks. N.R.), 254
Hornsea, 15, 55, 59–60, 161
Horsforth (Yorks. W.R.), 39
hospitals (medieval), see Folkton; Nafferton; Staxton
Hotham:
  Agnes, see Heslerton
  Durand, 255
  Sir Francis, 97, 276
  Sir John (d. 1370), 276
  Sir John (d. 1419), 97
  John (d. 1609), 97, 274, 276
  Rob. of, 180, 274
  Thos. of, 179–80
  fam., 255, 274, 276
Hought:
  Bessy, see Mosey
  Wm., 181
  fam., 181
Houghton (Houton):

Alice, see Bard
John, 193–4
Lettice, see Constable
Thos. de, 97
Wm. de, 97
Hovy, Rob., 122
Howard:
  Chas., earl of Carlisle, 173, 193, 218
  Eliz., see Dacre
  Fred., earl of Carlisle, 193
  Sir Geo., 294
  Hen., earl of Carlisle, 335
  Thos., duke of Norfolk (d. 1554), 46
  Thos. (fl. 18th cent.), 218
  Wm., Lord (d. 1640), 11, 193, 335
  Wm. (d. 1644), 11, 170
  fam., 167–9, 173, 190, 193, 195–6, 335
Howden, 318
Hoyle, Sam., 87
Huddersfield (Yorks. W.R.), 135
Huddleston, Edw., 77
Hudson:
  Anne, w. of Harrington, 21
  Benj., 87, 312, 316
  Chas., 92
  Geo., the 'Railway King', 22, 326
  Harrington, 18–19, 21, 91, 312, 314, 316
  John (fl. 1709), 314
  John (fl. 1760s), 18–19, 286
  Jos., 81, 286
  Wm., 81
  fam., 18, 21, 314, 316
Hugford:
  Cath., see Holles
  John, 217
Hugh (fl. 1086), 179, 184
Hugh, earl of Chester, 10, 83, 95, 97, 154, 160
Hugh s. of Norman, 154
Huitson, Wm., 87
Hull, Kingston upon, 58, 67, 140, 223, 227, 276, 310
  architects of, 65–6, 73–7, 79–80, 90, 96, 162, 207
  communications with, 2, 33, 51, 53–4, 59, 67, 143, 291, 315
  holiday-makers from, 58, 61, 144
  inhabitants of, 51, 61, 75, 134, 232, 283, 292
  priory, 183, 187, 246
Hull, riv., 185–6, 249, 283, 285, 288–9, 291
Hull Valley, 1, 176
Hulton, Thos., 115
Hume, Gladys, 167
Humphrey, Isabella, 130
hundreds and wapentakes, 2–5, 68, 101, 165, 319
Hunmanby:
  Joan of, m. And. Grimston, 234
  John s. of John of, 170, 235
  Rog. of, 234
  Wm. of, 167
Hunmanby, 3, 30, 55, 64, 103, 109, 131–2, 145, 172, **228–45**, 273, 297, 303
  alms-houses, 244
  castle, 229
  chars., 81, 244–5
  ch., 7, 122–4, 148, 174–5, 241–3, 280–2, 299, 301–2, 307–9
  econ. hist., 236–40
  educ., 244, 310
  gasworks, 230
  Hall, 232
  loc. govt., 240–1
  mans. and other estates, 4, 138, 141–2, 146, 148, 167–8, 173, 181, 192, 228, 231–6, 240, 278–9, 281, 298–300, 305
  mkt. and fairs, 142–3, 229, 240
  mills, 239
  nonconf., 75, 229, 243–4
  poor-law union, 241

351

Hunmanby (cont.)
 Primrose Valley, 228–30, 233
 vicars, 242; and see Littell
 workhouse, 234, 241
 and see Bartindale; Fordon; Fowthorpe; Ledemare
Hunter, Ric., vicar of Foston on the Wolds, 188
Hunthou hundred, 3–4, 101
Huntingdon, earl of, see Hastings, Hen.
Huntley, Ric., 335
Huntoudale, 3
Huntow (pasture), 3, 46–7, 85, 88
Hurt, Frances, 280
Hussey:
 Joan, see Pigot
 Sir Giles, 139
Hustler:
 Eleanor (Ellen), later m. Edw. Beaucock, 35, 98, 218
 Evereld, 97–8
 Jas., 88–9
 Wm. (d. 1644), 25, 35 n, 78–9, 97, 169, 217
 Wm. (fl. mid 17th cent.), 218
 ——, 65
 fam., 88, 97–8
Hutchinson:
 C. F., 83
 Chris. (fl. 1813), 282
 Chris. (fl. 1872), 45
 Edw. (fl. 1637), 299, 301, 307–8
 Edw. (fl. c. 1700), 301, 307–8
 F. A., 83
 Frances, see Osbaldeston
 J. H., 45
 Jane, m. R. S. Robson, 232
 Kath., see Osbaldeston
 Ric. (fl. 1547), 87
 Ric. (d. c. 1755), later Ric. Langley, 301, 307–8
 Rob., sr. (fl. 1776), 300
 Rob., jr. (fl. 1776), 300
 Thos., 87
 Wm., 298, 300
 fam., 239, 299
 and see Medforth
Huttoft (Lincs.), 8
Hutton:
 Chas., 287
 Thos., 235
 Tim. (fl. 1596), 255
 Sir Tim. (fl. 1617), 255
Hutton Cranswick, 221

Ibbitson, Gabriel, 204
improved husbandry, 26, 89, 185, 213, 238–9
Incorporated Church Building Soc., 15
Independents, 75, 77, 295
industry and trade, see brick-making; Bridlington; corn-milling; eggcollecting; Filey; fishing; fulling mills; iron foundry; lime-burning; malting; markets and fairs; pottery-making; rope-making; sand and gravel working; seaborne trade; seaside holidays; shipbuilding; woollen mills
infield-outfield system, 88, 212, 220, 256, 267
Ingilfeld, Alice, see Rossale
Inglefield, Beatrice, Lady, later Baroness von Haugwitz, 236
Ion, Revd. Geo., 286
Ireland, Francis, 285 n
Ireland, 1
iron foundry, 195
Iron-Age remains, 87, 119, 152, 216, 249, 310, 332
Italy, see Rome
Iveson:

 Eliz., dau.-in-law of Wm., 252
 Wm., 252

Jackson:
 Ant., 202
 Chris., 193
 G. R., 145
 Geo., 8
 John, 115
 Jos., 83
 Revd. T. N., 148
 Wm., 83
James I, King, 109, 231, 285–6
Jarratt (Jarrett):
 Betty, m. Hen. Broadley, 11, 13, 265, 268
 Hen. (d. 1721), 9, 11
 Hen. (fl. 1727), 265
 John (d. 1648), 11–12
 John (fl. 18th cent.), 6, 11, 265
 Wm., 92
 fam., 6, 12
Jefferson:
 R. J., 322
 Thos., 297
Jegon:
 Anne, see Metcalfe
 Art., 286
 fam., 286
Jenkinson, Wm., 183
Jessopp (Jessup):
 Doris, 306
 Thos., 180
 Wm., 180–1
Joan, queen of Scots, 181
John, King, 51, 252
John, Saint, of Beverley, 224, 264
John, Saint, of Bridlington, see Thwing
Johnson:
 Amy, 61
 Edw., 255
 F. F., 67, 306
 G. A., 181
 Jas., 182
 John, 252
 Rob., 286–7
 Thos. (fl. 1602), 255, 291
 Thos. (fl. 1807), 96
 Tim., 182, 184
Jones:
 Mrs. E. S., 139
 G. F., 198, 318
 Hugh, 273–4
 John Paul, 32, 153
Jordan:
 Francis, 306
 G. J., 305
 Jas., 170
 John, 310
 Ric., 7, 235
 Rob., 306
 Sam., 306
 Wm. (fl. early 16th cent.), 306
 Wm. (fl. 1565), 170
 Wm. (d. 1623), 305–6
 Wm. (fl. 1705), 306
 Wm. (fl. 1760), 306
 Wm. (fl. 1828), 7
 fam., 306
Jowitt, Wm., 155

Katherine of Braganza, queen of Charles II, 326
Keble College, see Oxford
Keck, Mat., 154
Keddy:
 John, 63
 Thos., 63
Keldholme (in Kirkbymoorside, Yorks. N.R.), 71, 89
Kelk:
 Chris., 182
 Rob. of, 183

 Wm. of, 187
 fam., 182
Kelk (unspecified), 55, 176, 179, 190, 245, 277, 297
Kelk, Great (in Foston on the Wolds), 3, 176–7, *178*, 179, 182–90, 245, 305
Kelk, Little, 3, 176, 179, 225, **245–7**, 272
 ch., 247, 276
 econ. hist., 246–7
 loc. govt., 247
 man. and other estates, 245–6
 nonconf., 247
 water-mills, 245, 247
Kempe and Tower, glass-painters, 261, 270
Kendall, M. T., 145
Kent, Wm., 24, 28
Kent, earl of, see Neville, Sir Wm.
Kent, see Sandwich
Kenyon, Wm., vicar of Boynton, 29
Kerdiston:
 Rog. of, 233
 Wm., 233
Keyworth, W. D., 73
Kildale (Yorks. N.R.), 215, 325
Kilham:
 Agnes, m. Thos. Mountford, 254–5
 Alan of, 245, 260
 Edm. of, 254
 John of (fl. c. 1200), 254
 John of (? fl. 15th cent.), 254–5
 Ric. of, 254
 Steph. of, 245–6, 254
Kilham, 2, 4–5, 30, *128*, 223, **247–263**, *248*, 273, 312,
 chars., 263
 ch., 259–61, 276, 318
 econ. hist., 255–9
 educ., 260, 262–3
 hosp., 260
 loc. govt., 259
 lunatic asylum, 251
 mans. and other estates, 251–5
 mkt. and fairs, 247, 249–50, 257–9, 277
 mills, 251, 258
 nonconf., 75, 261–2
 Rope Co., 258
 vicar, see Fellowes
 West End, 249–50
 and see Swaythorpe
Killingholme:
 And. of, 168
 Isabel, see Boythorpe
 John of, 192
 Rob. of, 192
Kilnwick Hall, 306
King:
 Alan, 154
 Nic., 86
Kirby, John, 45
Kirby Grindalythe, 221
Kirby Underdale, 129
Kirk, R. D., 252
Kirkbride (Cumb.), 20
Kirkby:
 Hen., 218
 Mark, 91, 219
 Wm., 218
Kirkby in Cleveland (Yorks. N.R.), 197
Kirkbymoorside, see Keldholme
Kirkcaldy (Scot.), 53
Kirkham priory, 167, 173–4, 219, 221
Kirkleatham (Yorks. N.R.), 325; and see Coatham
Kirkstall abbey (Yorks. W.R.), 327
Kitching, Art., 334
Knaggs, Jas., 145
Knaresborough, Forest of (Yorks. W.R.), 186
Knights Hospitallers, 25, 168, 192–4, 203, 211–12, 313, 327, 335; and see Beverley

INDEX

Knights Templars, 25, 168, 211–12, 219, 235, 334
Knottisford, John, 326
Knowles, Sir Francis, 71, 116
Knowsley:
  Anne (fl. 1603), see Pearson
  Anne (fl. mid 17th cent.), m. John Knowsley, 120–1
  Eliz. (fl. mid 17th cent.), m. Chas. Stutville, 7, 120–1
  Eliz. (d. 1800), 263, 270
  Frances, m. Cuthbert Lascelles, 120–1
  Isabel, m. 1 Rob. Ellis, 2 Alan Lamont, 120,
  John (fl. 17th cent.), 121–2
  John (fl. 1769), 121–3
  Ric. (fl. 1590), 122
  Ric. (d. 1774), 266, 270
  Ric. (d. 1790s), 268
  Rob. (? d. 1638), 7–8, 120–2, 312
  Rob. (fl. c. 1800), 121, 268, 270
  Wm., 122
  fam., 121–2, 266
Knyvett, Sir Ant., 246
Kyllyn, John, 138
Kyme, fam., 86

Lacy:
  Brian, 170, 172, 175
  Edm., 167
  Everild, m. Herb. St. Quintin, 167
  Gillian, see Folkton
  John (fl. 1346), 167
  John (fl. 1604–5), 167
  Marm. (d. 1578), 192, 210, 212, 214, 234
  Marm. (fl. 1586), 210
  Mary, m. Wm. St. Quintin, 167
  Ric. de, 167–8, 172
  Rob., 167–8
  Thos. (fl. 1346), 167
  Thos. (fl. 1428), 167
  Thos. (d. 1525), 167
  Wm. (fl. 1428), 167
  Wm. (fl. 1580), 170
  fam., 167, 234
Lademan, Thos., 192
Lady Fisholme, see Fisholme
Lake, Thos., 260
Lakeland:
  Eliz., w. of Rob., 219
  Rob., 219
Lakin, Rob., 335
Lambert, Jas., 127
Lamont:
  Alan (fl. 1640s), 120–2
  Alan (fl. 1733), 121–2
  Isabel, see Knowsley
Lamplough (Lamplugh):
  John, 16, 223, 271
  Thos., abp. of York, 293, 330
  Wm. (d. 1624), 139
  Wm. (fl. 1743), 139
Lancashire, see Blackburn; Liverpool; Manchester; Ringley
Langdale:
  Ambrose, vicar of Ganton, 214
  Marm., 192–4, 273–4, 285
  Rob., 182
  Thos. (fl. 1554), 97
  Thos. (fl. 18th cent.), 182
  Wm., vicar of Ganton, 214
  fam., 97
Langdale's Chemical Manure Co., 49
Langford, Wm., 315
Langley:
  Dorothy, 193–4
  Marm., see Dawnay
  Ric. (d. c. 1755), see Hutchinson
  Ric. (d. 1817), 300–1
Langthorne:
  Frances, 204
  Hen., 204
  Sim., vicar of Boynton, 27

Langtoft, Pet. of, chronicler and canon of Bridlington priory, 264
Langtoft, 4, 5, 124, 263–71, 309
  chars., 271
  ch., 198, *257*, 269–71
  econ. hist., 266–8
  educ., 271
  loc. govt., 268–9
  mans. and other estates, 107, 265–6
  mills, 264, 268
  nonconf., 271
  prebend of, see York, Cath. ch. of St. Peter
  and see Cottam
Langton:
  Denise, see Anstey
  Wal., 180
Lascelles:
  Cuth., 121–2
  Frances, see Knowsley
Lastingham (Yorks. N.R.), 294
Lathere, Ralph, 219
Latimer, Lords, see Neville, Sir John
Laton, John, 233
Lawrence, John, 204
Lawson:
  Edw., 102
  Rob., 139
Laybourne:
  Anne, 287, 294
  Chris., 291
  Jacob, 284, 294
  Ric. (d. 1820), 284, 291, 294
  Ric. (fl. 1895), 294
  Rob. (fl. 1609), 294
  Rob. (fl. 1772), 291
  Wm., 291
Laycoke, Westrope, 301
Layton:
  Chas., 126 *n*
  Thos., 126
  fam., 126
Leadbeater, Ric., 310
Leake (Yorks. N.R.), 73
Leatham, Isaac, 109, 238–9
Lebberston (in Filey), 4, 55, 131–2, 134, 137–41, 146–7, 150–1
Leckenby, Steph., 86, 161
Ledemare (in Hunmanby), 3, 228, 235–6
Leeds (Ledes):
  Ric., 286
  Rob., 286
  Thos., 255
  fam., 286
Leeds:
  duchess of, see Townshend
  duke of, see Osborne, Geo.
Leeds, 37, 39, 59, 67, 96
Leeds Regional Hospital Board, 66
Legard:
  Sir Algernon W., 192, 210, 255, 334
  Sir Chas., 255
  Sir Digby (d. 1773), 209, 212–13, 215
  Sir Digby (d. 1822), 215
  Frances, 215
  Sir Francis D., 192
  Geo., 215
  J. D., 280
  Jas., 158
  John (d. 1587), 210, 212, 234
  John (d. 1643), 214–16, 233, 238
  Sir John (d. 1678), 211, 214–15
  Sir John (d. 1719), 334
  John (d. 1738), 215
  Sir John (d. 1807), 212–13, 336–8
  Mary (fl. 1630), see Dawnay
  Mary (fl. 20th cent.), see L'Estrange Malone
  Sir Thos. (d. 1830), 215
  Sir Thos. D. (d. 1860), 121, 144, 215
  Sir Thos. D. (b. 1905), 225
  Revd. W., 215
  fam., 121, 210, 212, 215, 334–6

Leicestershire, 299; *and see* Loughborough
Leighton, Brian, 19
Leland, John, 155
Lennox, earl of, see Stewart, Mat.
Leppington:
  Edw. (fl. 1611), 138
  Edw. (fl. 1775), 220
  Francis, 219
  Jos., 233
  Rob., 231
  Wm., 233, 237, 239–40
  fam., 231
L'Estrange Malone:
  Lt. Col. E. G. S., 224
  Margery V., see St. Quintin
  Mary, m. Sir Thos. Legard, 224, 246, 273, 286, 321
Leven, see White Cross
Levens, Ric., 287
Lewes, Griffith, 120
ley farming, 13, 47, 98, 112, 157, 184, 195, 238, 267
life-boats, see Bridlington; Filey; Flamborough
lighthouses, 153, *208*
Lighting and Watching Act (1833), 292–3
Ligulf (fl. 1066), 10, 101, 202, 298, 311 *n*, 313
lime-burning, 20, 99, 128, 155, 160, 239, 268, 291, 308, 323
Lincoln, 51, 198
Lincolnshire, 32, 319; *and see* Bardney; Barrow; Barton; Clixby; Grimsby; Huttoft; Lincoln; Thornton
Lind, Jenny, 144, 230
Lindley:
  Chas., Vct. Halifax, 127
  John, 25, 27
Lisbon, 53
Lissett, 3, 118
Littell, Chris., vicar of Hunmanby, 243
Liverpool, 283
Lloyd:
  Alicia (d. 1867), see Greame
  Alicia, dau. of Alicia, 66
  Yarburgh G., later Y. G. Lloyd Greame, 50, 66, 74–5, 90, 95
Lloyd Greame:
  Yarburgh G., see Lloyd
  Yarburgh (d. 1965), 95, 182, 322
  fam., 7–8, 87, 90, 93, 182, 322
Lockwood, H. F., 96
Lofthouse, Seth, 21
Londesborough, Baron, see Conyngham
Londesborough, earls of, see Denison
London:
  bellfounders of, 100, 163, 215, 227, 282
  bishop of, see Grey
  City of, 231, 285
  inhabitants of, 21, 75, 81, 144, 283, 318, 329
  Lincoln's Inn, 329
  plate made in, 15, 21, 28, 90, 149, 163, 175, 188, 198, 222, 243, 277, 282, 294, 323, 339
  trade with, 50–4
Longbottom, C., 284
Loughborough (Leics.), 74, 198, 222
Lound:
  Thos. (fl. 1428), 25
  Thos. (fl. 16th cent.), 25
Louvain:
  Agnes of, see Percy
  Hen. of, later Hen. de Percy, 211, 325
  Joscelin of, 210
Lovel (Lovell):
  Francis, Vct., 299
  Sir John, 299
  Phil., 139
  Ric., 288

Low Countries, 53
Lowish, fam., 330
Lowson:
  Rob., 138, 279
  Wm., 279
Lowther, see Brodrick, Lowther, and Walker; Smith, Brodrick, and Lowther
Lowthorpe:
  Cecily, m. Rob. of Heslerton, 96, 204, 273
  Hawise, see Neville
  Margery, m. John of Heslerton, 96, 204, 273
  Thos. of, 96, 225, 273, 276
  Wal. of, 96, 273, 276
  fam., 204, 273
Lowthorpe, 4, 5, 110, 116, 185, 223, 245, **271–7**, 286 n, 290–1, 320, 322
  Cattleholmes, 272, 274
  chars., 190, 277, 297
  ch., 221, 247, 259–60, 273, 275–7, 294, 320, 323
  coll., 225, 272–7, 322–3
  econ. hist., 274–5
  educ., 277
  loc. govt., 275
  Lodge, 272
  man. and other estates, 225, 272–4, 321–2
  nonconf., 277
  perpetual curates, 276
  water-mills, 272, 274–5
Luck, Wm., perpetual curate of Bridlington, 71, 75, 77
Luckins, ——, 288
Lumb, M. G., 280
Lumley:
  Geo., 325
  Sir John (d. 1421), 326, 329
  John, Lord (d. 1544), 326
  John, Lord (d. 1609), 253, 326
  Lucy, see Thwing
  Marm., 11
  Sir Ralph, 11, 326, 331
  Sir Rob. (d. 1325), 326
  Rob. (d. 1374), 326
  fam., 11, 107, 191, 253, 313, 325–6, 330, 334
Lund, 214
Lundie, see Nundie
Lundy, Francis, 121, 123
Lutterell, fam., 312–13, 317
Lutton:
  Anne (fl. c. 1700), see Buck
  Anne (fl. 1713), m. John Headlam, 193
  Ralph, 193
  Ric., 299
  Rob., 140, 236
  Wm. (fl. 16th cent.), 140, 204, 308
  Wm. (fl. 1662), 193
Lutton, East and West, 196
Lyndall, Sam., 77

Macdonald:
  Sir Alex., 314
  Eliz., see Bosville
  Sir Godfrey, later Godfrey Bosville Macdonald, 314, 319
  J. W., 121, 312
McFarland, Rob., 286, 290–1
Machin, A. V., 149, 151
Madyson, Ant., 273
Maheu, Wm., 266
Mainforth, John, 193
Mainprise:
  Ellice, dau. of Geo., 253
  Geo., 253, 327
  Ric., 253
Maister:
  Art., 11–12
  Hen. (d. 1744), 11
  Hen. (d. 1812), 11, 13
  Mary, see Tymperon
Malbis:
  Eliz., m. Adam Beckwith, 279
  John, 170
  Maud, see Neville
  Ric., 96, 142–3
  Wm. (? two of this name), 96, 170, 235
  fam., 138, 235, 279, 305
Malet, June, 286
Maley, Nic., 147
Malger, 102
Mallore (Mallory):
  Anketin, 327
  Denise, 180
Maltby:
  Cath., m. Mic. Warton, 279
  Chris. (fl. c. 1580), 10, 84, 279–80
  Chris. (d. 1618), 10, 279
  Everild, m. Sir Geo. Wentworth, 279
  Frances, m. Thos. Tankard, 279
  fam., 138
malting, 56, 95, 258, *272*, 284, 291–2
Malton (Yorks. N.R.), 55
Manchester, 283, 295
Mangey, Chris., 104
Mann (Man):
  Rob., 273
  Thos., 21, 277, 319
Manners:
  Edw., earl of Rutland, 23, 233
  Eleanor, see Ros
  Eliz., Lady Roos, m. Lord Burghley 233
  Geo., 217
  Hen., earl of Rutland, 203
  Rob., 217
  Thos., Lord Ros, earl of Rutland, 203–4, 217, 313
Mansfield (Notts.), 198
Mapleton, Hen., 7
Marche, J. B. La, 252
Margaret, queen of Alexander III, 72 n
Margison, Chris., 322
markets and fairs, 2, 111, 126, 128, 158, 247, 275, 288; *and see* Bridlington; Filey; Hunmanby; Kilham
Marks, Ric., 84
Marmion:
  Avice (fl. 13th cent.), 237
  Avice (fl. 14th cent.), sis. of Rob., 233
  Joan, m. 1 Sir John Beruake, 2 Sir John de Folvill, 233
  Maud, w. of Rob., 233
  Rob., 233
  fam., 233, 240
Marr:
  A. L., 286
  Abel, 6
  H. W., 83
  L. J., 252, 286
  Stella, 286
  W. A., 83
  fam., 6
Marriott:
  C. H., 23
  Jas., later Jas. Strickland, 23
Marris, E. G., 280
Marsden, Hugh, 337
Marshall (Marshal):
  Edw., 117
  John, 121, 123
  Ric., 123
  Wm. the, 180
Marten, Thos., 127
Martin:
  Edwin, 135–6, 144, 279–80
  Eliz., 76
  Isabel, see Bard
  Rob., 193–4
  Sibyl, 246
Martinson, Wm., 273, 286
Marton:
  Ernald of, 97
  John of, 97
  fam., 97
Marton (Yorks. N.R.), 8
Marton (in Bridlington), 3, 30, 71, *94*, 180, 218, 254, 312; *and see* Sewerby and Marton
Martyrs' Memorial Trust, 123, 173, 241, 281
Marvell, And., perpetual curate of Flamborough, 162
Mason:
  John (fl. 1748), 322
  John (fl. 1794), 322
  R. H., 170
Matson:
  Francis, 328
  John, 41, 96, 153
Matthew (fl. 12th cent.), 91
Matthew, Hugh, 120
Matthews, Dav., 48
Maucovenant, Geof., 329
Mauleverer:
  Colin de, 127
  Joan, see Strangeways
  Nic., 127
  Rog., 127
  fam., 127
Mauley (Merlay):
  Alice, see Stutville
  Constance, m. Sir John Bigot, 233
  Eliz., m. Geo. Salvin, 233
  Isabel (fl. 1214), see Turnham
  Isabel (fl. 1265), m. Rob. de Somerville, 107, 110
  Mary, m. Wm. de Greystock, 107–8, 110
  Pet. (d. by 1241), 193, 326
  Pet. (d. by 1279), 193
  Pet. (d. after 1348), 233
  Pet. (d. 1355), 233
  Pet. (d. 1383), 26
  Pet. (d. 1415), 233
  Rog. de (d. 1188), 107
  Rog. de (d. 1239), 109
  Rog. de (d. 1265), 11, 84, 107, 110–11
  fam., 11, 24, 84, 109–10, 193, 313, 334
Mawburne, Wm., 154
Mawde:
  Major, dau. of Wm., 252
  Mary (fl. 1692), see Savile
  Mary (fl. 1730) m. Darcy Preston, 252
  Rosamond, dau. of Wm., 252
  Wm., 252
Mawe, Ric., 127
Maxwell, Ant., 319
Mears:
  C. & G., 100
  T., 227
  ——, 163
Mears and Stainbank, bellfounders, 163
Meaux:
  John of (or John of Dringhoe), 202, 205
  Thos. of, 202
  fam., 202
Meaux abbey, 287–9, 293, 299, 313, 325, 327–8
Medforth, Rob., 57, 70, 74
Medforth & Co., Medforth and Hutchinson, corn etc. merchants, 57
Meeke, Leon., 206
Megginson:
  Carol, 140
  Diana, 140
  J. D. T., 23, 140
  Kath., 192
Megson, Chris., 321
Mellish, Thos. C., 334
Melton:

INDEX

Dorothy, m. Geo. D'Arcy, 252
Joan, w. of Wm. s. of Hen. of, 252
Sir John, 252
Wm. s. of Hen. of, 252
Wm. of, abp. of York, 252, 254–5, 258
fam., 252
Merlay, *see* Mauley
Merlesuain, 312
Metcalfe (Metcalf):
  Anne, later m. Art. Jegon, 274, 286, 288
  Sir Chris., 95
  Jas., 95, 139
  Marg., *see* Pigot
  Ralph, 286
  Wm., 286
Metham:
  Geo., 95
  Thos., 102
Methodists, *see under places*, s.v. nonconf.
Methorpe, Jas., 288
Meynell:
  Alice, m. 1 Rob. of Bolton, 2 —— Percy, 23, 181
  Eliz., m. John D'Arcy, 23, 325
  John de, 181
  Lucy, *see* Thwing
  Nic. de (d. 1299), 10, 44, 83, 314, 325
  Nic. de (d. 1342), 23, 202, 325
  Rob. de, 255
  Steph. de, 12
  fam., 6, 10, 23, 25, 44, 83, 95, 181, 202–4, 273, 314
Michelbourne:
  John, 182
  Ric. (fl. 1549), 182
  Sir Ric. (fl. 1614), 182
  fam., 182
Middlesborough (Midelesburg) (Yorks. N.R.), 160 *n*
Middleton:
  Baron, *see* Willoughby
  John of, 195
Middleton (Yorks. N.R.), 103, 174
Middlewood, Harry, 252
Millington, 124, 318
Milne, Benj., 58, 64, 66, 153
Milner:
  Jas., 338
  John, 121
  Rob., 208
  Thos. (fl. 1590s), 254
  Thos. (fl. 1769), 121, 123
  fam., 121
Milner and Craze, architects, 227
Milton, Vct., *see* Damer
Ministry of Defence, 333
Ministry of Works, 108
Minithorpe:
  Edwin, 175
  Jane, dau. of Sam., 169
  Revd. John, 169, 175
  Sam., 169
  Revd. Wm., 169, 175
Mirfield:
  Dorothy, m. Thos. Grant, 92
  Hester, *see* Rickaby
Misson (Notts.), 148
Mitford:
  Bertram, later Bertram Osbaldeston-Mitford, 142, 192, 195, 232, 280
  Marg., m. W. A. T. Amherst, 305
  Admiral Rob., 144, 148, 168, 175, 232, 243–4, 282, 305
  fam., 138, 243, 279
Moffatt, *see* Scott
Moira, earl of, *see* Rawdon-Hastings
Monceaux, *see* Mounceaux
Monkton, Nun, priory (Yorks. W.R.), 170, 334
Monson, Sir John, 286
Montagu, fam., 218

Moore (Moor, More):
  Anne, w. of Chris., later m. —— Routh, 47, 71
  Chris., 71
  Edw., 21
  Essex, *see* Ricard
  Hen., 252
  John (? two of this name), 18, 71
  Ric., 127, 129, 274, 276
  Sam., 193
  T. L., 21, 222, 227, 330
  Thos., 296
Mora, Hugh de, 245
Morcar (fl. 1066), 44, 86, 91, 105, 107, 192, 210–11, 335
Morcar (fl. 12th cent.), 11–12
More, *see* Moore
Morgan, Rob., 294
Morley, Alex., 212
Morpeth:
  Rob. of, 139
  Rog. of, 138
  Wm. of, 139
  fam., 138
Morrice, Francis, 13, 19, 44, 218–19, 225, 318
Morris, Francis, vicar of Nafferton, 294
Mortain, count of, *see* William
Mortimer:
  Eleanor, *see* Rossale
  Sir John, 234
Mosey:
  Bessy, m. Wm. Hought, 181
  Frances, niece of Ric., 181
  Ric., 181, 185
  Wm., 335
Mounceaux (Monceaux):
  Alan de, 24, 306
  Ingram de (fl. 1200), 24
  Ingram de (fl. 1284), 314
  Joan, 129
  Sir John (fl. *c*. 1350), 91, 105
  John (fl. 1392), 183
  John (fl. *c*. 1420), 105, 314
  Juette, 170
  Maud, m. Brian del See, 105
  Pet. de, 306
  Thos. (d. 1345), 180
  Thos. (fl. 15th cent.), 105
  fam., 24, 180, 306, 314
Mountford:
  Agnes, *see* Kilham
  Thos., 254
Mowbray:
  John, 266
  Rog. de, 202
  fam., 202, 218
Mowthorpe, Wm. of, 327
Moyser:
  Jas., 287, 290
  John, 194
  Rob., 170
Mulcaster, Ric., 312
Mule (fl. 1066), 217
Munchensy:
  Denise, *see* Anstey
  Warin de, 180
Munro, Wm., 143
Muscamp, Hugh de, 121
Musgrave, Sam., 76
Muston, 3, 55, 64, 131, 145–6, 241, **278–82**, 305, *321*, 333
  chars., 151, 282
  ch., 174–5, 241–2, 281–2
  econ. hist., 280–1
  educ., 282
  Hall, 279
  loc. govt., 281
  mans. and other estates, 138, 140, 142, 170, 235–6, 278–80
  nonconf., 282
  vicars, 281
  windmills, 278–9, 281
  and see Ricstorp, Sclofstone

Muston Drainage Act, 141, 172, 213, 280–1, 332, 337

Nafferton, 3, 55, 176, 185, 188, 221, 275–6, **283–97**, *320*, 322–3
  alms-houses, 297
  chars., 190, 277, 284, 291, 296–7
  chs., 276, 293–5
  econ. hist., 288–92
  educ., 295–6
  Hall, 284
  hosp., 283
  loc. govt., 292–3
  mans. and other estates, 179, 186, 285–8
  mills, 247, *272*, 283–6, 288, 291–2
  Nether Hall, 284, 287, 289
  nonconf., 295
  vicars, 293–4; *and see* Somers
  Windersome, 283–4, 288, 294
  and see Pockthorpe; Thornholme; Wansford
Napoleonic War, 32
Nassington, John of, rector of Ruston, 318
National Fire Service, 66
National Health Service, 66
National Soc. (and National schools), 16, 78–80, 150–1, 164, 176, 223, 228, 244, 262, 271, 282, 295, 319, 331, 339
National Telephone Co., 66, 146
Naylor Vickers & Co., 74
Neolithic remains, 151, 216, 310
Nesfield:
  Theophilus (fl. 1721), 335
  Theophilus (fl. 1806), 170, 173
  Wm., 335
  ——, 173
  fam., 170
Ness, Wm., 194–5
Nettleton:
  J. W., 266
  John, 274
Neville:
  Alice, m. Sir John Conyers, 192
  Eliz., *see* Pigot
  Francis, 139, 233
  Geof. de, 96
  Hawise, m. Wal. of Lowthorpe, 96, 170, 235, 279
  Isabel, *see* Percy
  Joan, *see* Fauconberg
  Sir John, Lord Latimer (d. 1543), 170, 334
  Sir John, Lord Latimer (d. 1577), 171, 334
  Maud, m. Wm. Malbis, 96, 170, 235, 279
  Phil. de, 126
  Ralph de (fl. mid 12th cent.), 96, 138, 140, 306
  Ralph de (fl. 13th cent.) (two or more of this name), 132, 142, 279
  Rog. de, 96, 235, 279
  Wm. de (fl. 13th cent.), 96, 143
  Sir Wm., earl of Kent (d. 1463), 192
  fam., 96, 138, 170, 188, 192, 235, 279, 305, 334
Newbiggin (in Filey), 131–2, 138–40
Newcastle upon Tyne (Northumb.), 48, 52, 215
Newenham, Thos., 204
Newport:
  Chris., 102
  Eliz., *see* Boynton
  Sir Rob., 28
  Thos. (fl. 1428), 25, 218
  Thos. (fl. 16th cent.), 23, 314
  fam., 23, 25, 28
Newsham (in Bempton), 5, 8–14, 83, 155
newspapers, 58, 63–4, 144–5
Newsted, Wm., 202

Newton:
Agnes of, 155
Foord, 257
Mic., 102–3, 138, 141, 279–80, 282, 305, 307
P. M., 70
Ric., 328
Susanna, see Wharton
fam., 134
Newton upon Ouse, see Beningbrough
Newton, Wold (Newton Rocheford), 3, 228–9, 231, **297–303**
ch. 241, 301–2, 309
econ. hist., 300
educ., 199, 244, 302–3, 331
Hall, 298
loc. govt., 300–1
man. and other estates, 236, 298–300
mills, 300
nonconf., 244, 302
Nicholson:
Ant., 286
Thos., 191
Wm., 191
Noble:
Eliz. (fl. 1735), see Ellis
Eliz. (fl. 1767), m. J. R. Greenhill, 7
Mat., 7
Noell, Hen., 287
Norfolk, duke of, see Howard, Thos.
Norfolk, see Dickleburgh; Yarmouth
Norman (fl. 1066), 273
Normanvill, John, 186
Nornabell, Mathias, 291–2
North, Alice, 74
Northend, Geo., 225
Northumberland, earls of, see Percy, Hen. and Thos.
Northumberland, 127, 155; and see Newcastle upon Tyne; Shields
Norton:
John (d. 1489), 180
John (fl. 1524), 180
John (fl. 1628), 182
Sampson, 192
Sam., 182
Thos., 110
Wal., 312
Wm., 265
Norton, 338
Norton Conyers (Yorks. N.R.), 218
Norway, 53
Norwood:
John, 136
Mary, 136
Nostell (Yorks. W.R.):
priory, 121
Priory (mansion), 208
Nottingham, 66, 329
Nottinghamshire, see Mansfield; Misson; Nottingham
Nun Appleton, see Appleton
Nun Monkton, see Monkton
Nunburnholme, Baron, see Wilson, C. H. W.
Nundie (Lundie), Jas., 139
Nunkeeling priory, 121–2, 274, 327
Nunnington (Yorks. N.R.), 115, 218

Octon:
Hen. of, 327
John of (several of this name), 327–8, 330
fam., 326
Octon (in Thwing), 4, 124, 174, 300, 324–31
Oddy:
J. H., 254
Thos., 254, 312
fam., 254
Ogle:
Geo., 155
Revd. H. L., 155

J. F., perpetual curate of Flamborough, 164, 185
John (d. 1605), 155
John (fl. 1767), 155, 158
Revd. P. D. H., 156
Thos., 83
Wm., 155, 158
fam., 155, 163
Oldfield, Hen., 261
Oliver, fam., 322
Ombler:
Thos., 327–8
fam., 327
Orby:
Isabel of, see Tattershall
John of, 231
Marg., 231
Orm (fl. 1066), 217
Osbaldeston:
P. W., 121–3, 140, 168, 231–2, 235, 280
Frances, m. Edw. Hutchinson, 308
Humph., see Brooke
John, 243
Kath., m. Wm. Hutchinson, 232, 298
Sir Ric. (d. 1640), 122–3, 234, 241, 307–8
Sir Ric. (d. 1728), 192, 232, 234, 236–7
Ric., vicar of Hunmanby, dean of York, and bp. of Carlisle, 175, 242–3, 282
Theodosia, later Theodosia Brooke, 140, 148, 232, 279–80
Wm. (d. 1707), 231, 233, 244, 281
Wm. (d. 1765), 173, 237, 266, 305
fam., 121, 123, 138, 173–4, 192, 196, 228, 231–2, 235, 237–8, 240–241, 243–4, 279–81, 299, 301, 305, 308
Osbaldeston-Mitford:
Bertram, see Mitford
E. L., 136
J. P., 144, 266
Rob., 121, 144, 195
fam., 122–3, 138, 140, 147, 173, 192, 228, 232, 279, 299, 327
Osborne:
Geo., duke of Leeds, 58
Hen., 273
Osgodby, Wm. of, 139
Osgodby (Yorks. N.R.), 139, 241
Otes, John, vicar of Carnaby, 129
Otre (fl. 1066), 166, 169, 266
Otterburn, Revd. Ralph, 187
Outram:
Benj., 253
Sir Francis, 253
John, 253–4, 257
fam., 253, 261
Overend:
Jane, see Towse
Tim., 219
Owston:
Francis, 253
Thos., 82
Oxford, 217
Keble Coll., 196
Oxfordshire, see Cokethorpe
Oxtoby, 'Johnny', 149

Palmer:
Dudley, 180
John (fl. 1428), 203
John (fl. 16th cent.), 180, 312
Rob., 44
Palmes:
Anastasia, see Willesthorpe
Brian, 210–11, 335
Parker:
F. W., 239
H. J., 67
R. B., 236
fam., 239

Parkin:
Geo., 81
Thos., 183, 187
Patrington, see Frismarsh
Patten, Wm., 180
Paul:
Chris., 294
Wm., sr. (fl. 1772), 291
Wm., jr. (fl. 1772), 291
Wm. (fl. 1805), 268
Paulet:
Eleanor, see Ros
John, 233
Sir Wm., 233
Paulin (Paulyn, Pawling):
John (fl. 1379), 233
John (fl. 1579), 280
Pet. (fl. 1545), 170
Pet. (fl. 17th cent.), 6
Wm., 233
fam., 233
Payne:
John, 217
Wm. (fl. 1573), 217
Wm. (fl. 1634), 217
Paynel (Paynell):
Jordan, 44
Ralph, 181, 312, 315
Thos., 138
fam., 6, 10, 22, 44, 83, 95, 181, 202, 312
Peacock, Nath., 127; and see Pycock
Pearson:
Anne, m. Rob. Knowsley, 7
Frances, m. —— Rokeby, 277
J. F., 214
J. L., 222
John (fl. 17th cent., d. 1665, ? two of this name), 111, 231, 246, 273–5, 277, 286–8, 322
John (d. 1712), 277
Mallory, 182
Sir Mat., 273, 277, 322
Pet., 15
Ric., 182
Susanna, w. of Wm. (d. 1668), 21
Thos. (d. 1603), 7, 192, 266, 286, 313
Thos. (fl. 1630s), 7, 273–4, 291
Thos. (fl. 1669), 19
Thos. (fl. 1743), 222
Wm. (fl. 1624), 19
Wm. (d. 1668), 21
Wm. (d. 1717), 277, 287
fam., 110, 272–3, 276–7, 286–7, 291
Pease (Pese):
Edw., 20, 196, 336
J. R., 232
Peasegood, Marm., 81–2
Pecket (Peckitt):
Phil., vicar of Nafferton, 294
Wm., 28, 227
Pelham, Eliz., see Wharton
Pembroke, earls of, see Hastings, fam.; Valence
Pennyman, Mary, see Wharton
Percy:
Agnes, m. Joscelin of Louvain, 210
Alan de, 210, 298–9
Alice, see Meynell
Eleanor, see Arundel
Eliz. (fl. 14th cent.), see Strabolgi
Eliz. (fl. 15th cent.), m. Thos. Burgh, 180, 254
Emme, see Gant
Eustacia, m. Wal. of Heslerton, 126, 129
Hen. de (d. by 1196), see Louvain
Hen. de (d. 1272), 179
Hen. de (d. 1314), 288, 290
Hen. de (d. 1352), 127, 290
Hen. (d. 1368), 204, 335
Hen., earl of Northumberland (d. 1408), 126, 181, 204
Hen. (d. 1432), 180, 254

INDEX

Hen., earl of Northumberland (d. 1455), 231
Hen., earl of Northumberland (d. 1537), 231, 285, 334
Isabel (fl. 12th cent.), *see* Brus
Isabel (fl. 14th cent.), w. of Pet. de Percy, later m. Phil. de Neville, 126
John (two of this name), 325
Mary, m. John Ros, 231
Pet. de, 126, 204
Picot de, 126
Ralph de, 126
Ric. de (fl. 12th cent.), 336
Ric. de (d. 1244), 285
Rob. s. of Picot de (fl. *c.* 1150), 126, 129
Rob. de (fl. *c.* 1220), 126, 128
Rob. de (fl. 1305), 127–8
Thos., earl of Northumberland, 241, 334
Wal. de, 299, 325
Wm. de (d. 1096), 126, 179, 285, 287–8
Wm. de (d. 1168), 210, 335
Wm. de (d. 1245), 126–7, 129, 285
Wm. de (fl. 14th cent.), 23
fam., 126–7, 148, 179, 192, 203–4, 210–11, 215, 231, 234, 240, 285–9, 293, 298, 321, 325, 334–5
Perkins:
    Alice, 14
    Francis, 11
Pese, *see* Pease
Pettitt, Revd. Art., 147
Peverell, Wm., 311, 317
Philips (Phillips):
    Francis, 13, 19, 44, 127, 129, 218–19, 225, 274, 276, 291, 318
    Herb., rector and vicar of Folkton, 174–5
Pickering, fam., 121
Pickering (Yorks. N.R.), 138–9, 263
    honor, 168
    Vale of, 1, 131, 140, 164, 166, 208, 228, 278
Pickfurth:
    John, 12
    Thos., 12
Piers, Reynold Fitz, 266
Pigot:
    Eliz., m. 1 Sir Jas. Strangeways, 2 Francis Neville, 3 Sir Chas. Brandon, 95, 139, 181, 233–4, 312
    Sir Geof., 95, 234
    Joan, m. 1 Sir Giles Hussey, 2 Sir Thos. Folkingham, 139, 234
    Marg. (d. 1485), *see* Sewerby
    Marg. (fl. 1503), m. Jas. Metcalfe, 95, 139, 181, 234
    Margery, 139
    Sir Ranulph, 95, 181
    Thos., 95, 139, 181, 234
    fam., 181
Pistor, Rob., 14, 20
Pitt, J. W., 39, 61, 91–2
Pitts, Col., 58
Place:
    Francis, 286
    Marg., m. —— Sewerby, 139
    Rob. of, 138
    Sir Wm. (d. by 1387), 138
    Wm., s. of Sir Wm., 139
plague, 231, 265; *and see* Black Death
Plummer, Jas., 270
Pockley, Geo., 234
Pocklington, Hen. of, 202
Pocklington, 25, 263, 318
    Grammar Sch., 23, 25–6
Pockthorpe, Wal. of, 294
Pockthorpe (in Nafferton), 3, 283–291, 293–4
    chap., 293–4
    Hall, 285–6

Pococke, E., 163
Pole:
    Sir Mic., 187
    Sir Wm. de la, 180, 187
Ponsonby, Charlotte, Countess Fitzwilliam, 58
Porter, Ralph, 182
Portington:
    Thos., 102, 306
    fam., 102
Portland, earl of, *see* Bentinck
Portmore, earl of, *see* Colyear
Portugal, *see* Lisbon
Post Office, 66, 146
Potter, John, vicar of Nafferton, 293
pottery-making, 208, 213, 337
Povey, Justinian, 97
Powell:
    Eliz., *see* Cottrell
    Hen., 246
    Revd. Richmond, 246
    Sam., 246
Poynton:
    Joan, w. of Thos. de (d. 1299), 207
    John de (fl. early 14th cent.), 202
    John (fl. 1397), 202
    Thos. de (fl. 1226), 202 *n*
    Thos. de (d. 1299), 202, 207
Prendergast:
    Beatrice, *see* Rossale
    Sir John, 234
Presbyterians, 71, 75, 77, 163
Preston:
    Beatrice (fl. 14th cent.), m. John of Brompton, 203
    Beatrice (fl. 1940), 183
    Darcy, 252
    F. N., 288
    Hen., 183, 185
    John, 252, 257
    Mary, *see* Mawde
    Ric., 97, 155
    Thos. (fl. 16th cent.), 97, 155
    Thos. (fl. 18th cent.), 183, 185
    Sir Wm. of, 203
    fam., 183
Preston, Vct., *see* Graham, Sir Ric.
Prickett:
    Anne, w. of Marm. (d. 1765), 261
    Marm. (d. 1765), 261
    Marm. (fl. 1782), 88–9
    Rob., 326, 330–1
    Thos. (d. 1885), 69, 74
    Thos. (d. 1935), 74
    fam., 41, 56, 73, 261, 263
Primrose Valley, *see* Hunmanby
Prince Frederick, H.M.S., 329
Pritchard, ——, 96
Proctor, Wm., 336
Prodham:
    Blanche, 102
    Hen., 279, 334
    Valentine, 102
    fam., 279
protestant nonconformity, *see* Baptists; Congregationalists; Friends; Independents; Methodists; Presbyterians; Salvation Army; *and see under places, s.v.* nonconf.
Prudom:
    Dav., 75
    Mat., 77
    Rob. (fl. early 17th cent.), 69, 81
    Rob. (fl. 1698), 75
Puckering, Rob., 13, 102, 154, 158, 161
Pulley:
    Hen., 18
    Thos., 120
Putman, W. E. Y., 109
Pycock, ——, 73; *and see* Peacock

Quakers, *see* Friends

rabbit warrens, 7, 157, 212, 225, 237, 247, 256, 264, 267–8
Raikes, Rob., 114, 117
railways, 35, 54, 68
    Bridlington–Seamer Junction, 2, 9, 59, 67, 82, 95, 101, 132, 135, 143, 159, 229–30, 239, 278, 303
    Hull–Bridlington, 2, 17, 30, 33, 59, 61, 67, 107, 126, 245, 272, 284, 291, *320*
    Malton–Gt. Driffield, 216
    Market Weighton–Gt. Driffield, 67
    projected York–Bridlington, 22
    York–Scarborough, 209
Raine, Ric., 100
Rampston, Rob., 140
Ramsay:
    Sir Geo., 44
    Sir John, 44
Rank, Rob., 235
Ranson, Pet., 23
Rant:
    John, 115, 235
    Rog., 212, 214, 236, 241, 287
Ranulf s. of Mayolf, 245
Ranulph s. of Walter, 167, 169–70
Raper, Mary, 328
Rastrick (Yorks. W. R.), 135
Raunson, Rob., 322
Rawdon-Hastings, Francis, earl of Moira, 58
Rawghton, Wm., 219
Raygate, fam., 280
Rayner:
    J. M., 334
    fam., 334
Raynnowe, Thos., 92
Raysing, Ralph, 95
Readett Bayley:
    Sir Hen. D., 121, 123, 173, 192, 232
    T. D. R., 121
    fam., 147, 229, 235, 241, 281
Readhead:
    Wm., 6–7
    fam., 7
Reed, John, 7
Reekie, Lister, 145
Reeve, Joshua, 335
Reighton, Mauger of, 306
Reighton, 3, 101, 131–2, 184 *n*, 278, 303–10, *304*, 311, *321*, 322
    char., 310
    ch., 20, 90, 103, *193*, 241, 243, 301, 308–9
    econ. hist., 307–8
    educ., 103, 310
    Hall, 303, 306
    loc. govt., 241, 308
    mans. and other estates, 6, 182, 235, 279, 305–7
    mills, 308
    nonconf., 309–10
    vicar, *see* Rowley
Reveley, Willey, 7
Rhodes:
    Abraham, 299, 302
    Edw., 156
    Godfrey, 37, 60
Riby, Mary, 74
Ricard:
    Art., 252
    Cath., dau. of John, 252
    Dorothy, *see* Savile
    Eliz., dau. of John, 252
    Essex, m. Hen. More, 252
    John, 252
    Richard (fl. 1086), 95
Richmond, earl of, *see* Brittany
Rickaby:
    Cornelius, perpetual curate of Bridlington, 73, 78
    Hester, m. —— Mirfield, 92
    John (d. 1717), 35, 53, 91
    John (fl. 1780), 180, 185
    John (fl. 19th cent.), 74, 180
    Thos., 92

Rickaby (cont.)
   fam., 53, 73, 91, 180
Rickinson, Wm., 300
Ricstorp (in Muston), 3, 236, 278, 280
Rievaulx abbey (Yorks. N.R.), 139, 165, 167, 169, 171, 173–4, 235, 237, 306, 334, 337
Riggs, Edw., 116
Rillington:
   ch., 276
   poor-law union, workhouse, 301
Ringley (Lancs.), 12, 156
Ringrose:
   Chas., 173, 192, 195
   Rob., 233
Ripon (Yorks. W. R.), 73, 162
Riston, Long, 320
Rivis:
   G. D., 193
   T. W., 169
roads:
   mile-stones, 67, 165–6, 201, 229, 278, 303
   prehistoric trackways, 1, 31
   turnpike trust, 67, 201
   and see Bridlington, s.v. transport; Romano-British remains
Robert s. of Hugh, 245
   his dau., see Elizabeth
   his w., see Friboys, Philippa
Roberts:
   Anne, 168
   Eliz., m. Edw. Dowsett, 168
   John, 168
   Revd. Wm., 196
   fam., 168
Robinson:
   Hannah, m. Sir Wm. Foulis, 83
   H. P., 127
   Hen., 10, 83
   Humph., 84
   John (fl. 1690s), 98
   John (fl. 1740s), 83–4
   John (d. 1769), 10, 83
   Revd. John (fl. 1870s), 114
   Rob., 10, 111
   Thos. (d. c. 1698), 296
   Thos. (fl. 18th cent.), 76, 138
   Wm., 76
   fam., 83
Robson:
   Albert, 315
   G. S., 266
   Hen., 315
   Jane, see Hutchinson
   R. S., later R. S. Brooke, 232
   Sam., 18
   Thos., 89
   fam., 315
Rochford:
   Joan, m. —— Rogerson, 299
   Sim. of, 299
   Sir Walbran de, 299
   fam., 299
Rockley, John, 123
Rodebestorp (in Filey), 138
Rogers, E. P., 64
Rogerson:
   Dav., 102
   Joan, see Rochford
   Rob., 102
Rokeby:
   Frances, see Pearson
   Joan, see Arden
Roman Catholicism, see Bridlington; Filey
Romano-British remains, 17, 21, 31, 92, 119, 165, 208, 216, 332–3
   roads, 1, 31, 92, 132, 249; and see High Street; Wold Gate
   signal stations, 31, 153, 333
   villas, 1, 87, 223, 310
Rome, 215
Romeyn, John le, 221
Romford (Essex), 15
rope-making, 57, 143, 239–40, 258

Roper, Chas., 327–8
Ros (Roos):
   Adelina, see Espec
   Edm., Lord, 217
   Edw., 203
   Eleanor (fl. 15th cent.), m. John Paulet, 232–3
   Eleanor (fl. 16th cent.), m. Rob. Manners, 217
   Jas., 232
   John, 231
   Marg. de, 325 n
   Margery, m. —— Wittilbury, 232–3
   Mary, see Percy
   Rob. (fl. 1150s), 217
   Rob. de (fl. 13th cent.), 139
   Sir Rob. (d. 1441), 232
   Rob. (fl. 1541), 233
   Wm., Lord, 233
   fam., 217, 219, 236–7, 240
Ros (Roos), Lord and Lady, see Manners, Eliz. and Thos.; Ros., Edm. and Wm.; and see Helmsley
Rose, Thos., 242
Rossale:
   Alice, m. —— Ingilfeld, 234
   Beatrice, m. Sir John Prendergast, 234
   Eleanor, m. 1 —— Dagworth, 2 Sir John Mortimer, 234
   John, 234
   Vivian de, 234
   Sir Wal., 234
Rotherham and District Children's Convalescent Home, 230
Rotsea, Agnes, see Gras
Rotterdam (Holland), 53
Rouen:
   abp. of, 252, 254, 258–9
   chapter of, 252, 258
Roulin, Revd. E., 149
Routh:
   Amand of, 182
   Anne, see Moore
   fam., 182
Routh, 182
Rowley, Wm., vicar of Reighton, 308
Royal Air Force, 9, 49
Royal National Life-boat Institution, 49–50, 142, 153
Rudston:
   John of (fl. 1216), 126
   John (fl. 1623), 19
   John the knight of, 84
   Malger of, 313
   Rob. of (fl. 1166), 313
   Rob. of (fl. 14th cent.), 18
   Thos., 18
   Turold of, 313
   Wm. of (fl. 13th cent.), 11, 84, 313
   Wm. of (fl. 14th cent.), 313
   Wm. (fl. 1423), 18
   fam., 18, 312–13, 321
Rudston, 4, 7–8, 21, 27, 119, 132, 153, 254 n, 310–20, 321, 329
   chars., 320
   ch., 7, 27, 89–90, 124, 207, 260, 317–19
   econ. hist., 315–17
   educ., 29, 319–20
   loc. govt., 241, 317
   mans. and other estates, 311–15, 317
   mills, 316–17
   monolith, 5, 33, 310, 319
   nonconf., 319
   rectors and vicars, 318
   and see Caythorpe; Thorpe
Russell:
   Chris., 151, 279
   Lord John, Earl Russell, 144
Ruston, Edw., 19
Ruston Parva (Little Ruston), 4–5, 223, 246, 271–2, 311, **320–4**
   Braceford, 320
   Bracey bridge, 224, 320
   ch., 221, 260, 275–7, 294, 323

   econ. hist., 322–3
   educ., 277, 324
   loc. govt., 323
   man. and other estates, 186, 273, 306, 308, 321–2
   nonconf., 277, 323–4
   perpetual curate, see Somers
   water-mills, 272, 320–3
Ruston Parva Lime Co., 323
Rutland, earls of, see Manners, Edw., Hen., and Thos.
Rymer:
   Sir Jos., 183
   T. G., 180
   Wal., 183
Ryse, Thos., 299

Sadler, Thos., 15
Sage, John le, 28
St. Liz, Sim. de, 97
St. Quintin:
   Agnes (fl. c. 1200), see Stutville
   Agnes (fl. 14th cent.), see Wyerne
   Alex. de, 111
   Ant., 12, 139, 226
   Charlotte, 227
   Everild, see Lacy
   Gabriel, 12, 116, 138–9, 227
   Sir Geof., 225
   Geo., 116, 226
   Hen., 225
   Sir Herb. (fl. c. 1200), 107, 224
   Herb. (fl. 16th cent.), 18
   Herb. (d. 1634), 167
   Joan, 227
   Sir John (d. 1471), 112
   John (d. 1515), 226
   John (d. 1746), 227
   Margery V., m. E. G. S. L'Estrange Malone, 224
   Mary, see Lacy
   Mat. (d. 1785), 227
   Mat. (d. 1876), 227
   Sir Thos. (d. 1418), 139, 227
   Thos. (d. 1445), 227
   Violet H., w. of Wm. H., 110, 224
   Sir Wm. (d. 1349), 225–7
   Sir Wm. (d. 1379), 115
   Sir Wm. (fl. 1449), 115
   Sir Wm. (d. 1550), 115, 226
   Sir Wm. (d. 1649), 111, 116, 138, 167, 176, 225, 227–8
   Sir Wm. (d. 1723), 111–13, 117, 227, 247, 273–4, 276, 286–7, 290, 292
   Sir Wm. (d. 1770), 182–3, 186, 227, 246, 321, 323
   Sir Wm. (d. 1795), 109, 167, 169, 181, 185–6, 224, 226, 276, 288, 290, 306
   Wm. (d. 1859), 110–11, 113, 182, 184–5
   Wm. H. (d. 1933), 107, 224, 227, 272
   Wm. T. (d. 1805), see Darby
St. Quintin:
   fam., 106, 109–11, 113–14, 138, 167, 171, 181–4, 186, 223–7, 246–7, 272, 275, 279, 286–8, 297, 321–3
Saltmarsh:
   Marg., see Thornholme
   Rob., 110
Salton (Yorks. N.R.), 338
Salvation Army, 28, 62, 77, 262, 295
Salvin (Salvan):
   Eliz., see Mauley
   Sir Geo. (fl. 1344), 203, 274
   Geo. (d. 1417), 277
   Geo. (fl. 1428), 203
   Geo. (fl. 1537), 306
   Gerard (d. 1320), 180, 203, 254, 266, 273, 286, 306
   Gerard (fl. 1344), 273
   Gerard (fl. 1428), 254

INDEX

Hen., 140
John, 233
Marg., 246
Dame Mary, 272
Ralph (fl. 1502), 286
Ralph (fl. late 16th cent.), 254, 286
Rob. (fl. 13th cent.), 254
Rob. (fl. 1611), 287
Sybil, see Wake
Wm., 111, 255, 286
fam., 111, 203, 255, 266, 272–4, 286, 306
Sancton, see Cliffe
sand and gravel working, 113, 160, 220, 245
Sands, see Sandys
Sandwich (Kent), 52
Sandys (Sands), Sir Miles, 156, 288
Saunderson, John, 326
Savage:
  Jas., 23
  Wm., 219
Savile:
  Anne (fl. mid 17th cent.), see D'Arcy
  Anne (fl. 1692), m. John Smithson, 252
  Dorothy, m. John Ricard, 252
  Mary, m. Wm. Mawde, 252
  R. A., 280
  Wm. (fl. 1633), 252
  Wm. (d. 1692), 252
Sawdon:
  John, 121
  Thos., 125
Sawyer, Edw., 56
Saxo (fl. 12th cent.), 18
Scagetorp (in Filey), 138
Scaife, F. E., 12
Scampston, 224
Schankes, Wal., 169
Scarborough, Rob. of, dean of York, 263
Scarborough (Yorks. N.R.), 64, 132, 143, 146, 239, 282
  communications with, 54, 67, 143
  fishing at, 50, 141, 159
  gaol, 197
  inhabitants of, 43, 55, 75, 135, 282, 329
  resort, 59
  poor-law union, 146, 173, 214, 281, 338
Scargill:
  Marg., m. Sir John Gascoigne, 312
  Wm., 312
Scloftone (Scolfstona, Sleeton, Slocton) (in Muston) 3, 236, 278, 280
Scoresby, Wm., 20
Scothorpe, Thos., 313
Scotland, 51, 53, 75, 158, 191, 207, 238, 291; and see Alexander III; Kirkcaldy; Margaret
Scots, queen of, see Joan
Scott, Sir G. G., 73–4, 93, 100
Scott and Moffatt, architects, 74
Scrope:
  Agnes, dau. of Ancelin, 168, 173
  Alice, granddau. of Rob., 168
  Ancelin, 168
  Hen. (Scrope or Wolf), 168, 171
  Sir John, 254
  Maud, granddau. of Rob., 168
  Rob., 168
  Sim., 168–9
  Wal., 168
  fam., 168, 254
Scruton:
  John, 195
  fam., 195
Scudamore, Thos., 255
Sculcoates, 132, 329
sculptors, see Deare; Earle; Falsgrave; Fisher, John (fl. 1773) and fam.; Forsyth; Keyworth; Mann,
Thos.; Marshall, Edw.; Pycock; Skelton, fam.; Wilton; Wyatt
sea-bird colonies, 9, 152
Sea Birds Preservation Act, 9, 158
seaborne trade, 2, 33, 48, 158; and see Bridlington; Filey; s.v. shipping
Seadale Brick Co., 143
Seamer (Yorks. N.R.), 132, 197
seaside holidays, building for, etc., 2, 105–6, 228, 240, 305; and see Bridlington; Filey; Flamborough; Scarborough, s.v. resort
Seaton, Julia of, 155
Seaton (in Sigglesthorne), 55
See:
  Brian del, 105, 314
  Joan, m. Pet. Hildyard, 91, 105, 183, 204
  Marg., m. Sir Hen. Boynton, 24, 180, 314
  Sir Martin del, 24, 91, 105, 180, 183, 204, 314, 316
  Maud, see Mounceaux
  fam., 91, 105
Selby (Yorks. W.R.), 67
Sellar, Wm., 76
Seller, E., 198, 330
Sellers:
  Alf., 7
  Eliz., 180
  Ern., 7
  J. A., 180
  Marm., 180
  Wm., 180
  fam., 180
Severs, Wm., 220
Sewerby:
  Eliz. of, 99
  John of (fl. early 14th cent.), 203
  John of (fl. later 14th cent.), 10, 98
  Marg. (fl. c. 1400), see Place
  Marg. (fl. 1453), m. Geof. Pigot, 95, 139, 234
  Osbert of, 95
  Rob. of (fl. 1234), 95
  Rob. of (fl. 14th cent.), 95, 97–9
  Sir Thos., 234
  Wm. (fl. 1299), 95
  Wm. (fl. 15th cent.) (two of this name), 95, 139, 181, 234
  fam., 10, 95–7, 181
Sewerby with Marton (in Bridlington), 3, 8, 30–1, 35, 47, 60, 64, 69, 71, 81, 92–100, 94, 159, 185
  chars., 81, 100
  ch., 7–8, 69–70, 74, 89, 99–100, 330
  econ. hist., 98–9
  educ., 100, 164
  loc. govt., 99
  mans. and other estates, 95–8, 181
  Marton Hall, 93, 97
  nonconf., 100
  Sewerby Ho., 48, 61, 93, 95–6
  windmills, 95, 99
  and see Marton
Seymour, Sir Edw., duke of Somerset, 265
Sharp, John, abp. of York, 293
Sharpe:
  Edm., 73
  Ric., 14, 334
Shaw:
  Irene, 279
  J. A., 279
Sheffield, 35, 59–60, 74, 208
Sheperdson, Jos., 77
Shepherd:
  H. J., 134, 138
  John, 273–4
  R. J. (Engineers), 54
  Rob., 149
  T. H., 138
Sherburn, 201–2, 214
Sherman, Ralph, 156
Shields, North (Northumb.), 76
shipbuilding, 54, 57
Shipley, G. R., 266
Shippabotham (Shippabottom):
  Anne, m. Edw. Elrington, 169–70
  Dorothy, dau. of Ric., 169 n
  Eliz., dau. of Ric., 169 n
  Marg., dau. of Ric., 169 n
  Ric., 97, 169
  Rob., 97, 169
Shipton:
  Geo., 234
  Thos., 234
Shotton, Thos., 116
Shouler:
  H. L., 287
  J. A., 180
Shrewsbury, countess of, see Talbot
Sidney, Thos., 336
Sigglesthorne, 187; and see Catfoss; Seaton; Wassand
Sillito, Frank, 279
Silton, Over (Yorks. N.R.), 73
Silver, Hen., 202
Simeon, Chas., 71
Simpson:
  Chris., 183
  Francis, vicar of Carnaby, 131
  Jas., 219
  L. J., 334
  Mary, dau. of Francis, 29, 131, 207
  Wm., 194
Sinclair:
  Anne, m. John England, 253
  Cath., see Ewbank
  Eliz., m. Benj. Glossop, 253
  Enoch, perpetual curate of Fraisthorpe, 207
  Geo., 253
  John (fl. 17th cent.), 253
  John (fl. 1748), 322
  fam., 253
Singleton, John, 255
Sinnington (Yorks. N.R.), 338
Skelton:
  Francis, 97, 102
  Greg., 102
  fam., 73, 149, 215
Skerne, 103, 221, 283, 287, 293
Skeryn, Edw., 109
Skinner, Jas., 116
Skipsea, 241; and see Bonwick; Cleeton; Dringhoe
Skirpenbeck, 254 n
Sleat, see Bosville Macdonald
Sledmere, 58
Sleeton, see Scloftone
Slingsby (Yorks. N.R.), 197
Slocton, see Scloftone
Smalewood, Adam, 274
Smayles, Zachary, 76
Smeaton, John, 48
Smith:
  Alf., 66
  Art., 169
  Edw., 199
  Francis, 135
  John (fl. 1697), 121
  John (fl. c. 1750), 77
  Leon., 273
  Mat. (fl. earlier 18th cent.), 155, 306–8
  Mat. (fl. later 18th cent.), 12–13, 265, 306–7
  Pigot, 146
  R. G., 90, 162
  R. W., 233
  Rob., 193
  Sam. (d. 1709), 149, 175, 215, 261, 309, 319
  Sam. (d. 1731), 124, 175, 319, 330
  Sarah, 140
  Thos. (fl. 1560), 314
  Thos. (d. 1856), 294
  Tom, 140
Smith and Brodrick, architects, 65–6, 74, 90, 207

Smith, Brodrick, and Lowther, architects, 75
Smithson:
  Anne, *see* Savile
  Edm., 12, 192
  Eleanor, mother of John, 252
  Eliz., 120
  John, 252
  Wm., 92
Smythson, Rob., 108
Snainton, John of, 318
Snainton (Yorks. N.R.), 318
Snell, Hen., 287
Somers, Jos., perpetual curate of Lowthorpe and Ruston Parva, and vicar of Foston on the Wolds and Nafferton, 276, 295
Somerset:
  duke of, *see* Seymour
  earl of, *see* Beaufort
Somerville (Somervile):
  Isabel, *see* Mauley
  Joan, m. Rhys ap Griffith, 108
  Sir Phil. de, 108, 117
  Rob. de, 108, 110–11
  Sir Rog. de, 24, 111, 115–17
  fam., 11, 108, 110, 313
Sonulf (fl. 1066), 217
Sotherton, Chris., 299
Speeton:
  Gilb. of, 102
  John of, 102
  Thos. of, 102
Speeton (in Bridlington), 3, 5, 9, 30, 101–4, 159, 241, 303
  char., 104
  ch., 15, 69–70, 90, 103–4, 175, 225, 242, 308
  Clay, 101, 337
  econ. hist., 102–3
  educ., 90, 104, 310
  loc. govt., 103
  mans. and other estates, 101, 202
  nonconf., 104
  windmills, 101, 103
Spencer, fam., 266
Spink (Spinke):
  Francis, 56
  Hen., 135
  Jane, 148, 150
  Wm., 274
  ——, 274
Spofforth, J. D., 183
Spurn Head (in Kilnsea), 53
Stables, Sam., 189
Stafford, Rob., 326 n
Stainbank, *see* Mears and Stainbank
Stainfield, Ralph of, abbot of Bardney, 7
Stainforth, Dr. Wm., prebendary of Langtoft, 269
Stainton, John, 173
Standy, Ric., 252
Stane, fam., 234
Stanhope:
  Geo., 123
  John, Lord, 44, 71, 116
  Sir Mic., 71, 318
Stanley:
  Sir Edw., 235
  Wm., 286
Stapleton, John of, 155
Starkey, ——, 25
Statham, Ric., 127
Staveley:
  Mic., 18
  Ric., 18, 20
  fam., 243
Staxton, fam., 335
Staxton (in Willerby), 3, 216, 278, 332–3, 335–9
  St. Mary's hosp., 333, 336
Stead:
  C. D. H., 266
  Julia, *see* Booth
  Mary, 81

Steele, Wm., 87
Stephenson (Stevenson):
  Anne, *see* Bainton
  Gamaliel, 127
  John, 331
  Thos., 138
  Wm. (fl. 1670), 181
  Wm. (fl. 1724), 181
Steward:
  Zachariah (fl. 1616), 193
  Zachariah (fl. 1662), 193
Stewart:
  Mat., earl of Lennox, 204, 231, 285–6
  W. B., 43
  fam., 142, 205, 231–2, 236–8, 240, 289–90
Stillington (Yorks. N.R.), 265
  prebend of, *see* York, Cath. ch. of St. Peter
Stocks:
  Ric., 7
  Ric. Holtby, 7
Stockton, Thos., 83
Stockwith, John of, 123
Stokesley, Mat., 335
Stork, T. R., 180–1, 183
Storour, Thos., 84
Story, Wal., 253
Strabolgi:
  Dav. de (fl. 1323), earl of Atholl, 180
  Dav. de (d. 1375), 180
  Eliz., m. Sir Hen. Percy, 180
  Joan, w. of Dav. de (fl. 1323), 180
Strangeways (Strangways):
  Eliz. (fl. 1418), *see* D'Arcy
  Eliz. (d. 1580), *see* Pigot
  Sir Jas. (fl. 15th cent.), 23
  Sir Jas. (d. 1541), 139, 233
  Joan, m. —— Mauleverer, 233
'Straxton' (unidentified), 241 n
Street, G. E., 222, 295–6
Strensall (Yorks. N.R.), 265
  prebend, *see* York, Cath. ch. of St. Peter
Strickland:
  Art., 59
  Sir Chas., 23, 28–9, 105, 131, 203, 207
  Eliz. (fl. 1557), w. of Wm. (d. 1598), 6
  Eliz. (d. 1674), w. of Sir Thos., 28
  Eliz. (fl. 1685), 130
  Eliz. (d. 1803), w. of Sir Geo. (d. 1808), 29, 208
  Frances, m. Chas. Cottrell-Dormer, 74, 154–5, 167
  Sir Geo. (d. 1808), 22–9, 97, 121–3, 126, 128, 154, 203–4, 208, 306–8
  Sir Geo. (d. 1874), later Sir Geo. Cholmeley, 88–9, 121, 123
  Grace, m. John Grimston, 203
  Hen. E., agriculturalist, 305–6, 308
  Hugh E., naturalist, 306
  Revd. J. E., 203
  Jas., *see* Marriott
  Kath., 162
  Mary, *see* Constable
  Rob., 203
  Sir Thos., 28, 154, 164
  Wal. (d. 1635), 23, 27, 86, 126–7, 129, 204
  Wal. (d. 1671), 154, 163
  Wal. (d. 1780), 154, 157
  Wal. (d. 1793), 154
  Wal. (d. 1839), 154, 156, 161
  Wal. (d. 1870), 154, 161–4
  Wal. (d. 1938), 23
  Wm. (d. 1598), 6, 9, 23–5, 86, 186, 203–4
  Wm. (fl. early 17th cent.), 186, 204
  Sir Wm. (d. 1673), 27–8, 105, 129, 202, 206

Sir Wm. (d. 1724), 25, 199 n, 203–4, 269
Sir Wm. (d. 1735), 23–4, 26–8, 121–2, 208
Sir Wm. (d. 1834), 18, 26, 28, 128, 131, 305–9
  fam., 22, 26, 28, 86, 88, 91, 93, 97, 105, 126, 128, 163, 201, 206, 235, 306–8
Strickland-Constable:
  Hen., 121
  fam., 121, 306, 308
Strowbridge, Wm., 221
Sturges Bourne Act (1819), 292
Stutville:
  Agnes, m. Herb. de St. Quintin, 107, 111, 224
  Alice, m. Rog. de Mauley (d. 1188), 107, 109–11, 224
  Anselm de, 107, 109–10, 224, 245
  Chas. (d. 1621), 234–5
  Chas. (fl. 1630s), 7, 234, 237, 239
  Chas. (fl. *c.* 1700), 7–8, 121, 234, 236–8
  Eliz., *see* Knowsley
  Geof. de, 329
  Gunnore, *see* Aubigny
  Jane, m. John Close, 7
  Nic. de, 333
  Rog. de, 107–8, 224
  fam., 109–10
Styring:
  Edw., 18
  Francis (fl. *c.* 1600), 18–19
  Francis (fl. 1659), 18, 20
  Thos., 18–19
Suckling, Sir John, 273–4, 286, 291
Suffolk, duke of, *see* Brandon
Sunderland (co. Dur.), 48, 52
Sunderlandwick, Wm. of, 182
Sunley, A. E., 163
Surdeval, Ric. de, 181, 202, 273, 311
Sutcliffe, G. G. O., 70
Sutton upon Derwent, 126
Swanne, Sim., 204
Swanthorpe, Alice of, 145
Swaythorpe (in Kilham), 4, 247, 249, 251, 255–7, 259–60, 325 n
Sweden, 53
Swillington, Geo., 306
Swine priory, 91, 105, 121–2, 202, 205, 313
Swinton, Thos., 312
Switzerland, 26
Swynford, Thos., Lord, 23
Sykes:
  C. A. V., 193
  C. P., 196
  Sir Chris., 91, 181, 218–20, 252–3, 262, 265, 283, 286, 292
  Jos., 193, 196
  Revd. Mark (fl. 1768), 265
  Sir Mark M. (d. 1823), 91, 220, 252, 265, 268
  Sir Mark (d. 1919), 265
  Mary, 222
  Ric. (b. 1678), 91, 219
  Ric. (d. 1870), 193, 195
  Sir Tatton (d. 1863), 182, *208*, 217–18, 220, 222–3, 296
  Sir Tatton (d. 1913), 188, 222–3, 264, 270, 285, 293, 295–7
  fam., 58, 92, 181–2, 198, 218, 220, 265, 267, 286, 292–3
Sylvester, Thos., 274

Talbot, Eliz., countess of Shrewsbury, 183
Talun:
  Joan, m. 1 Hugh de Capella, 2 Wm. de Boyville, 183, 245
  Rob. (fl. early 13th cent.), 245–7
  Rob., grandson of Rob., 245–6

INDEX

Tancred:
  Sir Ric., 273
  fam., 273, 327
Tankard (Tanckard):
  Frances, see Maltby
  Thos., 279
  Wm., 105
Tassell, Mary, 74
Tate:
  Emily, 167
  Francis, 169
  Hannah, 282
  J. B., 167, 174
  Wm. (fl. 1600), 279
  Wm. (fl. 1789), 167, 169 *n*
  fam., 167
Tatham, Susanna, 138
Tattershall:
  Emma, m. —— de Cailly, 231
  Isabel, m. —— of Orby, 231
  Joan (d. 1335), w. of Rob. (d. 1306), 231-2
  Joan (fl. early 14th cent.), m. —— of Driby, 167, 231-2
  Phil. FitzRobert, 231
  Rob. FitzHugh (d. by 1185), 231
  Rob. of (d. 1298), 231
  Rob. of (d. 1306), 231-2, 298
  Rog. FitzHugh, 231
  fam., 6, 11-13, 18, 24-5, 84, 86-7, 91, 96, 101, 105, 120, 138, 167-8, 170, 181, 192, 202, 210, 233, 235, 278, 280, 305, 333, 335
Taylor:
  A. H., 109
  Dav., 192, 195
  Edwin, 143-4
  Eliz., 138
  Ern. (*alias* Andie Caine), 145
  Francis, 192
  H. J., 23, 64
  John, 204
  Minnie, 169
  Rob., 223
  Thos., 204
  Wm., 64
Taylor, J., Ltd., timber merchants, 23
Taylor & Son (J. & Co.), bell-founders, 74, 198, 222
Tempest:
  Francis, 271
  Isabel, see Clitheroe
  Sir Ric., 180
  fam., 180
Tennant:
  P. N., 180
  S. R., 183
Tero (fl. 12th cent.), 102
Thirkleby:
  Lettice, m. Nic. Wake, 254
  Wal. of, 254-5
  fam., 273
Thirsk & Sons, flour millers, 291
Thomas *nepos capellani*, 219
Thompson:
  Anne, 253
  Beilby, 158
  Eliz., 263
  Francis, 255
  G. H., 252
  Gustavus, 253
  Hen., 255
  Revd. Jas., 35
  John (fl. 1588), 183
  Sir John (fl. 18th cent.), 321, 323
  Jonas (fl. 17th cent.), 253
  Jonas (d. 1739), 250, 253, 259, 263
  M. E., 312
  Ric. (d. 1653), 253
  Ric. (d. 1713), 253
  Ric. (fl. later 18th cent.), 253, 255, 257
  Rob., 253 *n*, 259
  Thos., 121
  fam., 250, 252-5, 261

Thornholme:
  Cath., m. Sir Wm. Calverley, 110
  Hugh of, 286
  John of (fl. *c*. 1400), 110, 293
  John (d. 1599), 110, 287, 312
  Marg., m. Rob. Saltmarsh, 110
  Thos., 286
  fam., 110, 116, 286, 290
Thornholme (in Burton Agnes), 4-5, 106-16, 118-19
Thornholme (in Nafferton), 283, 286-7, 290
Thornton:
  G. E. C., 193
  Thos. (fl. early 19th cent.) (of Willerby), 336-7
  Thos. (d. 1823) (of Foxholes), 191, 193
  W. D., later W. D. T. Duesbery, 109, 111, 113, 116
Thornton abbey (Lincs.), 138, 168
Thorny:
  Geof. de, 255
  Ric., 254
Thorpe (Thorp):
  John (fl. 1535), 203
  John (fl. 1826), 299
  Rob. of (fl. 1305), 314
  Rob. of (fl. 1379), 314
  Rob. (fl. 1569), 255
  Steph. of, 97
  fam., 314
Thorpe (in Rudston), 4, 310-11, 314-17
  Hall, 121, *209*, 310-12, 314-15
Thorpe Bassett, 276
Throckmorton, Sir Geo., 274
Thurley, Ric., 274
Thwaite (Thwayt):
  Marm., 95
  Thos., 95, 218, 314
Thwing:
  Barth., 255
  Cath., 213
  Cecily, m. Wm. the constable, 252
  Chris., 95
  Eliz., m. Wm. of Botreaux, 11, 325 *n*
  Hugelin of, 327
  John of (St. John of Bridlington), prior of Bridlington, 15, 32, 45
  Lucy (fl. 1272), see Brus
  Lucy (fl. *c*. 1300), m. Nic. de Meynell, 325
  Lucy (fl. 1374), m. Rob. Lumley, 326
  Marm. of (d. after 1234), 252
  Marm. of (d. 1282-4), 107, 325, 327
  Marm. of (d. 1323), 255, 327, 330, 334, 336
  Ralph, 211
  Rob. of (d. by 1166), 326
  Rob. of (fl. 1166), 326
  Rob. of (fl. 1268), 11
  Thos., Lord, 11, 260, 325 *n*, 326, 329
  Ursula, m. Cuth. Dawnay, 211
  Wm. of, 329-30
  fam., 107, 191, 252-3, 255, 313, 325-7, 330, 334
Thwing, 4, 253, **324-31**
  chars., 331
  ch., 260, 301, 329-31
  econ. hist., 300, 327-8
  educ., 303, 331
  loc. govt., 328
  mans. and other estates, 107, 191, 253, 325-8, 331
  mills, 328
  nonconf., 331
  rectors, see Adam; Constable, Rob. (fl. 1667); Fowler, Edw.
  and see Fornetorp; Octon
Tibbald s. of Reinfrid, 167
Tilney, Chas., 69
Tindall, Wm., 241
Tipper, Wm., 204, 274

Todeni, Berenger de, 305
Tof (fl. 1066), 305
Toox (? Towse), Thos., 219
Topham, Edw., 219, 325
Topping, Rob., 170
Torchil (fl. 1066), 22, 44, 95, 217
Toreshou hundred, 4
Torfin (fl. 1066), 335-6
Torulf (fl. 1066), 326
Tosti (fl. 1066), 138
Toucotes, John de, 12
Tournai (Belgium), 73
Tournay (Tournai):
  Ant., 321
  Avice, 313
  Geof. of, 313, 321
  John (fl. 1331), 313
  John (d. 1404), 321
  Ric. of, 313
  fam., 321
Tovie, Rob., 115
Tower, see Kempe
Townsend:
  Anne, Marchioness, 58
  Lady Harriet, 58
Townshend, Charlotte, duchess of Leeds, 58
Towry, Mary, 169
Towse:
  Brian (d. 1680), 219-20, 253
  Brian (fl. 18th cent.), 219
  Isabel, see Ewbank
  Jane (fl. 1692), m. Tim. Overend, 219
  Jane (fl. 1770s), m. —— Cooke, 219-20, 222-3
  Jeremiah, 219
  John, 192, 219
  Thos., see Toox
  Tim., 219, 222
  Wm. (at least two of this name), 218-19
  fam., 219
Travis, G. W., 35, 37, 43
Treaty of Peace Order (1924), 236
Tress, Muriel, 156
Triffitt:
  J. W., 170
  W. K., 169
Trinity House, 153
Trott, Elisha, 151, 282
Truelove, Geo, 76
Tucker, Ralph, 127
Tunstall:
  Brian, 187
  Isabel, 187
Turbar hundred, 3, 4, 165
Turner:
  Christiana, m. Benj. Ashton, 219
  Chris., 219
  John, 219
Turnham, Isabel of, m. Pet. Mauley (d. by 1241), 326
Tympercon:
  Hen., 11
  Mary, m. Hen. Maister, 11
Tymperton:
  Jane, m. Rob. Hodgson, 91
  John, 91
  fam., 91-2
Tyndale, Marg., 312
Tyrwhitt:
  Sir Wm., 299
  fam., 299

Uctred (fl. 1086), 202, 204, 245, 311 *n*, 313, 315
Uerske, John, 161
Ughtred:
  Dorothy, m. —— Constable, 180
  Rob. (fl. 1290), 180, 186, 274
  Rob. (d. *c*. 1590), 180
  Thos., 187
Ulf (fl. 1066), 24, 265

361

Ulrome:
　Adam, 86
　Hugh, 86
　fam., 86
Ulrome, 81
Ulviet (fl. 1066), 182, 218, 305
Unett:
　Geo., 135
　John, 135
　J. W., 134–6, 138, 143–4, 146, 149
　fam., 136
Uppiby:
　Wal., 130
　fam., 127, 130
Upton, J. H., 154

Val . . . , Alina de, 270
Valence, Aymer de, earl of Pembroke, 180, 187
Varley:
　H., 63
　Jas., 300
　John, 63
　T. F., 63
Vavasour:
　Jas., 192
　Lady, 58
　Sir Thos., 58
Venables, Ric., 183
Vere:
　Denise, 180, 203, 254
　Hugh de, 180, 203, 254, 273, 286
Vescy, fam., 202
Vicarman (Vickarman, Vickerman):
　Hen., 203
　Jos., 268
　Ralph, 12, 203
　Rob. (d. 1565), 12, 118, 138, 204
　Rob. (fl. 1769), 328
　Thos., 331
Victoria, Queen, 100
Villiers, Geo., later duke of Buckingham, 18, 120–1, 202
Voase, Wm., 134, 143–4

Wade, Wm., 261
Wadsworth, Geo., 196–7
Waferer, Thos., 44
Wailes, Wm., 215
Waind, Wm., 12
Waite, Wm., 198
Wake:
　Lettice, see Thirkleby
　Nic., 254
　Sybil, m. Rob. Salvin, 254
　Thos., Lord, 182
　fam., 333, 335
Wakefield, Revd. Thos., 183
Walker:
　Anne, 189
　Geo., 238
　Jas., 49
　John, 238
　Rob., 189
　Wm., 140
　and see Brodrick
Walker, W. S., Son and Field, architects, 75
Wall, Isaac, 81–2
Walmsley:
　Eliz., 16, 83
　Francis, 16, 164
　Geo. (fl. 1786), 12
　Geo. (fl. 1857), 12
　Luke, 306
　Thos., 12
　fam., 12
Walter s. of Ives, 167
Walter s. of Ranulf s. of Mayolf, 245
Walters, Edm., 204
Walworth:
　Nathan, 12, 156
　Thos., 191
Wandesford, Rowland, 312, 315

Wansford, Ellis of, 293
Wansford (in Nafferton), 3–5, 185, 274, 283, 285–97, 315
wapentakes, see hundreds
Warcop (Warcopp, Warcoppe):
　Edw., 312
　John (fl. 1595), 19
　John (fl. 1768), 121
　Thos., 84, 102
Ward, Geo., 294
Wardell, Francis, 306
Warner:
　J., & Sons, 215
　Wm., 185–6
Worrall, Rob., 294
Warren, see Wyerne
Warter:
　John of, 327
　Thos., 99
　Wal. of, 255
Warter, 8
　priory, 203–4, 313
Warters, Luke, 92
Warton, see Wharton
Warwickshire, see Birmingham; Coventry
Wassand, Jas. of, 120
Wassand (in Sigglesthorne), 108, 111, 121, 255
Watford, John, 327
Watson:
　Anne, 81
　Edw., 263
　Mrs., 150
Watt, Wm., 149
Walton, 221
　priory, 91, 219
Watts, John, 286
Weaver, John, 92, 105
Weaverthorpe, 197, 199
Webster:
　Anne, w. of Wm. (d. 1575), 6
　John, 76
　Wm. (d. 1575), 6, 8, 11–12
　Wm. (d. 1619), 6, 11
　Wm. (fl. 1632), 11–12
　fam., 12
Wedall, Hen., 289
Weeton, Eliz., 71
Weighton, Market, 67
Welbury:
　Anne, see Bulmer
　Ant., 12, 266
Weldon, John, 233
Welfit (Welfitt):
　Anne, 204
　Everell, 204
　Tim., vicar of Burton Agnes, 116
Wells (Welles):
　John, 196, 235
　T. E., & Son, 121
Welton, 117, 309
Wentworth:
　Darcy, 287
　Everild, see Maltby
　Sir Geo., 279
　Isabel, see Willesthorpe
　Thos., 204, 211
　fam., 211
Welsley, John, 76–7, 228
Westingby, Wm., 155
Westmorland, 154
Weston, Wm., 334
Westow, see Firby
Westrop:
　Ralph (fl. late 16th cent.), 123, 234, 238, 241, 273
　Ralph (fl. 1616), 241
　Thos., 234, 241, 281, 308
　fam., 240, 299, 301
　and see Laycoke
Wetwang, 109
Weycoe, ——, 105
Whalley:
　Ric., 25, 92
　Wal., 25, 92

Wharram:
　J. C., 266, 326
　T. M., 121
　Thos., 121–4
Wharton (Warton):
　Cath., see Maltby
　Eliz., m. C. A. Pelham, 102, 279
　Mary, m. Sir Jas. Pennyman, 102, 279
　Mic. (d. c. 1590), 306
　Sir Mic. (d. 1655), 102, 279
　Sir Mic. (d. 1725), 102, 194, 279
　Rob., 84
　Susanna, m. Mic. Newton, 102, 279
　fam., 102, 138, 279, 305
Wheelhouse, C. G., 149
Whitaker Bros., 39, 60
Whitby (Yorks. N.R.), 50–1, 140–1
　abbey, 140, 193–4, 196, 235, 287–8, 299, 336
White, Ellen, 119
White Bus Co., 67
White Cross (in Leven), 67, 201
Whitehurst, Ric., 77
Whitmore, Wm., 56
Whitwell, see Barber
Whixley (Yorks. W.R.), 273
Wichard transmontanus, rector of Rudston, 318
Wickham:
　Cycely M., see Boynton
　Thos. L., later T. L. Wickham-Boynton, 108
Wickham-Boynton:
　Marcus W., 108, 110, 115
　Thos. L., see Wickham
　fam., 107, 206
Widdrington:
　Lady Cath., 218
　Sir Thos., 241
Wilberforce:
　Mary, w. of Ralph, 188
　Ralph, 188
　Rob., vicar of Burton Agnes and archdeacon of the E.R., 116–17
　Thos., 182
　Wm. (fl. 1767), 185
　Wm. (d. 1833), philanthropist, 182
　Wm. (fl. 1835), 287
　fam., 182, 185, 287
Wilberfoss, Wm., 285
Wiles:
　R. E., 286
　Rob., 254–5
Wilkinson:
　Caleb, vicar of Carnaby and rector of Foxholes, 129, 197
　Chris., 121
　Hen., 286
　Jas., 181
　Joan, w. of John, later m. John Glyn, 326
　John, 326
　Wm., 181
Willatt, W. H., 306
Willerby:
　Adelard the hunter (fl. early 12th cent.), 214, 334, 338
　Adelard of (fl. late 12th cent.), 336
　Hen. of, 334, 338
　fam., 212, 333–4
Willerby, 4, 216, **332–9**
　ch., 175, 214, 216, 338–9
　econ. hist., 336–8
　educ., 339
　loc. govt., 338
　mans. and other estates, 333–6, 338
　mills, 337
　nonconf., 339
　vicar, see Day
　and see Binnington; Staxton
Willesthorpe (Wilsthorpe):
　Agnes, m. —— Bennet, 210
　Anastasia, m. Brian Palmes, 210, 335

INDEX

Isabel, m. 1 Rob. Creyke, 2 Thos. Wentworth, 210–11, 335
Wm. (? two of this name), 192, 210–11, 335
fam., 215, 335
William IV, King, 227, 277
William, count of Mortain, 6, 10, 22, 44, 83, 91, 95, 98, 101, 181, 193, 202, 217–19, 285, 311, 313–15, 326, 334
William s. of Richard, 196
William s. of Robert, 168
William s. of Roger, 211
William s. of Tibbald, 167
Williamson:
  Ann, m. Wm. Cayley, 117
  Bart., 254, 274
  John, 335
  Ralph, 192
  fam., 67
Williamson & Son, 67
Willos, John, 158
Willoughby:
  Hen., Baron Middleton, 319
  Julia, 319
Wilsford:
  Edw., 156, 161
  Rob., 156, 158
  Sir Thos., 156
  fam., 161, 163
Wilson:
  C. H. W., Baron Nunburnholme, 232
  Chris., 121
  H. C. B., 253
  Prof. J. M., 62
  Jas. (fl. 1549), 196, 336
  Jas. (fl. 1918), 300
  John (? two of this name), 141, 300
  Joshua, 253, 255, 257
  Thos. (fl. 1600), 219
  Thos. (fl. 1717), 286
  Wm. (fl. 1549), 20 n
  Wm. (fl. 1601), 25, 204
  Wm. (d. 1792), 215
  fam., 253
Wilsthorpe, see Willesthorpe
Wilsthorpe (in Bridlington), 3, 5, 30, 91, **104–6**, 125, 199, *200*, 201
  ch., 69, 92, 106
  econ. hist., 105
  loc. govt., 91
  mans. and other estates, 44, 105
Wilton, J., 227
Wilton, Bishop, 265
  prebend, see York, Cath. ch. of St. Peter
Wiltshire, see Fisherton Anger
Windersome, see Nafferton
Wingate:
  Edm., 182
  Edw. (d. 1597), 111, 156, 183, 233, 299, 305, 327
  Edw. (fl. c. 1600), 299, 305
  Geo., 233, 299
  Rog., 182
  ——, 6
  fam., 182–3, 299
Winn (Winne):
  Rob., 92
  Sir Rowland, 208
Winteringham, Thos., 121
Wise, A. J., 288
Wiseman, Nic., cardinal, 144
Withernsea, 60
Wittie, Rob., 129
Wittilbury, Margery, see Ros
Wodehouse:
  A. T., 193
  E. T., 193
Wold Gate, 1, 17, 21, 24, 26, 31, 106, 125, 216, 223, 247, 249, 264, 310
Wolds, Yorkshire, 1
Wolf, Hen., see Scrope; Woolfe
Wollaston, Sir John, 288
Wood:

Anne, see Buck
Barnay, 312
Sir Francis L., 71, 127
John, 312, 314
Mat., 306
Thos. (fl. 1560s), 105, 168, 170, 187, 212, 219, 235, 274, 334
Thos. (d. c. 1695), 170, 314
Wm. (d. 1537), prior of Bridlington, 32
Wm. (fl. 1595), 44
fam., 314
Woodall:
  Eliz., 168
  J. W., 168
  John, 168, 173–4
  W. E., 135, 168
Woodcock:
  Nellie, 67
  Tom, 121
Woodhouse:
  Gerald, 161
  Herb., 154–5
  Nic., 201, 204
Woodnett, Lawr., 187
Woolfe (Wolf):
  Benj., 81
  Hen. (fl. 13th cent.), see Scrope
  Hen. (fl. 1705), 155
  Jane, 81
  Ric., 53, 56, 81, 155
  Tim., 81
  fam., 53
woollen mills, 22, 26, 285, 291–2, 295; *and see* fulling mills
workhouses, see Bridlington; Hunmanby; Rillington
Worm, Wm., 289
Worth & Frith, 59
Wotton, John, 299
Wragby (Yorks. W.R.), 207
Wrangham:
  Francis, vicar of Hunmanby and archdeacon of the E.R., 230, 242
  G. R., 10
Wright:
  A. G. W., 18, 75, 127
  Alf., 21
  Chris., 171
  G. W. J. H., 18, 91
  Geo., 18, 21, 91
  John (fl. 1538), 156, 161
  John (d. 1606), 6, 171, 313–14
  Jos., 77
  Rob., 335
  Wm., 183, 187
  ——, 86
  fam., 171
Wrigley:
  E. W., 192
  Harold, 121, 192, 209–10, 255, 334
  Mic., 214
  fam., 210, 255, 334
Wyatt, R. J., 21
Wyerne (Warren):
  Agnes, m. Thos. de St. Quintin, 139
  Ralph de, 24
  Rob. (fl. 1284), 139
  Rob. (fl. 14th cent.), 139
  fam., 139
Wykeham (Yorks. N.R.), 214, 301
  priory, 170, 327
Wynlove, Wm., 20

Yarburgh, Yarburgh, see Greame
Yarmouth, Gt. (Norf.), 50, 141, 159
Yates:
  Ann, 81
  Hen., 158
  Thos., 19
York, 32, 120
  abps., 144, 160, 174, 259, 265–6, 318, 323, 328–30

  as owners of estates, 70, 87–8, 95, 97–8, 110–11, 168, 182–3, 217–19, 221, 226, 272–5, 288, 305, 313, 315, 321–2
  as patrons of churches, 27, 74, 89, 100, 103, 114, 123, 129, 140, 161, 187, 214, 241, 269, 276, 293, 301, 308, 317
  and see Gray; Lamplough; Melton; Sharp
  architects of, 28, 69, 96, 137,
  bellfounders of, 124, 149, 175, 198, 215, 261, 270, 309, 319, 330
  Cath. ch. of St. Peter:
    canons, 116, 318
    deans, 255, 259, 263; *and see* Grey, Wm.; Osbaldeston, Ric.; Scarborough
    dean and chapter, 265–9, 315
    furnishings from, 74
    liberty, 313
    prebends, 242
      Apesthorpe, 197
      Bishop Wilton, 265, 267
      Bugthorpe, 97
      Grindale, 88–9, 103
      Langtoft, 265–9
      Stillington, 265–7
      Strensall, 265, 267
    St. William's coll., 255
    sub-treasurer, 197
    treasurer, 265
    vicar-choral, 318
  communications with, 1–2, 59, 67
  corporation, 293
    alderman, 255
    lord mayor, 253
  inhabitants of, 28, 51, 227, 239, 277, 283, 292, 318
  Museum, 175
  plate made in, 15, 21, 28, 90, 104, 130, 149, 198, 222, 243, 270–1
  St. Leonard's (formerly St. Peter's) hosp., 127–9, 138–9, 143, 194, 211, 225, 239, 255, 327
  St. Mary's abbey, 3, 107, 111, 114–115, 194, 196–7, 218, 226, 311–13, 315, 317
  St. Peter's hosp., *see* York, St. Leonard's hosp.
  sculptors of, 21, 73, 149, 215, 227, 243, 319
Yorkshire, 32, 51, 58–9, 144, 162, 257, 273, 286, 299, 334
Yorkshire, East Riding, 54, 238
  archdeacon of, *see* Wilberforce, Rob.; Wrangham, Francis
  constabulary, 65, 146
  county council, 45, 47, 66–7, 71, 78–80, 90, 105, 125–6, 128, 145–6, 160, 189, 253, 257, 306
Yorkshire, North Riding, 131, 137, 168, 172; *and see* Ampleforth; Arden; Beningbrough; Bossall; Brafferton; Broughton; Cayton; Coatham; Falsgrave; Farlington; Foston; Guisborough; Handale; Hinderwell; Hornby; Keldholme; Kildale; Kirkby in Cleveland; Kirkleatham; Lastingham; Leake; Malton; Marton; Middlesborough; Middleton; Norton Conyers; Nunnington; Osgodby; Pickering; Rievaulx; Salton; Scarborough; Seamer; Silton; Sinnington; Slingsby; Snainton; Stillington; Strensall; Whitby; Wykeham
Yorkshire, West Riding, 9, 33, 58–9, 61, 67, 134, 144; *and see* Appleton, Nun; Bolton Percy; Bradford; Burghwallis; Doncaster; Fewston; Haworth; Horsforth; Huddersfield; Kirkstall; Knaresborough; Leeds; Monkton, Nun; Nostell;

Yorkshire, West Riding (cont.)
    Rastrick; Ripon; Selby; Sheffield;
      Whixley; Wragby
Yorkshire Central Agricultural Soc., 257
Young:

Art., agriculturalist, 54, 58
Cath., *see* Duesbery
Freman, 140
Geo., 13
Ric., 25, 260
Revd. Rob., 336 *n*

Smithson, 279

Zouche:
    Rog. la, 234
    fam., 234

CORRIGENDA TO VOLUME I

Page 120, line 33, *for* '1665' *read* '1685'
" 317*b*, lines 17–18 from end, *for* 'rebuilt Zion, Beverley Road, their chief meeting-place, in 1869' *read* 'built Stepney, Beverley Road, later their chief meeting-place, to replace Zion in 1869'
" 317*b*, lines 14–15 from end, *for* 'built in that year, became their headquarters' *read* 'was built in that year'
" 320*a*, lines 31–2, *delete* 'it had been built in 1840 privately;'
" 322*b*, line 23 from end, *replace line by*: '*Argyle Street, Queen's Road (later Maple Street)*: registered by the Primitives in 1872'
" 322*b*, line 20 from end, *replace line by*: '*Argyle Street, Anlaby Road*: built by the Wesleyans in 1895; (3) 1,000'
" 322*b*, line 14 from end, *for* 'Wesleyans' *read* 'United Methodists'
" 323*b*, lines 21–2, *delete whole entry*
" 326*a*, lines 16–19, *replace entry by*: '*South Street*: built *c.* 1840 privately and licensed by the 'Primitive Methodist New Connexion' in 1843. (4) Opened by the Baptists in 1847.'
" 326*a*, lines 6–8 from end, *delete* 'The Primitives . . . same building.'
" 326*a*, line 6 from end, *for* 'destroyed' *read* 'demolished'
" 326*a*, after line 5 from end, *add new entry*: '*Sykes Street*: a mission used by the Primitives from 1892 to 1900.'
" 326*b*, line 23 from end, *for* 'Wesleyans' *read* 'Primitives'
" 425*a*, line 25, *for* 'Shppiing' *read* 'Shipping'
" 467*a*, line 9, *for* 'east' *read* 'west'